D0789373

For Reference
DISCARD
Not to be taken from this room

MARSHALLESE-ENGLISH DICTIONARY

PALI LANGUAGE TEXTS: MICRONESIA

Social Sciences and Linguistics Institute
University of Hawaii

Donald M. Topping
Editor

MARSHALLESE-ENGLISH DICTIONARY

TAKAJI ABO
BYRON W. BENDER
ALFRED CAPELLE
TONY DEBRUM

DISCARD
L.C.C.C. LIBRARY

The University Press of Hawaii
Honolulu

The publication of this book is subsidized
by the government of the
Trust Territory of the Pacific Islands.

Copyright © 1976 by The University Press of Hawaii

All rights reserved. No part of this work may be reproduced or transmitted in any form or by any means, electronic or mechanical, including photocopying and recording, or by any information storage or retrieval system, without permission in writing from the publisher.

Manufactured in the United States of America

Library of Congress Cataloging in Publication Data
Main entry under title:

Marshallese-English dictionary.

(Pali language texts : Micronesia)
Bibliography: p.
1. Marshall language—Dictionaries—English.
2. English language—Dictionaries—Marshall. 3. Names, Geographical—Marshall Islands. 4. Marshall language—Etymology—Names. I. Abo, Takaji, 1936– II. Series: Pali language texts.
PL6255.Z5M3 499′.5 76-26156
ISBN 0–8248–0457–0

This is one in a series of dictionaries compiled and edited with the aid of a specially developed system of computer programs, which also formatted the text for composition and produced the tapes to drive a digital character-generating phototypesetter.

For the
students and teachers
in the
schools
of the
Marshall Islands

CONTENTS

PREFACE

Although this work represents the most complete collection of information on the words of Marshallese yet compiled, it is still far from a complete listing of all the words of the language. Nor is the information given for the words that have been included always complete or entirely accurate. But interest in the study of the language is probably greater today than ever before, and rather than delay publication any longer in the interests of completeness and precision, the authors offer it in its present form in the hope that its appearance may stimulate others to join in producing a more nearly complete future edition.

Many of the words will appear in their usual form, while others will look familiar but changed slightly in various ways—by the inclusion of marks beneath some letters, by the use of one or two new letters, or by the use of different letters that more regularly and accurately show the sound of a word than others that have sometimes been used. These changes follow the recommendations made by a committee of Marshallese in 1971. Basically there are four changes:

1. Two consonant letters that have always been in the Marshallese alphabet but seldom used have been put to work to represent their intended sounds wherever they occur. These are the light *p*, and the light *d* (without an accompanying and redundant *r*), as in *ḷap* 'big' and *dik* 'small' (instead of *lab* and *drik*).
2. Two vowel letters that were not in the alphabet but were nevertheless sometimes used have been added to share the burden of representing the many vowel sounds of the language. These are the *ǫ* of *tǫ* 'sugar cane' and the *ū* of *ūlūl* 'adze'. Although the letter *ā* was included in the alphabet to represent the sound of the vowel in a word such as *mā* 'breadfruit', this sound has also sometimes been written with *e*. Only *ā* is used for this sound in this dictionary, since *e* is needed for two other vowel sounds, those of *me* 'which' and *me* 'fortress, fish weir'.
3. Double consonants and double vowels are written with double letters, so that a double *t* now distinguishes *bōtta* 'to bat' from *bōta* 'butter', and a double *a* distinguishes *maañ* 'pandanus leaf' from *mañ* 'brown coconut'.
4. Special marks beneath the letters *l*, *m*, and *n* are used to show when they have a heavy *(eddo)* sound as opposed to a light *(emera)* sound. Thus *ḷe*

'Sir' is distinguished from *le* 'Ma'am', *am̧* 'your' from *am* 'our', and *ņe* 'that by you' from *ne* 'leg, foot'.

It is not the authors' intention to propose one and only one correct spelling for each word. In fact, common alternative spellings are given for many words. Rather, they have attempted to show what the language would look like if the recommendations of the committee are eventually adopted. The final decision as to how the language should be written remains appropriately with those to whom this book is dedicated.

The names of many places in the islands have been included in a special section at the end of the volume. (The names listed in this section are spelled as they might have been if the early mapmakers had themselves been speakers of Marshallese rather than some other language. But the intent is not to change the spellings on the maps, for Bikini, Eniwetok, Kwajalein, Majuro, Ebeye, and so forth, will no doubt remain the official spellings of the names of such places for many years to come.) On the other hand, very few names of people are included. This contrast in treatment of the names of places and the names of people seems appropriate for a society in which land is held dearly and each small tract named, while people's names are treated with great delicacy and seldom mentioned in their presence.

The authors are deeply indebted to a number of organizations and people who have been of great help in compiling the lexical file on which the dictionary is based. Early work was supported in part by University of Hawaii Peace Corps Micronesia training projects, and by a grant from the University of Hawaii Office of Research Administration. The College of Arts and Sciences and the Social Sciences and Linguistics Institute (formerly the Pacific and Asian Linguistics Institute) have helped support the use of the University of Hawaii Computer Center from year to year. The participation of Lan̄lōn̄ Alik in 1971 and of the third author in 1971–1972 was made possible as part of the Pacific Language Development Program of the Culture Learning Institute of the East-West Center, under the coordination of Gregory Trifonovitch. Publication of the dictionary in this form has been made possible through a grant from the Government of the Trust Territory of the Pacific Islands.

The scientific identification of flora and fauna was assisted by the scientists mentioned in section 6. Keypunching for the computer and other editorial tasks were carried out by Olga Caldwell, Cindy Dalrymple, Melody Moir Actouka, and Doreen Yamamoto. Their participation was supported by the Social Sciences and Linguistics Institute and the Department of Linguistics of the University of Hawaii.

The authors are especially indebted to Donald M. Topping for organizing and guiding the overall project in which this and other reference works on Micronesian languages could be produced, for the help and encouragement received from him over the years, and for his editorial assistance as we approached publication. Finally, this dictionary could never have reached or appeared in its present form without much time, effort, and creative thinking on the part of Professors Robert W. Hsu and Ann Peters, who mediated between the authors and the computer. Lexicographers everywhere would do well to learn from them.

INTRODUCTION

1. How the Dictionary Was Compiled

The project that has resulted in the publication of this edition of a Marshallese dictionary extended over the better part of ten years. It began in 1966 when the first and second authors, Abo and Bender, compiled the 2,000-word glossary that appeared in *Spoken Marshallese* (Bender 1969), a set of language lessons designed primarily to assist Peace Corps volunteers in learning the language. In preparing that glossary, Abo began by consulting what was known as the original Navy dictionary (Carr and Elbert 1945) and the later version of it (Feeney 1952). A card file was established that included all the words of that dictionary that were known by Abo. The words were written in a phonemic transcription (see section 4 below) that could later be converted to a standard spelling when such had been determined. English translations were included on each card, and grammatical information and example sentences were also included on many of the cards. Various forms of a word and closely related words were all written on the same card. Abo read through the Marshallese translation of the Bible and other materials written in Marshallese in search of additional words to be added to the file. The total number of cards in the file was about 4,500 at this point.

DeBrum, the fourth author, who had helped write the early Peace Corps lessons in 1966, joined the dictionary project in 1967 and added hundreds of additional words that occurred to him. He also worked intensively on the scientific identification of the many fish names in the file. The entire file was placed in computer storage at the University of Hawaii in 1968 because of the many ways in which the computer could be of help to the project. The computer was able to alphabetize the entries automatically, and to print out new listings of the file without errors. It received new words as they were found and put them in their proper alphabetic places. Its greatest service was the automatic compilation of an English finder list (see section 8 below) from the English translations that were given for each word. By October 1968, the computer file contained almost 5,000 Marshallese entries and a total of over 6,000 English words in their finder list. The 2,000 most useful Marshallese words were selected for incorporation in the *Spoken Marshallese* glossary, and their accompanying finder list contained over 3,000 English words.

The third author, Capelle, joined the project later that year and added more words that had been overlooked by the previous authors. Many of these were discovered by comparing the English finder list with the *Thorndike-Barnhart Junior Dictionary*. When a word from this English dictionary was not found in the finder list, it was either added as another possible translation for a Marshallese entry already in the file, or it reminded the third author of a Marshallese word to be added to the file. By the middle of 1973, there were 6,200 Marshallese entries, and 11,000 English words in the finder list. (There are more English words than Marshallese entries because one Marshallese entry usually contains a number of different but related words.) Later in 1973, more than 3,000 names of places in the Marshallese islands collected by Bender (1963*b*) were included, and other words continued to be added up until the time of publication to increase the number of Marshallese entries to the present total of almost 12,000.

The name of yet a fifth co-author could have appeared on this dictionary with considerable justification. The late Johnny Silk spent many of his free hours during 1958 and 1959 helping Bender analyze the place names. This analysis helped uncover hundreds of older words that are contained in the place names. (Many of these appear in the dictionary labeled as "archaic.") His knowledge of the geography and lore of the islands was boundless, and has helped to enrich this work in many ways.

2. The Structure of an Entry

A minimal entry consists of a Marshallese headword and an English translation or definition. Many entries contain additional information. The various types of information that may be included and their order are as follows: (Technical terms used in the following discussion are followed by a reference to the section of the *Marshallese Reference Grammar* [abbreviated MRG; Bender 1976] in which they are explained.)

a. *Headword.* Each entry begins with a headword in italic type, and all entries are ordered according to the alphabetization of their headwords. One of the various words or forms of words included in an entry is selected as the headword of the entry. This is usually the word with the most basic form, one that does not have affixes or optional reduplications included in it. The infinitive forms of transitive verbs (MRG 3.4.8) are chosen as headwords, but where there are major differences between the infinitives and the transitive forms, a separate cross-entry is made with the transitive form as its headword.

> *m̧wijit* (**m̧ijit**). Transitive form of *m̧wijm̧wij* (**m̧ijm̧ij**).
> *kan̄* (**kag**). Transitive form of *m̧ōn̄ā* (**m̧egay**).
> *kiil* (**kiyil**). Transitive form of *kkiil* (**kkiyil**).

The same is true of the construct forms (MRG 3.1.6) of some nouns.

> *bawōn* (**bahwen**). Construct form of *bao* (**bahwew**).
> *kituon* (**kitiwen**). Construct form of *kōto* (**kętęw**).

Further details concerning the selection of headwords are given in section 7, Finding Words in the Dictionary.

b. *Phonemic Transcription.* The phonemic transcription (MRG 2) of each headword is given immediately following the headword. The transcription is in boldface type and enclosed in parentheses, as in the examples above. The relation of the phonemic transcription to the spelling of the words as they appear as headwords is discussed in section 4 below, and in MRG 2.1, 2.2, and 2.6.

c. *Dialect Information.* When a word has different pronunciations in the Rālik and Ratak dialects, or when two completely different words are used for the same meaning in the two dialects, this information is given after the abbreviation "Dial." following the phonemic transcription. The abbreviations W and E are used for the Rālik and Ratak dialects, respectively.

> *bae* (**bahyey**). Dial. E only; see *koba* (**kewbah**). Bamboo.
> *ellōk* (**yȩllȩk**). Dial. W, E: *m̧o̧le* (**m̧awley**). Rabbitfish.
> *m̧m̧an* (**m̧m̧an**). Dial. W: *em̧m̧an* (**yem̧m̧an**), E: *m̧ōm̧an* (**m̧em̧an**). Good.

The first example indicates that the word *bae* 'bamboo' is limited to the Ratak dialect, and that *koba* is used for 'bamboo' in the Rālik dialect but may also be used in the Ratak. The second example indicates that *ellōk* is used in the Rālik and *m̧o̧le* in the Ratak for a certain species of fish. The third example is a double consonant word (MRG 2.3.1) which is pronounced *em̧m̧an* in the Rālik but *m̧ōm̧an* in the Ratak. (The selection of a headword for double consonant words that is not identical to either dialectal pronunciation is discussed in section 7 below.)

d. *Variant Pronunciations.* When more than one pronunciation has been recorded for a headword, and when the pronunciations are not known to be especially connected with the geographic dialect areas, one pronunciation is arbitrarily chosen as the headword, and the others are listed following the phonemic transcription of the headword (or following the dialect information, if there is any).

> *alikkar* (**halikkar**). Also *allikar* (**hallikar**). Clear

This example shows that there are two pronunciations of the word meaning 'clear'. It should be emphasized that the choice of the one as headword is arbitrary, and does not indicate that it is in any way more correct than the other, or that the other is less preferable.

e. *Status Information.* When there is something special about the usage of a word that the reader of the dictionary should be made aware of, this is given following the phonemic transcription of the headword (or following any dialect or variant information). This is done by giving one of four words that best describes the special status of the word:

Archaic. Such words are old words that are no longer generally used, and may not be known to all speakers, especially younger ones.

Idiom. Such expressions are proverbs, sayings, or other phrases that have a special meaning beyond the literal meaning of each of the words.

Slang. Such words are generally newer words that may call attention to themselves when used, and which may not be appropriate for more formal speaking or writing.

Vulgar. Such words are avoided in conversation when any taboo relatives may be present. The words are themselves taboo in such situations. The second author takes full responsibility for their inclusion in the dictionary for the sake of completeness and because of their possible use for scientific purposes, such as the tracing of cognate words in various related languages.

f. *Etymological Information.* Next in order in an entry, information may be given concerning the history of a word—where it comes from. Words that are known to have come from some other language are so indicated:

> *jaajmi* (**jahajmiy**). From Japn. *sashimi*. A food, raw fish.
> *m̧aak* (**m̧ahak**). From Germ. Money.
> *tim̧a* (**tiym̧ah**). From Engl. *steamer*. Ship.

Words that do not come from other languages are sometimes accompanied by information concerning their origin within the Marshallese language.

> *dāpijbok* (**dapijbeq**). From *dāpij* (**dapij**) "hold", *bok* (**beq**) "sand", "to hold onto the sand".

It is hoped that much more of this latter sort of information concerning the derivation of words within the language can be included in a future edition of the dictionary.

g. *Grammatical Information.* Many entries include a numbered key that gives grammatical information for the various forms of the word included in the entry. The key consists of one or more of the Arabic numerals from 1 to 11, separated by commas. Some of the numbers may be followed by parentheses containing other forms of the word, or affixes to be added to it. The code meaning for each of the numbers used in the key is given in section 3.

h. *Definitions.* English translations for the various forms of the word included within an entry are given next, in roman type. Marshallese words, words from other languages, and the scientific names of flora and fauna are italicized within the definitions.

i. *Example Sentences.* Finally within an entry, one or more example sentences may be given in italic type, together with English translations in roman type. (Occasionally an example may be given that is not a complete sentence, but it has been punctuated as if it were a sentence for reasons having to do with its computer storage.) The example sentences are chosen to exemplify the relation between some of the forms indicated in the grammatical information and some of the English translations given as definitions. It is hoped that this part of the entries can also be enriched in a future edition.

3. The Grammatical Key

The grammatical information referred to in section 2 is given in the form of a key containing various coded numbers. The information given for a typical entry may look something like the following:

2, 3(inf, tr *-ik*), 4, 6(*-i*).

Notice that there are numbers given in order, but with some missing, and that some of the numbers are followed by material enclosed in parentheses, while others are not. The meanings of each of the numbers used in the key, those from 1 to 11, and of the material that may follow them within parentheses are discussed in order below.

Code 1. This means that the headword of the entry may be used as an INALIENABLE NOUN (MRG 3.1.2), combining with some or all of the POSSESSIVE PERSONAL PRONOUN SUFFIXES. The material in parentheses following the 1 shows the stem vowel that must be added to the headword in order for it to combine with these suffixes, or it may show the whole combining form if it differs from the headword by more than the addition of a vowel.

āt. 1(*-i*). Eyebrow.
āt. 1(*eta-*). Name.

These are portions of two different entries that have identical headwords, both of which may be used as inalienable nouns. The combining stem for 'eyebrow' is formed by adding the high stem vowel **i** to give **yati-**, so that the word for 'his eyebrow', with the 3s pronoun suffix *-n* is *ātin* (**yatin**). The combining stem for 'name' is as given in parentheses following the 1: *eta-* (with a different first vowel, so that the word for 'his name' is *etan* (**yetan**).

The hyphen following a headword indicates that it (as an inalienable noun) does not occur without one of the possessive suffixes (indicated by the Code 1):

daa-.	1.	Portion of pandanus.

No additional vowels need to be added to such headwords before attaching the suffixes. Thus *daan* means 'his portion of pandanus'.

Note however that headwords occurring without a hyphen and having the Code 1 need to add a vowel before attaching the possessive suffixes. This vowel PHONEME is shown in parentheses following the Code 1, as in the following examples:

ñat.	1(*-i*).	Palate.
mọọr.	1(*-e*).	Bait.
ñilep.	1(*-a*).	Molar.
wa.	1(*-a*).	Canoe.

Note that the vowel phoneme shown in the parentheses may be spelled in different ways, depending on which suffix is added: *n̄atūm̧* 'your palate' but *n̄atin* 'his palate', *mǫǫrō* 'my bait' but *mǫǫreer* 'their bait', *n̄ilepa* 'my molar' but *n̄ilepān* 'his molar', etc. The consonants on either side of this vowel phoneme (the last consonant of the headword and the first consonant of the suffix) determine the spelling of the vowel according to the rules given in MRG 2.2. The vowel phoneme shown after the Code 1 serves to show whether the various suffixed forms of the inalienable noun are spelled according to the I-STEM, E-STEM, SHORT A-STEM, or LONG A-STEM patterns shown in MRG 3.1.2.

Code 2. This means that the headword of the entry may be used as a VERB (MRG 3.4), combining with some or all of the SUBJECT PERSONAL PRONOUN PREFIXES (MRG 3.2.2).

maron̄. 2. Be able.

This portion of an entry containing the number 2 as part of the grammatical key indicates that the headword *maron̄* may be used as a verb and combined with subject pronoun prefixes such as the 3s *e-*, as in *emaron̄* 'he is able'.

When both the INFINITIVE and the TRANSITIVE forms of verbs (MRG 3.4.8) may be derived from the same headword, this is shown in the material in parentheses following the number 2.

m̧wijm̧wij. 2(inf, tr *m̧wijit*). Cut.

This portion of an entry containing the number 2 as part of the grammatical key with the abbreviations INF and TR in parentheses following the number illustrate this type of headword. The abbreviation "inf" followed by a comma (rather than by a Marshallese form) indicates that the headword of the entry is the infinitive form. Thus the infinitive form of this entry is *m̧wijm̧wij*, as in *em̧wijm̧wij* 'he cut(s)'. (If the infinitive form were different from the headword, it would be given in the key after the abbreviation *inf* and before the comma.) The transitive form of this headword is given after the abbreviation *tr*: *m̧wijit*, as in *em̧wijit* 'he cut(s) something'. The only other information sometimes given in parentheses following the Code 2 concerns those few verbs that have different transitive forms for singular and plural objects.

meme. 2(inf, tr sg. obj. *me*, pl. obj, *mei*). Chew.

This indicates that the following would be the 3s transitive forms:

eme	**yemey**	'he chewed it'
emei	**yęmęyiy**	'he chewed them'

Code 3. This means that the headword of the entry may be combined with the CAUSATIVE PREFIX *ka-* to form causative verbs (MRG 3.4.11). When the resulting form of the causative verb is different from the prefix joined

to the headword (ignoring vowel changes in the prefix), this form is given in the material enclosed in parentheses following the number 3. When both infinitive and transitive causative verbs may be formed, this is also indicated in the parentheses, just as described for verbs that are not causative under Code 2 above. When a special STATIVE CAUSATIVE verb may be derived, this is shown in the same way.

jook. 3(st inf *kajjookok,* tr *kajook*). Shame.

This portion of an entry shows that both stative infinitive causative and transitive causative verbs can be formed from the headword, and that their shapes with the 3s subject prefix would be as follows:

ekajjookok	**yekajjewekwek**	'it is shameful'
ekajook	**yekajewek**	'he humiliated (someone)'

A simpler entry of which the following is a portion indicates that a causative verb can be formed by adding *ka-* (or one of its variant forms: *ke-*, *kō-*, *kǫ-*) to the headword.

jerbal. 3, 4.

Wōn ņe ej kōjerbal eok.
'Who is employing you?'

Occasionally the parentheses following a Code 3 contain the abbreviation "reflex" to indicate that a causative form is used only reflexively, that is, with the object of the verb referring to the same individual as the subject of the verb:

perper. 1(*-i*), 2(inf, tr *pere*), 3(reflex only). Doubt.

Kwōn jab kaperpere eok bwe kwōj naaj etal wōt.
'Stop balking (doubting yourself) because you're destined to go.'

The same abbreviation may appear after the Code 2 of causative verbs that are headwords:

kakōl. 1(*-i*), 2(inf, tr reflex *kakile*). Be spoiled.

Aolep ajri raņ nājin lieņ rōkakileik er.
'All her children are spoiled.'

Code 4. This means that the headword of the entry may be combined with the person prefix *ri-* to form PERSON NOUNS (MRG 3.1.4). The 4 following *jerbal* above shows the possibility of deriving:

rijerbal	**rijerbal**	'worker'

Code 5. This means that a DISTRIBUTIVE verb (MRG 3.4.5) may be formed from the headword. The form of the distributive verb is shown in parentheses following the number 5.

ek.	5(*ike*).	Fish.
maroro.	5(*mmaroro*).	Green.
lokjak.	5(*llokjakjak*).	Be busy.

These portions of three different entries show the possibility of forming the following distributive verbs: *ike* 'be teeming with fish', *emmaroro* (W), *memaroro* (E) 'be greenish', and *ellokjakjak* (W), *lelokjakjak* (E) 'be continually tied down'. The special meanings of the distributive verbs thus formed are often brought out by an example sentence included in the entry.
Code 6. This means that a CONSTRUCT noun (MRG 3.1.6) may be formed from the headword by adding the construct suffix *-n* together with the stem vowel shown in the following parentheses. Irregular construct nouns are spelled out fully in the parentheses.

bao.	6(*bawūn, bawōn*).	Bird.
m̧anit.	6(*m̧antin*).	Custom.
koot.	6(*-i*).	Goat.

These portions of three different entries show the following construct forms: *bawūn* or *bawōn* 'bird of', *m̧antin* 'custom of', and *kootin* 'goat of'.
Code 7. This means that the DIRECTIONAL POSTPOSITIONS (MRG 3.4.3) may be used following the headword when it is used as a verb in one of its Code 2 forms. The three postpositions are:

tok	**teq**	'hither'
waj	**waj**	'toward you'
ļǫk	**ļaq**	'thither'

kōkajoor.	2, 7.	Excursion.
lukor.	2(inf, tr *-e*), 7.	A food.
m̧m̧ōkaj.	2(inf, tr *-e*), 7.	Precede.

These portions of three different entries show the possibility of forming sentences such as the following:

Kwōn lukor tok kijerro.
'Make some *lukor* for us.'

Koņro eņm̧ōkaj waj bwe eboñ.
'The two of you go on ahead before it gets dark.'

Kōmro ar kōkajoor arļǫk.
'The two of us took an excursion to the shore.'

Codes 8 and 9. These mean that the COMPARATIVE and SUPERLATIVE POSTPOSITIONS respectively *ļǫk* 'more' and *tata* 'most' (MRG 3.4.4) may be used following the headword when it is used as a stative verb.

kūk. 1(*-i*), 2, 3, 8, 9. Unripe.

This portion of an entry shows the possibility of forming sentences such as the following:

Ekūk ļǫk mā ņe jān mā e.
'That breadfruit is less ripe than this one.'

Ekūk tata mā eņ.
'That breadfruit is the ripest.'

Code 10. This code is used to show special PERFECTIVE (MRG 3.4.4) forms of certain headwords. (Perfective verbs are a special type of stative verb.)

pinej. 2(inf, tr (*-e*)), 10(*penjak*). Conceal.

This portion of an entry shows that *pinej* may be used as an infinitive or as a transitive verb (with an optional *e* at the end of the transitive form), and it also shows the related perfective verb *penjak.* The following two sentences illustrate the transitive and perfective verbs:

Ear pinej m̧aanū.
'He obstructed my view.'

Epenjak wa eo.
'The boat is out of sight.'

Code 11. This code is used to show special ADJECTIVAL forms of STATIVE verbs (MRG 3.4.4). These forms are used within noun phrases, coming in the position after the noun they modify but before the demonstrative that belongs with the noun.

bat. 2, 11(*batbōt*). Slow.

This portion of an entry shows that the headword may be used as a (stative) verb (Code 2), and that it has the special postpositional form *batbōt* (Code 11). Following is an example sentence for each:

Ebat wa eņ.
'That canoe is slow.'

Kwōlo ke wa batbōt eņ?
'Do you see that (very) slow canoe?'

Combination Codes. Occasionally the grammatical key shows two code numbers connected by a plus sign:

baru. 3, 6(*-i*), 3+7. Crab.

The 3+7 code indicates that this word may be followed by the directional postpositions *tok*, *ļǫk*, or *waj* (signified by Code 7) only if the word is also preceded by the causative prefix (signified by the Code 3): *kōbaru tok* 'find and bring crabs'. Following is an example of a grammatical key containing several combination codes:

bale. 3, 4+3, 5(*bbalele*), 3+7, 5+8, 5+9. Starry flounder.

The forms signified by each of these codes are as follows:

3	*kōbale*	'fish for starry flounder'
4+3	*rūkōbale*	'flounder fisherman'
5	*ebbalele* (W)	'teeming with flounder'
	bōbalele (E)	'teeming with flounder'
3+7	*kōbale tok*	'catch and bring flounder'
5+8	*ebbalele ļǫk*	'more plenteous in flounder'
5+9	*ebbalele tata*	'most plenteous in flounder'

The 4+3 code indicates that the person prefix *ri-* (*rū*) (Code 4) combines with *bale* only when the causative prefix *ka-* (*kō-*) (Code 3) is also combined. (The numbers are combined with pluses in the code in the same order as their respective prefixes occur in the word: the 4 prefix precedes the 3 prefix.) The 3+7 code means the same as it does for *baru* above. The 5+8 and 5+9 codes indicate that the comparative (Code 8) and superlative (Code 9) postpositions are used only with the distributive (Code 5) form of *bale*.

4. The Sounds of Marshallese

The letters used to show the sounds of the language and spell the words in this dictionary are listed here in the alphabetical order used in the dictionary. It is the same order used in English dictionaries, except that a letter with a mark follows the same letter without a mark. A brief phonetic description and a phonetic symbol are given for the sound of each letter, followed by several example words. (The term LIGHT is used to describe consonants that are pronounced with the body of the tongue in an "at rest" position for such consonants; the term HEAVY is used for consonants that have the back of the tongue raised (velarized) and the root of the tongue retracted (pharyngealized) so as to elongate the oral cavity, thereby giving the consonant a "heavier" or "darker" sound. The rounding referred to is that of the lips. This and the other phonetic terminology are explained in greater detail in MRG 2.)

a	a low back unrounded vowel	[ɑ]	*at* *bat* *ta*	'hat' 'slow' 'what?'
ā	a low front vowel	[æ]	*āj* *māj* *pā*	'thatch' 'eye' 'arm, hand'
b	a heavy bilabial stop	[bᵚ]	*ba* *bwe* *ob*	'say' 'because' 'chest'
d	a light retroflex trill	[ɹ]	*di* *addi* *ad*	'bone' 'finger' 'our'
e	a mid front vowel	[e] or [ɛ]	*ae* *ae* *nen* *ded*	'gather' 'current' 'a tree' 'size'

i	a high front vowel	[i]	*ip* *nin* *ni*	'crooked' 'pound' 'coconut'
j	a light dental stop or affricate	[t^{y}] or [c]	*jañ* *bajjek* *m̧aj*	'cry' 'just' 'eel'
k	a velar stop, unrounded or rounded	[k] or [k^{w}]	*ke* *kwe* *akki* *bōk* *bok*	'porpoise' 'you' 'fingernail' 'bring, take' 'sand'
l	a light lateral	[l^{y}]	*leddik* *pālle* *al*	'girl' 'Caucasian' 'sing'
ļ	a heavy lateral, unrounded or rounded	[l^{ɯ}] or [l^{w}]	*ļaddik* *ļwe* *ļōļļap* *ļōļ* *toļ*	'boy' 'pond' 'old man' 'moldy' 'mountain'
m	a light bilabial nasal	[m^{y}]	*maañ* *am*	'pandanus leaf' 'our'
m̧	a heavy bilabial nasal	[m^{ɯ}]	*m̧aan* *m̧weo* *kōm̧m̧an* *am̧*	'front' 'the house' 'make, do' 'your'
n	a light dental nasal	[n^{y}]	*ne* *enno̧* *en*	'leg, foot' 'taste good' 'let him'
ņ	a heavy dental nasal, unrounded or rounded	[n^{ɯ}] or [n^{w}]	*ņe* *eņņōjņōj* *ņo̧b* *eņ* *tōņ* *toņ*	'that' 'cracking sound' 'popping sound' 'that' 'ton' 'tune'
ñ	a velar nasal, unrounded or rounded	[ŋ] or [ŋ^{w}]	*ña* *aeñwāñwā* *iññā* *añ* *boñ*	'I' 'clamor' 'yes' 'wind' 'night'
o	a mid back rounded vowel	[o] or [ɔ]	*oror* *jojo* *jojo* *rūkōbbaoo* *roro*	'fence' 'chick' 'flying fish' 'chicken thief' 'chant'

ǫ	a low back rounded vowel	[ɒ]	*ǫǫj* *kǫǫt* *jǫ*	'horse' 'steal' 'start'
ō	a mid back unrounded vowel	[ə] or [ʌ]	*ōrōr* *ō* *tōōļ* *ļōļō* *aō* *aō*	'cut in strips' 'lionfish' 'comb tooth' 'wreathe' 'my' 'swim'
p	a light bilabial stop	[pʸ]	*pata* *ippān* *jaap*	'war' 'with him' 'red snapper'
r	a heavy retroflex trill, unrounded or rounded	[rᵚ] or [rʷ]	*rōk* *rot* *rorror* *ar*	'south' 'kind' 'to bark' 'lagoon beach'
t	a heavy dental stop	[tᵚ]	*tata* *etto* *atat*	'very' 'long ago' 'wear a hat'
u	a high back rounded vowel	[u]	*um̧* *kuum̧* *bu*	'earth oven' 'comb' 'gun'
ū	a high back unrounded vowel	[ɯ]	*ūrōj* *būb* *būbū*	'bother' 'trigger fish' 'grandchild'
w	a rounded velar glide	[w]	*wiwi* *jowan* *uwi*	'blubber' 'lazy' 'delicious'
y	an unrounded palatal glide	[y]	*yiō* *yokwe* *yuk*	'year (*iiō*)' 'aloha (*iǫkwe*)' 'you (*eok*)'

Note: The last letter is used in only a few words, such as those given as examples.

Phonemic Transcription. The actual structure of a word is often better portrayed by the phonemic transcription, which appears in boldface type enclosed in parentheses immediately following each headword. The details of the relation between the phonemic transcription and the spelling are given in MRG 2, but the main differences are the following:

a. The phonemic transcription shows the semiconsonants that are omitted from the usual spelling, and thereby brings out more clearly how words containing them have the same pattern as words containing full consonants at the same places:

jāje.	**jayjęy.**	Sword.
rarō.	**rahręh.**	Clean an area.

pǫpo.	**pawpęw.**	Bind.
eǫeo.	**yawyęw.**	Lash.
bakbōk.	**bakbęk.**	Knife.

Thus the first four words above as spelled in the first column do not appear to have the same consonant-vowel pattern as the fifth word, whereas in the phonemic transcription in the second column they do.

b. The phonemic transcription shows each vowel phoneme in just one way, rather than with the three different letters that may be used to spell it. Thus all five words above have the same vowel phoneme in their first syllables, and the same (but different from that of the first syllables) vowel phoneme in their second syllables. This is shown clearly in the phonemic transcription, while three different letters (*ā*, *a*, *ǫ*) are used to spell the vowel phoneme in the first syllable, and three other letters (*e*, *ō*, *o*) are also used to spell the vowel phoneme in the second syllable. This is because when all the consonant and semiconsonant phonemes are fully specified, as they are in the phonemic transcriptions, the front, back, and rounding distinctions between various vowel letters turn out not to be significant. They can be predicted according to Tables 4, 5, and 6 in MRG.

The phoneme:	*stands for the letters:* (*front*)	(*back*)	(*rounded*)
i	*i*	*ū*	*u*
e	*e*	*ō*	*o*
a	*ā*	*a*	*ǫ*

c. The phonemic transcription shows one additional vowel phoneme not shown in spelling, the **ę** phoneme, which is spelled the same as the **e** phoneme:

The phoneme:	*Example words:*		
ę	*ke*	*aō*	*to*
e	*ke*	*aō*	*to*

These example words are shown below together with their phonemic transcriptions and English translations:

ke **kęy** 'porpoise'	*aō* **hahęh** 'my'	*to* **tęw** 'get off'
ke **key** 'yes or no?'	*aō* **haheh** 'swim'	*to* **tew** 'rope'

Thus the reader who wants to know whether any *e*, *ō*, or *o* in the spelling stands for the mid or high-mid vowel should look at the phonemic transcription to see whether or not the **e** is marked. If it is, the vowel has the sound of one of the words in the first row; if not, it has the sound of one of the words in the second row.

d. The rounded consonants (except for some *w*'s) are spelled with the same letters as their related heavy consonants. Their rounding is shown by either a preceding or following rounded vowel letter (*u*, *o*, or *ǫ*) or by a following *w*. In the phonemic transcription, they are differentiated as follows:

Unrounded (heavy) phoneme:	Spelled:	Rounded phoneme:	Spelled:
k	*k*	**q**	*uk, ok, ku, ko, kw*
g	*n̄*	**g°**	*un̄, on̄, n̄u, n̄o, n̄w*
ŋ̧	*ŋ̧*	**ŋ̧°**	*uŋ̧, oŋ̧, ŋ̧u, ŋ̧o, ŋ̧w*
ļ	*ļ*	**ļ°**	*uļ, oļ, ļu, ļo, ļw*
r	*r*	**r°**	*ur, or, ru, ro, rw*

e. The phonemic transcription uses entirely different letters in a few cases: **g** for *n̄*, and **q** for rounded *k*, as can be seen in the preceding chart.

5. Place Names

More than 3,000 names of islets, land tracts, and other named entities in the Marshall Islands are included in a special section at the end of this volume. These were collected by students at the Marshall Islands Intermediate School under the supervision of Byron W. Bender in 1957 at the request of E. H. Bryan, Jr., of the Bishop Museum. The names collected were later analyzed in Bender 1963*b*, where they were classified as to whether or not they had some meaning in addition to being the name of a geographical entity. The various types of meanings found in that analysis are given together with the names in this dictionary, in abbreviated form.

Four main types were found, beginning with those that were completely grammatical and meaningful on the one hand, and shading off into those that were completely unanalyzable and meaningless on the other. The abbreviations used for these four types are:

Gramm.	Fully grammatical and meaningful.
Recur. form.	Contains recurring formants, but not fully meaningful.
Reminisc. gramm.	Reminiscent of grammatical constructions, but not fully meaningful.
Unanalyz.	Unanalyzable and meaningless, except for being the name of a place.

Examples of fully grammatical names are *M̧ōnōbbō* 'house of spear fishing at the edge of the reef', *M̧ōn-ekkōn̄* 'house of the *Terminalia litoralis* tree', and *Jabōn-bar* 'end of the rock'.

Several subtypes of the general grammatical category are also indicated with the following abbreviations:

Gramm. distort.	Grammatical and meaningful, but with some distortion in the form of the word.

Pers. name.	Meaningful, involving the name of a person.
Loan.	Meaningful, involving a loanword borrowed from another language.

Examples of distorted names are *M̧win-kipin-pat* 'house of the bottom of the swamp', which has vowel sounds changed from the fully grammatical *M̧ōn-kapin-pat, M̧ōnikkūn̄* 'house of the *Terminalia litoralis* tree' but with the last two vowel sounds changed (compare with the unchanged fully grammatical example above); and *Jabwe-ņo* 'end of the waves' and *Jabwi-ņa-eņ* 'end of that shoal', in which the word for 'end of' has archaic forms rather than the *jabōn* that would be the grammatical form in the present-day language. Examples of place names that involve the name of a person are *M̧ōttam̧ōj* (from *M̧ōn-Tam̧ōj*) 'house of Thomas', *M̧ōn-Waju* 'house of Waju'; a number that are recognizable as the names of famous or legendary persons: *Jebro̧, Jiruullōn̄, Jemaluut;* and others that are recognizable as the names of persons because they contain the *Li-* or *Ļa-* person prefixes (MRG 3.1.1): *Limarpe, Limādbōb, Lim̧wijlo̧k, Ļan̄i-daan, Ļajo̧utoļ, Ļajum̧aat,* etc. Examples of borrowed names include *Jotōm̧* 'Sodom', *Jerea* 'Syria', *Jinai* 'Sinai', *Jipein* 'Spain', *Jiruujlem* 'Jerusalem', *Julu* 'the Sulu sea', etc.

Examples of words that contain recurring formants that are less than fully meaningful include the following: *M̧wi-tete, Teteļabuk, Teteļan̄-rak, Tiete,* and *Tiete-eņ,* all of which contain the formant *tete* or *tiete*, which probably once meant something but no longer does. A similar example includes *Pieo, Pieoļe-eņ, Pienļwe, Pienmej, Pienm̧ōn, Piiooļļe, Piiooņļwe-rālik,* etc., all of which include the recurring formant *pieo* or *pien*.

One subtype of the recurring formant category is labeled as:

Part. recur. form.	Contains recurring formants, but only partially so, or with them combined in an unusual way.

Examples of this sort include *Buoj-kōp*, with the recurring formant *buoj*, but with the remainder of the word uncertain in identification, possibly coming from *kōpkōp* 'struggle'; *Kobūkōr*, in which the last part of the word is identical to the name of a variety of pandanus (*Būkōr*), but which does not especially make sense together with the *ko-* 'you are' subject pronoun; and *M̧ōtbaru*, which can be identified as *m̧ōt* 'what house?' and *baru* 'crab' which do not make sense when combined in this way.

Examples of the third major type, those which are reminiscent of grammatical constructions, but are not fully meaningful, include the following: *Kepin-le*, reminiscent of *kapin ļwe* 'bottom of the pond'; *Lo̧n̄lon̄*, reminiscent of *lan̄lōn̄* 'joy'; *M̧ōn-kure*, reminiscent of *m̧ōn ikkure* 'house of play'; *M̧wil-lukubwe*, reminiscent of *em̧ ilo kūbwe* 'house in the feces'; *M̧ōllokmar*, reminiscent of *em̧ ilukōn mar* 'house in the middle of the bushes'; and *Reo*, reminiscent of *erreo* 'clean'.

One subtype of the reminiscent category is labeled as:

Part. reminisc. gramm. Reminiscent of a grammatical construction, but only partially so, or with unidentifiable formants.

This is the last subcategory in which any shade of meaning may be seen, and all other names not in it or one of the preceding categories have been labeled "unanalyzable." Examples of the partially reminiscent category include: *Denikden*, reminiscent of *dān i kiden* 'water at the *Messerschmidia* tree'; *M̧an̄in-bōōt*, with the first part possibly meaning 'pate of'; *Penial̦*, with the last part identical to the word for 'road'; *M̧win-kipillo*, 'house at the bottom of the *lo*', with no clear meaning for the last syllable.

There has of necessity been some indeterminacy in the assigning of all the intermediate categories, between those labeled "grammatical" and those labeled "unanalyzable." On the one hand there is danger of reading into a name meanings that were never there, the process known as "folk etymologizing," and on the other hand one hopes not to lose sight of meanings that have become obscured through changes in the language or changes in the pronunciation of the names. The authors have tried to steer a middle course in this matter, but many of their decisions are deserving of some questioning.

An attempt has been made to provide possible translations for the names. The reader should be careful not to accept as certain the translations given for names that are not labeled as grammatical. Translations given for names labeled as containing recurring formants (or as being only reminiscent of the grammar of the language) are nothing more than educated guesses as to what these names might have meant originally.

6. Flora, Fauna, and Stars

The authors have attempted to be as inclusive as possible with respect to the names of plants and animals of the Marshalls, and to be as accurate as possible with respect to their scientific identification. In carrying out both these aims they have had the kind assistance of a number of specialists. Of most help with respect to plant names has been Professor Benjamin C. Stone of the Department of Botany at the University of Malaya, who began his fieldwork with the plants of the islands, especially pandanus, in 1955, as a graduate student at the University of Hawaii, when he was soon given the affectionate title "L̦abōb", Mr. Pandanus, by the people with whom he worked. Most of the plant identifications are taken from a manuscript "A Short Dictionary of Marshallese Plant Names" provided by Professor Stone while he was at the University of Guam (then the College of Guam) in 1964. In it he indicates that the botanical names were taken from a manuscript prepared by Dr. Harold St. John of the University of Hawaii, "Checklist of Marshallese Plants," a compilation from the literature and a record of his original exploration. Professor Stone also notes that "as in every language, there are cases where the same name applies to more than one species of plant; further, there are numbers of species which have received no precise Marshallese name. These last for the most part are weeds, introduced plants, or inconspicuous plants, especially the lower orders—fungi, lichens, etc."

The other main source for plant names and plant identifications is the handbook compiled by teachers and students at the Marshall Islands Intermediate School (Takeuchi 1959). The sources for this work in turn included Anderson (1950), Neal (1948), Taylor (1950), and Fosberg (1955).

Concerning pandanus, Professor Stone (personal communication) has the following to say:

> All the pandanus cultigens known in the Marshall Islands belong to one of two botanical species, *Pandanus fischerianus* Martelli (abbr. P. f.) or *Pandanus carolinianus* Martelli (abbr. P. c.). Even these two could reasonably be regarded as merely forms of a single species, to which the first name should apply. They are in turn very closely related to *Pandanus tectorious* Park. ex Z. For a full botanical discussion and classification of pandanus in the area, see Stone (in press).

Identification of land vertebrates was done with the help of Marshall (1950). Birds were identified chiefly by A. Binion Amerson, Jr., research biologist with the Pacific Ocean Biological Survey Program of the Smithsonian Institution in 1968. Dr. Amerson brought to Hawaii various frozen and mounted specimens from the northern atolls and worked with Bender and various Marshallese persons in Hawaii at that time to correlate the scientific names with the Marshallese names.

Identification of fish was accomplished primarily by DeBrum, using illustrated volumes available in the Pacific Collection of the University of Hawaii Library. Other fish identifications were taken primarily from Goo and Banner (1963). Shells were identified primarily by Mr. Kanchi Ibbino of Arno Atoll while he was in Hawaii in 1973, using Kira (1962) and Habe (1964).

Star and constellation identifications are based almost entirely on Erdland (1910), even though they are at variance with some modern-day identifications made by amateur astronomers. Erdland had the assistance of several of the most knowledgeable navigators of four generations ago, and his identifications are internally consistent. However, it should be noted that even then Erdland found differences among the experts he consulted.

7. Finding Words in the Dictionary

Many words in the language are not listed as the headword of an entry. In general only the simplest and most basic form of a group of grammatically related words has been chosen to serve as the headword of the entry that covers them all. The more complex words that are formed by adding affixes or by reduplication are shown in the grammatical key of the entry, and some are exemplified in the sentences given. For example, the following words are all included in the entry that has the headword *ttā*:

1. *ettāū, ettāim̧, ettāin*, etc.	'my, your, his, etc. lowness (W)'
tōtāū, tōtāim̧, tōtāin, etc.	'my, your, his, etc. lowness (E)'

2. *ettā, rōttā,* etc.	'it is short, they are low, etc.'
3. *kōttā*	'cause to be low'
kōttāik	'cause something to be low'
4. *rūttā*	'lowly person'
6. *ettāin*	'lowness of (W)'
tōtāin	'lowness of (E)'
8. *ettāḷǫk*	'lower'
9. *ettātata*	'lowest'
11. *ettāte*	'low (postposition) (W)'
tōtāte	'low (postposition) (E)'

The numbers preceding the examples are those that appear in the grammatical key of the entry to refer to the various forms.

The changes in form that will give a dictionary user the most trouble are those that occur at the front end of a word. These are of three main types: (a) the addition of a prefix to the headword, (b) a double consonant at the beginning of the headword, and (c) words that begin in **w** or **y**. The first two types are illustrated above: the (2) forms of *ttā* involve subject pronoun prefixes such as *e-* and *rō-*, and the (3) forms involve the causative prefix, which has the form *kō-* with this word. And since the headword *ttā* begins with the double consonant *tt*, there are different W and E forms for (1), (6), and (11).

7.1. The Causative Prefix ka-, kā-, ke-, kō-, kǫ-. If a word that cannot be found in the dictionary begins with a *k* and one of the above vowel sounds, there is a good possibility that the *k* and the vowel are a prefix which has been added to the basic form of the word, which follows. This prefix often has the meaning 'to cause to' or 'to cause to be', and is thus called "the causative prefix":

deḷǫn̄	'enter'	*kadeḷǫn̄*	'cause to enter; put in'
wōtlǫk	'fall'	*kǫwōtlǫk*	'cause to fall'
būroṃōj	'sorrow'	*kabūroṃōj*	'cause to be sad; sadden'
ememej	'memory'	*keememej*	'remember'
jerbal	'work'	*kōjerbal*	'use'
dik	'small'	*kadik*	'make small'

Since many words like those in the second column are not listed as headwords in the dictionary, they must be found by looking for the word without the prefix, the form in the first column. An entry with a headword like one of those in the first column will have grammatical Code 3 if it can form a word together with the causative prefix, and the 3 will be followed by any special information about the causative form, if there is more than one form, or if it is irregular in some way. Quite often the entry will also contain an example sentence illustrating a use of the causative form.

Some causative forms double the first consonant of the headword. For example, there are two causative forms for *deḷǫn̄* 'enter':

> *Iar kaddeḷǫn̄ aō ṃaak ilo pāān̄.*
> 'I deposited my money (indefinite amount) in the bank.'

Iar kadeļo̧n̄ m̧aak ko aō ilo pāān̄.
'I deposited my money (definite amount) in the bank.'

If one is trying to find the first form (*kaddeļo̧n̄*) in the dictionary, it will be necessary to remove both the causative prefix and the first *d* (*kad-*) and look for the word under the remainder (*deļo̧n̄*). As part of the entry headed by *deļo̧n̄*, one finds the following: 3(inf *kaddeļo̧n̄*, tr *deļo̧n̄*). This means that the first form is the causative infinitive (used to refer to an indefinite object), and the second is the causative transitive form (used for definite objects).

7.2. *Other prefixes.* Another common prefix has the shape *ri-*, *rū-*, or *ru-* as in *rieo̧n̄ōd* 'fisherman', *rūkaki* 'teacher', and *ruwa* 'sailor', and is used to form these and other PERSON NOUNS (MRG 3.1.4). Only a few of the most common such nouns are listed as headwords, and the number 4 in the Grammatical Key labels other words that can have this prefix added to form person nouns. Thus if a person noun cannot be found under the letter *r* including the prefix, it can probably be found by looking for the remainder of the word, without the prefix. Since a number of person nouns have their first consonant doubled when this prefix is added, it may be necessary to look under the single consonant. For example, *rūttariņae* 'soldier' will be found under *tariņae*, not under *ttariņae*.

The other derivational prefixes of the language do not form as many different words as do the causative and person prefixes, and the authors have attempted to include all words containing these prefixes as headwords to their own entries. Such prefixes include the negative prefix *ja-* (or *j* plus another vowel) (MRG 3.4.6) as in *jowan* 'lazy', the instrumental (MRG 3.4.7) *le-* as in *leinjin* 'use an engine', and the provisional (MRG 3.4.12) *ņa-* as in *ņakijen* 'to feed'.

7.3. *Double Consonant Words.* There are many words that begin with *i* or *e* followed by a double consonant in the pronunciation of the Rālik dialect, such as *illu* 'angry' or *em̧m̧an* 'good', for example. In the pronunciation of the Ratak dialect, these same words do not begin with *i* or *e*, but have the identical consonants separated by a vowel: *lilu*, *m̧ōm̧an*. Instead of listing each of these words at two different places in the dictionary, under *i* or *e* for the Rālik pronunciation, and under the consonant that appears twice for the Ratak pronunciation, they have been listed only once under the CONSONANT that appears twice, but in a form that is not exactly like either pronunciation. The form used as the headword contains the letters that are common to both the Rālik and Ratak pronunciations, but omits the vowels that are different. Thus *em̧m̧an* and *m̧ōm̧an* can both be found under *m̧m̧an*, and *illu* and *lilu* under *llu*, just as in the example above the entry for *ettā* and *tōtā* was headed by *ttā*. This same dialect-neutral form is also used in example sentences so that readers of either dialect can give the word their customary pronunciation.

There is an additional complication for some Rālik users of the dictionary concerning words that begin with ROUNDED double consonants, as for example the words which are pronounced and written *kukure* 'play' and *kokwaļ* 'sennit' in the Ratak dialect. Some Rālik speakers spell the first word *ikkure* and other spell it *iukkure*, inserting an extra *u* before the *k*'s to show how the vowel changes its sound before these rounded consonants. Similarly, for the second word, some Rālik speakers spell it *ekkwaļ* and others spell it *eokkwaļ*, inserting an *o*. Rālik speakers attempting to look up such words must ignore not only the *i* or *e* at the beginning, but the *u* or *o* that follows as well. Thus these two words are listed under *kkure* and *kkwaļ*. However, the Rālik dialectal spellings that follow such headwords contain the extra *u*'s and *o*'s as they were put there by the computer following the spelling conversion rules.

The most common pattern for forming distributive verbs (MRG 3.4.5) involves the doubling of the first consonant and reduplicating the final syllable of a word. Most such distributives are not given as headwords, but are listed under the form without consonant doubling or reduplication. Thus a word such as *kkijdikdik* (W: *ikkijdikdik*, E: *kūkijdikdik*) 'teeming with rats' will be found together with the Grammatical Key Code 5 under *kijdik*. Thus it is a good general rule to look for any word with double consonants under the single consonant if it cannot be found under the double.

7.4. Words That Begin in **w**. Many words that begin with the **w** phoneme and have *u, ū, o, o̧,* or *ō* as the first vowel have often been spelled in two different ways, with or without the *w*:

wōnm̧aanļo̧k	or	*onm̧aanļo̧k*	'go forward'
wōrwōr	or	*oror*	'fence'
wūtdikdik	or	*utdikdik*	'to sprinkle'

The tendency has been to write the *w* when the next consonant in the word is light, but to omit the *w* when the next consonant is heavy:

Light Second Consonant		Heavy Second Consonant	
wōp	'a tree'	*ob*	'chest'
wōj	'toward you'	*otobai*	'motorbike'
wōmak	'to duck'	*um̧*	'earth oven'
wōn	'who'	*oņān*	'its price'
wūllepān	'his uncle'	*uļūtļūt*	'plump'
wūddik	'tiny'	*urur*	'flame'
		ok	'net'
		on̄	'homesick'

This is the pattern that has been followed for the headwords in this dictionary, although other common spellings and cross references are given for the common exceptions to the pattern. [The **w** phoneme has generally been written before all the other vowels (*i, e, ā,* and *a*) regardless of the second consonant.] Thus, if a word beginning with **w** cannot be found under *w*, the reader should look under *o*, *ǫ*, or *u*. If a word often spelled with *o* or *u* at the beginning cannot be found under these vowel letters, the reader should look under *wo-*, *wō-*, *wu-*, or *wū*.

7.5. Words That Begin with **y**. The **y** phoneme at the beginning of words is generally not shown in writing before the vowels *i*, *e*, or *ā*. Before *u* and *ū* it is written as an *i*, and before *o*, *ǫ*, *ō*, and *a* it is written as an *e*, as in *iu* 'coconut apple', *iiūn̄* 'yes', *eo* 'the', *eǫr* 'carve', *eō* 'me', and *eakeak* 'skin ulcer'. When the **y** phoneme is at the beginning of a word before *a* (or *ā*), there have been some differences in spelling practices, although the most common pattern has been to show the **y** as an *e* preceding the *a* when the next consonant is heavy (but not rounded), and to write the *a* as an *ā* when the next consonant is light:

Heavy Second Consonant		Light Second Consonant	
eaab	'no'	*ām*	'to tip'
eake	'about it'	*āj*	'weave'
ean̄	'north'	*āne*	'islet'
eaḷ	'coconut milk'	*āl*	'shave'

Two exceptions to this pattern are words in which the second consonant is *r* or *t*, as in *ār* 'lung' and *āt* 'name', where even though *r* and *t* are heavy consonants, the light pattern of the second column is followed. There is also some tendency not to follow this pattern when the second consonant is *k*, (a heavy consonant), as in *ākil* 'to peel' and *ākūt* 'delouse'. The pattern is usually followed if the *k* is at the end of the word or followed by another consonant, but *ā* is often written when a vowel follows. This is well illustrated by the spellings of the two pronunciations of the transitive verb meaning 'to unload something': *eaktuwe* vs. *ākūtwe*. The best rule to follow in looking for words that begin in **ya** is to look in both places: under *ā*, and under *ea*. (And although many such words have also been spelled with simply *e* [as in *elikin* vs. *ālikin* 'after'], the reader should remember to look for them under *ā* or *ea* in this dictionary.)

7.6. Vowel Changes. Finally, some problems in locating words may be caused by changes in vowel letters brought about by the use of new vowel letters such as *ǫ* and *ū*, or by the more regular use of letters such as *ā* for the sounds they stand for. The reader may be thinking of the causative prefix in its basic shape of *ka-* and not be thinking of how its vowel sound changes before a word such as *wiin* 'to win' to form a word such as *kǫwiinin* 'award'. Or the reader may not think of how its sound changes before the number *emān* 'four' to give *kein kāāmān* 'the fourth'.

Such changes usually involve a move of one square to the right or left (or up or down) in the basic vowel chart of the language (MRG 2.2), and it may be well to keep this chart in mind as a means of remembering possible vowel changes.

	Front		Back: Unrounded		Back: Rounded
High	*i*	⟷	*ū*	⟷	*u*
	↕		↕		↕
Mid	*e*	⟷	*ō*	⟷	*o*
	↕		↕		↕
Low	*ā*	⟷	*a*	⟷	*o̧*

The examples given above of the causative prefix show right-left change among the low vowels. The third person plural subject pronoun prefix of verbs, which varies between *re-*, *rō-*, and *ro-*, is an example of right-left change among the mid vowels, as in *reitok* 'they come', *rōm̧m̧an* 'they are good', and *rokkut* 'they are close together'. The person prefix which varies between *ri-*, *rū-*, and *ru-* as discussed in section 7.2 is an example of left-right change among high vowels.

Change between high and mid vowels is caused by several of the rules of the language discussed in MRG 2.4.3. Examples of different forms of the same word with changes caused by these rules are *pet-piten* 'pillow', *ōn-ūnen* 'nutrition', and *ob-ubōn* 'chest'. Change between mid and low vowels is caused by several other rules, especially the low-vowel dissimilation rule (MRG 2.4.5), as shown by the following pairs: *māj-mejān* 'eye', *bar-bōran* 'head', and *ļo̧n̄-ļon̄an* 'canoe roller'. Because of these many possible changes, it is well to try to find a word one is looking for with a neighboring vowel in the chart if it cannot be found containing the first expected one.

8. The English Finder List

The list of English words in the second main section of this dictionary was compiled by computer by tagging key English words in the translations and definitions given for Marshallese words in the first section. It can be of help in two main ways.

First of all, it can help the reader find the Marshallese words that might be used to translate a given English word. It can also help find a familiar word that cannot be remembered at the moment if the general meaning of the word is remembered. In either event, it serves to help find a Marshallese word in the Marshallese-English section.

The list was also compiled with another type of user in mind, the student of Marshallese culture interested in seeing the total set of vocabulary associated with important topics of life in the islands. Such readers can find pulled together in one place many of the words associated with subjects such as fish and fishing methods; breadfruit, pandanus, and coconut culture; other plant names; games; winds, tides, sailing terms, canoe parts; foods, smells, and so forth. These groupings present an avenue to the culture of the islands through the words of its language.

BIBLIOGRAPHY

Anderson, D. 1950. The plants of Arno Atoll, Marshall Islands. Unpublished SIM (Studies in Micronesia) report. Used by Takeuchi as source for plant identifications.

Bailey, Charles-James N. 1967. Transformational outline of Marshallese syntax. Unpublished M.A. thesis. University of Chicago.

Bender, Byron W. 1963*a*. Marshallese phonemics: Labialization or palatalization. Word 19:335–341.

______. 1963*b*. A linguistic analysis of the place-names of the Marshall Islands. Unpublished Ph.D. dissertation. Indiana University. (Available on microfilm from University Microfilms, Ann Arbor, Michigan.)

______. 1968. Marshallese phonology. Oceanic Linguistics 7:16–35.

______. 1969. Spoken Marshallese. Honolulu: University of Hawaii Press.

______. 1976. Marshallese Reference Grammar. Honolulu: The University Press of Hawaii.

Carr, Denzel. 1945. Notes on Marshallese consonant phonemes. Language 21:267–270.

[Carr, Denzel, and Samuel H. Elbert.] 1945. Marshallese-English and English-Marshallese dictionary. 14th Naval District, District Intelligence Office, Marshall-Gilbert Area: United States Navy Department, vol. 30, no. 136, 121 pp. Mimeographed. Notes on pronunciation and grammar in introduction. 4000 entries.

English-Marshallese Dictionary. [c. 1963.] [Kwajalein, Marshall Islands.] xvii, 164 pp. No title page. Contains abbreviated entries from Carr and Elbert, English-Marshallese section. Introduction contains one-page table of sounds and selected entries grouped topically: adjectives, verbs, numbers and time, animals and insects, etc. Hawaiian and Pacific Collection, University of Hawaii Library.

Erdland, August. 1906. Wörterbuch und Grammatik der Marshall-Sprache nebst ethnographischen Erläuterungen und kurzen Sprachübungen. Berlin: Reimer. x, 247 pp. German-Marshallese 1–71 (3500 entries), Marshallese-German 73–180 (5000 entries), ethnographic notes 181–191, grammar 193–228, language practice 229–247. The New York Public Library.

______. 1910. Die Sternkunde bei den Seefahrern der Marshall-Inseln. Anthropos 5:16–26.

[Feeney, Thomas J., S. J.] [c. 1952.] [Likiep, Marshall Islands: Catholic Mission] 306 pp. No title page. Mimeographed. Contains entries from Marshallese-English section of Carr and Elbert, with some modifications, and some additional entries, especially of a religious nature.

Fosberg, F. R. 1955. Northern Marshall Islands expedition, 1951–52. Atoll Research Bulletin 38. 36 pp. Washington: Pacific Science Board. Used by Takeuchi as source for plant identifications.

Goo, C. C., and Albert H. Banner. 1963. A preliminary compilation of Marshallese animal and plant names. Honolulu: University of Hawaii, Hawaii Marine Laboratory.

Grace, George W. 1969. A Proto-Oceanic finder list. Working Papers in Linguistics 1:39–84. Honolulu: University of Hawaii, Department of Linguistics.

Habe, Tadashige. 1964. Shells of the Western Pacific in color. Osaka: Hoikusha.

Howells, William. 1973. The Pacific islanders. xvi, 299 pp. London: Wiedenfield and Nicolson.

Kira, Tetsuaki. 1962. Shells of the Western Pacific in color. Osaka: Hoikusha.

Ko, Young Kuk, 1962. The segmental phonemes of Marshallese including spectrographic study of the vowels. Unpublished M.S. thesis. Georgetown University.

Kotzebue, Otto von. 1821. Voyage of Discovery in the South Sea . . . 1815–18. 3 vols. London: Longmans.

Kroeber, A. L. 1911. Phonetics of the Micronesian language of the Marshall Islands. American Anthropologist 13:380–393.

Marshall, Joe T. 1950. Vertebrate ecology of Arno Atoll, Marshall Islands. Unpublished SIM (Studies in Micronesia) report 6.

Mason, Leonard E. 1947. The economic organization of the Marshall Islands. Typescript. Honolulu: U.S. Commercial Company.

Mason, Leonard [and Samuel H. Elbert]. 1952. Anthropology-geography study of Arno Atoll, Marshall Islands. Atoll Research Bulletin 10. 21 pp. Washington: Pacific Science Board.

Matsuoka, Shizuo. 1929. Study of the language of the Marshall Islands. 267 pp. Tokyo: Kyodo Kenkyusha.

Neal, Marie Catherine. 1948. In gardens of Hawaii. Honolulu: Bishop Museum. Used by Takeuchi as source for plant identifications.

Nida, Eugene A. 1952. Report on orthographic problems in Marshallese. Unpublished M.S. thesis. New York: American Bible Society.

Smith, Alfred G. 1951. Wahween jibehhleh kajin Marshall [Guide to Marshallese spelling]. Mimeographed. Department of Education, Office of the High Commissioner of the Trust Territory of the Pacific Islands.

Spoehr, Alexander. 1949. Majuro: A village in the Marshall Islands. 265 pp. Fieldiana, Anthropology 39. Chicago Natural History Museum.

Stone, B. C. (in press). The wild and cultivated pandanus of the Marshall Islands. Monographiae Phanerogamarum. Lehre, Germany: J. Cramer.

Takeuchi, Clarence E. 1959. Handbook of Marshallese plant names. Majuro: Education Department.

Taylor, C. R. H. 1965. A Pacific bibliography. 2nd ed. xxx, 692 pp. London: Oxford University Press.

Taylor, W. R. 1950. Plants of Bikini and other Northern Marshall Islands. Used by Takeuchi as source for plant identifications.

Tikjinere-Dictionary: Kajin Majōl & Kajin Iñlij: Marshallese & English. 1968. Kwajalein, Marshall Islands: Kwajalein Education Committee. xxxix, 170 pp. Content identical to introductory and Marshallese-English sections of Carr and Elbert, except for addition of preface by chairman of Kwajalein Education Committee which states that discrepancies and questions of original text copy were resolved by Rev. Jude Samson. Hawaiian and Pacific Collection, University of Hawaii Library.

Tobin, J. E. 1952. Land Tenure in the Marshall Islands. 36 pp. Atoll Research Bulletin 11. Washington: Pacific Science Board.

Tsuchida, Shigeru. 1965. Velarization in Marshallese. Unpublished M.S. thesis. Honolulu: University of Hawaii.

Wiens, Herold J. 1962. Atoll environment and ecology. xxii, 532 pp. New Haven: Yale University Press.

______. 1962*a*. Pacific island bastions of the United States. v, 127 pp. Princeton: Van Nostrand.

MARSHALLESE-ENGLISH DICTIONARY

aa- (**haha-**). Also *a-* (**ha-**). 1. Belonging to; possessive classifier, alienable objects and general possessive.

aaet (**hhayẹt**). Also *aet.* Yes; dialectal variant of *iññā* (**yiggay**) and *iiūñ* (**'yiyig**).

ab in et (**hab yin yẹt**). Also *aabinet* (**hhabinyẹt**). Idiom. But what can I do. *Ab in et ñe edike eok.* But what can I do if she doesn't like you.

aba (**habah**). From Engl. Harbor; anchorage; port. *Eṃṃan tata aba eṇ iarin Likiep.* Likiep has the best anchorage.

abba (**habbah**). From Japn. *happa*. 2(inf, tr *-ūk*), 4, 6(*-i*), 7. Dynamite. *Eerbooj ear abbaiki pedpedin Ānewātak.* The air force was dynamiting the Eniwetak reef.

abbwilōñlōñ (**habbilegleg**). Variant form of *aploñloñ* (**hapleg°leg°**).

abja (**habjah**). Archaic. 1(*-a*). Peculiarity; habit; principle.

abjāje (**habjayjẹy**). 1(*-i*), 2(inf, tr *-ik*, *abjāik*), 3, 4. Carry tucked under arm.

abje (**habjey**). 1(*abjei-*), 2, 3(inf, tr *abjeik*), 4, 5(*aabjeje, abbōjeje*). Flirting; shy; bashful. *Eabbōjeje.* She's bashful.

abḷajtiiñ (**habḷajtiyig**). From Engl. *everlasting.* 3, 6(*-i*). A plant, *Gomphrena globosa.*

abṇōṇō (**habṇehṇeh**). 1(*-i*), 2(inf, tr *-ik*), 3(inf, tr *-ik*), 4, 5(*aabṇōṇō*). Nervous; upset; disturbed; uncomfortable; bothered; nagged; gripe; complain. *Ta ṇe kwōj abṇōṇō eake?* What are you complaining about? *Iabṇōṇōik an mmakijkij an itok.* I am disturbed at how often he comes.

abor (**habẹr°**). 1(*-i*), 2, 3(inf *kaaborbor,* tr *kaabore*), 11(*aborbor*). Impeded; encumbered.

abọ (**habaw**). 1(*-i*). Fender; hood; cowling.

abōb (**habẹb**). Dial. E, W: *abwin* (**habin**). 2. Refuse; hate; decline. *Iabōb in roñ aṃ jañ.* I hate to hear you cry.

abōbbōb (**habẹbbẹb**). Also *eabōbbōb* (**yahabẹbbẹb**). 3. Hurry; quickly.

abōblep (**habẹblep**). Dial. W, E: *ṃakokolep* (**ṃakẹwkẹwlep**). 2, 3(inf, tr *-e*), 6(*-i*), 7, 8, 9, 11(*abōblep*). Always refuse. *Āinwōt baj tipen ḷaddik abōblep men ṇe.* That boy looks like the stubborn type.

abōḷ (**habeḷ**). From Engl. 3. Apple.

Abōḷ (**habeḷ**). 6(*-i*). A plant, banana variety.

abōn (**haben**). 1(*abōna-*). Spiritual power. *Ekajoor wōt abōnān rūanijnij eo.* The sorcerer has such great powers.

abōne- (**habene-**). 1, 6. Characteristics.

abōṇtọun (**habeṇtawin**). From Engl. *up and down*. 1(*-i*), 2(inf, tr *-i*), 3, 4. Teeter-totter; see-saw.

abwin (**habin**). Dial. W, E: *abōb* (**habẹb**). 2, 4. Refuse; dislike to do.

abwin bōk (**habin bek**). Reject. *Ear abwin bōk ṃōñā.* He rejected food.

abwinmake (**habinmakẹy**). 1, 2, 3(st inf *kaabwinmakeke,* tr *kaabwinmakeik*), 4, 5(*aabwinmakeke, abbinmakeke*). Afraid of ghosts; fear of being alone in the dark or at sea. *Ekaabwinmakeke wūleej in.* This graveyard is eerie.

abwinmakelep (**habinmakẹylep**). 2, 6(*-i*), 8, 9. Great fear of ghosts and the dark.

ad (**had**). Ours; our, inclusive; our soul.

ad (**had**). Archaic. Cloud formation or star; associated with storms. *Ad eṇ an Tiṃur.* A cloud formation signifying an approaching storm.

Ad (**had**). A star; Arcturus in Bootes; fourthborn of *Lōktañūr.*

addeboulul (**haddebewilwil**). 1(*-i*), 2, 3, 4. Rotate; whirl; dizzy; giddy; reel. *Iaddeboulul im iṃōḷañḷōñ.* I'm dizzy and nauseated. *Kwōn jab addeboulul bwe kwōnaaj ṃōḷañḷōñ.* Don't whirl around or you'll get dizzy.

addemlōkmej (**haddẹmlẹkmẹj**). Archaic. Inalienable rights or property. *Bwidej ko ad rej addemlōkmej.* Our land belongs to us until death.

addi (**haddiy**). 1(*-i*). Finger; toe; shell of larger clams.

addi-dik (**haddiy-dik**). 1(*-i*), 6(*-i*). Pinky; little finger. *Edik jān addi dikū.* It's smaller than my little finger.

addi-eoḷap (**haddiy-yewḷap**). 1(*-i*). Middle finger.

addi-kọọtot (**haddiy-kawatwẹt**). 1(*-i*). Index finger.

addi-lep (**haddiy-lep**). 1(*-i*), 6(*-i*). Thumb; big toe. *Addi lepin peiū.* My thumb. *Addi lepin neō.* My big toe. *Addi lepū.* My thumb (or big toe).

addikdik (**haddikdik**). 2(inf, tr *-i*), 4, 6(*-i*), 7. Look out of the corner of the eye; covet; squint. *Ej addikdiki eok.* She's looking at you out of the corner of her eye. *Ej addikdiki waj ņe aṃ.* He's got his eyes on your watch.

addimej (**haddimẹj**). 1(*-i*), 2, 3(inf *kaaddimejmej*), 4, 5(*addimejmej*). Feeble; lethargic; chronically sickly. *Eļap an ļadik eņ addimejmej.* That boy is sickly. *Kwōn jab kaaddimejmej eō.* Don't bother me.

addiṃakoko (**haddiṃakẹwkẹw**). Also *addiṃakoko* (**haddiyṃakẹwkẹw**). 1(*-i*), 2(inf, tr *-ik*), 3(inf, tr *-ik, -uk*), 4, 7, 8, 9. Lethargic; uneasiness; sluggishness; dullness (of people); listless, melancholy. *Eļap an bwil rainin im kaaddiṃakokoik eō.* It is so hot today it gives me a lethargic feeling. *Eļap aō addiṃakoko rainin im iabwin jerbal.* I'm sluggish today and don't feel like working.

adebdeb (**hadẹbdẹb**). 1(*-i*), 2(inf, tr *adibwij(i)*), 4, 7. Move something closer by using a stick; prodding. *Ļeo ej adebdeb waini.* He is moving copra nuts with a stick. *Ļeo ej adibwij waini eo.* He is moving the copra nut with a stick.

aded (**haded**). Also *aded* (**hadẹd**). 3, 6(*-i*). Clam shell, large; small *Tridacna.*

aden (**haden**). Archaic. Old word related to *addi.*

adenpe (**hadenpẹy**). Variant form of *arōnpe* (**harenpey**).

adibwij (**hadibij**). Transitive form of *adebdeb* (**hadẹbdẹb**).

adik (**hadik**). Archaic. First quarter of the moon.

adipā (**hadipay**). Also *addipā* (**haddipay**). A fish.

adpā (**hadpay**). 2, 6(*-i*), 7. Strut of a rooster. *Etke kwōadpā?* Why do you strut?

aduwado (**hadiwadew**). 1(*-e*), 2(inf, tr *-ok*), 3, 4, 7. Carry in a basket with long handle slung over shoulder; kind of basket. *Kwōn aduwadouk bōb e.* Put this pandanus in the basket and carry it.

ae (**hayẹy**). 1(*-i*), 2(inf, tr *ain*), 4, 7. Gather; collect; pool. *Kwōn ae waini.* Gather coconuts. *Kwōn aini waini kaņe.* Gather those coconuts. *Jen aini ṃani kein ad im wiaiki juon injin.* Let's pool our money to buy an engine.

ae (**hayey**). 1(*-i*), 2. Current. *Eae lọjet.* There is a current in the ocean.

aear (**hayeyhar**). Also *aewaar* (**hayewahar**). 1(*-i*), 2, 3. Current flowing into lagoon.

aebōj (**hayẹbẹj**). Rain water; a well; drinking water.

aebōj jimeeņ (**hayẹbẹj jimeyeņ**). Cistern.

aebōj laļ (**hayẹbẹj laļ**). Well water.

aebōjbōj (**hayẹbẹjbẹj**). 1(*-i*), 2, 3(inf, tr *-e*), 8, 9. Tasteless; not salty.

aejek (**hayẹjẹk**). 2(inf, tr *-e*), 4, 6(*-i*), 7. Fishing method, using surrounding net on dark nights. *Eban jab jeraaṃṃan ad eọñōd ilo aejekin ibwijtok.* We're bound to be lucky when we fish with a surrounding net on a dark night with the tide coming in.

aejemjem (**hayẹjẹmjẹm**). Also *aejemjem* (**hayejemjem**). 1, 2, 6(*-i*). Powerful in speech; persuasive; weighty in words; articulate. *Eaejemjem an irooj eņ naan.* That chief carries power in his words.

aejet (**hayẹjẹt**). Surface of the ocean. *Waan tulọk eņ ewaļọk i aejet.* The submarine is surfacing.

aekijek (**hayekijẹk**). Currents around a passage.

aekōrā (**hayekeray**). Canoe part, foot of sail, edge fastened to the boom.

ael (**hayel**). 3, 4+3, 6(*-i*), 3+7. A fish, unicorn fish, *Hepatus olivaceus* Schneider Bloch; a fish, orange spot tang, *Acanthurus olivaceus.*

aelaļ (**hayeylaļ**). Vulgar. 1(*-i*), 2(inf, tr *-e*), 4. Sexual act; movement of hips during sexual intercourse; women only.

aelbūrōrō (**hayelbirehreh**). A fish.

aelel (**hayẹlyẹl**). 1(*-i*), 2, 3, 6(*-i*). Smell of fish, lingering on hands, body, or utensils.

aelellaļ (**hayelellaļ**). Also *aelellọļ* (**hayelellaļ°**). 1, 2(inf, tr *-e*), 3, 4, 6(*-i*), 8, 9. Covet another's spouse, steal another's spouse; expectant; impetuous; uncontrolled desire. *Ļeetao ear aelellaļe Jemāluut.* Etao stole Jemaluut's wife. *Kwōjab* *aelellaḷ bwe kwōnāj jorrāān.* Control your lust before it ruins you. *Kadik ḷọk aṃ aelelḷọḷ.* Don't be too expectant. *Jab aelelḷọḷe bwe enaaj kọọle eok.* Better not fool around with his wife or he'll put a spell on you.

aelik (**hayelik**). Also *ailik* (**hayilik**). 1(*-i*), 2, 3. Current flowing out. *Kōjro kaaelik im jerak.* Let's wait for the current to flow out to set sail.

aelmeej (**hayelmeyej**). A fish, surgeonfish, *Acanthurus nigricans.*

Aelok (**hayẹlẹq**). 3, 6(*-i*). A plant, *Pandanus carolinianus* cultigen (Majuro). (Stone). Majuro, etc.

aelor (**hayẹlẹr°**). Also *allor, llor.* 1(*-i*), 2, 3, 5(*aelellor*). Shade. *Eḷap an aelellor iuṃwin wōjke eṇ.* It's very shady under that tree. *Pād ilo aelor ṇe.* Stay in that shade.

aelọk (**hayelaq**). 1(*-i*), 2, 3, 4. Hidden; obscure; invisible. *Ej jab aelọk.* It's quite obvious.

aelōñ (**hayẹlẹg**). 4. Land; country; island; atoll.

Aelōñ-kein (**hayẹlẹg-kẹyin**). From "these islands". 4. A plant, banana variety (Takeuchi).

aelōñin kiiñ (**hayẹlẹgin kiyig**). 4. Kingdom. *Aelōñin kiiñ ñan aelōñin kiiñ rōnaaj juṃae doon.* Kingdom shall rise against kingdom.

aelōñin pālle (**hayẹlẹgin palley**). From "land of the white man". 4. Europe; America; foreign country.

aelōñin-lañ (**hayẹlẹginlag**). 4. Heaven.

aemed (**hayẹmẹd**). 1(*-i*), 2, 3, 6(*-i*). Coolness; shade. *Eḷap an aemed iuṃwin mā eṇ.* It is quite shady beneath that breadfruit tree.

aemedḷọk (**hayẹmẹdḷaq**). 1(*-i*), 2, 3. Cool of the evening. *Kōjro kōttar an aemedḷọk im etal.* Let's (the two of us) wait for evening (until it cools off) to go.

aemọkkwe (**hayemaqqẹy**). Also *ḷodekā* (**ḷewdekay**). 1, 2, 7, 8, 9. Always following people around. *Kwōj aemọkkweik eō ñan ñāāt?* When are you going to stop following me around?

aeṃaan (**hayeṃahan**). 1(*-i*). Canoe part, edge of sail fastened to the gaff; back of a fish.

aeṃṃan (**hayeṃṃan**). 3. Good current; period between tides. *Kōjro kaaeṃṃan im jerak.* Let's wait for a good current to set sail.

aeṃōḷọḷo (**hayẹṃẹḷẹwḷẹw**). Also *aiṃōḷọḷo* (**hayiṃẹḷẹwḷẹw**). From *ṃōḷo* (**ṃẹḷẹw**) "cold". 1(*-i*), 2, 3(inf, tr *-uk*), 6(*-i*). Coolness; cool air. *Epaak an kwōj bwe ejjino aeṃōḷọḷo.* It'll freeze soon for it's beginning to get cool. *Eḷap an aeṃōḷọḷo mejatoto in jota.* The air is very cool in the evening.

aen (**hayen**). From Engl. 1(*-i*), 2(inf, tr *-(e)*), 3, 4, 6(*-i*), 7. Iron.

aeniñeañḷọk (**hayeynigyagḷaq**). Also *aeniñaḷọk* (**hayenigahḷaq**). 1(*-i*), 2, 3. Current flowing northward.

aenōṃṃan (**hayẹnẹṃṃan**). 1(*-i*), 2, 3, 6(*-i*), 8, 9. Peace; peaceful; pacified. *Kiki aenōṃṃan.* A peaceful sleep. *Kwōn kaaenōṃṃane.* Pacify him. Please quiet the baby.

aeṇak (**hayeṇak**). 1(*-i*), 2, 3, 4, 6(*-i*), 8, 9. Dripping wet; drenched to the skin.

aeñwāñwā (**hayeg°ayg°ay**). 1(*-i*), 2, 3(inf, tr *-ik*), 4, 6(*-i*). Chatter; gabble; clamor; noise; row; turbulence; turmoil. *Eḷap an aeñwāñwā ajri raṇ.* Those children are awfully noisy.

aeo (**hayew**). Archaic. Lower sides of back, kidney area.

aepedped (**hayepedped**). Also *aepādpād* (**hayepadpad**), *aipādpād* (**hayipadpad**). 1(*-i*), 2, 3, 4. Hesitate; procrastinate; be slow to decide; delay; tarry.

aepokpok (**hayẹpẹqpẹq**). 1(*-i*), 2(inf, tr *-e*), 3, 8, 9. Complex; complicated. *Eaepokpok wūn eo.* That was a complex mathematical problem. *Kwōn jab kōaepokpoke aṃ kōmḷeḷe.* Don't complicate your explanation.

aer (**hayẹr**). 1(*-i*), 2, 3(st inf *kaaerer,* tr *kaaer*). Tight; stretched; pressure; possessive. *Eḷap an aer jedọujij e aō.* My trousers are too tight. *Kwōn jab kaaerer (kōkkaaerer).* Don't be so possessive.

aer (**hayẹr**). Theirs. *Ta ṇe kwōj ba aer kake?* Why do you say it's theirs?

aer (**hayer**). Variant form of *aerā* (**hayeray**).

aerar (**hayerar**). 1(*-i*), 2, 3, 5. Yellow or brown leaves; scorched.

aerā (**hayeray**). Also *aer* (**hayer**). 1(*aera-, aerāi-*). Shoulder.

aerār (**hayeryar**). Touch shoulders. *Kwōn jab aerār ippa.* Don't touch shoulders with me.

aerār (**hayeryar**). Dialectal variant of *kōtkōt* (**ketket**).

aere (**hayẹrẹy**). A storm.

aereañ (**hayẹryag**). Dial. W, E: *aermān* (**hayẹrman**). Also *aerjeañ* (**hayẹrjeyag**). Theirs (four persons).

aerin bōtōktōk (**hayẹrin betektek**). Blood pressure.

aerjeañ (**hayẹrjeyag**). Variant form of *aereañ* (**hayẹryag**).

aerjeel (**hayẹrjẹyẹl**). Dial. W, E: *aerjel* (**hayẹrjẹl**). Theirs (three persons).

aerjel (**hayẹrjẹl**). Dialectal variant of *aerjeel* (**hayẹrjẹyẹl**).

aermān (**hayẹrman**). Dialectal variant of *aereañ* (**hayẹryag**).

aerṃwe (**hayẹrṃẹy**). 2(inf, tr *-ik*), 3, 4, 5(*aerṃweṃwe*), 6(*-i*). Taking care of relatives. *Kōjparok ṃantin Ṃajeḷ im jeḷā aerṃwe.* Preserve the Marshallese custom of taking care of your relatives by practicing it. *Ij aerṃweiki.* I'm treating him like a relative should.

aerōkeañḷọk (**hayeyrẹkyagḷaq**). Also *aerōñaḷọk* (**hayerẹgahḷaq**). 3. Current flowing southward.

aerro (**hayẹrrew**). Theirs (two persons).

aerwōj (**hayẹrwẹj**). Theirs (five or more persons).

aet (**hayẹt**). 2, 3(inf, tr *-e*), 6(*-i*), 7, 8, 9. Current. *Eaete ḷọk kōrkōr eo ñan lik.* The current drifted the canoe out to the ocean side.

aetak (**hayetak**). 1(*-i*), 2, 3. Current flowing eastward.

aeto (**hayẹtẹw**). 1(*-i*), 2, 3. Current flowing westward. *Eḷap an kajoor aeto in.* This easterly current is quite strong.

aeto (**hayẹtẹw**). 1, 2, 3, 4. Haunted; spooky; dreary. *Eḷap an aeto wūleej eṇ.* That graveyard is very spooky.

aetok (**hayeteq**). Dial. W, E: *aitok* (**hayiteq**). 1(*-a*), 2, 3(inf *kaaettoktok*, tr *kaaetok(e)*), 8, 9, 11(sg. *aetoktok*, pl. *aettok*). Long; tall; length. *Ḷeeṇ ear kaetokḷọk wa eṇ.* He made the canoe longer. *Eṃōj kaetoktok nuknuk iiō in.* This year's dresses have been lengthened.

aetọ (**hayetaw**). 4, 6(*-a*). Small islets of an atoll; name of a section of some atolls, usually the windward, northeast part. *Ij etal ñan aetọ kaṇ.* I'm going to those small islets.

aetōktōk (**hayẹtẹktẹk**). 6(*-i*). Stalk of arrowroot plant; drinking straw made from *aetōktōk; male arrowroot, of no food value.*

aetōl (**hayẹtẹl**). Variant form of *iāetōl.*

aewaar (**hayewahar**). Variant form of *aear* (**hayeyhar**).

aewanlik (**hayewanlik**). Archaic. 2, 3, 6(*-i*). Good in fishing, expert in fishing. *Ḷōḷḷap eṇ jemāmro eaewanlik.* My father-in-law is an expert fisherman.

aia (**hayyiyah**). Also *aiio* (**hayyiyẹw**). Slang. Interjection: "Good grief!"; "Nuts!"

aiaea (**hayiyahyah**). Slang. Interjection: dismay.

aibooj (**hayibẹwẹj**). Glory.

aiboojoj (**hayibẹwẹjwẹj**). 1(*-i*), 2, 3, 4. Glorious; splendid; marvelous; pretty; gorgeous; lovely; magnificent; wonderful.

aidik (**hayidik**). Also *ainiñ* (**hayinig**). 1, 2, 3(inf *kaaidikdik*, tr *kaaidik(i)*), 6(*-i*), 8, 9, 11(sg. *aidikdik*, pl. *aiddik*). Skinny; thin of body; narrow. *Eaidik mejān.* He has slanted eyes. *Liṃaraṇ rej kaaidikdik.* The women are reducing.

aij (**hayij**). Also *aej* (**hayẹj**). From Engl. 2(inf, tr *-i*), 3, 6(*-i*). Ice; frost. *Kōjro etal in kaaej.* Let's the two of us go get ice. *Aiji dān ṇe limed.* Put ice in the drinking water. *Kwōn ṃōk aiji bōra bwe en jab bbōj.* Would you press some ice cubes to my head to prevent swelling?

Aij (**hayij**). A plant, pandanus variety.

aij kudiiṃ (**hayij qidiyiṃ**). Also *aej kudiim* (**hayẹj qidiyim**), *aij kudiim* (**hayij qidiyim**), *aej kudiiṃ* (**hayẹj qidiyiṃ**). 1(*-i*), 2, 3, 4, 6(*-i*). Ice cream.

aijo (**hayijẹw**). A plant with a single leaf. *Aijoon kino.* A fern with one leaf.

aik (**hayik**). 3, 6(*-i*). Cedar driftwood. *Jen etal in kaaik.* Let's go and look for cedar driftwood.

aik (**hayik**). 1, 2(inf, tr *-e*). Tow, as a boat; pull; draw. *Kwōn aike booj eṇ.* Tow that boat.

aikiu (**hayikiyiw**). From Japn. *haikyuu*. 1(*-i*), 2(inf, tr *-uk*), 4, 7. Share food equally; ration. *Jenaaj aikiuuk ṃōñā e* *bwe aolep en ṃōñā.* We shall share this food equally so everyone can eat. *Aikiu eo aṃ ṇe.* That's your ration.

aikiu (**hayikiyiw**). Slang. 6(*-i*). A food, soup, spongy coconut and arrowroot.

aikne (**hayikney**). Archaic. On the north side of; see *eọọtle.*

aikuj (**hayiqij**). 1, 2(inf, tr *-i*), 4, 6(*-i*), 7. Desire; need; lack; must; deserve; necessity; necessary; obligated; should. *Iaikuj in etal.* I must go. *Kwōaikuj ṃōñā.* You need food. *Ej aikuj or oṇeaṃ.* You deserve some reward.

aikūtōkōd (**hayikiteked**). A fish.

aililōk (**hayiliylẹk**). 2(inf, tr *-e*), 7. Accompany; go around with; associate with. *Jab aililōk rinana bwe kwōnaaj jorrāān.* Don't go around with bad company for you'll get into trouble. *Kwōn jab aililōke ḷadik eṇ bwe kwōnāj po ilo rinana kaṇ an.* Don't associate with that boy or his bad manners will rub off on you.

ailparo (**hayilparew**). Also *ailparok* (**hayilpareq**). Cumbersome; troublesome; burdensome; very busy; work overtime.

ailparok (**hayilpareq**). Variant form of *ailparo* (**hayilparew**) and *parok* (**pareq**).

ailuwannañnañ (**hayiliwwannagnag**). Dial. Bikini only. Clamor, noise. *Pikinni ailuwannañnañ.* Bikini, the land of noisy people.

ailwaro (**hayilwarew**). Variant form of *airuwaro* (**hayiriwarew**).

aiḷip (**hayiḷip**). 2, 3(inf *kaaiḷḷip*, tr *kaaiḷip(i)*), 6(*-i*), 8, 9, 11(sg. *aiḷipḷip*, pl. *aiḷḷip*). Thick, of long and round objects.

ain (**hayin**). Transitive form of *ae* (**hayẹy**).

ainbat (**hayinbat**). From Engl. 1(*-i*), 2(inf, tr *-e*), 4, 6(*-i*). Iron pot; cooking utensil. *Iar ainbat bōb.* I was cooking (boiling) pandanus. *Iar ainbate juon bōb.* I was cooking (boiling) one pandanus (fruit).

ainikie- (**hayinikiye-**). 1, 2. Voice; sound; noise; melody.

ainikien bōklōkōt (**hayinikiyen bẹklẹkẹt**). Voice of conscience. *Roñjake ainikien aṃ bōklōkōt.* Follow the dictates of your conscience.

ainikien Etao (**hayinikiyen yetahwew**). Echo.

ainiñ (**hayinig**). Also *aidik* (**hayidik**). 1(*-i*), 2, 3(inf *kāiniñiniñ*, tr *kāiniñ*), 8, 9, 11(sg. *ainiññiñ*, pl. *ainniñ*). Thin; narrow. *Eḷap aṃ ainiñ ñan joñan aitok ṇe aṃ.* You are too thin for your height. *Liṃaraṇ rej kaainiññiñ.* The women are on a diet.

ainṃak (**hayinṃak**). 6. Leaves near pandanus stem; portion of fruit near stem of pandanus or breadfruit. *Enana ainṃakin bōb.* The pandanus keys near the stem are not good (to eat).

aintiin (**hayintiyin**). From Engl. *iron tin.* 1(*-i*), 2(inf, tr *-i*), 4, 7. To boil pandanus; cook in a tin pan; cook in a sea biscuit container. *Kwōn aintini bōb kaṇe bwe ren pidodo ad wōdwōd.* Boil those pandanus so that they will be soft for us to chew.

aiṇokko (**hayiṇeqqew**). From Japn. *ainoko.* Mixed blood; mixed ancestry.

aio (**hayyiyẹw**). Variant form of *aia* (**hayyiyah**).

aire (**hayirey**). 2, 6(*-i*). Tornado.

airuwaro (**hayiriwarew**). Also *ailwaro* (**hayilwarew**). 1(*-i*), 2, 3(inf, tr *-uk*), 4. Confusion; trouble; noisy; quarreling; conflict. *Eḷap airuwaro ilo kuḷab eṇ.* There's a lot of fighting at the club.

ait (**hayit**).. Sew together a rip in cloth; tackle someone, pulling their knees together like ripped cloth.

aitok (**hayiteq**). Dialectal variant of *aetok* (**hayeteq**).

aitwerōk (**hayitwẹyrẹk**). Also *aitwe.* 1(*-i*), 2(inf, tr *-e*), 3, 4, 6(*-i*). Compete; contest; dispute; conflict; controversy. *Eḷap an kar kumi in iakiu ko aitwerōk.* The baseball teams had a highly disputed game. *Elōñ rej aitwe doon kōn elōn men ko.* There are many who compete among themselves for many things.

aitwōnmej (**hayitwẹnmẹj**). 1, 2, 6(*-i*). Atmosphere in which death is certain. *Ealikkar an pojakin jako bwe eaitwōnmej.* He is ready to go as death broods over him.

aj (**haj**). 1, 3. Liver; spleen; seat of bravery. *Ejjeḷok ajin.* He is not brave.

aj (**haj**). 3, 6(*-i*). Thatch. *Liṃaro rej kōmaañ ajin ṃweo.* The women are looking for pandanus leaves to thatch this house.

aj (**haj**). Also *booraj* (**bewerhaj**). From Engl. *hatch*, *fore hatch*. Hatch. *Rej kiil aj kaņ an wa eņ bwe ewōt.* They are closing the hatches on that ship because it's raining.

ajaj (**hajhaj**). 1(*-i*), 5(*ajaje*). Calf of leg; substance of clam shell; hard rock; marble.

ajañ (**hajag**). Archaic. Place where birds, fish, or clams gather.

ajādik (**hajadik**). 1(*-i*), 2, 3, 4, 5(*ajjādikdik*), 7. Walk slowly; sneak. *Kwōn ajjādikdik ļok bwe ren jab lo eok.* Walk away very softly and slowly so they don't notice you. *Kwōn ajādik ļok bwe ren jab lo eok.* Walk away slowly so they don't notice you. *Kōjeañ ajādik.* Let's be on our way. *Rej ajjādikdik ļok kiiō.* They're sneaking up now.

ajāl (**hajal**). 2(inf, tr *-e*), 4, 6(*-i*), 7. Round up fish or animals. *Raar ajālitok ek ko ñan me eo.* They rounded up the fish into the trap.

ajāllik (**hajallik**). 6(*-i*). Consequence; result; aftermath; offshoot. *Enāj lo ajāllikin jab pokake.* He'll find out the result of disobedience.

Ajbwirōk (**hajbiyrȩk**). 3, 6(*-i*). A plant, *Pandanus fischerianus* cultigen.

aje (**hajȩy**). 4, 6(*-i*). Drum. *Eṃṃan ajein Ṃajeļ.* Marshallese drums are good.

aje (**hajey**). 1(*-i*), 2, 4, 7. Give away without remuneration; devote presents to the gods; dedicate; offer. *Koṃwin ajeļọk mour ko ami ñan Anij.* Dedicate your lives to God. *Jijej ear aje mour eo an ñan kōj.* Jesus offered his life for our salvation.

ajeeded (**hajeyedyed**). 1(*-i*), 2, 3(inf, tr *-e*), 7, 8, 9. Dispersed; scattered; see *jeeded*.

ajej (**hajyȩj**). 1(*-i*), 2(inf, tr *-e, -i*), 4, 6. Divide; distribute. *Kwōn ajeji ṃōñā kaņe.* Divide up that food.

ajej in kabwebwe (**hajyȩj yin kabȩybȩy**). From *ajej* (**hajyȩj**) "divide", *kabwebwe* (**kabȩybȩy**) "to fool". 2(inf, tr *-ik*), 4, 6(*-i*). Gyp. *Ear ajej in kabwebweik eō.* He gypped me.

ajejin Jowa (**hajyȩjin jewwah**). Be an Indian giver, supposed to be typical of members of the Jowa clan; give as present and ask for its return.

ajejin Ļōktab (**hajyȩjin ļektab**). Be an Indian giver; give as present and ask for its return.

ajeļkā (**hajeļkay**). 1(*-i*), 2, 3(inf *kaajeļkākā*, tr *-ik*), 4, 5(*aajeļkākā*). Weak feeling, usually from hunger; stiffness of a corpse.

ajeļļā (**hajeļļay**). Also *eojaļ*. Archaic. A pile of corpses or fish or people.

ajerre (**hajȩrrȩy**). Archaic. Work alone.

ajerwawa (**hajerwahwah**). 1(*-i*), 2, 3(inf *kaajjerwawa*, tr *kaajerwaik*). Openings in a house causing drafts. *Kwōn jab kaajerwawaik ṃwiin.* Don't let a draft into this house. *Ejjeļọk ajerwawa in ṃwiin.* This house is full of holes.

ajet (**hajet**). 2(inf, tr *-e*), 3, 6(*-i*). Drift nut, sweet smelling, used with coconut oil to make perfume. *Kwōn ajete pinneep ņe.* Put *ajet* in that coconut oil.

ajet (**hajet**). From Engl. *acid.* 2, 5(*ajete*), 6(*-i*), 8, 9. Acid; acidity. *Eajet penkō ņe.* That vinegar has already become acid. *Eajete penkō ņe.* That vinegar is acidic.

aji (**hajiy**). From Japn. *hashi*. Chopsticks. *Ijaje ṃōñā kōn aji.* I don't know how to use chopsticks.

ajilowōd (**hajiylewwed**). 2. Herd of bonitos that enters lagoon and can't find its way out. *Koṃwin kōttar an ajilowōd im aļeļeiki.* Wait till it's lost it's way before breaking out the *aļeļe*.

ajjādikdik (**hajjadikdik**). 2, 4, 6(*-i*), 7. Tiptoe; sneak. *Ear ajjādikdiktok em kailbōk eō.* She tiptoed up to me and startled me.

ajjen (**hajjen**). Hand of bananas; bunch of pandanus keys.

ajjibanban (**hajjibanban**). 1, 2(inf, tr *-e*), 3, 6(*-i*), 8, 9. Be overburdened; weighted down, of people only; to lug. *Eajjibanban kōn pāāk in waini eo.* He was weighted down with a sack of copra.

ajjikad (**hajjikad**). 1, 2(inf, tr *-e*), 4. Throw stones repeatedly at an object or person.

ajjiļapļap (**hajjiļapļap**). 1(*-i*), 2, 3, 4. Smell, body odor, disagreeable; rotten (of wood). *Eļap an bwiin ajjiļapļap.* He smells like rotten wood.

ajjimālele (**hajjimaylęylęy**). Also *kajjimālele.* 2, 4, 6(*-i*), 7. Talk of something one is not certain about; predict something and thereby cause it to happen. *Einwōt iļak lale kwōj ajjimālele.* You sound as if you're not sure of what you're saying. *Kwōn jab kajjimālele bwe enaaj wōt.* Don't say it will rain, or it will.

ajjim̧aalal (**hajjim̧ahalhal**). Also *ajjim̧alm̧al* (**hajjim̧alm̧al**). 1(*-i*), 2, 3(inf, tr *-ōk*), 4. Sway back and forth; nod; dizzy.

ajjinono (**hajjinewnew**). Also *ajjinono* (**hajjinęwnęw**). 1, 2, 6(*-i*), 7. Whisper; talk very quietly. *Kwōn ajjinono bwe ekiki baba.* Speak softly for my father is sleeping.

ajjipek (**hajjipęk**). 6(*-i*). Best part of pandanus fruit reserved for chiefs. *Daan irooj ajjipek. Ajjipek* is for chiefs.

ajjiwewe (**hajjiyweywey**). Archaic. 2, 3, 6(*-i*), 7. Sneak out. *Erro ar kōm̧ad eō innem ajjiwewe ļǫk ñan m̧ōn kadek eo.* They got me distracted and then sneaked out to the bar.

ajjuknene (**hajjiqneyney**). 1, 2, 3(inf, tr *-ik*), 4, 6(*-i*), 7. Hop on one foot; stand on tiptoes. *Ear ajjuknene em alwōj.* He stood on tiptoes in order to see. *Ear kaajjukneneik ļadik eo.* He made the boy hop around on one foot.

ajjukub (**hajjiqib**). Also *ajukub* (**hajiqib**), *ajukuk* (**hajiqiq**), *ajjukuk* (**hajjiqiq**), *ajjukok* (**hajjiqęq**). 1(*-i*), 2, 3, 4. Limp.

Ajjuunun (**hajjiwinwin**). Archaic. Legendary turtle.

ajjuur (**hajjiwir**). Hut; lean to. *Ajjuur eo im̧ōrro e.* Here is our hut.

ajļǫk (**hajļaq**). 2, 3(st inf *kaajļǫkļǫk,* tr *kaajļǫk*), 6(*-i*), 8, 9. Regret; recall with grief. *Jab kǫkkure am̧ jikuuļ bwe kwōnaaj ajļǫk.* Do not be careless about your schooling or you'll regret it.

ajokļā (**hajeqļay**). Dial. E, W: *ākā* (**yakay**). Heap of stones; mound of stones; trap for crabs; see *jokļā.*

ajokļā (**hajeqļay**). Archaic. Either end of an island. *Iar lo an kadkad ajokļā iōñ.* I saw him throw-netting at the northern end of the island.

Ajoļ (**hajeļ°**). 3, 6(*-i*). A plant, pandanus cultigen; Ebon atoll. N.F.

ajoļjoļ (**hajeļ°jeļ°**). 1(*-i*), 2(inf, tr *-e*), 3, 4. Gnaw. *Kijdik eo ej ajoļjoļe bōb eo.* The rat is gnawing the pandanus.

ajorm̧aan (**hajer°m̧ahan**). 2, 5(*ajorm̧aane*), 6(*-i*). Exceptionally big fish. *Juon eo koņa ajorm̧aan.* I hooked an exceptionally big fish.

ajri (**hajriy**). 1(*-i*), 2, 3(inf *kaajjiriri,* tr *-ik*). Child; kid; toddler.

ajriin uwaak (**hajriyin wiwahak**). Dial. W, E: *jiliktūr* (**jiliktir**). Idiom. 2. Rely on children to accomplish errands or chores. *Ejerata ļokwan an jerbal kōn an kijoñ ajriin uwaak.* Whatever he does always gets fouled up in the end because he relies on child help.

ajwewe (**hajweywey**). Also *ajjowewe* (**hajjeweywey**). 1(*-i*), 2(inf, tr *-ik*), 4, 6(*-i*), 7. Whistle; whistling, long continued. *N̄e ij etetal ilo marok eitok wōt bwe in ajwewe.* When I walk in the dark I have to whistle.

ak (**hak**). Dial. W, E: *akō* (**hakeh**). But; or.

ak (**hak**). Also *toorlōñ* (**tewerlęg**). 3, 5(*ake*), 6(*-i*). A bird, great frigate bird, *Fregata minor*; a bird, lessor frigate bird, *Fregata ariel.*

akade (**hakadęy**). Also *akajok, alekǫ.* Dial. W, E: *jende* (**jęndęy**). 1, 2(inf, tr *-ik*), 4. Watch birds to locate roost; roosting place of birds; rookery; to watch patiently. *Kwaar akadeik ke bao ko?* Did you watch the birds locating their roost?

akadik (**hakadik**). New building; new canoe.

akaje (**hakajey**). From Japn. *hakase (hakushi)* "expert, knowledgeable, scolar, holder of doctorate". Renowned; V.I.P. *Ia eo akaje eo eetal ie ļǫk?* Where did the V.I.P. go?

akajin (**hakajin**). 3, 4+3, 5(*-i*), 6(*-i*), 3+7, 5+8, 9. A fish, bass, *Plectropomus truncatus.*

akajok (**hakajeq**). Also *akade, alekǫ.* 1, 2(inf, tr *-e*), 4. Watch birds alight to locate roost. *Jen ilān akajoki ak kaņ bwe en kab pidodo ad jjǫñ.* Let's go locate the frigate birds' roost so we can easily catch them tonight.

akake (**hakhakey**). Also *aō kake* (**haheh kahkey**). 1(*-i*), 2, 3, 4. Tow while swimming; hold up from water.

akā (**hakay**). 1(*-i*), 2, 3(*kaakā, kaakāik*), 4, 5(*akeke*). Palsy; stiffness in joints; inaccessible. *Eakā am̧ etetal.* You walk stiff-leggedly. *Eļap an akā ñan delǫñ.* It's too inaccessible to try and enter. *Iban ellolo jikka kiiō bwe eļap an akā ñan koṃbani.* I can't get any cigarettes because the companies can't get any.

akeke (**hakęykęy**). 2, 3(inf, tr *-ik*), 6(*-i*), 7, 8, 9. Uncomfortable feeling about the stomach from being overstuffed with food. *Eakeke lǫjiō kōn an ļap aō kar ṃōñā.* I have an uncomfortable feeling in my stomach from overeating.

akeǫ (**hakeyaw**). Harvest first fruit of coconut, breadfruit, or pandanus.

akjijen (**hakjiyjen**). From Engl. *oxygen*. 2(inf, tr *-e*), 4, 6(*-i*). Scuba tank; oxygen. *Rej akjijene rūṃwijṃwij eṇ.* They're giving oxygen to the patient undergoing surgery.

akki (**hakkiy**). Also *akūk* (**hakik**). 1, 6(*-i*). Fingernail; toenail; claw; talon.

akkiin ne (**hakkiyin ney**). 1, 6(*...nein*). Toenail.

akkiin pā (**hakkiyin pay**). 1, 6(*...pein*). Fingernail.

akkǫun (**hakkawin**). From Engl. *account*. 1, 2(inf, tr *-i*), 3, 4. Charge on account.

akkōjdat (**hakkęjdat**). Also *akōjdat* (**hakęjdat**). 1(*-i*), 2(inf, tr *-e*), 3, 4. Hate; contempt; scorn; abhor. *Etke kwōakōjdate?* Why do you hate him?

akļañ (**hakļag**). 2(inf, tr *-e*), 3, 6(*-i*), 8, 9. To fish before everyone else and also before it is the right time to start. *Iļak etal in eǫñōd ettoot ke ear akļañe ek eo.* When I reached the spot to fish, he had already started fishing hours before.

akō (**hakeh**). But; how about; but what; dialectal variant of *ak* (**hak**). *Iar idaak akō iar jab kadek.* I drank but did not get drunk. *Akō kwe?* How about you? *Akō?* But what?

akōjdat (**hakęjdat**). Variant form of *kōjdat* (**kęjdat**).

akōr (**hakęr**). Also *akūr* (**hakir**). A fish, mullet, *Chelon vaigiensis.*

aktal (**haktal**). 1, 2(inf, tr *-e*), 4, 7(*aktaleļǫk*). A group of people going to a place for a specific purpose. *Jen aktale lǫk iroojeṇ emej.* Let's go as a group to pay our respects to the dead king.

akūk (**hakik**). Dialectal variant of *akki* (**hakkiy**).

akwāāl (**haqayal**). Also *iakwāāl* (**yihaqayal**). 1, 2(inf, tr *-e*), 3, 4. Strife; quarrel; bicker; argue.

akweļap (**haqeyļap**). 1(*-i*), 2, 3, 4. Strongly urge; beg insistently; insist.

akwōlā (**haqelay**). 3, 4+3, 5(*-e*), 6(*-i*), 3+7. A fish, chub mackerel, *Ragistrella.*

al (**hal**). 1(*-i*), 2, 3, 4, 6. Song; music; sing; carol.

al (**hal**). 3, 6(*-i*). A fish, kingfish.

alal (**halhal**). Also *alkarkar* (**halkarkar**). 1(*-i*), 2(inf, tr *-e*), 4. Watch over; care for.

albakbōk (**halbakbęk**). Archaic. 1, 2(inf, tr *-e, albakbūke*), 4, 6(*-i*). Carry tucked under arm. *Jonan an mera iep eo, lio ear albakbōke.* The basket was light enough for her to carry under her arm.

albok (**halbęq**). 2, 3, 5(*albokwe*), 6(*-i*). Bud; flower, about to bloom. *Kwōn ļōļō albok bwe ren ļak bbōl ekoṇ mejān ut ṇe utūṃ.* Make a garland with buds so when they bloom they'll fit closer together. *Ealboke raan wōjke eo.* The tree sported lots of buds.

albokbōrǫro (**halbęqberawręw**). 3, 6(*-i*). A plant, *Russelia juncea* (Scrophulariaceae); Cult. Orn. (Ebon) (see *kwōdeak* (**qedyak**)).

ale (**haley**). Provisions; storehouse.

aleak (**haleyak**). Also *aleañ* (**haleyag**). 1(*-i*), 2(inf, tr *-e*), 3, 4, 6(*-i*), 7. Wear hair loose on one's back, of women.

aleañ (**haleyag**). Also *aleak* (**haleyak**). A fish, grouper; *Epinephelus striatus.*

alebabu (**halęybahbiw**). Also *allebabu* (**hallęybahbiw**). 1, 2, 4, 6(*-i*), 8, 9. Inclined to recline; always lie down. *Kwōn jab alebabu bwe kwōnaaj ļōļļap ṃōkaj.* Don't be always lying down if you don't want to grow old fast.

alej (**halęj**). 1, 2(inf, tr *-e*), 4. Aim a gun; aim at; measure joints at an angle in construction work.

alekǫ (**halęykaw**). Also *akajok, akade.* 2(inf, tr *-ik, -uk*). Watch birds to locate roost.

alen (**halen**). Also *annen* (**hannen**). 5(*alenlen*), 6(*-i*). Time; turn; occasion;

times, in multiplication; sheet of paper; page; row of houses; story of a house; layer; phase; division of a land tract. *Elōñ alenin bok ne.* That book has many pages.

alijerļọk (**haliyjerļaq**). Archaic. 2, 3. Walk in a happy mood; sprightly; prance. *Alikkar ke etōprak jerbal eo an bwe etke ealijerļọk.* He must have landed the job since he's walking with a happy gait.

alikkar (**halikkar**). Dial. E, W: *allikar* (**hallikar**). Also *alkarkar* (**halkarkar**). 1(-*i*), 2, 3, 6(-*i*), 7. Clear; understandable; apparent; define; definite; legible; manifest; obvious; plain; visible. *Kaalikkare ṃōk ta eo kwōj ba.* Will you clarify what you're saying?

alin jar (**halin jar**). Hymn.

alin ṃaina (**halin ṃahyinah**). 2(inf, tr -*i*), 4, 6(-*i*), 7. Love song. *Kwōn jab alin ṃainaik alin jar ṇe.* Don't sing that hymn like a love song. *Ej alin ṃaina.* He's singing a romantic song.

alin ṃur (**halin ṃir°**). 1(-*i*), 2, 3, 4. Steering song.

aljek (**halję̧k**). 1(-*i*), 2(inf, tr -*e*, *aljike*), 3, 4, 6(-*i*), 7. Carry; transport. *Kwōj aljek ṃweiuk ñan ia?* Where are you taking those goods?

aljet (**halję̧t**). 1, 2, 3, 6(-*i*), 8, 9. Cross-eyed; pie-eyed; squint. *Ej mejān det bwe ealjet.* He wears dark glasses because he's cross-eyed. *Dān in kadek eo ekaaljete.* The strong liquor made him pie-eyed.

alkarkar (**halkarkar**). Variant form of *alikkar* (**halikkar**).

alle (**hallęy**). 3, 6(-*i*). A fish, wrasse, *Coris gaimardi*; *Anampses caeruleopunctatus*; *Thalashona ballieui.*

allejjor (**hallęjjęr°**). Variant form of *jjor* (**jjęr°**).

allijāljāl (**hallijaljal**). Also *aljāljāl* (**haljaljal**). 1, 2, 3. Hang. *Kwōn jab kaallijāljāle tọọļ ṇe bwe ettoon.* Don't hang that towel up because it's dirty.

allikar (**hallikar**). Dialectal variant of *alikkar* (**halikkar**).

allimōmō (**hallimehmeh**). 1(-*i*), 2(inf, tr -*ik*, -*ūk*), 3, 4, 6(-*i*), 7. Peep; peek. *Kwōn jab allimōmō ilo wūntō ṇe.* Don't look into that window.

allitoto (**hallitewtew**). Also *toto* (**tewtew**). 2, 3(inf, tr -*ik*), 4, 6(-*i*). Dangle. *Iar lo an kaallitotoik ļọk ijuweo ļọk.* I saw him dangle it in that direction.

allo (**hallęw**). Go around looking for something; search.

allo (**hallew**). 1(-*i*), 2, 3, 4, 6(-*i*), 8, 9. Stammer; tongue-tied; stutter. *Ij jab kanooj meļeļe an kōnnaan bwe eallo.* I can't quite understand what he says because he stammers.

allok (**hallęq**). 1(-*i*), 2(inf, tr *allukwe*), 3, 4, 6(-*i*), 7. Noose; snare. *Kaubowe eṇ ej allukwe kau eṇ.* The cowboy is roping the cow.

allolo (**hallęwlęw**). Also *allolo* (**hallewlew**). 1(-*i*), 2(inf, tr -*uk*), 3, 4. See; meet. *Enañin to ad allolouk eok.* We haven't seen you for a long time. *Etke ejọkkutkut ad allolouk eok?* Why don't we see you more often?

allor (**hallęr°**). Variant form of *llor* (**llęr°**).

allọk (**hallaq**). Also *anlọk* (**hanlaq**). 1(-*i*), 2(inf, tr -*e*), 4, 6(-*i*). Stand back and study critically, as an artist; survey critically; pause to admire; scrutinize, examine; compare; sight along a board to see if it is straight. *N̄e kwōallọke enaaj alikkar bōd kaṇe.* If you survey it critically, the mistakes will be obvious.

allọk (**hallaq**). Also *anlọk* (**hanlaq**). 2, 3, 6(-*i*). On target; within range. *Kōttar an allọk em buuki.* Wait till it comes within range, then shoot it. *Kakkōt kaallọke ṃaan aṃ bu.* Aim well before shooting. *N̄e jebar diak juon alen enaaj allọk ānen.* One more tacking and the island will be within range.

allōk (**hallęk**). 2(inf, tr -*e*), 4, 6(-*i*). To chant; invoke a spirit; perform an incantation. *Ear allōke rinañinmej eo.* He performed an incantation over the sick person.

allōñ (**hallęg**). 1(-*i*), 2(inf, tr -*e*), 6(-*i*). Month; moon. *Juon de allōñū ṇa ānin.* I have been on this islet one month now. *Ear allōñe eō ṇai Ṃajeļ.* I was in the Marshalls for a month.

allōñ iju (**hallęg yijiw**). 2(inf, tr -*uk*), 3, 4. Monthly contribution; tithe. *Kwōnañin door ke allōñ iju eo aṃ?* Have you made your monthly contribution (to the church) yet?

Kwaar allōñ ijuuk ke m̧ween̄ im̧ōm̧? Did you make the contribution for your land?

allōñ in laļ (**hallęg yin laļ**). Next month.

alluke (**halliqey**). Transitive form of *allok* (**hallęq**).

alluwaļǫk (**halliwahļaq**). Also *aluwaļǫk* (**haliwahļaq**). 1(-*i*), 2(inf, tr -*e*), 3, 4. Stare after; look at a distance. *Wōn n̄e kwōj alluwaļǫke?* Who are you staring at (over there)?

almaroñ (**halmareg°**). 1(-*i*), 2(inf, tr -*e*), 3, 4. Join in; do in common. *Kwōn itok jen almaroñ im m̧ōñā ilo peejin.* Come let's all join in and eat out of this bowl.

alñūrñūr (**halgirgir**). Also *alliñūrñūr* (**halligirgir**). 1, 2, 3, 4. Mumble; murmur; mutter. *Ij roñ wōt an alñūrñūr ak ij jab roñ naan ko ej ba.* I heard him mumbling but I didn't hear what he said.

aloklok (**haleqleq**). 1(-*i*), 2, 3(inf, tr -*e*). Appear; display. *Enañin aloklok ke bao eo ear jako.* Have you seen that lost chicken? *Kwōn jab aloklok.* Don't show yourself. *Ej kaalokloki m̧weiuk kan̄ an.* He's displaying his merchandise.

alǫk (**halaq**). Archaic. Variant form of *ttino* (**ttinęw**).

alu (**haliw**). 3, 6(-*i*). A shell, *Ellobiidae*; *Cassidula plecotrematoides japonica*; used in head leis. Also *Melampus nuxcastanea*; *Pythia cecillei*; *Melampus fasciatus.*

aluej (**haliwyęj**). 2, 4. Sing upon trees or in places above. *Ilo m̧antin M̧ajeļ, emǫ aluej ñe ej or irooj.* It's forbidden to be singing up above when there is an *irooj* around according to Marshallese custom.

aluje (**haliwjey**). Transitive form of *alwōj* (**halwęj**).

alwor (**halwer**). 3, 6(-*i*). A fish, parrotfish, *Callyodon microrhinos.*

alwōj (**halwęj**). 1(-*i*), 2(inf, tr *aluje*), 3(inf *kaalwōjwōj,* tr *kaalwōj*) , 4. Watch; look at; audience; admire. *Rūalwōj ro raar kabbokbok.* The audience clapped their hands. *Ejjeļǫk en̄ ej aluje eok.* No one's admiring you.

alwōj bajjek (**halwęj bajjęk**). 1(-*i*), 2, 4. Stroll; sight-seeing; taking in the view.

aļ (**haļ**). Sun.

aļ (**haļ**). Copra harvesting period. *An wōn in aļ kwōj kowaininiiki?* Whose copra harvesting period is it you're working?

aļak (**haļak**). Phosphorescent; name of legendary man.

aļakiia (**haļakiyyah**). 1(-*i*), 2, 7, 8, 9. Scarce; hard to find (see *aļakiie* (**haļakiyyęy**)).

aļakiie (**haļakiyyęy**). 1(-*i*), 2, 7, 8, 9. Plentiful; easy to find (see *aļakiia* (**haļakiyyah**)).

aļaļ (**haļhaļ**). 3, 6(-*i*). Stick; wood; plank; lumber.

aļaļ (**haļhaļ**). Meaty part of the clam.

aļaļ in deñdeñ (**haļhaļ yin degdeg**). Club; weapon.

aļap (**haļap**). 1, 2, 3(inf *kaaļapļap,* tr *kaaļap*), 6(-*i*). Lineage head; uncle on the mother's side; old man, term of respect. *Kwōn kaaļapļap.* Respect your elders. *Eļap an kaaļape.* He's feigning age when he's really young.

aļapļǫk (**haļapļaq**). 1(-*i*), 2, 3. Aged; doddering. *Iaļapļǫk im immālele.* I am old and absent minded.

aļbapeet (**haļbahpeyet**). Alphabet. *Ripālle raar kōm̧m̧an an kajin M̧ajeļ aļbapeet.* White men gave the Marshallese language its alphabet.

aļe (**haļey**). 6(-*i*). Closed circle of fish surrounded by *aļeļe* (**haļeyļey**) method. *Elōñ ke kobban aļe en̄?* Are there lots of fish in that circle?

aļe (**haļey**). Also *ļe* (**ļey**). Salutation; Mister. *Aļe kwaar lo ke joob eo arro?* Mister, did you see my soap?

aļeek (**haļeyek**). Transitive form of *aļeļe* (**haļeyļey**).

aļeļe (**haļeyļey**). 1(-*i*), 2(inf, tr *aļeek,* -*ik*), 4, 6(-*i*), 7. Fishing method, many men surround a school in shallow water using a coconut leaf chain as scarer; cf. Hawaiian *hukilau. Ļōm̧aro rōmoot in aļeļe.* The men have gone to fish with a scarer. *Ļōm̧aro rej aļeek m̧ǫle eo.* The men are surrounding the rabbit fish.

aļjer (**haļjer**). From Engl. 1(-*i*), 2, 3(inf, tr -*e*), 7, 8, 9. Ulcer. *Rej ba ke jikka ej kaaļjere kōj.* They claim that cigarettes cause ulcers.

aļkita (**haļkiytah**). From Engl. 3, 6(-*i*). Alligator; crocodile. *Eko tok* *kilū n̄e ij ellolo al̦kita.* Seeing an alligator gives me the creeps.

al̦koot (**hal̦kewet**). 2(inf, tr *-e*), 3, 6(*-i*), 7. Raincoat. *Inaaj al̦koote l̦ok eok.* You'll share my raincoat with me to your house.

al̦kōnar (**hal̦kenar**). 1, 2, 4(*riaal̦kōnar*), 6(*-i*). Look pretty at sunset. *Jen kam̧ōj ad jerbal im pojak in al̦kōnar.* Let's finish up our work and get ready to look nice at sunset. *Ij lewōj jatū bwe en am̧ rial̦kōnar in jota.* I'll let you take my sister for a sunset stroll.

al̦kwōjeje (**hal̦qejeyjey**). 2, 4, 6(*-i*). Sunbathing. *Kadikdik al̦kwōjeje bwe kwōnaaj ākilkil.* You'd better go slow or you'll peel from sunbathing.

al̦l̦an̄ (**hal̦l̦ag**). 1(*-i*), 2, 3, 4, 6(*-i*). Stare open-mouthed; gape; be slow witted. *Kwōn jab al̦l̦an̄ bwe kwōnaaj m̧ōn̄ā l̦ōn̄.* Don't stare with your mouth open or you will eat flies. *Al̦l̦an̄ im m̧ōn̄ā l̦ōn̄.* Stare and eat flies (a proverb).

Al̦l̦an̄inwa (**hal̦l̦aginwah**). 3, 6(*-i*). A plant, pandanus cultigen.

Al̦l̦orkan̄ (**hal̦l̦er°kan̄**). 3, 6(*-i*). A plant, pandanus cultigen.

al̦o (**hal̦ew**). Dial. E, W: *rum̧wij* (**r°im̧ij**). 1(*-i*), 2(inf, tr *-ik*), 3, 4, 6(*-e*), 7. Late; formant in place names. *Ial̦o.* I'm late. *Iwōj bwe ij baj al̦o waj wōt.* Go ahead because I'm coming later.

al̦ok (**hal̦eq**). 2(inf, tr *-e*), 3, 4, 6(*-i*). Break taboos attendant to certain medicines while under treatment. *Lale am̧ al̦ok bwe enāj ro̧ol utōn wūno kan̄e arro.* Beware of breaking the taboos or our medicines will bring on adverse effects.

al̦okbad (**hal̦eqbad**). 1(*-i*), 2, 3. Always late; delay. *Ejjel̦ok al̦okbadiier.* Boy, aren't they always late!

al̦ōm̧n̦ak (**hal̦em̧n̦ak**). Also *kōlan̦ta* (**kelan̦tah**). Almanac; calendar. *Kwōn m̧ōk lale al̦ōm̧n̦ak n̦e jete raan rainin.* Would you check the calendar and see what date today is.

am (**ham**). Our soul; ours; our, exclusive.

amān (**haman**). 2(inf, tr *-e*), 3, 7. Use; spend; consume. *Kwōn amān jāān kan̦e am̧ bwe kwōnaaj mej jāni.* Spend your money now because you can't take it with you.

Amedka (**hamedkah**). From Engl. 4. America.

amej (**hamẹj**). Dial. E only; see *ukood.* 1, 2, 3(inf, tr *-e*), 6(*-i*), 8, 9, 11(*amejmej*). Raw; uncooked; half-cooked; not well done. *Idike kanniōkin kau n̄e ej amej.* I don't like rare steaks. *Eor ke pilawā amej m̧wiin?* Do you have any flour? *Ekōmatte raij eo im kaameje.* He half cooked the rice.

amentakla̧l (**hamentakla̧l**). Archaic. Sorry consequences. *Lale am̧ kūbbon̦ bwe amentakla̧l eo enaaj urōt eok.* Keep it up and your stinginess will reap unhappy consequences for you.

ametōm̧a (**hameytem̧ah**). 2, 3, 4, 6(*-i*). Coconut candy.

ami (**hamiy**). Your souls; your; yours, plural.

ami (**hamiy**). From Engl. Army. *Elōn̄ uwaan ami eo an Amedka.* The U.S. Army has a lot of men.

amiian̄ (**hamiyyag**). Dial. W, E: *amimān* (**hamiyman**). Your; yours (four persons).

amijeel (**hamiyjẹyẹl**). Dialectal variant of *amijel* (**hamiyjẹl**).

amijel (**hamiyjẹl**). Dial. E, W: *amijeel* (**hamiyjẹyẹl**). Your; yours (three persons).

amimān (**hamiyman**). Dialectal variant of *amiian̄* (**hamiyyag**).

amim̧ōn̦o (**hamiym̧en̦ew**). 1(*-i*), 2, 3, 4, 6(*-i*). Handicraft; make handicraft. *Jete on̦āān amim̧ōn̦o n̦e am̧?* How much does that handicraft of yours cost? *Lim̧aro ran̦ rej amim̧ōn̦o.* Those women are making handicraft.

amiro (**hamiyrew**). Your; yours (two persons).

amiwōj (**hamiywẹj**). Your; yours (three or more persons).

aml̦ap (**haml̦ap**). 1(*-i*), 2, 3, 4. Own much land. *El̦ap an al̦ap en̦ aml̦ap.* That old man has lots of land. *Al̦ap en̦ eaml̦ap.* That old man has lots of land.

amn̦ak (**hamn̦ak**). 1(*-i*), 2, 3, 4. Inheritance; bequest; own much land or real estate. *Em̧ōj an l̦ōl̦l̦ap eo jim̧m̧aō kaamn̦ak eō kōn ijo jikin.* My grandfather gave me his land. *Eamn̦ak kōn an kar peran jim̧m̧aan ilo pata.* He has a lot of land as a result of his grandfather's bravery in battles.

amñe (**hamgey**). Although; even if; despite. *Ebwe an maroñ amñe edik.* He's quite able despite his young age.

aṃ (**haṃ**). Your soul; your; yours, singular.

aṃ (**haṃ**). From Engl. Ham.

aṃa (**haṃah**). From Engl. *hammer*. 1(*-a*), 2(inf, tr *-ik*), 4, 6(*-i*), 7. Hammer. *Lale kwōaṃaik peiṃ.* Be careful you don't hammer your finger.

aṃak (**haṃak**). From Engl. *hammock*. 1(*-i*), 2(inf, tr *-e*), 3, 6(*-i*), 7. Hammock. *Niññiñ eo eṇ ej kiki ilo aṃak eṇ.* The baby is sleeping in the hammock. *Wōn eṇ ear aṃake niññiñ eṇ?* Who put the baby in the hammock?

aṃaṃ (**haṃhaṃ**). 1, 2, 3, 6(*-i*), 7, 8, 9. Attract fish or flies with scraps. *Eaṃaṃ pako.* Something's attracting the sharks. *Jab kwōpejpej jeṇe bwe enaaj aṃaṃ.* Don't throw garbage there or you'll attract sharks. *Jab kaaṃaṃ.* Don't attract fish (flies) with garbage.

aṃbai (**haṃbahiy**). From Engl. 2(inf, tr *-ik*), 6(*-i*), 7. Umpire; referee.

aṃbōḷ (**haṃbeḷ**). From Engl. 6(*-i*). Anvil. *Kwōn noe ioon aṃbōḷ ṇe.* Pound it on the anvil.

aṃbwidilā (**haṃbidiylay**). From Engl. 1(*-i*), 2(inf, tr *-ik*), 3, 4, 6(*-i*). Umbrella; parasol.

aṃonika (**haṃewnikah**). From Engl. Harmonica.

aṃoot (**haṃewet**). Variant form of *anoot* (**hanewet**).

aṃōn (**haṃen**). Dialectal variant of *aṃwin* (**haṃin**).

aṃtōk (**haṃtẹk**). 1(*-i*), 2, 3. Bite lips. *Aolep iien ḷeeṇ ej aṃtōk ñe ej llu.* He always bites his lips when he's angry.

aṃwin (**haṃin**). Dial. E, W: *aṃōn* (**haṃen**). 1(*aṃwini-, aṃōna-, aṃōṇa-*), 6(*aṃōnān, aṃōṇan*). Water for washing hands. *Kwōn itōktok aṃōnān ripālle rā.* Draw water for these Americans to wash their hands with. *Dān eo aṃwiniṃ eo.* Here's some water for you to wash your hands with.

aṃwin (**haṃin**). 1(*-i*), 2(inf, tr *-i*), 3, 4. Wash hands. *Kwōn aṃwin(i) peiṃ ṃokta jān aṃ ṃōñā.* Wash your hands before eating.

an (**han**). His soul; her soul; his; her; hers; its.

an (**han**). 2(inf, tr *-e*), 4, 6(*-i*), 7(*ane tok, ḷọk, waj*). Overhaul; tune-up; get into prime running condition; work on a boat to make it sail fast. *Kwōmaroñ ke kab ane tok riwut e waō?* Would you then work on my toy canoe to make it fast? *Eṃōj an injinia eṇ ane tok injinḷọk e aō im elukkuun ṃṃan an jerbal.* My outboard engine has been tuned up by that mechanic and it's working perfectly.

an armeje doon (**han harmẹjẹy dewen**). Idiom. Feud; fight between relatives. *Koṃro en jab an armeje doon bwe enaaj or bwijerro.* You shouldn't fight each other or a great misfortune will result.

an mej eṇ (**han mẹj yeṇ**). 1. Weakness; shortcoming; disadvantage. *Aṃ mej ṇe kọkkure ṃaak.* That's your weakness, spending money. *An mej eṇ kiki in raan.* That's his shortcoming, taking naps.

anan (**hanhan**). 1(*-i*), 2(inf, tr *ane*), 4, 7. Bait; lure; to chum for fish; decoy. *Kwōn ane tok pako eṇ bwe jen dibōje.* Lure that shark here so we can spear it. *Kwōn anan ḷọk bwe jen eọñōd.* Go ahead and chum so that we can fish.

anbōro (**hanbẹrẹw**). 1, 2(inf, tr *-uk*), 4, 6(*-i*). Curry the favor of men or women with gifts. *Kwōn jab anbōro kōn jāān kaṇe aō.* Don't use my money to get in good with the girls.

Anbūri (**hanbiriy**). 3, 6(*-i*). A plant, pandanus cultigen.

anbwe (**hanbẹy**). 5(*anbwebwe*), 6(*-i*), 7. Coral finger extending out of a main coral head or reef. *Kwōn kōjere wa in bwe enaaj itaak ilo anbwe ṇe.* Change the course of this boat or it'll go aground on the *anbwe*.

anbwijban (**hanbijban**). 1(*-i*), 2(inf, tr *-e*). Left; left hand. *Kwōn anbwijbane.* Use your left hand.

anbwijmaroñ (**hanbijmareg°**). 1(*-i*), 2(inf, tr *-e*). Right; right hand. *Epidodo aō naaj anbwijmaroñe.* It'll be easy for me to use my right hand.

Anbwilwa (**hanbilwah**). 3, 6(*-i*). A plant, pandanus cultigen; Rongelap.

ane (**haney**). Transitive form of *anan* (**hanhan**).

anekane (**haneykahney**). Also *anōkkane* (**hanekkahney**), *ankane* (**hankahney**). 1(-*i*), 2(inf, tr -*ik*), 4, 7. Refuel a fire.

anemkwōj (**hanemqej**). 1(-*a*, -*i*), 2(inf, tr -*e*), 3, 4, 7. Freedom; liberty; independence; permission. *Jab anemkwōje aṃ tutu iar.* Don't swim without asking permission.

anen Etao (**hanen yetahwew**). From "soul of Etao". 2, 4, 6(-*i*). Epilepsy.

aneptok (**hanepteq**). 1(-*i*), 2. Attractiveness; popularity.

anidep (**haniydep**). 1(-*i*), 2(inf, tr -*e*), 3, 4. Ball made from pandanus leaves; native ball game; play kickball. *Rej anidepe bọọḷ eo nejiṃ.* They're kicking your kick-ball.

Anidep (**haniydep**). From "native football game (ball made from pandanus leaves)". 3, 6(-*i*). A plant, pandanus cultigen. Eniwetok.

anien (**haniyen**). From Engl. *onion*. 2(inf, tr -*e*), 5(-*e*), 6(-*i*). Onion. *Eaniene iiōk ṇe.* That recipe uses lots of onions.

Anij (**hanij**). God.

Anij in Inelep (**hanij yin yineylep**). Lord of Hosts.

Anij Ḷapḷap (**hanij ḷapḷap**). Almighty God.

anij raṇ (**hanij raṇ**). Idols; half gods, literally "those gods."

anijnij (**hanijnij**). 1(-*i*), 2(inf, tr -*i*), 3, 4. Spell, enchantment; magic; sorcery; witchcraft. *Ejeḷā anijnij.* He knows how to make magic.

anil (**hanil**). Archaic. Area from which soil has been taken.

anilen (**haniylen**). Slang. 1(-*i*), 2, 3, 4. Fate; destiny. *Jide im anilen bwe jen bar lo doon.* It's lucky and our fate to see each other again.

anilen (**haniylen**). 1(-*i*), 2, 3. Infected. *Eanilen kinej e peiū.* This cut on my hand is infected.

anilik (**haniylik**). 1(-*i*), 2(inf, tr -*i*), 3, 4. Outer clothes; external.

anilowa (**haniylewah**). 1(-*i*), 2(inf, tr -*ik*), 3, 4. Underclothes; underwear. *Kwōn anilowaik eok.* Put on your underclothes.

animro- (**hanimrew-**). Also *anmiro-* (**hanmirew-**). 1(-*a*, -*e*), 6(-*i*). Glimpse; glance. *Animroon wōt eo ij lo an ettōrḷọk.* I just caught a glimpse of him running.

anitta (**hanittah**). 1(-*i*), 2, 4. Ability to cast spell. *Eḷap an anitta.* He has the power to cast spells.

Anjeer (**hanjeyer**). 3, 6(-*i*). A plant, pandanus cultigen.

anjejjo (**hanjẹjjẹw**). Known by only a few. *Anjejjo wōt kapen.* Few people know navigation.

anji (**hanjiy**). 1(-*i*), 2(inf, tr -*ik*), 4. Use witchcraft.

anjidik (**hanjiydik**). Variant form of *anjilik* (**hanjiylik**).

Anjiio (**hanjiyyew**). 3, 6(-*i*). A plant, pandanus cultigen. Rongelap.

anjilik (**hanjiylik**). Also *anjidik* (**hanjiydik**). 2, 4, 6(-*i*). Sickness, constant running nose; constant sneezing.

anjin (**hanjin**). 2(inf, tr -*i*), 4, 5(*anjinjin, anitta*), 6(-*i*). Cast a spell on. *Eanjinjin lōḷḷap eṇ.* The old woman is always casting spells.

anjọ (**hanjaw**). 1(-*i*), 2, 3, 4. Victory; win a victory; conquered; defeat; overcome; subdue; triumph; prevail. *Irooj eo eṃōj an bōk anjọ.* The chief won the battle. *Kōm ar anjọ ioer.* We conquered them.

ankaan (**hankahan**). Also *ṇakaan* (**ṇahkahan**), *anōkkaan* (**hanekkahan**). 1, 2(inf, tr -*e*), 4, 6(-*i*). Feed a fire. *Ankaane kijek ṇe bwe en jab kun.* Put wood on the fire so it doesn't die out.

ankane (**hankahney**). Variant form of *anekane* (**haneykahney**).

ankeke (**hankẹykẹy**). 1(-*i*), 2(inf, tr *ankiij*), 3(inf, tr -*ik*), 4. Crooked; gaff.

ankiij (**hankiyij**). 1(-*i*), 2(inf, tr -*i*). Hook and pull.

ankiij (**hankiyij**). Transitive form of *ankeke* (**hankẹykẹy**).

ankilaa- (**hankilaha-**). 1. Will; desire; faculty. *Ej jab ankilaō.* It's not in my will.

ankilaak (**hankilahak**). 1(-*i*), 2(inf, tr -*e*). Give away freely.

ankiliriab (**hankiliyriyab**). Also *ankilriab* (**hankilriyab**). 1(-*i*), 2, 3, 4, 6(-*i*), 8, 9. Hypocrisy; deceit; pretense; false-hearted. *Elukkuun ankilriab.* He's an absolute hypocrite.

ankoṇak (**hanqeṇak**). Variant form of *aṇokṇak* (**haṇeqṇak**).

ankōmājur (**hankemajir°**). Variant form of *ankōṃad* (**hankeṃad**).

ankōm̧ad (**hankem̧ad**). Also *ankōmājur* (**hankemajir°**). 2(inf, tr *-e*), 4, 6(*-i*). Take by surprise in hand combat. *Ear ankōm̧ade em baiti.* He hit him when he wasn't looking. *Ear ankōm̧ade em ejjeļǫk an m̧aroñ.* He was unable to do anything for he was taken by surprise. *Enana ankōmājur.* I don't like being taken by surprise.

Ankōnār (**hankẹnyar**). From *Ļōkōnear* (**ļẹkẹnyar**) "name of Ralik chief who lived on Rongelap". 3, 6(*-i*). A plant, pandanus cultigen. Rongelap.

Anlojet (**hanlẹwjẹt**). 3, 6(*-i*). A plant, pandanus cultigen.

anlǫk (**hanlaq**). Steer a course with land on one's bow.

anlǫk (**hanlaq**). Variant form of *allǫk* (**hallaq**).

anmiiñ (**hanmiyig**). 1(*-i*), 2, 4. Left hand; left half of human body.

anmiro- (**hanmirew-**). Variant form of *animro-* (**hanimrew-**).

anmooņ (**hanmeweņ**). 1(*-i*), 2, 4. Right hand; right half of human body.

Anm̧ōden (**hanm̧edyen**). 3, 6(*-i*). A plant, *Pandanus fischerianus* cultigen. (Stone). Likiep.

anm̧ōkadede (**hanm̧ekadẹydẹy**). 3, 6(*-i*). A plant, *Nephrolepis acutifolia* similar to the familiar "Boston fern"; found on the moister (more southerly) islands.

annañ (**hannag**). 1(*-i*), 2(inf, tr *-e*), 4, 6(*-i*). Shadow; reflection; picture; diagram; plan; shape; silhouette; outline; caricature; image; profile; replica; statue; example. *Kwōj lo ke annañūm̧ ilo kilaaj eņ?* Do you see your reflection in the mirror? *Annañe tok m̧ōk ļōmān wa eo waam̧.* Draw me a picture of your boat.

annañ (**hannag**). 6(*-i*). A bird, small, about the size of a butterfly, lives in rocks around the shores of the Northwest Marshalls, smells sweet.

annañinmej (**hannaginmẹj**). Shadow of death.

Annānu (**hannaniw**). 3, 6(*-i*). A plant, *Pandanus fischerianus* cultigen.

annen (**hannen**). Also *alen* (**halen**). One more time. *Annen eo in im kōjro etal.* Once more before we go.

Annenep (**hannenep**). A plant, *Pandanus fischerianus* cultigen (Takeuchi). (Stone). Utirik.

anniabeab (**hanniyabyab**). 1(*-i*), 2, 3, 4, 8, 9. Flighty; emotionally unstable. *Kwōn jab kkure ippān ļeeņ bwe eanniabeab.* Don't play with him because he's unstable.

annor (**hannẹr°**). 2(inf, tr *-e, annire*), 4, 6(*-i*), 7. A special kind of knot. *Juon e kain annor koban jeļā.* This is a special kind of knot you'll never learn.

anoot (**hanewet**). Also *am̧oot* (**ham̧ewet**). 2, 4, 6(*-i*). A game, tag.

anōk (**hanek**). 1(*-i*), 2, 4, 7. Trace; pattern; follow trail or track; imitate; copy. *Ļōm̧aro rej anōkļǫk jinok eo jinokwan wōn eo.* Those fellows are following the trail of a turtle. *Kwōn jab anōk aō jeje.* Don't imitate my writing. *Kwōn anōk joñak e.* Follow this pattern.

anōļ (**haneļ**). 1(*-i*), 6(*-i*). Dial. *Ejorrāān anōļin waj e aō.* The dial of my watch is broken.

anōr (**hanher**). 1(*-i*), 2(inf, tr *anōre*), 3, 7. Graze; just touch. *Bǫǫļ eo eanōr(e) pijja eo.* The ball grazed the pitcher.

anpakolu (**hanpakewliw**). 6(*-i*). Left-overs of a shark. *Jenaaj itene anpakolu e?* What are we going to do with the leftovers of the shark?

Anperia (**hanpẹyriyah**). 3, 6(*-i*). A plant, *Pandanus fischerianus* cultigen.

anri- (**hanri-**). Vulgar. 1, 6(*-i*). Anus.

Antakļōñar (**hantakļegar**). From *Takļōnar* (**takļegar**) "name of wife of *Ļōkōnear*". 3, 6(*-i*). A plant, *Pandanus fischerianus* cultigen. Rongelap, Jaluit, Likiep, and Arno. (Stone).

antena (**hantẹynah**). From Engl. 2(inf, tr *-ik*), 6(*-i*). Antenna. *Enaaj m̧m̧an ñe kwōnaaj antenaiki.* It's going to work once you put up an antenna for it.

Anuujeep (**haniwijjeyep**). 3, 6(*-i*). A plant, pandanus cultigen.

Anuwōt (**haniwwet**). 3, 6(*-i*). A plant, pandanus cultigen.

aņokņak (**haņeqņak**). Also *ankoņak* (**hanqeņak**). 1, 2(inf, tr *-e*), 3, 4, 6(*-i*), 8, 9. Covet; appropriate others' property; covetousness; take by force that which one does not own. *Jab aņokņake pālen rūturum̧.* Don't covet your neighbor's wife.

aņtǫǫn (**haņtawan**). From "man named Anton noted for calculating prowess".

2(inf, tr *-e*), 4, 6(*-i*). Use one's head; do mental arithmetic; estimate; reckon. *Iar aṃtọọne wūn eo.* I worked the problem in my head.

añ (**hag**). 1(*-i*), 6(*-i*). Wind; breeze. *Añ ōt in?* Where is the wind coming from?

añak (**hagak**). 6(*-i*). Live at home of deceased during the week following death, relatives and spouse. *Iien añak ilju.* The period of *añak* starts tomorrow. *Kōjro ilān añak ippān rimej eṇ.* Let's go *añak* with the deceased.

añal (**hagal**). 1(*-i*), 2(inf, tr *-e*), 3, 4, 7. Attracted. *Ta in ej kaañal tok ḷọñ?* What is attracting the flies?

añañe (**haghagey**). 1(*-i*), 2, 8, 9. Drowsy; groggy; hungry; see *uwaañ añ*. *Ilukkuun añañe.* I'm really hungry.

añijwiwi (**hagijwiywiy**). Also *añjuwiwi* (**hagjiwiywiy**). 1(*-i*), 2, 3. Gust; whirlwind. *Eañijwiwi tok.* The wind is coming in gusts.

añinene (**haginyẹnẹy**). Uneven sailing wind in lee of an islet.

añinlur (**haginlir°**). A breeze forecasting calm weather. *Epaak tok wōt rak ke eñin eañinlur.* Summer is very near as we can tell from the breeze.

añinraanjitbōnmar (**haginrahanjitbenmar**). Wind that gathers strength as it reaches the treetops.

añinwoḷā (**haginweḷay**). Also *aunwōḷā* (**hawinweḷay**). 1(*-i*), 2(inf, tr *-ik*), 4, 6(*-i*), 7. Roof brace. *Eṃṃan ñe kwōañinwoḷāiki bwe en pen.* It would be better if you put braces to strengthen it.

añjarjar (**hagjarjar**). Archaic. 1, 2, 5(*añjarjare*), 7, 8, 9. Gusty wind; talk that hurts the feelings. *Ij kajineete eok ke eañjarjar an lōḷḷap eṇ kōnnaan.* I'm warning you beforehand that she is an old lady with a sharp tongue.

añjānjān (**hagjanjan**). From *añ* (**hag**) "wind". 2, 6(*-i*). Steady light breeze.

añjebwāālel (**hagjebayalyẹl**). 1(*-i*), 2, 3. Lost; not know which way to go. *Iañjebwāālel.* I'm confused and don't know which way to go.

añjerak (**hagjerak**). 1(*-i*), 2, 3, 5(*añjerake*). Exposed to wind and air. *Eañjerake ṃwiin.* This house is exposed to the wind.

añkidid (**hagkidid**). From *añ* "wind", *kidid* "wandering tattler", which spends winter months in the islands. Onset of calm season; April or May.

añkijep (**hagkijyep**). Also *añkōj* (**hagkẹj**). Handkerchief.

añkō (**hagkeh**). From Engl. *anchor*. 1(*-i*), 2(inf, tr *-ūk, -ik*), 3, 4, 6(*-i*). Anchor.

añkwōl (**hagqel**). From *añ* "wind", *kwōl* "sanderling". Onset of the windy season; November or December.

añlọkwi- (**haglaqi-**). 1. Outward appearance.

añḷap (**hagḷap**). From *añ* (**hag**) "wind", *ḷap* (**ḷap**) "big". 1(*-i*), 2, 3, 4. Exaggerate. *Eṃōj aṃ añḷap.* Why don't you stop exaggerating.

aññat (**haggat**). Violent storm.

añōltak (**hageltak**). 1(*-i*), 2, 3. Westerly breeze.

añōlto (**hageltẹw**). 1(*-i*), 2, 3. Easterly breeze.

añōltok (**hagelteq**). 6(*-i*). Appearance; material quality.

añōneañ (**hagenyag**). 3. Wintertime; harvest time for arrowroot; windy season; autumn; season of drought; dry season.

añōppāl (**hagẹppal**). 2, 3(inf, tr *-e*), 6(*-i*), 7. A canoe with its sail flapping. *Aḷe, ta wūnin an wa eṇ añōppāl?* Mister, why is that canoe's sail flapping.

añōt (**hagẹt**). 1(*-i*), 2, 3(inf, tr *-e*), 6(*-i*), 8, 9. Drawing much water causing it to be hard to paddle or sail, nautical. *Eḷap an añōt wa in.* This boat is drawing a lot of water (and being impeded thereby).

añōtñōt (**hagẹtgẹt**). 1(*-i*), 2, 3, 4. Request; importunate; entreat. *Iar añōtñōt ñane im ṃōk ak ear jab uwaak.* I importunated him so much that I got tired, but he didn't answer.

añtūkli (**hagtikliy**). 6(*-i*). Canoe part, waveguard on both sides of sailing canoe.

añur (**hag°ir**). Variant form of *uññūr* (**wiggir**).

añūr (**hagir**). From Engl. *hanker*. 1(*-i*), 2, 3(inf *kaañūrñūr*), 6(*-i*), 8, 9. Crave cigarettes. *Eḷap añūr in kōn an jañin itok wa.* People here are craving cigarettes since the ship hasn't come yet. *Ij kaañũrñũr m̧okta im ļak m̧ōj, kōbaatat.* I'm going to wait till I'm really dying before having a cigarette.

añũrlep (**hagirlep**). 1(*-i*), 2, 4. Smoking addict.

ao (**hahwew**). 2, 6(*-i*). Halo; white spot on the head of the brown noddy (*pejwak*) bird; oil found under the shell of a turtle; legendary power given by Jebro to Jekad; a legendary bird. *Joñan an jjetōbtōb, eao.* He is so spiritual, he has a halo on his head. *Aon irooj eņ ekǫkkure.* The special power of that chief can make you sick (if you have displeased him).

aod (**hawed**). Also *aode* (**hawedey**). 1(*aodei-*), 2, 3, 6(*-a*). Wake of a boat; challenge. *Ear naajdik wa eo juon aod.* He passed in front of the other boat. (He fed the other boat a wake.) *Kijem̧ eo aod.* Let's see you try this.

aoj (**hawej**). Bed (old word used in Bible).

Aojañ (**hawejag**). 3, 6(*-i*). A plant, pandanus cultigen.

aol (**hawel**). Also *awal* (**hawal**). 3, 6(*-i*). A fish, *piha*, *Spratelloides delicatulus*; minnow.

aolep (**hawelep**). 1(*-a*), 3, 6(*-a*). All; total; every; both; entire.

aolep iien (**hawelep 'yiyen**). Also *iien otemjej* (**'yiyen wętęmjęj**). Always. *Etke ej kakũtōtōik eok aolep iien?* Why is she always teasing you?

aolep raan (**hawelep rahan**). From *aolep* (**hawelep**) "all", *raan* (**rahan**) "day". Daily.

aolōk (**hawęlęk**). 1, 2(inf, tr *-e, aolike*), 3, 5(*-e*), 6(*-i*). A coelenterate, Portuguese man-o-war; genus *Physalia.*

aoļ (**haweļ**). 1(*-i*), 2(inf, tr *-e*) 3, 4, 6(*-i*). Dispute; complain; bewail one's state; quarrel; legendary fish banished by Jebro to be eaten by other fish.

aoļōt (**hawęļęt**). A fish, leather-jack, *Scomber*oides lysan.

Aoļōt (**hawęļęt**). See *aoļōt* "leather-jack". A constellation; stars in Draco; shaped like leather-jack fish (theta, eta, zeta) whose head (theta) has been pierced by a spear (18, 19): *M̧ade-eo-an-Aoļōt.*

aop (**hawep**). Dial. W, E: *aweep* (**haweyep**). 3, 6(*-i*). An animal, tree lizard, green and black, *Dasia smaragdina.*

aor (**hawer**). 2(inf, tr *-e*), 6(*-i*). Door; entrance; threshold; gateway. *Kwōnaaj aore m̧ōņe ñāāt?* When are you installing a door in that house?

aorak (**hawerak**). 3, 5(*-e*), 6(*-i*). A shell, *Strombidae*; *Lambis crocata/scorpius/ lambis*; spider shell.

aorōk (**hawęręk**). 1(*-i*), 2, 3, 4, 8, 9. Valuable; precious; essential; important; vital.

aotak (**hawetak**). 3, 6(*-i*). A fish, striped mullet, *Chelon vaigiensis.*

aō (**hahęh**). My soul; my; mine.

aō (**haheh**). 1(*-i*), 2(inf, tr *aũn*), 3, 4. Swim.

aō in kijdik (**haheh yin kijdik**). From "swimming of rats". 2, 4, 6(*-i*). Tread water.

aōņōņ (**hahenheņ**). 1(*-i*), 2(inf, tr *-e*), 3, 4. Paddle; row.

ap (**hap**). Way or manner of doing something; method. *Ikōņaan ap jab ņe wōjam̧.* I like your method.

apa (**hapah**). Formant in place names.

apañ (**hapag**). 1(*-i*), 2, 3(st inf *kaapañpañ*, tr *kaapañ(e)*), 4, 6(*-i*), 8, 9. Harass; hem in; crowded; cramped; balk; hindered; hassle. *Eapañ kōn ajri eo nājin.* His child is getting in his way. *Ajri eo nājin ej kaapañ an jerbal.* His child is impeding his work. *Ejjeļam apañin.* What a hassle.

apap (**haphap**). Also *apep* (**hapyęp**). 1(*-i*), 2(inf, tr *apij*), 3, 4, 6(*-i*). Pinching, with finger; nip. *Lale bwe apapin ekōmmetak.* (Behave, children), or he'll pinch and hurt you. *Etke kwaar apij ajiri eo?* Why did you pinch the child?

apaproro (**haphaprẹwrẹw**). Also *aproro* (**haprẹwrẹw**). 1(*-i*), 2(inf, tr *-ik, -uk*), 3, 4, 6(*-i*). Dubious; indecisive; conscience; undecided; in a dilemma. *Ejjeļǫk wōt apaproroū.* My conscience is really troubled. *Men eo ear ba ear kaapaproroik eō.* What he said troubled my conscience. *Iaproro in kōm̧m̧ane men eņ.* I don't think I should do that. *Kwōn jab apaproro.* Don't be undecided. (Make up your mind.) *Ta ņe ej kaapaproroūk eok?* Why can't you decide?

apar (**hapar**). 1(*-a*), 3, 4. Put alongside; rim; edge; border on mat or stone edge of road; prop. *Pet eo aparaṃ eo.* Here is a pillow to put alongside you.

apar (**hapar**). From *apar* (**hapar**). 2, 4. Witnesses in marriage. *Wōn ej apar ñan koṃro?* Who will be your witnesses?

apar (**hapar**). From *apar* (**hapar**) "stone markers along road". 2(inf, tr *-e*), 4, 7. Escort. *Jentoki ko raar apare inej in waan baaṃ ko.* The fighters flew escort for the bombers. *Bwilijmāāṇ ro raar apare būrejtōn eo.* The police escorted the president.

apā (**hapay**). Cave under reef shelf.

apād (**hapad**). 2(inf, tr *-e*), 4(*riapād*), 7. Lie in wait for; ambush; waylay; snoop; stalk someone or something. *Ij apād kake bu e.* I am waiting with a gun. *Ij apāde ḷeeṇ kōn bu e.* I am waiting for him with a gun.

apdik (**hapdik**). 3, 3+5, 5(*apdikdik*), 8. Less in quantity; diminish; lessen. *Eapdikḷọk jidik menọknọk ko.* The junk is getting cleaned up bit by bit. *Kwōn jino im kaapdikdik aṃ jerbal.* Start getting your work out of the way little by little.

apeltak (**hapeltak**). Dial. W: *rāpeltak* (**raypeltak**), E: *rapeltak* (**rahpeltak**). 1(*-i*), 2, 3, 4. Cramped; clumsy. *Ejjeḷọk apeltakin an jeje.* The way he writes is really clumsy. *Ejjeḷọk (ot) apeltakū.* I am clumsy. *Ij jab apeltak.* I am not clumsy. *Iapeltak kōn men kākaṇ.* I am cramped by those things.

apeñāñā (**hapegaygay**). 1(*-i*), 2, 3(inf, tr *-ik*), 4. Wasted away; emaciated; very thin.

apep (**hapyẹp**). Variant form of *apap* (**haphap**).

apep (**hapyẹp**). 2(inf, tr *-e*), 4, 6(*-i*), 7. Fishing method, using woven brown coconut fronds to catch sardines and minnows as they are chased ashore by bigger fish. *Kōm ar apep im booḷ iep eo.* We caught sardines using the *apep* method and filled the basket.

apet (**hapẹt**). Also *apit* (**hapit**). 1(*apeti-*), 6(*apetin*). Canoe part, curved piece connecting outrigger to hull.

apkaaj (**hapkahaj**). From Engl. *half-caste*. 3, 4, 6(*-i*). Half-caste; hybrid.

aplep (**haplep**). 1(*-i*), 2, 4, 6(*-i*). Wilful disobedience; lasciviousness.

aplo (**haplew**). 1, 2, 3(inf, tr *-uk*), 5(*aapelolo*), 6(*-i*), 8, 9. Slur one's words; babble; incoherent. *Jimañūñ eban jab kaaplouk an kōnnaan.* Toddy always slurs his speech. *Eaplolo an jipij.* The speech he made was slurred from beginning to end. *Eaplolo jipij eo an.* The speech he composed was such that it was slurred no matter who read it.

aploñloñ (**hapleg°leg°**). Also *appelōñlōñ* (**happelẹglẹg**), *abbwilōñlōn* (**habbilegleg**). 1(*-i*), 2, 3(inf, tr *-e*), 4. Aggravation; disturbance; enervate; discomfort; bothered; nagged; vexed. *Jab kōṃṃan aploñloñ bwe enaaj or tariṇae.* Stop causing a disturbance or a war may erupt.

appelōñlōñ (**happelẹglẹg**). Also *abbwilōñlōñ* (**habbilegleg**). 1(*-i*), 2, 3(inf, tr *-e*), 4. Variant form of *aploñloñ* (**hapleg°leg°**).

aproro (**haprẹwrẹw**). Variant form of *apaproro* (**haphaprẹwrẹw**).

ar (**har**). 2. Past tense.

ar (**har**). Lagoon beach; directional, enclitic, toward the lagoon side. *Ej mmaan iar.* It's anchored on the lagoon side. *Eṃweeaar wa eo.* The boat has entered the lagoon.

ar (**har**). 1(*-i*), 2(inf, tr *arin, ari*), 6(*-i*). Class; category; segment; image; copy; imitate actions of others; mock. *Arōt ṇe?* What class is that? *Arōṃṃan.* High class. *Kwōn jab lo ar.* Don't mock. *Kwōn jab arin ḷeeṇ bwe enaaj jook.* Don't imitate him or he'll be ashamed.

arar (**harhar**). 2(inf, tr *aruj(i)*), 6(*-i*), 7. Poke with something; stir food or fire with a stick. *Kwōn aruji kōn aḷaḷ ṇe.* Poke it with that stick.

arar (**harhar**). Also *arọr* (**harhar°**). 1(*-i*), 2(inf, tr *aruj*), 7. Pick out food from teeth; pick out splinters; extricate, as meat from clam. *Eor ke kein arar ñi?* Do you have a toothpick? *Ṃọjin an ṃōñā ear aruj ñiin.* After he ate he picked his teeth. *Kwōn aruj tenaḷ e peiū.* Pick the splinter out of my hand.

are (**harey**). Also *ari* (**hariy**). Archaic. Lagoon beach of; old construct form of *ar; modern form, arōn.*

ari (**hariy**). Transitive form of *ar* (**har**).

ari- (**hari-**). 1, 2, 6(-*i*). Like; similar to; imitate; mimic; emulate; simulate. *Ear al im arin Eḷbōj Būrejle.* He sang and mimicked Elvis Presley. *Etke kwōj jab arin rukkwōjarjar?* Why aren't you like a saint? *Kwōn jab arū bwe ña rinana.* Don't follow my example for I'm a bad model.

arin (**harin**). Transitive form of *ar* (**har**).

Arin-Mājlep (**harin-majlep**). See *ar:* "image of *Mājlep*". A constellation; epsilon, zeta, omega Aquilae.

arkooḷ (**harqeweḷ**). 1(-*i*), 2(inf, tr -*e*), 3. Alcohol. *Nōōj ro raar arkooḷe niññiñ eo bwe en dik ḷọk an pipa.* The nurses rubbed alcohol on the baby to reduce its fever.

armej (**harmẹj**). 3, 5(*armije*), 6(-*i*). Person; people; human being; folk; individual. *Earmije ānin.* This island has lots of people. or This island is inhabited.

armej jeedwa (**harmẹj jeedwah**). Also *armej jaduwa* (**harmẹj jahdiwah**). 6(-*i*), 7, 8, 9. Stranger, tramp, vagabond. *Armej jeedwaan in ia raṇe?* Where are those strangers from? *Iarmej jeedwaḷọk iānin jān eok.* I'm more of a stranger on this island than you.

armej waan (**harmẹj wahan**). Common people; commoner; riffraff.

arṃwe (**harṃey**). 3, 6(-*i*). A plant, tree *Pipturus argenteus* (Forst. f.) Weddell. (Urticaceae). A rather common tree with simple, acuminate leaves; almost palmately nervose; and minute flowers borne in pendent axillary racemes. The fruits are small, soft, whitish berries. The best fibres provide good cordage. (See *Loarṃwe* (**lewharṃey**).)

arokrā (**hareqray**). Variant form of *arorā* (**harewray**).

aroñ (**hareg°**). 3, 3+4, 6(-*i*), 3+7. A fish, African pompano; *Hynnis cubensis.*

arorā (**harewray**). Also *arokrā* (**hareqray**). Archaic. 2(inf, tr -*iki*), 3, 4. Carry in one hand. *Kwōn jab arorāiki niññiñ ṇe bwe enaaj wōtlọk.* Don't carry the baby with one hand or you'll drop it.

arot (**har°et**). Archaic. A game, similar to "drop the handkerchief"; circle around a pandanus tree, with person who is "it" dropping a discarded pandanus key behind someone.

arōk (**harek**). 1(-*i*), 2(inf, tr -*e*), 4. Miserly; covetous; greedy; stingy. *Arōk ṃweiuk.* Greedy for wealth. *Arōk jāān.* Greedy for money. *Arōk ṃaak.* Greedy for money. *Arōk ṃani.* Greedy for money.

arōk kōrā (**harek keray**). Jealous; possessive of women. *Eḷap an arōk kōrā ḷeeṇ.* He is jealous and possessive of his wife.

arōk menọknọk (**harek menaqnaq**). Miserly, even of worthless objects. *Earōk menọknọk ḷeeṇ.* He is a pack rat--saves any old thing--even trash.

arōk naan (**harek nahan**). Gossip. *Kōrā eḷap aer arōk naan.* Women like to gossip.

arōṃṃan (**hareṃṃan**). Well born; well-bred; high-born person; high-class person.

arōnpe (**harenpey**). Also *adenpe* (**hadenpẹy**). A fish, a shark.

arro (**harrew**). Our souls; ours; our, dual inclusive.

arrom (**har°r°em**). 1(-*i*), 2(inf, tr -*e*), 6(-*i*), 8. Eyes dim with age; perceive indistinctly; peer. *Ḷōḷḷap eo ear arrome wōt an armej eo deḷọñ tok.* The old man could hardly recognize the person who came in.

arrukwikwi (**har°r°iqiyqiy**). 1(-*i*), 2, 3(inf, tr -*ik*), 4. Ticklish; squeamish. *Kwōn jab kaarrukwikwiik katū.* Don't tickle my side.

aruj (**har°ij**). Transitive form of *arar* (**harhar**).

aruṃwijṃwij (**har°iṃijṃij**). Variant form of *aruñijñij* (**har°igijgij**).

aruñijñij (**har°igijgij**). Also *aruṃwijṃwij* (**har°iṃijṃij**), *arruñijñij* (**har°r°igijgij**), *aorñijñij* (**hawergijgij**). 1(-*i*), 2(inf, tr -*i*), 3, 4. Wake up, unwillingly; sleepy; groggy. *Eḷap aō kar aruñijñij ke ej jibboñ.* I didn't feel like waking up this morning. *Kwōn jab kaaruñijñiji eok make.* Stop making yourself sleepy.

at (**hat**). From Engl. 3, 6(-*i*). Hat. *Epād ia at eo aō?* Where is my hat? *Ña ij kaat.* I'm looking for a hat. *Atin ia ṇe aṃ?* Where did you get that hat from?

at (**hat**). 1(-*i*). Gall bladder; seat of brave emotions; seat of ambition; bile. *Ekajoor atin ñan kōṃṃane men eṇ.*

He's not afraid to do that. *Ekajoor atin ñan kkōnono ñan armej.* He's not afraid to speak to people.

at (**hat**). 5(*ate*), 6(-*i*). Bow waves from a ship. *Wa ņe ļe eate.* The boat cuts through the water beautifully.

atabuñ (**hathabig°**). 3. Ripe fruit, fallen to the ground. *Būki waj atabuñ kā im kōmatti.* Take these fruit and cook them.

atad (**hatad**). Also *ļōļ* (**ļeļ**). 2(inf, tr -*e*), 4, 6(-*i*), 7. Wire leader, used in fishing. *Bōlen kwōn atade bwe en jab jako kāāj ņe.* Maybe you should use a wire leader so you won't lose the hook. *Atadin ilarak.* Trolling wire leader.

atajinemjen (**hatajinemjen**). 1(-*i*), 2, 4, 6(-*i*). Orphan.

atak (**hatak**). 1(-*i*), 2(inf, tr -*e*), 4, 6(-*i*), 7. Tow; pull. *Kwōn atake wa ņe.* Tow that boat.

atake (**hatakęy**). From Japn. *hatake*. Farm; garden. *Ennǫ kobban atake eņ an.* The fruits of his farm are delicious.

atakiia (**hatakiyyah**). 1(-*i*), 2, 7, 8, 9. Hard to drag in water (see *atakiie* (**hatakiyyęy**)).

atakiie (**hatakiyyęy**). 1(-*i*), 2, 7, 8, 9. Easy to drag in water (see *atakiia* (**hatakiyyah**)).

atanijo (**hataniyjew**). Archaic. 1(-*i*), 2, 4, 6(-*i*). Work together. *Koṃwin itok jen atanijo im bwillǫke wa e.* Come let's work together and launch this boat.

atar (**hatar**). 2(inf, tr -*e*), 3, 4, 7. Go alongside of. *Atare ṃōk wa ņeņe.* Go alongside of that canoe there.

atar (**hatar**). Slang. 2(inf, tr -*e*), 7. Compare oneself with another; match; compete; paint or chop up to a line in canoe building. *Koban atare likao eņ.* You can't compare youself with him. *Itok kōjro jekab em atar doon.* Let's see which of us is better at checkers. *Atar erran.* Paint or chop up to the charcoal mark (older expression for *atarļain*).

atartar (**hatartar**). 1(-*i*), 2, 3, 4, 4+3, 7, 3+7, 10(*atōrak*). Lean upon; lean back; adjoining; depend on people; rest on; come alongside; sit close together. *Wa eo eņ eatartar ṃaan wab.* The ship is tied up at the end of the pier.

atat (**hathat**). From *at* (**hat**). 1(-*i*), 2, 3(inf, tr *kaatat(e)*), 4+3, 7. Wear a hat. *Kwōn atat bwe edet.* Wear a hat because the sun is hot. *Ewi wāween atatin Toni?* How does Tony wear his hat? *Kwōn kaatate ļadik ņe.* Put a hat on that boy.

atat (**hathat**). 3, 6(-*i*). A plant, vine, *Triumfetta procumbens* Forst. F. (Tiliaceae). A creeping woody herb with yellow 5-petaled flowers. The stems are dried and used for light cordage; the roots provide a brownish dye. N.

atbǫkwōj (**hatbaqej**). Also *bǫkwōj* (**baqej**). 1(-*i*), 2(inf, tr -*e*), 3, 4, 7. Embrace; cuddle; strain. *Kwōn atbǫkwōj niññiñ e bwe epiǫ.* Cuddle this baby because it's chilly.

atebar (**hatęybar**). 1(-*i*), 2(inf, tr -*e*), 3(st inf *kaatebarbar*, tr *kaatebar*), 4, 5(*aattebarbar*). Impatient; tense; jealous. *Eļap aō atebar kōn an luujļǫk wōt tiim e aō.* I am impatient because my team keeps losing. *Kwōn jab kaatebare bwe emaroñ bwebwe.* Stop making him jealous or he'll go crazy.

ati (**hatiy**). Also *atiti* (**hatiytiy**). Rack for heat or smoke drying. *An wōn in ati?* Whose *ati* is this?

atiļǫǫr (**hatiyļawar**). Variant form of *ļwaar.*

atin kǫǫnjeļ (**hatin kawanjeļ**). Variant form of *ṃǫkwōd* (**ṃaqed**).

Atinek (**hatinyęk**). From *atin* (**hatin**) "gall bladder of", *ek* (**yęk**) "fish". 3, 6(-*i*). A plant, pandanus cultigen.

atiti (**hatiytiy**). 1(-*i*), 2(inf, tr -*ik*), 3, 4, 6(-*i*). Smoke; dry fish or copra by heat; parch. *Kwōn atitiik waini kaņe bwe ren ṃōrā ļǫk.* Smoke that copra so that it will get drier.

atkadu (**hatkadiw**). A fish, *moi, Polydactylus sexfilis.*

atlaļ (**hatlaļ**). 1(-*i*), 6(-*i*). Lower jaw.

atlo (**hatlew**). 1(-*i*), 2, 4. Magical power of speech; sorcerer whose speech has magical power. *Eļap an kajoor atlo in ļeeņ.* He can enchant people with his words.

atlōñ (**hatlęg**). 1(-*i*). Upper jaw.

ato (**hatęw**). 1(-*i*), 2, 3(inf *kaatoto*, tr *kaatuwe*), 7. Take off of fire; come out of water. *Kwōn kaatuwe ainbat ņe.* Take that pot off the fire.

atok (**hateq**). Dial. E only; see *itok* (**yiteq**). 2. Come.

atōrak (**haterak**). 1(-*i*), 2, 3, 4, 7. Lean; perfective form of *atartar* (**hatartar**). *Kwōn jab atōrak bwe jebane eok.* Don't lean (on me) because I can't support you.

atōrej (**hateryej**). From Engl. *address*. 2(inf, tr -*e*), 6(-*i*), 7. Address a letter. *Iar atōreje lōta eo aō ñan ledik eo jera.* I addressed the letter to my girl. *Kwōmaroñ atōrejetok ñan ña.* You can address it to me.

atro (**hatrew**). 1(-*i*), 2(inf, tr -*uk*), 3, 4. Pandanus mat for sail cover; cover a sail. *Kwōn atrouk wōjḷā ṇe bwe en jab ute.* Cover that sail so that it doesn't get rained on.

attūkoko (**hattikewkew**). 1(-*i*), 2(inf, tr -*uk*, -*ik*), 3, 4, 6(-*i*). Eat garbage; eat left-overs. *Kwōn jab attūkoko bwe enaaj metak ḷọjieṃ.* Don't eat scraps or you will get a stomach ache.

atūñ (**hatig**). 3, 6(-*i*). Land crab, brown.

aubō (**hawibẹh**). 1, 4, 6(-*i*), 7. Fishing method, spearfishing on reef. *Eṃṃan bōkā in ñan aubō.* The tide is just right for spearfishing on the reef.

audaṃ (**hawidaṃ**). 3, 6(-*i*). A fish, parrotfish, *Callyodon bataviensis*; Batavian parrotfish.

audik (**hawidik**). Steer canoe with paddle on right of stern to keep bow straight; paddle is usually on left of stern.

auj (**hawij**). From Engl. *out.* 2, 3(inf *kawūjwūj*, tr -*i*), 4, 6(-*i*). Get nabbed; caught; reach a goal. *Ear auj jān jemān ledik eo.* He was caught by the girl's father. *Ear kawūjwūj im auj.* He played solitaire and reached his goal.

aujek (**hawijẹk**). Also *aojek* (**hawẹjẹk**). 1(-*i*), 2(inf, tr -*e*, *aujike*), 3, 4, 6(-*i*), 7. Stir. *Ear aujek ṃakṃōk.* She made some starch. *Kwōn aujeke bwe en jab tuḷar.* Stir it so it doesn't burn.

aujepaḷ (**hawijephaḷ**). 1(-*i*), 2, 3(inf, tr -*e*), 7, 8, 9. Clumsy; lanky; unwieldy; gangling. *Eaujepaḷ wōt eṇ ḷaddik.* What a gangling boy he is.

aujiid (**hawijiyid**). Also *aujid* (**hawijid**). 1(-*i*), 2(inf, tr -*i*), 4, 6(-*i*), 7. Trap; snare. *Eor ke koṇan aujiid eo aṃ?* Did you catch any birds in your snare? *Kwōn aujidi bao eṇ.* Snare that bird.

aujọjọ (**hawijawjaw**). Also *aojọjọ* (**hawejawjaw**). 3, 6(-*i*). Disturbance caused in water by canoe or fish. *Ek rot eṇ ej aujọjọ ijjuweo?* What kind of fish is that stirring up the water over there?

aujpitōḷ (**hawijpiteḷ**). From Engl. 4, 6(-*i*). Hospital.

aujrọñrọñ (**hawijrag°rag°**). 1(-*i*), 2(inf, tr -*e*), 3, 7. Bristle; stick up, on head or canoe. *Ta ṇe ej aujrọñrọñ eoon bōraṃ?* What's that on top of your head?

Aujtōrōlia (**hawijtereliyah**). From Engl. 4. Australia.

aujwe (**hawijwẹy**). A fish.

auḷakḷak (**hawiḷakḷak**). 6(-*i*). Spoon made from chip of green coconut husk.

auḷeḷe (**hawiḷeyḷey**). Also *aoḷeḷe* (**haweḷeyḷey**). 2, 6(-*i*), 7. Mill around, of small fish.

aunel (**hawinyẹl**). 3, 6(-*i*). A fish.

aunij (**hawinij**). From Engl. Ounce. *Jete aunijin ek eo?* How many ounces did the fish weigh?

aunwōḷā (**hawinweḷay**). Variant form of *añinwōḷā*.

Aunwōḷān-lañ (**hawinweḷayan-lag**). A constellation; sigma in Sagittarius and beta Librae; an arc drawn between these two stars and extended to Polaris in the north and Hydrus in the south is called "the diagonal timber of heaven" which divides the summer sky into east and west.

auretam (**hawireytam**). Archaic. 1, 2(inf, tr -*e*), 4. To paddle a canoe on the starboard side to change course. *Kwōn auretame wa ṇe bwe en jab itaak.* Paddle on the starboard to keep the canoe from hitting the coral head.

aut (**hawit**). Formant in place names; see *out.*

autak (**hawitak**). 3, 4+3, 6. A fish. *Autakin ia ṇe?* Where did you get that *autak*?

aū (**hahih**). 1, 2, 4. Be dying; near death. *Juon eṇ rinañinmej eaū.* A sick person is dying there.

aūn (**hahin**). Transitive form of *aō* (**haheh**).

awa (**hawah**). From Engl. 1(-*a*), 2(inf, tr -*ik*), 3(*kaawawa*), 6(-*a*). Hour; clock; time. *Ij etal kiiō bwe eawaūk eō.* I'm going now because I'm late. *Kōjro kaawawa ijin.* Let's kill time here.

Awai (**hawahyiy**). 4. Hawaii.

awal (**hawal**). Variant form of *aol* (**hawel**).

aweep (**haweyep**). Dialectal variant of *aop* (**hawep**).

awetak (**haweytak**). 2(inf, tr *-e*), 3(inf, tr *-e*), 6(*-i*). Part. *Eban peljo bwe ealikkar awetak eṇ an.* You can't miss him because of his outstanding part.

awi (**hawiy**). Archaic. Chiefly carriage and demeanor.

awiia (**hawiyyah**). 1(*-a*), 2, 3(inf, tr *-ik*), 4, 8, 9. Wild; undomesticated; barbaric; savage (see *awiie* (**hawiyyẹy**)). *Kwōn jab kaawiiaik bao eṇ.* Don't make that chicken wild.

awiia (**hawiyyah**). A game, dare base (two bases).

awiie (**hawiyyẹy**). 1(*-i*), 2, 3(inf, tr *-ik*), 4, 8, 9. Tame; domesticated (see *awiia* (**hawiyyah**)).

awōj (**hahwẹj**). Dialectal variant of *iwōj* (**yiwẹj**).

ā (**yay**). Formant in place names.

ābukwi. See *eabukwi.*

āe (**yayẹy**). 1(*-i*), 2(inf, tr *-ik*), 4, 7. Carve; repair a boat; fix; overhaul.

āe (**yayẹy**). Name of the letter *e.*

āi- (**yayi-**). 1. Same as; similar to; different from. *Āin wōt men e.* It's the same as this. *Āin ḷọk wōt jemān.* He's similar to his dad. *Āin juon jān e.* He's different from him.

āibukwi (**yayibiqiy**). Also *iāebukwi* (**yiyayebiqiy**). 3, 6(*-i*). A fish, ray fish (poisonous). *Kōjro etal in kāiāebukwi.* Let's go and catch some ray fish.

āierḷọkwōt (**yayiyẹrḷaqwet**). Et cetera; etc.

āindein (**yayindẹyin**). 7. Thus; as; so; just as; therefore; likeness.

āinjuon (**yayinjiwen**). 7. Different; unlike; otherwise. *Āinjuon aerro ḷōmṇak jān doon.* Those two have differing opinions.

āinḷọk (**yayinḷaq**). More similar to; almost alike.

āinwōt (**yayinwet**). Too; also; same; equal; like; resemble; seem. *Lukkuun āinwōt.* Exactly the same. *Ejjeḷọk āinwōt ilo bōnbōn.* In mathematics she has no equal.

āinwōt juon (**yayinwet jiwen**). Same; alike; never mind; that is all right; identical. *Āin ḷadik raṇe wōt juon.* Those two boys are identical. *Āinwōt juon ñe kwōjab etal.* It's all right if you don't go.

āj (**yaj**). 1(*-i*), 2(inf, tr *-e*), 3, 4. Weave; darn; knit. *Ear āj jaki.* She wove the mat. *Ear āje juon jaki.* She wove a mat. *Ear āje juwain ṇe.* She knit that lace.

āj (**yaj**). 6(*-i*). Fit for (always followed by construct particle *in*). *Āj in ṃōñā.* Fit for consumption. *Āj in kāine.* Good for breeding. *Āj in uṃuṃ.* Right for baking. *Āj in karūtto.* Ripe for deflowering. *Āj in jaajmi.* Just right for eating raw.

āj (**yaj**). 6(*ājin, āji*). Bunch of bananas. *Ājin keeprañ.* A bunch of bananas.

ājāj (**yajyaj**). 1, 2, 3, 4. Vicious; mischievous; naughty.

ājinkōj (**yajinkẹj**). A share; inheritance.

ājḷor (**yajḷẹr°**). 2(inf, tr *-e*), 4, 6(*-i*), 8, 9. Take as much as possible from a person; exploit. *Ājḷor kōn jeḷā kaṇ an ke ej ja mour.* Exploit what he knows while he's still around.

ājmuur (**yajmiwir**). Also *ājmour* (**yajmẹwir**). 1(*-i*), 2, 3, 4, 7. Healthy; robust; energetic; frisky, sound, vigorous.

ākā (**yakay**). Dialectal variant of *ajokḷā* (**hajeqḷay**).

ākil (**yakil**). Transitive form of *ākilkil* (**yakilkil**).

ākilkil (**yakilkil**). Also *kakilkil* (**kakilkil**), *kakkil* (**kakkil**), *ākkil* (**yakkil**), *ākil* (**yakil**). 1(*-i*), 2(inf, tr *ākil(i), kakil(i)*), 4, 7. To skin; to peel. *Ākili (kakili) piteto kaṇe.* Peel the potatoes. *Eākilkil likūṃ.* The skin on your back is peeling.

ākkil (**yakkil**). Variant form of *ākilkil* (**yakilkil**).

ākor (**yayqer**). Archaic. Forty pairs, fish or copra.

ākūt (**yakit**). 1(*-i*), 2(inf, tr *-i*), 3, 4. Delouse; sort out bad copra.

ākūtwe. Transitive form of *eakto* (**yaktẹw**).

āl (**yal**). 1(*-i*), 2(inf, tr *-e*), 4. Shave.

Āl-im-kobban (**yal-yim-qebban**). From *āl,* archaic word referring to a type of hut with no posts, and *kobban* "contents": "hut with contents". A constellation; stars in Centaurus (1, 2, 3) or Corvus.

ālāl (**yalyal**). 1(*-i*), 2(inf, tr *ālōk(e)*), 4, 6(*-i*), 7, 10(*ālkōk*). Turn over or up; pull out; raise; turn pages or leaves. *Kwōn ālōkļǫk m̧ōk peij ņe.* Please turn your book to the next page.

āle (**yalẹy**). Roll up mats, etc. *Kwōn āle m̧ōk jake ņe.* Please roll that mat up.

ālij (**yalij**). 1(*-i*), 2(inf, tr *-i*), 7. Repeat; review; quote; recite; reiterate. *Kwōn bar āliji m̧ōk jāntōj eo kwaar ba.* Please say that sentence again.

ālijinmen (**yalijinmen**). 1(*-i*), 2, 3. Repetitious; repeat over and over. *Em̧ōj ņe am̧ ālijinmen.* Don't keep on saying the same thing over and over.

ālik (**yalik**). Later. *Inaaj iwōj ālik.* I'll come later.

āliki- (**yaliki-**). 1, 6. After; outside; back; behind; last. *Ta in rej kōm̧m̧ane ālikin m̧wiin?* What are they doing outside (the house)? *Emetak ālikū.* My back hurts. *Kwōn bar itok ālikin juon wiik.* Come back again in a week. *Inaaj iwōj ālikin jet minit.* I'll be back in a few minutes.

ālikinjepjep (**yalikinjepjep**). Also *ālikinjepjep* (**yalikinjẹpjẹp**). 1(*-i*), 2(inf, tr *-e*), 6(*-i*), 7. Defraud; cheat; treat unfairly; take for granted. *Kwōn jab ālikinjepjepe eō bwe em̧ool iǫkwe in aō.* Don't be unfair for my love is true. *Etke kweālikinjepjepe eō?* Why are you cheating me?

āliklik (**yaliklik**). 1(*-i*), 2, 3, 4. Ashamed, concerning food; embarrassed. *Iāliklik kōn m̧ōñā kā kōnke jejjab naajdik er.* I am ashamed that we're not sharing this food with them.

āliktata (**yaliktahtah**). 1(*-i*), 2, 7. Very last; final; finally.

ālim (**yalim**). Transitive form of *ānen* (**yanyẹn**).

ālkōk (**yalkẹk**). 1(*-i*), 2, 3, 7, 10(*ālkōk, alkōk*). Bent back; perfective form of *ālāl* (**yalyal**). *Ealkōk akkiin peiū.* My fingernail got bent back.

ālkur (**yalqir**). Transitive form of *ālkurkur* (**yalqirqir**).

ālkurkur (**yalqirqir**). 1(*-i*), 2(inf, tr *ālkur(i)*), 3, 7. Turn the back on someone. *Etke kwōjaam jijet im ālkurkur?* Why are you sitting with your back turned? *Kwōn jab ālkuri eō.* Don't turn your back on me.

ālkūm̧ur (**yalkim̧ir°**). 1, 3(inf, tr *-i*), 6(*-i*), 8, 9. Fruit of aged trees. *Rej jab nnǫ mā kaņe kōnke reālkūm̧ur.* Those breadfruit are not good because they're from an old tree.

ālkwōj (**yalqej**). 1(*-i*), 2(inf, tr *-e*), 7, 10(*ālokjak*). To fold; to bend.

ālokjak (**yaleqjak**). 1(*-i*), 2(inf, tr *-e*), 3, 7. Bent over; crimped; perfective form of *ālkwōj* (**yalqej**); buckled. *Eālokjak jaki eo.* The mat is crimped. *Eālokjak neō.* I turned my ankle. *Joñan an kadek eļak tan jutak eālokjak neen.* He was so drunk when he tried to stand his legs buckled.

ālokorkor (**yalẹqẹrqẹr**). 2(inf, tr *ālokor*). Look back. *Kwōn jab ālokor kōj.* Don't look back at us.

ālōk (**yalek**). Transitive form of *ālāl* (**yalyal**).

ālu (**yaliw**). Tacks in sailing. *Em̧m̧an kōto in naaj bōlen ruom jilu wōt ālū.* The wind is good and two or three tacks should be enough.

ālur (**yalir°**). 2(inf, tr *-i*), 4, 6(*-i*), 7. Bail out. *Ta wūnin am̧ ālurļǫk ļwe ņe?* Why are you bailing out the pond?

ām (**yam**). 2, 3, 7. To tip, as of canoe; sail with outrigger out of water. *Eām wa eo.* The canoe is tipping.

ām (**yam**). Sennit used for tying canoes.

āmej (**yamẹj**). 2(inf, tr *-e, āmije*), 4, 6(*-i*), 7. Mourn a deceased; pay respects to a deceased; see *ilomej*. *Kōpooj rimej ņe bwe riāmej ro rā tok.* Get the deceased ready because the mourners are coming.

āmje (**yamjẹy**). From Engl. 2(inf, tr *-ik*). Empty; devoid. *Eor ke āmje bato?* Do you have an empty bottle? *Eāmje bato e.* This bottle is empty.

ānbwin (**yanbin**). 1(*ānbwinni-*). Body; frame; hull; physical.

āne (**yanẹy**). Also *ene* (**yẹnẹy**). 1(*āne-*), 7. Islet; island; land; directional, enclitic, islandward or shoreward. *Kwōn wōnānetak.* Come ashore.

āne-jem̧aden (**yanẹy-jem̧aden**). Wilderness; desert isle; desert.

ānen (**yanyẹn**). 1(*-i*), 2(inf, tr *ālim, ānene, ānine*), 3, 4, 7. Bail out water from canoe or boat. *Kwōn ānen ļǫk bwe enaaj douj wa ņe.* Bail faster or the canoe will ship water. *Kwōn* *ālim wa ņe bwe enaaj douj.* Bail the canoe or it will ship water.

ānin (**yanyin**). 4(*riānin, riinin*). This islet. *Kwe ke riānin (riinin)?* Are you from this islet?

ānine (**yaniney**). Transitive form of *ānen* (**yanyęn**).

āñiia (**yagiyyah**). 1(-*i*), 2, 3, 4. Slow when called (see *āñiie* (**yagiyyęy**)).

āñiie (**yagiyyęy**). 1(-*i*), 2, 3, 4. Quick when called (see *āñiia* (**yagiyyah**)).

āñin (**yagin**). 1(-*i*), 2(inf, tr -*i*). Escort; lead; show where to go. *Kwōn āñini koṃro ṃōñā.* Escort him to the table.

āñinñin (**yagingin**). Variant form of *āñiñin* (**yagiygin**).

āñiñin (**yagiygin**). Also *āñinñin* (**yagingin**). 2, 7. Calling someone by name. *Kairḷọk bwe rej āñiñin eok.* Hurry on for they're calling you.

āñiñintok (**yagiyginteq**). 1(-*i*), 2. Call to come.

āpil (**yapil**). A fish.

āpta (**yaptah**). Also *epta.* Archaic. Do something twice; redo; reread; rewrite; pour water through strainer twice in making arrowroot starch.

ār (**yar**). 1(-*i*), 2(inf, tr -*ek*), 3, 4, 7. Haul canoe or vessel up on shore; to beach canoe or vessel. *Itok jen ār.* Come let's haul ashore. *Itok jen ārōk wa eņ.* Come let's haul that canoe ashore.

ār (**yar**). 1(-*i*). Lung.

ār (**yar**). 6(-*i*). Pandanus core; discarded pandanus key.

ār (**yar**). Variant form of *kiār* (**kiyar**).

ārār (**yaryar**). Come closer. *Kwōn ārār tok ijeņe.* Come closer (called by leader in *aḷeḷe* fishing).

ārpej (**yarpęj**). 1(-*i*), 2, 3, 4, 7, 8, 9. Weakling; invalid. *Ejjeḷọk wōt ārpej in ņe eṃṃaan.* That fellow is really a weakling.

āt (**yat**). 1(*eta-*). Name; reputation. *Eṃṃan ke etan?* Has he a good reputation?

āt (**yat**). 1(-*i*). Eyebrow.

ātāt (**yatyat**). Dial. E: *ātoñ(ū-)* (**yateg°(i-)**), W: *ātuñ(ū-)* (**yatig°(i-)**). 1(*ātoñi-*), 2(inf, tr *ātoñ*), 3(inf, tr *kāātet*). Smell. *Bwiin ta in ij āt?* What's this odor I smell? *Kwōn ātoñ ṃōk pein eaelel ke.* Smell his hands and see if they smell like fish.

ātbwe (**yatbęy**). 1(-*i*), 2, 3, 4, 6(-*i*), 8. Sty on the eye. *Eātbwe mejān.* He's got a sty on his eye.

ātdik (**yatdik**). 1, 2, 3, 4. Pet name; nickname.

āte (**yatey**). Transitive form of *ātet* (**yatyęt**).

āteo (**yatyew**). Also *ātin* (**yatyin**). As expected; deserving of. *Āteo rinana.* Now that's a rascal for you. (What he's done is his expected behavior.) *Kwōj kab āteo jorrāān.* Now you've really had it. (You were already in trouble but now....) *Āteo bwebwe.* Now that's what I call stupid.

ātet (**yatyęt**). 1(-*i*), 2(inf, tr *āte*), 4, 7. Pack; put in container; impound. *Kwōn ātetḷọk bwe enaaj jerak wa eņ.* Pack up because the boat is sailing soon. *Kwōn āti nuknuk kaņe.* Pack those clothes. *Jab kōrōḷọk piik ņe kijeṃ bwe enaaj ātet.* Don't let your pig roam free or it'll be impounded.

ātin (**yatyin**). Also *āteo* (**yatyew**). From *āt in* (**yat yin**) "this name" (deserving of this description). Really; extremely; true to fact. *Lukkuun baj ātin taibuun.* Now that's what I call a typhoon. *Emake naaj kar baj lukkuun ātin jorrāān.* He would have really had it.

ātlep (**yatlep**). 1(-*i*), 2(inf, tr -*e*), 3, 4. Name with *Li-* or *Ḷa* prefix; address someone using *Li-* or *Ḷa-* prefix on name.

ātņaake (**yatņahakey**). Variant form of *etņake* (**yetņakey**).

ātņak (**yatņak**). 2(inf, tr -*e*). Be named after; take the name of another. *Ej ātņake jemān.* He's named after his father.

ātoñ (**yateg°**). Transitive form of *ātāt.*

ātōk (**yatek**). Lesser royal rank; conferred by chief as reward for service or bravery in battle. *Ḷeātōktōk.* Title of male in *ātōk* rank. *Liātōktōk.* Title of female in *ātōk* rank.

ba (**bah**). 2, 7. Say. *Ta ņe kwōj ba?* What are you saying? *Kwōn ba ḷọk ñan ṃaṃa ke ij jab etal.* Tell mother that I'm not going.

ba (**bah**). Dial. E only; see *uwur* (**wwir**). 1(-*i*), 2(inf, tr -*ik*), 3, 4, 7. Runny nose; mucous; blow the nose. *En jab jabde aṃ ba.* Don't blow your nose carelessly.

ba (**bah**). From Engl. Syllable "fa" of musical scale.

ba (**bah**). Dialectal variant of *bōḷa* (**beḷah**).

ba kajjie- (**bah kajjiye-**). 1, 2, 4. Show; point out; introduce. *Kwōmaroñ ke ba kajjien ṃweo iṃōn Robōt?* Can you show me where Robert's house is? *Eṃōj ke aṃ ba kajjien ñane?* Have you introduced him?

ba pata (**bah pahtah**). 1(*-i*), 2, 3, 4. Say in vain. *Kwōn jab ba pata etan aṃ Irooj.* Thou shalt not take the name of the Lord thy God in vain. *Kwōn jab ba pata eta.* Don't call me for nothing.

baab (**bahab**). 2. Suppose; have an opinion; think. *Ibaab kwōnaaj kar itok im iar kōttar.* I thought you would come and I waited for you.

baaj (**bahaj**). Slang. From Engl. 2, 3. Taken aback; halted; give up; pass, in card games; surrender. *Etal wōt bwe ibaaj.* I pass (in poker). *Ibaaj...Ibaaj.* I give up (in fighting).

baajkōḷ (**bahajkeḷ**). Also *baajikōḷ* (**bahajikeḷ**). From Engl. 1(*-i*), 2(inf, tr *-e*), 3, 4, 6(*-i*), 7. Bicycle. *Kwōmaroñ ke baajkōḷe juon pāāk in raij?* Can you carry a bag of rice on your bicycle? *Kwōn kōbaajkōle bwe en jab jañ.* Let him ride the bike so he doesn't cry.

baak (**bahak**). From Span. *barco*. 4, 6(*-i*). Ship; barque; frigate.

baak (**bahak**). From Engl. 1, 2(inf, tr *-e*), 7. To park. *Baake tūrak ṇe im ḷoor eō.* Park the truck and follow me.

baal (**bahal**). 6(*-i*). Coral species; reef edge. *Eike baal in Ṃajeḷ.* There are a lot of fish in the reef edges of the Marshalls.

baaṃ (**bahaṃ**). From Engl. 2(inf, tr *-e*), 3, 4, 6(*-i*). Bomb. *Eṃōj aer baaṃe tiṃa eo.* They bombed the ship. *Kobaaṃ ke?* Are you contaminated with radioactive fallout? *Rūbaaṃ ro jān Roñḷap raṇe.* Those are the radiation victims from Rongelap.

baaṃle (**bahaṃḷẹy**). From Engl. 2, 3(inf, tr *-ik*), 4, 5(*bbaaṃlele*), 6(*-i*). Family. *Kwōn jab kapoiki bwe rūbaaṃle e.* Don't tempt him because he's a family man.

baankeek (**bahankẹyẹk**). From Engl. 1(*-i*), 2(inf, tr *-e*), 4, 7. Pancake. *Kab baankeeke pilawā ṇe ilju.* Be sure to make some pancakes out of that flour tomorrow.

baantuun (**bahantiwin**). From Engl. 6(*-i*). Pontoon. *Kwōj lo ke baantuunin dān eṇ?* Do you see that water tank?

baañke (**bahagkẹy**). From Engl. 3, 6(*-i*). A plant, vine, *Cucurbita pepo* L. (Cucurbitanceae); also *Lagenaria siceraria* (Molina) Standley; the gourd; pumpkin; squash.

baar (**bahar**). 1(*-i*), 2(inf, tr *-e*), 4, 10(*bbaar, bbarōk*). Prevent; guard. *Kwōn baare pein jān an deñōt eok.* Put your guard up so he doesn't hit you. *Enjeḷ in bbaar.* Guardian angel. *Ebbarōk jān rijorrāān ro.* He was protected from the hoodlums.

baar (**bahar**). From Engl. 6(*-i*). Crowbar.

baar (**bahar**). From Engl. *bar*. 6(*-i*). Saloon; tavern; bar.

baar (**bahar**). From Engl. *bar*. 6(*-i*). Metal insignia, military.

baat (**bahat**). 1(*-i*), 6(*-i*), 7. Smoke.

baatat (**bahathat**). 1(*-i*), 2(inf, tr *baate*), 3, 4+3, 7, 8, 9. Smoke; steam. *Eḷap an baatat injin eo ilo wa eo.* The engine of that ship is smoking. *Emọ kōbaatat (i) ṃwiin.* No smoking (in this building). *Kwōn jab baate mejaṃ.* Don't get smoke in your eyes. *Eḷap an baatat tok uṃ eṇ an lieṇ.* Her oven is making a lot of smoke come this way. *Kwe rūkōbaatat ke ak jaab?* Are you a smoker or not?

baate (**bahatey**). Transitive form of *baatat* (**bahathat**).

bab (**bab**). 1(*-i*), 2, 3(inf *kababbab*, tr *kabab*), 5(*aibabbab*), 6(*-i*), 7, 8, 9. Fit tightly; full; clinging; tight; lock in combat. *Eḷap aō bab.* I am full. *Eḷap an bab jedọujij e.* My trousers are too tight. *Eḷap aṃ kar kōbab jedọujij e aō.* You made my trousers too tight. *Eḷap an kōbabbab an keke nuknuk.* She always sews things too tight. *Ear bọkwōj lio im bab.* He embraced and clung to her. *Eban ein dein ḷọk wōt arro aibabbab in deo.* We can't go on clinging to each other forever. *Iruṃwij jān aerro bab.* I missed when they were locked in fight.

bab (**bab**). 3, 6(*-i*). A fish, kind of shark, no teeth; holotype of *Hemigaleops fosteri*. *Kwōn ilen kōbab tok.* Go catch some *bab*.

bab-laļ (**bab-laļ**). From *lǫļe* (**laļ°ey**) "quick-minded". 1(*-i*), 2+1, 3(inf *kabab(bab)-laļ,* tr *kabab-laļi-*), 4(*rūbab-laļ* "inspired person", *rūkababbab-laļ* "person who arouses enthusiasm"). Arouse; enthuse; inspire. *Eļap an bab-laļū kōn jipiij eo an* Kennedy. I am enthused about Kennedy's speech. *Eļap an kababbab-laļ an jipiij.* His speeches are rousing. *Eļap an kar kabab-laļū jipiij eo an.* His speech aroused my enthusiasm.

baba (**bahbah**). Father; daddy.

babbūb (**babbib**). 3, 6(*-i*). Butterfly; moth. *Ajri raņ rej kōbabbūb.* Those children are looking for butterflies.

babu (**bahbiw**). 1(*-i*), 2, 3(inf *kōbbabu,* tr *-uk, -ik*), 4, 6(*-i*), 7. Lie down. *Kwōn kōbabuuk niñniñ ņe ņai raan peet ņe.* Put the baby down on the bed there.

bad (**bad**). Archaic. Place for divination.

Bad (**bad**). A star.

badej (**bạdej**). 3, 6(*-i*). A fish, flounder, *Bothus mancus.*

badet (**badet**). 3, 6(*-i*). A fish, sergeant major, *Abudefduf septemfasciatus*; a fish, *maomao, Abudefduf abdominalis.*

badik (**badik**). 1(*-i*), 2, 3, 5(*bbadikdik, badikdik*), 7. Duck; lower the head, humble oneself; bow down. *Badik jān raan mā ņe bwe enaaj itaak bōraṃ ie.* Duck under the branch of that breadfruit tree or your head will bump it. *Kwōn badikdik im kabuñ ñan eō.* Humble yourself and bow down before me.

bae (**bahyey**). Dial. E only; see *koba* (**kewbah**). 3, 6(*-i*). Bamboo. *Ekije bae in Jepaan.* Japanese bamboo is strong.

bae (**bahyey**). From Engl. Pie. *Ennǫ an iiōk bae.* She cooks delicious pies.

baeļ (**bahyeļ**). From Engl. 2(inf, tr *-e*), 4, 6(*-i*). File. *Jerbal eo an eņ baeļi peba kaņ.* He's employed as a fileclerk.

baeoliin (**bahyewliyin**). From Engl. 6(*-i*). Violin.

baib (**bahyib**). From Engl. 2(inf, tr *-i*), 6(*-i*). Pipe; plumbing; duct; muffler. *Kwōn baibi injin ņe bwe en dik ainikien.* Put a pipe (muffler) on the engine to cut down the noise.

Baibōļ (**bahyibeļ**). Also *Bāibōļ* (**bayibeļ**). 2(inf, tr *-e*), 4, 5(*bbaibōļbōļ*), 6(*-i*). Bible; religious instruction; catechism. *Iar roñ an jinen Baibōļe bwe en kajiṃweik an mour.* I heard his mother give him religious instruction so that he would lead a straight life. *Ebbaibōļbōļ an kōnnaan.* He's always quoting scripture.

baid (**bahyid**). From Engl. *briar*. 3, 5(*bbaidid*). Smoking pipe; cigarette. *Emake bbaidid ļōņe.* That guy is a chain smoker. *Eṃṃan tata baidin pālle.* American smoking pipes are the best.

baidik (**bahyidik**). 3, 4+3 6(*-i*). A plant, *Nephrolepis biserata* (Sw.) Schott. Namorik. Boston fern. *Rej kōjerbal baidik i Ṃajeļ ñan kāinōknōk.* They use *baidik* in the Marshalls for decorations.

baidtōñtōñ (**bahyidtegteg**). 1(*-i*), 2, 3, 4, 6(*-i*). Chain smoke. *Ejjeļǫk wōt baidtōñtōñ in ļeeņ.* He is a great chain smoker.

baij (**bahyij**). From Engl. 2(inf, tr *-i*), 4, 6(*-i*). Vise.

baijin (**bahyijin**). From Engl. 1(*-i*), 2(inf, tr *-i*), 3, 4, 6(*-i*). Poison; harmful substances. *Kwōn jab ṃōñā jān laļ bwe kwōnaaj ṃōñā baijin.* Don't eat something that has fallen on the ground or you will eat something harmful. *Raar jorrāān jān baijin in baaṃ eo.* They were contaminated by the poison from the bomb.

baijin (**bahyijin**). From *baijin* (**bahyijin**) "poison". 2(inf, tr *-i*), 4, 6(*-i*). Discredit someone to gain favor with another, or as revenge. *Ear baijini eō ñan lio ippa.* He tried to turn my wife against me. (By telling her bad things about me). *Ejool bwe erūbaijin.* He is shunned because he habitually discredits people.

baiklaaj (**bahyiklahaj**). Also *jibaiklaaj* (**jibahyiklahaj**), *jibweiklaaj* (**jibẹyiklahaj**). From Engl. *spy glass*. 2(inf, tr *-e*), 4, 6(*-i*), 7. Telescope; binoculars; spyglass. *Baiklaaje tok ṃōk wa eņ.* Take a look at the boat through the binoculars.

baiļat (**bahyiļat**). From Engl. 2(inf, tr *-e*), 6(*-i*), 7. Pilot.

bait (**bahyit**). From Engl. 1(*-i*), 2(inf, tr *-i*), 3, 4, 7. Hit with fists; box; punch. *Wōn ņe ear baiti mejaṃ?* Who gave you a blackeye? *Rōnaaj kabaiti erro buñniin.* They will make them fight tonight.

baj (**baj**). Vulgar. 1(*-i*), 6(*-i*). Lower abdomen, triangular area; loins; pubis.

baj (**baj**). Also *bōj* (**bẹj**). 2. Almost; just; nearly; anyway. *Ibaj mej wōt jidik.* I almost killed myself. I almost got killed. *Kobaj et?* What's the matter with you? *Iar baj ḷōmņak wōt in itok.* I just thought I would drop by. I thought of dropping by anyway.

baj (**baj**). From Engl. 1(*-i*), 2(inf, tr *-e*), 3, 5(*bbajbaj*), 6(*-i*), 7. Bus. *Jen baj ḷọk ñan Bootbuuḷ.* Let's take the bus to the Boat Pool. *Kwōn uke ḷadik e im kōbaje.* Take this boy and put him on the bus. *Kwōn baje ḷọk ajri raņe ñan jikuuḷ.* Bus those children to school. *Ij jab wia bajin Jepaan.* I'm not buying Japanese buses.

baj (**baj**). Then, denoting diversion from one activity, person, or situation to another. *Eṃōj ņe kwe, baj ña.* Enough for you, my turn. *Kwōn jerbal em ḷak ṃōk, baj ña.* Work and when you're tired, I'll work. *Baj letok ṃōk juon jikka?* Say, how about giving me a cigarette? *Eo, baj lewaj.* Here, hold this (for a while).

baj ke (**baj key**). Also *bake* (**bahkey**), *make* (**mahkey**). But how about; interrogative generally countering previous statements. Following are three possible responses to *Ij ilān ektake.* I'll go pick her up. *Baj ke emmoottok?* But how can you when she's already here? *Baj ke enañinmej?* How can you when she's sick? *Baj ke ejako ṃweeņ iṃōn?* How since she's not at home? *Bake ij jerbal?* But how about my work?

baja (**bahjah**). From Engl. *purser*. 2, 6(*-i*), 7. Purser, ship; supercargo. *Ear bajaḷọk ñan Nawōdo.* He went to Nauru as purser. *Ej kōbajaik ḷeeņ nukun.* He's making his relative the purser.

bajbaj (**bajbaj**). Busy.

bajet (**bajet**). From Engl. 1(*-i*), 2(inf, tr *-e*), 6(*-i*). Budget; money; finance. *Kwōj aikuj jeḷā bajete oņāāṃ bwe kwōn jab bbūrookok.* You have to know how to spend your money so you aren't constantly broke.

bajinjea (**bahjinjeyah**). From Engl. 1(*-i*), 2, 3, 4, 6(*-i*), 7. Passenger; go as a passenger. *Kwōn je etaṃ ñan bajinjea.* Write your name as a passenger. *Kwōmaroñ ke kōbajinjeaik ledik ņe?* Can you take her along as a passenger?

bajjek (**bajjẹk**). A little; just; only, indicating relative unimportance of activity. *Ij jijet bajjek.* I'm just sitting.

bajke (**bajkey**). Variant form of *make* (**mahkey**).

bakbōk (**bakbek**). 3, 6(*-i*). Knife, small, not folding. *Kwaar kōbakbōk ke?* Did you look for a knife?

bakbōk (**bakbek**). Dialectal variant of *di* (**diy**).

bake (**bahkey**). Variant form of *make* (**mahkey**).

bake (**bakẹy**). A shell; *Spondius; disks used to make necklaces.*

Bake-eo (**bakẹy-yew**). See *bake* and *debwāāl-eo.* A star; gamma in Ophiuchus; possibly alpha in Canis Minor.

bakke (**bakkey**). 1(*-i*), 2, 4, 5(*bakkeke*) 6(*-i*), 8, 9. Yaws, ulcerated. *Etke kwōj jab taktō kōn bakke ņe neeṃ?* Why don't you see the doctor about that ulcer on your leg? *Ear bakke iiō eo ḷọk.* He had the yaws last year . *Idike lieņ bwe rūbakke eo ilo kar Mājro eņ.* I abhor her because she was the one with the yaws in Majuro sometime back.

bakkiiñ (**bakkiyig**). From Japn. *bakkin* "fine". 2(inf, tr *-i*), 4, 6(*-i*). Fine; bail. *Ear bakkiiñ kōn an kar buuḷ.* He paid a fine for speeding. *Jāj eo ear bakkiiñi rūkọọt ro.* The judge fined the burglars. *Bakkiiñ e aō bakkiiñin ke iar ire.* My fine is a result of my having gotten into a fight.

bakkito (**bakkiytẹw**). Also *baakkito* (**bahakkiytẹw**). 2, 4, 5(*bbakkitoto*), 6(*-i*), 8, 9. Yaws, ulcerated. *Ebakkito jet ajri in Ṃajeḷ.* Some Marshallese children have yaws.

bakōj (**bakej**). From Engl. 3, 4+3, 6(*-i*). Bucket; pail. *Kwōmaroñ ke jouj in kōbakōj arro bakōj iṃōn wia eņ an Robōt?* Can you please buy us some buckets at Robert's store?

bakōj (**bakej**). 3, 6(*-i*). A fish, *Pomacentrid*; *Abudefduf saxatilis.*

bakōḷ (**bakeḷ**). From Engl. *buckle*. 2(inf, tr *-e*), 6(*-i*). Buckle. *Ejaje bakōḷe kañūr eņ an.* He doesn't know how to buckle his belt.

baktōk (**baktẹk**). Variant form of *bọktōk* (**baqtẹk**).

bakūk (**bakik**). 1(*-i*), 2, 7. Well built body. *Eḷap an bakūk ajri ṇe nejiṃ.* Your child is well built.

bal (**bal**). 2(inf, tr *-e*), 4, 6(*ballin*). Covered over. *Enañin bal ke uṃ eo?* Has the earth oven been covered? *Koṃwin bale uṃ eṇ.* Cover that oven.

bale (**baļẹy**). Also *parij* (**parij**). 3, 4+3, 5(*bbalele*), 3+7, 5+8, 5+9. A fish, starry flounder, *Platichthys stellatus. Kwaar kōbale ia?* Where did you fish for *bale* at? *Enana bale bwe edidi. Bale* fish are not good to eat because they are very boney.

balle (**balley**). 1(*balli-*), 2, 4(*ripālle*), 5(*bballele*), 6(*ballin*). Covering; clothing; costume. *Eṃṃan ballin lieṇ.* She is well dressed. *Iballe kōn nuknuk.* I have lots of clothes. *Eḷap an balle kōn ṃweiuk.* He has lots of possessions. *Kwōn etal in ṇa balliṃ.* Go put on your clothes.

ballin (**ballin**). Construct form of *bal* (**bal**) *balle* (**balley**).

balu (**bahliw**). Also *balo* (**bahlẹw**). 1, 2, 3(inf, tr *-ik*), 5(*bbalulu*), 6(*-i*). Rebuffed; hurt as result of rejection; shotdown; rejected. *Ke ledik eo ej ba jaab joñan an mejān balu.* He had such a hurt expression on his face when the girl said no. *Jab kōbaaḷuuki.* Don't rebuff him. *Ḷeo ebbalulu eṇ.* He's always rebuffed.

baḷ (**baḷ**). Canoe part, end of yard, boom (*rojak ṃaan*).

baḷebọọḷ (**bahḷẹybawaḷ**). From Engl. *volleyball*. 2, 4, 6(*-i*). Play volleyball; volleyball. *Jọọn ej baḷebọọḷ kiiō.* John is playing volleyball now.

baḷuun (**baḷiwin**). Also *baḷwūn* (**baḷwin**). From Engl. *balloon*. 3, 4, 6(*-i*). Airplane; plane. *Kōm ar kōbaḷuun boñ.* We went to the airport last night to meet the airplane. *Rūbaḷuun ro raar itaak.* The fliers had a smash-up.

baṃ (**baṃ**). From Engl. 1(*-i*), 2(inf, tr *-e*), 4, 6(*-i*), 7. To bum. *Eṃōj ṇe aṃ baṃe eō bwe enāj maat jikka kā kijō.* You'd better stop bumming my cigarettes before I run out.

baṃ (**baṃ**). From Engl. 1(*-i*), 2(inf, tr *-e*), 4, 6(*-i*), 7. Pump; pulse; heart. *Kwōn baṃe neen baajkōḷ ṇe bwe edik kūtuon.* Pump up that bicycle tire because there is only a little air in it. *Baṃin Jepaan baṃ in.* This is a Japanese pump. *Eṃōjṇọ baṃ e aō.* My pulse is weak.

baṃbaṃ (**baṃbaṃ**). From "onomatopoeia". 2(inf, tr *-e*), 6(*-i*). Spanking, child speech. *Jab bōt bwe kwōnaaj baṃbaṃ.* Don't be naughty or you'll get a spanking.

baṃbōr (**baṃber**). From Engl. Bumper. *Ejorrāān baṃbōrin wa e waō.* My car's bumper is busted.

baṃpe (**baṃpẹy**). From Japn. *bampei*. 2, 6(*-i*). Sentinel; guard; sentry. *Baṃpe eo ad ṇe ilo meḷan in.* That's our security guard in this area. *Kwōn baṃpetok i ar tok.* Guard around the lagoon beach. *Ij baṃpeik meḷan in.* I'm guarding this area.

ban (**ban**). 1(*-i*), 2(inf, tr *-e*), 3, 4, 5(*bbanban*), 6(*-i*). Unable; cannot; impossible; weak; not have the ability to; never will do; negative future tense.

ban (**ban**). 1(*-i*), 2(inf, tr *-e*), 5(*bbanban*). Envious. *Kwōn jab bane lieṇ kōn jerbal eṇ an.* Don't envy her job. *Eṃōj ṇe aṃ bbanban.* Why don't you stop being so envious of everybody?

ban (**ban**). From Engl. 6(*-i*). Punch, beverage. *Kwōj idaak ke ban?* Would you like some punch? *Banin ea ṇe limōṃ?* Where did you get that punch from?

ban jjeor (**ban jjẹyẹr°**). Idiom. 2. Indelible. *Eban jjeor eọ ṇe.* That tattoo is indelible.

banban (**banban**). 1(*-i*), 2, 3, 4, 7. Weak, permanent condition; invalid. *Kōrā ebanban jān ṃṃaaṇ.* Women are weaker than men. *Iḷōḷḷap im banban ñan tallōñ kiō.* I'm old and now too weak to climb trees. *Kwōn jab kōbanban eok make.* Don't pretend to be a weakling.

baninnur (**baninnir°**). Also *banennoor* (**banẹnnẹwẹr**). Dialectal variant of *banonoor* (**banẹwnẹwẹr**).

banonoor (**banẹwnẹwẹr**). Dial. E, W: *baninnur* (**baninnir°**). Also *banennoor* (**banẹnnẹwẹr**), *baninnoor* (**baninnẹwẹr**). 3+7, 6(*-i*). Small basket, two handles, made from fronds. *Kwōmaroñ ke kabaninnur tok arro?* Can you find some small baskets for us?

banōḷ (**banẹḷ**). From Engl. 2(inf, tr *-e*), 6(*-i*), 7. Funnel. *Kwōn banōḷe tok* *ļalem kōļanin kiaaj.* Use the funnel and pour me five gallons of gas.

bañ (**bag**). From Engl. Bunk. *Bañ eo aō ṇe ippaṃ.* That's my bunk you're lying on.

bañij (**bagij**). Variant form of *ūrōrmej* (**hirhẹrmẹj**).

bao (**bahwew**). 3(*kōbao, kōbbaoo*), 4+3, 6(*bawūn, bawōn*). Bird; chicken; fowl. *Iar jibwe rūkōbbaoo ro boñ.* I caught the chicken thieves last night.

bar (**bar**). Also *libar.* 5(*barbare*), 6(*-i*). Rock. *Eļap an barbare arin Mājro.* The lagoon shore of Majuro is very rocky. *Lale aṃ etetal bwe ejjir barin ānin.* Watch your step for the rocks on this island are slippery.

bar (**bar**). 2. Again; more; also. *Jenaaj bar lo doon.* We'll see each other again. *Ibar bōk mej in.* I have a cold again.

bar (**bar**). 1(*-i*), 2, 3. Empty. *Ebar aebōj jimeeṇ eo.* The cistern is empty.

bar (**bar**). 1(*bōra-*), 6(*bōra-*). Head, top, tip. *Emetak bōra.* I have a headache. *Wōn ṇe ear ṃwijbare bōran ledik eṇ?* Who gave her a haircut? *Ejok i bōran kiju eo.* It landed on the top of the mast.

Bar (**bar**). Variant form of *Ļāātbwiinbar.*

bar jet (**bar jet**). Other; others.

bar jidik (**bar jidik**). A little more. *Bar jidik wōt ikōṇaan ba.* I want to say a little more.

bar juon (**bar jiwen**). Another.

barāinwōt (**barayinwet**). Also *barļanwōt* (**barļanwet**), *bareinwōt* (**barẹyinwet**). 2. The same; also; likewise. *Ebarāinwōt kōṇaan itok ijellọkun an kōṇaan ṃōñā.* Besides wanting to eat, he also wants to come.

bareinwōt (**barẹyinwet**). Variant form of *barāinwōt* (**barayinwet**).

barļanwōt (**barļanwet**). Variant form of *barāinwōt* (**barayinwet**).

barļọk (**barļaq**). From *bar* (**bar**) "rock", *ļọk* (**ļaq**) "away, further, more". Sand hardened together.

barōk (**bahrek**). 2, 3, 4, 6(*-i*). Shielded; protected. *Ebarōke jān rijorrāān ro.* He shielded her from the hoodlums.

barōk (**bahrek**). Transitive form of *bbaar* (**bbahar**).

baru (**bariw**). 3, 6(*-i*), 3+7. Crab, general term. *Kwōj kōbaru ke rainin?* Are you hunting for crabs today?

baru (**bariw**). 2(inf, tr *-ik*). Bulldozer; tractor. *Rej baruuk pij eṇ bwe en ṃṃan jepaan.* They are bulldozing the airfield to make it level.

baru (**bariw**). 2, 6(*-i*). School of fish on reef, herd of animals; shoal, of fish; batch; bevy; feeling that one can catch many fish. *Edoom baruun ek mouj eṇ.* That's a big school of *ek mouj*.

baru waan (**bariw wahan**). 3, 6(*-i*). Land crab, inedible. *Jej ṃōñā baru waanin Ṃajeļ.* We eat land crabs in the Marshalls.

barulep (**bariwlep**). 3, 6(*-i*). Coconut crab. *Ennọ tata barulepin Likiep.* Likiep Atoll has the tastiest coconut crabs.

bat (**bat**). 1, 2, 3, 4, 8, 9, 11(*batbōt*). Slow. *Ebat tipñōl eo waan Toni.* Tony's sailing canoe is slow. *Etke kwōj kōbate injin ṇe?* Why are you letting the engine run slow? *Ebat ļọk Jọọn jān ṃokta.* John is slower than before.

bat (**bat**). 5(*batbate*), 6(*-i*). Hill; mound; knoll. *Eļap an batbate ānin.* This islet has lots of mounds.

bat (**bat**). From Engl. *pot*. 6(*-i*). Container, usually five-gallon paint bucket. *Kobōk ia batin wūno mouj ṇe aṃ?* Where did you get your five-gallon bucket of white paint?

bata (**bahtah**). From Engl. *Father*. 2, 6(*-i*). Priest. *Ebata.* He's become a priest. *Bata in Amedka men raṇe.* Those are American priests.

batakļaj (**bahtakļaj**). 3, 4+3, 6(*-i*), 3+7. A fish, unicorn fish, *Naso brevirostris*. *Kwōmaroñ ke in etal in kabatakļaj kijeerro ilo juubōrṃakōt eṇ?* Can you go buy unicorn fish for us at the supermarket?

batbat (**batbat**). Vulgar. 1(*-i*), 2, 3(inf, tr *-e*), 6(*-i*), 7, 8, 9. Need to relieve oneself. *Alikkar an batbat bwe ear kajju ñan ṃōn bwidej eo.* She was obviously in dire need to relieve herself since she made a bee-line for the restroom. *Ebatbat wōn eṇ.* The turtle is going to lay eggs.

bate (**batẹy**). From Engl. 2(inf, tr *-ik*), 4, 5(*bbatete*), 6(*-i*), 7. Putty. *Enana aṃ kar bateik wa e bwe ej ettal wōt.* You didn't putty the cracks in the boat well as it still leaks.

bati (**batiy**). Archaic. Hill of; old construct form of *bat; modern form, batin.*

batin (**batin**). Slang. 2(inf, tr *-i*). Secret lover; sweetheart. *Ej batini lieṇ.* He's having her as a secret lover.

batin (**batin**). From Engl. 1, 2(inf, tr *-i*), 3, 6(*-i*). Button; pill; tablet, medicine; capsule. *Etūṃ batin in jōōt e aō.* The button is off my shirt. *Etke kwōj jab idaak batin in metak kā ñe emetak bōraṃ?* Why don't you take these aspirin pills if you have a headache? *Kwōn batini jōōt ṇe aṃ.* Button your shirt.

batin (**batin**). Construct form of *bat.*

bato (**batew**). From Engl. 2(inf, tr *-uk*), 3, 5(*bbatoto*), 6(*-i*). Bottle; jar; broken glass. *Kwōn juujuj bwe ren jab batoik neeṃ.* Wear shoes so that pieces of glass don't get in your feet. *Ebbatoto turun ṃwiin.* This house has a lot of bottles around it.

batoñtoñ (**bahteg°teg°**). Also *ṃōtato* (**ṃetahtęw**). 1(*-i*), 2, 3, 7. Sob. *Eḷap an kar jañ ledik eo im batoñtoñ ke ej roñ ke emej jemān.* That girl really cried and sobbed when she heard that her father had died. *Ej batoñtoñ tok wōt jān kweilọk eo.* He's sobbing from the meeting.

batur (**batir°**). 1, 2, 3(inf *kabbaturtur, kabatur*), 4, 6(*-i*). Crave fish; crave. *Eḷap aō batur bwe eto aō jañin ṃōñā ek.* I'm hungry for fish because I haven't eaten any for a long time. *Ij kōbbaturtur im ḷak ṃōñā enaaj lukkuun nnọ.* I'll refrain from eating (fish) for awhile so that when I do it will be so much more delicious.

baūjō (**bahihjeh**). 1(*-i*), 2, 3, 4. Always smiling or laughing; giddy; see *ūjō. Ebar baūjō kōn an tab.* He's giddy again from drinking. *Ebaūjō wōt ṇe kōrā.* I've never seen a woman who is always laughing like her.

bawūn (**bahwin**). Also *bawōn* (**bahwen**). Construct form of *bao* (**bahwew**).

bbaar (**bbahar**). Dial. W: *ebbaar* (**yebbahar**), E: *bōbaar* (**bebahar**). Also *bbarōk.* 1(*-i*), 2(inf, tr *barōk, baare*), 4. Blockade; inhibit; perfective form of *baar* (**bahar**). *Inej eo an Amedka ear barōk wa ko waan riRojia jān aer itok ñan Kiuba.* The American fleet blockaded Russian ships from coming to Cuba. *Inej eo an Amedka ear bbaar wa.* The American fleet set up a blockade. *Ebbaar kadede.* It has already been guarded.

bbadede (**bbadeydey**). Dial. W: *ebbadede* (**yebbadeydey**), E: *bōbadede* (**bebadeydey**). 1(*-i*), 2, 3, 4. Rough skin. *Ebbadede kiliṃ kōn aṃ kōjeje.* Your skin is rough because you got sunburned. *Kobbadede.* Your skin is rough.

bbaidid (**bbahyidyid**). Dial. W: *ebbaidid* (**yebbahyidyid**), E: *bōbaidid* (**bebahyidyid**). From *baid* (**bahyid**) "smoking pipe". 1(*-i*), 2, 3, 5(*bbāidid*), 6(*-i*). Smell of smoke on breath, body, or clothing, etc.; chain-smoking; distributive form of *baid* (**bahyid**).

bbaḷokḷok (**bbaḷẹqḷẹq**). Dial. W: *ebbaḷokḷok* (**yebbaḷẹqḷẹq**), E: *bōbaḷokḷok* (**bebaḷẹqḷẹq**). 1, 2, 3(inf *kōbbaḷokḷok,* tr *kōbaḷokwe*), 5(*bbaḷokḷok*), 7, 8, 9. Bulge. *Ebbaḷokḷok eoon tebōḷ eṇ.* The top of that table is bulgy.

bbat (**bbat**). Dial. W: *ebbat* (**yebbat**), E: *bōbat* (**bebat**). 1, 2(inf, tr *-e*), 5(*bbatbat*), 7, 8, 9. Late; tardy; too late for something. *Kobbat tok jān im eo.* You missed the verbal skirmish. *Ijeḷā ke ibbate.* I know I was too late for it.

bbā (**bbay**). Dial. W: *ebbā* (**yebbay**), E: *bōbwā* (**bebay**). 1(*-i*) (inf, tr bayik). Tend fish traps. *Enañin ṃōj ke bwāik u eo?* Has the fish trap been brought up yet? *Ḷōṃaro rej bbā.* The men are tending the traps.

bbeer (**bbeyer**). Dial. W: *ebbeer* (**yebbeyer**), E: *bōbweer* (**bebeyer**). 1(*-i*), 2, 3, 6(*-i*). Give up, as in war; lose hope; despair; frustrated; discouraged; pessimism; surrender. *Kwōn jab bbeer ṃōkaj.* Don't give up too soon. *Jab kabbeere eō.* Don't discourage me.

bbeik (**bbeyik**). Variant form of *bbōk* (**bbẹk**).

bbetok (**bbeyteq**). Dial. W: *ebbetok* (**yebbeyteq**), E: *bōbwetok* (**bbeyteq**). Archaic. 1(*-i*), 2, 3(inf, tr *-e*), 4, 6(*-i*). Give up; lose hope. *Kwōn jab bbetok ṃōkaj bwe wūnin an ban* *tōprak ņe.* Don't give up so fast or you won't get it done.

bbiddikdik maroñroñ (**bbiddikdik mareg°reg°**). Dial. W: *ibbiddikdik maroñroñ* (**yibbiddikdik mareg°reg°**), E: *būbwiddikdik maroñroñ* (**bibiddikdik mareg°reg°**). Idiom. From *tūbbwiddidik* (**tibbiddikdik**) "many crumbs, grains, morsels (distributive)" *maroñroñ* (**mareg°reg°**) "lots of power (distributive)" *maroñ* (**mareg°**). Proverb: "We share the little food we have, but thereby gain much power (many friends)."

bbidetdet (**bbidetdet**). Dial. W: *ibbidetdet* (**yibbidetdet**), E: *būbdetdet* (**bibdetdet**). From *det* (**det**) "sunshine". 1(*-i*), 2, 3, 6(*-i*). Smell of clothing or mats under sun.

bbijetjet (**bbijętjęt**). Dial. W: *ibbijetjet* (**yibbijętjęt**), E: *būbjetjet* (**bibjętjęt**). 1(*-i*), 2, 3, 6(*-i*). Smell of the sea.

bbijinjin (**bbijinjin**). Dial. W: *ibbijinjin* (**yibbijinjin**), E: *būbjinjin* (**bibjinjin**). Also *ppijinjin* (**ppijinjin**). 1(*-i*), 2, 3(inf, tr *-i*), 6(*-i*), 8, 9. Spotted, dotted, spotty. *Ebbijinjin kilin kuuj in ioon toļ.* Leopards are spotted. *Bok eo ekabbijinjin mejān.* The measles made his face all spotted. *Rej kappijinjini jiiñlij kaņ aer.* They are putting spots all over their T-shirts. *Kidu ppijinjin.* A spotted dog.

bbilwōdwōd (**bbilwedwed**). Dial. W: *ibbilwōdwōd* (**yibbilwedwed**), E: *būbwilwōdwōd* (**bibilwedwed**). From *wōd* (**wed**) "coral". 1(*-i*), 2, 3(inf, tr *-e*), 6(*-i*), 3+7, 8, 9. Smell of exposed reef.

bbilwōnwōn (**bbilwęnwęn**). Dial. W: *ibbilwōnwōn* (**yibbilwęnwęn**), E: *būbwilwōnwōn* (**bibilwęnwęn**). 1, 2, 3(inf, tr *-e*), 6(*-i*), 8, 9. Smell of turtles. *Kwōn jǫ jān bbilwōnwōnim̧.* Wash the turtle smell off of yourself.

bbiroro (**bbiyręwręw**). Dial. W: *ibbwiroro* (**yibbiyręwręw**), E: *būbwiroro* (**bibiyręwręw**). From *bwiro* (**biyręw**) "preserved breadfruit". 1(*-i*), 2, 3(inf, tr *-ik*), 4+3, 6(*-i*), 7. Smell of preserved breadfruit; distributive form of *bwiro* (**biyręw**). *Ebwiin bbwiroro peim̧.* Your hands smell of *bwiro*.

bbo (**bbęw**). Variant form of *bok* (**bęq**).

bbool (**bbewel**). Dial. W: *ebbool* (**yebbewel**), E: *bōbool* (**bebewel**). 2, 3, 5(*bboolol*), 6(*-i*), 8, 9. Expand, as a balloon; inflated; swell. *Kabboole m̧ōk bujeeñ ņe.* Will you please blow the balloon? *Ebboolol pein ālikin aer lōke.* His arm was swollen all over after he got stung. *Kōttar an bbool em kōtļǫke.* Wait till it expands then let it go.

bbǫk (**bbaq**). Dial. W: *ebbǫk* (**yebbaq**), E: *bōbǫk* (**bebaq**). 1(*-i*), 2, 3, 7. Swollen; swell. *Ta eņ ej ebbǫk tok ioon wa eņ?* What's that we see piled up on that ship?

bbǫk (**bbaq**). Dialectal variant of *bǫk* (**baq**).

bbō (**bbeh**). Dial. W: *ebbō* (**yebbeh**), E: *bōbō* (**bebeh**). 1(*-i*), 2, 3, 4. Fishing method, with spear at reef edge.

bbōj (**bbej**). Dial. W: *ebbōj* (**yebbej**), E: *bōbōj* (**bebej**). 1(*-i*), 2, 3(st inf *kabbōjbōj*, tr *kabbōj*), 5(*bbōjbōj*), 6(*-i*). Swollen; swell; lump. *Baijin in ņo eo ekabbōj neen.* The poison from the stone fish made his foot swell. *Baijin in ņo ekabbōjbōj.* Stone fish poison causes swelling. *Ebbōjbōj peiū.* My arm is swollen in many places.

bbōj (**bbej**). Dial. W: *ebbōj* (**yebbej**), E: *bōbōj* (**bebej**). Slang. 1(*-i*), 2, 3(inf, tr *-e*), 8, 9. Thin; emaciated. *Nañinmej eo an ekabbōje.* His recent illness emaciated him. *Ijakile kōn an bbōj.* He was so thin I didn't recognize him.

bbōk (**bbęk**). Dial. W: *ebbōk* (**yębbęk**), E: *bōbōk* (**bębęk**). Also *bbeik* (**bbęyik**). 2(inf, tr *bōk*), 4, 7. Take; carry. *Iar bōk pinjeļ eo.* I took the pencil. *Bōktok juon aō pinjeļ.* Bring a pencil for me.

bbōk (**bbek**). Dial. W: *ebbōk* (**yebbek**), E: *bōbōk* (**bebek**). 1(*-i*), 2, 4, 6(*-i*), 8, 9. Nosey; gossip; bear tales; blabbermouth; not able to keep secrets. *Kōrā eņ ej make wōt bbōk iaan kōrin ānin.* That woman is the nosiest on this island. *Jab ba ñane bwe ebbōk.* Don't tell him cause he is a blabbermouth. *Āteo rūbbōk.* What a blabbermouth.

bbōl (**bbęl**). Dial. W: *ebbōl* (**yębbęl**), E: *bōbōl* (**bębęl**). 1(*-i*), 2, 3. Blossom; bloom. *Ekanooj aiboojoj bbōl in ut* *eņ.* The blossoms of that bush are really beautiful. *Ebbōl ut eņ.* That flower is opening.

bbōl (**bbęl**). Dial. W: *ebbōl* (**yębbęl**), E: *bōbōl* (**bębęl**). 1, 2, 3(inf, tr *-e*), 4, 6(*-i*), 7. Lights on. *Lale koṃ ar kabbōle ļaṃ ņe bwe rōnaaj lo kōj.* Don't light the lamp or it will give away our position.

bbōņōjņōj (**bbeņejņej**). Dial. W: *ebbōņōjņōj* (**yebbeņejņej**), E: *bōbņōjņōj* (**bebņejņej**). Also *ṃōņōjņōj* (**ṃeņejņej**). 2, 3, 6(*-i*), 8, 9. Itchy.

bbōōlōl (**bbehelhel**). Dial. W: *ebbōōlōl* (**yebbehelhel**), E: *bōbōōlōl* (**bebehelhel**). 2, 3(inf, tr *-e*), 6(*-i*), 7. Wobble; wiggle. *Ebbōōlōl an etetal.* She wiggles when she walks.

bbōroro (**bbęręwręw**). Dial. W: *ebbōroro* (**yębbęręwręw**), E: *bōbroro* (**bębręwręw**). From *bōro* (**bęręw**) "throat, heart". 1(*-i*), 2, 3, 7. Unstable; fickle; indecisive. *Eļap aō bbōroro in etal in tariņae.* I am very indecisive about going to war.

bbūkbūk (**bbikbik**). Dial. W: *ibbūkbūk* (**yibbikbik**), E: *būbūkbūk* (**bibikbik**). 2, 6(*-i*), 8, 9. Half-cooked (as rice when inadequate water is used). *Kōļap dānnin bwe en jab bbūkbūk.* Make sure there's enough water so it doesn't come out half-done.

bbūļapļap (**bbiļapļap**). Dial. W: *ibbūļapļap* (**yibbiļapļap**), E: *būbļapļap* (**bibļapļap**). 1(*-i*), 2, 3, 6(*-i*). Smell; body odor, disagreeable. *Enaaj bbūļapļap kǫǫj ņe ippaṃ.* You'll make the blanket all smelly.

bbūra (**bbirah**). Dial. W: *ibbūra* (**yibbirah**), E: *būbūra* (**bibirah**). 2, 6(*-a*). Sickness, swollen lymph glands.

bbūramejmej (**bbirahmęjmęj**). Dial. W: *ibbūramejmej* (**yibbirahmęjmęj**), E: *būbramejmej* (**bibrahmęjmęj**). 1(*-i*), 2, 3(inf, tr *-e*), 6(*-i*), 7, 8, 9. Smell and taste of uncooked meat. *Ebbūramejmej piik in.* The pork tastes raw.

bbūriri (**bbiriyriy**). Dial. W: *ibbūriri* (**yibbiriyriy**), E: *būbriri* (**bibriyriy**). From *būru* (**biriy**) "uvula" (distributive). 1, 2, 3(inf, tr *-ik*), 6(*-i*), 7, 8, 9. Desire food. *Ibbūriri ļok wōt kōn aō lali ṃōņā kaņe.* Looking at your food makcs me want to taste it.

bbūrǫrǫ (**bbirawraw**). Dial. W: *ibbūrǫrǫ* (**yibbirawraw**), E: *būbrǫrǫ* (**bibrawraw**). Vulgar. From *būrǫ* (**biraw**) "male child", *rǫ* (**raw**) "scrotum". 1(*-i*), 2, 3, 6(*-i*). Smell of scrotum.

bbūtbūt (**bbitbit**). Dial. W: *ibbūtbūt* (**yibbitbit**), E: *būbūtbūt* (**bibitbit**). 1, 2, 3, 6(*-i*), 7. Sprinkle; dripping; drops of water. *Ia in ej bbūtbūt tok?* Where are all those drops coming from?

bbūtūktūk (**bbitiktik**). Dial. W: *ibbūtūktūk* (**yibbitiktik**), E: *būbtūktūk* (**bibtiktik**). From *būttūk* (**bittik**) "spurt" (distributive). 1(*-i*), 2, 3(inf, tr *-i*), 6(*-i*), 7(*bbūtūkļǫk, bbūtūktūkļǫk*). Splash; spray; spurt; gush. *Kwōn jab kabūtūktūki tok dān ņe bwe kōm jādbūtūktūk.* Don't spray the water or we'll get all wet. *Eļak bbūtūkļǫk kinej eo eko.* She took off when blood gushed from the wound.

bo (**bęw**). 1(*buo-*), 6(*-i*). Missile, for throwing only; stones in a sling. *Kwōn kappok buoṃ bwe jen kad bao eņ.* Get yourself something so we can throw at that bird.

bo (**bew**). Dial. W, E: *piro* (**pirew**). Twins. *Bo ledik raņ.* Those girls are twins. *Juon eo kōrā eor nājin bo.* The lady has twins.

bo (**bęw**). Variant form of *bok* (**bęq**).

bo (**bęw**). Also *bwe* (**bęy**). Knot in divination; see *bubu.*

bo (**bew**). Dialectal variant of *piro* (**pirew**).

bobo (**bęwbęw**). 1(*-i*), 2(inf *bobo,* tr *booj*), 3, 4, 6(*-i*), 7, 10(*bobo*). Assemble; fit together, put together an engine or piece of machinery; braid, tie; perfective form of *bobo* (**bęwbęw**) and of *bubu* (**biwbiw**). *Kwōjeļā ke bobo injin ļǫk.* Can you assemble an outboard engine? *Booje ṃōk baajikōļ ņe.* Will you please put the bike together. *Ear boojetok wa eo waō.* He assembled my boat for me. *Ejaje bobo injin.* He doesn't know how to put an engine together.

bobo (**bewbew**). 1(*-i*), 2, 4. Make balls. *Lio ej kōṃṃan bobo in raij.* She is making rice balls. *Lio ebobo raij.* She is making rice into balls.

bobo (**bęwbęw**). Variant form of *bujek* (**biwjęk**).

boboor (**bewbewer**). Also *popoor* (**pewpewer**). 2(inf, tr *-e*), 4, 6(*-i*), 7. To pat gently; to rub gently. *Kwōmaroñ ke boboore bwe en bar kiki.* Could you please pat him gently so he can go back to sleep?

boea (**bewyah**). From Engl. *boy*. 2, 6(*-a*). Adolescent; youngster; delinquent; rascal. *Aolep kumi eṇ ilo kilaaj emān boea wōt.* Class four has nothing but delinquents.

boeṃ (**bewyeṃ**). From Engl. Poem.

bojin (**bẹwjin**). From Engl. 2(inf, tr *-i*), 3, 6(*-i*), 7. Boatswain. *Ear bojini tok wa eṇ.* He was the boatswain on that ship when it came in.

bok (**bẹq**). 1(*-i*), 2, 3, 5(*-e, bokboke*). Blister, chicken pox. *Ebok peiū kōn an to aō jabōḷ.* I have a blister on my hand from shoveling so long. *Ear bok(e) ilo iiō eo ḷọk.* He had chicken pox last year. *Eboke ānbwinnin.* His body is covered with pox.

bok (**bẹq**). Also *bo* (**bẹw**), bbo (**bbẹw**). 1(*boku-, bowū-, bukwō-*). Bladder.

bok (**bẹq**). 1(*-i*), 2, 3(inf, tr *-e*), 6(*-i*), 7. Warped; saturated with water. *Ebok bwilāwut e.* This plywood is warped. *Ebok būreej ṇe.* The biscuit is saturated with water.

bok (**bẹq**). Warmed up, in games; heated contest. *Kwōjako jān an bok keem eo.* You missed the part when the contest reached a climax.

bok (**bẹq**). From Engl. 2(inf, tr *-e*), 6(*-i*). Book. *Kwōn boke ḷadik eṇ nejū.* Book my boy.

bok (**beq**). 1(*-a*). Sand; sandspit; sandbar, usually not covered even at high tide.

bok aidik (**bẹqhayidik**). 1(*-i*), 2, 4. Prickly heat; heatrash; measles; chicken pox.

bok ajaj (**beq hajhaj**). Coarse sand.

bok allōñ (**beq hallẹg**). Sand disks.

bokbok (**beqbeq**). 1(*-i*), 2(inf, tr *bokwe*), 3, 5(*bokbokwe, kabokbok, bokwe*), 6(*-i*), 8. Be sandy. *Ebokboke lowaan ṃwiin.* There is lots of sand in this house. *Jab ikien bwe kwōnaaj kabokbok mejāer.* Don't horse around or you'll get sand in their eyes. *Ear boke bōran likao eo.* He threw sand in the man's hair. *Ebokbok meja.* My eyes have sand in them. *Ekabokbok arin ānin.* This island has lots of sand in its lagoon. *Ekadik (bok)boke mọọr ṇe mọọrōṃ.* Your bait has too much sand.

bokbok (**beqbeq**). Slang. 2. Rebuffed; unsuccessful in one's love advances. *Ear wadu im bokbok.* His proposition was rejected.

boke (**beqey**). Transitive form of *bokbok* (**beqbeq**).

bokkoḷọk (**bẹqqẹḷaq**). Also *ebbokḷọk* (**yẹbbẹqḷaq**). From "onomatopoeia". 1(*-i*), 2, 3, 5(*bbokbok*), 6(*-i*). Pop; noise; retort; boom; explode; sound of an explosion; bang, as of gun; blast; clap. *Eḷap aō ilbōk kōn bokkoḷọk in bu eo.* The sound of the gun startled me. *Ainikien ta in ej bbokbok?* What is the sound that keeps booming there? *Ebokkoḷọk baaṃ eo.* The bomb exploded. *Ejāpem bokkoḷọk kabbokbok eo.* The firecracker did not go off. *Koroñ ke bokkoḷọkun bọkutañ eo?* Did you hear the explosion of the bomb?

bokkwelep (**beqqeylep**). Also *bokwāelep* (**beqayelep**). From *bok* (**beq**) "sand", *ekilep* (**yekilep**) "it is big". Coarse sand.

bokkwidik (**beqqiydik**). From *bok* (**beq**) "sand", *edik* (**yedik**) "it is small". Fine sand.

bokḷọk (**bẹqlaq**). 2, 6(*-i*), 7. Movement of fish near surface; tight clustering of fish when attracted by bait or chum.

bokḷap (**bẹqḷap**). 2, 6(*-i*). Small pox.

bokoṃṇa (**beqemṇah**). Stony islet without trees.

bokpā (**beqpay**). From *bọk* (**baq**) "wrap torch", *pā* (**pay**) "arm". 1(*-i*), 2, 3, 4, 6(*-i*). Fold arms in front. *Ña ij bokpā bwe ipiọ.* I am folding my arms because I'm chilly.

boktak (**beqtak**). 1(*-i*), 2(inf, tr *-(e)*), 3, 7. Protect from rain or spray at sea with mat; shelter with mat at sea. *Itok kōjro boktak jān wōt kein.* Come let's protect ourselves from the rain. *Kwōn boktake ajri ṇe jān wōt kein.* Protect that child from the rain.

boktañ (**beqtag**). Variant form of *bọkutañ* (**baqitag**).

bokun pija (**bẹqin pijah**). Photo album. *Imaroñ ke aluje bokun pija ṇe aṃ?* May I take a look at your album?

bokwan (**beqan**). Also *bokwōn* (**beqen**). Sandspit of; construct form of *bok.*

bokwā (**beqay**). Archaic. Sandspit of; old construct form of *bok; modern form, bokwan.*

bokwārijet (**beqayriyjęt**). Archaic. 2(inf, tr -*i*), 3. Scrub self with coconut husk or oil. *Rej bokwārijet iar.* They are scrubbing themselves at the lagoon beach.

bokwe. See *boke.*

boḷ (**bęl°**). Also *ḷoboḷ* (**lawbęl°**). 1(*buḷō-, ḷobuḷō-*), 6(*buḷōn, ḷobuḷōn*). Heart of tree; root of matter; core; pith. *Jek wōjke ņe bwe en waḷok buḷōn.* Chop that tree so that the heart of it appears.

boḷan (**bewḷan**). Also *boḷōn* (**bewḷen**). From Engl. *bowline*. 2(inf, tr -*e*), 6(-*i*), 7. Tie securely; a knot. *Boḷane to ņe.* Tie that line well.

boḷio (**bęwḷiyew**). From Engl. *polio*. 1(-*i*), 2, 3, 4, 6(-*i*), 7. Polio.

boḷot (**bel°et**). 1(-*i*), 2, 3. Damp. *Eboḷot nuknuk kaņe aṃ.* Your clothes are damp.

boņ (**beņ°**). 1(-*i*), 2, 3(st inf *kabboņboņ,* tr *kaboņ*), 4, 6(-*i*). Stymied; dumbfounded; blocked; obstructed; constipated; clogged; indigestion. *Eboņ ḷeo im jaje ta eo en kōṃṃane.* He is stymied and doesn't know what to do. *Eboņ baib eo im jaje toọr dān.* The pipe is stopped up and the water can't flow.

boņōj (**bewņej**). From Engl. Bonus. *Eor ke aṃ boņōj jān jerbal eņ aṃ?* Do you get bonuses from your work?

boñ (**beg°**). 2(inf, tr -*e*), 3(*kabboñboñ*), 6(*buñōn, boñūn*), 8. Night; last night. *Iar itaak tok boñ.* I got here last night. *Kwōn kāiur bwe enaaj boñe eok.* Hurry up before it gets dark. *Jen kaboñboñ.* Let's wait until it gets dark.

boñōn eo turun inne eo ḷok juon (**beg°ęn yew tir°in yinney yew ḷaq jiwen**). Four nights ago.

booj (**bęwęj**). Knot; be knotted; see *bubu* and *bobo.*

booj (**bewej**). 6(-*i*). Shuttle. *Ejorrāān booj in mejiin e aō.* The shuttle in my sewing machine is busted.

booj (**bewej**). From Engl. Boat; skiff.

booj (**bewej**). Transitive form of *bobo* (**bewbew**).

booḷ (**bęwęl**). From Engl. 1(-*i*), 2, 3(inf *kabbooḷoḷ,* tr *kabooḷe*), 4. Filled up; full; lustful, males only; replete. *Ebooḷ bato eo.* The bottle is full. *Kwōn kabooḷe kab ņe.* Fill up that cup.

booḷkeno (**beweḷkeynew**). From Engl. Volcano.

booḷoḷ (**beweḷwel**). Also *bbooḷoḷ* (**bbeweḷwel**). 1(-*i*), 2, 3. Poorly fitting; loose. *Ebooḷoḷ jikūru ņe.* That screw is loose.

booḷtōñtōñ (**bęwęltegteg**). 2, 3, 6(-*i*). Overflow, water. *Joñan an to an wōt, ebooḷtōñtōñ tāāñ eo.* It rained so hard, the tank overflowed. *Kwōn kabooḷtōñtōñ kaḷan ņe.* Fill that gallon can to the brim.

Boonpe (**bęwęnpęy**). From Engl. 4. Place name; Ponape.

boor (**bęwęr**). 2, 5(*bbooror*), 6(-*i*), 8, 9. Wild, in throwing. *Rōnaaj kar wiin ak eboor pijja eo.* They would have won but their pitcher was wild. *Ibwilōñ an bbooror pijja eo.* I'm surprised at how often the pitcher threw wildly.

booraj (**bewerhaj**). Variant form of *aj* (**haj**).

bor (**ber°**). 2(inf, tr -*e*), 4, 5(*borbor*), 6(*borborun*), 7. Throw sand at. *Kwōn bore mejān.* Throw sand at it's eyes. *Eborbore lowaan bōjọ e aō.* There's sand inside my pants pocket.

boraañ (**bęwrahag**). 3, 5(*bbouraañañ*), 6(-*i*). A fish, great devilfish, manta; sting ray. (Wt. to 1,000 lbs.; poisonous). *Ebbouraañañ ar in ānin.* These waters are infested with sting rays.

borborun (**ber°ber°in**). Construct form of *bor* (**ber°**).

boub (**bęwib**). Also *bouk* (**bęwik**), *bou* (**bęwiw**). 3, 6(-*i*). An insect, dragonfly. *Ḷadik eo nejū ej kaboub.* My son is catching dragon flies.

bouk (**bęwik**). Variant form of *boub* (**bęwib**).

bouk in iiep (**bęwik yin 'yiyep**). 3, 6(-*i*). An insect; large dragonfly.

bout (**bęwit**). From Engl. 2(inf, tr -*i*), 4, 6(-*i*). Vote, vote for. *Kab bouti ḷeeņ.* Be sure and vote for him. *Wōn eo kwaar bouti?* Who did you vote for? *Erki bout ko?* Where are the votes?

boutḷọk (**bewitḷaq**). 1(-*i*), 2, 3, 4. Smoke; steam; spray; issue forth; emit. *Eboutḷọk kijek eņ.* That fire is smoking. *Ej kōboutḷọk raj eņ.* That whale is spouting.

bowōd (**bewwed**). 2(inf, tr -*e*), 6(-*i*). Argument; bickering; quarreling among siblings. *Jei im jati ro raar* *bowōde doon.* The brothers quarreled with each other.

bǫbo (**bawbęw**). 1(*-i*), 2(inf, tr *bǫur(i)*), 4, 6(*-i*). Fishing method, flying fish at night with torch and net; catch. *Ļōṃaro raṇ rej bǫbo.* The fellows are fishing for flying fish. *Ejeļā bǫbo (bǫǫļ).* He's a good (baseball) catcher.

bǫjet (**bawjet**). From Engl. Faucet; spigot. *Idaak jān bǫjet ṇe.* Drink out of the faucet.

bǫk (**baq**). Dial. E, W: *ebbǫk* (**bbaq**). 1(*-i*), 2(inf, tr *-e*), 4, 7. Make torches from brown fronds. *Kōjro etal in bǫk pāle in kabwil.* Let's go make torches for torch fishing. *Bǫke pāle ṇe.* Make a torch. *Rūbbǫk eo ṇe tok.* The man who makes torches is coming.

bǫktōk (**baqtęk**). Also *baktōk* (**baktęk**). 1(*-i*), 6(*-i*). Small house on canoe.

bǫkuj pedped (**baqij pedped**). Also *bǫkwōj pedped* (**baqej pedped**). From *bǫkwōj* (**baqej**) "hug", *pedped* (**pedped**) "reef". Giant lobster; crayfish.

bǫkutañ (**baqitag**). Also *boktañ* (**beqtag**). From Japn. *bakudan* "bomb". 1(*-i*), 2(inf, tr *-e*), 4, 6(*-i*). Bomb; dynamite. *RiAmedka raar bǫkutañe!* North Vietnam. The Americans bombed North Vietnam. *Rūboktañ eo ilo baļuun eo ṇe.* That's the bombardier on the airplane.

bǫkwōj (**baqej**). Also *atbǫkwōj* (**hatbaqej**). 1(*-i*), 2(inf, tr *-(e)*), 3, 4, 7. Embrace; hug; clutch. *Kwōn bǫkwōj niñniñ ṇe bwe epiǫ.* Hug that baby because he's cold.

bǫļōj (**baļ°ej**). From Engl. *ballast*. Ballast. *Kwōn etal in bǫļōje wa eṇ.* Go put ballast on the boat.

bǫñur (**bag°ir**). Vulgar. 2, 6(*-i*). Having well-developed Venus mound; pubis.

bǫǫj (**bawaj**). From Engl. *boss*. 2(inf, tr *-e*), 3+5, 4+3+5, 5(*bbǫǫjǫj*), 6(*-i*). Leader; boss. *Ej bǫǫj ñan kombani in.* He's this company's boss. *Ta ļe eṃṃan an bǫǫje eok ke?* Do you let him boss you around? *Eļap an kōbbǫǫjǫje.* He's always very pushy. *Kwōj kōbbǫǫjǫj.* You're acting like a boss. *Kwōn jab kōbbǫǫjǫj.* Don't act like a boss.

bǫǫjpet (**bawajpet**). From Engl. Phosphate.

bǫǫk (**bawak**). From Engl. 1(*-i*), 2(inf, tr *-e*), 6(*-i*). Box. *Ewi bǫǫkin dila eo?* Where is the box of nails? *Ej bǫǫke bok kaṇ an.* He's putting his books in a box.

bǫǫk (**bawak**). From Engl. 6(*-i*). Fork. *Jibwe tok ṃōk juon arro bǫǫk.* Could you pass me a fork?

bǫǫk aij (**bawak hayij**). From Engl. 2(inf, tr *-i*), 6(*-i*). Refrigerator; ice-box. *Bǫǫk aiji ek ṇe bwe en jab jorrāān.* Refrigerate that fish so it won't spoil. *Kab bǫǫk aiji ek eo.* Be sure to refrigerate the fish.

bǫǫkǫk (**bawakwak**). From *bǫǫk* (**bawak**). 1(*-i*), 2, 3(inf, tr *-e*), 6(*-i*). Use a box. *Ij ja bǫǫkǫk kōn bǫǫk e aṃ.* I'll use your box for now.

bǫǫkǫk (**bawakwak**). From *bǫǫk* (**bawak**). 1(*-i*), 2, 3(inf, tr *-e*), 6(*-i*). Use a fork. *Kwōn jab kabǫǫkǫke bwe ebōt.* Don't give him a fork because he's disobedient.

bǫǫļ (**bawaļ**). From Engl. 6(*-i*). Ball. *Bǫǫlin iakiu eo nejū ṇe.* That's my baseball.

bǫǫntōn peen (**bawanten peyen**). From Engl. Fountain pen. *Juon e aō bǫǫntōn peen.* I have a fountain pen.

bǫǫr (**bawar**). 1(*-i*), 2(inf, tr *-ōk*), 6(*booran*). Stopper; cork; cap; plug. *Kwōn bǫǫrōk mejān bato ṇe bwe en jab lutōk.* Put a cork in that bottle so it doesn't spill. *Ejako bǫǫr eo boran bato e.* The bottle's cork is missing.

bǫǫror (**bawarwęr**). Also *bǫǫrǫr* (**bawarwar**). From *bǫǫr* (**bawar**). 2(inf, tr *bǫǫrōk, bǫrōk*), 3(inf, tr *kabǫǫrǫr(e), kōbǫrōk*), 6(*-i*), 10(*bǫǫrǫr(e), bǫǫror(e)*). Top; cap; cork; covered. *Bǫrōk bato ṇe.* Put a cork in the bottle. *Ebǫrōk.* It's covered. *Bato eṇ ej bǫǫror kōn wūj.* The bottle is capped with a piece of cork. *Raar bǫrōke mejān bato eo.* They capped the bottle. *Ñe kwōnaaj kabǫǫrǫre eban lutōk.* If you cork it, it won't spill.

bǫǫt (**bawat**). Variant form of *bǫti* (**bawtiy**).

bǫro (**bawręw**). Long fish trap, for sprats, net with handle.

Bǫro (**bawręw**). See *bǫro* "sprat net." A constellation; stars in Pisces; theta, iota, mu, 15.

bǫrōk (**bawręk**). 2(inf, tr *-e, bǫrūke*), 3, 7. Covered; plugged.

bọrōk (**bawręk**). Transitive form of *bọọror* (**bawarwęr**).

bọti (**bawtiy**). Also *bọọt* (**bawat**). 1(*bọti-*), 6(*bọọtin*). Nose; snout; beak.

bọtin nee- (**bawtin neye-**). 1. Shin.

bọto (**bawtęw**). 1(*-i*), 2(inf, tr *-uk*), 3. Cover; protect from rain or wind. *Bōktok juon tiin in bọtouk kijek e.* Bring a piece of tin to protect this fire.

bọun (**bawin**). 1(*-i*), 2(inf, tr *-i*), 3, 4. Pound; scales; weight; weigh. *Jete bọunim̧?* How much do you weigh? *Imaroñ ke kōjerbal bọun ņe am̧?* May I use your scales? *Kwōn bọuni piik ņe.* Weigh that pig.

bọur (**bawir**). 1(*-i*), 2(inf, tr *-(i)*), 4, 7. Catch with net or basket; lift; hold up or catch with both hands; receive by radio; transitive form of *bọbo* (**bawbęw**). *Kwōn bọur ek ņe kōn ok ņe.* Catch that fish with that net. *Iar bọuri kōjeļā eo aō ilo retio.* I received my message by radio.

bọurok (**bawireq**). From Engl. (?). 3. Gunpowder.

bọuta (**bawitah**). Also *bouta* (**bęwitah**). From Engl. 1(*-i*), 2(inf, tr *-ik*), 3, 4, 6(*-i*). Powder. *Kwōn bọutaik niññiñ eo.* Powder the baby.

bōb (**beb**). 3, 6(*-i*). A plant, pandanus, a general name for any pandanus plant; also a ripe key of pandanus. *Bōb-in-M̧ajeļ.* Pandanus of the Marshalls.

bōb-. See *bb-*.

Bōb-bōņwa (**beb-beņwah**). 3, 6(*-i*). A plant, pandanus cultigen; Eniwetok.

Bōb-irooj (**beb-yiręwęj**). From *bōb* (**beb**) "pandanus", *irooj* (**yiręwęj**) "chief". 3, 6(*-i*). A plant, *Pandanus fischerianus* cultigen.

bōbrae (**bebrahyey**). 1(*-i*), 2(inf, tr *-ik*), 3, 4. Hinder; prevent; forbid; stop; avert; avoid. *Kwōn bōbrae ļadik eo jān an tutu iar.* Stop the boy from swimming in the lagoon.

bōbtowa (**bebtewah**). Archaic. Perceive correctly. *Ibōbtowa kiiō.* Oh, now I see.

bōd (**będ**). 1, 2, 6(st inf *kabōdbōd*, tr *kabōd*), 6(*-i*). Mistake; error; wrong; fault; sin; crime; defect; flaw; false; guilty. *Jete eo am̧ bōd ilo teej eo?* How many mistakes did you make on the test? *Kwōn jab kabōdbōd.* Don't overstep your boundaries. *Kobōd.* You're wrong.

bōd (**bed**). 6(*-i*). Turtle shell; plastic. *Bōdin wūnen Jemọ menin.* This is turtleshell from *Jemọ*.

bōdañ (**bedag**). 1, 2(inf, tr *-e*). Inherit, physical or mental characteristics; resemble, parent and child; heredity. *Eļap an ļadik eņ bōdañe jemān.* The boy resembles his father.

bōj (**bęj**). Variant form of *baj* (**baj**).

bōj (**bęj**). 1(*-i*), 2, 3, 6(*-i*), 8, 9. Swollen corpse. *Ejjeļam bōjin.* It's really a swollen corpse. *M̧ōkaj im kalbwini bwe ebōj.* Better hurry up and bury the corpse because it's swollen.

bōjbōj (**bejbej**). 1(*-i*), 2, 3, 7. Viscous. *Ebōjbōj iiōk ņe am̧.* That mixture is thick.

Bōjbōj (**bejbej**). From *bōjbōj* (**bejbej**) "viscous" (probably referring to mashed dish made from it). 3, 6(*-i*). A plant, pandanus cultigen.

bōjen (**bęjęn**). Dialectal variant of *bwijin* (**bijin**).

bōjin (**bęhjin**). From Engl. Virgin; nun.

bōjjāān (**bejjayan**). From Engl. Percent.

bōjọ (**bejaw**). 3(inf *kōbbōjọjo*, tr *kōbbōjọjouk, kōbbōjọjoik*), 6(*-i*). Pocket; hand basket of fine weave; pouch. *Ej kōbbōjọjo jikka.* He carries cigarettes in his pockets.

bōjrak (**bęjrak**). 1(*-i*), 2, 3(inf *kabbōjrak*, tr *kabōjrak*), 4+3(*rūkabbōjrak*), 6(*-i*). Stand still; pause; stop; perfective form of *kabwijer* (**kabijęr**); quit; cease; discontinue; halt; intermission; interruption. *Wa eo eņ ebōjrak.* The ship is stopping. *Kwōn kabbōjrak.* Hold on. *Ļeeņ rūkabbōjrak an irooj.* He's the praetorian guard for the chief.

bōk (**bek**). 2(inf, tr *(-e)*), 7. Take; carry; receive; get; capture; subtract; acquire; bring; obtain; occupy; transitive form of *bbōk* (**bbęk**).

bōk aļ (**bek haļ**). From "take sun". Celestial navigation; sextant. *Kwōjeļā ke bōk aļ?* Do you know how to use the sextant?

bōk bar (**bek bar**). Look up after nodding, sleeping, or reading.

bōk ddo (**bek ddew**). 4. Assume responsibility for; care for; be responsible for. *Wōn ņe ej bōk ddo in jerbal ņe?* Who is taking the responsibility for that job?

bōk iju (**bek yijiw**). From "take star". Celestial navigation; sextant.

bōk jikin (**bek jikin**). Supplant; take the place of; substitute for; replace. *Kwōnaaj bōk jikin.* You'll replace him.

bōk kakkije (**bek kakkijęy**). Idiom. Pass away. *Ļōļļap eo ear bōk an kakkije inne.* The old man passed away yesterday.

bōk koņaa- (**bek qeņaha-**). Dial. W, E: *bōk kuņaa-* (**bek qiņaha-**). 1, 2, 4. Participate; take part in; do one's duty, do one's share. *Kwōn etal in jerbal im bōk kuņaam.* Go do your share of the job.

bōk ob (**bek węb**). From *bōk* (**bek**) "take", *ob* (**węb**) "chest". 2(inf, tr *bōk ubō-*). Dying breath. *Ļeo enañinmej eņ ej bōk-ubōn.* That sick person is drawing his last breath.

bōka- (**beka-**). 1, 6. Just sufficient. *Letok wōt bōkan aō ṃōñā.* Just give me enough to eat. *Kōmat bōkāer.* Cook enough for them.

bōkan (**bekan**). Construct form of *bwe* (**bey**).

bōkā (**bekay**). Tide. *Eṃṃan ke bōkā in ñan eoñōd?* Is the tide good for fishing?

bōkā (**bekay**). Small bottle or jar; container for liquids, of coconut shell; canteen; jug; lotion; perfume. *In baj lale ṃōk bōkā ņe kaptōṃ?* May I please see your oil (or perfume) container?

bōkāñaj (**bekaygaj**). From *bōkā* (**bekay**) "bottle", *ñaj* (**gaj**) "fragrant", "bottle of fragrance". 2(inf, tr *-e*), 3, 6(*-i*). Perfume, imported only. *Bōkāñaje nuknuk ņe aō.* Spray some perfume on my dress.

bōkāro (**bekayrew**). From Japn. *baka yaroo* "stupid fellow". Interjection: "Stupid!"

bōke (**bękęy**). 5(*bbōkeke*), 6(*-i, būkien, būkie, būkōn, būke*). Cape, geographical; knot, in wood; horn. *Ebbōkeke aļaļ ņe.* That piece of wood is full of knots. *Lale eitaak wa ņe ilo bōke ņe.* Be careful the canoe doesn't go aground on that cape. *Wa eo eitaak ilo bōke eo ļok jān Kōļaļ-eņ ñan to eņ.* The canoe went aground on the cape that sticks out from *Kōļaļ-eņ* towards the pass.

bōkjab (**bekjab**). From *bōk* (**bek**) "take", *jab* (**jab**) "not". 1(*-i*), 2, 3, 4. Overstep authority. *Eļap aṃ bōkjab kōn men ko ej jab tōllọkuṃ.* You are going ahead with things that are not your business.

bōkkāāj (**bekkayaj**). A fish, wrasse, *Thalassoma umbrostigma.*

bōkkōk (**bękkęk**). Interjection: Wow! (Expression of surprise).

bōkkōrā (**bekkeray**). From *bōk* (**bek**) "take, carry", *kōrā* (**keray**) "woman". 1(*-i*), 2(inf, tr *-ik*), 3, 4, 6(*-i*). Carry female to or from vessel. *Kwōn bōkkōrāik metoļọk lieņ.* Carry her out to the canoe.

bōklaļļọk (**beklaļļaq**). 1(*-i*), 2, 4. Take downwards. *Kwōn bōklaļļọk ajri ņe.* Get that child down from there.

bōklōkōt (**bęklękęt**). 1(*-i*), 2, 3, 4. Expect; predict. *Ejiṃwe wōt aō kar bōklōkōt ke kwōnaaj kar itok.* My prediction was correct that you would come.

bōklōkōt (**bęklękęt**). 6(*-i*). Conscience; attitude; mind; intellect. *Aṃ jerbal nana enaaj kāeñtaan aṃ bōklōkōt.* Your evil deeds shall torment your conscience.

bōklōñļọk (**beklęgļaq**). 1(*-i*), 2, 4. Take upward.

bōkļamleļọk (**bekļamleyļaq**). Idiom. From *bōkļọk im leļọk* (**bekļaq yim leyļaq**). Deliver. *Bōkļamleļọk men ņe ñan Jọọn.* Deliver that thing to John.

bōkļap (**bekļap**). Also *bōklep.* 1(*-i*), 2(inf, tr *-e*), 4. Take more than one's share. *Eļap aṃ bōkļap bwe kiiō ejabwe.* You took too much and now there isn't enough.

bōktak (**bektak**). Slang. 2, 3(inf, tr *-e*), 4, 6(*-i*), 8, 9. Make out; make the grade; succeed in work, play, school, or with the opposite sex; catch up, in a game. *Iban luuj bwe inaaj bōktak.* I won't lose, I'll catch up.

bōl (**bęl**). 6(*-i*). Taro patch.

bōl (**bel**). Bloom; see *didbōlbōl, bbōl.*

bōlbōl (**bęlbęl**). 2, 4, 6(*-i*), 7. Gather green pandanus leaves from trees; see *ppel. Raar bōlbōl maañ in amiṃōņo.* They gathered pandanus leaves for making handicraft.

bōlej (**belej**). Slang. 2, 6(*-i*), 7, 8, 9. Extravagant; too much; expensive; excessive; exorbitant. *Ejjeļọk baj bōlejin oņān ṃweiuk raan kein.* The price of goods nowadays is really extravagant. *Ebōlej wōt.* How exorbitant.

bōlen (**bẹlẹn**). Perhaps; probably; maybe. *Bōlen enaaj itok ilju.* Maybe he'll come tomorrow.

bōlkōk (**belkek**). Also *bōlkōk* (**bẹlkẹk**). 1(*-i*), 2(inf, tr *-e*). Cracks in skin of soles of feet. *Emetak bōlkōk kaṇ neen.* The cracks on his feet hurt.

bōlōk (**bẹlẹk**). 1(*bwilikō-*), 3, 5(*bbōlōklōk*), 3+7. Leaf. *Ebbōlōklōk iumwin mā eṇ.* There are lots of leaves under that breadfruit tree. *Ij kabōlōk waj ñan kwe.* I'm picking leaves for you.

bōlōk (**bẹlẹk**). Vulgar. Vulva.

bōḷa (**beḷah**). Dial. E only; see *ba* (**bah**). Say. *Ta ṇe kwōj bōḷa?* What are your saying?

Bōḷaide (**beḷahyidey**). Variant form of *Bōraide* (**berahyidey**).

bōḷaḷ (**beḷaḷ**). Also *mera* (**merah**). 1(*-i*), 2, 3, 6(*-i*), 7, 11(*bōḷaḷḷōḷ*). Light in weight. *Eḷap aṃ bōḷaḷ ḷọk jān ke kwaar jino itok.* You don't weigh as much as you did when you first came.

Bōḷau (**beḷahwiw**). From Engl. 4. Place name; Palau.

bōḷbōḷ (**beḷbeḷ**). Vulgar. From Engl. Vagina; vulva.

bōḷeak (**beḷyak**). Also *bōḷāāk.* From Engl. 6(*-i*). Flag; ensign.

bōḷñak (**beḷgak**). 1(*-i*), 2, 3(inf, tr *-e*), 7. Split open; spread legs wide open. *Ebōḷñak kapin booj eo.* The bottom of the boat is split open. *Ej kōbōḷñake ke aḷaḷ eṇ āinwōt aō kar ba?* Is he splitting the board open like I said?

bōḷoñar (**bẹḷẹwgar**). 2, 3(*kabōḷoñar(ñar)*). Kernel of spongy meat inside coconut that has just started to sprout; see *per*. *Ebōḷoñar waini e.* This copra nut has started to form a spongy kernel.

bōn (**bẹn**). Archaic. Place from which corpses were floated away to sea; place where members of the *Ripako* clan exercise their power to control storms.

bōna (**benah**). 1(*-i*), 2, 3(inf, tr *-ik*), 4, 7. Flat, music; off key, voice. *Kwōn jab al bwe kobōna.* Don't sing because you're flat.

bōnbōn (**bẹnbẹn**). 1(*-i*), 2(inf, tr *bwini, bwine*), 4, 6(*-i*), 7. Arithmetic; count; audit; compute; mathematics; score. *Kwōjeḷā ke bōnbōn?* Do you know arithmetic? *Bwini ṃōk mā kaṇe.* Please count those breadfruit. *Kwōn bwini ek kā.* Count these fish.

bōnej (**benyej**). A fish, snapper, *Lutjanus vitta.*

bōnja- (**benja-**). 1. Heritage; quality; inherited characteristics; personality. *Enta kwōj eḷḷọk ke baj eo bōnjān eṇ.* Don't let that bother you; it's just the way he is.

bōōj (**bẹhej**). Also *bōōj* (**behej**). From Engl. First base. *Ttōr ñan bōōj.* Run to first base.

bōōjōj (**behejhej**). Also *bōkto-bōktak.* Archaic. Broadcast; spread the word. *Ej tar bōōjōje naan ko ñan armej ro.* He is starting to spread the word to the people.

bōōr (**bẹhẹr**). Also *bōōr* (**beher**). From Engl. 3, 6(*-i*). Pearl. *An kōrā jerbal kabōōr i Jepaan.* In Japan, diving for pearls is a woman's job.

Bōraide (**berahyidey**). Also *Bōḷaide* (**beḷahyidey**), *Būḷāide* (**biḷayidey**). From Engl. Friday.

bōraṃṃaajidak (**beraṃṃahajidak**). Dialectal variant of *bōraṃṃaanō* (**beraṃṃahanẹh**).

bōraṃṃaanō (**beraṃṃahanẹh**). Dial. E, W: *bōraṃṃaajidak* (**beraṃṃahajidak**). Archaic. From "your head, by my sacred male relative". Exclamation, of surprise.

bōran aelōñ (**beran hayẹlẹg**). 4+6(*-i*), 6(*-i*). Main islet of an atoll. *Jero jerak ḷọk ñan bōran aelōñin.* Let's sail up to the main island.

bōran baal (**beran bahal**). Outer edge of reef where large coral heads are. *Eḷap ṇo bōran baal.* The waves are big at the edge of the reef.

bōranṃaajidake (**beranṃahajidakẹy**). Interjection: expression of wonder or delight.

bōrā (**beray**). Archaic. Head of; old construct form of *bar; modern form, bōran.*

bōro (**bẹrẹw**). 1(*būruo-*), 2. Seat of the emotions; throat; "heart"; gills. *Emetak būruō kōn aō pokpok.* My throat hurts from my coughing. *Ḷeeṇ ej juon armej erreo būruon.* He's an honest man. *Ḷeeṇ enana būruon.* He has an ugly disposition.

bōro (**berew**). 2(inf, tr *-ik*), 6(*-i*). Rag. *Kwōn bōroik ijeņe ettoon ilo injin ņe.* Wipe that dirty spot off the engine with a rag.

bōro-jepel (**bẹrẹw-jẹpẹl**). 1(*-i*), 2, 3, 4. Disagree; not cooperative. *Ļeeņ ej make wōt kijoñ kōm̧m̧an bōro-jepel.* He is the least cooperative.

bōro-kadu (**bẹrẹw-kadiw**). Also *jidimkij* (**jidimkij**). 1(*-i*), 2, 3, 4. Short tempered. *Jab kōjak ippān bwe ebōro-kadu.* Don't joke with him because he has a short temper.

bōro-kōrkōr (**bẹrẹw-kẹrkẹr**). Also *būro-kōrkōr* (**birẹw-kẹrkẹr**). From *bōro* (**bẹrẹw**) "throat", *kūrkūr* (**kirkir**) "tickle, itch". 1(*-i*), 2, 3, 7. Hungry; have an appetite for. *Eļap aō bōro-kūrkūr kōn ek kaņe.* I would really like to taste some of your fish.

bōro-kuk (**bẹrẹw-qiq**). 1(*-i*), 2, 3, 4. Form a united group; agree among selves. *Em̧m̧an an aolep rūbukwōn in bōro-kuk.* It is good that the people of this district are united. *Ereañ ej jab bōro-kuk.* They can't agree among themselves.

bōro-ļap (**bẹrẹw-ļap**). 1(*-i*), 2, 3, 4. Wasteful; spendthrift; prodigal. *Ļeo ebōro-ļap.* He is a spendthrift.

bōro-pejpej (**bẹrẹw-pẹjpẹj**). 1(*-i*), 2, 3, 4. Fickle; indecisive; unstable. *Lieņ ebōro-pejpej.* She is fickle.

bōrojoļọk (**bẹrẹwjewļaq**). 2, 6(*-i*). Absent-minded; forgetful. *Kwōn joļọk aō bōd ak elukkuun ļap ļọk aō bōrojoļọk jān m̧okta.* Forgive me but I'm getting awfully forgetful.

Bōrọk (**beraq**). From name of Rongelap islet. 3, 6(*-i*). A plant, pandanus cultigen, Rongelap.

bōrọro (**berawrẹw**). 1(*-i*), 2, 3(inf, tr *-uk*), 4, 6(*-i*). Pregnant; budding. *Kwōn kōbōrọrotok.* Pick the budding flowers for us.

bōrōj (**berej**). A white sea bird.

bōrran (**bẹrran**). Construct form of *būrar* (**birar**).

bōrrā (**berray**). Also *bōrrā* (**bẹrray**). 1(*-i*), 2(inf, tr *-ik*), 3, 4, 6(*-i*), 7. Cut lengthwise; split; ripsaw; cleave, cut in half. *Kwōn bōrrāiktok aļaļ e.* Rip that piece of wood for me. *Eor ke am̧ (jidpān) bōrrā?* Do you have a rip saw? *Ewi bōrrā eo am̧?* Where is your rip saw? *Ebōrrā waini eo.* The coconut was cut in half.

bōrwaj (**berwaj**). 1(*-i*), 2(inf, tr *-e*), 3, 4, 6(*-i*). Roof ridge. *Itok jen bōrwaje m̧we bwe ettal.* Come let's cap this roof because it leaks.

bōrwaj (**berwaj**). 2(inf, tr *-e*), 4, 6(*-i*). Coating, of paint; phases in medical treatment starting with the second. *Kwōn wātin (wātok in) jipañ eō bōrwaje wa e waarro.* Come and help me put another coating of paint on our boat. *Bōrwaj eo āliktata in.* This is the final phase of the treatment.

bōt (**bẹt**). 1(*bōt-*), 2(inf, tr *bōte, būte*), 4, 6(*-i*), 8, 9. Disobedient; naughty; mischievous; obdurate; obstinate. *Kwōn deñōt ļadik ņe bwe eļap an bōt.* Spank that boy because he's naughty. *Eļap an ļadik eo būte jinen.* The boy is constantly disobeying his mother.

bōta (**betah**). From Engl. 1(*-i*), 2(inf, tr *-ik*), 3, 4, 5(*bbōtata*), 6(*-i, -a*), 7. Butter. *Kwōn bōtaik ļọk pilawā ņe kijen ledik eņ.* Put butter on that bread and give it to the girl to eat.

bōtab (**bethab**). However; nevertheless. *Ij jilkinļọk eok bwe kwōn m̧upi bōtab kwōnaaj make kōļļā oņeam̧.* I'm sending you to the movies, but you'll have to pay your own way.

bōtata (**betahtah**). Very great; exceedingly rare; eminent; majestic. *Anij eutiej bōtata.* God is most high.

bōtōktōk (**betektek**). 1(*-i*), 2, 3, 6(*-i*). Blood; bleed; menstruation.

bōtōktōk allōñ (**betektek hallẹg**). Idiom. 2, 3(inf, tr *-e*), 6(*-i*), 8, 9. Eclipse of the moon. *Ej bōtōktōk allōñ ñe laļ in ej pinej meramin aļ jāne.* An eclipse of the moon comes about when the earth blocks off the sunlight from it.

bōtta (**bettah**). From Japn. (from Engl. *batter*). 1(*-i*), 2(inf, tr *-ik*), 3, 4, 6(*-a*), 7, 8. Bat, baseball. *Ejeļā bōtta.* He's a good hitter. *Wōn eo ear bōttaik om̧rawūn eo?* Who hit the homerun? *Ekōjak bōttain kijak eņ.* His hitting is laughable.

bu (**biw**). 1(*-i*), 2(inf, tr *-uk*), 4, 6(*-i*), 7, 8. Gun; shoot; rifle. *Kwōn buuk bao eņ.* Shoot that bird.

bubu (**biwbiw**). 1(*-i*), 2(inf, tr *buuj(i)*), 3, 5(*bubuji*), 7, 8, 10(*bobo*). Tie a knot in string or rope; divination method, using knots in pandanus leaf. *Kwōn buuji jabōn to ņe.* Tie the end of that rope. *Eṃōj aer bubuji to eo.* They have knotted the string carelessly.

bubu (**biwbiw**). 1(*-i*), 2(inf, tr *buji*), 3, 4, 8. Tell fortunes; wizardism; divination. *Eṃṃan ke bwe in bubu eo.* Is the result of the divination good?

budeñ (**biwdeg**). 2, 3, 6(*-i*). Overflow; surplus.

bujeeñ (**biwjeyeg**). From Japn. *fuusen*. 6(*-i*). Balloon.

bujek (**biwjęk**). Also *bobo* (**bęwbęw**). 1(*-i*), 2(inf, tr *-e*), 3, 4, 5(*bbujekjek*), 6(*-i*), 8, 10(*bujeke*). Knot of hair, women; twist the hair into a knot; perfective form of *bubu* (**biwbiw**); braid. *Lio ear bujeke bōran ṃokta jān an kōṃṃan ṃōñā.* She tied her hair in a knot before cooking. *Ebbujekjek lieṇ.* She always wears her hair in a knot.

bujen (**biwjen**). Agreement; contract; compact. *Ekkar ñan bujen eo kōtaan Amedka im Maikronejia,....* According to the agreement between the United States and Micronesia,....

bujentōṃa (**biwjenteṃah**). From Japn. *fuusendama*. 6(*-i*). Balloon.

buji (**biwjiy**). Transitive form of *bubu* (**biwbiw**).

bukbuk (**biqbiq**). Dial. W, E: *laklak* (**laklak**). 3, 6(*-i*). A shell, Cassididae, *Cassis cornuta*, helmet shell.

Bukdọḷ (**biqdaḷ°**). 3, 6(*-i*). A plant, breadfruit variety; seedless.

bukduul (**biqdiwil**). 6(*-i*). Cut crosswise; crosscut saw.

bukun (**biqin**). Also *bukwi* (**biqiy**). Grove; cluster; forest. *Bao eo eko ñan bukun wōjke ko.* The chicken ran to the forest. *Bukun mā.* Breadfruit grove. *Bukun ni.* Coconut grove. *Bukun mar.* Boondocks.

bukun iju (**biqin yijiw**). Constellation.

bukwaarar (**biqaharhar**). 1(*-i*), 2(inf, tr *-e*), 3, 6(*-i*), 7. Wake, ship or fish; foam. *Ejjeḷọk ḷap in an wa kaṇ bukwaarar.* Those ships are really stirring up a lot of wake.

bukwabok (**biqabeq**). Dial. E only; see *ṃwijṃwij* (**ṃijṃij**). Also *bukwabok* (**biqabęq**). 1(*-i*), 2(inf, tr *bukwe*), 4, 5(*bbukbukwe, bukbukwe*). Cut; operate. *Ta ṇe ebukwe neeṃ?* What cut your foot? *Ñāāt ṇe raar bukwe lọjieṃ?* When did they operate on your stomach? *Eṃōj ṇe aṃ bbukbukwe ek ṇe.* Why don't you stop cutting that fish carelessly (or into small pieces).

bukwe (**biqęy**). Also *bukwie* (**biqiyey**). 1(*bukwie-*). Knee.

bukwe (**biqey**). Transitive form of *bukwabok* (**biqabeq**).

bukwekwe (**biqęyqęy**). 6(*-i*), 8, 9. Thick; dense, as of hair or bushes; lush. *Elukkuun bukwekwe bōran ledik eo.* The girl had very thick hair.

bukwelep (**biqeylep**). 1(*-i*), 2(inf, tr *-e*), 3, 7. Thick; dense; luxuriant. *Eḷap aṃ bukwelepi piteto kaṇe.* You cut those potatoes too thick.

bukwelōlō (**biqeylehleh**). Also *bukwelōlō* (**biqęylehleh**). 1(*-i*), 2, 3(inf, tr *-ūk*), 6(*-i*), 7. Kneel. *Ear kabukwelōlōik ḷeo im kkwōjarjare.* He made the man kneel and blessed him. *Kwōn bukwelōlō em jar.* Kneel and pray. *Rej bukwelōlō im jar.* They are kneeling and praying.

bukwi (**biqiy**). Hundreds of. *Emootḷọk jān bukwi rūttariṇae eṃōj aer mej.* More than a hundred soldiers died.

bukwi. See *bukun*.

bukwōn (**biqen**). 3(inf *kabbukwōnkwōn*, tr *kabbukwōnkwōne*), 4, 5(*bbukwōnkwōn*). District; division of an atoll or islet; chunk; province; town; village. *Etke kwōj kabbukwōnkwōne ek ṇe?* Why do you cut the fish up into chunks? *Eḷap an baj bbukwōnkwōn piik in.* This pork is too chunky.

buḷabọḷ (**biḷ°abeḷ°**). A plant, *Sonneratia caseolaris* (Takeuchi).

buḷọkwōjkwōj (**biḷ°aqejqej**). 1(*-i*), 2(inf, tr *-e*), 3, 7. Bulging; wrapped sloppily; bulky. *Eḷap an bwilọkwōjkwōj aṃ kar limi pakij e.* You wrapped this package sloppily.

buḷōn (**biḷ°en**). Also *lọbuḷōn* (**lawbiḷ°en**). From *bol* (**bęḷ°**) "heart, core". Middle of; center of; in the midst of; core; through; construct form of *boḷ* (**bęḷ°**). *Elōñ kidu awiia buḷōn ānin.* There are wild animals in the middle of the island. *Emetak buḷōn bōra.* My head hurts from deep inside.

buḷōn mar (**biḷ°en mar**). Wilderness; jungle; forest; woods.

buḷuḷḷuḷ (**biḷ°iḷ°ḷ°iḷ°**). From "onomatopoeia". 1(*-i*), 2, 3, 8. Boil, of water only; bubble; fizz. *Kōjro kōttar an buḷuḷḷuḷ dān e im katuwe.*

Let's wait until this water boils and take it off the fire.

buñ (**big°**). 1(*-i*), 2(inf, tr *buñtake, buñut*), 3, 5(*bbuñbuñ*), 7. Fall down. *Lañ eo ebuñut eok.* The sky will fall on you--you can't escape (proverb). *Ebbuñbuñ ļeeņ.* He's always falling down. *Ear buñtake pāāk eo ej ineke.* He fell carrying the sack.

buñ (**big°**). 1(*-i*), 2, 7. Be off course. *Ebuñ wa in jān āneņ.* The canoe won't make the island (on this tack).

buñ (**big°**). 2, 3, 6(*-i*). Come into appearance; beginning; occurrence. *Ear buñ pata ilo 1941.* The war started in 1941. *Jen rọọl ṃokta jān an buñ kōto.* Let's go back before the storm begins.

buñ (**big°**). 1(*-i*), 2, 3, 4. Lose virginity; be excommunicated.

buñ (**big°**). 2(inf, tr *-i*), 6(*-i*). Spear handle. *Buñūn ṃade.* Spear handle. *Inaaj buñi ṃade e aṃ ilju.* I'll make a handle for your spear tomorrow.

buñ (**big°**). 1(*-i*). Season. *An wōn in buñūn kowainini?* Whose turn is it to harvest the coconuts?

buñ kake (**big° kahkey**). 1(*-i*), 2, 7. Pull together, on rope, almost falling; stumble and fall while carrying. *Lale kobuñ kake ajri ņe.* Be careful you don't fall with that child. *Itok jen jiṃor buñ kake to e im kanōk wa eņ.* Come let's all pull together on this rope and pull the boat.

buñ-bōro (**big°-bẹrẹw**). From *buñbuñ* (**big°big°**) "famous", *bōro* (**bẹrẹw**) "throat, heart". 1(*buñ-būruo-*), 2, 3. Happy; proud. *Eļap an buñ-būruo kōn kwe.* I am very proud of you.

buñ-kōļowa- (**big°-keļewa-**). 1, 2, 3, 7. Arouse passion. *Ļeo eņ ebuñ-kōļowan im ej ilān ire.* His passion is aroused and he is going to fight.

buñ-pāļọk (**big°-payļaq**). From *buñ* (**big°**) "fall", *pāļọk* (**payļaq**) "float away", "There is so much food it is falling off the trees and floating away". 1(*-i*), 2, 3, 4, 7. Abundant. *Ebuñ-pāļọk ānin kōn ṃōñā.* This islet has an abundance of food.

buñ-pedo (**big°-pedew**). From *buñ* (**big°**) "fall down", *pedo* (**pedew**) "lie on stomach". 1(*-i*), 2, 3, 4, 7. Fall face downward; worship. *Rūttariṇae eo ej buñ-pedo im apād.* The soldier is lying in ambush.

buñ-peltak (**big°-peltak**). Also *buñūmpeļtak* (**big°impeļtak**). From *buñ* (**big°**) "fall", *peltak* (**peltak**) "jump up". 1(*-i*), 2, 7. Stumble and rise again to run; nimble. *Kōn an jeļā buñūmpeļtak ear jab jorrāān.* He is so nimble he did not get hurt when he fell down.

buñbuñ (**big°big°**). 1(*-i*), 2, 3, 4, 7, 8, 9. Famous; fame; honor; notorious; prestige; renown. *Eļap an buñbuñ ilo jerbal eņ an.* He is very famous in his field of study.

Buñbuñ (**big°big°**). From *buñbuñ* (**big°big°**) "famous". 3, 6(*-i*). A plant, *Pandanus fischerianus* cultigen; (Stone). Majuro, Arno.

buñi (**big°iy**). Make a handle for a spear; transitive form of *buñ*.

buñlik (**big°lik**). 1(*-i*), 2, 3, 4, 5(*bbuñliklik*), 7. Sail out to sea; depart. *Wa eo eņ ebuñlik.* That ship is sailing out to sea. *Wa eo ebbuñliklik eņ.* That ship makes a lot of voyages.

buñlọk (**big°laq**). Dial. E only; see *wōtlọk* (**wẹtlaq**). 1(*-i*), 2, 3, 5(*bbuñlọklọk*), 7. Fall down; topple. *Lale wōt ebuñlọk ajri ņe.* Watch it, that child might fall. *Ebbuñlọklọk ajri eņ.* That child always falls down. *Ebuñlọk oņān waini.* The price of copra has gone down.

buñṃaan (**big°ṃahan**). From *buñ* (**big°**) "fall", *ṃaan* (**ṃahan**) "in front of". 2, 6(*-i*), 7. Remain ahead of a wave when sailing following the wind.

buñniin (**big°niyin**). Tonight. *Jenaaj etal buñniin.* We will go tonight.

buñņo (**big°ņew**). 3, 5(*bbuñņoņo*), 7. Breaking waves; high surf. *Eļap an buñņo rainin jān inne.* The surf is higher today than yesterday. *Ebbuñņoņo likin ānin.* The surf is always high on the ocean side of this islet.

buñōn (**big°en**). Construct form of *boñ* (**bẹg°**).

buñraak (**big°rahak**). 6(*buñraakkin*). Breaking of waves; falling of words from lips. *Buñraakkin ṃaan tieṃ ear kabwebweik eō.* Your sweet lips fooled me completely.

buñraakkin (**big°rahakkin**). Construct form of *buñraak* (**big°rahak**).

buñtake (**big°tahkey**). Transitive form of *buñ* (**big°**).

buñto-buñtak (**big°tęw-big°tak**). 1(*-i*), 2, 3. Sway back and forth. *Eļap an* MIECO QUEEN *buñto-buñtak ilo iien an ļap ņo.* The MIECO Queen really rolls when there are big waves.

buñtokeañ (**big°teqyag**). Also *buñtokiōñ* (**big°teqyiyęg**). 3. Northerly swell. *Ekajoor buñtokeañ in.* This northerly swell is strong.

buñtokrear (**big°teqręyhar**). 3. Easterly swell.

buñtokrilik (**big°teqriylik**). 3. Westerly swell.

buñtokrōk (**big°teqręk**). 3. Southerly swell.

buñtōn (**big°ten**). 3, 7. Steps; taps; nods; beat regular time to music, pace. *Naaj jete buñtōn neem̧ jān ijin ļǫk ñan m̧weiieņ?* How many steps will it take you from here to that house? *Ej kabuñtōn ippān an jañ al eo.* He's tapping his foot in time to the music.

buñtōn ne (**big°ten ney**). 1(*...nee-*), 3, 7. Steps.

buñut (**big°it**). Transitive form of *buñ* (**big°**).

buñūn ilju (**big°in yiljiw**). Tomorrow night.

buñūn inne (**big°in yinney**). Also *buñinne* (**big°inney**). Night before last.

buñūn inne eo ļǫk juon (**big°in yinney yew ļaq jiwen**). Three nights ago.

buñūn jekļaj (**big°in jekļaj**). Night of the day after tomorrow.

buñūnpāp (**big°inpap**). 1(*-i*), 2(inf, tr *-e*), 3, 4, 7. Wrestling hold for throwing over shoulder.

buoj (**biwęj**). Also *booj* (**bęwęj**). Archaic. Chief's land; capital; navigation "knot" where two waves meet.

bur (**bir°**). 1(*-i*), 2(inf, tr *-i*), 3, 8, 9, 11(*burbur*). Unripe. *Ebur mā ņe.* That breadfruit isn't ripe.

burak (**bir°hak**). 1(*-i*), 2(inf, tr *-e*), 3, 7. Spew out chewed food. *Niññiñ eo ear burake ļǫk m̧ōñā eo jān lǫñiin bwe edike.* The baby spit out the food because it didn't like it.

burum̧ (**bir°wim̧**). From Engl. 1(*-i*), 2(inf, tr *-i*), 3, 4, 6(*-i*), 7, 8. Broom; to sweep.

buuj (**biwij**). Transitive form of *bubu* (**biwbiw**).

buuļtōñtōñ (**biwiļtegteg**). Also *booļtōñtōñ*. 2, 6(*-i*), 7. Move at highest possible speed. *Ear buuļtōñtōñ im itaak.* He crashed at a high speed.

buum̧ (**biwim̧**). From Engl. 6(*-i*). Boom. *Eaettok buum̧in wa eņ.* That ship's booms are normally long.

buwaddel (**biwaddel**). 1(*-i*), 2(inf, tr *-e*), 3, 4, 7. Firebrands; a game, pelting one another with lighted pandanus keys or coconut husks. *Jen etal in buwaddel.* Let's go play firebrands. *Kwōn buwaddele ke ej ja epaak.* Throw a firebrand at him now while he's still close.

buwae (**biwahyęy**). From Engl. Buoy. *Rej kōm̧m̧an buwae ilo to eņ.* Buoys are being installed in the channel.

buwae (**biwahyęy**). From Engl. *boy*. 2, 6(*-i*), 7. Waitress; waiter; servant; serve; cabin boy. *Ej buwae ilo m̧ōn m̧ōñā eņ.* He's a waiter at the restaurant. *Kwōn buwaeļǫk ñan rūm̧ōñā raņ.* Serve the diners.

buwaj (**biwaj**). Spot; bruise.

buwaj (**biwaj**). Also *kuwaj* (**qiwaj**). A fish, halfbeak, *Hemiramphus depauperatus.*

buwak (**biwak**). 1(*-i*), 2(inf, tr *-e*), 4, 5(*buwake, bbuwakwak*), 6(*-i*). Spot, as on dog; birthmark, dark; mole, hairy. *Ebuwake turun mejān lieņ.* She has a lot of birthmarks on her face. *Ebuwak ubōn ļadik eņ.* The boy has a birthmark on his chest. *Ebbuwakwak neen ļadik eņ.* The boy has birthmarks all over his leg.

buwar (**biwar**). Also *bar.* Archaic. A basket.

buwat (**biwat**). 1(*-i*), 2(inf, tr *-e, buwatte*), 3, 4, 6(*-i*), 7. Slingshot. *Kwōn buwate bao eņ.* Hit that bird with your slingshot. *Jab buwatte bao kaņ.* Don't shoot those birds.

būb (**bib**). 3, 6(*-i*). A fish, black triggerfish, *Melichthys ringens.*

būb-. See *bb-*.

būbnini (**bibniyniy**). Dial. E, W: *bwiin-ni* (**biyin-niy**). Smell of coconuts.

būbū (**bihbih**). From *jibū* (**jibih**). Grandmother, child speech; grandchildren.

Būbwin Epoon (**bibin yepewen**). Also *Būb.* From *būb* (**bib**) "black triggerfish thought to be cross-shaped". A constellation; Crux; the Southern

Cross; shows the course from Jaluit to Ebon.

būke (**bikẹy**). Also *būkie* (**bikiyey**). Archaic. Cape of; old construct form of *bōke.*

būkie (**bikiyey**). Also *būke* (**bikẹy**). Archaic. Cape of; old construct form of *bōke.*

būkien (**bikiyen**). Also *būkōn* (**biken**), *bōkein* (**bẹkẹyin**). Cape of; see *bōke.*

Būkien (**bikiyen**). 3, 6(*-i*). A plant; pandanus cultigen.

būkōn (**biken**). Also *būkien* (**bikiyen**), *bōkein* (**bẹkẹyin**). Cape of; see *bōke.*

būkōr (**bikẹr**). A plant, *Cyperus ferax.*

Būkōr (**bikẹr**). 3, 6(*-i*). A plant, *Pandanus fischerianus* cultigen. (Stone). Utirik.

būḷ (**biḷ**). 3, 6(*-i*). A fish, boxfish, *Ostracion cubicus.*

būḷaajpiim (**biḷahajpiyim**). From Engl. 1(*-i*), 2(inf, tr *-i*), 4, 7. Blaspheme. *Jab būḷaajpiimi bwe enaaj llu.* Don't blaspheme him or he'll get angry.

būḷab (**biḷab**). From Engl. 1(*-i*), 2(inf, tr *-e*), 4, 6(*-i*), 7. Bluff. *Kiiō ijeḷā ke kwōj būḷabe eō.* Now I know that you're bluffing.

būḷajtiik (**biḷajtiyik**). From Engl. *plastic*. 6(*-i*). Plastic.

būḷak (**biḷak**). 2(inf, tr *-e*), 5(*bbūḷakḷak*), 6(*-i*). Raise; increase; make high. *Būḷake ainikieṃ.* Raise your voice. *Rōkadek em būḷake al eo.* They got drunk and sang high and loud. *Eḷak epaak an maat jikka, ebūḷake oṇān.* When the cigarettes were nearly sold out, he raised the price. *Kwōn būḷake ḷaaṃ ṇe.* Make that lantern real bright.

būḷak (**biḷak**). From Engl. 2(inf, tr *-e*), 6(*-i*). Block; pulley.

būḷak (**biḷak**). From Engl. 2(inf, tr *-e*), 6(*-i*), 7. Concrete block; brick. *Jete būḷakin ṃweeṇ ṃōṃ?* How many blocks did you use on your house?

būḷañ (**biḷag**). From Engl. 2(inf, tr *-e*), 3, 4, 6(*-i*). Flunk. *Enana ad mour ñe jej būḷañi katak ko ad.* We don't feel well whenever we flunk any of our courses.

būḷañkōj (**biḷagkej**). From Engl. Blanket. *Būḷañkōjin ia ṇe kinieṃ?* Where did you get your blanket?

būḷāāt (**biḷayat**). From Engl. 1(*-i*), 2, 3, (inf, tr *-e*), 4, 8, 9. Flat music or voice, usually out of tune. *Kwōn jab al bwe kobūḷāāt.* Don't sing because you're flat. *Enta kwōj kabūḷāāt aṃ al?* Why are you singing out of tune?

būḷāwut (**biḷaywit**). From Engl. 2(inf, tr *-i*), 6(*-i*), 7. Plywood. *Eṃōj būḷāwuti tōrakin ruuṃ in.* The ceiling in this room has been covered with plywood.

būḷu (**biḷiw**). From Engl. 1(*-i*), 2(inf, tr *-uk*), 3(inf, tr *-uk*), 5(*bbūḷuḷu*), 6(*-i*), 7, 8, 9, 11(*būḷuḷu, būḷu*). Bluing; blue. *Ej kōṇak juon nuknuk ebbūḷuḷu mejān.* She's wearing a bluish dress.

būḷu (**biḷiw**). From Engl. 1, 2, 3(tr *-uk*), 4, 6(*-i*), 7. Flu. *Kwōj būḷutok jān ia ke kwōnaaj kabūḷuuk riānin?* Where did you contract the flu from? Now everybody on the island will get it.

būḷukaṃ (**biḷiwkaṃ**). From Engl. 2(inf, tr *-e*), 6(*-i*), 7. Bluegum; a type of imported lumber from the bluegum (eucalyptus) tree. *Rej būḷukaṃe kapin wa eṇ.* They are putting bluegum planks on the bottom of that boat.

būḷuuddik (**biḷiwiddik**). 1(*-i*), 2, 5(*būḷuuddik(i)*), 6(*-i*). Perspiration beads. *Ebūḷuuddik turun mejaṃ.* There are beads of perspiration on your face. *Ebūḷuuddiki turun mejān.* His face was covered all over with beads of sweat.

būḷūkkañ (**biḷikkag**). Also *bwilikkañ* (**bilikkag**). Vulgar. 1(*-i*). Clitoris.

būḷūtteej (**biḷitteyej**). Vulgar. 1, 6(*-i*). Clitoris.

būṇo (**biṇẹw**). Vulgar. 1(*-i*), 2, 3, 5(*bbūṇoṇo*). Smell of unwashed sexual organs.

būñal (**bigal**). 1(*-i*), 2(inf, tr *-e*), 3, 5(*būñalñal*), 7, 8, 9. Dust; dusty. *Eḷap an būñal(ñal) rainin.* It's very dusty today. *Kwōn jab būñale eok bwe kwōnaaj bōk mejin.* Don't get dust on yourself or you'll catch cold.

būraaj (**birahaj**). From Engl. Brass. *Ejeja būraaj iṂajeḷ.* Brass is hard to come by in the Marshalls.

būrabōḷ (**birabeḷ**). From Engl. 1(*-i*), 2, 4, 7. Parable.

būrae (**birahyey**). From Engl. 1(*-i*), 2(inf, tr *-ik*), 3, 4, 8. Fry. *Kwōn būraeiktok juon ek.* Fry me a fish.

būraj (**biraj**). From Engl. 1(*-i*), 2(inf, tr *-e*), 3, 4, 6(*-i*), 7, 8. Brush; scrub. *Kwōn būraje raan tebōļ ņe bwe ettoon.* Brush off the top of that table because it's dirty. *Kabūraje ajri raņ.* Make the children brush their teeth.

Būranij (**birahnij**). From Engl. 4. France.

būrar (**birar**). 1(*-i*), 2(inf, tr *-e*), 3, 5(*bbūrarrar*), 6(*-i, bōrran*), 8. Smear; stains; remnants; traces. *Ebūrar nuknuk ņe aṃ.* Your clothes are smeared. *Wōn ņe ear būrare nuknuk ņe aṃ?* Who smeared your clothes? *Ebbūrarrar ļam jako ijeņe.* That area there by you is all smeary. *Eor bōrran ṃōñā ilo nuknuk ņe aṃ.* There are food stains on your clothes. *Kwōn jab būrare nuknuk ņe aṃ.* Don't stain your clothes. *Ebūrar pilej e.* This plate isn't clean.

būrawūn (**birahwin**). From Engl. 1(*-i*), 2(inf, tr *-i*), 3, 5(*bbūrawūnwūn*), 6(*-i*), 7, 8. Brown. *Ebbūrawūnwūn mejān nuknuk eo ej kōņake.* The clothes he wears have brownish colors.

būreej (**bireyej**). Also *petkōj* (**pętkęj**). From Engl. *bread*. 3, 6(*-i*). Biscuits; crackers.

būreejtōn (**bireyejten**). From Engl. 1(*-i*), 2, 3, 6(*-i*). President.

būreek (**bireyek**). From Engl. 1(*-i*), 2(inf, tr *-e*), 3, 4, 5(*bbūreekek*), 6(*-i*), 7. Brake. *Eṃṃan ke an būreekin wa ņe waaṃ jerbal.* Do the brakes on your car function well? *Kwōn būreeke.* Step on the brakes. *Ebbūreekek an kijak eņ kattōr.* He's always braking when he drives.

būreek (**bireyek**). From Engl. *brig*. 2(inf, tr *-e*), 4, 5(*bbūreekek*), 6(*-i*). Prison. *Ear būreek boñ.* He got put in jail last night. *Ebbūreekek ļeeņ.* He's always in jail.

būreit (**birẹyit**). Also *būreet* (**birẹyẹt**). From Engl. Freight. *Kwōnañin kōļļāik ke būreitin ṃweiuk kaņe aṃ?* Have you paid the freight on your goods?

būri (**biriy**). 1(*-i*), 5(*bbūriri*), 6(*-i*). Uvula; esophagus.

būrij (**biryij**). From Engl. 6(*-i*). Priest. *Epen an būrijin Jāmne kien jān būrijin Amedka.* German priests are stricter than American priests.

būrij (**biryij**). From Engl. 6(*-i*). Bridge of ship.

būrijōōt (**biriyjehet**). From Engl. *breeches.* 2, 3(inf, tr *-e*), 4, 6(*-i*), 7. Bib-overalls. *Ekōjak būrijōōt eņ an.* He has on funny looking bib-overalls. *Wōn ņe ear kabūrijōōte?* Who gave him the bib-overalls?

būrinjibōļ (**birinjibeļ**). From Engl. 2, 3(inf, tr *-e*), 6(*-i*). Principal. *Eor ke būrinjibōļin jikuuļ in?* Does this school have a principal?

būrojāāk (**birewjayak**). From Engl. Project; enterprise.

būroṃōj (**birẹwṃẹj**). 1(*-i*), 2, 3(st inf *kabūroṃōjṃōj,* tr *kabūroṃōj*), 4, 5(*bbūroṃōjṃōj*), 7, 8, 9. Sorrow; sadness; sorry; mourn; bereave; grief; pity; sad. *Eļap an lio būroṃōj kōn ļeo ippān emej.* She is mourning her dead husband. *Ebbūroṃōjṃōj ļeeņ.* He has a tendency toward melancholy. *Ekabūroṃōjṃōj ṃupi eo.* The movie is sad.

būroñ (**bireg°**). 1(*-i*), 2(inf, tr *-e*), 4, 7, 8, 9. Talk harshly; scold. *Kwōn jab būroñ bwe armej enaaj mijak eok.* Don't talk harshly or people will be afraid of you.

būroojki (**birẹwẹjkiy**). From Japn. *furoshiki*. 2(inf, tr *-ik*), 3, 4, 5(*bbūroojkiki*), 6(*-i*), 7. Bundle of goods wrapped with a square of cloth; cloth for wrapping bundle of goods. *Etke kwōj jañin būroojkiiki nuknuk kaņe?* Why haven't you bundled up the clothes? *Kabūroojkiiki ippaṃ.* Let her share the bundle with you.

būrook (**birewek**). Also *būrok* (**birwek**). Slang. From Engl. 1(*-i*), 2, 3, 4, 5(*bbūrookok*), 8. Broke, financially; out of money; bankrupt. *Ebūrook kombani eņ.* That business went bankrupt.

būrooklep (**bireweklep**). Dial. E, W: *mattiia* (**mattiyyah**). 1(*-i*), 2, 3, 4, 8, 9. Greedy eater; glutton; voracious.

būrookraaṃ (**birewekrahaṃ**). From Engl. Program.

Būrotijen (**birewtiyjen**). From Engl. 1(*-i*), 2, 3, 4. Protestant, religion.

būrọ (**biraw**). Also *ļabbūrọ* (**ļabbiraw**). Sonny; vocative to boys.

būrọk (**biraq**). From Engl. 3, 6(*-i*). Frog.

Būrōk (**birẹk**). 3, 6(*-i*). A plant, pandanus cultigen (Takeuchi).

būrōrō (**birehreh**). 1(*-i*), 2(inf, tr *-ūk*), 3, 5(*bbūrōrō*), 7, 8. Red. *Ej kōņak juon nuknuk bbūrōrō mejān.* She is wearing a reddish dress. *Ej kabūrōrō.* She's wearing lipstick.

būrudik (**biriwdik**). Dial. E, W: *mattiie* (**mattiyyęy**). Also *biruukdik* (**biriwikdik**). 1(*-i*), 2, 3, 4, 8, 9. Light eater.

būruon kūro (**biriwen kiręw**). From *būruon* (**biriwen**) "heart of", *kūro* (**kiręw**) "rock cod, grouper". 2, 8, 9. Selfish; inconsiderate; stubborn. *Kwōn jab būruon kūro.* Don't be selfish.

būto (**bitęw**). 1(*-i*), 2, 3, 5(*bbūtoto*). Smell of pit for soaking coconut husks. *Kwōn jab uñūri eō bwe kwōnaaj kabūtouk iō.* Don't touch me or you'll make me smell all of *būto*.

būtoñ (**biteg°**). From Japn. *futon* "quilt". 2(inf, tr *-i*), 6(*-i*). Mattress. *Enañin būtoñe ke peet eņ?* Has a mattress been put on the bed?

būtoñtoñ (**biteg°teg°**). From *būtoñ* (**biteg°**). 1(*-i*), 2, 3, 4. Sleep on mattress. *Eṃṃan wōt būtoñtoñ ippa bwe emeoeo.* I like to sleep on a mattress because it's smooth.

būtti (**bittiy**). 1(*-i*), 2, 4, 5(*bbūttiti*), 6(*-i*), 8, 9. Wart; bump; projection. *Ebbūttiti ļeeņ.* He has warts all over him.

būtti kakūtōtō (**bittiy kakitęhtęh**). From *būtti* (**bittiy**) "wart", *kakūtōtō* (**kakitęhtęh**) "stubborn, naughty". 6(*-i*). Wart, bushy type.

būttiwaļ (**bittiywaļ**). 3, 6(*-i*). Small sandworm.

būttiwoļ (**bittiywеļ**). Also *bwittiwaļ* (**bittiywaļ**). 2, 6(*-i*). Small mole with a hair sticking out; wart.

būttǫǫr (**bittawar**). Fountain. *Juon eo būttǫǫr iturun ṃweo.* There was a fountain near the house.

būttūk (**bittik**). 1(*-i*), 2(inf, tr *-i*), 3, 5(*bbūtūktūk*), 7. Spurt; squirt. *Ia in ej bbūtūktūk tok?* Where is that spray coming from?

bwā (**bay**). 6(*-i*). Fish pole.

bwā (**bay**). 1, 2. Enlargement of breasts at puberty. *Ebwā ittin.* Her breasts are beginning to grow.

Bwā-eņ-an-Joktak (**bay-yeņ-an-jeqtak**). From Joktak, an *ekjab* that inhabits *Bokwan-ake,* Jaluit; "Joktak's fish pole". A constellation; Grus; alpha, the hook; nu, delta, beta and epsilon, the rod.

bwābwe (**baybęy**). 1, 2(inf, tr *-ik*), 3, 7. Tack windward; luff. *Kwōn bwābweik wa ņe.* Tack into the wind. *Jeņro kabwābweik wa in.* Let's two of us tack this canoe windward.

bwe (**bey**). 2, 6(*bwein, bōkan*). Left over; remainder; balance; excess; odd; residual; residue; surplus. *Eļap bwe in ṃōñā rainin.* There is lots of food left over today. *Lutōkļǫk bwe ņe.* Pour off the excess.

bwe (**bey**). Also *eb* (**yeb**), *-ōb* (**-eb**). Because; so that; for; why? *Ikōņaan idaak wūno bwe emtak bōra.* I want some medicine because I have a headache. *Kwōn jabōb (jab eb) iṃōk.* Don't do that because I'm beat.

bwe (**bey**). From *bwe* (**bey**) "left over". 1(*-i*), 6(*-i*). Result of divination.

bwe (**bey**). 2, 3(st inf *kabbwebwe,* tr *kabwe*), 6(*-i*), 8. Enough; sufficient; adequate; decent; fair. *Ebwe ke juon taļa ñan aṃ ṃōñein raelep?* Is one dollar enough for your lunch? *Ej et aṃ mour? Jej, ej bwe wōt.* How are you? ...Oh, so, so. *Kwōn bōk ruo pāāk em kabbwebwe ñan jilu allōñ.* Take three sacks to make sure you've got enough for three months. *Kōmat jitu bwe ekabbwebwe.* Make stew cause it goes further. *Letok ļalem jāān em kabweļǫk oņān juon jikka.* Lend me a nickel so I'll have enough money for some cigarettes. *Ebwe ņe.* That'll do.

bwe (**bęy**). Also *bo* (**bęw**). Knot in divination; see *bubu; fact; symbol. Ejejjet bwe eo.* "That's the true knot (the correct symbol) in divination.

bwe bōta (**bey betah**). Assuming that. *Eṃṃan ke tūrep eo aṃ ñan Amedka?...Bwe bōta iar etal.* Did you have a good trip to America?...(You're)assuming I went. *Ñāāt eo kwōj etal ñan Ṃajeļ? ...Bwe bōta inaaj etal.* When are you going to the Marshalls?...(You're) assuming I'm going. *Epād ke Toni i ṃōņe? ...Bwe bōta ej jokwe ṃwiin.* Is Tony in your house there?...(You're) assuming he lives here.

bwebwe (**bęybęy**). 1, 2, 3(inf, tr *-ik*), 4, 6(*-i*), 8, 9. Crazy; silly; foolish; giddy; thick-headed; demented; fool; insane; mad; imbecile; stupid. *Eṃōj aṃ* *bwebwe.* That was a silly thing you did. *Kwōn jab kabwebweiki bwe edik.* Don't call him crazy because he's still a child. *Ļeo ekabwebweik eō.* The man fooled me. *Im̧ōn rūbwebwe.* Lunatic's house.

bwebwe (**beybey**). 3, 6(*-i*). A fish, tuna, *Neothunus macropterus.*

bwebwenato (**beybeynahtew**). 1(*-i*), 2, 3(inf, tr *-ik, -uk*), 4, 6(*-i*), 7. Talk; conversation; story; history; article; episode; lore; myth; tale. *Ta ņe kom̧ean̄ ej bwebwenato kake?* What are you four talking about? *Em̧m̧an ke bwebwenato eo ilo pija eo bon̄?* Did the movie last night have a good story? *Kabwebwenato.* Make conversation with a stranger.

bwebwenato bajjek (**beybeynahtew bajjęk**). 1(*-i*), 2, 3, 4. Chat.

bwebwenatoon etto (**beybeynahtewen yettew**). 4. Legend.

bwebwenatoun mour an juon armej (**beybeynahtewin mẹwir han jiwen harmẹj**). Biography. *Ear je bwebwenatoun mour eo an.* He wrote his own biography--his autobiography.

bweetkōn (**bẹyẹtkẹn**). 2, 3, 5(*bbweetkōnkōn*), 6(*-i*), 8, 9. Discouraged; give up hope. *Kwōn jab bbweetkōnkōn bwe wūnin am̧ jerata ņe.* Don't be discouraged so easily; that is the reason why you have misfortunes.

bweo (**bẹyẹw**). Also *debeo* (**dẹbẹyẹw**). 6(*-a*). Pile of husks near husking stick.

bweǫ (**beyaw**). 3, 5(*bbweǫeǫ*), 6(*-i, -a*). Coconut husk; coconut fibre. *Ejjeļǫk wōt bbweǫeǫun m̧ōn kuk eņ.* That cooking house is full of coconut husks.

bweradik (**beyrahdik**). 2, 7. To begin going. *Jen jino bweradikļǫk n̄an keemem eņ.* Let's start moseying along to the party.

bwi (**biy**). Rack for heat or smoke drying. *Epād ioon bwi eņ.* It's on the drying rack.

bwiaea (**biyahyah**). Also *piaea* (**piyahyah**). 6(*-a*). Fish eggs.

bwiār (**biyar**). 1(*-i*), 2(inf, tr *-(e)*), 4, 7. Pierce with knife; stab. *Em̧ōj an ļeo bwiāre piik eo.* He has stabbed the pig.

bwibwi (**biybiy**). Egg yolk. *Bwibwi takin al.* The yellowness of the sunrise.

bwibwitakaļ (**biybiytakhaļ**). Egg yolk.

bwidak (**bidak**). Also *iroojiddik* (**yirẹwẹjiddik**). Half prince, royal father but commoner mother.

bwidak irooj (**bidak yirẹwẹj**). Quarter prince, royal father but mother half-princess.

bwidak lerooj (**bidak lẹyrẹwẹj**). Quarter princess, royal father but mother half-princess.

bwiddik (**biddik**). From *bwidej edik.* Small land tract.

bwidej (**bidẹj**). 1(*-i*), 2(inf, tr *-e*), 3(inf *kabwidejdej, -e*), 5(*bbwidejdej*), 6(*-i*). Earth; ground; soil; dirt; real estate. *Ebwidejdej nuknuk e aō.* My clothes are soiled. *Ebbwidejdej ļeeņ.* He's real estate minded.

bwiden (**biden**). Rather than; instead of. *Ebwiden kadek ak ej jab katak.* He spends his time drinking rather than studying. *Wūnin an jab m̧ōn̄ā ebwiden jerbal.* He didn't eat because he was busy working.

bwii- (**biyi-**). 1, 2+6, 6. Smell; odor. *Ebwiin nana.* It smells bad. *Bwiin n̄aj.* I smell something fragrant.

bwiin-ennǫ (**biyin-yennaw**). 1(*-i*), 2, 3. Savory smell.

bwiin-jin̄ (**biyin-jig**). 1(*-i*), 2, 3. Smell of breaking wind.

bwiin-juwapen (**biyin-jiwahpẹn**). Also *bwiin-kuļuļ* (**biyin-kiļ°iļ°**). 1(*-i*), 2, 3. Smell of cockroaches.

bwiin-kūbween-alōr (**biyin-kibeyen-halhẹr**). 1(*-i*), 2, 3, 5(*-e*). Smell of chicken manure.

bwiin-nana (**biyin-nahnah**). 1(*-a*), 2, 3(inf, tr *-ik*). Bad odor. *Ta wūnin am̧ jin̄ im kabwiin-nanaik ruum̧ in?* Why do you fart and make this room smell bad?

bwiin-ni (**biyin-niy**). Dial. W, E: *būbnini* (**bibniyniy**). Smell of coconuts.

bwiin-ppāllele (**biyin-ppalleyley**). From *pālle* (**palley**) "white man". 1(*-i*), 2, 3. Smell of new things; smell of imported goods.

bwiin-puwaļ (**biyin-piwaļ**). 1(*-i*), 2, 3(inf, tr *-e*), 5(*ppuwaļoļ*), 7, 8 9. Bad odor; foul odor stench; smell of decayed flesh; stink. *Ebwiin-puwaļ bakke ņe ineem̧.* The sore on your foot has an offensive odor. *Ejāālel bwiin-puwaļiier.* We can smell their offensive odor everywhere they go.

bwiin-tōñal (**biyin-tegal**). 1(*-i*), 2, 3, 5(*bwiin-ttōñalñal*). Sweet smell, of ripe pandanus fruit.

bwij (**bij**). 1(*-i*), 5(*-lep*), 6(*bwijjin*). Lineage; crowd; family; tribe.

bwij (**bij**). 6(*-i*). Canoe part, two pieces of ironwood support that attach the *kie* to the outrigger.

bwijbwij (**bijbij**). 1(*-i*), 2(inf, tr *bwijlọkwe, bwijilọkwe, bwijjike*), 3. Kick; a dance. *Lale wōt kobwijlọke lọjien ḷadik ṇe.* Be careful you don't kick that boy's stomach.

bwije- (**bije-**). 1. Navel.

bwijeae (**bijyahyey**). Dial. W, E: *bwijeaea* (**bijyahyah**). 2, 4, 6(*-i*), 7. Tread water; thrash the arms and legs around while in water; kick feet in swimming. *Ear jab aōḷọk jān ijo ak ear bwijeae wōt.* He didn't swim away but treaded water at that spot. *Iṃōk in bwijiaea.* I'm tired of treading water.

bwijenro (**bijẹnrẹw**). Superstition that cat crying at night portends death of someone.

bwijerro (**bijẹrrẹw**). 1(*-i*), 2(inf, tr *-ik*), 3, 4. A quarrel between two related persons which will result in misfortune; disaster; omen; tragedy. *Koṃro en jab bwijerro.* You two shouldn't quarrel--you're related and something evil will happen if you do.

bwijil (**bijil**). Dial. E, W: *bwijij* (**bijij**). Also *lijib* (**lijib**). 1(*-i*), 2, 3(inf *kabwijiljil*, tr *kabwijili*), 6, 8, 9, 11(*bwijiljil*). Blunt. *Ebwijil bōran doon eo.* The end of the husking stick is blunt. *Wōn eo ear kabwijil bōran doon eo?* Who made the end of the husking stick blunt?

bwijilọkwe (**bijilaqẹy**). Transitive form of *bwijbwij* (**bijbij**).

bwijin (**bijin**). Dial. E, W: *bōjen* (**bẹjẹn**). 6(*bwijinin*). Flock; a crowd of; school of fish; group. *Bwijin in armej ro wōj rā tok.* Here come several groups of people. *Bwijin in armej eo e tok.* Here comes a group of people. *Juon e bwijin in ṃọle iar.* Here's a school of rabbitfish at the lagoon beach. *Bōjen in ek ko kā tok.* Here come several schools of fish.

bwijin (**bijin**). Dial. E only. Many; multiple. *Bwijin aō ṃaak.* I've got lots of money.

bwijinbwije (**bijinbijey**). 2(inf, tr *-ik*), 6(*-i*). Coir fibre, fine, not woven, left over from weaving, used as wash cloth. *Eṃṃan tutu kōn bwijinbwije ippa.* I like using a coir fibre when bathing.

bwijjik (**bijjik**). 1(*-i*), 2(inf, tr *-e*), 4, 6(*-i*), 7. Kick. *Kwōjaaṃ bwijjike eō?* Why do you keep kicking me? *Eṃōjṇọ an bwijjik.* He doesn't kick hard. *Raar bwijjike jān jikuuḷ kōn an kkadekdek.* He was kicked out of school because he was a drunk.

bwijjike (**bijjikey**). Transitive form of *bwijbwij* (**bijbij**).

bwijjin (**bijjin**). Construct form of *bwij* (**bij**).

bwijlep (**bijlep**). Distributive form of *bwij* (**bij**).

bwijlọkwe (**bijlaqey**). Transitive form of *bwijbwij* (**bijbij**).

bwijọkorkor (**bijaqerqer**). 2, 6(*-i*), 7. Rush; hurry. *Ia ṇe kwōj bwijọkorkor ḷọk ñane?* Where are you rushing to?

bwijteoḷeoḷ (**bijteyeḷ°yeḷ°**). 1(*-i*), 2, 3, 4. Nomad. *Bwij eo ebwijteoḷeoḷ ṇe.* That lineage is always changing homes.

bwijuwe (**bijiwwẹy**). 1(*-i*), 2, 3(inf, tr *-ik*), 5(*bbijowewe*), 6(*-i*), 7, 8, 9. Uneven; dune; lump.

bwijwoḷā (**bijweḷay**). 1(*-i*), 2, 3, 7. Aged; doddering. *Ibwijwoḷā ḷọk.* I'm getting old. *Bwijwoḷā men eṇ.* He's a doddering old man.

bwil (**bil**). 1(*-i*), 2, 6(*-i*), 8, 9, 11(*bwilbwil*). Burn; hot; fever; temperature. *Ebwil nuknuk ko.* The clothes are burning. *Ie joñan bwil ṇe an?* What is his temperature?

bwil (**bil**). 3, 6(*-i*). Sap; chewing gum.

bwil (**bil**). 2(inf, tr *bwilli*), 4, 6(*-i*), 7. Launching. *Raar bwilli waan Toke.* They launched Toke's boat.

bwil (**bil**). Slang. 1, 2, 3, 6(*-i*). Head over heels in love; intimate. *Kōṃro lieṇ lukkuun bwil ippān doon.* She and I are madly in love.

bwil-bōro (**bil-bẹrẹw**). From *bwil* (**bil**) "heat", *bōro* (**bẹrẹw**) "heart, seat of emotion". 1(*bwil-būruo-*), 2+1, 6(*bwillin-bōro*). Revenge. *Ebwil būruon.* He is seeking revenge.

bwilak (**bilak**). Also *bwilaklak* (**bilaklak**). 3, 6(*-i*). A fish, unicorn fish, *Naso lituratus*; surgeonfish.

bwilbwil (**bilbil**). 2(inf, tr *bwili*), 3, 5(*bwilbwili*). Gummy; cover with gum; resin. *Ebwilbwil juuj ṇe aṃ.* There is gum on your shoes. *Wōn ṇe* *ear bwili juuj ṇe aṃ?* Who put gum on your shoes?

bwilbwil (**bilbil**). Also *wabwilbwil* (**wahbilbil**). 1(-*i*), 2(inf, tr *bwilli*), 3, 7. Sail model canoes. *Ḷadik ro raṇ rej bwilbwil riwut.* The boys are sailing model canoes.

bwilbwilikkaj (**bilbilikkaj**). A plant, *Sybedrella nodiflora* (L.) Gaertn. (see *kinwōj*) (compositae); also a species of *Euphorbia.*

bwili (**biliy**). Transitive form of *bwilbwil* (**bilbil**).

bwilijmāāṇ (**bilijmayaṇ**). From Engl. *policeman.* 2(inf, tr -*e*), 3, 4, 6(-*i*). Police; guard. *Rej bwilijmāāṇe pāāñ eo.* They are guarding the bank.

bwilik ṃaan (**bilik ṃahan**). Idiom. 2(inf, tr *bwiliki ṃaan*), 4, 7. Initiate; begin. *Kijak eo enaaj bwilik tok ṃaan al eo ṇe.* That's the chap who'll initiate the song.

bwilitudek (**biliytiwdek**). 2(inf, tr -*e*), 4, 6(-*i*). A food; sliced unripe breadfruit cooked in coconut milk. *Ennọ ke bwilitudek ippaṃ?* Do you like *bwilitudek? Kwōn bwilitudeki mā kaṇe.* Make *bwilitudek* with those breadfruit.

bwilji- (**bilji-**). Also *bwilij, ḷọbwilej.* 1, 2, 6, 7. Middle of many things or people; among. *Ḷadik eo eṇ ibwiljin armej raṇ wōj.* The boy is in the midst of all those people.

bwilkōn-utilomar (**bilken-wityilewmar**). Variant form of *utilomar.*

bwilli (**billiy**). Transitive form of *bwilbwil* (**bilbil**) and *bwil* (**bil**).

bwillọk (**billaq**). 1(-*i*), 2(inf, tr -*e*), 3, 7. Launch forth; push forth. *Wa eo eṇ emōj bwillọke.* That canoe has been launched.

bwilmeleeñ (**bilmęlęyęg**). 1(-*i*), 2, 3, 8. Heartburn. *Enana wōt aō bwilmeleeñ.* How I hate this heartburn.

bwilọk (**bilaq**). 1(-*i*), 2(inf, tr -*e*), 3, 6(-*i*), 7. Break; crease; fracture. *Ebwilọk aḷaḷ eo.* The piece of wood is broken. *Wōn ear būḷọke aḷaḷ eo?* Who broke the piece of wood? *Bwilọkun jedọujij ṇe aṃ eṃṃan.* You've got neat creases in your trousers.

bwilọk māj (**bilaq maj**). Idiom. Be embarrassed; lose face. *Kōṃṃan ko an rōkabwilọklọk māj.* Her actions are embarrassing.

bwilọklañ (**bilaqlag**). Also *wōtlọklañ.* Idiom. 2. Death of a chieftain. *Ebwilọklañ.* A chieftain has died.

bwilōñ (**bileg**). 1(-*i*), 2, 3, 7. Wonder; amaze; surprise; impress. *Eḷap aō bwilōñ kōn baḷuun eo.* The airplane amazes me.

bwiltoonon (**biltęwęnwęn**). 1(-*i*), 2, 3, 4, 7. Filthy; dirty. *Ij jab iwōj in jar bwe ibwiltoonon.* I'm not going to church with you because I'm dirty.

bwiltōñtōñ (**biltegteg**). 6(-*i*). Hottest time of day; piping hot. *Ear ḷap kwōle ilo bwiltōñtōñin pata eo.* There was a great famine when the war was in full-swing.

bwine (**binęy**). A fish, butterfly fish, *Chaetodon ornatissimus.*

bwini (**biniy**). Transitive form of *bōnbōn* (**bęnbęn**).

bwinimjaad (**binimjahad**). Archaic. Forbidden; taboo. *Bwinimjaad popoṃanit.* Do not go ashore on islands that do not belong to you.

bwio (**biyew**). 6(-*i*), 11(*bwioeo*). King; noble. *Irooj bwioeo eo ṇe tok.* The noble king is on his way.

bwiro (**biyręw**). 3, 5(*bbwiroro*), 6(-*i*). A food, preserved breadfruit. *Ebbwiroro nuknuk e aō.* My clothes smell of preserved breadfruit. My clothes have scraps of preserved breadfruit on them. *Lale ebbwiroro nuknuk ṇe aṃ.* Be careful you don't get preserved breadfruit on your clothes.

bwiro iiōk (**biyręw 'yiyęk**). 3, 6(-*i*). A food, preserved breadfruit mixed with arrowroot and coconut sap or sugar, wrapped in breadfruit leaves and baked.

da (**dah**). Also *dda.* 1(-*a*). Blood. *Ear tọọrḷọk da eo daan ioon debwāāl.* His blood flowed on the cross.

Da (**dah**). A star; Spica in Virgo; the sixthborn of *Lōktañūr.*

daa- (**daha-**). 1. Pandanus of. *Daō bōb ṇe.* That's my pandanus there by you. *Daan wōn bōb e?* Whose pandanus is this?

Daam-Ad (**daham-had**). From *Da im Ad.* The pair of stars Spica and Arcturus.

daan (**dahan**). Dial. E only. (Not) so very much (used only in the negative). *Ej jab daan m̧ōḷo.* It's not very cold. *En jab daan utiej.* Don't make it so high. *Ij jab daan jeḷā kajin Boonpe.* I don't know too much Ponapean.

daat (**dahat**). Archaic. Covered with blood.

dak (**dak**). From Engl. 3, 5(*-e*), 6(*-i*). Duck.

dakke (**dakkẹy**). Slang. 1, 2, 6(*-i*), 8, 9. Ugly, of people; homely. *Ejjeḷọk dakke in ḷeen̄.* That man is very ugly.

dakōlkōl (**dakẹlkẹl**). 1(*-i*), 2, 3, 4, 8. Ugly; homely. *Eḷap an dakōlkōl.* He is very homely. *Edakōlkōl wa en̄ waan.* His canoe is ugly.

dam̧ (**dam̧**). 1(*dem̧a-*). Forehead; brow; gable; edge.

dam̧dem̧ (**dam̧dẹm̧**). 1(*-i*), 2(inf, tr *dam̧wij*), 4, 5(*dam̧dim̧wij, ddam̧dem̧wij*), 7. Lick. *Lale kidu n̄e ej dam̧wij pilej n̄e.* Watch out, that dog is licking your plate. *Kidu ko rej dam̧dem̧ ilo pilej ko.* The dogs are licking at the plates. *Ear bajjek dam̧dim̧wij ḷọḷe eo.* He just kept licking the lollipop. *Jab dam̧wij ḷọḷe n̄e bwe etoon.* Don't lick that lollipop cause it's dirty. *Jab dam̧dem̧wij peim̧.* Don't lick your hand (continuously).

dam̧dim̧wij (**dam̧dim̧ij**). Distributive form of *dam̧dem̧* (**dam̧dẹm̧**).

dam̧ok (**dam̧eq**). Also *dam̧o* (**dam̧ew**). 1(*-i*), 2(inf, tr *-e*), 3, 6(*-i*), 7. Jutting out from the rest; extra; appendage, usually to a house (always used with directional postpositions). *Juon en̄ aḷaḷ ej dam̧okḷọk jān m̧ween̄.* A piece of wood is sticking out from that house. *Ij jerbal in kōm̧m̧an aō dam̧oḷọk.* I work to make some extra money. *Wōn n̄e ej jokwe ilo dam̧oḷọk n̄e?* Who is living in the small room?

dam̧wij (**dam̧ij**). Transitive form of *dam̧dem̧* (**dam̧dẹm̧**).

dao (**dahwew**). 1(*-i*), 2, 3, 8. First food after fast; break a fast. *Kwōnañin dao ke?* Haven't you broken your fast yet? *Ij jañin dao jān inne.* I haven't eaten since yesterday.

dapitōk (**dahpitẹk**). 2, 3, 5(*ddapitōktōk*), 6(*-i*). Tangled. *Jab juri bwe kwōnaaj kōdapitōke.* Don't step on it or you'll entangle it. *Em̧m̧an eke bwe rōjjab ddapitōktōk.* Nylon lines are good because they don't tangle often.

dāde (**daydẹy**). Also *ddāit* (**ddayit**). 2(inf, tr *dāit*), 6(*-i*), 7. Twist and pull hair; tangled; mesh. *Ekkā an kōrā dāde bar ñe rej ire.* Women usually pull hair when they fight. *Ear dāit bōran em ukōje.* He grabbed his hair and pulled him down.

dāik (**dayik**). Transitive form of *dāndān.*

dāit (**dayit**). Transitive form of *dāde* (**daydẹy**).

dān (**dan**). 1(*dānni-*), 5(*dāne, dāndān*), 6(*dānnin*). Water; liquid; beverage; fluid; juice; sap of coconut tree. *Edāne oran eo.* The orange was juicy. *Dānnin wōt.* Rain water.

dāndān (**dandan**). 2(inf, tr *dāne, dāik*), 3(inf, tr *-e*), 5(*dāndān, dāndāne*), 6(*-i*), 8, 9, 11(*ddāndān*). Watery; slimy. *Edāndān m̧ōñā en̄.* That food is watery. *Dāne raij n̄e.* Put water in the rice. *Kōdāndāne juub n̄e.* Dilute the soup.

dāne (**daney**). Transitive form of *dāndān* (**dandan**).

dānnin (**dannin**). Construct form of *dān* (**dan**).

dānnin aebōj (**dannin hayẹbẹj**). Rain water.

dānnin idaak (**dannin yidahak**). Drinking water.

dānnin kadek (**dannin kadek**). Strong liquor, alcoholic beverage.

dānnin kōmjaaḷaḷ (**dannin kemjahaḷhaḷ**). Tears.

dānnin laḷ (**dannin laḷ**). Well water.

dānnin lọjet (**dannin lawjẹt**). Salt water.

dānnin ni (**dannin niy**). Coconut juice.

dānnin wōt (**dannin wẹt**). Rain water.

dāp (**dap**). 3, 5(*-e*), 6(*-i*). A fish, eel, large and black; *Gymnothorax* sp.; moray eel.

Dāp-eo (**dap-yew**). A constellation; dark spot in the Milky Way beside theta in Ophiuchus; Coalsack.

dāpdep (**dapdẹp**). 5(*dāpdipe*), 6(*-i*). Trunk of a tree; stump.

dāpdep (**dapdẹp**). 1(*-i*), 2(inf, tr *dāpij*), 3, 5(*dāpdipij*), 7, 8, 10(*dāpijek*). Hold; grip; resist; clasp; control; keep; linger; maintain; negative; retain; adhere. *Kate eok dāpdep bwe wa in ej buuḷ.* Do your best to hold on because this vehicle is going fast. *Kate eok dāpij* *bao ṇe bwe en jab kelọk.* Do your best to hold that bird so that it doesn't fly away. *Kwōn dāpdipiji wōt piik ṇe bwe eṇ jab ko.* Keep on holding the pig so that it doesn't run away. *Jikin dāpdep.* Handle. *Edāpdep ippān.* He's negative about it.

Dāpdep (**dapdẹp**). Clan name.

dāpdipe (**dapdipey**). Distributive form of *dāpdep* (**dapdẹp**).

dāpdipij (**dapdipij**). Distributive form of *dāpdep* (**dapdẹp**).

Dāpeij (**dapẹyij**). Period of storms; associated with the ascendancy of *Jebrọ* (Pleiades) in early July.

dāpi- (**dapi-**). Also *dipi-* (**dipi-**). 1, 6. Base, foundation, bottom, stem, trunk. *Jāje eo eṇ idipin ni eṇ.* The machete is at the bottom of that coconut tree.

dāpij (**dapij**). Transitive form of *dāpdep* (**dapdẹp**).

dāpijbok (**dapijbeq**). From *dāpij* (**dapij**) "hold", *bok* (**beq**) "sand," "to hold on to the sand". 3, 6(*-i*). A plant, *Euphorbia thymifolia* L. (Ebon.)

dāpijdekā (**dapijdẹkay**). From *dāpij* (**dapij**) "hold", *dekā* (**dẹkay**) "rock", "to hold on to a rock". A plant, *Peperomia volkensii* C.; DC. (Piperaceae); Ebon. Also applied on most atolls to *Boerhavia duffusa* L.

dāpijek (**dapijẹk**). 1(*-i*), 2, 3, 7. Join; attach; link; fasten; perfective form of *dāpdep* (**dapdẹp**); mesh. *Edāpijek peba ko ippān doon.* The papers are fastened together.

dāpilpil (**dapilpil**). 1(*-i*), 2, 3(inf *kaddāpilpil,* tr *kadāpili*), 5(*ddāpilpil*), 7. Roll. *Kajiliñ eo ej ddāpilpil i raan wa eo.* The drum is rolling around on the deck of the ship.

Dāpilpil (**dapilpil**). From *dāpilpil* (**dapilpil**) "to roll". 3, 6(*-i*). A plant, pandanus cultigen. (Stone).

ddāil (**ddayil**). Dial. W: *eddāil* (**yeddayil**), E: *dedāil* (**dedayil**). 1(*-i*), 2(inf, tr *-i*), 4, 6(*-i*), 7. Make a hole; poke; drill; bore; awl. *Letok ṃōk kein ddāil eo aṃ.* May I have your awl? *Kwōn dāili men ṇe.* Bore a hole in it. *Dāilitok ṃōk bōd e.* Please drill a hole in this tortoise shell for me. *Imaroñ ke kōjerbal ddāil eo aṃ?* May I use your awl?

ddāp (**ddap**). Dial. W: *eddāp* (**yeddap**), E: *dedāp* (**dedap**). 1(*-i*), 2, 3, 7. Cling to; stick to; adhere; sticky; welded. *Lale eddāp nuknuk ṇe aṃ ilo bwil ṇe.* Be careful you don't get your chewing gum stuck on your clothes. *Kaddāp.* Welding.

dde (**ddẹy**). Dial. W: *edde* (**yẹddẹy**), E: *dede* (**dẹdẹy**). 1(*-i*), 2(inf, tr *-ik, ddiek, diek*), 7. Splice; lengthen. *Etke kwōj jab dieklọk to ṇe ke ekadu?* Why don't you lengthen that rope, because it's short.

ddeb (**ddẹb**). Dial. W: *eddeb* (**yẹddẹb**), E: *dedeb* (**dẹdẹb**). 1(*-i*), 2(inf, tr *dibōj*), 3, 4, 5(*dibdibōj*), 7, 8. Husk coconuts; pierce with husking stick or spear; jabbing. *Ḷeo ej ddeb waini.* He is husking copra nuts. *Ḷeo ej dibōj waini eo.* He is husking the copra nut. *Kwōn jab dibdibōj waini ṇe.* Don't make so many punctures in that copra husk. *Kwōn jab dibdibōj ek ṇe.* Don't spear so many holes in that fish.

ddek (**ddek**). Dial. W: *eddek* (**yeddek**), E: *dedek* (**dedek**). 1(*-i*), 2, 3, 7. Grow; develop; germinate; progress. *Eddek ṃōn wia eṇ an.* His store is progressing.

ddep (**ddẹp**). Dial. W: *eddep* (**yẹddẹp**), E: *dedep* (**dẹdẹp**). A fish.

ddiil (**ddiyil**). Variant form of *diil.*

ddipikpik (**ddipikpik**). Dial. W: *iddipikpik* (**yiddipikpik**), E: *didpikpik* (**didpikpik**). 1(*-i*), 2, 3, 7. Flutter; flop around. *Kwōn ṃan ek ṇe bwe eddipikpik.* Kill that fish because it's still flopping around.

ddipiñpiñ (**ddipigpig**). Dial. W: *iddipiñpiñ* (**yiddipigpid**), E: *didipiñpiñ* (**didipigpig**). 2, 3(inf, tr *-i*), 6(*-i*), 8, 9. Throb; pound. *Kwōn jab ddipiñpiñ bwe jouwaroñ.* Quit pounding cause you're getting on my nerves.

ddo (**ddew**). Dial. W: *eddo* (**yeddew**), E: *dedo* (**dedew**). 1(*-i*), 2, 3(st inf *kaddodo,* tr *kaddouk*), 4, 5(*ddodo*), 8, 11(*ddodo*). Heavy; burden; responsibility; tensed up; despondency; melancholy; sluggish. *Eḷap aō ddodo rainin.* I feel sluggish today. *Pāāk ddodo men eṇ.* That bag is very heavy. *Naan eo ekōṃṃan an ddodo.* The news made him feel melancholy.

ddoor (**ddewer**). Dial. W: *eddoor* (**yeddewer**), E: *dedoor* (**dedewer**). 2(inf, tr *door(e)*), 6(*-i*), 7, 10(*dorōk*). Put; put down; leave; consider; let down; let down carefully;

deposit; install; set, sell oneself short. *Kwōn door ņaib ņe.* Put down that knife. *Raar nieddoor.* They let down a bunch of coconuts by rope. *Jab door naan ko aō naan jekdọọn.* Don't disregard my words (don't consider my words lies). *Kwōn door wōt bok ņe.* Leave that book there. *Dodoor laļļọk ṃukko ņe.* Let the cargo net down carefully. *Etke kwōj dodoorļọk ijeņe aṃ?* Why are you selling yourself short? *Kwōj ddoor ia aṃ bok?* Where do you keep your books?

ddọdo (**ddawdẹw**). Also *dọdo* (**dawdẹw**). 1(*-i*), 2(inf, tr *dọuk(i)*), 7, 8. Close; to lower something. *Kwōn dọuk wūntō ņe.* Close that window. *Kwōn dọuk bwā ņe.* Lower that pole.

de- (**dey**). Facing; with directionals.

de (**dẹy**). Just. *Eṃōj de aō jino riiti bok eo.* I just started reading the book. *Eļọk de juon allōñū ņai ānin.* I have just completed my first month on this island.

de (**dẹy**). Dial. E, W: *edde* (**yẹddẹy**). 2, 3. Sleep, chickens only; rookery; defecate from trees, of birds. *Bao en ej de raan mā eņ.* The chicken is sleeping on the branch of the breadfruit tree.

debakut. See *debọkut.*

debbōn (**debben**). 1(*-i*), 2, 6(*-i*). Giant size; enormous; huge; large. *Ear buuk juon debbōn piik.* He shot a huge pig.

debdeb (**dẹbdẹb**). From *ddōb* (**ddẹb**) "to husk". 1(*-i*), 2(inf, tr *dibōj*), 5(*dibdibōj(e)*), 7. To spear; poke; prod; ram. *Kwōn dibōj ek eņ.* Spear that fish. *Letok ṃade ņe bwe in etal debdeb ek.* Give me that spear so that I can go spear fish. *Pako eo eņ eṃōj dibdibōje.* The shark has been speared many times.

deblọk (**dẹblaq**). 1(*-i*), 2(inf, tr *-(e)*), 3, 7. Pass through; go through; break through; penetrate. *Koṃ nañin deblọk ke lik.* Haven't you gotten through to the ocean side yet?

debokļọk (**dẹbẹqļaq**). 2, 3(inf, tr *-e*), 5(*debokbok*), 6(*-i*), 7. Explode. *Wōn eo ear kadebokļọke?* Who exploded it?

debọkut (**debaqit**). 6(*-i*). Coconut stump; pandanus stump; stump of any tree; remains of a tree especially if covered with fern growth; grass; etc.; a bush; a shrub; boondocks; heavy growth; thick beard; underground section of a plant. *Jọñan an ļap kōto, ekiōk tūṃ debọkut.* It was so windy the tree stumps nearly came off the ground.

debwāāl (**debayal**). 1(*-i*), 2(inf, tr *-e*), 3, 4. A cross; a drill.

Debwāāl-eo (**debayal-yew**). From *debwāāl:* "the drill", used to drill holes in the disks of *Spondius* mussels found at Namorik to make "*puka* shell" necklaces; *Bake,* the name of the mussel, is also the name of a nearby star, gamma in Ophiuchus. A constellation; stars in Ophiuchus; 67, 68, 70; possibly stars in *Hydra; delta, epsilon, theta, eta, sigma.*

debweiu (**debẹyiw**). Group of sprouted coconuts past the eating stage.

ded (**ded**). Stage of growth; size; age; amount; dimension; rate; share. *Ewi ded ļadik eņ?* How old is that boy? *Eṃṃan ded.* He is old enough. *Rōṃṃan ded.* They're old enough. *Ewi ded bọọk ņe?* What are that box's dimensions?

ded-. See *dd-.*

dede (**dẹydẹy**). 1(*-i*), 2, 3(inf *kadede,* tr *kadedeik*), 7. Ready; prepared; completed; entirely finished; implemented. *Edede ļọk men wōtōmjej.* Everything is ready. *Edede ļọk aō ṃōñā.* I've finished eating. *Jab jino juon jerbal eļañe kwōjāmin kadedeiki.* Do not undertake a project unless you can finish it.

dedeinke (**dẹydẹyinkey**). Because, already. *Iar ilim juon bato im jorrāān, dedeinke eṃōj aō ilim de juon keej.* I drank one bottle and passed out, because I had already drunk a case. *Iar piọ boñ dedeinke iar ṃōrābōt.* I was cold last night because I had wet clothing on.

deekto (**deyektew**). Also *rekoot* (**reykewet**). From Japn. (from Engl.) 3, 6(*-i*). Phonograph record.

deel (**deyel**). 6(*-i*). A fan.

deel (**deyel**). Transitive form of *deelel* (**deyelyel**).

deelel (**deyelyel**). 1(*-i*), 2(inf, tr *deel(e)*), 3, 6(*-i*), 7. To fan; use a fan. *Kwōn deele niññiñ ņe bwe emenokadu.* Fan that baby because it's sweating. *Lewaj deel ņe im deelel.* Take this fan and fan.

deelel (**deyelyel**). 4, 6(*-i*). A dance, using fans.

deenju (**dẹyẹnjiw**). From Japn. *renshuu*. 2(inf, tr *-uk*), 4, 6(*-i*). Practice; warm up; drill.

dej (**dej**). 2, 5(*ddejdej*), 7(*dejjeḷọk*). Steal away; flee. *Eḷak lo eō, edejjeḷọk em ko.* When he saw me, he took off like a flash. *Ke ej ju kijek eo, eddejdej armej.* When the fire broke out, people were running in all directions.

dejeñ (**dejeg**). 2, 5(*dejeñjeñ*), 6(*-i*), 7, 11(*dejeñjeñ*). Strong, of wind or storm; physically strong; expensive; severe; stubborn. *Edejeñḷọk kōto in.* This wind is growing stronger. *Ejjeḷọk dejeñjeñ in ānbwinnin.* He has such a strong body. *Ejjeḷọk dejeñjeñ in kōto in.* This wind is really strong. *Ejjeḷọk dejeñjeñ in oṇān ṃweiuk kaṇe.* Those goods are awfully expensive. *Ejjeḷọk dejeñjeñin ṇe ajri.* That child is really stubborn.

dek (**dek**). 2, 7. Hold one's breath. *Kwōn dek menowaṃ.* Hold your breath.

dekakkak (**dekakkak**). 1(*-i*), 2, 3(inf, tr *-e*), 6(*-i*), 7. Cackle. *Ta eṇ ej kadekakkake bao eṇ?* What's causing that chicken to cackle?

dekakḷọk (**dekakḷaq**). Slang. 2, 3(inf, tr *-e*), 6(*-i*). Outburst of laughter. *Kōmwōj dekakḷọk ke kōm roñ an jiñ.* We all burst into laughter when we heard him break wind.

dekā (**dekay**). 1(*-i*), 5(*ddekāke*), 6(*-i*). Stone; rock; gravel; flint. *Edekāke iarin ānin.* The lagoon side of this island has lots of gravel.

dekā (**dekay**). 1(*-i*), 2, 4, 5(*ddekākā*), 8, 9. Yaws; skin ulcer. *Ejjeḷọk wōt ddekākā in ḷadik eṇ.* That boy is really covered with yaws.

dekā aorōk (**dekay hawẹrẹk**). Gem.

dekā in jibke (**dekay yin jibkẹy**). Also *dekein jibke* (**dẹkẹyin jibkẹy**). 3, 5(*-e*), 6(*-i*), 3+7. Stones used in *jibke* fishing method for porpoises.

dekā lọḷ (**dekay laḷ°**). 6(*-i*). *Luau* stones; heavy volcanic rocks.

Dekā-Lijone (**dekay-lijewney**). A star; Canopus.

dekāke (**dekaykẹy**). From *dekā* (**dekay**). 2, 3(inf, tr *-ik*), 5(*ddekāke*), 6(*-i*), 7, 8, 9. Stony; rocky. *Kōto eo ekōdekākeik arin ānin.* The storm washed ashore gravel on the lagoon side of this island.

deke in jibke (**dẹkẹy yin jibkẹy**). 1(*-i*), 3, 6(*-i*). Kidney.

dekenin (**dẹkẹynin**). Also *dekeinnin* (**dẹkẹyinnin**), *dekāānnin* (**dekayannin**). 3, 6(*-i*). Mallet made from clam shell.

dekōṃkōṃ (**dekeṃkeṃ**). Dial. E, W: *kakōṃkōṃ* (**kakeṃkeṃ**). 2, 4, 6(*-i*), 7, 8, 9. Vociferous; noisy. *Ta eṇ ej dekōṃkōṃ eake?* What's he so noisy about?

del (**dẹl**). 1(*-i*), 2(inf, tr *-e*), 4, 6(*-i*)8 7. A food, pandanus pudding cooked in hot rocks. *N̄e kwōjelā del kwōn del tok kijed.* If you know how to prepare and cook pandanus pudding in hot rocks, then make some for us.

deldelbwij (**dẹldẹlbij**). A fish, eel with no teeth.

deltokrōk (**delteqrẹk**). A fish, skip jack, *Caranx melampygus*, Hawaiian *ulua*.

deḷọñ (**dẹyḷag°**). 1(*-i*), 2, 3(inf *kaddeḷọñ*, tr *kadeḷọñ*). Enter; runs, in a baseball game; admit; insert; enroll; import; deposit; income; inning. *Iar kaddeḷọñ aō ṃaak ilo pāāñ.* I deposited my money in the bank. *Iar kadeḷọñ ṃaak ko aō ilo pāāñ.* I deposited my money (definite) in the bank. *Raar kadeḷọñ rinañinmej eo.* They admitted the patient. *Edeḷọñ wa eo.* The ship has entered the lagoon. *Edeḷọñ.* He's enrolled.

dem (**dẹm**). Firm. *Edem im pen.* "Firm and strong".

demāju (**demajiw**). 6(*-i*). Cornice or gable of a Marshallese house. *Ejjeḷọk aj ilo demājuun iṃōn Ṃajeḷ.* There's no thatch in the gable of Marshallese houses.

deṃak (**deṃak**). 1(*-i*), 2(inf, tr *-e*). Oppose; prevent. *Iar deṃak pepe eo an.* I opposed his decision.

deṃwā (**deṃay**). Also *deṃōn* (**deṃen**). Edge of.

deñ (**deg**). Formant in place names.

deñdeñ (**degdeg**). 1(*-i*), 2(inf, tr *deñōt(e), deñḷọk(e)*), 3, 4, 5(*deñdeñōte*), 7, 8. Spank; slap; pound; lash; thrash; whip. *Kwōn jab bōt bwe kwōnaaj deñdeñ.* Don't be naughty or you'll get spanked. *Ḷeo ear deñōt ḷadik eo.* He spanked the boy. *Kwōn jab deñdeñōte ḷadik ṇe.* Don't spank the boy (all over his body).

deñdeñin mājlep (**degdegin majlep**). 2. Forecast predicting the onset of prevailing northeast trade winds.

deñļǫk (**degļaq**). 6(-*i*). Canoe part, decorations of feathers on masthead, boomtips, and sail. *Rōpeļļǫk deñļǫk ko ilo utǫr jidik eo.* The feather decorations blew away during the sqall.

deñōt (**deget**). Transitive form of *deñdeñ* (**degdeg**).

deñtak (**degtak**). 2(inf, tr -*e*), 4, 6(-*i*), 7. Fishing method, striking needlefish with a long piece of wood or a paddle as they float on the surface of the water on moonlit nights. *Deñtake tak eo waj.* Strike the needlefish that's going in your direction. *Kwōn deñtak waj ikōja ak ña iretam.* You strike needlefish on the leeside while I do so on the outrigger side.

deor (**deyer°**). 1(-*i*), 2, 3, 7. Escape; leave unnoticed. *Edeor jān pein Kaminij.* He escaped from the Communists. *Edeor jān bōd eo an.* He escaped from his sin. *Euwāween aṃ deor jān pade eo?* How did you manage to slip out from the party? *Ia eo edeor ie?* Where did he slip off to?

deǫ (**deyaw**). 1(-*i*), 2, 8, 11(*deǫeo*). Pretty, of women; beautiful. *Kokanooj deǫ.* You are very beautiful.

depakpak (**depakpak**). 1(-*i*), 2, 3(inf *kaddepakpak,* tr *kadepakpak(e)*), 7, 8, 9, 11(sg. *depakpak*, pl. *(d)depakpak*). Wide; broad; diameter; width. *Ej make wōt depakpak an riab.* His exaggerations are out of this world.

depdep (**depdep**). Also *depdep* (**dȩpdȩp**), *dep* (**dep**). 1(-*i*). Huge. *Lukkuun depdep in pako men eṇ.* That's a very huge shark.

depdep (**depdep, dȩpdȩp**). 1(-*i*), 2(inf, tr *depete*), 4, 6(-*i*), 7, 8. Spank; knock off; slap; to swing at someone wildly; beating of the waves. *Lale wōn ṇe edepet eok.* Look out or that turtle will slap you. *Ekātok juon bwebwe im depete kōrkōr eo waō.* A tuna jumped out of the water and slapped my canoe. *Eļak depdeptok iṃōkaj im baare.* As he swung at me I suddenly parried his blow.

depet-doon (**depet-dewen**). Slang. From "slap each other". 3, 4, 6(-*i*), 7. Compete; competition. *Erro depet-doon lǫkuṃ boñ ak ejjeļǫk eṇ ewiin.* They contested until dark but no one won.

depetdoul (**depetdȩwil**). Also *ļōbōtdoul* (**ļebetdȩwil**). 1(-*i*), 2, 3, 4, 8. Short and fat, of people; roly-poly. *Eṃōj ṇe aṃ ṃōñā bwe kwōdepetdoul.* You'd better stop eating because you're five by five.

depete (**depetey**). Transitive form of *depdep* (**depdep**).

depiio (**dȩpiyyȩw**). 1(-*i*), 2, 3(inf, tr -*ik*), 8, 9. Whole; mass.

depñat (**depgat**). From *ddāp* (**ddap**) "stuck", *ñat* (**gat**) "gums". 2, 5(*ddepñatñat*), 6(-*i*), 8, 9, 11(*depñat*). Viscid, sticky, of food; gooey, as bread not fully cooked. *Jab kaatuwe kiiō bwe enaaj depñat.* Don't take it out of the oven now or it'll be sticky. *Eddepñatñat pilawā e.* This bread is gooey all over.

depouk (**dȩpȩwik**). 6(-*i*). Flight of a group of birds or planes. *Ear peļļǫk juon depouk jān Kuwaaṃ.* A flight of planes took off from Guam.

det (**det**). 1(-*i*), 2(inf, tr -*e*), 3, 5(*ddetdet*), 8, 9, 11(*detdet*). Sunshine. *Eļap an det rainin.* It's very sunny today. *Eddetdet ānin.* This islet is always sunny.

detak (**dȩytak**). Blow, of the wind.

detñil (**detgil**). 6(-*i*), 8, 9, 11(*detñil*). Sunny day without wind. *Eļap an detñil rainin.* It's calm and sunny today.

detta- (**dȩtta-**). 1. Size; amount; quantity. *Ewi dettan?* How big is she?

di (**diy**). 1(-*i*), 5(*didi*), 6(-*i*). Bone. *Edidi ek ṇe.* That fish has lots of little bones.

di (**diy**). Dial. E, W: *bakbōk* (**bakbek**). 6(-*i*). Knife.

di (**diy**). Oyster.

diak (**diyak**). 1(-*i*), 2(inf, tr -*(e)*), 3, 4, 5(*ddiakek, ddiakeak*), 6(-*i*), 7, 8. Tack, change sail from one end of canoe to the other to tack. *Ediak wa eṇ.* That canoe is tacking. *Kwōn diake wa ṇe.* Tack your canoe. *Eddiakeōk wa eṇ.* That canoe is always tacking. *Raar diake wa eo ṃokta jān an itaak.* They tacked the boat before it hit the reef. *Eddiakeak wa eṇ kōn an ṃōkaj.* The boat tacks often on account of its speed.

diaka (**diyakah**). Also *diaka* (**diyahkah**). 1(-*i*), 2(inf, tr -*ik*), 6(-*i*), 7. Push cart.

dibab (**dibab**). Dial. W, E: *rūbōb* (**ribẹb**). 3, 6(-*i*). A fish, butterfly fish, *Chaetodon ocellatus.*

dibdibōj (**dibdibej**). Distributive form of *ddeb* (**ddẹb**).

diboñ (**dibẹg°**). Also *dibuñ.* 2, 3(inf, tr -*e*), 6(-*i*), 7, 8, 9. Pitch black; dark night. *Ediboñļọk jān inne.* It's darker than last night. *Ij jañin kar llolo boñ āinwōt in an diboñ.* I've never seen such a dark night as this.

dibōj (**dibej**). Transitive form of *ddeb* (**ddẹb**) and *debdeb* (**dẹbdẹb**).

dibuk (**dibiq**). 2(inf, tr -*i*), 3, 4, 6(-*i*), 7. Penetrate; go through; pierce; infiltrate. *Edibuki mar em ļak etal kōm jab bar loe.* It took off into the boonies and that was the last we saw of it. *Ridibuk mar ro raṇe.* Those are the boony trekkers. *Inaaj kadibuki wa in ilo ṇo ṇe tok.* I'll let this boat nose into the oncoming wave.

dibukae (**dibiqhayey**). 2, 6(-*i*), 7. Ocean currents that are farther away from an island than the *juae* currents; the second zone of currents. *Jetōpar dibukae.* We're in the zone of the *dibukae* currents. *Edibukae jikōt?* In what direction is this *dibukae* current flowing?

did (**did**). Small flowers of pandanus, coconut, or other plants; see *didbōlbōl.*

did-. See *dd-.*

didak (**didak**). Also *didak* (**diydak**). A fish.

didbōlbōl (**didbelbel**). From *did* "small flowers", *bōl* "bloom". 2. Grow well; to flower; flourish. *Edidbōlbōl an mā e kōtka ddek.* My breadfruit plant is growing well.

dide (**didẹy**). From Engl., or see *dde* (**ddẹy**). 1(-*i*), 2, 3, 4, 7, 8. Relay race. *Wōn eo ewiin ilo dide eo.* Who won the relay?

didiiñ (**diydiyig**). 2(inf, tr -*i*), 4, 6(-*i*). A cult; medicine women; medical treatment by members of the cult (*didiiñ*). *Maroñ kaṇ an didiiñ rōkabwilōñlōñ.* The powers of the *didiiñ* cult are miraculous.

didiṃakōl (**diydiyṃakel**). 2, 6(-*i*), 7. A toy; pandanus rocket; fly a pandanus rocket. *Eṃṃan tōllọkun didiṃakōl eo waan.* His *didiṃakōl* flew very well.

didmej (**didmẹj**). Variant form of *dumej* (**diwmẹj**).

die- (**diye-**). 1. Possessive classifier, earrings and other things worn on ear.

diede (**diyẹdẹy**). Also *dede* (**dẹydẹy**). 1(-*i*), 2(inf, tr *diek*), 3(inf, tr -*ik*), 4, 6(-*i*), 7, 8. Wear earring. *Eṃṃan diede ṇe dieṃ.* Your earring looks nice. *Kwōn diek diede ṇe dieṃ.* Wear your earrings. *Kwōn kadiedeik ledik ṇe.* Put some earrings on that girl. *Diedein Ṃajeļ.* Marshallese earrings.

diek (**diyek**). Transitive form of *diede* (**diyẹdẹy**).

dienbwijro (**diyenbijrẹw**). Also *dienbwijrok* (**diyenbijrẹq**), *deenbwijro.* Final meal together before an impending disaster; last dinner. *Riāneo raar dienbwijro ke raar roñ ke enaaj buñļọk Likabwiro.* The islanders ate their last meal together when they heard that typhoon *Likabwiro* would ravage their island.

diil (**diyil**). Also *ddiil* (**ddiyil**). 2(inf, tr -*i*), 4, 6(-*i*), 7. Fishing method, fishing for squirrel fish in small holes on reef during low tide using a two or three-foot-long leader fastened onto a piece of wood about the same length. *Eowi ikōn diil.* Fish caught using the *diil* method of fishing are tasty.

diin kat (**diyin kat**). Rib.

diiñko (**diyigkẹw**). From Japn. *ringo* "apple". Phosphate.

dijiñ (**dijig**). 3, 6(-*i*). A fish, scavenger, *Lethrinus variegatus.*

dik (**dik**). 1(-*i*), 2, 3(*kaddikdik, kadik*), 5(*jjidikdik, jjiddikdik*), 8, 9, 11(sg. *dikdik, jidikdik*, pl. *ddik, jiddik*). Small; young; little.

dik oṇea- (**dik weṇya-**). 1, 2, 3, 8, 9. Cheap; low salary. *Edik oṇān ṃweiuk ṃweeṇ.* The goods in that store are cheap. *Edik oṇān jerbal ṃweeṇ.* Working at that place doesn't pay much.

dikāāļāļ (**dikayaļyaļ**). Also *dikāāļāļ* (**diykayaļyaļ**). 1(-*i*), 2, 3, 4, 6(-*i*), 8, 9. Frustration; thwart. *Eļap an dikāāļāļ kōn an bane ledik eo.* He was frustrated over his vain attempts to impress the girl. *Eba jaab em* *kadikāāḷāḷ kōṇaan ko an.* She said no and thwarted his desires.

dike (**dikey**). 1(*-i*), 2, 8, 9. Hate; abhor; strongly dislike; disapprove; reject; resent. *Idike eok.* I hate you. *Idike ṃweiukun ṃweeṇ.* I don't like the goods at that store. *Rōdike kajjitōk eo am.* Our request was rejected by them.

diklōñ (**dikleg̣**). 1(*-i*), 2(inf, tr *-e*), 6(*-i*). Bosom; chest measurement. *Kwōn diklōñe ṃōk nuknuk e aō.* Would you measure the upper front of my garment?

dikḷọk (**dikḷaq**). Idiom. From *dik* (**dik**) "small", *ḷọk* (**ḷaq**) "comparative". Decrease; discount; subside. *Edikḷọk wōt.* It's subsiding. *Jete dikḷọkun oṇān men e?* What's the discount on this item? *Edikḷọk kōto in.* The wind has subsided.

dila (**diylah**). 1(*-i*), 2(inf, tr *-ik*), 3, 4, 5(*ddilala*), 6(*-i*), 7, 8. Nail. *Ebwe ke dila kaṇe aṃ?* Do you have enough nails? *Kwōn dilaik rā ṇe.* Nail that board. *Eddilala rā ṇe.* The board has lots of nails in it.

dile (**diylẹy**). 1(*-i*), 2, 3, 6(*-i*), 8. Barnacles; ship worm; termite; damage caused by termites or bookworms. *Edile kapin wa eṇ.* The boat has barnacles underneath. *Edile ḷọk tebōḷ ṇe.* That table is termite-eaten.

dilep (**diylep**). 1(*-i*). Backbone; spine.

dim (**dim**). 1(*-i*), 2, 3, 8, 9. Tight. *Eḷap an dim aṃ kar lukwōje.* You tied it very tight. *Edim jedọujij eṇ an.* His trousers are tight.

dimtak (**dimtak**). 1, 2(inf, tr *-e*), 4, 6(*-i*), 7. Jerk a fishline to hook a fish. *Jab kijer in dimtake.* Don't jerk it yet.

dimuuj (**dimiwij**). 3, 6(*-i*). A shell; clam, medium large.

diṃōṃ (**diṃẹṃ**). Vulgar. 1(*-i*), 2, 3(st inf *kaddiṃōṃṃōṃ*, tr *kadiṃōṃ*), 8. Orgasm; itchy.

dipāākāk (**diypayakyak**). Also *ḷadipāākāk* (**ḷadiypayakyak**). 6(*-i*). Canoe part; socket for end of boom (one at each end of canoe).

Dipāākāk (**diypayakyak**). See *dipāākāk* "boom socket". A star; epsilon Aurigae.

dipāl (**dipal**). Crouch. *Eruṃwij aō jibwe jān an dipāl em peḷḷọk.* Before I could grab him he had already crouched and sprang away.

dipen (**diypẹn**). From *di* (**diy**) "bone", *pen* (**pẹn**) "strong". 1(*-i*), 2, 3(st inf *kaddipenpen,* tr *kadipen*), 4, 8, 9, 11(*dipenpen*). Physically strong; husky. *Idipen jān kwe.* I am stronger than you. *Idaak ni bwe en kadipen eok.* Drink coconuts makes you strong. Drink a coconut so that it will strengthen you. *Ṃōn kaddipenpen.* Health gym. *Jero kaddipenpen em tallōñ.* Let's test our strength and climb.

ditōb (**ditẹb**). 2, 4, 6(*-i*), 8, 9. Dark; black. *Editōb wōt in armej.* I've never seen a blacker individual.

diwōj (**diywẹj**). Also *duoj* (**diwẹj**). 1(*-i*), 2, 3, 5(*dduojoj*), 7. Get out; go out; exit; secede; discharged. *Eṃōj ṇe aṃ ddiwōjwōj.* You stop going out so frequently. *Ear duoj jān aujpitōḷ.* He was discharged from the hospital.

diwōjḷọk (**diywẹjḷaq**). 2, 3(inf *kadduojḷọk*). Graduate. *Ear kadduojḷọk jān U. H..* He graduated from the U.H..

do (**dẹw**). Also *mādo* (**maydẹw**). 6(*-i*). Net, large-meshed, bag-shaped, for washing arrowroot and soaking breadfruit.

doebeb (**dewyebyeb**). 1(*-i*), 2, 4, 7, 8, 9, 11(*doebeb*). Meddlesome; mischievous. *Kwōn jab doebeb im kōṃṃane injin ṇe bwe enaaj jorrāān.* Don't mess around with that engine and foul it up. *Ejjeḷọk wōt doebeb in ṇe ajri.* That's the most mischievous child I've ever seen.

dokweer (**deqeyer**). A fish.

dokwōj (**deqej**). 2+7, 3+7, 5(*ddokwōjkwōj*), 7(*dokwōjḷọk*). Snap, as a branch. *Ta eṇ ej ddokwōjkwōj buḷōn mar eṇ?* What causes the continual snapping (of branches) inside the bush?

doñ (**dẹg°**). 1(*-a*), 2, 6(*-a*), 7. Pelvis; movement of pelvis; hip. *Ejeḷā doñ.* She can really shake it. *Ebwiḷọk doñan.* She broke her hip.

doom (**dewem**). 1(*-i*), 2, 3, 8, 9, 11(*doom*). Many, as a school of fish; teeming with. *Edoom tōū eṇ i ar.* The lagoon beach is teeming with mackerel.

doon (**dẹwẹn**). 2(inf, tr *-e*). Sharp stick for husking coconuts; horn of an animal. *Ej jañin ddek an doon.* It hasn't grown a horn yet. *Raar doone* *piik eo.* They killed the pig with a husking stick.

doon (**dewen**). 7. Each other; one another. *Itok kōjro kōrwaan doon.* Come, let's keep each other company.

doon (**dewen**). 1(*doo-*). Subjects; followers. *Doon wōn kwe?* Who is your chief? or Whose side are you on?

doonon (**dẹwẹnwẹn**). From *doon* (**dẹwẹn**). 2, 3(inf, tr *kadoonon(e)*), 6(-*i*). Use a coconut husker. *Jenaaj doonon eake ta?* What will we use for a husker? *Raar doonon kōn piik eo.* They used the pick as a husker. *Kwōn kadoonon(e) kōn doon eo am̧.* Let him use your coconut husker.

door (**dewer**). Transitive form of *ddoor* (**ddewer**).

douj (**dẹwij**). 1(-*i*), 2, 3(st inf *kaddoujuj*, tr *kadouj*), 7, 8, 9. To ship water; be overcrowded, of boats or vehicles (see *kaddoujuj*). *Eitok ņo eo em kadouj wa eo.* A wave covered the boat. *Ejjelọk emaroñ bar uwe bwe edouj wa e.* No more can get on as this boat is overcrowded as it is.

doulul (**dẹwilwil**). Also *douluul* (**dẹwiliwil**). 1(-*i*), 2(inf, tr -*i*), 3(inf *kaddoulul*, tr *kadoulul*), 8, 9, 11(*doulul*). Round; circle; club of people; organization; association.

dọlel (**dawlel**). Also *dọọlol* (**dawalwel**), *dọọlol* (**dawalwẹl**). 1(-*i*), 2, 3, 4, 8, 9. Serious illness; degenerate. *Likao eņ edọọlol.* He's really beyond help.

dọlin (**dawlin**). Also *dọli* (**dawliy**). From *dọlel in* (**dawlel yin**). Really; extremely; seriously. *Edọlin būrom̧ōj kōn men in.* He's really downhearted about the affair. *Edọlin (dọlel in) bōt.* He's very naughty.

dọọj (**dawaj**). Also *dọ* (**daw**). Argue. *Edọọj an ļōm̧aro kōnono ñan doon.* Their conversation is developing into an argument.

dọọl (**dawal**). 2(inf, tr -*e*), 6(-*i*). Dye. *Lieņ ear dọọle koolan bōran.* She dyed her hair.

dọuk (**dawik**). Transitive form of *ddọdo* (**ddawdẹw**).

du (**diw**). 1(-*i*), 2, 3, 8. Boil; have convulsions; simmer. *Edu dān eo.* The water is boiling. *Edu bao eo.* The chicken is having convulsions.

du (**diw**). Archaic. Gather to dance.

dujebwābwe (**diwjebaybẹy**). 2, 3(inf, tr -*ik*), 6(-*i*), 7. Mistake in performing a dance, song, or chant. *Edujebwābwe jebwa eo.* The *jebwa* dance was fouled up.

dujẹjjet (**diwjẹjjẹt**). 1(-*i*), 2, 3, 6(-*i*), 8, 9. Full to the brim. *Ejjeļam dujẹjjetiier.* They're overflowing. *Kadujẹjjete bwe eaetok iaļ in.* Fill it up because this is a long journey.

dukwal (**diqal**). 2(inf, tr -*e*), 3, 6(-*i*), 8, 9. Bow one's head; bend. *Kwōn kadukwale jidik bōram̧ bwe in lo m̧aan.* Bow your head a bit so I can see the front.

dukwaļ (**diqaļ**). Slang. 2(inf, tr -*e*), 6(-*i*). Punch; clenched fist; slug. *Jab keroro bwe kwōnaaj dukwaļ.* Shut up or you'll get a punch in the nose. *Edukwaļe.* He slugged him.

dukwaļ booļoļ (**diqaļ beweļweļ**). 3, 6(-*i*). A food; preserved breadfruit; cooked.

dumej (**diwmẹj**). Also *didmej* (**didmẹj**). 2(inf, tr -*e*), 5(*dumeje*), 6(-*i*), 7. Stake; picket. *Kwōn dumeje em̧ nuknuk ņe bwe en jab peļļok.* Stake down the tent so it won't blow away.

dunen (**diwnen**). Construct form of *doon* (**dẹwẹn**).

Dunen-eañ (**diwnen-yag**). Also *Lim̧anm̧an.* Polaris; called "husking stick of the north" as it stands motionless in the northern sky.

duoj (**diwẹj**). Variant form of *diwōj* (**diywẹj**).

duuj (**diwij**). 1(-*i*), 2, 7. Stick in; insert; jab.

e (**yẹy**). He; she; it; pronoun, absolute, third person singular; him, her, it; pronoun, object, third person singular.

e (**yẹy**). This; demonstrative, first person exclusive singular.

eaab (**yahab**). Dial. E, W: *jaab* (**jahab**). No.

eaab (**yahab**). Dialectal variant of *jaab* (**jahab**).

eaabōbbōb (**yahabẹbbẹb**). Variant form of *abōbbōb* (**habẹbbẹb**).

eabukwi (**yabiqiy**). Also *ābukwi.* 3, 7. Four hundred. *Jen kāābukwi kuņaad waini.* Let's each of us gather four hundred copra nuts.

eak (**yak**). Archaic. Legendary pile of copra brought to Mwineak on Ebon by man from the Gilbert Islands.

eake (**yakey**). Dial. E only; see *kake* (**kahkey**). With it; about it.

eake (**yakey**). Dialectal variant of *kake* (**kahkey**).

eakeak (**yakyak**). 1(*-i*), 2(inf, tr *-e*), 4. Skin ulcer.

eakeak (**yakyak**). 5(*eakeake*). Ghost; monster; hobgoblin. *Eļap an eakeake āneņ* That islet has lots of ghosts.

eaklep (**yaklęp**). Also *iakalep* (**yiyakalep**). 2(inf, tr *-e, eaklipe*), 4, 6(*-i*). Rob sitting hen of her eggs. *Jab eaklepe bao eņ bwe ennejnej.* Don't rob the hen of her eggs so she can have chicks.

eakļe (**yakļęy**). Pile of stones. *Eṃōj an ņo tọọre eakļe ilik; kwōn ejouji dekā kaņe ippān doon.* The waves have washed over the stone barrier on the ocean side; please stack the stones together again.

eakpel (**yakpęl**). 1, 2(inf, tr *-e, eakpile*), 4. Jettison; unload; lighten ship. *Koṃwin eakpel jān wa ņe bwe edouj.* Throw out something because your boat is shipping water.

eakto (**yaktęw**). 1(*-i*), 2(inf, tr *ākūtwe, eaktuwe*), 3, 4, 7. Discharge; unload. *Jibuunin eakto.* Serving spoon.

eaktuwe (**yakitiwey**). Transitive form of *eakto* (**yaktęw**).

eaļ (**yaļ**). 1(*-i*). Coconut milk.

eañ (**yag**). Also *iōn* (**yi'yęg**). 1(*-i*), 6(*eañin, eañi*), 7. North.

eañ (**yag**). 3, 6(*-i*). A shell, *Strombidae, Lentigo lentiginosus* or *Tricornis sinuatus/thersites/latissimus.*

eañ (**yag**). 1(*-i*), 2, 3, 6(*-i*). Urinate, of children only. *Eañ ajri eņ.* That child is urinating. *Kwōn keañ ajri eņ.* Help that child urinate.

eañ (**yag**). What do you say?; Do you hear me?

eañden (**yagden**). Dial. E only; see *kwōle* (**qęlęy**). 1(*-i*), 2. Hungry.

eañrōk (**yagręk**). Dial. W, E: *ṃọņe* (**ṃaņ°ęy**). A fish, surgeonfish, *Naso unicornis.*

eañtak (**yagtak**). 1(*-i*). North side.

earap (**yeharap**). Archaic. 6(*-i*). Four thousand.

eb (**yeb**). 1(*-i*), 2, 3, 4, 6(*-i*), 7. Dance.

eb (**yeb**). Variant form of *bwe* (**bey**).

ebaje (**yebajey**). Transitive form of *ebeb* (**yebyeb**).

ebajeet (**yebajęyęt**). Also *eita* (**yęyitah**). What's the matter.

ebajjeet (**yebajjęyęt**). More like it; proper. *Ebajjeet ke kokatak.* That's more like the way to study (you weren't studying before). *Ekwā ebajjeet.* Now that's more like it.

eban (**yeban**). Expression: "Impossible!"; "I don't believe it!"; "It can't be!"

ebb-. See *bb-.*

ebbokļọk (**yębbęqļaq**). Variant form of *bokkoļọk* (**bęqqęļaq**).

ebeb (**yebyeb**). 1(*-i*), 2, 3(inf, tr *-e*), 7. Shiver; shudder; vibrate. *Eļap aō ebeb kōn aō piọ.* I'm so chilly I'm shivering. *Ṃōļo in ekāebebe eō.* This cool weather makes me shiver.

ebeb (**yebyeb**). Also *eabeb* (**yabyęb**). 2(inf, tr *ebaje*), 5(*ebebaj*), 7, 10(*ebjak*). Scatter; throw down; scratch, of chickens. *Eṃōj an baru ko ebebaj ijo.* The bulldozers have dug things up there and made the land uneven. *Bao eņ ej ebaje ļā kaņ.* That chicken is scattering that gravel. *Kajjitōk jān ia kako en; jān lo mar eņ; kwaar et, iar eabeb kijō ṃōñā.* A query: "whence came that rooster?", "From those boondocks."; "What did you there?", "Scratched for my food.".

ebjak (**yebjak**). 2(inf, tr *-e*), 4, 6(*-i*), 7. Dug up; scattered; burst; perfective form of *ebeb* (**yebyeb**). *Eṃōj ebjake ijo.* The place was completely dug up. *Eebjak boktañ eo.* The bomb burst.

ed (**yęd**). 3. A mat for wearing; aboriginal women's skirts, now used as baby's mat.

ed (**yęd**). 1(*-i*). Fabric. *Eṃṃan edin (iden) nuknuk ņe aṃ.* Your dress is of good fabric.

ed (**yed**). Archaic. Become red, of leaves.

edd-. See *dd-.*

edde (**yęddęy**). Dial. W, E: *de* (**dęy**). 2, 3(inf, tr *-ik*), 6(*-i*). Roost; defecate from trees, of birds. *Ia eo bao in ej edde ie?* Where's this chicken roosting?

edded (**yęddęd**). Exclamation: "Oh my!" *Edded, ejjeļọk ṃṃan in.* Oh boy, that was good.

eddo ippa- (**yeddew yippa-**). 1, 2. Insulted; disappointed. *Men in eddo ippa.* I take this as a personal insult. *Enaaj eddo ippān ñe kwōjab kūri.* He'll be insulted if you don't invite him.

eded (**yedyed**). 1, 2(inf, tr *-e*), 3, 4, 8, 9. Snooping; prying; nosey; rummage; investigate. *Idike armej rot eṇ eeded.* I despise a person who is nosey. *Jej ilān eded i āneṇ.* We are going to get food from that island.

Edinij (**yedinij**). 3, 6(*-i*). A plant, pandanus cultigen; Arno.

edjoñ (**yẹdjẹg°**). 1(*-i*), 2(inf, tr *-e*), 4, 7. Taste food or drink; savor; sample. *Kwōn edjoñe ṃōk iiōk ṇe ennọ ke?* Taste this mixture--is it good?

Edṃaṃo (**yedṃahṃew**). 3, 6(*-i*). A plant, *Pandanus fischerianus* cultivar. (Stone).

edouṃ (**yẹdẹwiṃ**). 6(*-i*). Baked pandanus; cooked pandanus. *Itōm wōdwōd edouṃ.* Come chew some (cooked) pandanus.

edwaan (**yedwahan**). From *waan* (**wahan**) "without purpose". 3, 6(*-i*). A plant, *Edwaan*; any wild pandanus, i.e. a mature tree grown up from seed; riffraff.

Edwaan-eṇ-an-Limaan (**yedwahan-yeṇ-han-limahan**). From *Limaan* "a woman's name". 3, 6(*-i*). A plant, pandanus cultigen (Takeuchi).

Edwaan-eṇ-an-Luwaju (**yedwahan-yeṇ-han-liwajiw**). 3, 6(*-i*). A plant, pandanus cultigen; Ailinglapalap.

Edwaan-eṇ-an-Nelu (**yedwahan-yeṇ-han-neyliw**). From "the wild pandanus of Nelu (a Ralik chief)". 3, 6(*-i*). A plant, *Pandanus fischerianus* cultigen. (Stone).

Edwaan-in-Būkōr (**yedwahan-yin-bikẹr**). From "wild *Būkōr* (**biker**) (another cultigen)". 3, 6(*-i*). A plant, pandanus cultigen (Takeuchi).

Edwaan-in-Jọibeb (**yedwahan-yin-jawyibyẹb**). From "wild *Jọibeb*" (**jawyibyẹb**) (another cultigen)". 3, 6(*-i*). A plant, pandanus cultigen (Takeuchi).

Edwaan-in-likin-Ṃōnkwōlej (**yedwahan-yin-likin-ṃenqelyej**). From *Ṃōnkoleej* (**ṃenqelyej**) "Ebon place name", *likin* (**likin**) "ocean side of". 3, 6(*-i*). A plant, pandanus cultigen; Ebon.

Edwaan-in-lọurō (**yedwahan-yin-lawireh**). From *ḷọurō* (**lawireh**) "bad soil". 3, 6(*-i*). A plant, pandanus cultigen; Ebon.

Edwaan-in-Matoḷej (**yedwahan-yin-mateḷ°yẹj**). From *Matoḷiej* (**mateḷ°yẹj**) the name of an islet in Wotje atoll". 3, 6(*-i*). A plant, pandanus cultigen (Takeuchi).

Edwaan-in-Ṃwejok (**yedwahan-yin-ṃeyjeq**). From *Ṃwejok* (**ṃeyjeq**) the name of a land tract, *ṃwe* (**ṃey**) "house of", *jok* (**jeq**) "alight". 3, 6(*-i*). A plant, pandanus cultigen (Takeuchi).

eeo (**yẹyyew**). That's right.

eeọñōdñwōd (**yyag°edg°ed**). Dial. W: *eeọñōd* (**yeyyag°ed**), E: *eọñōdñōd* (**yeyag°edg°ed**). 1(*-i*), 2, 3, 4, 7, 8, 9. Go fishing frequently; distributive form of *eọñōd*.

eermeeḷ (**yeyermeyeḷ**). From Engl. 2(inf, tr *-e*), 4, 6(*-i*), 7. Airmail; send by airmail. *Lōta e aō ear itok ilo eermeeḷ tok.* My letter came by airmail. *Kab eermeeḷe ḷọk.* Be sure to send it by airmail.

eieṇ (**yẹyiyeṇ**). Variant form of *iieṇ* (**'yiyeṇ**).

Eijia (**yẹyijiyah**). From Engl. 4. Asia.

eiō (**yẹyiyẹh**). Variant form of *iiō* (**'yiyẹh**).

eita (**yẹyitah**). Variant form of *ebajeet* (**yebajẹyẹt**).

eitōn (**yẹyiten**). 7. Almost. *Eitōn maat dānnin aebōj eṇ.* The water in that cistern is almost all gone. *Reeitōn maat men kā.* These things are almost all gone.

ej (**yẹj**). Formant in place names; upper; eastern; see *-ej* of *utiej.*

ejaak (**yejahak**). 1(*-i*), 2(inf, tr *-e*), 7. Pile up; heap; build; construct form and perfective form of *ejej* (**yejyej**); evolve. *Wōn ṇe ear ejaake ṃōṇe?* Who built your house? *Kwōn ejaaki dekā kaṇe ṇai ijeṇe.* Pile up those stones there by you. *Armej ear ejaak jān menin mour ko jet.* Man evolved from other animals.

eje (**yejey**). Transitive form of *ejej* (**yejyej**).

ejej (**yẹjẹj**). Also *ejjej* (**yẹjjẹj**), *ejjeej* (**yẹjjẹyẹj**). Nothing; none; not any; nil; see *jej.*

ejej (**yejyej**). 2(inf, tr *eje*), 4, 6(-*i*), 7, 10(*ejaak*). Build up; erect; pile up; build. *Rej eje lōn̄ļǫk m̧ween̦.* They're building the house higher. *N̄e eejaak enaaj lukkuun utiej.* When it is built (completely), it will be very tall.

ejej (**yejyej**). Also *ōjōj* (**hejhej**). 2(inf, tr *ejek*). Use mouth to husk coconuts; husking of coconuts by coconut crabs; strip or peel off one layer at a time.

ejj-. See *jj-*.

ejja (**yejjah**). Archaic. Harbor.

ejjab aelǫk (**yejjab hayelaq**). Idiom. From "It's not obscured.". Obviously; conspicuously. *Ej jab aelǫk mālōtlōt.* He's definitely a genius.

ejjabdaan (**yejjabdahan**). Not many; not much; not exactly. See *daan*. *Ejjabdaan lōn̄ bōb ānin.* There are not many pandanus on this island.

Ejje (**yẹjjẹy**). Name of a navigational sign; a giant red shark.

ejjebaō (**yẹjjẹbahẹh**). From *ejjab* (**yejjab**) "it is not", *aō* (**hahẹh**) "mine". 2, 4, 6(-*i*), 7. A game, Marshallese women's baseball. *Leddik wōt rej ejjebaō M̧ajeļ.* Only girls play *ejjebaō* in the Marshalls. *Raar ejjebaō ļǫk em bon̄.* They played *ejjebaō* till nightfall.

ejjeej (**yẹjjẹyẹj**). Variant form of *ejej* (**yẹjẹj**).

ejjeļā (**yejjeļay**). Archaic. To anchor. *Ejjeļā toon bōbtowa (words from chant).* Anchor until everything is clear to me.

ejjeļǫk (**yejjeļaq**). Dial. W, E: *jej* (**jẹj**). Nothing; nobody; without; destitute of; nil; none.

ejm̧aan (**yejm̧ahan**). 6(-*i*). Large stone; rock; boulder.

ejouj (**yẹjẹwij**). Also *ejoujik* (**yẹjẹwijik**). 1(-*i*), 2(inf, tr -*ik*), 7. Pile; stack; aggregate. *Kwōn aljektok waini im ejouj tok n̦a ijjien̦.* Gather copra nuts and pile them up over there.

ejoujik (**yẹjẹwijik**). Variant form of *ejouj* (**yẹjẹwij**).

ek (**yẹk**). 5(*ike*), 6(*ikōn, ekin*). Fish. *Eike ānin.* There are lots of fish around this islet.

ek m̧ōn̦akn̦ak (**yẹk m̧en̦akn̦ak**). 6(-*i*). Smoked fish.

ek-bōlōk (**yẹk-bẹlẹk**). A fish, thread-backed butterfly fish, *Heniochus acuminatus.*

ek-bōļāāk (**yẹk-beļayak**). A fish.

ekajet (**yekajet**). Also *eakjet* (**yakjet**). 1(-*i*), 2(inf, tr -*e*), 3, 4, 7. Judge; try in court; to grill someone. *Raar ekajete ļǫk im bon̄.* They grilled him until it got dark.

ekbab (**yekbab**). 1(-*i*), 2(inf, tr -*e*), 7. Throw down, as in wrestling.

eke (**yẹkẹy**). 1(-*i*), 2, 5(*ekeke, ikikie* (**yikyikiye'y**)). Blood vessel; vein; artery. *Eekeke pein ļeen̦.* One can see lots of veins on his arm.

eke (**yẹkẹy**). From *eke* (**yẹkẹy**) "vein". 6(-*i*). Nylon fishline.

Eken̦ (**yẹkyen̦**). From "that fish". A plant, pandanus cultigen; Aur.

ekin bon̄ jab lo raan (**yẹkin bẹg° jab lew rahan**). Idiom. Fish that aren't sufficient for the next day. *Ear ba kōmin kan̄ ek ko bwe ekin bon̄ jab lo raan.* He told us to finish the fish because they were too few to be left for the next day.

ekjab (**yekjab**). Idol; statue.

ekk-. See *kk-*.

ekkan (**yekkan**). Dial. W only. 2, 4, 6(-*i*), 7. Bring food to a chief; tribute. *Kom̧win ekkan ļǫk n̄an irooj en̦.* Bring food to the chief.

ekkan (**yekkan**). Dialectal variant of *eǫjek* (**yawjẹk**).

Ekke (**yẹkkẹy**). 3, 6(-*i*). A plant, pandanus cultigen (Takeuchi).

ekkeitaak (**yẹkkẹyitahak**). Variant form of *kōkkeitaak* (**kẹkkẹyitahak**).

ekkejel (**yẹkkẹyjẹl**). 2, 6(-*i*), 7. Hang on; latch on to. *Ekkejel ippa n̄e kweitan wōtlǫk.* Hang on to me if you are about to fall.

ekkokowa (**yẹkkẹwkẹwah**). Dial. W only; see *lejǫn̄jǫn̄* (**leyjag°jag°**). Also *ekkokouwa* (**yekkewkewiwah**). 1(-*i*), 2(inf, tr -*ik(i)*), 4, 6(-*a*), 7. Juggling contest; juggle. *Ledik ro raar ekkokowa.* The girls had a juggling contest.

ekkoonak (**yẹkkẹwẹnhak**). 2(inf, tr -*e*), 4, 6(-*i*), 7. Fishing method, surround a school of rainbow runners with plain sennit. *Kōpooj kijeek ko bwe riekkoonak ro rā tok.* Get the cooking fires ready because those who went to fish for rainbow runners are on their way back. *Raar ekkoonaki ia ikaidik kein?* Where did they catch these rainbow runners?

eklejia (**yẹklẹyjiyah, yẹklẹjiyah**). From Engl. (from Greek *ekklesia*). 4. Members of the church; ecclesia; laity.

ekḷọk (**yẹkḷaq**). 2. Get spoiled, of fish. *Kwōn kōmatti ek kaṇe bwe rōnaaj ekḷọk.* Cook those fish before they spoil.

ekmouj (**yẹkmẹwij**). From *ek* (**yẹk**) "fish", *mouj* (**mẹwij**) "white". 3. A fish, parrotfish, *Scarus harid.*

ekōjka- (**yẹkẹjka-**). 1, 7. How. *Ekōjkan aṃ mour?* How are you?

ekōjkan (**yẹkẹjkan**). Certainly; "You bet!"; "And how!"

ekōḷōk (**yẹkẹḷẹk**). Exclamation: "Wow!"; "Ouch!"

ekpā (**yekpay**). 1(*-i*), 2, 7. Change clothes, from good to dirty. *Kwōn ekpā ḷọk bwe jen ilān eọñōd.* Put on old clothes because we're going fishing. *Ekpā ko aō kaṇe.* Those are my working clothes.

ekpā (**yekpay**). Also *ekpā* (**yẹkpay**). A fish.

ektak (**yektak**). 1(*-i*), 2(inf, tr *-e*), 7. To load; haul; wrestling maneuver, Marshallese style only. *Wa eo eṇ ej ektak ṃweiuk.* That boat is loading trade goods.

ekwe (**yeqey**). 1(*-i*), 7. Well; okay. *Ekwe inaaj iwōj.* Okay, I'll be there.

ekwekwe (**yeqeyqey**). Also *kwōjabṃōk* (**qejabṃek**). Interjection: "If that's so, then continue."; showing interest; keep on. *Ekwekwe bwe jen etal ḷọk.* Don't stop now; keep at it so we can leave soon.

el (**yẹl**). 1(*ile-, eli-*), 2, 6(*ilen, elin*). Nest; clothing (in construct only). *Ej el ia bao eṇ.* Where is that hen making its nest?

el (**yel**). Cut off.

ele (**yeley, yẹlẹy**). 6(*elen, ele*). Variant form of *ile* (**yilẹy**). *Elelōñ.* Upper part of fish string. *Elelaḷ.* Lower part of fish string.

Elej (**yelej**). From Engl. 4. Ellice Islands.

elianij (**yeliyahnij**). 7. Darkness that follows a cloud coming over the horizon at night. *Enaaj wōt bwe etke elianijtok.* It looks like rain as it is darker.

ell-. See *ll-*.

ellowetak (**yelleweytak**). 2, 3(inf, tr *-e*), 4, 6(*-i*), 7, 8, 9. Enthusiasm; earnest; excited; inspired. *Rej kab tan ellowetak ke rej roñ ainikien.* They began to get enthused when they heard his voice.

ellōk (**yẹllẹk**). Dial. W, E: *ṃọle* (**ṃawlẹy**). A fish, rabbitfish, *Siganus rostratus/puellus.*

ellōkan (**yellekan**). About, approximately.

elmaroñ (**yẹlmareg°**). 1(*-i*), 2, 7. Able to throw hard. *Eḷap an elmaroñ Sandy Koufax.* Sandy Koufax can really throw hard.

elme (**yelmey**). Dial. E, W: *kabbok* (**kabbẹq**). Breadfruit flower.

elmen (**yẹlmẹn**). Archaic. Man's skirt made from coconut fronds.

elmọkot (**yẹlmaqet**). 2(inf, tr *-e*), 4, 6(*-i*). Sample; experiment. *Jenaaj elmọkote ṃōk lale eṃṃan ke.* We'll experiment with it to see if it works.

Elmọñ (**yẹlmag°**). Also *Mọñ.* A constellation; Aries; alpha, beta, and gamma.

Elṃad (**yẹlṃad**). A star name, Vega.

Elpeekdu (**yelpeyekdiw**). From *peekdu* (**peyekdiw**) "a fish". 3, 6(*-i*). A plant, pandanus cultigen; Ebon; similar to *Jọṃwinjoñ* (**jawṃinjeg°**).

eḷ (**yẹḷ**). Also *el* (**yẹl**). 2, 7. Pay attention to; take seriously (with directionals). *Jab eḷḷọk bwe ajri men eṇ.* Don't pay any attention to him for he is just a child. *Jab eḷḷọk.* Don't let your attention wander. *Ear jab eḷtok ñan eō.* He didn't pay attention to me.

eḷ (**yeḷ**). Archaic. Cult that tattooed and practiced magic.

eḷ (**yeḷ**). Canoe part, place where one sits, just behind middle.

eḷañe (**yeḷaggey**). If. *Eḷañe eṃṃan mour inaaj iwōj.* If I feel all right, I'll be there.

eḷbōn (**yeḷben**). 3, 5(*-e*), 6(*-i*). Elephant. *Ḷōṃaro raar kaeḷbōn.* The men went elephant-hunting. *Eeḷbōne buḷọṇ Intia.* There are elephants all over India.

eḷḷ-. See *ḷḷ-*.

eḷḷa (**yeḷḷah**). 1(*-i*), 2(inf, tr *-ik*). Ribs, nautical.

eḷḷọk (**yeḷḷaq**). 1, 2(inf, tr *-e*), 4, 5(*eḷḷọkḷọk*), 6(*-i*). Lay out; spread out; lie; recumbent; stretch. *Eḷḷọke diiṃ.*

Lie down and relax. (Stretch out your backbone). *Eļļǫke peiṃ.* Hold out your hand. *Rej eļļǫk jaki.* They are laying out mats.

eļļǫk jān (**yęļļaq jan**). Avert; turn away from. *Kwōn jab eļļǫk jān e bwe enaaj mej.* Don't turn away from her or she'll die.

eļtan pā (**yeļtan pay**). 1(*...pei-*). Workmanship; penmanship. *Ekanooj eṃṃan eļtan pein.* His workmanship is fine. His penmanship is fine.

em (**yem**). Variant form of *im* (**yim**).

emān (**yeman**). 3, 7. Four.

emān ṃōttan ruwalitōk (**yeman ṃettan riwahliytęk**). Four eighths.

emān-awa (**yeman-hawah**). From *emān* (**yeman**) "four", *awa* (**hawah**) "hour, clock". 3, 6(*-i*). A plant, *Mirabilis jalapa* L. (Nyctaginaceae). The common tropical "four o'clock."

emej (**yemej**). Transitive form of *emjak* (**yęmjak**).

ememej (**yęmyęmęj**). Dial. E, W: *ememej* (**yemyemej**). 1(*-i*), 2(inf, tr *-(e)*), 3(*keememej*). Memory; remember; recall; recollect. *Kwōn keememej in kab itok.* Don't forget to come. *Iememej raan ko.* I remember the days. *Ememej.* Remember--no active attempt to remember--just sort of comes to mind. *Keememej.* Remember--there is a definite effort to bring it back to mind.

ememļǫkjeṇ (**yemyemļaqjeṇ**). 1(*-i*), 2. Remember with sorrow; reminisce. *Ememļǫkjeṇ ko aō kōn eok.* My sad memories of you (words from love song).

emjak (**yęmjak**). Also *emja* (**yęmjah**). 1(*-i*), 2(inf, tr *emje, emej, -e*), 3, 7, 10(*emjak*). Ride at anchor; tie up to a buoy; anchor; anchor line; moor. *Wa eo eṇ ej emjak i ar.* The boat is anchored close to the lagoon beach. *Eṃōj emje wa eo.* The boat has anchored. *Kōṃanṃan aṃ emjake wa ṇe.* Anchor the boat carefully. *Kwōn emjak kōn dekā.* Use a rock for an anchor.

emje (**yęmjęy**). Transitive form of *emjak* (**yęmjak**).

emļǫk (**yemļaq**). 1(*-i*), 2(inf, tr *-e*), 3, 4, 7. Nostalgia; speak fondly of a person or place where one has been; have fond memories of; reminisce; reverie. *Eban jeṃļǫk aō emļǫke tok ijin.* I can't stop being nostalgic about this place. *Ij emļǫk tok Ṃajeļ.* I have fond memories of the Marshalls.

emm-. See *mm-*.

eṃ (**yęṃ**). Also *ṃwe-*, *ṃō*, *ṃo-* (**ṃe-**); *ṃwi-*, *ṃū-*, *ṃu-* (**ṃi-**). 1(*iṃō-*), 4(*rūṃwiin*), 5(*iṃwe*). House; household; home; building; possessive classifier, houses or other buildings.

eṃ nuknuk (**yęṃ niqniq**). Idiom. Tent. *Jen kajuur eṃ nuknuk in ijin.* Let's pitch the tent here.

eṃṃ-. See *ṃṃ-*.

eṃṃōļō (**yemṃęļęh**). 1, 2, 3, 6(*-i*), 7. Excited, agitated, energized. *Eṃṃōļō armejin aelōn̄ eo ke rej ron̄ ke enāj itok.* The people of the atoll got excited when they heard he was coming.

eṃōj (**yęṃej**). From *ṃōj* (**ṃęj**) "finished". And so (in narratives).

eṃpiļoob (**yeṃpiyļeweb**). Variant form of *impiļoob* (**yimpiyļeweb**).

ene (**yęnęy**). Variant form of *āne.*

enjeļ (**yenjeļ**). From Engl. Angel.

enkanaode (**kęnkanhawedey**). Idiom. From *enkan* (**yęnkan**) "decoration of", *aode* (**hawedey**) "wake of a canoe". 6(*-i*). Something that has fallen from a canoe underway. *Jab rǫǫl n̄ane bwe enkanaode.* Do not turn back for it or it will bring misfortune.

enliklik (**yenliklik**). 1(*-i*), 2, 4, 7. Walk with the hands clasped behind the back. *Kwōj enliklik ļǫk n̄an ia.* Where are you walking with your hands behind your back.

enn-. See *nn-*.

ennāp (**yennap**). 4. Olden times; ancient. *Waan ennāp im ennāp men ṇe.* That's an old fashioned canoe.

enne (**yęnnęy**). Open field; see *maaj.*

enneok (**yenneyeq**). 1(*-i*), 2(inf, tr *-e*), 4, 5(*enneokeok*), 6(*-i*), 7. Twine for sewing up the mouth of a bag. *Enneoke tok mejān pāāk ṇe.* Sew up the mouth of that bag for me.

ennōk (**yęnnęk**). Also *ennōk* (**yennek**), *nōkkan* (**nekkan**). 1, 2(inf, tr *-e*), 4, 6(*-i*), 7. Gather food. *Ia ṇe kwaar ennōk ie?* Where did you gather the food from?

enōk (**yenek**). 1(*-i*), 2, 4, 7. Pick coconuts; transitive form of *nnōk* (**nnek**). *Ļeo eṇ ej enōktok ni eṇ.* He is knocking down some coconuts.

enrā (yęnray). 6(-*i*). Small tray, made from fronds for food.

enrā (yęnray). Variant form of *jepe* (jepey).

enta (yentah). Why?; What for? *Enta kaņe kwaar wiaiki?* What did you buy those things for?

entak (yęntak). Dial. E, W: *entak* (yentak). 1(-*i*), 2, 3, 4, 7. Pick green coconuts from tree.

ento (yentew). 1(-*i*), 2(inf, tr -*uk*), 4, 6(-*i*). Climb coconut tree with ankles tied. *Ear entouk ni.* He climbed the tree with his ankles tied.

eņ (yeņ). That (close to neither of us); demonstrative, third person singular.

eņak (yeņak). 1(-*i*), 2(inf, tr -*e*). Suspect. *Bwilijmāāņ ro rej eņake ļeo ke e eo ear kọọti ṃani ko.* The police suspect that he is the one who stole the money.

eņņ-. See *ņņ-*.

eņọ (yeņaw). Also *enọ* (yenaw). 1(-*i*), 7. Scold; punish; spank; suspect. *Kwōn jab kakūtōtō bwe rōnaaj eņọuk eok.* Don't horse around or they will be suspicious of you.

eñ-rear (yęg-ręyhar). Northeast.

eñak (yegak). 2, 7. Occur to; realize. *Eļak eñaktok aō ke eiọkwe eō, etto wōt ke ear moot.* When I finally realized she was in love with me, she had been long gone.

eñe (yęgęy). Also *iōñe* (yiyęgęy), *iōe* (yiyęhęy). Here he or it is; sentence demonstrative, first person exclusive singular.

eñeņ (yegyeņ). That over there; sentence demonstrative, third person singular.

eñeo (yegyew). Also *ieo* (yi'yew). This; here it is; sentence demonstrative, remote singular.

eñieņ (yęgyiyeņ). Also *iieņ* ('yiyeņ). 7. That over there; sentence demonstrative, third person singular, singling out.

eñin (yegyin). Also *eñin* (yęgyin). This thing here between us; thus; that's it; here it is; sentence demonstrative, first person inclusive singular.

eñiō (yęgyiyęh). Also *iiō* ('yiyęh). Here he or it is; sentence demonstrative, first person exclusive singular, singling out.

eñjake (yęgjahkey). 1(-*i*), 2, 7. Feel; emotion; experience; sense. *Iar jab eñjaake aer kōteep ñiū.* I didn't feel anything when they pulled my tooth. *Ejjeļọk an ļeeņ eñjake.* He has no feelings.

eñņe (yegņey). There it is; that (close to you); sentence demonstrative, second person singular; that's it.

eñņeņe (yegņeyņey). 7. That (close to you), singling out; sentence demonstrative, second person singular, singling out.

eñ (yęg). 6(*eñin*). Fin; dorsal fin; smaller fish.

eññ-. See *ññ-*.

eñoul (yęgęwil). 3(inf, tr -*i*), 7. Forty. *Kwōn kāeñouli bōnbōn ņe.* Make it forty.

eñoweo (yęgęwweyew). Also *eñuweo* (yęgiwweyew), *eñuwo* (yęgiwwew), *eñowo* (yęgęwwew). That thing (close to neither of us); that person (close to neither of us); sentence demonstrative, remote singular, singling out; there it is.

eñtaan (yęgtahan). 1(-*i*), 2, 3, 4, 6. Suffering; agony; torment; persecution; scourged. *Eļap aō eñtaan kōn aō katak.* I have a hard time with my studies.

eñuweo (yęgiwweyew). Variant form of *eñoweo* (yęgęwweyew).

eo (yęw). 7(*eowaj*). Here it is; take it. *Eo mā eo kijeṃ eo.* Here is breadfruit for you to eat. *Eo--bōke im etal.* Here--take it and go.

eo (yęw). 2, 3(inf, tr -*uk(i)*), 6(-*i*), 8, 9. Very wet; saturated. *Eļap an eo pen ņe.* That grated coconut is saturated.

eo (yew). The (often for entities not present); demonstrative, remote singular.

eo (yew). 6(*eoun*). Line; fishline. *Eoun ļatippān.* Line for deep tuna fishing. *Eoun ilarak.* Trolling line. *Eoun liklọk.* Line for bottom fishing on ocean side. *Eoun urōk.* Line for bottom fishing in lagoon. *Eoun kaṃōṃō.* Line for catching grouper, from bamboo pole on reef. *Eoun kadjo.* Line for catching goatfish, from bamboo pole on lagoon beach. *Eoun kāāpil.* Line for catching *āpil*, from bamboo pole on lagoon beach. (Smaller tackle).

eo eke (**yew yękęy**). From *eke* (**yękęy**) "blood vessel". Nylon fishline.

eoeo (**yewyew**). 1(*-i*), 2(inf, tr *-ok*), 3, 4, 7. Rub back and forth gently or caressingly; caress; stroke. *Kwōn eoeok peiū bwe emetak.* Rub my arm because it hurts.

eojaļ (**yewjaļ**). 1(*-i*), 2, 3, 5(*eojaļjaļ*), 7. Scattered; spread out; plentiful; variant form of *ajeļļā*. *Eojaļļok menọknọk i nōbjān m̧wiin.* Trash is scattered around outside the house. *Eojaļjaļ ļọk nuknuk ṇai lowaan m̧weeṇ.* Clothes are strewn all around inside that house.

eojojo (**yewjewjew**). From *eo* (**yew**) "fish line", *jojo* (**jewjew**) "soak". 1(*-i*), 2(inf, tr *-uk*), 3, 4, 7. Fishing method, throw out line from lagoon beach. *Iar eojojouk ļañe e.* I caught this *ļañe* by the *eojojo* method.

eok (**yęq**). Also *yok, yuk.* You; pronoun, object, second person singular.

eolaļ (**yewlaļ**). 1(*-i*), 2(inf, tr *-e*), 3, 4, 7. Fishing method, bottom fishing in lagoon.

eolọk (**yęwlaq**). Also *eoļañ* (**yęwļag**). 2(inf, tr *-e*), 6(*-i*), 7. Pull at it; pull down. *Kwōn kakkōt eolọke to ṇe.* Pull at it all you can. *Baru eo ear eolọke ni eo.* The bulldozer pulled down the coconut tree.

eoļap (**yewļap**). Dialectal variant *ioļap* (**yi'yewļap**).

eoļōpa- (**yewļepa-**). 1, 7. Middle of; center.

eomeļañ (**yewmeļag**). Land reserved for chiefs.

eom̧wi- (**yewm̧i-**). Variant form of *ium̧wi-* (**yi'yiwm̧i-**).

eoṇ (**yeṇ°**). Also *eọṇ* (**yaṇ°**), *eọr* (**yar°**). 1(*-i*), 2, 3, 5(*eoṇeoṇ*), 7. Go aground; scrape bottom; strike a shoal. *Eoṇ wa eo ilo juon wōd.* The boat struck a coral head. *Eeoṇeoṇ wa eṇ.* That boat is always going aground.

eoo- (**yewe-**). Variant form of *ioo-* (**yi'yewe-**).

eoojjaak (**yewejjahak**). 1(*-i*), 2, 7. Fishing method, at night from a canoe near lagoon shore.

eoon (**yęwęn**). Verse; stanza.

eoonene (**yęwęnęnęy**). Also *eoonene* (**yewenęnęy**). 4. Main islet of an atoll.

eoonkappe (**yewenkappęy**). Dialectal variant of *ioonkappe* (**yi'yewenkappęy**).

eoonļā (**yewenļay**). Also *eoweļā* (**yeweyļay**). 6(*-i*). Household. *Jenaaj le eoweļā ilo kakkuṇaṇa in laļ.* We'll contribute next time according to household.

eoonpālōñ (**yewenpaylęg**). Archaic. 2, 4, 6(*-i*). Putting the forearm on the forehead while lying down. *Aolep ro rej eoonpālōñ rej kwaļọk ke rōkelọk.* Those that lie and put their arms on their foreheads show that they are lovesick.

eor (**yęr°**). 1, 2, 6(*-i*), 8. Bleached; fading of color. *Eto an libbukwe eo kōjeje innem eor jān m̧m̧an in.* The shell stayed out so long in the sun that it was bleached.

eoreak (**yer°yak**). 1(*-i*), 2(inf, tr *-e*), 4, 7. Level off; ceremony performed six days after burial, gravel is spread over grave. *Baru eo em̧ōj an eoreake ijo.* The bulldozer has leveled off that area.

eotaak (**yęwtahak**). Dial. E only; see *oktaak* (**węktaak**), *uñtaak* (**wigtahak**). 1(*-i*), 2(inf, tr *-e*), 3, 4, 7. Wrestling.

eọ (**yaw**). 1(*-i*), 2. Start to bear fruit, of coconuts. *Enañin eọ ke ni eṇ?* Has that coconut tree started to sprout yet?

eọ (**yaw**). 1(*-i*), 2(inf, tr *eọuk(i)*), 3, 4, 6(*-a*), 7. Tattoo. *Wōn eo ear eọuk eok?* Who tattooed you?

eọeo (**yawyęw**). 1(*-i*), 2(inf, tr *eọut*), 5(*eọiuti*), 7. Bind with sennit; lash. *Ļeo ear eọut wa eo.* He lashed the canoe. *Ļeo ear eọeo wa.* He was lashing canoes. *Kwōnañin eọut(i) ke ni jekaro eṇ am̧?* Did you lash that coconut sap sprout of yours yet? *Em̧ōj aer eọiuti aļaļ eo.* They have lashed the piece of wood carelessly.

eọiuti (**yawyiwtiy**). Distributive form of *eọeo* (**yawyęw**).

eọjek (**yawjęk**). Dial. E only; W: *ekkan* (**yekkan**). 2(inf, tr *-e*), 4, 6(*-i*), 7. Bring food to a chief or lineage head; tribute. *Jemān eọjekļọk ñan irooj eṇ.* Let's bring food to the king. *Raar eọjekeļọk irooj eo.* They took food to the chief.

eọkur (**yaqir**). 1(*-i*), 2(inf, tr *-i*), 6(*-i*), 7. Scoop, dirt or sand; throw by handfuls. *Eọkurļọk jidik bok im* *kōm̧m̧an jikin kijek.* Scoop away some sand and make a fireplace. *Kwōn jab eo̧kur bok kaņe.* Don't throw that sand.

eo̧n̄ (**yag°**). 1(*-i*), 2, 3, 7. Sprout; grow. *Ejjeļo̧k wōt eo̧n̄ m̧ōkaj in ni ņe.* That coconut tree really grew fast.

eo̧n̄ōd (**yag°ed**). 1(*-i*), 2(inf, tr *-e*), 3, 4, 5(*eeo̧n̄ōdn̄wōd*). Go fishing. *Rieo̧n̄ōd ro raņe tok.* Here come the fishermen.

eo̧o̧j (**yawaj**). Dialectal variant of *iooj* (**yiyęwęj**).

eo̧o̧ļ (**yawaļ**). Flow.

eo̧o̧n wōt juon (**yawan wet jiwen**). 3, 7. Flat; level. *Kwōn eoreake jeņe bwe en eo̧o̧n wōt juon.* Smooth it out there so that it's level.

eo̧o̧t (**yawat**). 1(*-i*), 2(inf, tr *-e*), 3, 5(*eo̧o̧to̧te*), 6(*eo̧o̧tōn*), 7. Striped or spotted, as in ancient tattoo. *Eo̧o̧to̧te jedo̧ujij eņ an ļeeņ.* His trousers are striped. *Eor eo̧o̧tin jedo̧ujij eņ an ļeeņ.* His trousers are striped.

eo̧o̧tle (**yawatlęy**). Archaic. On the south side of; see *aikne.*

eo̧r (**yar°**). 1, 2(inf, tr *-e*), 4, 6(*-i*). Carve; smooth with a knife; pare; whittle. *Ļōļļap eņ ej eo̧re juon raanke.* The old man is carving a coconut grater.

eo̧r (**yar°**). Oyster.

eo̧r (**yar°**). Also *eo̧ņ, eoņ.* Go aground.

eo̧reor (**yar°yęr°**). Vulgar. 1(*-i*), 2, 3(inf, tr *kārure, kāārerwe*), 4, 7. Wash anus after defecating, especially women and children, usually in ocean. *Em̧ōj ke an ajri eo eo̧reor?* Has that child's bottom been washed? *Kwōn kāeo̧reore ajri eņ.* Wash that child's bottom.

eo̧ron̄ (**yawreg°**). Also *āron̄* (**yareg°**). 2, 6(*-i*). Respond to; find out; answer to call; seek news; report when called. *Kwaar eo̧ron̄ ke jinōm̧ ke ear kūr eok?* Did you go when your mother called? *Em̧ōj ke am̧ eo̧ron̄ lōta eo am̧?* Did you read your letter? *Ilām eo̧ron̄ ta eo raar kūr eok kake.* Go find out what they were calling you about. *Kōjan̄ retio ņe bwe jen āron̄.* Turn the radio on so we can listen to the news. *Kwōn ilān ārone bwe ear kūr eok.* You better report to him for he was calling you.

eo̧ron̄ naan (**yawreg° nahan**). 1(*-i*), 2, 4, 7. Gather news or information. *Kom̧win etal eo̧ron̄ naan in wa eņ.* Go find out what news that ship brought. *Ļeo emoot in eo̧ron̄ tok naan (eo̧ron̄ naan tok).* He went to get the news.

eo̧tōk (**yawtęk**). 1(*-i*), 2, 3, 7. Drift ashore; stranded, of canoes, boats or ships; shipwrecked. *Wa eo eņ eeo̧tōk.* That canoe is stranded.

eo̧uk (**yawik**). Transitive form of *eo̧* (**yaw**).

eo̧ut (**yawit**). Transitive form of *eo̧eo* (**yawyęw**).

eo̧wilik (**yawiylik**). 2. Retreat in war; sleep close to fire all night, especially old people. *Jar in tariņae eo ear eo̧wilik.* The troop retreated. *Ļōļļap eo ear eo̧wilik bon̄.* The old man slept close to the fire last night.

eō (**yęh**). Me; pronoun, object, first person singular. *Kwōn jab den̄ļo̧ke eō.* Don't hit me.

eōō (**yeheh**). Variant form of *ōō* (**heheh**).

ep (**yęp**). Also *m̧ur* (**m̧ir°**). 1(*ipe-*), 6(*-i*). Hip; loin.

epaak (**yepahak**). 1(*-i*), 2(inf, tr *-e*), 3, 7, 8, 9. Near; soon; nearly; immediate; next to; close to. *Epaak an jepļaaktok.* He'll be back any moment. *Eļap aerro epaake doon.* They (two) are immediate relatives.

epat (**yepat**). Archaic. Bottom.

epepen (**yepyepen**). Also *epepen* (**yępyępęn**), *epepen* (**yępęypęn**). Age; generation. *Dekā in epepen.* Rock of ages. *Epepen eo an jim̧m̧aad.* Our grandfather's generation. *Epepen kaņe rej itok enaaj kanooj oktak mour.* The way of life of coming generations will be greatly changed.

epje (**yępjęy**). Variant form of *peje* (**pęjęy**).

epliklik (**yepliklik**). Usually, mostly.

epp-. See *pp-*.

eppānene (**yeppanyęnęy**). Archaic. On dry land. *Pio̧ in eppānene.* Only the sort of chill one gets on dry land, where a fire can soon warm, not like a chill at sea.

Eprōļ (**yepreļ**). From Engl. April.

epta (**yeptah**). Also *āpta.* 2(inf, tr *-ik*), 4, 6(*-i*). To sieve arrowroot; second time; see *jepta. Bar eptaiki m̧akm̧ōk ņe.* Sieve the arrowroot a second time.

er (**yęr**). They; pronoun, absolute, third person plural, them; pronoun, object, third person plural.

er- (**yer-**). Come about, begin to have; see *erōm*.

era- (**yera-**). Sitting mat; see *erer*.

eran jebwe (**yeran jebey**). From *erer* (**yeryer**) "protector", *jebwe* (**jebey**) "paddle". 6(*-i*). Canoe part, piece of wood on leeside as guard against rubbing from steering paddle. *Eran jebwe eo ṇe.* That's the paddle protector.

eran tebōḷ (**yeran teybeḷ**). Tablecloth. *Eḷḷọke eran tebōḷ ṇe.* Spread the tablecloth.

ere (**yerey**). Canoe part, outrigger platform.

erer (**yeryer**). 1(*era-*), 2(inf, tr *ere*), 5(*ererak*), 6(*-i*), 7, 10(*erōk, erer*). Protector; mat; rug; covering; padding for comfort or for protection from dirt; canoe keel made from *kōñe* wood. *Ewi jaki eo eran lowaan ṃwiin?* Where is the mat that belongs in this room? *Kwōn ere lowaan wa ṇe.* Put some protection in that canoe (from dirt or for comfort). *Eererak jaki ilowaan ṃweo.* Mats were all over the floor in the house.

erkaṇ (**yerkaṇ**). Those things (close to neither of us); sentence demonstrative, third person plural nonhuman.

erkaṇe (**yerkaṇey**). There they are (things close to you); sentence demonstrative, second person plural nonhuman.

erkā (**yerkay**). Here they are (things close to me); sentence demonstrative, first person exclusive plural nonhuman. *Erkā ilowi.* I found them.

erkākaṇ (**yerkaykaṇ**). Those things (close to neither of us); sentence demonstrative, third person plural nonhuman, singling out.

erkākaṇe (**yerkaykaṇey**). There they are (things close to you); sentence demonstrative, second person plural nonhuman, singling out.

erkākā (**yerkaykay**). Here they are (things close to me); sentence demonstrative, first person exclusive plural nonhuman, singling out.

erkein (**yẹrkẹyin**). Here they are (things close to both of us); sentence demonstrative, first person inclusive plural nonhuman.

erki (**yerkiy**). Where are they? (of things); demonstrative, interrogative plural nonhuman. *Erki bok ko aṃ, kwōnañin loi ke?* Where are your books; haven't you found them yet?

erko (**yerkew**). These things (close to me); sentence demonstrative, remote plural nonhuman; here they are.

erko (**yerkew**). Variant form of *irko* (**yirkew**).

erkoko (**yerkewkew**). Those things (close to neither of us); sentence demonstrative, remote plural nonhuman, singling out; there they are.

erḷọk (**yerḷaq**). 1(*-i*), 2(inf, tr *-e*), 3, 7. Open; spread out; stretch out. *Kwōn etal ilo peet eṇ im erḷọke diiṃ.* Go lie down and relax.

erṃwe (**yẹrṃẹy**). 1(*-e*), 3(inf *kāerṃweṃwe*, tr *kāerṃweik(i)*), 6(*-e*). Relatives; family; kin. *Erṃwe eo aō ṇe.* That person (just named) is my relative. *Erṃweō ḷeeṇ.* He's my relative. *Ear kāerṃweiki koṃro.* He showed you how you are related. He is a relative you have in common.

erom (**yẹr°ẹm**). 2. Become; change from one thing to another. *Eṃōj an erom rūkadek.* He has become a drunkard.

erōk (**yerek**). Also *erak*. 1(*-i*), 2(inf, tr *-e*), 7. Spread mats; perfective form of *erer* (**yeryer**). *Kwōn eraki jaki kaṇe.* Spread out those mats.

err-. See *rr-*.

Erra (**yẹrrah**). Name of a navigational sign; one of a pair of whales; near Namorik; other named *Kerara*.

erraṇ (**yerraṇ**). Those people (close to neither of us); sentence demonstrative, third person plural human.

erraṇe (**yerraṇey**). There they are (people close to you); sentence demonstrative, second person plural human.

errā (**yerray**). Here they are (people close to me); sentence demonstrative, first person exclusive plural human.

errāraṇ (**yerrayraṇ**). Those people (close to neither of us); sentence demonstrative, third person plural human, singling out.

errāraṇe (**yerrayraṇey**). There they are (people close to neither of us); sentence demonstrative, second person plural human, singling out.

errārā (**yerrayray**). Here they are (people close to me); sentence demonstrative, first person exclusive plural human, singling out.

errein (**yẹrrẹyin**). Here they are (people close to us both); sentence demonstrative, first person inclusive plural human.

erri (**yerriy**). Also *erri* (**yẹrriy**). Where are they? (of humans); demonstrative, interrogative plural human.

erro (**yerrew**). These (people close to me); sentence demonstrative, remote plural human; here they are.

erro (**yerrew**). 7. They, two people.

Erroja (**yẹrrẹwjah**). Clan name.

Erroja-kijeek (**yẹrrẹwjah-kijeyek**). Clan name.

Erroja-pakolikaelaļ (**yerrẹwjah-pakewlikhayelaļ**). Clan name.

Erroja-rilikin-bwilujo (**yẹrrẹwjah-rilikin-biliwjew**). Clan name.

Erroja-rūbūkien-jekjekeṇ (**yẹrrẹwjah-ribikiyen-jẹkjẹkyeṇ**). Clan name.

erroro (**yerrewrew**). Those people (close to neither of us); sentence demonstrative, remote plural human, singling out; there they are.

Errūbra (**yẹrribrah**). Clan name.

ertak (**yertak**). Put something on top of; cover an earth oven with stones.

ertak (**yertak**). Ripen.

et (**yẹt**). Dial. W, E: *ita* (**yitah**). 2(inf, tr *itene*). Do what? *Eet?* What's the matter with it? *Ej et?* What's he doing? Howzit? *Kwaar itene?* What did you do to it? *Ej et aṃ mour?* How are you?

etal (**yetal**). 1(-*i*), 2, 4, 7. Go.

etal iene (**yetal yiyẹnẹy**). Walk between islands at low tide.

etal in wōt juon (**yetal yin wet jiwen**). Steadily; continuously. *Etal in wōt juon an wōt.* It keeps on raining. *Eruṃwij ak etal in wōt juon.* Slowly but surely.

etal laļ (**yetal laļ**). Walk; go on foot.

etal ļore (**yetal ļewrey**). 7. Follow after. *Kwōn etal ļore wōt bao eṇ.* Follow that chicken.

etal wōt (**yetal wet**). Idiom. From *etal* (**yetal**) "go", *wōt* (**wet**) "still". Continue; proceed; keep going. *Jab bōjrak ak etal wōt im bwebwenato.* Don't stop but continue with your story.

etale (**yetaley**). 1(-*i*), 2, 3, 4, 7. Go over; look over; inspect; examine; diagnose; investigate. *Kwaar etale ke bok e iar je?* Did you look at this book I wrote? *Kwōmarōn̄ ke etale nan̄inmej e aō?* Can you diagnose my illness?

etale-liktōmān (**yetaley-likteman**). Idiom. From woman named *Liktōmān* who had this characteristic. Do something for (or against) someone anonymously.

etalju (**yetaljiw**). 2(inf, tr -*(i)*), 8, 9. Ordeal. *Eetalju(i) mour in.* Life is an ordeal.

etalpeet (**yetalpẹyẹt**). Dial. E only. 2(inf, tr -*e*), 4, 6(-*i*), 7. Fishing method, searching for fish at low tide over the reef. *Etalpeete ṃōk lik ṇe im lale kwōlo ke ṃọle eo.* How about taking a walk over the ocean side reef and see if you locate the school of *ṃọle*.

etan wōt n̄e (**yetan wet gey**). Pretend that; imagine; as if. *Etan wōt n̄e kōjro ej pād Amedka.* Pretend that we are in the United States. *Etan wōt n̄e kon̄ak.* As if you don't know.

Etao (**yetahwew**). Also *etao* (**yetahwew**). 1(-*i*), 2(inf, tr -*uk*), 4, 7. Name of legendary trickster; sly; outwit; outsmart, swindle. *Enaaj etaouki.* He'll swindle him.

etetal (**yetyetal**). 1(-*i*), 2, 3, 4, 7. Walk; step on. *Jab etetal ioon wūjooj kaṇe.* Don't walk on the grass.

etke (**yetkey**). Why? *Etke kwaar jab itok n̄an bade eo?* Why didn't you come to the party?

etṇake (**yetṇakey**). Also *ātṇaake* (**yatṇahakey**). 1(-*i*), 2, 3, 4, 7. Be named for a person; namesake. *Ļadik eṇ ej etṇake jiṃṃaan.* That boy is named after his grandfather.

eton̄ (**yetegº**). Dial. E, W: *it* (**yit**). 1(-*i*), 2, 4, 7. Make fire by rubbing sticks.

ett-. See *tt-*.

etto (**yettew**). 4, 7. A long time ago; ancient times; olden times.

ettōbok (**yẹttẹbeq**). Also *tūbok*. 2(inf, tr -*e*), 4, 6(-*i*), 7. Fishing method, line fishing in lagoon from canoe at night. *Koṃ naaj bar ettōbok n̄āāt?* When will you fish the *ettōbok* method again? *Tipen rūttōbok.* He has the look of a man who knows how to fish the *ettōbok* method.

ettōl (**yẹttẹḷ**). 1(-*i*), 2, 6(-*i*), 8, 9. Charismatic, person who is always attracting people around him or her. *Ejjeḷam ettōlin ke eḷak mej aolepān aelōn̄ eo im ilomeje.* He was so charismatic that when he died the entire atoll mourned for him.

ettōnaak (**yettenahak**). Variant form of *tōn̄aak* (**tegahak**).

ettōn̄aak (**yettegahak**). Variant form of *tōn̄aak* (**tegahak**).

ettōū (**yẹttẹhih**). Dial. W, E: *tōū* (**tẹhih**). A fish, mackerel, *Trachurops crumenopthalmus.*

eub (**yẹwib**). 2, 4, 6(-*i*). A game, dare base (one base).

ewae (**yewahyey**). Dial. E, W: *ḷọom* (**ḷawẹm**). 3, 6(-*i*). A fish, snapper, *Aprion virescens.*

ewan (**yewan**). A time for being engaged in special activity. *Ej kab ewan an pād im̧wiin.* He just started to live here. *Jej kkure im m̧ōn̄ōn̄ō bwe ej kab ewan rainin.* Today is the time for those who like to participate in special events (U. N. Day, for example).

ewe (**yewey**). Archaic. On; surface of; old form of *eoon.*

Ewerōk (**yẹwẹyrẹk**). Also *Eọwerōk* (**yawẹyrẹk**). From *ewe* (**yewey**) "on", *rōk* (**rẹk**) "south". Legendary place where human spirits are said to go after death.

ewi (**yẹwiy**). Where?; How much?; Demonstrative, interrogative singular. *Ewi m̧weo im̧ōm̧?* Where is your house? *Ewi jon̄an raij eo kwōj bōke?* How much rice do you want? *Ewi wāween ba naan eo ilo kajin In̄lij?* How do you say this word in English?

i (**yiy**). Also *i-* (**yi-**). At; in; on. *Epād i lowaan pāāk ņe.* It's in that bag.

ia (**yi'yah**). 7. Where?; How? *Kwōj etal ia ḷọk?* How are you going? *Kwaar itok ia tok?* How did you get here? *Inaaj iwōj ia wōj?* How will I get there (where you are)? *Ia ņe kwōj kōnnaan tok jāne?* Where are you calling from?

iaa- (**yi'yaha-**). 1, 5(*iaea*). With someone. *Kwe āt iaam̧ ilo m̧upi eo bon̄?* Who was with you at the movie last night? *Iaarro ilo jerbal jab in.* We'll be partners in this job. *Jej iaea ke?* Are we going to split into teams? *Ej iaam̧?* What did you say?

Iaab (**yi'yahab**). From Engl. 4. Place name, Yap.

iaam̧ (**yi'yaham̧**). From Engl. Yam.

iaat (**yi'yahat**). From Engl. 6(-*i*). Yard. *Letok m̧ōk juon iaat in nuknuk.* Please give me a yard of cloth.

iabaru (**yiyabariw**). Dial. W: *iiabaru* (**yiyyabariw**), E: *iabaru* (**yiyabariw**). 1(-*i*), 2. Poisoned by eating crab. *Iar m̧ōn̄ā baru im iabaru.* I ate crab and got poisoned.

iabon̄ (**yiyahbeg°**). Dial. W: *iiabon̄* (**yiyyabeg°**), E: *iabon̄* (**yiyabeg°**). 4, 7. Raid at night; attack at night.

iabun̄ (**yi'yahbig°**). 2(inf, tr -*i*), 6(-*i*). Catch up with, overcome, overwhelm; burden; laden. *Jab inepata kōn an iien iabun̄i kom̧.* Don't worry about time catching up with you. *Eban kanooj ḷap an ekkeini kōj bwe eḷap an iabun̄ kōn ajri raņ nājin.* We don't see very much of him because he's so busy with his children.

iakalep (**yiyakalep**). Variant form of *eaklep* (**yaklẹp**).

iakiu (**yi'yakiyiw**). From Japn. *yakyuu.* Baseball; play baseball.

iakwāāl (**yihaqayal**). Also *akwāāl* (**haqayal**). 2(inf, tr -*e*), 4, 5(*iakwāālāl*), 6(-*i*). Quarrel; argue.

iaḷ (**yiyaḷ**). Dial. W: *iiaḷ* (**yiyyaḷ**), E: *iaḷ* (**yiyaḷ**). 1(-*a*), 6(-*i*), 7. Road; path; street; way; itinerary; journey; lane; route; transportation.

iaḷ aidik (**yiyaḷ hayidik**). Idiom. From *iaḷ* (**yiyaḷ**) "road, way", *aidik* (**hayidik**) "narrow". 2, 4, 6(-*i*), 7. Sneak away; go one at a time; come one at a time. *Ear kōttar aer m̧ad im iaḷ aidikḷọk.* He waited until they were not paying attention and sneaked away. *Jen iaḷ aidik jāne.* Let's go away from him one at a time.

iaḷ kadu (**yiyaḷ kadiw**). 6(-*i*), 7. Shortcut. *Kōjro iaḷ kaduḷọk n̄an tawūn.* Let's take the shortcut to town.

iaḷan bōtōktōk (**yiyaḷan betektek**). 1(-*i*), 6(-*i*). Blood vessel; artery; vein.

iaḷan jọọr (**yiyaḷan jawar**). A way made clear for escaping; escape route.

iaḷan juon (**yiyaḷan jiwen**). 2(inf, tr -*e*), 3, 4, 7. Examine; test; a game; a trial. *Raar iaḷan juone eō m̧okta jān aō ilān jikuuḷ.* They tested me before

I went to school. *Jen iaḷan juone doon.* Let's play *iaḷan juon*.

iaḷap (**yiyaḷap**). Dial. W: *iiaḷap* (**yiyyaḷap**), E: *iaḷap* (**yiyaḷap**). Period of great tidal variations; spring tide.

iaḷo (**yiyaḷẹw**). Dial. W: *iiaḷo* (**yiyyaḷẹw**), E: *iaḷo* (**yiyaḷẹw**). 1(-*i*), 2, 3, 5(*iaḷoḷo*), 7. Yellow. *Eiaḷoḷo mejān nuknuk eo an.* Her dress is yellowish.

iañak (**yiyagak**). Dial. W: *iiañak* (**yiyyagak**), E: *iañak* (**yiyagak**). 7. Come to one's senses. *Ej kab iañaktok aō im ikōṇaan etal jikuuḷ.* I just came to my senses and I want to go to school.

iar (**yiyhar**). From *i* (**yiy**) "locative", *ar* (**har**) "lagoon beach". 1(-*i*), 6(-*i*), 7. At the lagoon beach.

iaraj (**yiyaraj**). 3, 6(-*i*). A plant, taro, general term; *Cyrtosperma chamissonis*; taro.

iaroñroñ (**yiyahreg°reg°**). Dial. W: *iiaroñroñ* (**yiyyahreg°reg°**), E: *iaroñroñ* (**yiyahreg°reg°**). 1(-*i*), 2(inf, tr -*e*), 4, 6(-*i*), 7. Spy; reconnoiter; eavesdrop; wiretap; monitor secretly; investigate. *Wa eo emoot in iaroñroñ tok.* That ship has gone to spy. *Raar jilkinḷọk ña bwe in iaroñroñe lọk ṃṃakūtkūt ko an rinana ro.* They sent me to spy on and report the enemy movements.

iawewe (**yiyahweywey**). Dial. W: *iiawewe* (**yiyyahweywey**), E: *iawewe* (**yiyahweywey**). 1, 6(-*i*). Coral lime. *Kwōn raakutake ḷọk iawewe kaṇe jān lowaan upaaj ṇe.* Please rake out the coral lime from the fireplace.

iā (**yiyay**). Dial. E, W: *ūō* (**hihẹh**). Interjection: "Ouch!"

iādatōltōl (**yiyadateltel**). Dial. W: *iiadatōltōl* (**yiyyadateltel**), E: *iadatōltōl* (**yiyadateltel**). 1(-*i*), 2, 3. Saliva; spit; slobber; drool. *Eiādatōltōl ḷadik eṇ.* That boy is slobbering.

iāekwōj (**yiyayẹqẹj**). Dial. W: *iiāekwōj* (**yiyyayẹqẹj**), E: *iāekwōj* (**yiyayẹqẹj**). 1, 2. Race.

iāetōl (**yi'yayẹtẹl**). Also *aetōl.* Associate with.

iāllulu (**yiyalliwliw**). 1(-*i*), 2, 7. Foot race. *Ḷōṃaro raṇ rej iāllulu ippān ek kaṇ.* Those boys are racing to catch the fish (on the reef).

iāne (**yiyanẹy**). From *i* (**yiy**) "at", *āne* (**yanẹy**) "islet". Ashore. *Epād iāne.* He's ashore.

Ibae (**yibahyey**). From Engl. pronunciation of the spelling "Ebeye". Variant form of *Epjā* (**yepjay**).

ibb-. See *bb-*.

ibbuku (**yibbiqiw**). From Japn. *ippuku* "one swallow". Take a break; rest; recess. *Jemaroñ ke ibbuku jidik bwe jeṃōk?* Could we take a short break since we're tired?

ibeb (**yibyẹb**). 1(-*i*), 2, 3, 4, 6(-*i*), 7. Storm; overrun; overflow; overcome; onrush; onset; onslaught; flow, series of larger waves; waves of ships or planes; a sortie of planes; series of waves, usually three to six at a time, counted by good navigators before launching oceanward. *Ṃōttan wōt jidik ebar ibeb tok.* A series of waves will be coming soon. *Ia ṇe ej ibeb tok?* Where's that water coming from? *Raar ibebḷọk ñan ṃōn kiiñ eo.* They stormed the palace. *Ebooḷ em ibebḷọk.* It filled up and overflowed. *Raar ibeb em wiin ilo teeñ eo āliktata.* They turned on the pressure and came back to win in the last quarter. *Eibeb.* Here comes a large wave--warning to crew of small boat that a wave is about to break on them.

ibkij (**yibkij**). Variant form of *ikbwij* (**yikbij**).

ibnene (**yibnẹynẹy**). Also *ipnene* (**yipnẹynẹy**). 6(-*i*). Stump; rooty soil.

ibwij (**yibij**). 2(inf, tr -*i*), 3+7, 6(-*i*). High tide. *Eibwij tok.* The tide is coming in (rising). *Jen kaibwijḷọk.* Let's wait for the tide to come in. *Eibwiji wa eo im peḷọk.* The tide came up and the canoe drifted away.

ibwijleplep (**yibijleplep**). 1(-*i*), 2(inf, tr -*e*), 3(inf, tr -*e*), 7, 8, 9. Flood; deluge; highest tide. *Nowa wōt im bwij eo an raar mour ilo ibwijleplep eo ilo Baibōḷ.* Only Noah and his family survived the great flood in the Bible.

id (**yid**). 3, 6(-*i*). Strands for weaving garlands or stringing leis. *Rej kōṃṃan idin ḷōḷō jān maañ.* Weaving strands are made of pandanus leaves.

ida (**yidah**). Band, used for tying torch made from frond.

idaak (**yidahak**). Also *daak* (**dahak**), *ilim* (**yilim**). 1(-*i*), 2(inf, tr *ilim, inim, limi*), 3, 4, 7. Drink. *Kwōj daak ke?*

Do you want a drink? *Ilimi im kōmaate.* Drink it all up.

idaaptōk (**yidahaptẹk**). 1(*-i*), 2, 3, 7. Crossed in weaving or plaiting; tangled; ajar. *Ettōr im idaaptōk neen.* As he ran, his legs got tangled. *Ḷōmņak kein arro reidaaptōk (ippān doon).* Our opinions are ajar.

idajoñjoñ (**yidahjeg°jeg°**). 2(inf, tr *-e*), 4, 6(*-i*), 7. Try; examine; inspect; investigate. *Kwōn ṃōk idajoñjoñe tok ñan kōjro.* How about trying it out for us. *Riidajoñjoñ eo ņe tok.* Here comes the inspector. *Idajoñjoñin rūkapeel.* Investigation of an expert.

idd-. See *dd-*.

ide (**yidey**). Transitive form of *idid* (**yidyid**).

iden (**yiden**). Weaving strips; strands; fibre. *Eṃṃan iden nuknuk ņe.* That cloth has good fibers.

iden-oņe (**yiden-weņey**). 1, 2(inf, tr *-ik*), 4, 6(*-a*), 7. Revenge; avenge; retaliate; punish; even out; recompense for evil deed. *Anij enaaj iden-onieik eok kōn nana kaņe aṃ.* God will punish your evil deeds.

idepdep (**yidẹpdẹp**). 1, 2(inf, tr *-e*), 3, 7. Crowded; grow together as plants. *Eḷap an idepdep niin wāto ņe.* The trees on that tract are crowded. *Eidepdep armej ilo kweilọk eo.* The meeting is crowded.

idid (**yidyid**). 1(*-i*), 2(inf, tr *ide*), 7. Stinging sensation; to sting. *Lale aolōk eide eok.* Be careful or that Portuguese man-o'-war might sting you. *Eḷap an idid aolōkin likin ānin.* The Portuguese men-o'-war on the ocean side of this islet really sting.

idik (**yidik**). 3, 7. Period of neap tides.

idik (**yidik**). 2(inf, tr *-i*), 4, 5(*idikdik*), 6(*-i*). Shake. *Ejaje idik pein armej.* He never shakes hands. *Jab idiki ut ņe.* Stop shaking the tree. *Eidiki ut eo im mej.* He shook the flower tree and it withered.

idimkwi (**yidimqiy**). 1, 2, 3(inf, tr *-i*), 5(*iddimkwi*), 6(*-i*). Easily angered; be on edge, of people; edgy. *Kwōn jab kōkjakjek ippān bwe eiddimkwi.* Don't joke with him as he's edgy.

idiñ (**yidig**). 1(*-i*), 2, 3, 7. Sudden; abrupt decision; suddenly; change of plans; instantaneous. *Ejjeḷọk wōt idiñ in aṃ uwe.* That was an abrupt decision for you to travel.

ieṃa (**yiyeṃah**). Dial. W: *iieṃa* (**yiyyeṃah**), E: *ieṃa* (**yiyeṃah**). From Japn. *yama* "mountain". 5(*iieṃaṃa*), 6(*-i*). Stripes showing military rank. *Jilu an ḷeeņ ieṃa.* He's got three stripes. *Eieṃaṃa pein ḷeeņ.* His arm is covered with stripes.

ieñe (**yiyẹgẹy**). Here it is (close to me).

ieñe (**yiyẹgẹy**). Variant form of *eñe* (**yẹgẹy**).

ieñņe (**yiyegņey**). That's it.

iep (**yiyep**). Dial. W: *iiep* (**yiyyep**), E: *iep* (**yiyep**). 6(*-i*). Basket. *Wōn ņe ear āje iep ņe?* Who wove that basket?

iep (**yiyep**). Dial. W: *iiep* (**yiyyep**), E: *iep* (**yiyep**). Sheet, nautical.

iep jaḷḷọk (**yiyep jaḷḷaq**). Said of male children; see *iep jāltok*.

iep jāltok (**yiyep jalteq**). From "a basket whose opening is facing the speaker". Said of female children; a female married to a chief or householder. In her position she represents a basket whose contents are available to her relatives. Said of families with girl children (in matrilineal society); see *iep jaḷḷọk*. *Iep jāltok ajri ņe.* You are fortunate to have a girl child.

iepān ṃaal (**yiyepan ṃahal**). 6(*-i*). Large basket.

ieplik (**yiyẹplik**). 6(*-i*). Rope from sheet line forward and aft.

iia (**'yiyah**). Dial. W only; see *jemaluut* (**jemaliwit**). Rainbow.

iiaak (**'yiyahak**). 1(*-i*), 2(inf, tr *-e*), 3, 4, 6(*-i*), 7. Remove bones from fish; remove thorns from pandanus leaves; explain something in detail. *Kanooj iiaake ek ņe bwe edidi.* Be careful in taking the meat off that fish for it has lots of bones.

iiaeae (**'yiyahyahyey**). Rainbow-colored; distributive of *iia* (**'yiyah**).

iiaḷañe (**'yiyaḷagey**). 2(inf, tr *-ik*), 3, 6(*-i*). Moonrise. *Jen kaiaḷañe.* Let's wait for the moon to rise. *Enaaj iiaḷañeiki kōj ṃokta jān ad tōprak ḷọk.* We won't make it to there before moonrise.

iiāio (**'yiyayiyẹw**). Reunion. *Eṃṃan adwōj iiāio.* It's good for all of us to get together again.

iie ('yiyẹy). Needle. *Iie in aj.* Needle for sewing thatch. *Iie in kōtak.* Needle for tying on thatch.

iie ('yiyẹy). An animal, centipede.

iie ('yiyey). Archaic. Time; old form of *iien.*

iie rak ('yiyey rak). Variant form of *iien rak.*

iien ('yiyen). 7. Time; chance; occasion. *Elōñ iien tokālik.* There will be lots of time later.

iien kijone ('yiyen kijẹwnẹy). 2, 6(-*i*). Period of adjustment; Lent; religious period.

iien m̧m̧an ('yiyen m̧m̧an). Dial. W: *iien em̧m̧an* (yiyyen yem̧m̧an), E: *ien em̧m̧an* (yiyen yem̧m̧an). Opportunity; a chance.

iien rak ('yiyen rak). Also *iie rak* ('yiyey rak). Idiom. 2, 6(-*i*), 7. Summertime; time of fair weather. *Ļōm̧a e eiie rak tok bwe edik lọk kōto in.* Men, summertime is near as the wind is fairer.

iien wōtemjej ('yiyen wẹtẹmjẹj). Variant form of *aolep iien.*

iieņ ('yiyeņ). Also *eieņ* (yẹyiyeņ). That (close to neither of us); demonstrative, third person singular, singling out.

iiet ('yiyẹt). 1(-*i*), 2, 3(inf, tr -*e*), 7. Few; less; several. *Eļap an iiet aō nuknuk.* I have only a few clothes. *Kwōn jab kāiete am̧ bbōk.* Don't take so few.

iij (yiyij). Also *ij* (yij). From Engl. 2(inf, tr -*i*), 5(*iji, iijij*), 6(-*i*). Yeast; yeast beverage. *Eiijij iiōk eo an.* His batter came out having too much yeast. *Kōmij kōm̧m̧an dānnin kadek jān ij.* We make liquor from yeast.

iim̧ (yiyim̧). Also *im̧* (yim̧). 1, 2, 3(inf, tr -*i*), 7, 8, 9. Swift; fast; catch a glimpse of, because of fast motion. *Eim̧ wōt wa eo.* The boat was very fast. *Eļap an iim̧ wa eo.* That canoe is very swift.

iio ('yiyẹw). 1(-*i*), 2, 3(inf, tr *kaiouk*), 7. Whole; entirety; gross; intact. *Iar kaiouk mā eo im leļọk.* I gave him the whole breadfruit.

iioon ('yiyewen). 2(inf, tr -*e*). Meet; encounter; run into. *Iar iioon jera inne.* I ran into my friend yesterday.

iiō ('yiyẹh). Also *eiō* (yẹyiyẹh), *eñiō* (yẹgyiyẹh). 7. This (close to me); here it is; demonstrative, first person exclusive singular. *Bao eo kwōj pukot iiō.* The chicken you're looking for is right here.

iiō ('yiyeh). Also *yiō.* 1(-*i*), 2(inf, tr -*e*), 3, 6(-*i*). Year. *Jete iiōūm̧ ņai ānin?* How many years have you been on this island? *Iar kaiōeō ņai Amedka.* I spent years in America.

iiōk ('yiyẹk). 1(-*i*), 2(inf, tr -*e*), 4, 6(-*i*), 7. Mixture; mix; stir up; batter. *Kwōjeļā ke iiōk pilawā?* Do you know how to mix dough?

iiōk dakdak ('yiyẹk dakdak). 2, 4, 6(-*i*). Sloppy; hasty; slovenly. *Em̧ōj ņe am̧ iiōk dakdak.* Stop being sloppy.

iiūñ ('yiyig). Dial. E, W: *aet* (hayẹt). Also *iññā* (yiggay). Yes.

ijā (yijay). Dial. Mejit Island only. Exclamation: "Goodness!" *Ijā, emake baj m̧m̧an an lur.* Goodness, it's so nice and calm.

ije (yijẹy). Also *je* (jẹy). 7. Here; this place; locative demonstrative, first person exclusive singular.

ijekaņ (yijekaņ). Also *jekaņ* (jekaņ). There; those places (close to neither of us); locative demonstrative, third person plural.

ijekaņe (yijekaņey). Also *jekaņe* (jekaņey). Thereabouts (close to you); locative demonstrative, second person plural.

ijekā (yijekay). Also *jekā* (jekay). 7. Somewhere here around me; hereabouts; locative demonstrative, first person exclusive plural.

ijekākaņ (yijekaykaņ). Also *jekākaņ* (jekaykaņ). There; those places (close to neither of us); locative demonstrative, third person plural, singling out.

ijekākaņe (yijekaykaņey). Also *jekākaņe* (jekaykaņey). Somewhere around you; thereabouts; locative demonstrative, second person plural, singling out.

ijekākā (yijekaykay). Also *jekākā* (jekaykay). Somewhere here around me; hereabouts; locative demonstrative, first person exclusive plural, singling out.

ijekein (yijẹkẹyin). Also *jekein* (jẹkẹyin). 7. Somewhere here around us; hereabouts; locative demonstrative, first person inclusive plural.

ijeko (yijekew). Also *jeko* (jekew). Here; where; there; locative demonstrative, remote plural. *Em̧ōj etale ijeko ear etal ie ḷọk.* The places where he went have been investigated.

ijekoko (yijekewkew). Also *jekoko* (jekewkew). Yonder; over there; at that place (close to neither of us); locative demonstrative, remote plural, singling out.

ijellọkwi- (yijẹllaqi-). 1. Except; instead of; save. *Kab itok aolep raan ijellọkun wōt Jabōt.* Come every day except Sunday.

ijeṇ (yijeṇ). Also *jeṇ* (jeṇ). 7. There; that place (close to neither of us); locative demonstrative, third person singular.

ijeṇe (yijeṇey). Also *jeṇe* (jeṇey). 7. There by you; locative demonstrative, second person singular.

ijeṇeṇe (yijeṇeyṇey). Also *jeṇeṇe* (jeṇeyṇey). There by you; locative demonstrative, second person singular, singling out.

iji (yijiy). Transitive form of *ijij* (yijyij).

ijij (yijyij). Vulgar slang. 1(-*i*), 2(inf, tr *iji*), 4, 6(-*i*), 7. Sexual intercourse.

ijin (yijin). Also *jin* (jin). Here; this place; locative demonstrative, first person inclusive singular. *Jen kakkije ijin.* Let's rest here.

Ijitō (yijiteh). From Engl. Easter.

ijj-. See *jj-*.

Ijjidik (yijjiydik). Dial. W, E: *Jidikdik* (jiydikdik). Clan name.

Ijjidikin-kapinmeto (yijjiydikin-kapinmetew). Clan name.

ijjiieṇ (yijjiyiyeṇ). Also *jiieṇ* (jiyiyeṇ), *ijiieṇ* (yijiyyeṇ). Yonder; at that place (close to neither of us); locative demonstrative, third person singular, singling out.

ijjiiō (yijjiyiyẹh). Also *(i)jieō* ((yi)jiyeyẹh), *ijiiō* (yijiyyẹh). Here; this place (close to me); locative demonstrative, first person exclusive singular, singling out.

ijjurpe (yijjir°pẹy). Also *ijurpe* (yijir°pey). 1(-*i*), 7. Hold hands while walking.

ijjuweo (yijjiwweyew). Also *(i)juuweo* ((yi)jiwiweyew), *ijuweo* (yijiwweyew). Yonder; over there; at that place (close to neither of us); locative demonstrative, remote singular, singling out.

ijo (yijew). Also *jo* (jew). 7. Here; where; there; locative demonstrative, remote singular. *Raar kakkije ijo.* They rested there. *Imeḷọkḷọk bok eo aō ṇai ijo jaar kakkije ie.* I forgot (and left) my book there where we rested. *Ijo wōt kwōj ba.* Anything you say.

ijo (yijẹw). Archaic. Good soil.

ijoke (yijewkey). However; nevertheless; but as; maybe.

ijoko (yijeqew). 7. Those places.

ijoḷ (yijeḷ°). 1(-*i*), 2, 3, 7. Like; have an appetite for; to relish something.

iju (yijiw). 5(*ijujuwi*), 6(-*i*). Star; comet; planet; any celestial body other than the sun and the moon. *Iju Raan.* Morning Star. *Ej ijujui jọteen in.* There are lots of stars tonight.

Iju Raan (yijiw rahan). See *Jurōn Jemān Kurlōñ.*

iju rabōḷḷọk (yijiw rabeḷḷaq). Also *iju kāḷọk* (yijiw kayḷaq). Meteor; falling star.

Iju-ilo-bok-ajaj (yijiw-yilew-beq-hajhaj). See *bok ajaj* "coarse sand". A star; in the Magellanic cloud.

Iju-ilo-raan-kubōk (yijiw-yilew-rahan-qibẹk). See *kubōk:* "star in the branches of the *kubōk* tree. A star.

Iju-kuwaj-aiḷip (yijiw-qiwaj-hayiḷip). See *kuwaj, aiḷip:* "thick halfbeak fish". A constellation; Castor and Pollux in Gemini.

Iju-māj-roumuṃ (yijiw-maj-rẹwiṃwiṃ). A star; nebula in perseus; possibly the double cluster NGC 869 and 884.

Iju-pilo (yijiw-pilẹw). Also *Liiju-pilo.* A constellation; stars in Cancer; 44 is a blind woman led by her two granddaughters gamma and delta.

ijuboñ-ijuraan (yijiwbẹg°yijiwrahan). 2(inf, tr -*e*), 4, 6(-*i*). Move with steady and deliberate purpose; do something persistently. *Raar ijuboñ-ijuraane wa eo ñan ṃōjin.* They kept at it night and day until they finished the canoe.

ijur (yijir°). 3, 6(-*i*). Incense. *Raar kāijurtok lik tok.* They were collecting incense (wood) by the shore.

ijurwewe (yijir°wẹywẹy). 1, 2, 3(inf, tr -*ik*), 6(-*i*), 8, 9. Dilapidated; run-down condition. *Joñan an to aō jako jān ṃweo eijurwewe ḷọk.* I had been away from my house for so long that it was dilapidated.

ijuun māj (**yijiwin maj**). 1(...*meja*-), 6(...*mejān*). Pupil of the eye; eyeball.

Ijuun Rak (**yijiwin rak**). A star, possibly Achernar (alpha Eridani).

ik (**yik**). 2, 3, 7. Healing together of a wound; joining; coming together. *Eiktok mejān kinej ṇe peiṃ.* The center of the wound on your arm is starting to heal shut. *Eiktok kōtaan rā kaṇe.* The crack between those boards is closing up now. *Kaiktok me ṇe.* Close the weir.

ikaarar (**yikaharhar**). 1(-*i*), 2(inf, tr -*e*), 3, 6(-*i*), 7. Poisonous fish. *Eḷap an ikaarar ikōn ānin.* The fish around this islet are very poisonous. *Eikaarare ikōn ānin.* The fish around this islet poison people.

ikabwe (**yikabęy**). A fish, mackerel, *Grammatorcynus bicarinatus.*

ikade (**yikadęy**). 3, 6(-*i*). A fish, *Chelon vaigiensis.*

ikallo (**yikallęw**). A fish; used as bait for tuna.

ikāidik (**yikayidik**). A fish, rainbow runner, *Elagatis bipinnulatus.*

ikbwij (**yikbij**). Dial. W, E: *ḷañe* (**ḷagęy**). Also *ibkij* (**yibkij**). A fish, crevally, *Caranx stellatus.*

ikdeelel (**yikdeyelyel**). 1(-*i*), 2, 3, 7. Desire something; obsession; have something on one's mind; be bothered by something; eager; anxious; frantic. *Kwōjiktōm ikdeelel ilo būruō.* You have finally come and created desire in my heart. (From a love song). *Ij kab ikdeelel in jikuuḷ.* I have just decided that I want to go to school. *Ta ṇe ekaikdeelel eok?* What's on your mind?

ike (**yikey**). Distributive form of *ek* (**yęk**).

ikeruṃwij (**yikeyr°iṃij**). Variant form of *ikiruṃwij* (**yikiyr°iṃij**).

ikiddik (**yikiddik**). 1, 3(inf, tr -*i*), 4, 6(-*i*), 7. Sultry mannerisms. *Ikiddik kaṇ an lieṇ rōkọkkure aō ḷōmṇak.* Her sexy ways are driving me crazy.

ikien (**yikiyen**). 1(-*i*), 2(inf, tr -*e*), 3, 4, 7. Frolic; play; pester; bother; play practical jokes. *Ekanooj kiliddāp an ikien.* His pestering really gets under my skin.

ikiruṃwij (**yikiyr°iṃij**). Also *ikeruṃwij* (**yikeyr°iṃij**). 1(-*i*), 2, 3, 4, 6(-*i*), 7. Slow moving; very slow; chronically tardy; absenteeism. *Eṃōj ṇe aṃ ikiruṃwij.* I want you to stop being tardy.

ikjet (**yikjęt**). 6(-*i*). Depths of the ocean; the deep; point beyond which one cannot dig further; rock bottom. *Raar kōb im po ikjet.* They dug till they reached rock-bottom.

ikjin (**yikjin**). 1(-*i*), 2(inf, tr -*i*), 3, 4. Cook fish on stones.

ikk-. See *kk-*.

ikkwetōr (**yikqeyter**). From Engl. Equator. *Ṃajeḷ epād iturun ikkwetōr.* The Marshalls are situated near the equator.

ikmid (**yikmid**). Dial. W, E: *oḷaḷo* (**weḷaḷęw**). A fish, bass, *Variola louti.*

ikoeaak (**yikęwyahak**). Variant form of *ikueaak.*

ikōk (**yikek**). Variant form of *kōk* (**kek**).

ikōlood (**yikelewed**). A fish, electrid, *Valenciennesia strigata/violifera.*

ikōḷ (**yikeḷ**). From Engl. 6(-*i*). Eagle.

ikōn (**yiken**). Construct form of *ek* (**yęk**).

ikōn aḷe (**yiken haḷey**). Slang. Riffraff; a slovenly person; a ne'er-do-well. *Lale kwaar leḷọk aṃ ḷōmṇak ñan ikōn aḷe eṇ.* Don't you worry your head over that riff-raff.

ikōn-ae (**yiken-hayey**). A fish.

ikōn-wōd (**yiken-wed**). A fish, wrasse, *Thalassoma lunare.*

ikōnālkinṃwio (**yikenyalkinṃiyew**). Idiom. Fish that wanders outside coconut leaf chain scarer; belongs solely to the one who catches it; person who is not "in" or "with it"; deviant. *Kwōj jab aikuj kobaiki bwe ikōnālkinṃwio.* You don't have to put it with the rest because you caught it outside the scarer. *Jab inepata kake bwe ikōnālkinṃwio.* Don't worry about him because he's not with it.

ikōñ (**yikęg**). 1(-*i*), 2, 3. Silence; keep silent; quiet; dumb; mum; mute; taciturn. *Kwōn ikōñ wōt im jab keroro.* Be quiet and don't make any noise.

ikrooḷ (**yikreweḷ**). Also *ikūrooḷ.* Dissatisfied. *Armej in ṃweeṇ reikrooḷ ippān doon.* The people from that house are dissatisfied with each other.

ikudej (**yiqidęj**). A fish, scrawled file fish, *Alutera scripta.*

ikueaak (**yikiwyahak**). Also *ikoeaak.* 1(-*i*), 2, 3, 4, 6(-*i*), 7. Walk back and forth; ride back and forth; promenade; fellowship; traverse to and fro. *Ikueaakin ta kaņe ami?* Why are you people riding (walking) back and forth? *Eṃōj ņe aṃ ikoeaak bwe kwōj rippālele kiiō.* Stop running around for you're now a married man. *Kōm ar ikoeaak bajjek imeļan āneo.* We just sort of roamed around the island.

ikuut (**yikiwit**). A fish, pilot fish, *Naucrates ductor.*

ikūr (**yikir**). 2(inf, tr -*i*), 3, 5(*ikikūr*), 7. Change; rearrange; distort. *Eṃōj aō ikūr karōkin lowaan ṃwe.* I rearranged the room. *Kwōmake kijoñ ikikūr lowaan ṃōņe.* Your always rearranging the room. *Eṃōj ikūri bwebwenato eo.* The story has been distorted.

ikwōd (**yikwed**). Dialectal variant of *ukood* (**wikwed**).

il (**yil**). 3, 6(-*i*). Taro sprout; immature taro plant.

il (**yil**). Also *ilil* (**yilyil**). 2(inf, tr -*i*), 4, 6(-*i*), 7. Pierce; make a hole; pierce ears. *Wōn ņe ear ili ļọjilñūṃ?* Who made a hole in your earlobe? *Edikļọk ilil raan kein.* People don't pierce ears as much nowadays.

il (**yil**). 2, 3(inf, tr -*i*), 5(*ilil*), 6(-*i*), 8, 9. Small blisters from over exposure to sun. *Kwōmaroñ ke kāilili likū?* Can you please pop the blisters on my back?

il meej (**yil meyej**). 2, 6(-*i*). Beauty spot; mole.

ilar (**yilar**). 1(-*i*), 2(inf, tr -*e*), 3, 7. Fancy; pretty; bright colored. *Eļap an ilar jōōt eņ an.* His shirt is certainly fancy.

ilarak (**yilahrak**). 1(-*i*), 2, 3, 4, 7. Fishing method, trolling outside lagoon; trolling. *Ļōṃaro raņ rej ilarak lik.* Those fellows are trolling along the ocean side.

ilām (**yilam**). Contraction of *ilok im* (**yilaq yim**).

ilān (**yilan**). Contraction of *ilok in* (**yilaq yin**).

ilbōk (**yilbęk**). 1(-*i*), 2, 3, 7. Scared; startled; surprised; shocked. *Iilbōk kōn ainikien bu eo.* The sound of the gun scared me.

ile (**yilęy**). Also *ele* (**yeley, yęlęy**). 6(-*i*). String; wire for stringing fish. *Juon e ilein ek.* Here is a string of fish. *Eor ke aṃ ile?* Do you have a string (for stringing fish)?

ileek (**yileyek**). Transitive form of *ilele* (**yilęylęy**).

ilel (**yilyęl**). Pile of rubble; formant in place names.

ilele (**yilęylęy**). From *ile* (**yilęy**). 1(-*i*), 2(inf, tr *ileek*), 3(inf, tr -*ik*), 4, 7. String fish, coconuts, flowers, etc. *Kwōn ileek ek kaņe.* String those fish. *Rej ilele ek.* They are stringing fish. *Inaaj kāileleik eok ippa.* I'll let you string your fish with my stringer.

ilen (**yilen**). Construct form of *el* (**yęl**).

iliik (**yiliyik**). 1(-*i*), 2, 7. Walk swinging the arms. *Ia ņe kwōj iliik ļọk ñane?* Where are you walking to swinging your arms?

ilil (**yilyil**). Distributive form of *il* (**yil**) 'blisters'.

ililju (**yilyiljiw**). Early tomorrow. *Inaaj iwōj ililju.* I'll come there the first thing in the morning.

ilim (**yilim**). Transitive form of *idaak* (**yidahak**).

ilju (**yiljiw**). Tomorrow.

ilju im men (**yiljiw yim men**). Near future; within the next few days.

ill-. See *ll-*.

ilmeej (**yilmeyej**). 1(-*i*), 2. Mole on the skin; beauty spot.

ilmek (**yilmęk**). 3, 6(-*i*). A fish, silverfish, *Gerres baconensis.*

ilo (**yilew**). Dial. E, W: *ilo* (**yilęw**). At; in.

ilomej (**yilęwmęj**). 1(-*i*), 2(inf, tr -*e*), 3, 4, 7. Mourn the dead; visit the bereaved; visit home of dead person with gifts; grief; lament; see *āmej.*

ilowa (**yilewah**). 1(-*a*). Inside; in. *Bwil ņe an epād ilowa.* He has a fever (although he doesn't feel hot).

ilọk (**yilaq**). Dial. W, E: *wālọk* (**waylaq**). 1(-*i*), 2, 4, 6(-*i*). Go away (of humans).

ilọk (**yilaq**). 2, 3, 5(*ilọklọk*), 8, 9. Dilute food or drink to make it stretch; water down. *Kwōn jitu bwe eilọk.* Make a stew so we'll have more. *Eilǫk lǫjien.* He's got diarrhea.

ilǫklǫje (**yilaqlawjęy**). From *ilǫk* (**yilaq**) "dilute", *lǫje* (**lawjęy**) "stomach". 1(*...jie-*), 2, 3, 4, 7. Diarrhea; loose bowels.

ilūlōt (**yilhilet**). Variant form of *ūlūlōt.*

iḷḷ-. See *ḷḷ-.*

iḷoñ (**yiḷeg°**). Depth. *Ie iḷoñ in kinej eo?* How deep is the wound?

im (**yim**). Also *em* (**yem**), *-m* (**-m**). And. *Ṃṃaanem kōrā.* Men and women.

im (**yim**). 6(*-i*). A skirmish; bout; brawl; duel; riot; hassle. *Juon eo im ear waḷok ilo weta jab ṇe iōñ.* A verbal skirmish took place in the house next door north.

imen (**yimen**). 3, 6(*-i*). A fish, spotted eagle ray fish, poisonous, *Aetobatus narinari.*

imkili (**yimkiliy**). Transitive form of *imkilkil* (**yimkilkil**).

imkilkil (**yimkilkil**). Also *imkil* (**yimkil**). 1(*-i*), 2(inf, tr *imkili*), 3, 7. Tear into fine pieces; pluck feather or hair (Ralik only). *Jab imkili peba ṇe.* Don't tear that paper up.

imm-. See *mm-.*

impiḷoob (**yimpiyḷeweb**). Also *eṃpiḷoob* (**yeṃpiyḷeweb**). From Engl. 6(*-i*). Envelope.

iṃ (**yiṃ**). See *iiṃ.*

iṃaajaj (**yiṃahajhaj**). Also *iṃaaj* (**yiṃahaj**). 1(*-i*), 2(inf, tr *-e*), 3, 6(*-i*), 7. Strike aginst each other; smash into each other; bump into each other; collide head on; clash, physical as well as philosophical; smash-up. *Ruo eṇ kaar reiṃaajaj.* Those two cars smashed into each other. *Eiṃaajaj ainikien ko mejatoto.* Voices filled the air.

iṃiṃ (**yiṃyiṃ**). 3, 6(*-i*). A fish, reef triggerfish, *Balistapus rectangulus/ aculeatus*; Hawaiian *humu-humu nuku-nuku a-puaa.*

iṃṃ-. See *ṃṃ-.*

iṃōn aje (**yiṃen hajey**). Gift land; land given by chief as reward for services.

iṃōn bwebwe (**yiṃen bęybęy**). Asylum; house for the demented.

iṃōn kōppād (**yiṃen keppad**). Temporary shelter.

iṃōn utaṃwe (**yiṃen witaṃęy**). Asylum. *Iba kwaar pād iṃōn utaṃwe eṇ?* Could it be that you were in the asylum?

iṃtō- (**yiṃte-**). 3, 6. Dance steps. *Ej lukkuun kāiṃtōn.* He's actually making up dance steps.

iṃuk (**yiṃiq**). 1(*-i*), 2(inf, tr *-i*), 3, 7. Shake a bush or tree. *Iṃuk jān leen ut ṇe.* Shake the flowers off the bush. (lit. Shake from its fruit that flowering bush.) *Kwōn iṃuki jān leen oran ṇe.* Shake the oranges off that tree.

iṃwe (**yiṃey**). Distributive form of *eṃ* (**yęṃ**).

in (**yin**). To. *Kwōj etal in jikuuḷ ia?* Where do you go to school? *Kokanooj in ṃṃool.* Thank you very much.

in (**yin**). Dial. W, E: *ōr* (**her**). Grass skirt.

in (**yin**). This (thing close to us both); demonstrative, first person inclusive singular. *Men in eṃṃan.* This thing is good.

in (**yin**). Also *-in* (**-in**). Of; from; for; construct particle or suffix.

indeeo (**yindęyyew**). Forever; perpetual. *Ejjeḷọk eṇ enaaj mour ñan indeeo.* No one will live forever. *Indeeo im indeeo.* Forever and ever.

ine (**yiney**). 1(*-e*), 3(inf, tr *-ik*). Seed; breed; spawn; seedling. *Kako eṇ ej kāineik lǫlǫ eṇ.* The rooster is covering the hen. *Ineen rinana.* Spawn of the wicked.

ine (**yinęy**). Also *ineek.* Long stick placed on shoulders of two persons to carry burden suspended between; see *inene* (**yinęynęy**).

ine- (**yine-**). 1. Sisters of a male; female parallel cousins of a male; taboo female relatives of the same generation. *Liṃarein rej inem.* Our sisters and female parallel cousins.

ineea (**yinęyyah**). 1(*-i*), 2, 4, 6(*-i*), 7, 8, 9. Giant; of great stature; tall. *Enaaj kanooj ineea ñe erūttoḷọk.* He'll be very tall when he grows up.

ineek (**yineyek**). Transitive form of *inene* (**yinęynęy**).

ineeṃṃan (**yinęyęṃṃan**). 1(*-i*), 2, 3, 4, 7. Serene; meek; gentle; cheerful, resigned; soft-hearted; easy-going; carefree; mellow; benign. *Jet armej eḷap aer ineeṃṃan.* Some people don't have anything to worry about. *Enana ñe ej ḷe jān joñan ad* *ineemman.* It's not good to be too easy going.

inej (**yinẹj**). 6(*-i*). Fleet of canoes, ships, or planes.

inelep (**yineylep**). Multitude. *Naajdikin inelep eo.* Feeding of the multitude.

inene (**yinẹynẹy**). 1(*-i*), 2(inf, tr *ineek*), 3, 4, 6(*-i*), 7. Carry on shoulders; bear a burden. *Kwōmaroñ ke ineek pāāk e?* Can you carry this bag on your shoulder? *Rej inene pāāk in waini.* They are carrying bags of copra on their shoulders.

inepata (**yinẹypahtah**). 1(*-i*), 2, 3, 4, 6(*-i*), 7. Worry; anxious; troubled; angered; displeased; perturbed.

inij (**yinij**). From Engl. 1(*-i*), 6(*-i*), 7. Inch.

inik (**yinik**). Also *inōk* (**yinẹk**). From Engl. 1(*-i*), 2(inf, tr *-i*), 3, 6(*-i*), 7(*inikitok, ḷọk, waj*). Ink.

inim (**yinim**). Transitive form of *idaak* (**yidahak**).

inin (**yinyin**). From *in* (**yin**). 1(*-i*), 2, 3(inf, tr *kāinin(i)*), 4, 7. Wear a skirt; grass skirt. *Rōnañin kāinin(i) ke rieb ro?* Have they adorned the dancers with grass skirts?

injej (**yinjẹj**). From Engl. 1(*-i*), 2(inf, tr *-e*), 4. Hinge; hasp. *Kwōn injeje kōjām eṃ.* Install the hinges on that door.

injin (**yinjin**). 4, 6(*-i*). Engine; motor. *Injin jarom.* Generator. *Injinin kwaḷkoḷ.* Washing machine. *Injin ḷọk.* Outboat motor. *Injin batbat.* Japanese one-cylinder engine (putput).

injin ḷọk (**yinjin ḷaq**). Outboard motor.

injinia (**yinjiniyah**). 1(*-i*), 2(inf, tr *-ik*), 3, 4, 6(*-i*), 7. Engineer; mechanic. *Wōn eṇ ej injinia in wa eṇ?* Who is the engineer on that boat? *Wōn eṇ ear injiniaik tok wa eṇ?* Who was engineer on that ship when it came here?

innām (**yinnam**). Also *innem* (**yinnem**). Then. *Innem ta?* Then what?

inne (**yinney**). Yesterday.

inne eo ḷọk juon (**yinney yew ḷaq jiwen**). Also *raan eo ḷọk juon* (**rahan yew ḷaq jiwen**). The day before yesterday.

innem (**yinnem**). Variant form of *innām* (**yinnam**).

innijek (**yinniyjẹk**). Also *innijek* (**yinnijẹk**). 3(inf, tr *-e*), 6(*-i*), 8, 9. Pitch black, said of nights. *Buñūn bọbo men in bwe einnijek.* This should be an ideal night for catching flying fish because it's pitch black.

Innintok (**yinninteq**). From *nnin* (**nnin**) "to pound, smash", *tok* (**teq**) "toward me". 3, 6(*-i*). A plant, pandanus cultigen (Takeuchi).

ino (**yinew**). 1(*-i*), 6(*-i*). Lashing cord.

inojeik (**yinewjẹyik**). 7. Ignore; drift away from. *Kwōjab inojeikḷọk jāni wa kein, iaḷ in mour ko kein.* Don't drift away from these canoes, these are your passes to life. (Don't take things for granted.)

inọñ (**yinag°**). Also *inoñ* (**yineg°**). 1(*-i*), 2, 4, 6(*-i*), 7. Legend; folkloristic story; fiction; lore; myth; day-dream. *Inọñūn ia ṇe kwōj inọñ kake?* Where does that legend you're telling come from?

inọñ (**yinag°**). Euphemism used on sailing vessels to notify men to stay out of sight when women need to relieve themselves.

inōk (**yinẹk**). Variant form of *inik* (**yinik**).

inōknōk (**yineknek**). Also *inōknōk* (**yinẹknẹk**). 1(*inōka-*), 2(inf, tr *inōke*), 3(inf, tr *-e*), 4(*riinōk*), 5(*inōke, inōknōke*), 6(*inōka-*). Adorn; decorate; embellish; ornament, trimmings; decked out. *Eḷap an inōknōk ṃōn jar eṇ.* That church is decorated. *Wōn eṇ ear kāinōknōk ṃōn jar ṇe?* Who decorated that church? *Wōn ṇe ear inōke ṃōn jar ṇe?* Who decorated the church with those colors of paint? *Ledik ro rej kāinōknōk lōb.* The girls are decorating graves. *Ledik eo ear kāinōknōke ruuṃ eo.* The girl decorated the room. *Einōknōke ubōn opija eo.* The officier was much decorated.

inpel (**yinpẹl**). 3, 6(*-i*). Coconut cloth. *RiṂajeḷ rej kōjerbal inpel ñan kāāḷāḷ.* Marshallese use *inpel* for straining coconut milk.

inwijet (**yinwiyjẹt**). 2(inf, tr *-e*), 4, 6(*-i*), 7. Lashing technique used on canoes. *Raan kein ejejā eṇ eṃṃan an inwijet.* Few people nowadays can perform a good lashing job.

iņoņooj (**yiņewņewej**). 2(inf, tr *-e*), 6(*-i*). Manipulate; tamper with.

iñ (**yig**). 6(*-i*). Spines on fish.

iñ (**yig**). Angry.

iñ lọjien (**yig lawjiyen**). 6(*-i*), 7, 8, 9. Strain one's abdominal muscles; hernia. *Eiñ lọjien kōn an kate kotak men ddodo eo.* He strained his abdominal muscles lifting the heavy weight.

iñimmaļ (**yigimmaļ**). 1(*-i*), 2, 3, 7. Writhe in pain. *Eļap an kar iñimmaļ kōn lọjien.* He writhed in pain from the stomach (ache).

iñiñ (**yigyig**). 2(inf, tr *iñūti*), 4, 6(*-i*), 7, 10(*iñtōk*). Twirl; turn, around and around; wind; kinky, of hair. *Iñūti waj ņe aṃ.* Wind your watch. *Ear iñiñ im jotok bọọļ eo.* He wound up and threw me the ball. *Eiñ lọjien ļadik eņ.* That boy's got a hernia.

iñiñ (**yigyig**). 1, 2(inf, tr *iñūr(i), ikūr*), 4, 6(*-i*), 7, 10(*iñrōk*). Sprain; change; turn for worse. *Ear iñūr injin eo.* He threw the engine's tuning off.

iñiñtōk (**yigyigtẹk**). 1(*-i*), 2, 3(inf, tr *-e*), 7. Wiggle; wriggle.

iñjālle (**yigjalley**). 1(*-i*), 2(inf, tr *-ik*), 3, 7. Toss a line by means of weight tied to end.

Iñlen (**yiglen**). From Engl. 4. Place name, England.

Iñlij (**yiglij**). From Engl. 4. English; England. *Ejeļā kajin Iñlij.* He knows the English language. *RiIñlij men ņe.* That's an Englishman.

iññ-. See *ññ-*.

iññā (**yiggay**). Dial. E only; see *aet* (**hayẹt**). Also *iiñ* (**'yiyig**). Yes.

iñrōk (**yigrẹk**). 1(*-i*), 2, 3, 7. Sprain; perfective form of *iñiñ* (**yigyig**); twisted. *Ittōr im iñrōk neō.* I ran and sprained my ankle.

iñtōk (**yigtẹk**). 2, 3, 5(*iñtōktōk, iñiñtōk*), 6(*-i*), 7, 8, 9. Twisted; perfective form of *iñiñ* (**yigyig**); squirm. *Ālkin baaṃ eo, eiñtōktōk māāl ilo jikin eo.* After the bomb, the city was a wreck of twisted steel. *Eṃōj ņe aṃ iñtōk.* Stop squirming.

iñūti (**yigitiy**). Transitive form of *iñiñ* (**yigyig**).

io (**yiyẹw**). Interjection: "Shucks!", "Darn!" *Io ewōt.* It is raining now (period of expecting rain implied). *Io kwōnaaj et?* Now what are you going to do?

io (**yi'yew**). Variant form of *eñeo* (**yegyew**).

io- (**yi'yew-**). Interjection: "See what you've done!" (always used with personal demonstratives). *Ioļe.* See what you (a man) have done. *Ioliṃa.* See what you gals have done.

iok- (**yiyeq-**). Also *iook-* (**yiyeweq-**). 7. Go directly to or towards; come directly.

ioļap (**yi'yewļap**). Dial. E, W: *eoļap* (**yewļap**). 1(*-i*), 3, 7. Middle.

ioo- (**yi'yewe-**). Also *eoo-* (**yewe-**). 1, 1+7. On; upon; top; surface; over.

iooj (**yiyẹwẹj**). Dial. E, W: *eọọj* (**yawaj**). 1(*-i*), 7. Middle of an island; interior of an island. *Piik ko rōpād iooj.* The pigs are in the middle of the island.

ioonkappe (**yi'yewenkappẹy**). Dial. E, W: *eoonkappe* (**yewenkappẹy**). 6(*-i*), 7. Landward side of beach; on the shore.

ioot (**yiyewet**). Dial. W: *iioot* (**yiyyewet**), E: *ioot* (**yiyewet**) . From Engl. *yacht.* Sloop.

iọkiọkwe (**yi'yaqyi'yaqey**). 2(inf, tr *-ik*), 4, 6(*-i*), 7. Greet; bid farewell to. *Etke ej jab iọkiọkwe armej?* Why doesn't he greet people?

iọkwe (**yi'yaqey**). Also *yokwe.* 1(*-i*), 4, 5(*iọkiọkwe*), 6(*-i*), 7. Greet; to love; bid farewell; sympathize.

iọkwe in eọ (**yi'yaqey yin yaw**). From *iọkwe* (**yi'yaqey**) "love", *eọ* (**yaw**) "tattoo". 2, 4, 6(*-i*). True love.

iọkwe in kij (**yi'yaqey yin kij**). Idiom. From *iọkwe* (**yi'yaqey**) "love", *kij* (**kij**) "louse". 2(inf, tr *-i*), 4, 6(*-i*). Infatuation; false love; pretentious care; puppy love. *Erro ej iọkwe in kij bajjek.* Theirs is just a puppy love. *Ekaannuoj ļap an allikar an iọkwe in kiji eok.* Her love for you is so obvious that it is a put-on.

iọọt (**yi'yawat**). From Engl. Yacht.

iọuwọ (**yiyawiwwaw**). Dial. W: *iiọuwọ* (**yiyyawiwwaw**), E: *iọuwọ* (**yiyawiwwaw**). Interjection: "Beware!"

iō (**yiyeh, yiyẹh**). Formant in place names; variant form of *iu* (**yiw**) "sprouted coconut".

iōñ (**yi'yẹg**). Variant form of *eañ* (**yag**).

iōōe (**yiyẹhẹy**). Variant form of *eñe* (**yẹgẹy**).

iōōļ (yiyeheļ). Dial. W: *iiōōļ* (yiyyeheļ), E: *iōōļ* (yiyeheļ). 3, 6(-*i*). A fish, mullet, *Crenmugil crenilabis.*

ip (yip). 1(-*i*), 2, 3, 7. Awry; askew; crooked; distorted. *Enana aļaļ ņe bwe eip.* That piece of lumber is no good because it's crooked.

ip (yip). 1(-*i*). Hips; waist.

ipep (yipyęp). 1(-*i*), 2(inf, tr *iper*), 7. Drag; haul. *Kwōn iper arļǫk kimej kaņe.* Drag those fronds to the lagoon beach. *Rej ipep arļǫk kimej.* They are dragging fronds to the lagoon beach.

ipep (yipyęp). 1(-*i*), 2, 3, 6(-*i*). Women's full-length dress; Mother Hubbard. *Ipepin ia ņe aṃ?* Where did you get your long dress? *Kab baj ipepū.* This is the first time I wore a long dress.

iper (yiper). Transitive form of *ipep* (yipyęp).

ipnene. See *ibnene.*

ipp-. See *pp-.*

ippa- (yippa-). Dial. W, E: *pepa-* (ppa-). 1, 7. With; spouse of. *Lio ippa e.* Here's my wife.

ippān doon (yippan dewen). Together; cooperate.

iptu (yiptiw). From Engl. 2(inf, tr -*ik*), 4, 6(-*i*), 7. Heave to; lay to, nautical. *Wa eo eņ ej iptu ilik.* The ship is heaving to outside.

ir (yir). 2, 3(inf, tr -*i*), 6(-*i*), 7. Dislocated; out of joint; displaced; sprained; deviate. *Eir bok kaņe jān ke iar karki.* Those books are changed from the way I arranged them. *Eirļǫk neō.* My leg is sprained. *Lale bwe kwōn jab ir jān men eo iaar ba.* Be careful not to deviate from my instructions. *Eirļǫk diin aeran.* He dislocated his collar bone.

ir (yir). Transitive form of *irir* (yiryir).

irar (yirar). Contact, constant and physical. *Aō ekōņan bwin (ekōņaan bwe in) irar ippaṃ le raan im boñ.* I'd love to have her cuddle close to me night and day--words from a love song.

ire (yirey). Also *ire* (yirȩy). 1, 2, 3(inf, tr -*ik*), 4, 5(*irere*), 6(-*i*). To fight; duel; brawl. *Raar ire ippān doon.* They fought among each other. *Jab kāireik ajri raņ.* Don't make the children fight. *Enaaj kalbuuj kōn an irere (ļaire).* He'll end up in jail from fighting all the time.

iri (yiriy). Transitive form of *irir* (yiryir).

irir (yiryir). 1(-*i*), 2(inf, tr *ir(i)*), 3, 4, 7. Rub; friction; scrape.

irir (yiryir). Also *ir* (yir). 2(inf, tr *iri*), 4, 6(-*i*), 7. Wipe.

irko (yirkew). Also *erko* (yerkew). Here they are, nonhumans only. *Irko bok ko aṃ ko.* Here are your books.

irļǫk (yirļaq). Also *irlǫk* (yirlaq). 2, 3(inf, tr -*e*), 6(-*i*), 8. Flaw; defect; dislocated; not all there. *Eor jidik irļǫk ilo kōmālij eņ an.* He's got a bit of a mental defect.

irooj (yirȩwȩj). Dial. E, W: *irooj* (yirewej). Also *irwōj* (yirwȩj), *irooj* (yirewej), *irwōj* (yirwej). 3, 6(-*i*). Chief; king.

Irooj (yirewej). Clan name.

irooj rilik (yirȩwȩj riylik). 2, 3, 6(-*i*). A god of fish.

irooj-eṃṃaan (yirȩwȩj-yeṃṃahan). 1(-*i*), 2, 3, 6(-*i*). Commoner married to royal woman.

iroojiddik (yirȩwȩjiddik). Variant form of *bwidak* (bidak).

irr-. See *rr-.*

iruj (yir°ij). 1(-*i*), 2, 3, 7. Alarm; excitement. *Ta eņ rej iruj ļǫk kake?* What are they getting excited about?

iruj lǫjie- (yir°ij lawjiye-). 1, 2, 3(inf, tr -*i*). Thrilled; inspired; intrigued. *Nnaan eo ekāiruji lǫjiō.* The news thrilled me.

it (yit). Dial. W only, see *etōñ* (yȩtȩg). 1(-*i*), 2, 3, 4, 7, 8. Make fire by rubbing sticks.

it (yit). Also *jit* (jit). 2(inf, tr -*i*), 4, 6(-*i*), 7. Strike a match. *Ij iti ak eban tok bwe eṃōļǫwi.* I keep striking the match but it won't light up because it's wet.

ita (yitah). Dialectal variant of *et* (yȩt).

itaak (yitahak). 1(-*i*), 2, 3, 7. Clash; strike against; collide with; arrive at; bump into. *Lale eitaak bōraṃ.* Watch that you don't bump your head. *Wa eņ ear itaaktok ñāāt?* When did that ship get here?

itak kipilōñ (yitak kipiylȩg). Wind from the west.

itaka- (yitaka-). Variant form of *ļokwa-* (ļeqa-).

itakļǫk (**yitakļaq**). Also *itaļǫk* (**yitahļaq**). 2. Go eastward.

itaļǫk (**yitahļaq**). Variant form of *itakļǫk* (**yitakļaq**).

item̧am̧ōj (**yiteym̧am̧ȩj**). 2(inf, tr *-e*), 6(*-i*). Rub in black carbon on tattoos. *Eiñimmaļ ke rej item̧am̧ōje.* He writhed in agony as black carbon was rubbed into his tattoos.

itene (**yitȩynȩy**). Transitive form of *et* (**yȩt**).

itileñeñ (**yitilyȩgyȩg**). Variant form of *tileñeñ* (**tilyȩgyȩg**).

itileoñeoñ (**yitilyeg°yeg°**). 2, 7. A large crowd passing backwards and forwards; milling about of a crowd; jostling; see *tileñeñ. Eitileoñeoñ armej ilowaan m̧ōn wia eo.* A lot of people are milling around in the store.

itkaap (**yitkahap**). 2, 7. Make fire; method in which one person squeezes two sticks while another moves a third back and forth between. *Kōjro itkaap.* Let's make fire by the *itkaap* method.

ito (**yitȩw**). 2, 4, 7. Go westward.

ito-itak (**yitȩw-yitak**). 1(*-i*), 2, 3, 4. Travel; go around; go back and forth; journey. *Rej ito-itak bajjek.* They are just walking around. *RiAmedka rōkijoñ ito-itak.* Americans are accustomed to traveling.

itok (**yiteq**). Dial. W, E: *wātok* (**wayteq**), *atok* (**hateq**). Also *tok* (**teq**). 1(*-i*), 2, 4, 6(*-i*). Come here (of humans).

itok (**yiteq**). 1, 6(*-i*). Whale meat. *Ekane m̧ōñā mā ippān itok.* Breadfruit with whale meat is a tasty combination.

itok reeaar (**yiteq rȩyyahar**). Wind from the east.

itok-limo (**yiteq-limew**). From "comes interest". 1(*-i*), 2+1, 3(st inf *kāitoktok-limo,* tr *kāitok-limowi-*), 4(*riitok-limo* "interested person, *rūkāitoktok-limo* "person who arouses interest). Arouse interest; enjoy; enthusiasm. *Eļap an itok-limoū ilo jerbal in.* I am very interested in this job. *Eļap an kāitoktok-limo an jipij.* He makes interesting speeches. *Eļap an kar kāitok-limoū jipij eo an.* His speech really interested me.

itōk (**yitȩk**). Also *ititōk.* 1(*-i*), 2(inf, tr *-e*), 3, 4, 7, 8. Draw water; dip up water. *Rej itōk dān.* They are drawing water.

itōm (**yitem**). Come and; contraction of *itok im* (**yiteq yim**).

itōn (**yiten**). Come in order to; contraction of *itok in* (**yiteq yin**); intend; mean; about to. *Eitan wōt.* Looks like rain. It's about to rain.

itt-. See *tt-*.

ittūt (**yittit**). Dial. W, E: *tūttūt* (**tittit**). 1(*itti-*). Breast; nipple; teat.

itūk (**yitik**). 1(*-i*), 2(inf, tr *-i*), 3, 4, 5(*ititūk*), 7. Pluck out eyes; rub ones eye. *Raar itūk(i) mejān Jam̧jen.* They plucked out Samson's eyes. *Jab ititūk(i) mejam̧.* Don't rub your eyes.

itūñ (**yitig**). 2(inf, tr *-i*), 7. Rub ones eye. *Jab itūñi mejam̧.* Don't rub your eye.

itweļǫk (**yitweyļaq**). 2. Hesitate (reflexive); waver; falter; balk. *Jab itweļǫk eok.* Don't hesitate.

iu (**yiw**). 3(*kaiuiu*), 5(*-i*), 6(*-i*). Spongy meat of sprouted coconut; sprouted coconut; coconut "apple". *Eļap an iui āneņ.* There are lots of sprouted coconuts on this islet.

iuiuun dekein jinme (**yiwyiwin dȩkȩyin jinmey**). Idiom. 2, 4. Tamper with the status quo. *Jet armejin M̧ajeļ rōdike kain eņ ej iuiuun dekein jinme.* Some Marshallese don't take kindly to those who are trying to advocate changes.

ium̧wi- (**yi'yiwm̧i-**). Also *eom̧wi-* (**yewm̧i-**), *eǫm̧wi-* (**yawm̧i-**), *iǫm̧wi-* (**yi'yawm̧i-**). 1(*-i*), 4, 6(*-i*), 7. Under; beneath; underneath; below.

iupej (**yiwpȩj**). Also *iuwapej* (**yiwahpȩj**). 3(inf, tr *-e*), 4, 6(*-i*), 3+7. Overgrown and inedible sprouted coconut; worthless person or thing. *Rej kaiupeje wāto eņ.* They are cleaning that tract of *iupej*.

iur (**yir°**). 6(*-i*). Flock of birds.

iur (**yir°**). 1(*-i*), 2, 3, 7, 8, 9, 11(*iur, iuriur*). Swift; fast; quick; immediate; prompt; rapid. *Juon uwaak iur.* An immediate reply.

iurjet (**yir°jȩt**). 1(*-i*), 2, 3, 4, 8, 9. Quick in action; sprightly; rapid. *Ekadik iurjet am̧ kōnono.* But you speak so rapidly.

iutūr (**yiwtir**). 2(inf, tr *-i*), 3, 4, 5(*iiutūrtūr*), 6(*-i*), 7. A food, bundled and baked spongy meat of sprouted coconut. *Kwōn iutūri iu kaņe.* Bundle and bake the coconut apples. *Ear* *iutūri ļok ñane.* She made *iutur* for him.

iuun (**yiwin**). 1(-*i*), 2(inf, tr -*i*), 4, 6(-*i*), 7. Push; poke; boost. *Kwōmaroñ ke jipañ eō iuuni kaar e?* Could you help me push the car? *Kwōjaam iuun katū?* Why don't you stop poking my side?

iuwumum̧ (**yiwwim̧wim̧**). 2(inf, tr -*i*), 4, 6(-*i*), 7. A food, spongy meat of sprouted coconut baked in its shell. *Kwōmaroñ ke iuwumum̧i iu kā kijerro?* Could you do me a favor and bake these sprouted coconuts for us?

iwapej (**yiwahpęj**). Variant form of *iupej* (**yiwpęj**).

iwōj (**yiwęj**). Dial. W, E: *wawōj* (**wahwęj**), *awōj* (**hahwęj**). Also *wōj* (**węj**). 1(-*i*), 2, 4. Go to you; come to you (of humans). *Iwōj kōjro etal.* Let's go. *Iwōj m̧okta bwe ij iwōj wōt.* You go first and I'll come later. *Kwōn awōj ļok.* Come on, step on it.

ja (**jah**). Still; for the time being; now. *Ta nnaan bajjek?...Ej ja jjeļok wōt.* Any news yet?...Nothing yet. *Enañin or ke eņ eitok?...Ej ja jjeļok wōt.* Has anyone showed up yet?...No one yet. *Kokōņaan ke bar m̧ōñā?...Kom̧m̧ool ak ej ja m̧ōj.* Do you want something more to eat?...Thanks but I've had enough for now. *Ej ja m̧ōj in.* Let's call it quits for now. *Kōjro ajādik....Kwōn ja m̧ōñā m̧okta.* Let's get going....Why don't you eat first. *Jen kam̧ōje ke ej ja or wōt iien.* Let's finish it while there is still time to do it.

ja (**jah**). See *ejja*. Formant in place names; harbor; men's house (?); small thing. *Ja eo jān em̧m̧aan.* (words from a chant). *Bōk tok ja in markūbwebwe eņ.* Bring that small plant here.

ja- (**ja-**). Also *jā, je-, jo-, jǫ-, jō-*. Negative prefix. *Jarroñroñ.* Hard of hearing.

jaab (**jahab**). Dial. W only; see *eaab* (**yahab**). No.

jaad (**jahad**). A fish.

jaad (**jahad**). Also *jaadin* (**jahadin**). Rather; fairly; somewhat; slightly. *Ejaad m̧ōkajļok aerro jerbal.* They're working somewhat faster--fairly fast. *Kom̧ro iwōj wōt bwe ij jaad m̧ōk.* You two go on ahead as I am a bit tired.

jaaj (**jahaj**). From Engl. 2(inf, tr -*e*), 4, 5(*jjaajaj*). Charge a battery; charge on account. *Jaaje pāātre ņe.* Charge the battery. *Enaaj jjaajaj bwe em̧or.* That old battery will have to be charged all the time. *Kab jaaje akkawūn eo aō.* Be sure to charge it to my account.

jaajmi (**jahajmiy**). From Japn. *sashimi*. 1(-*i*), 2(inf, tr -*ik*), 3, 4, 6(-*i*). A food, raw fish. *Kwōn jaajmiik juon ek.* Cut up a fish and make sashimi.

jaak (**jahak**). 2, 3, 3+7, 10(*jaaki, jaaklǫk*). Attempt; undertake; done; achieved; reached. *Ij kōjaake jilubukwi taļa allōñ in.* I'm aiming to earn 300 this month. *Emaroñ jaaki.* It could be done (achieved). *Ejaak tǫujin eo raar kōttōpare.* Their thousand dollar goal was reached.

jaaļ (**jahaļ**). 2, 3(inf *kōjjaaļaļ*, tr *kōjaaļ*), 5(*jjaaļaļ*), 6(-*i*), 7. Turn a vehicle. *Kōjaaļe wa ņe.* Turn the boat. *Ejjaaļaļ kaar eo waan rūkadek ro.* The drunkards' car couldn't go straight.

jaam̧ (**jaham̧**). Also *jaam* (**jaham**) before light consonants. Why still?; Why persist in ...?; Why again? *Etke kwōjaam etal?* Why do you persist in going? *Ejaam marok m̧wiin im̧ōm̧?* Why is your house still dark? *Ijaam̧ bar metak bar?* Why did I get a headache again?

jaam̧ (**jaham̧**). From Engl. 2(inf, tr -*e*), 4, 5(*jjaam̧am̧*), 6(-*i*), 7, 8, 9. Jam; jelly. *Jaam̧e pilawā ņe.* Put jam on your bread. *Ejjaam̧am̧ eoon tebōļ eņ.* There is jam all over the table.

Jaam̧ (**jaham̧**). From Engl. The Psalms. *Em̧m̧an kōnono ko ilo bokun Jaam̧ ippa.* I like the readings in the Book of Psalms.

jaanpeba (**jahanpęybah**). From Engl. 2(inf, tr -*ik*), 4, 6(-*i*), 7. Sandpaper. *Kwōn jaanpebaik rā ņe.* Sandpaper that board.

jaañke (**jahagkęy**). From Japn. *jankenpon*. 1(-*i*), 2, 3(inf, tr -*ik*), 4, 6(-*i*). A game, scissors, paper, and stone; a game; jun ken po. *Jaañke in lale wōn in m̧okta.* Let's play *jaañke* to see who goes first.

jaap (**jahap**). Dial. W, E: *jato* (**jahtęw**). 3, 6(-*i*). A fish, red snapper, *Lutjanus vaigiensis.*

jaar (**jahar**). Archaic. Private place reserved for chiefs.

jaat (**jahat**). From Engl. 6(-*i*). A shot of whiskey. *Letok juon jaatin wōjke.* Give me a shot of whiskey.

jaat (**jahat**). From Engl. 1(-*i*), 2(inf, tr -*e*), 3, 4, 6(-*i*), 7. Chart.

jab (**jab**). Intensifier used with demonstratives; direction. *Tujab ieṇ.* Right over there. That side.

jab (**jab**). 2. Not. *Ij jab iwōj.* I am not coming.

jab (**jab**). Full of. *Ejab kōn dān.* It's full of water.

jab bar (**jab bar**). 2. Not again; do not. *Jab bar kakūtōtōūki e tokālik bwe kwōnaaj deñdeñ.* Don't ever anger him again because next time you'll get spanked.

jab dodoorḷọk (**jab dewdewerḷaq**). Idiom. Not to sell oneself short; underestimate one's potential. *Kwōn kate eok im jab dodoorḷọk ijeṇe aṃ.* Do your best and don't sell yourself short.

jab juur laḷ (**jab jiwir laḷ**). Idiom. Be very happy. *Ke ej roñ ke ewiini teej eo ear jab juur laḷ.* When he heard that he passed the exam, he was very happy.

jab meḷọkḷọk (**jab meḷaqḷaq**). From "don't forget". A plant, flower, *Angelonia salicariaefolia* (Takeuchi).

jab po bōro (**jab pew bẹrẹw**). Discontent; dissatisfy. *Ej jab po būruō kōn ṃōñā in.* I'm not terribly excited about this meal.

jab ruṃwij (**jab r°iṃij**). From *jab* (**jab**) "don't", *ruṃwij* (**r°iṃij**) "late". 7. Immediately; hurry up. *Jab ruṃwijtok.* Come at once. Hurry up and come.

jabalur (**jabalir°**). Shade. *Pād ilo jabalur in ānṇe.* Abide in the shade of your islet.

jabar (**jabhar**). Also *jebar* (**jebhar**). 1(-*i*), 4, 6(-*i*), 7, 9. Lagoon side of an island.

jabawōt (**jahbahwet**). From Bibl. *Sabaoth.* 1(-*i*), 2, 3, 4, 6(-*i*), 8. Church offering. *Iaikuji roñoul ḷalem jāān ñan aō jabawōt.* I need a quarter for my church offering.

jabde (**jabdey**). 1, 2, 4, 5(*jjabdede*), 6(-*i*), 8, 9. Careless; sloppy; easy-going; carefree; irresponsible; reckless; slipshod. *Ekadik jabde likao eṇ.* The young man is very careless. *Eṃōj ṇe aṃ jjabdede ak kwōn jino koortokjān aṃ mour.* Stop being so carefree and start making something of your life.

jabdetakwōt (**jabdeytakwet**). At random. *Jabdetakwōt an bbōk.* He takes on a wife at random.

jabdewōt (**jabdeywet**). Any; anything; miscellaneous; whatever; each; every. *Eṃṃan jabdewōt ippa.* Anything is OK with me.

jabdik (**jabdik**). 1(-*i*), 2, 6(-*i*), 7. Sailing port to wind; canoe part, afterpart when outrigger is on port side; starboard tack.

jabjab (**jabjab**). 1(-*i*), 2, 3, 6(-*i*), 8. Be short of; out of reach. *Ejabjab neō jān laḷ.* I can't touch the bottom with my feet. *Ejabjab peiū jān raan mā e.* I can't reach this breadfruit branch with my hands. *Iar joḷọk to eo ak ejabjab.* I threw the rope but it fell short.

jabjabmenowa- (**jabjabmenewa-**). 1, 2, 3, 8. Short of breath; out of breath. *Iban tulọk ḷọk wōt bwe enaaj jabjabmenowa.* I can't dive further or I'll run out of breath.

jabjen menowa- (**jabjen menewa-**). 1, 2, 3. Suffocate; smothered; stifled. *Ejabjen menowan ajri eo ṇa ilowaan bọọk eo.* The child suffocated in the box.

jabjet (**jabjet**). Five pairs, fish or copra.

jablik (**jablik**). 1(-*i*), 7. Ocean side of an island.

Jabloed (**jablewyed**). From *jab* (**jab**) "not", *lo* (**lew**) "see", *ed* (**yed**) "veins on a leaf". 3, 6(-*i*). A plant, *Pandanus fischerianus* cultigen.

jablọk (**jablaq**). Also *jebḷọk* (**jeblaq**). 3, 6(-*i*). Butt of cigarette; tail half of fish. *Kwōn bōk jablọkun ek ṇe.* Take the tail half of that fish.

jablur (**jablir°**). 1(-*i*), 2(inf, tr -*i*), 3, 7, 9. Leeward side where there is no wind; sheltered. *Itok im pād jablurū eḷañnē kwōpiọ.* Come and stay beside me so I can shelter you from wind if you are cold.

jabḷap (**jabḷap**). 1(-*i*), 2, 6(-*i*), 7. Sailing starboard to wind; canoe part, forward part when outrigger is on port side; port tack.

jabneejej (**jabneyejyej**). 2, 7. Cry on someone's shoulder. *Eitok inne im jabneejej tok ñan ña kōn aer kar jab kōjeļāik kake keemem eo.* She came and cried on my shoulder yesterday saying they did not let her know about the birthday party.

jabok (**jabeq**). Archaic. Part.

jaboņke (**jabeņ°kęy**). Dialectal variant of *m̧ōjañūr* (**m̧ejagir**).

jabōļ (**jabeļ**). From Engl. 1(*-i*), 2(inf, tr *-e*), 4, 6(*-i*), 7, 8. Shovel.

jabōm̧ (**jabęm̧**). Variant form of *podem.*

jabōn (**jaben**). From "construct form of *jab* as in *jabar* (**jabhar**), *jablik*, *jablap*, *jablọk* (**jablaq**)". 7, 9. Point; corner; at the end of; extreme; tip of.

jabōn (**jaben**). From Engl. *serpent.* 6(*-i*). Serpent; snake; viper.

jabōn pe (**jaben pęy**). Stick for stirring fire, turning breadfruit while cooking, etc.

Jabōn-bok (**jaben-beq**). From *jabōn* (**jaben**) "edge of", *bok* (**beq**) "sand". 3, 6(*-i*). A plant, *Pandanus fischerianus* cultigen.

jabōnke (**jabenkęy**). Dial. E only; see *m̧ōjañūr* (**m̧ejagir**). A fish, porcupine fish, *Diodon hystrix.*

jabōnkōnnaan (**jabenkennahan**). 4, 6(*-i*). Proverb; saying.

jabōt (**jabet**). 6(*-i*). Shepherd. *Jabōtin Ijdiiel ro raar lo iju eo.* The shepherds from Israel saw the star.

Jabōt (**jabet**). From Engl. Sunday; the Sabbath.

Jabroñjake (**jabreg°jakey**). From *jab* (**jab**) "not", *roñjake* (**reg°jakey**) "listen". A plant, pandanus cultigen.

Jabtōkā (**jabtekay**). 3, 6(*-i*). A plant, pandanus cultigen.

jabuk (**jabiq**). 1(*-i*), 2(inf, tr *-i*), 4, 7. Fishing method, using long net at day time along reef ridge. *Ļōm̧aro raņ rej jabuk* lik. The men are fishing by the *jabuk* method on the ocean side. *Kom̧wij etal ke in jabuki baruun merā eņ ej lọklọk ioon pedped?* Are you going to use the *jabuk* method and catch the school of fish feeding on the reef?

jabwatōr (**jabwater**). Variant form of *jebwatōr* (**jebwater**).

jabwe (**jabey**). 1(*-i*), 2, 3, 8. Not enough; insufficient; meager (see *bwe* (**bey**)). *Ejabwe m̧ōñā eo.* The food is insufficient.

jabwe (**jabey**). Also *jabwi* (**jabiy**). Archaic. Tip of; end of; point of; old form of *jabōn.*

jabwea (**jabeyah**). Archaic. Get ready for battle.

jabwi (**jabiy**). Archaic. Taboo.

jabwi. See *jabwe.*

jabwilbwil (**jabilbil**). 1(*-i*), 2, 3(inf *kōjjabwilbwil*, tr *kōjabwil(i)*), 5(*jjabwilbwil*), 7. Roll back and forth. *Kwōn jab jabwilbwil ioon bok kaņe bwe kwōnaaj bokbok.* Don't roll around on the sand there or you'll get all sandy. *Kwōn jab jjabwilbwil ijeņe bwe kwōnaaj ttoon.* Don't roll all over the place there or you'll get dirty (said to baby having tantrum).

jade (**jahdęy**). Tree in which birds roost and defecate; see *edde, de.*

jaidiñ (**jahyidyig**). Also *jāidiñ* (**jayidyig**). From Engl. 1(*-i*), 2, 6(*-i*), 7. Siren. *Jaidiñin jino jerbal eo in ejañ.* The siren for starting work is blowing.

jaij (**jahyij**). Also *jāij* (**jayij**). From Engl. 1(*-i*), 2(inf, tr *-i*), 6(*-i*). Size. *Ekōjaij Oļka.* Olga is a doll.

jaike (**jahyikey**). Also *jāike* (**jayikey**). 1(*-i*), 2, 3, 6(*-i*), 8, 9. Scarcity of fish (see *ike* (**yikey**)).

jain (**jahyin**). From Engl. 2(inf, tr *-i*), 4, 6(*-i*). Sign; endorse. *Kwōj aikuj jaini jāāk ņe bwe ren maroñ kōļļāiki.* You must endorse the check before it can be cashed.

jain (**jahyin**). Variant form of *jañin* (**jahgin**).

Jaina (**jahyinah**). Variant form of *Jeina* (**jęyinah**).

jaintiij (**jahyintiyij**). From Engl. 2(inf, tr *-i*), 6(*-i*), 7, 8, 9. Scientist. *Ej jaintiiji ļọk ñane.* He's explaining it scientifically to him.

jaja (**jahjah**). 1, 2, 3(inf, tr *-ik*), 4, 5(*jjaja*), 7, 8. Carry a child on the hip. *Ejjeļọk wōt jjaja in eņ ajri.* That child is always being carried (on the hip). *Jab kajajaik ajri ņe.* Don't carry the child on your hip.

jaja (**jahjah**). 2, 6(*-i*). Keeping a ball in the air by kicking (*anidep* (**haniydep**)). *Eto an jaja bọọļ eo.* The ball remained in the air for a long time.

jaje (**jahjęy**). Dial. W only; see *ñak* (**gak**). 1(-*i*), 2, 3(inf, tr -*ik*), 4, 8, 9. Not know. *Ijaje ia eo ear ilọk ñan e.* I don't know where he went.

jaje kuṇaa- (**jahjęy qiṇaha-**). 1, 2. Thoughtless.

jaje ḷōmṇak (**jahjęy ḷemṇak**). 1(-*i*), 2, 6(-*i*), 7, 8, 9. Illogical; not able to reason; inconsiderate. *Ibūroṃōj kōn an jaje ḷōmṇak.* I'm so sorry for his inability to reason. *Rōjaje ḷōmṇak.* They are inconsiderate.

jajeḷọkjeṇ (**jahjęyḷaqjeṇ**). 1(-*i*), 2, 3, 4, 7, 9. Ignorant; silly; innocent; unconscious. *Edik im ejajeḷọkjeṇ.* He is young and innocent. *Rijajeḷọkjeṇ.* Uneducated person. *Ijab metak kōn aō kar jajeḷọkjeṇ.* It didn't hurt because I was unconscious.

jak (**jak**). Part of a net. *Jaklōñ.* Top part of net. *Jaklaḷ.* Bottom part of net.

jak (**jak**). Archaic. Killed in battle.

jakapen (**jakapen**). Also *jekapen* (**jekapen**). 1(-*i*), 2, 3, 5(*jjekapenpen*), 7, 8, 9. Less than half full. *Aolep ni jekaro kaṇ im jjekapenpen.* The bottles on all those coconut trees being tapped for sap are all less than half full. *Ejakapen aebōj jimeeṇ e.* This cistern is less than half full.

jake (**jahkey**). 2+7, 7, 7+8. Give (polite form); hand over; offer; hold out, as a baby for another to take; grant; transitive form of *jjaak* (**jjahak**). *Kwōn jake ḷọk ḷọk ajri ṇe.* Hurry up and hand that child over. *Jaketok ṃōk niññiñ ṇe.* Would you please let me hold the baby?

jake (**jahkey**). Not in line; uneven, as racing canoes. Place the lee canoe more ahead than the windward one at the start so as not to be backwinded.

jake jibwil (**jahkey jibil**). Also *jake jebōl* (**jahkey jębęl**). Idiom. From *jake* (**jahkey**) "pass", *jibwil* (**jibil**) "molded arrowroot starch". Be considerate of others; cooperative. *Koṃwin jake jibwil eo im letok peimi.* Be considerate and give us a helping hand.

jakeiie (**jakęyiyyęy**). 1(-*i*), 2, 4, 7, 8, 9. Not strong; not useful; not serviceable (see *keiie* (**kęyiyyęy**)).

jaketo-jaketak (**jahkeytęw-jahkeytak**). Distribute; pass something around; share.

jaki (**jakiy**). 6(-*i*). Mat.

jakile (**jakiley**). 1(-*i*), 2, 7. Not recognize (see *kile* (**kiley**)).

jakimej (**jakimęj**). Variant form of *jakimuur* (**jakimiwir**).

jakimuur (**jakimiwir**). Also *jakimej* (**jakimęj**). 1(-*i*), 2, 8. Unproductive coconut tree (see *kimuur* (**kimiwir**)). *Eḷap an jakimuur niin wāto in.* The coconut trees on this tract are not productive.

jakkijeje (**jakkijęyjęy**). 1(-*i*), 2, 3, 4, 8, 9. Seldom tire (see *kkijeje* (**kkijęyjęy**)).

jakkōl (**jakkęl**). Also *jakkōlkōl* (**jakkęlkęl**). 1(-*i*), 2, 3, 4, 5(*jakkōlkōl*), 7+5, 8, 9. Not scare easily (see *kkōl* (**kkęl**)); reckless. *Ejakkōlkōl ḷeeṇ.* He isn't scared easily. He's reckless.

jakkōlkōl (**jakkęlkęl**). 2, 3. Unrecognizable; disguised.

jakkōlkōl (**jakkęlkęl**). Slang. 2, 3, 6(-*i*). Women's panties. *Kwaar wia ia jakkōlkōl.* Where did you buy panties?

jakkurere. See *jọkkurere.*

jakkutkut. See *jọkkutkut.*

jakkūk (**jakkik**). 2, 3(inf, tr -*i*), 6(-*i*), 8, 9. Not biting, of fish (see *kūk* (**kik**)). *Eḷap an jakkūk iarin ānin.* The fish are not biting in the lagoon off this islet.

jakkūramen (**jakkirahmen**). From Engl. 6(-*i*). Sacrament. *Jakkūramenin Peptaij.* The Sacrament of Baptism.

jakkwikwi. See *jọkkwikwi.*

jakmeej (**jakmeyej**). 1(-*i*), 2, 3(inf, tr -*e*), 5(*jjakmeejej*), 6(-*i*), 7, 8, 9. Brunette; darkskinned. *Ireel ippān jakmeej eṇ.* I'm hung up on that dark beauty.

jako (**jakęw**). 1(-*i*), 2, 3(inf, tr -*uk*), 5(*jjakoko*), 7(*jakoḷọk*). Gone; missing; lost; away; vanish; evaporate; disappear; out; pass away; dead; vanished; absent. *Ejako pinjeḷ eo aō.* My pencil is missing. *Ia ṇe kwaar jjakoko ie.* Where have you been that I haven't seen you for so long? *Ejako.* He's away. *Kwōj kab nāj jako ak kiiō.* You're definitely finished this time.

jakoṇ. See *jọkoṇ.*

jakoṇkoṇ. See *jọkoṇkoṇ.*

jakōl (**jakęl**). 2, 4, 6(-*i*), 8, 9, 11(*jakōl*). Unattractive;

uncoordinated in dancing (see *kōl* (**kẹl**)); sloppy; clumsy; rude. *Kwōn jab jakōl.* Don't be clumsy.

jakōḷ (**jakeḷ**). From Engl. *shackle*. 2(inf, tr *-e*), 6(*-i*). Handcuffs; shackles. *Raar jakōḷe rūkọọt eo.* They handcuffed the thief.

Jakōmen (**jakemen**). Also *Jakmen* (**jakmen**). 3, 6(*-i*). A plant, pandanus cultigen (Takeuchi).

jakur. See *jọkur.*

jalen (**jahlen**). Single, unmarried. *Ejalen lieṇ.* She's unmarried. *Ejalen men e.* This thing is by itself.

jalenpā (**jahlenpay**). 2(inf, *tr-ik(i)*), 3, 4, 6(*-i*), 7. Singlehanded; use one hand. *Jab jalenpāik(i) niñniñ ṇe bwe emaroñ wōtlọk.* Don't carry that baby with one hand because you might drop it.

jalōb (**jahlẹb**). 5(*jjalōblōb*). Shallow pool on reef. *Lale ek eṇ ilo jalōb eṇ.* Look at the fish in that pool. *Eḷap an jjalōblōb likin ānin.* There are lots of pools on the ocean side of this islet.

jalōb (**jahlẹb**). 1(*-i*), 2(inf, tr *-e, jalibwe*). Barb. *Kwōn jalōbe kāāj ṇe.* Make a barb on your hook.

jaḷ (**jaḷ**). Also *jāl* (**jal**). 2, 3, 6(*-i*), 7. To face (with directional). *Ej jaḷtok.* He's facing me. *Kōjaḷtoke.* Make it face me. *Kwōn jaḷḷọk.* Face the other way.

jaḷiia (**jahḷiyyah**). 1(*-i*), 2, 3, 8, 9. Hard to turn (see *jaḷiie* (**jahḷiyyẹy**)). *Ejaaḷiia wa eṇ.* This canoe is hard to turn.

jaḷiia (**jahḷiyyah**). 3, 6(*-i*). A fish, scavenger, *Lethrinus miniatus.*

jaḷiie (**jahḷiyyẹy**). 1(*-i*), 2, 3, 8, 9. Easy to turn (see *jaḷiia* (**jahḷiyyah**)).

jaḷjaḷ (**jaḷjaḷ**). 1(*-i*), 2(inf, tr *jeḷate, jeḷati*), 3, 4, 5(*jaḷjaḷate*), 7, 8, 10(*mejaḷ*). Loosen; unwind; unsnarl; take apart. *Kwōn jeḷate ṃōk to ṇe.* Please unsnarl that string. *Ḷōṃaro rōmoot in jaḷjaḷ injin.* The men went to take the engine apart. *Emōj aer jaḷjaḷate injin eo.* They have taken the engine apart carelessly. *Jeḷate korak in juuj ṇe.* Loosen your shoestring.

jaḷḷọk (**jaḷḷaq**). Variant form of *jeḷḷọk* (**jeḷḷaq**).

jaḷtak (**jaḷtak**). Also *jeltak* (**jẹltak**). 1(*-i*), 2, 3, 7. Facing east.

jaḷtok (**jaḷteq**). 2(inf, tr *-e*), 6(*-i*). Adze. *Inaaj jaḷtoke ḷọk ijeṇe enana ilo jouj ṇe.* I'll use the adze and whittle off the bad part of the canoe bottom.

jaṃ (**jaṃ**). 2(inf, tr *-e*), 4, 6(*-i*), 7. Kick. *Jaṃe bọọḷ ṇe.* Kick that ball.

jaṃ (**jaṃ**). Slang. 2(inf, tr *-e*), 4, 6(*-i*), 7. Steal; pilfer; swipe. *Ijaje jaṃ men rot ṇe.* I never learned how to steal that kind of thing. *Kwaar jaṃe ia?* Where did you swipe it from?

jaṃbo (**jaṃbẹw**). From Japn. *sanpo* "walk, stroll". 1(*-i*), 2, 3, 4, 5(*jjaṃbobo*), 7. Hike; travel on a vacation; go away for a change of scene; saunter; excursion; ramble; stroll; walk aimlessly. *Rōjaṃbo tọḷọk ñan Ḷora.* They are hiking westward to Laura. *Ejjaṃbobo jar eṇ.* That couple is always vacationing.

jaṃbōḷ (**jaṃbeḷ**). From Engl. 2(inf, tr *-e*), 6(*-i*). Sample.

jaṃjaṃ (**jaṃjaṃ**). 1(*-i*), 2(inf, tr *-e*), 3(st inf *kōjaṃjaṃ*), 8. Desire more, of a delicious food, music, or game; not satisfied; want more. *Ijaṃjaṃe ek eo.* I want more of that fish. *Ijaṃjaṃe kkure eo.* I want to watch the game some more. *Ekadik kōjaṃjaṃ kōl ko nājin.* His ways were such that people never tired of seeing or listening to him.

jaṃlik (**jaṃlik**). 2(inf, tr *-i*), 4, 6(*-i*). Backkick in kickball. *Epen jaṃlik ñe kwōj jab kamminene.* It's hard to back-kick if you don't practice.

jaṃṃōk (**jaṃṃek**). From *ṃōk* (**ṃek**) "please". 3. Please show it to me; let's see. *Kōjaṃṃōk nuknuk ṇe aṃ.* Show me your clothes.

jaṃṃōṇōṇō (**jaṃṃeṇehṇeh**). 1, 2, 3(inf, tr *-ūk*), 4, 6(*-i*), 8, 9. Sour faced; a kill-joy; straightlaced.

jaṃōṇ (**jaṃeṇ**). From Engl. 3, 2(inf, tr *-e*), 5(*jjaṃōṇṃōṇ*), 6(*-i*). A fish, salmon. *Bwiin jjaṃōṇṃōṇ.* Smell of salmon. *Jenaaj jaṃōṇe raij e bwe en nnọ.* We'll mix salmon with the rice to make it tasty.

jaṃōṇōṇō (**jaṃeṇehṇeh**). 1(*-i*), 2, 3, 4, 8, 9. Not interesting (see *ṃōṇōṇō* (**ṃeṇehṇeh**)). *Ejaṃōṇōṇō bade eo.* The party was uninteresting.

jaṃōñā (**jaṃegay**). From *jab* (**jab**) "not" *ṃōñā* (**ṃegay**) "eat". 2, 8, 9. Not biting, of fish. (See *ṃōñā* (**ṃegay**)). *Ejaṃōñā kōn an liṃ.* The fish aren't biting on account of the murky water.

jaṃtiltil (**jaṃtiltil**). 2(inf, tr *-i*), 4, 6(*-i*). A move in game of checkers whereby one jump captures many pieces. *Kōjparok aṃ kkure ippān bwe rijaṃtiltil eo ṇe.* Be careful how you play checkers with him because he's a champion.

Jaṃuwa (**jahṃiwwah**). 4. Place name; Samoa.

jaṇtōj (**jaṇtej**). From Engl. Sentence.

jañ (**jag**). 1(*-i*), 2(inf, tr *jañūt(i)*), 3, 5(*jjañjañ*), 6(*-i*), 7, 8. Cry; play music on radio or phonograph; lament; mourn; weep; wail. *Kwōn kōjañ alin kaubowe kaṇe.* Play those cowboy songs (on the phonograph). *Etke ejañ ajri eṇ.* Why is the child crying? *Ejjañjañ ajri eṇ.* That baby is always crying. *Wōn ṇe kwōj jañūti.* Who are you crying for? *Jedike kain eṇ ejjañjañ.* We don't like cry-babies. *Kwaar roñ ke jañin jāidiiñ eo?* Did you hear the siren wail?

jañai (**jahgahyiy**). Boom; used as onomatopoeia for explosive sound.

jañij (**jagij**). 3, 4+3, 5(*-i*), 6(*-i*), 5+7, 5+8, 5+9. A fish, jellyfish.

jañin (**jahgin**). Also *jain* (**jahyin**). 2. Not yet; never. *Ejjañin itok.* He hasn't come yet. *Ij jañin ṃwijbar.* I didn't get a haircut yet.

jañin kkaan (**jahgin kkahan**). Intact; unused. *Joñan eo ej jañin kkaan ṇe.* That's the unused portion of it.

jañiñi (**jahgiygiy**). 6(*-i*). Sleeping mat.

jañnuwaad (**jagniwwahad**). Also *jañinuwaad.* 1(*-i*), 2(inf, tr *-e*), 3, 4, 7. Lonesome; yearn for; long for; wait for anxiously. *Ij jañnuwaade tok eok.* I am lonesome for you.

jaññiñi (**jaggiygiy**). 1(*-i*), 2, 3, 4, 8, 9. Slow to anger in debate (see *ññiñi* (**ggiygiy**)).

jaññōr (**jagger**). 1, 2(inf, tr *-e*), 6(*-i*). Canvas drop; windbreak. *Kwōn jaññōre.* Make a canvas-drop there.

jañūt (**jagit**). Transitive form of *jañ* (**jag**).

jao (**jahwew**). Archaic. 2, 6(*-i*). Light birthmark.

jar (**jar**). 1(*-i*), 2(inf, tr *-e*), 3, 4, 5(*jjarjar*), 7, 8. Pray; go to church. *Alin jar.* Hymn. *Iṃōn jar.* Church. *Eḷap an jjarjar rōplen eo.* The reverend is always praying. *Jen jar.* Let us pray.

jar (**jar**). 6(*-i*). Crowd; any group of people, as a class, unit or division. *Jarin tariṇae.* Army. *Jarin kōjañjañ.* Band, orchestra. *Jarin kadduojḷọk.* Graduating class.

jar (**jar**). 1(*-i*), 2, 3(st inf *kōjjarjar,* tr *kōjar*), 5(*jjarjar*), 6(*-i*), 7. Split; torn off; broke, out of money. *Lale ejar aḷaḷ ṇe.* Look out, that piece of wood might split. *Ejar peiū.* My hand is scratched. *Ilukkuun jar.* I am really broke. *Ejjarjar aḷaḷ ṇe.* That piece of wood is always splitting off. *Taij ekadik kōjjarjar.* Crap shooting is expensive. *Lio ear kōjjarjar nuknuk ko.* The lady spread the clothes out to dry. *Keem eo elukkuun kōjare eō.* The game left me busted. *Wūliaṃ ej make wōt jjarjar.* William is always broke.

jar eke (**jar yẹkẹy**). 1(*-i*), 2, 3, 6(*-i*). Varicose veins.

jar ṃajeḷ (**jar ṃajeḷ**). 1(*-i*), 2, 3, 6(*-i*). Flexed muscles. *Ejar ṃajeḷin ḷeeṇ.* He's flexed his muscles.

jarin kōjeraaṃṃan (**jarin kejerahaṃṃan**). Idiom. Benediction. *Wōn enaaj kōṃṃane jarin kōjeraaṃṃan eo?* Who will give the benediction?

jarin kōtḷọk (**jarin ketḷaq**). From *jar* (**jar**) "pray", *kōtḷọk* (**ketḷaq**) "release". 2(inf, tr *-e*), 6(*-i*). Excommunicate. *Raar jarin kōtḷọke kōn an koba waan.* They excommunicated him for promiscous cohabitation.

jarjar (**jarjar**). 1(*-i*), 2(inf, tr *jarōk(e)*), 3, 4, 7, 8. Raise fish net from water; take coconut husks from water after soaking to make sennit; draft (fishing); start a song. *Enañin jarjar ke ok eo?* Hasn't the net been taken from the water yet? *Kwōn jarōk ok ṇe.* Take that net out of the water. *Wōn enaaj jarōk al eo?* Who'll start the song?

jarkaju (**jarkajiw**). Variant form of *jedkaju* (**jedkajiw**).

Jarkul (**jarqil**). Name of a navigational sign; a giant shark.

jarlepju (**jarlepjiw**). Also *jāllepju* (**jallepjiw**). 1(*-i*), 3, 6(*-i*), 8. Large crowd; majority; mob; throng; multitude; in the public eye; congregation; society.

jarleplep (**jarleplep**). Also *jālleplep* (**jalleplep**), *jelleplep* (**jelleplep**). 1(*-i*), 2, 3(inf, tr *-e*), 4, 6(*-i*), 7. Fall on one's back; lie on one's back with no regard to surroundings or people. *Ear jālleplep nabōjān m̧ōn m̧upi eo.* He lay face up outside the movie theatre. *Ekajjookok an jālleplep bul̦ōn armej ro.* He made a spectacle of himself lying face up in the crowd. *Ripālle eo ej jarleplep im al̦kōjeje.* The American is lying on his back and sunbathing.

jarom (**jar°em**). 1(-*i*), 2(inf, tr -*e*), 3, 4, 5(*jjaromrom*), 6(-*i*), 7. Electricity; lightning; electric shock; punch; hit. *Lale toon jarom n̗e ejarome eok.* Watch out that you don't get a shock from that cord. *El̦ap an jjaromrom buñūnin.* There's lots of lightning this evening. *Jab keroro bwe kwōnāj jarom.* You'd better shut up or get punched.

jarōb (**jareb**). Dial. W only; see *m̧ōkaj* (**m̧ekaj**). Also *jerab* (**jerab**). 1(-*i*), 2, 7, 8. Quickly; hurry up (with directional). *Kwōn jarōb tok.* Hurry and come here. *Jarōbl̦ok.* Go quickly.

jarōj (**jarej**). Tiny bumps on glans penis.

jarōjrōj (**jarejrej**). Slow to lose temper.

jarōk (**jarek**). Transitive form of *jarjar* (**jarjar**).

jarroñroñ (**jarreg°reg°**). 1(-*i*), 2, 3, 4, 8, 9. Deaf; unable to hear (see *roñ* (**reg°**)).

jarrōñrōñ (**jarręgręg**). Sexually impotent (male) (see *rrōñ* (**rręg**)).

jaruk (**jariq**). 2(inf, tr -*i*), 3, 8. Reanimate; restore; revive; resurrect; resuscitate; safe.

jat (**jat**). Deep water.

jat (**jat**). Archaic. Surface, sod. *Ium̧win jat.* Submerged.

jata (**jahtah**). From Engl. *charter.* 2(inf, tr -*ik*), 4, 6(-*i*). Rent; charter; borrow. *Ear jataik juon kaar.* He rented a car. *Ear jata kake wa eo waō.* He borrowed my boat.

jatak (**jatak**). Wave ready to break.

jatal̦e (**jatal̦ęy**). 1(-*i*), 2, 3, 4, 8, 9. Lacking sex appeal (see *tal̦e* (**tal̦ęy**)).

jatāāñ (**jatayag**). 1(-*i*), 2, 3, 4, 8, 9. Lacking sex appeal; coconut tree that cannot give more fresh toddy (see *tāāñ* (**tayag**)).

jatbo (**jatbew**). 1(-*i*), 2, 3, 5(*jjatbobo*). Smell of damp clothing.

jatdik (**jatdik**). 1(-*i*), 2, 3, 4, 6(-*i*), 7. Deceptively; surprisingly; having hidden qualities; trying. *Ejatdik an m̧ōkaj wa en̗.* That canoe is deceptively fast. *Ejatdik wōt eo jem̧nājin.* That was a trying exam.

jati (**jatiy**). 2(inf, tr -*ik*), 3, 6(-*i*). Duty that an older sibling is expected to give to younger siblings. *Ij jatiik eok jān kiiō im etal.* From now on you're my younger sibling. *Jatiin riM̧ajel̦.* Marshallese way of caring for younger siblings.

jati- (**jati-**). 1. Younger sibling; younger brother; younger sister; younger cousin (parallel).

jatiin (**jahtiyin**). From Engl. 3, 6(-*i*). Sardines.

jatiraito (**jahtiyrahyitęw**). From Japn. *saachiraito* (from Engl. *searchlight*). 2(inf, tr -*ik*), 4, 6(-*i*), 7. Searchlight; beacon. *Rej jatiraitoiki bal̦uun eo.* They're using a searchlight to search for the airplane.

jatloñ (**jatleg°**). 2. Unfavorable tide, neither high nor low. *Enana ñan eo̧ñōd kiiō bwe ejatloñ.* It's not good to go fishing at this time because the tide is not favorable.

jato (**jahtęw**). Dial. E, W: *jaap* (**jahap**). 3, 6(-*i*). A fish, *Lutjanus gibbus.*

jato (**jatew**). Not rain. *Ejato kiiō.* The rain is over.

jatokwōj (**jateqej**). 1(-*i*), 2, 3, 8, 9, 11(*jatokwōj*). Fire starting slowly; not ignited easily (see *tokwōj* (**teqej**)). *Ejatokwōj al̦al̦ n̗e.* That piece of wood is hard to burn. *Ejatokwōj mājet kā.* These matches are hard to light. *Ejatokwōj injin eiō.* This engine does not start easily.

jatol̦ (**jahtel̦°**). 1(-*i*), 2(inf, tr -*e*), 3, 4, 7. Grope; explore. *Emarok im iar jatol̦e aō etal.* It was dark and I felt my way.

jatōk (**jatek**). 1(-*i*), 2, 3, 8. Salty; not sweet, of beverages. *Ejatōk ni n̗e.* That coconut is not sweet.

jatōltōl (**jateltel**). Also *jjatōltōl* (**jjateltel**). 1(-*i*), 2(inf, tr -*e*), 3, 7, 8, 9, 11(*jatōltōl*). Shiny; brilliant; polish (with causative prefix). *El̦ap an jjatōltōl juuj kan̗e am̧.* Your shoes are very shiny. *Kōjjatōltōli juuj kan̗e am̧.* Polish your shoes.

jatōptōp (**jateptep**). Surrender, give up.

jatōr (**jater**). 1(-*i*), 2, 3, 4, 8, 9, 11(*jatōr*). Not greedy (see *tōr* (**ter**)).

jatpe (**jatpey**). 1, 2, 3(inf, tr *-ik*), 6(*-i*), 8, 9, 11(*jatpe*). Clumsy; awkward. *Ejatpe lieṇ ilo eb.* She's clumsy in dancing. *Kwōjatpeḷọk jān ña.* You're more awkward than I.

jattapepe (**jattapẹypẹy**). Vulgar. 1(*-i*), 2, 3, 4, 8, 9, 11(*jattapepe*). Not have intercourse often (see *tape* (**tapẹy**)).

jattutu (**jattiwtiw**). 1(*-i*), 2, 3, 4, 7, 8, 9, 11(*jattutu*). Seldom bathe (see *tutu* (**tiwtiw**)).

Jatūrwe (**jatirwey**). 3, 6(*-i*). A plant, pandanus cultigen (Takeuchi).

jauñ. See *jọuñ.*

jauwi. See *jọuwi.*

jauwōta. See *jọuwōta.*

jawiia. See *jọwiia.*

jawiie. See *jọwiie.*

jawōd (**jahwed**). 1, 2(inf, tr *-e*), 3, 4, 5(*jjawōdwōd*), 6(*-i*), 7. Girl hunting; seduce; woo. *Ear jawōde juon leddik.* He seduced a girl. *Likao eṇ ejjawōdwōd.* The young man is always girl-hunting.

jawōtwōt. See *jọwōtwōt.*

jā (**jay**). 1(*-i*), 2, 3, 8. Eye cataract; membrane; hymen. *Juon ṇe jā ejino waḷọk mejaṃ.* A cataract is starting to form on your eye.

jā (**jay**). 1(*-i*), 2, 3(inf, tr *-ik*), 5(*jjājā*), 7, 8. Windward overlay of sail. *Ejā wa eo.* The sail of the canoe is falling (toward the outrigger). *Wa eo ejjājā eṇ.* The sail of that canoe is always falling (toward the outrigger).

jā (**jay**). 6(*-a*). Contents of newborn's intestines.

jā (**jay**). Thick cloud formation of cumulus type covering a large portion of the sky.

jāāk (**jayak**). From Engl. *check*. 6(*-i*). Check, money order.

jāāk (**jayak**). 2(inf, tr *-e*), 4, 5(*jjāākāk*), 6(*-i*). Check; examine. *Rōnaaj jāāke peet kaṇ buñniin.* They'll have a bed check tonight. *Ej jāākāk waj eṇ.* The guard is always checking or rechecking.

jāāk (**jayak**). Fishing method, using diving mask and fishline outside.

jāāk (**jayak**). 2(inf, tr *-e*). To jack up something. *Ej jāāke tūrak eṇ.* He's jacking up the truck.

jāāk. See *jjāāk.*

jāāl (**jayal**). Transitive form of *jjāāl* (**jjayal**).

jāālel (**jayalyẹl**). Waft. *Nemān ta in ej jāāleltok?* What is this smell wafting this way?

jāān (**jayan**). From Engl. 6(*-i*). Cent(s); money; finance; fund.

jāān dekā (**jayan dekay**). From *jāān* (**jayan**) "cent", *dekā* (**dekay**) "stone". Coin. *Kwōn jab kattōñtōñi jāān dekā kaṇe bwe jouwaroñ.* Stop clinking those coins because we're annoyed by the noise.

jāānkun (**jayanqin**). 1(*-i*), 2(inf, tr *-i*), 3, 4, 5(*jjāānkunkun*), 6(*-i*). A food, dried overripe breadfruit; in Ralik Chain, dried pandanus paste. *Ejjāānkunkun nuknuk ṇe aṃ.* Your clothes are covered with *jāānkun*.

jāānwūj (**jayanwij**). From Engl. 1(*-i*), 2(inf, tr *-i*), 4, 5(*jjāānwūjwūj*), 6(*-i*), 7. Sandwich.

jāār (**jayar**). 2(inf, tr *-e*), 6(*-i*), 7. A food, method of cooking fish: take fish eggs (roe) out and squeeze on fish and cook half done.

jād (**jad**). 6(*-i*). Platform for drying copra; rack.

jādbūtbūt (**jadbitbit**). Variant form of *jādbūtūktūk* (**jadbitiktik**).

jādbūtūktūk (**jadbitiktik**). Also *jādbūtbūt* (**jadbitbit**), *jjādbūtbūt.* 1(*-i*), 2, 3, 7. Spray; wet with spray. *Ia in ej jādbūtūktūk tok?* Where is that spray coming from?

jāde (**jadẹy**). 1(*-i*), 2, 3(inf *kōjjādede,* tr *kōjādeik*), 5(*jjādede*), 7. Appear; show; be in sight. *Ine ko kaṇ ejjādede mejāer.* Some of those seeds are beginning to sprout. *Kwōn jab kōjjādede bwe kwe leddik.* Don't show yourself in public too much for you're a girl. *Wa eo eṇ ejāde.* The ship's in sight.

Jādede (**jadeydey**). From Engl. 3. Saturday. *Kōjeañ kōJādede em kōppojak ñan ilju.* Let's do our Saturday chores and prepare for tomorrow.

jādeiaarḷap (**jadẹyyiyaharḷap**). Variant form of *jerakiaarḷap* (**jerakyiyaharḷap**).

jādipen (**jadiypẹn**). 1(*-i*), 2, 3, 4, 8, 9. Not strong physically (see *dipen* (**diypẹn**)).

jādṃūṃ (**jadṃiṃ**). 6(*-i*). A bird, sleeps in holes, similar to *pejwak.*

jāibo (**jayibew**). Also *jaibo* (**jahyibew**). 1(-*i*), 2(inf, tr -*ik(i)*), 3, 4, 5(*ijāibobo*), 6(-*i*), 7, 8, 9. A food, unleavened dough cooked by boiling; dumpling. *Iijoļ jāibo.* I want to eat *jāibo*. *Ejjāibobo nuknuk kaņe aṃ.* Your clothes have scraps of dumplings on them.

jāibo (**jayibew**). 3, 5(*ijāibobo*), 6(-*i*), 3+7. Sea cucumber, *Holothuroidea*, *Opheodesoma*; found close to shore at low tide, soft, light in color, two cm. in diameter and ca. 30 cm. in length; eel-like in appearance; edible. *Ejjāibobo arin Arņo.* There are lots of *jāibo* along the lagoon shores of Arno.

jāik (**jayik**). Transitive form of *jjā* (**jjay**).

jāike (**jayikey**). 2, 3(inf, tr -*ik*), 6(-*i*), 8, 9. Not many fish, of a place (see *ek* (**yẹk**)). *Ejāike wōd jab in.* This particular coral head hasn't got many fish.

Jāipaan (**jayipahan**). From Engl. 4. Place name; Saipan.

jāiur (**jayir°**). Also *jaiur* (**jahyir°**). 2, 3(inf, tr -*i*), 6(-*i*), 8, 9, 11(*jāiur*). Not fast; slow; not quick (see *iur* (**yir°**)). *Kwōn jab jāiur bwe jenaaj ruṃwij.* Don't be slow or we'll be late.

jāiurjet (**jayir°jẹt**). Also *jaiurjet* (**jahyir°jẹt**). 1(-*i*), 2, 3(inf, tr -*e*), 6(-*i*), 8, 9. Not speedy; not fast; not quick in action (see *iurjet* (**yir°jẹt**)).

jāj (**jaj**). A fish, snapper, *Lutjanus flavipes.*

jāj (**jaj**). From Engl. 2, 6(-*i*), 7. Judge.

jāje (**jayjẹy**). 2(inf, tr -*ik*), 6(-*i*). Long knife; sword; machete; bayonet. *Jājeik tok juon kimej.* Cut a coconut frond for me with a machete.

jājiṃaat (**jajiṃahat**). 2, 3(inf, tr -*e*), 6(-*i*), 8, 9, 11(*jājiṃaat*). Not smart; dull; not clever (see *jiṃaat* (**jiṃahat**)). *Ijājiṃaat jān kwe.* I'm not as smart as you are.

jājiniet (**jajiniyẹt**). Also *jājineet* (**jajineyet**). 1(-*i*), 2, 3, 4, 7, 8, 9. Unacquainted (see *jiniet* (**jiniyẹt**)). *Ijājiniet in itoitak eoon ānin.* I don't know my way around this island.

jājjāj (**jajjaj**). 1, 2(inf, tr *jājek*), 4, 6(-*i*), 7, 8, 9. Boast; boastful; brag about one's self; egotism; show-off; pompous. *Jab jājjāj kake lieņ pāleṃ.* Don't boast about your wife. *Eļap aṃ jājek eok.* You boast too much. *Likao eņ ejājeke.* He's boastful.

jājjāj (**jajjaj**). 2, 3(*kōjjājjāj, kōjājjāj*), 4, 6(-*i*), 7. Skip; skim across a surface; ski; skid; ricochet. *Ijeļā jājjāj ioon dān.* I know how to water-ski. *Kōjājjāje dekā kaņe.* Skip those stones over the water. *Ear jājjāj tok im okjak otobai eo waan.* His motorcycle skidded and fell over.

jājjiñjiñ (**jajjigjig**). 1(-*i*), 2, 3, 4, 8, 9. Not break wind often (see *jiñ* (**jig**)).

jājjookok (**jajjewekwek**). 1(-*i*), 2, 3, 4, 8, 9. Hard to embarrass (see *jjookok* (**jjewekwek**)); shameless.

jājjō (**jajjẹh**). 1(-*i*), 2, 3, 4, 5(*jājjōjō*), 8, 9. Not nauseated easily; having strong stomach (see *jjō* (**jjẹh**)); not squeamish. *Ejājjō ļeeņ.* He isn't easily nauseated. *Ejājjōjō ļeeņ.* He's never nauseated by anything.

jājļọk (**jajḷaq**). 1(-*i*), 2, 3, 7. Separate from; slip; glance off. *Rōjaje jājļọk jān doon.* They are inseparable. *Lale bwe kwōn jab jājļọk.* Be careful you don't slip. Be careful you don't get separated (from us).

jāl (**jal**). Variant form of *jaļ*.

jāle (**jalẹy**). Transitive form of *jāljel* (**jaljẹl**).

jāle- (**jalye-**). 1. Sauce; gravy; possessive classifier, sauces; meat course to go with rice or other staple. *Ta ņe jāleṃ?* What do you have for gravy there?

jāleek (**jaleyek**). Transitive form of *jālele* (**jalẹylẹy**).

jālele (**jalẹylẹy**). 1(-*i*), 2(inf, tr *jāleek*), 3, 5(*ijālele*), 6(-*i*), 8. A food, meat course; sauce; gravy. *Ta ņe kwōj jālele?* What are you eating as a meat course? *Kwōn jāleek mā ņe kijeṃ.* Put some sauce on your breadfruit. *Rej ijālele aolep iien.* They always eat sauce with their food.

jāli (**jaliy**). 3, 6(-*i*). Kind of basket.

Jāli (**jaliy**). Also *Bar.* See *Ļāātbwiinbar.* A constellation; lambda, phi 1, phi 2 Orionis.

jāliñiñ (**jalyigyig**). 2, 3(inf, tr -*i*), 6(-*i*), 7. Wrapped around, of string; kink; coil. *Eban tọọr ooj ņe bwe ejāliñiñ.* Water won't come out of the hose because it is kinked. *Jabōn eo ear jāliñiñ ilo ra eo.* The serpent coiled around the branch.

jālirara (**jaliyrahrah**). 2, 3(inf, tr *-ūk, -ik*), 5(*ijālirara*), 6(*-i*). Swing; inertia; flop. *Itipiji im jālirara kōn an iiṃ an itok.* I tripped him and sent him flying because of his tremendous speed.

jālitak (**jaliytak**). 1(*-i*), 2(inf, tr *-e*), 6(*-i*). Bulwark; defense; protection. *Kwōn jālitake kōrā im ajri raṇe jān būñalñalin ṇo.* Put up something to protect the women and children from the sea spray.

jāljel (**jaljẹl**). 1(*-i*), 2(inf, tr *jāle, jāli*), 3, 4, 7, 8. Roll up, as dried pandanus leaves; coil; reel; roll of film. *Rej jāljel maañ.* They are rolling up pandanus leaves. *Rej jāli maañ kaṇ.* They are rolling those pandanus leaves up.

Jāljel (**jaljẹl**). Variant form of *Ḷōmānkoto.*

jāllo (**jallew**). 1(*-i*), 2, 3, 4, 5(*ijāllolo*), 8, 9. Not able to see well (see *llo* (**llew**)).

jāllulu (**jalliwliw**). 1(*-i*), 2, 3, 4, 8, 9. Not angered easily (see *llu* (**lliw**)).

jālōke (**jalẹkẹy**). 1(*-i*), 2, 7, 8, 9. Not believe; not trust in; not depend on (see *lōke* (**lẹkẹy**)); distrust; mistrust.

jālōt (**jalet**). Loose.

jālōt (**jalet**). 1(*-i*), 2, 3, 7, 8, 9. Not well-sifted; not well-cleaned; not thoroughly done (see *lōt* (**let**)). *Ejālōt aṃ rakij meḷaṇ in.* You did not clean up the grounds thoroughly.

jāmeej (**jameyej**). 1(*-i*), 2, 3, 8, 9. Light colored (see *meej* (**meyej**)).

jāmilur (**jamilir°**). 6(*-i*). Mirage, optical illusion, illusion. *Jāmilur bajjek men eo kwaar baab kwaar loe.* It was only a mirage or illusion that you thought you saw.

jāmin (**jamin**). 2. Will not, determination or simple future. *Ijāmin ilọk ñan Jālwōj.* I will never go to Jaluit.

jāmmijakjak (**jammijakjak**). 1(*-i*), 2, 3, 4, 8, 9. Hard to scare; fearless (see *mijak* (**mijak**)).

jāmminene (**jamminẹynẹy**). 1(*-i*), 2, 3, 4, 8, 9. Unaccustomed; inexperienced (see *mminene* (**mminẹynẹy**)).

jāmmourur (**jammẹwirwir**). 2, 3(inf, tr *-i*), 6(*-i*), 7, 8, 9, 11(*jāmourur*). Not lively; sluggish; sickly (see *mour* (**mẹwir**)). *Ejāmmourur kōn an jowan.* He's not lively on account of his laziness.

Jāmne (**jamney**). From Engl. 4. Germany.

jāṃōd (**jayṃed**). 2(inf, tr *-e*), 6(*-i*), 8, 9. Careless; prodigal; unscrupulous; unruly. *Koban teru kōn aṃ jāṃōd.* You won't get anywhere with your unscrupulous behavior.

jān (**jan**). Since; from; than; off. *Ñāāt ṇe kwaar itok jān Ṃajeḷ?* When did you come from the Marshalls? *Jān ñāāt in aṃ pād ānin?* Since when have you been on this islet?

jān (**jan**). 1(*-i*), 2(inf, tr *-e*), 4, 6(*-i*), 7. Snare. *Rej jān bao.* They are snaring birds.

jān (**jan**). 1(*-i*), 2, 4, 5(*jāne*), 8, 9. Skin disease, white spots on body; *Tinea versicolor*; psoriasis. *Eḷap aṃ jāne.* You have a bad case of psoriasis.

jān-aelōñ-ñan-aelōñ (**jan-hayẹlẹg-gan-hayẹlẹg**). From "from island to island". A plant, *Vernocia cinerea* (L.) Less. A weedy Composite herb.

jāndik (**jandik**). Variant form of *jendik* (**jendik**).

jānel (**janyẹl**). 6(*-i*). Canoe part, board that runs lengthwise on the leeside, above the *jouj* (the bottom half). *Epaḷḷọk jānelin wa eo.* The *jānel* on the canoe got torn off.

jānij (**janij**). From Engl. 1(*-i*), 2(inf, tr *-i*), 4, 7. Make change; trade; exchange; swap; switch. *Kwōmaroñ ke jānijitok jāān e?* Can you change this money for me? *Kōjro jānij at bwe edik at e jān bōra.* Let's trade hats because this one is too small for me. *Eor ke jānij ippaṃ?* Have you got any change on you?

jāniknik (**janiknik**). 1(*-i*), 2(inf, tr *-i*), 3, 4, 8, 9. Not perservering (see *niknik* (**niknik**)); not industrious; lazy; neglect. *Ejānikniki ajri eṇ nejin.* She's constantly neglecting her child.

jānindeeo-ñanindeeo (**janyindẹyyew-ganyindẹyyew**). Eternal; everlasting. *Anij Jānindeeo-ñanindeeo.* God Eternal.

jānit (**janit**). 1(*jānti-*), 6(*jāntin*). Finger; claw of crab. *Jāntin barulep.* Claw of a coconut crab.

jānnibadbad (**jannibadbad**). Archaic. Land; birthplace dear and inherited.

jānruk (janriq). 1(-*i*), 2, 3, 8. Sprain. *Ejānruk peiū.* My arm is sprained.

jāntin (jantin). Construct form of *jānit* (janit).

jāntōj (jantej). 6(-*i*). Sentence. *Jete jāntōj ilo pāārokōrāāp ņe?* How many sentences does that paragraph have? *Jāntōjin Iñlij.* An English sentence.

Jānwōde (janwedey). From Engl. January.

jāp (jap). Also *jepā* (jepay), *jepe* (jepey). 1(*jepa-, jepe-*). Cheek.

jāpakij (japakij). Also *jāppakij* (jappakij), *jeppakij* (jeppakij). 1(-*i*), 2, 3, 4, 8, 9. Inability to stay underwater long (see *pakij* (pakij)).

jāpe (japẹy). Dial. E and W; W also *jokmej* (jẹqmẹj). 6(-*i*). A small dug-out bowl for pounding food; wooden bowl; wooden tub.

Jāpe (japẹy). From *jāpe* "bowl". A constellation; stars in Delphinus; alpha, beta, and gamma; ninthborn of *Lōktañūr. Jeban lo Jāpe bwe ekkōdọdo.* We can't see the constellation *Jāpe* because of the heavy overcast.

jāpek (japẹk). A fish.

jāpo (japẹw). In between. *Epād ilo jāpo.* It's in between.

jāppim (jappim). Variant form of *podem* (pẹwdẹm).

jāppiọeo (jappiyawyẹw). 1(-*i*), 2, 3, 8, 9. Not get chilly easily (see *piọ* (piyaw)).

je (jẹy). 1(*jie-*). Belly; stomach; innards. *Emetak jiō.* My stomach hurts. *Kwōmetak je ke?* Do you have a stomach ache?

je (jey). 1(-*i*), 2, 3(inf, tr -*ik*), 4. Avoid because of unfortunate experience; change actions in future; punish (with causative prefix). *Ije in etal eọñōd.* I am not going fishing again (because of what happened last time). *Rōnaaj kajeik kōn an kar kọọt.* They will punish him for his stealing. *Rej kajeik eok bwe kwōn je.* They are punishing you so you won't do it again.

je (jẹy). Variant form of *ije* (yijẹy).

je (jey). Transitive singular form of *jeje* (jẹyjẹy).

jea (jeyah). Also *jeea* (jeyyah). From Engl. 6(-*i*). Chair; bench; pew; seat; bleacher.

jeb- (jeb). To reach; see *jabjab* and *likjab. Ej jeb ioon āneņ.* He reached the island. *Ej jeb i Epoon inne.* It got to Ebon yesterday.

jebake (jebakey). Kind of turtle; beautiful multi-colored shell.

jeballe (jeyballey). To rock something. *Ņo ej jeballe wa eo.* The waves are rocking the boat.

jeban (jẹyban). Head of; at the top of. *Wōn eņ ej jeban jikuuļ.* Who is the Director of Education? *Lale bao eņ ej pād jeban kiju eņ.* Look at the bird on the top of the mast.

jeban (jeban). 1(-*i*), 2, 3, 4, 8, 9. Rich; well supplied with food and property; have it made; affluent. *Kwōmake jeban.* You sure have it made.

jebar (jebar). 2, 3. Sprout, of leaves; produce; bear fruit; originate; flourish; grow; stem from. *Ejino jebar mā ņe.* That breadfruit is beginning to sprout leaves. *Wōn eo ear jebar pepe in jāne?* Who originated that decision?

jebata (jebahtah). Idiom. Interjection: "No wonder!" "It stands to reason." *Jebata wūnin aṃ jorrāān ņe.* No wonder you are in trouble.

jebbar (jebbar). 1(-*a*), 2+1, 6(-*i*), 7. Head part in lying down, as the head of the bed; front half of fish. *Kwōn bōk jebbarin ek ņe.* Take the front half of that fish.

jebbar (jebbar). 1(-*i*), 2(inf, tr -*e*), 4. Behead. *Ļeo eņ rej pojak in jebbare.* They are getting ready to cut off his head. *Raar jebbare Jọọn Peptaij.* They beheaded John the Baptist.

jebbōro (jẹbbẹrẹw). From *jep* "cut, bōro* "throat, heart". 2(inf, tr -*ik*). Steal another's spouse.

jebjeb (jẹbjẹb). 1(-*i*), 2(inf, tr *jibwe*), 4, 5(*jjibjibwe, jibjibwe*), 7, 10(*po*). Seize; hold; capture; grasp; fondle. *Emōj aer jibwe rūkọọt eo.* They have captured the thief. *Rej jebjeb piik.* They are catching pigs. *Kwōn jab jjibjibwe ajri ņe.* Don't fondle that baby all the time.

jebkwanwūjọ (jebqwanwijaw). 1(-*i*), 2(inf, tr -*ik(i)*), 4, 6(-*i*), 7. Coconut oil used for frying. *Jibwe tok mōk jebkwanwūjọ eo ilo pāāntōre ņe.* Could you hand me the coconut oil from the pantry?

jeblaak (jeblahak). 1(-*i*), 2, 3, 4, 5(*jjeblaakak*), 6(-*i*), 7. Go; sail away;

leave. *Wa eo eņ ejeblaak.* The boat has left. *Wa eo ejjeblaakak eņ.* That ship is continually making trips.

jeblokwa- (**jęblęqa-**). Also *jebōlkwa-* (**jębęlqa-**). 1, 2+1, 3+1, 5(*jjebōlǫklǫk, jjebōlkwankwan*), 7. Half; be half full. *Bōk jeblokwan kijeṃ.* Take your half of the food for yourself. *Ejebōlkwan bato eo.* The bottle is half full. *Ejjeblǫklǫk bato kaņ.* Those bottles are all half full.

jeblǫk (**jeblaq**). Variant form of *jablǫk* (**jablaq**).

jebļaak (**jebļahak**). Variant form of *jepļaak* (**jepļahak**).

jebo (**jębęw**). 2, 3(inf, tr *-uk*), 6(*-i*). Tie in a game; a draw. *Erro kkure im jebo.* They played to a draw. *Keem eo inne jebo.* Yesterday's game was a tie.

jebokwōn (**jębęqęn**). 2, 4, 6(*-i*). Spend the night with friends who are departing; wake. *N̄e kwōj uwe ilju inaaj jebokwōn ippaṃ bun̄ūnin.* If you are leaving tomorrow, I'll come and spend the night with you.

jebon̄ōn (**jębęg°ęn**). Custom of spending the last night with people before they depart; also done the night after observing the custom of *eǫreak* after a death.

jeboulul (**jebewilwil**). 1(*-i*), 2, 3, 5(*jjeboulul*), 7. Turn the head slowly from side to side; shake the head in disagreement. *Eṃōj ņe aṃ kijon̄ jjeboulul.* Why don't you stop shaking your head in disagreement all the time.

jebōlkwa- (**jębęlqa-**). Variant form of *jeblokwa-* (**jęblęqa-**).

jebōnmāl (**jębęnmal**). 6(*-i*). Piece of wood on which coconut husk is beaten to yield fibre for sennit. *Ewi jebōnmālin iiō eo ļǫk eo aṃ?* Where's your *jebōnmāl* that you made last year?

jebōn̄ (**jębęn**). Very small amount; very little. *Jebōn̄ wōt dān ilo kab in.* There's very little water in this cup.

jebrano (**jebrahnew**). From Engl. Soprano.

Jebrǫ (**jebraw**). Also *Jeļeilōn̄.* A star, eta in Taurus (Pleiades); a legendary hero; youngest brother of *Tūṃur* and king of the stars; tenthborn of *Lōktan̄ūr; Jebrǫ* was also known by other names: *Mājdik* as a lad, *Buonṃar* when he began the contest with his brothers, *Jeļeilōn̄* when he became king, *Dāpeej* as an old man, and also sometimes as *Jetakdik.*

jebta (**jebtah**). From Engl. *chapter.* 4, 6(*-i*). Chapter; group within a Protestant congregation.

jebta (**jebtah**). 2, 4, 6(*-i*). Christmas song fest (Protestant groups). *Rōnaaj jebta ilo ṃōn jikuuļ eņ.* They will hold a song fest in the school building. *Enaaj or jebta Kūrijṃōj in.* There will be a song fest this Christmas.

jebwa (**jebwah**). 2, 4, 6(*-a*). Marshallese stick dance.

jebwatōr (**jebwater**). Also *jabwatōr* (**jabwater**). 1(*-i*), 2(inf, tr *-e*), 4, 6(*-i*). A food, grated taro mixed with coconut milk, wrapped in taro leaves and baked in oven.

jebwā (**jebay**). A coral.

jebwāālel (**jebayalyęl**). 1(*-i*), 2, 3, 7. Stagger; go to and fro.

jebwābwe (**jebaybęy**). 1(*-i*), 2, 3(inf, tr *-ik*), 4, 7. Stray; wander; be lost; deviate; mislead; perverted.

jebwe (**jebey**). 3, 6(*-i*). Oar; paddle; rudder; steering wheel.

jebwe (**jebey**). Tombstone.

jebwebwe (**jebeybey**). Also *kōjbwe.* From *jebwe* (**jebey**). 1(*-i*), 2(inf, tr *-ik*), 3(inf, tr *kajebwebwe(ik)*), 4, 7. Steer; use a paddle. *Jebwebwein Jiļap ekōṃṃan bwe en rōļǫk wa in.* Jilap's steering caused the boat to miss the island. *Kwōn kajiṃwe aṃ (ka)jebwebweik wa ņe.* Steer the boat on the right course. *Kwōn kajebwebweiki n̄an ṃweo iṃōn.* Steer him to his house. *Kwōn kajebwebweiki ippaṃ.* Let him use one of your paddles.

jebwij (**jebij**). 1(*-i*), 2(inf, tr *-i*), 3, 7. Spur; cut with spurs; kick. *Lale bao ņe ejebwiji eok.* Be careful that chicken doesn't cut you with its spurs. *Iar jebwiji anrin.* I kicked him in the rear end.

jedan̄ (**jedag**). 1(*-i*), 2, 4, 8, 9. Unskilled person; incompetent; amateur; naive.

jedao (**jedahwew**). 1(*-i*), 6(*-i*). Unfortunate. *Kwōn jab kanooj inepata ippān bwe jedao bajjek.* Don't worry too much over him because he's just an unlucky kid. *Jedaoun pālle men eņ.* He's a sorry American.

jedān (**jedan**). Dial. E only; see *jekaro* (**jekarẹw**). 3, 6(-*i*). Coconut sap, toddy.

jeddam̧ (**jeddam̧**). 1, 2, 3, 4, 6(-*i*), 9. Rebuffed; repelled; obstructed; rejected. *Iar kajjioñ im jeddam̧.* I tried but ran into an obstacle. *Ledik eo ekōjeddam̧ Maik.* The girl rebuffed Mike. *Ear lōkātok em jeddam̧.* He surfed in and got wiped out.

jede (**jẹdẹy**). Transitive form of *jedjed* (**jẹdjẹd**).

jedelañ (**jedeylag**). 1(-*i*), 2, 3(inf *kōjjedelañ,* tr *kōjedelañ*), 7. Lie face up; supine. *Ejirilọk lio im jedelañ.* She slipped and fell on her back. *Kōjedelañe wōn kaņe.* Turn the turtles face up.

jedjed (**jẹdjẹd**). 2(inf, tr *jede*), 4, 6(-*i*). Observe from a distance. *Rijedjed iju.* Astronomer. *Raar jede m̧weo m̧okta jān aer deļọñe.* They kept a lookout on the house before raiding it.

Jedjed (**jedjed**). Clan name.

jedjed iju (**jẹdjẹd yijiw**). Astronomy; observing stars. *Ejeļā jedjed iju ļōļļap e.* This old man is good at observing stars.

jedkaju (**jedkajiw**). Also *jarkaju* (**jarkajiw**). 1(-*i*), 2(inf, tr -*uk*), 3, 4, 7, 8, 9. Sudden; transitory; of short duration; fleeting. *Enañin jedkaju am̧ pād ānin?* Why are you staying on this island for such a short time? *Enañin jarkaju ami itok im etal.* Your comings and goings are sudden.

jedkā (**jẹdkay**). Choose.

jedọujij (**jedawijij**). From Engl. 1(-*i*), 2, 3, 6(-*i*), 8. Trousers; pants. *Kōjedọujiji ļadik ņe.* Put some pants on the boy.

jedpānit (**jedpanit**). Also *jedpanit* (**jẹdpanit**). From Engl. 3, 6(-*i*). Serpent; snake.

jedtak (**jedtak**). Also *jertak* (**jertak**). 1(-*i*), 2, 3, 5(*jjedtaktak*), 7. Lie on back as result of accident; fall on one's back; turn over. *Ettōr im jedtak.* He ran and fell on his back. *Ļeo ejjedtaktak eņ. Ejjertaktak ļeeņ.* That man is always falling on his back. *Ittōr im jertak.* I ran and slipped on my back.

jeeaaļ (**jeyyahaļ**). 1(-*i*), 2(inf, tr -*e*), 4, 6(-*i*), 7, 8. Beckon with the hand, downward motion; beckon by waving arms. *Kwōn jeeaaļe wa eņ bwe en itok.* Beckon that canoe to come here. *Jeeaaļe bwe en itok.* Wave him over.

jeeded (**jeyedyed**). Also *ajeeded.* 1(-*i*), 2, 3(inf, tr -*e*), 5(*jjeeded*), 7, 8, 9. Spread out; dispersed; scattered. *Eļap an jjeeded ripālle meļan āne in.* The Americans are all over this islet.

jeej (**jẹyẹj**). Also *wōjej* (**wẹjyẹj**). Interjection: "Heck!"; "Darn it!"

jeek (**jeyek**). Transitive form of *jeje* (**jeyjey**).

jeekļọk (**jẹyẹkļaq**). 2, 3(inf, tr -*e*), 6(-*i*). Short of breath. *Kōmij tōprakļọk wōt raan toļ utiejej eo ak ejeekļọk.* He started gasping for air upon our reaching the high mountain top.

jeeknaan (**jeyeknahan**). From Engl. *second hand*. 2, 6(-*i*). Common; commoner; low-class people. *Jeeknaan rej jijet laļ.* Commoners sit on the floor. *Jeeknaan in buļōn mar.* A bush native (*kanaka*).

jeeļ (**jeyeļ**). From Engl. Cell, biological.

jeen (**jeyen**). From Engl. 6(-*i*). Chain.

jeeọñōd (**jeyyag°ed**). 1(-*i*), 2, 3, 4, 8, 9. Seldom go fishing.

jeep (**jẹyẹp**). Also *jeep* (**jeyep**). From Germ. (?). Shake hands to make a promise binding.

jeepepļọk (**jeyepyepļaq**). Also *jeepepļọk* (**jẹyẹpyẹpļaq**). 1(-*i*), 2, 3, 6(-*i*). Ruin; destroy; annihilate; overthrow; disintegrate; fall apart; disappear. *Ear kōk laļ em jeepepļọk āneo.* There was an earthquake and the island disappeared. *Baam̧ kaņe rōnaaj kajeepepļọk laļ in.* The bombs will disintegrate the earth. *Ejeepepļọk pād eo aerro.* Their marriage is ruined. *Em̧ọj bọkutañe wa eo im ejeepepļọk.* The ship was bombed and destroyed.

jeer (**jeyer**). Also *jeer* (**jẹyẹr**). Variant form of *jeor* (**jeyer°**).

jeerinbale (**jeyerinbaļẹy**). 2(inf, tr -*ik*), 3(tr -*ik*), 4, 5(*jjeerinbakele*), 6(-*i*), 7. Evade; run in a zigzag fashion; make quick sharp turns.

jei (**jẹyiy**). 2(inf, tr -*ik*), 3, 6(-*i*). Duty that a younger sibling is expected to give to older siblings.

jei (**jẹyiy**). Transitive plural form of *jeje* (**jẹyjẹy**).

jei- (**jẹyi-**). 1. Older sibling; older brother; older sister; older cousin (parallel).

jeib (**jẹyib**). 3, 6(*-i*). Bottle used for coconut sap.

jeik (**jẹyik**). To turn.

jeim̧ōta (**jẹyim̧etah**). 3, 6(*-i*). A plant, *Caesalpinia pulcherrima* L.; (Leguminosae). A leguminous tree; said to be named for *Jeim̧ōta*, the grandfather of Amata Kabua; contemporary Marshall Islands leader. An ornamental shrub; with bipinnate leaves and conspicuous red and yellow flowers.

Jeina (**jẹyinah**). Also *Jaina* (**jahyinah**). From Engl. *China*. 4. China.

Jeina (**jẹyinah**). From Engl. A plant, banana variety (Takeuchi).

jeinae (**jẹyinahyey**). 2, 3(*-ik*), 6(*-i*). Mat woven from coconut fronds.

jej (**jẹj**). Dial. E only; see *jjeļọk* (**jjeļaq**). None; no more; lacking. *Ejej jikka im̧wiin.* There are no cigarettes in this house.

jej uwaan (**jẹj wiwahan**). Unparalleled.

jej-. See *jj-*.

jeja (**jẹyjah**). 1(*-i*), 2, 7. Scarce; seldom; rare. *Ejeja kain wōjke rot in.* This kind of tree is scarce.

jeja (**jeyjah**). Also *eja* (**yejah**). Make a sound of pleasure while sleeping because of good dreams.

jeje (**jẹyjẹy**). 1(*-i*), 2(inf, tr sg. obj. *je*, pl. obj. *jei*), 3, 4, 6(*-i*),7, 8. Write; edit; record.

jeje (**jẹyjẹy**). Also *jieje* (**jiyẹjẹy**). 1(*-i*), 2, 3, 4. Disease characterized by swollen belly and emaciated limbs as a result of malnutrition; kwashiorkor; swollen abdomen. *Ejeje ļeeņ.* He's got the *jeje* disease.

jeje (**jeyjey**). Also *jeje* (**jẹyjẹy**). 1(*-i*), 2(inf, tr sg. obj. *jeek(e)*, pl. obj. *jeik(i)*), 3, 6(*-i*), 7. Sail into the wind, tacking often. *Jej aikuj jeje im jibadekļọk āneņ.* We need to sail into the wind and try to reach that islet. *Jej jeek āneņ.* We are sailing into the wind to that islet. *Kōm ar jeik bōke ko.* We tacked around the capes.

jeje (**jeyjey**). Make room for; avoid.

jejer (**jẹjẹr**). Look for.

jejjat (**jejjat**). Dry; no water. *Ejejjat ioon pedped.* There is no water on the reef.

jejjet (**jẹjjẹt**). 1(*-i*), 2(inf, tr *jitūk(e, i)*), 3, 4, 8. Clean a fish or chicken. *Rōnañin jejjet ke ek ko?* Haven't those fish been cleaned yet? *Kwōn jitūke ek ņe.* Clean that fish.

jejjet (**jejjet**). Also *jijjet* (**jijjet**), *jejjet* (**jẹjjẹt**). 1(*-i*), 2, 3, 7, 8, 9. Proper; straight; accurate; right; correct; specific; concise; precise; exact. *Enañin jejjet ke ruwalitōk awa?* Is it exactly eight o'clock? *Ejejjet aō uwaak kajjitōk ko ilo teej eo.* I answered the questions on the test correctly.

jejjet kūtie- (**jẹjjẹt kitiye-**). 1, 2+1, 3+1. Enforce. *Enañin jejjet ke kūtien kien ņe.* Has that ordinance been enforced?

jejjo (**jẹjjẹw**). 3, 5(*jejjojo*), 3+5. Few; several. *Eor jejjojo riM̧ajeļ Awai.* 'There are Marshallese scattered throughout Hawaii. *Eor jejjo riM̧ajeļ Awai.* There are a few Marshallese in Hawaii.

jejļōma- (**jẹjļema-**). 1, 2, 3, 8, 9. Shapeless.

jek (**jẹk**). Transitive form of *jekjek* (**jẹkjẹk**).

jekab (**jekab**). 2, 5(*jjekabkab*), 6(*-i*), 11(*jekabkab*). Checkers; play checkers; be checkered. *Ejjekabkab jōōt eo an.* He was wearing a checkered shirt.

jekaboot (**jekabewet**). From Engl. *checkerboard*. 2(inf, tr *-e*), 4, 5(*jjekabootot*), 6(*-i*). Checker board; to maneuver; plan; scheme. *Ejjekabootot jōōt eo an.* He wore a checkered shirt. *Ej jekaboote an etal.* He's scheming his move.

jekad (**jekad**). 3, 6(*-i*). A bird, black noddy, *Anous tenuirostris.*

jekad- (**jekad-**). 2+7, 3+7, 7. Fling.

jekade (**jekadey**). Transitive form of *jekadkad* (**jekadkad**).

jekadkad (**jekadkad**). 1(*-i*), 2(inf, tr *jekade*), 3, 5(*jjekadkad*), 7, 8. Scattered; pieces flying in every direction. *Ear lel ilo jekadkadin baam̧ eo.* He got hit by shrapnel (from the bomb).

jekajeje (**jekajeyjey**). 1(*-i*), 2(inf, tr *-ik*), 4, 5(*jjekajeje*), 6(*-i*), 7, 8. A by-product of *jekaro*; (coconut sap), white; keeps only two days without fermenting. *Kwōn jekajejeik jekaro kaņe.* Cook that sap to make it thicker.

jekak (**jekak**). 3, 5(*-e*), 8+3. Copra pieces, taken out of the shell.

jekak (**jekak**). 1(-*i*), 2, 3, 5(*jekake*), 6(-*i*), 8, 9. Dandruff. *Eor ke jekak bōraṃ?* Do you have dandruff? *Eḷap an jekake bōra.* I have lots of dandruff.

jekaka (**jekahkah**). 3, 2(inf, tr -*ik*), 6(-*i*). A food, pandanus chips. *Eṃōj am jekakaik bōb ko.* We have made chips out of the pandanus.

jekaṇ (**jekaṇ**). Variant form of *ijekaṇ* (**yijekaṇ**).

jekaṇe (**jekaṇey**). Variant form of *ijekaṇe* (**yijekaṇey**).

jekapeel (**jekapeyel**). 1(-*i*), 2, 4, 8, 9, 11(*jekapeel*). Unskillful; immature (see *kapeel* (**kapeyel**)), not clever. *Ej jekapeel wōt.* He's still immature.

jekapen (**jekapen**). Variant form of *jakapen* (**jakapen**).

jekar (**jekar**). Formant in place names; see *jekad.*

jekaro (**jekarẹw**). Dial. W, E: *jedān* (**jedan**). 1(-*i*), 2(inf, tr -*uk*), 4, 5(*jjekaroro*), 6(-*i*), 7, 8. Coconut sap, toddy. *Ennọ ke jekaroun ni (jekaro) eṇ?* Is the sap from that coconut sapling delicious? *Lale eḷap an jjekaroro raij ṇe.* Be careful not to put too much toddy all over that rice.

jekā (**jekay**). Variant form of *ijekā* (**yijekay**).

jekāān (**jekayan**). Archaic. Its trunk; formant in place names; variant form of *kāān.*

jekāiōōj (**jekayiyehej**). Also *jekāiro* (**jekayirẹw**). 1(-*i*), 2(inf, tr -*e, -ik*), 4, 8. Notches cut in a tree for climbing.

jekāiro (**jekayirẹw**). Variant form of *jekāiōōj* (**jekayiyehej**).

jekākaṇ (**jekaykaṇ**). Variant form of *ijekākaṇ* (**yijekaykaṇ**).

jekākaṇe (**jekaykaṇey**). Variant form of *ijekākaṇe* (**yijekaykaṇey**).

jekākā (**jekaykay**). 7. Anywhere around here; variant form of *ijekākā* (**yijekaykay**).

jekdọọn (**jekdawan**). 2+3, 3(inf, tr -*e*), 11(*jekdọọn*). Not matter; never mind; disregard; regardless; ignore. *Jab kōjekdọọn kōṇaan ko aō.* Don't disregard my wishes. *Jekdọọn ta.* Regardless of what happens.

jekea- (**jekeya-**). Also *jekāā-*. Variant form of *kea-, kā.*

jekeidaak (**jẹkẹyidahak**). 1(-*i*), 2(inf, tr -*e*), 3, 4, 7. Steal and drink coconut toddy (off a tree).

jekein (**jẹkẹyin**). Variant form of *ijekein* (**yijẹkẹyin**).

jekjek (**jẹkjẹk**). 1(-*i*), 2(inf, tr *jek(e), jek*), 4, 5(*jjekjeke*), 7, 8. Cut; hew; chop; to prune; salute with the hands. *Jek tok juon limō ni.* Cut a coconut open for me to drink. *Rej jekjek waini.* They are chopping copra nuts (in two lengthwise). *Kwōn jab jjekjeke waini ṇe.* Don't keep chopping that copra nut.

jekjek wa (**jẹkjẹk wah**). 1(-*i*), 2, 3, 4, 7. Build a canoe or boat. *Wōn ṇe ear jek wa ṇe waaṃ?* Who built your canoe?

jekkar (**jekkar**). 1(-*i*), 2, 3, 6(-*i*), 8, 9, 11(*jekkar*). Ill matched; unbecoming; improper; contrary to; unsuitable; ridiculous; absurd (see *kkar* (**kkar**)). *Ejekkar juuj kā ñan neō.* These shoes don't fit my feet. *Erro jekkar ñan doon.* They are unsuited for each other. *Kwōn jab jekkar.* Don't be ridiculous.

jeklaḷ (**jeklaḷ**). 6(-*i*). Part of net where weights are attached.

jeklep (**jeklep**). 1(-*i*), 2(inf, tr -*e*), 3, 4. Cut it large or thick. *Eḷap aṃ jeklepe kane kaṇe.* You cut that firewood large.

jeklep (**jeklep**). 1(-*i*), 2(inf, tr -*e*), 3, 4. Insult; expose one's faults before his face.

jekḷaj (**jekḷaj**). The day after tomorrow.

jekṃai (**jekṃahyiy**). 1(-*i*), 2(inf, tr -*ik*), 3, 4, 5(*jjekōṃaiṃai*), 6(-*i*). Coconut syrup boiled down from sap. *Lale ejjekōṃaiṃai nuknuk ṇe aṃ.* Be careful, coconut syrup might get spilled on your clothes.

jeko (**jekew**). Variant form of *ijeko* (**yijekew**).

jekoko (**jekewkew**). Variant form of *ijekoko* (**yijekewkew**).

jekōbwa (**jẹkẹbwah**). A food, meat of *mejoub* coconut mixed with sugar or sap.

jekōn (**jeken**). From Engl. A second of time; second base.

jekōnāān (**jekenayan**). From Engl. Second-hand.

jekōt (**jẹkẹt**). Also *jikūt.* 1, 2(inf, tr -*e*), 6(-*i*), 7. To weave the edges of a mat or hat. *Kwōn jekōte at ṇe bwe en ṃōj.* Give it the final weaving so the hat is completed.

jekōt (**jękęt**). Variant form of *jikōt.*

jekpād (**jekpad**). 2(inf, tr *-e*), 4, 5(*jjekpādpād*), 6(*-i*), 7. Rafters. *Enañin m̧ōj ke jekpāde m̧weo?* Have the rafters been put on the house?

jekpen (**jękpęn**). 1(*-i*), 2, 4. Make false excuses; pretend; feign; blame someone or something.

jel (**jel**). Curved.

jel (**jęl**). Grown over. *Ejel kōn wūjooj im mar.* It's grown over with grass and bushes.

jelae (**jelhayey**). Archaic. Not on the current; see *ae* and *jelbōn.*

jelba (**jęlbah**). From Engl. 6(*-i*). Silver.

jelbōn (**jelbęn**). Archaic. On the current; see *bōn* and *jelae.*

jele (**jęlęy**). Also *jel* (**jęl**). Archaic. Harvest fruit. *Kom̧win jeli ni kaņ ņa ilaļ.* Harvest those coconuts.

jeljel (**jęljęl**). Stone axe.

Jeljel (**jęljęl**). From *jeljel* "stone axe". A constellation; delta, epsilon, zeta, sigma Orionis. Legend says its rising brings powerful storms such as the typhoon of June 30, 1905. *Jeljel i raan mā kaņ.* Jeljel is in the branches of the breadfruit trees: it has shaken the fruit from the trees and the season is over.

Jeljel-im-Kouj (**jęljęl-yim-kęwij**). The constellations *Jeljel* and *Kouj.*

Jeljeltak (**jęljęltak**). Storms associated with the ascendancy of *Jeljel* (stars in Orion).

jellen (**jellen**). Position of. *Enana jellen ļōkar eņ.* That locker isn't standing straight.

jelm̧ae (**jelm̧ahyey**). Also *jālm̧ae* (**jalm̧ahyey**). 1(*-i*), 2(inf, tr *jelm̧aik*), 3, 4, 7. Face to face; meet; confront. *Erro ar jelm̧aik doon ilo kweļọk eo.* They confronted each other at the meeting. *Jenaaj bar jālm̧ae doon juon iien.* We'll meet again sometime.

jelōk (**jelek**). From Engl. 5(*jjelōklōk*), 6(*-i*). Silk.

jelōñlōñ (**jęlęglęg**). Also *jilōñlōñ* (**jilegleg**). Very, intensifier, of limited use: for time, tide, or weather. *Edet jelōñlōñ.* Bright sunshine. *Raelep jelōñlōñ.* High noon. *Raan jelōñlōñ.* Broad daylight. *Pāāt jelōñlōñ.* High and dry (low tide, reef exposed).

jelōt (**jelet**). 2(inf, tr *-e*), 7. Touch unexpectedly by accident; implicate; affect; concerned; involved. *Ijelōt bato eo raan tebōļ eo em wōtlọk.* I bumped the bottle off the top of the table and it fell. *Mejin ejelōte aolep.* The (common) cold is affecting everyone. *Jorrāān eo ejelōte.* He was involved in the trouble.

jelpa- (**jelpah**). Archaic. 1. A parent-in-law. *Jelpān kōrā.* Mother-in-law. *Jelpān m̧aan.* Father-in-law.

jelpaak (**jelpahak**). 2(inf, tr *-e*), 7. Put arm around waist of another while standing side by side. *Ear jelpaake ledik eo jeran.* He put his arm around his girlfriend's waist.

jelpaak (**jelpahak**). 1, 2(inf, tr *-e*), 6(*-i*), 7. Swing something or someone around in a circle, as a child. *Jab jelpaake niññiñ ņe bwe enaaj m̧ōļañļōñ.* Don't swing the child around in a circle or it'll want to throw up.

jeltak (**jęltak**). Variant form of *jaļtak* (**jaļtak**).

jeļa (**jeyļah**). From Engl. 1(*-i*), 2(inf, tr *-ik*), 3, 4, 6(*-i*), 7. Sailor. *Wōn enāj jeļaik wa ņe?* Who will be the crew of the boat?

jeļaar (**jeļahar**). Pine driftwood.

jeļañ (**jeyļag**). A big storm.

jeļañ (**jeļag**). Replace the bottom part (*jouj*) of a canoe.

Jeļapļap (**jęļapļap**). Clan name.

jeļatae (**jeļathayey**). 2(inf, tr *-ik(i)*), 6(*-i*), 7, 8, 9. Ocean currents that are farther away from an island than the *juae* or *dibukae* currents; the third zone of currents. *Ejeļataeiki booj jerakrōk eo im pen an m̧m̧akūt jān ijo.* The sailboat got caught up in the third current zone and hardly made any headway.

jeļate (**jeļatey**). Transitive form of *jaļjaļ* (**jaļjaļ**).

jeļā (**jeļay**). 1(*-i*), 2, 3, 4, 7. Know; well-informed; know how to; aware. *Ļadik eo ejeļā tata ņe.* That's the most well-informed chap.

jeļā jabjab (**jeļay jabjab**). Idiom. Insufficient knowledge. *Ejeļā jabjab kōn an kar jab kam̧ōj an jikuuļ.* His insufficient knowledge stems from his not having completed his schooling.

jeļā kōppeļak (**jeļay keppeļhak**). Also *jeļā kōpļaak* (**jeļay kepļahak**). 2. Know how to maneuver; a smart move; good tactic; good strategy;

tactful; poised. *Ejeḷā kōppeḷak lieṇ.* She's got poise. She's tactful.

jeḷā kuṇaa- (**jeḷay qiṇaha-**). 1, 2, 4, 8, 9. Considerate; thoughtful; diplomacy; knack. *Kwōmake jeḷā kuṇaaṃ.* You sure are thoughtful. *Ejeḷā kuṇaan ñan raṇ nukun.* He takes care of his responsibilities toward his relatives. *Ejeḷā kuṇaan ñan ruwamāejet.* She has diplomacy with her visitors.

jeḷā ḷọkjeṇ (**jeḷay ḷaqjeṇ**). 1(*-i*), 2, 3, 4, 6(*-i*), 8, 9. Conscious; sober; come to; wisdom; knowledge; educated; sane. *Enañin jeḷā ḷọkjeṇ ke ālikin an kar ḷotḷọk?* Has she come to since she passed out?

jeḷāṇae (**jeḷayṇahyey**). 1(*-i*), 2, 3, 4, 8, 9. Know how to take care of; be kind to. *Kwōn jeḷāṇae jinōṃ im jemaṃ.* Know how to take care of your mother and father.

Jeḷeilōñ (**jeḷẹyilẹg**). Also *Jebrọ.* A star; eta in Taurus (Pleiades); name of the youngest son (tenthborn) of *Lōktañūr* (**lẹktagir**), legendary.

jeḷḷọk (**jeḷḷaq**). Also *jaḷḷọk* (**jaḷḷaq**). 1(*-i*), 2, 3, 8. Face away from.

jeḷmāne (**jeḷmaney**). 1(*-i*), 2, 3, 4, 8, 9. Unruly; self-willed; unscrupulous; reckless. *Kwōn jab jeḷmāne.* Don't be unruly.

jeḷo (**jẹyḷẹw**). Also *jeḷo* (**jeyḷew**). 2, 3, 5(*jjeḷoḷo*), 6(*-i*). An insect, grasshopper. *Ejjeḷoḷo ānin.* There are lots of grasshoppers on this island.

jeḷo (**jẹyḷẹw**). From Engl. "*sail ho*!". 2, 3(*kajjeḷoḷo*), 5(*jjeḷoḷo*), 6(*-i*), 7. Cry an arrival, of ship or plane. *Jeañ lọk in kajjeḷoḷo.* Let's go see if there's a boat coming. *Ejjeḷoḷo Mājro.* There are always boats arriving in Majuro. *Jen wōnarḷọk bwe ejeḷo.* Let's go to the beach for there's a ship coming in.

jeḷọk (**jẹyḷaq**). 1(*-i*), 2(inf, tr *-e*), 3, 6(*-i*), 7, 8. Crutch used for pushing boom of canoe away. *Jeḷọke wōjḷā ṇe.* Push the sail away there.

jem (**jẹm**). Transitive form of *jemjem* (**jẹmjẹm**).

jema- (**jema-**). 1. Father; uncle, father's brother.

jemā (**jemay**). 2(inf, tr *-ik*), 3, 6(*-i*). Duty of taking care of a father.

jemājirok (**jemajirẹq**). Rope used for climbing trees.

jemāluut (**jemaliwit**). Dial. E only; see *iia* (**yiyyah**). Also *jeṃāluut* (**jemayliwit**). Rainbow.

Jemāluut (**jemayliwit**). Clan name.

jemān aj (**jeman haj**). 1(*-i*), 2, 3, 4, 7. Pass thatch to one tying. *Kwōn itōn jemān aj.* Go pass thatch.

jemān bo (**jeman bẹw**). 2(inf, tr *-ik*), 7. Select stones for missiles; throw stones at. *Raar jemān boik Jọọn inne.* They threw stones at John yesterday.

Jemān Kurlōñ (**jeman qirlẹg**). See *Jurōn Jemān Kurlōñ.*

jemān-āe (**jeman-yayẹy**). Example; model; charter.

jemānji- (**jemanji-**). 1. One who has taken care of another's child; relation between two brothers-in-law who are married to two sisters.

Jemānuwe (**jemaniwwẹy**). A constellation; stars in Ursa Minor; gamma, beta, 5.

jemej (**jẹymẹj**). 2, 3, 6(*-i*). Slip; wear a slip. *Kwōn jemej bwe emāni nuknuk ṇe aṃ.* Wear a slip because your dress is thin.

jememe (**jemeymey**). 1, 2(inf, tr *-ik*), 4, 6(*-i*), 8, 9. Anti-social; introversion; unkind; inconsiderate; sober; reserved; apathetic; grimace; hostile; pout. *Joḷọk jememe im kōpeḷḷọk būruoṃ.* Stop being unkind and have a heart. *Kwōn jab jememeik eō.* Don't be unkind to me.

jemetak (**jẹymetak**). Also *jiemetak* (**jiyemetak**). 1(*-i*), 2, 3, 4, 7. Stomach ache.

jemjati (**jẹmjatiy**). Also *jeimjati.* 2(inf, tr *-ik*), 3(*kajemjatiik*), 6(*-i*). Siblings.

jemjem (**jẹmjẹm**). 1(*-i*), 2(inf, tr *jem(e)*), 3, 4, 5(*jjemjeme*), 7. Whet; sharpen. *Kwōn jeme bakbōk ṇe.* Sharpen that knife. *Rej jemjem bakbōk.* They are sharpening knives.

jemjem māāl (**jẹmjẹm mayal**). Idiom. From *jemjem* (**jẹmjẹm**) "sharpen", *māāl* (**mayal**) "adze". To bring foods with songs as refreshments to a group of men building a canoe or house to keep their morale up, usually done by the womenfolk of a community.

jemḷam (**jemḷam**). Also *jjeḷam.* 2. So; such a. *Ejemḷam ḷap aṃ nana.* You're awful. *Ejemḷam aiboojoj an tulọk aḷ.* What a beautiful sunset. *Ejemḷam ḷap.* It's so large. *Ejemḷam tōñal.* How sweet it is. *Kwōjemļam jouj.* You are so kind. *Ejemļam m̧m̧an in am̧ al.* You sing so beautifully.

jempaan (**jempahan**). From Engl. 6(*-i*). Sampan.

jem̧aan (**jeym̧ahan**). Some time ago. *Ij jañin jeje jān jem̧aan.* I haven't written for some time. *Iar loe jem̧aan.* I saw her some time ago.

jem̧aden (**jem̧aden**). Wasteland.

jem̧ar (**jem̧ar**). From Engl. 2, 4, 6(*-i*), 7. Summer; summer vacation.

jem̧jerā (**jęm̧jeray**). Also *jem̧jerā* (**jęm̧jęray**). 2(inf, tr *-ik*). Be friends; friendship; friendly relationship. *Erro ej jem̧jerā.* They are friends. *Ear jem̧jerāik baam̧le eo.* He befriended the family.

jem̧jǫ (**jęm̧jaw**). Variant form of *jim̧jǫ* (**jim̧jaw**).

jem̧kat (**jem̧kat**). Also *jam̧kat* (**jam̧kat**). 1, 2(inf, tr *-e*), 4, 6(*-i*), 7. Sidekick in kickball. *An jejjo wōt jam̧kat.* Not very many people can side-kick. *Ear jam̧kate bǫǫļ eo.* He side-kicked the ball.

jem̧ļǫk (**jem̧ļaq**). 1(*-i*), 2, 3(inf *kōjjem̧ļǫk, kōjem̧ļǫk*), 7. End; finish; conclusion; limit; pass out; aftermath. *Ejem̧ļǫk pija eo.* The movie is over. *Ejem̧ļǫk koontōreak eo.* The contract is terminated.

jem̧m̧a (**jem̧m̧ah**). From Japn. *sanma*. 3, 4+3, 5(*jjem̧m̧am̧a*), 6(*-a*), 3+7. Canned sardines. *Kōjro tōn kōjem̧m̧a tok.* Let's go get some canned sardines. *Kobwiin jjem̧m̧am̧a.* You smell of sardines.

jem̧m̧aan (**jem̧m̧ahan**). Slang. From *m̧m̧aan* (**m̧m̧ahan**). Top man in organization; chief; boss; host. *Jab keroro bwe jem̧m̧aan ņe tok.* Shut up for the boss is coming.

jem̧nājin (**jęm̧najin**). Parent-child relationship; brother-sister relationship; taboo relationship. *Lieņ im ļadik eņ rej jem̧nājin.* She and that boy are taboo relatives.

jem̧nājin (**jęm̧najin**). From Engl. 2, 3. Examination day at end of term; review day program.

jem̧ōnna (**jem̧ennah**). 2(inf, tr *-ik*), 4, 6(*-i*). Stick used for clubbing fish. *Kwōnañin jem̧ōnnaik ke jilo ņe?* Have you clubbed the white tuna fish?

jen (**jęn**). 1(*-i*), 2, 3, 7. Shrink; grow smaller; fall short of, in length. *Ekwaļkoļ nuknuk e aō im jen.* This clothing of mine was washed and shrank.

jen (**jen**). Let's, we are to.

jen (**jęn**). Transitive form of *jenjen* (**jęnjęn**).

jen ba (**jen bah**). Supposing; let's say.

jende (**jęndęy**). Dialectal variant of *akade* (**hakadęy**).

jendik (**jendik**). Also *jāndik* (**jandik**), *jendik* (**jęndik**). 3, 6(*-i*). Young chicken.

jenjen (**jęnjęn**). 1(*-i*), 2(inf, tr *jen(e)*), 4, 8. Start a fire. *Kwōn jen kijek ņe.* Light a fire there. *Enañin jenjen ke kijek eo?* Has the fire been started yet?

jenjen (**jęnjęn**). Variant form of *jinjin* (**jinjin**).

jenliklik (**jęnliklik**). 1(*-i*), 3, 4, 7. Go backward; retreat; lag; hold back, not do one's best; deviate.

jenļap (**jęnļap**). 3, 6(*-i*), 8, 9. Old chicken; to mature, of poultry; brood hen. *Ewi jenļap in lala eo?* Where is the mother hen?

jennade (**jennahdęy**). From Japn. *sen nadi* "...cents is..."(uttered between entries by abacus users). 1(*-i*), 2(inf, tr *-ik*), 4, 6(*-i*), 7. Calculate. *Jennadeik m̧ōk m̧uri eo aō ippam̧.* Would you calculate how much I owe you?

jennōb (**jęnnęb**). Dial. W, E: *rǫkrok* (**raqręq**). 2(inf, tr *-e*), 3, 5(*jjennōbnōb*), 6(*-i*). A food, pandanus custard mixed with water. *Lale ejjennōbnōb nuknuk ņe am̧.* Be careful you don't slop pandanus custard on your clothes. *Jennōbe tok m̧ōk jidik kijō iu.* Make some *jennōb* for me.

jeno (**jenew**). Dialectal variant of *mejānwōd* (**mejanwed**).

jenok (**jęnęq**). Also *kin* (**kin**). 1(*jenkwa-*), 3(inf *kajjenoknok,* tr *kajenokwe*), 5(*(j)jenoknok*), 6(*-i*). Footprints; tracks; traces; fingerprint; print. *E(j)jenoknok arin ānin.* The beach on this island has a lot of footprints.

jenokwōn (**jęnęqęn**). Related to each other.

jenoļǫk (**jenewlaq**). 1(*-i*), 2(inf, tr *-e*), 3(inf, tr *-e*), 6(*-i*). Separate; isolate;

discreet; distinct; conspicuous; disconnected; segregated. *Ejenolọk jān ṃōko jet.* It was isolated from the rest of the houses. *Kōjenolọk ruo aō jedọujij.* Put aside two pairs of pants for me. *Kōjenolọke raij ṇe jān jālele ṇe.* Separate the rice from the meat course.

jenọ (**jenaw**). Dial. E only; see *mejānwōd* (**mejanwed**). 3, 6(*-i*). A clam, bivalve.

jenwaan (**jenwahan**). Archaic. Common things.

jenwōd (**jenwed**). 2, 6(*-i*), 7. Tacking. *Kōn an nana kōto in wa eo eṇ ej jenwōd tak wōt.* Because of this unfavorable wind, the canoe is doing plenty of tacking to get here.

jeṇ (**jeṇ**). Variant form of *ijeṇ* (**yijeṇ**).

jeṇe (**jeṇey**). Variant form of *ijeṇe* (**yijeṇey**).

jeṇeṇe (**jeṇeyṇey**). Variant form of *ijeṇeṇe* (**yijeṇeyṇey**).

jeṇro (**jeṇrew**). We two are to; let's the two of us.

jeṇtoki (**jeṇtẹwkiy**). From Japn. *sentooki*. 4, 6(*-i*). Fighter plane.

jeñak (**jẹygak**). 1(*-i*), 2(inf, tr *-e*), 3, 7. Filled up, of a hole; perfective form of *jjioñ* (**jjiyẹg°**). *Ejeñak rọñ eo.* The hole is filled up. *Wōn ṇe ear jeñake rọñ ṇe?* Who filled that hole there?

jeor (**jeyer°**). Also *jeer* (**jẹyẹr**), *jeer* (**jeyer**). 1(*-i*), 2(inf, tr *-e*), 3, 5(*jjeoreor*), 7. Turn. *Ejjeoreor wa eo.* The vehicle keeps turning this way and that. *Kwōn jeor ilo iaḷ ṇe.* Turn into that street.

jeor (**jeyer°**). Also *jeer* (**jeyer**). 1, 2(inf, tr *-e*), 6(*-i*). Sideburns; trim hair with a razor. *Letok juon reja bwe in jeore bōraṃ.* Hand me a razor so that I can trim your hair. *Eaitok jeor kaṇ an likao eṇ.* That young man's sideburns are long.

jeor (**jeyer°**). Transitive form of *jjeor* (**jjeyer°**).

jep (**jẹp**). Working place.

jep (**jẹp**). Also *jep* (**jep**). 1(*-i*), 2, 3, 4, 5(*jjepjep*), 6(*-i*). Biased; take sides; prejudiced; bigot; nepotism; partial. *Ej jep ippān ḷōṃaraṇ nukun.* He's taking his relatives side. *Kwōn jab kōṇaan jjepjep.* Don't always be so biased. *Kwōn jab jep.* Don't take sides.

jep (**jep**). 2(inf, tr *-e*). Determine. *Eṃōj aō jep ippa bwe ij kate eō kiiō.* I'm determined to do my best now.

jep (**jep**). Transitive form of *jepjep* (**jẹpjẹp**).

jepa (**jepah**). 1(*-i*), 2, 3, 4, 6(*-i*), 8, 9. Disease; ugly; plain; homely. *Ejepa ḷadik eṇ.* That boy is ugly.

jepaa- (**jepaha-**). 1, 6. Arrangement. *Eṃṃan jepaan ut kein.* These flowers are nicely arranged.

jepaake (**jepahakey**). From Engl. Tobacco. *Jepaake jaake.* We share tobacco.

Jepaan (**jepahan**). From Engl. 4. Japan.

jepak (**jepak**). 1(*-i*), 2(inf, tr *-e*), 3, 4, 7. Support; hold up. *Kwōn jepak ḷọk ajri ṇe.* Carry that baby there.

jepak (**jepak**). 2(inf, tr *-e*), 4, 6(*-i*), 7. Cut, hack, chop off, split, slash. *Juon iaan ri Wōleai ro ear jepake bōran Lipepe.* One of the Woleaians hacked off Lipepe's head.

jepak (**jepak**). Tip of coconut frond; cloud formation resembling tip of frond.

jepar (**jepar**). Also *jinnipran̄* (**jinniprag**). 1(*-i*), 2, 3, 5(*jeparpare*), 6(*-i*). Stem of coconut bunch from which nuts have fallen; open spathe of coconut tree.

jeparujruj (**jepar°ijr°ij**). 1(*-i*), 2, 3, 5(*jjeparujruji*). Be excited; in a flutter; excitement during unexpected happenings. *Raar jeparujruj im ko ke ej bwil ṃweo.* They got excited and escaped when the house burned.

jepā (**jepay**). Variant form of *jāp* (**jap**).

jepāde (**jepadẹy**). Land used for preserving food, esp. pandanus.

jepāl (**jẹypal**). Sporadic in bearing, of trees. *Ejepāl ni eṇ.* That coconut tree bears sporadically.

jepāp (**jepap**). 3, 6(*-i*). A fish, kind of shark.

jepāpe (**jepaypẹy**). 1(*-i*), 2, 3(inf, tr *jepāpeik*), 7. To list; slope; careen. *Ejepāpe wa eo.* The boat is listing. *Kwōn jab kōjepāpeik wa ṇe.* Don't make that canoe list.

jepāppāp (**jepappap**). 1(*-i*), 2, 3, 5(*jjepāppāp*), 7. Stagger; stumble but not fall.

jepdak (**jępdak**). 1(*-i*), 2, 3, 4, 5(*jjepedakdak*), 7. Lie with head propped on elbow; crushed in; perfective form of *jjiped* (**jjiped**). *Ejepdak tibat eo.* The tea kettle is crushed in. *Ejjepdakdak kuwat ko.* The cans are all smashed.

jepe (**jepey**). Also *enrā* (**yęnray**). 6(*-i*). Small basket.

jepe rūr (**jepey rir**). Also *jepen rūr* (**jepen rir**). 1(*-i*). Buttocks.

jepekōļan (**jepeykeļan**). 2(inf, tr *-e*), 6(*-i*), 7. A steady procession. *Inej eo an Amedka ear jepekōļane tok loṃaļoun Mājro im lutōkļǫk.* The U.S. fleet came in such huge numbers to the Majuro lagoon that it literally overflowed.

jepel (**jępęl**). 1(*-i*), 2, 3, 4, 4+3, 7. Apart; divorced; separate; diverge. *Ejepel jar eņ.* That couple is divorced. *Kwōn kōjepel rūkadek raņ rej ire.* Separate those drunks that are fighting.

jepelien (**jępęliyen**). From Engl. Civilian. *Jepelien men raņ.* They're civilians.

jepeliklik (**jepeyliklik**). Variant form of *jepliklik* (**jepliklik**).

jepeļā (**jepeļay**). 1(*-i*), 2, 3, 5(*jjepeļāļā*), 7. Glide in the air; wings outstretched in flying.

jepen rūr (**jepen rir**). Variant form of *jepe rūr* (**jepey rir**).

jepet (**jepet**). Archaic. Shell of many colors, used as lure for tuna; variety of *di* or *eǫr*.

jepewa (**jepeywah**). 1(*-i*), 2, 3(inf, tr *-ik*), 7, 8, 9. Careen; keel over. *Ej jepewa ļǫk ñan an jorrāān.* It's careening towards its destruction.

jepjep (**jępjęp**). 2(inf, tr *jep(i), jepe*), 4, 7. Cut off; shorten; mow. *Kwōn jep jedǫujij e aō bwe eaitok.* Cut off my trousers because they're too long. *Ej jepjep wūjooj.* He's mowing the grass.

jepjep (**jępjęp**). 1(*-i*), 2, 3, 7. Move away; change domicile; emigrate; evacuate; migrate; vacate. *Eṃōj aer jepjep ļǫk jān ṃweeņ.* They have moved out of that house.

jepjep (**jepjep**). Elliptical in shape.

jepjep (**jępjęp**). 5(*-e*), 6(*-i*). Bundle; package. *Ejepjepe lowaan wa ņe.* The inside of that vehicle is cluttered with packages. *Jepjep eo aō ņe.* That's my bundle. *Jepjepin nuknuk.* A bundle of clothes.

Jepjep-eo-an-Lōktañūr (**jępjęp-yew-han-lęktagir**). See *jepjep*: "*Lōktañūr*'s bundle". A constellation; stars in Taurus; gamma, delta, epsilon.

jepkǫ (**jępkaw**). 5(*jjepkǫkǫ*), 6(*-i*). Floor mat, coarse. *Ejjepkǫkǫ lowaan ṃwiin.* There are lots of floor mats in this house. This house smells of floor mats.

jeplej (**jeplej**). From Engl. 1, 2, 3(inf, tr *-e*), 4, 5(*jjeplejlej*), 6(*-i*), 7, 8, 9. Syphilis; gonorrhea; venereal disease. *Jab men ippān lieņ bwe enaaj kōjepleje eok.* Do not have sexual intercourse with her or you'll contract syphilis from her.

jepliklik (**jepliklik**). Also *jepeliklik* (**jepeyliklik**). 1(*-i*), 2, 3, 5(*jjepliklik*), 6(*-i*), 7, 8, 9. Swaying from side to side, as a ship rolling. *Eļap an jjepliklik wa eņ.* That ship is really rolling.

jeplōklōk (**jepleklek**). Also *jeplōklōk* (**jęplęklęk**). 1(*-i*), 2, 3(inf *kajjeplōklōk, kajeplōk*), 5(*jjeplōklōk*), 7. Scattered; spread about; straggle. *Jab kajeplōklōk bok kaņe.* Don't scatter those books around. *Kuk im jab jeplōklōk.* Bunch up and don't straggle.

jepļaak (**jepļahak**). Also *jebļaak* (**jebļahak**). 1(*-i*), 2, 3(inf *kōjjepļaak,* tr *kōjepļaak*), 4, 5(*jjepeļaakak*). Return. *Ejepļaak wa eo.* The boat returned. *Wa eo ejjepļaakak eņ.* The ship is continually returning.

jepooj (**jepewej**). A fish, cornet fish, *Fistularia petimba.*

jepta (**jeptah**). To sieve arrowroot: first time; see *epta.*

jeptak (**jeptak**). 1(*-i*), 2(inf, tr *-e*), 4, 5(*jepjeptake*), 7, 8. Slap. *Raar jeptake ļadik eo.* They slapped the boy.

Jeptōṃba (**jepteṃbah**). Also *Jebtōṃba* (**jebteṃbah**). From Engl. 2(inf, tr *-ik*), 6(*-i*). September. *Emaroñ Jeptōṃbaik kwe ņa ānin.* September might still see you on the island.

jepukpuk (**jepiqpiq**). Also *jepukpuk* (**jępiqpiq**). 6(*-i*). Barrel; bushel; keg.

jepwaļ (**jepwaļ**). 1, 2(inf, tr *-e*), 4, 5(*jjepwaļwaļ*), 6(*-i*). Slap on the back of the head. *Jiṃṃaan ear jepwaļe.* His grandfather slapped him on the back of the head. *Rūkaki eo* *ejjepwaḷwaḷ ṇe.* That's the teacher who's always slapping (his students) on the back of the head.

jera (**jerah**). 3, 6(*-i*). A fish, squirrel fish, *Holocentrus* sp.; *Myripristis* sp.

jeraaṃṃan (**jerahaṃṃan**). Also *ṃaju* (**ṃajiw**). 1(*-i*), 2, 3, 4, 7, 8, 9. Wealth; lucky; blessed; fortunate; congratulation; luck; successful. *Eor iien jeraaṃṃan im eor iien jerata.* There are good times and bad times. *Anij eṇ kajeraaṃṃan eok.* May God bless you. *Eḷap an jeraaṃṃan ḷeeṇ.* He is very fortunate.

jerab (**jerab**). Variant form of *jarōb* (**jareb**).

jerajko (**jerajkew**). From Japn. *sarashiko* "bleach powder". 2(inf, tr *-uk*), 5(*jjerajkoko*), 6(*-i*). Bleach. *Jerajkouk nuknuk mouj kaṇe.* Bleach those white clothes. *Ejjerajkoko ṇo ear kwaḷkoḷ ie.* There was bleach all over the spot she washed the clothes at.

jerak (**jerak**). 2(inf, tr *-e*), 3, 4, 5(*jjerakrōk*), 6(*-i*), 7. Sail away; be underway, nautical; hoist sails.

jerakiaarḷap (**jerakyiyaharḷap**). Also *jādeiiaarḷap* (**jadẹyyiyaharḷap**). 2, 6(*-i*). Point of no return; too late. *Etal kake bwe eṃōj an jerakiaarḷap.* Might as well continue since he's gone and spilled the beans.

jerakrōk (**jerakrẹk**). 1(*-i*), 2(inf, tr *-e, jerakrūke*), 3, 4, 5(*jjerakrōk*), 7, 8. Go sailing. *Waat kaṇe rej jerakrōk iar?* What canoes are those sailing in the lagoon? *Wōn eṇ ej jerakrūke wa eṇ?* Who is sailing that canoe? *Ejjerakrōk lọjilñin.* He's got elephant ears.

jeraṃōl (**jeraṃel**). 1(*-i*), 2, 3(inf *kōjjeraṃōlṃōl,* tr *kōjeraṃōl*), 4(*rijjeraṃōl*), 6(*-i*), 8, 9, 11(*jeraṃōlṃōl*). Poor; lonely; poverty.

jerapen (**jerapen**). Archaic. 2, 3(inf, tr *-e*), 6(*-i*). Thousand.

jerata (**jerahtah**). 1, 2, 3(inf, tr *-ik*), 4, 6(*-i*), 8, 9. Misfortune; bad luck; unfortunate; calamity; disaster; tragedy. *Eḷap an jerata peejnej eo an.* His business venture was a flop. *Kadek enaaj kōjerataik eok.* Your drinking will be the end of you.

jerawiwi. See *jerọwiwi.*

jerā (**jeray**). 1(*jera-*), 2, 3(inf, tr *-ik*), 4, 7. Befriend; friend. *Inaaj kōjerāik koṃro kiiō.* Now I'll make you two friends.

jerbal (**jerbal**). 1(*-i*), 2(inf, tr *-e*), 3, 4, 5(*jjerbalbōl*), 6(*-i*), 8. Work; affair; career; chore; deed; duty; employ; employee; enterprise; project; function; task; undertaking; labor; occupation; operate; serve; do. *Ejjerbalbōl ḷeeṇ.* He's always working. *Kwōn kōjerbale.* Use it. *Wōn ṇe ej kōjerbal eok?* Who's employing you? *Rijerbal e.* He's an employee. *Ta ṇe kwōj jerbale?* What are you doing?

jerjer (**jerjer**). Swing arms while walking.

jerkak (**jerkak**). Dial. W, E: *waḷọk.* 1(*-i*), 2, 3(*kōjjerkak, kōjerkak*), 5(*jjerkakkak*), 7, 8. Arise; get up. *Kwōn jerkak.* Get out of bed. *Kwōn kōjerkake.* Get him up. *Iar kanooj jjerkakkak boñ kōn aō abṇōṇō.* I kept getting up all night because I was uncomfortable.

jerkakpeje (**jerkakpẹjẹy**). 1(*-i*), 2, 3, 4, 7. Rise from the dead; resurrection. *Jijej ear jerkakpeje ilo raan eo kein kajilu.* Jesus rose from the dead on the third day.

jerkan (**jerkan**). From *jerkak* (**jerkak**) "rise", *in* (**yin**) "of". 6(*-i*), 7. Begin; become. *Jerkan raan.* Break of day. *Ejkab jerkantak an mour bade in.* The party is just coming to life.

jerọ (**jeraw**). 1(*-i*), 2, 3(inf *kōjjerọro,* tr *kōjerọuk*), 4, 7, 11(*jerọro*). Good marksmanship in shooting or throwing. *Eḷap aō jerọ jān kwe.* I am a better marksman than you. *Kōjro etal in kōjjerọro.* Let's go have a shooting contest.

jerọwiwi (**jerawiywiy**). 1(*-i*), 2, 3, 4, 7, 8, 9. Sin.

jerọwiwiin jolōt (**jerawiywiyin jẹwlẹt**). From *jerọwiwi* (**jerawiywiy**) "sin", *jolet* (**jẹwlẹt**) "inheritance". 6(*-i*). Original sin.

jerọwiwiin mej (**jerawiywiyin mẹj**). Mortal sin. *Jerọwiwiin mej ḷōñ.* Lust is a mortal sin.

jerpentain (**jerpentahyin**). From Engl. Turpentine.

jerta (**jertah**). 1(*-i*), 2, 3, 4, 8, 9. Not good marksman, with gun, slingshot, or by throwing stones (see *jerọ* (**jeraw**)).

jertak (**jertak**). Variant form of *jedtak* (**jedtak**).

jeruru (**jẹyriwriw**). Dial. E only. 1(*-i*), 2(inf, tr *-ik(i)*), 4, 6(*-i*), 7. A beverage, diluted coconut sap. *Ij idaak wōt jeruru kōn aō bane tōñal.* I take only diluted coconut sap because I can't stand sweets. *Jeruru ļọk limen niñniñ eņ.* Give the infant some diluted coconut sap.

jerwaan (**jerwahan**). 1(-*i*), 2(inf, tr -*e*), 4, 8, 9. Prodigal; waste; careless. *Kwōn jab jerwaane ien ṃṃanṃōn kein.* Don't squander the ripe times.

jerwōt (**jerwet**). 3, 6(-*i*). A fish, stripey, *Kuhlia taeniura.*

jet (**jet**). Few; several; a few others; some. *Eor wōt jet armej raar itok ñan kweilọk eo.* Only a few people came to the meeting.

jet (**jet**). 2, 3(inf, tr -*e*), 6(-*i*), 7. Spin. *Kajjioñ ṃōk kajete likaeb(eb) ņe.* Try and spin that top.

jet ien (**jet yiyen**). Sometimes.

jetaar (**jetahar**). Also *jetaad* (**jetahad**). 3, 6(-*i*). A fish, snapper, *Lutjanus kasmira forskal.*

jetak (**jetak**). 2, 3, 7. Heaping up of waves.

jetak (**jetak**). Dial. E, W: *wetaa-*. 1(-*i*), 6(-*i*), 7. On the east side of; see *rāātle. Itok im jijet jetakū.* Come sit on my eastside. *Ear ettōrtok jetakin ṃweotok.* He ran over on the east side of the house.

jete (**jetey**). 3(*kajete, kajjette*), 7. How many? *Jete ņe aṃ pinjeļ?* How many pencils do you have? *Kein kajete in?* How many does that make?

jetļādik (**jetļaydik**). 2, 6(-*i*), 7. Lightning as a sign of fair weather. *Ṃa e enaaj lur bwe ejetļādik.* Know ye by this lightning that there will be calm weather.

jetļọk (**jetļaq**). To vanish over the horizon; disappear. *Iṃad em ļak bar reilọk ejetļọk wa eo.* I got occupied for a while and when I tried to find the boat it had vanished over the horizon.

jetmar (**jẹtmar**). Night after full moon; night after *jetñil* (**jẹtgil**); first moon phase.

jetņaak (**jetņahak**). Also *jetñaak* (**jetgahak**). 2(inf, tr -*e*), 4, 6(-*i*). Nurture a love affair; protect with jealousy. *Ta wūnin aō jetņaake iọkwe eo arro?* Oh why did I let our love get so deep?

jetñaak (**jetgahak**). Variant form of *jetņaak* (**jetņahak**).

jetñak (**jetgak**). Dial. W, E: *jorñak* (**jergak**). Go fast.

jetñōl (**jẹtgẹl**). Night of full moon; day of month when moon comes over the horizon just as sun sets.

jetōb (**jẹtẹb**). 1(*jitūbō-*), 2, 4, 5(*jjetōbtōb*), 6(-*i*). Spirit. *Jetōb Kwōjarjar.* Holy Ghost. *Ejjetōbtōb ānin.* This islet is full of spirits. *Jitūbōn Kūrijṃōj.* Christmas spirit.

jettal (**jettal**). 1(-*i*), 2, 3, 8, 9. Not leak; water-tight (see *ttal* (**ttal**)). *Ejettal wa eņ.* The canoe is water-tight.

jettokja- (**jẹtteqja-**). 1, 2, 3, 7, 8, 9. Worthless; of no value; no good; unprofitable; useless; trivial (see *tokja-* (**teqja-**)). *Ejettokjān aṃ wiaik wa ņe.* There's no reason for you to buy that boat. *Etke kokajettokjān aō wiaik wa e?* Why do you think there's no reason for me to buy this boat?

ji (**jiy**). From Engl. Syllable "ti" of musical scale.

jiab (**jiyab**). 1(-*i*), 6(-*i*). Heart of palm.

jiadel (**jiyadel**). Archaic. A taboo place reserved for chiefs; place for bathing. *Jiadel eo an irooj eņ ņe.* That's the taboo spot for the chief.

jiāe (**jiyayẹy**). Also *jiāi* (**jiyayiy**). From Japn. *shiai* "tournament, contest". 2(inf, tr *jāiik*), 3(inf, tr -*ik*), 4, 6(-*i*). Contest; compete; rivalry. *Kōṃro ar jiāe in lale wōn eo eṃōkaj.* We had a contest to see who was faster. *Erro ej jiāiiki doon.* They're competing with each other.

jiāi (**jiyayiy**). Variant form of *jiāe* (**jiyayẹy**).

jib (**jib**). 1(-*i*), 2, 3(inf, tr -*i*), 5(*jjibjib*), 6(-*i*), 7, 8. Rise, of bread; swell up; fizz; effervesce; have an epileptic attack; water rises in a well or swamp. *Jab kurkuri bwe kwōnaaj kajibi.* Don't shake it up or it'll fizz all over. *Pia māāņāņ ejjibjib.* Warm beer always fizzes.

Jibabwāi (**jibahbayiy**). A plant, taro variety, *Colocasia* (Takeuchi).

jibadbad (**jibadbad**). Endeavor; attempt; ambition; try hard; quest. *Jej aikuj jibadbad im jab aipādpād ñe jekōņaan ļe.* We have to have ambition and not be phlegmatic if we want to succeed.

jibadede (**jibahdẹydẹy**). Dial. Namu only. 2(inf, tr -*ik(i)*), 4, 6(-*i*), 7. Fishing method, catching flying fish when they enter lagoon at a certain location at Namu. *Ejeparujruj armej ñe ej iien jibadede iNamo.* People on Namu get excited when they prepare to catch flying fish there.

jibadek (**jibadek**). Also *kōttōpar* (**kettepar**). 1(*-i*), 2(inf, tr *-e*), 3(*kajjibadek*), 7. Try to reach; proceeding toward destination. *Ta ṇe kwōj jibadekḷọk Amedka kake.* Why are you trying to go to the States? *Iar jibadektok eok.* I came to see you. *Wa eṇ ej jibadekḷọk āneṇ.* The ship is going to the island.

jibadek jidik (**jibadek jidik**). From *jibadek* (**jibadek**) "try to reach", *jidik* (**jidik**) "a little bit". 2. Be on one's way; get ahead. *Kōjro jibadek jidik.* Let's be on our way. *Eṃṃan aō roñ tok ke kwōj kakkōt jibadek jidik.* I'm glad to hear that you are getting ahead.

jibai (**jibahyiy**). 1(*-i*), 2, 4, 6(*-i*). Magic trick; perform a trick.

jibai (**jibahyiy**). From Engl. *spy*. 2(inf, tr *-ik(i)*), 4, 6(*-i*). Spy. *Raar jilkinḷọk bwe en jibaik(i) rūkōjdat ro.* He was dispatched to spy on the enemy.

jibaik (**jibahyik**). From Engl. Spike.

jibaiklaaj (**jibahyiklahaj**). Variant form of *baiklaaj* (**bahyiklahaj**).

jiban (**jiban**). 1(*-i*), 2, 6(*-i*), 8, 9. Unable to throw far; short of money. *Kwōjja wia kijerro bwe ijiban.* You buy our food cause I'm a little short of money. *Ejekkar ñan pijja bwe ejiban.* He won't make a good pitcher because he can't throw far.

jibana (**jibahnah**). From Japn. *supana* (from Engl. *spanner*). A wrench.

jibañūñ (**jibahgig**). 5(*jjibañūññūñ*), 6(*-i*). Edible portion inside certain nuts or seeds.

jibbaḷañ (**jibbahḷag**). 3, 4+3, 5(*-e*), 6(*-i*), 3+7. A fish, general term for all blenny.

jibbatūñtūñ (**jibbahtigtig**). 1(*-i*), 2, 3, 6(*-i*). Very small; minute; tiny; microscopic. *Ṃōttan wōt jibbatūñtūñ.* Just a wee bit more.

jibbin-bōran-bōb (**jibbin-beran-beb**). Also *luo.* From *jib* "rise". A shell, conical and longer than trochus.

jibboñ (**jibbęg°**). 2(inf, tr *-e*), 3, 6(*-i*), 7, 8, 9. Morning.

jibboñōn eo turun inne (**jibbęg°ẹn yew tir°in yinney**). Three mornings ago.

jibboñōn ilju (**jibbęg°ẹn yiljiw**). Tomorrow morning.

jibboñōn inne (**jibbęg°ẹn yinney**). Yesterday morning.

jibboñōn inne eo ḷọk juon (**jibbęg°ẹn yinney yew ḷaq jiwen**). Three mornings ago.

jibboñōniin (**jibbęg°ẹniyin**). This morning.

jibboñōnin jekḷaj (**jibbęg°ẹnin jekḷaj**). Morning of the day after tomorrow.

jibbūñ (**jibbig**). 6(*-i*), 11(*jibūñbūñ*). Minute; tiny; microscopic; little bit; joy. *Idaak wōt jibbūñ in men ṇe em kwōmej.* Just take a tiny bit of that and you'll die.

jibke (**jibkẹy**). 1, 2(inf, tr *-ik*), 4, 6(*-i*), 7. Fishing method, for porpoises. *Ḷōṃaro raar jibkeik rōñoul ke.* They caught twenty porpoises by the *jibke* method.

jibọkjeep (**jibaqjeyep**). From Engl. 2(inf, tr *-e*), 4, 6(*-i*), 7. Spokeshave. *Kwōn jibọkjeepe ijeṇe eṃōdṃōd.* Use the spokeshave and shave off the frayed section.

jibōr (**jiyber**). From Engl. 2(inf, tr *-e*), 6(*-i*), 7. Zipper; to zip.

jibriiñ (**jibriyig**). From Engl. 2, 3(inf, tr *-i*), 6(*-i*). Spring.

Jibuklik (**jibiqlik**). Clan name.

jibukwi (**jibiqiy**). 2, 3, 5(*kajjibkwi*), 7. One hundred.

jibuñ (**jiybig°**). 2, 5(*jjibuñbuñ*), 6(*-i*). Stillbirth. *Ejibuñ.* It's a stillbirth. *Ejjibuñbuñ nājin.* She's always delivering stillbirths.

jiburi (**jibir°iy**). Transitive form of *jjibur* (**jjibir°**).

jiburlep (**jibir°lep**). 2(inf, tr *-e*), 4, 6(*-i*), 7. Bear hug.

jibuun (**jibiwin**). From Engl. 1(*-i*), 2(inf, tr *-i*), 3. Spoon; fork. *Kwōn ṃōñā kōn jibuun.* Eat with a spoon. *Kwōn jibuuni jān pilej ṇe.* Spoon it off your plate. *Eor ke ñiiṃ jibuun bọọk.* Do you have a fork?

jibuut (**jiybiwit**). From Engl. *sea boot*. Boot. *Kobbōk ia aṃ jibuut?* Where did you get your boots?

jibūkbūk (**jibikbik**). 6(*-i*). A sloop. *Kwaar lo ke jibūkbūkin Likiep eo?* Did you notice the sloop from Likiep?

jibūñ (**jibig**). 7. Little bit; jot.

jibwe (**jibey**). Transitive form of *jebjer* (**jębjęb**).

jibwe doon (**jibey dewen**). Also *kabwijer doon* (**kabijer dewen**). Idiom. To clash in a fight; to square off. *Erro baj jibwe doon wōt jidik.* They almost clashed.

jibwe turin jerbal (**jibey tiwrin jerbal**). Idiom. Leave a chore undone and start another. *Kwōn jab jibwe turin aṃ jerbal.* Don't do another chore before you finish the first.

jibweiklaaj (**jibęyiklahaj**). Variant form of *baiklaaj* (**bahyiklahaj**).

jibwi (**jibiy**). 2(inf, tr *-ik*), 3, 6(*-i*). Pet; duty of taking care of a grandson, granddaughter, a grandparent, or a pet.

jibwi- (**jibi-**). 1. Grandmother, grandchild, of; pet of; possessive classifier, grandmother or grandchild or pet.

jibwil (**jibil**). 2(inf, tr *-i*), 4, 5(*jjibwilbwil*), 6(*-i*). Molded arrowroot starch. *Kwōj ļōmņak in jibwili ñāāt ṃakṃōk eņ.* When do you intend to mold the arrowroot starch?

Jibwiļuļ (**jibiyļ°iļ°**). Clan name.

jidaak (**jidahak**). 2, 3(inf, tr *-e*), 6(*-i*), 7. To touch sand; to land; to arrive, of a canoe; beach a canoe to the water line. *Ejidaak wa ko.* The canoes have arrived. *Kwōn kajidaake wa ņe.* Pull the canoe on the sand.

jiddik (**jiddik**). Petty; small; minor.

jidduul (**jiddiwil**). 3, 6(*-i*). A shell, *Patellidae*, *Collisella grata*. Also *Cellana nigrolineata*, *Notoacmea gloriosa/concinna* and *Patelloida saccharina* lanx. A shell, *Trochidae*, *Bathybembix aeola*, top shell; limpet snails with nonconical shells. *Rej kajidduul ilik.* They're hunting for top shells in the ocean side.

jide (**jidęy**). From Japn. *shitsurey* "lose courtesy" (words of apology when one wins at a game through luck). 1, 2, 3+5(*kajjidede*), 5(*jjidede*), 6(*-i*). Fate; chance; by accident. *Ejide im bōk jerbal eo.* He was lucky to get the job. *Eṃōj ņe aṃ kajjidede.* Stop depending on chance. *Wūnin an wiin kōn an jjidede em ṃṃan pein.* He won because of the cards falling in place often by accident.

jidep (**jidep**). 2(inf, tr *jideppe*). Burn a tree. *Kwōn jab jideppe mā ņe.* Don't burn that breadfruit tree.

jidik illǫk jidik (**jidik yillaq jidik**). Idiom. Gradually, little by little, piecemeal.

Jidikdik (**jiydikdik**). Dialectal variant of *Ijjidik* (**yijjiydik**).

jidimkij (**jidimkij**). Also *bōro-kadu* (**bęręw-kadiw**). 1(*-i*), 2, 3, 4, 5(*jjidimkijkij*), 7, 8, 9. Hot tempered; sudden; in a hurry; abrupt. *Ejidimkij an uwe.* He left in a hurry. *Ļeo ejjidimkijkij ņe.* He has a short temper. That fellow gets angry easily.

jidjid (**jidjid**). 3, 4(*rūkkajidjid*), 5(*jjidjid*), 6(*-i*), 7, 8. Cricket; grasshopper; locust. *Ejidjide turun ṃwiin.* There are a lot of crickets around this house.

jidjid (**jidjid**). 2(inf, tr *-i*), 6(*-i*). Club used for beating coconut husk for sennit. *Imaroñ ke kōjerbal jidjid eo aṃ?* Can I use your coconut husk beating club?

jidkok (**jidqęq**). A plant.

jidpaļ (**jidpaļ**). 1(*-i*), 2, 3, 5(*jjidpaļpaļ*), 7. Sprain. *Ejidpaļ neō.* My ankle is sprained. *Ejjidpaļpaļ neen ļeeņ.* His ankle is always getting sprained.

jidpān (**jidpan**). 1(*-i*), 2(inf, tr *-e*), 3, 4, 6(*-i*), 7, 8. Saw. *Wōn e ear jidpāne aļaļ e?* Who sawed this piece of wood?

Jidpān (**jidpan**). From *jidpān* (**jidpan**) "a saw". 3, 6(*-i*). A plant, pandanus cultigen.

jidpān aen (**jidpan hayen**). From *jidpān* (**jidpan**) "saw", *aen* (**hayen**) "metal". 2(inf, tr *-e*), 4, 6(*-i*), 7. Hacksaw. *Jemaroñ jidpān aene men ņe.* We can cut it with a hacksaw.

jieb- (**jiyęb-**). 2+7, 3+7, 7. Be running over; overflow; erupt. *Ejiebļǫk dānnin jekaro eņ.* The *jekaro* on that coconut tree is running over.

jieje (**jiyęjęy**). Swollen abdomen; see *jeje*.

jiemetak (**jiyemetak**). Variant form of *jemetak* (**jęymetak**).

jieñ (**jiyeg**). Also *jiōñ* (**jiyęg°**). 2(inf, tr *-e*), 6(*-i*), 7. Cover up a hole; erase footprints. *Jieñe lōb ņe.* Cover up the grave.

jiieņ (**jiyiyeņ**). Variant form of *ijjieņ* (**yijjiyeņ**).

jiij (jiyij). From Engl. 2(inf, tr *-i*), 6(*-i*). Cheese. *Enņo jiij.* I like cheese. *Jiiji jāānwūj ņe.* Put cheese in that sandwich.

jiilñij (jiyilgij). Variant form of *jiiñlij* (jiyiglij).

jiin (jiyin). From Engl. Gin. *Idike nemān jiin.* I don't like the taste of gin.

jiiñlij (jiyiglij). Also *jiilñij* (jiyilgij). From Engl. *singlet.* 1(*-i*), 2(inf, tr *-i*), 3(inf, tr *-i*), 5(*jjiiñlijlij*), 6(*-i*), 7. Undershirt; T-shirt. *Ejjiiñlijlij ļeeņ.* He always wears an undershirt. *Kajiiñliji niñniñ ņe.* Put an undershirt on the baby.

jiip (jiyip). From Engl. 2(inf, tr *-i*), 5(*jjiipip*), 6(*-i*), 7. Jeep. *Kwōmaroñ ke jiipiļok eō ñan tawūn?* Can you take me to town in the jeep?

jiip (jiyip). From Engl. 5(*jjiipip*), 6(*-i*). Sheep. *Ejjiipip meļaaj eņ an.* His pasture is crawling with sheep.

jiipip (jiyipyip). From *jiip* (jiyip). 1(*-i*), 2, 3(inf, tr *kajiipip(-i)*), 6(*-i*), 7. Drive a jeep. *Kwōn kipeddikdik im jab mmakijkij aṃ jiipip bwe eļap oņāān kiaaj raan kein.* You'd better cut corners and not use the jeep all the time because gas is expensive these days.

jiipkako (jiyipkahkẹw). From Engl. *supercargo, chief cargo.* 2, 6(*-i*), 7. Supercargo; purser; wallet; purse; cash box. *Ej jiipkako ilo wa eņ.* He's the supercargo on the ship. *Ejako jiipkako eo aō.* I lost my wallet.

jiit (jiyit). From Engl. 2(inf, tr *-i*), 5(*jjiitit*), 6(*-i*). Sheet. *Jiiti būtoñ ņe.* Put a sheet on the mattress.

jiitit (jiyityit). From *jiit* (jiyit). 1(*-i*), 2, 3(inf, tr *kajiitit(-i)*), 6(*-i*), 7. Use a sheet. *Kwōj jiitit ke?* Are you using a sheet? Do you want to use sheets?

jij-. See *jj-.*

jijāj (jiyjaj). From Engl. 2(inf, tr *-e*), 6(*-i*), 7. Shears; scissors; cut with scissors. *Kwōn jijāje nuknuk ņe.* Cut that cloth.

Jijej Kūraij (jiyjẹj kirahyij). From Engl. Jesus Christ.

Jijer (jiyjer). From Engl. Caesar.

jijet (jiyjet). 1(*-i*), 2, 3(inf *kajjijet,* tr *kajijete*), 5(*jjijetjet*), 7, 8. Sit down. *Kwōn jab jjijetjet bwe eboñ.* Don't keep sitting down all the time because

it's almost night. *Kwōn jab kajijete bwe ejaje jijet.* Don't make him sit because he doesn't know how yet. *Etke kwōj jab jijet wōt?* Why don't you settle down?

jijidiiñ (jijidiyig). From Japn. *shichirin.* Broiler. *Enņo kōṃattin jijidiiñ e wōja.* My broiler cooks real well.

jijimmarok (jijimmareq). Variant form of *jimmarok* (jimmareq).

jijjet (jijjet). Variant form of *jejjet* (jejjet).

jijo (jijẹw). Also *lukwej.* A plant, *Calophyllum inophyllum* L. (Guttiferae).

jik (jik). 1(*jikki-*), 3, 6(*-i*). Place for making love, usually in bushes; bower; den.

jikeet (jikeyet). Also *jiket* (jikyet). From Engl. 2, 3(inf, tr *-e*), 4, 6(*-i*), 7. Skate; slip.

jiki- (jiki-). 1. Place of; property of; land of; position; territory; possessive classifier, position or property.

jikin ioon doon (jikin yiyewen dewen). A rendezvous. *Naaj jikin ioon doon eo ad in.* This will be our rendezvous.

jikin kallib (jikin kallib). Farm; garden.

jikin kweļok (jikin qẹylaq). From *jikin* "place of", *kweļok* "assembly". City; town.

jikin menin mour (jikin menin mẹwir). Zoo. *Iar alwōj ilo jikin menin mour eņ.* I went sightseeing at the zoo.

jikin niñniñ (jikin nignig). Womb; uterus. *Ejorrāān jikin niñniñ eņ an.* Her womb is malignant.

jikin uwe (jikin wiwẹy). Ladder; staircase; climb a ladder or a staircase; uneven; ratline; stairway. *Ear jikin uwe lōñļok ñan po eņ.* He climbed up stairs to the attic. *Ejikin uwe an ṃwijit bōraṃ.* Your hair was trimmed quite sloppily.

jikip (jikip). Archaic. Dancing place.

jikipkip (jikipkip). Variant form of *jipikpik* (jipikpik).

jikka (jikkah). 3, 5(*jjikkaka*), 6(*-i*). Cigarette. *Ebwiin jjikkaka lowaan ruuṃ in.* I smell cigarette odor all over this room.

jikmeed (jikmeyed). Variant form of *ļajikmeed* (ļajikmeyed).

jikorōj (**jiykewrej**). Variant form of *jipkorōj* (**jipkewrej**).

jikōḷ (**jikeḷ**). From Engl. 2(inf, tr *-e*), 4, 6(*-i*). Sickle.

Jikōpeo (**jikepyew**). 3, 6(*-i*). A plant, pandanus cultigen.

jikōt (**jikẹt**). (**jikẹt, jiket**). Also *jekōt* (**jẹkẹt**). 2. In what direction; to do what. *Ej ettōrjikōt?* Which way is he running? *Baḷuun eo ear jokjikōt?* Which way did the plane land? *Kwōj wajjikōt? Kwōj wajekōt?* Where are you heading? What are you coming here to do? *Kwōj wajjikōt Mājro?* What are you going to do in Majuro? *Ej jitjikōt?* Which way is it facing?

jikraip (**jikrahyip**). From Engl. 3(inf, tr *-i*), 5(*jjikraipip*), 6(*-i*). Scribe.

jikrōk (**jikrẹk**). 2, 7. Approach; draw near; arrive. *Batok ñe ejikrōk.* Tell me when he draws near. *Wa eo eṇ ejikrōk.* The ship has arrived.

jiktok (**jikteq**). 2, 6(*-i*). Become an obsession. *Ilo iien aṃ jiktok, iitōn bwebwe.* When you come into my mind, I nearly go crazy. *Ejiktok aō kōṇaan idaak.* I'm dying for a drink. *En jab bar jiktok aṃ ajri nana.* Now don't you go and be naughty again. *Ebar jiktok an nana.* He's becoming naughty again.

jikuna (**jikiwnah**). From Engl. *schooner*. 6(*-i*). Schooner; ketch.

jikur (**jikir°**). Also *jukur* (**jiqir°**). 5(*jjikurkur*), 6(*-i*). Ditch; trench. *Ejjikurkur iooj in ānin.* The interior of this islet is full of ditches.

jikut (**jiqit**). Also *jukut, jikūt* (**jikit**). Archaic. One hundred pairs, fish or copra.

Jikut-im-rukut (**jiqit-yim-riqit**). A constellation; stars in Centaurus; alpha and beta.

jikuuḷ (**jikiwiḷ**). Also *jukuuḷ* (**jiqiwiḷ**). From Engl. 1(*-i*), 2(inf, tr *-i*), 3, 4, 7. School; teach. *Ṃōn jikuuḷ.* School house. *Jabōt jikuuḷ.* Sunday school. *Itok bwe in jikuḷi eok.* Come to me and I'll teach you.

jikūru (**jikiriw**). From Engl. 1(*-i*), 2(inf, tr *-uk*), 3, 6(*-i*), 7, 8. Screw; bolt.

jikūt (**jikit**). Variant form of *jekōt.*

jil (**jil**). 1(*-i*), 2, 3, 7. Dark colored. *Ejil an maroro nuknuk ṇe aṃ.* Your clothing is dark green. *Ejil an maroro nuknuk kaṇe aṃ.* Your clothes are dark green.

jila (**jilah**). From Engl. *tiller*. 6(*-a*). Tiller, nautical.

jilej (**jilẹj**). Place where the *wūlej* grows.

jilel (**jilẹl**). 2(inf, tr *-e*), 3, 4, 6(*-i*), 7. A shell, *Cymatiidae*; *Charonia tritonis*; triton shell. A shell, *Cassididae*; *Morum macandrewi/teramachii* or *Bezoardicella decussata/areola* or *Phalium glauca*; trumpet, horn, siren, conch. *Tiṃa eo ear jilele an jerak.* The ship blew its horn to signal its departure.

Jilelwōj (**jilẹlwẹj**). From *jilel* (**jilẹl**) "helmet shell, blow a conch shell", *wōj* "toward you". 3, 6(*-i*). A plant, pandanus cultigen.

jilikiia (**jilikiyyah**). 1(*-i*), 2, 8, 9. Slow to obey; disobedient (see *jilikiie* (**jilikiyyẹy**)).

jilikiie (**jilikiyyẹy**). 1(*-i*), 2, 8, 9. Obey readily and cheerfully; obedient (see *jilikiia* (**jilikiyyah**)).

jilikor (**jiliqer**). Also *jilor* (**jilwer**). Archaic. Thirty pairs, fish or copra.

jiliktūr (**jiliktir**). Dialectal variant of *ajriin uwaak* (**hajriyin wiwahak**).

jilirap (**jilirap**). Also *jilirab* (**jilirab**). Archaic. 2, 3(inf, tr *-e*), 6(*-i*). Three thousand.

jiljilimjuon (**jiljilimjiwen**). Also *jijilimjuon* (**jijilimjiwen**), *jimjuon* (**jimjiwen**). 3, 5(*kajjijilimjuon*), 6(*-i*), 7. Seven.

jiljilimjuonñoul (**jiljilimjiwengẹwil**). 2, 3, 6(*-i*). Seventy.

jiljino (**jiljinew**). 3(*kajiljino*), 5(*inf kajjiljino*, tr *kajjiljinouk*), 7. Six. *Kōjro ej kajjiljino bok.* We each have six books.

jiljino awa (**jiljinew hawah**). From "six o'clock". A plant, flower, *Phyllantus niruri* (Takeuchi).

jiljinokor (**jiljinewqer**). Archaic. Sixty pairs, fish or copra.

jiljinoñoul (**jiljinewgẹwil**). Also *jiljinōññoul* (**jiljinẹggẹwil**). 2, 3, 6(*-i*). Sixty.

jilkin (**jilkin**). Transitive form of *jjilōk* (**jjilẹk**).

jillǫk (**jillaq**). Also *jinlǫk*. 1(*-i*), 2, 3, 4, 5(*jjillǫklǫk*), 7, 8. Bend forward and down; bow the head, as in prayer.

Etetal jillọk ko aṃ rōkarel eō. The way you always walk with your head down attracts me (words from love song). *Eṃōj ṇe aṃ jjillọklọk.* Stop hanging your head all the time.

jilñuul (**jilgiwil**). 3, 5(*kajjilñuul*), 7. Thirty.

jilo (**jilẹw**). 3, 4+3, 5(*-e*), 6(*-i*), 3+7. A fish, dog-tooth tuna, *Gymnosarda nuda.*

jilōñlōñ (**jilegleg**). Variant form of *jelōñlōñ* (**jẹlẹglẹg**).

jilu (**jiliw**). 3, 5(*inf kajjillu*, tr *kajjiluuk*), 7. Three.

jilubukwi (**jiliwbiqiy**). Also *jilibukwi* (**jilibiqiy**). 3, 5(*inf kajjilubukwi*, tr *kajjilubukwiik*), 7. Three hundred.

Jilubukwi (**jiliwbiqiy**). From "three hundred" (because of the abundance of the fruits). 3, 6(*-i*). A plant, banana variety.

jiḷait (**jiḷahyit**). From Engl. 1(*-i*), 2(inf, tr *-i*), 4, 6(*-i*), 7. Slice; carve. *Kwōn jiḷaiti ḷoob ṇe bwe jen ṃōñā.* Would you slice up the loaf so we can have some bread?

Jiḷōbbar (**jiḷebbar**). From "a fish". 3, 6(*-i*). A plant, pandanus cultigen; Jaluit.

jimañūñ (**jimagig**). Also *jemañūñ* (**jemagig**). 1(*-i*), 2(inf, tr *-i*), 3(inf *kajjimañūññūñ*, tr *kajimañūñi*),5(*jjimañūññūñ*),E 6(*-i*). Fermented coconut toddy; sour toddy. *Kwōnañin jimañūñi ke jekaro eo.* Have you fermented the coconut toddy?

jimaroñ (**jimareg°**). 1(*-i*), 2, 3(inf *kajjimaroñroñ*, tr *kajimaroñ*), 4, 7. Throw far. *Eḷap aō jimaroñ jān kwe.* I throw farther than you. *Kōjro etal in kajjimaroñroñ.* 'Let's go have a throwing contest.

jimattan (**jimattan**). 1(*-i*), 2, 3(inf *kajjimattantan*, tr *kajimattan*), 5(*jjimattantan*). Half. *Ejjimattantan pilawā kā.* These loaves of bread are all cut in half.

jimeeṇ (**jimeyeṇ**). Also *jimāāṇ* (**jimayaṇ**). From Engl. 1(*-i*), 2(inf, tr *-e*), 3, 4, 5(*jjimeeṇeṇ*), 6(*-i*), 7, 8. Cement; concrete. *Wōn ṇe ear jimeeṇe ijeṇe.* Who cemented that place there? *Kwaar wia tok jimeeṇ jān ia?* Where did you buy this cement from?

jimmarok (**jimmareq**). Also *jijimmarok* (**jijimmareq**). 1(*-i*), 2(inf, tr *-e*), 3, 5(*jijimmarok*), 7, 8, 9. Period before dawn. *Iar ruj wōt ke ej jimmarok.* I woke up before dawn.

jimmiḷọk (**jimmiḷaq**). From *jeṃḷọk* (**jeṃḷaq**). 6(*-i*). End (used in songs); eternity. *Naaj kōjro wōt ñan jimmiḷọkun aō mour.* It'll just be the two of us till I die.

jimni (**jimniy**). From Engl. 6(*-i*). Lamp chimney.

jiṃ (**jiṃ**). 6(*-i*). Coconut shell, lower half, without eye.

jiṃ (**jiṃ**). 1(*-i*), 2(inf, tr *-i*), 6(*-i*). Canoe part, two end pieces of canoe. *Ej jiṃi wa eṇ.* He's working on the two end pieces of the canoe.

jiṃ (**jiṃ**). 6(*-i*). A bunch of dried pandanus leaves for thatch.

jiṃa (**jiṃah**). Beyond; above; more than; some; always used with numerals. *Inaaj kālọk joñoul jiṃa raan in allōñ in.* I will leave on the plane shortly after the tenth of this month.

jiṃaat (**jiṃahat**). From Engl. 1(*-i*), 2, 3(inf *kajjiṃaatat,* tr *kajiṃaate*), 6(*-i*), 8, 9. Smart; intelligent; shrewd; cunning; clever. *Ejjeḷọk wōt jiṃaatin.* He's so clever. *Ijaje kajjiṃaatat.* I wouldn't know how to act smart. *Eḷap an kajiṃaate e.* He's putting on airs.

jiṃalejlej (**jiṃahlẹjlẹj**). 1(*-i*), 2, 3, 7. Giddy; dizzy. *Ejiṃalejlej meja kōn an to aō riit.* My head is giddy from my reading so long. *Ear jiṃalejlej meja ṇai raan ni utiej eo.* I felt giddy in the tall coconut tree.

jiṃañko (**jiṃagkẹw**). 3, 6(*-i*). Coconut cup.

jiṃjọ (**jiṃjaw**). Also *jeṃjọ* (**jẹṃjaw**). 3, 6(*-i*). A fish, a species of skate.

jiṃṃa (**jiṃṃah**). 1(*-a*). Grandfather, child speech; grandfather (with possessive suffixes).

jiṃṃūḷọk (**jiṃṃiḷaq**). Eternity.

jiṃor (**jiṃer°**). 7. Together; both. *Komro jiṃor itok.* The two of you both come.

jiṃōkṃōk (**jiyṃẹkṃẹk**). 2, 4, 6(*-i*). Marshallese women's stick dance.

jiṃwe (**jiṃẹy**). 1(*-i*), 2, 3(st inf *kajjiṃwe,* tr *kajiṃwe, -ik*), 4, 7, 8, 9, 11(*jiṃwe*). Straight; correct; right; honest; amend; scrupulous; precise;

rightly; straightforward. *Kwōn kajimweik mour ņe aṃ.* You must amend your life.

jiṃwin ne (**jiṃin ney**). 1(*...nee-*). Heel.

jiṃwin ñi (**jiṃin giy**). 1(*...ñii-*). Chin.

jiṃwin ñi (**jiṃin giy**). Slang. From *jiṃwin-ñi* (**jiṃin-giy**) "chin". 1(*-i*). Spokesman; closest advisor. *Ļeo jiṃwinñiin irooj eņ ņe.* He's the closet adivsor to the chief.

jiṃwin pā (**jiṃin pay**). 1(*...pei-*). Elbow.

jin (**jin**). Variant form of *ijin* (**yijin**).

jinaketa (**jinahkeytah**). From Japn. *shina geta* "Chinese geta". 2(inf, tr *-ik*), 3, 4, 6(*-i*), 7. Wooden clog, footwear. *Ijaje jinaketa.* I can't wear wooden clogs. *Kwōn ja kajinaketaiki ñan ilju.* Let him use the wooden clogs until tomorrow.

jinbaat (**jinbahat**). 1(*-i*), 2(inf, tr *-(e)*), 3, 4, 7, 8. Smoke out; smudge. *Kwōn jinbaate barulep ņe.* Smoke out that coconut crab.

jine (**jiney**). 2(inf, tr *-ik*), 3, 6(*-i*). Duty of taking care of a mother.

jine (**jiynęy**). 3, 5(*jjinene*), 6(*-i*). A crab. *Ejjinene ānin.* This island is full of crabs.

jine- (**jine-**). 1. Mother; aunt; older sister; female cousin.

jinenpokpok (**jinenpeqpeq**). 3, 4+3, 6(*-i*), 3+7. A shell, *Neritidae*; *Thliostyra albicilla*; sea snail.

jinibọọr (**jinibawar**). Also *jinnibọọr* (**jinnibawar**). Brass; tin roofing. *Eṃōj aō erōm jinibọọr ettōñtōñ.* I am become as pounding brass (Bible).

jiniet (**jiniyęt**). Also *jineet* (**jinęyęt**). 1(*-i*), 2(inf, tr *-e*), 3, 4, 7, 8, 9. Guide; familiar; acquainted with; direct. *Kwōn jiniete i ānin.* Show him around the island. *Ejiniet ānin.* He is familiar with this island. *Jiniete ļọk ñan jikin eọñōd eņ arro.* Direct him to our favorite fishing spot.

jiniñniñ (**jinignig**). Also *jiniñ* (**jinig**). From *niñ* (**nig**). 5(*jjinniñniñ*), 6(*-i*). Tiny; very small; slight.

jinjin (**jinjin**). Also *jenjen* (**jęnjęn**). From *jine-* (**jine-**) "mother". 1(*-i*), 2(inf, tr *-e*), 4, 6(*-i*), 7, 9. Curse; swear; cuss. *Wōn ņe kwōj jinjine?* Whom are you cursing? *Ellu ļōļļap eo im jinjini ajri ro.* The old man got mad and swore at the children.

Jinkabo (**jinkabew**). Clan name.

jinkadool (**jinkadwel**). 1(*-i*), 2(inf, tr *-e*, *-i*), 3, 4, 7. Broil, on hot stones; barbecue; grill. *Rej jinkadool ek.* They are broiling fish. *Kwōn jinkadoole ek ņe.* Broil that fish.

jinkōļar (**jinkeļar**). Dial. E, W: *norōbōtōñ* (**newrebeteg°**). 6(*-i*). A food, coconut bread, from copra and flour and sap or sugar.

jinlọk (**jinlaq**). Variant form of *jillọk*.

jinṃa (**jinṃah**). 2(inf, tr *-ik*), 6(*-i*). Stone upon which bait or chum is mashed; pound something or someone; clobber someone. *Kwōn jinṃaiki ļọk pajo ņe bwe jen eọñōd.* Hurry up and mash that chum so we can start fishing. *Ñe kobar kōṃṃane inaaj jinṃaik eok.* Do it one more time and I'll clobber you.

jinnibọọr (**jinniybawar**). 3, 6(*-i*). Roofing; corrugated iron.

jinnipran̄ (**jinniprag**). Also *jepar* (**jepar**). 3, 5(*jinnipran̄ran̄e*), 6(*-i*). Open spathe of coconut tree; stem of coconut bunch from which nuts have fallen. *Ejinnipran̄ran̄e raan ni eņ.* That coconut tree has lots of old bunch stems.

jino (**jinew**). Transitive form of *jjino* (**jjinew**).

jinōkjeej (**jinękjęyęj**). Also *jinōkjej* (**jinekjęj**). 2(inf, tr *-e*, *jinōkjeije*), 3, 7. Reward; merit; attribute. *Kwōnaaj bōk aṃ jinōkjeej ilañ.* You will receive your reward in heaven.

jinre (**jinręy**). 2(inf, tr *-ik*), 4, 6(*-i*), 7. Cooking and eating fish right after catching them, usually at night; eat secretly. *Ennọ jinre ek ilo bōñ.* Fish are more tasty when cooked right after catching them at night.

jintanji (**jintanjiy**). Slang. 2, 3(inf, tr *-ik*). Deteriorate; out of commission; broken. *Ejintanji injin ņe arro.* Our engine's deteriorating.

jintōb (**jintęb**). 1(*-i*), 2(inf, tr *-e*), 3, 4, 7. Go barefoot; eat only one food. *Emake jab metak neeṃ aṃ jintōb im etetal.* It doesn't seem to hurt your feet at all to walk around barefoot. *Etke kwōjintōb jatiin, ta ejjeļọk raij ke?* Why are you eating only sardines--isn't there any rice? *Iaar jintōbe ek eo.* I ate the fish alone without anything else.

jinwōd (**jinwed**). Collect coconuts or breadfruit.

jiṇo (**jiṇẹw**). 1(*-i*), 2, 3(*jjiṇoṇo*), 4+3, 5(*jjiṇoṇo*), 7. A sore, painful and malignant, usually located on the hands or feet; gangrene. *Elōñ riṂajeḷ rōlukkuun jeḷā kajjiṇoṇo.* There are Marshallese who are experts in treating *jiṇo*.

jiṇo (**jiṇẹw**). From Engl. 6(*-i*), 7, 8, 9. Snow.

jiñ (**jig**). 1(*-i*), 2(inf, tr *-ūt*), 3(st inf *kajjiñjiñ*, tr *kajiñ*), 5(*jjiñjiñ*), 7. Fart; break wind. *Ejjiñjiñ ḷeeṇ.* He's always breaking wind. *Kwōle ekajjiñjiñ.* Nuts are gas producing.

jiñap (**jigap**). 2(inf, tr *-e*), 4, 6(*-i*), 7. Laying gifts under a Christmas tree (at a Christmas song fest). *Raar jiñapeḷọk wōjke eo.* They put gifts under the tree.

jiookra (**jiyẹwẹkrah**). From Japn. *shiokara*. 2(inf, tr *-ik*), 4, 6(*-i*). A food, salted fish guts or clams. *Jen jiookraik mejānwōd kein.* Let's make *jiookra* out of these clams.

jioñ (**jiyẹg°**). Transitive form of *jjioñ* (**jjiyẹg°**).

jipañ (**jipag**). 1(*-i*), 2(inf, tr *-e*), 4, 5(*jipjipañ*), 7. Help; aid; benefit; pension. *Koṃwin itok jen jipjipañ doon.* Come let's help each other (and divide up the separate tasks). *Jipjipañ wōt doon.* Don't neglect to perform those tasks which are your contribution to the general welfare of your community.

jiped (**jiped**). Transitive form of *jjiped* (**jjiped**).

jipeeḷ (**jipeyeḷ**). From Engl. 1(*-i*), 2(inf, tr *-e*), 3. Spell; spelling.

Jipein (**jipẹyin**). From Engl. 4. Spain.

jipeit (**jipẹyit**). From Engl. 2, 6(*-i*). Spade. *Eijin jipeit.* An ace of spades. *Kwaar lo ke jipeit eo arro?* Did you see my spade?

jipeḷḷọk (**jipeḷḷaq**). 2, 7. Shove a person; push. *Raar jipeḷḷọk doon nabōjān ṃōn pija eo.* They shoved one another about outside the theater. *Jipeḷḷọktok.* Push him toward me.

jipenpen (**jipẹnpẹn**). Sea cucumber, *Holothuroidea*, *Holothuria leucospilo*ta; up to 20 cm. in length, black or gray, found in ankle-depth water at low tide; give forth sticky secretion. *RiRuk rej ṃōñā jipenpen.* Trukese eat sea cucumber.

jipij (**jipyij**). From Engl. 1(*-i*), 2(inf, tr *-i*), 3, 4, 5(*jjipijij*), 6(*-i*), 7, 8. Speech; make a speech; address; lecture. *Ear jipiji ledik eo.* He flattered the girl. *Emake jjipijij aḷap eṇ.* That old man is always preaching.

jipijuḷ (**jipiyjiḷ°**). 2(inf, tr *-i*), 4, 6(*-i*), 7. Walk with a limp; have one limb shorter than the other; prune a bush. *Ej jipijuḷ bwe ekadu juon ne.* He walks with a limp because one of his legs is short. *Iar lo juon jipijuḷ in kōtkōt.* I saw a turnstone with one leg missing. *Komaroñ jipijuḷi tirooj kaṇe.* Please prune that hedge plant.

jipikpik (**jipikpik**). Also *jikipkip* (**jikipkip**). 1(*-i*), 2, 3(inf, tr *-i*), 4, 5(*jjikipkip*), 6(*-i*), 7, 8, 9. Maimed; incomplete; partially finished; handicapped. *Ijipikpik jān jikuuḷ.* I dropped out of school. *Ear kajipikpiki an jikuuḷ.* He did not finish his schooling. *Ejjikipkip an jerbal.* He never finishes one job before going on to the next. *Ejipikpik.* He's handicapped.

jipikra (**jipikrah**). Waves receding from shore slapping against incoming waves.

jipila (**jipilah**). Baby bird, sooty tern, *mmej*.

jipkorōj (**jipkewrej**). Also *jikorej* (**jiykewrej**). A bird, white-tailed tropicbird, *Phaethon lepturus*.

jipkōn (**jipken**). Roost of.

jipḷeḷe (**jipḷẹyḷẹy**). Variant form of *pijḷeḷe* (**pijḷẹyḷẹy**).

jipọkwe (**jipaqẹy**). 1(*-i*), 2, 3, 4, 6(*-i*), 7, 8. Take captive; refugee; loss of royal status through defeat in war.

jippapa (**jippahpah**). 1, 2, 3(inf, tr *-ik*), 4, 6(*-i*), 7. A game, holding a child up with one's feet while flat on one's back (parent-child game). *Kajippapaik būrrọ ṃokta jān an kiki.* Play *jippapa* with the youngster before he goes to sleep.

jippuḷe (**jippiḷ°ẹy**). From *jibuk* (**jibig**) "small", *ḷwe* (**ḷ°ẹy**) "pond". 3, 6(*-i*). A fish, general term for all goby.

jiraak- (**jirahak-**). Also *raak* (**rahak**), *ruwaak* (**riwahak**), *uraak* (**wirahak**). 2, 7. Move (with directional); push. *Jiraaktok iturū.* Move over close to me.

jiraal (**jirahal**). 1, 2(inf, tr *-e*), 4, 6(*-i*). A food, coconut eaten with another dish, esp. salt fish or miso. *Iar jiraal ek jo̧o̧ļ.* I ate salt fish with coconut. *Bōktok juon ek bwe in jiraale.* Bring me a fish to eat with coconut.

jiraan (**jirahan**). Dawn.

jirab (**jirab**). 2(inf, tr *-e*), 4, 6(*-i*), 7. Hoist; lift by rope; winch. *Raar jirabe lōn̄ļo̧k booj eo.* They hoisted the skiff aboard.

jirilo̧k (**jiriylaq**). Also *jirillo̧k* (**jirillaq**). 1(*-i*), 2, 3, 5(*jjirilo̧klo̧k*), 7. Slip; slide accidentally; skid; accident; unintentionally; error. *Lale kwōjirilo̧k bwe ejjir ijeņe.* Be careful you don't slip because it's slippery there. *Ettōr em jirilo̧k.* He ran and slipped. *Ļeo ejjirilo̧klo̧k eņ.* He keeps slipping. *Kwōn jab llu bwe ejirillo̧k peiū.* Don't get mad because my arm accidently bumped you.

jirok (**jirȩq**). 2, 7. Hold on to keep from falling; hang on. *Kakkōt jirok n̄e ettōr wa in.* Hang on tight when this boat moves.

jiron̄ (**jireg°**). 1(*-i*), 2, 3, 5(*jiron̄e*), 7. Nickname for baby girl; unmarried adolescent girl; maid; vocative to girls.

jiron̄ (**jireg°**). 1(*-i*), 2(inf, tr *-e*), 7. Tell; invite; notify; assure. *Iar jiron̄e bwe en itok.* I invited him to come. *Ij jiron̄ eok ke koban tōprak.* I assure you that you won't make it.

jirōm̧rōm̧ (**jiyrȩm̧rȩm̧**). 1, 2, 3, 4, 6(*-i*), 7. Dancing a jig. *Jon̄an an m̧ōņōņō ear jutak im kajirōm̧rōm̧.* He was so happy he got up and did a jig. *Eļap jirōm̧rōm̧ ilo eb in etto.* There was a lot jigging in old dances.

jirukli (**jiriqliy**). 2(inf, tr *-ik(i)*), 4, 6(*-i*), 7. Canoe part, cleat for tying sheet. *Ij ja tan jirukliiki wa eņ waō.* I think I'll install the sheet cleats on my canoe now.

jirūm̧le (**jirim̧lȩy**). 1(*-i*), 2, 3, 5(*jirūm̧lele*), 7, 8, 9. Steep slope; sharp drop off on bottom of ocean or lagoon; bold water; steep close to shore; precipitous. *Ejjeļo̧k wōt jirūm̧lele in iar in ānin.* The lagoon bottom of this islet drops off exceptionally steeply. *Jab wanmetoļo̧k bwe ejirūm̧le.* Don't go out far for it gets steep.

jit (**jit**). 2+7, 3+7, 7. Head in a certain direction. *Kwōn jitlo̧k.* Lie with your head that way. *Wa eņ ej jit jekōt.* Which way is that canoe headed?

jit (**jit**). 2(inf, tr *-i*), 6(*-i*), 7. Tinder; punk.

jit (**jit**). Variant form of *it* (**yit**).

jitaak (**jitahak**). 2, 3. Arrive; approach. *Raar jino jitaak tok m̧aan āneo.* They began to approach the lagoon shore of the islet. *Kwōn kajitaak tok wa ņe bwe jen ārōke.* Bring the canoe here so we can beach it.

jitaam̧ (**jitaham̧**). From Engl. 2(inf, tr *-e*), 6(*-i*). Stamp.

jitable (**jitablȩy**). Slang. 1, 2(inf, tr *-ik*), 4, 6(*-i*), 7. Mix together a variety of ingredients; smothered, of food; scramble. *Kanniōk jitable anien.* Meat smothered with onions. *Ear jitableik iiōk eo.* He used a variety of ingredients in his recipe.

Jitata (**jitahtah**). A constellation; stars in Aquarius; gamma, zeta, and pi; seventhborn of *Lōktan̄ūr.*

jitdam̧ (**jitdam̧**). 2(inf, tr *-i*), 3, 4, 6(*-i*), 7. Seek knowledge; look for the true pedigree; study one's genealogy; inquire of an authority. *Jitdam̧ kapeel.* Seeking knowledge guarantees wisdom (a proverb). *Jitdam̧e ke ej ja mour.* Inquire of him (who has the knowledge) while he's still around.

jitlo̧k (**jitlaq**). Archaic. Plantation plantings.

jitlo̧k (**jitlaq**). 2, 3, 4, 6(*-i*). To fast; abstain; religious retreat. *Ear jitlo̧k jān kadek ium̧win ruo iiō.* He abstained from intoxicating liquor for two years. *Lio ear kajitlo̧k ajri eo.* The woman deprived the child of food.

jitlōn̄ (**jitlȩg**). 1(*-i*), 2, 3(inf *kajjitlōn̄*, tr *kajitlōn̄*), 6(*-i*), 7. Stand upward from below (seen from above, as looking down in water). *Jāje eo ej jitlōn̄ ļo̧k mejān.* The sharp edge of the machete is turned up.

jitm̧anm̧an (**jitm̧anm̧an**). 2, 3, 6(*-i*). Recline, stretched out. *Jenaaj aolep jitm̧anm̧an ilo lōb.* We will all be laid in our graves.

jitnen m̧ōm̧ō (**jitnen m̧ehm̧eh**). 2. Arranged head to tail, of fish; euphemism for sexual position. *Jatiin rej jitnen m̧ōm̧ō ilowaan kāān.* Sardines are packed head to tail in cans.

jitniñeañ (**jitnigyag**). 1(*-i*), 2, 3(inf *kajjitniñeañ*, tr *kajitniñeañ*), 6(*-i*), 7. Head northward. *Ni eo eolǫk im jitniñeañ.* The tree fell with its top pointing northward. *Ļeeņ ej babu im jitniñeañ.* He is lying with his head pointing northward.

jitoja (**jitewjah**). From Japn. *jidoosha.* 2(inf, tr *-ik*), 4, 6(*-i*), 7. Automobile; truck; drive. *Iar jitoja in jota.* I went for an evening drive. *Jitojaik ļǫk men kaņe ñan Rita.* Drive those things over to Rita. *Rej jitojaik(i) ļǫk aļaļ kaņ ñan ia?* Where are they trucking the lumber to? *Jitojain ia ņe waaṃ?* Where was your automobile made?

jitoob (**jiteweb**). From Engl. 6(*-i*). Stove.

jitǫkin (**jitawkin**). Also *takin* (**takin**). 1(*-i*), 2, 3, 6(*-i*). Stockings; socks.

jitōk (**jitẹk**). 2, 3, 6(*-i*), 7. Ask; alternant form of *kajjitōk* (**kajjitẹk**).

jitōnbōro (**jitenbẹrẹw**). 1(...*būruo-*), 2, 4, 8, 9. Dear; darling; beloved; sweetheart; favorite one.

jitōñ (**jitẹg**). 3, 6(*-i*). Firewood, for keeping warm only.

jitōñ (**jiteg**). Also *jitōñ* (**jitẹg**), *jitōñe* (**jitegey**). 1(*-i*), 2(inf, tr *-e*), 5(*jjitōñtōñe*), 7. Point out something (to someone); appoint; assign; delegate; designate. *Ta ņe kwōj jjitōñtōñe ļǫk.* What is that you keep pointing at? *Ij jitōñ eok bwe kwōn etal.* I appoint you to go.

jitōñ (**jitẹg**). 6(*-i*). Large sailing canoe. *Juon eo jitōñ raar lo ilowaan to eņ.* They saw a large sailing canoe in the pass.

jitpeeļeļ (**jitpeyeļyeļ**). 1(*-i*), 2, 3(inf *kajjitpeeļeļ*, tr *kajitpeeļeļ*), 4, 5(*jjitpeeļeļ*), 7. Lie crosswise. *Ni eņ ejitpeeļeļ ioon iaļ eņ.* That tree is lying across the road. *Kwōn jab kkein jitpeeļeļ ioon peet ņe.* Don't always lie crosswise on the bed there.

jitrōkeañ (**jitrẹkyag**). 1(*-i*), 2, 3(inf *kajjitrōkeañ*, tr *kajitrōkeañ*), 6(*-i*), 7. Head southward.

jittak (**jittak**). 1(*-i*), 2, 3(inf *kajjittak*, tr *kajittak*), 6(*-i*), 7. Head eastward. *Kwōn jittak ļǫk.* Lie with your head eastward.

jitto (**jittẹw**). 1(*-i*), 2, 3(inf *kajjitto*, tr *kajitto*), 6(*-i*), 7. Head westward. *Kwōn jitto ļǫk.* Lie with your head westward.

jitūk (**jitik**). Transitive form of *jejjet* (**jẹjjẹt**).

jitūūl (**jitihil**). Also *ṃakneet* (**ṃakneyet**). From Engl. 2(inf, tr *-i*), 3, 6(*-i*), 7. Steel; magnet. *Kwōmaroñ ke jitūūli nitōļ eo ear wōtlǫk ilo rǫñ e.* Would you pick up the needle that fell in the hole with the magnet.

jja (**jjah**). Dial. W: *ejja* (**yejjah**), E: *jeja* (**jejah**). 1(*-a*), 2, 3(inf, tr *-ik(i)*), 6(*-i*), 7. Talk or walk in one's sleep. *Ekkein jja ļeeņ.* He used to talk in his sleep.

jjaak (**jjahak**). Dial. W: *ejjaak* (**yejjahak**), E: *jejaak* (**jejahak**). 2(inf, tr *jake*), 4, 6(*-i*), 7. Pass something to someone; polite form of *letok* (**leyteq**). *Jake ļǫk mā ņe ñane.* Pass him the breadfruit.

jjatōltōl (**jjateltel**). Variant form of *jatōltōl* (**jateltel**).

jjā (**jjay**). 2(inf, tr *jāik*), 4, 6(*-i*), 7. Catch a falling object or fruit. *Kwōn jāik mā e.* Catch this breadfruit.

jjāāk (**jjayak**). Also *jāāk.* Archaic. Overeat on fruitful land. *Ijāāk.* I'm stuffed.

jjāāl (**jjayal**). Dial. W: *ejjāāl* (**yejjayal**), E: *jejāāl* (**jejayal**). 1(*-i*), 2(inf, tr *jāāl(e)*), 3, 4, 7. Follow with the eyes; observe; see something pass by. *Rej jāāle baļuun eo.* They are following the plane with their eyes. *Rijjāāl baļuun.* A lookout for planes. *Iar jāāleļǫk em jako.* I watched him till he disappeared in the distance.

jjānene· (**jjaneyney**). Dial. W: *ejjānene* (**yejjaneyney**), E: *jejānene* (**jejaneyney**). 1(*-i*), 2, 3, 4, 7. Moving; commotion; excitement. *Ta ņe koṃwij jjānene kake?* What are you so excited about?

jjed (**jjed**). Dial. W: *ejjed* (**yejjed**), E: *jejed* (**jejed**). 1(*-i*), 2, 3, 7. Look up.

Jjed (**jjed**). Clan name.

jjedmatmat (**jjẹdmatmat**). Dial. W: *ejjedmatmat* (**yẹjjẹdmatmat**), E: *jejedmatmat* (**jẹjẹdmatmat**). 1, 3(inf, tr *-e*). Conspicuous; obvious. *Ejjeļǫk jjedmatmatin an kǫǫte piik eo.* It's so obvious he stole the pig.

jjedwawa (**jjedwahwah**). Dial. W: *ejjedwawa* (**yejjedwahwah**), E: *jejedwawa* (**jejedwahwah**). Also *jjerwawa.* 1(*-i*), 2, 3(inf, tr *-ik*, *-ūk*), 6(*-i*), 8, 9. To air out; ventilate; expose; unsheltered; unconcealed.

Kwōn jab kajjedwawaik(i) pilawā ņe bwe enaaj kijñeñe. Don't leave the loaf out in the open because it'll get hard. *Kwōn jab jerwawa bwe kwōnañinmej.* Don't go around exposed for you are sick. *Ejekkar an ledik raņ kōjjerwawaik anilowa kaņ aer.* It is not proper for the girls to leave their underthings in the open.

jjeikik (jjęyikyik). Dial. W: *ejjeikik* (yęjjęyikyik), E: *jejeikik* (jęjęyikyik). Also *jekiik.* 1, 2, 3(inf, tr -*i*), 4, 6(-*i*), 7. Excited; agitated; walk in an excited mood. *Ejjeikik riāneo ke ejeļo.* The island populace were agitated by the sighting of a sail. *Etke kwōj jjeikik; ta eor men eo ke?* Why are you walking around excitedly; is something big coming up?

jjeļok (jjęylaq). Dial. W: *ejjeļok* (yęjjęylaq), E: *jejeļok* (jęjęylaq). 2, 3, 6(-*i*), 7. Break loose, as boat from sand; float loose. *Eļak ibwij ejjeļok wa eo.* When the tide came in, the boat floated loose. *Raar kanōk em kōjjeļok wa eo.* They pulled the boat off the reef.

jjelōblōb (jjelebleb). Dial. W: *ejjelōblōb* (yejjelebleb), E: *jejelōblōb* (jejelebleb). Also *jjiliblib* (jjiliblib). 1(-*i*), 2, 3, 4, 7. Splash. *Ek rot eņ ej jjelōblōb ijjuweo?* What kind of fish is that splashing way over there?

jjeļok an naan (jjęlaq han nahan). Idiom. Taciturn; quiet; not talkative.

jjeṃ (jjeṃ). Dial. W: *ejjeṃ* (yejjeṃ), E: *jejeṃ* (jejeṃ). Brittle.

jjeor (jjeyer°). Dial. W: *ejjeor* (yejjeyer°), E: *jejeor* (jejeyer°). 1(-*i*), 2(inf, tr *jeor, jeer(e)*), 7, 8. Erase; delete; obliterate; eliminate.

jjeraak (jjerahak). Nautical term; correct point for tacking in order to reach an island.

jjerwawa (jjerwahwah). Dial. W: *ejjerwawa* (yejjerwahwah), E: *jejerwawa* (jejerwahwah). Variant form of *jjedwawa.*

jjeurur (jjeywirwir). Dial. W: *ejjeurur* (yejjeywirwir), E: *jejeurur* (jejeywirwir). From *je* (jey) "stomach", *ur* (wir) "lump". 1(-*i*), 2, 3, 5(*jjeurur*), 7. Stir up; commotion; excited; aroused to excitement. *Eļap kar jjeurur ke ej bwil ṃweo.* There was a great commotion when the house burned. *Ta eņ rej jjeurur eake?* What are they excited about?

jjibjibwe (jjibjibey). Dial. W: *ijjibjibwe* (yijjibjibey), E: *jijibjibwe* (jijibjibey). Distributive form of *jebjeb* (jębjęb).

jjibur (jjibir°). Dial. W: *ijjibur* (yijjibir°), E: *jijbur* (jijbir°). 1(-*i*), 2(inf, tr *jiburi*), 4, 5(*jjiburbur*), 6(-*i*), 7. Hug; embrace while sleeping; cuddling; nestle. *Eṃṃan jjibur ñe kwōj piọ.* It's good to cuddle when you're cold. *Ejjiburbur lieņ.* The young lady likes to cuddle.

jjiliblib (jjiliblib). Variant form of *jjelōblōb* (jjelebleb).

jjilōk (jjilęk). Dial. W: *ijjilōk* (yijjilęk), E: *jijlōk* (jijlęk). 2(inf, tr *jilkin*), 4, 6(-*i*), 7. Send; errand; dismiss; dispatch. *Kab jjilōktok aō juuj.* Send me some shoes. *Jilkinļok ñan Ṃajeļ.* Send him to the Marshalls. *Kwōn jilkinļok ļadik ņe bwe en bōktok bok eo.* Send that boy to bring the book.

jjino (jjinew). Dial. W: *ijjino* (yijjinew), E: *jijino* (jijinew). 1(-*i*), 2(inf, tr *jino(e)*), 4, 7. Begin; commencement; initial; initiate; institute; origin; originate; start; resume. *Kwaar jino aṃ jerbal jān ñāāt?* When did you start work? *Kwōn jinoe jān rainin.* Begin from today. *Jinoe al eo.* Start the music.

jjioñ (jjiyęg°). Dial. W: *ijjiōñ* (yijjiyęg°), E: *jijiōñ* (jijiyęg°). Also *jjiōñ* (jjiyeg). 2(inf, tr *jioñ*), 4, 6(-*i*), 7, 10(*jeñak*). Refill a hole with dirt; erase footprints or traces. *Jioñ lōb ņe.* Cover up the grave. *Ejeñak.* It's covered up.

jjipdodo (jjipdęwdęw). Dial. W: *ijjipdodo* (yijjipdęwdęw), E: *jijipdodo* (jijipdęwdęw). 1(-*i*), 2, 3(inf, tr -*ik*), 8, 9. Limp; soft; supple. *Ejjipdodo neō.* My legs have gone limp.

jjiped (jjiped). Dial. W: *ijjiped* (yijjiped), E: *jijped* (jijped). Also *jjiped* (jjipęd). 2(inf, tr *jiped(e)*), 4, 6(-*i*), 7, 10(*jepdak*). Press down on; run over; weigh down; oppression; flatten; smash. *Kein jjiped peba.* Paper weight. *Raar jipede.* He was run over (by an automobile).

jjir (jjir). Dial. W: *ijjir* (yijjir), E: *jijir* (jijir). 1(-*i*), 2, 3, 7, 8, 9. Slippery;

lubrication. *Eor ke kajjirin?* Has it any lubrication?

jjo (**jjew**). Dial. W: *ejjo* (**yejjew**), E: *jejo* (**jejew**). Also *ḷōjo* (**ḷejew**). 1(*-i*), 2, 3(*kajjo*), 7. Rusty.

jjon̄ (**jjeg°**). Dial. W: *ejjon̄* (**yejjeg°**), E: *jejon̄* (**jejeg°**). 1, 2(inf, tr *jon̄e*), 6(*-i*). Catch sleeping birds by hand. *Ikōn jjon̄ ke iar dik.* I used to catch birds by hand when I was young.

jjon̄jon̄ (**jjeg°jeg°**). Dial. W: *ejjon̄jon̄* (**yejjeg°jeg°**), E: *jejon̄jon̄* (**jejeg°jeg°**). 2(inf, tr *jjon̄jon̄ kake*), 6(*-i*). Pick off someone; annihilate one-by-one; kill singly. *Ḷan̄e ear jjon̄jon̄ kake er. Ḷan̄e* killed them all singly.

jjookok (**jjewekwek**). Dial. W: *ejjookok* (**yejjewekwek**), E: *jejookok* (**jejewekwek**). 1(*-i*), 2, 3, 4, 7, 8, 9. Always ashamed; distributive form of *jook* (**jewek**); bashful.

jjor (**jjẹr°**). Dial. W: *ejjor* (**yẹjjẹr°**), E: *jejor* (**jẹjẹr°**). Also *allejjor* (**hallẹjjẹr°**). 1(*-i*), 2(inf, tr *jure*) 4, 7. To shade the eyes with the hand and watch for a school of fish.

jjoram (**jjewram**). Dial. W: *ejjoram* (**yejjewram**), E: *jejoram* (**jejewram**). 1, 2, 3(inf, tr *-e*), 4, 5(*jjoramṃramṃ*), 6(*-i*), 7. Flashing light. *Waan eọn̄ōd eo ear kōjjoramram ilik bon̄.* The fishing boat was flashing its searchlight on the oceanside last night.

jjọjọ (**jjawjaw**). Dial. W: *ejjọjọ* (**yejjawjaw**), E: *jejọjọ* (**jejawjaw**). 1, 2, 6(*-i*). Bold; unconcerned about consequences. *Eḷap an jjọjọ likao eo ilo jipij eo an.* The young man was very bold in his speech.

jjọn̄ (**jjag°**). Dial. W: *ejjọn̄* (**yejjag°**), E: *jejọn̄* (**jejag°**). 1(*-i*), 2(inf, tr *jọn̄e*), 4, 7. Kill in the night; catch birds at night. *Kōjro etal in jjọn̄ bao.* Let's the two of us go catch birds (tonight). *Rōmoot in jjọn̄ bao.* They went to catch birds. *Ear jọn̄e bao eṇ.* He caught that bird. *Kwōn jab etal bwe rōnaaj jọn̄e eok.* Don't go or they'll kill you.

jjō (**jjẹh**). Dial. W: *ejjō* (**yẹjjẹh**), E: *jejō* (**jẹjẹh**). 2(inf, tr *jōjōḷe*), 5(*kajjōjō*). Get nauseated by; loathe; queasy; squeamish. *Ijōjōḷe kkan in Ruk.* I can't eat Trukese food. *Ekadik kajjōjō an iiōk.* He nauseates people with his doings (his mixtures are nauseating). *Ejekkar n̄an kain eṇ ejjō.* It's not for the squeamish.

jjuok (**jjiwek**). Dial. W: *ijjuok* (**yijjiwek**), E: *jijuok* (**jijiwek**). Also *jokā* (**jẹwkay**). 1(*-i*), 2(inf, tr *juok(e), jokak(e), jokāik(i)*), 4, 5(*jjokākā*), 7, 8, 10(*jokak*). Chop down; cut down; trees; dismantle. *Eṃōj an juoke ni eo.* He cut the coconut tree down. *Eṃōj juoke ni eo.* The coconut tree has been chopped down. *Rōjuoke ṃweo.* They dismantled the house. *Kwōn jokāik ni ṇe.* Cut down that coconut tree.

jjurjur (**jjir°jir°**). Dial. W: *ijjurjur* (**yijjir°jir°**), E: *jijurjur* (**jijir°jir°**). Also *jurjuri*. Archaic. 1, 2, 8, 9. Fading of color or shade. *Ejurjuri wūnokan jōōt e aō.* The color of my shirt is fading.

jjurpe (**jjir°pẹy**). Dial. W: *ijjurpe* (**yijjir°pẹy**), E: *jijurpe* (**jijir°pẹy**). Also *lijjurpe* (**lijjir°pẹy**). 2, 6(*-i*), 7. Walk hand in hand. *Itok kōjro ijjurpeḷok eọọj ḷọk.* Come let's walk hand in hand toward the ocean.

jjuur (**jjiwir**). Dial. W: *ijjuur* (**yijjiwir**), E: *jijuur* (**jijiwir**). Also *jujuur* (**jiwjiwir**). 1(*-i*), 2(inf, tr *juur(i)*), 3(inf, tr *-i*), 4, 5(*jjujuuri*), 6(*-i*), 7. Step on; set foot on; tread on; kick. *Kwōn jab jujuuri jaki ṇe.* Don't step on that mat there.

jjuurore (**jjiwirwẹrẹy**). Also *jjuururi* (**jiwirwiriy**). Full of. *Ejjuurore (ejjuururi) ṃweeṇ kōn ṃṃaan.* That house is full of men.

jo (**jẹw**). Also *jo* (**jew**). 2, 3(inf, tr *-uk*), 6(*-i*). Cast loose; float loose, of ships. *Ejo wa eo.* The boat floated loose. *Kajouk an̄kō ṇe.* Cast the anchor loose.

jo (**jew**). 3, 6(*-i*). A fish, goatfish, *Mulloidichthys samoensis*; goatfish.

jo (**jew**). Fishing method, stand beside weir and watch for mackerel; a place where one watches and waits for tides favorable to fishing.

jo (**jew**). Also *ju* (**jiw**) (for plural objects). 2+7. Throw (always with directional postpositions).

jo (**jew**). Interim period between stormy seasons, usually a calm spell. *Jen jerak ke ej ja jo men in.* Let's sail while there is a calm spell.

jo (**jew**). Variant form of *ijo* (**yijew**).

jo (**jew**). Appear; as in *joraantak.*

jo (**jew**). Muddy. *Ejo kōn bwidej pidodo.* It's muddy with soft soil.

joba (**jewbah**). From Engl. 2, 3(inf, tr *-ik*), 4, 6(*-i*). Sofa; couch; lawn chair with canvas back. *Kwōn kōjobaik ļadik ņe ippaṃ.* Let that boy sit on the sofa with you.

jobai (**jewbahyiy**). From Japn. *shoobai* "business". 1, 2, 4, 6(*-i*). Sell; trade; dicker; barter; peddle. *Ear jobai kake (kōn) ek ko koņan.* He sold the fish he caught.

joda (**jewdah**). Also *jakoņkoņ* (**jaqeņqeņ**). 1(*-i*), 2, 3, 4, 8, 9. Inability to catch many fish (see *wōda* (**wedah**)).

jodi (**jewdiy**). From Japn. *zoori*. 1(*-i*), 2, 3(inf, tr *-ik*), 6(*-i*), 7. Zorie(s); wear a zori; slipper; go-ahead.

jodik (**jęwdik**). 2(inf, tr *-i*), 4, 6(*-i*), 7. To invade; to land; to raid. *RiAmedka raar jodiki Kuwajleen im pād ie ṃae rainin.* The Americans invaded Kwajalein and have stayed on it ever since.

joiu (**jęwyiw**). From Japn. 2(inf, tr *-(i), -(uk)*), 5(*jjoiuiu*), 6(*-i*). Soy sauce; shoyu. *Joiuuk ek ņe.* Put shoyu on that fish. *Ejjoiuiu jaajmi eo kijō.* My sashimi had shoyu all over it.

jojaab (**jewjahab**). From Engl. *soursop*. 3, 6(*-i*). A plant, *Annona muricata* L. (Annonaceae). The soursop, a tree bearing edible fruits. F. Introduced.

jojo (**jęwjęw**). 3, 5(*jojoe*), 6(*-i*). Chick. *Ejojoe lowaan oror eņ.* There are lots of chicks in that pen.

jojo (**jewjew**). 1(*-i*), 2(inf, tr *joon(e)*), 4, 7. Soak. *Bweọ ko kaņ rej jojo i ar.* Those coconut husks are soaking along the lagoon beach. *Kwōn joon bweọ kaņe.* Soak those coconut husks.

jojo (**jewjew**). 3, 5(*jojoe*), 6(*-i*), 8. A fish, flying fish, family *Exocoetidae. Ejojoe likin Mājro.* There are lots of flying fish on the ocean side of Majuro.

jojo (**jewjew**). Also *kabaj* (**kahbaj**). Canoe part, outrigger spar; canoe part, ties between spar and outrigger.

jojoļāār (**jęwjęwļayar**). 2, 6(*-i*), 7. Someone who has no one to take care of him; alone; abandoned; destitute. *Ekabūroṃōjṃōj kōn an jojoļāār bajjek.* He's in a pitiful situation to have no one to turn to.

jojomar (**jęwjęwmar**). 2, 4. Intercede; defend; pacify. *Rijojomar.* Public defender.

jojoon (**jewjewen**). Put on top of; pile up; stack up.

jojoon (**jewjewen**). Slang. From *joon* (**jewen**). 2, 4. Pacify; solace. *Lieņ rijojoon būruō.* She's my consolation.

jojoon bōro (**jewjewen bęręw**). Idiom. Appease; pacify. *Ej make wōt rijojoon būrwōn jinen.* He's the only one left to pacify his mother's grief.

jok (**jeq**). 2, 3(*kajjokjok, kajok*), 5(*jjokjok*), 6(*jokkun*), 7. To land; alight; perched; settle, of liquids. *Ear kajoke baļuun eo bwe ejorrāān juon pikpik.* He landed the plane because an engine wasn't working properly. *En baj jjokjok wōt bao eņ?* Why is that bird always landing? *Rej etal in wōnṃae komja eņ ilo jikin kajokjok eņ.* They are going to meet the administrator at the airport. *Eṃṃan jokkun ut ņe ņa ioon bōraṃ.* The flower looks nice in your hair. *Waan kajjokjok.* Crash boat. Aircraft carrier. *Jikin kajjokjok.* Air strip.

jok (**jeq**). 2, 3, 6(*-i*), 8, 9. Heavily loaded boat; keep a boat steady. *Ejok wa eņ kōn waini.* The boat is full of copra. *Ej jab ṃōt kōn an waini kaņ kajoke.* It doesn't roll because the copra is keeping it steady.

jokak (**jęwkak**). Chopped down; dismantled; perfective form of *jjuok* (**jjiwek**); transitive form of *jjuok* (**jjiwek**).

jokankan (**jewkankan**). 2, 3, 6(*-i*). Dress. *Kajokankane ajri ņe.* Dress that child.

jokā (**jęwkay**). 6(*-i*). A pile of coconuts. *Kwōnañin jeke ke jokāin waini eo iar aini?* Have you chopped the coconuts in the pile I made?

jokā (**jęwkay**). Variant form of *jjuok* (**jjiwek**).

jokāik (**jęwkayik**). Transitive form of *jjuok* (**jjiwek**).

jokālōt (**jewkaylet**). 2(inf, tr *-e*), 4, 6(*-i*). Candidate. *Ear wiini jokālōt eo.* He won the election for candidacy.

jokdād (**jeqdad**). 1(*-i*), 2, 3(inf, tr *-e*), 4, 7, 8, 9. Filthy; very dirty; foul. *Aolepem dike ledik eņ bwe ejokdād.* Nobody likes that girl because she's filthy.

jokiae (**jewkiyhayey**). Young stage of coconut growth, after *debweiu.*

jokiin̄ (**jewkiyig**). From Japn. *zookin* "cloth for scrubbing". 1(-*i*), 2(inf, tr -*i*), 4, 7. Scrub, using wet cloths. *Elōt am̧ kar jokiin̄i raan tebōļ e.* Your cleaning of the table top was well done.

jokko (**jeqqew**). From Japn. *jokoo*. 6(-*i*). Commoner; tramp; youngster. *Jab eļļok n̄an jokko ņe bwe ej jaad bwebwe.* Don't let the tramp bother you as he is a bit crazy. *Jokkoun Likiep ro raņe tok.* Here come the Likiep youngsters.

jokkun (**jeqqin**). Construct form of *jok* (**jeq**).

jokkun wōt juon (**jeqqin wet jiwen**). Stabilized; well-balanced.

jokkwi (**jeqqiy**). From Japn. Rice bowl. *Jokkwi eo n̄iū ņe.* That's my ricebowl.

jokkwōp (**jeqqep**). 1(-*i*), 2(inf, tr -*e*, -*i*), 3, 4, 5(*ijokkwōpkwōp*), 6(-*i*), 8. A food, soup of soft rice or breadfruit. *Kwōn jokkwōpi mā kā.* Make these breadfruit into soup. *Ennǫ ke jokkwōp in mā ippam̧?* Do you like breadfruit soup?

jokkwōpin mā (**jeqqepin may**). 3, 6(-*i*). A food, breadfruit soup.

jokļā (**jeqļay**). Also *jokoļā* (**jeqeļay**). Wind from the north.

jokmej (**jȩqmȩj**). Dialectal variant of *jāpe* (**japȩy**).

joko (**jeqew**). 6(-*e*). Tentacles; octopus.

joko (**jewkew**). From Japn. *sooko*. 6(-*i*). Storehouse; warehouse.

jokoņ (**jeqeņ°**). Also *jokoņ* (**jeqeņ**). 1(-*a*), 6(-*a*). Cane; crutches; staff; walking stick. *Jokoņan wōn e?* Whose cane is this?

jokoņkoņ (**jeqeņ°qeņ°**). From *jokoņ* (**jeqeņ°**). 2, 3(inf, tr *kajokoņkoņ(e)*), 4, 6(-*i*), 7. Use a cane; use crutches. *Ej jokoņkoņ bwe ebūļǫk neen.* He's using crutches because he's got a broken leg. *Taktō ro raar kajokoņkoņe.* The doctors made him use a cane.

jokoojwa (**jȩqȩwȩjwah**). Grated coconut.

jokutbae (**jewqitbahyey**). From Engl. *goodbye.* 2(inf, tr *jokutbwaik*), 3(inf, tr -*ik*), 4, 6(-*i*), 7. Wave goodbye. *Ear jokutbwaeik eō.* She waved goodbye to me. *Ear kajokutbwaeik ajri eo.* She made the child wave goodbye.

jokwa (**jeqah**). 1, 2, 6(-*a*), 8, 9. Uncoordinated; clumsy; homely; lack rhythm. *Ejokwa an eb.* He dances without rhythm. *Eban pālele bwe ejokwa.* She won't get married for she's very homely.

jokwadikdik (**jeqadikdik**). 2, 6(-*i*), 7. Fly low. *Baļuun eo ear jokwadikdiktok em jok.* The plane made a low approach and landed.

jokwajok (**jeqajeq**). 5(-*e*), 6(-*i*), 7, 8, 9. Gnat; mosquito; (in Ratak dialect; see *ņam̧* (**ņam̧**). *Ejokwajokwe ļǫk ānin jān Likiep.* The island is more infested with gnats than Likiep.

jokwane (**jeqaney**). 1(-*i*), 2, 3(inf, tr -*ik*), 8, 9. Pacified; calm.

jokwā (**jeqay**). Also *kājokwā* (**kayjeqay**). 3(inf, tr -*ik*), 5(*ijokwākwā*), 6(-*i*). Driftwood (small). *Eijokwākwā likin ānin.* The ocean side of this islet is littered with driftwood. *Iaar kōjokwāik bato eņ ilik.* I found that bottle on the ocean side shore.

jokwe (**jȩqȩy**). 2, 3, 7. Live somewhere; dwell; inhabit; reside; transitive form of *jukjuk* (**jiqjiq**). *Ewi m̧wiin kwōj jokwe ie?* Which house do you live in? *N̄a ij jokwe Wūlka.* I live on Uliga.

jokwōd (**jeqed**). 1, 2, 5(*ijokwōdkwōd*), 6(-*i*). Miss constantly; lose contact with; neglect. *Jab jokwōd jān kilaaj.* Don't be absent from class. *Lale kwaar jokwōd jān ro rej jipan̄ eok.* Don't lose contact with those who help you. *Kememej im jab jokwōd in jejetok.* Remember not to neglect writing to me.

jolǫk (**jewlaq**). 2(inf, tr -*e*), 6(-*i*), 7. A pointed stick rubbed up and down on another stick to make a fire. *Kwōn jolǫketok m̧ōk jidik m̧ōttan aļaļ bwe kōjro eton̄.* How about making a little piece of wood as *jolǫk* so we can hustle up a fire using the *eton̄* method.

jolōt (**jȩwlȩt**). 1(-*i*), 2, 3, 4. Inheritance; souvenir; keepsake. *Wāto in ej aō jolōt jān jema.* This tract is my inheritance from my father.

Joļ (**jeļ°**). Clan name.

joļǫk (**jewļaq**). 2(inf, tr -*e*). Discard; eradicate; throw away; excommunicate; expel; kick out; forsake. *Kwōn joļǫk Jetan jān ippam̧.* Renounce Satan. *Raar joļǫke jān jar* *kōn an nana.* She's excommunicated from church for being a whore. *Jab joļǫk nukuṃ.* Don't forsake your kinsfolk.

joļǫk bōd (**jewļaq będ**). Idiom. Apologize; to excuse; forgive. *Joļǫk aō bōd.* Excuse me. *Joļǫk aō bōd, Jema, bwe iar jerawiwi.* Forgive me, Father, for I have sinned.

joļǫkṃōōr (**jewļaqṃeher**). A fish, goatfish, *Upeneus tragula.*

jomām (**jęwmam**). Also *mām.* Any large fish.

jome (**jewmey**). A fish, goatfish, *Mulloidichthys auriflama.*

jona (**jewnah**). From "Jonah in the Bible". 1(*-i*), 2, 3, 4, 7, 8, 9. Person or thing that causes trouble or bad luck.

joniak (**jęwniyak**). 1(*-i*), 2(inf, tr *-e*), 7. Press oil out of grated copra.

joņak (**jewņak**). Also *leņak* (**leyņak**). 1(*-i*), 2, 3(inf, tr *-e*). Sleep soundly. *Wūno eo ekōjoņake.* The medication caused him to sleep soundly.

joñ (**jeg°**). 3, 5(*joñe*), 6(*-i*). A plant, mangrove, *Bruguiera conjugata* (L.) Merrill; (Rhizophdraceae). One of several mangrove species. This is frequently a large tree, with dark, glossy leaves; firm red flowers which envelop a long, slender fruit. The trees grow only in wet, swampy depressions; in company with other mangrove species, or alone; or with *Hibiscus tiliaceus* and *Barringtonia.*

joñ (**jeg°**). 2, 3(inf, tr *-e*), 6(*-i*), 8, 9. Pain in the arm caused by throwing. *Kadkad jab eo ekajoñe peiū.* That throwing method caused this pain in my arm.

joña- (**jeg°a-**). 1, 6. Size; extent; par; quantity; amount. *Ewi joñan?* How much should it be? *Joñan an ļap an nañinmej ebaj mej.* He was so sick, he almost died. *Eļap jān joñan.* More than enough. *Joñan wōt juon.* Equal. *Ejjeļǫk joñan.* Unexcelled. *Ej jab joñāer wōt juon.* They are not on a par.

joñak (**jeg°ak**). 2(inf, tr *joñe, -e*), 4, 6(*-i*), 7. Measure; survey. *Raar joñe joñan bwidej eņ an.* They surveyed his land. *Rijoñak raņ an kien.* The government surveyors.

joñak (**jeg°ak**). Also *joñǫk.* 6(*-i*). Pattern; style (clothes). *Eṃṃan joñǫkun nuknuk eņ an.* Her dress was made from a beautiful pattern.

joñe (**jeg°ey**). Transitive form of *joñak* (**jeg°ak**) and *joñjoñ* (**jeg°jeg°**).

joñe aorōkin (**jeg°ey hawęrękin**). Assess the value of. *Kwōmaroñ ke joñe aorōkin mour?* Can you assess the value of life?

joñjoñ (**jeg°jeg°**). 2(inf, tr *joñe*), 4, 6(*-i*), 7. Measure; compare size; try on clothes. *Kōjro joñjoñ.* Let's see which of us is taller. *Iar joñe jōōt eo.* I tried the shirt on.

joñoul (**jęg°ęwil**). Also *joñoul* (**jeg°ewil**). 3, 5(*kajjoñoul*), 7. Ten.

joñoul emān (**jęg°ęwil yeman**). 2, 3(inf, tr *-e*), 6(*-i*). Fourteen. *Ejoñoul emān an iiō rainin.* He reaches fourteen today.

joñoul jilu (**jęg°ęwil jiliw**). 2, 3(inf, tr *-i*), 6(*-i*). Thirteen.

joñoul ruo (**jęg°ęwil riwew**). 2, 3, 6(*-i*). Twelve.

joñouljiljilmjuon (**jęg°ęwiljiljilmjiwen**). 2, 3, 6(*-i*). Seventeen.

joñouljiljino (**jęg°ęwiljiljinew**). 2, 3, 6(*-i*). Sixteen.

joñouljuon (**jęg°ęwiljiwen**). 2, 3(inf, tr *-e*), 6(*-i*). Eleven. *Kwōn kajoñouljuone ek ņe koņaṃ ṃokta jān aṃ rǫǫl.* You must catch eleven fish before you return.

joñoulļalem (**jęg°ęwilļalęm**). 2, 3(inf, tr *-e*), 6(*-i*). Fifteen. *Kwōn kajoñoulļaleme bōnbōn ņe.* Make that number fifteen.

joñǫ (**jeg°aw**). Also *jeñǫ* (**jegaw**). 1(*-i*), 2, 3(inf, tr *-uk*), 5(*jjoñǫñǫ*), 6(*-a*), 8, 9. Fish odor; smell of fish—lingering on hands, body, or utensils. *Ejoñǫ peiṃ.* Your hands are fishy. *Ejjoñǫñǫ jikin wia ek eņ.* The fish market is smelly with fish odors.

joob (**jeweb**). From Engl. 1(*-i*), 2(inf, tr *-e*), 3(inf *kajjoobob*), 5(*jjoobob*), 5+1, 6(*-i*), 8. Soap. *Joobin tutu.* Bathing soap. *Joobin kwaļkoļ.* Washing soap. *Joob bǫuta.* Powdered soap. *Ejjoobob dān eņ.* That water is soapy. *Joobe peiṃ.* Wash your hands with soap.

joobņōj (**jewebņej**). 2, 3, 6(*-i*). Tie. *Kōmro jiāi im joobņōj.* We had a contest but no one won. *Raar kōjoobņōje keem eo.* They deliberately kept the scores even.

joobob (**jewebweb**). From *joob* (**jeweb**). 2, 3(inf, tr *-e*), 5(*jjoobob*), 6(*-i*), 7. Use soap. *Ej ja joobob eake joob eṇ arro.* Let him use our soap for now. *Kwōn kajoobobe ke eō ippaṃ ñe emaat joob e aō?* Will you let me share your soap if I run out of mine?

jook (**jewek**). 1(*-i*), 2, 3(st inf *kajjookok*, tr *kajook*), 5(*jjookok*), 8, 9. Ashamed; embarrassed; shy; disgrace; dishonor; humiliate; shame. *Ejjookok ļeeṇ.* He is easily embarrassed--very shy. *Ekajjookok men eo kwaar kōṃṃane.* You did a shameful thing. *Jab kajook eō.* Don't shame me. *Kwōn jab kajooke jinōṃ im jeṃaṃ.* Don't humiliate your parents.

jool (**jewel**). 1(*-i*), 2, 3, 4, 7, 8, 9. Unwanted; ignored; neglected. *Ejool ajri eṇ.* That child is neglected.

jooļ (**jeweļ**). From Engl. Syllable "sol" of musical scale.

jooṃuṃ (**jeweṃwiṃ**). A fish, mullet, *Crenmugil crenilabis* (Eniwetak).

joon (**jewen**). 2, 5(*jojoon*), 7. Press down on. *Kwōn jab joon ña.* Don't put your weight on me.

joon (**jewen**). Transitive form of *jojo* (**jewjew**).

joonjo (**jewenjew**). From Japn. *sonchoo*. 3, 4, 6(*-i*). Magistrate.

Joonmāāṇ (**jewenmayaṇ**). From *joon* (**jewen**) "to soak it", *māāṇ* (**mayaṇ**) "burning sensation". 3, 6(*-i*). A plant, prob. *Pandanus fischerianus* cultigen. Ebon, Jaluit.

jooṇ (**jeweṇ**). 2(inf, tr *-e*), 5(*jooṇe*), 6(*-i*). Ballast. *Ejooṇe wa eṇ.* The boat is carrying a lot of ballast. *Jenaaj jooṇe wa in rainin.* We'll put ballast on the boat today.

joor (**jẹwẹr**). 2(inf, tr *-e*), 3(tr *kajuur(ōk)*), 5(*jure*), 6(*-e, jurōn*). Pillar; column; pole; post; staff. *Aolep jurōn ṃwiin kōṃṃan jān mā.* All of this house's pillars are made of breadfruit timber. *Kajurōk aļaļ kaṇe.* Put up (stand) those timbers. *Ej joore ṃweeṇ.* He's installing posts in the house.

joor (**jẹwẹr**). Tall tree where seabirds sleep.

joor (**jewer**). 2, 3, 4, 6(*-i*). Escape, usually from getting hurt; get away clean.

joorkatkat (**jẹwẹrkatkat**). 1(*-i*), 2, 3, 4, 6(*-i*), 7. Stand ready; mobilize (military); fighting stance. *Raar joorkatkat ke rej roñ kōn an po wa eo.* They mobilized when they heard of the boat's capture.

joortak (**jẹwẹrtak**). 7. Gift; present; sacrifice; a food gift offered at a grave to the ghosts of dead.

joortoklik (**jẹwẹrteqlik**). Also *jortoklik* (**jer°teqlik**). 1, 6(*-i*). Security, land or goods or money put away for future use or for children; insurance; mortgage; surety; guarantee; collateral; savings. *Ear llik jortoklik ñan ajri ro nājin.* He left securities for his children. *Eor ke aṃ joortoklik.* Have you any savings?

joot (**jewet**). 1(*-i*), 3, 5(*joote*), 6(*-i*), 7. Bullet.

jopāl (**jewpal**). 2, 3, 5(*jjopālpāl*), 6(*-i*). Shake, of a sail in the wind; wave, of a flag; flap; flutter. *Ejjopālpāl bōļāāk ilo* U. N. Day *eo.* Flags were waving all over tha place on U. N. Day. *Jopāl em kōttar wa kaṇ jet.* Flap your sails and wait for the other boats.

jor (**jer°**). Archaic. Can; be able to.

joraantak (**jewrahantak**). 3, 6(*-i*), 7. Dawn.

jorbañ (**jer°bag**). From Japn. *soroban*. 1, 2(inf, tr *-e*), 4, 6(*-i*), 7. Abacus; to compute. *Eor ke aṃ jorbañ?* Have you got an abacus? *Kwōn ṃōk jorbañe tok jete oṇāān ṃweiuk kaṇe.* How about computing the price of the merchandise for me?

jore (**jẹwrẹy, jẹr°ẹy**). Look for fish.

jore (**jẹwrẹy, jẹr°ẹy**). Taboo relationship.

jorjor (**jer°jer°**). 1(*-i*), 2, 3, 4, 6(*-i*), 7. Walk fast. *Ia ṇe kwōj jorjor ñane?* Where are walking so fast?

jorjor (**jer°jer°**). 1, 2(inf, tr *-e*), 6(*-i*). Speed up when rubbing sticks to make fire. *Kōttar an māāṇāṇ im jorjore.* Wait till it gets a little warm and speed it up.

jorṃōta (**jer°ṃetah**). From Japn. *sarumata*. 2, 3(inf, tr *-ik*), 6(*-i*), 7. Underpants, men's. *Kōjorṃōtaik ajri ṇe bwe epiọ.* Make the child wear underpants because he's cold.

jorñak (**jer°gak**). Dial. E, W: *jetñak* (**jetgak**). Go fast.

jorobbā (**jer°ebbay**). A fish, goatfish, *Parupeneus sp.*

Jorobbā (**jer°ebbay**). From *jorobbwā* "goatfish". A plant, *Pandanus fischerianus* cultigen. Rongelap.

jorom (**jer°em**). 1(*-i*), 2(inf, tr *-e*), 7. Suck up; drink up; absorb.

jorrāān (**jer°r°ayan**). 1(*-i*), 2, 3, 4, 5(*jjorrāānān*), 7, 8. Broken; accident; damaged; crime; harm; ruined; trouble; out of order; out of commission. *Ejorrāān waj e nājū.* My watch is broken. *Ejjorrāānān waj eṇ nājin.* His watch is always broken. *Ta jorrāān?* What's the trouble?

jortoklik (**jer°teqlik**). Variant form of *joortoklik* (**jẹwẹrteqlik**).

jota (**jẹwtah**). 3, 7. Evening.

jota (**jewtah**). 7. Last evening.

jotal (**jewtal**). 1(*-i*), 2, 3, 4, 7. Food or drink eaten while walking; eat or drink while walking. *Kwōn jab jotal.* Don't eat or drink while you walk.

joto (**jewtew**). From Japn. *choodo* "looks fitting". 6(*-i*). Look fitting. *Ejjeḷam jotoun jōōt ṇe ṇa ippaṃ.* That shirt really looks fitting on you.

jotoiñ (**jewtewyig**). Also *jotouñ* (**jẹwtẹwig**). From Japn. *soodooin* "community working party". 2(inf, tr *-i*), 4, 6(*-i*). General clean up. *Jen jotoiñi ānin āned.* Let's give our island a general clean up.

jou (**jẹwiw**). Dialectal variant of *jowi* (**jẹwiy**).

jouj (**jẹwij**). 1(*-i*), 2, 4, 8, 9. Kind; kindhearted; kindness; benevolence; benign; charity; favor; grace.

jouj (**jẹwij**). Also *jooj* (**jẹwẹj**). 2(inf, tr *-i*), 6(*-i*). Canoe part, bottom part of canoe. *Kwōmarōñ ke jouji kōrkōr iiō waō?* Can you attach the bottom part of my canoe to the upper part?

joujo (**jẹwijew**). 7. Right here.

jouneak (**jẹwinyak**). 2(inf, tr *-e*), 4, 6(*-i*), 7. Coconut cloth used to squeeze and extract oil from grated coconut. *Kwōn jouneake pen ṇe ṇa ilowaan raij ṇe.* Use the coconut cloth to squeeze and extract the oil from the grated coconut into the rice.

jourur (**jẹwirwir**). Also *jourur* (**jewirwir**). 2, 5(*jjourur, joururi*), 6(*-i*), 7. Thunder. *Eḷap an kar jourur boñ.* It kept thundering all (last) night.

jourur (**jẹwirwir**). A fish, Moorish idol, *Zanclus canescens.*

jourur (**jẹwirwir**). 6(*-i*). An insect.

Jowa (**jewwah**). Clan name.

jowaanroñ (**jewahanreg°**). Dial. E, W: *kōlọṃōrṃōr* (**kelawṃẹrṃẹr**). 1(*-i*), 2(inf, tr *-e*), 4, 6(*-i*), 7. A food, juice extracted from fresh pandanus.

jowakin (**jewwahkin**). 3, 4+3, 6(*-i*), 3+7. A shell, *Fissurellidae*; *Diodora (austroglyphis) sieboldii* or *Montfortula pulchra* or *Tugali vadososinuata*; a shell, *Siphonaridae*; *Siphonaria atra/japonica/sirius*; a shell, *Patellidae*; *Cellana nigrisquamata*; a shell, *Acmaeidae*; *Acmaea pallida*; limpet shell.

jowan (**jewwan**). 1(*-i*), 2, 3, 4, 6(*-i*), 7, 8, 9. Lazy (see *owan*); idle.

jowanurọñ (**jewahniwr°ag°**). 3, 4+3, 5(*-e*), 6(*-i*), 3+7, 5+8, 9. A fish, bass, *Plectropomus truncatus.*

jowālel (**jewaylẹl**). Also *jowāleel* (**jewaylẹyẹl**). 1(*-i*), 2, 3, 4, 8, 9. Not good marksman with spear (see *wālel* (**waylẹl**)).

jowāme (**jewaymey**). Also *jowāme* (**jewaymẹy**). A fish, giant sea bass, *Promicrops truncatus.*

jowāmuur (**jewaymiwir**). 2(inf, tr *-i*), 6(*-i*). Live bait. *Eor ke aṃ jowāmuur?* Have you got any live bait?

jowe (**jewwey**). Harvest pandanus.

jowi (**jẹwiy**). Dial. E only; see *jou* (**jẹwiw**). 6(*-i*). Matrilineal kin; clan; race.

jǫ (**jaw**). 2, 3, 5(*jjǫjǫ*), 7. Ignite; run, of engines; start, of fire; to crank an engine (with causative prefix). *Ejjǫjǫ injin eṇ.* That engine is easy to start. *Ejǫ kijeek eo.* The fire has started. *Kōjǫ injin ṇe.* Crank up the engine.

jǫ (**jaw**). 1(*-i*), 2, 3(inf, tr *kōjjǫuj*), 5(*jjǫjǫ*), 7. Slip under ground or sand; place in sand where turtle lays eggs or coconut crab molts. *Ejǫ ek eo buḷōn bok.* The fish is slipping into the sand. *Ejjǫjǫ kain ek rot ṇe.* That kind of fish is always slipping into the sand.

jǫ (**jaw**). Be formerly, used to be. *Ejǫ riakiu raan ko an riNibboñ.* He used to be a baseball player during Japanese times. *Ejǫ kōn kilep ak kiiō eaidik.* He used to be fat but now he is skinny.

jǫ (**jaw**). Formant in place names; locative particle.

jǫej (**jawyẹj**). Variant form of *jǫweej*.

Jǫibeb (**jawyibyẹb**). From *jǫ* (**jaw**) "(a formative)", *ibeb* (**yibyẹb**) "saliva running down chin". 3, 6(-*i*). A plant, *Pandanus fischerianus* cultigen.

Jǫilokwaar (**jawyilewqahar**). 3, 6(-*i*). A plant, *Pandanus fischerianus* cultigen. Jaluit.

Jǫinin (**jawyinyin**). 3, 6(-*i*). A plant, pandanus cultigen; Ailinglaplap.

jǫjej (**jawjej**). From Engl. Sausage.

jǫjo (**jawjẹw**). 1(-*i*), 2(inf, tr *jǫun(i), jǫ*), 4, 6(-*i*), 7. Splash water on; dash. *Iar jǫuni kōn dān im kǫruji.* I splashed water on him to wake him up. *Jǫuntok mǫk peiū.* Will you throw some water on my hands? *Jǫuni kidu kaṇe.* Throw water on those dogs. *Kwōn jǫ jān jǫǫļūm.* Wash the salt water off of yourself.

jǫkden (**jaqden**). Archaic. Ten pairs, fish or copra.

jǫkkurere (**jaqqirẹyrẹy**). Also *jakkurere.* 1(-*i*), 2, 3, 4, 8, 9. Seldom play (see *kkure* (**qqirẹy**)); not athletic. *Ejǫkkurere.* He's not athletic.

jǫkkutkut (**jaqqitqit**). Also *jakkutkut.* 1(-*i*), 2(inf, tr -*i*), 3, 4, 8, 9, 11(*jǫkkutkut*). Not often; not close together; not frequent (see *kut* (**qit**)). *Ejǫkkutkut(i) an jar.* He doesn't go to church often. *Ejǫkkutkuti jemān.* He rarely visits his father.

jǫkkwikwi (**jaqqiyqiy**). Also *jakkwikwi.* 1(-*i*), 2, 3, 4, 8, 9, 11(*jǫkkwikwi*). Slow to cry; slow to anger in debate (see *kwi* (**qiy**)).

jǫkleej (**jaqleyej**). From Engl. Chocolate; candy. *Kijen wōn e jǫkleej?* Whose chocolate candy is this?

jǫkoṇ (**jaqeṇ**). Also *jakoṇ.* 1(-*i*), 2, 3, 8, 9. Fit poorly (see *koṇ* (**qeṇ**)); not neat. *Ejǫkoṇ aṃ kar kōṃṃane wūntō eṇ.* You didn't close that window tightly. *Ejǫkoṇ tōptōp ṇe aṃ.* Your footlocker isn't neat.

jǫkoṇkoṇ (**jaqeṇqeṇ**). Also *jakoṇkoṇ, joda* (**jewdah**). 1(-*i*), 2, 3, 4, 8, 9. Inability to catch many fish (see *koṇkoṇ* (**qeṇqeṇ**)).

jǫkooļoļ (**jaqeweļweļ**). Also *jakooļoļ.* 1(-*i*), 2, 3, 8, 9, 11(*jǫkooļoļ*). Not hairy (see *kooļ* (**qeweļ**)).

jǫkpej (**jaqpẹj**). 1(-*i*), 2(inf, tr -*e, jǫkpije*), 4, 6(-*i*), 7. Trash; rubbish; dump; reject. *Wōn e ear jǫkpeje bok e?* Who dumped this book in the trash? *Rōjǫkpeje.* He was rejected. He was dumped.

jǫkur (**jaqir**). 6(-*i*). Turtle shell; shell of a crab.

Jǫlije (**jawlijẹy**). From *jǫ* (**jaw**) "a formative)", *lije* (**lijẹy**) "to pound". 3, 6(-*i*). A plant, pandanus cultigen.

Jǫliō (**jawliyẹh**). 3, 6(-*i*). A plant; pandanus cultigen.

Jǫmōdān (**jawmedan**). 3, 6(-*i*). A plant, pandanus cultigen. Rongelap.

jǫmur (**jawmir°**). Also *kaak* (**kahak**). 2(inf, tr -*i*), 6(-*i*), 7. Ropes that go from top of the mast down to both ends of sailing canoe.

jǫmwin (**jawmin**). Archaic. Under; old form of *iumwin.*

Jǫmwin-atak (**jawmin-hatak**). From *jǫ* (**jaw**) "(a formative)", *mwinatak* (**minhatak**) "place name meaning 'house of towing a boat'". 3, 6(-*i*). A plant, *Pandanus carolinianus* cultigen.

Jǫmwin-jekad (**jawmin-jekad**). From *jǫ* (**jaw**) "(a formative)", *mwinjekad* "place name meaning 'house of the *jōkad* (**jekad**) (name of a bird)'". 3, 6(-*i*). A plant, pandanus cultigen.

Jǫmwin-joñ (**jawmin-jeg°**). From *jǫ* (**jaw**) "(a formative)", *mwinjoñ* (**minjeg°**) "place name meaning 'house of mangrove'". 3, 6(-*i*). A plant, pandanus cultigen.

jǫñe (**jag°ey**). Transitive form of *jjǫñ* (**jjag°**).

jǫǫb (**jawab**). From Engl. 2, 4. Get a job; work on a job, employment. *Kwōj jǫǫb ke?* Are you working? *Eor ke aṃ jǫǫb?* Do you have a job?

jǫǫk (**jawak**). From Engl. 1(-*i*), 2(inf, tr -*e*), 3, 5(*jjǫǫkǫk*), 6(-*i*). Chalk. *Ejjǫǫkǫk peiū.* My hands are covered with chalk.

Jǫǫk (**jawak**). From Engl. *chalk* (because of the whitish, waxy covering of the fruits). 3, 6(-*i*). A plant, banana variety.

jǫǫļ (**jawaļ**). From Engl. 1(-*i*), 2(inf, tr -*e*), 3, 4, 5(*jǫǫļǫļe, jjǫǫļǫļ*), 6(-*i*), 7, 8, 9, 11(*jǫǫļǫļ*). Salt. *Jǫǫļ kwaar wia ia jǫǫļ?* Where did you buy salt? *Kwōn jǫǫļi ek kaṇe.* Salt those fish. *Ek jǫǫļ/jǫǫļin ek.* Salt fish. *Piik jǫǫļ/*

jǫǫļin piik. Salt pork. *Wōn jǫǫļ/ jǫǫļin wōn.* Salted turtle. *Eļap an jǫǫļǫļe ek ņe.* That fish is very salty.

jǫǫr (**jawar**). 1(*-i*), 2, 3, 7. Escape; be released from.

jǫre (**jawr°ẹy, jar°ẹy**). Dial. E only; W: *jorrāān.* Also *jǫrwe.* Broken.

Jǫrukwōd (**jar°ikwed**). 3, 6(*-i*). A plant, banana variety.

jǫteen eo turun inne eo ļǫk juon (**jawtẹyẹn yew tir°in yinney yew ļaq jiwen**). Four evenings ago.

jǫteen ilju (**jawtẹyẹn yiljiw**). Tomorrow evening.

jǫteen inne (**jawtẹyẹn yinney**). Yesterday evening.

jǫteen inne eo ļǫk juon (**jawtẹyẹn yinney yew ļaq jiwen**). Three evenings ago.

jǫteen jekļaj (**jawtẹyẹn jekļaj**). Evening of the day after tomorrow.

jǫtiinin (**jawtiyinyin**). This evening.

jǫun (**jawin**). Transitive form of *jǫjo* (**jawjẹw**).

jǫuñ (**jawig**). Also *jauñ.* 1(*-i*), 2, 3, 7, 8, 9. Incomplete; not enough of counted things; not add up; not paired off (see *uñ* (**wig**)). *Ejǫuñ jān bōnbōn eo.* There are not as many here as there are supposed to be. *Ejǫuñ kōj e.* This share is short.

jǫut (**jawit**). From Australian Engl. *shout*. 2, 4, 6(*-i*), 7. Buy gifts for; buy drinks and food for a group; treat. *Ij jǫut.* The drinks are on me. *Kwōn jǫuttok.* Treat me.

jǫuwi (**jawwiy**). Also *jauwi.* 1(*-i*), 2, 3, 8, 9. Not tasty, of fish (see *uwi* (**wwiy**)).

jǫuwōta (**jawiwetah**). Also *jauwōta.* 2, 4, 5(*jǫuwōtata*), 6(*-i*), 8, 9. Not scare easily (see *uwōta* (**wiwetah**)).

jǫwe (**jawẹy**). A fish, giant sea bass, *Promicrops lanceolatus/truncatus*; a fish, bass, *Plectropomus truncatus.*

jǫweej (**jawẹyẹj**). Also *jǫej* (**jawyẹj**). 2(inf, tr *-e*), 3, 6(*-i*). Late, time of day or tide. *Elukkuun jǫweeje an etal.* He was terribly late in going.

jǫwiia (**jawiyyah**). Also *jawiia.* 2, 3(inf, tr *-ik*), 6(*-i*), 8, 9. Not start easily; not flammable (see *jǫwiie* (**jawiyyẹy**)).

jǫwiie (**jawiyyẹy**). Also *jawiie.* 2, 6(*-i*), 8, 9. Start easily; inflammable (see *jǫwiia* (**jawiyyah**))).

jǫwōtwōt (**jawwẹtwẹt**). Also *jawōtwōt, jawōttuot* (**jawẹttiwẹt**). 1(*-i*), 2, 8, 9. Drought; dry spell; not rainy; seldom rains (see *wōt* (**wẹt**)).

jōjōļe (**jẹhjẹhļẹy**). Transitive form of *jijō* (**jijẹh**).

jōōt (**jehet**). From Engl. 6(*-i*). Shirt.

jōōtōt (**jehethet**). From *jōōt* (**jehet**). 1(*-i*), 2, 3(inf, tr *-e*), 7, 8. Wear a shirt. *Ta kwōjaje jōōtōt ke?* Don't you know how to wear your shirt?

ju (**jiw**). 1(*-i*), 2, 3, 4, 5(*jjuju*), 6(*-i*), 7, 8, 9. Perpendicular; erect; stand on one's hands; stand on one's head; vertical; steep; straight up, of tall trees; precipitous; walk on hands. *Lale wōn in eto an ju.* Let's see who can stand on his hands the longest. *Emake ju limaakak ņe waaṃ.* Your kite can fly vertically. *Ekadik ju toļ eņ.* The mountain is very steep. *Epen tallīñe ni ņe bwe eju.* It's hard to climb that coconut because it's standing exactly vertical. *Kwōjeļā ke ju?* Can you walk on your hands?

ju (**jiw**). 2. Numerous (of insects). *Eju ņaṃ.* There are a lot of mosquitoes.

ju-bōro (**jiw-bẹrẹw**). 1(*ju-būruo-*), 2+1, 3+1, 7. Satisfied. *Eju-buruō kōn ṃōñā ko.* I am satisfied with the meal.

juae (**jiwhayey**). 2, 6(*-i*), 7. Ocean currents nearest to an island; the first zone of currents. *Ejuae ijin.* We're in the currents closest to the island. *Ej jab aelǫk juaein turun Epoon.* It's not difficult to notice the currents closest to *ebon*.

juakak (**jiwhakhak**). Look for birds; variant form of *kōbao.*

jubwij (**jiwbij**). 2(inf, tr *-i*), 4, 6(*-i*), 7. Signal made on the end of the *kie* of a canoe signifying battle; visual signal such as fire to notify of death or other natural disasters. *Ruwa eo waan Ļoeaak rejubwijiļǫk inej eo.* The people on Loeaak's canoe signalled to the rest of the fleet to get ready for battle. *Tile kijeekin jubwij eo.* Light the fire to signal for help. *Rōtar āneļǫk ke rej jubwiji er jān āneo.* They headed toward the island when they noticed the islanders signaling them.

judel (**jiwdẹl**). Dialectal variant of *juunbōñ* (**jiwinbẹg°**).

judu (**jiwdiw**). 1(*-i*), 2, 3, 4, 7. Hives, from eating spoiled fish.

juel (**jiwyẹl**). Dialectal variant of *kabuñpet* (**kabig°pẹt**).

jueoonmǫñ (**jiwyewenmag°**). Idiom. From *ju* (**jiw**) "stand on one's hands", *eoon* (**yewen**) "on", *mǫñ* (**mag°**) "pate". 1, 2, 4, 6(*-i*). Chew out someone; reprimand; scold. *Bǫǫj eo an ear jueoonmǫñūn kōn an rrum̧wijm̧wij.* His boss chewed him out for his tardiness.

juip (**jiwyip**). From Engl. *sweep*. 2, 3, 4, 6(*-i*). A card game.

jujaļ (**jiwjaļ**). Variant form of *juunm̧aad* (**jiwinm̧ahad**).

jujāl (**jiwjal**). Also *jujaļ* (**jiwjaļ**). 2+7, 3+7, 7. Look; direct; turn toward (always used with directional postpositions). *Kwōn jujāl ļǫk im ekkōnono.* Look right at him while you're speaking.

Juje (**jiwjey**). From Engl. Tuesday.

jujem (**jiwjem**). Variant form of *jujen* (**jiwjen**).

jujen (**jiwjen**). Also *jujem* (**jiwjem**). Then; consequently; and so; might as well. *Ļak ke eibwij, erro jujen pād wōt āneo.* The tide came in so they stayed on the island. *Ñe eitok enaaj jujen bōktok lōta eo.* As he is coming he might as well bring the letter.

jujukap (**jiwjiwkap**). Variant form of *jujukōp* (**jiwjiwkẹp**).

jujukōp (**jiwjiwkẹp**). Also *jujukap* (**jiwjiwkap**), *tutukōp* (**tiwtiwkẹp**). 3, 4+3, 5(*-e*), 6(*-i*), 3+7, 5+8, 9. A fish, barracuda, *Sphyraena barracuda.*

jujuur (**jiwjiwir**). Variant form of *jjuur* (**jjiwir**).

jujuurļǫk (**jiwjiwirļaq**). 2, 3. To get rid of; interfere in order to avoid; evade, verbally.

juk (**jiq**). Transitive form of *jukok* (**jiqẹq**).

juk jetōb (**jiq jẹtẹb**). Spirit dwelling within a person, good or bad.

jukjuk (**jiqjiq**). 1(*-i*), 2(inf, tr *jokwe*), 6, 7. Live with; residence; community; colony; dwell; inhabit; municipality; settle; settlement, village. *Jukjukun pād.* Community.

jukjuk (**jiqjiq**). 1(*-i*), 2(inf, tr *-i, -e*), 4, 5(*jjijukjuk*), 6(*-i*), 7. Pound breadfruit or taro; massage. *Kwōn jukjuke neō bwe emetak.* Massage my leg because it hurts. *RiAelok rōkadik jjijukjuk.* Ailuk people are always pounding breadfruit. *Itok bwe in jukjuki diim̧.* Come let me massage your back.

jukkwe (**jiqqẹy**). 1(*-i*), 2(inf, tr *-ik*), 7. Scratch. *Kwōn jukkweik m̧ōk ālikū.* Please scratch my back.

jukkwe (**jiqqẹy**). Dial. W only; see *kūkōr* (**kikẹr**). 3, 4+3, 6(*-i*), 3+7. Sand clam, bivalve.

juknen (**jiqnen**). Live forever. *Ijo ij pād im juknen ie.* Where I dwell and live forever and ever.

juknene (**jiqneyney**). 2, 4, 6(*-i*), 7. Walk on heels. *Ear kōm̧m̧an kōjak im juknene lōñļǫk.* He clowned about and walked up on his heels.

jukok (**jiqẹq**). 1(*-i*), 2(inf, tr *jukoke, juk(i)*), 4, 7, 8. Uncover an earth oven, usually when food therein is cooked. *Em̧ōj ke an jukok um̧ eo?* Has the oven been uncovered? *Ļeo eņ ej juk (jukoke) um̧ eņ.* That fellow is uncovering the oven.

jukoñki (**jiqegkiy**). From Japn. *chikuonki*. 2, 6(*-i*). Phonograph; gramophone; record player.

jukur (**jiqir°**). Variant form of *jikur* (**jikir°**).

jukuuļ (**jiqiwiļ**). Variant form of *jikuuļ* (**jikiwiļ**).

jukwa (**jiqah**). From Engl. 1(*-i*), 2(inf, tr *-ik(i)*), 3, 5(*jjukwakwa*), 6(*-i*), 7, 8. Sugar. *Ejjukwakwa tebōļ ņe.* The table has sugar all over it. *Kwōmake jjukwakwa.* You use sugar too often.

jukweea (**jiqeyyah**). From Engl. 2(inf, tr *-ik*), 3, 4, 6(*-i*), 7, 8, 9. Square.

Julele (**jiwlẹylẹy**). From "stand on tip toes". A plant, pandanus cultigen (Takeuchi).

juļ (**jiļ°**). Also *ļor* (**ļẹr°**). 1(*-i*), 2, 3, 6(*-i*), 7. Core of coconut tree at upper end; bud forth; sprout; growth from old root or branch; young shoot. (Not used for coconuts or pandanus. *Ejuļ mejān ine eo.* The seed sprouted.

Juļae (**jiwļahyey**). From Engl. July.

juļļwe (**jiļ°ļ°ẹy**). Archaic. Form a triangle shape with scarer (*m̧wieo*) in fishing by the *jurōk* method.

jumej (**jiwmẹj**). 1(*-i*), 2(inf, tr *-e*), 3, 7, 8, 9. Sudden; premature; untimely; abrupt. *Ejumej an uwe.* He decided to go all of a sudden.

jum̧ae (**jiwm̧ahyey**). 1(*-i*), 2(inf, tr *-ik*), 4, 7. Protest; resist; argue against; contrary; defy; interfere; oppose. *Raar jumaeik doon.* They argued among themselves.

juñaidi (jiwgahyidiy). From Japn. *chuugaeri*. 1(-*i*), 2, 3(inf, tr -*ik*), 6(-*i*), 7. Dive, of a plane; fall headlong, in wrestling; somersault. *Baluun ko raar kātōm juñaidi.* The planes dove.

juñurñur (jig°ir°g°ir°). 1(-*i*). Eardrum.

juok (jiwek). Transitive form of *jjuok* (jjiwek).

juon (jiwen). 3, 5(st *kajjojo*, inf *kajjo*, tr *kajjouk*). One; other; somebody; someone.

juon alen (jiwen halen). Once. *Juon alen ebwe.* Once is enough.

juon iien (jiwen 'yiyen). Sometime; one time; once.

juon im rājet (jiwen yim rayjet). Variant form of *ruo mōttan jilu* (riwew mettan jiliw).

juon jāān (jiwen jayan). Penny.

juon men (jiwen men). Something. *Juon men e ej kaabōņōņōik eō.* Something's bothering me.

juoñ (jiwęg). 1(-*i*), 2, 3, 5(*jjuoñoñ*), 6(-*i*). Smell of dead plants in water; smell of a swamp; smell of decayed flesh. *Kōkāāl dānnin nien ut ņe bwe ejuoñ.* Change the water in the vase because it is getting smelly.

jurbak (jir°bak). From Engl. 2, 3(inf, tr -*e*), 4, 5(*jjurbakbak*), 6(-*i*), 7. Jitterbug; tap-dance. *Ejjurbakbak likaoun Mājej.* Young men of Mejij island are known as good tap dancers.

jure (jiwręy). 3(inf *kajurere*, tr *kajure*), 4+3, 5(*jjurere*), 3+7, 5+8, 9, 6(-*i*). A fish, barracuda, *Sphyraena forsteri*.

jure (jiwrey). Also *juululin-Pikaar* (jiwilwilin-pikahar). From *joor* (jęwęr). 6(-*i*). Teeming with. *Ejure ānin kōn bao.* This island is teeming with birds.

jure (jir°ey). Transitive form of *jjor* (jjęr°).

Juriātak (jir°iyatak). 3, 6(-*i*). A plant, pandanus cultigen (Takeuchi).

juro- (jir°e-). 2(tr *jure*), 6(-*i*). Handle, as of a knife or shovel. *Ekadik aetok juron jabōļ ņe.* The handle on that shovel is too long. *Kwōn jure bakbōk e.* Make a handle for this knife.

juron bōļeak (jir°en beļyak). Also *juron bōļāāk*. Flagpole. *Eokjak juron bōļāāk eo.* The flagpole fell down.

jurōk (jiwręk). 1(-*i*), 2(inf, tr -*e*), 4, 7. Fishing method, use long net and mwio (miyew) during high tide and wait for low. *Kōjro jurōke mejje eņ mokta jān an pāāt.* Let's use this fishing method at that opening between those islets before low tide comes.

jurōk (jiwręk). Also *jurōk* (jiwrek). 2(inf, tr -*e, e*), 3(inf *kajjurōk*, tr *kajurōk*), 6(-*i*), 7. Standing; erected; perfective form of *kajjuur* (kajjiwir); stand. *Jurōke ņa ieņe.* Stand it over there near you.

jurōn (jiwren). Construct form of *joor* (jęwęr).

Jurōn-aodet-kaņ-rilik (jiwren-hawedet-kaņ-riylik). A star; possibly 2 in Ursa Minor; one of the four "posts of Polaris" (*Jurōn-Limanman*); pairs with gamma Cephei to point to Polaris.

Jurōn-Jemān-Kurlōñ (jiwren-jeman-qirlęg). Also *Iju Raan* (yijiw rahan), *Jemān-Kurlōñ* (jeman-qirlęg). A star (planet), Morning Star, Venus (mornings only).

Jurōn-Limanman (jiwren-limanman). Posts of Polaris; two pairs of stars that point to the North Star; one pair is the two stars of *Wātalkaņ,* and the other is *Limanman-eņ-an-Ñinjib* and *Jurōn-aodet-kaņ-rilik.*

jurub (jir°ib). From Engl. 2(inf, tr -*i*), 3, 6(-*i*). Syrup. *Emōj jurubi dān eo.* The water has been mixed with the syrup.

jutak (jiwtak). 1(-*i*), 2, 3(inf, tr -*e*), 5(*jjutaktak*), 7, 8. Stand up. *Emōj ņe am jjutaktak.* Why don't you stop standing up all the time. *Kajutake jurōn bōļāāk eņ.* Stand the flagpole up.

juub (jiwib). 1(-*i*), 2(inf, tr -*i*), 3, 4, 5(*jjuubub*), 6(-*i*), 8. Soup; stew. *Ejjuubub nuknuk ņe am.* Your clothes have soup slopped on them.

juubkwe (jiwibqęy). Also *juubke* (jiwibkęy), *jubukwe* (jiwbiqęy). 1(-*i*), 2, 3, 4, 5(*jjuubkwekwe*), 7. Kneel; genuflect. *Ejjuubkwekwe ļeeņ.* He's always kneeling. *Juubkwe im jar.* Kneel and pray.

juubub (jiwibwib). 1(-*i*), 3, 6(-*i*). Shoot of coconut, pandanus; etc.

juuj (**jiwij**). From Engl. 6(*-i*). Shoes; hoof.

juuj (**jiwij**). 2(inf, tr *-i*), 7. Kick. *Juuji nabōjļǫk kidu ņe.* Kick that dog out.

juujuj (**jiwijwij**). From *juuj* (**jiwij**). 1(*-i*), 2, 3(inf, tr *-i*), 5(*jjuujuj*), 6(*-i*), 7. Wear shoes. *Kajujuuji ļadik ņe.* Put on his shoes for him.

juululin-Pikaar (**jiwilwilin-pikahar**). Variant form of *jure* (**jiwrey**).

Juun (**jiwin**). From Engl. June.

juunbon̄ (**jiwinbęg°**). Dial. W, E: *judel* (**jiwdęl**). 2, 4, 6(*-i*), 7. Fishing method, pole fishing on barrier reef edge at low tide on dark nights. *Juunbon̄ eṃṃan n̄an bon̄ūn marok.* It is best to use the *juunbon̄* fishing method when it's dark. *Ekōņaan iwōj in judel.* He wants to go pole fishing with you. *Ekōppaļpaļ judelin riMejeej.* It's fascinating to watch people from Mejit pole fishing.

juunṃaad (**jiwinṃahad**). Also *jujaļ-* (**jiwjaļ-**). 2(inf, tr *-e*), 3, 4, 7. Envy; jealousy.

juur (**jiwir**). Transitive form of *jjuur* (**jjiwir**).

juwa (**jiwah**). 2, 3(inf, tr *-ik(i)*), 4. Proud; egotism. *En dik ļǫk aṃ juwa.* Lessen your pride. *Lale bwe jeban ņe aṃ en jab kajuwaik eok.* Don't let your success make you too proud.

juwabōļ (**jiwahbeļ**). From Engl. Swivel.

juwadel (**jiwwahdel**). Royal bathing pool in old days.

juwain (**jiwahyin**). From Engl. *twine*. 2(inf, tr *-i*), 3, 6(*-i*). Lace; embroider. *Ṃwejo ej juwaini jemej eņ an.* M'wejo is sewing lace on her slip.

juwajo (**jiwajew**). Also *juwajo* (**jiwajęw**). 3, 6(*-i*). A fish, snapper, *Lutjanus monostigmus.*

juwaļōn̄ļōn̄ (**jiwahļęgļęg**). 1(*-i*), 2, 3, 6(*-i*), 7, 8, 9. Show off; gloat. *Kwōn jab juwaļōn̄ļōn̄.* Don't show off. *Emake juwaļōn̄ļōn̄.* He's such a show off. *Ejuwaļōn̄ļōn̄ kōn ṃweiuk kaņ an.* He's gloating over his possessions.

juwape (**jiwahpęy**). From Engl. 5(*jjuwapepe*), 6(*-i*). Swabby; sailor. *Jet wōt kaņe baj ṃūtōn juwape.* Sailors have some style.

juwapin (**jiwahpin**). Dial. E, W: *kuļuļ* (**qiļ°iļ°**). Also *juwapen* (**jiwwapęn**), *jowapin* (**jewahpin**). 2, 3, 5(*jjuwapinpin*), 6(*-i*), 8, 9. Roach; cockroach; cricket.

juwi (**jiwiy**). Dialectal variant of *mejǫ* (**mejaw**).

juwōne (**jiwwęnęy**). 2(inf, tr *-ik*), 4. See off on a voyage. *Rōmoot in juwōneik jar ko rej uwe.* They went to see off the group that is making the voyage.

ka (**ka-**). Formant in place names.

ka- (**ka-**). Also *ke-*, *kō-*, *ko-* (**ke-**). Causative prefix.

kaab (**kahab**). From Engl. 6(*-i*). Gaff. *Ebwilǫk kaab eo kaabin wa eo.* The gaff of the sailboat is broken.

kaab (**kahab**). Variant form of *kōōb* (**kęhęb**).

kaabraita (**kahabrahyitah**). Variant form of *kaabreta* (**kahabreytah**).

kaabreta (**kahabreytah**). Also *kaabraita* (**kahabrahyitah**). From Engl. Carburetor. *Ejorrāān kaabretain injin eo an.* His engine's carburetor is out of commission.

kaadikdik (**kahadikdik**). Variant form of *kadikdik* (**kadikdik**).

kaaj (**kahaj**). From Engl. 1(*-i*), 2, 3, 4, 6(*-i*), 8. Play cards; playing cards.

kaajiriri (**kahajiriyriy**). Also *kōkkaajiriri* (**kekkahajiriyriy**), *kaajjiriri* (**kahajjiriyriy**), *kōkajiriri* (**kekahjiriyriy**), *kōkaajjiriri* (**kekahajjiriyriy**). 1(*-i*), 2(inf, tr *-ik*), 3, 4, 7. Raise children; adopt children; babysit; nurture; nurse a baby (or a situation).

kaajliin̄ (**kahajliyig**). From Engl. 6(*-i*). Empty gasoline barrel; oil drum, 50-gallon.

kaak (**kahak**). Variant form of *jǫṃur* (**jawṃir°**).

kaal (**kahal**). Transitive form of *kkaal* (**kkahal**).

kaallo (**kahallęw**). A fish.

kaalwōjwōj (**kahalwęjwęj**). Also *kaloojoj* (**kahlęwęjwęj**). From *alwōj* (**halwęj**). Exhibit; show. *Jikin kaalwōjwōj.* Museum. Fair.

kaaļapļap (**kahaļapļap**). From *aļap* (**haļap**). Respect elders. *Ejeļā kaaļapļap.* He knows how to respect elders.

kaamijak (**kahamijak**). Variant form of *kaammijak* (**kahammijak**).

kaammeǫeo (**kahammeyawyęw**). Also *kammeǫeo* (**kammeyawyęw**), *kōmmeǫeo* (**kemmeyawyęw**). 2(inf, tr

-*uk*), 4, 8, 9. Cheat. *Raar peǫǫt peba eo an kōn an kaammeǫeo.* They tore up his paper because he was cheating.

kaammijak (**kahammijak**). Also *kaamijak* (**kahamijak**). 1(-*i*), 2, 8, 9. Horrible; frightening; terrifying. *Ekaammijak an mej.* His was a horrible death.

kaaṃtō (**kahaṃteh**). From Engl. 1(-*i*), 2(inf, tr -*ūk*), 4, 6(-*i*), 8. Carpenter; carpentry. *Kaaṃtōūk ṃōk men ṇe.* Fix that thing.

kaan (**kahan**). 2, 6(-*i*). Fuel; use as fuel. *Emaat kaan wa eo.* The boat ran out of fuel. *Injin e kaan tijeḷ.* This motor runs on diesel. *Emaat kaan kijek eṇ.* That fire doesn't have any more fuel.

kaane (**kahaney**). Transitive form of *kkaan* (**kkahan**).

kaapooḷ (**kahapeweḷ**). Variant form of *kōpooḷ* (**kepeweḷ**).

kaar (**kahar**). 3, 5(*kkaarar, kkaarōr*) 6(-*i*). A plant, tree, *Premna corymbosa* (Burm. F.) Rottl. + Willd. Var. *Obtusifolia* (R. Br.) Fletcher.

kaar (**kahar**). From Engl. 6(-*i*). Car. *Kaarin ia ṇe waaṃ?* Where was your car made?

kaarar (**kaharhar**). From *kaar* (**kahar**). 1(-*i*), 2, 3(inf, tr -*e*), 6(-*i*), 7. Drive a car. *Kwōj kaarar ḷǫk ñan ia?* Where are you driving the car?

kaarmejjet (**kaharmęjjet**). 1(-*i*), 2(inf, tr -*e*), 3, 4, 6, 7. Deny; disavow; repudiate; defy; renounce; abjure; refuse to recognize. *Koṃwin katak kaarmejjete kōṇaan ko an kanniōk.* You must learn to renounce the temptations of the flesh. *Ear kaarmejjete kallimur in pālele ko an.* He defied his marriage vows. *Pita ear kaarmejjete Jijej.* Peter denied Jesus.

kaat (**kahat**). Variant form of *katin* (**katin**).

kaatat (**kahathat**). Also *pitpit.* Prepare bait.

kaatat (**kahathat**). A plant.

kaattilekek (**kahattilyękyęk**). Variant form of *kaattilōklōk* (**kahattilęklęk**); causative form of *tilekek* (**tilyękyęk**).

kaattilōklōk (**kahattilęklęk**). Dial. E only; see *kūttiliek* (**kittiliyęk**). Also *kaattileklek* (**kahattilyękyęk**). 1(-*i*), 2, 3, 4, 7. Hide-and-seek; lurk; hide.

kaatuwe (**kahatiwey**). Causative transitive form of *ato* (**hatęw**).

kab (**kab**). And; too; also; just; finally. *Kwōn kab itok.* Come when you can. *Kab bar kwe, kwōn kab itok.* You come too. *Ej kab wōt.* It finally started to rain. *Ej kab jejjet.* It's finally correct.

kab (**kab**). From Engl. 6(-*i*). Cup; drinking glass.

kab (**kab**). 1(-*i*), 2. Paddle a canoe so as to hold it against current.

kabaj (**kahbaj**). 3, 6(-*i*). A bird, reef heron, *Egretta sacra*; crane.

kabaj (**kahbaj**). 2(inf, tr -*e*), 6(-*i*). Crane, mechanical. *Rej kabaje injin eṇ jān lowaan wa eṇ.* They're using the crane to take the engine out of that ship.

Kabaj (**kahbaj**). 3, 6(-*i*). A plant, pandanus cultigen; Rongelap.

kabba (**kabbah**). Also *kōbba* (**kebbah**). From Japn. *kappa* (from Portuguese *capa* "cape"). 2(inf, tr -*ik*), 6(-*i*). Raincoat; overcoat; canvas cover. *Koṃwin kabbaik waini kaṇe bwe ren jab ṃōḷǫwi.* Cover the copra so it won't get wet.

kabbe (**kabbey**). 1(-*i*), 2(inf, tr -*ik*), 7. Tack canoe to leeward; sail westward; sail with the wind.

kabbil (**kabbil**). 1, 2, 6(-*i*), 8, 9, 11(*kabbil*). Dandy; ingrate; arrogant; show-off; pride; stuck-up. *Kabbil men eṇ.* He's a dandy. *Ekabbil ñan eō ak iar kaḷe.* He's such an ingrate but I'm the one who put him ahead.

kabbok (**kabbęq**). Dial. E, W: *elme* (**yelmey**). Breadfruit flower.

kabbok (**kabbęq**). 2(inf, tr -*e*). Cut tree trunk into pieces, as breadfruit for making canoe. *Ej kabboke wōjke eṇ.* He's cutting up that tree.

kabbok (**kabbęq**). 3, 6(-*i*). A plant, *Asclepias curassavica* (Ebon).

kabbokbok (**kabbęqbęq**). 1(-*i*), 2(inf, tr *kabbukwe*), 4, 7. Clap hands; applaud; applause; firecracker; ovation. *Kwaar lo ke kabbokbok eo aō?* Did you see my firecracker anywhere?

kabbōjrak (**kabbęjrak**). Idiom. From *bōjrak* (**bęjrak**). 2, 4, 6(-*i*), 7. Return gift; hold on to keep from falling; reciprocating of gifts. *N̄e rej kaṃḷo ñan eok kwōj aikuj kabbōjrak.* When you are being honored at a feast you should give away little presents to show your appreciation.

kabbōk (**kabbęk**). Variant form of *tōbak* (**tebak**).

kabbōl (**kabbęl**). Transitive form of *kabōlbōl* (**kabęlbęl**).

kabbukwe (**kabbiqey**). Transitive form of *kabbokbok* (**kabbęqbęq**).

kabbūroṃōjṃōj (**kabbiręwṃejṃęj**). Also *kabūroṃōjṃōj* (**kabiręwṃejṃęj**). From *būroṃōj* (**biręwṃęj**). 1(-*i*), 2, 4, 6(-*i*), 7, 8, 9. Sorrowful; saddening; pitiful; pathetic. *Ekabbūroṃōjṃōj wāween jab eo.* That was a pathetic situation. *Ekabūroṃōjṃōj kōn an jako jinen im jemān.* His being an orphan is pathetic.

kabkab (**kabkab**). From Engl. 1(-*i*), 2, 3(inf, tr -*e*), 6(-*i*), 7. Use a cup. *Imaroñ ke kabkab kōn kab ṇe ñiiṃ?* May I use your cup?

kabkūbjer (**kabkibjęr**). Archaic. 2(inf, tr -*e*), 4, 6(-*i*), 7. Advise someone to lead a conventionally good clean life. *Iar kabkūbjere em ṃōk ak kōn an kar bōd katakini eban ṃṃan.* I gave him all the advice I could but he's been so spoiled that I doubt if he'll ever reform.

kabkūbwijer (**kabkibijer**). Distributive form of *kabwijer* (**kabijer**).

kabna (**kabnah**). From Engl. 6(-*i*). Governor. *Kabna eo ad ṇe.* That's our governor. *Kabnain injin eṇ men ṇe.* That governor belongs to that engine.

kabodān (**kabęwdan**). Also *kōbodān* (**kebewdan**). 1(-*i*), 2(inf, tr -*e*), 3, 4, 7. Dilute; mix with water. *Enañin kabodān ke jekaro ṇe?* Hasn't that toddy been diluted yet? *Eṃōj kabodāne jekaro eo.* That toddy has been diluted.

kabodān (**kabęwdan**). Also *kōbodān* (**kebewdan**). 2, 7. Mix sail power with engine power. *Wa eṇ ej kabodān.* The boat is using both its sails and its engine.

kabōlbōl (**kabęlbęl**). 1(-*i*), 2(inf, tr *kabbōl*), 3, 6(-*i*), 7. Bright; shining. *Ej kabōlbōl mejān ilo boñ.* It's eyes shine at night.

kabōlbōl (**kabęlbęl**). 2, 6(-*i*), 7. Shine in the distance; twinkle, as stars; glow. *Ej baj to, ęlok em bar kabōlbōl iju.* After a while, the rain stopped and the stars came out again. *Iar lo juon meram ej kabōlbōl.* I saw a light shining in the distance.

kabōllaḷ (**kabęllaḷ**). 1, 2, 4, 6(-*i*), 7, 8, 9. A grandstander; a dandy; show-off. *Aḷe, ekabōllaḷ wōt.* Man, he's such a grandstander. *Rūkabōllaḷ men raṇ.* They're notorious for putting on airs.

kabro (**kabręw**). 3, 4+3, 5(*kkabroro*), 6(-*i*), 3+7. A fish, rock cod, *Anyperodon leucogrammicus.*

kabroñḷok (**kabreg°ḷaq**). Warn.

kabuñ (**kabig°**). 2, 4, 6. Worship; religion; adoration; rite. *Jabōt raan in kabuñ.* Sunday is a day of worship. *Likao eṇ ej rūkabuñ wōt.* He's still a catechumen.

kabuñpet (**kabig°pęt**). Dial. E, W: *juel* (**jiwyęl**). 2, 4, 6(-*i*). Intuition and knowledge possessed by certain expert Marshallese navigators using traditional methods. *Kōn an jeḷā kabuñpet emaroñ pād ilowaan juon wa im jeḷā ke ebōd kooj eo an.* Because he possesses the intuition and knowledge of Marshallese navigation, he can sense that a boat is off its course even while he's inside the boat.

kabūrōrō (**kabirehreh**). 2, 5(*kkabūrōrō*), 6(-*i*), 7. Wide-eyed; eyes wide open. *Ear kabūrōrō ke ij ba ejorrāān wa eo waan.* His eyes went wide when I told him his car had broken down. *Ekkabūrōrō Eaṃōṇ.* Herman is always wide-eyed.

kabūt (**kabit**). 6(*kabtōn, kabte*). Prepare bait from a plant.

kabwijer (**kabijer**). 1(-*i*), 2(inf, tr -*e*), 7, 10(*bōjrak*). Take by the hand; hold; control. *Kwōn kabwijertok bok ṇe.* Hand me that book. *Kwōn kabwijere bwe enaaj buñ.* Hold him because he'll fall. *Wōn eṇ ej kabwijer jebwe eṇ?* Who's controlling the wheel?

kabwijer (**kabijer**). 2, 5(*kabkūbwijer*), 7. Keep a canoe or boat full-sailing. *Kwōn kabkūbwijer ḷok wa ṇe.* Keep the sail of the canoe full there.

kabwijer doon (**kabijer dewen**). Variant form of *jibwe doon* (**jibey dewen**).

kabwijeran (**kabijeran**). Customary reimbursement given by anyone in return or exchange for food, living, or payment for medicine or priest-craft; foods prepared for visitors before their arrival.

kabwijlōñ (**kabijlęg**). 3, 6(-*i*). A plant, *Soulamea amara* Lam. (Simarubaceae). A large, simple-leaved shrub of the beaches. Leaves approach 6" in length. N.

kabwil (**kabil**). 1(*-i*), 2(inf, tr *-i*), 4, 7. Fishing method, fishing with a torch; slash with machete.

kabwilǫklǫk māj (**kabilaqlaq maj**). 2, 6(*-i*), 8, 9. Causing public embarrassment; scandalize; hurt feelings of some by showing favoritism to others. *Eļap an kabwilǫklǫk māj kōn an ire kōrā.* He caused great public embarrassment by beating his wife. *Ekabwilǫklǫk māj ad naajdik wōt Ļajiļap ak jej jab naajdik Jeeklik.* Our support of *Ļajiļap* but not of *Jeeklik* is causing hurt feelings.

kabwilōñe (**kabilegey**). Transitive form of *kabwilōñlōñ* (**kabilegleg**).

kabwilōñlōñ (**kabilegleg**). 1(*-i*), 2(inf, tr *kabwilōñe*), 3, 4, 7, 8, 9. Amazing; surprising. *Eļap an kabwilōñlōñ tiṃa eņ ear potok.* Everyone is amazed by that ship that arrived.

kad (**kad**). Transitive form of *kadkad* (**kadkad**).

kaddejdej (**kaddejdej**). 2(inf, tr *-e*), 3, 4, 6(*-i*), 7. To tire a fish after it is hooked. *Kōjparok aṃ kadejdeje ek ņe bwe en jab ļǫrak.* Be careful while tiring the fish so it won't get entangled with a coral head. *Kaddejdeje ṃokta jān aṃ tōbwe.* Let it tire before you haul it in.

kaddikdik (**kaddikdik**). Reduce. *Iaikuj kaddikdik bwe eļap aō tebu.* I have to reduce because I'm overweight.

kaddipenpen (**kaddiypęnpęn**). From *dipen* (**diypęn**). 4, 6(*-i*). Lift weights to build up body.

kaddoļ (**kaddeļ°**). 3, 6(*-i*). A shell, *Neritidae*; *Puperita japonica* or *Amphinerita polita*; sea snail, top shell.

kaddouj uj (**kaddęwijwij**). From *douj* (**dęwij**) "ship water". 2, 6(*-i*). Space-filling. *Bōk wōt kobban dimwūj kaņe bwe ekaddoujuj aded kaņe.* Just take the meat out of the clams because the shells will only be (undesirable) added weight. *Ejab maattok rukkure ro bwe raalwōj ro rouwe em kaddoujuj.* Not all the players came because the spectators got on and took up all the room.

kade (**kadey**). Transitive form of *kadkad* (**kadkad**).

kadek (**kadek**). 1(*-i*), 2(inf, tr *-e*), 3, 4, 5(*kkadekdek*), 6(*-i*), 7, 8. Intoxicating; drunk; poisonous, of fish; intoxicated; inebriated. *Ļeo ekkadekdek eņ.* That fellow is always drunk. *Iar kadeke ek eo.* I got poisoned by the fish.

kadeǫeo (**kahdeyawyęw**). Dial. E only; see *kauļaļo* (**kahwiwļaļęw**). 3(*kōkadeǫeo, kōkadeǫeouk*), 6(*-i*). Spider; cobwebs. *Ear kōkadeǫeouk tōptōp eo.* He got the cobwebs off the chest.

kadikdik (**kadikdik**). Also *kaadikdik* (**kahadikdik**). 1(*-i*), 2, 3(inf, tr *-i*), 7, 8, 9. Slow; take it easy; ease something. *Ñe kwōj ttōr iturun aujpitōļ kwōj aikuj kadikdik.* Slow down when you drive by a hospital. *Kwōn kkadikdiki ļadik ņe bwe enaaj bwilǫk diin.* Take it easy with that boy or you'll break his bones.

kadjo (**kadjew**). Also *karōjo* (**karejew**). 2(inf, tr *-uk(i)*), 3, 4, 6(*-i*), 7. Fishing method, pole fishing for goatfish. *Iar kadjouki ilo jikin eǫñōd eņ aō makmake.* I caught this goatfish at my favorite fishing spot. *Ia eo ear kōkadjouk eok ie?* Where did he take you pole fishing for goatfish?

kadkad (**kadkad**). 1(*-i*), 2(inf, tr *kad(e)*), 4, 5(*kkadkade*), 7. Throw; pitch; large stone used as an anchor. *Kwōn kade bao eņ.* Throw something at that bird. *Wōn ņe ej kadkad ñan kumi ņe?* Who is the pitcher on your team? *Kwōn jab kkadkade bao eņ.* Don't keep throwing stones at that bird.

kadkad (**kadkad**). 1(*-i*), 2(inf, tr *-e*), 3, 4, 7. Fishing method, use throwing net.

kadkad (**kadkad**). 1(*-i*). Family relationship; position; status; description; contents (of a book); genealogy; pedigree.

kadkad (**kadkad**). 2(inf, tr *kade*), 4, 6(*-i*). Bloodletting; phlebotomy. *Eļap an aļap kōjerbal kadkad ñan nañinmej kaņ aer.* Older people often resort to bloodletting to cure their ailments. *Ruuno eo ear kade rinañinmej eo.* The medicine man treated the sick man by bloodletting. *Ej kadkad kōn ñiin pako.* He lets blood with shark teeth.

kadkadajaj (**kadkadhajhaj**). 2, 4, 6(*-i*). Attempt the impossible; push one's luck. *Rūtto ro rōkein ba jab* *kadkadajaj bwe enaaj or jerata.* The old folks used to say to never attempt the impossible or sorry consequences might follow. *Kwōn jab kadkadajaj bwe eanitta.* Don't try him because he's a voodoo expert.

kadkadmootot (**kadkadmewetwet**). 2, 4, 6(*-i*). Neglect one's primary responsibility. *Eļañe juon ṃṃaan ej jab lale bwe en tōprak aikuj ko an baaṃle eo an ṃokta jān an lale ro jet, ej kadkadmootot.* If a man doesn't make sure that his family's needs are met before he helps others, we say he's neglecting his primary responsibilities.

kadu (**kadiw**). Also *kanu* (**kaniw**). 1(*-i*), 2, 3(inf *kōkkaddudu,* tr *kōkaduuk*), 4, 5(*kkadudu, kkadu*), 7, 8, 9, 11(*kkadudu*). Short; brief. *Ļakkadudu eo ņe tok.* There comes Shorty. *Lio ekkadu an nuknuk eņ.* She always wears short skirts. *Rūttariņae raņ rej kōkkaddudu.* The soldiers all have crew-cuts.

kadulele (**kadiwleyley**). 2, 3(inf, tr *-ik(i)*), 4, 5(*kkadulele*), 6(*-i*). Decorations made from feathers of frigate birds, one on each tip of the sail on a chief's canoe. *Raar kōkaduleleiki wa eo im ļak kadulele, epeļļọk.* They readied the canoe with all kinds of feather decorations before she sailed away.

kae (**kahyey**). From Engl. 1(*-i*). Guy rope or cable; band around ankles used in climbing trees.

kae (**kahyey**). From Engl. *guy.* 2(inf, tr *-ik*), 4, 6(*-i*), 7. Special twine made from skin of coconut frond midrib for climbing coconut trees. *Ļeo ejeļā kae ni ņe.* He is the man expert in climbing coconut trees with a guy.

kaerer (**kahyẹryẹr**). 1(*-i*), 2, 3, 4, 7, 8, 9. Pamper a child so as to create undue attachment; a pampered child; cling to one another; embrace.

kaijoļjoļ (**kahyijeļ°jeļ°**). 2(inf, tr *-e*), 4, 6(*-i*), 7, 8, 9. Luscious; tantalize or tease, of food only. *Bọọļ, kwōn jab kaijoļjoļe jatūṃ.* Paul, don't tease your brother with that candy.

kaik (**kahyik**). Also *kāik* (**kayik**). Transitive form of *kkāke* (**kkaykẹy**).

kaikai (**kahiykahiy**). From Melanesian Pidgin. Eat. *Kwōn kaikai ļọk bwe jen etal.* Eat up so we can leave.

kaikikūt (**kahyikiykit**). Also *kaikūtkūt* (**kahyikitkit**). 2(inf, tr *-i*), 4, 6(*-i*), 7. Fishing method, search for fish on the reef at low tide. *Rainin inaaj kaikikūt niñaļọk.* Today I'll walk northward over the reef searching for fish.

kailar (**kahyilar**). Variant form of *kāilar* (**kayilar**).

kaiṃak (**kahyiṃak**). Variant form of *kōṃṃak* (**keṃṃak**).

kain (**kahyin**). From Engl. Kind; type; sort.

kaiņņe (**kahyiņņey**). From *kain ņe* (**kahyin ņey**) "that kind". Sort of; act in a certain way. *Ejaad kaiņņe maroro.* It's sort of green. *Kwōn jab kaiņņe.* Don't act that way.

kaiñ (**kahyig**). 1(*-i*), 2(inf, tr *-(i)*), 4, 7. To send a command to; to inform. *Eṃōj ke aṃ kaiñ er?* Have you informed them?

kaiok (**kahyiyeq**). Also *kaiook* (**kahiyeweq**). 2+7, 3+7, 7. Steer directly for; go toward.

kaiuiu (**kayiwyiw**). Also *kāiuiu.* Causative form of *iu.*

kaj (**kaj**). 1(*-i*), 5(*kkajkaj*), 6(*-i*). Idiom; language; motto; pun; saying; slang; slogan; jargon; lingo. *Liṃaroro rej kkajkaj.* Those women are using fancy language.

kaj (**kaj**). Variant form of *kajkaj* (**kajkaj**).

kajdo (**kajdẹw**). 3, 6(*-i*). A plant, tree, *Ixora carolinensis* (Val.) Hosokawa (Rubiaceae). Known on Majuro, Jaluit, and Ebon as well as in the Carolines.

kaje (**kajey**). 1(*-i*), 2(inf, tr *kajeik*), 4, 6(*-i*). Punish; penalize; penalty. *Rōnaaj kajeik eok ñe kobōt.* You will be punished if you are naughty.

kajek (**kajek**). Transitive form of *kkaj* (**kkaj**) and *kajkaj* (**kajkaj**).

kajet (**kajet**). Spin. *Ekajet likaep eņ.* The top is spinning.

kajikia (**kajikiyah**). 1(*-i*), 2, 3, 4, 6(*-i*), 7. Move hips from side to side while dancing; bump and grind. *RiKilbōt rōjeļā kajikia.* Gilbertese swing their hips well.

kajikur (**kajikir°**). Transitive form of *kajjikur* (**kajjikir°**).

kajin (**kajin**). Language; dialect; construct form of *kaj* (**kaj**). *Kajin Pālle.* English. *Kajin Ratak.* The eastern dialect. *Kajin Rālik.* The western dialect. *Kajin Boonpe.* The Ponapean language.

kajipedped (**kajipędpęd**). A food, preserved breadfruit or *peru* flattened and covered with breadfruit leaves and baked.

kajitūkin (**kajitikin**). Slang. 2. Ask; find out about; query; interrogate; grill verbally; transitive form of *kajjitōk* (**kajjitęk**). *Kwōn m̧ōk kajitūkini ļeņe ear wajjikōt?* How about asking that man why he came?

kajje (**kajjey**). 1(-*i*), 2, 4, 7. To swear by.

kajjeor (**kajjeyer°**). 4, 6(-*i*), 7. A game, contest to see who can throw a sharp-pointed piece of dried pandanus root, about a yard long, farthest by skimming it on the ground once. *Ajriin raan kein rejaje kajjeor.* Modern day Marshallese children do not know how to play *kajjeor*.

kajji (**kajjiy**). Also *kiaj* (**kiyhaj**). From Japn. *kyaccha*. 2, 6(-*i*), 7. Baseball catcher. *Kwōj kajji rainin.* You'll be the catcher today. *Kwōn kajji tok ñan kōj.* You be our catcher.

kajjidede (**kajjidęydęy**). 1(-*i*), 2(inf, tr -*ik*), 4. Guess; conjecture; speculate. *Idike kajjidedeiki uwaak eo.* I don't want to guess the answer.

kajjie- (**kajjiye-**). Variant form of *kijjie-* (**kijjiye-**).

kajjikur (**kajjikir°**). 1(-*i*), 2(inf, tr *kajikur(i)*), 4, 5(*kajjikurkur*), 7. Dislike; a feeling against; pessimistic. *Ļeo ej make wōt kijoñ kajjikurkur eņ.* He's always the most negative.

kajjimalele (**kajjimahlęylęy**). Also *ajjimalele* (**hajjimahlęylęy**), *kajjimālele* (**kajjimalęylęy**). 1(-*i*), 2(inf, tr -*ik*), 4, 7. Foretell; predict; surmise; guess; speculate.

kajjim̧we (**kajjim̧ęy**). From *jim̧we* (**jim̧ęy**). 1(-*i*), 2, 4, 6(-*i*), 8, 9. Strict; rigid; inflexible; stern; rigorous; hairsplitting. *Joñan an kajjim̧we ear kōm̧o̧ an lio nājin alwōj pija.* He was so strict he forbade his daughter to see a movie.

kajjinōk (**kajjinęk**). 1(-*i*), 2, 3, 4, 5(*kkajjinōknōk*), 7, 8, 9. Tired out; fatigued; weary; winded; be beat. *Ekkajjinōknōk ļeeņ.* He gets tired easily. He isn't strong.

kajjioñ (**kajjiyeg°**). 1(-*i*), 2(inf, tr -*e*), 4, 5(*kajjioñeoñ*), 7. Endeavor; try; attempt; mock; imitate; emulate. *Inaaj kajjioñ iwōj.* I'll try to come to your place. *Em̧ōj ņe am̧ kajjioñeoñ.* Stop imitating me. *Ña ij rūkajjioñe.* I am a member of the Endeavor Society. *Ej kajjioñeoñe jemān.* He's emulating his father. *Kwōn jab kajjioñeoñ.* Don't be a conformist.

kajjirere (**kajjireyrey**). 1(-*i*), 2, 3, 4, 7, 8. Laugh at; ridicule; mock; deride; insult; sneer.

kajjitōk (**kajjitęk**). 1(-*i*), 2(inf, tr *kajitūkin(i)*), 4, 5(*kkajjitōktōk*), 7. Ask; question; inquire; petition; plea; problem; request. *Kwōn m̧ōk kajitūkini ear pād ia?* Inquire of him where he was.

kajjo (**kajjęw**). 1(-*i*), 2(inf, tr -*uk*), 5(*kajjojo*), 7. Each; divide among each; distributive form of *juon* (**jiwen**). *Aolep kajjo mā.* Each person take a breadfruit. *Kwōn kajjoukļo̧k mā kaņe ñan aolep.* Divide up those breadfruit among everyone. *Aolep ej kajjojo ļo̧k wōt mā.* Everybody has a breadfruit.

kajjo (**kajjew**). 2(inf, tr -*uk(-i)*), 4, 6(-*i*), 7. Chip or scrape rust off; make rusty. *Ij kajjouk bu e aō.* I'm cleaning the rust off of my rifle. *Ta ņe ekajjouk jōōt ņe am̧?* What smeared your shirt with rust?

kajjojo (**kajjęwjęw**). From *kajjo* (**kajjęw**). 2, 6(-*i*). Take turns; separately; singly. *Kōjro kajjojo tūraip.* Let's take turns driving.

kajjookok (**kajjewekwek**). Scandal; shameful behavior. *Ear kōm̧m̧ane juon kajjookok ļapļap.* He made a big scandal.

kajjōjō (**kajjęhjęh**). From *jjō* (**jjęh**). 1(-*i*), 2, 4, 7, 8, 9. Nauseating; very ugly; very hateful; despicable; mean; revolting. *Kokajjōjō.* You're revolting.

kajju (**kajjiw**). 2(inf, tr -*uk*), 6(-*i*), 7. Go directly toward. *Kajjuuk wa ņe ñan Kuwajleen.* Steer the boat directly to Kwajalein. *Inaaj kajju ļo̧k ñan ippān bo̧o̧j eņ.* I'll go direct to the boss.

kajjuur (**kajjiwir**). 2(inf, tr *kajuuri*), 4, 6(-*i*), 7, 10(*jurōk*). Erect; put up; stand; establish; institute; locate; build. *Rej kajjuur joor.* They are putting up posts. *Ejurōk joor ko.* The pillars have been put up.

kajkaj (**kajkaj**). Also *kaj* (**kaj**). 1(-*i*),
2(inf, tr *kajek*), 7.   Be jarred; be
shaken; bumpy. *Ewōtlok jān tūrak eo
im kajkaj ṇai laḷ.* He fell off the truck
and was shaken by hitting the ground.
Ekaj wa in. This boat is bumpy. *Ekaj
iaḷ eṇ ilo* Kaena Point. The road
around Kaena Point is bumpy.

kajḷor (**kajḷer°**). 1(-*i*), 2(inf, tr -*e*), 3, 4,
7.   Get the last drops of water from a
water container. *Kwōn kajḷore bato
ṇe.* Get all the water out of that
bottle.

kajnōt (**kajnet**). 1(-*i*), 2, 4, 7, 8, 9.
Curious; inquisitive; talkative.

kajṇoṇ (**kajṇ°eṇ°**). 1(-*i*), 2, 3, 4, 7, 8, 9.
Talk through the nose.

kajokkor (**kajęqqer**). 1(-*i*), 2(inf, tr -*e*), 3,
7.   Place a bottle (*kor*) at the end of
coconut shoot to collect sap initially.
Ni jekaro eo aō eṇ ekajokkor. My
coconut sapling has a bottle on it now.

kajoor (**kajęwęr**). 1(-*i*), 2, 3, 4, 7, 8, 9,
11(*kajooror*).   Strong; force; strength;
power; might.

kajoor (**kajęwęr**).   Common people;
commoner.

kaju (**kajiw**). Dial. E only; see *kiju*
(**kijiw**). 1(-*i*).   Mast.

kajukur (**kajiqir**). 2(inf, tr -*i*), 6(-*i*).
Neglect; ignore. *Jab kajukur ajri raṇe
bwe ḷōṃaro ilju raṇe.* Don't ignore the
children for they are the men of
tomorrow.

kajumej (**kajiwmęj**). 1(-*i*), 2, 4, 7.   Keep
watch all the time, as on board a ship
or at a bedside, without taking a rest;
to bear some hardship; withstand
hardships.

kajuuri (**kajiwiriy**).   Transitive form of
kajjuur (**kajjiwir**).

kajuurōk (**kajiwiręk**).   Causative
transitive form of *joor* (**jęwęr**).

kaka (**kahkah**). 7.   To drink water, child
speech.

kake (**kahkey**). Dial. W only; see *eake*
(**yakey**).   With it; about it; because of.
Eake men e. Because of this thing
here.

kakememej (**kakęymęymęj**). 2(inf, tr -*e*,
kakememije), 4, 6(-*i*).   Remind. *Kab
kakememeje eō.* Be sure to remind me.

kaki (**kahkiy**). From Engl.   Khaki.

kakiaaj (**kakiyahaj**). 1, 2, 4, 6(-*i*), 7.   Jog;
run lightly. *Emṃan kakiaaj in

jibboñ ñan kammourur. Jogging in the
morning is excellent exercise.

kakidiej (**kakidiyęj**). 1(-*i*), 4, 7.   Fishing
method, use fishpole at the reef edge
and fish for *kidiej.*

kakidwaan (**kakidwahan**). From *edwaan*
(**yedwahan**).   Pick wild pandanus.

kakijdikdik (**kakijdikdik**). Also
kakkijdikdik (**kakkijdikdik**). Idiom.
From *kijdik* (**kijdik**).   Pretty; alluring.
Eḷap an ledik eṇ kakijdikdik. She's
very alluring.

kakijen (**kakijen**). 1(-*i*), 2, 4, 7.   Gather
food. *Ḷōṃaro rōmoot in kakijen tok.*
The men went to gather food.

kakil (**kakil**).   Transitive form of *kakilkil*
(**kakilkil**).

kakile (**kakiley**).   Transitive form of
kakōl (**kakel**).

kakilen (**kakilen**).   Transitive form of
kakōlkōl (**kakęlkęl**).

kakilkil (**kakilkil**). Also *ākilkil*
(**yakilkil**). 1(-*i*), 2(inf, tr *kakil(i)*), 4, 7.
To peel; to skin; sunburned. *Rej
kakilkil piteto.* They are peeling just a
few potatoes. *Jab kōjeje bwe kwōnaaj
kakilkil.* Stay out of the sun or you'll
get sunburned.

kakkiāmem (**kakkiyamyęm**). 1, 2(inf, tr
-*e*), 4, 6(-*i*), 7.   To bring up outrigger
and hold it at 45 degrees while
sailing. *Likao jiddik in Ṃajeḷ eḷap aer
iokwe kakkiāmem. Kakkiāmem* is a
favorite pastime among Marshallese
youngsters.

kakkije (**kakkijęy**). 1(-*i*), 2(inf, tr -*ik*), 4,
7.   To rest; to expel; to resign;
vacation; holiday; recess; take a break.
Emōj kakkijeik jān an Kūrjin. He's
been expelled from the Church.
Ikōṇaan kakkije jān aō rijeje. I wish to
resign as scribe.

kakkil (**kakkil**).   Variant form of
ākilkil (**yakilkil**).

kakkilaajaj (**kakkilahajhaj**). From *kilaaj*
(**kilahaj**). 1(-*i*), 2, 4, 7.   Reflect a bright
light; signal with a mirror. *Ta eṇ ej
kakkilaajaj?* What is that reflecting
the sun?

kakkōnkōn (**kakkęnkęn**).   Distributive
form of *kkōn.*

kakkōt (**kakket**). Dial. E, W: *kate*
(**katey**). Also *kaññōt* (**kagget**). 1(-*i*),
2(inf, tr *kate*), 4, 5(*kattūkat*), 6(-*i*).
Struggle; try hard; persevere;
endeavor; persist; strive; stand ready;

exert oneself; apply oneself; effort. *Ej kakkōt bwe en m̧m̧an an kūreit.* He's trying hard for good grades. *Kwōn kakkōt iuuntok.* Push it hard. *Kakkōt ilo jikuuļ.* Work hard in school. *Eļap an kate katak.* He's trying hard to learn. *Kwōn kate eok m̧ōñā.* Eat all you can. *Ļeo ej kattūkat im pojak in ire.* He's standing poised to fight.

kakkōt (**kakket**). 6(-*i*). Very; really (only in negative usage); quite. *Ej jab kakkōt pen.* It's not very hard. It's quite easy. *Eban kakkōt ibwij.* The tide will not be very high.

kakkūm̧kūm̧ (**kakkim̧kim̧**). A plant, grass, *Thuarea involuta.*

kakkūm̧kūm̧ (**kakkim̧kim̧**). Suspenseful; risky.

kako (**kahkęw**). 6(-*i*). Rooster; cock.

kako (**kahkęw**). Vulgar slang. 2, 6(-*i*), 8, 9. Said of a male who ejaculates prematurely in sexual intercourse.

kakōl (**kakel**). Also *kakōl* (**kakęl**). 1(-*i*), 2(inf, tr reflex *kakile*), 4, 7, 8, 9. Show-off; stuck-up; be spoiled, of a pampered child; nagging; style-setter; causative form of *kōl*. *Ej kakōl kōn nuknuk kaņ an.* She's showing off her dresses. *Kwōmake kakōl.* You're stuck up. *Aolep ajri raņ nājin lieņ rōkakileik er.* All her children are spoiled.

kakōlkōl (**kakęlkęl**). 1(-*i*), 2(inf, tr *kakilen*), 4, 7. Examine, physically. *Em̧ōj an rijikuuļ ro kakōlkōl.* The students have been given their physicals. *Wōn eo ear kakilen rijikuuļ ro?* Who gave the students their physicals?

kakōlkōl (**kakęlkęl**). 2(inf, tr *kakilen*), 7. Try to recognize; scanning; scrutinizing; examine. *Kwōn kakilen m̧ōk wōn eņ ej eoñōd ilo kōrkōr eņ.* Try to recognize who that is fishing in that canoe. *Taktō eo ear kakilen eō inne.* The doctor examined me yesterday.

kakōļ (**kahkeļ**). 1(-*i*), 2, 6(-*i*). Hermaphrodite; hybrid; eunuch.

kakōļļe (**kakeļļey**). Also *kakkaļļe* (**kakkaļļey**), *kōkaļļe* (**kekaļļey**). 1(*kakōļļa*-), 2(inf, tr -*ik*), 4, 6(-*i*), 7. Sign; symbol; punctuation; check mark; uniform insignia; miracle; signal; signify; brand; emblem; hint; indication; landmark; monument; omen; symptom.

kakōm̧kōm̧ (**kakem̧kem̧**). Inspiring; full of ideas. *Ekakōm̧kōm̧ an kōnono.* His speech is inspiring.

kakūtōtō (**kakitęhtęh**). 1(-*i*), 2(inf, tr -*ik*), 4, 8, 9. Teasing; taunt; aggravate; mischievous; annoy; nit-pick.

kakwōj (**kahqej**). Legendary cruel sea men with long fingernails.

kalbuuj (**kalbiwij**). From Engl. *calaboose*. 1(-*i*), 2(inf, tr -*i*), 4, 5(*kkalbuujuj*), 7. Jail; to be thrown in jail; to be in jail; confine; penetentiary; prison; stockade. *Ekkalbuujuj ļeeņ.* He's always getting put in jail.

kalbwin (**kalbin**). Transitive form of *kallib* (**kallib**).

kalemeej (**kaļęymeyej**). Also *kālemeej* (**kaylęymeyej**). 6(-*i*). A fish, blue-spotted grouper, *Cepahalopholis argus.*

kalenen (**kahlęynęn**). A plant, *Morinda citrifolia* L. (Rubiaceae); female tree.

kalia (**kaliyah**). 2(inf, tr -*ik*), 4, 6(-*i*). Banish; remove from land; ostracize; disinherit; repudiate. *Kōn aer kar jipǫkwe, raar kaliaik er.* As a result of their defeat in battle and loss of royal status, they lost all their land. *Jemān ear kaliaik ļadik eo nejin.* The father disinherited his son from his land.

kalibbañ (**kahlibbag**). 3, 6(-*i*). White sand crab.

kalibok (**kahliybęq**). Dial. E only; see *kǫnōt* (**kawnet**). 3, 6(-*i*). A shell, small bivalve clam.

kalijekļǫk (**kalijękļaq**). 1, 2, 4, 6(-*i*). Bias; partial; prejudice. *Kwōn jab kalijekļǫk ilo am̧ jerbal ippam̧.* Don't be partial in your dealings with us. *Ejjeļǫk kalijekļǫk ippān ñan jidik.* He has no inclination to bias whatsoever.

kaliklik (**kaliklik**). Bear offspring.

kalikūrōk (**kalikirępk**). A fish, spot snapper, *Lutjanus fulviflamma.*

kalimjek (**kalimjęk**). Transitive form of *kallimjek* (**kallimjęk**).

kallep (**kallep**). 3, 5(*kkalleplep*), 6(-*i*), 7, 8, 9. An insect, big black ant. *Ekkalleplepe ijeņe.* That place there is swarming with ants.

kallib (**kallib**). 1(-*i*), 2(inf, tr *kalbwin(i)*), 4, 7. Bury; plant; funeral. *Em̧ōj kalbwin rimej eo.* They have buried the dead person. *Enañin m̧ōj ke kallib?* Isn't the planting finished yet? Isn't the burial over yet?

kallimjek (**kallimjęk**). Also *kallimjek* (**kallimjek**). 1(*-i*), 2(inf, tr *kalimjek(e)*), 4, 5(*kallimjekjek*), 7, 8, 9, 11(*kallimjek*). To gaze at; look at steadfastly; stare at; regard. *Eḷap an kallimjekjek lieṇ.* She's always staring at people.

kallim̧ur (**kallim̧ir°**). 1(*-i*), 2(inf, tr *-i*), 4, 7. Promise; testament; covenant; guarantee; oath; obligated; pledge; vow. *Em̧ōj aō kallim̧ur ke inaaj bar itok.* I promised that I would come again.

kallor (**kaller°**). Shadow, shade.

kalmadok (**kalmadeq**). Variant form of *kaḷmarok.*

kalo (**kalew**). 3, 8, 9. Ripe, of breadfruit; mature; mellow.

kaloojoj (**kahlęwęjwęj**). Variant form of *kaalwōjwōj* (**kahalwęjwęj**).

kalōk (**kalek**). Transitive form of *kkal* (**kkal**).

kalōlō (**kalehleh**). 1(*-i*), 2(inf, tr *kalōōr*), 3, 4, 7. Point head downwards; turn upside down. *Kwōn kalōōr ajri ṇe bwe emaḷoñ.* Turn that baby upside down because it has swallowed some water.

kalōōr (**kaleher**). Transitive form of *kalōlō* (**kalehleh**).

kalwor (**kalwęr**). Dial. E, W: *kawor* (**kawęr**). Also *kaloor, kalor.* 1(*-i*), 2, 4, 7. To hunt lobsters. *Rōmoot in kalwor.* They went to look for lobsters.

kaḷ (**kaḷ**). 6(*-i*). Diaper; loin cloth.

kaḷan (**kaḷan**). Also *kōḷan* (**keḷan**). From Engl. *gallon*. 6(*-i*). Gallon; column.

kaḷkaḷ (**kaḷkaḷ**). From *kaḷ* (**kaḷ**). 1(*-i*), 2, 3(inf, tr *kōkaḷkaḷ(e)*), 6(*-i*). Wear a diaper; wear a loin cloth. *RiRuk rōkein kaḷkaḷ etto.* Trukese used to wear loin cloths.

kaḷḷaḷḷaḷ (**kaḷḷaḷḷaḷ**). Also *kǫḷḷoḷḷoḷ* (**kaḷ°ḷ°ęḷ°ḷ°ęḷ°**). 1(*-i*), 2, 4, 7, 8. To knock. *Kōḷḷaḷḷaḷ im inaaj kōpeḷḷok.* Knock and I will open.

kaḷmarok (**kaḷmareq**). Also *kōlmarok* (**kelmareq**), *kōḷmarok* (**keḷmareq**), *kalmadok* (**kalmadeq**). 2, 4, 6(*-i*), 8, 9. Covetousness. *Ekaḷmarok.* He's covetous.

kaḷo (**kahḷew**). Dial. W, E: *tǫḷ* (**taḷ°**). Also *kaḷǫ* (**kahḷaw**). A bird, brown booby, *Sula leucogaster.*

kaḷǫ (**kaḷaw**). Also *kōḷǫ* (**keḷaw**). 6(*-i*). A food, very ripe breadfruit mixed with coconut milk; wrapped in breadfruit leaves, and baked.

kaḷǫ (**kahḷaw**). Variant form of *kaḷo* (**kahḷew**).

Kaḷǫ (**kahḷaw**). Clan name.

kaḷǫk (**kaḷaq**). Also *kōḷǫk* (**keḷaq**). 2(inf, tr *-e*), 4, 6(*-i*). Commemorate; wait under shelter for rain to stop. *Raar kaḷǫke raan in keemem eo.* They commemorated the birth. *Kōjro kaḷǫk wōt kein.* Let's wait for the rain to stop.

kameḷ (**kameḷ**). From Engl. 5(*kkameḷmeḷ*), 6(*-i*). Camel. *Ejjeḷǫk kameḷ M̧ajeḷ.* There aren't any camels in the Marshalls.

kamiti (**kamiytiy**). From Engl. Committee.

kam̧bōj (**kam̧bej**). From Engl. 6(*-i*). Compass.

kam̧m̧oolol (**kam̧m̧ewelwel**). 1(*-i*), 2(inf, tr *-e*), 4, 7. To thank; be grateful.

kam̧o (**kam̧ew**). 1(*-i*), 2(inf, tr *-uk*), 4, 5(*kkam̧om̧o*), 7, 8, 9, 11(*kkam̧om̧o*). Jealous; envious. *Ekkam̧om̧o lieṇ.* She gets jealous easily.

kam̧ool (**kam̧ewel**). 2(inf, tr *-e*), 4, 6(*-i*), 7. Fulfill; testify; confirm; proof; evidence. *Kūraij ear kam̧ool naan eo an ke ear jerkakpeje ilo raan eo kein kajilu.* Christ fulfilled his word when he rose on the third day.

kam̧ōj (**kam̧ęj**). 2(inf, tr *-e*). Resign; terminate. *Ear kam̧ōj jān jerbal eo an.* He resigned from his job.

kam̧ōḷo (**kam̧ęḷęw**). 1(*-i*), 2(inf, tr *-uk*), 4, 5(*kkam̧ōḷoḷo*), 6(*-i*), 7. Party, Marshallese style. *Kom̧win kōppojak bwe ejako iien kam̧ōḷo.* Get ready because it's almost time for the party. *Ekkam̧ōḷoḷo riM̧ajeḷ.* Marshallese are always having parties.

kam̧ōm̧ō (**kam̧ehm̧eh**). Variant form of *kōbwābwe* (**kebaybęy**).

kam̧ōṇōṇō (**kam̧eṇehṇeh**). 1(*-i*), 2(inf, tr *-ik*), 8, 9. Entertain; amuse; lively; jolly; merry; jovial; pleasant; be a good sport; happy. *Ḷoor eō im inaaj kam̧ōṇōṇōik eok.* Follow me and I'll entertain you.

kan (**kan**). Transitive form of *m̧ōñā* (**m̧egay**).

kanaan (**kahnahan**). 4. Prophesy.

kanbōj (**kanbej**). From Engl. *canvas.* 6(*-i*). Canvas. *Eor aō juuj kanbōj.* I have canvas shoes.

kanbōk (**kanbek**). 3, 4+3, 5(*-e*), 6(*-i*), 3+7, 5+8, 9. A fish, bass, *Variola louti.*

kane (**kanẹy**). 1(*-i*), 3, 5(*kkanene*), 6(*-i*). Fuel; firewood. *Kwaar kōkane ke?* Did you gather firewood? *Kwōn jek kane ṇe.* Chop that firewood there.

kane (**kaney**). 1, 2, 8, 9. A tasty combination of foods. *Ṃool ke ekane bwiro ippān wōn.* I believe that preserved breadfruit goes with turtle meat deliciously.

kanejnej (**kanẹjnẹj**). Also *kōnājnej* (**kenajnẹj**), *kanijnij* (**kanijnij**). 1, 2(inf, tr *-e, kanejnije*), 4, 5(*kkanejnej*), 6(*-i*). Curse; swear; cuss. *Ellu bwe raar kanijniji.* He's angry because they cursed him.

kanijnij (**kanijnij**). Variant form of *kanejnej* (**kanẹjnẹj**).

kaniọkwe (**kaniyaqey**). Sufficient even if it's little, of food; food given with love.

kankan (**kankan**). 1(*-i*), 2(inf, tr *kanōk(e)*), 3(intr *kōkankan*, tr *kōkankane*), 5(*kkanōknōke*), 7. Stretch; pull; stand at attention; tug; taut; tight; full sail, nautical. *Kankan to.* Tug o' war. *Kwōn kōkankane ḷọk to ṇe.* Stretch that rope so it's really tight. *Ekankan nuknuk ṇe aṃ.* Your dress is too tight. *Wa eo uweo ej kankan ḷọk.* There goes the canoe with a full sail.

kankan kōj (**kankan kẹj**). Slang. From *kankan* (**kankan**) "stretched", *kōj* (**kẹj**) "share". 2, 3(inf, tr *-e*), 8, 9. Stretched luck; lucky. *Ekankan kōj eṇ an ippān lieṇ.* He's getting to first base with her.

kankan to (**kankan tew**). 1(*-i*), 2, 3, 4, 7. Tug of war.

kanmat (**kanmat**). 1, 2(inf, tr *-e*), 3, 4, 6(*-i*), 7. Cooked food.

kanne (**kanney**). 1(*-i*), 2, 3, 4, 7. To fill. *Eṃōj aō kanne wa eo kōn ṃweiuk.* I have loaded the ship with trade goods (or provisions).

kanniōk (**kanniyẹk**). 1(*-i*), 2(inf, tr *-e*), 5(*kkanniōkeōk*), 6(*-i*), 7. Meat; flesh. *Eḷap an kkanniōkeōk piik eṇ raar ṃane.* The pig they killed had much lean meat.

kanniōkin kau (**kanniyẹkin kahwiw**). Beef. *Jej jab ṃōñā kanniōkin kau iaelōñ ko ilikin iṂajeḷ kōn an jjeḷọk.* We don't eat beef on the outer islands of the Marshalls because there isn't any.

kanniōkin piik (**kanniyẹkin piyik**). Pork.

kanooj (**kahnẹwẹj**). 2. Very.

kanōk (**kanek**). Transitive form of *kankan* (**kankan**).

kanōōn (**kahnẹhẹn**). Variant form of *kaōnōn* (**kahẹnhẹn**).

kanpil (**kanpil**). 4. Wise man; sage.

kanu (**kaniw**). Dial. E only; see *kadu* (**kadiw**). 1(*-i*), 2, 3, 4, 5(*kkanunu*), 7, 8, 9, 11(*kkanunu*). Short; brief. *Juon eṇ ṃṃaan kkanunu ear itok ilo baḷuun eo.* A dwarfed man came on the plane.

kanwōd (**kanwed**). 1(*-i*), 2(inf, tr *-e*), 3, 4, 5(*kkanwōdwōd*), 7, 8. Mend a net. *Eṃōj ke aṃ kanwōde ok eo?* Have you mended the net? *Ḷeo ekkanwōdwōd eṇ.* He's always mending nets.

kaṇ (**kaṇ**). Those (things close to neither of us); demonstrative, third person plural nonhuman.

kaṇe (**kaṇey**). Those (things close to you); demonstrative, second person plural nonhuman. *Komaroñ ke jibwi tok men kaṇe (i)turuṃ?* Can you hand me those things near you?

kañ (**kag**). Transitive form of *ṃōñā* (**ṃegay**).

kañal (**kahgal**). A plant, tree, *Pisonia grandis* R. Br. (Nyctaginaceae). A large hard wood tree. N.

kañkañ (**kagkag**). 2(inf, tr *-e*), 4, 6(*-i*), 7. To chip off rust; to sponge off of someone; to bum. *Jeḷa ro rej kañkañe tiṃa eo.* The sailors are chipping off rust from the ship. *Lale aṃ aetōl ippān bwe enāj kañkañe eok.* Beware of associating with him or he'll bum everything off of you.

kañkōñ (**kagkẹg**). A fish, squirrel fish, *Holocentrus microstoma.*

kaññōt (**kagget**). Variant form of *kakkōt* (**kakket**).

kañōr (**kagẹr**). Variant form of *kañūr* (**kagir**).

kañurñur (**kahg°irg°ir**). 1(*-i*), 2(inf, tr *kañur(i)*), 7. Grind with the teeth, noisily; crunch; munch.

kañūr (**kagir**). Also *kañōr* (**kagẹr**). 2(inf *kañūrñūr*, tr *-e*), 6(*-i*). Belt; strap. *Kwōn kañūre bọọk ṇe bwe en jab rup.*

Wrap that box with a belt so it doesn't burst.

kañūrñūr (**kagirgir**). Also *kañōrñōr* (**kagẹrgẹr**). From *kañūr* (**kagir**). 1(*-i*), 2(inf, tr *-e*), 3(inf, tr *kakañōrñōr(e)*), 6(*-i*), 7. Wear a belt; put a belt on. *Ej ke kakañōrñōre ḷadik eṇ?* Is he letting the boy wear a belt? Is he putting a belt on the boy?

kaōnōn (**kahẹnhẹn**). Also *kanōōn* (**kahnẹhẹn**). 3, 6(*-i*). A plant, vine, *Cassytha filiformis* L. (Lauraceae); a leafless green or brown twining parasite; common on most atolls. N.

kaōrōr (**kaherher**). 2(inf, tr *-e*), 3, 4, 6(*-i*), 7. A plant, herb, *Phsalis angulata*; grate one's teeth.

kap (**kap**). 6(*-i*). Roll of cloth; bolt of cloth.

kapāl (**kapal**). 1(*-i*), 2(inf, tr *-e*), 4. Make magic.

kapdik (**kapdik**). 1(*-i*), 2, 3, 6(*-i*), 7, 8, 9, 11(*kapdik*). Having a shallow draft, of ships (see *kaplep*). *Emaroñ wōnāneḷọk bwe ekapdik.* It can go close to shore because it has a shallow draft.

kapeel (**kapeyel**). 1(*-i*), 2, 4, 7, 8, 9, 11(*kapeelel*). Skillful; clever; craft; knack; wise; astute. *M̧m̧aan kapeelel men eṇ.* He's definitely an astute fellow.

kapej (**kapẹj**). Also *kāpej* (**kaypẹj**). From Engl. Cabbage. *Ennọ kapej.* I like cabbage.

kapejlọk (**kapẹjlaq**). Also *kōpejlọk* (**kepẹjlaq**). From *pejlọk* (**pẹjlaq**) "go through". 2(inf, tr *-e*), 6(*-i*), 7. Dilute paint; add liquid to substance such as starch; jello; penetrate; pierce. *Kapejlọk wūno ṇe kōn jerpāntain.* Dilute the paint with turpentine.

kapel (**kahpel**). From Germ. *Gabeḷ*. 2(inf, tr *-e*), 6(*-i*), 7. Fork. *Kwōn kapele tok juon wūdin kanniōk.* Fork out a piece of meat for me.

kapen (**kapen**). 2(inf, tr *-e*), 7. Captain; officer of high rank.

kapi (**kapiy**). Archaic. Bottom of; west side of; old form of *kapin*.

kapi- (**kapi-**). 1, 6(*kapin, kapi*). Bottom of. *Erreo ke kapin ainbat ṇe?* Is the bottom of that kettle clean? *Jab jijet laḷ bwe enaaj ttoon kapim̧.* Don't sit on the ground or the seat of your pants will get dirty.

Kapi-Ḷak (**kapiy-ḷak**). See *Ḷak*: "west of *Ḷak*". A constellation: stars in Perseus; alpha, beta, delta.

kapije (**kapiyjẹy**). Dial. E, W: *kapijje* (**kapijjẹy**). 1(*-i*), 2(inf, tr *-ik*), 3, 7. Eat before working; grub. *Eor ke kapije jekaṇe?* Is there any grub around?

kapijje (**kapijjẹy**). Dialectal variant of *kapije* (**kapiyjẹy**).

kapijjule (**kapijjiwlẹy**). Dial. E, W: *kapinbōklik* (**kapinbẹklik**). 2(inf, tr *-ik(-i)*), 4, 6(*-i*), 8, 9. Fishing term, said of a coconut leaf chain used as scarer that is strung out unevenly. *Ekapijjule.* The scarer is not even. *Jab kapijjuleik m̧wio ṇe bwe enaaj jejeḷọk kobban.* Better not string that scarer unevenly or it won't catch any fish.

kapijpij (**kapijpij**). 1(*-i*), 2, 3, 7. Kneel or bend over.

kapijukune- (**kapiyjiqine-**). 1. Home of; property of; land inherited by.

kapilōk (**kapiylẹk**). 2(inf, tr *-e*), 4, 5(*kkapilōklōk*), 6(*-i*). Advise; admonish. *Kwōn kapilōke ḷadik eṇ nājim̧ bwe eḷap an kadek.* Give your boy some advice--he drinks too much.

kapilōñ (**kapiylẹg**). Also *kipilōñ* (**kipiylẹg**). 4. Western sky; Caroline Islands; Mariana Islands. *Ebūrōrō kapilōñ.* The western sky is red.

kapilōñ iōñ (**kapiylẹg yi'yẹg**). Northwestern sky.

kapilōñ rōk (**kapiylẹg rẹk**). Southwestern sky.

kapiḷak (**kapiyḷak**). Tropical storm similar to typhoon in strength.

kapin lañ (**kapin lag**). Horizon. *Ekkōdọdo kapinlañ.* There are clouds on the horizon.

Kapin-marok (**kapin-mareq**). Hades; depths of darkness.

kapinbōklik (**kapinbẹklik**). Dialectal variant of *kapijjule* (**kapijjiwlẹy**).

kapipā (**kapiypay**). 2(inf, tr *-ik*), 4, 6(*-i*). Pound food; mash; pulverize; beat; spank. *Kapipāik mā kaṇe.* Pound the breadfruit.

kapit (**kapit**). Transitive form of *kkapit* (**kkapit**).

kapitō- (**kapite-**). Also *kapte-* (**kapte-**). 1. Oil belonging to; possessive classifier, perfume or lotion, or containers thereof.

kapitōn būriij (**kapiten biriyij**). Ordination.

kapjer (**kapjẹr**). Also *kilaaj* (**kilahaj**), *kapjor* (**kapjẹr°**). 6(*-i*). Mirror.

kapjulaļ (**kapjiwlaḷ**). 1(*-i*), 2, 3, 6(*-i*), 7, 8, 9, 11(*kapjulaļ*). Unable to go in shallow water, of vessels; having a deep draft. *Ekapjulaļ wa eņ im emaroñ eoņ ilo wōd eņ.* That boat can't go in shallow water, and it may go on the reef. *Jab kepaak āne bwe ekapjulaļ wa in.* Don't go too close to shore for the boat has a deep draft.

Kapjulaļ (**kapjiwlaḷ**). 3, 6(*-i*). A plant, pandanus cultigen.

kaplep (**kaplep**). 1(*-i*), 2, 7, 8, 9, 11(*kaplep*). Low keel; canoe that cannot go in shallow water.

kaplo (**kaplew**). 1(*-i*), 2(inf, tr *-uk*), 4, 5(*kkaplolo*), 7. To spit; saliva; spittle; slobber; expectorate. *Ekkaplolo niññiñ eņ.* That baby is always slobbering.

kapo (**kapew**). 1, 2(inf, tr *kapouk, -ik*), 4, 5(*kkapopo*), 6(*-i*). Tempt; temptation. *Jab kadeļoñ kōm ilo kapo.* Lead us not into temptation. *Ear kapouk eō bwe in kōbaatat.* He tempted me to smoke. *Tepiļ ekkapopo.* The devil is always trying to tempt someone.

kapopo (**kapewpew**). 1(*-i*), 2, 4, 7, 8, 9, 11(*kapopo*). Contagious. *Ekapopo mej in.* This disease is contagious. *Mej kapopo men ņe ippaṃ.* Your sickness is quite contagious.

kappe (**kappẹy**). 1(*-i*), 7. Seacoast; shore; land edge of beach. *Ej jijet ioon kappe.* He is sitting on the bank.

kappej (**kappẹj**). 1(*-i*), 2, 4, 7. Fishing method, use fishpole at night. *Ļōṃaro raņ rej kappej lik.* The men are fishing with poles at the ocean side.

kappetpet (**kappetpet**). 2, 4, 6(*-i*), 7. A game, hop-scotch. *Ledik ro raar kappetpettok ilowaan iaļ eo tok.* The girls were playing hop-scotch along the path.

kappiñ (**kappig**). 2, 4, 6(*-i*), 7. A game, high jump or broad jump. *Rej kappiñ.* They're doing the high jump. *Rūkappiñ men raņ.* Those are high jumpers.

kappok (**kappẹq**). 1(*-i*), 2(inf, tr *kappukot*), 4, 6(*-i*), 7. Look for; search for; hunt for. *Kwōn kappukottok juon pinjeļ.* Try to find me a pencil. *Kwaar kappok ke ṃōn wia eņ?* Did you look for it (them) at that store?

kappok jide (**kappẹq jidẹy**). Slang. Apple-polishing; curry favor with someone; snobbish. *Ej kappok an jide.* He's apple-polishing. *Koṃwin jab kappok ami jide im āinwōt ñe koṃ ajri.* Stop being like children polishing apples.

kappokpok (**kappẹqpẹq**). Also *ṃōjjero* (**ṃẹjjẹyrẹw**). A food, very ripe breadfruit baked in coconut oil.

kappukot (**kappiqet**). Transitive form of *kappok* (**kappẹq**).

kaptō- (**kapte-**). Variant form of *kapitō-* (**kapite-**).

kapwor (**kapwẹr**). 3, 6(*-i*). A shell, giant clam.

kar (**kar**). Also *kōrat.* Scratch; scrape. *Ear kar kūbwe eo jān laļ.* He scraped up the droppings.

kar (**kar**). Past tense; conditional, contrary to fact; had; ought to have.

karbōb (**karbeb**). 1(*-i*), 2, 3, 4, 5(*kkarbōbbōb*), 7, 8, 9. Neat; well-formed; perfect; elegant; decent; tidy. *Ekkarbōbbōb ajri raņ nājin.* She always bears healthy children. *Kōrā eo ekkarbōbbōb eņ.* She's always smartly dressed.

kare (**karẹy**). From Japn. *karee* (from Engl. *curry*). 1(*-i*), 2(inf, tr *-ik(i)*), 4, 5(*kkarkare*), 6(*-i*), 7, 8, 9. Curry. *Kareik(i) jidik.* Throw a dash of curry in it.

karere (**kareyrey**). 2(inf, tr *-ik*), 4, 6(*-i*), 7. Flatten pandanus leaves. *An kōrā jerbal karere.* It's a woman's job to flatten pandanus leaves. *Karereiktok juon tūrtūr in aj.* Flatten a bundle of pandanus leaves for me.

kariab (**kariyab**). 2(inf, tr *-e*), 4. Refute; disprove.

kariwutut (**kariywitwit**). 6(*-i*). A game, racing toy outrigger canoes.

karjin (**karjin**). From Engl. 1(*-i*), 2(inf, tr *-i*), 3, 5(*kkarjinjin*), 6(*-i*), 7. Kerosene. *Ekkarjinjin nuknuk e aō.* There is (the smell of) kerosene all over my clothes. *Kwōn karjini ṃokta jān aṃ tile.* Throw some kerosene on it before you light it.

karkar (**karkar**). 1(*-i*), 2(inf, tr *kōrat(e), kōrat(i)*), 4, 5(*karkarōte*), 7. Cut out copra meat from shell. *Ļōṃaro raņ rej* *kōrate waini ko.* Those men are cutting the meat out of those copra nuts.

karko (**karkew**). 2, 3(inf *kōkkarkoko,* tr *kōkarkouk*), 4, 5(*kkarkoko*), 6(*-i*). Skin disease; white acne-like fungus under skin. *Ekkarkoko ānbwinnin.* He has lots of fungi under his skin. *Raar kōkkarkokouk ānbwinnin kōn nitōḷ.* They picked fungi off his skin with needles.

karo (**karew**). From Japn. *karoo* "chamberlain". Head of a household; head man.

Karoḷāin (**karewḷayin**). Caroline; place name; Caroline Islands.

karōk (**karek**). 5(*kkarōkrōk*), 6(*-i*). Turtle nest. *Ekkarōkrōk arin Jemo̧.* Jemo's shores are always full of turtle nests.

karōk (**karek**). Transitive form of *kkar* (**kkar**).

karpen (**karpȩn**). 1(*-i*), 2(inf, tr *karpine*), 3, 4, 5(*kkarpenpen*), 7, 8, 9. Mend; patch. *Ekkarpenpen jōōt eo an.* His shirt has patches all over it.

karpine (**karpiney**). Transitive form of *karpen* (**karpȩn**).

karreelel (**karrȩyȩlyȩl**). Advertise; campaigning; a commercial; propaganda. *Etke kwōj jab karreelel kake m̧weiuk kaņ ilo m̧ōn wia eņ am̧.* Why don't you advertise the merchandise in your store?

karro̧n̄ro̧n̄ (**karrag°rag°**). Also *kōrran̄ran̄* (**kerrag°rag°**). 2(inf, tr *-e*), 4, 6(*-i*). Perforate.

kartōp (**kartep**). 3(inf, tr *-e*), 5(*kkartōptōp*), 6(*-i*), 7. A plant, *Asplenium nidus* L. (Pteridophyta). The birds' nest fern. This epiphyte has long, simple leaves up to six feet in length. The sori are borne in slanted rows on the back of the fern.

karuk (**kariq**). 3, 5(*kkarukruk*), 6(*-i*). White sand crab. *Eḷap an kkarukruk iarin ānin.* There are lots of sand crabs on the lagoon beach of this islet.

karuwanene (**kariwanȩynȩy**). Also *karwainene* (**karwahyinȩynȩy**). 2(inf, tr *-ik*), 4, 6(*-i*). Welcome; make someone feel welcome; hospitality. *Jen ilān karuwaneneik ruwamāejet raņ.* Let's go welcome the strangers.

karūtto (**karittew**). Vulgar. From *rūtto* (**rittew**) "mature". 2(inf, tr *-uk*), 4, 6(*-i*). Make mature; deflower; initiate sexually; cause to come of age.

karwaan (**karwahan**). Also *kōrwaan* (**kerwahan**). 2(inf, tr *-e*), 4, 7. Be with; accompany; chaperon; escort. *Itok kōjro karwaan bwe iabwinmake.* Come let's go together because I'm afraid to go alone.

karwainene (**karwahyinȩynȩy**). Variant form of *karuwanene* (**kariwanȩynȩy**).

karwūn (**karwin**). 1(*-i*), 2(inf, tr *-i*), 4, 7. Scale fish. *Kwōn karwūni ek kaņe.* Scale those fish there. *Em̧ōj ke an karwūn ek ko?* Have the fish been scaled?

kat (**kat**). 1(*-i*), 6(*-i*). Side of man or animal.

kat (**kat**). 1(*-i*), 2(inf, tr *-e*). Stand a coconut husking stick in the ground. *Kwōn kate doon ņe ņa iturun bōb eņ.* Stand the husking stick in the ground by that pandanus tree.

kat (**kat**). From Engl. 2(inf, tr *-e*), 6(*-i*), 7. Cut cards. *Kwōnan̄in kate ke kaaj kaņe?* Have you cut (the cards) yet?

katabuuk (**katahbiwik**). Also *kōtabuuk(i)* (**ketahbiwik(iy)**). Causative form of *tabu* (**tahbiw**).

katak (**kahtak**). 1(*-i*), 2(inf, tr *-in(-i)*), 3, 4(*rūkkatak*), 7. Study; learn; to teach; discipline; instruction; lesson; moral. *Iar ķatakini kūta.* I taught him how to play the guitar. *N̄a rūkkatak bajjek.* I'm just beginning to learn.

katak kōn menin mour (**kahtak kȩn menin mȩwir**). Zoology.

katak kōn mour (**kahtak kȩn mȩwir**). Biology. *Rej katak kōn mour ilo jikuuḷ.* They're studying biology in school.

kate (**katey**). Transitive form of *kakkōt* (**kakket**).

katejukjuk (**katȩyjiqjiq**). From *kate* (**katey**) "try", *jukjuk* (**jiqjiq**) "stay put, live, make a community". 3, 6(*-i*). A plant, *Eleusine indica* (L.) Gaertn. A digitate grass resembling the digitarias. Prob. W.

katiej (**katiyȩj**). Jump up.

katiin (**kahtiyin**). Also *katiin̄* (**kahtiyig**). From Japn. *kaaten* (from

Engl. *curtain*). 1(-*i*), 2(inf, tr -*i*), 3, 6(-*i*). Curtain; drape.

katiiñ (**kahtiyig**). Variant form of *katiin* (**kahtiyin**).

katin (**katin**). Also *kaat* (**kahat**). From Engl. 5(*kkatintin*), 6(-*i*). Carton. *Iar wiaik ļalem katin in jikka kameļ.* I bought five cartons of Camel cigarettes.

katkijm̧uuj (**katkijm̧iwij**). From Latin. Catechism.

Katlik (**katlik**). From Engl. 1(-*i*), 2, 3, 4, 6(-*i*). Catholic.

Katlik (**katlik**). From Engl. 2, 6(-*i*). A Catholic. *Ekatlik ñāāt?* When did he become a Catholic?

katļo̧k (**katļaq**). From Engl. 6(-*i*). Catalogue. *Letok m̧ōk katļo̧k eo am̧ bwe in lale.* May I see your catalogue?

katmāne (**katmaney**). Also *kōtmāne* (**ketmaney**). 2. Expect; propose to do; hope, trust, look forward to. *Ña ij katmāne bwe enaaj itok ilo baļuun eo ilju.* I expect him to come on the plane tomorrow. *Ij kōtmāne aō etal ñan M̧ajeļ iiō in laļ.* I expect to go to the Marshalls next year. *Iar jab kōtmāne am̧ itok.* I did not expect you to come.

katnok (**katneq**). Put thatch on walls.

katok (**kateq**). From *tok* (**teq**) "catch fire". 1(-*i*), 2(inf, tr -*e*), 4, 7. Offer sacrifice; sacrifice; incantation.

katoļo̧k (**katęwļaq**). Archaic. Divest of all property; purge; purify; expurgate; cleanse; catharsis.

katooj (**katewej**). From *tooj* "conspicuous". Fishing method, hunt lobster or coconut crab when the moon is right.

katōk (**katek**). Dial. E only; see *mō* (**meh**). A fish, wrasse, *Epibulus insidiator.*

katrar (**katrar**). 2(inf, tr -*e*), 4, 6(-*i*), 7. Dry pandanus or coconut leaves over fire in preparation for weaving.

katriiñ (**katriyig**). From Engl. (or Germ.) *Catherine*. 3, 6(-*i*). A plant, *Ocimum sanctum* L. (Labiatae). A cult. mint.

katro (**katrew**). Vulgar. 1(-*i*), 2(inf, tr -*uk*), 4. Sexual act; rapid up and down movement of hips.

kattal (**kattal**). Also *kōttal* (**kettal**). 6(-*i*). Rafters; horizontal.

kattar (**kattar**). Also *kōttar* (**kettar**). 1(-*i*), 2(inf, tr -*e*), 4, 7. Wait for; bide; await.

kattoojoj (**kattewejwej**). 1, 2, 4, 6(-*i*), 7, 8, 9. Flirt; show-off before the opposite sex. *Ledik eņ ej kattoojojwaj ñan eok.* The girl is trying to flirt with you. *Lieņ ļōm̧a rūkattoojoj.* Gentlemen, she's a flirt.

kattōñtōñ (**kattęgtęg**). 1, 2, 6(-*i*), 8, 9. Pleasant; popular; graceful; charming; provoking laughter. *M̧antin kattōñtōñ kaņ an rōkabwebweik eō.* Her charming movements drive me crazy. *Ekattōñtōñ an bwebwenato.* He tells laugh-provoking stories.

kattōrak (**kattęhrak**). Variant form of *tōrak* (**tęhrak**).

kattu (**kattiw**). 1(-*i*), 2(inf, tr -*ik, -uk*), 4, 6(-*i*). Dip food; dunk. *Pilawā kattu ko̧pe.* Bread dipped in coffee. *Kwōn kattuuki.* Dip it. *Enno̧ kattu mā ilo wiwi in wōn.* Dipping breadfruit in turtle fat is scrumptious. *Kattu eo ilo pade eo, kōm̧m̧an jān jukkwe.* The dip at the party was made from oysters.

kattūkat (**kattikat**). 2, 4, 6(-*i*), 7. Do one's best; try hard; persevere; distributive form of *kakkōt* (**kakket**). *Kattūkat wōt bwe ejako ejem̧ļo̧k.* Do your best for it's almost over.

katu (**katiw**). From *kōto* (**kętęw**) "wind". 1(-*i*), 2, 4, 7. Check the weather; weather lookout; forecast weather.

katūbtūb (**katibtib**). 1(-*i*), 2, 3. Hail; call to. *Jen al em kōkatūbtūb etan Irooj.* Let's sing and hail the name of the Lord.

kau (**kahwiw**). 1(-*i*), 2(inf, tr -*ik, -uk*), 4. Look after a sick person; nurse a patient. *Rōmoot in kauuk rinañinmej eo.* They went to care for the sick person. *Ij ilān kauuk rinañinmej eņ.* I am going to nurse that sick person.

kau (**kahwiw**). From Engl. 6(-*i*). Cow; beef.

kaubowe (**kahwiwbewey**). From Engl. 1(-*i*), 2(inf, tr -*ik*), 4, 6(-*i*), 7. Cowboy. *Ļadik eo ear kauboweik peikab eo.* The boy jumped on the pick-up truck while it was still moving (just like a cowboy). *Āin kwe wōt kaubowe bwe kwaar kauboweik wa eo.* You're like a cowboy because of the way you mounted the vehicle.

kaujuuj. See *kawūjwūj.*

kauḷaḷo (**kahwiḷahḷęw**). Dial. W only; see *kadeọeo* (**kahdeyawyęw**). Also *kọuḷaḷo* (**kawiḷahḷęw**). 3, 5(*kkauḷaḷoḷo*), 5+8, 5+9. Spider. *Jab bōktok kọuḷaḷo bwe enāj kkọuḷaḷoḷo ṃwiin.* Don't bring spiders to this house or you'll cause it to be crawling with them.

kaurur baib (**kahwirwir bahyib**). Also *kọurur baib* (**kawirwir bahyib**). Slang. Illicit drinking; smoking marijuana. *Iar jibwe aerro kọurur baib.* I caught them smoking pot.

kaurur jiañ (**kawirwir jiyag**). 2, 4, 6(*-i*). Black magic performed by a sorcerer using a husked coconut; pacify the winds and cause winds favorable for a sailing expedition. *Rijọubwe eo eṇ ej kaurur jiañ.* The sorcerer is doing his thing to cause good sailing winds.

kauwe (**kahwiwęy**). Also *kọuwe* (**kawiwęy**). 2(inf, tr *-ik*), 4, 6(*-i*). Leaven. *Kwōnañin kọuweiki ke pilawā eo?* Have you put leaven in the dough?

kauwe (**kahwiwęy**). Also *kọuwe* (**kawiwęy**). 1(*-i*), 2(inf, tr *-ik*), 4. Scold; warn; reproach; advise; punish; reprove; admonish; reprimand.

kauwe (**kahwiwęy**). Dial. E only; see *ṃōḷọjetak* (**ṃeḷęwjeytak**). Also *kọuwe* (**kawiwęy**). A fish, pompano, *Trachinotus bailloni*; a fish, *opelu, Cecapterus* sp.

kauwiinin. See *kọwiinin.*

kauwōtata (**kahwiwetahtah**). Also *kọuwōtata* (**kawiwetahtah**). From *uwōta* (**wiwetah**). 1(*-i*), 2(inf, tr *-ik*), 3, 4, 7, 8, 9. Dangerous; hazardous; risky; endanger; jeopardize. *Ekọuwōtata jerbal eo an.* His work is dangerous. *Kwōn jab kọuwōtataiki mour kein ad.* Don't endanger our lives.

kaū (**kahih**). 2(inf, tr *-ūk*), 7. Draw lips to one side in contempt; pout; make a face. *Raar kaūūk bwilijmāāṇ eo.* They made faces at the policeman.

kawal (**kahwal**). A fish.

kawal (**kahwal**). Watch for enemies.

kawiiaea (**kahwiyyahyah**). From *awiia* (**hawiyyah**). 1(*-i*), 2, 3, 4, 6(*-i*), 7. Avoid; stay away from. *Jab kawiiaea jān eō.* Don't avoid me.

kawor. See *kọor.*

kawūjwūj (**kahwijwij**). Also *kaujuuj.* 2(inf, tr *-i*), 4, 6(*-i*). Predict, using cards; foretell; solitaire. *Ear kawūjwūji an ḷōḷḷap eo mej.* He predicted the old man's death.

kawūno (**kahwinew**). Also *kauno, kọuno* (**kawinew**). 1(*-i*), 2(inf, tr *-ik*), 4, 5(*kkọunono*), 6(*-i*), 7, 8, 9. Dye; coloring. *Eor ke aṃ kọuno?* Have you any coloring?

kā (**kay**). These (things close to me); demonstrative, first person exclusive plural nonhuman.

kā (**kay**). 1(*kea-*). Torso; figure; frame; trunk. *Eṃṃan kāān.* She has a good figure. He is well built.

kā (**kay**). 1, 2, 6(*-i*), 8, 9. Stiffness of a corpse.

kā (**kay**). Turn; change; shift. *Kōto in ekā iōñ.* The wind is shifting to the north.

kā- (**kay-**). Also *ke-* (**key-**). 1(*-i*), 2, 3, 4, 5(*kkālọklọk*), 7. Ride on a plane; fly; to spring; take-off; form of *kkāke* (**kkaykęy**) that combines with directional postpositions.

kāāj (**kayaj**). Little stones used to make necklaces.

kāāj (**kayaj**). 3, 6(*-i*). Hook; barb; gaff. *Kāājin kabwebwe, kāājin ḷatippān, kāājin kadejo, kāājin kaṃōṃō, kāājin kōbwābwe, kāājin ilarak, etc.* Names of hooks for specific fish or types of fishing.

kāāj in kabwebwe (**kayaj yin kabeybey**). Idiom. Slim-waisted and broad-shouldered. *Likao eṇ ekāāj in kabwebwe.* That young man has a slim waist and broad shoulders.

kāājāj (**kayajyaj**). 6(*-i*). Big shot; dignitary; person who is notable; V.I.P. *Ebooḷ baḷuun eo kōn kāājāj.* The plane was loaded with dignitaries.

kāājej (**kayajyej**). Really.

Kāājejen-Tūṃur (**kayajyejen-tiṃir°**). A constellation; stars in Scorpius; theta, eta, zeta, mu, epsilon; the torso of *Tūṃur.*

kāājrabōl (**kayajrabel**). 2(inf, tr *-e*), 4, 6(*-i*), 7. Fishing method, pole or line fishing using no bait but simply jerking the line in the hope of hooking a fish by chance. *Kwōmaroñ ke kāājrabōle tok juon mọọrū mamo?* Could you hook me a sardine for bait?

kāāl (**kayal**). 1(-*i*), 2, 3, 7, 11(*kāleel, kāālel*). New; fresh.

kāālōt (**kayalet**). Transitive form of *kkāālel* (**kkayalyẹl**).

kāām (**kayam**). From Engl. *camp*. 4, 6(-*i*). Camp; low-cost housing.

Kāām-anij (**kayam-hanij**). A constellation; stars in Ursa Major; mu and lambda.

Kāām-armej (**kayam-harmej**). A constellation; stars in Ursa Major; theta, chi(or kappa), iota.

Kāām-kaṇ (**kayam-kaṇ**). The constellations *Kāām-anij* and *Kāām-armej*.

kāāṃbōj (**kayaṃbej**). From Engl. Campus. *Eḷap peḷaakin kāāṃbōj eṇ an U. H.* The U. H. has a big campus.

kāān (**kayan**). Also *kein* (**kẹyin**), *jekāān*. Trunk of a tree; torso of a person; tree; construct form of *kea-*, *kā*. *Ejjeḷǫk kāān wāto eṇ.* There are no trees on that tract. *Kein ni.* Trunk of a coconut tree. *Kein mā.* Trunk of a breadfruit tree. *Kein bōb.* Trunk of a pandanus tree.

kāān (**kayan**). From Engl. Can of meat.

kāānjeḷ (**kayanjeḷ**). From Engl. 2(inf, tr -*e*). Cancel. *Raar kāānjeḷe kkure eo kōn an wōt.* The game was cancelled on account of the rain.

kāāntōḷ (**kayanteḷ**). From Engl. 2(inf, tr -*e*), 3, 6(-*i*). Candle. *Kwōn kāāntōḷe.* Melt some of the candle on it.

kāāntōḷ (**kayanteḷ**). A fish.

kāāñ (**kayag**). From Engl. Gang. *Kwōn etal ippān kāāñ eṇ ṃōttaṃ.* Go join your own gang.

kāāp (**kayap**). 6(-*i*). Trigger.

kāātet (**kayatyẹt**). 2(inf, tr -*e*), 4, 6(-*i*), 7. Sniff around; trace scent; smell; sniff; snuff. *Kidu ko raar kāātet nemān rūkalbuuj eo.* The dogs traced the scent of the fugitive. *Ta ṇe kwōj kāātete nemān.* What are you sniffing?

kāboṇ (**kaybeṇ°**). Variant form of *kāpoon* (**kaypewen**).

kābwil (**kaybil**). Also *kiabōl* (**kiyahbẹl**). Baby birds.

kādik (**kaydik**). 1(-*i*), 2, 3, 4, 7, 8, 9. Small waisted; petite; slender; slim.

kādikdik (**kaydikdik**). 6(-*i*). Frame of a house. *Enañin kōṃṃan ke kādikdikin ṃweeṇ?* Has the frame for the house been fixed?

kāeǫreore (**kayar°yẹr°ẹy**). Causative transitive form of *eǫreor* (**yar°yẹr°**).

kāiiuiu (**kayiyyiwyiw**). Variant form of *keiiuiu* (**kẹyiyyiwyiw**).

kāik (**kayik**). Also *kaik* (**kahyik**). 1(-*i*), 2, 7. Jump on; jump over, transitive form of *kkāke* (**kkaykẹy**).

kāilar (**kayilar**). Also *kailar* (**kahyilar**). From *ilar* (**yilar**). 6(-*i*), 7, 8. Splendor; elegance; shine; polish. *Kwe aō rooj in kāilar ilueaḷ.* You're my rose that stands out in the crowds (words from a love song). *Ej baj jeḷā ṃantin kāilar.* He surely is an elegant gentleman.

kāiuiu. See *kaiuiu*.

kājekḷǫkjeṇ (**kayjekḷaqjeṇ**). Variant form of *kejakḷǫkjeṇ* (**keyjakḷaqjeṇ**).

kājokwā (**kayjeqay**). Variant form of *jokwā* (**jeqay**).

kājoon (**kayjewen**). 2(inf, tr -*(e)*), 7. Jump over; hop; skip over; cross over. *Ear kājoone pedkat eo.* He jumped over the mud puddle. *Iar kājoon jea eo.* I jumped over the chair.

kājōjō (**kayjehjeh**). 2(inf, tr -*ik*), 3, 5(*kkājōjō*), 6(-*i*), 7. Louver, fixed and opaque; sliding window. *Kwōn kōḷaak kājōjō ṇe ewōtlǫk.* Install that louver which fell off.

kākaṇ (**kaykaṇ**). Those (things close to neither of us); demonstrative, third person plural nonhuman, singling out.

kākaṇe (**kaykaṇey**). Those (things close to you); demonstrative, second person plural nonhuman, singling out.

kākā (**kaykay**). These (things close to me); demonstrative, first person exclusive plural nonhuman, singling out.

kākemǫǫj (**kaykẹymawaj**). 1(-*i*), 2, 4, 7, 8, 9. To be here and there; very active person; sprightly.

kālemeej (**kaylẹymeyej**). Variant form of *kalemeej* (**kalẹymeyej**).

kālik (**kaylik**). 2, 3, 4, 5(*kkāliklik*), 7. Go to the ocean side.

kālikrōk (**kaylikrẹk**). 3, 6(-*i*). A fish, perch, *Lutjanus fulviflamma*; go to the ocean side on the southern end of an island.

kālǫk (**kaylaq**). Also *kelǫk* (**keylaq**). 1(-*i*), 2, 3(*kōkkelǫk, kōkālǫk*), 4, 5(*kkālǫklǫk*), 7, 8. Fly away; jump down; jump into the sea; fly; jump; lovesick; fond; hop. *Ekkālǫklǫk* *baḷuun eṇ.* That plane makes lots of flights. *An jerbal eṇ kōkkālǫk baḷuun.* His job is preparing planes for take-off. *Ear kōkālǫk baḷuun eo.* He got the plane off. *Emejān kālǫk.* She displays a fond look.

kālǫk iḷǫkwan (**kaylaq yiḷaqan**). Also *kālǫk ilokwan* (**kaylaq yileqan**). Idiom. To pine after. *Jǫñan an kālǫk iḷǫkan ledik eo ewūdeakeak.* He pined after the girl so much that he went delirious.

kālōklōk (**kaylęklęk**). From *lōklōk* (**lęklęk**) "thorn". 3, 5, 6(*-i*). A plant, *Ximenia americana* L. (Oclacaceae). A thorny-stemmed tree. Also applied to other spiny or thorny plants, such as *Achyranthes aspera* L. on Eniwetok, or, in the shorter variant *lōklōk*; applied to a cultigen of *Cyrotosperma* (the large "taro"), also to *Cenchrus enchinatus*, or other species of *Cenchrus*, a weedy grass with obnoxious burred fruits, also, on Ebon, to Caesapinia bonduc, a leguminous shrub.

kālōklōk (**kaylęklęk**). 3(inf, tr *-e*), 5(*kkālōklōk*), 6(*-i*). Thorns; brambles. *Raar kōkālōklōke bōran.* They crowned him with thorns. *Jab tallōñe wōjke ṇe bwe ekkālōklōk.* Don't climb that tree because it has lots of thorns.

Kālōklōk (**kaylęklęk**). A plant, taro variety (Takeuchi; Xanthosoma).

kāmeej (**kaymeyej**). 3, 6(*-i*). Redwood.

kāmeñ (**kaymęg**). A plant; a tree.

kāpej (**kaypęj**). Variant form of *kapej.*

kāpin (**kaypin**). From Engl. 6(*-i*), 7. Cabin. *Kōm ar kāpin tok.* We stayed in a cabin during our trip here.

kāpoon (**kaypewen**). Also *kāboṇ* (**kaybeṇ°**). 1(*-i*), 6(*-i*). Intersection of roads; corner.

kāre (**kayrey**). 1(*-i*), 2(inf, tr *kāreik*), 4, 5(*kkārere*), 6(*-i*), 7. Mix with water; dilute; ingredient; blend. *Kwōn kāreik jekaro ṇe.* Dilute that toddy. *Ta ṇe kāre in juup ṇe?* What are the soup ingredients?

kāre kāāj (**kayrey kayaj**). Idiom. Fishing contest. *Kōjrooj kab kāre kāāj.* Now the two of us are really going to have a fishing contest.

kāre lǫwob (**kayrey lawwęb**). Idiom. Contest, fighting or wrestling. *Kokōṇaan ke kāre lǫwob?* Would you like to take me on?

kāroñjak (**kayreg°jak**). Also *keroñjak* (**keyreg°jak**). From *roñjake* (**reg°jakey**). 2(inf, tr *-e*). Listen intently; monitor. *Kwōn kakkōt kāroñjake retio ṇe.* Listen closely to the radio. *Ear kōḷaak kein kāroñjake ko.* He put on the earphones.

kātilmaak (**kaytilmahak**). 2. Fly up and down. *Bao kaṇ rej kātilmaak iṃaan wa in.* Those birds are flying up and down in front of this boat.

kātōk (**kaytek**). 2(inf, tr *-(e)*). Assert oneself. *Ear kātōke ñan ḷōṃaro.* He provoked the men. *Jab kātōk eok bwe kooḷaḷo.* Don't assert yourself for you are a weakling.

kāwur (**kaywir**). 3, 6(*-i*). Young chicken; bird just getting first wing feathers and not big enough to eat.

ke (**kęy**). 3, 6(*-i*). Porpoise; dolphin, *Delphinus roseiventris.*

ke (**key**). Yes-no question particle; past tense subordinate clause introducer; that; as. *Rōbuuki ke ej duojtok.* He was shot as he stepped out.

kea- (**keya-**). Also *kāā-, jekea-, jekāā-.* 1, 6. Trunk; shape; figure; see *kāān, kā.*

kear (**keyhar**). Also *keeaar* (**keyyahar**). Go from sea side of an island to lagoon side.

keār (**keyyar**). Also *kear, keear-dik* (**keyyar-dik**). A bird, black-naped tern, *Sterna sumatrana*; gull.

keār (**keyyar**). Dial. W: *keār-ḷap* (**keyyar-ḷap**), E: *keār-ṃōt* (**keyyar-ṃęt**). A bird, crested tern, *Thalasseus bergii.*

keār-ḷap (**keyyar-ḷap**). Dialectal variant of *keār* (**keyyar**).

keār-ṃōt (**keyyar-ṃęt**). Dialectal variant of *keār* (**keyyar**).

kebeban (**keybeyban**). 1(*-i*), 2(inf, tr *-e*), 3, 7. Shiver; shudder, as with cold.

kebōḷ (**keybeḷ**). From Engl. 2(inf, tr *-e*), 6(*-i*), 7. Cable; strong wires twisted together. *Jen kebōḷe rikin kein.* Let's use cable for the riggings.

keeaar (**keyyahar**). 1(*-i*), 2, 3(inf, tr *-e*), 4, 6(*-i*), 7. Go to the lagoon side; fly to the lagoon side. *Kwaar lo ke an Liṃwejo keeaar iṃwiin?* Did you notice Limwejo walking to the lagoon side here?

keeañ (**keyyag**). 2, 3, 4, 6(-*i*), 7. Announcement; proclamation; news; report of official matters; inform; notify. *Koṃ keeañļọk kōn naan ṇe ñan Rita.* Spread the news over to Rita.

keej (**kẹyẹj**). From Engl. 2(inf, tr -*e*), 5(*kkeejej*), 6(-*i*). Case, as of food; case, as of legal matter.

keek (**kẹyẹk**). From Engl. 6(-*i*). Cake.

keelwaan (**keyelwahan**). 1(-*i*), 2, 3, 4, 6(-*i*), 7. Naked; badly dressed; uncovered; exposed; bare. *Kanuknuk ro rōkeelwaan.* Clothe the naked.

keeļ (**keyeļ**). 1(-*i*), 2, 3(inf, tr -*e*), 5(*keeļeļ*), 6(-*i*), 8, 9. Muscle. *Ekeeļeļ ļọk jān Jọọn.* He's more muscular than John. *Eļļap keeļ kaṇe aṃ.* You have big muscles. *Kwōj kakeeļe eok kōnke epād jeṃaṃ ijin.* You're acting big because you have your father here.

keemem (**keyemyem**). 1(-*i*), 2(inf, tr -*e*), 3, 4, 6(-*i*), 7. Feast; birthday party; anniversary; banquet; celebration.

keememej (**kẹyẹmyẹmẹj**). 2(inf, tr -*e*), 3(inf, tr -*e*), 7. Remember. *Kwōn keememeje ta eo iaar ba ñan kwe.* Remember what I told you.

keeṇ (**keyeṇ**). Transitive form of *kkeeṇ* (**kkeyeṇ**).

keeñjak (**keyegjak**). 1(-*i*), 2(inf, tr -*e, keñaj*), 3, 5(*kkeeñjakjak*), 7. Bump a sore or wound. *Ekeeñjak kinej e neō.* I bumped the sore on my leg. *Ekkeeñjakjak kinej eṇ pein.* He is always bumping the wound on his hand.

keeñki (**kẹyẹgkiy**). Also *keiñki* (**kẹyigkiy**). From Japn. *genki*. 1(-*i*), 2, 3(inf, tr -*ik*), 4, 6(-*i*), 8, 9. Energy; energetic; good health; vivacious; active; lively; hearty; pep. *Jekdọọn ñe eļōļļap ak ej keiñki wōt.* Despite his being old, he's still very active. *Jiroñ eṇ ej loe ekakeiñkiiki.* His new girl has brought new life into him. *Eļap wōt an keeñki.* He's so energetic.

keepep (**kẹyẹpyẹp**). 1, 2, 6(-*i*), 7. Yank; apply constant powerful pressure on a rope; snare for catching birds. *Kōttar an allok neen em keepep.* Wait till his foot gets in the noose then yank. *Jekdọọn ñe ekankan to eo ak pen in deo an keepep.* Even though the rope was pulled taut, he continued to hold it.

keeprañ (**keyeprag**). 3, 6(-*i*). A plant, general term for bananas, *Musa sapientum* L. (Musaceae); banana.

keid (**kẹyid**). 1(-*i*), 2(inf, tr -*i*), 3, 4, 6(-*i*). Compare; take a rooster to a cock-fight; cause to fight. *Keidi ṃōk waļọk e aō ippaṃ.* Please compare my results (figures) with yours. *Ajri raṇ rej keid bao.* The children are having a cock-fight. *Jab keidi bao kaṇe.* Don't make those chickens fight. *Kwōn keidi ṃōk ewi wōt ṃweo eṃṃan ian ṃōkaṇ.* Please compare which of those houses is best.

keiie (**kẹyiyyẹy**). 1(-*i*), 2, 4, 7, 8, 9. Strong; useful; serviceable. *Eļap an keiie wa eṇ.* That boat is very useful. *Ekeiie lieṇ.* She is a great help.

keiiuiu (**kẹyiyyiwyiw**). Also *kāiiuiu* (**kayiyyiwyiw**). Swamp spring; hole in a swamp where the water rises and falls with the tide.

keikōb (**kẹyikẹb**). 6(-*i*). Bucket or can for drawing water from a well; variant form of *kekōb* (**kẹykẹb**).

keilupako (**kẹyiliwpakew**). 2(inf, tr -*ik(i)*), 4, 6(-*i*), 7. Fastest method of righting a canoe after it has capsized in order to escape sharks. *Ej okjak wōt wa eo ak rōkeilupakoiki.* As soon as the canoe capsized they performed the *keilupako*.

kein (**kẹyin**). These (things close to us both); demonstrative, first person inclusive plural nonhuman.

kein (**kẹyin**). Word used to form phrases and ordinal numbers; instrumental; thing for doing something. *Kein ṃōñā.* Eating utensils. *Kein kajilu.* The third.

kein (**kẹyin**). Variant form of *kāān* (**kayan**).

kein aō (**kẹyin haheh**). Life jacket; life preserver.

kein jerbal (**kẹyin jerbal**). Also *keijerbal* (**kẹyijerbal**). Tool; apparatus; implement; instrument. *Eor ke aṃ kein jerbal?* Have you any tools?

kein juṃae (**kẹyin jiwṃahyey**). Idiom. Objection.

kein kajilu (**kẹyin kajiliw**). The third.

kein kajuon (**kẹyin kajiwen**). The first.

kein kakeememej (**kẹyin kakẹyẹmẹymẹj**). Reminder; momento; souvenir; memorandum.

kein kaḷalem (**kẹyin kaḷalẹm**). The fifth.

kein kaṃool (**kẹyin kaṃewel**). Also *keikaṃooḷ* (**kẹyikaṃeweḷ**). Certificate; evidence; proof. *Eor ke aṃ kein kaṃool?* Do you have a certificate? Do you have any evidence?

kein karuo (**kẹyin kariwew**). The second.

kein katu (**kẹyin katiw**). Also *keikatu* (**kẹyikatiw**). Barometer. *Ta ņe kein katu ņe ej ba?* What's the reading on the barometer?

kein kāāmen (**kẹyin kaymen**). Also *kein kāmen.* The fourth.

kein kōjjọ (**kẹyin kejjaw**). Also *keikōjjọ* (**kẹyikejjaw**). Ignition switch; crank. *Ewi kein kōjjọ eo an injin in?* Where's the ignition switch for this engine?

kein kōṃ (**kẹyin keṃ**). Also *keikōṃ* (**kẹyikeṃ**). Stick for picking breadfruit.

kein kōttōbalbal (**kẹyin kettebalbal**). Instrument for plotting courses, nautical.

kein liklik (**kẹyin liklik**). Also *keiliklik* (**kẹyiliklik**). Sieve.

keinabbu (**kẹyinabbiw**). 3, 6(*-i*). A plant, papaya, *Carica papaya* L. F.; introd. from Central America; papaya.

keinikkan (**kẹyinikkan**). 5(*-e*), 6(*-i*). Plants. *Ekeinikkane ānin.* This island is full of all kinds of plants.

keiñki (**kẹyigkiy**). Variant form of *keeñki* (**kẹyẹgkiy**).

keiwa (**kẹyiwah**). 2, 6(*-a*). Cock-fight, in water.

kejakḷọkjeņ (**keyjakḷaqjeņ**). Also *kājekḷọkjeņ* (**kayjekḷaqjeņ**). 1(*-i*), 2, 3, 4. Be silent and pensive; mute; be in a trance. *Ta ņe kwōj kejakḷọkjeņ kake?* What are you being so silent and pensive about?

kejau (**keyjahwiw**). 2, 4, 6(*-i*), 7. Juggle. *Ilo raan eņ an* United Nation, *eor jiāl in kejau.* There is a juggling contest on U.N. Day.

kekaak (**keykahak**). Transitive form of *ekkekaak* (**yekkeykahak**).

kekaake (**keykahakey**). Transitive form of *kkekaak* (**kkeykahak**).

keke (**kẹykẹy**). 1(*-i*), 2, 3, 7, 10(*kijek*). Mature; strong; enough, of goods or needs; competent. *Ekeke ni eņ.* That coconut tree is mature. *Joñan ņe ekeke peiṃ im kwōmaroñ jutakḷọk iaaṃ.* You have enough capital to go into business on your own.

keke (**kẹykẹy**). 1(*-i*), 2(inf, tr *kiij(i)*), 3, 4, 7, 10(*kijek*). Sew; stitch. *Lio ej keke.* She is sewing. *Ej kiij nuknuk eo an.* She is sewing her dress.

keke (**keykey**). Also *keko* (**keykew**). 3, 6(*-i*). A bird, crane, white *kabaj.*

keke ņa ireeaar (**kẹykẹy ņah yirẹyyahar**). Idiom. Mature and capable of taking care of oneself. *Kwōn jab inepata bwe ekeke ņa ireeaar kiiō.* Don't worry about him; he's mature now and can take care of himself.

kekebuona (**keykeybiwenah**). A bird, crane, black and white spotted *kabaj.*

kekeel (**keykeyel**). Dial. W, E: *peoeo* (**peyewyew**). Also *kekōl* (**keykel**). 1(*-i*), 2(inf, tr *-e*). Tear; rend; rip. *Kekōle tok ṃōk ṃōttan e.* Would you tear this piece of cloth for me?

keko (**keykew**). Variant form of *keke.*

kekōb (**kẹykẹb**). Also *keikōb* (**kẹyikẹb**). 1(*-i*), 2(inf, tr *-e*), 3, 4, 6(*-i*), 7. Dipper.

kekōl (**keykel**). Variant form of *kekeel* (**keykeyel**).

kelọk (**keylaq**). Variant form of *kālọk* (**kaylaq**).

keḷe (**kẹyḷẹy**). 2, 4, 6(*-i*), 8, 9. Bad case of skin disease (*koko* (**kewkew**)). *Ñe kokeḷe, ej baj pen mour.* When your skin disease gets really bad, you have a hard time staying alive.

kena (**keynah**). From Engl. Gehenna; hell.

kenabōj (**keynabẹj**). 1(*-i*), 2, 3, 7. Jump out of.

kenato (**keynahtew**). 2, 5(*kkenatoto*), 6(*-a*). A very tall coconut tree. *Ekkenatoto ānin.* This islet has lots of tall coconut trees.

kenọkwōl (**keynaqel**). 1(*-i*), 2(inf, tr *-e*), 3, 4, 7. Start a fire. *Kwōn kenọkwōl kijek ņe.* Start that fire there.

keņaak (**keyņahak**). 2, 3, 5(*kkeņaakak*), 6(*-i*), 7, 8, 9. Hemmed in; trapped; cooped up. *Ikeņaak ņa ilowaan jōōt e.* I feel hemmed in in this shirt. *Ear keņaak ņa ioṃwin kaar eo.* He was trapped under the car. *Ekkeņaakak* *juuj kā aō.* My shoes are tight in several places. *Ikeņaak.* I'm stuck. *Kōm ar jijet em kkeņaakak ilo ruuṃ eo.* We sat crowded in the room.

keñaje (**keygajey**). Transitive form of *kkeñaj* (**kkeygaj**).

keotak (**kẹyẹwtak**). 2(inf, tr *-e*), 4, 6(*-i*). Beget; give birth. *Epereaaṃ ear keotake Aijek.* Abraham begot Isaac.

kepaak (**keypahak**). 1(*-i*), 2(inf, tr *-i*, *-e*), 3, 4, 7. Move closer; approach. *Kwōn kepaaki tok men kaņe.* Move those things closer here.

Kerara (**kẹyrahrah**). Archaic. Name of a navigational sign; one of a pair of whales; other named *Erra.*

keroñjak (**keyreg°jak**). Variant form of *kāroñjak* (**kayreg°jak**).

keroro (**kẹyrẹwrẹw**). 1(*-i*), 2, 3(inf, tr *-ik*, *-uk*), 4, 5(*kkeroro*). Be noisy; clatter; racket. *Jab keroro.* Don't make noise. *Eļap an ajri ro kkeroro.* The children make lots of noise.

ketak (**kẹytak**). 1(*-i*), 2(inf, tr *-(e)*), 4, 6(*-i*). Betray. *Jutōj ear ketake Jijej.* Judas betrayed Jesus. *Jibai eo ear ketake aelōñ eo an.* The spy betrayed his country.

kewa (**keywah**). 1(*kewa-*). Match; equal; peer. *Ļeo kewa ņe.* He's my match.

kewā (**kẹyway**). Archaic. Compete. *Ruo jar rej kewā doon.* Two groups compete with each other.

kewe (**kẹywẹy**). Dialectal variant of *ṃōdkowak.*

ki (**kiy**). From Engl. 6(*-i*). Key.

kiaj (**kiyhaj**). Also *kiaaj* (**kiyahaj**). 5(*kkiaajaj*), 6(*-i*). Gasoline. *Emootļọk waan kiaaj eo.* The gas truck left already. *Ekkiaajaj ioon pein baļuun eo.* There was gas all over the plane's wings.

kiaj (**kiyhaj**). Also *kajji* (**kajjiy**), *kiaaj* (**kiyahaj**). 6(*-i*), 7. Baseball catcher. *Ear kiaaj ñan kumi eo.* He was catcher for the team. *Kwōnaaj kiaaj tok ñan kōj.* You'll be our catcher.

kiaļe (**kiyaļẹy**). From Engl. Galley. *Ij jerbal ilo kiaļe eņ.* I'm working in the galley.

kiāptōļ (**kiyapteļ**). From Engl. 1(*-i*), 2(inf, tr *-e*), 6(*-i*), 7. Print by hand with manuscript style; capital city; capital letters.

kiār (**kiyar**). Also *ār* (**yar**). 3, 6(*-i*). Inner end of a single pandanus key. *Kakiāre bōb ņe.* Bite off the end of the pandanus.

kiddik (**kiddik**). 1, 5(*kkidikdik*), 6(*-i*). Memories of those little things we used to do. *Ij idpeenen im emļọk kōn kiddik ko arro.* I toss and turn reminiscing about those little things we used to do. *Iban meļọkļọk kiddikūrro.* I'll never forget those little things we used to do. *Ejjeļọk joñan kkidikdik in raan ko arro.* One cannot enumerate the little things we did in days gone by.

kideddelbwij (**kidẹddẹlbij**). A fish, moray eel; *Gymnothorax rupelli/petelli*; *Myrichthys bleekeri.*

kidel (**kidẹl**). Also *kiden* (**kidẹn**). 2, 3. Tired of staying in one place; stir-crazy; rock-happy; bored. *Ikidel ņa ānin.* I'm stir-crazy of staying on this island. *Ikiden ņa iAwai.* I got bored staying in Hawaii.

kiden (**kidẹn**). 2, 3, 6(*-i*). A plant, *Messerschmidia argentea* (L.f.) I. Johnston. The beach borage.

kiden (**kidẹn**). Variant form of *kidel* (**kidẹl**).

kidid (**kidid**). A bird, wandering tattler, *Heteroscelus incanum.*

kidiej (**kidiyẹj**). A fish, spotted hawkfish, *Cirrhitus pinnulatus.*

kidu (**kidiw**). 3, 5(*kkidudu*), 6(*-i*). Dog. *Ekkidudu ānin.* This island is full of dogs.

kidu (**kidiw**). Slang. 1, 2, 6(*-i*). Promiscuous; bitch. *Emake kidu lieņ.* She's a bitch.

kidudujet (**kidiwdiwjẹt**). A fish, sea horse, *Hippocampus kuda; legendary monster.*

kiduun lọjet (**kidiwin lawjẹt**). Walrus.

kie (**kiyẹy**). 6(*-i*). Canoe part, two beams to which *apet* (**hapẹt**) are lashed; the large cross timbers forming foundation work of the outrigger in a canoe.

kie (**kiyẹy**). 3, 4+3, 5, 6(*-i*), 3+7, 5+8, 9. A fish, big-eye or burgy; *Monotaxis grandoculis.*

kieb (**kiyẹb**). Also *kiōb.* 3, 6(*-i*). A plant, *Crinum asiaticum* L. (Amaryllidacea). The large common spider lily cultivated as hedges; or ornamental groups. Large white flowers.

kiebin wau (**kiyębin wahwiw**). From "Oahu spider lily". A plant, *Hymenocallis littoralis*. (Takeuchi).

kieȷ (**kiyęj**). Dial. E, W: *kiejor* (**kiyejer°**). A plant, *Pemphis acidula* Forst.

kiejor (**kiyejer°**). Dial. W, E: *kieȷ* (**kiyęj**). A plant, *Pemphis acidula* Forst. (Takeuchi).

kiel (**kiyel**). Also *kkiel* (**kkiyel**). 1(-*i*), 2(inf *kkiel*, tr -*e*), 7. To bend. *Kwōn jab kiel aļaļ ņe bwe enaaj bwilọk.* Don't bend that piece of wood or it will break. *Kwōn jab kiel kāāp ņe.* Don't pull the trigger.

kien (**kiyen**). 1(*kie*-), 3, 4, 6, 7+3. Government; law; commandment; ordinance; politics; rule; regulations; policy. *Kien Amedka.* U. S. Law. *Kien an Amedka.* U. S. Government. *Kien anemkwōj.* Democratic government. *Kien ko an Anij.* Commandments of God.

kietak (**kiyęytak**). 1(-*i*), 2(inf, tr -*(e)*), 7. To bend down, of coconut shoots only.

kii- (**kiyi-**). 6. Side of a house; wall. *Ear kajutak aļaļ ko ikiin ṃweo.* He stood the boards up against the house. *Kiin eṃ.* House wall.

kiibbu (**kiyibbiw**). From Japn. *kippu*. 6(-*i*). Permit; pass; ticket. *Ikōņaan bwe in bōk aō kiibbuun anemkwōj ioon tawūn aṃ.* I'd like to take my liberty pass in your town--words from a love song.

kiij (**kiyij**). Transitive form of *keke* (**kęykęy**).

kiijbaal (**kiyijbahal**). 1, 2, 4, 6(-*i*). Fishing method, hanging on to reef while spearing.

kiil (**kiyil**). Transitive form of *kilōk* (**kiylęk**).

kiiļ (**kiyiļ**). From Engl. Keel.

kiin (**kiyin**). Dial. E only; see *kiiō* (**kiyyeh**). 7. Now.

kiin (**kiyin**). See *kii-*.

kiin jeṃaanļọk (**kiyin jeyṃahanļaq**). Recently. *Ear jako kiin jeṃaanļọk.* He passed away recently.

kiinkiin (**kiyinkiyin**). Dialectal variant of *kiiō-kiiō* (**kiyyeh-kiyyeh**).

kiiñ (**kiyig**). From Engl. 2, 3(inf, tr -*i*), 6(-*i*). King. *Juon pea kiiñ.* A pair of kings.

kiiñkiiñ (**kiyigkiyig**). 2, 4, 6(-*i*). A game, jacks.

kiiō (**kiyyeh**). Dial. W only; see *kiin* (**kiyin**). 7. Now.

kiiō-kiiō (**kiyyeh-kiyyeh**). Dial. W, E: *kiinkiin* (**kiyinkiyin**). Immediately; very soon.

kij (**kij**). 1(-*i*), 5(*kijkij(i)*). Louse; bacteria; bug; flea; germ; parasite. *Ekijkij bōran lieņ.* Her hair is full of lice.

kij (**kij**). From Engl. *kiss*. 5(*kkijkij*), 6(-*i*). Light touching in billiards.

kij (**kij**). Transitive form of *kūk* (**kik**).

kij jān pid (**kij jan pid**). Variant form of *ļatuṃa* (**ļatiwṃah**).

kij-ļọkwan-doon (**kij-ļeqan-dewen**). Occur one after another, consecutively, bumper-to-bumper. *Ajri raņ nejin rej kij wōt ļọkwan doon.* Her children close one after the other. *Wa rej kij ļọkwan doon.* Cars were bumper-to-bumper.

kijak (**kijak**). Fellow; guy; lad; usually used with demonstratives. *Kijak eņ ļe eļap an kadek.* Say, that guy seems to be extremely intoxicated.

kijbadbad (**kijbadbad**). 1(-*i*), 2(inf, tr *kijibadke*), 4, 7. Try hard to reach; endeavor. *Rūkanpil ro raar kijbadbad im kōttōparļọk ijo niññiñ eo ear ļotak ie.* The wise men tried hard to reach the place where the child was born.

kijbo (**kijbęw**). 1(-*i*), 2(inf, tr -*ik(i)*), 3, 4, 7. Throw stones at. *Ta ņe kwōj kijboiki?* What are you throwing stones at?

kijdepak (**kijdepak**). 1, 2, 8, 9. Crab louse, *Phthirius pubis. Ekijdepake lieņ.* She's got the crabs.

kijdik (**kijdik**). 3, 5(*kkijdikdik(e)*), 6(-*i*), 7. Mouse; rat, *Rattus rattus* or *Rattus exulans. Ekkijdikdik ānin.* This island is full of rats.

kije (**kijey**). 1(-*i*), 2, 4, 7, 8, 9. Hardwood; determination; durable; enduring; optimistic; rugged; stalwart; sturdy. *Eļap an kije ļeeņ ilo jerbal.* He works hard. *Ekije aļaļ ņe.* That lumber is hardwood.

kije- (**kije-**). 1. Food of; cigarettes of; possessive classifier, food or cigarettes. *Ta ņe kijeṃ?* What are you eating? *Ta eņ kijeer?* What are they eating? *Kijen wōn e jikka?* Whose cigarette is this?

kijeek (**kijeyek**). 3+5(*kakijeekek*). Fire. *Ta uweo ej kakijeekek?* What's causing all that fire light way over there?

kijejeto (**kijẹyjẹytẹw**). 1(-*i*), 2, 3, 4, 6(-*i*), 7. Persevere; zealous; zeal; earnest; effort. *Eḷap an kijejeto ilo jerbal in.* He is very zealous in this work. *Jen kijejeto ilo m̧m̧an.* Let us persevere in what is good.

kijek (**kiyjẹk**). Also *kijōk, keke* (**kẹykẹy**), *kejek* (**kẹyjẹk**). From *keke* (**kẹykẹy**). 2, 3(inf, tr -*e*), 6(-*i*), 7. Sewn; snagged; hooked; fastened; perfective form of *keke* (**kẹykẹy**). *Ekijek mejān pāāk eo.* The sack's been sewn. *Ekijek nuknuk eo an.* Her dress got snagged. *Kajjioñ in kakijeke añkō ṇe.* Try to make that anchor fast.

kijen jidpān (**kijen jidpan**). From *kijen* (**kijen**) "food of", *jidpān* (**jidpan**) "saw". 6(-*i*). Sawdust.

kijen niñniñ (**kijen nignig**). Slang. From *kijen* (**kijen**) "food of", *niñniñ* (**nignig**) "infant". 6(-*i*). Cinch; easy; "duck soup"; pushover. *Kijen niñniñ teej eo.* The test was a cinch. *Jab inepata bwe kijen niñniñ.* Have no fear for it'll be a cinch.

kijen peto (**kijen pẹytẹw**). Slang. From "food of drifting westward". Leeway; allowance for error. *Kwōn kōm̧m̧an kijen peto bwe ekajoor aeto in.* Provide for some leeway because of the strong westward current.

kijenmej (**kijẹnmẹj**). 1(-*i*), 2, 3, 4, 7. Persevere; patience; endurance; optimism. *Kwōn kijenmej wōt im jikuuḷ.* Keep on trying in your school work.

kijer (**kijẹr**). Not yet. *Jab kijer in katuwe bwe ejjañin mat.* Don't take it off the fire yet because it is not done. *Iban kijer in kajjitōk m̧ae iien ilukkuun ban.* I won't ask until I'm really stuck. *Etke kokijer im bu.* Why did you shoot before you were told to do so?

kijerjer (**kijẹrjẹr**). Also *kijooror* (**kijẹwẹrwẹr**). 1(-*i*), 2, 3, 6(-*i*), 7, 8. Impatient; in a hurry; eager; anxious; restless. *Kakijerjere bwe erum̧wij.* Hurry him up because he's late. *Ekijerjer kapen eṇ in jerak.* The captain is in a hurry to sail. *Kwōn jab kijooror.* Control your restlessness.

kiji (**kijiy**). Transitive form of *kkij* (**kkij**).

kijibadke (**kijibadkey**). Transitive form of *kijbadbad* (**kijbadbad**).

kijin (**kijin**). Reward for.

kijjie- (**kijjiye-**). Also *kajjie-* (**kajjiye-**), *kōbaajjie-* (**kebahajjiye-**). 1. Regarding; direction of; in line with; location of; identification of. *Kwōn reilọk ikijjeen ḷọk wōt ni eṇ im kwōnaaj lo wa eṇ.* Look over there in the direction of that coconut tree and you will see the ship. *Kwōmaroñ ke ba kajjien m̧weo?* Do you know where the house is? Could you show me where the house is?

kijlep (**kijlep**). 1(-*i*). Large louse.

kijḷat (**kijḷat**). 1, 2(inf, tr -*e*), 6(-*i*). Eat kernel of coconut out of shell with one's teeth.

kijñeñe (**kijgẹygẹy**). 1(-*i*), 2, 3(inf, tr -*ik*), 7. Firm; strong; tense; austere; strict; formal; grim; obdurate; rigid. *Jab kakijñeñeik peim̧.* Don't make your arm muscles tense. *Enañin baj kijñeñe am̧ kien?* Why do you make such strict rules?

kijoñ (**kijeg°**). Slang. 1(-*i*), 2, 3, 4, 7, 8, 9. Immoral; immorality; tough, of people; unlawful desire; brave; bold; promiscuous. *Kōrā kijoñ.* Promiscuous woman. *Ekijoñ ḷeeṇ.* He is brave.

kijoon (**kijewen, kijẹwẹn**). 1(-*i*), 2(inf, tr -*e*), 6(-*i*), 7. Skip; pass over; pass across; to cross. *Ear kijoone kilaaj jilu.* He skipped the third grade. *Kōjro kijoon iaḷ e.* Let's go across the road.

kijooror (**kijẹwẹrwẹr**). Variant form of *kijerjer* (**kijẹrjẹr**).

kijōk. See *kijek.*

kiju (**kijiw**). Dial. W only; see *kaju* (**kajiw**). 1(-*i*), 5(*kkijuju*), 6(-*i*). Mast.

kikanju (**kiykanjiw**). From Japn. *kikanjuu*. 2(inf, tr -*ik(i)*), 4, 6(-*i*), 7. Machine gun.

kiki (**kiykiy**). Dial. W only; see *mājur* (**majir°**). 1(-*i*), 2, 3, 7. Sleep; asleep; slumber. *Em̧ōj ṇe am̧ kijoñ kiki.* Why don't you stop sleeping all the time. *Ekiki.* He's asleep.

kil (**kil**). 1(-*i*), 3, 6(-*i*). Skin.

kil (**kil**). Variant form of *kilōne.*

kilaaj (**kilahaj**). See *kilaj.*

kilaak (**kilahak**). 1(*kilaa-*), 2(inf, tr *kilaak(e)*), 6, 7. Fate; result; desire; commit; be responsible for. *Inaaj jerbal wōt ñan kilaam̧.* Your wish is my command. *Wōn ear kilaaktok* *armej rein?* Who is responsible for these people being here?

kilaba (**kilahbah**). From *Kilaba* (**kilahbah**) "name of man who killed himself". 2, 4. Suicide; commit suicide. *N̄e riM̧ajeļ rej kilaba, rej kālǫk jān ni.* When Marshallese commit suicide, they jump off coconut trees.

kilaj (**kilhaj**). From Engl. 1(*-i*), 2(inf, tr *-e*), 3, 4, 6(*-i*), 7. Mirror; look in a mirror. *Eor ke kilaj bwe i̧n kilaj?* Do you have a mirror I can use? *Em̧ōj n̄e am̧ kilaje mejam̧.* Stop admiring yourself in the mirror.

kilaj (**kilhaj**). From Engl. 6(*-i*). Glass. *Wūntō rot eņ am̧ kilaj ke būļajtiik?* Are your windows glass or plastic?

kilaj (**kilhaj**). 2, 3, 6(*-i*), 7. Class; category. *Kilajin ta eo kwaar kilaj ie kiiō?* What class did you just have here?

Kilbōt (**kilbet**). From Engl. 4. Gilbert (Islands).

Kilbōt (**kilbet**). From Engl. *Gilbert (Islands)*. A plant, banana variety (Takeuchi).

kilbur (**kilbir°**). Also *kūblur* (**kiblir°**). 1(*-i*), 2(inf, tr *-(i)*), 3, 4, 7. Mat used as blanket or sheet; cuddle under a blanket. *Em̧m̧an wōt kilbur ippa.* I prefer sleeping in mats.

kilbūrōrō (**kilbirẹhrẹh**). 1(*-i*), 2, 3(inf, tr *-ik*), 6(*-i*), 7, 8, 9. Blush; flush. *Jon̄an an llu ekilbūrōrō.* He got so mad he turned red.

kile (**kiley**). 1(*-i*), 2, 7. Recognize; realize; aware; distinguish; familiar with; identify; notice; perceive. *Kwōj kile ke wōn eņ?* Do you recognize who that is? *Ij kile ippa make ke eban tōprak jerbal eņ.* I can see on my own that that job can never be finished.

kile (**kiley**). 2, 3(inf, tr *-ik*), 4+3. Choosy; particular; meticulous; nagging. *Emake kile kijen.* Isn't he choosy when it comes to food. *Kwōn jab kakileik eok arin kōrā.* Stop your feminine nagging.

kilen (**kilen**). Construct form of *kōl* (**kẹl**).

kilen jāje (**kilen jayjẹy**). 2(inf, tr *-ik*), 4, 6(*-i*), 7. Art of fencing. *Kilen jājeik m̧ōk e bwe in lale kwōjeļā ke.* Fence with him so I can see whether you're good or not.

kilep (**kilep**). 1(*-i*), 2, 3, 7, 11(sg. *kileplep*, pl. *(k)killep*). Big; large; maximum; vast; huge. *Juon eņ wa kileplep ej kab po tok.* There is a very large ship there that just arrived.

kili (**kiyliy**). Also *kiili.* Transitive form of *kkiil* (**kkiyil**).

kiliblib (**kiliblib**). 1, 6(*-i*). Placenta; afterbirth.

kiliblib (**kiliblib**). 2(inf, tr *-i*), 6(*-i*), 7. Heave. *Ekiliblibi ļǫk tūram̧ eo.* He lifted and threw the drum.

kiliddāp (**kiliddap**). 1(*-i*), 2, 3, 4, 7. Get under one's skin; persistent; stubborn.

kilin kau (**kilin kahwiw**). Leather.

Kilin-ek (**kilin-yẹk**). From *kilin* (**kilin**) "skin of", *ek* (**yẹk**) "fish". 3, 6(*-i*). A plant, pandanus cultigen.

kilkil (**kilkil**). A fish.

kille (**killẹy**). 3, 6(*-i*). A plant, *Sophora tomentosa* L. (Leguminosae). A hairy shrub; small tree with one-pinnate leaves and very numerous leaflets; yellow flowers; and pods which are elongate and constricted between the seeds.

kilmeej (**kilmeyej**). 1(*-i*), 2, 3, 4(*rūkkilmeej*), 5(*kkilmeejej*), 6(*-i*), 7. Black. *Ekkilmeejej lan̄.* The sky is gray and overcast.

kilmij (**kilmij**). Also *kimlij* (**kimlij**). From Engl. 2(inf, tr *-i*), 6(*-i*). Gimlet; auger; drill; spiral. *Ekimlij an kelǫk.* It flew in a spiral. *Kimliji aļaļ n̄e.* Drill a hole in that board.

kilmir (**kilmir**). 2, 3(inf, tr *-i*), 6(*-i*), 8, 9, 11(*kilmir*). Red.

kiloottōr (**kilẹwẹttẹr**). Archaic. Make perfume.

kilǫk (**kilaq**). 1(*-i*), 2(inf, tr *-e*), 3, 4, 6(*-i*), 7. Method of extracting pudding from cooked pandanus. *Kwōn kilǫki bōb kan̄e.* Press the juice out of those pandanus.

kilōk (**kilẹk**). 2, 3, 6(*-i*). Fastened, of anchors only. *Ekilōk ke an̄kō n̄e?* Is the anchor fastened? *Kajjion̄ kakilōke an̄kō n̄e.* Try to make that anchor fast.

kilōk (**kilẹk**). 2(inf, tr *-e*), 4, 5(*kkilōklōk*), 6(*-i*). Large basket. *Rōnan̄in kilōki ke m̧ōn̄ā ko?* Have they put the food in the *kilōk*?

kilōk (**kiylẹk**). 1(*-i*), 2(inf, tr *kiil(i)*), 3, 5(*kkilōklōk*), 7. Shut; perfective form of *kkiil* (**kkiyil**). *Ekkilōklōk kōjām eo.* The door is always closed.

kilōñe (**kilęgęy**). Variant form of *kōlñe* (**kęlgęy**).

kilperakrōk (**kilperakręk**). 1(*-i*), 2, 3, 7. Ticklish. *Ekilperakrōk neō.* My leg is ticklish.

kiltōn (**kilten**). 3(inf, tr *-e*), 3+4, 3+5(*kakiltōntōn*), 3+7. Method of doing something step by step; construct form of *kōl;* snitch; swipe. *Kwōjeḷā ke kiltōn eb jab ņe?* Do you know that dance? *Wōn ņe kwaar kakiltōne ḷait ņe aṃ jāne?* Who did you swipe that lighter from?

kilwōd (**kilwed**). Outer bark of tree.

kiḷij (**kiyḷij**). Also *kiḷūt* (**kiyḷit**), *kūḷḷij* (**kiḷḷij**). 3, 6(*-i*). An animal, green and black lizard, *Dasia smaragdina.*

kimā (**kimay**). Archaic. A tree; see *kimeme.*

kimej (**kimęj**). 1(*kōmeja-*, *-i*), 3, 5(*kkimejmej*), 6(*-i*). Coconut frond. *Ekkimejmej nōbjān ṃwiin.* There are fronds all around (on the ground) outside this house.

kimeme (**kimeymey**). 3, 6(*-i*). A plant, *Lumnitzera littorea.*

kimij (**kimij**). Transitive form of *kkim* (**kkim**).

kimirmir (**kimirmir**). Vulgar. 1, 6(*-i*). Anus.

kimlij (**kimlij**). Variant form of *kilmij* (**kilmij**).

kimuur (**kimiwir**). 2, 6(*-i*), 8, 9. Rich, of soil or plant; fertile. *Emake kimuur ni ņe.* That coconut tree bears a lot of fruit.

kin (**kin**). Bed of fronds on which the tails of porpoises are placed.

kin (**kin**). Groove in piece of wood, for *etōñ* firemaking.

kin (**kin**). Also *jenok.* Footprints.

kina (**kinah**). Also *ņa* (**ņah**). Archaic. Shoal.

kinaak (**kinahak**). 2(inf, tr *-(e)*), 5(*kkinaakak*), 7. Tattle; complain of others; betray; accuse; reproach; snitch; telltale; tell on someone. *Inaaj kinaak eok.* I will report you. *Ekkinaakak ḷeo.* He's a tattle-tale. *Kwōn jab kkinaakak.* Don't be a snitch. Don't be a telltale.

kinaḷ (**kinaḷ**). 6(*-i*). An insect, smallest ant.

kinbo (**kinbęw**). A fish, red spot tang, *Acanthurus achilles.*

kinbūt (**kinbit**). Not ripe, of breadfruit.

kine (**kiney**). Compose songs or chants.

kinej (**kinęj**). 1(*kōnja-*). Wound; scar. *Eḷap kinej eņ pein.* There is a big wound on his hand.

kinejnej (**kinęjnęj**). 1(*-i*), 2, 3, 4, 5(*kkinejnej*), 7, 8, 9. Wounded; marred. *Ekinejnej pein.* His hand is wounded. *Eḷap an kkinejnej ānbwinnin.* His body has many wounds. *Ekinejnej ekjab in.* This statue is marred.

kinie- (**kiniye-**). 1. Mat of; possessive classifier, mat or blanket or mattress.

kinji (**kinjiy**). 2, 7. Pinch with fingernails.

kino (**kinew**). Also *kino* (**kinęw**). 3, 5(*kkinono*), 6(*-i*). A plant, fern, *Microsorium scolopendria* Burm. F. Copeland. The very common oak-leaf fern, epiphytic or terrestrial; the sori borne like tumours on the once-pinnate fronds.

kino (**kinew**). From *kino* (**kinew**). 3(inf *kakinono,* tr *kakinonoik*), 5(*kkinono*), 6(*-i*). Ingredient; decoration. *Kwōn kakkinonoik juub ņe kōn anien bwe en nnọ.* Add some onion to the soup to make it tasty.

kinọwea- (**kinaweya-**). 1, 6. Obstacle. *Epād ikinọwea.* He is in my way.

kinōr (**kinher**). 2(inf, tr *-(e)*), 7. Carry, of currents; waft, of waves. *Rōkinōr lik ḷọk wa eo.* The currents are taking the canoe out to sea.

kintak (**kintak**). 2(inf, tr *-e*), 6(*-i*), 7. Pick up bits of rubbish; pull up weeds or grass. *Koṃwin kintak bwe enaaj itok koṃja eo ilju.* Clean up because the Distad is coming tomorrow.

kinwōj (**kinwęj**). 3, 6(*-i*). A plant, *Synedrella nodiflora*, a small yellow fld. composite weed. Namorik. Hedyotis biflor.

Kinwuṃ (**kinwiṃ**). Also *Kinuṃ.* 3, 6(*-i*). A plant, pandanus cultigen.

kio (**kiyew**). Also *kieo.* 3, 6(*-i*). A plant, *Sida fallax* Walpers; a yellow-flowered herb; often planted around houses; N. Worn by "*lōrrọ*" women, women said to fly because of disappointment in love according to Marshallese belief. Eaten by warrior-trainees at their coming-out ceremonies.

kio (**kiyew**). Also *kieo.* 1(*-i*), 2, 3(inf, tr *-uk*), 5(*kkioeo*), 6(*-i*), 7. Orange colored.

kiojaḷjaḷ (**kiyewjaḷjaḷ**). 1(*-i*), 2, 3, 4, 7. Stir up; antagonize by tale-bearing; disagree; stir up trouble. *Kwōn jab kōṃṃan kiojaḷjaḷ.* Don't start trouble by spreading tales. Don't stir up trouble.

kior (**kiyẹr°**). Also *kiur* (**kiyir°**), *kōtteepiṇa.* 6(*-i*). Storm. *Ebuñlọk juon kior kijoñjoñ im kọkkure wa ko.* A big storm came and ravaged the canoes.

kiōk (**kiyẹk**). Also *ikiōk* (**yikyẹk**). Archaic. Grass skirt boys put on at puberty.

kiōk (**kiyẹk, kiyek**). Also *kiek.* 2. Nearly; practically; almost. *Ear dọlelḷọk em ḷak kiōk mej, ebar mour.* He was near death but recovered. *Joñan an ḷap kōto, kiōk taibuun.* The wind blew so hard it was practically a typhoon. *Wa eo kiōk okjak, ekwe ebar jiṃwe.* The boat would almost capsize but then would straighten up again.

kipdo (**kipdẹw**). Get one's comeuppance.

kiped (**kiped**). Paddle. *Kiped dikdik ṇe.* Don't move the stern paddle too much (when you're sailing close to the wind).

kipeddikdik (**kipẹddikdik**). 2, 4, 6(*-i*), 7. Manage to exist; get by; sail close to the wind; progress slowly but steadily; make do with what one has; cut corners; economize. *Kwōmake jeḷā kipeddikdik kōn oṇāān ṇe aṃ.* You really know how to make ends meet with your salary. *Ej jab kanooj ṃṃan oṇān ak ebwe an kipeddikdik.* He doesn't get paid too well, but he's progressing steadily.

kipel (**kipel**). 2(inf, tr *-(e)*). Lead; advise; persuade; instruction; train; scold; warn; reproach; compel; force; forbid; oblige. *Kwōn kipel er bwe ren itok.* You persuade them to come.

kipiliia (**kipiliyyah**). 1(*-i*), 2, 4, 7, 8, 9. Disobedient (see *kipiliie* (**kipiliyyẹy**)); obdurate; obstinate.

kipiliie (**kipiliyyẹy**). 1(*-i*), 2, 4, 7, 8, 9. Obedient (see *kipiliia* (**kipiliyyah**)); docile.

kipilōñ (**kipiylẹg**). Variant form of *kapilōñ* (**kapiylẹg**).

kipin (**kiypin**). 2(inf, tr *-i*), 7. Ram; force into. *Kipiniḷọk men ṇe ṇai kiin eṃ.* Push it against the wall.

kitak (**kiytak**). 2(inf, tr *(-e)*), 6(*-i*). Hem; lift dress; roll up pants. *Kitake nuknuk ṇe aṃ em tuwaak.* Raise your dress before you walk into the water.

kito (**kiytẹw**). 1(*-i*), 2, 5(*kkitoto*), 6(*-i*). Ringworm; fungus. *Ekito ḷeeṇ.* He's got ringworm. *Ekkitoto ānbwinnin ajri eo.* The child was covered with ringworm.

kiu (**kiyiw**). From Engl. Cue.

kiudi (**kiyiwdiy**). From Japn. *kyuuri*. 2(inf, tr *-ik*), 3, 4+3, 5(*kkiudidi*), 6(*-i*), 7. Cucumber. *RiNibboñ raar kkat kiudi iṂajeḷ jeṃaan.* The Japanese planted *kiudi* in the Marshalls during their time there.

kiwūl (**kiywil**). Archaic. End of an islet.

kkaadad (**kkahadhad**). Dial. W: *ekkaadad* (**yekkahadhad**), W: *kōkaadad* (**kekeahadhad**). 1(*-i*), 2, 3(*kōkkaadade*), 5(*kkaadad*), 6(*-i*), 7, 8, 9. Multicolored, spotted, usually brownish. *Ekkaadade mejān jōōt eo an.* He had on a multicolored brownish shirt.

kkaal (**kkahal**). Dial. W: *ekkaal* (**yekkahal**), E: *kōkaal* (**kekahal**). 1(*-i*), 2(inf, tr *kaal(e)*), 4, 7. Entice; lead; lure; call or entice animals or children to come near. *Kwōn kaal tok kidu eṇ.* Call that dog.

kkaan (**kkahan**). Dial. W: *ekkaan* (**yekkahan**), E: *kōkaan* (**kekahan**). 2(inf, tr *kaane*), 4, 6(*-i*). Use for the first time; break something in; take part of; use part of. *Eṃōj kaan keek eo.* Someone took some of the cake. *Ejjañin kkaan pāāk in pilawā ṇe.* That sack of flour has not been opened yet. (It is still intact.) *Kwōmaroñ kaane mājet kaṇe.* You may use those matches (which have never been used before).

kkaapap (**kkahaphap**). Dial. W: *ekkaapap* (**yekkahaphap**), E: *kōkaapap* (**kekahaphap**). 1(*-i*), 2(inf, tr *-e*), 4. Cast for broken bone; clamp.

kkaj (**kkaj**). Dial. W: *ekkaj* (**yekkaj**), E: *kōkaj* (**kekaj**). 1(*-i*), 2(inf, tr *kajek(e)*), 7, 8, 10. Bumpy; rough; to bump. *Emake kōkkaj iaḷ eṇ ñan Ḷora.* The road to Laura is very bumpy. *Ear kajek ḷantōn eo.* He bumped the lantern.

kkajkaj (**kkajkaj**). Dial. W: *ekkajkaj* (**yekkajkaj**), E: *kōkajkaj* (**kekajkaj**). Distributive form of *kaj* (**kaj**).

kkal (**kkal**). Dial. W: *ekkal* (**yekkal**), E: *kōkal* (**kekal**). 1(-*i*), 2(inf, tr *kalōk*), 3, 4, 7. Build; erect; structure. *Eṃṃan kkalin ṃween.* The structure of that house is good.

kkal (**kkal**). Dial. W: *ekkal* (**yekkal**), E: *kōkal* (**kekal**). 2. Imprint. *Ekkal jenkwan ñiin ṇa ipeiū.* She left her teeth marks on my arm.

kkan (**kkan**). Dial. W: *ekkan* (**yekkan**), E: *kōkan* (**kekan**). Food; grub; sustenance. *Eor ke kkan ṃōṇe?* Do you have any food in your house?

kkañ (**kkag**). Dial. W: *ekkañ* (**yekkag**), E: *kōkañ* (**kekag**). 1(-*i*), 2, 3, 7, 11(*kkañkōñ*). Sharp; pointed; keen. *Ekkañ pinjeḷ ṇe aṃ.* Your pencil is sharp. *Ekkañ jāje ṇe aṃ.* Your machete is sharp.

kkañ loo- (**kkag lewe-**). Dial. W: *ekkañ loo-* (**yekkag lewe-**), E: *kōkañ loo-* (**kekag lewe-**). 1, 2, 8, 9. Critical in speech; fluent; sharp-tongued. *Emake kkañ loon.* He's so critical when speaking. *Lale an kkañ looṃ bwe rōnaaj llu ippaṃ.* Watch your sharp tongue or people will get angry at you.

kkapit (**kkapit**). Dial. W: *ekkapit* (**yekkapit**), E: *kōkapit* (**kekapit**). 1(-*i*), 2(inf, tr *kapit(i)*), 4, 5(*kkapitpit*), 6(-*i*), 8. Oil oneself; put on perfume; anoint; ointment; rub. *Lōḷḷap eo ar anjin kkapitpiti ajri eo bwe en llejkōnkōn.* The old woman performed the anointing treatments on the child so that she would grow up popular.

kkapit (**kkapit**). Variant form of *pitpit* (**pitpit**).

kkar (**kkar**). Dial. W: *ekkar* (**yekkar**), E: *kōkar* (**kekar**). 1(-*i*), 2(inf, tr *karōk(e)*), 3, 4, 5(*kkarrūkarōk*, *kkarkarōke*), 7, 10(*kkar*). Suitable; fit; it is fitting; organize; appropriate; correspond; eligible; prescribe; qualified; plan; scheme; plot a course; match; relevant; proper; put in order; arrange; system. *Ekkar ke nuknuk kaṇe ñan kwe?* Do your clothes fit you? *Rej karōkḷọk eok ñan e.* They are trying to set you up with her. *Jab kkarrūkarōkḷọk eok bwe kwe jeeknaan.* Don't try and get yourself accepted (by doing different things) because you're only second class. *Kōmij kōṃṃan ta kien ej karōke.* We do what the law prescribes. *Eṃṃan aṃ kkar.* Your planning is good. *Ekkar ke?* Is it relevant? *Rej kkarkarōke lowaan ṃween.* They are rearranging the interior of that house this way and that way. *Eṃōj an karōk lowaan ṃweo.* She has tidied up the house.

kkarjinjin (**kkarjinjin**). Dial. W: *ekkarjinjin* (**yekkarjinjin**), E: *kōkarjinjin* (**kekarjinjin**). 1(-*i*), 2, 3. Smell of kerosene; distributive form of *karjin* (**karjin**).

kkarkarōke (**kkarkarekey**). Dial. W: *ekkarkarōke* (**yekkarkarekey**), E: *kōkarkarōke* (**kekarkarekey**). Distributive form of *kkar* (**kkar**).

kkarrūkarōk (**kkarrikarek**). Dial. W: *ekkarrūkarōk* (**yekkarrikarek**), E: *kōkarrūkarōk* (**kekarrikarek**). Distributive form of *kkar* (**kkar**).

kkat (**kkat**). Dial. W: *ekkat* (**yekkat**), E: *kōkat* (**kekat**). 1(*kkatti-*, *kōtka-*) 2(inf, tr *katōk*), 4, 6(-*i*), 7. To plant; to sow. *Kkatū mā ṇe.* I planted that breadfruit tree.

kkā (**kkay**). Dial. W: *ekkā* (**yekkay**), E: *kōkā* (**kekay**). 1(-*i*), 2, 7, 8, 9. Very often; repeatedly; common; usually; apt; inclined to; susceptible to; tend to; normally. *Ekkā wōt am teej in Bōḷaide.* We often have tests on Friday. We normally have tests on Fridays. *Ekkā wōt an ṃōñā raij.* He usually eats rice.

kkāālel (**kkayalyẹl**). Dial. W: *ekkāālel* (**yekkayalyẹl**), E: *kōkāālel* (**kekayalyẹl**). 1(-*i*), 2(inf, tr *kāālōt*), 4, 7. Select; elect; selection; election; pick out; choose; option; choice; pull. *Eṃōj ke aer kkāālel?* Is the election over yet? *Eṃōj ke aṃ kāālōt jet piteto?* Did you pick out some good potatoes yet?

kkāke (**kkaykẹy**). Dial. W: *ekkāke* (**yekkaykẹy**), E: *kōkāke* (**kekaykẹy**). 2(inf, tr *kaik*, *kāik*), 4, 6(-*i*), 7(*kātok*, *ḷọk*, *waj*). Fly; aviation; jump up and down. *Rūkkāke.* Pilot. *Rej kātok kiiō ḷọk jidik.* They'll fly here later. *Eṃṃan an rañ kkāke.* Wild ducks fly nicely (in formation). *Etke kwōj kkāke?* Why are you jumping up and down?

kkārere (**kkayreyrey**). Dial. W: *ekkārere* (**yekkayreyrey**), E: *kōkārere* (**kekayreyrey**). 1(*-i*), 2, 8, 9. Assorted; mixed; diverse; miscellaneous. *Ekkārere armej iAwai.* The people of Hawaii are diverse. *Kōļanin m̧weiuk kkārere ko ņe.* That's the column for the miscellaneous.

kkeeņ(e) (**kkeyeņ(ey)**). Dial. W: *ekkeeņ* (**yekkeyeņ**), E: *kōkeeņ* (**kekeyeņ**). 1(*-i*), 2(inf, tr *keeņ(e)*), 3, 5(*kekeeņ, kkekeeņ(e)*), 7, 10(*keņaak*). Squeeze; press; strain. *Kwōn jab kkekeeņe pein.* Don't keep on squeezing her hand. *Keeņe m̧ōk.* Try squeezing it.

kkeilǫk (**kkęyilaq**). Dial. W: *ekkeilǫk* (**yękkęyilaq**), E: *kōkeilǫk* (**kękęyilaq**). 2, 3(inf, tr *-e*), 6(*-i*), 7. Shout; yell; holler; shriek; whoop.

kkein (**kkęyin**). Dial. W: *ekkein* (**yękkęyin**), E: *kōkein* (**kękęyin**). 7. A while ago. *Ear etal kkein ļǫk jidik.* He went a little while ago. *Emoot kkein ļǫk jidik.* He left a little while ago.

kkein (**kkęyin**). Dial. W: *ekkein* (**yękkęyin**), E: *kōkein* (**kękęyin**). Also *kōn* (**kęn**). 2. Used to. *Ekkein jja.* He used to walk in his sleep. *Ikōn rūkadek.* I used to be a heavy boozer. *Ikkein kōbaatat ak kiin ij jab.* I used to smoke, but I don't anymore.

kkein wa (**kkęyin wah**). Dial. W: *ekkein wa* (**yękkęyin wah**), E: *kōkein wa* (**kękęyin wah**). Also *kkeiwa* (**kkęyiwah**). 1(*-i*), 2, 3, 4, 8, 9. Take good care of a canoe. *Ekkein wa ļeeņ.* He takes good care of canoes.

kkeini (**kkęyiniy**). Dial. W: *ekkeini* (**yękkęyiniy**), E: *kōkeini* (**kękęyiniy**). Also *kkeini* (**kkęyiniy**). 2(inf, tr *-ik*), 7, 8, 9. To frequent; keep in touch with; haunt. *Em̧ōj ņe am̧ kkeini m̧ōn kadek kaņ.* Stop frequenting the bars. *Jekdǫǫn ñe eļe ak ear jab jokwōd an kkeini jemān.* Despite his great success and fame he did not fail to keep in touch with his father.

kkeitaak. See *kōkkeitaak.*

kkeiwa (**kkęyiwah**). Variant form of *kkein wa* (**kkęyin wah**).

kkejel (**kkęyjęl**). Dial. W: *ekkejel* (**yękkęyjęl**), E: *kōkejel* (**kękęyjęl**). 1(*-i*), 2(inf, tr *-e*), 3, 4, 7. To unite with; hang upon; latch on to; hold on to; stuck on to; attached; link. *Ear ekkejel ippa.* She held on to me. *Kakkejele ņa ijabōn kiju ņe.* Tie it on to the top of the mast.

kkekaak (**kkeykahak**). Dial. W: *ekkekaak* (**yekkeykahak**), E: *kōkkekaak* (**kekkeykahak**). 1(*-i*), 2(inf, tr *kekaake*), 6(*-i*), 7. Pull out; drag; slip out; a drawer; draw out; pull as in dancing; withdraw. *Kekaake peim̧.* Pull your hand out of the way. *Kekaake nabōjtak.* Draw it out.

kkeñaj (**kkeygaj**). Dial. W: *ekkeñaj* (**yekkeygaj**), E: *kōkeñaj* (**kekeygaj**). 2(inf, tr *keñaje*), 4, 6. Bump a sore or wound. *Kwōjaam̧ keñaje peiū?* Stop bumping the sore on my arm!

kkeroro (**kkęyręwręw**). Dial. W: *ekkeroro* (**yękkęyręwręw**), E: *kōkeroro* (**kękęyręwręw**). Slang. 2, 3(inf, tr *-ik*), 4, 6(*-i*). Fuss; complain; grumble; noise; clamor; racket. *Ta ņe kwōj bar kkeroro kake kiiō?* Now what are you fussing about again?

kketaak (**kkęytahak**). Dial. W: *ekketaak* (**yękkęytahak**), E: *kōketaak* (**kękęytahak**). 1(*-i*), 2(inf, tr *-e*), 3, 4, 6(*-i*), 7. Attachment; joint. *Kōkāāle kketaak jab ņe bwe tipen m̧or.* Fix that one attachment as it seems old.

kkiel (**kkiyel**). Variant form of *kiel* (**kiyel**).

kkiil (**kkiyil**). Dial. W: *ikkiil* (**yikkiyil**), E: *kūkiil* (**kikiyil**). 2(inf, tr *kiili*), 5(*kkilōklōk*), 7, 10(*kilōk*). Close; shut. *Kili wūntō ņe.* Close the window. *Ekilōk wūntō eo.* The window is closed.

kkiil (**kkiyil**). Dial. W: *ikkiil* (**yikkiyil**), E: *kūkiil* (**kikiyil**). 2(inf, tr *kiili*), 3(*kakiil*), 6(*-i*), 10(*kilōk*). Memorize; know by heart. *Ej kili jipij eņ an.* He's memorizing his speech. *Ekili inǫñ eo.* He has memorized the tale. *Kakiil m̧ōk ajri raņe.* See if the children know their lessons. *Ekilōk al eo ippām.* We've memorized the song by heart.

kkij (**kkij**). Dial. W: *ikkij* (**yikkij**), E: *kūkij* (**kikij**). 1(*-i*), 2(inf, tr *kiji*), 4, 5(*kkijkij*), 6(*-i*). Bite. *Etke kwōj kiji wōt peim̧ im einwōt niññiñ.* Why do you keep biting your hand like a baby?

kkijeje (**kkijęyjęy**). Dial. W: *ikkijeje* (**yikkijęyjęy**), E: *kūkjeje* (**kikjęyjęy**). 1(*-i*), 2, 4, 7. Tire easily; short winded. *Eļap aō kkijeje ļǫk raan kein.* I get tired quickly these days.

kkilparakrōk (**kkilpahrakręk**). Dial. W: *ikkilparakrōk* (**yikkilpahrakręk**), E: *kūkilparakrōk* (**kikilpahrakręk**). Distributive form of *kūrkūr* (**kirkir**).

kkim (**kkim**). 2(inf, tr *kimij(i)*), 7. Close parts, as bivalve; to close tight, as a clam shell. *Kwōn kimij mejān mejānwōd ņe.* Close that clam.

kkinaļnaļ (**kkinaļnaļ**). Dial. W: *ikkinaļnaļ* (**yikkinaļnaļ**), E: *kūknaļnaļ* (**kiknaļnaļ**). 2, 3(inf, tr *-e*), 4, 5(*kkinaļnaļ*), 6(*-i*), 7, 8, 9. Pricking sensation of body limbs.

kkodaṃdaṃ (**kkewdaṃdaṃ**). Dial. W: *ekkodaṃdaṃ* (**yekkewdaṃdaṃ**), E: *kōkodaṃdaṃ* (**kekewdaṃdaṃ**). Having a receding hairline; having a protruding forehead.

kkootantōn (**kkewetantęn**). Dial. W: *ekkootantōn* (**yekkewetantęn**), E: *kōkootantōn* (**kekewetantaęn**). Distributive form of *wōtan* (**wetan**).

kkor (**qqer**). Dial. W: *eokkor* (**yeqqer**), E: *kokor* (**qeqer**). 1(*-i*), 2(inf, tr *kore*), 7. Tie; wrap up; bandage.

kkorkor (**qqerqer**). Dial. W: *eokkorkor* (**yeqqerqer**), E: *kokorkor* (**qeqerqer**). Also *kkorkor* (**qqer°qer°**). 1(*-i*), 2, 3, 5, 7. Rattle; jingle; jangle; distributive form of *kor*. *Ta kaņe rej kkorkor ilo bōjǫ ņe aṃ?* What is that jingling in your pocket?

kkotaak (**kkęwtahak**). Dial. W: *ekkotaak* (**yękkęwtahak**), E: *kōkotaak* (**kękęwtahak**). 2(inf, tr *kotaake*), 4, 6(*-i*). Preempt. *Koṃwin jab kkotaak.* Don't try to take more than your share. *Iar kotaake bato eo.* I grabbed the bottle before anyone else could get to it.

kkǫbōl (**kkawbęl**). Dial. W: *ekkǫbōl* (**yekkawbęl**), E: *kōkǫbōl* (**kekawbęl**). 1(*-i*), 2(inf, tr *kǫbwile*), 4, 6(*-i*), 7. Rebuke; harass; find fault with. *Kwōn kǫbwile wōt im enaaj ṃṃan.* Keep after him and he'll straighten up.

kkǫǫl (**qqawal**). Dial. W: *eokkǫǫl* (**yeqqawal**), E: *kokǫǫl* (**qeqawal**). Also *kkwaal* (**kkawal**). 1(*-i*), 2(inf, tr *kǫǫl(e)*), 3, 4, 6(*-i*). Put a curse on; put a spell on someone; bewitch. *Lale rokǫǫle eok.* Be careful, they might put a curse on you. *Kwōn jab kkǫǫl.* Don't praise me too much or it will bring me bad luck. *Jab ṃōñā luublej bwe rōnaaj kǫǫle eok.* Don't eat in public or someone will cast a spell on you.

kkōb (**kkęb**). Dial. W: *ekkōb* (**yękkęb**), E: *kōkōb* (**kękęb**). 1(*-i*), 2, 3, 7. Blunt; dull. *Eļap an kkōb bakbōk e.* This knife is dull.

kkōbaba (**kkebahbah**). Dial. W: *ekkōbaba* (**yekkebahbah**), E: *kōkōbaba* (**kekebahbah**). From Engl. 1(*-a*), 2, 3. Smell of copper; distributive form of *kōba* (**kebah**). *Wōn in ekkōbaba?* Who smells like copper?

kkōl (**kkęl**). Dial. W: *ekkōl* (**yękkęl**), E: *kōkōl* (**kękęl**). 1(*-i*), 2, 3, 5(*kkōlkōl*), 7. Scared; afraid, warn. *Eļap aō kkōl in uwe ilo baļuun.* I am afraid of riding in planes. *Ear kakkōl eō.* He warned me.

kkōļjake (**kkęļjahkey**). Dial. W: *ekkōļjake* (**yękkęļjahkey**), E: *kōkōļjake* (**kękęļjahkey**). 1(*-i*), 2, 3, 7. Suspect; distrust; suspicion; hunch. *Ikkōļjake ñe e eo ear kǫǫt.* I suspect that he might be the one that stole.

kkōṃ (**kkeṃ**). Dial. W: *ekkōṃ* (**yekkeṃ**), E: *kōkōṃ* (**kekeṃ**). 1(*-i*), 2, 3(inf, tr *-e*), 6(*-i*), 8, 9. Brittle; fragile. *Kōjparok nien ut ņe bwe ekkōṃ.* Be careful with that vase because it's brittle.

kkōn (**kkęn**). Dial. W: *ekkōn* (**yękkęn**), E: *kōkōn* (**kękęn**). 1(*-i, kōnea-*), 2(inf, tr *kine*), 3, 4, 5(*kakkōnkōn*) 7. Invent; compose; improvise; ad lib; make do. *Ļeo ejeļā kkōn al ņe.* That fellow there can compose songs. *Elōñ al eņ ear kine.* He has composed many songs. *Wōn in ear kine al in.* Who composed this song? *Ear kine lio jeran.* He composed a song about his girlfriend. *Kkōnān al in.* He composed this song. *Eṃṃan kūrepe bwe ekkōn.* Making gravy is a good way to stretch food. *Ear kine ta eo en ba.* He ad libbed what he said. *Jej aikuj kakkōnkōn bwe ejako emaat raij e.* We need to eat slowly because the rice is almost gone.

kkōņak (**kkeņak**). Dial. W: *ekkōņak* (**yekkeņak**), E: *kōkōņak* (**kekeņak**). 1(*-i*), 2(inf, tr *kōņak(e)*), 3, 4, 5(*kkōņakņak*), 7, 8, 9. Wear; be surrounded by; to love. *Kwōn kakōņake ajri eņ.* Dress that child. *Ekōņaan kakkōņak ajri.* She likes to dress children. *Kwōn kōņake jokankan* *eņ*. Put on that dress. *Kwōmake ruṃwij in kkōṇak aṃ nuknuk*. It takes you an awfully long time to get dressed. *Ikōṇak eok*. I love you. *Ekkōṇakṇak ḷeeņ*. He has a roving eye.

kkōñ (kkęg). Dial. W: *ekkōñ* (yękkęg), E: *kōkōñ* (kękęg). 3, 6(-*i*). A plant, tree, *Terminalia litoralis*. Said to be poisonous (to goats). Used to be "draw" boils and as a mash on wounds (see *kotōl* (qętęl)).

kkōōrōr (kkęhęrhęr). Dial. W: *ekkōōrōr* (yękkęhęrhęr), E: *kōkōōrōr* (kękęhęrhęr). 1(-*i*), 2, 3. Smell of dead flesh.

kkōpāl (kkepal). Dial. W: *ekkōpal* (yekkepal), E: *kōkōpal* (kekepal). 1(-*i*), 2(inf, tr *kōpāle*), 4, 7. Voodoo; black magic; to curse; using black magic.

kkōpeļ (kkepeļ). Dial. W: *ekkōpeļ* (yekkepeļ), E: *kōkōpeļ* (kekepeļ). 1(-*i*), 2(inf, tr *kōpeļ(e)*), 3, 4, 7. Chase. *Rej kkōpeļ bao*. They are chasing chickens. *Rej kōpeļ(e) bao eņ*. They are chasing that chicken.

kkōr (kker). Dial. W: *ekkōr* (yekker), E: *kōkōr* (keker). 1(-*i*), 2, 3, 7. Watery; messy; sweaty; slimy; filthy; oozy.

kkōt (kket). Dial. W: *ekkōt* (yekket), E: *kōkōt* (keket). 1(-*i*), 2, 3, 4, 7. Strong; great capacity. *Eḷap an kkōt ḷeeņ*. That fellow is really strong. *Eḷap an kkōt wa eņ*. That canoe has a large capacity. *Ej kakkōt ilo jikuuḷ*. He works hard in school.

kkubōl (qqibel). Dial. W: *iukkubōl* (yiqqibel), E: *kukbōl* (qiqbel). 1(-*i*), 2(inf, tr *kubōl(e)*), 4, 7, 10(*kob*). Bend; snap up. *Kwōn kubōl mōk aḷaḷ ņe*. Please bend that piece of wood. *Rej kkubōl teekkiiñ*. They're bending the decking material. *Kwōn kubōltok tiin ņe*. Bend the tin (roofing) this way.

kkumarmar (qqiwmarmar). Dial. W: *iukkumarmar* (yikkiwmarmar), E: *kukmarmar* (qiqwmarmar). 1(-*i*), 2, 3. Smell of leaves of bushes.

kkumatmat (qqimatmat). Dial. W: *iukkumatmat* (yiqqimatmat), E: *kukmatmat* (qiqmatmat). Distributive form of *kwōdmat* (qedmat).

kkuṃliklik (qqiṃliklik). Dial. W: *iukkuṃliklik* (yiqqiṃliklik), E: *kukuṃliklik* (qiqiṃliklik). 1(-*i*), 2,

3(inf, tr -*i*), 4, 7, 8, 9. Hunchback; curved; bent over. *Kkuṃliklik eo uweoḷọk*. There goes the hunchback.

kkun (qqin). Dial. W: *iukkun* (yiqqin), E: *kukun* (qiqin). 1(-*i*), 2(inf, tr *kune*), 4, 5(*kkunkun*), 7. Extinguish; go out, of a light; put out a fire; deflate. *Ekun ḷaaṃ eo*. The lamp went out. *Kwōn kune ḷaaṃ ņe*. Extinguish that lamp. *Kwōn kune kijek ņe*. Put out that fire. *Waan kkun eo*. The fire truck. *Eokkunkun ḷaaṃ eņ*. That lamp is always going out.

kkure (qqiręy). Dial. W: *iukkure* (yiqqiręy), E: *kukure* (qiqiręy). 1(-*i*), 2, 3, 4, 5(*kkurere*), 6(-*i*), 7. Play; game; drama; sport. *Eokkurere ḷeeņ*. He's always playing. He's athletic.

kkuujuj (kkiwijwij). Dial. W: *ikkuujuj* (yikkiwijwij), E: *kukuujuj* (kikiwijwij). 1(-*i*), 2, 3. Smell of cats; distributive form of *kuuj* (kiwij).

kkuul (qqiwil). Dial. W: *iukkuul* (yiqqiwil), E: *kukuul* (qiqiwil). 2(inf, tr *kuul*), 4, 5(*kkukuul, kukuul*), 6(-*i*), 7. Grab, squeeze; choke; grasp; embrace; hold tight. *Ekuuli peiū im emetak*. My hand hurt when he squeezed it. *Eñak kkuul*. It can't grasp things with its hands. *Rukkuul bōro*. A chronic spouse stealer. *Koṃro ej kkuul ḷọk ñan ñāāt?* How long are you two going to embrace? *Kwōn jab kkukuul bao ņe*. Don't keep squeezing that bird.

kkuul bōro (kkiwil bęręw). 1, 2(inf, tr *kuul būruo-*), 4, 6(-*i*). Steal another's spouse; choke; strangle, to throttle. *Ear kuul būruon ḷeo jein*. He stole his brother's wife. *Rōkuul būrwōn im mej*. They strangled him to death.

kkūṃkūṃ (kkiṃkiṃ). Dial. W: *ikkūṃkūṃ* (yikkiṃkiṃ), E: *kūkūṃkūṃ* (kikiṃkiṃ). 1(-*i*), 2, 3, 4, 7, 8, 9. Fast beating of heart in fear; palpitation; nervous; afraid. *Ta ņe kwōj kkūṃkūṃ kake?* What is your heart beating so fast about?

kkūr (kkir). Dial. W: *ikkūr* (yikkir), E: *kūkūr* (kikir). 1(-*i*), 2(inf, tr *kūr(i)*), 4, 7. Call; crow; invitation; summon. *Kwōn kūri bwe en itok*. Call him to come. *Rej kkūr rūttariņae*. They're calling for soldiers. *Ej (ik)kūr kako eņ*. That rooster is crowing. *Raar kūr ke koṃ?* Were you invited?

kkūtbuuj (**kkitbiwij**). Dial. W: *ikkūtbuuj* (**yikkitbiwij**), E: *kūkūtbuuj* (**kikitbiwij**). From *kūtim* (**kitim**) "covering", *buuj* (**biwij**) "tie". 2(inf, tr *kūtbuuj(i)*), 3, 4, 7. To cover; tuck in. *Kwōn kūtbuuj ajri ņe kōn juon kọọj.* Cover that baby with a blanket.

kkwaad (**qqahad**). Dial. W: *eokkwaad* (**yeqqahad**), E: *kokwaad* (**qeqahad**). 2, 8, 9. Fade away; distant, of sight and sound. *Ear etal wa eo im kkwaad ļọk.* The boat departed and slowly went out of sight. *Eṃṃan aō roñjake aer al ak men eo, eokkwaad.* I loved their singing but the thing is the sounds seemed so distant.

kkwaļ (**qqaļ**). Dial. W: *eokkwaļ* (**yeqqaļ**), E: *kokwaļ* (**qeqaļ**). 1(*-i*), 2(inf, tr *-e*), 4, 7. Coconut sennit; cord made from coconut fibre; make sennit.

kkwanjinjin (**qqanjinjin**). Dial. W: *eokkwanjinjin* (**yeqqanjinjin**), E: *kokwanjinjin* (**qeqanjinjin**). 1(*-i*), 2, 7. Smell of roasting breadfruit. *Ia in ej (bwiin) kkwanjinjin tok?* Where is the smell of roasting breadfruit coming from?

kkweetet (**qqẹyẹtyẹt**). Dial. W: *eokkweetet* (**yẹqqẹyẹtyẹt**), E: *kokweetet* (**qẹqẹyẹtyẹt**). Vulgar. From *kweet* (**qẹyẹt**) "octopus". 2. Possessing control of vaginal muscles.

kkwelep (**qqeylep**). Dial. W: *eokkwelep* (**yeqqeylep**), E: *kokwelep* (**qeqeylep**). 1(*-i*), 2, 3. Coarse.

kkwidik (**qqiydik**). Dial. W: *iukkwidik* (**yiqqiydik**), E: *kukwidik* (**qiqiydik**). 1(*-i*), 2, 3(inf *kọkkwidikdik*, tr *kọkkwidiki*), 5(*kkwidikdik*), 6(*-i*), 8, 9. Fine, not coarse; fine, of grated coconut. *Kọkkwidiki aṃ raanke.* Grate that coconut fine. *Eokkwidikdik mejān ok eo.* That was a small-meshed net.

kkwōjarjar (**qqejarjar**). Dial. W: *eokkwōjarjar* (**yeqqejarjar**), E: *kokwōjarjar* (**qeqejarjar**). 1(*-i*), 2, 3, 4, 7, 8, 9. Holy; sanctified; righteous; pure; spotless; clean; divine; eminent; sacred; immaculate.

ko (**kew**). The (often for entities not present); demonstrative, remote plural nonhuman.

ko (**kew**). 1, 2(inf, tr *koon*), 3, 4, 5, 6, 7. To fly the coop; flee; run away. *Ij ko jān rūkadek raņ.* I'm running away from the drunkards. *Ear kako piik ko.* He freed the pigs. *Etao ear koļọk ñan Amedka.* Etao fled to America. *Eko juon rūkalbuuj.* A prisoner has flown the coop.

ko (**kew**). 6(*-i*). Tentacle; strand of rope or wire.

ko (ro) jet (**kew (rew) jet**). Rest; what is left; remainder. *Kwōnaaj iteen men kaņe jet.* What're you going to do with the rest?

ko tok kili- (**kew teq kili-**). 1, 2, 3. Goose pimples; chills; be embarrassed for. *Eko tok kilū kōn aṃ jaje ṃanit.* Your actions give me goose pimples. *Aṃ kōnnaan rot ņe ekakotok kilin.* Your language gives her the chills. *Eko tok kilū kōn mānōt kaņe aṃ.* I'm embarrassed for your behavior.

ko-in-aļ (**kew-yin-haļ**). Rays of the sun.

ko-in-kweet (**kew-yin-qẹyẹt**). Octopus tentacles.

kob (**qẹb**). 2, 6(*-i*), 7, 8, 9. Bent; curved; buckled; stooped. *Ekob ṃade eo aō.* My spear was bent.

koba (**kẹwbah**). 1(*-i*), 2(inf, tr *-ik*), 3(inf *kakkobaba*, tr *kakobaik*), 4, 7. Add; cohabit; put together; get together; betroth; combine; engaged; incorporate; integrate; involve; join; merged; mingle; plus; sum; unified; unite. *Eṃōj kakobaik erro.* They are now betrothed.

koba (**kewbah**). Dial. W only; see *bae* (**bahyey**). 3, 6(*-i*). Bamboo.

kobaak (**kẹwbahak**). Variant form of *kubaak* (**kiwbahak**).

kobak (**qebak**). 1, 2(inf, tr *-e*), 6(*-i*). Hem a dress; cuff; pleat. *Inaaj kobake nuknuk e bwe ekadik aitok.* I'll hem this dress because it is much too long.

kobal (**kewbal, qebal**). 3, 4+3, 6(*-i*), 3+7. A shell, *Neritipsidae*; *Neritipsis radula.*

kobal (**qebal**). 2(inf, tr *-e*), 4(*rukobal*), 6(*-i*), 7. Cover up an earth oven with leaves and dirt.

Kobal (**qebal**). Name of two navigational signs; turtles off *Wōja* islet of Ailinglapalap atoll.

kobba- (**qebba-**). 1, 7. Contents of. *Ta ņe kobban bọọk ņe?* What's in that box there?

kobbā (**qebbay**). 2, 8, 9. Voluminous. *Ekobbā ļọk aebōj jimāāņ e aō jān ņe* *aṃ.* My water cistern holds more water than yours.

koboob (**kewbeweb**). Variant form of *koobob* (**kewebweb**).

kodaaj (**kewdaaj**). Go away. *Ekodaajļǫk ļeo.* He went away.

kodia (**kẹwdiyah**). From Japn. *korya korya* "expression uttered when inebriated". 2, 4, 6(*-i*). Bottoms up; hard drinking. *Emoot ļōṃaro in kodia.* They've gone to do some serious drinking. *Kodia.* Bottom's up.

kojuwa (**kẹwjiwah**). 2, 4, 6(*-a*). A game, king of the mountain; (played on floating raft). *Jeañ ilān kojuwa.* Let's play king of the mountain.

kok-. See *kk-*.

koko (**kẹwkẹw**). 6(*-i*). A fish, dolphin, *Coryphoena hippurus.*

koko (**kẹwkẹw**). Also *koko* (**kewkew**), *koko* (**qẹwqẹw**), *koko* (**qewqew**). From Engl. 2, 3(inf, tr *-ik, -uk*), 6(*-i*). Cocoa; chocolate. *Kwōj idaak ke koko?* Would you like to drink chocolate?

koko (**kewkew**). Those (things distant but visible); demonstrative, remote plural nonhuman, singling out.

koko (**kewkew**). Also *koko* (**kẹwkẹw**). 1(*-i*), 2, 3, 4, 6(*-a*), 8, 9. Disease, scaly and flaky skin; ringworm. *Epen kōmour koko.* This skin disease (koko) is hard to cure.

koko (**kewkew**). Drink after or together with another; see *limenkoko. Jero nini koko.* Let's share this coconut.

kokōrā (**kewkeray**). 3, 6(*-i*). Female, of animals; see *kōrā.*

kokōro (**kewkerew**). From Japn. *kokoro*. Mind. *Ekōṃōjņǫ aō kokōro.* She's torturing my mind (words from a lovesong).

kolied (**kewliyed**). 1(*-i*), 2(inf, tr *-e*), 4. Eat one kind of food not usually eaten alone; chew tobacco. *Kwōn jab kolied jukwa.* Don't eat sugar without anything else.

kolōkabwi- (**kewlekabi-**). 1, 2, 3. Disenchanted; estranged; alienated. *Jipij eo an ekakolōkabwiier.* They were disenchanted by his speech.

koļa (**kẹwļah**). 3, 6(*-i*). Coke; cola; soft drink.

koļaṃṃwā (**qeļaṃṃay**). Also *baru eņ nejin Lijǫkkwe.* Archaic. A land crab.

koļap (**qeļap**). Loud; noisy; boisterous; big-mouth. *Ekoļap aṃ kōnnaan.* You have a big mouth.

koļeiaat (**qẹļẹyiyahat**). From Engl. *Goliath*. 1(*-i*), 2, 3, 4, 6(*-i*), 7. Nude; shirtless; bare; a food, preserved breadfruit boiled or baked without wrapping. *Koļeiaatin ia ņe kijeṃ?* Where did you get your *koļeiaat*?

Koļeiaat (**qẹļẹyiyahat**). Goliath.

koļmān (**qeļman**). Characteristic; typical. *Ear kako rūkeemem ro, koļmān Kaaļ.* He chased away the guests--you know Carl. *Ear jab keroro ñan jidik, koļmān.* It was just like him to remain absolutely quiet.

komen (**kewmen**). From Engl. *corpsman*. 2, 6(*-i*). Corpsman; health aide. *Ej komen Mājro.* He works as a corpsman on Majuro.

koṃ (**qẹṃ**). Dial. W, E: *kōmi* (**kemiy**). You; plural; pronoun, absolute and object, second person plural.

koṃ make (**qẹṃ makẹy**). Yourselves.

koṃa (**qeṃah**). From Engl. 2(inf, tr *-ik*),5(*kkoṃaṃa*). Comma.

koṃaan (**kewṃahan**). 3, 6(*-i*). Male, of animals; see *ṃṃaan.*

koṃaaņta (**qeṃahaņtah**). From Engl. Commandant; commander.

koṃbani (**qeṃbaniy**). From Engl. Company, business usage; outfit.

koṃbani (**qeṃbaniy**). From Engl. 2. Buddy; friend; fellowship; partner. *Ej ilān idaak ippān koṃbani eņ an.* He's going out drinking with his buddy.

koṃja (**qeṃjah**). From Germ. *Kommissar*. 2, 6(*-i*). Head of a governmental organization; magistrate; District Administrator; Educational Administrator; District Director of Education.

koṃlaļ (**qẹṃlaļ**). 3, 5(*kkoṃlaļlaļ*), 7. Valley, depression; groove. *Eokkoṃlaļlaļ eoojin ānin.* There are lots of valleys in the interior of this islet.

koṃṃool (**qeṃṃewel**). Thank you.

koṃro (**qeṃrew**). Dial. W only; see *kōmiro* (**kemiyrew**). You, two persons.

kona (**kewnah**). From Engl. 6(*-i*). Corner. *Epād ilo kona eņ.* It's in the corner over there.

kona (**kewnah**). Slang. 1(*-i*), 2(inf, tr *-ik*), 3, 4, 5(*kkonana*), 7. Snitch; sneak away from; hide from work; malingering. *Rej kona jān aer jerbal.* They are goofing off from their work. *Iar konaik peen e aō.* I snitched this pen. *Erro ar kona.* They had a tryst. *Ekkonana ļeeņ.* That man always sneaks away. *Ej riab naññinmej bwe en kona.* He's malingering.

koņ (**qeņ**). 1(*-i*), 2, 3, 7. Tight; well-organized; fit; orderliness; orderly; safe; secured; compact. *Eļap an koņ lowaan ṃweeņ.* Everything is neatly arranged in that house. *Eļap an koņ būrokraaṃ eo.* The program was well planned. *Eļap an koņ kōtaan rā kaņ.* Those boards are fit together well. *En koņ ke ņa ijeņe?* Is it safe for it to stay there?

koņ (**qeņ**). Concurrence; agreement; compact, contract. *Enaaj or juon koņ kāāl ikōtaan Amedka im aelōñ kein.* There will be a new agreement made between the U. S. and these islands.

koņa- (**qeņa-**). 1. A catch of fish, crabs, or birds; possessive classifier, fish, crabs, or birds.

koņaa- (**qeņaha-**). Dialectal variant of *kuņaa-* (**qiņaha-**).

koņak (**kewņak**). Greed.

koņkoņ (**qeņqeņ**). 1(*-i*), 2, 4, 7. Able to catch many fish. *Eļap an koņkoņ ļeeņ ñe ej eoñōd.* He catches a lot of fish when he goes fishing.

koņkōtaa- (**qeņketaha-**). 1. Harmony; reconciled. *Ekoņ kōtaerro raan kein.* There's harmony between the two of them these days.

koñil (**kewgil**). From *ko* (**kew**) "flee". 1, 2, 4, 6(*-i*), 7, 8, 9. Run away far after losing a fight or because afraid; alienated. *Joñan aer koñil, raar jab bar rọọl.* The extent of their alienation was such that they didn't return.

koob (**keweb**). Variant form of *koub* (**kẹwib**).

koobob (**kewebweb**). Also *koboob* (**kewbeweb**). 1, 2(inf, tr *kobaj*), 4, 6(*-i*), 7, 9. Squeeze into a seat; occupy a lot of space; come very close. *Jab koobob.* Don't try to sit here cause there's no room. *Raar kooboblọk ņa ilowaan kaar jidikdik eo.* They squeezed into the small car. *Jab kepaake bwe kwōnaaj kobaje.* Don't go too close or you'll get in his way.

koobub (**kewebwib**). Eat raw fish.

koodpak (**kẹwẹdpak**). Variant form of *kọudpak* (**kawidpak**).

kooj (**kewej**). From Engl. *course*. 6(*-i*). Nautical course; academic course.

kooļ (**kẹwẹļ**). From Engl. Gold.

kooļ (**qeweļ**). 1(*-a, -i*), 5(*kooļoļ, kkooļoļ, kkooļoļe*), 6(*-i*), 7+5. Hair; feather. *Eokkooļoļ ļeeņ.* He's covered with hair trimmings.

kooļjejeļ (**keweļjeyjeļ**). Also *koorjejeļ* (**kewerjeyjeļ**). From Engl. 2(inf, tr *-e*), 4, 6(*-i*), 7. Cold chisel. *Kwōn kooļjejeļe tūraṃ ņe.* Cut up that drum with the cold chisel.

kooļoļ (**qeweļweļ**). From *kooļ* (**qeweļ**). 2, 3, 4, 6. Be hairy. *Ekooļoļ ļeeņ.* He is hairy.

koon (**kẹwẹn**). 3, 6(*-i*). Young birds or animals; squab. *Koon in kau.* Calf.

koonaļ (**kewenhaļ**). 5(*kkoonaļaļ*), 6(*-i*). Sunray; sunbeam. *Ñe ej det em ṃṃan lañ, ekkoonaļaļ buļōn lọjet.* When the weather is good and the sun is shining, one sees sun rays in the ocean.

koonțōreak (**keweņteryak**). From Engl. Contract.

kooral (**qewerhal**). 2(inf, tr *-e*), 4, 6(*-i*), 7. Fishing method, occasional jerking of line to lure a fish to the bait or jig. *Kwōn koorale wōt bwe enañin pen wōt jidik.* Keep jerking the line because pretty soon you'll feel it hooked.

koorjejeļ (**kewerjeyjeļ**). Variant form of *kooļjejeļ* (**keweļjeyjeļ**).

koorļọk (**kewerļaq**). From *orļọk* (**werļaq**). 1(*-i*), 2(inf, tr *-e*), 3, 7. Multiply; increase.

koot (**kewet**). From Engl. 3, 6(*-i*). Goat.

kopā (**kewpay**). 1(*-i*), 2, 3, 4, 5(*kkopāpā*), 6(*-i*), 7. Coat; jacket; overcoat. *Aolep iien ej kkopāpā.* He always wears a coat.

kopāp (**kewpap**). 2, 3(inf, tr *-e*), 4, 6(*-i*), 7. Wrestle. *Erro ar kopāp ļọk oom ar.* The two of them wrestled all the way up to the lagoon shore.

Koperwa (**kewperwah**). 3, 6(*-i*). A plant, pandanus cultigen.

kor (**qẹr**). 1(*-i*), 2, 3(inf *kọkkorkor*, tr *kọkor*), 5(*kkorkor*), 6(*-i*), 8, 9. Frightened; afraid; scared; terrified; dread; fear; horror; intimidated. *Ekor in uwe ilo baļuun.* He's afraid to fly on planes. *Kwōn jab riab em kọkore.* Don't lie just to scare him. *Kain rot m̧m̧aan ke eokkorkor.* What kind of a man is he that gets scared so easily? *Em̧ōj ṇe am̧ kkorkor.* Why don't you stop being frightened all the time.

kor (**qer**). 2, 3(inf *kọkkorkor*, tr *kọkorrōḷọk*), 5(*kkorkor*), 7(*korrōḷọk*). Crunch; rattle. *Ekorrōḷọk aḷaḷ eo iar juri.* The twig crunched under my weight. *Ta kaṇe rej kkorkor ilowaan bọọk ṇe.* What's rattling in the box?

kor (**qer**). Also *kor* (**qẹr**). 6(*kurōn*). Coconut shell for catching coconut sap, whole and empty. *Kurkure kor ṇe m̧okta jān am̧ kōjerbale.* Wash out the *kor* before you use it. *Kurōn ni eṇ aō men ṇe.* That's a *kor* for my coconut tree.

kor (**qẹr**). 6(*kurōn*). Abandoned unhatched egg, usually spoiled. *Kurōn lọlọọt ṇe?* Which hen left that egg unhatched?

koraal (**kẹwrahal**). 2(inf, tr *-e*), 4, 6(*-i*), 7. Pull fishing line rhythmically while trolling. *Kwōn koraale wōt bwe en m̧ōñā.* Keep pulling it to get a bite.

korak (**qerak**). 1(*-i*), 2(inf, tr *-e, kor(e)*), 3, 4, 6(*-i*), 7. Tie; wrap up; bandage; perfective form of *kwarkor* (**qarqẹr**); band; bond; shoestring knot. *Ta ṇe kwōj korake?* What are you wrapping up? *Em̧ōj ke am̧ korake pakij eo?* Have you wrapped the package yet? *Etūm̧ korak eo kōtaerro.* The bond that tied them together is severed. *Kwōn kore kinej ṇe neem̧ bwe eḷọñḷọñ.* Cover up your wound from the flies. *Korak in juuj.* Shoestring.

Korak-eṇ-an-Tūm̧ur (**qerak-yeṇ-han-tim̧ir°**). A constellation; stars in Scorpius; nu, beta, delta, pi, ro; the (hair)knot of *Tūm̧ur.*

korap (**qerap**). 3, 5(*kkoraprap*), 6(*-i*). An animal, kind of lizard, gecko, *Lepidodactylus pelagicus* or *Hemiphyllodactylus typus. Eokkoraprap tōrak in m̧wiin.* The ceiling of this house has lots of geckos.

korap kūro (**qerap kirẹw**). An animal, kind of lizard, big tree gecko, *Gehyra oceanica.*

kore (**qerey**). Transitive form of *kkor* (**qqer**).

korjak (**qẹrjak**). Vulgar. 2, 3, 5(*kkorjakjak*), 6, 8, 9. Circumcised.

korkor (**qerqer**). Bandaged, tied up, wrapped up; perfective form of *kwarkor* (**qarqẹr**).

koro (**qerew**). Variant form of *kōro* (**kerew**).

Korōjjaak (**qerejjahak**). 3, 6(*-i*). A plant, pandanus cultigen (Takeuchi).

korōt (**qeret**). 2, 3, 5(*kkorōtrōt*), 8, 9. Burn, of eyes; smart, irritated; slimy. *Eokkorōtrōt buḷōn meja.* My eyes smart.

kotaake (**kẹwtahakey**). Transitive form of *kkotaak* (**kkẹwtahak**).

kotak (**kewtak**). 1(*-i*), 2(inf, tr *-e*), 5(*kkotaktak*), 7. Lift; raise; jack up. *Em̧ōj kotak ḷọk oṇāān m̧weiuk.* The price of goods has gone up.

kotin (**qetin**). From Engl. *cotton*. 3, 6(*-i*). A plant, *Gossypium barbadense* L. (Malvaceae). Barbados cotton. Also, *Ceiba pentandra* (L.) Gaertn., the "kapok" tree. (Bombacaceae).

kotin (**qetin**). From Engl. 3, 5(*kkotintin*), 6(*-i*). Cotton.

kotōl (**qẹtel**). 3, 6(*-i*). A plant, *Terminalia catappa* L. (Combretaceae). The Indian Almond. Introd. The young leaves are commonly reddish; or red-veined; similar to the young leaves of *Barringtonia* but more rugose and different in shape. Note: another species of *Terminalis*, *T. Littoralis* Seemann; is called *kkōñ.*

kotūbtūb (**kewtibtib**). 1(*-i*), 2, 7. Return to fight again after having been repulsed.

Kou (**kẹwiw**). Also *Kounmaañ* (**kẹwinmahag**). A plant, probably *Pandanus fischerianus* cultigen; variant name for *Wūnmaañ. Used only for leaves (textile materials).*

koub (**kẹwib**). Also *koob* (**keweb**). 2(inf, tr *-e*), 4, 6(*-i*), 7. To puff a cigarette; inhale. *Ij jañin jeḷā koub.* I haven't learned to inhale.

koubub (**kẹwibwib**). 1(*-i*), 2(inf, tr *-i*), 3, 4, 6(*-i*), 8, 9. A food, fish eaten half broiled but still raw; half-done, of fish or meat. *Ennọ koububin jojo.* Lightly broiled flying fish are delicious. *Kwōn koububi tok m̧ōk ek ṇe.* Would you please broil that fish lightly for me. *Ennọ koubub m̧ōlm̧ōl.* Mackerel is good when only slightly cooked. *Kwōn koububi ek ṇe kijem̧.* Don't cook your fish too well.

koudpak (**kewidpak**). Variant form of *kǫudpak* (**kawidpak**).

kouj (**kẹwij**). Also *kouj* (**qẹwij**). 3, 6(-*i*). A fish, devilfish, giant octopus.

Kouj (**kẹwij**). A constellation; stars in Orion; iota, upsilon, and 49 form the head of this giant octopus, while eta, 27, psi 1, psi 2, 32, 52, etc. as the tentacles embrace the stone axe (*Jiljil*) which has killed it.

Kounm̧aan̄ (**kẹwinm̧ahag**). Variant form of *Kou* (**kẹwiw**).

kowa (**qẹwwah**). Also *uwa*. 2, 3(inf, tr *kōkowaik*), 6(-*i*), 8, 9. Fruit-laden. *Ekowa wōt in āne.* This island is full of fruit. *Ear kōkowaik m̧ā eo kōtkan wiik eo ļọk.* He treated his breadfruit tree last week so that it would bear more fruit.

kowadon̄ (**kewwadeg°**). 1, 2(inf, tr -*e*), 4, 6(-*i*). Rob; extort; murder; slay; assassinate. *Ear kowadon̄e lōļļap eo.* He robbed the old lady. *Rej pukot rūkowadon̄ eo.* They're looking for the robber. *Raar kowadon̄e ke ej kiki.* He was murdered in his sleep.

kowainini (**kewwahyiniyniy**). 1(-*i*), 2(inf, tr -*ik*), 4, 6(-*i*), 7. Make copra; harvest coconuts.

kowak (**kẹwwak**). Also *kowak* (**kewwak**). Curlew.

kowak (**kewwak**). A bird, whimbrel, *Numenius phaeopus*.

kowaļǫk (**kewwahļaq**). Also *kwaļok* (**qahļeq**). From *waļǫk* (**wahļaq**). 1(-*i*), 2(inf, tr *kowaļǫk, kwaļok*), 4, 7. Show; declare; reveal; preach; proclaim; expose; express; imply; indicate; locate. *Em̧m̧an an kowaļǫk naan.* He speaks well. *Kwaļǫk m̧ōk.* How about showing it to me.

kowawa (**kewahwah**). 2(inf, tr -*ik*), 6(-*a*), 7. Stand; cross the legs; prop up. *Ear kowawaik rā ko ioon kein ni eo.* He laid the boards up against the log. *Ripālle rej kowawa ne n̄e rej jijet.* Americans cross their legs when sitting.

kowāelel (**kewwayẹlyẹl**). Variant form of *wālel* (**waylẹl**).

kǫ (**kaw**). Fetus; embryo; stillborn baby. *Ear kōmmour kǫ bon̄.* She gave birth to a fetus last night.

kǫbaj (**kawbaj**). Push out; banish; expel.

kǫbōk (**kawbek**). 1, 2(inf, tr -*e*), 3, 6(-*i*). Wrestle; horse around. *Erro ar kǫbōk.* They were horsing around. *Iar kǫbōke likao eo rilikū.* I wrestled with my cousin. *Ear kōkǫbōke bo ro.* He made the twins wrestle.

kǫbwile (**kawbiley**). Transitive form of *kkǫbōl* (**kkawbẹl**).

kǫde (**kawdẹy**). A fish.

kǫje- (**kawje-**). Also *kǫjee-* (**kawjeye-**). 1(-*i*), 6(-*i*). Blanket of; possessive classifier, blankets and other things used as blankets. *Kǫjeō men ṇe.* That's my blanket.

kǫjek (**kawjẹk**). 1(-*i*), 2, 3, 7. Caught on a hook; get hooked. *Ekǫjek ek eo.* The fish is hooked. *Ekǫjek.* He got hooked.

kǫjek (**kawjek**). Transitive form of *kǫǫjoj* (**kawajwẹj**).

kǫkkoṇkoṇ (**kaqqeṇqeṇ**). 1(-*i*), 2(inf, tr *kǫkoṇ(i), kǫkoṇ(e)*), 4, 7. Put things away; put things in place; hoard. *Em̧ōj aō kǫkoṇ lowaan kōban̄ e aō.* I have straightened up the contents of my suitcase. *Em̧ōj ke an kǫkkoṇkoṇ?* Has he put things away? *Rej kǫkkoṇkoṇ pijin kwiir.* They're hoarding toilet paper.

kǫkkorōjrōj (**kaqqerejrej**). 1(-*i*), 2(inf, tr -*e*), 3. Shake a liquid so that it gurgles. *Kǫkkorōjrōje waini ṇe.* Shake that copra nut to see if it gurgles.

kǫkkure (**kaqqirey**). 1(-*i*), 2, 4, 5(*kǫkkurkure*), 7, 8, 9. To destroy; spoil; injure; demolish; ruin. *Em̧ōj aer kǫkkure jikin kweilǫk eo.* They completely demolished the city. *Jab kǫkkurkure bwe enaaj baj m̧m̧aan juon raan.* Don't harass him for he'll grow up someday.

kǫkkwidikdik (**kaqqiydikdik**). Vulgar. 4, 6(-*i*). Sexual technique; short, fast deliberate movements.

kǫkleejej (**qaqleyejyej**). Run at full speed.

kǫkoṇ (**kaqeṇ**). Transitive form of *kǫkkoṇkoṇ* (**kaqqeṇqeṇ**).

kǫkǫ (**kawkaw**). Vulgar. 6(-*i*). Penis, child speech; pet name for male child.

kǫkwe (**qaqẹy**). 3, 6(-*i*). Parrot.

kǫkwe (**qaqẹy**). 1, 2(inf, tr -*ik*), 5(*kkǫkwekwe*), 6(-*i*). Wear hair in bangs. *Ear kǫkweik bōran.* She combed her hair toward the front. *Eokkǫkwekwe bōran jiron̄ eṇ.* That young lady always wears bangs.

kǫkweet (**kaqęyęt**). 2, 6(-*i*), 7. Dive, of boats. *Ekǫkweet wa eo.* The boat's bow went under.

kǫkwōle (**kaqeley**). 2(inf, tr -*ik*), 4, 6(-*i*), 7. Castrate. *Eṃōj an kǫkwōle piik ṇe.* That pig has been castrated.

kǫkwōpej (**kaqępęj**). 2(inf, tr -*e*, *kǫkwōpije*), 4, 6(-*i*). Deselect; sort out. *Raar kǫkwōpeje ine ko.* They sorted the seeds.

kǫmijen. See *kwamijen*.

kǫnōt (**kawnet**). 3, 6(-*i*). A shell, small bivalve, clam.

kǫnōt (**kawnet**). Dialectal variant of *kalibok* (**kahliybęq**).

kǫob (**kaweb**). From *ob* "chest". Wrestle chest to chest.

kǫor (**kawęr**). Also *kawor*. Dialectal variant of *kalwor* (**kalwęr**).

kǫǫj (**kawaj**). 1(-*e*, -*ee*), 2(inf *kǫǫjoj*, tr *kǫjek*), 3, 6(-*e*, -*ee*). Blanket. *Kokōṇaan ke kǫjeke kǫǫj ṇe kǫǫjerro?* Would you like to use my blanket? *Ta ṇe kwōj kǫǫjoj kake?* What are you using for a blanket?

kǫǫjoj (**kawajwęj**). From *kǫǫj* (**kawaj**). 1(-*i*), 2(inf, tr *kǫje(e)*, *kǫjik(e)*), 3(inf, *(ka)kǫǫjoj*, tr *(ka)kǫǫjoj(e)*), 6(-*i*), 7. Use a blanket. *Ta ṇe kwōj kǫjeke?* What are you using for a blanket? *Eṃakoko in kǫǫjoj.* He doesn't want to use a blanket. *Kwōn kakǫǫjoje niñniñ ṇe.* Put a blanket around the baby.

kǫǫl (**qawal**). Transitive form of *kkǫǫl* (**qqawal**).

kǫǫn (**kawan**). From Engl. *corn*. 6(-*i*). Corn.

kǫǫnjeļ (**kawanjeļ**). From Engl. 2(inf, tr -*e*), 4, 6(-*i*). Council; deliberate; discuss. *Ta eṇ rej kǫǫnjeļe?* What are they deliberating? What are they discussing?

kǫǫnpiip (**kawanpiyip**). From Engl. 3, 5(*kkǫǫnpiipip*), 6(-*i*). Corned beef. *Ekkǫǫnpiipip iiōk eṇ.* That concoction is replete with corned beef.

kǫǫt (**kawat**). 1(-*i*), 2(inf, tr *kǫǫtte*, -*e*), 3, 4, 5(*kkǫǫtot*), 7, 8, 9, 11(*kǫǫtot*). Steal; burglarize; fraud; swindle; swipe; pilfer. *Addi kǫǫtot.* Index finger. (The stealing finger). *Kǫǫt eo ṇe.* That's the burglar.

kǫpe (**kawpęy**). From Engl. 1(-*i*), 2(inf, tr -*ik*), 3, 4, 5(*kkǫpepe*), 6(-*i*), 7. Coffee. *Ekkǫpepe tebōļ ṇe.* There is coffee all over that table there.

kǫpe jǫǫb (**kawpęy jawab**). From Engl. *coffee shop*. Restaurant. *Kōjro etal ñan kǫpe jǫǫb eṇ an Jera.* Let's go to Jera's restaurant.

kǫrōj (**kawrej**). From Engl. Chorus; a musical composition to be sung by all singers together.

kǫto (**kawtęw**). Northeast trade wind. *Kǫto iūñin aļ.* North northeast trade. *Kǫto irūkin aļ.* East northeast trade.

kǫudpak (**kawidpak**). Also *koudpak* (**kewidpak**), *koodpak* (**kęwędpak**). 1(-*i*), 2(inf, tr -*e*), 7. Peel off the end of a coconut shoot. *Eṃōj ke aṃ kǫudpake utak eṇ?* Did you peel off the end of that coconut shoot?

kǫuwe (**kawiwęy**). Also *kauwe*. Dialectal variant of *ṃōļojetak* (**ṃęļęwjeytak**).

kǫwiinin (**kawwiyinyin**). Also *kauwiinin*, *kǫuwiinin*. Award; prize; trophy. *Wōn eo ebōk kǫwiinin eo?* Who received the award?

kōb (**kęb**). 1(-*i*), 2(inf, tr *kūbwij(i)*), 4, 7. Dig. *Jen kūbwij juon rǫñ.* Let's dig a hole. *Ļōṃaro raṇ rej kōb.* Those men are digging.

kōb (**kęb**). Drinking water containers on a canoe or boat. *Eṃōj ke kanni kōb ko an wa ṇe.* Have the water containers for your boat been filled?

kōba (**kebah**). From Engl. *copper*. 3, 5(*kkōbaba*), 6(-*a*). Copper. *Ke raar wia kōba, aolep riānin raar kōkōba.* When copper (scrap) was being bought, everyone on this island went looking for copper.

kōba (**kebah**). Slang. 3, 4+3, 6(-*i*), 7. Old flame; easy woman. *Eṃōj ṇe aṃ kōkōba bwe an rūkien kwe.* Stop chasing women because you are married.

kōbaajjie- (**kebahajjiye-**). Variant form of *kajjie-* (**kajjiye-**).

kōbaatat (**kebahathat**). 1(-*i*), 2, 3, 4, 7. To smoke.

kōbañ (**kebag**). 6(-*i*). Suitcase; luggage.

kōbba (**kebbah**). Variant form of *kabba* (**kabbah**).

kōbbaal (**kebbahal**). 2, 4, 6(-*i*), 7. Forecast weather by observing clouds. *Kwōn kōbbaal tok ñan kōjro bwe kwōjaad jeļā iaarro.* Go ahead and predict the weather for us since you know more about clouds than I do.

kōbbat (**kebbat**). From *bbat* (**bbat**) "late". 2, 4, 6(*-i*). Preempt. *Erro ej kōbbat doon.* They are trying to get ahead of each other (while pursuing identical goals).

kōbbaturtur (**kebbatir°tir°**). From *batur* (**batir°**). 2, 4, 6(*-i*). Stop craving fish. *Lewaj eo kein aṃ kōbbaturtur.* Here's a fish to free you from your craving for one.

Kōbbok (**kębbęq**). A plant, pandanus cultigen; Rongelap and Kwajalein.

kōbbǫk (**kebbaq**). From *bbǫk* (**bbaq**). 2(inf, tr *-e*), 6(*-i*). Pompadour.

kōbbǫjǫj (**kebbawajwaj**). From *bǫǫj* (**bawaj**). 1(*-i*), 2(inf, tr *-e*), 4, 8, 9. Overbearing; be bossy; arrogant. *Kōm dike bwe ekōbbǫjǫj.* We don't like him because of his overbearing manners.

kōbbōkakkak (**kebbekakkak**). 2, 6(*-i*), 8, 9. Extraordinary healing powers, as in Marshallese native medicine. *Ekōbbōkakkak an wūno.* His medicines are extraordinarily strong.

kōbkōb (**kębkęb**). 2, 3(inf, tr *-e*), 6(*-i*), 8, 9. Digging of feet or tires into soft sand. *Ekōbkōbe arin Emejwa.* The lagoon beach of Emejwa Island is difficult to walk on.

kōbo (**kębęw**). Forever. *Jined ilo kōbo, jemād im jemān ro jet.* Our mothers forever; our fathers and the fathers of others. (A proverb extolling the matrilineal relation).

kōbobo (**kebewbew**). 1(*-i*), 2(inf, tr *kōbooj(e)*), 4, 7. Tie; fasten. *Enañin kōbobo ke wōjḷā eṇ?* Hasn't the sail been fastened yet? *Kwōn kōbobooj wōjḷā eṇ.* Fasten that sail.

kōbodān (**kebewdan**). Variant form of *kabodān* (**kabęwdan**).

kōbooj (**kebewej**). Transitive form of *kōbobo* (**kebewbew**).

kōbotuut (**kębęwtiwit**). 2, 6(*-i*), 7. Sniff, inhale, breathe. *Jeban kōbotuut turun rimej eo.* We couldn't breathe near the corpse.

kōbǫrōk (**kebawręk**). 1(*-i*), 2(inf, tr *-e, kōbǫrūke*), 4, 6(*-i*). Preserve; embalm. *Raar kōbǫrōke ānbwinnin.* His corpse was embalmed. *Mā kōbǫrōk.* Preserved breadfruit.

kōbǫur (**kebawir**). Causative form of *bǫbo* (**bawbęw**).

kōbǫuwe (**kebawiwęy**). Also *kōbauwe.* 1, 2, 4, 6(*-i*). Debate; argue; deliberate. *Raar kōbǫuwe kake an Amedka pād Pietnaaṃ.* They debated on America's presence in Viet Nam.

kōbōj (**kębęj**). Pole for poling in shallow water.

kōbōjbōj (**kębęjbęj**). 1(*-i*), 2(inf, tr *-e, kōbōjbwije*), 3, 4, 7. Poling in shallow water with a pole. *Kwōn poon wa ṇe im kōbōjbōj.* Put the sail on your canoe down and pole. *Ta ṇe kwōj kōbōjbōje wa ṇe kake?* What are you poling the canoe with?

kōbōjbōj (**kębęjbęj**). Slang. 1(*-i*), 2, 4, 7. Give gift to win favor, to opposite sex.

kōbwābwe (**kebaybęy**). Also *kaṃōṃō* (**kaṃehṃeh**). From *bwā* (**bay**) "fish pole". 1(*-i*), 2(inf, tr *-ik*), 4, 7. Fishing method, fish with a pole.

kōbwebwei- (**kębęybęyi-**). 1. Building materials; outfit; paraphernalia.

kōd (**ked**). Vulgar. 1(*-e*). Vagina.

kōdālōb (**kedaleb**). Also *kōddalōb* (**keddaleb**). 2(inf, tr *-e*), 4, 6(*-i*). Swallow; to bolt one's food.

kōddāpilpil (**keddapilpil**). 2(inf, tr *-i*), 4, 6(*-i*), 7. Fishing method, use hand line from canoe in deep ocean for fish other than tuna. *Elōñ rūkōdāpilpil rej eọñōd ilik.* There are a lot of fishermen doing the *kōddāpilpil* method of fishing.

kōdǫ (**kedaw**). 5(*kkōdǫdo*), 6(*-i*). Cloud; overcast. *Ekkōdǫdo rainin.* Today is cloudy.

kōdǫ jutak (**kedaw jiwtak**). From *kōdǫ* (**kedaw**) "cloud", *jutak* (**jiwtak**) "stand". Cumulus cloud.

kōj (**kęj**). We (incl.); us; (incl.); pronoun, absolute and object; first person plural inclusive.

kōj (**kęj**). Share of food; ration.

kōja (**kejah**). 1(*-a*), 6(*-a*), 7. Leeward side of a canoe; port side (see *retam* (**reytam**)).

kōjab (**kejab**). 1(*-i*), 2(inf, tr *-e*), 4, 7. To be on both sides; witness in marriage ceremony; stand beside.

kōjaij (**kejahyij**). Also *kōjāij* (**kejayij**). From *jaij* (**jahyij**). 1(*-i*), 2, 3(*kōkōjaij(i)*), 4, 5(*kkōjaijij*), 7, 8, 9. Beautiful; knock-out, pretty; handsome; good looking. *Nuknuk ṇe ṇe* *ekōkōjaij(i) eok liiō.* That dress merely makes you look pretty. You're only pretty because of that dress. *Ekkōjaijij an ttoṇ.* Her smile is captivating.

kōjak (**kejak**). 1(-*i*), 2, 4, 5(*kkōjakjek*), 7, 8, 9. Make fun; to joke; to kid; funny; clown; grotesque; humor; outlandish; strange; ridiculous. *Kwōn jab kōṃṃan kōjak?* Don't make jokes. *Ej kkōjakjek.* He makes jokes.

kōjakkōlkōl (**kejakkẹlkẹl**). 2. Disguise; camouflage. *Ear kōjakkōlkōl e make em lọk ñan pade eo.* He disguised himself and went to the party.

kōjaṃṃōk (**kejaṃṃek**). Interjection: "How about that!"

kōjañjañ (**kejagjag**). 1(-*i*), 2(inf, tr *kōjañ*), 3, 4, 6(-*i*), 7. Play music; musical instrument. *Kwōn kōjañ juon alin kaubowe.* Play a cowboy song. *Kōjañjañin ia ṇe nājiṃ?* Where did your instrument come from?

kōjat (**kejat**). 6(-*i*). A bird, found on Midway Island.

kōjatdikdik (**kejatdikdik**). 1(-*i*), 2, 3, 4, 7. Hope; potential.

kōjato (**kejatew**). 1(-*i*), 2, 3, 4, 7. Take shelter from the rain or sun. *Jen kōjato bwe ewōt.* Let's take shelter because it's raining.

kōjāl (**kejal**). Transitive form of *kōjjāl*.

kōjālli- (**kejalli-**). 1. Appearance; looks; description; figure (used negatively). *Enana kōjāllin.* She's homely. *Ein kōjāllin wōt ṃōrō.* He looks like a criminal.

kōjām (**kejam**). 1(-*i*), 6(-*i*). Door; doorway; entrance; gate.

kōjbar (**kẹjbar**). 3, 6(-*i*). A plant, *Ochrosia oppositifolia* (Lam.) K. Schum. (Apocynaceae). A large, glossy-leaved tree, with milky sap, white flowers, and fruits somewhat the shape of a small mango; but green.

kōjbwe (**kejbey**). Also *jebwebwe.* Steer.

kōjdat (**kẹjdat**). Also *akōjdat* (**hakẹjdat**). 1(-*i*), 2(inf, tr -*e*), 3, 4, 7. Hate; animosity; enemy; scorn. *Eḷap aō kōjdate eok.* I hate you very much. *Kwōn iọkwe aṃ rūkōjdat.* Love your enemies.

kōjea- (**kẹjẹya-**). Also *kōjeea-* (**kẹjẹyya-**), *kōjeiie-* (**kejẹyiye-**). 1. Comfort; condition; disposition. *Enana kōjeān.* He's uncomfortable. *Eṃṃan kōjeān an kiki laḷ.* He's comfortable sleeping on the floor. *Kōṃanṃan kōjeāmi ṇai ṃōṇe.* Make yourselves comfortable at the house.

kōjebare (**kejebarey**). Transitive form of *kōjjebar* (**kejjebar**).

kōjeek (**kejeyek**). Transitive form of *kōjeje* (**kejeyjey**).

kōjeje (**kejeyjey**). 1(-*i*), 2(inf, tr *kōjeek*), 3, 4, 7. Dry under sun; to sun; sunbathe. *Waini ko kaṇ rej kōjeje.* Those copra nuts are drying under the sun. *Kwōn kōjeek waini kaṇ.* Dry those copra nuts.

kōjelbabō (**kejelbahbẹh**). Also *kōjelbabo* (**kejelbahbẹw**). 1(-*i*), 2, 4, 7, 8, 9. Disregard; be careless; disobey; to risk. *Kwōn jab kōjelbabō im kadek bwe emọ aṃ kadek.* Don't disobey and get drunk, because it's forbidden for you to get drunk.

kōjerrā (**kejerray**). 2(inf, tr -*ik*), 6, 7. To carry things on hips. *Letok in kōjerrāiki.* Let me carry it. *Ear kōjerrāiktok iep eo.* He carried the basket over to me.

kōjjaad (**kejjahad**). 1(-*i*), 2(inf, tr -*e*), 4, 7. Observe; spy; lie in wait for; peek; peep. *Ta ṇe kwōj kajjaade?* What are you spying on?

kōjjaaḷaḷ (**kejjahaḷhaḷ**). 2(inf, tr -*e*), 4, 6(-*i*), 7. Wag; waggle. *Kidu eṇ ej kōjjaaḷaḷe ḷokwan.* The dog's wagging its tail.

kōjjaromrom (**kejjar°emr°em**). 2(inf, tr -*e*), 4, 6(-*i*), 7. Fishing method, line fishing at night, jerking the line to cause phosphorescence in water to attract fish to the bait.

kōjjarōk (**kejjarek**). Also *kōjjerak* (**kejjerak**). 1(-*i*), 2, 4, 7. Start a dispute.

kōjjād (**kejjad**). Also *kōjjed* (**kejjed**). From *jedtak* (**jedtak**). 1(-*i*), 2(inf, tr *kōjād(-e)*), 4, 6(-*i*), 7. Turn face up; open a bag or basket. *Kōjādi waini kaṇ bwe ren kōjeje.* Turn those copra (split shells) face up so they will dry in the sun.

kōjjājet (**kejjajet**). 1(-*i*), 2(inf, tr -*e*), 4. See off on a journey; bid farewell.

kōjjāl (**kejjal**). 2(inf, tr *kōjal(e)*), 4, 6(-*i*), 7. Hold open and up. *Kwōn kōjāl peiṃ.* Hold your hands palms upward. *Kōjāle pāāk ṇe bwe in kanne* *eake waini.* Hold that bag open so I can fill it with copra.

kōjjāl (**kejjal**). 1(*-i*), 2(inf, tr *kōjjālle*), 4, 7. Throw a line with a weight attached to the end; to lasso; throw in a wide sweeping motion. *Ear kōjālle nabōjļọk pileij ko.* He (angrily) threw out the plates.

kōjjeb (**kejjeb**). From Engl. 1(*-i*), 2(inf, tr *-e*), 4, 6(*-i*), 7, 8, 9. Catsup. *Kwōmaroñ ke kōjjebwe raij e kijō?* Could you please put some catsup on my rice?

kōjjebar (**kejjebar**). 1(*-i*), 2(inf, tr *kōjebare*), 3, 4, 7. Designate portions; make shares, of food, work, etc.

kōjjeļā (**kejjeļay**). 1(*-i*), 2(inf, tr *-ik*), 4, 6(*-i*), 7. Information; bulletin; notice. *Eor ke kōjjeļā kōn jiraik eo ke ejjibboñ?* Was there any news bulletin about the strike this morning?

kōjjemọọj (**kejjeymawaj**). 2(inf, tr *-e*), 4, 6(*-i*), 7. To appropriate; allot; allocate. *Jenaaj kōjjemọọje ṃani kein ekkar ñan joñan armej.* We'll appropriate the money according to population.

kōjjeṃ (**kejjeṃ**). 1(*-i*), 3, 6(*-i*). Muscle in a bivalve; cartilage; ligament.

kōjjeṃļọk (**kejjeṃļaq**). From *jeṃļọk* (**jeṃļaq**). Bon voyage; spend last moments together, farewell occasion, bring to a finish. *Ṃōñā in kōjjeṃļọk.* Farewell dinner. *Ij kōjjeṃļọk idaak im joļọk kadek.* I'll drink for the last time and go on the wagon. *Raar kōjjeṃļọk ippān ṃokta jān an etal.* They held a farewell get together with him before he left.

kōjjen (**kẹjjẹn**). Steal.

kōjjeraṃōlṃōl (**kejjeraṃelṃel**). Idiom. From *jeraṃōl* (**jeraṃel**). 2, 4, 6(*-i*), 7. Put on a long face; seek pity. *Ealikkar an kōjjeraṃōlṃōl.* It's obvious that he's putting on a long face.

kōjjerọro (**kejjerawrẹw**). From *jerọ* (**jeraw**). 2, 4, 6(*-i*), 7. Target practice; shooting contest.

kōjjoal (**kejjewhal**). Also *me* (**mẹy**). 6(*-a*). Stone fortress for trapping fish.

kōjjobaba (**kejjewbahbah**). 2, 4, 6(*-i*), 7. Play marbles. *Ledik in Ṃajeļ rōjeļā kōjjobaba.* Marshallese girls can really play marbles.

kōjjoram (**kejjewram**). Variant form of *kōmram* (**kemram**).

kōjļọr (**kejļar°**). 1(*-i*), 2(inf, tr *-e*), 3, 6(*-i*), 7, 8, 9. Stunned, of fish. *Ejej wōt kōjļọriier ke rej jab ko.* The fish are so stunned they don't run away. *Ewi kilen kōjļọri ṃọle kā?* How do we stun these rabbitfish?

kōjṃaal (**kejṃahal**). Dial. W, E: *tūñañ.* 1(*-i*), 2, 3, 4, 7. Watch and long for a bite of food while another is eating; beg for food. *Kwōn jab kōjeṃaal.* Don't watch people eating.

kōjool (**kejewel**). 1(*-i*), 2(inf, tr *-e*), 4, 7. Ignore.

kōjota (**kẹjẹwtah**). 1(*-i, -a*), 2, 3, 7. Supper; eat supper; to sup. *Koṃwin itok jen kōjota.* Come let's eat supper.

kōjọliṃ (**kejawliṃ**). 2(inf, tr *-i*), 4, 6(*-i*), 7. Fishing method, using weight with hook, octopus for bait, and dragging it on sandy bottom. *Kwaar aluje ke wāween an kōjọliṃ inne?* Did you observe the way he fished using the *kōjọliṃ* method yesterday?

kōjparok (**kejpareq**). 1(*-i*), 2(inf, tr *-e*), 4, 7. Protect; take care of; save; beware; careful; caution; conserve; economize; preserve. *Kōjparok aṃ mour.* Take care of yourself. *Kōjparok ṃani kaṇe nājiṃ.* Save your money. *Kōjbarok kiaaj.* Conserve gasoline.

kōjwad (**kejwad**). 3, 5(*kkōjwadwad*), 6(*-i*). Flock of birds. *Jabdewōt ien kwōj llo kōjwad, kwōn jeļā bwe eor ek ippāer.* Anytime you see a flock of birds on the ocean, you must know that there are fish with it.

kōk (**kek, kẹk**). Also *ikōk* (**yikek**), *likōk* (**likek**). 2, 3, 6(*-i*), 7. Cracked; split; chink. *Ekōk jimeeṇ ṇe.* The concrete is cracked. *Aṃaiki im kakōke.* Pound it till it cracks. *Kwōlo ke (i)kōk eo?* Did you find the crack?

kōk-. See *kk-*.

kōkki (**kẹkkiy**). Hold something tightly.

kōkajoor (**kekajẹwẹr**). From *kajoor* (**kajẹwẹr**). 2, 4, 6(*-i*), 7. Go away for some fresh air; excursion; saunter. *Kōmro ar kōkajoor arļọk.* The two of us took an excursion to the seashore.

kōkaļļe (**kekaļļey**). Variant form of *kakōļļe* (**kakeļļey**).

kōkāāl (**kekayal**). Also *kōkkāāl* (**kekkayal**). From *kāāl* (**kayal**). 2(inf *kōkkāāl,* tr *kōkāāle*), 4, 6(*-i*), 7. Renew; renovate; change; refurbish.

Kwōn kōkkāāl aṃ nuknuk. Change your clothes.

kōkālǫk (kekaylaq). 2(inf, tr *-e*). Oust; launch. *Raar kōkālǫk er jān ān eo.* They were ousted from the island. *Raar kōkālǫk rakōt eo.* They launched the rocket.

kōkkaajiriri (kekkahajiriyriy). Variant form of *kaajiriri* (kahajiriyriy).

kōkkau (kekkahwiw). 1(-*i*), 2, 4, 5(*kōkkauu*), 6(-*i*), 7, 8, 9. Beg for food. *Ij jain kar llolo kōkkauu āinwōt e.* I never saw a greater begger for food than he is.

kōkkāāḷāḷ (kekkayaḷyaḷ). 2(inf, tr *-e*), 4, 6(-*i*), 7. Fishing method, waiting along the usual path of fish on the reef to spear them, usually done at the beginning of ebb and flow tide. *Ḷōmen eṇ ej kōkkāāḷāḷ wōt.* That fellow is still standing out there with his spear hoping to waylay and spear some fish.

kōkkeilǫk (kekkẹyilaq). Also *kōkkeilǫk* (kẹkkẹyilaq). 1, 2, 4, 6(-*i*), 7. Scream; shout; shriek; yell; holler. *Ñe ej or jeḷo, aolep rej kōkkeilǫk.* When a boat is sighted the islanders all shout.

kōkkeitaak (kẹkkẹyitahak). Also *ekkeitaak* (yẹkkẹyitahak). From *itaak* (yitahak) "meet". 6(-*i*). Connection; contact.

kōkkekaak (kekkeykahak). See *kkekaak* (kkeykahak).

kōkkǫjekjek (kekkawjẹkjẹk). 1(-*i*), 2, 4, 7. Fishing method, trolling inside lagoon.

kōkkōk (kekkek). A bird, bristle-thighed curlew, *Numenius tahitiensis.*

kōkkōk (kekkek). Vulgar. 1, 2, 3(inf, tr *-e*), 8, 9. Uncircumcised penis.

kōkkōrārā (kekkerayray). Vulgar. From *kōrā* (keray). 1(-*i*), 2(inf, tr *-ik(i)*), 4, 7. Chase women.

kōkḷaḷ (kekḷaḷ). Navigational sign in Marshallese navigation. *Ñe juon enaaj jeḷā kōkḷaḷ eban peḷǫk.* If ones knows all the navigational signs he'll never get lost at sea.

kōkṃanṃōn (kekṃanṃẹn). Dialectal variant of *kōṃṃanṃen* (keṃṃanṃẹn).

kōkōṃṃanṃōn (kekeṃṃanṃẹn). Decorate, dress up.

kōl (kẹl). 2, 3, 6(*kilen, kiltōn*), 7. Technique; method; way or manner of

doing something; policy; procedure. *Ewi kilen kōṃṃane?* What is the way to do it? *Ekōl an kōṃṃan kōl.* He has wonderful technique. *Ear kilen kaubowe.* He did a cowboy trick.

kōl (kel). Fertile soil. *Kōl eo in, emaroñ ddek jabdewōt men ko.* This is fertile soil; anything can grow.

kōlaṇta (kelaṇtah). Variant form of *aḷōṃṇak* (haḷemṇak).

kōle (kẹlẹy). A basket for bearing tribute to a chief.

kōlla (kellah). Garbage dump.

kōllejar (kelleyjar). 1(-*i*), 2(inf, tr *-e*), 4, 6(-*i*), 7. Strategy; tactics; plan; scheme; alert; cautious. *Rōbane kōllejari er.* They couldn't outmaneuver them. *Kōllejar wōt jeṇe im pojak.* Stand by there and be alert.

kōllōkā (kellekay). 2(inf, tr *-ik*), 6(-*i*), 7. Sail following the wind; sail with the wind directly behind.

kōlmarok (kelmareq). Variant form of *kaḷmarok* (kaḷmareq).

kōlñe (kẹlgẹy). Dial. E only; see *mejā* (mejay). Also *kilōñe* (kilẹgẹy), *kōlōñe* (kẹlẹgẹy). 6(-*i*). Gashes in coral reef. *Jeañ ilān eǫñōd ilo kōlñe kaṇ lik.* Let's go fishing in the coral holes.

kōlǫṃōrṃōr (kelawṃẹrṃẹr). Dialectal variant of *jowǫanroñ* (jewahanreg°).

kōlǫtuwawa (kelawtiwahwah). Archaic. 2(inf, tr *-ik(i)*), 3, 6(-*i*), 7. To peer at; to see someone passing between clumps of trees. *Enta kwōj kōlǫtuwawaiki ijeṇe ke ej jab itok.* Don't waste your time trying to spot him passing through that opening because he's not coming.

kōlǫwutaktak (kelawwitaktak). Dial. E only. 1(-*i*), 2(inf, tr *-e*)), 4, 6(-*i*), 7. A food, diluted starch baked in coconut spathe in earth oven. *Rūkōlǫwutaktak eo ennǫ an iiōk ṇe.* That's the expert in making *kōlǫwutaktak.*

kōlōk (kelek). 2, 6(-*i*), 8, 9. Full. *Ekōlōk ḷwe eo kōn dān.* The pond is full of water.

kōḷ (keḷ). Also *kil; kilōñe, kōlñe.* Archaic. Stream running out of swamp.

kōḷa (**keḷah**). From Engl. Collar. *Ettoon kōḷaan jōōt ṇe aṃ.* Your shirt collar is soiled.

kōḷaak (**keḷahak**). 1(*-i*), 2(inf *kōḷḷaak,* tr *-e*), 4, 7. Put on; assemble; install. *Eṃōj kōḷaak injin eo.* The engine has been (re)assembled. *Ijaje kōḷḷaak injin.* I don't know how to assemble engines.

kōḷaebar (**keḷahyeybar**). 2, 3(inf, tr *-e*), 6(*-i*), 8, 9. Brackish, of water. *Etipen kōḷaebar dān ṇe.* It looks like it's brackish water.

kōḷan (**keḷan**). Variant form of *kaḷan* (**kaḷan**).

kōḷaoḷab (**keḷahwẹḷab**). Dialectal variant of *kōḷaoḷap* (**keḷahweḷap**).

kōḷaoḷap (**keḷahweḷap**). Dial. W, E: *kōḷaoḷap* (**keḷahwẹḷap**). A fish, rock cod, *Anyperodon leucogrammicus.*

kōḷā (**keḷay**). Also *kōḷe* (**keḷey**). 3, 5(*kkōḷāḷā*), 6(*-i*). Stem of a fruit; stalk, leafstem, petiole. *Kwōn joḷọk jān kōḷā in mā kaṇe.* Throw the stems of those breadfruit away. *Ekkōḷāḷā nōbōjān ṃwiin.* There are lots of fruit stems all around (on the ground) outside this house. *Bwilọke kōḷein bōlōk ṇe.* Break off the stem of that leaf.

kōḷe (**keḷey**). Variant form of *kōḷā* (**keḷay**).

Kōḷein-dipāākāk-eo (**kẹḷẹyin-diypayakyak-yew**). See *kōḷā, Dipāākāk:* "stem of the boom socket". A constellation; stars in Auriga; eta, zeta.

kōḷḷapḷap (**keḷḷapḷap**). From *ḷap* (**ḷap**) "large". 2, 4, 6(*-i*). Exaggerate. *Lale bwe armej rōkein kōḷḷapḷap.* Beware of exaggerations.

kōḷḷā (**keḷḷay**). 1(*-i*), 2(inf, tr *-ik*), 4, 7. Pay; get paid. *Eṃōj ke aṃ kōḷḷā?* Have you been paid? Did you get paid? *Eṃōj aō kōḷḷāik oṇeaṃ.* I paid you your wages. I was paid your wages.

kōḷḷā likjab (**keḷḷay likjab**). Reimburse; repay. *Iar itōn kōḷḷā aō likjab.* I came to pay my debts.

kōḷḷā oṇea- (**keḷḷay weṇya-**). 1. Recompense; remunerate; pay for; compensate. *Inaaj kōḷḷā oṇān aṃ jouj.* I'll recompense your kindness.

kōḷmānḷọkjeṇ (**keḷmanḷaqjeṇ**). 1, 2, 4, 6(*-i*). Meditate; concentrate; think; contemplate; reflect. *Kōḷmānḷọkjeṇ ṃokta jān aṃ etal.* Think twice before leaving. *Ej kōḷmānḷọkjeṇ kōn bōd ko an.* He's thinking about his mistakes.

kōḷo (**keḷew**). 1(*-a*), 3(inf *kakkōḷoḷo,* tr *kakkōḷoḷouk*), 5(*kkōḷoḷo*), 6(*-a*). Anger; physical stimulation; morale. *Ejiktok (euwetok) kōḷowan kōn al ko.* He was stimulated by the songs. *Raar kakūtōtōik im kakkōḷoḷouki.* They teased and angered him. *Ekkōḷoḷo.* She's mad.

kōḷo (**keḷew**). 1, 6(*-a*). Contractions during childbirth. *Euwe kōḷowan.* She's starting labor.

kōḷotōr (**kẹḷẹwtẹr**). Make perfume. *Kwōn kōḷotōre ut ṇe.* Make perfume from that flower.

kōḷọ (**keḷaw**). Variant form of *kaḷọ* (**kaḷaw**).

kōḷọk (**keḷaq**). 2, 3, 6(*-i*). Forest fire; fire out of control. *Raar tile em kōkōḷọke kijek eo.* They lighted the fire and let it burn out of control.

kōḷọk (**keḷaq**). Also *kaḷọk* (**kaḷaq**). 2(inf, tr *-e*). Celebrate an occasion in a rather unceremonial manner; wait for rain to subside. *Jej ja kōḷọk wōt kein.* Let's wait until this rain is over.

kōḷōjabwil (**keḷejabil**). 2(inf, tr *-i*), 4, 6(*-i*), 7. Fishing method, for bonitos. *Allōñin kōḷōjabwil ko kein.* This is the season for bonito fishing.

kōḷōnwa (**keḷenwah**). 6(*-i*). A game, hide behind a mat and have another guess.

kōḷōṇta (**keḷeṇtah**). From Engl. Calendar. *Eor ke ami kōḷōṇta in iiō in?* Have you (plural) a calendar for this year?

kōḷtak (**keḷtak**). 1, 2, 6(*-i*), 7. Squat with legs wide apart. *Enana an leddik kōḷtak.* Girls shouldn't squat with their legs apart.

kōm (**kẹm**). Dial. W, E: *kōmmem* (**kẹmmẹm**), *kōṃ* (**keṃ**). We (excl.); us (excl.); pronoun, absolute and object, first person plural exclusive.

kōmañmañ (**kemagmag**). From *mañ* (**mag**). 1(*-i*), 2(inf, tr *kōmañ(e)*), 4, 6(*-i*), 8, 9. Punish. *Ekadik kōmañmañ an riJāmene ro rūkaki.* The Germans used punishment a lot in teaching. *Ejaje kōmañmañ.* He's very cruel when punishing. *Iar kōmañ(e) rūkọọt eo.* I taught the thief a lesson in such a way that he's going to think twice before stealing again.

kōmaroñ (**kemareg°**). 2(inf, tr -*e*), 4. Enable; authorize. *Ta enaaj kōmaroñ eō etetal?* What'll enable me to walk? *Eṃōj kōmaroñ eō.* I've been authorized.

kōmat (**kemat**). 1(*kōmatti-*), 2(inf, tr *kōmatte*), 7. To cook; to distill. *Kōmrooj kōmat arkooḷ.* We're distilling alcohol. *Kōmattin wōn mā kein?* Who cooked these breadfruit?

kōmatōr (**kemater**). Transitive form of *kōmmatōr* (**kemmater**).

kōmatōrtōr (**kematerter**). From *matōrtōr* (**materter**). 1(-*i*), 2, 3, 4, 8, 9. Obnoxious; offensive; hateful. *Ekōmatōrtōr.* He has an obnoxious personality.

kōmādodo (**kemadewdew**). 1(-*i*), 2(inf, tr -*uk*), 3, 4, 7. Send another to do one's work; shirk.

kōmājmāj (**kemajmaj**). Also *kōmājjimāj* (**kemajjimaj**). 2, 6(-*i*). Eye-catching; attractive. *Lieṇ eḷap an kōmājmāj ippa.* She catches my fancy.

kōmālij (**kemalij**). 1(-*i*), 6(-*i*). Brain; mashed taro or potato.

Kōmālij (**kemalij**). From *kemālij* (**kemalij**) "brain". 3, 6(-*i*). A plant, *Pandanus fischerianus* cultigen.

kōmāltato (**kemaltahtęw**). Slang. 4, 6(-*i*), 7. Chew the fat; shoot the breeze; chat. *Kwōn wātok kōjro kōmāltato.* Come over and let's chew the fat.

kōmeḷeḷe (**kemeḷeyḷey**). Variant form of *kōmmeḷeḷe* (**kemmeḷeyḷey**).

kōmennañ (**kemennag**). 1(-*i*), 2(inf, tr -*e*), 4, 6(-*i*), 7. Eat fish while fishing, beat up someone badly. *Jen kijeekin kōmennañ eo.* Hustle up the fire so we can cook some fish and eat while we're fishing. *Raar kōmennañe Jāāk ṇa i tawūn boñ.* Jack got beaten up badly in town last night.

kōmi (**kemiy**). Dialectal variant of *koṃ* (**qęṃ**).

kōmiro (**kemiyrew**). Dialectal variant of *koṃro* (**qeṃrew**).

kōmja (**kemjah**). 2(inf, tr -*ik*), 4, 6(-*i*), 7. Watch; to keep awake during the usual hours of sleep; to ambush; waylay. *Kōjro tan kōmjaik wōn eo.* Let's go and keep watch for the turtle. *Inaaj kōmjaik ḷeeṇ ilju ej jibbōñ iturun ṃweeṇ iṃōn.* I'll waylay him tomorrow morning near his house.

kōmjaaḷaḷ (**kemjahaḷhaḷ**). 1(-*i*), 2, 3(inf, tr -*e*), 6(-*i*), 7. Sorrowful looking. *Kwōn jab kōmjaaḷaḷ tok ñan eō bwe ejjeḷọk men eṇ imaroñ kōṃṃane.* Don't look so sad at me because there's nothing I can do.

kōmjedeọ (**kemjedyaw**). 2, 6(-*i*). Fragile; flimsy; looks good but won't last; superficially fancy. *Ekōmjedeọ jet ṃweiukun Jepaan.* Some goods from Japan look good but are flimsy.

kōmlōt (**kemlet**). 2. Speak; say.

kōmḷan (**kemḷan**). Wait a spell; await. *Ij ja kōmḷan jidik ṃokta jān aō kakiaaj.* I'll wait a spell before I jog.

kōmmaanwa (**kemmahanwah**). 1(-*i*), 2, 4. Understand how to keep temper; keep one's cool. *Ejeḷā kōmmaanwa.* He knows how to keep his temper.

kōmmako (**kemmakew**). Wait for fruit to ripen.

kōmmatōr (**kemmater**). 1(-*i*), 2(inf, tr *kōmatōr(e)*), 3, 4, 7. Invite criticism; anger; vex; blame; objectionable; offensive; outrageous; to sabotage; urinate. *Eḷap an kōmmatōr an jerbal.* His work invites criticism. *Iar kōmatōre.* I put the blame on him. *Eduoj ḷọk wōt im kōmmatōr iturun mejān kōjām eo.* He stepped out and urinated right in front of the door.

kōmmāidik (**kemmayidik**). 1(-*i*), 2, 3, 4, 7. Primp; strut; appear sultry; ogle. *Kwōn jab kōmmāidik.* Don't primp and strut.

kōmmālmel (**kemmalmęl**). 1(-*i*), 2(inf, tr -*e*), 3, 4, 6, 7. Rehearse; practice; exercise; training. *Rej kōmmālmel al.* They're rehearsing songs.

kōmmālwewe (**kemmalweywey**). 1(-*i*), 2, 4, 6(-*i*), 7. Method of extracting coconut meat out of its shell without breaking the meat. *Kōmmālweweik tok ṃōk juon kijen bwe kwōjaad jeḷā iaarro.* Could you fix him one coconut since you know this method better?

kōmmejāje (**kemmejayjęy**). 1(-*i*), 2, 3, 4, 5(*kkōmmejāje*), 7. Puffed-up; boastful; show-off one's possessions or achievements.

kōmmeḷeḷe (**kemmeḷeyḷey**). Also *kōmeḷeḷe* (**kemeḷeyḷey**). 1(-*i*), 2(inf, tr -*ik*), 4, 7. Explain; make clear; disentangle; unsnarl a tangled fishline; demonstrate; describe; untangle; elaborate. *Kwōn kōmeḷeḷeik eo ṇe.*

Unsnarl that fishline there. *Kwōn kōmeļeļeik m̧ōk wūn ņe.* Please explain that problem.

kōmmem (**kęmmęm**). Dialectal variant of *kōm* (**kęm**).

kōmmeñ (**kęmmęg**). Also *kōmmōñ.* 1(-*i*), 2, 7. Make a sour face; grieve; have tears in the eyes; frown; grimace. *Ekōmmeñ jān aer kar lui.* She got tears in her eyes from being bawled out.

kōmmeo̧eo (**kemmeyawyęw**). Variant form of *kaammeo̧eo* (**kahammeyawyęw**).

kōmmerara (**kemmerahrah**). Vulgar slang. From *mera* (**merah**) "light", "to make light, relieve burden". 2, 4, 6(-*i*). Euphemism for sexual relations.

kōmmour (**kęmmęwir**). 1(-*i*), 2, 3, 4, 6(-*i*), 7. Give birth; bear offspring; bring forth; give life to. *Lio ippān ear kōmmour boñ.* His wife gave birth last night. *Em̧ōj an lio kōmmour.* She's had a baby.

kōmmo̧ (**kemmaw**). 1(-*i*), 2, 4, 7, 8, 9. Jealous; be possessive.

kōmour (**kęmęwir**). From *mour* (**męwir**). 2(inf, tr -*i*), 4, 7. Cure; make well. *Wūno eo ekōmouri eō.* The medicine cured me.

kōmram (**kemram**). Also *kejjoram* (**kejjewram**). Beacon; fireworks. *Kwaar lo ke kōmram eo?* Did you see the beacon?

kōm̧a (**kem̧ah**). From Japn. *kama*. 6(-*i*). Large pot; caldron; kettle.

kōm̧adm̧ōdin idiñ (**kem̧adm̧edin yidig**). First aid; emergency treatment.

kōm̧ajoñjoñ (**kem̧ajeg°jeg°**). 2, 6(-*i*), 7. Hop back and forth on both feet. *Eļap kōm̧ajoñjoñ ilo ebin etto.* There is a lot of back and forth hopping in ancient dances.

kōm̧akoko (**kem̧akęwkęw**). 2(inf, tr -*ik*), 4, 6(-*i*). Force someone to do some favor for one; servant (with person prefix *rū*-).

kōm̧anm̧an (**kem̧anm̧an**). 1(-*i*), 2, 3, 4, 7. Make good; create; creation; doing. *Ej jab kōm̧anm̧anū.* It's not my creation.

kōm̧anōt (**kem̧anęt**). Etiquette; manners; custom. *Ekkar ñan kōm̧anitin M̧ajeļ, kwōj aikuj pokake jeim̧.* According to Marshallese etiquette, you have to listen to your older siblings.

kōm̧aolaļ (**kem̧ahwewlaļ**). Slang. Dessert. *Ij ja edjoñe kōm̧aolaļ e am̧.* Let me taste your dessert.

kōm̧bade (**kem̧badey**). 1(-*i*), 2, 4, 6(-*i*), 7. Take care not to spoil a good thing; endure. *Ej kōm̧bade kōn lieņ ippān.* He's being very careful about his wife. *Kōm̧bade wōt.* Keep on, don't give up.

kōm̧kōm̧ (**kem̧kem̧**). 1(-*i*), 2(inf, tr *kōm̧ōj*), 4, 7. Pick breadfruit with a stick. *Em̧ōj ke aer kōm̧kōm̧?* Have they finished picking breadfruit?

kōm̧m̧aanan (**kem̧m̧ahanhan**). 1(-*i*), 2(inf, tr -*e*), 3, 4, 7. Chase men.

kōm̧m̧aejek (**kem̧m̧ahyęyjęk**). Fight. *Ej raan in kōm̧m̧aejek.* It's the day for the battle.

kōm̧m̧ak (**kem̧m̧ak**). Dial. W, E: *kōm̧ak* (**kem̧ak**), *kaim̧ak* (**kahyim̧ak**). From causative form of *m̧ak* "needlefish". 2(inf, tr -*e*), 4, 6(-*i*), 7. Fishing method, for needlefish (*m̧ak*). *Kōjro ej kaim̧akļo̧k ñan ia?* How far are we fishing for needlefish?

kōm̧m̧alijar (**kem̧m̧ahliyjar**). Contest. *Iien kōm̧m̧alijar.* It's the time for the contest.

kōm̧m̧an (**kem̧m̧an**). 1(-*i*), 2(inf, tr -*e*), 4, 6(-*i*), 7. Make; do; build; fix; earn; execute; operate; perform. *Jerbal eo an eņ kōm̧m̧an wa.* His job is building boats. *E eņ ear kōm̧m̧ane wa eņ.* He is the one that made that boat. *Jete ņe kwōj kōm̧m̧ane?* How much are you earning? How many are you making?

kōm̧m̧an (**kem̧m̧an**). Artificial. *Elukkuun aeboojoj ut kōm̧m̧an eņ.* That's a very pretty artificial flower. *Ejorrāān ne kōm̧m̧an ko neen.* He busted his artificial legs.

kōm̧m̧an (**kem̧m̧an**). Actions; behavior. *Kwōnaaj kalbuuj kōn wōt kōm̧m̧an kaņe am̧.* You'll get put in jail as a result of your actions.

kōm̧m̧anm̧ōn (**kem̧m̧anm̧ęn**). Dial. W, E: *kōkm̧anm̧ōn* (**kekm̧anm̧ęn**). 2(inf, tr -*e*, *kōm̧m̧anm̧wine*), 4, 6(-*i*), 7. Handle someone or something with care; take it easy. *Kōm̧m̧anm̧ōne ajri ņe bwe enāj wōtlo̧k.* Be careful with that child or you'll drop it. *Kwōj aikuj kōm̧m̧anm̧ōn.* You'd better take it easy.

kōm̧m̧ao (**kem̧m̧ahwew**). 1, 2, 3(inf, tr *-uk*), 4, 5, 6. To converse; conversation; keep company; chat. *Kōm̧ro ar kōm̧m̧ao.* We had a conversation. *Kōkōm̧m̧aouk ļōļļap eņ.* Talk with the old man (cause him to talk to you).

kōm̧ñūr (**kem̧gir**). Roar of an animal.

kōm̧ñūr (**kem̧gir**). Dial. E, W: *ere.* Dimension of a canoe between hull and outrigger; canoe part, outrigger platform.

kōm̧ōj (**kem̧ej**). Transitive form of *kōm̧kōm̧* (**kem̧kem̧**).

kōm̧ōttōņa (**kem̧etteņah**). From Japn. *komatta na* "I'm stuck". "Shucks!"; "Damn!"

kōm̧te (**kem̧tey**). Toss and pitch on the sea.

kōn (**kęn**). For; because; with; concerning.

kōn (**kęn**). Leave marks; imprinted; indelible; not removable; stuck; sunken in. *Ekōn jenkwan ñiin.* He left his teethmarks. *Ekōn jenkwan māj ņe mejam̧.* Your glasses have left marks. *Ikōn ņa ilo jikin in.* Nobody can chase me off this land. *Ekōn wa in ilo bok.* This canoe is stuck in the sand.

kōn (**kęn**). Variant form of *kkein* (**kkęyin**).

kōn menin (**kęn menyin**). Therefore; wherefore.

kōnana (**kenahnah**). From *nana* (**nahnah**). 2(inf, tr *-ik(i)*), 4, 6(*-i*), 7. Talk bad about someone; homely; ugly. *Ear kōnanaiktok eok ñan eō.* He said bad things about you to me. *Kōnana men ņe.* She's ugly.

kōnar (**kenar**). 1(*-i*), 2(inf, tr *-e*), 4, 6(*-i*), 7, 8. To girdle a plant; skin parts of a plant to ensure its bearing of fruit or flowers; strike the trunk of a tree so that the flowers may blossom forth quickly. *Em̧m̧an an mour bwe raar kōnare.* It is growing very well after being skinned. *Em̧ōj aō kōnar ut eņ.* I have struck the trunk of that bush.

kōnājnej (**kenajnęj**). Variant form of *kanejnej* (**kanęjnęj**).

kōnāmnām (**kenamnam**). 1(*-i*), 2(inf, tr *-e*), 4, 6(*-i*), 7. Smell; sniff; make odorous. *Kidu rōkanooj jeļā kōnāmnām.* Dogs have a keen sense of smell.

kōnān (**kenan**). A fish, Pacific sea perch, *Kuhlia taeniura* (Mejit.)

kōneo (**keneyew**). Trunk of a young tree; six or seven years old.

kōnke (**kęnkey**). Because; since; as.

kōnnaan (**kennahan**). 1(*-i*), 2(inf, tr *-ōk*), 4, 5(*kkōnnaanan*), 7. Talk; speak; tell; report; testify; declare; reveal; state. *Wōn in ej kkōnnaanan?* Who is this that keeps on talking? *Ñe ej kadek, ekadik kkōnnaanan.* When he's drunk he's very talkative. *Emake kijoñ kkōnnaanan.* She has a big mouth.

kōnnǫ (**kennaw**). 6(*-i*). Dish; plate.

kōnono (**kenewnew**). Also *kwōnono* (**qenewnew**). 1(*-i*), 2, 3, 4, 7. Read; talk; mention; oral; recite; speak; verbalize.

kōnpat (**kęnpat**). From *pat* (**pat**) "swamp". 3, 5(*kkōnpatpat*), 6(*-i*). A plant, mangrove, *Sonneratia caseolaris*. In mangrove depressions.

kōnwa (**kenwah**). 1(*-a*). Neck.

kōņ (**keņ**). 1(*-i*), 2(inf, tr *-e*), 3, 4, 6(*-i*). Fertilize; dry or decayed leaves used in fertilizing; caulk; manure; oakum, compost. *Rōnaaj kōņe wa eņ m̧okta jān an bwil.* They'll caulk the boat before launching it. *Kōņe atake ņe bwe en kimuur.* Fertilize your garden so it will be rich.

kōņaan (**keņahan**). 1(*-i*), 2, 7. Want; like; usually do something; desire; enjoy; please; wish. *Em̧ōj am̧ kōņaan rum̧wij.* Why don't you stop being late all the time. *En m̧ōj am̧ kōņaan rum̧wij.* I want you to stop being late all the time. *Kijak eņ ekōņaan rum̧wij.* He's usually late. *Kōm̧m̧an ta kokōņaan.* Do what you please. *Ekōņaan ke?* Does he like it? Does he want it?

kōņaanikien (**keņahanyikiyen**). From *kōņaan* (**keņahan**) "want", *ikien* (**yikiyen**) "frolic". 2, 4, 6(*-i*). Horse play; frolic. *Rūkōņaanikien eo ņe.* Here comes the guy who is always horsing around.

kōņak (**keņak**). Transitive form of *kkōņak* (**kkeņak**).

kōņakō (**keņahkeh**). From Engl. *kanaka*. 6(*-i*). Native; Kanaka, derogatory.

kōņauwe. See *kōņǫuwe.*

kōņkōm̧m̧an (**keņkem̧m̧an**). 1(*-i*), 2, 3, 4, 6(*-i*), 7, 8, 9. Boast; be proud; show-off; assert oneself; inconsiderate. *Kwōn jab kōņkōṃṃan.* Don't boast. *Eļap an kōņkōṃṃan ak epuwaļ.* He's quite boastful but actually he's a coward.

kōņņat (**kęņņat**). 3, 6(-*i*). A plant, *Scaevola frutescens* (Mill.) Krause. A common beach shrub of the Goodeniaceae. The flowers are split-tubular, white or purplish; the leaves bright yellowish-green; simple about 6-10 inches long.

kōņo (**keņew**). 3, 5(*kkōņoņo*), 6(-*i*). A plant, *Cordia subcordata* Lam. (Boraginaceae). A handsome large tree with subcordate, light green leaves and tubular orange flowers.

kōņo (**keņew**). 3(inf, tr -*ik*), 5(*kkōņoņo*). Pink.

Kōņọuwe (**keņawiwey**). 3, 6(-*i*). A plant, coconut variety.

kōñe (**kęgęy**). 3, 6(-*i*). A plant, *Pemphis acidula* Forst. A small, sclerophyllous-leaved shrub with scaly black branches and small white flowers, growing on the hottest open sandy beaches. (*Lythraceae*; the loose-strife family).

kōōb (**kęhęb**). Also *kaab* (**kahab**). 3(inf, tr -*e*), 7, 8, 9. Curve. *Ear kakōōbe an kadkad.* He threw curves.

kōp (**kęp**). Shoulder.

kōpa (**kepah**). 1, 2, 4, 5(*kkōpapa*), 6(-*i*). Incest. *Ekkōpapa ļeeņ.* That man is always falling in love with relatives.

kōpat (**kepat**). 3, 6(-*i*). A fish, surgeonfish, *Acanthurus dussumieri*; *Hepatus bariene.*

kōpādel (**kepadel**). A fish.

kōpāle (**kepaley**). Transitive form of *kkōpāl* (**kkepal**).

kōpālele (**kepaļęylęy**). 1(-*i*), 2(inf, tr -*ik(i)*). Pluck ripe coconuts.

kōpejlọk (**kepęjlaq**). Variant form of *kapejlọk* (**kapęjlaq**).

kōpeļ (**kepeļ**). Transitive form of *kkōpeļ* (**kkepeļ**).

kōpetaklik (**kepeytaklik**). Security; land or goods put away for future use or need; collateral. *Naaj ta aṃ kōpetaklik ñe inaaj kaṃuriik eok?* What will be your collateral should I give you the loan?

kōpin (**kepin**). Shoot with a sling. *Kwōn kōpin bao eņ.* Shoot that bird with your sling.

kōpjar (**kepjar**). 3, 6(-*i*). A food, breadfruit baked in earth oven.

kōpjeļtak (**kepjeļtak**). 1(-*i*), 2(inf, tr -*e*), 4, 6(-*i*), 7. A food, biscuits and flour cooked together in water. *Kōpjeļtakin wōn nnọno in?* Who prepared this delicious *kōpjeļtak?*

kōpkōp (**kępkęp**). 2. Struggle. *Iṃōk in dāpiji ak tōreo ekōpkōp.* The more I held him the more he struggled.

kōplọk (**kęplaq**). 2, 3, 4, 5(*kkōplọklọk*), 6(-*i*), 7. Escape; run away; move out swiftly; take off. *Ilaṃōj im ekōplọk.* I yelled and he lit out. *Ta eo ekakōplọke?* What made him run away". *Ekōplọkin pikōt.* He escaped like a coward. *Ekōplọkļọk ijjuweoļọk.* He took off in that direction.

kōpļe (**kepļey**). Also *lukwarkwar* (**liqarqar**). Chase.

Kōpnaan (**kępnahan**). 3, 6(-*i*). A plant, *Pandanus fischerianus* cultigen.

kōpooj (**kepewej**). Transitive form of *kōpopo* (**kepewpew**).

kōpooļ (**kepeweļ**). Also *kapooļ* (**kahpeweļ**). 2, 7. Surround; include; close in on; twist around; encircle; chase; contain. *Kōpooļ ut ņe ņa ioon bōraṃ.* Wrap the lei around your head. *Raar kōpooļ ek ko.* They encircled the fish. *Rōkōpooļe im jibwe.* They chased and caught him.

kōpopo (**kepewpew**). 2(inf, tr *kōpooj(e)*), 5(*kōpopooj(e)*), 7, 10(*pojak*). Prepare. *Kwōn kōpooj ṃōņe im karreouki.* Get the house ready and clean it up. *Wa eo eņ rej kōpopooje ñan an jerak.* They are doing everything necessary to prepare this ship for its voyage.

kōppajojo (**keppahjewjew**). 1(-*i*), 2, 4, 7. Fishing method, line fishing inside lagoon using hermit crab for bait, drift unanchored.

kōppaļpaļ (**keppaļpaļ**). 1(-*i*), 2, 3, 4, 7, 8, 9. Fantastic; extraordinary; fabulous; fascinating; amazing; spectacular.

kōppao (**keppahwew**). 1(-*i*), 2(inf, tr -*uk*), 3, 4, 5(*kōppaoo*) 6(-*i*), 7. Lie in waiting; watch with evil interest or hidden purpose; lie in ambush; wheel and deal; lie in wait to grab an opportunity. *Wōn ņe kwōj kōppaouk?* Who are you lying in wait for? *Ej kōppaouk an bōk jikūṃ.* He's waiting for a chance to take your place.

kōppāāt (**keppayat**). Shoal; shallow place in the water.

kōppeḷọk (**keppeyḷaq**). 2(inf, tr *-e*), 4, 6(*-i*), 7. Float used in fishing; fishing method, line fishing using floats. *Ij kōppeḷọkwaj ak kwōj kōppeḷọktok.* We'll fish towards one another. *Eọtōk kōppeḷọk ko an riJepaan ro ibaal.* The Japanese fishing floats washed up on the reef.

kōptata (**keptahtah**). 1(*-i*), 2(inf, tr *-ik*), 6(*-i*), 7. No return; beyond the point of; deeply involved; too late. *Koban bōjrak bwe kokōptata.* You can't stop now for you're too deeply involved. *Wa eo eban rọọl bwe ekōptata.* The boat won't turn back for it's passed the point of no return. *Ekōptata kiiō.* It's too late now.

kōrabōl (**kerabel**). Also *kōrrabōl* (**kerrabel**). 1, 2(inf, tr *-e*), 4, 6(*-i*), 7. Procure something by flattery or by "borrowing"; seduce a woman; smuggle; snitch; swipe. *Ear kōrabōle juon limen pia jān kuḷab eo.* He got the club to give him a free beer. *Ijaje wōn eo ekōrabōle kopā eo aō.* I don't know who took off with my coat. *Eor eṇ ekōrabōle jodi ko aō.* Somebody swiped my zories.

kōrabōl (**kerabel**). 2(inf, tr *-e*), 4(*kōrrabōl*), 7. Flip. *Kōrabōl ṃōk jāān e.* How about flipping this coin?

kōrajraj (**kerajraj**). 1(*-i*), 2, 3, 4, 7. Whaling. *Waan kōrajraj.* A whaling vessel.

kōrat (**kerat**). Transitive form of *karkar* (**karkar**).

kōrā (**keray**). 2, 3(*kōkkōrārā*), 5(*kkōrārā*), 6(*-i*). Woman; female; effeminate; lady. *Ejjeḷọk wōt kkōrārā in ānin.* This island is full of women. *Ekōrā ḷeeṇ.* He's effeminate.

kōrkaak (**kerkahak**). 1(*-i*), 2, 3, 4, 5(*kkōrkaakak*), 7. Fishing method, troll at night; paddling a canoe for pleasure. *Ekkōrkaakak ḷeeṇ.* That man is always trolling at night.

kōrkaakiia (**kerkahakiyyah**). 2, 6(*-i*), 8, 9. Not paddle easily, of canoes (see *kōrkaakiie* (**kerkahakiyyẹy**)).

kōrkaakiie (**kerkahakiyyẹy**). 2, 6(*-i*), 8, 9. Paddle easily, of canoes (see *kōrkaakiia* (**kerkahakiyyah**)).

kōrkōr (**kerker**). 6(*-i*). Paddling canoe.

kōrkōr ioon kūro (**kerker yiyewen kirẹw**). Idiom. Be choosy or particular. *Jab kōrkōr ioon kūro bwe kwōnaaj jerata.* You'd better not be choosy or you'll be sorry.

kōro (**kerew**). Also *koro* (**qerew**). From Japn. *goro* "ground ball" and *koro* "roller". 1(*-i*), 2(inf, tr *-ik*), 5(*kkōroro*), 6(*-i*), 7. Ground ball in baseball; roller. *Ear kōroukḷọk bọọḷ eo ñan jekōn.* He hit a ground ball to second. *Likūt koro ko eọṃwin.* Put the rollers under it. *Raar korouk ānetak wa eo.* They rolled the vessel toward the shore.

kōrōnāl (**kẹrẹnyal**). 2(inf, tr *-e*), 4, 6(*-i*), 7. Clean whiskers off of newly braided sennit. *Kwōn kōrōnāle tok kkwaḷ e.* Clean the whiskers off this sennit for me.

kōrraat (**kerrahat**). 1, 2(inf, tr *-e*), 4, 5(*kkōrraatat*), 6(*-i*). Criticize; skeptical; disappointed; disapprove; pessimistic. *Kwōn jab kōrraat ak kwōn jipañ eō.* Stop being skeptical and start helping me. *Eḷap aō kōraate eok kọn an ḷap aṃ kadek.* I'm very disappointed in your heavy drinking. *Koṃ kadik kkōrraatat ak ejjeḷọk men eṇ koṃwij kōṃṃane.* You're always so critical and yet never do anything.

kōrrabōl (**kerrabel**). Variant form of *kōrabōl* (**kerabel**).

kōrrā (**kerray**). 2(inf, tr *-ik*), 4, 7. Exchange.

kōrrọñrọñ (**kerrag°rag°**). Variant form of *karrọñrọñ* (**karrag°rag°**).

kōrwaan (**kerwahan**). Variant form of *karwaan* (**karwahan**).

kōt (**kẹt**). Ripe, of breadfruit.

kōt (**kẹt**). 2, 3, 6(*-i*), 8, 9. Spoiled fish or meat; rot; decayed; rotten. *Raar kakōti ek ko.* They let the fish spoil.

kōtaa- (**ketaha-**). 1, 7. Between; boundary line; dividing line; contrast; difference; distance; intermediate; possessive classifier, boundary or difference.

kōtaan wāto (**ketahan waytẹw**). Idiom. Feud; quarrel; land dispute. *Eto wōt aerro kōtaan wāto kōn āneṇ.* Their feud over the island is a protracted one.

kōtabañ (**ketahbag**). 1(*-i*), 2(inf, tr *-e*), 4, 5(*kkōtabañbañ*), 6(*-i*), 7. A food, cake doughnut.

kōtabtab (**ketabtab**). Large tree. *Kōtabtab in ni.* Large coconut tree. *Kōtabtab in mā.* Large breadfruit tree.

kōtabuuk (**ketahbiwik**). Variant form of *katabuuk* (**katahbiwik**).

kōtak (**ketak**). 1(*-i*), 2(inf, tr *-e*), 4, 6(*-i*), 7. Put thatch on roof; sew or tie on thatch. *Eṃōj kōtake ṃweo.* The house has been thatched. *Eṃōj an ṃweo kōtak.* The thatching of the house is finished. *An aolep armej jerbal kōtak.* Thatching a house is a community project.

Kōtak (**ketak**). 3, 6(*-i*). A plant, taro variety; *Colocasia esculenta* (L.) Schott. Var. Antiquorum (Schott.) Hubb. And Rehd. The true taro of Polynesia. F.

kōtal (**ketal**). 1(*-i*), 2(inf, tr *-e, -eke*). Sink something in water.

kōtaltōl (**ketaltẹl**). 2(inf, tr *-e, kōtaltile*), 4, 6(*-i*), 7. Fishing method, chasing mackerel into a throw net held upon one side.

kōtka- (**ketka-**). 1. Plant of; possessive classifier, plant or seedling.

kōtkōt (**ketket**). Dial. W: *nakdid* (**nakdid**), *aerār* (**hayeryar**), E: *na* (**nah**), *wūla* (**wilah**). 3, 6(*-i*). A bird, ruddy turnstone, *Arenaria interpres*, with red in breeding plumage.

kōtlaḷ (**ketlaḷ**). Stick something into the ground; as a husking stick; see *kat* and *kōtooj*.

kōtḷọk (**ketḷaq**). Also *kōtōḷọk* (**keteḷaq**), *katōḷọk* (**kateḷaq**). 1(*-i*), 2(inf, tr *-e*), 3, 7. To free; let go; allow; let out; relinquish; permit; release. *Kōtḷọke to ṇe.* Let go of the rope. *Eban kōtḷọktok ledik raṇ nājin.* He won't let his daughters come with us. *Ij kōtḷọkḷọk eo e.* I'm letting the fishing line out. *Eṃōj kōtḷọk rūkalbuuj eo.* The prisoner has been freed.

kōtmāne (**ketmaney**). Variant form of *katmāne* (**katmaney**).

kōto (**kẹtẹw**). 1(*kūtuo-*) 3(inf *kakkōtoto*, tr *-ik, -uk*), 5(*kkōtoto*), 6(*kūtuon*). Wind. *Ekkōtoto tok jān nabōj.* The wind keeps on blowing in from the outside. *Jab kakkōtotouk eok.* Don't expose yourself to the wind.

kōtooj (**ketewej**). Pull something out of the ground; as a husking stick; see *kōtlal*.

kōtōḷọk (**keteḷaq**). Variant form of *kōtḷọk* (**ketḷaq**).

kōtōmānlimpok (**ketemanlimpeq**). From Ponapean *ketemenlimpoak* "reminder of love". A plant, a shrub with red flowers.

kōtōṃ (**kẹtẹṃ**). Bundle of mats.

kōtra (**ketrah**). Land reserved for chiefs.

Kōtra (**ketrah**). Clan name.

kōtrai (**kẹtrahiy**). See *kōtrāe* (**ketrayyẹy**).

kōtrar (**ketrar**). Touch only part of something.

kōtrāāk (**ketrayak**). From Engl. Cataract; waterfall. *Ejjeḷọk kōtrāāk i Ṃajeḷ.* We have no cataracts in the Marshalls.

kōtrāe (**ketrayyẹy**). Also *kōtrai* (**ketrahyiy**). From *kōtra* (**ketrah**) "land which belongs only to chief (as *mọ* (**maw**) "taboo land"). 1(*kōtrei-*), 2, 4, 7, 8, 9. Disobey; despise people; sacrilegious; profane; break a taboo, desecrate. *Kwōnāj bwil ikena kōn aṃ kōtrai.* You'll burn in hell for being profane.

kōttadede (**kettahdẹydẹy**). Also *kōttāte, jokwadikdik*. 2, 6(*-i*), 7. Fly low; follow a zigzag course in running past obstacles. *Baḷuun eo ear kōttadedetok ioon lọjet tok.* The plane flew low above the water.

kōttal (**kettal**). Variant form of *kattal* (**kattal**).

kōttar (**kettar**). Variant form of *kattar* (**kattar**).

kōttāte (**kettaytẹy**). 2, 6(*-i*), 7. Fly low. *Bao eo ear kōttātetok ioon ṃweo tok.* The bird flew low over the house.

kōtteepiṇa (**ketteyepiyṇah**). Also *kior, kiur*. From *teep* "remove", *ṇa* "shoal". Storm.

kōttọọr (**kettawar**). 2(inf, tr *-e*), 4, 6(*-i*), 7. Fishing method, chasing fish into weir. *Jero etal in kōttọọri merā ko bwe bōkāiier kiiō.* Let's go chase the parrotfish into the weir because this is the right tide for them.

kōttōbalbal (**kettebalbal**). Slang. 1, 2(inf, tr *-e*), 3, 4, 6(*-i*), 7. Plot a course; maneuver; scheme; tactics. *Kwōjeḷā ke kōttōbalbal?* Do you know how to plot a course on the chart? *Lukkuun kwe rūkōttōbalbal.* You sure are a schemer.

kōttōmāle (**kettemalęy**). 2(inf, tr *-ik(i)*), 4, 6(*-i*), 7. Canoe-surfing, when sailing down wind. *Kōjparok aṃ kōttōmāleik(i) wa ņe bwe enāj kǫkweet.* Watch how you surf this canoe or it'll dive.

kōttōn (**kęttęn**). Put aside; lay away; to store.

kōttōpar (**kettepar**). Variant form of *jibadek* (**jibadek**).

kubaak (**kiwbahak**). Also *kobaak* (**kęwbahak**). 1(*-i*), 3, 6(*-i*). Outrigger; partner of opposite sex. *Ewi kubaak eo aṃ?* Where's your partner? *Eddo kubaakin kōrkōr eņ waan.* His canoe's outrigger is quite heavy.

kubaļ (**qibaļ**). 1(*-i*), 2(inf, tr *-e*), 4, 5(*kkubaļbaļ*), 6(*-i*), 7. A food, cooked preserved breadfruit smothered in grated coconut. *Kubaļe ṃōk im lale an kane.* Smother it in grated coconut and see how tasty the combination is.

kuborbor (**qibęr°bęr°**). Also *kūborbor* (**kibęr°bęr°**). 1(*-i*), 2(inf, tr *-e*), 4, 7, 8 9. Eat with oversize bites; much. *Kwōn jab kuborbor bwe kwōnaaj pǫk.* Don't eat with your mouth so full or you'll get food caught in your esophagus.

kubōk (**qibęk**). A plant, tree, *Intsia bijuga.*

kubōl (**qibel**). Transitive form of *kkubōl* (**qqibel**).

Kubwilkōn (**qiwbilken**). A plant, taro variety; inedible.

kude (**qidey**). From Japn. *tokkuri.* Tall bottle; Japanese *sake* bottle.

kudiil (**qidiyil**). A fish.

kudǫkwōl (**qidaqel**). A fish, blenny, *Istiblennius paulus* (Mejit).

Kujjae (**qijjahyey**). 4. Place name; Kusaie.

kuju (**kiwjiw**). From Japn. *kuushuu* "air raid". 2, 6(*-i*). Invasion; landing of soldiers; air raid.

kuk (**qiq**). From Engl. 1(*-i*), 2, 6(*-i*). Work as a cook.

kuk (**qiq**). 2, 3, 7. Gathered together; huddle; congregated, aggregated. *Ekuk ek ko ņa ippān doon.* The fish are all gathered together. *Wōn e ear kǫkuk waini kā?* Who gathered these copra nuts together?

kuk-. See *kk-*.

kukkuk (**qiqqiq**). 6(*-i*). Dog, child speech; penis, child speech.

kuku (**kiwkiw**). 1(*-i*), 2, 3, 4, 7. Carry a person on one's back. *Eṃōj ņe aṃ kijoñ kuku.* Why don't you stop wanting to be carried all the time.

kul (**qil**). Formant in place names; an animal or an insect which makes its nest in thatch and said to be the color of the ruling clan; land where only chiefs and certain women are allowed.

kulālā (**qilaylay**). Vulgar. 6(*-i*). Penis, child speech.

kuli (**qiliy**). From Engl. *coolie*. 2, 3(inf, tr *-ik*), 6(*-i*). Slave; servant. *Ej kuli ñan irooj raņ.* He is a slave to the royalty. *Ļōļļap eo ear kǫkuliik (kuli kake) ledik eo.* The old man enslaved the girl.

kuļab (**qiļab**). 1(*-i*), 2, 3, 4, 5(*kkuļabļab*), 6(*-i*), 7. Club; go drinking at a club. *Eokkuļabļab ļeeņ.* He's always at the club.

kuļatļat (**qiļatļat**). 2(inf, tr *-e*), 6(*-i*), 7. Coconut shell for scrubbing clothes. *Kōṃṃanetok juon aō kuļatļat.* Make a coconut scrub-shell for me. *Kwōn kuļatļate bwe en rreo.* Scrub it with a coconut shell so it will really come clean.

kuļuļ (**qiļ°iļ°**). Dial. W only; see *juwapin* (**jiwapin**). 3, 5(*kkuļuļļuļ*). An insect, cockroach, roach. *Eokkuļuļļuļ ṃwiin.* This house is full of cockroaches.

kumat (**qimat**). Variant form of *kwōdmat* (**qedmat**).

kumi (**qimiy**). From Japn. *kumi* "group". 6(*-i*). Work gang; company, team, group.

kumi (**qimiy**). From Germ. *Gummi*. 6(*-i*). Small rubber tube. *Kumiin Jepaan men ņe.* That's a Japanese rubber tube.

kumit (**qimit**). From Engl. *committee* (?). 1, 2(inf, tr *-i*), 6(*-i*). Work on something as a group. *Raar kumiti waini eo im kōmate ṃokta jān an boñ.* They worked together on the copra and finished it before nightfall.

kun an ļaaṃ (**qin han ļahaṃ**). Idiom. 1, 2, 3. Lose temper; sightless; blind; lose one's cool; become angry. *Ekun aō ļaaṃ ippān rūkadek ro.* I lost my temper with those drunkards. *Raar kakūtōtōūki ak ear jab kun an* *ļaam̧.* They provoked him but he did not lose his temper.

kune (**kiwney**). 2, 3. Fertilized egg, ready to hatch; (see *tabwil* (**tabil**)). *Ekune lep ko.* The eggs are ready to hatch.

kune (**qiney**). Transitive form of *kkun* (**qqin**).

kuņa (**qiņah**). 2(inf, tr *-ik(i)*), 4, 6(*-i*), 7. Fishing method, surrounding edges of shoals with net. *Kom̧win kōpooļi ļọk ñan turun ņa uweo im kuņaiki.* Chase them to that shoal over yonder and catch them with the surrounding net.

kuņaa- (**qiņaha-**). Dial. E, W: *koņaa-* (**qeņaha-**). 1. Contribution; duty; responsibility; spouse. *Ejeļā kuņaan.* He does his share. or He knows what to do.

kuņaņa (**qiņahņah**). 3(*kọkkuņaņa*). Contribution, share; chip in. *Kwōj kuņaņa kōn ta?* What (thing) are you contributing? *Raar kọkkuņaņa.* They collected the contributions. They contributed.

kuņōk (**qiņẹk**). 1(*-i*), 2, 3(inf, tr *-e*), 5(*kkunōknōk*), 7, 8, 9. Dwindle; shrivel; shrink; limp; wilt, contract. *Ekuņōk.* It's shrunk. *Ejino kuņōk.* It's beginning to contract.

kupañ (**qipag**). A fish, convict tang or banded surgeonfish, *Hepatus triostegus*; a fish, banded surgeonfish, *Acanthurus triostegus* triostegus Linnaeus.

kupi (**qipiy**). 2(inf, tr *-ik*), 3(inf, tr *-ik*), 4, 6(*-i*). Disqualify; put someone out of a competition; dismiss, fire. *Raar kupiiki kōn an ikirum̧wij.* He was disqualified on account of his tardiness. *Em̧ōj kupiik jān kar jerbal eo an.* He's been fired from his job.

kupkup (**qipqip**). A fish, skip jack, immature form, *Caranx lessonii.*

kur (**qir**). 3, 6(*-i*). A fish, squirrel fish, *Holocentrus binotatus/scythrops.*

kuraañañ (**qirahaghag**). Also *kurañāñā* (**qirahgaygay**). 1(*-i*), 2, 3, 4, 7, 8, 9. Dry hair, not oily. *Etke kwaar jab kkapit ke eļap am̧ kuraañañ?* Why didn't you put oil on your hair, because it's very dry?

kuraj (**qiraj**). Vulgar. 1, 2(inf, tr *-e*), 5(*kkurajraj*), 6(*-i*). Pull back the foreskin.

kurar (**qirar**). 1(*-i*), 2(inf, tr *kuratte*), 7. Small cut, scratch. *Juon ņe kurar peim̧.* You've got a scratch on your hand. *Ta ņe ekuratte neem̧?* What scratched your leg?

kuratte (**qirattey**). Transitive form of *kurar* (**qirar**).

kurbalōklōk (**qirbalẹklẹk**). Also *kurm̧alōklōk* (**qirm̧alẹklẹk**). 1(*-i*), 2, 3, 5(*kkurbalōklōk*), 7, 8, 9. Rough; surface; callous; thorny; splintered. *Ekurbalōklōk raan jaki ņe.* The surface of that mat there is rough. *Eļap an kkurbalōklōk raan jaki eņ.* The surface of that mat is rough all over. *Ekurm̧alōklōke rā ko.* The boards have splinters all over.

kurere (**qirẹyrẹy**). 2, 3(inf, tr *-ik*), 5(*kkurere*), 6(*-i*), 8, 9. Scratchy; rough; not smooth. *Jab iri māj ņe mejam̧ kōn rāāk bwe kwōnaaj kọkurereiki.* Don't wipe your glasses with rags or you'll scratch them. *Eokkurere tōrerein wa eo.* The side of the car was all scratched up.

kuriļa (**qiriyļah**). From Engl. Gorilla.

kurjep (**qirjep**). Also *urjep* (**wirjep**). 3, 6(*-i*). Reel for fishline.

kurkur (**qir°qir°**). Also *rukruk* (**r°iqr°iq**), *rukruk* (**riqriq**). 1(*-i*), 2(inf, tr *-i, -e*), 4, 5(*kkurkur, rrukruk*), 7. Gargle; brush teeth; rinse one's mouth. *Kwōn kurkure ñiim̧ ñe ej m̧ōj am̧ m̧ōñā.* Brush your teeth when you finish eating.

kurm̧a (**qirm̧ah**). 2(inf, tr *-ik*), 6(*-i*), 7. Cart; haul by cart; wagon. *Ear kurm̧aikļọk waini ko an ñan Rita.* He hauled his copra to Rita by cart.

kurm̧alōklōk (**qirm̧alẹklẹk**). Variant form of *kurbalōklōk* (**qirbalẹklẹk**).

kurob (**qir°eb**). From Japn. *guroobu* (from Engl.). 6(*-i*). Baseball glove.

kurobrob (**qir°ebr°eb**). From *kurob* (**qir°eb**). 1(*-i*), 2, 3(inf, *kọkurobrob(e)*), 6(*-i*), 7. Wear a baseball glove. *Enañin kọkurobrob(e) ke kiaaj eņ.* Has he let the catcher use a glove?

kurōn (**qiren**). Construct form of *kor* (**qẹr**).

kut (**qit**). 1(*-i*), 2, 3(inf *kọkkut(kut),* tr *kọkuti*), 5(*kkutkut(i)*), 7, 8, 9. Thick; dense, of shrubbery; crowded, of people; close together; often; frequent. *Eokkutkut im̧ōn ānin.* The houses on this islet are very close together.

Kwōn jab kǫkuti jea kaṇe. Don't put those chairs so close together. *Eokkutkut an wa itok.* Ships come often. *Ikōṇaan babu ikōtaan ittūt kaṇ rokkut.* I want to lay my head between those heavenly orbs (line from a love song). *Jab kkutkuti ļǫk kuļab eṇ.* Stop frequenting the pub.

kutak (**qitak**). 1(*-i*), 2(inf, tr *-e*), 3, 4, 5(*kkutaktak*), 7. Rake; scratch; scrape; brush. *Kwōn kutake ļǫk ttoon ṇe jān ṃōñā ṇe.* Brush the dirt off your food. *Lōļļap eo ej kutak iu.* The old woman is scraping sprouted coconuts. *Eokkutaktak iu lōļļap eṇ.* That old woman is always scraping sprouted coconuts.

kutiltil (**kiwtiltil**). 2(inf, tr *-i*) 3, 4+3, 5(*kkutiltil*), 6(*-i*), 3+7, 8, 9. Ugly-looking lizard. *Raar kakutiltili āneo im raan kein ekanooj kkutiltil.* They put lizards on the island and nowadays it's crawling with lizards.

kutiñ (**qityig**). 1, 2, 3(inf, tr *-i*), 6(*-i*), 7. A game, skip-rope. *Rej kǫkutiñi ippāer.* They're letting her skip-rope with them.

kuuj (**kiwij**). 5(*kkuujuj*), 6(*-i*). Cat; pussy. *Ekkuujuj ānin.* This islet has lots of cats.

kuul (**kiwil**). Transitive form of *kkuul* (**qqiwil**).

kuuṃ (**kiwiṃ**). From Engl. 1(*-i*), 2(inf, tr *-i*), 3, 5(*kkuuṃuṃ*), 6(*-i*), 7. Comb. *Ekkuuṃuṃ lieṇ.* She's always combing her hair.

kuuṃuṃ (**kiwiṃwiṃ**). From *kuuṃ* (**kiwiṃ**). 1(*-i*), 2, 3(inf, tr *-i*), 6(*-i*), 7. Use a comb. *Imaroñ ke kuuṃuṃ eake kuuṃ ṇe aṃ?* May I use your comb? *Kwōn kab kakuuṃuṃi ippaṃ.* See that you share your comb with her.

kuur (**kiwir**). Birdcall.

kuwaj (**qiwaj**). Variant form of *buwaj.*

kuwat (**qiwat**). 5(*kkuwatwat*), 6(*-i*). Can of food; tin can. *Eokkuwatwat ṃwiin.* This house is full of cans. This house smells like tin cans.

kuwata (**kiwatah**). From Engl. Quarter. *Juon kuwata in juon awa ej joñoul ļalem minit.* A quarter of an hour is 15 minutes.

kuwi (**qiwiy**). Also *kwi* (**qiy**). A fish, surgeonfish, *Acanthurus lineatus.*

kūbboṇ (**kibbeṇ°**). 1(*-i*), 2, 4, 8, 9. Stingy; very miserly; selfish. *Kwōn jab kūbboṇ.* Don't be so stingy.

kūblur (**kiblir°**). Variant form of *kilbur* (**kilbir°**).

kūborbor (**kibẹr°bẹr°**). 3, 6(*-i*). A plant, pandanus cultigen.

kūborbor (**kibẹr°bẹr°**). Variant form of *kuborbor* (**qibẹr°bẹr°**).

kūbu (**kibiw**). A fish, halfbeak, *Hyporhamphus laticeps.*

kūbur (**kibir°**). A fish; see *kūbu.*

kūbwe (**kibey**). Also *kibwe.* Vulgar. 1(*-e*), 5(*kūbwebwe*), 6(*-i*). Excrement; manure; feces. *Kūbween wūpaaj.* Ashes. *Ekūbwebwe nuknuk eo an.* There are feces all over his clothes.

Kūbwedoul (**kibeydẹwil**). From *kūbwe* (**kibey**) "feces", *doulul* (**dewilwil**) "round". A plant, breadfruit variety (Takeuchi).

kūbween aļ (**kibeyen haļ**). From *kūbwe* (**kibey**) "feces", *aļ* (**haļ**) "sun". 6(*-i*). Slimy moss.

kūbween kijdik (**kibeyen kijdik**). From *kūbwe* (**kibey**) "feces", *kijdik* (**kijdik**) "rat". 1, 2, 6(*-i*). Drawing lots; raffle. *Raar kūbween kijdik in lale wōn eo ej etal.* They drew lots to see who would go.

kūbween lǫlǫ (**kibeyen lawlaw**). Dial. W, E: *kūbween lala.* From *kūbwe, lǫlǫ:* "hen's feces". Dirty waste water from arrowroot straining process.

kūbween ļǫñ (**kibeyen ļ°ag°**). From *kūbwe* (**kibey**) "feces", *ļǫñ* (**ļ°ag°**) "fly". 6(*-i*). Freckles.

kūbween uṃ (**kibeyen wiṃ**). From *kūbwe* "feces", *uṃ* "earth oven". Cinders.

kūbween upaaj (**kibeyen wiwpahaj**). From *kūbwe* (**kibey**) "feces", *wūpaaj* (**wipahaj**) "fireplace". 2, 6(*-i*). Ashes from fireplace; gray colored; tan colored.

Kūbwejeñōn (**kibeyjẹgẹn**). From *kūbwe* (**kibey**) "feces". 3, 6(*-i*). A plant, *Pandanus fischerianus* X *Pandanus carolinianus* (hybrid) cultigen. (Stone).

kūbwij (**kibij**). Transitive form of *kōb* (**kẹb**).

kūk (**kik**). 1(*-i*), 2, 3, 8, 9. Not ripe, of fruit; unripe. *Ekūk mā ṇe.* That breadfruit isn't ripe.

kūk (**kik**). 1(*-i*), 2(inf, tr *kij(i)*), 3, 4, 5(*kkijkij*). Bite; peck; nip. *Kwōn jab kūk.* Don't bite. *Kwōn jab kij(i) peiṃ.* Don't bite your fingers. *Kwōn* *jab kkijkij pinjeļ ņe.* Don't chew on your pencil.

kūk-. See *kk-*.

kūkōr (**kikẹr**). Dial. E, W: *jukkwe* (**jiqqẹy**). 3(*kakkōr*), 6(*-i*). Small clam, oyster, a shell, *Arcidae*, *Scapharca inequivalvis* or *Anadara pilulu*; a shell, *Veneridae*, *Veremilpa minuta/micra/costellifera/scabra* or *Dosinia histrio/abyssicola*; a shell, *Solemyidae*, *Acila schencki*; a shell, *Cadiidae*, *Corculum impressum/monstrosum/cardissa*; a shell, *Tellinidae*, *Tellinella philippii/staurella/virgata*.

kūkōr-in-ar (**kikẹr-yin-har**). 3, 4+3, 6(*-i*), 3+7. A shell, *Arcidae*, *Anadara (scapharca) satowi/broughtonii*.

kūļaabreej (**kiļahabreyej**). Slang.. Gadget.

kūļaṃwe (**kiļaṃẹy**). 2, 6(*-i*), 8, 9. Off beat; stupid; absent-minded; eccentric; loony; freak; moron; odd; clumsy; imbecile. *Ejouj ak ej jaad kūļaṃwe.* He's kind but slightly stupid.

kūļarōj (**kiļarej**). Also *kūrarej* (**kirarej**). Vulgar. 6(*-i*). Roughness around penis.

kūļatļat (**kiļatļat**). 2, 6(*-i*). Spoon cut from coconut husk. *Ej kūļatļat.* He's using a coconut husk spoon.

kūļiit (**kiļiyit**). From Engl. 2(inf, tr *-i*), 6(*-i*). Cleat.

kūļinij (**kiļiynij**). From Engl. 2(inf, tr *-i*), 4, 6(*-i*), 7. Clinch. *Kwōn kūļiniji dila kaņe.* Clinch the nails.

kūļļij (**kiļļij**). Variant form of *kiļij* (**kiyļij**).

kūļōj (**kiļẹj**). Smell of urine; stench.

kūļu (**kiļiw**). From Engl. 2(inf, tr *-ik*, *-uk*), 3, 4, 5(*kkūļuļu*), 6(*-i*), 7. Glue. *Ta ņe kwōj kūļuuki?* What are you gluing?

kūṃake (**kiṃakẹy**). A bird, gull.

kūṃaļṃaļ (**kiṃaļṃaļ**). 2, 3(inf, tr *-e*), 5(*kkūṃaļṃaļ*)+1(-i), 6(*-i*), 7, 8, 9. Frill; ornaments; insignia. *Eļak jādetok lio eto an kūṃaļṃaļ.* When she appeared, she was laden with frills.

Kūṃlujen (**kiṃliwjen**). 3, 6(*-i*). A plant, *Pandanus fischerianus* cultigen. (Stone).

kūṃṃūļọk (**kiṃṃiļaq**). 1(*-i*), 2, 3, 7. Shock. *Ear kūṃṃūļọk ke ej roñ ke emej ļeo nājin.* He was shocked when he heard that his son died.

kūṃōōr (**kiṃeher**). Trap for catching birds; esp. golden plover (*kwōlej*) and ruddy turnstone (*kōtkōt*).

kūṃur (**kiṃir°**). 1(*-i*), 2(inf, tr *-i*), 3, 4, 5(*kūṃurṃur*), 6(*-i*), 7. Ointment of leaves and oil, put on heads or chests of those allegedly attacked by ghosts to repel later attacks; herb.

kūñ (**kig**). 1(*-i*), 2, 3. Smell of feces.

kūr (**kir**). Transitive form of *kkūr* (**kkir**).

kūraaj (**kirahaj**). From Engl. Garage. *Epād ilo kūraaj eņ.* It's in the garage.

kūraaṃ (**kirahaṃ**). From Engl. Gram.

kūraaṇto (**kirahaṇtew**). From Japn. *gurando* (from Engl. *grounds*). Baseball field; playground.

kūrababboon (**kirahbabbewen**). From Engl. *gramaphone*. 6(*-i*). Phonograph.

kūrae (**kirahyey**). 2, 6(*-i*). Woman who just gave birth; pregnant woman. *Ej jab kanooj ājmour bwe kūrae.* She's not very active for she just gave birth.

kūrak (**kirak**). A plant, *Inocarpus edulus*. (Takeuchi).

kūrañ (**kirag**). A plant, *Portulaca*. (Takeuchi).

kūrañ (**kirag**). 1, 2, 3, 5(*kkūrañrañ*), 6(*-i*). Shocked; startled; stunned. *Ekūrañ kōn ainikien kabokbok eo.* He was startled by the firecracker. *Ear ṃōjjo em kakūrañ eō.* He hid and startled me. *Rilaab rōkkūrañrañ.* Yapese get startled easily.

Kūrañ (**kirag**). 3, 6(*-i*). A plant, pandanus cultigen.

kūrarōj (**kirarej**). Variant form of *kūļarōj* (**kiļarej**).

kūrawūn (**kirahwin**). From Engl. 2(inf, tr *-i*), 6(*-i*). Crown; corona; ground wire. *Enaaj or aṃ kūrawūn ilañ.* You'll wear a crown in heaven.

kūre (**kirẹy**). From Engl. 1(*-i*), 2(inf, tr *-ik*), 3, 5(*kkūrere*), 6(*-i*), 7, 8, 9, 11(*kūre, kkūrere*). Gray colored. *Ekkūrere mejān nuknuk eo an.* Her dress is grayish.

kūreep (**kirẹyẹp**). From Engl. 2(inf, tr *-e*), 5(*kkūreepep*), 6(*-i*), 7. Grape. *Rej kōṃṃan wain jān kūreep.* Wine is made from grapes.

kūrepe (**kirẹypẹy**). From Engl. 1(*-i*), 2(inf, tr *-ik(-i)*), 3, 4, 6(*-i*), 8, 9. Gravy. *Kwōn kūrepeik(i) ļọk jālele ņe bwe jen ṃōñā.* Hurry up with the gravy on the meat so we can eat.

kūriij (**kiriyij**). From Engl. 1(*-i*), 2(inf, tr *-i*), 3, 4, 5(*kūriji*), 6(*-i*), 8, 9. Grease; fat, of meat; blubber; lard. *Eḷap an kūriiji ek kā.* The fish here are too greasy.

kūriijin kkapit (**kiriyijin kkapit**). Hair pomade.

kūriin (**kiriyin**). From Engl. 1(*-i*), 2(inf, tr *-i*), 3, 5(*kkūriinin*), 6(*-i*), 7. Green.

Kūrijm̧ōj (**kirijm̧ẹj**). From Engl. 1(*-i*), 2, 3, 6(*-i*), 7. Christmas.

Kūrjin (**kirjin**). From Engl. 1(*-i*), 2(inf, tr *-i*), 3, 4, 6(*-i*), 7. Christian; church member in good standing.

kūrkaboņ (**kirkabeņ°**). From Engl. *carbuncle* (?) 2, 6(*-i*). Corns.

kūrkūr (**kirkir**). 1, 2(inf, tr *-e*), 5(*kkilparakrōk*). To tickle. *Kwōn jab kūrkūre niññiñ ņe bwe ekkilparakrōk.* Don't tickle the baby because it is ticklish.

kūrkūrbale (**kirkirbahlẹy**). Dial. E only; see *kūrūble* (**kiriblẹy**). Giant spider.

kūrm̧ool (**kirm̧ewel**). 1(*-i*), 2, 3, 7, 8, 9. Fulfill, as a prophecy.

kūro (**kirẹw**). 3, 6(*-i*). A fish, grouper, *Epinephelus fuscoguttatus*; a fish, rock cod, *Serranus fuscoguttatus.*

kūro (**kirẹw**). Variant form of *kūru* (**kiriw**).

kūrǫǫjti (**kirawajtiy**). Variant form of *kūrǫtiik* (**kirawtiyik**).

kūrǫtiik (**kirawtiyik**). Also *kūrǫǫjti* (**kirawajtiy**). From Engl. *cross-stick.* 6(*-i*). Cross-stick on ship's mast.

kūrōn (**kiren**). Also *kūrōn* (**kirẹn**), *kōrōn* (**kẹrẹn**). 2(inf, tr *-e*), 6(*-i*), 7. Speed up; accelerate. *Ear kūrōne wa eo em ko.* He sped away.

kūrro (**kirrẹw**). 1(*-i*), 2, 3, 4, 5(*kkūrroro*), 7. Gout; rheumatism; arthritis; lame; crippled. *Ekkūrroro an etetal.* He walks with a limp.

kūru (**kiriw**). Also *kūro* (**kirẹw**). From Engl. Crew. *Ewi kūru eo an wa in?* What happened to the crew of this ship?

kūrūble (**kiriblẹy**). Dial. W only; see *kūrkūrbale* (**kirkirbahlẹy**). 3, 5(*kkūrūblele*), 6(*-i*). Giant spider.

kūrwaan (**kirwahan**). 3. Food in time of famine. *Jen ilān kakūrwaan bwe jekwōle.* Let's go look for food before we starve.

kūta (**kitah**). From Engl. 1(*-i*), 2, 4, 6(*-i*), 7. Guitar. *Eḷap an jeḷā kūta.* He plays guitar well.

kūtaak (**kitahak**). 3, 6(*-i*). A plant, tree, *Allophylus timorensis* (DC.)

kūtak (**kitak**). 2, 5(*kkūtaktak*), 6(*-i*). Wind from southwest. *Ekkūtaktak allōñ jab in.* The wind generally comes from the southwest during this month.

kūtañtañ (**kitagtag**). 3, 6(*-i*). Caterpillar.

kūtarre (**kitarrey**). 1(*-i*), 2, 3, 4, 7, 8, 9. Strong; patient; diligent; perseverance. *Ekūtarre ḷeeņ ilo jerbal.* He works hard and long.

kūtim (**kitim**). Mat used to cover corpses; casket; transitive form of *kūtimtim* (**kitimtim**).

kūtimtim (**kitimtim**). 1(*-i*), 2(inf, tr *kūtim(i)*), 3, 5(*-i, kūktimtim*), 7. Wrap the body; swaddle; cover. *Em̧ōj ņe am̧ kūtimtimi ajri ņe aolep iieņ.* Why don't you stop wrapping that baby up all the time.? *Kūtimi m̧ōñā ņe bwe en jab ḷōñḷōñ.* Cover that food so that the flies don't get on it.

Kūtko (**kitkew**). Also *KITCO.* Acronym for Kwajalein Islands Trading Company; KITCO.

kūtkūt (**kitkit**). Diaḷ. Bikini only. Vulgar. 1(*-i*), 2, 3, 4, 5(*kūtkūti*), 6(*-i*), 7, 8, 9. Smell of unwashed genitals. *Bwiin kūtkūt.* There is the smell of unwashed genitals in the air.

kūtkūtijet (**kitkitiyjẹt**). A fish.

kūtōb (**kiteb**). 2(inf, tr *-e*). Wrap pandanus fruit with coconut leaves to make it ripen.

kūtōk (**kitẹk**). A fish, goby (Mejit).

kūtōm (**kitẹm**). Archaic. Large bundle of mats; see *kūtimtim.*

kūtōtō (**kitẹhtẹh**). 1(*-i*), 2(inf, tr *-ik*), 3(inf, tr *-ik*), 7, 8, 9. Very angry; furious; anger; hate; heckle; irritation; malice; rage. *Eḷap an kūtōtō ḷeo.* He is very angry. *Raar kakūtōtōiki ke ej kwaḷọk naan.* He got heckled as he gave a speech.

Kūtroro (**kitrewrew**). From *tūroro* (**tirewrew**) "wrap wtih breadfruit leaves for cooking". A plant, breadfruit variety (Takeuchi).

kūttiliek (**kittiliyẹk**). Dial. W only; see *kaattilōklōk* (**kahattilẹklẹk**). 1(*-i*), 2, 3, 4, 7. Hide-and-seek; to hide. *Wōn ņe*

BEMIS PUBLIC LIBRARY
303-795-3961
www.littletongov.org/bemis

User ID: 21393003742230

Title: Interlibrary loan materials
Item ID: 31813002298973
Date due: 3/26/2009,23:59

RENEW 24/7, 303-797-0566
or http://bemis.sirsi.net
Thank you

kwōj kūttiliek jāne? Who are you hiding from?

kūttūk (**kittik**). A game, making holes in sand and covering them; saying *kūttūke* when they cover them.

kūtuon (**kitiwen**). Construct form of *kōto* (**kętęw**).

kwaal. See *kkǫǫl.*

kwaar (**qehar**). You, plus particle of past tense singular. *Kwaar itok ñāāt?* When did you come?

kwadikdik (**qadikdik**). Put in order; put in good shape.

kwaļ (**qaļ**). Transitive form of *kwaļkoļ* (**qaļqęļ**).

kwaļini (**qaļiyniy**). Dial. E only; see *kwaļinni* (**qaļinniy**). 3, 6(*-i*). Tiny coconut not fully grown.

kwaļinni (**qaļinniy**). Dial. W only; see *kwaļini* (**qaļiniy**). 3, 6(*-i*). Tiny coconut not fully grown.

kwaļkoļ (**qaļqęļ**). 1(*-i*), 2(inf, tr *kwaļ(e)*), 4, 6(*-i*), 7. Wash; launder. *Kwōn kwaļ kōnnǫ kaņe kōn dān bwil.* Wash the dishes there with hot water. *Dān rot eo kwaar kwaļkoļ kake?* What kind of water did you use to wash with?

kwaļm̧we (**qaļm̧ęy**). 5(*kkwaļm̧wem̧we*). Fall prematurely, of coconuts. *Kwaļm̧we men e ij idaak.* This nut I'm drinking came down prematurely. *Eokkwaļm̧wem̧we leen ni eņ.* The nuts of that coconut tree are always falling down prematurely.

kwaļǫk (**qahļeq**). Also *kwaļǫk* (**qahļaq**). Transitive form of *kowaļǫk* (**kewwahļaq**).

kwaļǫk (**qahļaq**). Causative form of *waļǫk* (**wahļaq**).

kwaļǫk bōro (**qahļaq bęręw**). Slang. From *kwaļǫk* (**qahļaq**) "show", *bōro* (**bęręw**) "throat". 2, 3(inf, tr *-ik*), 4, 6(*-i*). Confession. *Kwōnañin ke kwaļǫk bōro?* Have you gone to confession yet?

kwaļǫk kadkadi- (**qahļaq kadkadi-**). 1, 2, 4, 7. Portray; describe; characterize.

kwaļǫk m̧ool (**qahļaq m̧ewel**). Confess; own up; tell the truth.

kwaļǫk naan (**qahļaq nahan**). 2, 4, 6(*-i*), 7. Oration; preach; speech; lecture. *Rukwaļǫk naan eo ewājepādik ņe.* That's the eloquent orator.

kwamijen (**qamiyjen**). Also *kǫmijen.* From Engl. Commission. *Enaaj or am̧ kwamijen.* You'll get a commission.

kwanjin (**qanjin**). 1(*-i*), 2(inf, tr *-i*), 4, 5(*kkwanjinjin*), 6(*-i*), 7. A food, breadfruit cooked on coals and scraped; to roast breadfruit. *Eokkwanjinjin lowaan m̧wiin.* The inside of this house smells of baked breadfruit. There is lots of baked breadfruit in this house. *Kwōn kwanjini mā ņe.* Roast that breadfruit.

kwañkurōj (**qagqirej**). Also *kǫñkorōj* (**kag°qerej**). From Engl. 2, 4, 6(*-i*). Congress.

kwarkor (**qarqęr**). 1, 2(inf, tr *kore*), 6(*-i*), 7, 10(*korak, korkor, kwarkor*). Bandage; tie up; wrap up. *Kore kinej ņe.* Bandage up your wound.

kwarkor (**qarqęr**). 1(*-i*), 2(inf, tr *kwarkore*), 6(*-i*), 7, 10(*kwarkor*). Roll a cigarette; pandanus leaf used for rolling cigarettes; cigarette paper. *Kwōn kwarkore jepake ņe.* Roll up that cigarette.

kwarkwar (**qarqar**). 3, 6(*-i*). A fish, sardine, *Sardinella* sp.

kwe (**qey**). You; pronoun, absolute, second person singular.

kwe (**qey**). Transitive form of *kwekwe* (**qęyqęy**).

Kwe (**qęy**). Archaic. Name of a navigational sign; a big sea bird.

kwe make (**qey makęy**). Yourself.

kweejej (**qeyejyej**). 1, 2, 3, 5(*kkweejej*), 8, 9. Fuzzy, of hair; head devoid of hair. *Emake kkweejej bōran.* His hair is so fuzzy. *Raar piļōļe rūkalbuuj ro im ear kweejej bōrāer.* The heads of the prisoners were clipped and shaved.

kweet (**qęyęt**). 3, 6(*-i*). Octopus.

kweilǫk (**qęyilaq**). Also *kwelǫk* (**qęylaq**). 1(*-i*), 2, 3(inf, tr *-e*), 4, 5(*kkweilǫklǫk*), 7. To assemble; assembly; meeting; to meet together; conference; to congregate. *Eokkweilǫklǫk kǫǫnjeļ ro.* The councilmen are always having meetings. *Kǫkwelǫk er ijeņe.* Congregate them there.

kwekwe (**qęyqęy**). 1(*-i*), 2(inf, tr *kwe*), 4, 5(*kkwekwe*), 7. Scrape; scratch. *Em̧ōj ņe am̧ kkwekwe.* Why don't you stop scratching all the time.

kwelo̧k (**qe̜ylaq**). Variant form of *kweilo̧k* (**qe̜yilaq**).

kwi (**qiy**). 1(*-i*), 2(inf, tr *-ik*), 3, 4, 5(*kkwikwi*), 6(*-i*), 7, 8, 9. Anger through jealousy; angry about injuries received; short tempered, cry-baby, provoked. *Kwōn ko̧kwiiki Jo̧o̧n m̧ōk im lale ellu ke.* Provoke John and see if he gets mad. *Eokkwikwi ļadik ņe.* The boy is a cry-baby. *Eokkwikwi ļeeņ.* That man gets angry easily.

kwi (**qiy**). Also *kuwi* (**qiwiy**). 3, 6(*-i*). A fish, surgeonfish, *Acanthurus lineatus.*

kwiin (**qiyin**). From Engl. 2, 3(inf, tr *-i*), 6(*-i*). Queen. *Ej kwiin kiiō.* She's a queen now. *Raar ko̧kwiini inne.* She was crowned queen yesterday. *Kwiinin at.* A queen of hearts.

kwiir (**qiyir**). Vulgar. 1, 2(inf, tr *-i*), 3, 6(*-i*). To wipe oneself after defecating.

kwōd (**qed**). 6(*-i*). Husk fibre.

kwōdaelem (**qedhaye̜le̜m**). Land given by a chief to a commoner as a bounty for bailing out the chief's canoe in battle expeditions.

kwōdeak (**qedyak**). 1(*-i*), 2, 3, 4, 5(*kwōdeake*), 7, 8, 9. Beard; whiskers; mustache. *Ekwōdeake ļeeņ.* That man has lots of whiskers--a big beard.

kwōdkwōdi (**qe̜dqe̜diy**). Slang. 2, 3(inf, tr *-ik*), 5(*(k)kwōdkwōdi*), 7, 8, 9. Scabby; scaly skin. *Ekwōdkwōdi kilin neen lieņ.* Her legs are scabby.

kwōdmat (**qedmat**). Also *kumat* (**qimat**). 1(*-i*), 2(inf, tr *-e*), 3, 4, 5(*kkwōdmatmat, kkumatmat*), 7. Clip all of the hair off. *Wōn ņe ear kwōdmate eok?* Who shaved your head? *Eokkwōdmatmat ļeeņ.* That man always shaves his head.

kwōdmat (**qedmat**). Also *reja* (**reyjah**). Slang. To strip of money or property by fraud or threat; to fleece someone; to sponge off of someone.

kwōj (**qej**). You, singular progressive. *Kwōj etal ñan ia?* Where are you going?

kwōj (**qej**). 1(*-i*), 2, 3, 7, 8, 9. Congeal; solidify; thicken; stiffen; freeze; hardening of starch or tallow or lead.

kwōj (**qej**). 1(*-i*), 2(inf, tr *kwōje*), 5(*kkwōjkwōj(e)*), 7(*kwōjjeļo̧k*). Break, sticks or bones; snap; break, as a branch. *Jab kepaak jabōn ra ņe bwe enaaj kwōjjeļo̧k.* Don't go near the end of the branch or it will give way. *Em̧ōj kkwōjkwōje aļaļ eo.* The stick has been broken into pieces.

kwōjabkwōjab (**qejabqejab**). Variant form of *kwōjabm̧ōk* (**qejabm̧ek**).

kwōjabm̧ōk (**qejabm̧ek**). Also *kwōjabkwōjab* (**qejabqejab**), *ekweekwe* (**yeqeyyeqey**). Interjection: "You don't say!"

kwōje (**qejey**). Wrap up; to coil.

kwōje dunen meļaaj (**qejey diwnen meļahaj**). Idiom. 2, 4. Neglect the commoners. *Jab kwōje dunen meļaaj.* Don't neglect the commoners because that's where the strength lies.

kwōjenmeto (**qejenmetew**). 2, 6(*-i*). Sea demon. *Ekwōjenmeto lieņ.* She's possessed by a sea demon.

kwōjkwōj (**qejqej**). 2, 3(inf, tr *-e*), 4, 6(*-i*). Communion, church usage; feast. *Kwōjkwōj an Irooj.* Holy Communion. *Bata eo ear ko̧kwōjkwōje rinañinmej ro.* The priest gave holy communion to the sick people.

kwōjkwōjin pālele (**qejqejin pale̜yle̜y**). Idiom. Matrimony; marriage feast; wedding; marrige ceremony.

kwōl (**qel**). A bird, semi-palmate sandpiper, *Ereunetes pusillus*; a bird, sanderling, *Crocethia alba.*

kwōle (**qe̜le̜y**). Dial. W, E: *eañden* (**yagden**). 1(*-i*), 2, 3(inf *ko̧kkwōlele,* tr *ko̧kwōleik*), 5(*kkwōlele*), 7. Hungry; starved; underfed; undernourished; famine. *Eokkwōlele ļeeņ.* That man gets hungry easily. *Ij ko̧kkwōlele ļak m̧ōj m̧ōñā.* I'll fast before eating. *Raar ko̧kwōleik rūttariņae ro.* They starved the soldiers. *Ear or kwōle ilo 1901.* There was a famine in 1901.

kwōle (**qeley**). 1(*-e*), 3(inf *ko̧kwōle, ko̧kkwōlele,* tr *ko̧kwōleik*), 5(*kkwōlele*), 6(*-i*). Kernel; fruit; seed; nut; testicle; berry. *Em̧ōj ko̧kwōleik piik eo.* The pig has been castrated. *Eokkwōlele mā e.* This breadfruit is full of nuts.

kwōlej (**qe̜lye̜j**). Also *kwōlej* (**qelyej**). 3, 5(*kkwōlejej*), 6(*-i*). A bird, golden plover, *Pluvialis dominica; snipe. Eokkwōlejej ānin.* This island has lots of snipe.

kwōlej (**qe̜lye̜j**). A fish, snapper, *Scolopsis cancellatus.*

kwōlejiped (**qeleyjiped**). Also *kwōlemat* (**qeleymat**). 6(*-i*). A food, nuts of breadfruit, cooked.

kwōmej (**qẹmẹj**). Fishing method, using scarer and weir.

kwōn (**qen**). Stand a torch in the ground.

kwōnono (**qenewnew**). Variant form of *kōnono* (**kenewnew**).

kwōp (**qep**). Slang. 2, 7(*kwōppeḷọk*). Smashed; wiped out, busted, stoned. *Ear idaak im kwōppeḷọk.* He drank till he got stoned.

kwōpej (**qẹpẹj**). 1(*kupiji-*), 3, 7. Trash; garbage; junk; offal; refuse; rubbish; waste; litter. *Ewi waan jọkwōpej eo ke elōn̄ kwōpej.* Where's the garbage truck; there's lots of garbage.

kwōpejpej (**qẹpẹjpẹj**). 1(*-i*), 2, 7. Throw waste food or trash somewhere; litter. *Kwōn kwōpejpej ṇa ilo iep eṇ.* Put the waste food in that basket. *Jab kọkwōpejpeje iaḷ ṇe.* Don't litter the road.

kwōpra (**qẹprah**). A fish, goby (Mejit).

la (**lah**). Dial. W, E: *le* (**ley**). Ma'am; vocative, feminine singular.

la (**lah**). From Engl. Syllable "la" of musical scale.

la (**lah**). Also *wūnaak*. 6(*laan*). Attraction of big fish to smaller fish; a flock of birds flying over a school of fish. *Laan bao.* A flock of birds (fishing). *Laan ek.* A school of fish (chasing another school.)

laajrak (**lahajrak**). 1(*-i*), 2, 3(*kōllaajrak*), 7. Line; order; rank; list. *Eṃṃan laajrak in ṃokaṇ.* Those houses are lined up nicely. *Laajrak eo eo.* Here's the list.

laklak (**laklak**). Dial. E, W: *bukbuk* (**biqbiq**). 3, 6(*-i*). A shell, Cassididae, *Cassis cornuta*, helmet shell.

lala (**lahlah**). A fish, parrotfish, *Callyodon pulchellus.*

lala (**lahlah**). Dialectal variant of *lọlọ* (**lawlaw**).

lale (**lahley**). 1(*-i*), 2(inf, tr sg. obj. *lale*, pl. obj. *lali*), 4, 7. Look; see; look at; look after; observe; summon; take care of; supervise; manage. *Lale tok taktō eo.* Summon the doctor. *Kwōnāj lale ṃōṇe ṃōrro n̄e ijako.* You'll manage our house when I'm gone.

laḷ (**laḷ**). 1(*-i*), 4, 7. World; on the ground; country of the world; below; down; earth; nation; directional, enclitic, downward; bottom. *Ipād laḷūṃ ilo teej eo.* I scored below you on the test. *Laḷ ta ko raar tariṇae ilo pata eo kein karuo?* What countries fought in the second world war? *Baḷuun eo eṇ laḷḷọk.* There goes the plane downward.

laḷ (**laḷ**). 2, 6(*-i*), 7. Ante, in poker.

laḷḷọk (**laḷḷaq**). Downward. *Baḷuun eo uweo laḷḷọk.* There's that plane going downward.

laṃōj (**laṃẹj**). 1(*-i*), 2(inf, tr *-e*), 5(*llaṃōjṃōj*), 7. To shout; call; holler. *Kwōn laṃōje tok.* Call him to come. *Kwōn jab llaṃōjṃōj.* Don't keep shouting. *Wōn eo ear laṃōj?* Who hollered?

lan̄ (**lag**). 4. Sky; weather; heaven. *Eṃṃan lan̄.* The weather is nice. *Kwōnaaj mej ilan̄.* You're on the road to perdition.

lan̄lōn̄ (**lagḷẹg**). 1(*-i*), 2, 3, 4, 7. Joy; merriment.

Lan̄lōn̄ (**lagḷẹg**). 3, 6(*-i*). A plant, *Pandanus fischerianus* cultigen. (Stone). Majuro.

lan̄ṃwijidjid (**lagṃijidjid**). Also *lōn̄ mejidjid* (**leg mejidjid**). 2, 8. Overwhelmed (usually with negative emotion). *Ledik eo ear lan̄ṃwijidjid kōn būroṃōj.* The girl was overwhelmed with grief.

lā (**lay**). 2, 3(st *kōllāle*, inf *kōlā*, tr *kōlāik*), 5(*llāle*), 6(*-i*), 7. To bank, of airplanes; to roll, of ships; to list; to capsize. *Elā wa eo.* The boat capsized. *Waini lōn̄lōn̄ eo ekalāik wa eo.* The great quantity of copra made the boat list. *Ellāle wa eṇ.* The boat is top-heavy (rolls a lot). *Ellāle wa eo.* The boat rolled a lot. *Elā baḷuun eo ke ej jeer.* The plane banked when it turned.

lāj (**laj**). 1(*-i*), 2, 3, 4, 7, 8, 9. Cruel; fierce; mean; ferocious; grim; harsh; hostile. *Elāj kidu eṇ.* That dog is ferocious. *Kwōn jab lāj.* Don't be mean.

lām (**lam**). Crystalline style; organ of giant clam.

lān̄wi (**layg°iy**). Variant form of *lọn̄i* (**lawg°iy**).

lāwūn Pikaar (**laywin pikahar**). Variant form of *lọun Pikaar* (**lawin pikahar**).

le (**lęy**). 3, 6(*-i*). A bird, black-footed albatross, *Diomedea nigripes*; a bird, laysan albatross, *Diomedea immutabilis*; albatross.

le (**ley**). Ma'am; vocative, feminine singular.

le (**ley**). Use; be equipped with; with. *Wa eṇ ej leinjin.* That boat has an engine. *Jitob eṇ ej lekarjin.* That stove uses kerosene.

le (**ley**). 1(*-e*), 2, 3(*kalle*), 6(*-e*), 7. Bear fruit; fruit. *Ejjañin le bōb eṇ.* That pandanus hasn't borne fruit yet. *Kwōj ṃōñā ke leen wōjke?* Do you like fruits?

Le (**lęy**). Formant in place names; name of legendary bird banished by *Jebrọ* along with the *aol* fish because of their tardiness; said to be isolated on the ocean today and die when it gets to land; see *lia.*

le- (**ley-**). 1+7, 2+7, 7. Give; offer; administer; grant; render.

leak- (**leyhak-**). Also *lōkake.* 2, 4, 7. Take; carry; transfer; ferry; transport. *Ej leakḷọk jemān ñan Rita.* He's taking his father to Rita. *Rōnaaj lōkaketok tūraṃ eo kōn juon tūrak.* They'll bring over the drum by truck.

lear (**leyhar**). 1(*-i*), 2, 4, 7. To drag or tow from ocean side to lagoon side. *Wa eo eṇ rej lear tak.* They are dragging that canoe up from the ocean to the lagoon side.

leāne (**leyyanęy**). 1(*-i*), 2, 7. Set ashore. *Leāne tak wa ṇe.* Set that boat ashore.

leddik (**leddik**). Also *leddik* (**lęddik**), and *ledik* (**lędik**) or *ledik* (**ledik**) preceding demonstratives. 3, 6(*-i*). Girl. *Ledikin ia eṇ?* Where is that girl from?

Ledik-raṇ-nājin-Jebrọ (**ledik-raṇ-najin-jebraw**). A constellation; stars in Taurus; pi and 71; *Jebrọ*'s daughters, said to be running away from *Ḷoojḷapḷap* (**ḷewejḷapḷap.**

Ledikdik (**ledikdik**). Archaic. A star; sister of *Liṃanṃan* and *Lijṃaan.*

leea (**lęyyah**). 1(*-i*), 2, 3(inf, tr *-ik*), 4, 6(*-i*), 7. Laugh hysterically; laugh long and loudly. *Iar kiki im roñ ainikien al im leea.* While I was asleep, I heard the sound of song and laughter. *Rūkōṃṃan kōjak eo ear kaleeaik rūalwōj ro.* The comedian really made the audience laugh. *Koṃwin jab ttōñ leea bwe rej kiki.* Don't laugh so loudly because they are sleeping.

leelle (**leyelley**). Also *lele* (**leyley**). Far; a great distance. *Ijuweo leelle.* Way over there.

leep (**leyep**). 2, 3(inf, tr *-e*), 4, 5(*lleepep*), 6(*-i*), 7. Marshallese folk dance; usually done in groups; slow moving. *Jej aikuj jaruki ṃanit ko ad rōmājkunḷọk im katakin ajri ro nājid leep ñe re jañin kar jeḷā.* We must revive some of our waning customs such as *leep* dancing by teaching our children if they don't already know how.

leet (**leyet**). From Engl. 3, 6(*-i*). Lead.

leinjin (**lęyyinjin**). 2(inf, tr *-i*), 4, 6(*-i*), 7. Use an engine; operate an engine. *Ej leinjin ke wa eṇ?* Is that boat using an engine? *Ijaje leinjin.* I can't use (operate) a motor. *Juon in ear leinjinin wūdkabbeiki.* Some jerk must have operated this motor.

lejān (**leyjan**). 1(*-i*), 2, 4, 6(*-i*), 8, 9. Adultery. *Ejjeḷọk wōt lejāniier.* They're so adulterous. *Rilejān.* Adulterer. *Elejān ḷọk jān e.* He's more adulterous than that other person. *Kwōn jab lejān.* Thous shalt not commit adultery.

lejjibjib (**lejjibjib**). Female of quarter royal descent; father a *bwidak* (**bidak**); mother a *kajoor* (**kajwęr**).

lejḷā (**lęjḷay**). 6(*-i*). Chief's wife, may or may not be of royal blood.

lejnono (**lejnewnew**). Unmarried woman; spinster; maid.

lejọñjọñ (**leyjag°jag°**). Dial. E only; see *ekkokowa* (**yekkewkewwah**). Also *lejoñjoñ* (**leyjeg°jeg°**). 1(*-i*), 2(inf, tr *-e*), 3, 4, 7. A game, juggling; juggle.

lekarjin (**leykarjin**). 2(inf, tr *-i*), 4, 6(*-i*), 7. Use kerosene. *Jeban lekarjin bwe emaat.* We won't be using kerosene anymore because there's no more left. *Rilekarjin eo ṇe.* That's the guy who uses a lot of kerosene.

lekōn (**lęykęn**). 2(inf, tr *-e*), 4, 5(*llekōnkōn*), 6(*-i*), 7. To poke into a hole persistently at something, usually an octopus. *Kwōn lekōne wōt bwe en waḷok.* Keep poking at it so it'll come out.

lekōto (**leykętęw**). 1(*-i*), 2(inf, tr *-ik*, *-uk*), 3, 4, 6(*-i*), 7. To shoot the breeze; soft sell; to proposition; chat idly. *Jab lekōto bwe elōñ jerbal.* Don't chat idly--there's lots of work to be done.

lel (**lęl**). 1(*-i*), 2, 3, 5(*llellel*), 7. Struck; hit; hit the mark; shot down. *Elel bao eo.* The bird has been hit. *Ellellel baḷuun eṇ.* That plane always gets hit. *Elel kōn jipij eo aṃ.* He was shot down by your speech.

lel-. See *ll-*.

lele (**lęlęy**). From Engl. Lily.

lele (**leyley**). Variant form of *leelle* (**leyelley**).

lelik (**lęylik**). 1(*-i*), 2, 4, 7. To drag or tow from lagoon side to ocean side; hand something to the rear or back. *Kwōn lelik ḷọk wa ṇe.* Drag that canoe to the ocean side.

lelkan (**lelkan**). Also *lelñan* (**lelgan**). Series; a batch.

lelñan (**lelgan**). Variant form of *lelkan* (**lelkan**).

lelōñ (**lęylęg**). 1, 2, 4, 7. Lift. *Lelōñḷọk aḷaḷ ṇe.* Lift that piece of wood.

leḷọk (**leyḷaq**). 1(*-i*), 2, 8. Give away.

leḷọk-letok (**leyḷaq-leyteq**). From *le* (**ley**) "give", *tok* (**teq**) "hither", *ḷọk* (**ḷaq**) "away". 2. Argument; misgiving; quarrel; spat. *Erro leḷọk-letok bajjek ak ejjeḷọk tōprak.* They argued and never agreed on anything. *Iban etal im ejjeḷọk bar leḷọk-letok.* I won't go, and there are no if's, and's or but's about it.

leḷōmṇak (**leyḷemṇak**). 1(*-i*), 2, 7. Guess; estimate; speculate; surmise; conjecture. *Kwōn jab leḷōmṇak ak kwōn bwine.* Don't guess--figure it out exactly.

lem (**lęm**). 6(*-i*). Bailer.

lemlem (**lęmlęm**). 1(*-i*), 2(inf, tr *lim(i)*), 3, 4, 7, 8, 10(*limek*). Fold; wrap; packed; package. *Eṃōj ke aṃ lemlem?* Have you finished folding? *Kwōn lim(i) jaki kaṇe.* Fold those mats. *Lemlem in ta ṇe?* What's in the package?

lemḷat (**lęmḷat**). 3. An animal, white land crab.

lemñoul (**lęmgęwil**). 2, 3(inf, tr *-e*), 5(*kallemñoul*), 7. Fifty.

leṃōṇōṇō (**leyṃeṇehṇeh**). 1(*-i*), 2, 4, 7, 8, 9. Cheerful; merry. *Eḷap an leṃōṇōṇō mour eṇ an.* He leads a cheerful existence.

lennab (**lęnnab**). 1(*-i*), 2, 3, 7, 8, 9. Hives; allergy; rash. *Ilennab kōn kieb ko iar būki.* I got the hives from those spider lilies I carried.

leṇak (**leyṇak**). Also *joṇak* (**jewṇak**). Sleep soundly.

lep (**lęp**). 1(*lipe-*, *lepi-*). Egg.

lepā (**leypay**). Vulgar slang. From *le* (**ley**) "use", *pā* (**pay**) "hand". 1, 2, 4, 5(*llepāpā*). Masturbate.

Lepni (**lepniy**). From *lepi-* (**lepi-**) "egg", *ni-* (**niy**) "coconut" (?). A plant, *Pandanus fischerianus* cultigen (Takeuchi). (Stone). (Utirik).

lerooj (**lęyręwęj**). 6(*-i*). Daughter of a queen; high chieftess; queen.

letak (**leytak**). Vulgar slang. Have sexual relations.

leto (**leytew**). 1(*-i*), 2(inf, tr *-ik(i)*), 4, 7. Use a rope.

letok (**leyteq**). 1, 2, 8. Give to the speaker.

letōñ (**lęytęg**). Blow sharply, of wind.

lewōj (**lęywęj**). Also *lewaj* (**leywaj**). 1(*-i*). Give to you.

lewōjḷā (**lęywęjḷay**). 2(inf, tr *-ik*), 4, 6(*-i*), 7. Use a sail. *Emaroñ ṃōkaj ḷọk ñe kwōnaaj lewōjḷāiki.* It may run faster if it uses a sail. *Kwōj lewōjḷā ḷọk ñan ia?* Where are you sailing?

Li- (**li-**). Prefix to feminine names.

lia (**liyah**). Archaic. Be estranged from; see *le*.

liaajḷọḷ (**liyahajlaḷ°**). Also *liaajḷoḷ* (**liyahajḷ°eḷ°**). 1, 2, 3(inf *kalliaajḷọḷ*, tr *kaliaajḷọḷ*), 6(*-i*), 8, 9. Afflicted; distressed; lament; mourning; lamentation. *Eḷap an liaajḷọḷ kōn aer kọkkure.* She was greatly distressed by their jeers. *Etke kwōj eḷḷọk jān aō liaajḷọḷ?* Why do you turn away when I'm so distressed?

liaakḷọk (**liyahakḷaq**). 1(*-i*), 2, 4. Condemn; betray; be railroaded. *Eṃōj liaakḷọk ñan mej.* They condemned him (or them) to die. *Eṃōj liaakeḷọk ñan mej.* They condemned him to die.

lianij (**liyhanij**). 2(inf, tr *-i*), 3(inf, tr *-i*), 6(*-i*), 7. Dark cloudy night; somber; gloomy. *Einwōt enaaj wōt ke elianij tok.* Looks like a rainy night as it is dark and cloudy.

liāp (**liyap**). 1(*-i*), 2(inf, tr *-e*), 4, 7. Tie up a person or animal; bind. *Kwōn liāpe piik ṇe.* Tie up that pig.

liāp (**liyap**). 1(*-i*), 2, 3, 4, 8, 9. Funny; joke. *Eḷap an liāp* Bob Hope. Bob Hope is very funny.

libar (**libar**). Variant form of *bar.*

libbukwe (**libbiqẹy**). 3, 6(-*i*). A shell, *Cypraeidae*; *Arabica scurra/eglantina/couturiera/asiatica* or *Cyraea tigris*, etc. A shell, *Ovulidae*; *Ovula costellatum*. Any cowrie shell, any shell.

libbūn̦ōj (**libbin̦ej**). Also *lūbbun̦ōj* (**libbin̦°ej**). 3, 6(-*i*). Shrimp.

libbūn̦ōj (**libbin̦ej**). Also *lūbbun̦ōj* (**libbin̦°ej**). 1, 2(inf, tr -*e*), 4, 6(-*i*), 7. To flick someone or something with the fingers. *Kwōn jab libbūn̦ōje eō bwe imetak.* Stop flicking me with your fingers because it hurts.

libobo (**libẹwbẹw**). 1(-*i*), 2, 3(inf *kalbubu*, tr *kalbubuuk(i)*), 7, 8, 9, 11(*libobo*). Cover; lid. *Kwōn kalbubuuk wa n̦e.* Cover that canoe. *Ewi libobo eo an kōm̧a n̦e?* What happened to that cauldron's lid?

libooror (**libẹwẹrwẹr**). 1(-*i*), 2(inf, tr -*e*), 3, 4, 7. Chase; a chase. *L̦oon eo ear liboorore tim̧a eo.* The launch chased the ship.

libōntōr (**libenter**). Variant form of *libwetōr* (**libeyter**).

libwetōr (**libeyter**). Also *lūbōntōr* (**libenter**). 5(*libwetōre*), 6(-*i*). Dimples. *Elibwetōre jiron̄ en̦.* She's got double dimples.

lidid (**liydid**). 3, 4+3, 6(-*i*), 3+7. A shell, *Muricidae*; *Drupa ricina/morum* or *Purpura* (mancinella); *Distinguenda/echinata*; common snail.

lie (**liyẹy**). This woman (close to me); this girl (close to me); personal demonstrative, first person exclusive singular feminine.

liele (**liyẹlẹy**). 6(-*i*). A fish, triggerfish, *Rhinecanthus aculeatus.*

lien̦ (**liyen̦**). That woman (close to neither of us); that girl (close to neither of us); personal demonstrative, third person singular feminine.

lien̦e (**liyen̦ey**). That woman (close to you); that girl (close to you); personal demonstrative, second person singular feminine.

lien̦en̦e (**liyen̦eyn̦ey**). That woman (close to you); that girl (close to you); personal demonstrative, second person singular feminine, singling out.

liien̦ (**liyiyen̦**). That woman (close to neither of us); personal demonstrative, third person singular feminine, singling out.

liin (**liyin**). This woman (close to us both); this girl (close to us both); personal demonstrative, first person inclusive singular feminine.

liiō (**liyiyẹh**). This woman (close to us both); this girl (close to us both); personal demonstrative, first person exclusive singular feminine, singling out; vocative, familiar, feminine singular. *Liiō kwōn kōtl̦ok eō.* Let me go, girl.

liit (**liyit**). 2(inf, tr -*i*), 5(*lliitit*), 7. Yank a fishline; jerk. *Liit eo n̦e.* Yank on the line. *Kokadik lliitit.* You're always jerking the line (even though there's no fish on it).

lij (**lij**). 2(inf, tr -*i*), 6(-*i*), 7, 11(*lij*). Beat; mash; pound; grind; digest; whip; transitive form of *lijlij* (**lijlij**). *Raar liji mā ko.* They mashed the breadfruit. *Kwōn lukkuun liji bwe en mālij.* Pound it well so it becomes paste.

lij (**lij**). Also *rōm̧* (**rẹm̧**). Crumble; scatter.

lijaakkwōlele (**lijahakqeleyley**). Ankle bones. *Emetak lijaakkwōlelein neō.* My ankle bones are painful.

lijadoul (**lijadẹwil**). Anything small and round; see *ja.*

lijakkwe (**lijakqẹy**). 3, 6(-*i*). Cotton coral.

lijā (**lijay**). Gal; lass; miss; usually used with demonstratives.

lijāludik (**lijaliwdik**). Also *lijidduul* (**lijiddiwil**). Slang. 1, 2, 3(inf *kallijāludik*, tr *kalijāludik*), 4, 6(-*i*). Smoke illicitly. *Ej kalbuuj bwe ear lijāludik.* He's being punished for smoking. *Ear kalijāludiki ajri ro.* He unlawfully gave cigarettes to the youngsters. *Raar rupe kien jikuul̦ im lijidduul.* They broke school rules and smoked.

lije (**lijey**). Rinse bait. *Ej lije m̧ọọr eo n̦ai l̦ọjet. Ej liji m̧ọọr ko n̦ai l̦ọjet.* He's rinsing the bait in the sea.

Lijebake (**lijebakey**). A legendary turtle.

lijekl̦ọk (**lijẹkl̦aq**). 3. Very great; greatest; exalted above another.

lijeljelm̧ak (**lijẹljẹlm̧ak**). Wiggler larvae of mosquitoes.

lijem̧ao (**lijẹym̧ahwew**). 3, 6(-*i*). A bird, short-eared owl, *Asio flammeus;* female; see *m̧ao.*

lijeṃōrṃōr (**lijęyṃęrṃęr**). 1(*-i*), 2(inf, tr *-e*), 3, 7, 8, 9. Foam. *Elijeṃōrṃōr ioon ņoon baal.* It's quite foamy on the breaker's crests.

lijeñūrñūr (**lijęygirgir**). Also *lijeñūrñūr* (**lijeygirgir**), *lijeñōrñōr* (**lijęygęrgęr**). 2, 6(*-i*), 7. Distant rumbling of waves; sound of waves pounding on reef.

Lijepen (**lijeypęn**). A plant, pandanus cultigen (Takeuchi).

lijib (**lijib**). Dial. E, W: *bwijij* (**bijij**). Also *ļijib* (**ļijib**), *bwijil* (**bijil**). 2, 3(*kallijibjib*), 5(*llijibjib*), 6(*-i*), 8, 9. Blunt. *Elijib bōraņ doon e.* The point of the husking stick is blunt. *Wōn ar kalijibi bōran doon e.* Who made the point of this husking stick blunt?

lijidduul (**lijiddiwil**). Variant form of *lijāludik* (**lijaliwdik**).

lijjapillo (**lijjahpillęw**). 6(*-i*). A game, with blindfolds.

lijjibūbū (**lijjibihbih**). Affectionate term for grandmother; granddaughter.

lijjidwaļọk (**lijjidwahļaq**). 1, 2, 3(inf *kallijjidwaļọk*, tr *kalijjidwaļọk*), 4, 6(*-i*). A swing. *Ear kalijjidwaļọke ledik eo nājin.* He pushed his daughter on the swing.

lijjikin (**lijjikin**). Also *lijjikōn* (**lijjikęn**). 2, 4, 6(*-i*). A game, child's play using pebbles and shells as imaginary objects and characters.

lijjikwōlkwōl (**lijjiyqelqel**). Variant form of *lijjukwōlkwōl* (**lijjiqelqel**).

lijjipdo (**lijjipdew**). 1, 2, 3(inf, tr *-uk*), 7, 8, 9. Weak in the legs. *Joñan an lijjipdo jidik wōt iuuni ak eokjak.* He's so weak in the legs that even a little push would make him fall down.

lijjọọn (**lijjawan**). Gal; dame.

lijjukul (**lijjiqil**). Vulgar. 2(inf, tr *-e*), 4, 6(*-i*). Fondle sexually.

lijjukwōlkwōl (**lijjiqelqel**). Also *lijjikwōlkwōl* (**lijjiyqelqel**). Peashooter; shotgun; pistol; revolver. *Eṃṃan wōt lijjukwōlkwōl ņe aṃ.* Your shotgun sure looks beautiful.

lijjurpe (**lijjir°pęy**). Variant form of *jjurpe* (**jjir°pęy**).

lijlij (**lijlij**). 2(inf, tr *lij(e)*), 4, 6(*-i*). Pound food; mash.

lijunaṃnaṃ (**lijiwnaṃnaṃ**). 2, 4, 6(*-i*). A game, diving for pandanus.

lik (**lik**). 1(*-i*), 6(*-i*), 7, 9. Behind; in back of; outside; ocean side of; exterior; external; rear; directional, enclitic, backward or toward the ocean side. *Aolep uraak likļọk.* Everyone move to the rear. *Kōjro wanlikļọk.* Let's go to the oceanside.

lik (**lik**). 2, 3, 5(*lliklik*). To set, of hens; to lay eggs. *Elik bao eo.* The chicken is setting. *Elliklik bao eņ.* That chicken is always setting. *Eato wōn eo em lik.* The turtle crawled ashore and laid eggs.

likaabdoulul (**likahabdęwilwil**). Also *likaadboulul* (**likahadbęwilwil**), *likaaddeboulul* (**likahaddębęwilwil**). 3, 4+3, 6(*-i*), 3+7. Trochus, a shell, *Pleurotomariidae*; *Perotrochus teramachii* or *Mikadotrochus schmalzi.*

likaadboulul (**likahadbęwilwil**). Variant form of *likaabdoulul* (**likahabdęwilwil**).

likaakrak (**likahakrak**). 1(*-i*), 2, 3, 5(*likaakrake*), 6(*-i*), 8, 9. Have maggots; as dead matter; worm, maggot. *Eļap an likaakrake bwiro ņe.* That preserved breadfruit is full of maggots. *Elikaakrak ek eo.* The fish had maggots.

likaaļļaj (**likahaļļaj**). A food, *peru* cooked in certain shapes.

Likabwiro (**likabiyręw**). Name of a storm that usually comes in the summer. *Allōñin rak ej iien Likabwiro.* The summer months are Likabwiro's months.

likaebeb (**likahyebyeb**). Also *likaeb* (**likahyeb**). 2, 3, 5(*llikāebeb*), 6(*-i*). Cone shell; a shell, *Conidae*; *Conasprella praecellea/comatosa/sowerbii* or *Profundiconus profundiconus*. Also *Hermes mitratus/cylindraceus/auriconus/clavus*; *Leptoconus kawamurai/ammiralis*; *Lithoconus eburneus/litteratus/pardus*; *Conus marmoreus/bandanus*; etc. *Ellikaebeb likin ānin.* The ocean side of this islet has lots of cone shells.

likaebeb (**likahyebyeb**). Also *likaeb* (**likahyeb**). 2(inf, tr *-e*), 3, 6(*-i*). Top; a toy, of shells or wood; spin. *Kwōn kalikaebebe.* Spin it.

likajik (**likajik**). 2(inf, tr *-i*), 6(*-i*). Gun; pistol; revolver. *Likajikin ia ņe aṃ?* Where did your pistol come from?

likajjid (**likajjid**). 3, 4+3, 6(*-i*), 3+7. Money cowrie, a shell, *Cypraeidae*; *Erosaria helvola/erosa/flaveola* or

Monetaria annulus harmandiniana/ moneta rhomboides. Also *Notadusta martini katsuae*; *Palmadusta lutea*; and *Perstolida coffea/ursellus.*

likakōj (likakej). 1(-*i*), 2(inf, tr -*e*), 3, 5(*llikakōjkōj*), 6(-*i*), 7. To pine; to long; yearn; reminisce. *Emōj ņe aṃ llikakōjkōj bwe eban or men etōprak.* Quit your wistful yearning if you want to accomplish anything.

likao (likahwew). 1(-*i*), 2, 3, 5(*likaoe*), 6(-*i*). Young man. *Elikaoe ānin.* This islet has lots of young men. *Likao in ia eņ?* Where is that young man from?

likapijwewe (likahpijwẹywẹy). 2. Cowlick; whorl; whirlpool; vortex. *Elikapijwewe bōran.* He's got a cowlick.

likarkar (likarkar). 2(inf, tr -*e*), 6(-*i*), 8, 9. A shell, *Macrophragma tokyeense* (*Turritellidae*).

likatōttōt (likatettet). 2. Stay where one is at patiently; stay put. *Likatōttōt wōt bwe enañin iien ṃupi wōt jidik.* Be patient and stay where you are because it's almost time for the movie.

likbad (likbad). 2(inf, tr -*e*), 4, 6(-*i*), 7. Test drive a new or overhauled vehicle; test sail a new or overhauled vessel.

liki (likiy). Archaic. Ocean side of; outside; behind; old construct form of *lik.*

likiej (likiyẹj). 1(-*i*), 6(-*i*), 7. Windward side of an atoll; eastern side.

likiio (likiyyẹw). 1(-*i*), 2, 3, 7. Whole; all present; get together; intact. *Ear kalikiio juon pāākin mā im wiaiki.* He bought a whole bag of breadfruit.

Likin-Buwame (likin-biwamẹy). See *Buwame,* a tract of land on *Piñlep* islet, Jaluit; "ocean side of Buwame". A star; Rediculus (alpha Pavonis).

likipia (likipiyah). 6(-*i*). Fish eggs; roe.

likjab (likjab). 1(-*i*), 2, 3, 4, 5(*llikjabjab*), 7, 8, 9. Fall short of; be too late; not reach; less than; owe; debt; deficit; due; fail; liability; moron. *Ilikjab jān laļ.* I can't reach the ground. *Ellikjabjab ļeo.* He's always in debt. *Elikjab jān wa eo.* He missed the boat.

likjerjer (likjẹrjẹr). Variant form of *lipjerjer* (lipjẹrjẹr).

likko (likkẹw). 1(-*i*), 2(inf, tr -*ik(i)*), 6(-*i*). Petticoat; slip; gown; skirt.

Likkūr (likkir). From *ikūr* "mixed up". Name of waves caused by typhoon; fifth largest.

liklaļ (liklaļ). Leeward side of an atoll; western and northwestern island northwestern islands in an atoll.

liklep (liklep). Pain in testicles.

liklik (liklik). 1(-*i*), 2(inf, tr -*i*), 7. Strain; sift; digest; filter. *Kwōn likliki pilawā ņe bwe ekijkij.* Sift that flour because it has lots of bugs in it.

liklọk (liklaq). Fishing method with a canoe and line on the ocean side.

liko (likẹw). 2(inf, tr -*ik*), 4, 6(-*i*). Rubber band. *Kwōn likoik bōraṃ bwe en jab jjopālpāl.* Use a rubber-band to hold your hair from flapping in the wind.

likōb (likẹb). A fish, wrasse, *Coris gaimardi*; *Xyrichthys taeniouris*; *Cymolutes praetextatus.*

likōbla (likeblah). 1(-*i*), 2(inf, tr -*ik(i)*), 4, 6(-*i*), 7, 8, 9. A food, three to one combination of arrowroot starch and water cooked together. *Ejejjet utōn likōbla in.* This *likōbla* is well prepared. *Likōblaiki ṃakṃōk jidik ņe bwe en kabwebwe.* Make *likōbla* out of the little starch that's left so that all of us can partake of it.

likōk (likẹk). Preparedness; vigilance; perseverance.

likōmjāje (likemjayjẹy). Also *likōmmejāje* (likemmejayjẹy). 1(-*i*), 2(inf, tr -*ik*), 4, 7, 8, 9. Show-off; boast.

likōpejñak (likẹpẹjgak). Also *likōppejñak* (likẹppẹjgak). Shield; protection; guardian. *Anij ej aō likōpejñak jān Jetan.* God is my shield from satan.

likōppejdat (likẹppẹjdat). 3, 6(-*i*). Trochus, a shell, *Trochidae, Omphalius pfeifferi* or *Tristichotrochus haliarchus.* A shell, *Pleurotomariidae*; *Perotrochus teramachii* or *Mikadotrochus schmalzi.*

liktak (liktak). 2(inf, tr -*e*), 4, 6(-*i*). To trick; cheat; obtain surreptitiously. *Juon eo eliktake jiipkako eo an.* Someone snatched his wallet.

liktūt (liktit). 1, 2, 3(inf *kalliktūt,* tr *kaliktūt*). Wean. *Kōrein Ṃajeļ rej kaliktūt kōn bōlōk meọ.* Marshallese women wean their babies with bitter leaves.

likūt (**likit**). Transitive form of *llik* (**llik**).

likūtōn (**likiten**). Leave so that it...(contraction of *likūt bwe en* (**likit bey yen**)).

lil (**lil**). Vulgar. 6(*-i*). String under penis.

lil-. See *ll-*.

lim (**lim**). Transitive form of *lemlem* (**lẹmlẹm**).

limabukwi (**limabiqiy**). 3, 5(*kallimabukwi*). Five hundred.

limakor (**limaqer**). Archaic. Fifty pairs, fish or copra.

limādep (**limadep**). Archaic. 2, 3(inf, tr *-e*), 6(*-i*). Five thousand.

lime- (**lime-**). Also *nime-* (**nime-**). 1. Drink of; beverage of; possessive classifier, water, soft drinks, or juice of coconuts, etc. *Eor liṃō (limō) koḷa.* I have some coke. *Eor ke liṃōṃ koḷa?* Have you got some coke?

limek (**limẹk**). 2, 4, 6(*-a*), 7. Perfective form of *lemlem* (**lẹmlẹm**); folded; package; wrapping; pack; packing up. *Eṃōj limek jaki.* The mats have been folded. *Ta kobban limek ṇe aṃ?* What have you got in your package? *Ear llu im limek.* She got angry and packed. *Ta limekan men kā?* What shall we wrap these with? *Ia ṇe kwōj limek ḷọk ñane?* Where are you packing up to go to?

limen ninnin (**limen ninnin**). Land given by a king to a commoner woman as a bounty for suckling a royal baby.

limenkoko (**limenkewkew**). Two babies suckling from the same woman.

limi (**limiy**). Transitive form of *idaak* (**yidahak**).

limo (**limew**). 1(*-i*), 2, 3, 6(*limou-*), 7. Interest; enthusiasm; fad. *Rōjino bōk limoun doon.* They are becoming interested in each other. *Limo eo raan kein ṇe.* That's the current fad.

limtak (**limtak**). 1, 2(inf, tr *-e*), 6(*-i*). Roll up shirt sleeves or trousers. *Limtake peiṃ bwe enaaj tutu jōōt ṇe.* Roll up your sleeves or your shirt will get wet.

liṃ (**liṃ**). 1(*-i*), 2, 3, 5(*liṃliṃ*), 6(*-i*), 7, 8, 9. Murky water; stirred up; dirty water; fine sand in sea; roiled; turbid. *Eliṃ iar kōn an ḷap ṇo.* The water along the lagoon side is all murky from the big waves.

liṃa (**liṃah**). You, to many women in general, not specific; vocative, feminine plural.

liṃaajṇoṇo (**liṃahajṇewṇew**). 1(*-i*), 2, 3(inf, tr *-ik, -uk,* st *kalliṃaajṇoṇo*), 6(*-i*), 7. Choppy seas; waves caused by something; ripple; agitate; rip. *Ta eṇ ej kōṃṃan liṃaajṇoṇo ijjuweo?* What is causing those big waves way over there? *Jab kaliṃaajṇoṇouk lowaan naṃ ṇe.* Don't agitate the water in that pond.

liṃaakak (**liṃahakhak**). 2, 5(*-e*), 6(*-i*), 7. Kite; fly a kite. *Eliṃaakake mejatoto.* The sky is full of kites. *Kwōn tan liṃaakak.* Go fly a kite.

Liṃaan (**liṃahan**). 3, 6(*-i*). A plant, pandanus cultigen.

Liṃanṃan (**liṃanṃan**). Also *Dunen-eañ* (**diwnen-yag**), *Ledikdik, Lijṃaan.* North Star; Polaris; Algedi; alpha Ursae Minoris.

Liṃanṃan-eṇ-an-Ñinjib (**liṃanṃan-yeṇ-han-ginjib**). Also *Liṃanṃan-eṇ-an-Ḷañinjib-reeaar.* A star; gamma in Cepheus; one of the four "posts of Polaris" (*Jurōn-Liṃanṃan*).

liṃaraṇ (**liṃahraṇ**). Those women (close to neither of us); those girls (close to neither of us); personal demonstrative, third person plural feminine.

liṃaraṇe (**liṃahraṇey**). Those women (close to you); those girls (close to you); personal demonstrative, second person plural feminine.

liṃarā (**liṃahray**). These women (close to me); these girls (close to me); personal demonstrative, first person exclusive plural feminine.

liṃarāraṇ (**liṃahrayraṇ**). Those women (close to neither of us); those girls (close to neither of us); personal demonstrative, third person plural feminine, singling out.

liṃarāraṇe (**liṃahrayraṇey**). Those women (close to you); those girls (close to you); personal demonstrative, second person plural feminine, singling out.

liṃarārā (**liṃahrayray**). Also *liṃarere* (**liṃahrẹyrẹy**). These women (close to me); these girls (close to me); personal demonstrative, first person exclusive plural feminine, singling out; vocative, familiar, feminine plural. *Weeak, liṃarārā.* Gracious, girls.

liṃarein (**liṃahreyin**). These women (close to us both); these girls (close to us both); personal demonstrative, first person inclusive plural feminine.

liṃaro (**liṃahrew**). The women (often not present); these women (close to me); these girls (close to me); personal demonstrative, remote plural feminine.

liṃaroro (**liṃahrewrew**). Those women (close to neither of us); those girls (close to neither of us); personal demonstrative, remote plural feminine, singling out; vocative, familiar, feminine plural.

Limjeed (**limjeyed**). From *jeeded* "scattered". Name of waves caused by typhoon; sixth largest.

limḷim (**limḷim**). 1(-*i*), 2, 3(inf, tr -*i*), 5(*limḷimi*), 8, 9. Moss. *Elimḷimi kapin wa in.* This boat has a mossy bottom.

limotak (**limẹwtak**). 2, 6(-*i*). Provocation; agitation of feelings. *Naan ko an rōkōṃṃan limotak.* His words were a provocation.

limō (**limeh**). 1(-*i*), 2, 3(inf, tr -*ūk*), 7. Weep loudly; wail; bawl. *Eḷap an kar limō ke ej roñ ke emej jemān.* He wept loudly when he heard his father had died.

linọk (**linaq**). 1, 2, 6(-*i*). Gone for a long time. *Ear linọk Awai jiljino iiō.* He was in Hawaii for six years. *Eto wōt aṃ linọk.* You've been gone for such a long time.

liñña (**liggah**). Variant form of *lōñña* (**ḷeggah**).

liññar (**liggar**). Nit.

liñōr (**ligẹr**). 1(-*i*), 2(inf, tr -*e*). Look into; study; buckle down. *Kwōn liñōri katak kaṇ aṃ.* Study your subjects.

lio (**liyew**). The woman (often not present); this woman (close to me); this girl (close to me); personal demonstrative, remote singular feminine.

lioeo (**liyẹwyẹw**). Also *lieoeo.* 1(-*i*), 2, 7. Get together happily. *Eṃṃan ad kar lioeo ṇa ilo juon wōt jikuuḷ.* It's good that we all got together in one school.

liok (**liyẹq**). 3, 6(-*i*). Aerial roots of the pandanus.

lipaanto (**liypahantẹw**). 2(inf, tr -*ik(i)*), 4, 6(-*i*), 7. Fishing method, using a coconut leaf chain as a scarer at night to block off exit route of fish and waiting for low tide in order to trap them. *Etke koṃwij jab eañini bwe en kkaatak lipaanto?* Why won't you take him along so he may learn to fish by the *lipaanto* method?

liped (**liped**). Baked breadfruit.

lipjerjer (**lipjẹrjẹr**). Also *likjerjer* (**likjẹrjẹr**). 2(inf, tr -*e*). To hurry someone; hustle. *Kwōn lipjerjere bajinjea raṇe bwe jen jerak ḷọk.* Hurry those passengers up so we can sail right away.

Lipjinmede (**lipjinmẹdẹy**). From *Li-* (**li-**) "female name prefix", *pijinmede* (**pijinmẹdẹy**) "discarded coconut shell with soft meat remaining inside", *pijin* (**pijin**) "refuse of", *mede* (**mẹdẹy**) "soft coconut meat". A plant, *Pandanus fischerianus* cultigen. (Stone). Likiep, etc.

lipopo (**lipewpew**). 1, 6(-*i*), 7. Arrival of many canoes. *Ekōppaḷpaḷ wōt lipopotokun inej eo.* The arrival of the fleet was very impressive.

Lippidjọwe (**lippidjawẹy**). Marshallese goddess of speed.

lippin (**lippin**). 2(inf, tr -*i*), 4, 6(-*i*), 7. Shoot with rubber and spear; shoot with a rubber band. *Iar lippini ek e.* I shot this fish. *Jab lippini doon bwe koṃ naaj jorrāān.* Don't shoot (rubber) at each other because you'll get hurt.

lippiru (**lippiyriw**). Also *lippiruk* (**lippiyriq**). 3, 6(-*i*). Berry; fruit of *kōṇṇat, kkōñ, kitaak,* and *jidkok.*

lippọṇ (**lippaṇ°**). 1(-*i*), 2(inf, tr -*e*), 4, 6(-*i*), 7. Arrow; shoot a bow and arrow; bow.

lirawe. See *lirọuwe.*

lirọuwe (**lirawiwẹy**). Also *lirawe.* 2, 6(-*i*), 8, 9. Mold; fungus. *Elirọuwe pilawā ṇe.* The bread is moldy.

litōḷpi (**liteḷpiy**). 6(-*i*). Deuce of spades.

lladikdik (**llahdikdik**). Dial. W: *elladikdik* (**yellahdikdik**), E: *leladikdik* (**lelahdikdik**). 1(-*i*), 2, 3, 7, 8, 9. Coolness of a breeze; breezy; pleasantly cool; blow gently, of wind. *Eṃṃan an lladikdik.* The breeze is nice and cool. *Ej kōlladikdik iuṃwin mā eṇ.* He is getting some fresh air under the breadfruit tree.

llāle (**llaylęy**). Dial. W: *ellāle* (**yellaylęy**), E: *lelāle* (**lelaylęy**). 1(*-i*), 2, 3, 7. Roll of a ship. *Eḷap an llāle Mieko Kwiin.* The MIECO QUEEN always rolls.

lle (**lley**). Dial. W: *elle* (**yelley**), E: *lele* (**leley**). 1(*-e*), 2, 3(inf, tr *-ik*). Negative reward; to receive one's just desserts; be served right; comeuppance; get what one deserves. *Elle bwe ekōṇaan jab roñjake kōnnaan.* It serves him right because he didn't follow the advice.

llejkakkak (**llęjkakkak**). Dial. W: *ellejkakkak* (**yęllęjkakkak**), E: *lelejkakkak* (**lęlęjkakkak**). 1(*-i*), 2, 3, 4, 7, 8, 9. Laugh.

llejkōnkōn (**llęjkęnkęn**). Dial. W: *ellejkōnkōn* (**yellejkenken, e:** *lejkōnkōn* (**lelejkenken**). A girl or woman whose appearance makes everyone smile; pleasant; popular; see *ḷḷajkōnkōn. Aolep armej im iọkwe kōn an llejkōnkōn.* Everyone likes her because of her appealing personality.

llejlej (**llęjlęj**). Dial. W: *ellejlej* (**yęllęjlęj**), E: *lelejlej* (**lęlęjlęj**). 1, 2, 3(inf, tr *-e*), 4, 6(*-i*), 7. Boisterous; loud nonsense talk. *Kwōn jab llejlej bwe aṃ bōd eo.* No sense being boisterous about it because you're at fault.

lleḷọk (**lleyḷaq**). Be changed.

llemej (**llęmęj**). Dial. W: *ellemej* (**yęllęmęj**), E: *lelemej* (**lęlęmęj**). Archaic. 1, 3(inf, tr *-e*), 6(*-i*). To pass a crucial stage. *Ilōke wa e bwe eṃōj an llemej.* I trust my canoe now because it has successfully passed the trial run.

lleṃaj (**lleyṃaj**). Dial. W: *elleṃaj* (**yelleyṃaj**), E: *leleṃaj* (**leleyṃaj**). 1(*-i*), 2, 3(inf, tr *-e*), 5(*lleṃajṃaj*), 7, 8, 9. Jerk; jerky. *Jab kalleṃaje aṃ kanōk to ṇe.* Don't jerk the rope while you're pulling it in.

llik (**llik**). Dial. W: *illik* (**yillik**), E: *lilik* (**lilik**). 2(inf, tr *likūt(i)*), 7. Leave vehicle or vessel; put; place; consider; deposit; ferry. *Likūtḷọk eō ñan wa eṇ.* Carry me over to the ship. *Kwōn likūt wōt bok ṇe.* Lay your book down. *Ij likūt eok lukkuun nājū.* I consider you to be a real child of mine. *Kwōn likūt ḷọk ñan Ḷora.* Transport it to Laura. *Kwaar llik ke kuṇaaṃ ñan bade eṇ?* Did you contribute to the party? *Iar likūt juon kuṇaō taḷa.* I contributed a dollar as my share. *Likūt bok ṇe ṇai raan tebōḷ ṇe.* Put the book on the table.

llo (**llew**). Dial. W: *ello* (**yellew**), E: *lelo* (**lelew**). 1(*-i*), 2(inf, tr *lo(e)*), 4, 5(*llolo*). See; detect; discover; find; get; recover; unfaithful, as of spouse. *Inaaj lo waj eok.* I'll visit you. *Kwaar lo ke peen eo aō?* Did you see my pen? *Kwōnañin llo ke aṃ peen?* Haven't you found yourself a pen yet? *Ilo peen eo aō ear jako.* I recovered my pen that was lost. *Kwōllo ke jikka?* Did you get any cigarettes? *Lieṇ ej bar llolo.* She's unfaithful to her husband.

llok (**llęq**). Dial. W: *ellok* (**yęllęq**), E: *lelok* (**lęlęq**). Also *loklok* (**lęqlęq**). 1(*-i*), 2(inf, tr *lukwōj*), 7, 10(*lokjak, loklok*). Tie; attached; bind. *Lukwōj pein.* Bind his hands together.

llolo (**llewlew**). Dial. W: *ellolo* (**yellewlew**), E: *lelolo* (**lelewlew**). From *llo* (**llew**) "see". Easily attracted to anyone of the opposite sex; distributive form of *llo* (**llew**). *Ellolo ḷeeṇ riiṃ.* Your husband has a lover everywhere he goes.

llor (**llęr°**). Dial. W: *ellor* (**yęllęr°**), E: *lelor* (**lęlęr°**). Also *allor* (**hallęr°**), *aelor.* 1(*-i*), 2, 3, 5(*aelellor*), 7. Shade; shadow. *Kōjro etal in kōttar ilo llor eṇ.* Let's go wait in the shade there.

llotaan (**llęwtahan**). Dial. W: *ellotaan* (**yęllęwtahan**), E: *lelotaan* (**lęlęwtahan**). 1, 2, 3(inf, tr *kalotaan,* st *kallotaanan*), 5(*llotaanan*), 6(*-i*), 8, 9. Despise; gripe; complain; disappointed; displease; resent; worry. *Ellotaan kōn piik eo nājin ejako.* He's complaining about his lost pig. *Kwōn jab kallotaane.* Don't give him anything to gripe about. *Armej ro rōllotaanan raṇ.* Those are the people who are always griping.

llu (**lliw**). Dial. W: *illu* (**yilliw**), E: *lilu* (**liliw**). 1(*-i*), 2(inf, tr *lu*), 3(st inf *kallulu,* inf *kallulu,* tr *kalluuk*), 5(*llulu*), 7. Angry; displeased; fury; mad; offended; riled; provoked; scold; bawl out. *Ekallulu jipij eo an.* His speech was provocative. *Ear kalluuk eō.* He angered me. *Etke raar lu eok?* Why did they scold you? *Aolep iien rej lui ḷadik eṇ.* They are always scolding that boy. *Ellulu.* He's got a bad temper. *Jab kōṇaan kallulu aḷap.* Don't insult your elders.

llutōk (**lliwtęk**). Dial. W: *illutōk* (**yilliwtęk**), E: *lilutōk* (**liliwtęk**). 2(inf, tr *lutōk(e)*), 4, 5(*llutōktōk*), 7. Pour; overflow; slop out; drain; spill. *Ellutōktōk bakōj eņ kōn an m̧m̧akūtkūt wa in.* The bucket keeps slopping out because of the motion of the ship.

lo (**lęw**). Also *balu* (**bahliw**), *balo* (**bahlęw**). 1(-*i*), 2, 3(inf, tr -*ik*, -*uk*), 6(-*i*), 7, 8, 9. Disconcerted; abashed; embarrassed; disenchanted; ashamed. *Elo bwe rōkajooke.* He was disenchanted when they rejected him.

lo (**lew**). A fish, wrasse, *Thalashona vitidum.*

lo (**lew**). 1(-*e*). Tongue.

lo (**lew**). 2. Behold; witness; see, in Biblical usage. *Lo eļotak Rilǫm̧ǫǫr.* Behold the Redeemer is born.

lo (**lew**). Transitive form of *llo* (**llew**).

lo (**lew**). Also *lǫ* (**law**), *ilo* (**yilew, yilęw**). At; locative particle.

lo- (**lew-**). 7. Visit.

Lo-raan-m̧wām̧wā-ko (**lew-rahan-m̧aym̧ay-kew**). A constellation; stars in Octans; mu, chi.

loar (**lewhar**). Variant form of *lowaar.*

Loarm̧we (**lewharm̧ey**). 3, 6(-*i*). A plant, probably *Pandanus fischerianus* cultigen. (Stone). (Jaluit).

lodideañ (**lęwdidyag**). 2(inf, tr -*e*), 4, 5(*lodideañe*), 6(-*i*), 7. Windmill, pinwheel. *Rej kōm̧m̧an lodideañ jān kimjān ni i M̧ajeļ.* Pinwheels are made from coconut leaves in the Marshalls. *Ij lodideañ waj nejim̧.* I'm making you a pinwheel. *Elodideañ ilo kōto in.* It's spinning like a windmill in the wind.

lojojo (**lewjewjew**). Vulgar. From *lo* (**lew**) "tongue", *jojo* (**jewjew**) "soak". 1, 2(inf, tr -*uk*), 4, 6(-*i*). French kiss.

lok (**lęq**). From *lukwō-* (**liqe-**) "middle of". Formant in place names.

lokatok (**lewkateq**). Altar; shrine; sanctum.

lokjak (**lęqjak**). 1(-*i*), 2, 3, 4, 5(*llokjakjak*), 7. Be busy with; be involved; be tied down by a task; perfective form of *loklok* (**lęqlęq**); obsessed; be committed to perform a task; commitment. *Ij jab maroñ iwōj bwe ilokjak kōn ajri rā nājū.* I can't come because I'm tied down with my children. *Illokjakjak kōn ajri rā nājū.* I am continually tied down by these children of mine. *Joñan aō lokjak iar jab maroñ in iwōj ñan keemem eo.* I was so committed I was unable to come to your birthday party.

loklok (**lęqlęq**). 1(-*i*), 2(inf, tr *lukwōj(e)*), 3, 4, 7, 10(*lokjak*). Bind; tie on; variant form of *llok* (**llęq**).

lokm̧aan (**lęqm̧aan**). From *loklok* "tie", *m̧aan* "front". Bow line, used to tie up an anchor.

lokor (**lęqer**). Archaic. Wrap. *Lokore wōjļā ņe.* Wrap that sail.

loloorjake (**lęwlęwęrjahkey**). 1(-*i*), 2, 3, 4, 7. Take responsibility; urge; make sure; follow through; carry out; carry on; execute an order. *Wōn eo ej loloorjake tok kijen rijerbal.* Who has taken responsibility for bringing food for the workers? *Kwōn loloorjake bwe kwōn uwe ilo baļuun eo.* Make sure you are on the plane.

loļ (**lęļ°**). Also *ļwōl, ļol* (**ļ°ęl**). 3, 4+3, 6(-*i*), 3+7. A fish. *Ennǫ loļūn arin ānin.* This islet has some delicious *loļ* near its shore.

loļǫkjeņ (**lewļaqjeņ**). 1(-*i*), 2, 3, 4, 7, 8, 9. Have broadened horizons; long vision; receive sight; foresight; sensitive in perception; keen vision.

lomije- (**lewmije-**). 1, 2, 4. Intuition about a future misfortune or death. *Iar lomijen Jǫǫn.* I thought I saw John but it was only an omen.

lom̧aan (**lewm̧ahan**). 1(-*i*), 2, 3, 4, 5(*llom̧aanan*), 6(-*i*), 8, 9. Arrogant; haughty; stuck-up; conceited. *Joñan an lom̧aan ke ej rǫǫltok, iban ba.* I cannot describe how arrogant he was when he returned. *Aer likūti bwe en aer rūtōl ekalom̧aane.* Their making him their leader made him arrogant. *Kijoñ eņ ellom̧aanan.* That guy is always arrogant.

lom̧aļo (**lewm̧aļew**). 6(-*i*). Lagoon.

loñ (**leg°**). Archaic. Neither high nor low; in between.

Looj (**lęwęj**). Also *RiLoojrañ* (**rilęwęjraņ**). Clan name; name of legendary woman; mother of *Ļoeak.*

Look (**lęwęk**). Clan name.

lotaan (**lewtahan**). Also *lotaan* (**lęwtahan**). 1(-*i*), 2(inf, tr *llotaane*), 3, 4. Peeved; cross; chagrin; miffed; offended.

Lotọọn (**lewtawan**). Also *Lọtọọn* (**lawtawan**). 3, 6(-*i*). A plant, *Pandanus fischerianus* variety. (Stone). Likiep. *Lotọọnin ia ṇe daaṃ?* Where is that *Lotọọn* from?

lotōñā (**lewtegay**). Variant form of *lọtōñā* (**lawtegay**).

lowa (**lewwah**). 1(-*a*). Inside; interior; internal. *Epād ilowa.* It's inside the lagoon.

lowaar (**lewahar**). Also *loar* (**lewhar**). 1, 2, 6(-*i*) 2(inf, tr -*in*), 4. Make fun of; mock; mimic; criticize. *Lieṇ ekadik jeḷā loar.* She's a wiz at mimicking people. *Enana lowaarin armej.* It is bad to make fun of people. *Lowaar kōkōḷḷan ban.* Making fun of others is a sign of jealousy.

lowaṇwoṇ (**lẹwaṇwẹṇ**). Busy woman; see *ḷowaṇwoṇ*. *Juon eṇ lowaṇwoṇ.* There's a busy woman.

lọ (**law**). Also *lo* (**lew**). Archaic. At; locative particle.

lọboḷ (**lawbẹḷ°**). Variant form of *boḷ* (**bẹḷ°**).

lọbuḷōn (**lawbiḷ°en**). Variant form of *buḷōn* (**biḷ°en**).

lọbwij (**lawbij**). Also *lubwij* (**liwbij**). 6(-*i*). Canoe part, the area around the *bwij*. *Epād ilọbwij.* It's on the *bwij*.

lọbwilej (**lawbilẹj**). Also *bwilji-*. 4. Publicity; in public. *Armej in lọbwilej.* A public figure.

lọdiñi (**lawdigiy**). 1(*lọdiñi-*). Posterior; buttocks.

lọje (**lawjẹy**). 1(*lọjie-*). Stomach; abdomen.

lọjet (**lawjẹt**). Ocean; sea.

lọjien āne (**lawjiyen yanẹy**). Interior of an island.

Lọjikōt (**lawjiket**). From "name of legendary Northern Ratak chief (plant imported to Ebon from Northern Ratak)". A plant, pandanus cultigen. Ebon.

lọjilñi (**lawjilgiy**). 1(*lọjilñi-*). Ear.

lọjilñin jourur (**lawjilgin jẹwirwir**). 3, 4+3, 6(-*i*), 3+7. A shell, *Nautilidae*; *Nautilus pompilius*; chambered nautilus.

lọjilñin kijdik (**lawjilgin kijdik**). Dial. W, E: *ḷeen kijdik*. From "ear of rat". A plant, toadstool, *Auricularia ampla* Persoon and other earlike Basidiomycetes (fungi). Rogers; Pac. Science.

lọjiraan (**lawjirahan**). From *jiraan* "dawn". A bird that sings at dawn.

lọk (**laq**). 1(*lokwa-*), 6(*lokwa-*). Posterior, buttocks.

lọklọk (**laqlaq**). 2, 6(-*i*). Wave tail above surface, of fish.

lọkmej (**laqmẹj**). 1(-*i*), 2, 3(inf, tr -*e*), 4, 5(*llọkmejmej*), 7, 8, 9. Sickly; ill; ailing. *Einwōt kwōmejān lọkmej bajjek.* You look ill.

lọlọ (**lawlaw**). Dial. W only; see *lala* (**lahlah**). 6(-*i*). Hen.

lọḷe (**laḷ°ey**). 1(-*i*), 2, 3, 4, 7, 8, 9. Quick-minded; level-headed; able to keep wits during crisis. *Eḷap an lọḷe ḷeeṇ.* He is very level-headed.

lọḷin (**lawḷin**). Also *lọḷi* (**lawḷiy**). Form of, shape of.

lọmeto (**lawmetew**). 6(-*i*). Ocean; sea.

lọmọọr (**lawmawar**). Also *lomọọr* (**lewmawar**). 1(-*i*), 2(inf, tr -*e*, -*en(e)*), 4. Salvation; save; rescue; redeem. *Rilọmọọr.* Savior. *Waan lọmọọr.* Rescue boat.

lọñi (**lawg°iy**). Also *lāñwi* (**layg°iy**). 1(-*i*). Mouth.

lọpet (**lawpẹt**). Eastern side of a house; see *pet*.

lọpiden ne (**lawpiden ney**). 1(...*nee-*). Sole of foot.

lọpiden pā (**lawpiden pay**). 1(...*pei-*). Palm of hand.

Lọpiñpiñ (**lawpigpig**). 3, 6(-*i*). A plant, pandanus cultigen.

lọri. See *lọrun*.

lọrun (**lawr°in**). Also *lọri* (**lawr°iy**), *lori* (**lewriy**). Archaic. Under; sleeping place of.

lọtōñā (**lawtegay**). Also *lotōñā* (**lewtegay**). 1(*lọtōña-*). Inside of thigh; crotch. *Liiō kwōn lale aṃ jijet bwe ewaḷọk lotōñaṃ.* Lady, watch the way you're sitting because your exposing yourself.

lọudiñdiñ (**lawidigdig**). Also *wūdiñdiñ*. 2, 3. Ecstacy; rapture; delight; beatitude; bliss; glee. *Jen lọudiñdiñ im wūdiñdiñ.* Let's shout and cry for joy. *Elọudiñdiñ kōn an roñ al eo.* Hearing the song sent him into ecstacy.

lọun Pikaar (**lawin pikahar**). Also *ḷāwūn Pikaar* (**ḷaywin pikahar**). A bird, blue-gray noddy, *Procelsterna caerulea*.

lǫurō (**lawireh**). 2, 3(inf, tr *-ūk*), 6(*-i*), 7, 8, 9. Poor soil. *Ekkā an lǫurō turun bōl.* The soil near taro patches is normally poor. *Ta in ej kōlǫurōūk ijin?* What makes this soil poor?

lōb (**lęb**). 1(*libwi-, libō-*). Grave; tomb.

lōb (**lęb**). Pond with many fish.

lōba (**lebah**). From Engl. 1(*-i*), 2, 3(inf, tr *-ik*), 4. Leper; leprosy; Hansen's disease.

lōbbañij (**lębbagij**). Variant form of *ūrōrmej* (**hirhęrmęj**).

lōbdak (**lębdak**). Female whose father is a chief and whose mother is a commoner.

Lōbjañwūjooj (**lębjagwijęwęj**). From *wūjooj* "grass". Name of waves caused by typhoon; fourth largest.

lōbǫ (**lebaw**). 1(*-i*), 2, 3(inf, tr *-ik*), 7. Confine because of disease; come down with a sickness. *Koban loe bwe elōbǫ.* You won't find him because he's sick.

lōkake (**lekahkey**). 2, 7. To draw; drag; take; see *leak-*. *Lōkake ļǫk ñane.* Take it to him.

lōkā (**lekay**). Dial. W only; see *lōkōr* (**lękęr**). 1(*-i*), 2, 3(inf, tr *-ik*), 4, 7. Surf-boarding; dive of birds or planes.

lōkdoon (**lekdewen**). From *lōk* (**lek**) "prick", *doon* (**dewen**) "each other". 2, 4, 6(*-i*). Compete with each other. *Erro ej lōkdoon.* They are competing against each other.

lōke (**lękęy**). 1(*-i*), 2, 7, 8, 9. Believe; trust in; depend on; confidence; credit; faith; reckon; rely on. *Rōlōke ñan jerbal eņ.* They think that he can do that job.

lōkeed (**lekeyed**). 3, 4+3, 6(*-i*), 3+7. A shell, *Strombidae*; *Conomurex luhuanus*; murex shell.

lōkkalik.

lōkkūk (**lekkik**). 1(*-i*), 2, 3(inf, tr *-i*), 5(*lōkkūki*), 8, 9. Female aristocrat; female celebrity. *Lōkkūk ro jān Ṃōn-kūbwe raņe tok.* Here come the female aristocrats from *Ṃōn-kūbwe.*

lōklōk (**leklek**). 2(inf, tr *-e*), 5(*lōklōk(e)*), 6(*-i*). A plant, a grass, prickly; prick. *Elōklōk men ņe.* It's prickly. *Men ņe elōke eō.* That thing pricked me.

lōkōk (**lękęk**). Archaic. Be prepared for the task at hand.

lōkōr (**lękęr**). Dial. E only; see *lōkā* (**lekay**). 1(*-i*), 2, 3(inf, tr *-e*), 4, 7. Surf-boarding.

Lōktañūr (**lęktagir**). A star; Capella; mother of all great stars, including *Tūṃur,* the eldest, and *Jeļeilōñ* or *Jebrǫ,* the youngest, according to legend.

lōlō (**lehleh**). 2, 3(inf, tr *-ūk, -ik*), 6(*-i*). Stick with spear, knife, or needle, etc.; pierce; puncture; stand on one's head. *Elōlō neen ilo dila eo.* He stepped on a nail. *Kwōn kalōlō.* Stand on your head.

lōļļap (**lęļļap**). Also *leļļap.* 1(*-i*), 2, 3, 6(*-i*), 8, 9. Old woman.

lōļļap (**lęļļap**). 3, 6(*-i*). A bird, blue-faced booby, *Sula dactylatra.*

lōļñǫñ (**lęļg°ag°**). 1(*-i*), 2, 3, 4, 5(*llōļñǫññǫñ*), 7, 8, 9. Fright; terror; be afraid of; fear; amazed; awe; panic. *Eṃōj ņe aṃ llōļñǫññǫñ.* Why don't you stop being a coward.

Lōļtok (**lęļteq**). 3, 6(*-i*). A plant, pandanus cultigen. Rongelap.

Lōņomeme (**leņewmeymey**). From *meme* "foam" (?) Name of waves caused by typhoon; second largest.

lōñ (**lęg**). 1(*-i*), 7, 8, 9. Up; above; high; over; overhead; directional, enclitic, upward. *Wōn eņ lōñ tata ilo teej eo?* Who scored highest on the test? *Kwōj pād lōñū ilo teej eņ.* You are above me on the test. *Lelōñļǫk.* Raise it. *Emoot lōñļǫk.* He went up.

lōñ (**leg**). 1(*-i*), 2, 3(inf *kallōñlōñ,* tr *kalōñ*), 7, 8, 9. Many; much; plenty; full; lot; outnumber; abundant. *Ej kallōñlōñ an nuknuk ke ejja dik oņān.* He's buying up on clothes while the sale is on. *Rōlōñ jān kōm.* They outnumber us.

lōñ alen (**leg halen**). 2. Many times; often.

lōñ mājidjid (**leg majidjid**). 2. Full to the brim; see *lañṃwijidjid.*

lōñ ṃweñan (**leg ṃęygan**). From *lōñ mwiañin* (**leg ṃiyagin**) "It has many branches". 1, 2, 3. Ambiguous. *En jab lōñ ṃweñan aṃ kōnnaan.* Don't equivocate.

lōñña (**lęggah**). Also *liñña* (**liggah**), *lōññā* (**ięggay**). 1(*-i, -a*), 2, 3, 4, 5(*llōññaña*), 6(*-i*), 7. Riddle. *Liññaū liññaaṃ.* I made a riddle about you. *Lōññaan lieņ emaroñ bōk jilñuul minit ñan pukot uwaak eo an.* The riddle about that woman can take 30 minutes to solve. *Kalōññaiki bwe ejeļā.* Make him tell a riddle because he's good at it. *Rilōñña e.* He's a riddle teller. *Lōñña tok ṃōk.* Please tell me a riddle.

lōrak (**lehrak**). 1(-*i*), 2, 3, 5(*llōrakrak*), 7. Dive down; fall head down; upside down; dive, of planes. *Lale baļuun eņ elōrak.* Look at that plane diving. *Baļuun eo ellōrakrak eņ.* That plane is always diving. *Elōrak baļuun eo em dibōj laļ.* The plane dove and hit the ground. *Kalōrak bōraṃ bwe kwōn jab ļotļǫk.* Lower your head so you won't faint.

lōrro (**lȩrrȩw**). Variant form of *lōrrǫ* (**lerraw**).

lōrro (**lȩrrȩw**). Small empty shells that wash up and pile up on beach.

Lōrro (**lerrew**). 3, 6(-*i*). A plant, *Pandanus fischerianus* cultigen.

lōrrǫ (**lerraw**). Also *lōrro* (**lȩrrȩw**). 2, 6(-*i*). Fairy; legendary flying woman; woman who flies after loss of love or departure of loved one. *Ear or jineņ Jiņo Wait lōrrǫ.* Snow White had a fairy godmother. *Elōrrǫ lieņ.* That woman has "flown".

lōt (**let**). What woman?

lōt (**let**). 1(-*i*), 2, 3, 7, 8, 9. Well-sifted; well-cleaned; thoroughly done. *Elōt ke aṃ kar kwaļi pilej kaņ?* Did you wash the plates clean?

lōt (**lȩt**). Transitive form of *lōtlōt* (**lȩtlȩt**).

lōta (**letah**). From Engl. 3, 4+3, 6(-*i*), 3+7. Letter; mail. *Kōjro tōn kalōta ilo iṃōn lōta eņ.* Let's go see if we got mail at the post office.

Lōtbar (**lȩtbar**). From *bar* "rock". Name of waves caused by typhoon; third largest.

lōtlōt (**lȩtlȩt**). 1(-*i*), 2(inf, tr *lōt(e)*), 3, 4, 7. Wear a piece of clothing for the first time. *Ij kab lōt(e) jōōt e aō.* This is the first time I wore this shirt.

lōtlōt (**lȩtlȩt**). 2, 3, 7. Stretched tight, of lines, ropes, etc.; full sail, nautical. *Elōtlōt wōjļā eo.* The sail is full.

Lōttǫǫr (**lȩttawar**). From *tǫǫr* "flow". Name of waves caused by typhoon; largest.

lu (**liw**). Transitive form of *llu* (**lliw**).

lubwij (**liwbij**). Variant form of *lǫbwij* (**lawbij**).

lueaļ (**liwyaļ**). 4, 6(-*i*). In public. *Iar roñ ilueaļ.* I heard people talking about it.

luej (**liwyej**). Variant form of *lukwej* (**liqyej**).

lukkuun (**liqqiwin**). 2. Exact; true; certain; right; actual; extremely; indeed; main; really; surely. *Rōlukkuun jeļā kajin Ṃajeļ.* They really know the Marshallese language.

lukkuun (**liqqiwin**). From *lukkuun* (**liqqiwin**) "real". 2, 4, 6(-*i*), 7. Play marbles for keeps. *Iar lukkuun im luuji bǫǫļ ko nājū.* I played for keeps and lost my marbles.

lukor (**liqȩr**). 1(-*i*), 2(inf, tr -*e*), 4, 6(-*i*), 7. A food, pounded meat of sprouted coconut; coconut mixed with sap or sugar. *Kwōn lukor tok kijerro.* Make some *lukor* for us.

lukor (**liqȩr**). Slang. 2(inf, tr -*e*). Perform a feat. *Eļak lukore kūta eo aolep im ppaļ.* As he strummed on the guitar, everyone went agape.

luku (**liqiw**). Variant form of *lukwi.*

lukwar (**liqar**). 6(-*i*). Line used to decrease the sail on a canoe. *Kwōn lukwōje lukwar ņe bwe erōļǫk.* Tighten the *lukwar* because it's loose.

lukwarkwar (**liqarqar**). Also *kōpļe* (**kepļey**). 1(-*i*), 2(inf, tr -*e*), 3, 7. Chase. *Wōn eņ rej lukwarkware?* Who are they chasing?

lukweej (**liqeyej**). Variant form of *lukwej* (**liqyej**).

lukwej (**liqyej**). Also *luwej* (**liwyej**), *lukweej* (**liqeyej**), *jijo* (**jijȩw**). 3, 6(-*i*). A plant, *Calophyllum inophyllum* L. (Guttiferae). A large tree with simple glossy leaves, these with many parallel oblique lateral veins, yellow and white flowers, and round, hard fruits like golfballs.

lukwi (**liqiy**). Also *luku.* Authentic; real; fact; genuine. *Lukwi eo ņe.* That's the real one. *Pojak bwe lukwi eo in kiiō.* Get ready now for here comes the real thing.

lukwō- (**liqe-**). 1, 7. Middle of; waist. *Ewi lukwōn aļaļ e?* Where is the middle of this piece of wood? *Ewi dettan lukoṃ?* What size is your waist?

lukwōj (**liqej**). Vulgar slang. 2, 4, 5(*llukwōjkwōj*). Masturbate.

lukwōj (**liqej**). Transitive form of *loklok* (**lẹqlẹq**) and *llok* (**llẹq**).

lukwōn boñ (**liqen bẹg°**). Midnight.

lumọọrḷọk (**liwmawarḷaq**). Archaic. 1, 2, 3(inf, tr *-e*), 6(*-i*). Forsake; a child who deserts home through anger over parental coercion; a pet bird that flies away and never returns. *Kōn an nana aer lale elumọọrḷọk.* Because they did not treat him well, he left and never returned.

luo (**liwew**). Also *jibbin-bōran-bōb.* A shell, conical and longer than trochus.

lur (**lir°**). 1(*-i*), 2(inf, tr *-i*), 3, 7, 8, 9. Calm; quiet; still; serene. *Eḷap an lur allōñ kein.* These months are quite calm. *Eluri wa eo ṇai lọmeto.* The boat was becalmed in the middle of the ocean.

lutōk (**liwtẹk**). Transitive form of *llutōk* (**lliwtẹk**).

lutōkḷọk (**liwtẹkḷaq**). 1(*-i*), 2, 3. Overflowing; plentiful; abundant. *Elutōkḷọk kōn ṃōñā.* He has an abundant supply of food.

luuj (**liwij**). 1(*-i*), 2(inf, tr *-i*), 3(*kalluujuj, kaluuj*), 4, 5(*lluujuj*), 7, 8, 9. Lose. *Elluujuj ḷeeṇ ilo pile.* He always loses at poker. *Ekalluujuj.* He's an "icebox" (he causes losing). *Ear kaluuj eō.* He beat me. *Eluuji keem eo.* He lost the game.

luwa (**liwah**). Look for a vehicle. *Etke kwōj luwa?* Why are you looking for something to ride?

luwajet (**liwajẹt**). Also *ḷojat* (**ḷ°ejat**). From *Luwajet* (**Liwajẹt**) "name of a sea mermaid". 2, 3, 5(*luwajete*), 6(*-i*), 7, 8, 9. Get old and dilapidated due to continuous soaking in sea water. *Eluwajetḷọk kiiō kōnke eto an jojo iar.* It's old and corroded because it's been in the sea for so long.

Luwaju (**liwwajiw**). From "name of a woman". A plant, pandanus cultigen; Ebon.

luwap (**liwap**). Dial. E only; see *wat* (**wat**). 6(*-i*). A fish, puffer fish, *Tetraodon hispidus*; T.; *Canthigaster jactator/solandri.*

luwap-iaḷo (**liwap-yiyaḷẹw**). A fish, puffer, *Arothron nigropunctatus.*

luwap-kilmeej (**liwap-kilmeyej**). A fish, puffer, *Arothron meleagris.*

luweo (**liwiweyew**). That woman (close to neither of us); that girl (close to neither of us); personal demonstrative, remote singular feminine, singling out.

luwi (**liwiy**). 2, 6(*-i*). Charge of larger fish on minnows, sardines, etc.

luwo (**liwwew**). Archaic. Conical shell, larger than trochus.

Ḷa- (**ḷa-**). Also *Le-, Lō-, Lo-* (**le-**). Prefix to masculine names.

ḷaak (**ḷahak**). To fit. *Kōḷaake aḷaḷ ṇe.* Make that plank fit.

ḷaaṃ (**ḷahaṃ**). From Engl. Lamb.

ḷaaṃ (**ḷahaṃ**). From Engl. 6(*-i*). Lamp.

ḷaaṃ jarom (**ḷahaṃ jar°em**). 2(inf, tr *-e*), 4, 6(*-i*), 7. Flashlight; electric light. *Ear ḷaaṃ-jarome ajri eo ḷọk ñan ṃweo.* He used a flashlight and escorted the child to the house.

ḷaaṃ kaaj (**ḷahaṃ kahaj**). 2(inf, tr *-e*), 4, 6(*-i*), 7. Coleman lantern. *Ear ḷaaṃ-kaaje ajri eo ḷọk ñan ṃweo.* He used a Coleman lantern to escort the child to the house. *Rūḷaaṃ-kaaj eo ṇe tok.* Here comes someone using a Coleman lantern.

ḷaaṃaṃ (**ḷahaṃhaṃ**). 2(inf, tr *-e*), 4, 6(*-i*), 7. Use a lamp. *Kwōn ḷaaṃaṃ kōn ḷaṇtōn ṇe.* Please use the lantern when you come.

ḷaanriab (**ḷahanriyab**). Liar.

ḷaanwōtwōt (**ḷahanwetwet**). 1(*-i*), 2, 3, 7. Be hit by mistake as a bystander; get caught in crossfire; get involved accidently. *Lale koḷaanwōtwōt ilo bo kaṇ buon.* Be careful you don't get hit by the stones he's throwing.

ḷabbūrọ (**ḷabbiraw**). Variant form of *būrọ* (**biraw**).

ḷabuk (**ḷabiq**). Raise up.

ḷaddik (**ḷaddik**). Also *ḷadik* (**ḷadik**) preceding demonstratives. 6(*-i*). Boy.

ḷadikin eoon ere (**ḷadikin yewen yerey**). From *ḷadik in eoon ere* (**ḷadik yin yewen yerey**). Gusty wind. *Ear bat kōrkōr eo waō jinoun ak eḷak wōtḷọk juon ḷadikin eoon ere eliboorore wa ko jet im ḷe.* At first my canoe was behind but a gusty wind fell, I chased and passed the others.

ḷadipāākāk (**ḷadiypayakyak**). Variant form of *dipāākāk* (**diypayakyak**).

ḷae (**ḷahyey**). 1(*-i*), 2(inf, tr *-ik*), 3, 7, 8, 9. Smooth and calm, of water. *Eḷae lọjet kōn an lur.* The ocean is smooth because of the calm.

ļae (**ļahyey**). Archaic. Flock of birds fishing.

ļaikaalal (**ļahyikahalhal**). Also *ļeikaalal* (**ļẹyikahalhal**). 1(-*i*), 2, 3(inf, tr -*e*), 6(-*i*), 8, 9. Big shot; important. *Enaaj itok ñāāt ļaikaalalin Roojia eo?* When will the Russian big-shot come over?

ļaiṃ (**ļahyiṃ**). From Engl. 3, 6(-*i*). A plant, citrus, lime.

ļain (**ļahyin**). From Engl. 1(-*i*), 2(inf, tr -*i*), 4, 5(*ļļainin*), 7. Line; land tract (Likiep only). *Eļļainin peba eṇ.* That piece of paper is ruled.

ļaiōōn (**ļahyiyehen**). Also *ļaiōn* (**ļahyiyhen**). From Engl. Lion.

ļaire (**ļahyirey**). 2, 4. Pugnacious; given to wife-beating. *Kōrā eo ear joļọk ļeo ippān kōn an ļaire.* The woman divorced her husband because he beat her.

ļait (**ļahyit**). From Engl. Lighter.

ļaita (**ļahyitah**). From Engl. *lighter.* 2(inf, tr -*ik*), 4, 6(-*i*), 7. Lighter; flat-bottom barge. *Jero ļaitaik ļọk waini kā.* Let's haul the copra on the lighter.

ļaj (**ļaj**). Hit the mark; on target. *Bao eṇ ej ļaj bwe eṇ ioon allok eṇ.* The bird landed right on the spot of the snare.

ļajdeñ (**ļajdeg**). Archaic. Last fruits; smallest breadfruit or pandanus remaining on tree at end of season.

ļajiiñ (**ļahjiyig**). From Engl. *lashing*. 2(inf, tr -*i*), 4, 6(-*i*), 7. Tie or fasten with a rope or cord. *Kwōn ļajiiñi tūraṃ kaṇe.* Lash those drums down.

ļajikaj (**ļajikaj**). Slang. From "name of a man who was born a dwarf on Ebon". Midget; dwarf. *Ļajikaj eo nājin eṇ.* That's his dwarf child.

ļajikmeed (**ļajikmeyed**). Also *jikmeed* (**jikmeyed**). Vulgar. From "name of legendary masturbator". 1(-*i*), 2(inf, tr -*e*), 3, 4, 5(*ļļajikmeeded*), 6(-*i*), 7. Masturbate. *Kwōnañinmej kōn aṃ ļļajikmeeded.* You're sick because you masturbate a lot.

ļajinono (**ļajinewnew**). Unmarried man; bachelor.

ļajjibjib (**ļajjibjib**). Male of one-fourth royal descent; father a *bwidak* (**bidak**) and mother a *kajoor* (**kajwẹr**).

ļajjibūbū (**ļajjibihbih**). Grandson, affectionate term.

ļajjidik (**ļajjidik**). A coral; brown or white, two or three branches, smooth.

ļajjutak (**ļajjiwtak**). 6(-*i*). Chicken that walks upright.

ļajjuur (**ļajjiwir**). 2, 6(-*i*). Person who carries weight in his speech due to social status. *Eļajjuur wōt eṇ ṃṃaan.* He's such a powerful individual.

ļak (**ļak**). Then when; after; then after; what if. *Eļak ṃōj aō jerbal, elukwōn boñ.* When I finally got through working, it was midnight. *Iļak lale ejekkar aṃ etal.* After due consideration, I don't think you should go. *Ļak jorrāān?* What if it breaks?

ļak (**ļak**). From Engl. 1(-*i*), 2(inf, tr -*e*), 5(*ļļakļak*), 6(-*i*). To lock; latch; padlock. *Kwōn kab ļake ṃōṇe.* Lock the house then (when you leave.) *Eor ke aṃ ļak?* Do you have a lock?

Ļak (**ļak**). A constellation; stars in Pegasus; beta, mu, lambda.

ļakajeṃ (**ļakajeṃ**). Rash; speak taboo words that may bring bad luck.

ļakej (**ļakyẹj**). Also *ļakōj* (**ļakẹj**). Edge of reef.

ļakeke (**ļakẹykẹy**). A bird, golden plover, black variety, in breeding plumage.

Ļakeke (**ļakẹykẹy**). From *ke* "porpoise". A constellation; shaped like a porpoise whose head is *Elmọñ,* dorsal fin is *Ūlin-raj-eo,* belly fin is *Poob,* and tail is *Ļokwan-Ļakeke; see Ļakelōñ.*

Ļakelōñ (**ļakẹyleg**). Archaic. A star; member of a pair with *Ļakeke* that cause storms in April and May. *Ļakeke to, rooj iekūt, waan Elmọñdik.* Lakeke in the west, they (the sailors) stand by, vehicle of the storm called *Elmọñdik.* (A chant.)

ļakilulu (**ļakiyliwliw**). Also *ļatiptip* (**ļatiptip**). 2(inf, tr -*uk*), 4, 6(-*i*), 7. Pry; raise by lever.

Ļakiwa (**ļakiywah**). 3, 6(-*i*). A plant, pandanus cultigen.

ļakkūk (**ļakkik**). 1(-*i*), 2, 3(inf, tr -*i*), 6(-*i*), 5(*ļakkūki*), 8, 9. Male aristocrat; male celebrity; big wheel; important person; distinguished; V.I.P. *Eṃōj ṇe aṃ kaļakkūki eok.* Stop acting like a big wheel. *Eļakkūki ṃwiin.* This house is full of V.I.P.'s.

ļakkūrae (**ļakkirahyey**). A fish, grouper.

ļakļak (**ļakļak**). Swagger; strut. *Ealikkar an kabbil bwe eļakļak.* His swagger goes to show his arrogance.

Ļakmijtata (**ļakmijtahtah**). The constellations *Ļak* and *Jitata.*

ļalem (**ļalęm**). 3, 5(*kaļļaļļōm*), 7. Five.

laļļap (**laļļap**). Also *ļōļļap* (**leļļap**). 1(-*i*), 2, 3, 6(-*i*), 8, 9. Old man.

ļam (**ļam**). 5(*ļamļam*). Bay. *Eļamļam aelōñ in.* This atoll has lots of bays.

ļam (**ļam**). Also *tam* (**tam**), *rọkwōj* (**raqej**). 1(*ļōma-*), 2(inf, tr *ļōmak(ey)*, 4, 5(*ļame, ļamļame, ļļamļam*), 6(-*i*). Imagine; scheme; plot; determine; to shape. *Ej ļōmake an rūkkāke.* He's imagining himself a flier. *Inaaj ļōmake ta eo kwōnaaj kōṃṃane.* I'll determine what you should do. *Eļamļame bōke in Julel.* Julel Cape is quite prominent.

ļam jako (**ļam jakęw**). Extremely; entirely. *Etutu ļam jako.* He's wet to the bones. *Ewōt ļam jako.* It's raining cats and dogs.

ļam waan (**ļam wahan**). 2. Crude; of poor quality; informal; simple. *Wa eo waan eļam waan ak ebwe.* His boat was crude but served its purpose. *Ijook kōn waj e aō bwe ļam waan bajjek.* I'm ashamed of my watch, for it is of poor quality. *Ta wūnin an pen ke eļam waan?* How could it be so difficult when it's quite simple?

Ļaṃtōr (**ļaṃtęr**). 3, 6(-*i*). A plant, *Pandanus fischerianus* cultigen. (Mejit).

ļanno (**ļannęw**). From Engl. *land ho*. 2(inf, tr -*ik*), 6(-*i*). Cry announcing the sighting of land; sight land. *Raar ļanno ke ej joraantak.* They sighted land at dawn.

ļantōn (**ļanten**). From Engl. 6(-*i*). Lantern.

ļaṇtōna (**ļaṇtenah**). From Engl. 3(inf, tr -*ik(i)*), 5(*ļļaṇtōnana*), 6(-*i*). A plant, lantana. *Eļļaṇtōnana wāto jab in.* This particular spread is grown over with lantana.

ļañ (**ļag**). 1(-*i*), 2, 3, 7. To crack; open a crack; spread one's thighs.

ļañ (**ļag**). 1(-*i*). Storm; typhoon. *Ļañin wōn in?* Whose storm is this? (Based on belief that certain people can cause storms).

ļañe (**ļagęy**). Dial. E, W: *ikbwij* (**yikbij**). A fish, skip jack, *Caranx lessonii.*

ļañōn irooj (**ļagen yirewej**). Archaic. From *ļañ* "storm". A rain storm that is the sign of a chief coming.

ļaom. See *ļọom.*

ļap (**ļap**). Also -*lep* (**lep**). 1(-*i*), 2, 3, 8, 9, 11(sg. *ļapļap*, pl. *ļļap*). Big; great; large; plenty. *Ejjeļọk wōt ļapin eņ tiṃa.* That ship is outstandingly large. *Eļap aṃ iien.* You have plenty of time. *Eļap jorrāān eo.* The accident was fatal.

ļappo (**ļappęw**). A fish, hogfish, *Cheilinus undulatus.*

ļaptata (**ļaptahtah**). From *ļap* (**ļap**) "great", *tata* (**tahtah**) "superlative". Especially; particularly; greatest; biggest.

Ļapukor (**ļapiqęr**). From *Ļa-* (**ļa-**) "man's name prefix", *pukor* (**piqęr**) "a rough stone used for grinding arrowroot". A plant, pandanus cultigen (Takeuchi).

ļarere (**ļarẹyrẹy**). Archaic. Breeze.

ļat (**ļat**). 6(-*i*). Coconut shell; skull; reflector of flashlight or spotlight.

ļat-jiṃ (**ļat-jiṃ**). 6(-*i*). Coconut shell, lower half with sharp end.

ļat-mej (**ļat-męj**). 6(-*i*). Coconut shell, upper half next to stem, with eyes.

ļatipñōl (**ļatipgęl**). 2(inf, tr -*e*), 4, 6(-*i*). Trip someone; cause someone to fall; assault; rape; tempt. *Ij ja tan wōnṃaanļọk wōt ak eletok neen im ļatipñōle eō.* I was about to go forward but he tripped me with his foot.

ļatippān (**ļatippan**). 2, 4, 6(-*i*), 7. Fishing method, long line, deep ocean, for tuna. *Koban ļatippān ñe ejjeļọk waaṃ.* You can't *ļatippān* without a boat.

ļatiptip (**ļatiptip**). Variant form of *ļakilulu* (**ļakiyliwliw**).

ļatōļ (**ļateļ**). From Engl. 2(inf, tr -*e*), 3, 6(-*i*), 7. Ladle; dipper. *Kwōmaroñ ke ļatōļe tok jidik limō aebōj?* Could you pour me some water with the ladle?

ļattil pako (**ļattil pakew**). A fish, shark pilot, *Echeneis naucrates.*

ļattuñ (**ļattig°**). 2(inf, tr -*i*), 6(-*i*). Pack bags tightly; shake down a container to pack more solidly. *Ļattuñi pāāk ņe.* Pack that sack tight.

ḷatum̧a (**ḷatiwm̧ah**). Also *kij jān pid* (**kij jan pid**). 6(*-a*). A food, flying fish with pandanus stuffing.

ḷaum̧. See *ḷo̧om*.

Ḷawōden (**ḷahweden**). 3, 6(*-i*). A plant, pandanus cultigen. Mejit.

ḷā (**ḷay**). 6(*-i*). Gravel.

ḷā (**ḷay**). 2(inf, tr *-ik*), 6(*-i*). File. *Ḷāik jidik tōrerein.* File down the edges.

ḷāān (**ḷayan**). Have four of a kind in poker. *Eḷāān peiū.* I have four of a kind.

ḷāān (**ḷayan**). 2, 3(inf, tr *-e*), 6(*-i*). Ricochet; graze.

Ḷāātbwiinbar (**ḷayatbiyinbar**). From *ātet* "pack, *bwe* "leftovers", *buwar (bar)* "a basket": Mr. Pack-leftover-basket". A star; Bellatrix in Orion. Legend says *Ḷāātbweinbar* has a basket (*Jāli*) which he carries to *Ḷōkañebar,* who eats contents, thereby nourishing his bright face. The bearer however does not partake, hence his pale face.

ḷābōḷ (**ḷaybeḷ**). From Engl. 2(inf, tr *-e*), 4, 6(*-i*), 7. Carpenter's level.

ḷāibrāre (**ḷayibrayrẹy**). From Engl. Library.

ḷām̧oran (**ḷaym̧er°an**). Also *ḷām̧oran* (**ḷaym̧ewran**). Heritage of land.

ḷārooj (**ḷayrẹwẹj**). 6(*-i*). Island or atoll reserved for food gathering, usually for a chief and his immediate family. *Eor kilen kōnono ilo ḷārooj.* There's a certain manner in which we conduct a conversation when we are at a *ḷārooj* island. *Jemo̧, Pikaar, Tōke, im Ādkup rej jet iaan ḷārooj ko ilo aelōñin M̧ajeḷ.* Jemo, Bikar, Taka, and Erikub are some of the islands in the Marshalls reserved for chiefs strictly for food-gathering purposes.

ḷe (**ḷey**). Sir; vocative, masculine singular.

ḷe (**ḷey**). 1, 2, 3(inf, tr *-ik*), 4, 6(*-i*), 7. Pass; advanced; by-pass; achieve prominence; miss; outdo; overshoot; surpass. *Iar ettōr im ḷe jān e.* I ran and passed him. *Jemān ar kaḷeiki.* His father pushed him ahead.

ḷe (**ḷẹy**). Variant form of *ḷōe* (**ḷẹhyẹy**).

ḷe (**ḷey**). Variant form of *aḷe* (**haḷey**).

ḷe eoon em̧ (**ḷey yewen yẹm̧**). Illegal gathering of food on another's property; poach; trespass. *Emo̧ ḷe eoon em̧ ānin bwe rōnaaj lem̧adeik eok.* It's forbidden to gather food on another's property on this island under the risk of getting speared.

ḷeen kijdik (**ḷeyenkijdik**). Dialectal variant of *ḷo̧jilñin kijdik.*

ḷeeņ (**ḷeyeņ**). He, away from the speaker; that man (close to neither of us); that boy (close to neither of us); personal demonstrative, third person singular masculine.

ḷeepwal (**ḷeyepwal**). A star; zeta in Centaurus; thirdborn of *Lōktañūr.*

ḷeieņ (**ḷeyiyeņ**). That man (close to neither of us); that boy (close to neither of us); personal demonstrative, third person singular masculine, singling out.

ḷeikaalal (**ḷẹyikahalhal**). Variant form of *ḷaikaalal* (**ḷahyikahalhal**).

Ḷeikm̧aan (**ḷẹyikm̧ahan**). 3, 6(*-i*). A plant, *Pandanus fischerianus* cultigen.

ḷein (**ḷẹyin**). This man (close to us both); this boy; personal demonstrative, first person inclusive singular masculine.

ḷeiō (**ḷẹyiyẹh**). This man (close to us both); this boy (close to us both); personal demonstrative, first person exclusive singular masculine, singling out; vocative, familiar, masculine singular. *Kwōn jab men rot ņe ḷeiō.* Don't do that, pal.

ḷeņe (**ḷeyņey**). Variant form of *ḷōņe* (**ḷeņey**).

ḷeņeņe (**ḷeyņeyņey**). Variant form of *ḷōņeņe* (**ḷeņeyņey**).

ḷeo (**ḷeyew**). The man (often not present); this man (close to me); this boy (close to me); personal demonstrative, remote singular masculine.

ḷijib (**ḷijib**). Variant form of *lijib* (**lijib**).

ḷijji (**ḷijjiy**). Transitive form of *ḷḷijḷij* (**ḷḷijḷij**).

ḷipdeḷo̧k (**ḷipdẹyḷaq**). Go through.

Ḷipjenkur (**ḷipjenqir**). A plant, pandanus variety.

ḷḷaaj (**ḷḷahaj**). Dial. W: *eḷḷaaj* (**yeḷḷahaj**), E: *ḷōḷaaj* (**ḷeḷahaj**). 1(*-i*), 2, 3, 7, 8, 9. Dynamic voice; melodious sound; sonorous; loud. *Eḷap an ḷḷaaj ainikien an al.* The sound of his singing is very melodious.

ḷḷaaj (**ḷḷahaj**). Dial. W: *eḷḷaaj* (**yeḷḷahaj**), E: *ḷōḷaaj* (**ḷeḷahaj**). 1(*-i*), 2, 3, 7, 8, 9. Treble; high-pitched sound;

piercing sound; loud. *Eļap an ļļaaj ainikien am̧ al.* Your singing really carries.

ļļaak (**ḷḷahak**). Dial. W: *eļļaak* (**yeḷḷahak**), E: *ļōļaak* (**ḷeḷahak**). 2, 3(inf *kaļļaak,* tr *kaļaak(e)*), 6(-*i*). Fit. *Kwōnañin kōļaak ke?* Have you fit it?

ļļaeoeo (**ḷḷahyẹwyẹw**). 1(-*i*), 2, 3, 6(-*i*), 8, 9. Fast; swift, of canoes or boats, nautical term. *Tipñōl eo ij baj ba eļļaeoeo in.* I would call that a fast sailing canoe. *Eļļaeoeo ļok jān wa ņe waam̧.* It's faster than yours.

ļļajkōnkōn (**ḷḷajkẹnkẹn**). Dial. W: *eļļajkōnkōn* (**yeḷḷajkẹnkẹn**), E: *ļōļajkōnkōn* (**ḷeḷajkẹnkẹn**). 2, 3, 6(-*i*), 7, 8, 9. A boy or man whose appearance makes everyone smile; pleasant; popular; see *llejkōnkōn.*

ļļaļļaļ (**ḷḷaḷḷaḷ**). Dial. W: *eļļaļļaļ* (**yeḷḷaḷḷaḷ**), E: *ļōļaļļaļ* (**ḷeḷaḷḷaḷ**). 1(-*i*), 2, 3, 8, 9. Knocking; dryness, onomatopoetic. *Eļļaļļaļ aebōj eo.* The well went dry. *Lale m̧ōk wōn eņ ej kōļļaļļaļ.* See who's knocking at the door.

ļļao (**ḷḷahwew**). Dial. W: *eļļao* (**yeḷḷahwew**), E: *ļōļao* (**ḷeḷahwew**). 1(-*i*), 2, 3(inf, tr -*uk*), 4, 6(-*i*), 7, 8, 9. Seasick; motion sickness; disgusted. *Elōñ rūļļao bwe eļap ņo.* There are a lot of seasick people because it's rough. *Jab m̧ōñā kūriij bwe enaaj kōļļaouk eok.* Don't eat fat or it'll make you seasick. *Iļļao kōn m̧ōñā ņe.* That's a disgusting food.

ļļā (**ḷḷay**). Dial. W: *eļļā* (**yeḷḷay**), E: *ļōļā* (**ḷeḷay**). 1(-*i*), 2, 7. Cross; pass by; glance by; passed. *Eļļā piiļ eo.* The bill has been passed.

ļļāārār (**ḷḷayaryar**). Dial. W: *eļļāārār* (**yeḷḷayaryar**), E: *ļōļāārār* (**ḷeḷayaryar**). From *ļā* (**ḷay**). 1(-*i*), 2, 3, 6(-*i*), 7. Rattling of gravel. *Wōn in ej ļļāārār tok?* Who is this making noise on the gravel coming here?

ļļeoeo (**ḷḷeyewyew**). Dial. W: *eļļeoeo* (**yeḷḷeyewyew**), E: *ļōļeoeo* (**ḷeḷeyewyew**). 1, 2, 3(inf, tr -*ik*), 6(-*i*), 8, 9. Too fresh to be tasty, said of fish just caught that has not been allowed to settle sufficiently before being eaten raw.

ļļijļij (**ḷḷijḷij**). Dial. W: *iļļijļij* (**yiḷḷijḷij**), E: *ļūļijļij* (**ḷiḷijḷij**). 2(inf, tr *ļiji*), 3. Nibble, as fish on bait. *Eitok ek eo im ļiji eo eo aō.* A fish came and nibbled on my line. *Kōttar an ļļijļij im dimtake.* Wait till he nibbles on the bait and then jerk the line.

ļļōjo (**ḷḷejew**). Variant form of *ļōjo* (**ḷejew**).

ļļōko̧ (**ḷḷekaw**). Dial. W: *eļļōko̧* (**yeḷḷekaw**), E: *ļōļōko̧* (**ḷeḷekaw**). 2(inf, tr -*ik(i)*), 4, 6(-*i*), 7. Type of lashing applied to the *kie* section of a canoe. *Kwōmaroñ ke ļļōko̧ik tok wa e waarro?* Could you please lash the *kie* of our canoe?

ļļwūjļwūj (**ḷ°ḷ°ijḷ°ij**). Dial. W: *iļļwūjļwūj* (**yiḷ°ḷ°ijḷ°ij**), E: *ļuļwūjļwūj* (**ḷ°iḷ°ijḷ°ij**). Also *ļļujļuj.* 2, 3(inf -*(i)*), 4, 6(-*i*), 7. Pounding or thudding of canoes together. *Lali wa kaņe bwe roļļwūjļwūj.* Watch the canoes because they're hitting each other.

ļo- (**ḷew-**). 2, 3(inf *kaļļo-,* tr *kaļo-*), 7. Be at (always with directional). *Ekadik ļolōñ am̧ kañūrñūr.* You wear your belt too high. *Ekadik ļotok kōba eņ.* The outfielder is too shallow. *Ej make wōt ļolaļ ilo kilaaj eņ an.* He's the lowest student in his class.

ļoār (**ḷewyar**). From Engl. Lawyer; attorney. *Wōn ej am̧ ļoār?* Who's your lawyer?

ļobļoba (**ḷ°ebḷ°ebah**). Also *ļōbļaba* (**ḷebḷabah**). 1(-*i*), 2, 3, 4, 6(-*i*), 7. Lava-lava; wear a lava-lava; wear a towel as a lava-lava. *Ewi ļobļoba eo aō?* Where is my lava-lava? *Kwōn ļobļoba kōn to̧o̧l ņe.* Use your towel as a lava-lava.

ļobōrwa (**ḷewberwah**). 6(-*a*). Bowsprit; bow; prow.

ļodekā (**ḷewdekay**). Variant form of *aem̧o̧kkwe* (**hayemaqqẹy**).

ļojat (**ḷ°ejat**). Variant form of *luwajet* (**liwajẹt**).

ļokkorbar (**ḷeqqerbar**). 2(inf, tr -*e*), 3, 5(*ļokkorbarbar*), 6(-*i*), 7. Scarf. *Rej ļokkorbar ñe rej jar.* They wear scarves when they go to church. *Kwōn kaļokkorbare.* Make her wear a scarf. *Eļokkorbarbar lieņ.* She's always wearing scarves. *Ļokkorbare bōran.* Put a scarf around his head.

ļokļok (**ḷeqḷeq**). Vulgar. 1(-*i*), 2(inf, tr *ļokwe*), 3, 7 Wash private parts, female. *Kwōn ļokwe eok.* Wash yourself. *Kwōn etal in ļokļok.* Go wash yourself.

ļokot (**ḷeqẹt**). 5(-*e*). Pile of trash.

ļoktōk (**ļẹqtẹk**). 1(-*i*), 2, 3(inf *kaļļoktōk,* tr *kaļļoktōk,* st *kaļļoktōktōk*), 5(*ļļoktōktōk*), 6(-*i*), 7, 8, 9. Wrinkled; perfective form of *ļukut* (**ļiqit**); ruffled; rumpled; be down and out. *Eļļoktōktōk nuknuk ņe am̧.* Your clothes are all wrinkled. *Eļoktōk nuknuk kā aō.* My clothes are wrinkled. *Kwaar jijet ioon im kaļoktōke.* You sat on it and wrinkled it. *Eļļoktōktōk mejān ļōļļap eo.* The old man's face had lots of wrinkles. *Ilukkuun ļoktōk.* I'm definitely down and out.

ļokwa- (**ļeqa-**). Also *itaka-* (**yitaka-**). 1, 1+7. After; behind; bottom; hind; tail; aft.

Ļokwakōj (**ļeqakej**). 3, 6(-*i*). A plant, pandanus cultigen (Takeuchi).

ļokwan (**ļeqan**). Also *ļokwa-* (**ļ°eqan**). Idiom. 2. Happen to; should. *Eļañņe koļokwan itok kab bōktok ippam̧ tok.* If you should come, bring it with you.

Ļokwan-Ļakeke (**ļeqan-ļakẹykẹy**). Also *Ļo̧k.* See *ļakeke.* A constellation; stars in Cassiopeia: alpha, beta, gamma, delta and epsilon; eighthborn of *Lōktañūr.*

ļokwanwa (**ļeqanwah**). 2(inf, tr *-ik(i)*), 3, 6(-*i*), 7. Pine after someone or something; be homesick for. *Joñan an kar ļokwanwaik tok aeļōñ kein ke ear pād ijekaņ eļak ro̧o̧ltok elukkuun m̧ō.* He was homesick for the Marshalls while he was abroad that when he returned he was really skinny.

ļokwājek (**ļeqayjek**). Also *ļokwājek* (**ļeqayjẹk**). A bird, red-tailed tropicbird, *Phaethon rubricauda.*

ļokwe (**ļẹqẹy**). Transitive form of *ļokļok* (**ļẹqļẹq**).

ļolōñ (**ļẹwlẹg**). 1(-*i*), 2, 3(inf, tr *-e*), 4, 6(-*i*), 8, 9. Elevation; height; altitude. *Ewi ļolōñin allōñ?* How high is the moon?

ļoļātāt (**ļ°eļ°yatyat**). Also *loļātāt* (**leļ°yatyat**). 1, 6(-*i*). Mind; consciousness; essence; self; intellect; soul; wisdom. *Jetōb ej ļoļātāt im ankil anemkwōj.* Spirit is consciousness and free will.

ļoñ (**ļ°ẹg°**). 5(*ļoñļoñ*), 6(-*i*). Ant. *Kwōn kōjparok m̧ōñā kaņe kijen irooj eņ bwe ren jab ļoñļoñe.* Be careful not to let ants get on the chief's meal.

ļoñ (**ļeg°**). Deep.

ļoñanwa (**ļeg°anwah**). From *ļo̧ñan* (**lag°an**) "roller of", *wa* (**wah**) "canoe". Cirrus clouds.

ļoñtak (**ļeg°tak**). 1(-*i*), 2(inf, tr *-e*), 3, 7. Base; foundation; lever; roller for launching canoe; something that is put under something else to protect, lift, or support it. *Kwaar ļoñtake ke wa eo?* Did you put a roller under the canoe? *Kwōn ļoñtak kōn pet ņe.* Prop yourself with that pillow.

ļoob (**ļeweb**). From Engl. 3, 6(-*i*). Loaf of bread.

ļooj (**ļewej**). 3, 6(-*i*). A fish, false albacore or *kawakawa.*

Ļoojļapļap (**ļewejļapļap**). See *ļooj:* "big bonito". A star; Aldebaran in Taurus.

ļoon (**ļewen**). From Engl. *launch.* 6(-*i*). Picket boat; with outboard engine.

ļoor(e) (**ļewer(ey)**). 2, 3, 4, 5(*ļļoļoor*), 7. Follow; comply.

ļooribeb (**ļeweryibyẹb**). 2, 6(-*i*), 7. Follow a large wave in entering a lagoon; arrive in full force. *Ear douj kōn an jab ļooribeb.* He sank because he did not follow the large wave. *Rijikuuļ ro raar ļooribebtok ñan jikin iakiu eo.* The students arrived in full force at the baseball field.

ļor (**ļẹr°**). Also *jul* (**jiļ°**), *ļor* (**ļ°ẹr**). 2, 3(inf *kaļļor,* tr *-e*), 4+3, 6(-*i*), 7. Sprout; young shoot; plant or tree growth from old root or after old branch of tree has been cut down; shrub.

Ļora (**ļewrah**). Also *Laura.* 4. Place name; islet; main island of Majuro; from *Laura, U. S. Navy code name.*

ļorak (**ļewrak**). 2, 3, 5(*ļļorakrak*), 7. Caught; entangled. *Eļorak kāāj eo.* The hook is caught. *Eļļorakrak kāāj eo an.* The hook on his fishing pole always gets caught on the reef.

ļot (**ļ°et**). 1(-*i*), 2, 3, 7. Become extinct; die out, of plants, animals, or people; disappear. *Eļot bwij eņ.* That lineage is dying out. *Eļot ni eņ.* That coconut tree is not producing any more. *Eļot wa eo.* The boat disappeared.

ļot (**ļ°et**). 6(-*i*). Canoe part, mast top.

ļot (**ļ°et**). Transitive form of *ļotļot* (**ļ°ẹtļ°ẹt**).

ḷotak (**ļ°etak**). 2, 3. Birth; be born. *Iiō̄t eo kwaar ḷotak ie?* What year were you born?

ḷotḷot (**ļ°ẹtļ°ẹt**). 1(*-i*), 2(inf, tr *ḷot(e)*), 10(*ḷot*). Pick; pluck, of fruit; pull keys off pandanus. *Rej ḷotḷot bōb.* They are pulling keys off of pandanus. *Kwōn ḷot(e) tok juon daō bōb.* Pull me off a key of pandanus. *Eḷot juon ñiū.* One of my teeth came out.

ḷotḷọk (**ļ°etļaq**). 1(*-i*), 2, 3, 5(*ḷḷotḷọkḷọk*). Faint; disappear. *Ettōr lio im ḷotḷọk.* She ran and fainted. *Eḷotḷọk wa eo.* The canoe disappeared. *Eoḷḷotḷọkḷọk lieṇ.* She is always fainting.

ḷouj (**ļẹwij**). A fish; long fins.

ḷouweo (**ļewiweyew**). That man (close to neither of us); that boy (close to neither of us); personal demonstrative, remote singular masculine, singling out.

ḷowaṇwoṇ (**ļewaṇwẹṇ**). Busy man; see *lowaṇwoṇ.*

ḷọ (**ļaw**). 3, 6(*-i*). A plant, hibiscus, *Hibiscus tiliaceus* L. (Malvaceae). A large cordate-leaved, yellow-flowered tree; unmistakably a hibiscus, with very strong bast fibres. The Polynesian *hau.*

ḷọk (**ļaq**). The last; the most recent. *Pata eo ḷọk.* The last war. *Wiik eo ḷọk.* Last week.

ḷọk (**ļaq**). 2, 3, 6. Over; stop. *Kōjro kōḷọk wōt kein.* Let's wait for the rain to stop. *Eḷọk wōt ko.* The rain has stopped.

ḷọk (**ļaq**). Hurry; faster; accelerate. *Jeje ḷọk.* Hurry up and write. *Men ḷọk.* Hurry. *Ṃōñā ḷọk.* Hurry up and eat.

ḷọk (**ļaq**). Also *lọk* (**laq**) (obligatorily following the *i-* of *ilọk* (**yilaq**) and the *wā* of *wālọk* (**waylaq**)). Toward a third party, neither speaker nor addressee; directional, postposition, toward third party. *Ear ṃallọk ñan e.* He stooped toward him. *Kwōn tarniñaḷọk.* You must sail northward.

Ḷọk (**ļaq**). Variant form of *Ḷokwan-Ḷakeke.*

ḷọkdede (**ļaqdeydey**). Caudal fin.

ḷọkjenaa- (**ļaqjenaha-**). 1. Amazed; astonished; wonder; beside oneself with fear; distracted by some calamity. *Ear ḷọkjenaō ke ij roñ ke emej.* I was shocked when I heard that he died.

ḷọkun (**ļaqin**). 7. After. *Ḷọkun ḷọk pata eo.* Right after the war.

ḷọḷe (**ļawļẹy**). From Engl. 3, 6(*-i*). Candy.

ḷọḷōjjed (**ļaļ°ejjed**). 1(*-i*), 2(inf, tr *-e*), 3, 4. Envy. *Eḷọḷōjjede kōn jerbal eo an.* He envies him because of his job.

ḷọñ (**ļag°**). Also *ḷọñ* (**ļ°ag°**). 1(*ḷọña-*). Roller for launching canoe.

ḷọñ (**ļ°ag°**). Also *ḷọñ* (**ļag°**). 5(*ḷọñḷọñ*), 6(*-i*). A fly. *Eḷọñḷọñ ṃōñā ṇe.* There are flies all over that food there.

ḷọom (**ļawẹm**). Dial. W, E: *ewae* (**yewahyey**). Also *ḷaom, ḷaum; ḷọuṃ* (**ļawiṃ**). A fish, streaker, *Aprion virescens.*

ḷọr (**ļar°**). Sea anemone; black.

ḷọuṃ (**ļawiṃ**). Also *ḷauṃ.* Variant form of *ḷọom* (**ļawẹm**).

ḷọun (**ļawin**). Archaic. Magical power; one of two kinds, see *ṃọun.*

ḷōb (**ļeb**). 6(*-i*). Rooster tail feather; boat decorations.

ḷōbat (**ļebat**). 1(*-i*), 2(inf, tr *-e*), 5(*ḷōbḷōbate*), 6(*-i*), 7. Raise by lever; lift by lever; pry; pull up; raise. *Kwōn ḷōbate kōn juon aḷaḷ.* Raise it with a piece of wood.

ḷōbḷaba (**ļebļabah**). Variant form of *ḷobḷoba* (**ļ°ebļ°ebah**).

ḷōbọtin (**ļebawtin**). From *Lōbọtin* (**ļebawtin**) "name of a man". 2(inf, tr *-i*), 4, 6(*-i*). Fish out an area in order to spite those coming later. *Eṃōj ḷōbọtini arin ānin.* This lagoon has been fished out.

ḷōe (**ļẹhyẹy**). Also *ḷe* (**ļẹy**). This man (close to me); this boy (close to me); personal demonstrative, first person exclusive singular masculine.

ḷōjabwil (**ļejabil**). 3, 6(*-i*). A fish, bonito, *Katsuwonus pelamis*; *Sarda sarda.*

Ḷōjennoṃaj (**ļẹjẹnnewṃaj**). A plant, banana variety (Takeuchi).

ḷōjepjep (**ļejepjep**). 3, 6(*-i*). A fish, rock hind, *Epinephelus albofasciatus*; a fish, grouper, *Epinephelus adscenscionis.*

Ḷōjepkọ (**ļẹjẹpkaw**). From "name of former chief". 3, 6(*-i*). A plant, *Pandanus fischerianus* cultigen (Takeuchi). (Stone).

ḷōjjeptaktak (**ļejjeptaktak**). Also *ḷōjeppetaktak* (**ļejeppetaktak**). A fish.

ḷōjkaan (**ļejkahan**). A fish, swordfish, *Xiphia gladius*; marlin.

Ļōjm̧ao (**ļejm̧ahwew**). 3, 6(-*i*). A plant, pandanus cultigen. (Stone). Majuro.

ļōjo (**ļejew**). Also *jjo* (**jjew**). 1(-*i*), 2, 3, 6(-*i*), 7, 8, 9. Rust. *Ejjo.* It is rusty!

ļōjo (**ļejew**). Also *ļļōjo* (**ļļejew**). 1(-*i*), 2. Nosebleed. *Eļōjo bọtin.* His nose is bleeding.

Ļōjokdād (**ļejeqdad**). 3, 6(-*i*). A plant, *Pandanus carolinianus* cultigen.

Ļōjoor (**ļejewer**). 3, 6(-*i*). A plant, pandanus cultigen (Takeuchi).

ļōkajem̧ (**ļekajem̧**). 1(-*i*), 2(inf, tr -*e*), 4, 6(-*i*). Inconsiderate; do something that will result in misfortune, such as breaking a taboo; be rash. *Ejjeļam ļōkajem̧win ļeeņ.* He's such an inconsiderate fellow. He's always breaking taboos.

Ļōkañebar (**ļekageybar**). See *Ļāātbwiinbar.* A star; Betelgeuse in Orion.

ļōkatip (**ļekatip**). 1(-*i*), 2(inf, tr -*i*), 3, 4, 6. Mischievous; naughty; teasing; to tease; displease; pest; angry; chagrin. *Jab ļōkatipi jatūm̧.* Don't tease your brother.

ļōke (**ļẹkẹy**). Also *ļōke* (**ļekey**). 1(-*i*), 2, 3, 7. Step or go over; cross over. *Kwōn jab ļōke ļadik ņe.* Don't step over that boy there.

Ļōkoojņo (**ļekewejņew**). A star; Regulus.

ļōkōm̧ (**ļekem̧**). 1(-*i*), 2(inf, tr -*e*), 4, 7. Imagine; pretend; make believe; wish for; a game, to play house. *Em̧ōj ņe am̧ ļōkōm̧.* When are you going to stop kidding yourself. *Ajri raņ rej ļōkōm̧.* The kids are playing house.

Ļōkōtwa (**ļeketwah**). 3, 6(-*i*). A plant, *Pandanus fischerianus* cultigen; Mejit and Aur. (Stone). (Jaluit, Majuro, Likiep, Aelok, Utirik).

Ļōktaan (**ļektahan**). 3, 6(-*i*). A plant, banana variety.

ļōļ (**ļeļ**). 1(-*i*), 2, 3, 7, 8, 9. Moldy; smell moldy. *Ta in ebwiin ļōļ?* What smells moldy?

ļōļ (**ļeļ**). 1(-*i*), 2, 3. Smell of rotten copra or rancid coconut oil.

ļōļ (**ļeļ**). Also *atad* (**hatad**). 2(inf, tr -*e*), 6(-*i*). Wire leader, used in fishing. *Kab ļōļe kāāj ņe.* Be sure to use wire leader with that hook.

ļōļ-. See *ļļ-*.

ļōļļap (**ļeļļap**). Variant form of *ļaļļap* (**ļaļļap**).

ļōļō (**ļehļeh**). 1(-*i*), 2(inf, tr *ļōōt(e)*), 3, 4, 6(-*i*), 7. Weave flowers or shells into a lei; wreathe. *Lim̧aro raņ rej ļōļō.* Those women are making leis. *Kwōn ļōōt juon ñan ilju.* Make a lei for tomorrow.

ļōma- (**ļema-**). 1, 2. Characteristic; shape; fashion; feature; semblance. *Ļōmān rinana.* He's got the characteristics of a delinquent.

ļōmak (**ļemak**). Transitive form of *ļam* (**ļam**).

Ļōmānkōto (**ļemankẹtẹw**). Also *Jāljel* (**jaljẹl**), *limenkūttū.* See *kōto:* "Mr. Wind". A star; in Aries; 41.

Ļōmejdikdik (**ļẹmẹjdikdik**). A constellation; stars in Scorpius; lambda, upsilon, chi (or kappa), iota; secondborn of *Lōktañūr.*

ļōmmejne (**ļemmẹjney**). 2, 8. Crippled, of legs only. *Eļōļļapļọk em ļōmmejne.* He became old and crippled.

ļōmņak (**ļemņak**). 1(-*i*), 2, 8. Think; thought; assume; attitude; idea; intend; mean; mental; notion; opinion; plans; ponder; position; presume; suggestion.

ļōm̧a (**ļem̧ah**). Also *m̧a.* You, to many men in general, not specific; vocative, masculine plural.

ļōm̧araņ (**ļem̧ahraņ**). Those men (close to neither of us); personal demonstrative, third person plural masculine.

ļōm̧araņe (**ļem̧ahraņey**). Those men (close to you); those boys (close to you); personal demonstrative, second person plural masculine.

ļōm̧arā (**ļem̧ahray**). These men (close to me); these boys (close to me); personal demonstrative, first person exclusive plural masculine.

ļōm̧arāraņ (**ļem̧ahrayraņ**). Those men (close to neither of us); those boys (close to neither of us); personal demonstrative, third person plural masculine, singling out.

ļōm̧arāraņe (**ļem̧ahrayraņey**). Those men (close to you); those boys (close to you); personal demonstrative, second person plural masculine, singling out.

ļōm̧arārā (**ļem̧ahrayray**). Also *ļōm̧arere* (**ļem̧ahrẹyrẹy**). These men (close to me); these boys (close to me); personal demonstrative, first person exclusive plural masculine, singling out; vocative, familiar, masculine plural. *Koṃwin kaiur ḷọk ḷōṃarārā.* Step on it, you guys.

ḷōṃarein (**ḷeṃahrẹyin**). These men (close to us both); these boys (close to us both); personal demonstrative, first person inclusive plural masculine.

ḷōṃarere (**ḷeṃahrẹyrẹy**). Variant form of *ḷōṃarārā* (**ḷeṃahrayray**).

ḷōṃaro (**ḷeṃahrew**). The men (often not present); these men (close to me); these boys (close to me); personal demonstrative, remote plural masculine.

ḷōṃaroro (**ḷeṃahrewrew**). Those men (close to neither of us); those boys (close to neither of us); personal demonstrative, remote plural masculine, singling out; vocative, familiar, masculine plural.

ḷōṃṃak (**ḷeṃṃak**). Variant form of *ṃak* (**ṃak**).

Ḷōṃōeṇ (**ḷeṃehyeṇ**). From *Ḷōṃō* (**ḷeṃeh**) "man's name" *ṃō* (**ṃeh**) "thin". 3, 6(-*i*). A plant, *Pandanus fischerianus* cultigen; Arno and Wotje. (Stone).

ḷōnañ (**ḷenag**). 1(-*i*). Fake; pretend to be satisfied. *Ejjeḷam ḷōnañiier.* They're such fakes.

Ḷōṇa (**ḷeṇah**). See *ṇa*: "Mr. Shoal. A constellation; Hydrus; thought to show true south.

ḷōṇe (**ḷeṇey**). Also *ḷeṇe* (**ḷeyṇey**). That man (close to you); that boy (close to you); personal demonstrative, second person singular masculine.

ḷōṇeṇe (**ḷeṇeyṇey**). Also *ḷeṇeṇe* (**ḷeyṇeyṇey**). That man (close to you); that boy (close to you); personal demonstrative, second person singular masculine, singling out.

ḷōñ (**ḷẹg**). 1(-*i*), 2, 3, 4, 8, 9. Commit adultery; lust; fornicate. *Kwōn jab ḷōñ.* Don't lust.

ḷōōt (**ḷehet**). 2, 6(-*i*). Concoction; fabrication; recipe; combination. *Eṃṃan wōt in ḷōōt.* This is a great combination. *Wōn eo ej ḷōōt rainin?* Whose turn is it to make the recipe today?

ḷōōt (**ḷehet**). Transitive form of *ḷōḷō* (**ḷehḷeh**).

Ḷōpo (**ḷẹpẹw**). 3, 6(-*i*). A plant, *Pandanus fischerianus* cultigen. (Stone). Utirik.

ḷōppekañkūr (**ḷẹppẹykagkir**). 2, 6(-*i*). Picnic.

ḷōpper (**ḷẹppẹr**). 1(-*i*), 2, 3, 4. Mumps; tumor; swelling.

ḷōruk (**ḷeriq**). Archaic. Second crop of coconuts; a week or so after first collection. *Kōḷōruk waini.* Gather the second crop of copra nuts.

ḷōt (**ḷet**). What man? What boy?

Ḷōtōl (**ḷẹtẹl**). A plant, *Pandanus fischerianus* cultigen (Takeuchi).

ḷōttekōḷkōḷ (**ḷetteykeḷkeḷ**). Slang. 6(-*i*). Shooter marble; fatso. *N̄e kwōj bu ilo kōjjobaba, kwōj kōjerbal ḷōttekōḷkōḷ eṇ.* When you shoot while playing marbles, you use a shooter marble.

ḷubōr (**ḷiwber**). From Engl. 2(inf, tr -*e*), 5(*ḷḷubōrbōr*), 6(-*i*). Louver, movable and opaque or transparent. *Kwōnaaj ḷubōre ñāāt wūntō ṇe?* When are you going to put the louvers on that window?

ḷuj. See *ḷwūj.*

ḷuktūr (**ḷiqtir**). Dialectal variant of *ubwe* (**wibey**).

ḷuktūrri (**ḷiqtirriy**). Transitive form of *ḷuktūr* (**ḷiqtir**).

ḷukut (**ḷiqit**). 2(inf, tr -*i*), 7, 10(*ḷoktōk*). Rolled, as by surf; washed ashore; roll up sloppily, wrinkled. *Raar ḷukut ānetak kājokwā eo.* The log was washed ashore. *Eḷoktōk nuknuk kaṇe.* The clothes are wrinkled.

ḷukut (**ḷiqit**). Dialectal variant of *ubwe* (**wibey**).

ḷuḷ (**ḷiḷ°**). Also *ḷuḷ* (**ḷ°iḷ°**). 1, 6(-*i*). Sacrum; coccyx.

ḷuḷu (**ḷiwḷiw**). 2(inf, tr -*ik(i)*), 4, 6(-*i*). A game, played with pebbles and ball, similar to dice game; shake pebbles and ball or dice.

ḷūb (**ḷib**). Variant form of *ḷwūp* (**ḷ°ip**).

ḷūbbat (**ḷibbat**). 2, 6(-*i*), 8, 9. Grow slowly; stunted growth.

ḷūḷ-. See *ḷḷ-.*

ḷwaar (**ḷ°ahar**). Also *atiḷọọr* (**hatiyḷawar**). 2(inf, tr -*e*), 3, 5(*ḷwaare*), 6(-*i*). Mosquito coil. *Etke koṃwij jab ḷwaare (atiḷọọr) lowaan ṃwiin?* Why don't you people light up the mosquito coil to keep the mosquitoes out of the house?

ḷwe (**ḷ°ẹy**). 6(-*i*). Small pool on reef at low tide, or in interior of island.

ḷwiit (**ḷ°iyit**). 1(*-i*), 2(inf, tr *-i*). To slurp; drink noisily.

ḷwōjat (**ḷ°ejat**). Also *ḷojat.* 1(*-i*), 2, 3(inf, tr *-e*), 8, 9. Soggy; drenched; saturated; waterlogged. *Eḷwōjat im ddo.* It's waterlogged and extra heavy.

ḷwōjā (**ḷ°ejay**). Also *ḷojā.* 2(inf, tr *-ik(i)*), 4, 6(*-i*), 7. Spank. *Ḷeo eḷwōjāiki ḷadik eo nejin.* The man spanked his son.

ḷwōl (**ḷ°el**). Also *loḷ* (**leḷ°**). A fish, goggle-eye, *Priacanthus cruentatus.*

ḷwūj (**ḷ°ij**). Also *ḷuj.* 2(inf, tr *-i*), 4, 6(*-i*), 7. Mallet; hammer. *Kwaar kōjerbale ke ḷwūj eo arro?* Did you use our mallet? *Jāj eo ellu im ḷwūji eoon tebōḷ eo an.* The judge got mad and pounded the mallet on his desk.

ḷwūp (**ḷ°ip**). Also *ḷup, ḷūb* (**ḷib**). Vulgar. 2, 3, 4+3. Deflower. *Eṃōj an ḷwūp ledik eṇ.* That girl is not a virgin.

maaj (**mahaj**). 3(inf *kōmaajaj,* tr *kōmaajaj*), 5(*maajaj*), 6(*-i*), 8, 9. Cleared space; open field; pasture. *Jen kōmaajaje ḷain in.* Let's clear up this plot of land. *Emake maajaj ānin.* This island has been cleared very well.

Maalal (**mahalhal**). A star (planet), Evening Star, Venus (evenings only).

maalkan ne (**mahalkan ney**). 1(*-e*), 2, 3(inf, tr *kamaalkan-neek*). Footprints. *Emalkan-ne arin ānin.* There are footprints on the lagoon side beach of this islet. *Kwōnaaj kōmaalkan-neek lowaan ṃwiin kōn juuj kaṇe aṃ.* You'll soil the floor with your shoe prints.

maañ (**mahag**). 1(*-i*), 3, 5(*mmaañañ*), 6(*-i*). Pandanus leaf. *Emmaañañ nōbjān ṃwiin.* There are lots of pandanus leaves outside this house.

Maañurun (**mahagir°in**). From "name of a clan of handsome people who fade early in life". 3, 6(*-i*). A plant, *Pandanus fischerianus* cultigen; Ebon. Not used for thatch because it soon rots. (Stone). Utirik.

maat (**mahat**). 2, 3, 5(*mmaatat*), 7. Empty; no more; all gone; exhausted. *Emaat ṃōñā.* The food is all gone. *Aolep maat ḷọk ñan kweilọk eṇ.* Let's all go to the meeting.

mab (**mab**). From Engl. 6(*-i*). Map.

makak. See *mekak.*

makarta (**mahkartah**). Also *mekarta.* Nevertheless; so what. *Makarta ñe eitok.* So what if he comes?

make (**mahkey**). Also *bake* (**bahkey**), *bajke* (**bajkey**). Quite the contrary. *Make ij jerbal.* But I am working. *Make.* That's what I said.

make (**makẹy**). 1(*-i*), 2, 3(inf, tr *-ik*), 7. Alone; self; lonely; solitary; unaccomplished. *Ear make tok.* He came alone.

makijkij (**makijkij**). 1(*-i*), 2, 3, 5(*mmakijkij*), 7, 8, 9. Often; frequent; common.

makillō (**makilleh**). Dial. W, E: *pitōro* (**piyterew**). 1(*-i*), 2(inf, tr *-ik(i)*), 4, 5(*mmakillōlō ppitōroro*), 6(*-i*), 7. A food, balls of preserved breadfruit sweetened and boiled in coconut oil.

makmake (**makmakẹy**). Favorite. *Komaroñ kōjerbal pinjeḷ e aō makmake.* You are welcome to use my favorite pencil.

makōḷkōḷ (**makeḷkeḷ**). 1(*-i*), 2, 3, 5(*mmakōḷkōḷ*), 7. Stretch the body. *Kwōn jab mmakōḷkōḷ.* Don't be stretching all the time.

makōrlep (**makerlep**). Vulgar. 1, 2, 6(*-i*), 8, 9. Hypersensitive, sexually.

maḷko (**maḷkew**). 1(*-i*), 2, 3, 4, 5(*mmaḷkoko*), 8, 9. Straight hair. *Emmaḷkoko kooḷan bōran riJaina.* Lots of Chinese have straight hair.

maḷḷipen (**maḷḷipẹn**). 1(*-i*), 2, 3, 4, 5(*mmaḷḷipenpen*), 7, 8, 9. Oily. *Emmaḷḷipenpen pet kā.* These pillows are all oily.

maḷḷipen (**maḷḷipẹn**). 1(*-i*), 2, 3, 5(*mmaḷḷipenpen*). Smell of rotten copra on body.

maḷoñ (**maḷeg°**). 1(*-i*), 2, 3, 5(*mmaḷoñḷoñ*), 7. Drown. *Ajri eo emmaḷoñḷoñ eṇ.* That child is always (coming close to) drowning.

maḷto (**maḷtẹw**). 6(*-i*). Veranda; lanai; porch.

maḷtu (**maḷtiw**). Roof; overhang.

maḷūttōk (**maḷittẹk**). 2, 6(*-i*), 8, 9. Roll of fat around waist. *Emaḷūttōk.* He's got an overhang.

mamo (**mahmẹw**). A fish, sardine, *Sardinella* sp.; *Harengula kinzei.*

manōt (**mahnet**). A fish.

mañ (**mag**). Coconut beginning to turn brown; see *mañbōn.*

mañ (**mag**). 2, 8, 9. Negatively conditioned; know better; learn not to. *Kiiō ke eṃōj an kalbuuj, bōlen enaaj mañ.* Now that he has been in jail, maybe he will know better. *Emañ kako eo em jab bar ire.* The rooster got negatively conditioned and refused to fight.

mañbōn (**magben**). 1(-*i*), 2, 3, 4+3, 5(*mmañbōnbōn, mañbōne*), 6(-*i*), 8, 9. Coconut beginning to form hard meat and turn brown. *Emañbōne ni ṇe.* That coconut tree has a lot of *mañbōn* on it.

mañde- (**magde-**). 1. Children of a man's sister; nephew; niece.

mañko (**magkẹw**). From Engl. 3, 6(-*i*). Mango.

mañoño (**magẹwgẹw**). Variant form of *mañōtñōt* (**magẹtgẹt**).

mañōtñōt (**magẹtgẹt**). Also *mañoño* (**magẹwgẹw**). 1(-*i*), 2, 3, 7, 8, 9. Flexible; pliable; pliant.

mañūñ (**magig**). 1(-*i*), 2, 3, 8, 9. Old and sour coconut sap; fermented, of coconut sap. *Emañūñ jekaro eo.* The toddy is old and sour.

mao (**mahwew**). 1(-*i*), 2, 3, 5(*mmaoo*), 7, 8, 9. Bruised. *Ebaj et im mmaoo turun mejaṃ?* How did your face get all bruised?

mao (**mahwew**). Dial. W only; see *merā* (**meray**). 3, 6(-*i*). A fish, parrotfish, *Scarus jonesi/sordidus*; a fish, wrasse; *Cheilinus* sp.

mar (**mar**). 5(*mare, marmar(e)*), 6(-*i*). Bush; shrub; boondocks; thicket. *Eḷap an mare ānin.* This islet has much bush.

marere (**mareyrey**). From *rere* "laugh". Legendary game played by young women.

mariko (**mahriykẹw**). A plant, *Centella asiatica* (L.) Urban (Umbelliferae). A small ground-cover plant of moister areas. The flowers are borne at the base of the plant, hence are not seen unless looked for carefully. The leaves are similar to those of garden violets.

mariprip (**mariprip**). Devastation; calamity; harm; trouble; damage. *Jej jorrāān tok wōt jān maripripin ḷañ eo.* We are still down and out from the damage of the storm.

marjāj (**marjaj**). Variant form of *markūbwebwe* (**markibeybey**).

marjej (**marjej**). Variant form of *markūbwebwe* (**markibeybey**).

markinenjojo (**markinenjewjew**). From *mar* (**mar**) "bush, vine". 3, 6(-*i*). A plant, *Vigna marina* (Burm.) Merrill. (Leguminosae). A yellow-flowered leguminous vine climbing, or decumbent on beaches. Also; *Ipomoea pes-caprae.*

markūbwebwe (**markibeybey**). Also *marjāj* (**marjaj**), *marjej* (**marjej**). From *mar* (**mar**) "bush, vine", *kūbwebwe* (**kibeybey**) "covered with feces", "toilet paper vine". 3, 6(-*i*). A plant, *Wedelia biflora* (L.) DC. (Compositae). An opposite-leaved, yellow-flowered composite, quite common.

marḷap (**marḷap**). From *mar* (**mar**) "bush, vine", *ḷap* (**ḷap**) "big". 3, 6(-*i*). A plant, *Canavalia* spp. (Leguminosae); esp. *C. maritima* (Aubl.) Thou., A trifoliolate beach vine with pink sweet-pea-like flowers and large flat green pods. Also, *Ipomoea tuba*, (Convolvulaceae), a creeping viney morning-glory with white flowers.

maro (**mahrew**). From *maroro* "green". Formant in place names.

maro (**marẹw**). 1(-*i*), 2, 3(inf, tr -*uk*), 5(*mmaroro*), 7, 8, 9. Thirsty; thirst. *Raar kamarouk rūkalbuuj eo.* They made the prisoner thirsty. *Imaro kōn aō kar ṃōñā jọọḷ.* I'm thirsty from having eaten salt. *Immaroro kōn aō kar ṃōñā jọọḷ.* I keep on being thirsty because I ate salt.

marok (**mareq**). 1(-*i*), 2(inf, tr -*e*), 3, 4, 5(*mmarokrok*), 7, 8, 9, 11(*marokrok*). Dark; darkness; gloom. *Emarok ṃweeṇ.* That house is dark. *Buñūn marok.* Moonless night. *Emarok ḷeeṇ.* He is cruel. *Emarok būruon.* He has an evil heart. *Ear ruj wōt ke ej mmarokrok.* He woke as the darkness was vanishing.

marok jilōñlōñ (**mareq jilẹglẹg**). 8, 9. Thick darkness.

marokiddik (**mareqiddik**). Fifth moon phase; moon phase after *meḷọkḷọk.*

maroklep (**mareqlep**). 2, 6(-*i*), 8, 9. Moonless; pitchblack; sixth moon phase; moon phase after *marokiddik. Enana kawor ilo maroklep.* It's not good to hunt for lobsters on moonless nights.

maroñ (**mareg°**). 1(-*i*), 2, 3(inf *kammaroñroñ*, tr *kōmaroñe*), 7, 8, 9.

Can; be able to; ability; power; afford; authority; capable; claim; competent; delegated; may; possible. *Imaroñ kotak jibukwi-lemñoul bọun.* I can lift 150 lbs. *Kwōmaroñ ke kotak jibukwi-lemñoul bọun?* Can you lift 150 lbs? *Kōjro kōmmaroñroñ.* Let's (the two of us) have a contest. *Wōn ear kōmaroñ eok?* Who authorized you? Who delegated you that power?

maroñ ṃṃakūt (**mareg° ṃṃakit**). Removable. *Emaroñ ṃṃakūt men ṇe.* That's removable.

maroro (**mahrewrew**). 1(*-i*), 2, 3(inf, tr *-uk*), 5(*mmaroro*), 6(*-i*), 7, 8, 9, 10(*maroro, maro*). Green colored. *Ej kōṇak juon nuknuk emmaroro mejān.* She is wearing a greenish dress.

marpeḷe (**marpeḷey**). 3, 6(*-i*). A plant, vine, *Ipomoea tuba.*

martok (**marteq**). A plant, *Psilotum nudum.*

mat (**mat**). 1(*-i*), 2, 3(inf *kōmat,* tr *kōmatte*), 7, 8, 9. Cooked. *Emat mā ko.* The breadfruit are cooked. *Kwōn kōmatte ek ṇe.* Cook that fish.

mat (**mat**). 1(*-i*), 2(inf, tr *-e*), 3(inf, tr *-e*), 5(*kōmatmat*), 6(*-i*), 7, 8, 9. Full after eating; satisfied; satiated. *Kwōmat ke kiiō?* Are you satisfied now? *Ij kōmat niñniñ e.* I'm feeding the baby until it's full. *Ekōmatmat an kōrā e riū kōmat.* My wife's cooking is very delicious and thus satisfying. *Kwōn kañ ṃōñā ṇe matin.* Eat his leftovers. *Imate raij eo.* I couldn't eat any more of the rice. *Kwōn kōmate.* Feed him until he's satisfied.

matātōp (**mahtaytẹp**). 2(inf, tr *-e*), 6(*-i*). Canoe part, reinforcement close to both ends. *Inaaj matātōpe kōrkōr e bwe en pen.* I'll leave these as reinforcements for the canoe.

matmat (**matmat**). Dial. W only; see *oñoñ* (**weg°weg°**). 2(inf, tr *-e*), 3, 6(*-i*). Sponge; pad.

matoḷ (**mateḷ°**). Also *jemmatoḷ* (**jemmateḷ°**). Part; a third; see *jimmatan. Letok jemmatoḷun mā ṇe kijeṃ.* Give me a piece of your breadfruit.

matōk (**matek**). 1(*-i*), 2, 3, 7, 8, 9. Fat; fatten.

matōrtōr (**materter**). 1(*-i*), 2(inf, tr *-e*), 3, 4, 7, 8, 9. Very angry; furious; offended; rage.

mattiia (**mattiyyah**). 1(*-i*), 2, 4, 7, 8, 9. Hard to cook; (see *mattiie* (**mattiyyẹy**)).

mattiia (**mattiyyah**). Dial. W, E: *būrooklep* (**bireweklep**). 1(*-i*), 2, 3, 4, 8, 9. Greedy for food; hard to satisfy with food; greedy eater; glutton; voracious; (see *mattiie* (**mattiyyẹy**)).

mattiie (**mattiyyẹy**). 1(*-i*), 2, 3, 4, 8, 9. Easy to cook; (see *mattiia* (**mattiyyah**)).

mattiie (**mattiyyẹy**). Dial. W, E: *būrudik* (**biriwdik**). 1(*-i*), 2, 4, 7, 8, 9. Abstemious of food; of small appetite; easy to satisfy with food; light eater; (see *mattiia* (**mattiyyah**)).

mā (**may**). 3, 5(*mmāmā*), 6(*-i*), 7. A plant, general term for the breadfruit, *Artocarpus incisus* (Thunb.) L. F. Moraceae; or fig family); (identical with *A. altilis* (Park. ex z.) Fosberg.) *Emmāmā ḷam jako lowaan ṃwiin.* The inside of this house is really covered with breadfruit scraps. *Emmāmā nuknuk e aō.* My clothes have scraps of breadfruit on them.

māāl (**mayal**). 5(*mmāālāl*), 6(*-i*). Axe; hatchet; adze; iron; steel; metal. *Enemen mmāālāl.* It has the taste of iron.

māāl waan (**mayal wahan**). Alloy. *Wūnin an kkōṃ jāje ṇe kōnke māāl waan.* It's an alloy, that's why your machete is breakable.

māāṇ (**mayaṇ**). 1(*-i*), 2, 3, 5(*mmāāṇāṇ*), 8, 9, 11(*māāṇāṇ*). Burn; smart, as medicine on a sore. *Emāāṇ kinej e peiū.* The wound on my arm burns. *Emmāāṇāṇ kinej e peiū.* The cut on my hand keeps on burning.

māāṇāṇ (**mayaṇyaṇ**). Also *okmāāṇāṇ* (**wẹkmayaṇyaṇ**). 1(*-i*), 2, 3, 5(*mmāāṇāṇ*), 7, 8, 9. Warm; warmth; heat. *Ia in ej mmāāṇāṇ tok?* Where is that heat coming from?

māār (**mayar**). 1(*-i*), 2, 4, 7, 8, 9. Tell a lie. *Kwōn jab māār.* Don't lie.

māār (**mayar**). 1(*-i*), 2, 3(tr *kamāār*), 7. Stained; yellowish. *Lale emāār nuknuk ṇe aṃ.* Watch out, your clothes might get stained.

Mābat (**maybat**). From *mā* (**may**) "breadfruit", *bat* (**bat**) "hill". A plant, breadfruit variety (Takeuchi).

mābuñ (**maybig°**). 2, 3, 4+3, 6(*-i*). Breadfruit blown down by the wind; windfallen breadfruit.

mād (**mad**). Ripen. *Emād bōb kaṇ.* Those pandanus are ripening.

Mādak (**maydak**). A plant, breadfruit variety (Takeuchi).

mādepep (**madyepyep**). Scorpion.

Mādik (**maydik**). From *mā* (**may**) "breadfruit", *dik* (**dik**) "small". A plant, breadfruit variety (Takeuchi).

mādke (**madkęy**). From Engl. *America.* 1(*-i*), 2, 3, 5(*mmādkeke*), 6(*-i*), 7, 8, 9. Venereal disease. *Kōn an kar rūAmedka ro ilo waan kōrajraj ko jino bōktok nañinmej in ñan riṂajeḷ, raar ṇa etan mādke.* Because of the fact that venereal disease was first introduced to the Marshallese people by the American whaleship crewmen, they called it *mādke* ("America").

mādo (**madew**). Archaic. Sea crab.

mādo (**maydęw**). Variant form of *do* (**dęw**).

Māe (**mayęy**). From Engl. May; the month.

Māikwe (**mayiqey**). From *mā* (**may**) "breadfruit", *kwe* (**qey**) "scrape it (referring to the scraping off of charred skin of roasted breadfruit). A plant, breadfruit variety (Takeuchi).

māirrūb (**mayirrib**). 3, 6(*-i*). Unripe fallen breadfruit.

māj (**maj**). 1(*meja-*), 2. Eye; face; cutting edge; lid; opening of any container, hole, doorway, or cave, etc. *Mejān jāje.* Edge of the machete. *Emejān kālọk.* She displays a fond look.

māj (**maj**). 1(*meja-*), 3, 6(*-i*). Sunglasses; diving mask; eyeglasses.

māj kilaaj (**maj kilahaj**). Spectacles; eyeglasses.

mājet (**majet**). From Engl. 3, 6(*-i*). Match.

Mājetdikdik (**majetdikdik**). Also *Mājetdikin-Mājlep.* A constellation; stars in Sagittarius; alpha, beta, delta, gamma.

mājidjid (**majidjid**). 3. Full.

mājik (**majik**). Archaic. Harbor; secondary lagoon.

mājinmuur (**majinmiwir**). 1(*-i*), 2, 3, 4, 8, 9. Wake up early in the morning; an early-bird.

mājkun (**majqin**). 1(*-i*), 2, 3, 5(*mmājkunkun*), 7. Blink. *Etke kwōjaam mmājkunkun?* Why do you keep on blinking?

mājkun (**majqin**). 2, 3, 7. Fade; wane. *Emājkun wūnokan nuknuk ṇe aṃ.* The color of your dress is faded.

Mājlep (**majlep**). See *māj:* "big eye". A constellation; alpha, beta, gamma Aquilae; Altair; fifthborn of *Lōktañūr.*

mājḷwōj (**majḷ°ęj**). Also *mājḷoj.* 6(*-i*). An animal, a small black lizard with white stripes.

mājmāj (**majmaj**). From *māj* (**maj**). 1(*-i*), 2, 3(inf, tr *kamājmāj(e)*), 4, 6(*-i*), 7. To wear glasses; to cover with a lid. *Kwōn mājmāj bwe edet.* Wear your glasses because the sun is bright. *Kwōn kamājmāje ainbat ṇe.* Cover that pot with a lid.

mājojo (**majewjew**). 1(*-i*), 2, 3, 5(*mmājojo*), 7, 8, 9. Firm; strong; solid. *Kōkki im kōmājojoiki.* Hold it tightly and make it fit together more tightly (from a chant referring to the lashing of a canoe). *Ejjeḷọk mājojoon likao ṇe.* That lad is really strong.

mājur (**majir°**). Dial. E only; see *kiki* (**kiykiy**). Also *mejur* (**męjir°**). 1(*-i*), 2, 3, 4, 5(*mmājurjur*), 7. Sleep; asleep. *Emmājurjur ḷadik eṇ.* That boy is always sleeping. *Emājur.* He's asleep.

mājurlep (**majir°lep**). Also *mejurlep* (**męjir°lep**). 1(*-i*), 2, 3, 4, 8, 9. Sleep soundly; late in awakening; oversleep.

Mākinono (**maykinewnew**). 3, 6(*-i*). A plant, breadfruit variety; seedless.

Mākwōle (**mayqeley**). From *mā* (**may**) "breadfruit", *kwōle* (**qeley**) "testicle, seed (referring to seeds inside)". 3, 6(*-i*). A plant, breadfruit variety (Takeuchi).

māl (**mal**). Archaic. 6(*māllen*). Thing, creature. *Māllen eañ in, ebuñut ḷakijoñjoñ in.* Men from the north are strong (from a chant).

mālejjoñ (**malęjjęg°**). Also *mālijjoñ* (**malijjęg°**). 1(*-i*), 2(inf, tr *-e*), 4, 6(*-i*). Trial; test; acid test; parable; take as example, experiment; analogy, attempt; try; prove. *Jab llu bwe ej bajjek mālijjoñe atūṃ.* Don't get mad, he's just trying your patience. *Jenaaj mālijjoñ kake jerbal ko an.* Let's take his works for example. *Rej mālejjoñe wa eṇ.* They are testing the canoe.

mālij (**malij**). 1(*-i*), 2, 3, 5(*mmālijlij*), 6(*-i*), 7, 8, 9. Well chewed; smashed; mashed. *Emālijlij bao eo raar jipede.* The chicken they ran over is really smashed. *Enaaj nañinmej kōn an jab kōmālij kijen.* He'll get sick from not chewing his food well. *Emmālijlij ek eo kidu eo ear kiji.* The fish the dog stole was all chewed up.

mālij (**malij**). 3, 6(*-i*). A fish, squirrel fish.

mālijjoñ (**malijjęg°**). Variant form of *mālejjoñ* (**malęjjęg°**).

mālim (**malim**). 1(*-i*), 2, 3, 6(*-i*), 7. Permitted; allowed; lawful; permission; license; sanction. *Eor aō mālim in deļọñ.* I have permission to enter.

mālkwōj (**malqej**). 1(*-i*), 2, 3, 5(*mmālkwōjkwōj*), 8, 9. Having healing powers; potent. *Emālkwōj wūno rot eņ ñan kinej.* That kind of medicine is good for wounds. *Emmālkwōjkwōj an wūno.* His medicines have great healing powers.

mālle (**malley**). 3, 5(*mmāllele*), 6(*-i*). Coal; charcoal; coals of fire; embers. *Elōñ ke aṃ mālle?* Do you have any charcoal? *Ḷale emmāllele lowaan ṃọṇe.* Be careful not to spill charcoal all around inside that house. *Ej mmāllele wōt.* There are still some embers there in the ashes.

mālōtlōt (**maletlet**). 1(*-i*), 2, 3, 4, 6(*-i*), 7, 8, 9, 11(*mālōtlōt*). Smart; bright.

mālu (**maliw**). 1(*-i*), 2, 3, 8, 9, 11(*mālu*). Fragrant, of flowers; aroma. *Emālu leen ut eņ.* The flowers from that bush are fragrant.

mālwe (**malwey**). 2(inf, tr *-ik*), 3, 4, 6(*-i*), 7. Twine made from skin of coconut frond midrib; midrib of frond stripped for tying or for sewing copra sacks. *Kwōn mālweiki mejān pāāk ṇe.* Sew the sack close with *mālwe*.

māḷọk (**mayḷaq**). 1(*-i*), 2, 3. Overripe spoiled breadfruit.

māmet (**mamet**). 1(*-i*), 2, 8, 9. Fresh water; sweet coconut water; sweet; sweetish taste. *Emāmet leen ni eņ.* The fruit of that coconut tree is sweet.

Māṃwe (**maymęy**). 3, 6(*-i*). A plant, breadfruit variety (Takeuchi).

māni (**maniy**). 3(inf *kammānni,* tr *kamāniik(i)*), 8, 9, 11(sg. *mānini,* pl. *mmānni*). Thin; flimsy. *Nuknuk mānini men eo ej kōņake.* The clothing she is wearing is very thin. *Nuknuk māni men eo ej kōņake.* The clothing she is wearing is thin.

māniddik (**maniddik**). An insect, small, brown, often found around rotten breadfruit.

mānija (**maniyjah**). From Engl. 2(inf, tr *-ik*), 3, 6(*-i*). Manager; executive. *Ej mānijain koṃbani eņ.* He's the manager of that company.

mānnikiden (**mannikidẹn**). 3, 6(*-i*). An insect, moth.

Mānnikkiden (**mannikkidẹn**). 3, 6(*-i*). A plant, pandanus cultigen (Takeuchi).

mānnimar (**manniymar**). 1(*-i*), 2, 3, 4, 8, 9. Wild chicken; wild. *Jen etal kōmānnimar.* Let's go hunting for wild chickens.

mānnimuuj (**mannimiwij**). 3, 6(*-i*). A bird, white sea gull.

mānniñ (**mannig**). 2, 3, 6(*-i*). Young louse; nit; adolescent (derogatory); small fry; tot; minor. *Jab inepata bwe mānniñ men eņ.* Don't worry, he's a nobody. *Etke enana ak mānniñ?* Why is he so bad when he's just a kid?

mānnōt (**mannet**). Archaic. A fish.

mānnueaḷ (**manniwyaḷ**). 3, 6(*-i*). Lizard.

māntōl (**mantẹl**). A bird, sooty shearwater, *Puffinus griseus*; a bird, slender-billed shearwater, *Puffinus tenuirostris.*

māro (**mayręw**). 1(*-i*), 2, 6(*-i*), 8, 9. Weak-legged; bow-legged; knock-kneed; walk dragging a leg; disease characterized by emaciated legs; muscular distrophy. *Kwōn jab ilān iakiu bwe kwōmāro.* Don't play baseball for you have weak legs. *Emāro an rūkōṃṃan kōjak eo etetal.* The comedian walked knock-kneed. *Emāro an etetal.* He drags a leg when walking.

Māroñ (**mayreg°**). A plant, breadfruit variety (Takeuchi).

mātōrej (**mayteryej**). Also *būtoñ* (**biteg°**), *maatreej* (**mahatreyej**). From Engl. 6(*-i*). Mattress.

me (**mẹy**). Also *kōjjoal* (**kejjewhal**). Fort; fortified place; coral weir to trap fish; coral wall; barricade.

me (**mey**). That; which; who. *E juon armej eo me eḷap an jouj.* He is a person who is very kind.

me (**mey**). Transitive singular form of *meme* (**mẹymẹy**).

meanwōd (**meyhanwed**). 1(*-i*), 2, 4, 7, 8, 9. Long enduring; patience; longsuffering; soft-hearted; gentle. *Eḷap an meanwōd ḷeeṇ.* He is very patient.

mebbōḷa (**mebbeḷah**). 1(*-i*), 2, 3, 7. Yawn.

med (**mẹd**). 3, 8, 9. Cooled off, of food once hot. *Emed raij eṇ kiiō.* The rice is cool now.

medaekek (**medahyẹkyẹk**). 1, 2, 6(*-i*). Phlegm; pus; lymph; slime from slugs and fish.

medde (**meddey**). Reef in the lagoon just under the surface.

mede (**mẹdẹy**). 1(*-i*), 3, 5(*mmedede*), 6(*-i*). Young coconut meat. *Emmedede nuknuk ṇe aṃ.* There are scraps of coconut meat on your clothes.

mede (**medey**). Also *mede* (**mẹdẹy**). 1(*-i*), 2(inf, tr *-ik*). Chisel. *Kwōn medeik ṃōk tiek ṇe bwe en koṇ.* Chisel that notch so that it fits.

medek (**medek**). 1(*-i*), 2(inf, tr *-e*), 4, 5(*mmedekdek*), 7. To conciliate; reconcile; reconciliation; appease; coax. *Kwōn medeke bwe ellu.* Talk kindly to him because he's angry. *Kwōn ilān mmedekdeke jān an ilān kōṃṃan tūrabōḷ.* Go do anything you can to keep him from going and making trouble. *Kwōn ilān medeke jān an ilān kōṃṃan tūrabōḷ.* Go do something to keep him from going and making trouble.

medọḷ (**medaḷ°**). 1(*-i*), 2, 3, 7, 8, 9. Oily hair; hair smoothed with oil. *Emedọḷ bōraṃ.* Your hair is smoothed down with oil.

medwañ (**medwag**). 1(*-i*), 2, 3, 5(*mmedwañwañ*), 6(*-i*), 8, 9, 11(*mmedwañwañ*). Smell of armpits; armpit.

meej (**meyej**). 3, 5(*mmeejej*), 7, 8, 9. Dark in color; bright colored.

meej (**meyej**). 1(*-i*), 2, 3, 4, 7. Accustom oneself; habit. *Emeej in eọñōd ijeṇ.* He is used to fishing there.

meej (**meyej**). From Engl. 2, 6(*-i*), 7. Ship's mate. *Ear meejḷọk ñan Jepaan.* He went to Japan as mate.

mei (**mẹyiy**). Transitive plural form of *meme* (**mẹymẹy**).

meimed (**mẹyimed**). 1(*-i*), 2, 3(inf, tr *-e*), 4+3, 6(*-i*), 3+7, 8, 9. Overripe, of breadfruit with seeds; overripe breadfruit.

mej (**mẹj**). Also *mij* (**mij**). 1(*-i, mije-*), 2, 3, 4, 5(*mmejmej*), 6(*-i, mijen*). Dead; numb; death; disease; illness; peril; plague; wrath. *Emmejmej nājin lieṇ.* Her children all die. *Mejet ṇe aṃ?* What's your illness? *Iar lo mijen inne ṃokta jān an mej.* I saw his spirit yesterday before he died. *Ekeiñtaanan mejin (mijen) lōḷḷap eo.* The old lady's death was torturous.

mej (**mẹj**). Dial. E only; see *mejje* (**mẹjjẹy**). The opening between islets.

mej (**mẹj**). Place where turtles molt; taboo place inhabited by demons.

mej ānbwin (**mẹj yanbin**). 1(*mej ānbwinni-*). Palsy; paralyzed. *Ear waḷok juon mijen mej ānbwin.* A disease called *palsy* struck.

meja- (**meja-**). 1. Eye of; face of; cutting edge of; lid of; eyeglasses of; sunglasses of; opening of any container, hole, doorway, or cave, etc.; possessive classifier, eyes, lids, openings, eyeglasses, masks, or goggles.

mejabbe (**mejabbẹy**). 3, 6(*-i*). A fish, *Lethrinus* sp.

Mejabwil (**mejabil**). A star; Formalhaut in Pisces Austrinus.

mejaḷ (**mejaḷ**). 1(*-i*), 2(inf, tr *-e*), 3, 5(*mejaḷjaḷ*). Unsnarl; disentangle; perfective form of *jaḷjaḷ*; unravel; disconnect; unclasp; untie. *Emejaḷjaḷ ḷọk tōrej eṇ.* The thread is unsnarled. *Emejaḷ ḷọk jitọkin kā aō.* My stockings are running.

mejate (**mejatẹy**). Path from house to either beach. *Kwōn bar rakij mejate ṇe bwe eitan penjak.* Clear out the path again because it's overgrown. *Emejate ṃweeṇ.* That tract has a path to the beach.

mejatoto (**mejatewtew**). 1(*-i*), 2, 3, 6(*-i*), 7. Air; atmosphere; climate; possessed by ghosts; space. *Eṃṃan mejatotoun Awai.* The climate in Hawaii is nice. *Koṃro en ja mejatoto ḷọk em bar itok.* You two go get some fresh air and come back again. *Emejatoto lieṇ.* She's possessed by ghosts.

mejā (**mejay**). Dial. W only; see *kōlñe* (**kęlgęy**). Long gashes in the outside reef.

mejā (**mejay**). 6(*-i*). Small man-made channel through coral. *Jeañ rakij juon mejā.* Let's clear a channel.

mejādik (**mejadik**). 1(*-i*), 2, 3, 4, 8, 9. Skill; dexterity; knack; resourceful; shrewd; tactful. *Emejādik ḷeeṇ.* He is skillful.

mejāliraan (**mejaliyrahan**). 1(*-i*), 2(inf, tr *-e*), 4, 5(*mmejāliraanan*), 6(*-i*), 7. A food, plain baked ripe breadfruit. *Enaaj kar nnọ ñe kwaar jab mejāliraane ak kwaar pọḷjeje.* It would have tasted better if you had baked it in coconut oil instead of plain.

mejān jāje (**mejan jayjęy**). Idiom. Blade of machete. *Ebwilọk mejān jāje e.* The blade of this machete is chipped.

mejān turọñ (**mejan tiwrag°**). Goggles; diving mask.

mejānkajjik (**mejankajjik**). Prize; goal; objective; destiny.

mejānwōd (**mejanwed**). Dial. W, E: *jenọ* (**jenaw**), *jeno* (**jenew**). 3, 6(*-i*). A shell, a clam, *Tridacnidae*; *Tridacna (chametrachea) crocea.*

mejāro (**mejayrew**). Interjection: "Honestly, I swear it's so."

mejbak (**męjbak**). 1(*-i*), 2, 3, 6(*-i*), 7. Overripe, of breadfruit without seeds.

mejeik (**męjęyik**). A fish.

mejek (**mejek**). Also *mejek* (**męjęk**). 2(inf, tr *mejek(e)*), 7. Watch; keep watching; notice. *Kwōn mejek ṃōk ta eṇ ej kōṃṃane?* You watch to see what he does. *Ijab mejeke an etal.* I didn't notice him leaving.

mejel (**męjęl**). Variant form of *mijel* (**mijęl**).

mejel kil (**męjęl kil**). 1, 2. Bold; unconcerned about consequences; presumptuous; forward; thick-skinned; incapable of being hurt or embarrassed. *Emake mejel kiliṃ.* You're so bold. *Koṃwin ḷōmṇak kōn armej em jab mejel kilimi.* Be considerate and don't be so presumptuous. *Ejab eñjaake naan ko aṃ bwe emejel kilin.* He didn't feel your stinging remarks as he's quite thick-skinned.

mejeḷat (**mejeyḷat**). 2(inf, tr *-e*) 4, 6(*-i*), 7. Fishing method, line fishing using the front half of a coconut shell, in lagoon area. *Rej ilān mejeḷat iarin jittoeṇ.* They're going fishing using the *mejeḷat* method at the western end of the island.

mejen allōñ (**męjęn hallęg**). Also *mejān allōñ* (**męjan hallęg**). From *mej* (**męj**) "sickness", *allōñ* (**hallęg**) "moon". 2, 6(*-i*). Menstruation.

mejenkwaad (**męjęnqahad**). 2, 4. Witch who eats people; vampire.

mejenma (**męjęnmah**). 1(*-i*), 2(inf, tr *-ik*), 3, 4, 7, 8. Kiss; osculate.

Mejenwe (**mejenwey**). 3, 6(*-i*). A plant, breadfruit variety.

mejeto (**mejetew**). Also *mejate* (**mejatęy**). Path from house to beach.

Mejidduul (**męyjiddiwil**). From *mā* (**may**) "breadfruit", *jidduul* (**jiddiwil**) "a clam". A plant, breadfruit variety (Takeuchi).

mejin (**męjyin**). Common cold; flu epidemic. *Ibōk mejin.* I have a cold.

mejin (**męyjin**). From Engl. 6(*-i*). Sewing machine.

mejinede (**mejyineydey**). Also *mijinede* (**mijineydey**). From Engl. 6(*-i*). Missionary.

mejjani (**mejjahniy**). From Japn. *me ja nai* "he is no match for me", "it is too easy". 1, 2, 3(inf, tr *-iki*), 6(*-i*), 7, 8, 9. Weakling; lethargic; pushover. *Aolep jeḷa raṇe aṃ mejjani wōt.* Your crew members are a sorry bunch.

mejje (**męjjęy**). Dial. W only; see *mej* (**męj**). Also *mej* (**męj**). The opening between islets.

mejje (**męjjęy**). 2(inf, tr *-ik*), 6(*-i*). Fishline, on a pole. *Jonan an ḷap ek eo eetal eake mejje eo aō.* The fish I hooked must have been a big one since it broke my pole-line.

mejjeeḷ (**męjjeyeḷ**). Slang. 1(*-i*), 2, 6(*-i*), 7, 8, 9. Inactive; slow; phlegmatic; lethargic; lazy; be beat. *Āinwōt kobaj mejjeeḷ rainin.* You look beat today.

mejjiia (**męjjiyyah**). 1(*-i*), 2, 3, 4, 8, 9. Long in dying; slow to die (see *mejjiie* (**męjjiyyęy**)). *Emejjiia wōn eṇ.* That turtle is slow to die.

mejjiie (**męjjiyyęy**). 1(*-i*), 2, 3, 4, 8, 9. Quick to die (see *mejjiia* (**męjjiyyah**)). *Emejjiie bao eṇ.* That bird is quick to die.

mejkaiie (**męjkahiyyęy**). Also *mijkāiie* (**mijkayiyęy**), *mejkōnkōn* (**mẹjkẹnkẹn**). 1(*-i*), 2(inf, tr *-ik*), 3(inf, tr *-ik*), 4, 6(*-i*), 7, 8, 9. To lust in vain; lust for; lustful; lovesick. *Wūnin aṃ addimejmej ṇe kōn aṃ mejkaiie.* You've lost your coordination because you yearn after but can't get to first base with women.

mejki (**mẹjkiy**). 1(*-i*), 2, 3, 5(*mmejkiki*), 7, 8, 9. Sleepy. *Imejki kōn pija eo.* The movie has made me sleepy. *Emmejkiki ḷeeṇ.* He's always sleepy.

mejko (**mẹjkẹw**). Slang. 2, 3(inf, tr *-i*), 6(*-i*). Be embarrassed for. *Jọọn eñak ta eo en ba kōn an mejko kake Jemej ke ear buñ.* John didn't know what to say, being so embarrassed for James when he (James) fell down.

mejko (**mẹjkew**). Also *mejko* (**mẹjkẹw**). 1(*-i*), 2, 3, 7, 8, 9. Blinded with smoke. *Imejko kōn kijek ṇe aṃ.* Your fire is blinding me.

mejkōnkōn (**mẹjkẹnkẹn**). Extra mesh in a net; makes one row of mesh longer than the last.

mejkōnkōn (**mẹjkẹnkẹn**). Variant form of *mejkaiie.*

mejkōr (**mejker**). 1(*-i*), 2, 3, 4, 7, 8. Bleary-eyed; slimy-eyed.

mejḷat (**mẹjḷat**). Bird trap.

mejmej (**mẹjmẹj**). 3, 6(*-i*). A fish, snapper, *Gymnocranius microndon/ griseus*; a fish, scavenger, *Lethrinus microdon.*

mejmetak (**mẹjmetak**). 2, 3(inf, tr *-e*), 4, 6(*-i*), 8, 9. Have sore eyes. *Iaikuj mājmāj bwe imejmetak.* I've got to wear sunglasses because my eyes are sore.

mejoub (**mẹjẹwib**). 3. Coconut, nearly ripe.

mejọ (**mejaw**). Dial. W, E: *juwi* (**jiwiy**). 3, 6(*-i*). A bird, white tern, *Gygis alba.*

mejọkut (**mejaqit**). 3, 6(*-i*). A fish, big-eye or burgy, *Monotaxis grandoculis.*

mejpata (**mẹjpahtah**). From *mej* (**mẹj**) "die", *pata* (**pahtah**) "in vain". 1, 2, 4, 6(*-a*), 8, 9. Playboy; ladies' man (derogatory sense); romantic desires. *Emejpata ḷeeṇ.* He thinks he's God's gift to women. *Jab mejpata eake bwe eor pāleen.* Don't fall over her for she's married.

Mejwa (**mẹjwah**). 3, 6(*-i*). A plant, breadfruit variety (Takeuchi).

Mejwaan (**mẹjwahan**). 3, 6(*-i*). A plant, breadfruit variety; seeded; with five-lobed leaves.

mekak (**mekak**). 1, 2, 6(*-i*), 7, 8. To clot; thick blood; blood clot. *Joñan an ḷap kinej eo, eto mekak.* The wound was so severe that large blood clots came out.

mekarta (**meykartah**). Variant form of *makarta.*

Mekijko (**mekijkew**). Clan name.

melea (**meleyah**). A fish.

meliak (**mẹyliyhak**). 1(*-i*), 2(inf, tr *-e*), 3, 4, 7. To chew food and then throw it out of the mouth; take something from the mouth.

melkwaarar (**melqaharhar**). 1(*-i*), 2, 3, 5(*mmelkwaarar*), 6(*-i*), 7. Ashes; burn to ashes. *Emmelkwaarar lowaan ṃweeṇ.* Ashes are scattered all over the place inside that house.

melkwarkwar (**melqarqar**). 2, 3, 5(*mmelkwarkwar*), 6(*-i*), 8, 9. Phlegm; clear the throat. *Idaak wūno ṃokta jān an (m)melkwarkwar būruoṃ.* Take medicine before you start getting phlegm in your throat. *Bōlen wōjke eo kwaar ilimi ekamelkwarkware būruoṃ.* Maybe the whiskey you drank got your throat clogged up. *Emmelkwarkwar būruon.* He keeps coughing up phlegm.

melmelea (**melmeleyah**). A bird, crane, black *kabaj.*

meḷa (**meḷah**). 3, 7. Time between rain showers. *Jen etal kiiō ke ejja meḷa.* Let's go now while it has stopped raining.

meḷaaj (**meḷahaj**). Open space; field; pasture; outdoors.

meḷak (**meḷak**). 1(*-i*), 2, 3, 7, 8, 9. Not crowded; in good order; uncluttered; tidy; neat. *Eḷap an meḷak lowaan ṃwiin.* Everything is uncluttered in this house.

meḷaḷ (**meḷaḷ**). Archaic. Playground for demons; not habitable by people.

meḷan (**meḷan**). 7. Land surface; surroundings; environment. *Eṃṃan meḷan ānin.* This islet is a nice area. *Ej jepjep wūjooj ilo meḷan eṇ an.* He's mowing the grass on his lawn.

meḷañūr (**meḷagir**). Legendary food.

meḷeḷe (**meḷeyḷey**). 1(*-i*), 2, 3(inf, tr *-ik*), 4, 6(*-i*), 7. Understand; well-defined; well-ordered; information; comprehend; logic; meaning; plain;

rational; unsnarled. *Imeļeļe.* I understand. *Eļap an meļeļe lowaan bok eņ.* The book is well written. *Meļeļe in ia ņe aṃ?* Where did you get that information from?

meļļā (**meļļay**). 1(*-i*), 2, 3, 5(*mmeļļāļā*). Smell of blood.

meļoktak (**meļeqtak**). Period between setting of sun and rising or moon; second moon phase; moon phase after *jetmar.*

meļoktakōn (**meļeqtaken**). Also *tuujloñloñ* (**tiwijleg°leg°**), *tujiloñloñ* (**tiwjileg°leg°**). 2, 6(*-i*). Period between setting of sun and rising of moon; third moon phase; moon phase after *meļoktak. Emeļoktakōn ke buñūnin?* Is this the night of *meļoktakōn*?

meļo̧ (**meļaw**). Existence. *Eṃṃan ad meļo̧ ņa inin.* We have a good existence on this islet. *Meļo̧o̧ṃṃan.* A happy existence with plenty to eat.

meļo̧kļo̧k (**meļaqļaq**). 1(*-i*), 2(inf, tr *-e*). Forget; oblivious.

meļo̧kļo̧k (**meļaqļaq**). 2, 6(*-i*). Period between setting of sun and rising of moon; fourth moon phase; moon phase after *meļoktakōn.*

mem-. See *mm-*.

meme (**mẹymẹy**). 1(*-i*), 2(inf, tr sg. obj. *me,* pl. obj. *mei*), 7. Chew. *Ej meme bwil.* He's chewing gum.

meme (**mẹymẹy**). Eat, child speech.

meme (**meymey**). Archaic. Foam.

men (**men**). Thing; matter; object.

men (**men**). A person, unnamed. *Jo̧o̧n im men.* John and his wife. *Limen ņe tok.* Here comes Ms. What's-her-name.

Men-kaņ (**men-kaņ**). Also *Min-kaņ.* A constellation; stars in Leo Minor; beta, 29, 30, 34, 35, 38, 33, 37, 42.

menādik (**menadik**). 1(*-i*), 2, 3, 7, 8, 9. Moth; mildew. *Emenādik nuknuk ņe aṃ.* There are moths in your clothes.

menin aje (**menin hajey**). Idiom. Offerings. *Likūt menin aje ko ami ņa ioon tapnakōļ ņe.* Put your offerings on the tabernacle.

menin le- (**menin ley-**). 7. Gift (with directional postpositions).

menļo̧k (**menļaq**). Slang. Hurry up; do it fast. *Kwōn menļo̧k.* Hurry up.

menninmour (**menninmẹwir**). From *men* (**men**) "thing", *in* (**yin**) "of", *mour* (**mẹwir**) "life". Animal; living things. *Jet rej ba armej bar menninmour.* Some people say that man is also an animal.

menokadu (**menewkadiw**). 1(*-i*), 2, 3(inf, tr *-ik*), 4, 7, 8, 9. Perspiration; perspire; sweat; vapor. *Kwōn kamenokaduuk eok kōn to̧o̧l ņe.* Wipe the perspiration off yourself with that towel.

menono (**menewnew**). 1(*-i, menowa-*), 2, 3, 7. To breathe; heart; respiration; breath.

meno̧kno̧k (**menaqnaq**). 1(*-i*), 2, 3, 5(*-e*), 6(*-i*), 7. Debris; litter; clutter; rubbish; trash. *Ejjeļo̧k wōt meno̧kno̧kun nōbōjān ṃwiin.* There is an awful lot of debris outside this house. *Emeno̧kno̧ke nōbōjān ṃwiin.* There is trash strewn all around outside this house.

menrotkaņ (**menr°etkaņ**). Variant form of *mettorkaņ* (**metter°kaņ**).

mentorkaņ (**menter°kaņ**). Variant form of *mettorkaņ* (**metter°kaņ**).

meñ (**mẹg**). Also *mōñ.* 1(*-i*), 2, 3, 5(*mmeñmeñ*), 6(*-i*), 8, 9, 11(*meñmeñ*). Smell or taste sour or bitter, as milk, vinegar, or rice soup, etc.; fermented. *Jab ṃōñā jokkwōp ņe bwe emeñ.* Don't eat that soup because it's sour. *Emmeñmeñ jokkwōp in mā.* Breadfruit soup sours quickly.

meñe (**meygey**). Although; even if; even though; though.

meoeo (**meyewyew**). 1(*-i*), 2, 3, 7, 8, 9, 11. Soft to touch; smooth like fur; lenient; sleek; slick; velvety.

meo̧ (**meyaw**). 1(*-i*), 2, 3(inf, tr *-ik*), 7, 8, 9, 11(*meo̧eo*). Sour; bitter.

mera (**merah**). Also *bōļaļ* (**beļaļ**). 1(*-i*), 2, 3(inf, tr *-ik*), 7, 8, 9, 11(*merara*). Light in weight; bland; delicate; mild; subtle. *Kwōn kameraik ļo̧k kōbañ ņe.* Make your suitcase lighter. *Imera ļo̧k jān ṃokta.* I am lighter than before.

meraļo̧k (**merahļaq**). 1(*-i*), 2, 6(*-i*). Abate; subside; decrease. *Emeraļo̧k kōto in.* The wind has changed to a light breeze.

meram (**meram**). 1(*-i*), 2, 3, 5(*mmeramram*), 7, 8, 9, 11(*meramrōm*). Bright; light; flash; glow; illuminate; luminous. *Kwōn kabbōl ļaaṃ ņe bwe en meram.* Light the lamp there so that we can have some light.

meramin allōñ (**meramin halļeg**). Moonlight. *Erreo meramin allōñ buñūnin.* It's a clear moonlight night tonight.

meramin aļ (**meramin haļ**). Sunlight.

merā (**meray**). Dial. E only; see *mao* (**mahwew**). 3, 6(-*i*). A fish, parrotfish, *Scarus jonesi/sordidus; a fish, wrasse, Cheilinus* sp.

merā (**meray**). 2, 3, 5(*mmerārā*), 6. Capsize; let sail and mast fall while tacking. *Kajimwe kiju ņe bwe enaaj merā wa ņe.* Straighten the mast or the canoe will capsize.

meria (**meyriyah**). 3, 6(-*i*). Plumeria; a plant, *Plumeria acuminata* Ait. (Apocynaceae). Introd. Orn.

merrōļọk (**merreļaq**). 1, 2, 3(inf, tr -*e*), 6(-*i*), 7. Tear; rip. *Jab toto ilo jedọujij ņe aō bwe kwōnaaj kōmerrōļọke.* Don't hang on to my pants or you'll tear them.

Metaat (**metahat**). 3, 6(-*i*). A plant, pandanus cultigen (Takeuchi).

metak (**metak**). 1(-*i*), 2, 3, 7, 8, 9. Pain; hurt; ache; sore. *Emetak bōra.* I have a headache.

metal (**metal**). 1(-*i*), 2, 3, 5(*mmetaltōl*), 7, 8, 9, 11(*metaltōl*). Smooth; sleek; slick. *Eļap an lur im mmetaltōl eoon ļọjet.* The surface of the ocean is very calm and smooth.

Metete (**meteytey**). A plant, breadfruit variety.

meto (**metew**). 4, 6(-*i*), 7. Sea; ocean; navigation; navigate; directional, enclitic, seaward. *Kwōn aō metotak.* Swim oceanward toward me. *Metoon ia in?* These waters are close to what land? *Ejeļā meto.* He knows navigation.

metoļọk (**metewļaq**). Seaward.

metto (**mettew**). Archaic. Anchorage on ocean side of islet where one waits for more favorable winds.

mettorkaņ (**metter°kaņ**). Also *menrotkaņ* (**menr°etkaņ**), *mentorkaņ* (**menter°kaņ**). Euphemistic reference to any of a variety of activities, mostly off-color; you-know-what. *Kōmij ilān mettorkaņ.* We are going to do you-know-what.

Metwan Al (**metwan hal**). The waters between Jaluit and Ailinglaplap atolls.

mi (**miy**). From Engl. Syllable "mi" of musical scale.

miade (**miyahdẹy**). Also *miadi* (**miyahdiy**). From Japn. *mihari* "to guard". Watch-tower; lighthouse.

miar (**miyar**). Also *miār*. Small sitting mat. *Lewaj miār e im jijet raan.* Here's a mat for you to sit on.

midij (**midij**). 2, 3(inf, tr -*e*), 6(-*i*), 7. Slip; slide; skid.

Mieko (**miyeykew**). Also *MIECO*. Acronym for Marshall Islands Import-Export Company; MIECO.

mien (**miyen**). A place for fishing canoes on an island.

mieñ (**miyẹg**). Also *miōñ*. 1(-*i*), 2, 3, 5(*mmieñeñ*). Smell of urine.

miin (**miyin**). From Engl. *mean.* 1, 2, 4, 6(-*i*), 8, 9. Miserly; penny-pinching; stingy; uncharitable. *Eban lewaj aṃ jāān bwe emiin.* He won't give you any money because he is a miser.

mij (**mij**). Variant form of *mej* (**mẹj**).

mija (**miyjah**). From Engl. Mass service; Roman Catholic Missa.

mijak (**mijak**). 1(-*i*), 2(inf, tr -*e*), 3(st inf *kaamijak,* tr *kamijak*), 5(*mmijakjak*), 7. Fear; afraid; horror; scared; threatened; timid; dread. *Imijak in etal ñan Amedka.* I am afraid to go to America. *Ta ņe kwōj mijake?* What are you afraid of? *Eṃōj ņe aṃ mmijakjak.* Why don't you stop getting scared by everything. *Ekaamijak ṃupi eo.* The movie was scarey. *Ekaamijak eō.* It scared me.

mijak dān (**mijak dan**). Idiom. Seldom bathe. *Ebwiin bbūļapļap kōn an mijak dān.* He smells because he rarely bathes.

mije (**mijey**). Also *mije* (**mijẹy**). 1(-*i*), 2, 4, 7. Accompany either physically or spiritually while in great danger. *Kōmij pād wōt in mije eok.* We will stick with you come what will.

mijel (**mijẹl**). Also *mejel* (**mẹjẹl**). 1(-*i*), 2, 3, 5(*mmijeljel*), 8, 9, 11(sg. *mijeljel,* pl. *mmijel*). Thick; thickness. *Wōt mijeljel.* Raining cats and dogs. *Kōdọ mijel.* Thick clouds.

mijeļ (**miyjeļ**). From Engl. 6(-*i*). Missile.

mijen (**mijen**). Construct form of *mej* (**mẹj**).

mijen (**miyjen**). From Engl. *mission*. 4. Protestant; mission.

mijenatabuñ (**mijenhatabig°**). 2, 6(*-i*). Premature death. *Emijenatabuñ.* His was a premature death.

mijinede (**mijineydey**). Variant form of *mejinede* (**mejyineydey**).

mijjebwā (**mijjebay**). See *jebwā* "a coral". A fish; possibly a variant form of *mejabbe.*

mijkāie (**mijkayiyęy**). Variant form of *mejkaiie* (**męjkahiyyęy**).

mijmijelaļ (**mijmijeylaļ**). 2, 4. Persevere. *Kwōn mijmijelaļ wōt im jab bbeer.* Keep persevering and don't lose hope.

Mile (**milęy**). From *Mile* (**milęy**) "place name, a Ratak atoll". A plant, banana variety (Takeuchi).

milien (**miliyen**). From Engl. Million.

milik (**milik**). From Engl. 2, 3, 5(*mmiliklik*). Milk; cream. *Emmiliklik turun lọñiiṃ.* There's milk around your mouth.

mim-. See *mm-*.

mimuul (**mimiwil**). 3, 5(*mmimuulul*), 6(*-i*). A fish, sardine, *Sardine sardinella* (small).

minit (**minit**). From Engl. 1(*-i*), 2(inf, tr *-i*), 7. Minute.

minor (**minęr°**). Also *naṃonaṃo* (**naṃęwnaṃęw**). 1(*-i*), 2(inf, tr *-e*), 4, 5(*mminornor*), 6(*-i*), 7. Unleavened pancake. *Eijoḷḷap minor.* He likes to eat unleavened pancakes a lot.

mir (**mir**). 2, 3(inf, tr *-i*), 6(*-i*), 8, 9, 11(*mir*). Red colored, of reddish coconuts or sky.

miro (**mirew**). 1, 2, 3(inf, tr *-uk, -ik*), 5(*mmiroro*), 6(*-i*). Trace; put in an appearance; move fast so as to avoid detection; glance. *Kōm ar jab lo miroun.* We found no trace of him. *Enana an leddik mmiroro.* Girls should not be seen all over the place. *Ear kamirouk eō ak ear jab lo eō.* She kept an eye out for me but couldn't find me.

mmaan (**mmahan**). Dial. W: *emmaan* (**yemmahan**), E: *memaan* (**memahan**). 2(inf, tr *-ik, -ōk*), 3. Be at anchor; tie up a vessel. *Raar (kō)mmaanik wa eo.* They tied the canoe up.

mmadidi (**mmahdiydiy**). Dial. W: *emmadidi* (**yemmahdiydiy**), E: *memadidi* (**memahdiydiy**). 2, 3(inf, tr *-ik(i)*), 6(*-i*). Drowsy; sleepy; somnolent.

mmakijkij (**mmakijkij**). Dial. W: *emmakijkij* (**yemmakijkij**), E: *memakijkij* (**memakijkij**). Often; frequent; common; constant. *Emmakijkij an itok wa ñan ānin.* The ship comes to this islet often.

mmaļ (**mmaļ**). Dial. W: *emmaļ* (**yemmaļ**), E: *memaļ* (**memaļ**). 1(*-i*), 2, 3, 7. Heartburn caused by drinking fresh coconut sap on an empty stomach. *Immaļ in jibboñ.* I have the morning heartburn.

mmat (**mmat**). Dial. W: *emmat* (**yemmat**), E: *memat* (**memat**). 1(*-i*), 2, 3, 7. Be on top of a plane surface, water or land; protrude out from a surface thereby showing; emerge from water; come into view after being hidden. *Lale wōn eṇ emmat i aejet.* Look at that turtle on top of the water. *Ej mmatḷọk jān mar eo.* He emerged from the boondocks.

mmāālāl (**mmayalyal**). Dial. W: *emmāālāl* (**yemmayalyal**), E: *memāālāl* (**memayalyal**). From *māāl* (**mayal**) "axe". 1(*-i*), 2. Smell of iron.

mmāālel (**mmayalyęl**). Dial. W: *emmāālel* (**yemmayalyęl**), E: *memāālel* (**memayalyęl**). 1(*-i*), 2, 3, 7. Have a shiver sent up one's spine; the heebie-jeebies; unpleasant sensation; be given shivers. *Emmālel ñiū kōn aō ṃōñā aij.* My teeth hurt from eating ice. *Jab iper jea ṇe bwe jemmāālel.* Don't drag that chair because it gives us the shivers.

mmālele (**mmalęylęy**). Dial. W: *emmalele* (**yemmalęylęy**), E: *memalele* (**memalęylęy**). 1(*-i*), 2, 3, 4, 6(*-i*), 7, 8, 9. Absent-minded; forgetful; oblivious. *Erūttoḷọk em mmālele ḷọk.* He grew older and became absent-minded.

mmālwewe (**mmalweywey**). Dial. W: *emmālwewe* (**yemmalweywey**), E: *memālwewe* (**memalweywey**). 1(*-i*), 2, 3, 5(*mmālwewe*), 6(*-i*), 7, 8, 9. Embarrassment caused by actions of another; to cringe. *Ejjeḷọk wōt mmālweweid kōn ṃanōt ko an.* We were very embarrassed by his behavior. *Kwōj mmālwewe ḷọk ñan ia?* Where are you taking your embarrassment? Why don't you stop being embarrassed? *Emmālwewe naan ko an tok ñan eō.* His talk embarrassed me. *Ekōmmālwewe mānōt ko an.* His actions are embarrassing.

mmed (**mmed**). Dial. W: *emmed* (**yemmed**), E: *memed* (**memed**). Also *mād.* 1(-*i*), 2, 3(inf, tr -*e*), 7, 8, 9. Very ripe, overripe, of breadfruit only; phlegm; catarrh; sputum. *Eḷap an mmed mā e.* This breadfruit is very ripe. *Emmed mā e.* This breadfruit is overripe.

mmeej (**mmeyej**). Attractive. *Kommeej kōn aṃ kōṃṃan rot ṇe.* The way you do that is attractive.

mmej (**mmęj**). Dial. W: *emmej* (**yęmmęj**), E: *memej* (**męmęj**). 1(-*i*), 2(inf, tr *mmejrake*), 3, 4, 7. Keep awake; stay up. *Ta eo kwaar mmejrake?* What did you stay up for? *Enañin to aṃ mmej?* Why are you staying up so late?

mmej (**mmęj**). Dial. W: *emmej* (**yęmmęj**), E: *memej* (**męmęj**). A bird, sooty tern, *Sterna fuscata.*

mmejaja (**mmejahjah**). Dial. W: *emmejaja* (**yemmejahjah**), E: *memjaja* (**memjahjah**). 1, 2, 6(-*i*), 8, 9. Attractive; pleasing; charming; alluring; appealing; enchanting; lovely. *Lio emmejaja ippa eṇ.* That's the girl that caught my eye. *Iar ruj kōn ainikien ko rōmmejaja imejatoto.* I awoke to the sound of beautiful music about me.

mmejo (**mmejew**). Dial. W: *emmejo* (**yemmejew**), E: *memjo* (**memjew**). 1(-*i*), 2, 3, 5(*mmejojo*), 7, 8, 9. Far apart (see *kkut* (**qqit**)). *Emmejo ṃōkaṇ.* Those houses are far apart.

mmejǫkunkun (**mmęjaqinqin**). Dial. W: *emmejǫkunkun* (**yęmmęjaqinqin**), E: *memejǫkunkun* (**męmęjaqinqin**). 1(-*i*), 2, 4, 7, 8, 9. Not bold; modest.

mmejraalal (**mmęjrahalhal**). Dial. W: *emmejraalal* (**yęmmęjrahalhal**), E: *memejraalal* (**męmęjrahalhal**). 1(-*i*), 2, 3, 7. Sleepy; drowsy. *Eḷap aō mmejraalal kōn aō kar eọñōd boñ.* I'm awfully sleepy because I went fishing last night.

mmelkwarkwar (**mmelqarqar**). Dial. W: *emmelkwarkwar* (**yemmelqarqar**), E: *memelkwarkwar* (**memelqarqar**). 1(-*i*), 2, 3, 7, 8, 9. A raspy feeling in the throat, especially after a cold; to clear one's throat; distributive form of *melkwarkwar* (**melqarqar**). *Emetak būruō kōn aō mmelkwarkwar.* My throat hurts from its raspiness.

mmeḷo (**mmeḷew**). Dial. W: *emmeḷo* (**yemmeḷew**), E: *memeḷo* (**memeḷew**). 1(-*i*), 2, 3, 5(*mmeḷoḷo*), 7, 8, 9. Far apart (see *kkut* (**qqit**)). *Eḷap an mmeḷo kōtaan ni kā.* These coconut trees are widely spaced. *Wōn e ear kammeḷouk kōtan ni kā?* Who made the spaces between these coconut trees so wide? *Emmeḷo niin wāto in.* The coconut trees on this tract are far apart.

mmenonoun kijdik (**mmenewnęwin kijdik**). Dial. W: *emmenonoun kijdik* (**yemmenewnęwin kijdik**), E: *memenonoun kijdik* (**memenewnęwin kijdik**). Idiom. 2. Puff; breathe quick and hard. *Ta ṇe kwaar wōjake bwe kwōn emmenonoun kijdik?* What did you do to be puffing like that?

mmewiwi (**mmęywiywiy**). 2, 3(inf, tr -*ik*), 6(-*i*), 7, 8, 9. Rustling of leaves and branches. *Emmewiwi raan keinikkan bwe elladikdik.* The branches rustle in the breeze (words from a Wotje love song).

mminene (**mminęynęy**). Dial. W: *imminene* (**yimminęynęy**), E: *mimnene* (**mimnęynęy**). 1(-*i*), 2, 3(inf, tr -*ik*), 8, 9. Habit; practice; used to; accustomed to; have the habit of; experienced; practiced. *Eḷap an mminene ilo jerbal in injin.* He's an experienced mechanic. *Kwōn kammineneik eok ruj in jibboñ tata.* You ought to make it a practice to get up early. *Ear jino kamminene katak kūta.* He started to practice guitar.

mmourur (**mmęwirwir**). Dial. W: *emmourur* (**yęmmęwirwir**), E: *memourur* (**męmmęwirwir**). 1(-*i*), 2(inf, tr -*i*), 3, 7, 8, 9. Lively; living; active; sprightly. *Eḷap aō mmourur in jibboñ.* I am very lively in the morning. *Eḷap an mmourur ḷadik en.* That boy is very active.

mo (**mew**). 1(-*i*), 2, 3(st inf *kammomo, kamo*), 7. To heal. *Emo bakke eo neō.* The sore on my leg is healed. *Ekammomo wūno ṇe.* That medicine is very powerful.

mo (**mew**). Certain places for chiefs only and forbidden to the commoner. *Ānin ej ṃōttan mo ko an irooj raṇ ilo aelōñ in.* This islet is one of those restricted to the Irooj clan only.

mokwaṇ (**meqaṇ**). 3, 5(*mmokwaṇkwaṇ*), 6(*-i*). A food, pandanus juice cooked and preserved. *Emmokwaṇkwaṇ nuknuk ṇe aṃ.* Your clothes have scraps of pandanus pudding on them.

mokwaṇ dada (**meqaṇ dahdah**). 3, 6(*-i*). A food; pandanus juice mixed with grated coconut, uncooked.

mokwaṇ duul (**meqaṇ diwil**). 3, 6(*-i*). A food; pandanus juice mixed with grated coconut, cooked into custard.

mooḷ (**meweḷ**). 1(*-i*), 2, 3, 7. Smooth surf after a succession of rollers. *Wa ko kaṇ rej kōmmooḷ in ṃwelik.* The canoes are waiting for the period of smooth surf for going out to sea. *Ej kab mooḷ peiū.* I finally have a few free moments.

moot (**mẹwẹt**). 2, 8, 9. Familiar; expert; wiz. *Likao en emoot ilo bōnbōn.* He's a mathematical wiz.

moot (**mewet**). 2, 7. Gone forth. *Emoot kijak eo.* That guy is gone.

mouj (**mẹwij**). 1(*-i*), 2, 3(inf *kamoujuj,* tr *kamouj*), 4(*rimmouj*), 5(*mmoujuj*), 7, 8, 9, 11(*moujuj*). White. *Ej kōṇak juon nuknuk mmoujuj im bbūrōrō mejān.* She is wearing a whitish and reddish dress.

mour (**mẹwir**). 1(*-i*), 2, 3, 5(*mmourur*), 6(*-i*), 7. Live; life; existence; alive; recover; exist; cured. *Emmourur.* He's lively. *Ruuno eo ear kamour ledik eo.* The medicine-woman healed the girl. *Imour.* I'm cured.

mour-tak (**mẹwir-tak**). Be recovering.

mowi (**mẹwiy**). 5(*mmowiwi*). Wind squall.

mowiia (**mẹwiyyah**). 1(*-i*), 2, 3, 8, 9. Wound that is hard to cure or heal (see *mowiie* (**mẹwiyyẹy**)).

mowiie (**mẹwiyyẹy**). 1(*-i*), 2, 3, 8, 9. Wound that is easy to cure or heal (see *mowiia* (**mẹwiyyah**)).

mọ (**maw**). 1(*-i*), 2, 3, 8, 9, 10(*mọmo*). Taboo; forbidden; prohibited; ban; restricted; land reserved for chiefs. *Emọ an jabdewōt armej deḷọñ.* It is forbidden for any person to enter. *Emọ an jabdewōt armej etal ñan Kuwajleen.* No one is permitted to go to Kwajalein.

mọk (**maq**). 2, 3, 7. Take possession of; enter into. *Emọk tiṃọṇ ṇa ippān.* He is possessed by a demon.

mọk (**maq**). A fish; smaller than the *kōpat* surgeonfish.

mọkun (**maqin**). 1(*-i*), 2, 3, 5(*mmọkunkun*), 7. Decreasing in size; to droop; wane. *Emmọkunkun kain pilawā ṇe.* That kind of bread is always getting smaller.

mọkwōj (**maqej**). 1(*-i*), 5(*mọkwōjkwōj*), 6(*-a*). Joint, body; knuckle; wrist. *Emetak mọkwōjān peiū.* The joints of my arm hurt.

mọle (**mawlẹy**). Dialectal variant of *ellōk* (**yẹllẹk**).

mọṇ (**maṇ°**). 5, 6(*-i*), 8, 9. Hard, dry coconut meat still in shell. *Kōmọṇtok iuṃwin ni eṇ.* Go get a *mọṇ* under that coconut tree.

mọṇ (**maṇ°**). 5(*mọṇmọṇ*), 6(*-i*). Hard feces.

mọṇmọṇ (**maṇ°maṇ°**). 1(*-i*), 2, 3, 4, 7, 8, 9. Haunted; having supernatural powers; taboo. *Emọṇmọṇ wūliej eṇ.* That graveyard is haunted. *Elōñ ruuno eḷap aer mọṇmọṇ.* Many medicine men have supernatural powers. *Emọṇmọṇ lōb in irooj.* Kings' tombs are taboo.

mọñ (**mag°**). 1(*-i*). Pate of head; soft spot on baby's head.

Mọñ (**mag°**). Variant form of *Elmọñ.*

mọọl (**mawal**). Period between series of larger waves; see *ibeb. Eibeb kiiō; kōttar an mọọl.* The big waves are coming now; wait for the interim period.

mọọn (**mawan**). 2(inf, tr *-e*), 3, 4, 5(*mmọọnọn*), 6(*-i*), 7. Enter; sink into something; penetrate; go into. *Kwōn mọọn buḷōn mar ṇe.* Get into that shrub there. *Kwaar mọọn(e) ke iuṃwin ṃwe?* Did you crawl under the house? *Emọọn ibuḷōn bok.* It has sunk into the sand. *Emọọn bao eo buḷōn mar.* The chicken went into the bushes.

mọọn (**mawan**). Dried copra ready to be weighed. *Bọuni mọọn kaṇ.* Weigh those copra pieces.

mọọr (**mawar**). 1(*-e*), 3, 5(*-e*). Fish bait. *Mọọr rot ņe mọọrōm̧?* What kind of bait do you have there? *Imọọre.* I have lots of bait.

mọọrọr (**mawarwar**). 1(*-i*), 2, 3. To use bait.

mọun (**mawin**). Archaic. Magic to make soldiers brave; magical power; one of two kinds, see *ļọun*.

mō (**meh**). 2, 3, 7. Elastic; stretchy; extended. *Emō jiiñlij e aō.* My T-shirt is stretchy.

mō (**meh**). Dial. W only; see *katōk* (**katek**). A fish, wrasse, *Epibulus insidiator*.

mōōbōb (**mehebheb**). 1(*-i*), 2, 3, 7. Stretch the neck; straighten one's self up.

mū (**mih**). 1(*-i*), 2, 3(inf, tr *-uk*), 5(*mmūmū*), 6(*-i*), 7. To crane the neck to see better; look over one's shoulder. *Ej itan mū wōt ak rōbuuki im lel.* As he was craning his neck to see better, he got shot at and hit.

m̧a (**m̧ah**). Archaic. Crying sound; see *m̧ōjaan. Ij roñ an m̧a.* I hear its cry.

m̧a (**m̧ah**). Variant form of *ļōm̧a*.

m̧aa- (**m̧aha-**). 1, 1+7. Ahead; before; a place in front of. *Itok m̧aō.* Come in front of me.

m̧aab (**m̧ahab**). From Engl. 2(inf, tr *-e*), 3, 4, 6(*-i*), 7. Mop. *Rej m̧aabe lowaan jikin m̧ōñā eo.* They're mopping down the dining hall.

m̧aaj (**m̧ahaj**). From Engl. 2(inf, tr *-e*), 3, 4, 5, 7. To march, parade. *Jajen eņ ej kam̧aaje ļọk rūttariņae raņ ñan kāām eo aer.* The sergeant is marching the troops to their camp.

M̧aaj (**m̧ahaj**). From Engl. March; the month.

m̧aajta (**m̧ahajtah**). From Engl. *master*. Choirmaster, director of a choral group. *M̧aajta eo an jabta eo ņe.* That's the director of the chorus.

m̧aak (**m̧ahak**). From Germ. 6(*-i*). Money.

m̧aal (**m̧ahal**). 1(*-i*), 2, 3, 7, 8, 9. Give up; satiated; weakened from a blow; stunned; bloated. *Im̧aal jān m̧ōñā ko.* I'm so full I can't eat any more of that food. *Iar m̧ōñā wor ļọk oom m̧aal.* I ate lobsters till I was absolutely full. *Dān kajoor eo ekōm̧aal ļōm̧aro.* The hard liquor floored the gentlemen.

m̧aan (**m̧ahan**). 1(*-i*), 2, 7, 8, 9. Front; peak; fore; forward; onward; directional, enclitic, forward. *Waat eņ m̧aan tata?* What canoe is that at the very front? *Eñeņ m̧aanļọk.* He's moving forward.

m̧aanjāppopo (**m̧ahanjappewpew**). 1(*-i*), 2, 3, 4, 7. To prepare for the unexpected; be alert. *Ij baj m̧aanjāppopo wōt im kọkoņ jidik jāān.* I'll just be prepared for a rainy day and stash away some money. *Kom̧win m̧aanjāppopo wōt.* Get prepared for any eventuality.

m̧aanje (**m̧ahanjẹy**). 1(*m̧aanjie-*), 6(*-i*). First-born. *Emọ kanejneje bwe m̧aanje.* It is forbidden to swear at him because he is a first-born. *Likao eņ m̧aanjien jemān.* He is his father's first-born.

m̧aanjibaik (**m̧ahanjibahyik**). From Engl. *marlinespike*. 2(inf, tr *-i*), 4, 6(*-i*). Marlinespike.

m̧aanpā (**m̧ahanpay**). From *m̧aan* (**m̧ahan**) "front", *pā* (**pay**) "arm". 1(*m̧aanpei-*), 2(inf, tr *-ik*), 3, 4, 6(*-i*). Emergency equipment; Marshallese art of self-defense. *Ear bōk juon m̧aanpein jāje.* He took a machete along just in case. *Raar ebbōktok bu im m̧aanpāik (ņam̧aanpāān) kumi eo.* They brought guns and armed the group. *An jejjo wōt m̧aanpā.* The arts of self-defense are known by but a few.

m̧abuñ (**m̧ahbig°**). 1(*-i*), 2, 3, 8. Eat breakfast; breakfast.

m̧abwil (**m̧abil**). 1(*-i*), 2(inf, tr *-i*), 7. To roll in a kneading way; rub.

m̧ad (**m̧ad**). 1(*-i*), 2, 3, 4, 5(*m̧m̧adm̧ad*), 7. Loiter; distracted; busy; occupied. *Erum̧wij jān wa eo kōn an m̧m̧adm̧ad.* He missed the boat because of his loitering around. *Ej jab itok bwe em̧ad.* He isn't coming because he's busy. *Leļọk jidik wūno bwe en kōm̧ade jān an metak.* Give him a little medicine to ease his pain.

m̧ade (**m̧adẹy**). 1(*-i*), 6(*-i*). Spear; harpoon.

M̧ade-eo-an-Aoļōt (**m̧adẹy-yew-han-hawẹļẹt**). A constellation; stars in Draco; see *Aoļōt*.

M̧ade-eo-an-Tūm̧ur (**m̧adẹy-yew-han-tim̧ir°**). See *m̧ade*: "*Tūm̧ur*'s spear". A constellation; stars in Ophiuchus; theta, 36.

m̧adede (**m̧adȩydȩy**). From *m̧ade* (**m̧adȩy**). 2, 3(inf, tr *kōm̧adedeik(i)*), 6(-*i*), 7. Use a spear. *An wōn ņe m̧ade kwōj m̧adede kake?* Whose spear are you using? *Irooj eo ear kam̧adedeik rūttariņae ro an.* The king equipped his warriors with spears.

m̧adenļǫk (**m̧adenļaq**). Also *m̧ōdānļǫk* (**m̧edanļaq**). 1(-*i*), 2, 4. Sleep soundly; see a vision in sleep; fall asleep. *Iaar kiki im m̧ōdānļǫk.* I slept and dreamed.

m̧adeoñeoñ (**m̧adyeg°yeg°**). 1(-*i*), 2, 3(inf, tr -*e*), 8, 9. Disintegrate; dilapidated.

M̧adianna (**m̧adiyhannah**). From Engl. 4. Place name; Mariana islands.

m̧adjake (**m̧adjahkey**). 1(-*i*), 2, 7. Be busy with. *Iar m̧adjake rinañinmej eo.* I was busy with the patient.

m̧adm̧ōd (**m̧adm̧ȩd**). 1(-*i*), 2(inf, tr *m̧adm̧wide, -e*), 3(inf, tr -*e*), 4(+*3*), 6(-*i*), 7. Reap; harvest; make food; sorcery in medicine; working by some contrivance or other; labor; operate; perform; fix; repair; do. *Ta ņe kwōj kōm̧adm̧ōde?* What are you working on? *Iien kōm̧adm̧ōd.* It's harvest time.

m̧adm̧wide (**m̧adm̧idey**). Transitive form of *m̧adm̧ōd* (**m̧adm̧ȩd**).

m̧ae (**m̧ahyey**). Until; for; toward; against.

m̧aelǫk (**m̧ahyeylaq**). Archaic. Distinct. *Em̧aelǫk im alikkar.* It's clear and distinct.

M̧aidikdik (**m̧ahyidikdik**). From *m̧m̧aidikdik* (**m̧m̧ahyidikdik**) "whisper", or from land tracts of same name. 3, 6(-*i*). A plant, *Pandanus carolinianus* cultigen. (Stone). Ebon, Namu.

m̧aijek (**m̧ahyijȩk**). Also *m̧wājek* (**m̧ayjȩk**), *m̧ajek* (**m̧ahjek**). 2(inf, tr -*e*), 7. To help one another; to gang up on someone or something. *Kom̧win m̧aijek pāāk eņ im bōke.* Help each other carry that bag. *Raar m̧aijek ļeo im m̧ane.* They ganged up on him and killed him.

m̧aiļ (**m̧ahyiļ**). From Engl. 1(-*i*), 2(inf, tr -*i*), 4, 7. Mile.

m̧aina (**m̧ahyinah**). Minor; no big thing.

m̧aio (**m̧ahyiyȩw**). 3, 6(-*i*). A food, preserved breadfruit, formed into loaves, wrapped in coconut leaves, and cooked on fire.

m̧aj (**m̧aj**). 1(-*i*), 2, 3, 4, 5(*m̧aje*), 6(-*i*), 7. Eel, intestinal worm. *Em̧aje iarin ānin.* There are lots of eels along the lagoon side of this islet.

m̧aj (**m̧aj**). 1(-*i*), 2, 3(*kōm̧ajm̧aj*), 4, 5(*m̧aje*). Tumor; hemorrhoids. *Em̧ōj aer kōm̧ajm̧aje eō.* They gave me medicine for my tumor. *Wūno in kōm̧ajm̧aj.* Medicine for the treatment of hemorrhoids.

m̧aj-mouj (**m̧aj-mȩwij**). A fish, moray eel, *Gymnothorax pictus.*

m̧aj-waan (**m̧aj-wahan**). A fish.

m̧aje (**m̧ajȩy**). 1(-*i*), 2(inf, tr -*ik*), 3, 5(*m̧m̧ajeje*), 7. Sneeze. *Inaaj bōk mejin bwe im̧m̧ajeje.* I'm getting a cold because I'm sneezing all the time.

m̧aje (**m̧ahjȩy**). Variant form of *m̧ajō* (**m̧ahjȩh**).

m̧ajed (**m̧ajed**). 1(-*i*), 2, 3, 5(*m̧m̧ajedjed*), 7. Lift up the face. *Em̧ōj ņe am̧ m̧m̧ajedjed.* Why don't you stop looking up.

m̧ajeļ (**m̧ajeļ**). From Engl. 1(-*i*), 2, 5(*m̧m̧ajeļjeļ*). Muscle; brawny. *Eļap an m̧m̧ajeļjeļ ļeeņ.* He is very muscular.

M̧ajeļ (**m̧ahjeļ**). From Engl. *Marshall.* Marshall Islands.

m̧ajid (**m̧ajid**). 1(-*i*), 2(inf, tr -*i*), 3, 5(*m̧m̧ajidjid*), 6(-*i*), 7. To bow; nod assent (distributive only). *Em̧ōj ņe am̧ m̧m̧ajidjid.* Why don't you stop bowing and scraping. *Iba wōt emeļeļe kōn an m̧m̧ajidjid ke ij kōnono ñane.* I thought he understood my point because he nodded when I talked to him about it.

m̧ajid (**m̧ajid**). A fish, snake eel, *Myrichthys colubrinus.*

m̧ajidak (**m̧ahjidak**). Interjection: "By God!"

m̧ajkadāl (**m̧ajkadal**). Also *m̧ajkōdāl* (**m̧ajkedal**). 3, 6(-*i*). Earthworm.

m̧ajkōdāl (**m̧ajkedal**). Variant form of *m̧ajkadāl* (**m̧ajkadal**).

m̧ajñal (**m̧ajgal**). Also *m̧ōjñal* (**m̧ejgal**). 1(-*i*), 6(-*i*). Guts, intestines, bowels, offal, innards.

m̧ajoñjoñ (**m̧ajeg°jeg°**). 1(-*i*), 2, 3, 7. Hiccough.

m̧ajō (**m̧ahjȩh**). Also *m̧aje* (**m̧ahjȩy**). Interjection: "Gracious!"

m̧ajōjō (**m̧ajȩhjȩh**). 1(-*i*), 2, 3, 7, 8, 9. Stunned; almost knocked out; shock; jolted. *Ear kanooj m̧ajōjō ke raar* *patōk ņai laļ.* He was really stunned when they threw him on the ground.

m̧aju (**m̧ajiw**). Also *jeraam̧m̧an.* Wealth; lucky; fortunate.

m̧ak (**m̧ak**). Dial. E, W: *em̧m̧ak* (**yem̧m̧ak**). Also *ļōm̧m̧ak* (**ļem̧m̧ak**). 3, 6(*-i*). A fish, needlefish, *Strongylura marina.*

m̧ak (**m̧ak**). Inedible portion near stem of pandanus or breadfruit; butt of pandanus key.

m̧ak (**m̧ak**). 2, 6(*-i*), 8, 9. Cavity in teeth; hole in tree for catching rain water. *Em̧ak ñiin.* He's got cavities.

m̧akañ (**m̧ahkag**). A fish, moray eel, *Gymnothorax flavimarginatus.*

m̧ake (**m̧akęy**). Dial. E only; see *m̧akur* (**m̧akir°**). 1(*-i*), 2(inf, tr *-ik(i)*), 3, 5(*m̧m̧akeke*), 6(*-e*), 7. Thorns in a pandanus leaf; be pricked by pandanus thorns. *Em̧ake peiū.* I've got a thorn in my hand. *Jab etetal ium̧win bōb bwe em̧m̧akeke.* Don't walk under pandanus trees for there are thorns all over the place.

m̧akm̧ōk (**m̧akm̧ęk**). 1(*-i*), 2, 3, 5(*m̧akm̧ūke*), 6(*-i*). A plant, arrowroot, *Tacca leontopetaloides* (L.) Ktze., the Polynesian arrowroot. (Taccaceae). A source of starch for food (from the tubers). *Ejjeļok wōt m̧akm̧ūke in m̧wiin.* This tract has an awful lot of arrowroot.

m̧akm̧ōk (**m̧akm̧ęk**). 1(*-i*), 2, 3(inf, tr *-e*), 5(*m̧akm̧ōke*), 6(*-i*). Starch. *Kwaar kōm̧akm̧ōk ke nuknuk?* Did you starch clothes? *Kwōmaroñ ke kam̧akm̧ōke nuknuk kā aō?* Can you starch my clothes?

m̧akneet (**m̧akneyet**). Also *jitūūl* (**jitihil**). From Engl. 2(inf, tr *-e*), 6(*-i*). Magnet. *M̧akneete dila kaņ.* Pick up those nails with the magnet.

m̧akoko (**m̧akęwkęw**). 1(*-i*), 2, 3(inf, tr *-ik*), 5(*m̧m̧akoko*), 7, 8, 9. Refuse to do something; decline; unwilling. *Kwōn jab m̧akoko in jikuuļ.* Don't refuse to go to school. *Iar kam̧akokoiki bwe en je lōta eo aō.* I forced him to write my letter. I imposed upon him to write my letter.

m̧akokolep (**m̧akęwkęwlęp**). Dial. E, W: *abōblep* (**habęblep**). Always refuse.

m̧akokoun bōk (**m̧akęwkęwin bek**). Also *abwin bōk* (**habin bek**). Reject; refuse to accept or take. *Ear m̧akokoun bōk menin jipañ ko am.* He rejected our help.

m̧akōni (**m̧ahkeniy**). Variant form of *m̧aōkōni* (**m̧ahehkeniy**).

m̧akroro (**m̧akrewrew**). 5(*m̧m̧akroro*), 7, 8, 9. Fresh breeze; fair breeze; favorable; prosperous wind. *Em̧m̧akroro kōto raan kein.* The breeze is fresh these days. *Em̧akroro kūtwōn wa eo waan.* His boat sailed under a prosperous wind.

m̧akur (**m̧akir°**). Dial. W only; see *m̧ake* (**m̧akęy**). 1(*-i*), 2(inf, tr *-i*), 3. Thorns in a pandanus leaf.

m̧akūt (**m̧ahkit**). From Engl. 2(inf, tr *-i*), 6(*-i*). Market. *Kōjro etal ñan m̧akūt in ek eņ.* Let's go to the fish market. *Ij etal in m̧akūti amim̧ōņo kā aō.* I'm going to sell these handicraft items at the market.

m̧akūtkūt (**m̧akitkit**). Variant form of *m̧m̧akūt* (**m̧m̧akit**).

m̧al- (**m̧al-**). 5(*m̧m̧alm̧al*),7. Bend toward; stoop; sway; lean toward. *M̧al m̧aanļok.* Bend forwards. *Em̧m̧alm̧al an etal.* He sways when he walks.

m̧alen (**m̧ahlen**). From Germ. *malen* "to paint, portray". 1(*-i*), 2(inf, tr *-e*), 4, 6(*-i*), 7. Script; write; draw; engrave. *Ejeļā m̧alen.* He's a good artist. *M̧alene tok m̧ōk eta ilo juron jāje e aō.* Would you engrave my name on the handle of my machete.

m̧alik (**m̧alik**). Archaic. Custom.

m̧alōk (**m̧alek**). 2(inf, tr *-e*). Put in; call at. *Ia eņ wa eņ enaaj m̧alōke m̧m̧ōkaj?* What will be that ship's first port of call?

m̧aļo (**m̧aļew**). 6(*-e*). Lagoon. *Eļap m̧aļoon Kuwajleen.* Kwajalein has a large lagoon.

M̧aļo-eļap (**m̧aļew-yeļap**). Variant form of *M̧ōņooļļap* (**m̧eņeweļļap**).

m̧aļokļok (**m̧aļęqļęq**). A fish; sting ray.

m̧am̧a (**m̧ahm̧ah**). Mother; momma.

m̧am̧a (**m̧ahm̧ah**). 2, 4, 6(*-i*), 7. A gathering of people to celebrate the onset of breadfruit season in summer by making offerings to Jebro, the god of breadfruit. *Kōm ļak tōprakļok, kōm iioon aer m̧am̧a.* As we arrived at the place, we were in time to witness the celebration of the breadfruit season.

m̧am̧ōj (m̧am̧ej). 2(inf, tr *-e*), 5(*m̧am̧ōje*), 6(*-i*), 7.   Black carbon on lantern chimney, used to blacken tattoos. *Rej m̧am̧ōje eo en̄ an l̗een̄.* They're using black carbon on his tattoos.

m̧an (m̧an).   Transitive form of *m̧anm̧an* (m̧anm̧an).

M̧ande (m̧andey).   From Engl.   Monday.

m̧ani (m̧aniy).   From Engl. 6(*-i*).   Money.

m̧anit (m̧anit).   Also *m̧anōt* (m̧anet̗). 1(*m̧anti-*), 3, 4, 6(*m̧antin*).   Custom; behavior; conduct. *Ejel̗ā m̧anit.* He knows how to conduct himself. *Ejel̗ā kilen kōm̧anit.* He knows the workings of protocol.

m̧anm̧an (m̧anm̧an). 1(*-i*), 2(inf, tr *m̧an(e)*), 4, 7.   Kill; hit; beat; cross out writing; execution; extinguish; slaughter; slay. *Kwōn m̧ane l̗ok etan jān bok n̄e.* Cross his name out of that book. *Kwōn m̧ane kijeek n̄e.* Extinguish the fire.

m̧anol̗ (m̧anel̗°).   A fish, *Seriola purpurascens.*

m̧antin (m̧antin).   Construct form of *m̧anit* (m̧anit).

m̧antin etto (m̧antin yettew).   Slang. Old-fashioned. *Kwōn jab m̧antin etto.* Don't be old-fashioned.

m̧an̄ke (m̧agkey).   From Engl. *monkey.* 1(*-i*), 2, 3(inf, tr *-ik*), 6(*-i*), 7, 8, 9. Monkey; ape; naked; nude; bare; shirtless. *M̧an̄ke in ia n̄e nājim̧?* Where did you get your pet monkey? *Kwōn jab m̧an̄ke bwe elōn̄ kōrā.* Put on your clothes because there are females present. *Kwōn jab m̧antin m̧an̄ke.* Stop acting like a monkey. *Enana m̧an̄ke ilo im̧ōn jar.* It's not good to go to church shirtless.

m̧an̄ke jibana (m̧agkey jibahnah).   From Japn. *supana* (from Engl. *spanner*). 2(inf, tr *-ik*), 6(*-i*).   Monkey wrench.

m̧ao (m̧ahwew).   From *m̧a* "cry", *o.*   A bird, short-eared owl, *Asio flammeus;* male; see *lijem̧ao.*

m̧ao.   See *m̧oo.*

m̧aōkōni (m̧ahehkeniy).   Also *m̧akōni* (m̧ahkeniy).   From Engl.   Mahogany.

m̧are (m̧arey).   From Engl. 1(*-i*), 2(inf, tr *-ik*), 3(inf, tr *-ik*), 4, 7.   To marry. *Em̧ōj aer m̧are.* They are married. *Em̧ōj an m̧areik juon ripālle.* He married an American. *Em̧ōj an kōm̧are.* He finished conducting the

wedding ceremony. *Em̧ōj an kōm̧areik jar eo.* He married the couple.

m̧arm̧ar (m̧arm̧ar). 1(*-i*), 2(inf, tr *m̧arōk*), 3(inf, tr *kam̧arm̧ar(e)*), 4, 6(*-i*), 7.   Necklace; wear a necklace; wear around the neck; medal. *Raar kōm̧arm̧are wōt ke ij em̧m̧akūt.* They were putting the leis around his neck when I left.

m̧arō- (m̧are-).   Also *m̧ōra-* (m̧era-). Necklace of; medallion of; possessive classifier, flowers, medals, necklaces, or fishing baskets.

m̧arōk (m̧arek).   Transitive form of *m̧arm̧ar* (m̧arm̧ar).

m̧atan̄.   See *m̧ōtan̄.*

m̧m̧aan (m̧m̧ahan).   Dial. W: *em̧m̧aan* (yem̧m̧ahan), E: *m̧ōm̧aan* (mem̧ahan). 2(inf, tr *-ek*, *-e*), 3(*kōm̧m̧aanan*), 5(*m̧m̧aanan(e)*, *m̧m̧aane*), 6(*-i*).   Man; male; wife's brother. *Rōaikuj m̧m̧aan l̗ok n̄an tarin̄ae.* They need more men for fighting. *El̗ap an m̧m̧aane ānin.* There are lots of men on this islet. *M̧m̧aan eo aō n̄e tok.* Here comes my wife's brother. *Em̧m̧aanane.* He's manly.

m̧m̧aanan (m̧m̧ahanhan).   Dial. W: *em̧m̧aanan* (yem̧m̧ahanhan), E: *m̧ōm̧aanan* (mem̧ahanhan). 1(*-i*), 2, 3, 4, 7.   Manly; distributive form of *m̧m̧aan* (m̧m̧ahan). *El̗ap an l̗een̄ m̧m̧aanan(e).* He is very manly.

m̧m̧aelep (m̧m̧ahyelep).   Dial. W: *em̧m̧aelep* (yem̧m̧ahyelep), E: *m̧ōm̧aelep* (mem̧ahyelep). 1(*-i*), 2(inf, *-e*), 3, 4, 5(*m̧m̧aeleplep*), 8, 9. Desire for something, uncontrolled; brash; take more than one's share; overanxious. *Kwōn jab m̧m̧aelep in etal eon̄ōd.* Don't get carried away by your desire to go fishing. *Kwōn jab m̧m̧aelepe ek kan̄e kijen.* Don't take his fish too (in addition to yours). *Lale bwe em̧m̧aeleplep.* Watch out for him for he is always trying to take more than his share. *Kwōn jab m̧m̧aelep.* Don't be too anxious.

m̧m̧aidikdik (m̧m̧ahyidikdik).   Dial. W: *em̧m̧aidikdik* (yem̧m̧ahyidikdik), E: *m̧ōm̧aidikdik* (mem̧ahyidikdik).   Also *m̧m̧wāidikdik* (m̧m̧ayidikdik), *m̧m̧wādikdik* (m̧m̧aydikdik).   Whisper. *Kwōn m̧m̧aidikdik l̗ok n̄ane.* Whisper to him.

m̧m̧ak (**m̧m̧ak**). Dial. W: *em̧m̧ak* (**yem̧m̧ak**), E: *m̧ōm̧ak* (**mem̧ak**). A hole in a tree for catching water. *Eor ke dānnin m̧m̧ak eņ?* Is there any water in the hole in that tree?

m̧m̧akūt (**m̧m̧akit**). Dial. W: *em̧m̧akūt* (**yem̧m̧akit**), E: *m̧ōm̧akūt* (**mem̧akit**). Also *m̧akūtkūt* (**m̧akitkit**). 1(*-i*), 2, 3(intr *kōm̧m̧akūt*, tr *kōm̧akūti*), 5(*m̧m̧akūtkūt*),7. Unstable; move; budge; migrate; motion; pull up stakes. *Jab m̧akūtkūt.* Don't move. *Ta in ej kōm̧akūtkūt m̧wiin?* What is shaking this house?

m̧m̧al (**m̧m̧al**). Dial. W: *em̧m̧al*, E: *m̧ōm̧al*. Archaic. Place for beating coconut husks after soaking in preparation for making sennit.

m̧m̧al (**m̧m̧al**). Archaic. Stagger.

m̧m̧aļkaro (**m̧m̧aļkarew**). Dial. W: *em̧m̧aļkaro* (**yem̧m̧aļkarew**), E: *m̧ōm̧aļkaro* (**mem̧aļkarew**). Also *m̧m̧ōļkaro* (**m̧m̧eļkarew**). 1(*-i*), 2, 4, 6(*-i*), 7, 8, 9. Psychosis, of a latent nature; moody; sulky; bad disposition; rowdy; variable in temper; fickle; ornery; grouchy. *Jab kalluuki bwe em̧m̧aļkaro.* Don't make him angry because he's a latent psychotic. *Eor ien an m̧m̧ōļkaro.* There are times when he gets rowdy.

m̧m̧an (**m̧m̧an**). Dial. W: *em̧m̧an* (**yem̧m̧an**), E: *m̧ōm̧an* (**mem̧an**). 1(*-i*), 2, 3(*kōm̧m̧an*), 4, 5(*kōm̧anm̧an*), 6(*-i*), 8, 9, 10(*m̧m̧ane*), 11(*m̧m̧anm̧ōn*). Good; cute; favorable; fine; grand; nice; choice; opportune; pleasing; swell; great. *Em̧m̧ane ke injin ņe?* Has that engine been fixed? *Kōm̧m̧ane injin ņe.* Fix the motor. *Kōm̧anm̧an am̧ jerbal.* Work well. *Em̧ m̧m̧anm̧ōn men eņ.* That's a lovely house. *M̧ōm̧an kaņ.* That's great.

m̧m̧an ded (**m̧m̧an ded**). Dial. W: *em̧m̧an ded* (**yem̧m̧an ded**), E: *m̧ōm̧an ded* (**mem̧an ded**). 1(*-i*), 2, 6(*-i*). Of good size; youthful; of good age; maturity. *Em̧m̧an ded dettan piik eo.* The pig is just the right size. *Ļadik eo etōpar iien em̧m̧an ded.* The boy is reaching maturity.

m̧m̧an utōn (**m̧m̧an witen**). Dial. W: *em̧m̧an utōn* (**yem̧m̧an witen**), E: *m̧ōm̧an utōn* (**mem̧an witen**). 1(*-e*). Of good mixture; of right dilution; of right combination.

m̧m̧ar (**m̧m̧ar**). Dial. W: *em̧m̧ar* (**yem̧m̧ar**), E: *m̧ōm̧ar* (**mem̧ar**). 1(*m̧ōra-*). Fishing basket.

m̧m̧awi (**m̧m̧ahwiy**). Dial. W: *em̧m̧awi* (**yem̧m̧ahwiy**), E: *m̧ōm̧awi* (**mem̧ahwiy**). Also *m̧m̧ao*. 1(*-i*), 2, 3, 4, 5(*m̧m̧awiwi*), 6(*-i*). Adult conversation, informal and possibly trivial; talkative; precocious, of children. *N̄e ej kadek ekadik m̧m̧awiwi.* When he's high he's always talkative. *Ejjeļọk wōt m̧m̧aoun an ļadik ņe kōnnaan.* That boy sounds like an adult when he speaks. *Ļōm̧aro raņ rej kōm̧m̧ao bajjik.* Those fellows are chatting. *Em̧m̧an bwe em̧m̧ao.* She's good and talkative.

m̧m̧ool (**m̧m̧ewel**). Dial. W: *em̧m̧ool* (**yem̧m̧ewel**), E: *m̧ōm̧ool* (**mem̧ewel**). 1(*-i*), 2, 3, 4. To be thanked; generous; grateful; integrity; liberal; open-handed. *Eļap aō kam̧m̧oolol eok.* I'm grateful to you.

m̧m̧ōd (**m̧m̧ẹd**). Dial. W: *em̧m̧ōd* (**yẹmm̧ẹd**), E: *m̧ōd* (**m̧ẹd**). 1(*-i*), 2, 3, 4, 7. Provisions for a voyage. *Elōn̄ ke an wa in m̧ōd?* Does this ship have lots of provisions?

m̧m̧ōj (**m̧m̧ẹj**). Dial. W: *em̧m̧ōj* (**yẹmm̧ẹj**), E: *m̧ōm̧ōj* (**m̧ẹm̧ẹj**). 1(*-i*), 2(inf, tr *-e*, *m̧m̧ōjraake*), 3, 7. Vomit; spit; saliva.

m̧m̧ōjānjān (**m̧m̧ejanjan**). Dial. W: *em̧m̧ōjānjān* (**yem̧m̧ejanjan**), E: *m̧ōm̧jānjan* (**mem̧janjan**). 1, 2, 3, 6(*-i*), 7. Footsteps in gravel or dry leaves. *Ke ij ron̄ ainikien m̧m̧ōjānjānļọk, iba wōt kwōj eañiñin eō.* When I heard footsteps I thought you were calling my name.

m̧m̧ōkadkad (**m̧m̧ekadkad**). Dial. W: *em̧m̧ōkadkad* (**yem̧m̧ekadkad**), E: *m̧ōm̧kadkad* (**mem̧kadkad**). 1, 2, 4, 6(*-i*), 7. Wander; roam. *Em̧m̧ōkadkad riMājej.* Mejit people like to wander. *Kwōj em̧m̧ōkadkad ļọk ñan ia?* Where are you wandering to?

m̧m̧ōkaj (**m̧m̧ekaj**). Dial. W: *em̧m̧ōkaj* (**yem̧m̧ekaj**), E: *m̧ōm̧kaj* (**mem̧kaj**). 2(inf, tr *-e*), 5(*m̧m̧ōkajkaj*), 7. Go ahead; first; before; haste; precede, be in time for. *Kwōn m̧m̧ōkaj waj.* Go on ahead. *Ear m̧m̧ōkajļọk in kōm̧m̧an jikin baam̧le eo an.* He went ahead to prepare a place to stay for the family. *Kwe m̧m̧ōkaj.* You first. *Kom̧ro* *m̧m̧ōkaj waj bwe eboñ.* You two go on ahead before it gets dark. *Kwaar m̧m̧ōkaje ke kkure eo?* Did you get to the games early? *Ear m̧m̧ōkaje iij eo.* He got there in time for some yeast (drink).

m̧m̧ōļeiñiñ (**m̧m̧eļęyigyig**). Dial. W: *em̧m̧ōļeiñin* (**yem̧m̧eļęyigyig**), E: *m̧ōm̧ļeiñiñ* (**m̧em̧ļęyigyig**). 1(*-i*), 2, 3(inf, tr *-i*), 5(*m̧m̧ōleiñiñ*), 6(*-i*), 7, 8, 9. To bob; rock; roll; sway. *Ta eņ ej kam̧m̧ōleiñiñi?* What's causing it to bob?

m̧m̧ōļkaro (**m̧m̧eļkarew**). Variant form of *m̧m̧aļkaro* (**m̧m̧aļkarew**).

m̧m̧ōņm̧ōņ (**m̧m̧eņm̧eņ**). Dial. W: *em̧m̧ōņm̧ōņ* (**yem̧m̧eņm̧eņ**), E: *m̧ōm̧ōņm̧ōņ* (**m̧em̧eņm̧eņ**). 5, 7. Pitter-patter of rain.

m̧m̧ōt (**m̧m̧ęt**). Dial. W: *em̧m̧ōt* (**yęm̧m̧ęt**), E: *m̧ōm̧ōt* (**m̧em̧ęt**) . Also *m̧ōt* (**m̧ęt**). 2, 3, 6(*-i*). Pitch, of a boat. *Eļap an wa eo m̧m̧ōt.* The boat pitched very badly. *M̧okta jān am̧ m̧welik kōn kōrkōr, kwōj aikuj jeļā kam̧m̧ōt.* Before you can take a canoe out into the ocean you have to know how to control the pitch.

m̧m̧ōtm̧ōt (**m̧m̧ętm̧ęt**). From *m̧ōt* "drink using mouth directly". Sucking noise made in drinking green coconuts. *Em̧m̧ōtm̧ōt an idaak.* He drank noisily.

m̧m̧ūņm̧ūņ (**m̧m̧iņm̧iņ**). Dial. W: *im̧m̧ūņm̧ūņ* (**yim̧m̧iņm̧iņ**), E: *m̧ūm̧ūņm̧ūņ* (**m̧im̧iņm̧iņ**). 1(*-i*), 2, 3, 5, 7. Stamping; treading; sound of treading feet.

m̧ojo (**m̧ewjew**). From Japn. 2, 6(*-i*). Appendicitis. *Erup m̧ojo eo an.* His appendix is ruptured.

m̧okm̧ok (**m̧eqm̧eq**). Rinse.

m̧okta (**m̧eqtah**). Also *m̧ōm̧kaj* (**m̧em̧kaj**). 7. Before; former; precede. *Iar iioone m̧okta jān an etal.* I met him before he went. *Kwōn wātok m̧m̧ōkaj.* Come here for a minute. *Ien ko m̧okta.* The former times.

m̧oņ (**m̧eņ°**). 2(inf, tr *-e*), 7(*m̧oņetok, ļo̧k, waj*). Lie; deceive; trick; to stall. *Iar m̧oņe ļo̧k bwe en etal.* I tricked him into going.

m̧oñ (**m̧eg°**). From Japn. *mon*. 6(*-i*). Gateway, usually decorated with flowers and coconut fronds.

m̧ool (**m̧ewel**). 1(*-i*), 2, 3, 4(*rūkam̧ool*), 8, 9, 11(*m̧oolol*). Truth; true; right; correct; realistic; loyal; sincere; sure; fact; faithful; frank; honest. *Em̧ool ļo̧k m̧upi eo m̧okta jān eo ālik.* The first movie was more realistic than the second one. *Rūkam̧ooļ.* Witness. *Kwōj m̧ool ke?* Are you sure?

m̧ootka (**m̧ewetkah**). From Engl. *motor car*. 6(*-i*). Automobile; car; truck.

m̧or (**m̧er°**). 1(*-i*), 2, 3, 5(*m̧m̧orm̧or*), 7, 11(*m̧orm̧or*). Old, of things; rotten; worn out; dilapidated; obsolescent; obsolete; outdated; trite.

m̧or (**m̧er°**). Slang. 1(*-i*), 2, 3(inf, tr *-e*), 6(*-i*). Former lover. *Kwōn jab kabbil kake bwe m̧or lieņ.* Don't go showing off with her because she and I used to be intimate.

m̧or (**m̧er°**). Also *itaak*. Arrive at; sail onto land.

m̧oram̧or (**m̧er°am̧er°, m̧er°am̧ęr°**). Variant form of *m̧orm̧or* (**m̧er°m̧er°**).

m̧orm̧or (**m̧er°m̧er°**). Also *m̧oram̧or* (**m̧er°am̧er°**), *m̧oram̧or* (**m̧er°am̧ęr°**). 6(*-i*). A fish, rabbitfish, *Siganus* sp.

m̧oujlep (**m̧ęwijlep**). 1(*-i*), 2, 3, 7, 8, 9. Very wet; drenched; soaked.

m̧ouweo (**m̧ewiweyew**). That house (close to neither of us); house, demonstrative third person singular, singling out.

m̧o̧kulkul (**m̧aqilqil**). Also *uļūtlūt* (**wiļitļit**). 1(*-i*), 2, 3, 7, 8, 9. Fat and healthy, usually referring to a baby. *Eļap an m̧o̧kulkul ajri eņ.* That baby is healthy and fat.

m̧o̧kulkul (**m̧aqilqil**). 2, 6(*-i*), 8, 9. Cuddly; velvety.

m̧o̧kut (**m̧aqit**). Archaic. Grow close together (see *kkut*).

m̧o̧kwōd (**m̧aqed**). Also *tiek* (**tiyek**), *atin ko̧o̧njeļ* (**hatin kawanjeļ**), *reeļ* (**reyeļ**). Vulgar. 1(*-i*). Neck of the penis.

m̧o̧le (**m̧awlęy**). Dial. E, W: *ellek* (**yęllęk**). A fish, rabbitfish, *Siganus rostratus.*

m̧o̧ļweļwe (**m̧aļ°ęyļ°ęy**). Dial. E, W: *m̧o̧ļwōjļwōj* (**m̧aļ°ejļ°ej**). Archaic. Soak.

m̧o̧ļwōjļwōj (**m̧aļ°ejļ°ej**). Dialectal variant of *m̧o̧ļweļwe* (**m̧aļ°ęyļ°ęy**).

m̧o̧ņe (**m̧aņ°ęy**). Dial. E, W: *eañrōk* (**yagręk**). A fish, surgeonfish, *Naso unicornis.*

m̧o̧o (**m̧awęw**). Also *m̧ao.* Dance call, move.

m̧o̧roj (**m̧ar°ej**). Also *m̧aroj.* 6(*-i*). Cock's comb.

m̧o̧ruj (**m̧ar°ij**). 1(*-i*), 2(inf, tr *-i*), 5(*m̧o̧rujruj*), 7. Break, as a stick; broken. *Wōn ņe ear m̧o̧ruji bōtta ņe?* Who broke that bat?

m̧ō (**m̧eh**). 1(*-i*), 2, 3, 7, 8, 9. Thin, of animals or men; emaciated.

m̧ōd (**m̧ęd**). Dial. E, W: *em̧m̧ōd* (**yęm̧m̧ęd**). 3. Provisions for a voyage. *Em̧ōj ke aer kōm̧m̧an m̧ōd?* Have they prepared provisions for the voyage?

m̧ōd (**m̧ęd**). 1(*-i*), 2, 3(inf, tr *-e*), 6(*-i*), 8, 9. Lose leaves, of trees; lose hair. *Em̧ōd ni eo kōn an kar aerar.* The coconut tree is losing its leaves because it was singed by the fire. *Em̧ōd jān kooļan bōran.* He has lost his hair.

m̧ōdānļo̧k (**m̧edanļaq**). Variant form of *m̧adenļo̧k* (**m̧adenļaq**).

m̧ōdkowak (**m̧ędkewwak**). Dial. W, E: *kewe* (**kęywęy**). 6(*-i*). Snipe that has lost its feathers.

m̧ōdm̧ōd (**m̧edm̧ed**). 1(*-i*), 2, 3, 8, 9. Easy to break or tear; frayed; dilapidated. *Em̧ōdm̧ōd nuknuk in Jepaan.* Cloth made in Japan tears easily.

m̧ōj (**m̧ęj**). 1(*-i*), 2, 3, 3+7, 6(*m̧ōjin, m̧wijin, m̧wiji*). Finished; already; quit; completed; done. *Enañin m̧ōj ke m̧weo kwaar kalōke?* Is the house you were building almost finished? *Em̧ōj m̧weo iar kalōke.* The house I was building is finished. *Kwōn kam̧ōj ļo̧k m̧weo iar kalōke.* You finish the house I was building. *Ij kam̧ōj aō jerbal kiiō.* I'm quitting work now.

m̧ōjaan (**m̧ejahan**). Cry of; see *m̧a.*

m̧ōjab- (**m̧ejab-**). From *em̧* "house", *jab* "intensifier". House; used intensively with demonstratives. *M̧ōjabōt?* Which house? *M̧ōjabuweo.* That house right over there.

m̧ōjani (**m̧ejahniy**). A fish, big-eye or burgy, *Monotaxis grandoculis.*

m̧ōjañ (**m̧ejag**). 6(*-i*). Tail of lobster.

m̧ōjañūr (**m̧ejagir**). Dial. W only; see *jabōnke* (**jabenkęy**). 3, 6(*-i*). A fish, porcupine fish, *Diodon hystrix.*

m̧ōjawōnene (**m̧ejahwęnęynęy**). 2, 3, 6(*-i*), 7. Dawn. *Allikar an raan bwe em̧ōjawōnene tok.* Daylight is obviously near since dawn is breaking.

M̧ōjāl (**m̧ejyal**). 3, 6(*-i*). A plant, *Pandanus fischerianus* cultigen.

m̧ōjāliklik (**m̧ejaliklik**). Variant form of *m̧ōjālūlū* (**m̧ejalihlih**).

m̧ōjālūlū (**m̧ejalihlih**). Also *m̧ōjaliklik* (**m̧ejaliklik**). 1(*-i*), 2, 3(inf *kōm̧m̧ōjālūlū*, tr *-ūk, -ik*), 5(*m̧m̧ōjālūlū*), 8, 9. Curly; kinky; wavy. *Ear kōm̧m̧ōjālūlūūk bōran.* She set her hair. *Em̧m̧ōjālūlū bōran ledik eo.* She had curly hair.

m̧ōjālūlū (**m̧ejalihlih**). 2. Stunned; in a daze. *Em̧ajālūlū kōn nakōļ eo.* He was stunned by the blow.

m̧ōjbwe (**m̧ęjbęy**). Archaic. Sail of a certain shape.

m̧ōjjā (**m̧ejjay**). 2, 4. A game, slight-of-hand using shell and three holes in sand.

M̧ōjjelwōj (**m̧ęjjęlwęj**). From "house of Jaluit". A plant, *Pandanus fischerianus* cultigen (Takeuchi). (Stone). Jaluit.

m̧ōjjero (**m̧ęjjęyręw**). Also *kappokpok* (**kappęqręq**). A food, very ripe breadfruit baked in coconut oil.

m̧ōjjo (**m̧ęjjęw**). 2, 4, 6(*-i*). Hide; hide-and-seek. *Ear m̧ōjjo jān eō.* He hid from me. *Ajri raņ rej m̧ōjjo.* The children are playing hide-and-seek.

m̧ōjņo̧ (**m̧ejņaw**). 1(*-i*), 2, 3(inf, tr *-ik*), 4, 7, 8, 9. Weak; puny; feeble; impotent; invalid; powerless. *Em̧ōjņo̧ kōn an kar nañinmej.* He is weak from having been sick.

m̧ōjoud (**m̧ęjęwid**). A fish, eel, *Conger cinereus.*

m̧ōjo̧ (**m̧ejaw**). 2(inf, tr *-uk, -ik*). Urinate on. *Em̧ōj an m̧ōjo̧uk jaki eņ kinien.* He wet his mat.

m̧ōjo̧liñōr (**m̧ejawligęr**). 1(*-i*), 2, 3, 4, 8, 9. Sickness believed to be caused by sleeping at night under the moon; lunacy; lunatic; mentally unstable.

m̧ōk (**m̧ek**). Dial. E, W: *m̧ōk* (**m̧ęk**). 1(*-i*), 2, 3(inf *kam̧m̧ōkm̧ōk*, tr *kam̧ōk*), 5(*m̧m̧ōkm̧ōk*), 7, 8, 9. Tired; exhausted; fatigue; weary. *Im̧ōk in jutak.* I'm tired of standing. *Eļap aō m̧m̧ōkm̧ōk.* I get tired easily. *Ekam̧m̧ōkm̧ōk an jipij.* His speeches are long-winded.

m̧ōk (**m̧ek**). Please, would you kindly. *Itok m̧ōk.* Please come. *Kwōmaroñ ke itok m̧ōk?* Would you please come?

m̧ōkade (**m̧ekadȩy**). 1(*-i*), 2, 7, 8, 9. Wizard; ghost; expert; champion. *Em̧ōkade ilo piimboñ.* He is expert at ping pong.

M̧ōkadkad (**m̧ekadkad**). From "wander". 3, 6(*-i*). A plant, banana variety.

m̧ōkaj (**m̧ekaj**). Dial. E, W: *jarōb* (**jareb**), *jerab* (**jerab**). 1(*-i*), 2, 3, 4, 7, 8, 9, 11(*m̧ōkajkōj*). Fast; speedy; instantly; prompt; quick; speed. *Eļap an wa eo m̧ōkaj.* That boat is speedy. *Wa m̧ōkajkōj eo nȩ.* That boat is very speedy. *Kwōn m̧ōkajļo̧k jidik.* You'd better step on it.

m̧ōkaj jān om̧ (**m̧ekaj jan wȩm̧**). Idiom. Move slowly, snail's pace. *Joñan an m̧ōkaj jān om̧ eluuj ilo iāekwōj eo.* He was so slow he lost the race.

m̧ōkajkaj (**m̧ekajkaj**). 1(*-i*), 2, 3, 4, 7. First food brought to a chief that has just arrived.

M̧ōkaluoj (**m̧ekahliwej**). Variant form of *M̧ōkauleej* (**m̧ekahwilȩyȩj**).

m̧ōkan̄ (**m̧ekan̄**). Those houses (close to neither of us); houses, demonstrative third person plural.

m̧ōkanȩ (**m̧ekanȩy**). Those houses (close to you); houses, demonstrative second person plural.

M̧ōkauleej (**m̧ekahwilȩyȩj**). Also *M̧ōkaluoj* (**m̧ekahliwej**). Clan name.

m̧ōkā (**m̧ekay**). These houses (close to me); houses, demonstrative first person exclusive plural.

m̧ōkākan̄ (**m̧ekaykan̄**). Those houses (close to neither of us); houses, demonstrative third person plural, singling out.

m̧ōkākanȩ (**m̧ekaykanȩy**). Those houses (close to you); houses, demonstrative second person plural, singling out.

m̧ōkākā (**m̧ekaykay**). These houses (close to me); houses, demonstrative first person exclusive plural, singling out.

m̧ōkein (**m̧ekȩyin**). These houses (close to us both); houses, demonstrative first person inclusive plural.

m̧ōko (**m̧ekew**). The houses (often not present); these houses (close to me); houses, demonstrative third person plural abstract.

m̧ōkoko (**m̧ekewkew**). Those houses (close to neither of us); houses,demonstrative third person plural, singling out.

m̧ōleo̧ (**m̧eleyaw**). Also *pio̧* (**piyaw**). Chilly; cold; see *m̧ōlo.*

m̧ōlm̧ōl (**m̧elm̧el**). 3, 5(*m̧ōlm̧ōle*), 6(*-i*). A fish, mackerel, *Scomber japonicus. Em̧ōlm̧ōle ānin.* There are lots of mackerel around this islet.

m̧ōļajiktak (**m̧eļahjiktak**). Variant form of *m̧ōļojetak* (**m̧ȩļȩwjeytak**).

m̧ōļajutak (**m̧eļahjiwtak**). 3, 6(*-i*). A fish, skip jack, *Caranx lessonii.*

m̧ōļan̄ļōn̄ (**m̧eļagļȩg**). 1(*-i*), 2(inf, tr *-e*, *m̧ōļan̄ļūn̄e*), 3, 7, 8, 9. Nausea; nauseated; disgusted; seasick. *Im̧ōļan̄ļōn̄ im iabwin m̧ōn̄ā.* I'm nauseated and I don't feel like eating.

m̧ōļawi. See *m̧ōļo̧wi.*

m̧ōļe (**m̧eļey**). Sand crab.

m̧ōļejetak (**m̧eļeyjeytak**). A fish, redfin, *Argyrops spinifer.*

m̧ōļo (**m̧ȩļȩw**). 1(*-i*), 2, 3, 5(*m̧m̧ōļoļo*), 6(*-i*), 7, 8, 9, 11(*m̧ōļoļo*). Cool; cold. *Emm̧an an m̧m̧ōļoļo iarin ānin.* It's nice that the whole lagoon side of this islet is cool.

m̧ōļojetak (**m̧ȩļȩwjeytak**). Dial. W only; see *ko̧uwe* (**kawiwȩy**). Also *m̧ōļajitak* (**m̧eļahjiktak**). A fish, pompano, *Trachinotus bailloni.*

M̧ōļooļļap (**m̧eļeweļļap**). Variant form of *M̧ōn̄ooļļap* (**m̧en̄eweļļap**).

m̧ōļo̧wi (**m̧eļawiy**). 2, 6(*-i*), 8, 9. Retarded; giddy; dumb. *Jab eļļo̧k bwe ejaad m̧ōļo̧wi.* Don't pay him any attention because he's a bit dumb.

m̧ōļo̧wi (**m̧eļawwiy, m̧eļawiy**). Also *m̧ōļawi.* 1(*-i*), 2, 3, 7, 8, 9. Dew; mildew; damp; humid; moist; moisture; wet.

m̧ōļōbbā (**m̧eļebbay**). Archaic. Huge pile, as of coconuts; keep piling up.

m̧ōm̧ (**m̧em̧**). Also *m̧ōm̧* (**m̧em̧**). 1(*-i*), 2, 3, 4, 7, 8, 9. Lusty; to lust, overanxious. *Eļap aō m̧ōm̧ ke ij lo ek ko.* When I saw the fish I felt that I had to catch them.

m̧ōm̧-. See *m̧m̧-.*

m̧ōm̧kaj (**m̧em̧kaj**). Variant form of *m̧okta* (**m̧eqtah**).

m̧ōm̧lep (**m̧em̧lep**). Also *m̧ōm̧lep* (**m̧ȩm̧lep**). 1(*-i*), 2, 3, 4, 7, 8, 9. Impetuous.

ṃōṃō (**ṃehṃeh**). A fish, grouper, *Epinephelus hexagonatus.*

ṃōṃō in (**ṃehṃeh yin**). Idiom. From *ṃōṃō* (**ṃehṃeh**). Familiar with; know one's way around. *Jon̄an an to aṃ pād ānin, kiiō kwe ṃōṃō in jin.* You've been here so long, now you know the place inside out. *Kwōn jab inepata bwe kōjro ṃōṃō in jekein.* Don't be afraid; I know this place like the back of my hand.

ṃōn (**ṃẹn**). Also *ṃōn ed* (**ṃẹn yed**). A fish, squirrel fish, *Myripristis berndti.*

ṃōn bwidej (**ṃen bidẹj**). From *ṃōn* (**ṃen**) "house of", *bwidej* (**bidẹj**) "night soil". Toilet; latrine.

ṃōn jar (**ṃen jar**). Church (building).

ṃōn jikuuḷ (**ṃen jikiwiḷ**). Schoolhouse.

ṃōn kōppād (**ṃen keppad**). Temporary house, shack.

ṃōn kōppojak (**ṃen keppewjak**). Toilet; latrine.

ṃōn kuk (**ṃen qiq**). Kitchen; cook house.

ṃōn kweiḷọk (**ṃen qẹyiḷaq**). Townhouse; meeting house.

ṃōn ṃōn̄ā (**ṃen ṃegay**). Cafeteria; restaurant; mess hall. *Kōjro etal n̄an ṃōn ṃōn̄ā eṇ an Kūḷara.* Let's go to Clara's restaurant.

ṃōn taktō (**ṃen takteh**). Hospital; dispensary; health clinic.

ṃōn utḷaṃ (**ṃen witḷaṃ**). 4, 6(*-i*). Brothel; whore house.

ṃōn wia (**ṃen wiyah**). Store; shop.

ṃōn-kiden (**ṃẹn-kidẹn**). 3, 6(*-i*). A fish, *uu* or *panu*; *Myripristis bowditchae/ murdjan.*

ṃōnkọḷotḷot (**ṃenkaḷ°etḷ°et**). Land given to someone who took care of the head of the lineage owning the land during illness before death.

ṃōnwa (**ṃenwah**). From Engl. *man ọ war*. 6(*-i*). Warship; battleship.

ṃōṇakjān (**ṃeṇakjan**). A food, preserved dried breadfruit.

ṃōṇakjān (**ṃeṇakjan**). Hat block form, any mold, any form.

ṃōṇakṇak (**ṃeṇakṇak**). 1(*-i*), 2(inf, tr *-e*), 3, 6(*-i*), 7, 8, 9. Brown; withered; dry; spoiled from overexposure to air and sun. *Ek ṃōṇakṇak.* Dried fish. *Pāāt ṃōṇakṇak.* Low, low tide (dry).

ṃōṇakṇak (**ṃeṇakṇak**). A fish, file fish, *Amanses carolae*; *Aleutra scripta.*

ṃōṇe (**ṃeṇey**). That house (close to you); house, demonstrative second person singular.

ṃōṇeṇe (**ṃeṇeyṇey**). That house (close to you); houses, demonstrative second person singular, singling out.

ṃōṇōjṇōj (**ṃeṇejṇej**). Dial. E only; see *bbōṇōjṇōj* (**bbeṇejṇej**). 1(*-i*), 2, 3, 7, 8, 9. Itch.

ṃōṇōṇō (**ṃeṇehṇeh**). 1(*-i*), 2, 3(inf, tr *-ik*), 5(*ṃṃōṇōṇō*), 7, 8, 9. Happy; amusement; gay; glad; joy; pleasure. *Eḷap aō ṃōṇōṇō.* I'm very happy.

ṃōn̄ā (**ṃegay**). 1(*-i*), 2(inf, tr *kan̄ (W), kan(E)*), 3, 4, 5(*ṃṃōn̄āne*), 6(*-i*), 7. Food; eat; diet; grub; meal; nutrition; erode. *Eṃōj ṇe aṃ ṃṃōn̄āne?* Why don't you stop eating all the time? *Ear ṃōn̄ā ek eo koṇa.* He ate of my fish. *Ear kan̄ ek eo koṇa.* He ate my fish. *Kwōn lale aṃ ṃōn̄ā bwe kotōn̄al.* Watch your diet because you've got diabetes. *Ṇo ekan̄e āneo.* Waves eroded the island.

ṃōn̄āin kōjab (**ṃegayin kejab**). Also *ṃōn̄ein kōjab.* 4, 6(*-i*). Farewell dinner; last supper; banquet. *Rūkaḷoor ro raar ṃōn̄āin kōjab ippān Kūraij.* The apostles ate the last supper with Christ. *Raar ṃōn̄āin kōjab ippān ṃokta jān an ilān tariṇae.* They ate a farewell dinner with him before he went off to war.

ṃōn̄ān̄e (**ṃegaygẹy**). From *ṃōn̄ā* (**ṃegay**). 2, 3(inf, tr *-ik*), 6(*-i*). Expand; extend; increase. *Eṃōn̄ān̄e kijeek eo.* The fire expanded.

ṃōn̄ein kōtaan awa (**ṃẹgẹyin ketahan hawah**). Idiom. Snack.

ṃōn̄ka (**ṃegkah**). 1(*-i*), 2, 3, 4, 7. Cartoon; caricature; comic. *Ṃōn̄ka men eṇ.* He's a joker.

ṃōraṃrōṃ (**ṃeraṃrẹṃ**). 2, 3(inf *kōṃṃōraṃrōṃ,* tr *kōṃōraṃrōṃ*), 5(*ṃṃōraṃrōṃ*), 6(*-i*), 8, 9. Landslide; disintegrate; crumble; crumb; dilapidated. *Eṃōraṃrōṃ laḷtak tōrerein toḷ eo.* There was a landslide on the side of the mountain. *Enaaj ṃṃōraṃrōṃḷọk em maat.* It'll keep crumbling till it finally disintegrates.

ṃōrā (**ṃeray**). 1(*-i*), 2, 3(inf, tr *kōṃōrāik*), 5(*ṃṃōrāre*), 7, 8, 9, 11(*ṃōrāre*). Dry; withered; dehydrated. *Eṃōrā kane kaṇe.* Those pieces of firewood are dry. *Kane ṃōrāre men kā.* These pieces of firewood are very dry. *Ejino ṃṃōrāre nuknuk kā aō.* My clothes are beginning to dry (in certain places).

ṃōrā-bōjbōj (**ṃeray-bejbej**). 1(*-i*), 2, 3, 7, 8, 9. Dry throat; husky voice. *Eḷap aō ṃōrā-bōjbōj.* My throat is very dry.

ṃōrābōt (**ṃeraybet**). Also *ṃōrābat* (**ṃeraybat**). Wear wet clothing. *Kwōn jab ṃōrābōt bwe kwōnaaj nañinmej.* Don't wear wet clothes or you'll get sick.

ṃōre (**ṃeṛey**). Formant in place names; gone forth. *Eṃōre iōñ.* He went away northward.

ṃōrṃōr (**ṃeṛṃeṛ**). 1(*-i*), 2, 5(*ṃōrṃōre*), 7, 8, 9. Foam; foaming; froth. *Eḷap an ṃōrṃōr lik kōn an ḷap ṇo.* There is lots of foam at the ocean side due to the big waves.

ṃōrō (**ṃehreh**). From Engl. *murder*. 2, 3(inf, tr *-ik, -ūk*), 6(*-i*), 8, 9. Murder; to kill; murderer; murderous; to assassinate; criminal; mean. *Raar ṃōrōik ledik eo.* Someone murdered the girl. *Ein kōjällin wōt ṃōrō.* He looks like a criminal. *Jab etal ippān bwe eṃōrō.* Don't hang around with him because he's mean.

ṃōrōn (**ṃeren**). Color of. *Ṃōrōt?* What color".

ṃōt (**ṃeṭ**). Also *ṃṃōt* (**ṃṃeṭ**). 1(*-i*), 2, 3, 5(*ṃṃōtṃōt*), 7. Plunge of a canoe or ship; ride the waves; pitch, of a boat. *Eṃōt wa eṇ.* That vessel is riding the waves. *Eṃṃōtṃōt wa eṇ.* That ship keeps riding the waves.

ṃōt (**ṃeṭ**). 1, 2(inf, tr *-e*), 4, 6(*-i*). To drink from a well or a hole in a tree by bending over and using the mouth directly; birds feeding on surface of the ocean, diving and flying up again. *Jońan an kar maro, ej itok wōt ak eṃōt ilo aebōj eo.* He was so thirsty he dove his head into the well and started drinking.

ṃōt (**ṃet**). Also *ṃōta* (**ṃetah**). What house? *Ṃōta iaan ṃōkā?* Which one of these houses?

ṃōtal (**ṃetal**). A fish, goatfish, *Parupeneus barberinus.*

ṃōtañ (**ṃetag**). Also *ṃatañ* (**ṃatag**). 1(*-i*), 2, 4, 6(*-i*), 8, 9. Handsome; beautiful; attractive. *Jońan an ṃōtañ, ebōk jān menowa.* She was so beautiful, she left me breathless. *Kwōmake ṃōtañ.* How beautiful you are.

ṃōtato (**ṃetahtẹw**). Dial. W only; see *batōñtōñ* (**bahteg°teg°**). 1(*-i*), 2, 3, 7. Sobbing because of grief. *Eḷap an ṃōtato lio.* She is sobbing because of her grief.

ṃōto (**ṃetew**). Come up; rise.

ṃōtodān (**ṃetewdan**). From *ṃōto* "come up, *dān* "water". Name of a current.

ṃōtọdik (**ṃetawdik**). Drizzle; mist.

ṃōtta- (**ṃetta-**). 1, 7. Part; piece; fraction; partner; companion; associate; comrade; member; pal; portion; remnant; section of. *Eor ke ṃōttan nuknuk?* Is there a piece of cloth? *Eor ke ṃōttan aḷaḷ?* Is there a piece of wood?

ṃōttaalia (**ṃettahaliyah**). From Engl. Medallion; medal.

ṃōttan. See *ṃōtta-.*

ṃōttan jidik (**ṃettan jidik**). 7. Soon; almost; in a little bit; shortly.

ṃōttawi (**ṃettahwiy**). From *ṃōtta* "my partner", *ewi* where is (s)he? A game, making holes in sand and covering them; hiding black coral in one and saying *ṃōttawi.*

ṃukko (**ṃiqqẹw**). From Japn. *mokko* "basket". 2(inf, tr *-uk*), 4, 6(*-i*), 7. Sling for hoisting cargo; hoist by sling; cargo net. *Raar ṃukkouk ānetak juon tōn in waini.* They hoisted a one-ton sling of copra ashore.

ṃukṃuk (**ṃiqṃiq**). 1(*-i*), 2(inf, tr *ṃukwe*), 3, 4, 7. Rub clothes in washing; rinse clothes. *Kwōn ṃukwe nuknuk ṇe.* Rub that piece of clothing. *Lio eṇ ej ṃukṃuk nuknuk.* She is rubbing clothes.

ṃukwe (**ṃiqey**). Transitive form of *ṃukṃuk* (**ṃiqṃiq**).

ṃuḷe (**ṃiḷ°ẹy**). 3, 6(*-i*). A bird, Micronesian pigeon, *Ducula oceanica*; pigeon; dove.

ṃupi (**ṃiwpiy**). From Engl. 1(*-i*), 2(inf, tr *-ik*), 3, 4, 6(*-i*), 7. A movie; to see a movie. *Iiọkwe bwe in kar ṃupiiki koṃro.* I wish I had a movie camera so I could take a picture of you two.

ṃur (**ṃir°**). Also *ep* (**yẹp**). 1(*-i*). Hip; loin.

ṃur (**ṃir°**). Ancient chant; start fighting. *Jar eo ej itok in ṃur.* The group is coming to start fighting.

m̧ur (**m̧ir°**). Appear.

m̧ur (**m̧ir°**). 6(*m̧urun, m̧uri*). Flock, school. *M̧urun keār.* A flock of gulls. *M̧urun māntōl.* A flock of shearwater.

m̧uri (**m̧ir°iy**). 1(*-i*), 2(inf, tr *-ik*), 3(inf *kam̧m̧urirwi,* tr *-ik*), 4, 5(*m̧m̧urirwi*), 6(*-i*), 7. Owe; debt; liability. *Eļap am̧ m̧uri ippa.* You owe me quite a bit. *Imaroñ ke m̧uriik juon taļa ippam̧?* Can I borrow a dollar from you? *Kwōmaroñ ke kam̧uriik e juon taļa?* Can you loan him a dollar? *Kōjro etal in kam̧m̧urirwi.* Let's go collect debts. *Em̧m̧uriri ļeeņ.* He's always in debt.

m̧uriej (**m̧ir°iyęj**). Also *m̧urlōñ* (**m̧ir°lęg**). 1(*-i*), 2, 3, 4, 7, 8, 9. Wear pants high on hips. *Eļap an m̧uriej.* He wears his pants high on his hips.

m̧urlōñ (**m̧ir°lęg**). Variant form of *m̧uriej* (**m̧ir°iyęj**).

m̧uuj (**m̧iwij**). Pile up plant materials.

m̧ūļōñ (**m̧iļęg**). Shoot of the bird's nest fern (*kartōp*).

m̧ūm̧-. See *m̧m̧-*.

m̧ūrar (**m̧irar**). 1(*-i*), 2, 3, 4, 5(*m̧m̧ūrarrar*), 7, 8, 9. Reddish color. *Em̧ūrar kooļan bōran lieņ.* Her hair is red. *Em̧m̧ūrarrar kooļan bōran riAmedka.* Lots of Americans have blond hair.

m̧ūt (**m̧it**). Grip; hang on.

m̧ūtok (**m̧iteq**). Darkness.

m̧ūtō- (**m̧ite-**). 1, 6(*-e*). Style; actions; antics; disposition; behavior. *Kwōn bar lale m̧ūtōn bwebwe eņ.* Observe the antics of that nut. *Em̧m̧an m̧ūtōn an eb.* He's got good dancing form. *Ebar nana m̧ūtōn kijak ņe.* That chap's back in the dumps again.

m̧wājek (**m̧ayjęk**). Variant form of *m̧aijek* (**m̧ahyijęk**).

m̧wām̧wā (**m̧aym̧ay**). Eat, food, child speech.

m̧we (**m̧ęy**). This house (close to me); house; demonstrative first person exclusive singular.

m̧we (**m̧ęy**). Brown coconut leaves which fall. *Em̧we bōlōk kaņ.* Those leaves are brown.

Mwe-toļoñ.

m̧weawi (**m̧eyhawiy**). A sudden wind.

m̧weeaar (**m̧ęyyahar**). 1(*-i*), 2, 3, 7. Enter lagoon; go in a passage. *Em̧weeaar tim̧a eo.* The ship has entered the lagoon.

m̧weed (**m̧eyed**). 2, 3(st inf *kam̧m̧weeded,* tr *kam̧weed*), 5(*m̧m̧weeded*), 6(*-i*), 8, 9. Disenheartened; lose enthusiasm; be fed up; give up; alienated; disenchanted. *Im̧weed kōn m̧anit kaņ an.* I'm fed-up with his actions. *Kwōn jab kōņaan m̧m̧weeded.* Don't lose heart so easily. *Im̧weed.* I give up.

m̧weeņ (**m̧eyeņ**). That house (close to neither of us); house, demonstrative third person singular.

m̧weieņ (**m̧ęyiyeņ**). That house (close to neither of us); house; demonstrative third person singular; singling out.

m̧weiie (**m̧ęyiyyey**). 1(*-i*), 2, 3, 4, 7, 8, 9. Rich; wealthy; opulent; well-to-do.

m̧weiō (**m̧ęyiyęh**). This house (close to me); house; demonstrative first person exclusive singular, singling out.

m̧weiuk (**m̧ęyiq**). 1(*m̧weie-*), 3, 5(*kam̧m̧weiukiuk*), 6(*-i*). Goods; provisions; wealth; gifts; baggage; cargo; equipment; merchandise; property. *Ia ņe kwōj kam̧m̧weiukiuk ñane?* Where are you packing your belongings to go to?

m̧weiur (**m̧ęyir°**). 1(*-1*), 2, 3(inf, tr *-i*), 6(*-i*). Quake; jolted; shocked; startled; be shaken by recoil of a gun; jarred. *Kōm ar eñjake an m̧weiur laļ ke ej wōtlǫk baam̧ eo iPikinni.* We could feel the ground quaking when the H-bomb was dropped at Bikini Atoll. *Em̧weiur ke ej bu kōn bu eo.* He was shaken by the recoil of the gun when he shot it.

m̧weiur (**m̧ęyir°**). 6(*-i*). Canoe part, piece of wood between *apit* and *jojo, below the kie. Ej ļame m̧weiur eo m̧weirun akadik eo.* He's hewing the *m̧weiur* for the newly constructed canoe. *Kwōnañin kōm̧m̧ane ke m̧weiur eo?* Have you fixed the *m̧weiur*?

m̧welik (**m̧eylik**). 1(*-i*), 2, 3, 5(*m̧m̧weliklik*), 7. Leave lagoon; go out a passage. *Wa eo em̧m̧weliklik eņ.* That boat is always setting out to sea.

m̧weo (**m̧eyew**). The house (often not present); this house (close to me); house, demonstrative third person singular abstract.

m̧wi (**m̧iy**). 1, 2(inf, tr *-ik*), 5(*m̧m̧wim̧wi*), 6(*-i*). Defecate, of children; soft bits of feces. *Niñniñ eo* *ear m̧wiik kal̩ eo an.* The baby dirtied its diaper.

m̧wiañ (m̧iyag). 6(-*i*). Major branch of a tree and its contents. *Elōñ mā ilo m̧wiañ ņe ej jittol̩ok.* There are lots of breadfruit on the branch pointing westward.

m̧wid (m̧id). Archaic. Worn-out woven things.

m̧wiin (m̧iyin). This house (close to us both); house, demonstrative first person inclusive singular. *Ekāāl m̧wiin.* This house is new.

m̧wijbar (m̧ijbar). Also *m̧ōjbar* (m̧ejbar). 1(-*i*), 2(inf, tr -*e*), 3, 4, 5(*m̧m̧wijbarbar*), 7, 8. Cut hair; haircut; to shear; trim. *L̩eo em̧m̧wijbarbar ņe.* That fellow is always getting his hair cut. *Ewi rūm̧wijbar eo?* Where is the barber?

m̧wijit (m̧ijit). Transitive form of *m̧wijm̧wij* (m̧ijm̧ij).

m̧wijju (m̧ijjiw). 2, 4. A game, hide-and-seek. *Itok kōjro m̧wijju.* Come let's play hide and seek.

m̧wijkōk (m̧ijkȩk). 1(-*i*), 2(inf, tr -*e*), 3, 5(*m̧m̧wijkōkkōk*), 7. Break, as a rope; severed. *Em̧m̧wijkōkkōk to ņe.* That rope is always breaking.

m̧wijm̧wij (m̧ijm̧ij). Dial. W, E: *bukwabok* (biqabeq). Also *m̧ōjm̧ōj* (m̧ejm̧ej). 1(-*i*), 2(inf, tr *m̧wijit*), 4, 6(-*i*), 7, 10(*m̧wijm̧wij*). Cut; slit; incision; surgery. *Em̧wijm̧wij peiū.* My hand is cut. *Ta ņe ear m̧wijit peim̧?* What cut your hand? *El̩ap wōt ņe m̧wijm̧wij.* How big that incision scar is.

m̧wil (m̧il). 1(-*i*). Act; behavior; manner; conduct. *Em̧m̧an m̧wilin.* He is well behaved.

m̧wil in jiip (m̧il yin jiyip). Idiom. 1, 2, 6(-*i*), 8, 9. Hypocritical; two-faced. *Em̧wil in jiip lieņ.* She's a hypocrite. *Imake bwilōñ kōn an m̧wil in jiip.* I'm quite shocked at her two-facedness.

m̧wilal̩ (m̧ilal̩). 3, 6(-*i*), 8, 9. Deep; profound. *Em̧wilal̩ roñ ņe.* That hole is deep. *Juon ņe l̩ōmņak m̧wilal̩.* That's a profound thought.

m̧wilal̩ bōro (m̧ilal̩ bȩrȩw). Idiom. 1(...*būruo*-), 2. Inscrutable. *Em̧wilal̩ būruon.* He's inscrutable.

m̧wilik (m̧ilik). Place where frigate birds sleep in trees.

m̧wina (m̧inah). Also *awiia* (hawiyyah). 6(-*i*). A game.

m̧winam̧ōn (m̧inam̧en). 3, 6(-*i*). Caterpillar. *M̧winam̧ōn rej erom babbūb.* Caterpillars become butterflies.

m̧wio (m̧iyew). Also *m̧wieo.* Coconut leaf chain used in fishing as scarer.

m̧witaak (m̧itahak). 2, 3(inf *kam̧m̧witaak*, tr *kam̧witaake*), 4, 6(-*i*). Pitch; rock; yaw; go aground; strike a wave. *Alikkar an l̩l̩ap ņo jān an kajoor m̧witaakin wa in.* It's obviously choppy today from the pitching of the boat.

m̧witok (m̧iteq). Darkness; dark.

naaj (nahaj). Also *nāj* (naj). 2, 7. Will be; future tense marker; shall. *Kwōnaaj etal ñāāt?* When will you go?

naajdik (nahajdik). Also *naajdiñ* (nahajdig). 1(-*i*), 2(inf, tr -*i*), 4, 7. To feed; nourish. *Kwaar naajdik ke piik?* Did you feed the pigs?

naajdiñ (nahajdig). Variant form of *naajdik* (nahajdik).

naal̩ (nahal̩). Archaic. Splinter, chip.

naan (nahan). 5(*nnaan*), 7. Word. *Ewi nnaan?* What's new?

naan jekdoon (nahan jekdawan). 6(-*i*). Lies; false promises; gossip.

naan mera (nahan merah). Idiom. 1(-*i*), 2(inf, tr -*ik*), 6(-*i*). Soft spoken; euphemism. *Enaan mera likao eņ.* He's a soft-spoken man.

nabbe (nabbȩy). Archaic. Ugly.

nabōj (nabȩj). 1(-*i*), 7. Outside; exterior; open air. *Ajri ro raņ rej kkure nabōj.* The children are playing outside there.

nakdid (nakdid). Dialectal variant of *kōtkōt* (ketket).

Nakwōpe (nahqepey). Archaic. Name of a navigational sign; near *Wōja* islet, Ailinglaplap. *Kōm̧m̧akūtkūt ke dikdik ko, ilikin Nakwōpe em̧m̧an o.* The small porpoises are in motion, off *Nakwōpe* everything's fine for the *o* birds (to feed). (Words from a chant about the sign.)

nam̧ (nam̧). Secondary lagoon.

nam̧nam̧ (nam̧nam̧). 1(-*i*), 2, 3, 7. Wash bottles.

nam̧noor (nam̧nȩwȩr). 6(-*i*). Ramrod. *Wiaakl̩ok joot ņe am̧ kōn nam̧noor ņe.* Insert your bullet with your ramrod.

nam̧onam̧o (**nam̧ęwnam̧ęw**). Variant form of *minor* (**minęr°**).

nam̧ōļ (**nameļ**). 2(inf, tr *-e*), 4, 5(*nnam̧ōļmōļ*), 6(*-i*), 7. Ladle, scoop food. *Ejaje nam̧ōļ raij.* He can't scoop out rice properly. *Nam̧ōl(e) tok kijerro kūrepe.* Scoop out some gravy for us.

nana (**nahnah**). 1(*-i*), 2, 3(inf, tr *-ik*), 4, 7, 8, 9, 11(*nana*). Bad; wicked; evil. *Ear kōnanaik eō.* He corrupted me. He said bad things about me (which are not true).

nana (**nahnah**). 3, 6(*-i*). A bird, red-footed booby, *Sula sula.*

nana kobban lo̧ñii- (**nahnah qebban lawgiyi-**). 1, 2, 9. Foul-mouthed. *Kwōnaaj deñdeñ ñe enana kobban lo̧ñiim̧.* You'll get a spanking if you talk bad.

nana tam̧m̧wi- (**nahnah tam̧m̧i-**). 1, 2, 6(*-i*), 7. Grouchy; threatening; in a bad mood; moody; disadvantage; uneasy; wretched; awful; rowdy. *Āinwōt enana tam̧m̧win lañ.* The weather seems to be threatening. *Enana tam̧m̧win ñe ej kadek.* He gets moody when he's drunk.

nañin (**nahgin**). 2. Almost; ever; nearly. *Enañin m̧ōj ke wa eo?* Is the boat almost finished? *Kwōnañin ke pād Pikaar?* Have you (ever) been to Bikar atoll? *Enañin m̧ōj wōt jidik.* It's nearly finished.

nañinmej (**nahginmęj**). 1(*-i*), 2, 3, 4, 5(*nnañinmejmej*), 7, 8, 9. Sick; sickness; pregnant; ill; plague; disease; ailing. *Ennañinmejmej ļeeņ.* He is always getting sick.

Nawōdo (**nahwedew**). 4. Place name; Nauru.

nāj (**naj**). Variant form of *naaj* (**nahaj**).

nāji (**najiy**). Dial. E, W: *neji* (**nęjiy**). 1(*-i*), 2(inf, tr *-ik*), 3, 6(*-i*). Duty of taking care of a natural or adopted child or pet or domesticated animal. *Ij nājiik ak e.* I'm keeping this frigate bird as a pet. *Nājiin wōn bao e?* Who domesticated this bird? *Nājiū.* I raised it as a pet. I adopted it.

nāji- (**naji-**). Dial. E, W: *neji* (**nęji-**). 1. Son of; daughter of; child of; toy of; pet of; money of; offspring of; son or daughter-in-law of; possessive classifier, children, pets, money, watches, or Bible.

nājnej (**najnęj**). From *nāji-* (**naji-**). 1(*-i*), 2, 3, 4, 7. To keep as a pet; pet. *Ikōņaan wōt nājnej kidu jān kuuj.* I prefer dogs to cats as pets.

nāl (**nal**). 1(*-i*), 2, 3, 6(*-i*), 8, 9. Bone dry; dehydrated. *Enāl bwiro in.* This preserved breadfruit is dry. *Kwōjaam̧ kōnāle?* Why do you dehydrate it?

nām (**nam**). 1(*nema-*), 4(*rināme*), 5(*nāme*), 6(*nemān, nemā*), 7+1. Smell; taste; flavor; odor; scent; smelly. *Enno̧ nemān m̧ōñā ņe.* The taste of that food is delicious. *Nemān uwi in ea in ej jāālel tok?* Where is the smell of cooking fish wafting this way from? *Enāme ek ņe.* That fish is smelly.

nāmnām (**namnam**). 1(*-i*), 2(inf, tr nemak(ey), 3(inf, tr *-e*), 4, 5(*nemnemake*). Taste; smell. *Kwōn nemak m̧ōk m̧ōñā ņe enno̧ ke.* Taste that food to see if it's good. *Kidu eo ejeļā kōnāmnām ņe.* That's the dog with the good sense of smell. *Ta ņe kwōj kōnāmnāme?* What are you sniffing around for?

nānnān (**nannan**). 1(*-i*), 2, 3(inf, tr *-e*), 8, 9. Stale.

nāpe (**napęy**). From Japn. *nabe*. 6(*-i*). Cooking pan.

nāpnāpe (**napnapęy**). 1(*-i*), 2(inf, tr *-ik(i)*), 4, 6(*-i*), 7. A food, ripe breadfruit mixed with coconut oil and cooked in pots. *Kwaar kkatak ia nāpnāpe?* Where did you learn how to prepare *nāpnāpe*?

ne (**ney**). 1(*-e*). Leg; foot; wheel; paw; cartwheel.

ne m̧akūtkūt (**ney m̧akitkit**). 1(*-i*), 2, 3, 4, 7, 8, 9. Moving from one place to another; unable to keep still.

neen kōbkōb (**neyen kębkęb**). 2, 3, 6(*-i*), 7, 8, 9. Feet sink in sand making for difficult walking. *Eneen kōbkōb iarin ānin.* It's hard to walk along the lagoon beach of this islet.

neen kōtkōt (**neyen ketket**). From *neen* (**neyen**) "legs of", *kōtkōt* (**ketket**) "sea bird: noddy". 3, 6(*-i*). A plant, *Fleurya ruderalis* (Forst. F.) Gaudichaud. (Urticaceae). A red-stemmed weedy herb.

neen wūliej (**neyen wilyęj**). From *ne* (**ney**) "foot", *wūliej* (**wilyęj**) "graveyard" (Walking through graveyards is forbidden.) 2, 6(*-i*), 9. Taboo breaker. *Ear neen wūliej im ļōke irooj* *eo.* He broke a taboo and walked over the king.

neji (**nẹjiy**). Dialectal variant of *nāji* (**najiy**).

nel (**nel**). To dry under the sun; copra or fish. *Kanel waini ṇe.* Dry that copra under the sun.

nemak (**nemak**). Transitive form of *nāmnām* (**namnam**).

nemāmei- (**nemaymẹyi-**). 1, 7. Likeness; image; appearance; resemblance. *Enañin āin nemāmeen lieṇ wōt lio jein.* That girl is almost exactly the likeness of her older sister. *Ein nemāmein ledik eṇ wōt jinen.* That girl looks like her mother.

nemwak (**nemwak**). 1(*-i*), 2, 6(*-i*), 7, 8, 9. Not hairy, not feathery. *Enemwak bao eṇ.* That chicken doesn't have a lot of feathers. *Enemwak neen bwe ear reja.* Her legs are smooth because she shaved them.

nen (**nẹn**). 3, 6(*-i*). A plant, *Morinda citrifolia* L. (Rubiaceae). A tree with large simple leaves; flowers borne on a semispherical base; white fleshy fruits.

nen-. See *nn-*.

nep (**nep**). Deluge.

nepi (**nẹypiy**). From Engl. Navy.

netūbtūb (**neytibtib**). 1, 2, 4, 6(*-i*), 7, 8, 9. Quick short steps. *Enañin aolep kōrāin Jepaan rōnetūbtūb.* Most all Japanese women walk in quick, short steps.

ni (**niy**). 6(*-i*). A plant, general term for all varieties of coconut trees and fruit; a coconut tree.

Ni Bōn (**niy bẹn**). A plant, coconut variety.

Ni Būrōrō (**niy birehreh**). 6(*-i*). A plant, coconut variety.

Ni Iaḷo (**niy yi'yaḷẹw**). From Engl. *yellow*. A plant, coconut.

Ni Kadu (**niy kadiw**). 3, 6(*-i*). A plant, coconut variety.

ni kenato (**niy keynahtew**). A plant, tall coconut palm.

Ni Lọurō (**niy lawireh**). 6(*-i*). A plant, coconut variety.

Ni Lōklōk (**niy leklek**). From *lōklōk* (**leklek**) "thorn; name of a grass". A plant, coconut variety (Takeuchi).

Ni Maro (**niy mahrew**). 3, 6(*-i*). A plant, coconut variety.

Ni Mir (**niy mir**). 3, 6(*-i*). A plant, coconut variety.

Ni Mouj (**niy mẹwij**). From *mouj* (**mẹwij**). A plant, coconut variety (Takeuchi).

Ni M̧ōl (**niy m̧ẹl**). 3, 6(*-i*). A plant, coconut variety.

Ni Ram (**niy ram**). 3, 6(*-i*). A plant, coconut variety (Takeuchi).

nib (**nib**). 2, 5(*nnibnib*), 6(*-i*). Preemptive. *Ennibnib.* He's always trying to outdo everyone.

Nibboñ (**nibbeg°**). From Japn. *nippon.* 4. Japan.

Nibuñ (**nibig°**). 3, 6(*-i*). A plant, *Pandanus fischerianus* cultigen. (Stone). Wotje, etc.

nieded (**niyẹdyẹd**). 1(*-i*), 2, 3, 7. Mat worn as clothing.

nien (**niyen**). Construct form of *nne* (**nnẹy**).

niiddoor (**niyiddẹwẹr**). Also *niieddoor* (**niyyẹddẹwẹr**). 2(inf, tr *-e*), 4, 6(*-i*), 7. Coconuts still attached to spathe and lowered from tree by means of a rope. *Rej niiddoor ḷọk limen ruwamāejet raṇ.* They're doing the *niiddoor* method for the guests.

niikro (**niyikrẹw**). From Engl. Negro.

niiḷ (**niyiḷ**). From Engl. 6(*-i*). Needle; straight pin.

niim̧bu (**niyim̧biw**). From Japn. *ninpu*. 2, 6(*-i*). Laborer.

nikāi (**niykayiy**). From Japn. *nikai* "second floor". 6(*-i*). Two-story house.

niknik (**niknik**). 1(*-i*), 2, 3, 4, 7, 8, 9. Industrious; diligent; hard working. *Eḷap an niknik ḷeo.* He is quite industrious.

nikoko (**niykẹwkẹw**). Variant form of *ninikoko* (**niyniykẹwkẹw**).

nikōḷ (**nikeḷ**). From Engl. Nickel.

nime- (**nime-**). Variant form of *lime-* (**lime-**).

nimuur (**niymiwir**). Coconut tree loaded with nuts.

nin (**nin**). 1(*-i*), 2(inf, tr *-i*), 4, 7. Pound. *Em̧ōj ke an nin maañ kā?* Have these pandanus leaves been pounded? *Kwōn nini maañ kaṇe.* Pound those pandanus leaves.

ninārār (**ninyaryar**). 2, 3(inf, tr *-e*), 6(*-i*), 8, 9. Steady waves buffeting the shore.

nine (**ninẹy**). 1(*nie-*), 2, 3(*kanne*), 5(*kkanne*), 6(*nien*), 7. Container; use as a container; sheath. *Enaaj nine kōn at e aō.* He'll use my hat for a container. *Kanne bato ṇe kōn jimañūñ.* Fill that bottle with toddy. *Raar kkanne limeer dān jān aebōj eṇ.* They drew water from the well. *Eor nien ittūt in wia Mieko.* There are bras for sale at MIECO.

ninikoko (**niyniykẹwkẹw**). Also *nikoko* (**niykẹwkẹw**). 2(inf, tr *-uk*), 6(*-i*). Drink while eating; two or more persons sharing one coconut. *Itok kōjeañ ninikoko.* Come let's eat and drink.

ninjek (**ninjẹk**). 3, 8, 9. Very dark. *Eḷap an ninjek buñniin.* It's very dark tonight.

ninnin (**ninnin**). 1(*-i*), 2(inf, tr *-i*), 3, 4, 7. Suck; breast; suckle. *Niñniñ eo ej ninnin ilo ninnin ko limen.* The baby is getting its milk from the breasts.

ninninkoko (**ninninkewkew**). Also *ninkoko.* Share a drink.

niñ (**nig**). 1(*-i*), 2, 3, 7, 8, 9, 11(sg. *niñniñ, jiniñniñ,* pl. *nniñ, jinniñ*). Small; young; little; tiny; puny.

niña (**nigah**). Dial. W, E: *niñeañ* (**nigyag**). Northward; directional, enclitic, northward. *Kōjro jaṃbo niñawaj.* Let's take a stroll to the north end of the island.

niñeañ (**nigyag**). Dial. E, W: *niña* (**nigah**). Directional, enclitic northward.

niñniñ (**nignig**). 1(*-i*), 2, 3, 6(*-i*). Baby; infant. *Niñniñ eo ej ninnin ippān jinen.* The baby is sucking from its mother.

niñniñ (**nignig**). 2, 4, 6(*-i*). A game, underwater football using a rock for a ball.

nit (**nit**). 6(*-i*). Pit for bird fight; sunken enclosure.

nitbwil (**nitbil**). 1(*-i*), 2(inf, tr *nitbwilli*). Surround; beseige a city; assault; attack.

nitijeḷā (**nitiyjeḷay**). 1, 2(inf, tr *-iki*), 4, 6(*-i*). A law-making body; to legislate; legislature. *Ta eṇ rej nitijeḷāiki rainin?* What are they going to legislate upon today?

nitñil (**nitgil**). Also *ñilñil* (**gilgil**). 1(*-i*), 2, 3, 6(*-i*), 8, 9. Hot and close; stuffy. *Enitñil lowaan ṃwiin.* It is hot and close in this house.

nitōḷ (**niteḷ**). Also *nitōḷ* (**niyteḷ**). From Engl. 6(*-i*). Needle.

nnaan (**nnahan**). Dial. W: *ennaan* (**yennahan**), E: *nenaan* (**nenahan**). 1(*-i*), 7. News; message; distributive form of *naan* (**nahan**).

nnān (**nnan**). Dial. W: *ennān* (**yennan**), E: *nenān* (**nenan**). 1(*-i*), 2, 3, 7. Musty taste; moldy taste; stale; rancid. *Eḷap an nnān pilawā ṇe.* That bread is moldy.

nnọ (**nnaw**). Dial. W: *ennọ* (**yennaw**), E: *nenọ* (**nenaw**). 2, 3(inf, tr *-ik, -uk*), 6(*-i*), 8, 9, 11(*nnọno*). Delicious; taste good; luscious; tasty; scrumptious; delightful.

nnōk (**nnek**). Dial. W: *ennōk* (**yennek**), E: *nenōk* (**nenek**). 1(*-i*), 2(inf, tr *enōk(e)*), 4, 6(*-i*), 7. Knock down coconuts from tree; pile of coconuts knocked down from tree. *Nnōkin wōn in?* Who knocked these coconuts down?

nnōk (**nnẹk**). 1(*-i*), 2, 3(inf, tr *-e*), 4, 5(*nnōke*), 6(*-i*), 7. Provisions for a voyage. *Ennōkin wōn kein?* Who prepared these provisions? *Ennōke wa eo.* The canoe was well stocked.

nnōōr (**nneher**). Dial. W: *ennōōr* (**yenneher**), E: *nenōōr* (**neneher**). 1(*-i*), 2(inf, tr *nōōr(e)*), 5(*nōnōōr*), 6(*-i*), 7. Pull; withdraw. *Eḷap nnōōr ilo jurbak.* There's a lot of pulling in dancing the jitterbug. *Nōōre waj kimej ṇe.* Pull that frond over.

no (**new**). Transitive form of *nono* (**newnew**).

Nobōṃba (**newbeṃbah**). Also *Nopeṃba* (**newpeṃbah**). From Engl. November.

nokjek (**nẹqjẹk**). 1(*-i*), 2, 3, 5(*nnokjekjek*), 7, 8, 9. Mussed up; wrinkled; perfective form of *nukuj* (**niqij**); puckered. *Ennokjekjek peba e aō.* This paper of mine is all wrinkled.

nokwōn (**nẹqẹn**). 2, 4, 6(*-i*). Evening prayers (Protestant).

nono (**newnew**). Also *nono* (**nẹwnẹw**). 1(*-i*), 2(inf, tr *no(e)*), 7, 8. Pound.

noonon (**nẹwẹnwẹn**). From *nono* "to pound". Pounded stack of processed pandanus leaves. *Eor jete de noonon eṃōj aṃ noe?* How many stacks have you pounded?

noñ (**neg°**). 2, 3(*kannoñ*), 6(*-i*), 7(*noññōḷọk, nnoñōḷọk*). Popping sound made when squashing lice. *Enoññoḷọk kij eo.* The louse snapped when squashed. *Ennoñoḷọk.* It popped. *Rej kannoñ kij.* They are killing lice.

norōbōtoñ (**newrebeteg°**). Dialectal variant of *jinkōḷar* (**jinkeḷar**).

notoñ (**newteq**). Also *notōñ* (**newteg**), *notañ* (**newtag**). 2(inf, tr *-e*), 4, 6(*-i*), 7. Clobber; strike; hit; spank; pound. *Rōnotoñe rinana eo.* The bad guy got clobbered.

nọọj (**nawaj**). Interiorward of an island and from lagoon side only; directional, enclitic, interiorward. *Ij ja wenọọjtak.* I think I'll take a walk to the interior. *Ear wenọọjḷọk ekkein.* He went toward the interior a little bit ago.

nōbar (**nebar**). 1(*-i*), 2, 3, 4, 5(*nōbnōbare*), 7, 8, 9. Praise; admire; recommend; glorify; compliment; credit; revere.

nōbba (**nebbah**). From Japn. *nappa*. 2(inf, tr *-ik*), 3, 4+3, 5(*nnōbaba*), 6(*-i*), 7. Green vegetables. *Ejaje nōbba ṃōñā.* He can't combine greens with food. *Nōbbaik ḷọk ñan e.* Scramble it with greens for him.

nōkkan (**nekkan**). Variant form of *ennōk*.

nōḷ (**neḷ**). Make weapons. *Ej nōḷ ṃade ñan tariṇae.* He's making spears for battle.

nōṃaiki (**neṃahyikiy**). From Japn. *namaiki*. 1(*-i*), 2, 6(*-i*), 8, 9. Impertinent.

nōṃba (**neṃbah**). From Engl. 1(*-i*), 2(inf, tr *-ik*), 4, 7. Number; figure.

nōnōōr (**nehneher**). Distributive form of *nnōōr* (**nneher**).

Nōñnōñ (**negneg**). A plant, breadfruit variety (Takeuchi).

nōōb (**nẹhẹb**). From Engl. 6(*-i*). Nerve.

nōōj (**nehej**). From Engl. 6(*-i*). Nurse. *Nōōj in ia eṇ?* Where is that nurse from?

nōōr (**neher**). Transitive form of *nnōōr* (**nneher**).

nōr (**ner**). Start to bloom.

nōt (**net, nẹt**). 3, 5(*nnōtnōt*), 6(*-i*). Squid. *Ennōtnōt ar in ānin.* This lagoon is full of squid.

nōt (**net**). A fish, scavenger, *Lethrinus variegatus.*

nukne (**niqnẹy**). From Engl. "*New Guinea*". 3, 6(*-i*). A plant, *Euphorbia heterophylla* L. (Euphobiaceae). A common tropical herbaceous weed. The uppermost leaves are splotched with red at their bases, reminiscent of the poinsettia.

Nukne (**niqney**). From Engl. 4. Place name; New Guinea.

nuknuk (**niqniq**). 1(*-i*), 2, 3(inf, tr *kanuknuk(i)*), 6(*-i*), 7. Clothes; cloth; clothing; dress up; costume; garment. *Kwōn nuknuk bwe jen etal jar.* Dress up because we're going to church. *Kanuknuki bwe epiọ.* Clothe him because he's cold.

nuknukun kuk (**niqniqin qiq**). Apron. *Kōṇak nuknukun kuk eo aṃ.* Put on your apron.

nukuj (**niqij**). 2(inf, tr *-i*), 7, 10(*nokjek*). Fold in a sloppy manner; clench; crumble paper. *Jab nukuji peba kaṇe.* Don't crumble those papers.

nukwi (**niqiy**). 1(*nukwi-*), 2(inf, tr *-ik*), 3, 6(*-i*). Relatives; family; kin; duty towards ones relatives. *Ejjeḷọk nukū eoon ānin.* I don't have any relatives on this islet. *Ejeḷā nukwi.* He knows how to be a proper relative.

nuuj (**niwij**). From Engl. 1(*-i*), 2(inf, tr *-i*), 4. News. *Eṃōj nuuji eok.* You are in the news.

nuujpeba (**niwijpẹybah**). From Engl. 3, 6(*-i*). Newspaper.

ṇa (**ṇah**). Also *ṇai* (**ṇahyiy**). Locative particle. *Iar door bok eo ṇa ioon tebōḷ eo.* I put the book on the table.

ṇa (**ṇah**). Also *kina* (**kinah**). Shoal; exposed and stony bar. *Jen etal in kakkōr ilo ṇa eṇ.* Let's go clamming at that shoal.

ṇab (**ṇab**). Variant form of *ṇọb* (**ṇ°ab**).

ṇaballi- (**ṇahballi-**). 1. To clothe.

Ṇadepak (**ṇahdepak**). 3, 6(*-i*). A plant, pandanus cultigen. Mejit.

ṇae (**ṇahyey**). 7. Against.

ṇaeta- (**ṇahyeta-**). 1. To name; to christen. *Wōn ear ṇaetan wa eṇ?* Who named that boat?

ṇai (**ṇahyiy**). Variant form of *ṇa* (**ṇah**).

ṇaib (**ṇahyib**). From Engl. 2(inf, tr *-i*), 6(*-i*). Pocket knife.

ṇajiki- (**ṇahjiki-**). 1. Make room for.

ṇakaan (**ṇahkahan**). Also *ankaan* (**hankahan**). 2(inf, tr *-e*), 4, 6(*-i*), 7. Feed a fire with firewood; provide fuel for. *Enañin ṃōj ke ṇakaane?* Has somebody fed the fire?

ṇakije- (**ṇahkije-**). 1(-*i*), 4. Provide with food. *Wōn enaaj ṇakijed ṇa āneṇ ñe jenaaj kowainini?* Who'll feed us when we go make copra on that islet?

ṇakinee- (**ṇahkineye-**). 1. Provide a mat for.

ṇakṇōk (**ṇakṇęk**). Also *amam* (**hamham**). 2, 6(-*i*), 8, 9. Wizard; genius; expert; specialist; shaman; witchdoctor; skillful. *Eban jab jeḷā bwe ṇakṇōk.* He's bound to have the answer since he's a wizard.

ṇakọje- (**ṇahkawje-**). Also *ṇakọjee-* (**ṇahkawjeye-**). 1, 4. To provide with a blanket. *Raar ṇakọjen riāneo ālkin taibuun eo.* The islanders were provided with blankets after the typhoon. *Eor ke rūṇakọjeer?* Do they have anybody to give them blankets?

ṇalime- (**ṇahlime-**). 1. Provide drink for.

ṇaḷōma- (**ṇahḷema-**). Give shape to; formulate; provide a framework for.

ṇamāni (**ṇahmaniy**). 3, 6(-*i*). A fish, scavenger, *Lethrinus* sp.

ṇaṃ (**ṇaṃ**). Dial. W only; see *jokwajok* (**jeqajeq**). 2(inf, tr -*e*), 5(*ṇaṃṇaṃ, ṇaṃṇōṃ*), 7, 8, 9, 11(*ṇaṃṇaṃ*). Mosquito. *Eṇaṃṇaṃ ānin.* This islet is full of mosquitoes.

ṇaṃaanpāā- (**ṇahṃahanpaya-**). To arm.

ṇaṃweie- (**ṇahṃęyiye-**). 1. To enrich; give gift to someone; furnish.

ṇaṇ (**ṇaṇ**). Vulgar. 1, 5(*ṇaṇṇaṇ*), 6(-*i*). Smegma.

ṇaṇ (**ṇaṇ**). A fish, tiny surface minnow.

ṇaoṇea- (**ṇahweṇaya-**). Also *ṇawōnea-*. 1(-*i*), 4. Compensate; pay; provide with a wage or salary; to reciprocate. *Raar ṇaoṇān ekkar ñan jeḷā eo an.* He got paid according to his skills.

ṇapitō- (**ṇahpite-**). Provide a pillow for. *Kwōn ṇapitōn bwe ejjeḷọk.* Give him a pillow because he doesn't have any.

ṇaruo- (**ṇahriwe-**). 1, 2+1, 4. Blame. *An bōd eo ak ear ṇaruon likao eo jatin.* It was his fault but he blamed his brother. *Iban ṇaruoṃ.* I won't blame you.

ṇatoon (**ṇahtewen**). Also *ṇatọọn* (**ṇahtawan**). 1(-*i*), 2(inf, tr -*e*), 3, 7, 8. To sheet sails in. *Kwōn ṇatoone wōjḷā ṇe.* Sheet that sail in there. *Rōṇatọọne wa eo.* They sheeted the sails of their boat in.

ṇautō- (**ṇahwite-**). 1(-*i*), 4. Provide with bathing water. *Kwōn ṇautōn ḷọk bwe en tutu.* Give him some water so he can bathe right away. *Ej jab rūṇautōd.* He's not supposed to give us bathing water.

ṇawāwee- (**ṇahwayweye-**). Provide wherewithal; answer someone's question; fulfill someone's request.

ṇe (**ṇey**). That (close to you); demonstrative, second person singular.

ṇeṇe (**ṇeyṇey**). That (close to you); demonstrative, second person singular, singling out.

ṇṇooj (**ṇṇewej**). Dial. W: *eṇṇooj* (**yeṇṇewej**), E: *ṇōṇooj* (**ṇeṇewej**). 1, 2(inf, tr *ṇooj(e)*), 5(*ṇoṇooj*), 6(-*i*), 7, 10(*ṇojak*). Hide; conceal. *Ṇooje peba kaṇe.* Hide the papers. *Ṇoojtok juon limō pia.* Sneak in a beer for me. *Eṇojak.* It's hidden. *Kwōn ṇooj pija ṇe.* Hide that picture.

ṇṇōjṇōj (**ṇṇejṇej**). Dial. W: *eṇṇōjṇōj* (**yeṇṇejṇej**), E: *ṇōṇōjṇōj* (**ṇeṇejṇej**). 1, 2(inf *ṇṇōjṇōj*, tr *ṇōjje*), 3, 4+3, 5(*ṇṇōjṇōj*), 6(-*i*), 7. Snapping or cracking sound. *Jab kaṇṇōjṇōje peiṃ.* Stop cracking your knuckles.

ṇṇōk (**ṇṇek**). Dial. W: *eṇṇōk* (**yeṇṇek**), E: *ṇōṇōk* (**ṇeṇek**). 2, 5(*ṇṇōkṇōk*), 6(-*i*), 8, 9. Sharp pain as from a whip or a burn; sting; pang. *Eṇṇōk peiū ke rej wāiki.* My arm hurt when I got a shot. *Eṇṇōkṇōk ānbwinnū kōn aō kar kakōtkōt buḷōn wōt.* My body stung all over after running through the rain.

ṇo (**ṇęw**). 6(-*i*). A fish; scorpion fish or stone fish, *Scorpaenopsis diabolus/ gibbosa/novaeguineae/macadamsi/ cacopsis/albobrunnea/guamensis/ parvipinnis*; *Synanceja verrucosa*; *Teanianotus triacanthus.*

ṇo (**ṇew**). 1(-*i*), 6(-*i*). A wave; surf. *Lale ṇo kaṇe ṇoun wa eṇ.* Look at the waves coming toward you from that boat.

ṇoj (**ṇ°ej**). Also *ṇōj* (**ṇej**). 2, 3(inf *kaṇojṇoj* tr -*e*), 5(*ṇṇojṇoj*), 6(-*i*), 7(*ṇojjeḷọk*). Snapping sound. *Eor ke aṃ batin ṇṇojṇoj.* Have you got a snap fastener. *Eṇojjeḷọk addiin peiū.* My finger snapped.

ṇojak (**ṇewjak**). Hidden; obscured; perfective form of *ṇṇooj* (**ṇṇewej**).

ṇojọ (**ṇewjaw**). Bow spray; not cut waves well. *Eḷap an ṇojọ wa eṇ.* That boat makes a lot of bow spray.

ṇok (**ṇeq**). Dial. E only; see *tutu* (**tiwtiw**). 1(-*i*), 2, 3, 5(*ṇṇokṇok*), 7, 8, 9,

11(*ṇe*). Wet. *Eṇṇokṇok nuknuk eṇ an ajri eṇ.* That child's clothes are always getting wet.

ṇok (**ṇeq**). 6(*-i*). Midrib of a coconut leaf.

ṇokwanej (**ṇeqanyej**). Also *ṇokneej* (**ṇaqneyej**). 6(*-i*). An animal, centipede.

ṇomṇom (**ṇ°emṇ°em**). 1, 2(inf, tr *ṇome*), 4, 6(*-i*), 7. Suck in hard; siphon. *Ear ṇome kiaaj eo.* He siphoned the gasoline. *Ṇaṃ rej ṇomṇom bōtōktōk.* Mosquitoes suck blood.

ṇompe (**ṇ°ẹmpẹy**). 1, 2, 6(*-i*), 8, 9. Alcoholic; like alcoholic beverages. *Eban tōprak an jikuuḷ kōn an ṇompe.* He won't succeed in school because of his love for alcohol.

ṇoniep (**ṇẹwniyep**). Variant form of *ṇoonniep* (**ṇewenniyep**).

ṇoṇṇoṇmeej (**ṇ°eṇ°ṇ°eṇ°meyej**). 6(*-i*). Bone marrow.

ṇoonniep (**ṇewenniyep**). Also *ṇoniep* (**ṇẹwniyep**). Legendary fairies who fished for red snappers and sometimes fed people; fairy.

ṇop (**ṇ°ep**). Archaic. Container of oil or water for use with royal whetstone.

ṇota (**ṇ°etah**). 1(*-a*), 2(inf, tr *-ik*), 6. Fault; grudge. *Jab lo ṇotaan armej.* Don't criticize others. *Jab ṇotaik eō.* Don't hold a grudge against me.

ṇọb (**ṇ°ab**). Also *ṇab* (**ṇab**). 2, 3(*kọṇṇọbḷọk*), 5(*ṇṇọbṇab*), 6(*-i*). Popping sound. *Eoṇṇọbṇab buḷōn kōḷọk eo.* Popping sounds kept coming out of the forest fire.

ṇọkneej (**ṇaqneyej**). Variant form of *ṇokwanej* (**ṇeqanyej**).

ṇōj (**ṇej**). Variant form of *ṇoj* (**ṇ°ej**).

ṇōṇ-. See *ṇṇ-*.

ña (**gah**). I; pronoun, absolute, first person singular.

ñad (**gad**). 1(*-i*). Gums.

ñade (**gadey**). Transitive form of *ñadñad* (**gadgad**).

ñadñad (**gadgad**). 2, 6(*-i*). Fall on one's bottom; flop.

ñadñad (**gadgad**). 2(inf, tr *ñade*), 4, 6(*-i*). Design edges of canoes or boats.

ñaj (**gaj**). 1(*-i*), 2, 3(*kañajñōj*), 5(*ññajñōj*), 7, 6(*-i*), 8, 9, 11(*ñajñōj*). Fragrant smell. *Ia in ej bwiin ññajñōj tok?* Where is that pervasive fragrance coming from?

ñak (**gak**). Dial. E only; see *jaje* (**jahjẹy**). 1(*-i*), 2, 8, 9. Not know; amateur; novice. *Ñak men ṇe.* He's a lemon. *Iñak.* I don't know.

ñakḷọkjeṇ (**gakḷaqjeṇ**). 1(*-i*), 3, 4, 8, 9. Ignorance; unconscious; sleep soundly. *Eḷap an kar kiki im ñakḷọkjeṇ.* He really slept soundly. *Kwōn jab llu ippān ajri eṇ bwe eñakḷọkjeṇ.* Don't be angry with that child because he is ignorant.

ñal (**gal**). 2(inf, tr *-e*), 4, 6(*-i*), 7. Knead; buffet. *Ñale tok pilawā ṇe.* Knead the dough for me. *Epoktak dekā ko bwe ṇo ko rej ñali.* The stones have been displaced by the buffeting of the waves.

ñan (**gan**). To.

ñañ (**gag**). Dry and brittle.

ñar (**gar**). 1, 6(*-i*). Hard coconut meat remaining in half-shall of sprouted coconut after spongy core has been removed. *Aini ñar kaṇe ñariier.* Collect those *ñar* they left there.

ñarij (**garij**). Transitive form of *ñarñar* (**gargar**).

ñarñar (**gargar**). 2(inf, tr *ñarij*), 6(*-i*). Bite the dust; feed off a surface; take a nose dive. *Eñarñar ek.* The fish are feeding off the reef. *Iar ñarij laḷ.* I bit the dust. *Ear ñarij pileij eo an.* He ate his food without using his hands (or utensils).

ñat (**gat**). 1(*-i*). Palate of mouth. *Ij pojak in bōk mejin bwe emetak ñatū.* I'm about to get a cold because the roof of my mouth hurts.

ñate (**gatey**). Transitive form of *ñatñat.*

ñatñat (**gatgat**). 2(inf, tr *ñate*), 5(*ññatñat*). Unable to stomach something; unable to endure physically. *Iñate ṃupi eo.* I couldn't stomach the movie. *Kwōjjab ñate etal laḷ ke?* Are you able to endure walking?

ñāāt (**gayat**). When? *Ñāāt eṇ wa eṇ ej jerak?* When will the ship sail?

ñe (**gey**). When; if. *Ñe eṃōj aō tutu inaaj ṃōñā.* When I have finished bathing I will eat.

ñe (**gẹy**). A reef separate from main reef; see *kōlñe.*

ñeej (**gęyęj**). Transitive form of *ñeñe* (**gęygęy**).

ñeñe (**gęygęy**). Also *ñeñe* (**geygey**). 1(*-i*), 2(inf, tr *ñeej(e)*), 4, 7. Fathom. *Kwōn ñeej m̧ōk eo ņe im lale jete ñeñe.* Measure that fishline and see how many fathoms it is.

ñeñe (**gęygęy**). Also *ñe.* 3, 6(*-i*). A plant, *Suriana maritima* L. (Simarubaceae). A beach shrub of dryer area, with small yellow flowers and short-lance-ovate leaves in habit similar to *Pemphis* but closest related to *Soulamea* with much larger leaves.

ñi (**giy**). 1(*-i*). Tooth; fang.

ñi (**giy**). Also *kwi* (**qiy**). 1(*-i*), 2, 3, 4, 5(*kañiñi, kaññiñi*). So angry as to resort to revenge. *Ear ñi im m̧ane ļadik eo.* He revenged and killed the boy. *Ekañiñi an kōņanikien.* His horseplay is provoking.

ñiājo (**giyajew**). Archaic. 1(*-i*), 2, 3, 8, 9. To indulge; to gratify; praised; honored.

ñiban (**giyban**). 1, 2, 4, 6(*-i*), 8, 9. Weak teeth. *Eban m̧ōñā raj bwe eñiban.* He can't eat whale meat because he's got weak teeth.

ñiejo (**giyejew**). Favorite child; apple of one's eye. *Ñiejo eo nājin ņe.* That's his favorite daughter.

ñii- (**giyi-**). 1. Tooth of; possessive classifier, tooth or eating utensils.

ñiinpako (**giyinpakew**). 2(inf, tr *-ik(i)*), 4, 6(*-i*), 7. A method of tying sennit on the *m̧weiur* of a canoe. *Kwōmaroñ ke ñiinpakoik tok wa e waarro?* Could you please do the sennit work for our canoe's *m̧weiur*?

ñiitwa (**giyitwah**). Also *ñituwa* (**giytiwah**). 3, 4+3, 5, 6(*-i*), 3+7. A fish, barracuda, *Sphyraena forsteri.*

ñijir (**gijir**). 1(*-i*), 2(inf, tr *-i*), 3, 4, 7. To chant while drawing up a canoe or other such cooperative work.

ñijlǫk (**gijlaq**). 1(*-i*), 2, 3, 7. Groan; to grapple with; finish a task; groaning. *Ļeo eņ ej ñijlǫk kōn an metak bōraņ.* He is groaning from his headache.

ñijlǫk (**gijlaq**). Also *wūnlǫk.* 2, 6(*-i*). Dive after getting hooked, of fish. *Em̧wijm̧wij peiū ilo eo eo ke ek eo ej ñijlǫk.* I cut my hand on the line when the fish dove (down to break away).

ñil (**gil**). 6(*ñillin, ñilli*). Sound.

ñilep (**giylep**). 1(*-a*), 2, 6(*-a*). Wisdom tooth; molar. *Enañin eǫñ ke ñilepam̧?* Do you have your wisdom teeth yet?

ñillitok (**gilliteq**). 2, 6(*-i*). Faint; dizzy. *Eñillitok bōra kōn an m̧ōkaj aō jutak.* My head feels dizzy from getting up too fast.

ñilñil (**gilgil**). 2, 3, 6(*-i*), 8, 9. Solid; pressurized; packed; tight. *Eñilñil mejatoto kōn an m̧wilaļ.* The air is thick because of the depth. *Kwōn kañilñili am̧ lukwōje.* Tie it tight.

ñiņo (**giyņęw**). 2, 6(*-i*). Chisel-chin.

ñiñat (**giygat**). From *ñi* (**giy**) "tooth", *ñat* (**gat**) "palate". 2, 3(inf, tr *-e*), 4, 6(*-i*). False teeth. *Ejorrāān ñiñat kā ñiñatū.* My false-teeth are broken.

ññat (**ggat**). Dial. W: *eñeñat* (**yeggat**), E: *ñōñat* (**gegat**). 3, 5(*ññatñat*), 6(*-i*), 7, 8, 9. Storm. *Allōñin ññat ko kein.* These are the stormy months.

ññij (**ggij**). Variant form of *ññūr;* see also *ñijlǫk.*

ññiñi (**ggiygiy**). Dial. W: *iññiñi,* E: *ñūñiñi.* Easily angered.

ññurñur (**ggir°gir°**). Dial. W: *iññurñur* (**yiggir°gir°**), E: *ñūñurñur* (**gigir°gir°**). 1(*-i*), 2, 3(inf, tr *-i*), 6(*-i*), 8, 9. Crunch. *Kwōn jab kañurñuri am̧ m̧ōñā.* Avoid crunching when you're eating.

ññūr (**ggir**). Dial. W: *iññūr* (**yiggir**), E: *ñūñūr* (**gigir**). Also *ññij.* 1(*-i*), 2, 3, 5(*ññūrñūr*), 6(*-i*), 7. Groan; moan; rumble; growl; grunt. *Ej ññūr bwe emetak lǫjien.* He is groaning because he has a stomach ache. *Iar roñ an ññūr in metak.* I heard him moan in pain. *Ealikkar ainikien ññūrñūr in ņo.* One can clearly hear the distant rumble of waves.

ñoñ (**g°eg°**). A fish; small, found on reef.

ñoño (**gewgew**). Also *ñoño* (**gęwgęw**). Vulgar. 1(*-i*), 2, 3, 6(*-i*). Smell of feces on body or clothing.

ñortak (**g°ertak**). 1(*-i*), 2, 3, 4, 5(*ññortaktak*), 6(*-i*), 7. Snore. *Ļeo eoññortaktak eņ.* That fellow always snores.

ñōl (**gęl**). 6(*-i*). Ocean swell; mounting wave which does not break; billow. *Bao ko rej kātok wōt ioon ñōl.* The birds flew low over the waves.

ñōñ-. See *ññ-*.

ñūñ (**gig**). 2, 3, 6(*-i*), 8, 9. Packed solid; firm; compact; hard, ground. *Emake ñūñ kūraanto in.* This playground is very hard. *Kañūñ aṃ kanne pāāk ṇe.* Pack that sack solid.

ñūñ-. See *ññ-*.

ñūt (**git**). Sickness; dizziness.

ñūta (**gitah**). 1(*-i*), 2, 3, 7, 8, 9. Famine; starvation. *Eļap an ñūta āneo ṃōjin an taibuun.* There is much famine on the island since the typhoon.

o (**wẹw**). Dial. E only; see *u* (**wiw**). 1(*-i*), 2, 3, 7, 8, 9. Pale; wan.

o (**wẹw**). 6(*-i*). Refuse of scraped coconut after it is squeezed; dregs.

o (**wẹw**). From Engl. Woe. *O, o, o ñan ro rej jokwe ioon laļ.* Woe, woe, woe to the inhabitants of the earth. (Rev. 8:13).

o (**wew**). Interjection: "Oh. Oh my. Darn it." (exclamation of mild surprise or disappointment).

o (**wew**). Archaic. A bird.

ob (**wẹb**). 1(*ubō-*). Chest; bosom; thorax.

obab (**webab**). 1(*-i*), 2, 7. Bruised; collapsed; dented. *Eobab tibat eo.* The teapot is dented.

obab (**wewbab**). 3, 6(*-i*), 8, 9. Smashed. *Ear itaak kaar eo waan im obab.* His car was hit and got smashed.

obajañ (**webahjag**). From Japn. *obaachan*. Grandmother; old woman. *Ļōṃare ebar ita obajañ.* Now, what's the matter with grandma again?

obar (**webar**). 2, 3(tr *-e*), 8, 10(*obrak*). Force to fit; squeeze into. *Ear koobareļǫk ajri ro ṇailowaan ruuṃ eo.* He squeezed the children into the room. *Eobrak ruuṃ eo.* The room was crowded.

obataim (**wewbahtahyim**). Also *obataiṃ*. From Engl. 2(inf, tr *-i*), 4, 6(*-i*). Overtime. *Iar obataimi men e.* I worked overtime on this. *Kwōj obataiṃ ke buñinin?* Are you working overtime tonight?

obbar (**webbar**). Archaic. Fishing method involving fruit of the *wōp* (*Barringtonia asiatica* tree).

oboñ (**webeg°**). From Japn. *obon*. 6(*-i*). Tray. *Kwaar lo ke oboñūn Jāmne eo arro?* Did you see my German tray?

obrak (**webrak**). 1(*-i*), 2, 3, 7, 8, 9. Full; tight, not used with liquids; perfective form of *obar* (**webar**) and of *koobob* (**kewebweb**); replete; teem. *Eobrak wa eṇ kōn ṃweiuk.* The ship is full of trade goods. *Eobrak kōn kūṃaļṃaļ.* It's replete with decorations.

obwin (**webin**). Also *obwin* (**wẹbin**). From Engl. 6(*-i*). Stove; oven.

oda. See *wōda*.

oja. See *wōja*.

ok (**wẹk**). Also *ok* (**wẹq**). 1(*ukō-*). Net; netting; screen.

Ok-an-adik (**wẹk-han-hadik**). From *ok* "fish net", *adik* "first quarter of the moon": "net of the first quarter", when certain fish may be caught easily in large numbers in the ocean side. A constellation; stars in Bootes (beta, mu, nu) and mu in Corona Borealis.

okabur (**wekabir°**). 1(*-i*), 2, 4, 7. Pick unripe pandanus.

okaetok (**wẹkhayeteq**). 2(inf, tr *-e*), 4, 6(*-i*), 7. Long fishing net. *Jen tan okaetoki ṃǫle kaṇ.* Let's go use the long net and catch that school of rabbitfish.

okaj (**wekaj**). Transitive form of *okok* (**wekwek**).

okaliklik (**wekaliklik**). Cause pandanus to ripen; by picking and storing, or by pounding stem of fruit until pliable and leaving it hang three more days before picking.

okar (**wekar**). 1(*okra-*), 6(*-i*). Root.

okjak (**wẹqjak**). 1(*-i*), 2(inf, tr *ukwōj*), 3(inf *kǫokjakjak,* tr *kǫokjak*), 5(*okkwōjakjak, owokwōjakjak*), 7. Overturn; upset; upside down; fall, from erect position; capsize; perfective form of *ukok* (**wikwẹk**). *Tipñōl eo eokkwōjakjak eṇ.* That canoe is always capsizing. *Wōn ṇe ear ukōj wa ṇe?* Who capsized that canoe? *Eokjak rūkadek eo.* The drunk fell down.

okjānlañ (**wekjanlag**). Strong wind; gusty wind.

okjānļañ (**wekjanļag**). Archaic. 2(inf, tr *-e*), 4, 6(*-i*). Kill someone during a typhoon in anticipation of shortage of food; this custom may be abused to settle grudges. *Okjānļañin rinana.* Killing of a bad person. *Raar okjānļañe ļōļļap eo boñ.* They killed the old man last night. *Ruokjānļañ eo eko.* The killer escaped.

okkoļǫk (**wẹqqẹļaq**). From "onomatopoeia". 1, 3, 6(*-i*). Sound of a collision; slam, as of a door. *Iilbōk kōn okkoḷǫk in kōjām eo.* I jumped when the door slammed.

okḷā (**wẹkḷay**). 2(inf, tr *-ik*), 4, 6(*-i*), 7. Turn over small rocks when searching. *Okḷāik nabōjān ṃwiin im pukot riiñ eo aō.* Turn everything over in front of this house and look for my ring.

okḷe (**wẹqḷẹy**). Also *ǫkḷe* (**waqḷẹy**). Archaic. Hungry; variant form of *kwōle* (**qẹḷẹy**).

okmāāņāņ (**wẹkmayaņyaņ**). Variant form of *māāņāņ* (**mayaņyaņ**).

okok (**wekwek**). 1(*-i*), 2(inf, tr *okaj*), 3, 4, 7. Pick pandanus. *Rōmoot in okok.* They went to pick pandanus. *Eṃōj okaj bōb eo.* The pandanus have been picked off that tree.

okpej (**wẹqpẹj**). 1(*-i*), 2(inf, tr *-e, okpije*), 3, 4, 7. Scrounge around; scavenge; turn over rubbish hunting for something.

okraan (**wekrahan**). 2(inf, tr *-e*). Twilight; morning; dawn.

oktaak (**wẹqtahak**). Dial. W only; see *eotaak* (**yẹwtahak**). Also *uñtaak* (**wigtahak**). 1(*-i*), 2(inf, tr *-e*), 3, 4, 7. Wrestling.

oktak (**wẹktak**). 1(*-i*), 2, 3, 8, 9. Peculiar; unusual.

oktak (**wẹqtak**). 1(*-i*), 2, 3(inf *kǫwoktaktak,* tr *kǫoktak*), 5(*okoktaktak*), 7. Change; perfective form of *ukok* (**wikwẹk**); difference; contrast; turn around. *Ejjeḷǫk wōt oktakūṃ jān ke iar lo eok.* You have really changed from when I last saw you. *Kwōn oktak tok.* Turn around and face me.

oktak (**wẹktak**). Dialectal variant of *eotaak* (**yẹwtahak**).

Oktoba (**wektewbah**). From Engl. October.

okun bade (**weqin bahdẹy**). From Engl. 1(*-i*), 2, 3, 4, 6(*-i*), 7. Stevedore; working party. *Rej kappok okun bade ñan wa eņ i ar.* They are looking for stevedores for the ship in port.

okwa (**wẹkwah**). 1(*-i*), 2. Tripod for fishing; scaffold.

okwa (**wẹqwah**). 2(inf, tr *-ik(i)*), 4, 6(*-i*), 7. Fishing method, pole fishing from a raised platform or tripod used for fishing. *Jet raņ ṃṃaan rej okwa iaar.* I can see some men fishing from tripods on the lagoon shore. *Raar okwaik ek eo.* The fish was landed using the tripod method.

okwōjaja (**weqejahjah**). Shallow draft; ride high in water because not loaded. *Wa in eokwōjaja.* This canoe is riding high.

olǫk (**wewlaq**). Fall down.

oḷaḷo (**weḷaḷẹw**). 1(*-i*), 2, 3, 4, 7, 8, 9. Weakling; coward; invalid.

oḷaḷo (**weḷaḷẹw**). Dial. E, W: *ikmid* (**yikmid**). A fish, bass, *Variola louti.*

oḷaḷo (**weḷaḷẹw**). Dialectal variant of *ikmid* (**yikmid**).

oḷañi (**weḷagiy**). Variant form of *waḷañi* (**waḷagiy**).

oḷar (**weḷar**). Tiny; runt; general term for small things. *Oḷar in iu.* Sprouted coconut with small leaf. *Oḷar in matmat.* Small sponge.

oḷā (**weḷay**). 1(*-i*), 2, 3, 7, 8, 9. Out of perpendicular; askew; correct angle of handsaws. *Kwōn kooḷāik jidpān e aō.* Bend the teeth of my saw to the correct angle.

oḷeǫ (**weḷeyaw**). 1(*-i*), 2, 3, 4, 7. Beautiful. *Eḷap an oḷeǫ jikin kweilǫk eņ.* That city is beautiful.

oḷiaanta (**weḷiyahantah**). Also *oḷiaaņta* (**wẹḷiyahaņtah**). From Engl. 3, 6(*-i*). A plant, flower, *Nerium oleander.* L.

oḷiiñ (**wewḷiyig**). Also *oḷiñ* (**weḷyig**). From Engl. *all in* (poker). 1(*-i*), 2, 3, 4, 8. Broke, financially; out of money. *Ilukkuun oḷiiñ.* I am really broke.

oḷip (**weḷip**). From Engl. Wolf.

oḷkūñ (**weḷkig**). 1(*-i*), 3, 6(*-i*). Anus hair.

oḷǫk (**weḷaq**). 1(*-i*), 2, 3, 5(*owoḷǫkḷǫk*), 6(*-i*), 7. Tumble over; fall, as a tree; tipped over; fallen prostrate; felling of a tree; topple over. *Lale eoḷǫk ḷǫk ni ņe im buñut ṃweeņ.* Be careful the tree doesn't fall on that house. *Eoḷǫk ni eo.* The palm tree fell down. *Kǫoḷǫke (keoḷǫke) miade eņ.* Tear down the tower. *Eḷak baajkōḷ, eowoḷǫkḷǫk.* When he rides a bicycle, he falls all over the place.

oḷōt (**weḷet**). Small piece of land; of no value.

oḷūb (**weḷib**). 1, 2(inf, tr *-i*), 5(*-i*). Bald head; shaven head. *Eoḷūb bōran.* His hair has been shaved bald. *Ñe eor rijikuuḷ eņ ekōbaatat, rōnaaj oḷūbi.* If a student is caught smoking, his hair will be shaved off.

omom. See *wōmwōm.*

om̧ (wȩm̧). 3, 6(-*i*). Hermit crab.

om̧oja (wem̧ewjah). Slang. 2, 6(-*i*), 8, 9. Poor quality; fragile; rickety. *M̧weiuk in Oñkoñ roomoja.* Hong Kong products are of poor quality.

om̧rawūn (wem̧rahwin). Also *om̧rawūn* (wȩm̧rahwin). From Engl. 2(inf, tr -*i*), 3, 4, 6(-*i*), 7. Home run; run a complete circuit around a field.

onaji. See *wōnaji.*

oņaak (weņahak). 2(inf, tr -*e*), 4, 6(-*i*). Protect; provide for; oversee; look after; keep an eye on; auspices. *Oņaak an Anij.* Providence. *Anij ej oņaake kōj.* God looks over us. *Juon irooj ej aikuj oņaake armej ro an.* A king must provide for his people.

oņān jata (weņyan jahtah). Rental. *Oņān jata eo an m̧weȩn ij jokwe ie ej jibukwi ruwalitoññoul taļa.* The rental for my apartment is one hundred eighty dollars a month.

oņea- (weņya-). Also *wōnea-.* 1. Price of; salary of; cost of; fare; fee; hire; stipend; wages of. *Jete oņān jōōt n̄e am̧?* How much did your shirt cost? *Jete oņān am̧ rūkaki?* How much do you get paid for teaching?

oņeņak (weņȩyņak). Also *wōneņak* (wȩņȩyņak). 6(-*i*). A ghost, haunts and drives people mad, lives in dense forests.

oñ (weg°). Also *uñ* (wig). 1(-*i*), 2, 3, 4, 5(*owoñoñ*), 7, 8, 9. Homesick; longing for; nostalgia. *Eowoñoñ ajri eņ.* That child keeps on being homesick.

oñoñ (weg°weg°). Dial. E only; see *matmat* (matmat). 3, 6(-*i*). Sponge.

oo (wewew). Dialectal variant of *mmej* (mmȩj).

ooj (wewej). From Engl. 6(-*i*). Hose.

oom (wȩwȩm). Until; up to. *Ear idaak oom kadek.* He drank until he was drunk. *Kwōnaaj rum̧wij bajjek oom tūm̧.* You'll keep procrastinating until you're completely lost.

opene (wewpeney). 2, 3(inf, tr -*ik*), 6(-*i*), 8, 9. Dent; crush. *Kwōn jab koopeneik ainbat ņe.* Don't crush the pot.

opiem̧. See *wōpiem̧.*

opij. See *wōpij.*

opija. See *wōpija.*

or (wȩr). Also *wōr, wor.* 3(*kalwor*). Lobster.

or (wer). Also *wōr.* Fish gills.

or (wer). Also *wōr.* 7. Be; there is; there are; have; exist. *Eor juon im̧ō em̧.* I have a house. *Eortok armej ñan m̧wiin.* Someone is coming toward this house.

or (wer). Formant in place names; may be related to *or* "fish gill", or possibly to the *or* of *ora-* "quantity", *or* "exists", and *orļok* "grows, propagates"; or possibly related to *oror* "enclosure"; also possibly *war, orañe* "barren, sterile".

ora- (wera-). Also *wōra-.* 1. Number of; quantity.

oran (weran). From Engl. 3, 6(-*i*). Orange, the fruit.

orañe (weragey). Also *wōrañe, war* (war). 1(-*i*), 2, 8, 9. Sterile; barren; incapable of bearing offspring, of women only.

orañļok (weragļaq). Also *wōrañļok.* 1(-*i*), 2, 3. Swallow; devour; gulp.

orā (weray). Also *wōrā.* 1(-*i*), 2, 3, 6(-*i*), 8, 9. Tired; exhausted; beat; bushed; pooped; oppressed. *Ejjeļok wōt orāū jān jipiij eo an.* His sermon really oppressed me. I was very tired after his speech.

ore (wȩrȩy). Also *wōre.* Vulgar. 1, 2(inf, tr -*ik(i)*), 4, 5(*oworere*), 6(-*i*). Pull back the foreskin.

orjeb (wȩrjȩb). Variant form of *orjib* (werjib).

orjib (werjib). Also *wōrjib, orjib* (wȩrjib), *orjeb* (wȩrjȩb). 2, 3, 6(-*i*). Peel; molt. *Ibwil im orjib.* I burned and peeled. *Eorjib m̧winam̧ōn eo em erom babbūb.* The caterpillar molted and became a butterfly.

orjin (wȩrjin). Also *wōrjin.* 1(-*i*), 2(inf, tr -*i*), 3, 4, 7. To bolt one's food. *Kwōn kate eok meme im jab orjin.* Take care to chew your food and don't bolt it.

orļok (wȩrļaq). Also *wōrlok.* 1(-*i*), 2, 3, 4. Asthma.

orļok (werļaq). Also *wōrļok.* 1(-*i*), 2, 3. Increase; profit; interest money; invested money; propagate.

ormej (wȩrmȩj). Also *wōrmej.* 1(-*i*), 2, 3, 7. Wash one's face. *Kwōn ormej ṃokta jān aṃ ṃōñā in jibboñ.* Wash your face before eating breakfast.

oror (**werwer**). Also *wōrwōr.* 1(-*i*), 2(inf, tr -*e*), 3, 6(-*i*), 7. Pen; fence; enclosure; coop; corral. *Kwōn orore piik ṇe.* Put that pig in the pen. *Ororin bao.* Chicken coop.

ortabtab (**wẹrtabtab**). Also *wōrtabtab.* 1, 2, 3(inf, tr -*e*), 6(-*i*), 8, 9. Haphazard; careless manner. *En jab ortabtab aṃ kanne pāāk ṇe bwe enaaj booḷ wōt kiiō.* You'd better arrange the contents of that sack if you want it to contain more.

oru (**wẹriw**). Also *wōru.* From Japn. *ooru* (from Engl. *oar*). 1, 2(inf, tr -*uk*), 4, 6(-*i*), 7. Row a boat; scull. *Oruuk āneḷọk wa ṇe.* Row the boat ashore.

ot. See *wōt.*

ota (**wetah**). Variant form of *wata.*

otem. See *wōtōm.*

out (**wẹwit**). Archaic. Meeting place; place where many people live.

owan (**wwan**). Dial. W: *eowan* (**yewwan**), E: *owan* (**wewwan**). 1(-*i*), 2, 3, 4, 7, 8, 9, 11(*owan*). Industrious; hard working.

owar (**wwar**). 1(-*i*), 2(inf, tr -*e*), 4, 6(-*i*), 7. Beg; beseech; appeal; petition; plead; invoke. *Iar oware im kajjinōk ak ear jab kōtḷọk tok wa eo waan.* I begged him until I got tired but he never let us borrow his canoe. *Ij owar ñan eok bwe kwōn jouj in jab baere Jọọn.* I'm begging you please not to fire John. *Jijej ear oware Jemān.* Jesus invoked His Father.

owat (**wwat**). Dial. W: *eowat* (**yewwat**), E: *owat* (**wewwat**). 1(-*i*), 2, 3, 7, 8, 9. Ripe, of pandanus. *Enañin owat ke bōb ṇe?* Is that pandanus ripe yet?

owatrere (**wwatrẹyrẹy**). Dial. W: *eowatrere* (**yewwatrẹyrẹy**), E: *owatrere* (**wewwatrẹyrẹy**). From *watre* (**watrẹy**). 1(-*i*), 2, 3(inf, tr -*ik(i)*), 4, 6(-*i*), 7, 8, 9. Not ripe; green; undried copra. *Waini kein aṃ rej owatrere wōt.* Your copra still needs more drying. *Ij jab lōke bwe eowatrere.* I don't trust him cause he's green.

owe (**wwey**). Dial. W: *eowe* (**yewwey**), E: *owe* (**wewwey**). Also *wejeḷ* (**weyjeḷ**). 1(-*i*), 2, 3, 4, 5(*ajowewe, ajjowewe*), 7. Whistle. *Wōn in ej ajjowewe?* Who's that that keeps whistling?

owōj (**wwej**). Dial. W: *eowōj* (**yewwej**), E: *owōj* (**wewwej**). 1(-*i*), 2, 3, 4, 7. Tax; tribute. *Eṃōj aer tōltōl owōj.* They have finished collecting taxes.

Ọkwōj (**waqej**). From Engl. August.

ọkwōn (**waqen**). From Engl. 2, 4, 6(-*i*), 7. Organ, musical. *Ọkwōn in ia ṇe?* Where was that organ made?

ọo (**wawẹw**). From Engl. 1(-*i*), 2(inf, tr -*uk*), 7. Circle; zero; mark to show absence; name of the letter *o. Etke kwaar ọo jān jikuuḷ?* Why were you absent from school?

ọọj (**wawaj**). Also *ọwaj* (**wawwaj**). From Engl. 6(-*i*). Horse.

ọọjọj (**wawajwaj**). From *ọọj* (**wawaj**). 1(-*i*), 2, 3(inf, tr -*e*), 6(-*i*), 7. Ride a horse. *Ear ọọjọj eọọjḷọk.* He rode the horse toward the interior. *Kwōn kọọọjọje kurṃa ṇe.* Hitch the horse to the cart.

ōjek (**hejek**). Transitive form of *ōjōj* (**hejhej**).

ōjjej (**hẹjjẹj**). Also *ōjej* (**hẹjẹj**), *wōjej* (**wẹjẹj**). Interjection: surprise or disappointment.

ōjjeti- (**hẹjjẹti-**). 1. Interjection of displeasure used only by women. *Ōjjetūṃ.* Go to hell.

ōjōj (**hejhej**). Also *ejej* (**yejyej**). 1(-*i*), 2(inf, tr *ōjek*), 3, 4, 7. Husk a coconut with one's teeth. *Etke kwōōjōj ni ejjeḷọk doon ṇe?* Why are you husking coconuts with your teeth, isn't there a husking stick around?

ōkkōk (**hẹkkẹk**). Also *ōkōk* (**hẹkẹk**), *okōk* (**wẹkẹk**), *okkōk* (**wẹkkẹk**). Interjection: "Darn!" Or "God forbid!"

ōḷ (**heḷ**). Flow.

ōḷḷōḷ (**hẹḷḷẹḷ**). Also *ōḷōḷ* (**hẹḷẹḷ**), *oḷōḷ* (**wẹḷẹḷ**). Interjection: connotes unwillingness.

ōḷōḷ (**heḷheḷ**). 1(-*i*), 2, 3, 7, 8, 9. Grit the teeth; chattering of teeth. *Eḷap aō ōḷōḷ kōn aō piọ.* I'm so cold my teeth are chattering.

ōn (**hẹn**). 1(*ūne-*), 3, 5(*ūne*). Nourishing; substance; vitamin; nutrition.

ōne (**hẹnẹy**). From Engl. Honey.

ōnḷọk (**hẹnḷaq**). 1(-*i*), 2, 3. Dissolve; melt.

ōņņōņ (**hęņņęņ**). Also *ōņōņ* (**hęņęņ**), *oņōņ* (**węņęņ**). Interjection: connotes unwillingness.

ōō (**heheh**). Also *eōō* (**yeheh**). A fish, lionfish, *Pterois volitans*; a fish, scorpion fish, *Dendrochirus zebra.*

ōr (**her**). Dial. E, W: *in* (**yin**). Grass skirt.

ōrōr (**herher**). 1, 2(inf, tr *ōrōj*), 4, 6(*-i*), 7. Cut into strips; stab; slash. *Ōrōje piik ņe.* Stab the pig. *Ōrōje kōņọuwe kaņe.* Husk the *kōņọuwe* (with your teeth).

ōrrōr (**hęrręr**). Also *ōrōr* (**hęręr**), *orōr* (**węręr**). Vulgar slang. Interjection: "Darn!" Or "Heck!"; interjection: expression of sexual pleasure; interjection: "Ugh!"

ōttōt (**hęttęt**). Also *ōtōt* (**hętęt**), *otōt* (**wętęt**). Vulgar. Interjection: "Ouch!" (pain or sexual pleasure).

paaj (**pahaj**). Archaic. Small oven or stove; chief's land for making food.

paan (**pahan**). From Engl. 1(*-i*), 2, 3, 4, 6(*-i*), 7. Musical band; orchestra.

paan (**pahan**). 3, 6(*-i*). A fish, red snapper, *Lutjanus bohar.*

paan (**pahan**). From Engl. Cooking pan.

paane (**pahaney**). Archaic. Feed; give bait. *Paane paane raj eo.* Feed the whale (words from a chant).

paañ (**pahag**). Appear before an audience.

paarōr (**paharher**). Dial. E, W: *kōpaarōr* (**kepaharher**). Archaic. Illicit sexual intercourse; live licentiously; withdraw from society to follow one's own desires.

pajo (**pahjew**). 1, 2, 4, 6(*-i*). Prepare hermit crabs for bait. *Jenaaj ruj in jibbōñ tata im pajo.* We'll get up early and squash hermit crabs for bait.

pak (**pak**). 6(*-i*). Taro residue, used for seedling after the edible portion has been cut off, usually of a mature taro.

Pak (**pak**). A plant, taro variety (Takeuchi); Cyrtosperm.

pakij (**pakij**). Also *ppakij* (**ppakij**). 1(*-i*), 2, 3(*kōppakij*), 4, 3+5(*ppakijkij*), 6(*-i*), 8, 6, 11(*pakijkij*). Long-winded in diving; able to stay underwater long. *Eļap aō pakij jān kwe.* I can stay under longer than you. *Kōjro etal in kappakijkij.* Let's go see which of the two of us can stay under longer. *Ejjeļọk ppakijin ļeeņ.* He sure can stay long under the water. *Ippakij jān kwe.* I can hold my breath longer than you. *Kōmālij in ek enaaj kōppakij eok.* Eating fish brains will cause you to be able to hold your breath for a long time.

pakij (**pakij**). From Engl. 2(inf, tr *-i*), 4, 5(*ppakijkij*), 6(*-i*), 7. Package; pack; packet; parcel. *Kwōn pakiji nuknuk kaņe im eermeeļi.* Put those dresses in a package and airmail them.

pakke (**pakkęy**). Also *pakke* (**pakkey**). 1(*-i*), 2(inf, tr *-ik*), 3, 4, 6(*-i*), 7. Big gun; cannon.

pako (**pakew**). 3, 6(*-i*). A fish, general term for shark.

pako korak (**pakew qerak**). 3, 6(*-i*). A fish, shark, *Trisenodon obesus.*

pako mej (**pakew męj**). 3, 6(*-i*). A fish, shark grouper, *Carcharhinus melanopterus.*

pako tiltil (**pakew tiltil**). A fish, tiger shark, *Galeocerdo arcticus.*

pako tọrtọr (**pakew tar°tar°**). A fish, thresher shark, *Alopias vulpes.*

pakoon eoon pedped (**pakewen yewen pedped**). A fish, ground shark, *Carcharhinus melanopterus.*

paļ (**paļ**). 1(*-i*), 2(inf, tr *-e*), 3, 4, 5(*ppaļpaļ*), 8. Furious; angry; eager for revenge; envious; jealous. *Eļap an ļōmaraņ paļe doon.* They are both eager for revenge. *Eppaļpaļ ļeeņ.* He's always trying to get revenge.

paļ (**paļ**). 1(*-i*), 2(inf, tr *-e*), 3, 4, 5(*ppaļpaļ*), 6(*-i*), 8. Fishbone stuck in throat. *Eppaļpaļ ļeeņ.* He's always getting bones stuck in his throat.

paļ (**paļ**). A coral which can be used as sandpaper.

paļōj (**pahļej**). Variant form of *paļōt* (**pahļet**).

paļōt (**pahļet**). Also *paļōt* (**paļet**), *paļōj* (**pahļej**). 2(inf, tr *-e*), 4, 5(*ppaļōtļōt*), 6(*-i*), 7. Pallet. *Paļōji ṃweiuk kaņe bwe ren ṃukko.* Put the merchandise on the pallet so we may winch them up.

pañ (**pag**). 2(inf, tr *-e*), 3, 7. Prepare to strike; put up fists. *Ļeo ej pañ pein in itōn bait.* He is putting up his fists to fight.

pañijñij (**pagijgij**). 1(*-i*), 2(inf, tr *-i*), 3, 7, 8, 9. Tremor or vibration caused by sound of gun or thunder; loud, as of a burst. *Eļap an pañijñij ainikien pakke* *eṇ.* The noise of the cannon shook everything.

pao (**pahwew**). 1(-*i*), 7. Appearance; feature. *Eṃṃan pao tok in āneo.* The islet looks good from here (on a boat).

parij (**parij**). Variant form of *bale* (**baļęy**).

parijet (**pariyjęt**). 1(-*i*), 6(-*i*), 7. Lagoon shore; lagoon beach; seacoast; seashore. *Lali ek kaṇ parijet.* Look at those fish at the shore.

parok (**pareq**). Also *ailparok* (**hayilpareq**). 2, 3, 6(-*i*). Cumbersome; troublesome; burdensome; very busy. *Iparok kōn katak lōñlōñ kein aō.* I'm very busy with my many assignments.

parōk (**parek**). Faint; overworked. *Iṃōk im parōk, kwōn jipañ eō.* I'm tired and faint, please help me (from a hymn).

pat (**pat**). 1(-*i*), 5(*ppatpate*), 6(-*i*). Swamp. *Eppatpate iooj in ānin.* There are lots of swamps in the interior of this islet.

pata (**pahtah**). 2(inf, tr -*ik*), 3, 8. War; campaign. *Eļap an kar lōñ mej ilo pata eo kein karuo.* Very many died in world war two.

pata (**pahtah**). 1(-*i*), 2(inf, tr -*ik*), 6(-*i*), 7, 8, 9, 11(*pata*). Numerous; common. *Eļap an pata ṃōle eṇ.* Rabbitfish are very common there.

pata (**pahtah**). Useless; good for nothing; in vain; see *ba pata. Eļap aṃ rūtto pata.* You don't seem to have learned anything with the years. *Kwaar jukuuļ pata.* You went to school for nothing.

pate (**pahtey**). Variant form of *pāte* (**paytey**).

pati (**patiy**). Variant form of *pāti* (**paytiy**).

patōk (**patek**). Transitive form of *patpat* (**patpat**).

patōļ (**pateļ**). From Engl. 2(inf, tr -*e*), 6(-*i*), 7. Bicycle pedal. *Ia ṇe kwōj patōļ ļọk ñane?* Where are you pedaling to?

patpat (**patpat**). 1(-*i*), 2(inf, tr *patōk*), 4, 7, 1/. Throw down, as in wrestling; throw on the ground. *Rūkadek ro raar uñtaak im rōpatōk ļeo juon.* The drunks were wrestling and one threw the other down. *Eļap an kar patpat ļeo juon ṇai laļ.* The other one was thrown down hard.

patpat (**patpat**). 1(-*i*), 2(inf, tr *patōk(e)*), 4, 7, 8. Wash rice. *Ewi ledik eo bwe en etal patpat raij?* Where is the girl that is supposed to go wash the rice?

pā (**pay**). 1(*pei*-, *pāā*-). Arm; hand; wing; fin.

pāāk (**payak**). From Engl. 1(-*i*), 3, 5(*ppāākāk*), 6(-*i*). Bag; burlap sack; pouch.

pāāk (**payak**). From Engl. 1(-*i*), 2(inf, tr -*e*), 6(-*i*). Back up; reverse. *Imaroñ ke pāāk waj ñan jeṇe?* Can I back up to there?

pāāntōre (**payantęręy**). From Engl. Cupboard; pantry; food cabinet.

pāāñ (**payag**). From Engl. 1(-*i*), 2(inf, tr -*e*), 4, 6(-*i*). Bank, financial; safe; cash box. *Epeļļọk ke pāāñ eṇ?* Is the safe open? *Kwōn pāāñi ṃani kā nājū.* Put my money in the safe.

pāāñkōļ (**payagkeļ**). From Engl. 2, 3, 6(-*i*), 7. Bracelet; bangle; wear a bracelet. *Kwōn pāāñkōļ tok ñan bade eṇ.* Wear a bracelet to the party.

pāāñkōrab (**payagkerab**). From Engl. 1(-*i*), 2, 3(inf, tr -*e*), 7, 8, 9. Bankrupt; broke. *Epāāñkōrab ṃōn wia eo an.* His business went bankrupt.

pāār (**payar**). From Engl. 5(*ppāārār*), 6(-*i*). Bear.

pāāt (**payat**). 1(-*i*), 2(inf, tr -*e*), 3, 6(-*i*), 8. Ebb tide; stranded high-and-dry. *Enañin pāāt ke?* Is the tide low yet? *Jen kōpāātļọk.* Let's wait for the tide to go out. *Epāāte piiļ tūreep eo.* The field trip ship was stranded high and dry.

pāāt ṃōṇakṇak (**payat ṃeṇakṇak**). 1(-*i*), 2, 3, 6(-*i*), 8. Lowest ebb tide. *Jen ilān eọñōd bwe epāāt ṃōṇakṇak.* Let's go fishing because there's an extremely low tide.

pābōļ (**paybeļ**). From Engl. 1(-*i*), 2(inf, tr -*e*), 3, 4, 6(-*i*), 7, 8, 9. Bevel. *Kwōn jouj in pileini ekkar ñan pābōļ e an wūntō e.* Please plane it so it can fit the bevel of the window sill.

pād (**pad**). 2(inf, tr *pādjaake, pādkaake*), 4, 7. Be somewhere; stay; remain; be left; stop, in the sense of stay; attend; exist; presence. *Kwōn pād wōt.* Stay here. *Kwōnaaj pādjake peiṃ ļọk em eanilen.* You'll keep putting off getting your hand fixed until it gets infected. *Ear pādjake jemān aujpitōļ.* He stayed with his father at the hospital. *Iar jeļā ke epād ilo ruuṃ eo.* I knew of his presence in the room. *Kwaar pād ke ilo kwelọk eo?* Did you attend the meeting?

pād bajjek (**pad bajjẹk**). Idle; loaf. *Etke kwōj pād bajjek?* Why are you idling?

pād o (**pad wẹw**). Also *pāddo* (**paddẹw**). Off and on. *Pād o lio in.* Shucks, here she comes again. *Ej pāddo wōt.* It rains off and on.

pādādijṃaan (**padadijṃahan**). Variant form of *pādālijṃaan* (**padalijṃahan**).

pādāl (**padal**). Also *pedāl* (**pedal**). Archaic. Push up soil, of roots.

pādālijṃaan (**padalijṃahan**). Also *pādādijṃaan* (**padadijṃahan**). 3, 6(*-i*). A plant, a grass; refers to both *Fimbristylis atollensis* St. John and *Eleocharis geniculata* (L.) R **S., both of the** *Cyperaceae.*

pāddo (**paddẹw**). Variant form of *pād o* (**pad wẹw**).

pādjake (**padjahkey**). Transitive form of *pād* (**pad**).

pādkake (**padkahkey**). Transitive form of *pād* (**pad**).

pāin (**payin**). Transitive form of *ppāin* (**ppayin**).

pāin ni (**payin niy**). 6(*-i*). Green coconut fronds.

pāipjek (**payipjẹk**). Variant form of *pāpijek* (**paypijẹk**).

pāj (**paj**). Vulgar. From *pājrōk* (**pajrẹk**). 1(*-i*), 2, 3(inf, tr *-e*), 6(*-i*), 7, 8, 9. Circumcised penis.

pājeñ (**pajeg**). 1(*-i*), 3, 6(*-i*). Breastbone of a fowl.

pājrōk (**pajrẹk**). 3, 6(*-i*). A fish, chub or rudder fish, *Kyphosus vaigiensis.*

pāl (**pal**). 2, 6(*-i*). To die, of arrowroot, signaling time for digging the root; arrowroot season. *Epāl ṃakṃōk kaṇ.* The arrowroot are dying. *Kōpooj dunen kōb ko bwe epāl.* Prepare the shovels for it's arrowroot digging time.

pāl (**pal**). Archaic. Formant in place names; house; see *pelpel.*

pāl (**pal**). From *ppālpāl* "flutter". Formant in place names; blow.

pāl- (**pal-**). 1+7, 2+7, 3+7, 7, 7+8. Leap; jump; soar.

pāle (**palẹy**). 3, 6(*-i*). Torch made from dried fronds. *Kwōnañin bọk ke pāle?* Haven't you wrapped a torch yet?

pālee- (**paleye-**). 1. Spouse; wife; husband. *Pālen wōn kōrā eṇ?* Whose wife is she?

pālele (**palẹylẹy**). 1, 2(inf, tr *pāleek*), 3, 4(*rippālele*), 6(*-i*), 8. Marriage; married. *N̄āāt eṇ erro ar pālele jāne?* Since when have they been married?

pāleṃoron (**palẹyṃer°en**). 6(*-i*). Trusted friend of a chief; member of a clan a chief is especially fond of; favorite of a chief. *Pāleṃoron ro an irooj eṇ raṇe.* They are the chief's bosom friends.

pālep (**palep**). Dial. W, E: *wōllaañ* (**wellahag**). A fish, Moorish idol, *Zanclus cornutus.*

pālep (**palep**). Dialectal variant of *wōllaañ* (**wellahag**).

pālle (**palley**). 2+5(*ppāllele*), 3+5. Westernized; see *balle. Eppāllele ālkin an rọọltok jān Amedka.* He's acting westernized ever since he came from America. *Kwōn jab kōppālleleik eok.* Don't pretend to be an American.

pālli- (**palli-**). Also *pāli-*. 1(*-i*). Head wreath of; possessive classifier, flowers or wreaths worn on head. *Ej pālōk kūrawūn eo pāllin.* She's wearing her crown. *Pāllin ta ṇe kwōj ļōōte?* What's that lei you're stringing for?

pālmuuj (**palmiwij**). 6(*-i*). Cloud formation preceding storm.

pālo (**palew**). 1(*-i*), 2, 3, 4, 7, 8. Worn out; tired out; very busy; occupied; engaged; obsessed; weary. *Eļap an lio pālo kōn ajri ro nājin.* She is worn out from taking care of her children.

pālōk (**palẹk**). Transitive form of *pālpel* (**palpẹl**).

pālpel (**palpẹl**). 1(*-i*), 2(inf, tr *pālōk*), 3, 4, 6(*-i*), 7. Put wreath on one's head; wear flowers on head. *Ej pālōke ut eo pāllin.* She's putting on a wreath. *Ej pāliki ut ko pāllin.* She's putting flowers on as a wreath. *Ej pālpel (kōn) ut.* She has flowers on her head.

pālpilikio (**palpilikiyew**). A fish, parrotfish, *Callyodon pulchellus.*

pālu (**paliw**). Archaic. From man's name *Pālu.* V.I.P.; big shot; important person. *Ļeeṇ epālu ioon armej ro.* He's an important person.

pāḷōt (**payļet**). Variant form of *pǫḷot* (**paļ°et**).

pānāpnep (**paynapnęp**). Also *penabnōb* (**peynabnęb**). 1(*-i*), 2, 4, 8. Filch; steal; inquisitive, of hands only; kleptomania. *Ripānāpnep eo ṇe.* He has sticky fingers.

pānuk (**paniq**). 2(inf, tr *-i*), 5(*ppānuknuk*), 7. Pile up; gather; put clothes away carelessly; jumble; stow. *Eṃōj pānuk ḷọk jeṇ kōn kwōpej.* The trash has been piled up over there. *Raar pānuktok wōt nuknuk kā ṇa ije.* Someone just threw these clothes down here. *Ear llu im ppānuknuk ṇabōjḷọk nuknuk.* He got angry and threw clothes all over the place.

Pānuk (**paniq**). From *pānuk* (**paniq**) "pile up". 3, 6(*-i*). A plant, pandanus cultigen; Arno.

pāp (**pap**). 3, 5(*pāpe*), 6(*-i*). Coconut frond; midrib of coconut frond.

pāpijek (**paypijęk**). Also *pāipjek* (**payipjęk**). From *pā* (**pay**) "hand", *pijek* (**pijęk**) "defecate". 1(*-i*), 2, 3, 4, 8. Unlovable; revolting person; ill-bred; wretched. *Epāpijek kōn an nana.* He is revolting because of his bad character.

pāpjel ṃae (**papjel ṃahyey**). 1(*-i*), 2(inf, tr *-ik*), 3, 4, 7. Oppose; stop; meet and stop; waylay, accost. *Kwōn pọjak wōt in pāpjel ṃae rūkadek eo ñe enaaj itok.* Be ready to stop the drunk if he comes.

Pāpode (**papewdey**). From Engl. February.

pārājet (**payrayjet**). 1(*-i*), 2(inf, tr *-e*), 3, 4, 7. Carry in one hand. *Kwōn jab pārājete ajri ṇe bwe enaaj wōtlọk.* Don't carry that child with one hand or it will fall.

pārokōrāāp (**payrewkerayap**). From Engl. Paragraph.

pārokrā (**payreqray**). Variant form of *pārorā* (**payrewray**).

pārorā (**payrewray**). Also *pārokrā* (**payreqray**). 1(*-i*), 2(inf, tr *-ik*), 3, 4, 7. Carry with both hands. *Kwōn pārorāik bōb ṇe.* Carry that pandanus with both hands.

pāte (**paytey**). Also *pate* (**pahtey**). Slang. From *pāāt* (**payat**). 2, 3. Caught in the act; be stranded high-and-dry. *Epāte an ilen kọọt.* He was caught stealing. *Bwilijmāāṇ ro raar kōpāte an kọọt.* The police caught him stealing.

pāti (**paytiy**). Also *pati* (**patiy**). 3, 4+3, 6(*-i*). A fish, big-eyed or goggle-eyed scad fish or horse mackerel, *Trachurops crumenophthalmus.*

pātōñtōñ (**paytegteg**). 1(*-i*), 2, 3, 4. Active; vigorous. *Epātōñtōñ lieṇ.* She is active.

pātōre (**paytęręy**). From Engl. 3(inf, tr *-ik*), 6(*-i*). Battery. *Kōpātōreik teeñki ṇe.* Put batteries in that flashlight.

pea (**peyah**). From Engl. 3, 6(*-i*). Pair; couple. *Jete pea in jodi eo kwaar wiaiki?* How many pairs of zories did you buy?

peaut (**peyahwit**). From Engl. 2(inf, tr *-i*), 4, 6(*-i*), 7. Pay out, nautical; let out a rope to slacken it; let anchor line out to allow for tide change. *Peauti añkō ṇe.* Pay out the rope for the anchor.

peaut (**peyahwit**). 1(*-i*), 2(inf, tr *-i*), 4, 5(*ppeautut*), 6(*-i*), 7. A food, spongy meat of sprouted coconut cooked with arrowroot starch and diluted with water.

peba (**pęybah**). From Engl. 5(*ppebaba*), 6(*-i*). Paper; card. *Eppebaba nabōjān ṃwiin.* There is lots of paper (on the ground) outside this house.

peba (**pęybah**). Also *pepa* (**pepah**). 3, 6(*-i*). A plant, pepper, *Capsicum* sp.

peba (**pebah**). Variant form of *pepa* (**pepah**).

ped in pā (**ped yin pay**). Also *pedenpā* (**pedeṇpay**). 6(*-i*). Cloud formation predicting a typhoon.

pedakilkil (**pedakilkil**). 1(*-i*), 2, 3, 5(*ppedakilkil*). Crumbled; shattered; broken in bits; smithereens. *Erup bato eo im ppedakilkil.* The bottle broke into smithereens.

pedaṃwijiṃwij (**pedaṃijiṃij**). Variant form of *pedañwūjñwūj* (**pedag°ijg°ij**).

pedañōtñōt (**pedagętgęt**). 1(*-i*), 2(inf, tr *-e, pedañōtñūte*), 3, 5(*ppedañōtñōt*), 8, 9. Flexible; pliable. *Eḷap an pedañōtñōt būḷāwut ṇe.* That plywood is flexible.

pedañwūjñwūj (**pedag°ijg°ij**). Also *pedañutñut* (**pedag°itg°it**), *pedañotñot* (**pedag°etg°et**), *pedaṃwijṃwij* (**pedaṃijiṃij**). 2, 6(*-i*), 8, 9. Deafening; resounding. *Joñan an peran jañin baaṃ eo ekiōk* *pedañwūjñwūj.* The explosion was so loud it was nearly deafening.

pedāp (**pedap**). A fish, large eel; female eel.

peddejak (**peddeyjak**). Also *peddejak* (**peddejak**). 1(-*i*), 2(inf, tr -*e*), 3, 5(*ppeddejake*), 8. Spread abroad; covered with; replete with. *Eppeddejake ānin kōn mā.* This island is covered with breadfruit.

peddeJǫkwe (**peddejaqey**). Also *peddejake* (**peddejakey**). 2. Smashed; mangled; crushed. *Ewōtlǫk im peddejǫkwe ioon laḷ.* It fell and got smashed on the ground.

pedej (**pedej**). 2, 5(*ppedejdej*), 6(-*i*), 7(-*ḷǫk*). Fall and get squashed; fall flat. *Epedejḷǫk juon mā.* A breadfruit fell and got squashed. *Ilo iien rak eo, ear eppedejdej iuṃwin aolep mā.* During the summer there was squashed ripe breadfruit under all the breadfruit trees.

pedej (**pedej**). Expression, "Chicken!"; "Coward!"; "Yellow!"

pedenpā (**pedenpay**). Variant form of *ped in pā* (**ped yin pay**).

pedeǫ (**pedeyaw**). Also *peleǫ* (**peleyaw**). A fish, Moorish idol (?)

pedet armej (**pedet harmẹj**). Also *perōt armej* (**peret harmẹj**). 1, 2, 6(-*i*), 8, 9. Forward; presumptuous; imposing, conceited, inconsiderate. *Joñan an pedet armej, edeḷǫñ im kǫkkure kweilǫk eo.* He's so forward, he went in and broke up the meeting. *Eperōt armej kijak eṇ.* That fellow is inconsiderate of everyone.

pedetaij (**peydeytahyij**). From Engl. Paradise.

pedkat (**pẹdkat**). 1(-*i*), 2(inf, tr -*e*), 5(*ppedkatkat, ppedkate, pedkate*), 6(-*i*), 7, 8, 9, 11(*pedkatkōt*). Mud. *Eḷap an ppedkate lowaan iaḷ eo.* The road is muddy.

pedo (**pedew**). 1(-*i*), 2(inf, tr -*wan*), 3, 5(*ppedodo*), 7, 8. Lie on stomach; fall on face; turn over; capsize. *Eṃṃan wōt babu pedo ippa.* I like to sleep on my stomach. *Ettōr em pedo.* He ran and fell on his face. *Lale kottōr em pedowan ajri ṇe.* If you run with the baby you may fall with it on its face. *Ḷeo iba eppedodo ṇe.* This is the man that always falls on his face.

pedobar (**pẹdẹwbar**). Sea slug; *Nudibranchs, Onchidium* sp. *Epedobare pedpedin likin ānin.* There are plenty of sea-slugs on the ocean-side reef of this island.

pedowan (**pedewwan**). Transitive form of *pedo* (**pedew**).

pedǫḷ (**pedaḷ°**). A plant; see *pādāl* and *pādālijṃaan.*

pedped (**pedped**). 2(inf, tr -*e*), 4, 5(-*e*), 6(-*i*), 7, 8, 9. Foundation; reef; floor of house; slab; base; basis. *Emake pedpede likin ānin.* This island has quite a reef. *Bwidej ej pedped eo an aolep menin jeraaṃṃan.* Land is the basis of all wealth.

peed (**peyed**). Variant form of *peet* (**peyet**).

peejnej (**pẹyẹjnẹj**). From Engl. 1(-*i*), 2(inf, tr -*e*), 4, 6(-*i*), 8, 9. Business; to cheat. *Kwōn jab peejneje armej kōn waj nana kaṇe.* Stop cheating people with those poor quality watches.

peek (**peyek**). 2(inf, tr -*e*). Dominate; own; rule over. *Eban peek eō.* He'll never dominate me.

peek (**peyek**). Transitive form of *pepe* (**peypey**).

peekdu (**peyekdiw**). Also *peekdu* (**pẹyẹkdiw**). 3, 6(-*i*). A fish.

peeḷ (**peyeḷ**). From Engl. 6(-*i*). Bell.

peeḷ (**peyeḷ**). Dial. E only; see *tape* (**tapẹy**). Vulgar. 1(-*i*), 2(inf, tr -*e*), 3, 4, 5(*ppeeḷeḷ*). Sexual intercourse.

peen (**peyen**). From Engl. 6(-*i*). Pen.

peenen (**peyenyen**). From *peen* (**peyen**). 1(-*i*), 2, 3(inf, tr -*e*), 6(-*i*), 7. Use a pen. *An wōn ṇe peen kwōj peenen kake?* Whose pen are you using? *Jab inepata bwe inaaj kapeenen eok ippa.* Don't worry because I'll let you use my pen.

peenjej (**peyenjej**). Also *pinjej* (**pinjej**). From Engl. 6(-*i*). Pincers; pliers.

peeñka (**peyegkah**). From Engl. *banker*. 1, 2, 3(inf, tr -*ik*), 4, 6(-*i*). A card game. *Rej peeñka.* They are playing banker. *Inaaj kapeeñkaik eok.* I'll take you to a banker game.

peet (**pẹyẹt**). 2(inf, tr -*e*), 4, 6(-*i*), 7. To survey; oversee; search in a large area. *Rej ilān peet im kappukottok bao eo jibwin.* They're off to search for his pet bird.

peet (**peyet**). Also *peed* (**peyed**). From Engl. 6(-*i*). Bed.

peij (**pęyij**). From Engl. 6(-*i*). Page. *Jete peij in bok ṇe aṃ?* How many pages in that book of yours?

peij (**pęyij**). From Engl. 1(-*i*), 2, 3(inf, tr -*i*), 4, 7, 8, 9. Bass. *Ejjeḷam peijin.* He has a very deep voice.

peikan (**pęyikan**). From Engl. 1(-*i*), 2, 3(inf, tr -*e*), 4, 8, 9. Pagan; heathen.

peinabōḷ (**pęyinahbeḷ**). From Engl. 3, 6(-*i*). Pineapple.

pej (**pęj**). 3, 6(*pijin*). Discarded pandanus key; dry key of pandanus fruit.

pej (**pęj**). 1, 6(*pijin*). Placenta. *Ekaamijak pej eṇ pijin lieṇ.* She has a malignant placenta.

pej (**pęj**). Variant form of *pij* (**pij**).

pejaju (**pejahjiw**). 2(inf, tr -*uk*), 4, 6(-*i*). Pound; beat; spank; thrash; clobber. *Jemān ear pejajuuk kōn an kar jako boñ.* Her father spanked her for going out last night. *Rōpejajuuk kumi eo an.* His team got clobbered at the games.

pejao (**pejahwew**). 2, 4(*rippejao*), 6(-*i*). Method of casting lots; a shell, clam.

peje (**pęjęy**). Also *epje* (**yępjęy**). Formant in place names; capital; meeting place.

pejin (**pęyjin**). From Engl. 2(inf, tr -*i*), 6(-*i*). Basin. *Kwōn pejini dān ṇe.* Catch the water in the basin.

pejḷọk (**pęjlaq**). 1(-*i*), 2, 3, 5(*ppejḷọkḷọk*), 7. Go through; pierce; penetrate. *Elel ek eo im pejḷọk.* The fish was hit with the spear and pierced through. *Ek rot eo eppejḷọkḷọk ṇe.* This (kind of) fish is easy to pierce.

pejmām (**pęjmam**). 1, 2(inf, tr -*e*), 6(-*i*), 7. Spit out something. *Ñe kwōj ṃōñā tọ kwōj aikuj pejmām.* When you chew sugar cane you have to spit out the fibers.

pejpej (**pęjpęj**). Also *pijpij* (**pijpij**). 3, 8, 9, 11(*pejpej*). Shallow; superficial. *Eḷap an pejpej iarin ānin.* The lagoon beach of this island is very shallow. *Epejpej jeḷā eṇ an.* His knowledge is superficial.

pejpetok (**pęjpeyteq**). Idiom. 6(-*i*). A drifter; immigrant. *Ebooḷ ānin kōn pejpetok.* There are a lot of drifters on this island.

pejwak (**pęjwak**). 3, 6(-*i*). A bird, brown noddy, *Anous stolidus.*

pek (**pek**). 1(-*i*), 2(inf, tr -*e*), 3, 5(-*e*), 7, 8. Semen; sperm.

pek (**pęk**). Formant in place names; place.

peka (**peykah**). Dial. E, W: *wekañ* (**węykag**). 6(-*i*, -*a*). Scraper for pandanus with three wooden legs and bowl set beneath; tripod for juicing pandanus. *Ewi peka eo bwe jen kilọki bōb kā?* Go find the pandanus scraper so that we can extract the juice from these pandanus.

pekab (**pęykab**). From Engl. 2(inf, tr -*e*), 6(-*i*), 7. Pick-up truck. *Jenaaj pekabi ḷọk ñāāt ṃweiuk kā?* When will we deliver the merchandise with the pick-up?

pektaan (**pektahan**). 1, 2, 6(-*i*), 8, 9, 11(*pektaan, pektaanan*). Habitually defecate on ground. *Epektaan ḷeeṇ.* He's always defecating in odd places.

pel (**pęl**). A fish, boxfish, *Ostracion sebae*; a fish, trunkfish, *Ostracion tuberculatus.*

pelaḷ (**peylaḷ**). 1(-*i*), 2, 3, 7. Sink. *Kwōn kōpelaḷḷọk dekā ṇe.* Sink that stone to the bottom of the sea.

peleọ (**peleyaw**). Variant form of *pedeọ* (**pedeyaw**).

peljo (**peljew**). 1(-*i*), 2, 3(inf, tr -*uk*), 7. Mix in; be indistinguishable; blend in; integrated; assimilated; merged; mingle. *Kwōn peljoḷọk ippāer wōj.* Go mix in with all of them. *Eḷak to an pād Awai, epeljo ippān riBoodke raṇ.* After living a while in Hawaii he could pass for a Portuguese. *Epeljo ek ko koṇa ippān ko koṇan.* My catch got mixed in with his.

peloñloñ (**peleg°leg°**). Variant form of *piliñliñ* (**piliglig**).

pelọk (**peylaq**). 1(-*i*), 2, 5(*ppelọkḷọk*), 6(-*i*). Get something in one's eye. *Epelọk meja.* There's something in my eye.

pelọk (**peylaq**). Idiom. 1(-*i*), 2, 3. Be ashamed; embarrassed; lose face. *Ipelọk kōn an kar jab kūr eō.* I was embarrassed when he did not call my name.

pelōñ (**pęylęg**). 1(-*i*), 2, 3, 7. Float upwards to the surface of the water. *Ta ṇe ej pelōñtak?* What is that floating to the surface?

pelpel (**pęlpęl**). Also *archaic.* Small house on canoe; see *pāl.*

pelpel (**pẹlpẹl**). 2(inf, tr *-e*), 4, 6(*-i*), 7. Fishing method, using coconut leaf chain as scarer on dark nights. *Koṃ ar pelpeli ia ek kein?* Where did you use the scarer and catch these fish?

peḷ (**peḷ**). Coral; found on reef near lagoon beach and secondary lagoons.

peḷaak (**peḷahak**). 1(*-i*), 2, 6(*-i*), 1+7. Area; surrounding; around; vicinity; neighborhood. *Eṃṃan peḷaakin ānin.* This island is in a beautiful area.

peḷaak (**peḷahak**). 3, 7+3. Move a crowd; gather in a certain spot; congregate. *Kwōn kōpeḷaak jar kaṇe wōj ṇa ijeko jikiier.* Have all those groups assemble at their respective places.

peḷaak (**peḷahak**). Pass by, of clouds and rain. *Epeḷaak kōdọ eo.* The cloud passed by.

peḷaj (**peḷaj**). From Engl. 2, 3, 5(*ppeḷajḷaj*), 6(*-i*). A flush in poker. *Eitok juon taiṃoṇ em kōpeḷaje.* He drew a diamond which gave him flushes. *Eppeḷajḷaj.* He's always getting flushes.

peḷak (**peḷak**). 6(*-i*). A temporary shed; hut; lean-to; shack; shanty; cook shack. *Iṃōn wōn peḷak e?* Whose shack is this?

peḷan (**peḷan**). From Engl. 1(*-i*), 2(inf, tr *-e*), 8, 9. Balance. *Epeḷan ke ṃuri eo aṃ?* Did you get your debt squared away?

peḷḷọk (**peḷḷaq**). 2, 3, 5(*ppeḷḷọkḷọk*), 7. Open; blown; temporary; ajar. *Epeḷḷọk kōjām eo.* The door is open. *Eppeḷḷọkḷọk kōjām eṇ.* That door is always open. *Epeḷḷọk kōdọ eo.* The cloud is blown away. *Ripeḷḷọk kōm.* We're not going to stay long.

peḷo (**peḷew**). From Engl. *fellow.* 6(*-i*). Peer; contemporary; one of the same or nearly the same age as another. *Kwōn pukot juon peḷo ṇe aṃ.* Pick on your peer.

peḷo (**peḷew**). A plant, a tree; to be found on *Mājrwirōk* islet on Jaluit.

peḷọk (**peyḷaq**). 1(*-i*), 2, 3, 4, 7. Drift away; lose direction; miss destination. *Epeḷọk wa eo.* The canoe is drifting away. The ship missed the island. The ship lost its direction.

peḷọk (**peyḷaq**). 2, 6(*-i*), 7. Fishing method, using a canoe and drifting with the wind and current in a lagoon, line fishing. *Jeirro uweo ej peḷọk i ar.* Our brother is drifting and fishing on his canoe over yonder.

peḷọñ (**peḷag°**). Build attachments onto a canoe. *Rej jino peḷọñe wa eṇ.* They are beginning to put the other parts on the canoe.

pen (**pẹn**). 1(*-i*), 2, 3, 8, 9, 11(*penpen*). Solid; firm; strong; difficult; hard; strict; severe; stout; tough; rigid. *Eḷap an pen teej eo.* The test was very hard.

pen (**pẹn**). Encourage.

pen (**pẹn**). 5(*penpen*), 6(*-i*). Grated coconut.

pen būruo- (**pẹn biriwe-**). Idiom. From *pen* (**pẹn**) "hard", *bōro* (**bẹrẹw**) "throat, heart". 2+1, 3+1, 8. Stronghearted; determined; brave; stouthearted; intrepid; fearless. *Epen būruon wōt eṇ ṃṃaan.* He's such a fearless fellow.

pen in deo (**pẹn yin dẹyew**). At the same level; continue; keep on. *Iṃōk in ba en jab jañ ak pen in deo an jañ.* She kept crying despite my plea for her to stop. *Jekdọọn ñe rōṃane ak pen in deo an kakkōt.* Even though they beat him up, he kept trying.

penabnōb (**peynabnẹb**). Variant form of *pānāpnep* (**paynapnẹp**).

penawiia (**pẹnhawiyyah**). 1(*-i*), 2, 3, 4, 8, 9. Stupid; slow to learn (see *penawiie* (**pẹnhawiyyẹy**)).

penawiie (**pẹnhawiyyẹy**). 1(*-i*), 2, 3, 4, 8, 9. Smart; quick to learn (see *penawiia* (**pẹnhawiyyah**)).

penā (**penay**). Also *pene* (**peney**). 1(*-i*), 2, 3(inf, tr *-ik*), 8. Collapse; get smashed in; be dented. *Ewōtlọk tibat eo im penā.* The tea kettle fell and got dented.

penejeḷōn (**peneyjeḷẹn**). From Engl. 6(*-i*). Penicillin.

peniñeañ (**peynigyag**). Also *peniña-* (**peynigah-**). 1(*-i*), 2, 3, 7. Drift northward.

penja- (**pẹnja-**). 1, 6. Stopper; protector. *Men eo penjān kaajliiñ eṇ ṇe.* That is the stopper for that (gasoline) drum.

penjak (**pẹnjak**). 1(*-i*), 2, 3, 7, 8. Covered; out of sight; something in one's way or place; perfective form of *pinej* (**pinẹj**). *Epenjak mejān ainbat eo.* The top of the cooking pot is covered.

penkō (**penkeh**). From Engl. 3, 6(*-i*). Vinegar.

penkwe (**pęnqęy**). From *pen* (**pęn**) "grated coconut", *kweet* (**qęyęt**) "octopus". 1(*-i*), 2(inf, tr *-ik(i)*), 4, 5(*ppenkwekwe*), 6(*-i*), 7. A food, octopus smothered in grated coconut. *Penkweiki kweet ņe kijerro.* Smother our octopus in grated coconut.

penļwūj (**penļij**). From *penpen* "tap", *ļwūj* "mallet". Pound with a mallet or hammer.

penpen (**pęnpęn**). 1(*-i*), 2(inf, tr *pinik*), 3, 4, 8. Add sand or grated coconut. *Rej penpen raij.* They are adding grated coconut to rice(balls).

penpen (**penpen**). 1(*-i*), 2(inf, tr *pine*), 4, 5(*ppenpene*), 7, 8. Beat upon; tap on. *Ripenpen aje eo ņe.* That's the drummer. *Kwōn pine kapin ainbat ņe.* Tap on the bottom of that cauldron. *Kwōn ppenpene kapin ainbat ņe.* Keep banging on that kettle (held upside down--to make clean).

peñak (**pegak**). Archaic. Bay.

peñpeñ (**pegpeg**). 1(*-i*), 2, 3, 4, 8, 9, 11(*peñpeñ*). Strong; vigorous; muscular; husky, and usually quite tall. *Eļap an peñpeñ rūbait eņ.* That fighter is muscular.

peo (**peyew**). Torn; ripped; perfective form of *peoeo* (**peyewyew**).

peoeo (**peyewyew**). Dial. E, W: *kekeel* (**keykeyel**). 1(*-i*), 2(inf, tr *peo̧o̧t(e), potake*), 3, 4, 5(*ppeo̧eo̧o̧te*), 7, 8, 10(*potak, peo*). Tear; rend; rip. *Ļōmaro rej peoeo nuknuk.* The fellows tore clothes. *Rej peo̧o̧t nuknuk ko.* They tore the clothes.

peo̧o̧b (**pęyawab**). From Engl. *pay off*. Pay; refund.

peo̧o̧t (**peyawat**). Transitive form of *peoeo* (**peyewyew**).

pep-. See *pp-*.

pepa (**pepah**). Also *peba* (**pebah**). From Engl. 2(inf, tr *-ik(i)*), 3, 4, 6(*-i*). Pepper.

pepa- (**ppa-**). Dial. E only. Dialectal variant of *ippa-*.

pepe (**peypey**). 1(*-i*), 2(inf, tr *peek*), 3, 4, 7. Council; bargain; authority; decide; plan; confer; negotiate; deal. *Enañin or ke pepe eņ etōprak?* Has a decision been reached? *Ta eņ rej peke?* What are they conferring about?

pepe riab (**peypey riyab**). 1(*-i*), 2, 3, 4. False promise. *Eṃōj aṃ kōņaan pepe riab.* You've made your last false promise.

peptaij (**peptahyij**). From Engl. 1(*-i*), 2(inf, tr *-i*), 4, 6(*-i*), 7. Baptize. *Bata eņ ear peptaiji ajri e.* That priest baptized this child.

per (**pęr**). 1(*-i*), 2, 3, 5(*perpere*). Small sprouted coconut; tumor; swelling; wen; see *bōļoñar*. *Eperpere waini kā.* These copra nuts have lots of spongy growths inside (as a result of beginning to sprout).

perak (**perak**). 3, 6(*-i*). A fish, scavenger, *Lethrinus kallopterus.*

perakrōk (**peyrakręk**). 1(*-i*), 2, 3, 7, 8, 9, 11(*perakrōk*). Bow-legged; spread eagle; straddle.

peran (**peran**). Brave; courageous; bold; daring; heroic; undaunted; valiant; fearless. *Ļeeņ ej juon armej eperan.* He is a brave fellow.

peran (**peran**). 3, 7, 8, 9, 11(*peranrōn*). Loud; boisterous; noisy. *Eļap an peran ainikien bu eo.* The noise of the gun is loud.

perañ (**perag**). Stalk inside bunch of bananas or breadfruit; last part; basket in which chiefs store left-overs; person entitled to "throw it away" considered lucky. *Wūnōk i jabōn perañ.* Food stored at the edge of the special basket.

perar (**perar**). Put something over a fire.

pere (**peyrey**). From Engl. *beriberi*. 2, 6(*-i*). Beriberi.

pere (**perey**). Transitive form of *perper* (**perper**).

perōkeañ (**peyrękyag**). Also *perōña-* (**peyręgah-**). 1(*-i*), 2, 3, 7. Drift southward.

perōt armej (**peret harmęj**). Variant form of *pedet armej* (**pedet harmęj**).

perper (**perper**). Also *porpor* (**per°per°**). 1(*-i*), 2(inf, tr *pere*), 3(reflex only), 4, 5(*pperpere*), 8, 9, 11(*perper*). Doubt; underestimate; pessimistic; balking. *Kwōn jab pere wa eņ kōn an dik.* Don't underestimate that canoe because of its size. *Kwōn jab pperpere wa eņ.* Don't always underestimate the ability of that canoe (to get us there). *Kwōn jab kaperpere eok bwe kwōj naaj etal wōt.* Stop balking because you're destined to go. *Kwōn jab pere bwe juon eņ ṃṃaan.* Do not doubt him for he is also a man.

peru (**pęyriw**). 1(*-i*), 2(inf, tr *-uk*), 4, 5(*pperuru*), 6(*-i*), 8. A food, pandanus pulp and juice mixed with grated coconut and coconut oil (and optionally with arrowroot starch), wrapped in breadfruit leaves and boiled or baked. *Epperuru nuknuk ņe aṃ.* Your clothes are covered with *peru* food.

peru (**peyriw**). Vulgar slang. 1, 2(inf, tr *-ik*), 3, 4, 5(*pperuru*), 7. Sexual intercourse.

pet (**pęt**). 1(*pitō-*), 6(*-i*). Pillow; head; eastern side of a house; the side where people lay their heads while sleeping. *Jab etetal ijin bwe lọpet.* Don't walk here because it's the eastern side of the house.

pet (**pęt**). 6(*-i*). A bit, as used on boats. *Lukwōj emjak ņe ilo pet ņe.* Tie the anchor on the bit there.

pet (**pet**). From Engl. *bid.* 1, 2, 4, 6(*-i*). Bid.

pet (**pet**). 1, 2, 3, 5(*ppetpet*), 6(*-i*). Foul, in games. *Epet ilo rawūn eo kein kajuon.* He fouled in the first round. *Eļorak neen em kapete.* His foot got caught and caused him to foul. *Ekadik ppetpet an kkure.* He fouls often when playing.

pet pā (**pet pay**). 1, 2, 3, 8, 9. Warmed up, in games. *Epet pein.* He's warmed up. *Kwōn kōmmālmel im kapet peiṃ.* Practice and warm up for a while. *Epetļọk peimi jān ṃokta.* You're getting warmed up. You're getting better than before.

peta (**peytah**). From Engl. *bettor*. 2(inf, tr *-ik*), 4, 6(*-i*), 7. Bet; raise a bet. *Ear petaik eō.* He raised my bet.

peta (**petah**). Archaic. From *pat* "swamp". Small valley or depression.

peta- (**peytah**). See *petak* (**peytak**).

Petaaktak (**petahaktak**). 3, 6(*-i*). A plant, breadfruit variety; seedless variety of *Artocarpus incisus* (Thunb.) Linn.; the breadfruit tree.

petak (**peytak**). Also *peta-* (**peytah-**). 1(*-i*), 2, 3, 7. Drift eastward.

petkōj (**pętkęj**). Also *būreej* (**bireyej**). From Engl. 3, 6(*-i*). Biscuit; cracker.

peto (**pęytęw**). Dial. W, E: *pieto* (**piyętęw**). 1(*-i*), 2, 3, 7. Drift westward. *Wa eo eņ epetoļọk.* That canoe is drifting westward.

peto (**pęytęw**). Leeway.

peto-petak (**pęytęw-peytak**). 1(*-i*), 2, 3, 5. Drift about the sea.

petōk (**petek**). 6(*-a*). Fish's stomach.

petpet (**pętpęt**). 1(*-i*), 2(inf, tr *pitōk*), 3, 7. Use a pillow.

pi (**piy**). From Engl. Bee.

pia (**piyah**). Also *piaea* (**piyahyah**), *bwiaea* (**biyahyah**). 6(*-i*). Fish roe.

pia (**piyah**). From Engl. 6(*-i*). Beer.

piaea (**piyahyah**). Variant form of *bwiaea* (**biyahyah**), *pia* (**piyah**).

piano (**piyahnew**). From Engl. 1(*-i*), 2, 3, 4, 6(*-i*), 8. Piano; play piano.

piāpe (**piyapęy**). 3, 5(*ppiāpepe*), 6(*-i*). Sea slug; sea cucumber, *Holothuroidea*, *Thelonia* or *Actinopyga*; large, brown; found in water one fathom or more in depth at low tide. *Jen ilān kapiāpe.* Let's go gather sea slugs.

piba (**piybah**). From Engl. 1(*-i*), 2, 3, 4, 8. Fever; feverish; ague.

pid (**pid**). Vulgar. 6(*-i*). Posterior; butt; ass; buttocks; rump. *Raar wā-pidi ajri eo.* They gave the child an injection in the buttocks.

pidiiet (**pidiyyet**). From Engl. 2(inf, tr *-e*). Period.

piditte (**pidittey**). Also *pidikke* (**pidikkey**). From Japn. 2, 3(inf, tr *-ik*), 6(*-i*), 8, 9. Come in last in a race. *Enāj kar wiin ak wōjļā eo an ekapidikkeiki.* He would have won if his sail hadn't been torn, thus making him bring up the rear. *Ekar piditte wa eo waan ilo iāekwōj eo.* His canoe was the last in the race.

pidodo (**pidęwdęw**). 1(*-i*), 2, 3, 8, 9, 11(*pidodo*). Soft; tender; easy; frail; limber; simple; brittle; fragile; breakable. *Kwōn ṃōñā ṃōñā pidodo ñe emetak ñiiṃ.* Eat soft food if you have a toothache. *Epidodo teej eo.* The test was easy.

pidtoto (**pidtęwtęw**). Also *ppidtoto* (**ppidtęwtęw**). 1(*-i*), 2, 3(inf, tr *-ik*), 5(*ppiditoto*), 7, 8, 9, 11(*pidtoto*). Loose, of clothing or rope; flabby, of skin; sag; shabby; baggy. *Epidtoto nuknuk ņe aṃ.* Your clothing fits you loosely.

pieo (**piyew**). Also *pio.* Archaic. 6(*pien*). Formant in place names; place for making medicine.

piepe (**piyẹpẹy**). Variant form of *ppe.*

pieto (**piyẹtẹw**). Dialectal variant of *peto.*

piik (**piyik**). From Engl. 3(*kappiikik*), 5(*ppiikik*), 6(*-i*). Pig; hog; pork. *Eḷap an ppiikik ānin.* There are lots of pigs on this islet.

piiḷ (**piyiḷ**). From Engl. 2(inf, tr *-i*), 6(*-i*). Bill. *Kwōn kab piiḷi eō kōn m̧weiuk kā ij kaduoji.* Bill me later for the goods I'm taking out.

piiḷ tūrep (**piyiḷ tiryep**). From Engl. 1(*-i*), 2, 3, 4, 7. Field trip; field trip ship. *Kwōj piiḷ tūrep ḷọk ñan ia?* Where are you making a field trip to?

piin (**piyin**). From Engl. 5(*ppiinin*), 6(*-i*). Beans.

piin (**piyin**). From Engl. 1(*-i*), 2(inf, tr *-i*), 6(*-i*). Safety pin; oarlock; bobby pin. *Ewi piinin oru eo.* Where's the oarlock?

piinin (**piyinyin**). From *piin* (**piyin**). 1(*-i*), 2, 3(inf, tr *-i*), 6(*-i*), 7. Wear a pin; use an oarlock. *Kwōj piinin ḷọk ñan ia?* Where are you going with that pin? *Kwōn ja kapiinini ippān m̧okta.* Let her use your pins for the time being.

piiñ (**piyig**). From Engl. 1(*-i*), 2(inf, tr *-i*), 3, 5(*ppiiñiñ*), 6(*-i*), 8, 9, 11(*piiñ, ppiiñiñ*). Pink. *Eppiiñiñ pija ņe.* That picture has lots of pink in it.

piit (**piyit**). From Engl. *beat*. 1(*-i*). Rhythm; beat.

pij (**pij**). Also *pej* (**pẹj**). From Engl. *pitch*. 2(inf, tr *-i*), 4, 6(*-i*), 7. Tar; airfield.

pij in kwiir (**pij yin qiyir**). From *pej* (**pẹj**) "discarded pandanus keys". 6(*-i*). Toilet paper.

pija (**pijah**). 1(*-a, -i*), 2(inf, tr *-ik*), 3, 4, 6(*-a, -i*), 7, 8. Picture; camera; draw a picture; design; photo; portrait.

pija m̧akūtkūt (**pijah m̧akitkit**). 1(*-i*), 2, 3, 4, 6(*-i*), 7. Moving picture; movie.

pijek (**pijẹk**). Vulgar. 1(*ppijekjeki-*), 2(inf, tr *pekat(e)*), 3, 4, 5(*ppijekjek*), 6(*-i*), 7. Defecate. *Niñniñ eo epekate kaḷ eo an.* The baby soiled its diaper. *Ñe korap epekat bōram̧, kwōnaaj jeraam̧m̧an.* If a lizard defecates on your head, you will have good luck.

pijin (**pijin**). Construct form of *pej* (**pẹj**).

pijin (**pijin**). From Engl. 1(*-i*), 2, 4, 6(*-i*), 8, 9. Pidgin. *Iar roñjake an pijin ippān ripālle eo.* I heard him speaking broken English to that American.

pijja (**pijjah**). From Engl. Pitcher; container for liquids. *Tteiñ tok m̧ōk limō dān ilo pijja ņe.* Would you give me a drink of water from the pitcher?

pijja (**pijjah**). From Engl. Baseball pitcher. *Wōn naaj pijja ñan kōj?* Who'll be our pitcher?

pijḷeḷe (**pijḷẹyḷẹy**). Also *pijḷōḷō* (**pijḷẹhḷẹh**), *jipḷeḷe* (**jipḷẹyḷẹy**). 1(*-i*), 2, 3, 4, 7. Squat; sit on one's haunches. *Kwōj jab m̧ōk in pijḷōḷō ke?* Aren't you tired of squatting? *Kwōn pijḷeḷe bwe ettoon jeņe.* Squat because that place is dirty.

pijḷōḷō (**pijḷẹhḷẹh**). Variant form of *pijḷeḷe* (**pijḷẹyḷẹy**).

pijpij (**pijpij**). Variant form of *pejpej* (**pẹjpẹj**).

pijtoñ (**pijteg°**). From Engl. 6(*-i*). Piston.

pik (**pik**). 6(*pikōn, pike, pikin*). Plane surface; layer; stratum. *Em̧m̧an pikōn.* It (the ground) has a smooth surface.

pik (**pik**). From *pikpik* "flapping of wings". Formant in place names; to fly.

pikin (**pikin**). Also *pikōn* (**piken**), *pike* (**pikey**). 6(*-i*). Flat, of land only; construct form of *pik. Em̧m̧an pikin āneo.* That island is nice and flat.

pikḷọk (**piklaq**). 1(*-i*), 2, 3, 7. Fly off. *Epikḷọk bao eo.* The bird flew away.

pikmeto (**pikmetew**). 2, 3, 6(*-i*), 7. Fly off towards the sea. *Eḷak pikmetoḷọk bao ko, jeban lo lọjet.* When the birds flew out to sea, they blocked our view of it.

piknik (**piknik**). From Engl. 2, 3, 4, 5(*ppikniknik*), 6, 7. Picnic. *Iar kapikniki ajri ro jatū.* I took my brothers and sisters on a picnic. *Eppikniknik baam̧le eņ.* That family is always having picnics. *Kōm ar piknikḷọk ñan Ḷora.* We went on a picnic to Laura.

pikōḷ (**pikeḷ**). From Engl. 2(inf, tr *-e*), 4, 6(*-i*). Pickle. *Lale kwaar joḷọk pikōḷ ņe.* Don't throw away the pickle.

pikōt (**pikẹt**). 1(*-i*), 2, 3, 4, 8, 9. Coward; one who flees from battle; afraid to. *Āin kwe wōt ej jab m̧m̧aan kōn am̧* *pikōt.* You are too cowardly to be a man.

pikpik (**pikpik**). 1(-*i*), 6(-*i*). Propeller of plane or ship; flap; flutter, as of wings.

pikpikūr (**pikpikir**). 1(-*i*), 2(inf, tr -*i*), 3, 4, 5(*ppikpikūri, pikpikūri*), 7. Shake out; shake off. *Kwōn ppikpikūri jaki ņe.* Shake out that mat.

pikūr (**pikir**). 2(inf, tr -*i*), 7. Brush off. *Kwōn pikūri m̧ōttan raij ņe.* Brush off that piece of rice. *Kwōmaroñ ke pikūri ļǫk meņǫkņǫk ņe ñan nabōj?* Can you brush out that piece of dirt?

pil (**pil**). 2(inf, tr *pillit*), 5(*ppilpil, pilillil*), 5+7. Drop of liquid; dribble; trickle. *Kaidaak ajri ņe ļalem pil in wūnokan pokpok.* Give that child five drops of cough medicine. *Ia in ej ppilpil tok?* Where are those drops coming from? *Dān eo ej pil jidik jān bakōj ņe.* The water is leaking from that bucket.

pilawā (**pilahway**). 1(-*i*), 2(inf, tr -*ik*), 3, 4, 5(*pilawāwā*), 6(-*i*). Flour; bread; dough. *Eppilawāwā tebōļ ņe.* There is flour all over that table there.

pilawā mat (**pilahway mat**). 3, 6(-*i*). Bread.

pile (**pilęy**). From Engl. *play*. 1(-*i*), 2, 3, 4. Play cards for stakes; play poker; gamble.

pile (**piley**). Also *pile* (**pilęy**). 2(inf, tr -*ik*), 4, 6(-*i*), 7. Parry; ward off using Marshallese hand-to-hand combat defense techniques.

pileij (**pilęyij**). Also *pileej* (**pileyej**). From Engl. 6(-*i*). Plate.

pilein (**pilęyin**). From Engl. 2(inf, tr -*i*), 4, 6(-*i*), 7. Carpenter's plane. *Ta ņe kwōj pileini?* What are you planing?

pilej (**pilyej**). Variant form of *pileij* (**pilęyij**).

Pilele (**pileyley**). 3, 6(-*i*). A plant, pandanus cultigen (Takeuchi).

pilerab (**pilęyrab**). From Engl. *flare up*. Blowtorch; Coleman lantern. *Imaroñ ke kōjerbal pilerab eo wōjam̧?* May I borrow your blowtorch?

piliet (**piliyet**). From Engl. 2, 3(inf, tr -*e*), 6(-*i*), 7. Billiards; pool. *Jab kapiliete ñak ņe.* Don't let that novice play billiards.

pilim̧ (**pilim̧**). Also *jāljel.* From Engl. Film. *Eor ke am̧ pilim̧ kaļar?* Do you have a color film?

piliñliñ (**piliglig**). Also *peloñloñ* (**peleg°leg°**). 1(-*i*), 2, 3, 5(*ppiliñliñ*), 7, 8. Bleeding; drop; dripping. *Epiliñliñ ļǫk neen ļadik ņe.* That boy's leg keeps on bleeding.

pillit (**pillit**). Transitive form of *pil* (**pil**).

pilo (**pilęw**). 1(-*i*), 2, 3, 4, 7. Blind; trachoma; inflamed eye; not see well. *Ipilo.* I am blind.

piļōļ (**piļeļ**). 1(-*i*), 2(inf, tr -*e*), 3, 4, 8. Bald.

pinana (**pinahnah**). From Engl. 3, 6(-*i*). A plant, a general term for banana; (see also *keeprañ* (**keyeprag**)).

pine (**piney**). Transitive form of *penpen* (**penpen**).

pinej (**pinęj**). 2(inf, tr -*(e)*), 4, 6(-*i*), 7, 10(*penjak*). Hide; obstruct; cover; conceal; to block. *Kwōn jab pinej meja.* Don't block my view. *Ear pinej m̧aanū.* He obstructed my view. *Epenjak wa eo.* The boat is out of sight.

pinej jenkwa- (**pinej jęnqa-**). 1, 2+1, 4+1. Represent; replace; succeed; literally "cover the footsteps"; supersede; substitute for. *Kwōn ja pinej jenkwa ilo kweilǫk in.* Please take my place in this meeting.

pinid (**pinyid**). 3, 6(-*i*). Foreign beads.

pinik (**pinik**). 2(inf, tr -*i*), 4, 6(-*i*), 7. To throw grated coconut or sand at someone or something; transitive form of *penpen* (**pęnpęn**). *Ej jādetok wōt ak rōpiniki.* As he appeared they threw sand at him. *Piniki boboon raij kaņe.* Put some grated coconut on the rice balls.

piniktak (**piniktak**). 2(inf, tr -*e*), 4, 6(-*i*), 7. Chant and urge someone on by beating on a drum. *Raar piniktake rūttariņae ro bwe ren peran.* They chanted to the warriors to make them brave.

pinitto (**pinittęw**). Variant form of *pinnitto* (**pinnittew**).

pinjej (**pinjej**). Variant form of *peenjej* (**peyenjej**).

pinjeļ (**pinjeļ**). From Engl. 2(inf, tr -*e*), 3, 6(-*i*). Pencil.

pinju (**pinjiw**). 1(-*i*), 2(inf, tr -*uk*), 4, 6(-*i*), 7. Collect coconuts and husk them before making copra; gather many husked copra nuts. *Iar pinjuuk tok waini eo aō.* I gathered lots of my copra nuts here. *Jemān pinju bwe jen kab kōm̧m̧an mālle.* Let's husk before cutting copra so we can also make charcoal.

pinmuur (**pinmiwir**). 4. Redeem; ransom.

pinneep (**pinneyep**). Also *pinniep* (**pinniyep**). 1(-*i*), 2, 3, 5(*ppinneepep*), 6(-*i*). Coconut oil. *Eppinneepep nuknuk ņe am̧.* Your clothes are covered with coconut oil.

pinniep (**pinniyep**). Variant form of *pinneep* (**pinneyep**).

pinnik (**pinnik**). 1(-*i*), 2(inf, tr -*i*), 4. Urge on by cheers or other means; to cheer on. *Kom̧win pinniki kumi eņ ad bwe ren kkōļoļo im wiin.* You must cheer our team so they can be enthused toward winning.

pinnitto (**pinnittew**). Also *pinitto* (**pinittęw**). 2(inf, tr -*iki*), 4, 6(-*i*), 7. To struggle for; strive toward. *Ear pinittoiki juon an tiikri im tōprak.* He struggled for a degree and got one.

pinōt (**piynet**). From Engl. 3, 5(*ppinōtnōt*), 6(-*i*). Peanut.

piñpiñ (**pigpig**). 3, 6(-*i*). A plant, tree, *Hernandia nymphaeifolia* (Presl) Kubitzki (Hernandiaceae). A large, handsome, cordate-leaved tree with yellow inflated fruits. (See *Lọpiñpiñ* (**lawpigpig**)).

piolōt (**piyewlet**). From Engl. 2(inf, tr -*e*), 3(inf, tr -*e*)), 5(*ppiolōtlōt*), 6(-*i*), 8, 9, 11(*piolōt, ppiolōtlōt*). Violet. *Wōn iaami ear kapiolōte ijeņe?* Which one of you spilled the violet paint there? *Em̧m̧an an ppiolōtlōt nuknuk ņe.* The violetness of that dress is pleasing.

piọ (**piyaw**). Also *m̧ōleọ* (**m̧eleyaw**). 1(-*i*), 2, 3(inf *kappiọeo*, tr -*uk*), 5(*ppiọeo*), 8, 11(*piọeo*). Chilly; fever and chills; cold. *Eļap aō piọ kōn kōto in.* I am chilly because of this wind. *Eļap an kappiọeo kōto in.* This wind makes one chilly. *Jōōt e aō etutu ekapiọuk eō.* This wet shirt of mine makes me chilly. *Eļap aō ppiọeo.* I chill easily.

pip-. See *pp-*.

pipi (**piypiy**). Archaic. Nap. *Ej pipi ijeņ ium̧win jidik iien.* He's taking a short nap there.

pipi (**piypiy**). Vulgar. 6(-*i*). Vagina.

pir (**pir**). 1(-*i*), 2, 3, 5(*ppirpir*), 7. Slip down out of position, of things. *Epir kaļ eo an ajri eo.* The baby's diapers are slipping off. *Jidik wōt an pir dān eo jān mejān aebōj eo.* The water is down just a little from the top of the cistern. *Eppirpir kaļ eo an ajri eņ.* That baby's diapers keep slipping down.

pir (**pir**). 3, 6(-*i*). A fish, red spot tang, *Acanthurus achilles.*

pirañrañ (**piragrag**). 1(-*i*), 2, 3, 4, 5, 7, 8, 9. Criss-cross; jagged; unkempt; fuzzy-haired; stems of coconut tree that nuts are attached to. *Etke kwaar jab kuum̧wi bōram̧ ke epirañrañ?* Why didn't you comb your hair, for it looks a mess?

piro (**pirew**). Dial. E, W: *bo* (**bew**). Twins; double; grown together; joined; two pandanus keys joined together. *Piro ledik raņ.* Those girls are twins. *Āne kaņ repiro ippān doon.* Those islets are joined together.

pirōk (**pirẹk**). From Japn. (from Engl.) 2(inf, tr -*e*), 4, 6(-*i*). Concrete block; brick. *Inaaj pirōke m̧weeņ im̧ō.* I'll build my house using cement blocks.

pirōke (**pirẹkẹy**). Transitive form of *pirōkrōk* (**pirẹkrẹk**).

pirōkrōk (**pirẹkrẹk**). 1(-*i*), 2(inf, tr *pirōke*), 5(*ppirōkrōk*), 7, 8, 11(*pirōkrōk, ppirōkrōk*). Braid, of hair; braid a handle of a basket; plait. *Em̧m̧an pirōkrōk eņ an lieņ.* Her braids are nice.

pirūrrūr (**piririr**). 1(-*i*), 2, 3. Method of climbing down; slip down a tree or pole. *Kwōn pirūrrūr laļtak.* Slip down (the tree).

pit (**pit**). Shrink; to dry and become seasoned, of lumber, as in canoe building. *Epit wōjke eo.* The tree is cured.

pit (**pit**). 2(inf, tr *piti*). Twist sennit; make leis. *Kwōn pit ut ņe.* Please make the lei. *Kwōn piti kkwaļ ņe.* Please twist that sennit.

Pit (**pit**). 4. Gilbertese; clan name.

piteto (**piteytew**). 3, 6(-*i*). A plant, sweet potato, *Ipomoea batatas.*

piteto (**piteytew**). From Engl. 3, 4+3, 6(*-i*). Potato. *Kōjro ilān kapiteto.* Let's go shop for some potatoes.

piti (**pitiy**). Transitive form of *pitpit.*

pitōk (**pitek**). Transitive form of *petpet* (**pȩtpȩt**).

pitōro (**piyterew**). Dialectal variant of *makillō* (**makilleh**).

pitpit (**pitpit**). Also *kkapit* (**kkapit**). 1, 2, 3(inf, tr *piti*), 4, 5(*ppitpit*), 6(*-i*). Rub with oil as medical treatment; massage; osteopathy. *Ālikin aō wōtl̦o̧k, iar pitpit.* After I fell I got a good rub-down. *Jab kōtl̦o̧k an jabdewōt piti lo̧jiem̧.* Do not let just anybody massage your abdomen.

pitpit (**pitpit**). Also *kaatat* (**kahathat**). 1, 2(inf, tr *pit-(i)*), 4, 6(*-i*), 7. To chum for fish, usually in deep water. *Kwōn piti lal̦ bwe en m̧ōñā.* Make chum and sink it so the fish can bite. *Ij pitpit waj ak kwōj pitpit tok.* I'll throw chum in your direction and you throw chum in my direction.

pitto (**pittȩw**). 1(*-i*), 2(inf, tr *-ik*), 3, 4, 7. Climb or descend a rope; rappelling. *L̦adik eo ej pitto lōñl̦o̧k ñan raan mā eo.* The boy is climbing up a rope to the breadfruit branch. *Kwōn pitto lal̦l̦o̧k.* Climb down the rope.

piwūj (**piywij**). From Engl. Fuse. *Ebwil piwūj eo.* The fuse burned out.

po (**pȩw**). 1(*-i*), 2, 3(*kapo, kapopo*), 5(*ppopo*), 8. Fall off, of ripe pandanus keys. *Epo bōb eņ.* Some of the keys of that pandanus are ripe and falling. *Jen kapo bōb eņ.* Let's wait until that pandanus gets ripe and some of its keys fall. *Jen etal kapopo.* Let's go look for fallen ripe pandanus keys. *Eppopo leen bōb eņ.* That pandanus tree always has bunches with keys that fall easily.

po (**pȩw**). 3, 6(*-i*). A fish, wrasse, *Halichoeres trimaculatus*; *Cheilinus chlorourus/diagrammus/oxcephalus/trilobatus.*

po (**pew**). 1(*-i*), 2(inf, tr *-on*), 3, 5(*ppopo*), 7, 8. Lower sail; land, sailing vessel; arrive, of sailing vessel or airplane. *Kwōn poon wa ņe.* Lower the sail of your canoe. *Enaaj potok ñāāt wa eo?* When will the canoe get here (and lower sail)? *Wa eo eppopo eņ.* That canoe is stopping at many places. The sail of that canoe keeps coming down. *Epo bal̦uun eo.* The plane has arrived.

po (**pew**). 1(*-i*), 2, 3, 5(*ppopo*). Caught; capture; arrest; perfective form of *jebjeb* (**jȩbjȩb**); reach; nabbed; seized. *Epo bao eo.* The chicken is caught. *Epo rūko̧o̧t eo.* The thief is arrested. *Eppopo l̦eeņ.* He's always getting arrested. *Ear kōb l̦o̧k em po dān.* He dug until he hit water.

po (**pew**). 1(*-e*). Shelf; upper story of house; loft. *Jete poon m̧weeņ?* How many stories does that house have?

po bōro (**pew bȩrȩw**). Idiom. From *po* (**pew**) "reach", *bōro* (**bȩrȩw**) "throat". Content; satisfy. *Epo būrwōn kōn ledik eo pālen l̦eo nājin.* He's contented with his son's spouse.

po l̦ōma- (**pew l̦ema-**). 1, 2, 3, 4, 8, 9. Perfect; ideal. *El̦ap an po l̦ōmān būrookraam̧ eo.* The program was perfect.

podem (**pȩwdȩm**). Also *poom* (**pȩwȩm**), *jāppim* (**jappim**), *jāpim* (**japim**), *jāpem* (**japȩm**), *jabōm̧* (**jabem̧**). Not at all; not even. *Ear m̧m̧an aer kkure ak rōjab podem wiin.* They played well but didn't begin to win. *Iar pād Awai ak ijab poom lo Waikiki.* I was in Hawaii but didn't get near to Waikiki. *Ej jab podem tōprak m̧ōñā ko ñan jiljino awa.* The food wasn't ready by six o'clock. *Rōpodem m̧ōñā.* They haven't even begun to eat. *Ijabōm̧ etal.* I didn't even begin to go.

pojak (**pewjak**). 1(*-i*), 2, 3(*kōppojak*), 4+3, 5(*ppojakjak*), 6(*-i*), 7, 8, 9. Ready; prepared; secure; perfective form of *kōpopo* (**kepewpew**); alert; immune. *Kwōpojak ke?* Are you ready? *Kom̧win jino kōppojak.* Start to get ready. *L̦ōm̧aro raņ rej ppojakjak wōt in etal.* The men are still working at getting ready to go. *L̦ōm̧aro raņ rej pojak wōt in etal.* The men are ready to go. *Ipojak ñan mej in.* I've been immunized and won't get the flu.

pok (**pȩq**). 1(*-i*), 2(inf, tr *pukwōj*), 3, 4, 5(*ppokpok, aipokpok*), 6(*-i*), 7, 8, 9, 10(*poktak*). Entangle; disorder; confuse; trouble; messed up; baffled; bedlam; bewildered; intricate; jumbled; perplexed; snarled; elaborate; complex; complicated. *Epok tōrej eo.* The thread is tangled. *Kwōn jab kapok eō.* Don't make me confused. *Kwōn* *jab pukwōj eō.* Don't confuse me. *Ekijoñ ppokpok tōrej eo.* The thread is always tangled.

pokake (**pewkahkey**). 1(*-i*), 2, 3, 4, 8, 9. Obey; obedience. *Pokake eṃṃan jān katok.* Obedience is better than sacrifice (from Old Testament: Samuel to King Saul).

pokpok (**peqpeq**). 1(*-i*), 2, 3, 4, 5(*-e*), 7. Cough. *Emetak būruō kōn aō pokpok.* My throat hurts from coughing.

poktak (**pẹqtak**). Stirred up; stir; be messed up; disturb; displace; rolled; perfective form of *pok* (**pẹq**). *Kwōn poktake juub ņe.* Stir that soup. *Toni eņ ej kōṃṃan poktak ilo kuļab eņ.* Tony is making a disturbance in the club. *Kwōn jab pokpoktake nuknuk kaņe.* Don't strew your clothes all over the place.

polel (**pewlel**). 1(*-i*), 2, 3, 8, 9. Complete; satisfy; perfect. *Bwe en polel ami ļōmņak, koṃwij aikuj kwōnono ilo Baibōļ.* So that your minds may be satisfied, you need to read the Bible.

poļ (**peļ°**). Vulgar. 1, 6(*-i*). Rectum; anus.

poñpoñ (**peg°peg°**). 1(*-i*), 2(inf, tr *-e*), 3. Cover pandanus to ripen.

poob (**peweb**). Transitive form of *popo.*

Poobin-raj-eo (**pewebin-raj-yew**). See *poob* "sweep something": "belly fin of the whale (or porpoise)". A star; gamma Andromedae.

pook (**pewek**). Transitive form of *popo* (**pewpew**).

pooklim̧ (**peweklim̧**). 3, 6(*-i*). A fish, rock cod, *Epinephelus flavocaeruleus.*

pooļ (**peweļ**). 1(*-i*), 2(inf, tr *-e*), 3, 5(*jjepooļ(e)*), 7, 10(*pooļ*). Surrounded; encircled. *Ipooļ.* I am surrounded. *Rōpooļ ek ko.* The fish are surrounded. *Eṃōj aer jjepooļi ek ko.* The large group has surrounded the fish. *Eṃōj aer pooļi ek ko.* They (a small group) have surrounded the fish.

poom (**pẹwẹm**). Variant form of *podem* (**pẹwdẹm**).

poon (**pewen**). Transitive form of *po.*

popo (**pewpew**). 1(*-i*), 2(inf, tr *pook, poob*), 4, 7, 8. Sweep; brush off. *Kwōn pookļọk bok kaņe.* Sweep the sand away there. *Kwōn popo bwe ettoon ṃwiin.* Sweep, because the house is dirty.

popo (**pewpew**). 6(*-i*), 7. Turtle traces. *Ekilep wōn in ear ato bwe ealikkar jān popoun.* The turtle that came ashore here is obviously a big one from its traces.

popo ṃanit (**pewpew ṃanit**). Also *popo ṃanōt* (**pewpew ṃanẹt**). 1, 2, 4, 6(*-i*). Go ashore on islands belonging to others. *Kwōn jab popo ṃanit bwe rōnaaj ṃan eok.* Quit going to other peoples' land or they will kill you.

popoor (**pewpewer**). Variant form of *boboor* (**bewbewer**).

porpor (**per°per°**). Variant form of *perper* (**perper**).

potak (**pewtak**). 1(*-i*), 2(inf *peoeo,* tr *-e*), 3, 5(*ppotaktak*), 7, 8, 9, 11(*ppotaktōk, potak*). Tear; torn; perfective form of *peoeo* (**pewewyew**); tattered; ripped. *Epotak nuknuk ņe aṃ.* Your clothes are torn. *Eļap potak ņe ilo nuknuk ņe aṃ.* There is a big rip in your clothes. *Eppotaktak nuknuk kaņe aṃ.* Your clothes are torn in many places. *Etke kwōpotake?* Why did you rip it?

potake (**pewtakey**). Transitive form of *peoeo* (**peyewyew**).

poub (**pẹwib**). 1(*-i*), 2, 3, 4, 8, 9. Busy; occupied; engaged. *Eļap aō poub ilo raan jab kein.* I am very busy these days.

pǫ (**paw**). 2, 3(inf, tr *-uk*). Enter and hide inside coral, said of fish only. *Ear kǫjek ak kōn an pǫ, ejab mej.* I hooked it but it got inside the coral and I didn't land it.

pǫk (**paq**). 1, 2, 3, 5(*ppǫkpǫk*), 6(*-i*). Catch something in one's windpipe; choke on something, suffocate. *Jab babu im ṃōñā bwe kwōnaaj pǫk.* Don't eat while lying down or you'll suffocate. *Eppǫkpǫk kōn an ṃōñā kaiur.* He's always getting something in his throat from eating too fast.

pǫkwi (**paqiy**). From "onomatopoeia". 2+7, 5(*ppǫkwikwi*), 7. Sound of someone falling; thudding sound. *Iar roñ wōt ainikien an pǫkwiļǫk.* I only heard him falling to the ground. It seems as though I heard him fall. *Ļeo eņ epǫkwi ļǫk laļ.* The man has fallen to the ground. *Iar roñ pǫkwi ļǫk in an wōtlǫk.* I heard the sound of him falling.

pǫļjej (**paļ°jej**). Also *pǫļjej* (**paļ°jẹj**). 1(*-i*), 2(inf, tr *-e*), 3, 4,

5(*ppǫḷjejjej*), 6(-*i*), 8. A food, very ripe breadfruit baked in coconut milk. *Kwōn pǫḷjeji mā kaṇe.* Make those breadfruit into *pǫḷjej*. *Kwōn ṃōñā pǫḷjej.* Eat some *pǫḷjej*. *Eppǫḷjejjej lieṇ.* That woman is always making *pǫḷjej*.

pǫḷot (**paḷ°et**). Also *pāḷōt* (**payḷet**). From Engl. Ballot. *Rōnañin bwini ke pǫḷot ko.* Have the ballots been counted?

pǫpo (**pawpẹw**). 2(inf, tr *pǫut(i), pǫuni*), 6(-*i*), 7. Bind; tie; bound; coil. *Epǫpo jabōn eo ṇai neen.* The snake coiled around his leg. *Pǫutitok kkwaḷ ṇe ṇa ioon.* Tie that sennit around the top.

pǫputi (**pawpiwtiy**). Distributive form of *pǫpo* (**pawpẹw**).

pǫuni (**pawiniy**). Transitive form of *pǫpo* (**pawpẹw**).

pǫut (**pawit**). Transitive form of *pǫpo* (**pawpẹw**).

ppa- (**ppa-**). Dialectal variant of *ippa-* (**yippa-**).

ppakij (**ppakij**). Variant form of *pakij* (**pakij**).

ppaḷ (**ppaḷ**). Dial. W: *eppaḷ* (**yeppaḷ**), E: *pepaḷ* (**pepaḷ**). 2, 3(st inf *kōppaḷpaḷ, kōppaḷ*), 6(-*i*), 8, 9. Astonish; confound; absent-minded; senile; doddering; astound; gape; fascination; invalid. *Eḷap an kōppaḷpaḷ kōl ko nājin.* His tricks were fantastic. *Erūttoḷǫk em ppaḷ.* He's getting senile and absent-minded. *Eitok em kōppaḷ armej ro kōn an jeḷā kajin Pālle.* He returned and amazed the people with his knowledge of English.

ppat (**ppat**). Dial. W: *eppat* (**yeppat**), E: *pepat* (**pepat**). 1, 2, 3, 4, 6(-*i*), 8, 9. Feel unworthy; feel undeserving. *Ippat in etetal ippān.* I feel unworthy to walk beside her. *Aṃ deǫ ekōppat eō.* Your beauty makes me feel unworthy.

ppāin (**ppayin**). Dial. W: *eppāin* (**yeppayin**), E: *pepāin* (**pepayin**). 1(-*i*), 2(inf, tr *pāin(i)*), 3, 4, 7, 8. Insert. *Kwōn pāinḷǫk aḷaḷ ṇe ṇa iuṃwin ṃōṇe.* Put that piece of wood under the house there.

ppālpāl (**ppalpal**). Dial. W: *eppālpāl* (**yeppalpal**), E: *pepālpāl* (**pepalpal**). 1(-*i*), 2, 3, 7. Wave, of a flag or clothes; flap; flutter. *Eppālpāl bōḷeak eo.* The flag is waving.

ppānpān (**ppanpan**). Dial. W: *eppānpen* (**yeppanpan**), E: *pepānpen* (**pepanpan**). Also *ppānpen* (**ppanpẹn**). 1, 2, 3, 6(-*i*), 8, . Beautifully arranged; pleasing to the eye; well dressed. *Eppānpān wōt lijā eṇ.* She's quite an attractive girl. *Emaat maroñ in kōppānpen jiroñ eo ñan an ṃare.* They gave all they had to prepare the girl for her wedding.

ppārijet (**ppayriyjẹt**). Dial. W: *eppārijet* (**yeppayriyjẹt**), E: *pepārijet* (**pepayriyjẹt**). 1(-*i*), 2, 3, 4. A sickness supposed to come from eating *kǫnet* (**kawnet**). *Kwōn jab ṃōñā kǫnōt bwe kwōnaaj ppārijet.* Don't eat *kǫnet* shells or you will get this certain sickness.

ppe (**ppẹy**). Dial. W: *eppe* (**yẹppẹy**), E: *pepe* (**pẹpẹy**), *piepe* (**piyẹpẹy**). Also *ippe* (**yippẹy**). 6(-*i*), 7. Sandbank; build up a pile of rocks; build a platform. *Wa eo eṇ eṃōj ārōk ṇa ioon ippe.* The canoe has gone aground on a sandbank. *Wa eo eṇ ej pād ioon ippe eṇ.* The canoe is on that sandbank.

ppedikdik (**ppeydikdik**). Dial. W: *eppedikdik* (**yeppeydikdik**), E: *pepedikdik* (**pepeydikdik**). 1(-*i*), 2, 3, 4, 5, 7. Slow; tardy. *Jab ppedikdik bwe eboñ.* Don't be slow because it's almost night.

ppeerir (**ppẹyẹryir**). Dial. W: *eppeerir* (**yẹppẹyẹryir**), E: *pepeerir* (**pẹpẹyẹryir**). 1(-*i*), 2, 3, 7. Not in order; askew; disturbed.

ppej (**ppẹj**). Dial. W: *eppej* (**yẹppẹj**), E: *pepej* (**pẹpẹj**). 2, 3(inf, tr -*e*), 6(-*i*), 8, 9. Watery; flooded; diluted; float. *Kappej jidik wūno ṇe ṃokta jān aṃ kōjerbale.* Thin the paint a bit before using it. *Eppej lowaan ṃweo.* The house was flooded. *Eppej wa eo kiiō.* The canoe is floating now.

ppel (**ppẹl**). Dial. W: *eppel* (**yẹppẹl**), E: *pepel* (**pẹpẹl**), *bōlbōl* (**bẹlbẹl**). 1(-*i*), 2, 4, 7, 8. Gather fallen pandanus leaves from ground for thatch or handicraft. *Liṃaro rej ppel aj in ṃweo.* The women are gathering pandanus leaves for thatching the house.

ppepe (**ppeypey**). Dial. W: *eppepe* (**yeppeypey**), E: *pepepe* (**pepeypey**). 1(-*i*), 2, 3(inf, tr -*ik*), 7. Float. *Ta uweo ej ppepe iar?* What is that way over there floating near the lagoon beach?

ppiditoto (**ppidiytẹwtẹw**). Dial. W: *ippiditoto* (**yippidiytẹwtẹw**), E:

pipiditoto (**pipidiytęwtęw**). Distributive form of *pidtoto* (**pidtęwtęw**).

ppidtoto (**ppidtęwtęw**). Variant form of *pidtoto* (**pidtęwtęw**).

ppijinjin (**ppijinjin**). Variant form of *bbijinjin* (**bbijinjin**).

ppikaj (**ppikaj**). Dial. W: *ippikaj* (**yippikaj**), E: *pipkaj* (**pipkaj**). 1(-*i*), 2, 4, 6(-*i*). Ability to jump far; agile. *Ekkar ñan būtbǫǫļ bwe eppikaj.* He's made for football for he is very agile.

ppiñ (**ppig**). Dial. W: *ippiñ* (**yippig**), E: *pipiñ* (**pipig**). 1(-*i*), 2, 3, 4, 8, 9. Able to leap well. *Jen kappiñ in lale wōn in eppiñ.* Let's have a jumping contest to see who jumps best.

ppok (**ppęq**). Dial. W: *eppok* (**yęppęq**), E: *pepok* (**pępęq**). 1(-*i*), 2(inf, tr *pukot(e)*), 3(*kappok, kappukot*), 4, 5(*pukpukot*), 7, 8. Search for; look for; hunt for; find; quest; seek. *Ta ņe kwōj pukote?* What are you looking for? *Kwōn pukottok juon pinjeļ.* Please find a pencil for me. *Iar pukpukote em m̧ōk.* I hunted and hunted for it until I was tired.

ppoñ (**ppeg°**). Dial. W: *eppoñ* (**yeppeg°**), E: *pepoñ* (**pepeg°**). 1(-*i*), 2, 3, 4, 8. Hoarse. *Ebajet ke eppoñ ainikiem̧?* What is the matter that your voice is so hoarse?

pukor (**piqęr**). Stone used for grinding arrowroot; soft coral rocks found on beach.

pukot (**piqet**). Transitive form of *ppok* (**ppęq**).

pukpukot (**piqpiqet**). Distributive form of *ppok* (**ppęq**).

pukwōj (**piqęj**). Transitive form of *pok* (**pęq**).

puruk (**pir°ik**). Also *piruk* (**piriq**). From "onomatopoeia". 3+7, 5(*ppurukruk*), 7. Sound of stamping; fall with a thud. *Ta in epurukļǫk laļ?* What was that that made a noise falling down? *Kwōn jab ppurukruk.* Don't keep on making that thudding noise.

puwaļ (**piwaļ**). 1(-*i*), 2, 3, 4, 5(*kapuwaļoļ*), 7, 11(*puwaļoļ*). Coward; dastardly. *Kwōpuwaļ.* You are a coward. *Kwōn jab kapuwaļoļ eō.* Don't call me a coward.

ra (**rah**). 1(-*a*), 5(*rrara*), 7. Branch; bough; denomination; limb. *Eļap an rrara mā eņ.* That breadfruit tree has a lot of branches. *Raan kabuñ ta ņe am̧?* Which denomination is yours?

ra (**rah**). Formant in place names.

raab (**rahab**). From Engl. 2(inf, tr -*e*), 6(-*i*), 7. Raft. *Raar raabe āne tak m̧ootka eo.* The automobile was brought ashore on a raft.

raajkōļ (**rahajkeļ**). From Engl. Rascal.

raak (**rahak**). Also *ruwaak* (**riwahak**), *uraak* (**wirahak**), *jiraak* (**jirahak**). 2, 3(inf, tr *kōraake*), 7. Move (with directional).

raan (**rahan**). On top of.

raan (**rahan**). 1(-*i*), 3(*karraan*), 6(-*i*), 7. Day, date. *Jete raanim̧ ņai Kuwajleen?* How many days have you been on Kwajalein? *Juon wōt raanū ņai Kuwajleen.* I have been (I was) on Kwajalein only one day. *Kōrraan em etal.* Wait for daylight, then go.

raan eņ turun jekļaj (**rahan yeņ tir°in jekļaj**). The day after the day after tomorrow.

raan eo ļǫk juon (**rahan yew ļaq jiwen**). Variant form of *inne eo ļǫk juon* (**yinney yew ļaq jiwen**).

raan eo turun inne (**rahan yew tir°in yinney**). The day before yesterday.

raan ñan raan (**rahan gan rahan**). Idiom. Diary. *Ejako raanñanraan eo aō ilo pata eo ļǫk.* I lost my diary during the last war.

raanbat (**rahanbat**). Top of the hill.

raane-bōkāān (**rahaney-bekayan**). From "day of its bottle". Ready for a bottle, of coconut shoots only.

raanin ļotak (**rahanin ļ°etak**). Birthday. *Raanin ļotak eo am̧ in.* This is your birthday.

raanke (**rahankęy**). 1(-*i*), 2(inf, tr -*ik*), 3, 4, 6(-*i*), 7. Grate coconuts, grater; cog, gear, ratchet. *Kwōn raankeik ļǫk waini ņe.* Hurry up and grate that copra. *Ewi raanke eo bwe in raanke?* Where is the grater so that I can grate?

raantak (**rahantak**). 2, 6(-*i*). Daybreak; dawn.

Raarņo (**raharņew**). Clan name.

rabōlbōl (**rabelbel**). 1(-*i*), 2, 3, 5(*rrabōlbōl*), 7. Shiny; glitter; luster. *Eļap an rabōlbōl juuj kaņe am̧.* Your shoes are very shiny. *Eļap an rrabōlbōl juuj kaņe am̧.* Your shoes are awfully shiny.

rabwij (**rabij**). Vulgar. 1(*-i*), 2, 3, 4, 5(*rrabwijbwij*), 7. To warm one's bottom by the fire. *Errabwijbwij ļōļļap eņ.* That old man is always warming his bottom by the fire.

radikdik (**rahdikdik**). 6(*-i*). Twig; small branches. *Tūṃtok juon utū ilo radikdik ko.* Pick me a flower from the small branches.

Raej (**rahyẹj**). Clan name.

Rael (**rahyẹl**). Clan name.

raelep (**rahyelep**). 2(inf, tr *-e*), 3, 5(*rraeleplep*), 7. Noon. *Eraelep an ruj.* He woke up around noon. *Erraeleplep an ruj.* He usually wakes up at noon.

rai (**rahiy**). Variant form of *re* (**rẹy**).

raij (**rahyij**). From Engl. 3, 6(*-i*). Rice.

rainin (**rahyinyin**). Also *rainiin* (**rahyiniyin**). Today.

raj (**raj**). 3(*kōrajraj*). Whale.

rajāl (**rahjal**). 1, 2(inf, tr *-e*), 4, 7. Throw a rope over a branch; lasso a branch. *Kwōn rajāle mā ņe.* Lasso that breadfruit.

rajjiia (**rajjiyyah**). 1(*-i*), 2, 4, 5(*rrajjiiaea*), 7, 8, 9. Yaws; ulcerated framboesia. *Errajjiiaea ajri raņ nājin.* All of his children have yaws.

rak (**rak**). South; summer.

rakij (**rakij**). Transitive form of *rarō* (**rahrẹh**).

rakim (**rakyim**). 1(*-i*), 2(inf, tr *-i*), 3, 7. To plunder; destroy and take everything; ravage, ransack, loot. *Eṃōj rakimi jikin eo.* The place has been plundered.

rakka (**rakkah**). Also *rōkka* (**rekkah**). From Japn. *rakka* "drop down". 2, 4, 6(*-i*), 7. Parachute. *Enaaj rōkka laļtak.* He'll make a parachute jump. *Wōjļā ņe kōṃṃan jān rōkka.* That sail is made of parachute material.

rakōm (**rakẹm**). Archaic. Plunder after battle. *Koṃwin kab rakōme aolep ṃweiuk.* Now plunder all the goods.

rakōt (**raket**). From Engl. Rocket.

rakutak (**rahqitak**). 1(*-i*), 2(inf, tr *-e*), 3, 4, 5(*rrakutaktak*), 6(*-i*), 7. Scratch, as a cat; make marks with the fingernails; to rake, to claw. *Ajri eo ekijoñ rrakutaktak ņe.* That child is always scratching (people). *Kuuj eo ear rakutake jōōt eo aō em potak.* The cat clawed my shirt to shreds.

raļǫk (**rahļaq**). 1(*-i*), 2, 3, 4, 5(*rraļǫkļǫk*), 7, 8, 9. Slow; easy-going. *Eṃōj ņe aṃ rraļǫkļǫk.* Why don't you stop being so easy going.

rami (**ramiy**). From Engl. Rummy. *Kōjro rami.* Let's (the two of us) play rummy.

rane (**raney**). Transitive form of *rran* (**rran**).

raņ (**raņ**). Those (individuals close to neither of us); demonstrative, third person plural human.

raņe (**raņey**). Those (individuals close to you); demonstrative, second person plural human.

rañ (**rag**). 3, 6(*-i*). A bird, wild duck.

rañña|ǫk (**raggaļaq**). 1, 2, 3(inf, tr *-e*), 4+3. Astounded; astonished; be overcome. *Erañńaļǫk ke ej roñ ke rōjoļǫke.* He was almost overcome when he heard that his wife had left him.

rañrañ (**ragrag**). 1(*-i*), 2, 3, 4, 5(*rrañrañ*), 7. To warm oneself by the fire. *Ļōṃaro raņ rej rañrañ bwe rōpiǫ.* The men are warming themselves by the fire because they are chilly.

rap (**rap**). 2, 3(*karrapļǫk*), 5(*rraprap*), 6(*-i*). Voiceless bilabial affricate with a sudden, audible expulsion of sound (low); rasping sound. *Erraprap jañ in kaar eo kōn an jjeļǫk ṃabōļōrin.* The car made a loud rasping sound because it didn't have a muffler.

rapit (**rapit**). From Engl. 3, 6(*-i*). Rabbit.

rapit (**rapit**). Dial. Arno only. 6(*-i*). A bird.

raprap (**raprap**). Diarrhea.

rar (**rar**). 1(*-i*), 2(inf, tr *-e*), 3, 4, 7. To bleach pandanus leaves over the fire; to dry leaves by fire.

rarō (**rahrẹh**). 1(*-i*), 2(inf, tr *rakij*), 3, 7. Clean up an area. *Koṃwin rakij nōbōjān wōpij eņ.* Clean outside the office there. *Iien rarō kiiō.* It's clean up time now.

Raur (**rahwir**). Clan name.

raut (**rahwit**). Vulgar. 1(*-i*), 2(inf, tr *-i*), 3, 5(*rrautut*), 7. Urinate; urine. *Errautut ajri eņ.* That child is always urinating.

raut (**rahwit**). Dialectal variant of *taan* (**tahan**).

rawūn (**rahwin**). Also *raun.* From Engl. 1(*-i*), 2, 3, 4, 5(*rrawūnwūn*), 7. Go around; go on a field trip ship.

Erawūn Ratak eañ. He's making the Northern Ratak field trip. *Errawūnwūn ļeeņ.* He's always making field trips.

rā (**ray**). These (individuals close to me); demonstrative, first person exclusive plural human.

rā (**ray**). 3, 6(*-i*). Board; plank.

rāātle (**rayatlęy**). Dial. E, W: *rilik* (**riylik**). Archaic. On the west side of; see *jetak*.

rādik doon (**raydik dewen**). To cooperate; cooperative.

rājet (**rayjet**). 1(*-i*), 2, 3, 5(*rrājetjet*), 7. Apart, divided into two parts; partly; one-sided. *Errājetjet mā kā.* These breadfruit are all cut in two.

rājetak (**rayjetak**). 1(*-i*), 2(inf, tr *-e*), 2+7. Accompany; counterpart. *Boñ ej rājetake raan.* Night is the counterpart of day. *Kwōn rājetake ļọk.* Accompany him there.

rālik (**raylik**). 1(*-i*), 7, 8, 9. West.

rāpeļta- (**raypeļta-**). 1. Method of doing something; explanation of meaning of words. *Ewi rāpeļtan kōṃṃane wūn e?* What is the way to do this problem?

rāraņ (**rayraņ**). Those (individuals close to neither of us); demonstrative, third person plural human, singling out.

rāraņe (**rayraņey**). Those (individuals close to you); demonstrative, second person plural human, singling out.

rārā (**rayray**). These (individuals close to me); demonstrative, first person exclusive plural human, singling out.

rārōk (**rayręk**). Uninhabited land.

re (**ręy**). Also *rai* (**rahiy**). From Engl. Syllable "re" of musical scale.

reba (**ręybah**). From Engl. River.

reeaar (**ręyyahar, reyyahar**). Also *rear.* 1(*-i*), 2, 7, 8, 9. East.

reek (**reyek**). From Engl. 1, 2(inf, tr *-e*), 4, 5(*rreekek*), 6(*-i*), 7. Rake.

reel (**ręyęl**). Also *reil* (**ręyil**). 1(*-i*), 2, 3(st inf *karreelel*, tr *kareil*), 5(*rreelel*), 7, 8, 9. Gullible, attracted to; hung up on, sold on; persuaded; commercial; cajole; concur. *Eļap kareelel ilo tōlpijen.* There are a lot of commercials on T. V. *Ej kajjioñ kareele ledik eņ.* He's trying to attract that girl. *Likao eņ erreelel.* That boy is always finding something new that he likes. *Rūraan kein rōlukkuun rreelel.* People nowadays are gullible. *Erreelel ļeeņ.* He's always agreeable. He's got a roving eye.

reeļ (**reyeļ**). From Engl. 6(*-i*). Rails of boats; railings; bulwark; variant form of *ṃọkwōd* (**ṃaqed**). *Etūṃ reeļ in wa eo.* The boat's railings came off.

reil (**ręyil**). Variant form of *reel* (**ręyęl**).

reilik (**ręyilik**). Also *relik* (**ręylik**). 2, 3, 5(*rreiliklik*), 7. Look back. *Reito.* Look westward. *Reitak.* Look eastward. *Reiniñeañ.* Look northward. *Reirōkeañ.* Look southward. *Reilōñ.* Look upwards. *Reilaļ.* Look downwards. *Reito-reitak.* Look around. *Kwōn jab rreiliklik.* Don't keep looking back.

rein (**ręyin**). These (individuals close to us both); demonstrative, first person inclusive plural human.

reitaar (**ręyitahar**). Variant form of *retaar* (**ręytahar**).

rej (**rej**). They, progressive.

reja (**reyjah**). From Engl. 1(*-i*), 2(inf, tr *-ik*), 3, 4, 5(*rrejaja*), 6(*-i*), 7, 8. Razor; shave. *Kwōn rejaik kwōdeak kaņe aṃ bwe rōaittok.* Shave your whiskers because they are long. *Errejaja ļeeņ.* That man shaves often.

reja (**reyjah**). Also *kwōdmat* (**qedmat**). Slang. 2(inf, tr *-ik*). To strip of money or property by fraud or threat; to fleece someone; to sponge off of someone. *Rōnāj rejaik eok ņa ilo kuļab eņ.* You'll get fleeced if you go to that bar.

rejeta- (**reyjeta-**). 1. Supplementary part. *Ewi bok eo ej rejetan bok e ij riiti?* Where is the book to go with this one I'm reading?

rejetak (**reyjetak**). 1(*-i*), 2(inf, tr *-e*), 3, 7. To assist; ally; agree; to second, concur; help. *Elōñ ear rejetak būrejetōn eo.* There were many who agreed with the president.

rejin (**ręyjin**). From Engl. 6(*-i*). Raisin.

rekoot (**reykewet**). Variant form of *deekto* (**deyektew**).

ren (**ren**). They should.

rere (**ręyręy**). Peep.

rere (**reyrey**). Dial. E only; see *ttōñ* (**ttęg**). 1(*-i*), 2, 3, 7. Laugh; breaking of waves; smile, showing the white of the teeth.

rereenak (**reyreyenhak**). From *rere* (**reyrey**) "laugh", *in* (**yin**) "of", *ak* (**hak**) "frigate bird". 1, 2, 3(inf, tr *-e*). Sorrowful laughter. *Ibūroṃōj kake ke ij lo an rereenak.* I pitied him when I saw him laugh like that.

retaar (**rẹytahar**). Also *reitaar* (**rẹyitahar**). From Engl. 2(inf, tr *-e*), 6(*-i*), 7. Radar. *Raar retaare baḷuun eo im loe.* They searched and found the plane with the radar.

retam (**reytam**). 1(*-i*), 7. The outrigger side of a canoe.

retio (**rẹytiyẹw**). 1(*-i*), 2, 3, 6(*-i*), 7. Radio.

rewa (**reywah**). A fish, kingfish, *Caranx fulvoguttatus* Forskal.

ri- (**ri-**). Also *rū-, ru-*. Person from; person who.

riab (**riyab**). 1(*-i*), 2(inf, tr *-e*), 3, 4, 5(*rriabeb*), 7, 8, 9, 11(*riabeb*). Lie deny, dishonest; fake; false; liar; untrue. *Eṃōj ṇe aṃ rriabeb.* Why don't you stop fibbing all the time. *Kwōn jab kariabe men in.* Don't deny it.

riab nañinmej (**riyab naginmẹj**). 1(*riabwi-*), 2, 4, 6(*riabwin*). Feign sickness; malinger. *Ejjeḷọk wōt riabier nañinmej.* Never have we seen such great fakes about being sick. *Kwōj riab nañinmej ḷọk ñan ia?* Where are going with your malingering?

RiEpatōn (**riyepaten**). From place name: *Epatōn* (**yepaten**) islet in Kwajalein Atoll. Clan name.

rii- (**riyi-**). 1. Husband; wife; spouse. *Ewi lio riiṃ?* Where is your wife? *Ewi ḷeo riiṃ?* Where is your husband?

Riikjet (**riyikjẹt**). Clan name.

riiñ (**riyig**). From Engl. 3, 6(*-i*). Ring. *Ejako riiñ eo aō.* My ring is lost.

riiñiñ (**riyigyig**). From *riiñ* (**riyig**). 1(*-i*), 2, 3(inf, tr *-e*), 6(*-i*), 7. Wear a ring. *Ij jab kōṇaan riiñiñ bwe emetak peiū.* I don't like to wear a ring because my hand hurts. *Kwōn kariiñiñi bwe ekōṇaan riiñiñ.* Put a ring on her because she likes to wear a ring.

riitok (**riyiteq**). Guest; visitor.

rijekā (**rijekay**). 2, 6(*-i*). Possessed; characterized by chronic sinusitis.

RiJelwōj (**rijẹlwẹj**). From place name: *Jaluit Atoll*. Clan name.

rijerbal (**rijerbal**). Worker; employee; personnel; commoner.

rijjelōk (**rijjẹlẹk**). Also *rijjilek* (**rijjilẹk**). Apostle; disciple; servant. *Jete kar rijjelōk ro an Kūraij?* How many disciples did Christ have? *Rijjilōk eo an irooj raṇ ṇe tok.* Here comes the servant of the royalty.

rijjiit (**rijjiyit**). From Engl. Receipt.

rijjilōk (**rijjilẹk**). Variant form of *rijjelōk* (**rijjẹlẹk**).

rijorrāān (**rijer°r°ayan**). Slang. Delinquent; rascal. *Rijorrāān men ṇe.* He's a delinquent.

rijọubwe (**rijawiwbey**). 6(*-i*). Magician; sorcerer; kahuna. *Jen kōttar an rijọubwe eṇ rojak.* Let's wait for the magician to perform.

rikin (**riykin**). From Engl. 6(*-i*). Riggings of boats; shrouds. *Eitōk reeḷ em baatat rikin.* There's water over the rails and the riggings are smoking. (Sailor's description of a fast sailboat).

RiKuwajleen (**rikiwajleyen**). From place name: *Kwajalein Atoll*. Clan name.

rilik (**riylik**). Dial. W, E: *rāātle.* 1(*-i*), 4, 6(*-i*), 7. On the west side of; see *wetaa-*.

riliki- (**riyliki-**). 1. Cross cousin. *Koṃro ej rilikin doon.* You two are cross cousins.

Rilikijjine (**rilikijjinẹy**). Clan name.

Rilikin Jepakina (**rilikin jepakinah**). From place name: *Jepakina* (**jepakinah**). Clan name.

Rilobareṇ (**rilewbaryeṇ**). Clan name.

rilojet (**rilẹwjẹt**). 2, 3, 6(*-i*). Sickness, believed caused by sea-ghosts. *Erilojet ḷōḷḷap eṇ.* The old man has the sea-ghost sickness. *Rej karilojete.* They are treating him for sea-ghost sickness.

Rilokilōñe (**rilewkilegẹy**). Clan name.

Rilokōlañe (**rilewkelagey**). Clan name.

Riloṃaḷo (**rilewṃaḷew**). Clan name.

RiLoojraṇ (**rilẹwẹjraṇ**). Also *Looj* (**lẹwẹj**). Clan name.

rilotok (**rilewteq**). 6(*-i*). Visitor; guest. *Koṃwin karwaineneik rilotok raṇe.* Make the visitors feel welcome.

Rilotọbōn (**rilewtawbẹn**). Clan name.

Rilujien Naṃo (**riliwjiyen naṃẹw**). From place name: Namu Atoll. Clan name.

Riluut (**riliwit**). Clan name.

rimakaiio (**rimahkahiyyẹw**). Giant.

Rimatoḷeṇ (**rimateḷ°yeṇ**). Clan name.

Rimeik (**rimeyik**). Clan name.

rimmenanuwe (**rimmenahniwẹy**). Also *rūṃōkarraṇ* (**riṃekarraṇ**). 3, 6(*-i*). Menehune; leprechaun; dwarf; elf; midget. *Ajri in Ṃajeḷ rōkōn karimmenanuwe.* Marshallese children love to hunt for leprechauns.

RiNaṃo (**rinaṃẹw**). Clan name.

rinana (**rinahnah**). Outcast; outlaw; pest; naughty.

Ripako (**ripakew**). Clan name.

ripija (**ripijah**). Artist. *Ej juon ripija eṃṃan.* He's a good artist.

ripija annañ (**ripijah hannag**). Architect.

RiPikaarej (**ripikaharyẹj**). From place name: *Pikaarej* (**pikaharyẹj**) islet in Arno Atoll. Clan name.

RiPit (**ripit**). Clan name.

RiPitin-Mājro (**ripitin-majrẹw**). Clan name.

RiPitin-Naṃdik (**ripitin-naṃdik**). Clan name.

ripitwōdwōd (**ripitwedwed**). Archaic. 5(*ripitwōdwōde*), 6(*-i*). A barkentine. *Rūtto ro rōkōn ṇa etan baak ko etto ripitwōdwōd.* Our ancestors used to call the foreign barkentines *ripitwōdwōd*.

rirar (**riyrar**). 2(inf, tr *-e*), 4, 6(*-i*). Singe; burn hair off. *Kōm ar rirare piik eo.* We burned the hair off the pig.

Rita (**riytah**). Also *Jarej* (**jarej**). 4. Place name; islet; Majuro atoll.

RiWōjjā (**riwejjay**). Also *RuWōjjā.* Clan name.

riwut (**riywit**). 2, 3(*kariwutut*), 6(*-i*), 7. A toy, canoe made from very light wood; to sail a toy canoe. *Iar riwutḷọk (kariwututḷọk) ñan jitto-eṇ.* I sailed my *riwut* over to the south side of the island.

ro (**rẹw**). Also *rok* (**rẹq**). 2, 5(*rroro*). Angry; enraged; infuriated; jealous; disappointed. *Ero kōn naan ko aṃ.* He was enraged by your words. *Kwōn lale bwe erroro.* Watch it for he is easily angered.

ro (**rẹw**). Jump into the water.

ro (**rẹw**). Brood; litter. *Jojo ṇe ej ṃōttan ro eo jinoin.* That chick belongs to the first brood.

ro (**rew**). The (often for entities not present); demonstrative, remote plural human.

roba (**r°ebah**). From Engl. 3, 6(*-i*). Rubber.

robba (**r°ebbah**). 1(*-i*), 2, 3, 4, 6(*-i*), 7. Trumpet; flute. *Ejeḷā kōjañjañ robba.* He knows how to play the trumpet.

roj (**r°ej**). 1(*-i*), 2, 3, 6(*-i*), 8, 9. Ebb tide. *Ejej wōt rojin.* It's absolutely the lowest possible tide. *Eroj.* It's ebb tide. *Eroj ḷọk rainin jān inne.* The tide today is lower than yesterday.

rojak (**r°ejak**). 6(*-i*). Spar of sail; boom; gaff. *Rojak kōrā.* Boom. *Rojak ṃaan.* Gaff.

rojak (**r°ejak**). 2, 5(*rrojakjak*), 6(*-i*), 7. Sorcery; magic. *Ej ja rojak ṃokta.* Let him get the sorcery over with first.

roje (**r°ejey**). Transitive form of *rojroj* (**r°ejr°ej**).

rojeri (**rẹwjẹriy**). From Engl. Rosary. *Rej rojeri kiiō.* They're saying the rosary now.

Rojia (**rẹwjiyah**). From Engl. 4. Russia.

rojroj (**r°ejr°ej**). 1(*-i*), 2(inf, tr *roje*), 4, 6(*-i*). Wrap; bandage; bind. *Etiljek rojrojū.* I wrap things well. *Taktō eo ear roje peiū kōn juon korak.* The doctor bound my arm with a bandage.

rok (**rẹq**). Variant form of *ro* (**rẹw**).

roḷọk (**rẹwḷaq**). 1, 2, 3, 6(*-i*). Plunge into the sea. *Ear roḷọk iar.* He ran and plunged into the lagoon. *Raar karoḷọke.* They dunked him.

roḷọk (**rẹwḷaq**). 2(inf, tr *-e*). Praise. *Roḷọke etan Irooj.* Praise the Lord.

rom (**r°ẹm**). 1(*-i*), 2, 3, 5(*rromrom*), 7. Wink; blink.

romaak (**r°emahak**). 1(*-i*), 2, 3, 5(*rromaakak*), 7, 8, 9. Shine; to light; perfective form of *romrom* (**r°emr°em**); gleam; illuminate; luminous. *Meramin jatiraito eo eromaake kōdọ eo.* The searchlight illuminates the cloud. *Ta eṇ ej rrōmaakak tok ijjuweo?* What's that that keeps shining this way from way over there?

rome (**r°emey**). Transitive form of *romrom* (**r°emr°em**).

romrom (**r°emr°em**). 1(*-i*), 2(inf, tr *rome*), 3, 4, 7, 10(*romaak*). To have light. *Kwōmaroñ ke letok teeñki ṇe aṃ bwe in ja romromḷọk kake?* Can you give me your flashlight so that I can light my way with it? *Ta ṇe kwōj rome?* What are you shining a light on?

roñ (**reg°**). 2, 3, 5(*rroñroñ*), 7. To hear. *Kwaar roñ ke nuuj eo ilo retio eo?* Did you hear the news on the radio? *Kwaar karoñ ke er ke eor ad kweilǫk?* Did you inform them that we have a meeting? *Erroñroñ ļeeṇ.* He has good hearing. *Roñjake nuuj.* Listen to the news. *Ej jab roñļǫkjeṇ.* He can't hear.

roñ (**reg°**). 1(*-i*). Angle of the jaw.

roñ (**reg°**). Archaic. Hoop; made of wood for flying fish net.

roñ jaṃōṇ (**reg° jaṃeṇ**). 1(*-i*), 2, 3, 7. Dull of hearing.

roñanpat (**reg°anpat**). A bird, mallard, *Anas platyrhynchos*; a bird, northern shoveler, *Anas clypeata.*

roñiia (**reg°iyyah**). 1(*-i*), 2, 4, 7, 8, 9. Hard of hearing (see *roñiie* (**reg°iyyęy**)).

roñiie (**reg°iyyęy**). Also *roñļǫkjeṇ* (**r°eg°ļaqjeṇ**). 1(*-i*), 2, 4, 7, 8, 9. Good hearing (see *roñiia* (**reg°iyyah**)).

roñjake (**reg°jakey**). 1(*-i*), 2, 3(*keroñjake*), 4, 7. Listen. *Jouj im roñjake.* Please listen.

roñļǫkjeṇ (**r°eg°ļaqjeṇ**). Hear well; quick of hearing.

roñļǫkjeṇ (**r°eg°ļaqjeṇ**). Variant form of *roñiie* (**reg°iyyęy**).

roñoul (**reg°ewil**). Also *roñoul* (**ręg°ęwil**). 3, 5(*karrōñoul*), 7. Twenty.

rooj (**rewej**). 6(*-i*). Rose; hibiscus flower.

roojoj (**rewejwej**). 1(*-i*), 2, 3, 7. Wear a rose or hibiscus flower.

rook (**rewek**). Transitive form of *roro* (**rewrew**).

ropāj (**ręwpaj**). 2(inf, tr *-e*), 4, 6(*-i*). Plunder, clean out; loot. *Rōropāje ṃōn wia eo an boñ.* His store was looted last night.

ror-. See *rr-*.

ror (**r°er°**). Formant in place names; variant form of *rorror.*

roro (**ręwręw**). 1(*ruja-*), 2(inf, tr *ruoj(e), rooj(e)*), 4, 6(*rujān, rojān*), 7. Chant; shout rhythmically while doing a job requiring team work, as carrying a canoe. *Eor roro ñan aolep kain jerbal.* There is a chant for any type of work. *Ļōļļap eṇ ekanooj jeļā roro.* The old man can really chant. *Rej rooje aer jerbal.* They're chanting while working. *Elōñ rujān wa i lǫmeto.* There are many chants for a vessel in the lagoon. Anything goes at sea.

roro (**ręwręw**). Dust from coconut cloth (*inpel*). *Ewōtlǫk roro jān inpel eṇ.* Dust is falling from the coconut cloth.

roro (**rewrew**). 1(*-i*), 2(inf, tr *rook(e)*), 7. Hang on the line; clothesline; leave to dry. *Nuknuk ko kaṇ rej roro.* The clothes are hanging on the line. *Kobaak eo eṇ ej roro.* I've left the outrigger out to dry.

roro (**rewrew**). Those (individuals distant but visible); demonstrative, remote plural human, singling out.

rorror (**r°er°r°er°**). Also *ror* (**r°er°**). From "onomatopoeia". 1(*-i*), 2(inf, tr *-e*), 3, 6(*-i*), 7. Bow-wow; to bark, of dogs; roar, as of the wind or a monster. *Kidu eo ear rorrore ļadik eo.* The dog barked at the boy. *Jab kǫrorrore kidu ṇe.* Don't make that dog bark. *Kidu eo erorļǫk.* The dog is barking.

rot (**r°et**). Also *tor* (**ter°**). Kind; type; sort. *Ṃōñā rot eṇ kokōṇaan ṃōñā?* What kind of food do you like?

rotak (**rewtak**). 2, 3, 5(*rrotaktak*), 6(*-i*). Fall on one's back; tripped. *Ettōr tōm rotak.* He fell on his back running toward me. *Iar ektake em kōrotake.* I lifted him up and threw him on his back. *Errotaktak ñe ej kkure.* He's always falling on his back when he plays. *Erotak wōn eo.* The turtle's on its back.

Rouk (**ręwik**). A constellation; possibly a variant form of *Ok-an-adik.*

rowālǫk (**rewaylaq**). 1, 2, 3, 6(*-i*), 8, 9. Crazy; mad; moron; deviate. *Erowālǫk.* He's off his rocker. *Kwōn jab rowālǫk jān men eo iar ba.* Don't deviate from what I said.

rǫ (**raw**). Vulgar. 1(*rou-, rǫǫ-*). Scrotum; testicle.

rǫklep (**raqlep**). 2(inf, tr *-e*)8 4, 6(*-i*), 7. Scoop up more than one's share. *Kwōn jab rǫklep bwe elōñ armej.* Don't scoop up too much and be considerate of the others.

rǫkrok (**raqręq**). 1, 2(inf, tr *rǫkuj*), 4, 6(*-i*). Scoop up; scratch. *Raar rǫkrok bok im boke.* They scooped up sand and covered him with it. *Lale bwe kuuj ṇe en jab rǫkuj eok.* Be careful that the cat doesn't scratch you.

rǫkrok (**raqręq**). Dial. E, W: *jennōb* (**jęnnęb**). 1(*-i*), 2(inf, tr *-e*), 4, 5(*rrǫkrokrok*), 6(*-i*), 7. A food, watered down pandanus preserves. *Ear kwaļ ke pein ṃokta jān an rǫkroke* *mokwaṇ eo?* Did he wash his hands before he worked on the pandanus preserves?

rǫkwōj (**raqej**). Also *ḷam* (**ḷam**), *tam* (**tam**). 1(*-a*), 6(*-a*). Physique; body shape, looks. *Ein rǫkwōjān wōt enjeḷ.* She's built like an angel.

rǫñ (**r°ag°**). 1(*-i*), 2, 3, 5(*rrǫñrǫñ*), 6(*-i*), 7. Hole; shelter pit, air raid; cave, orifice, pit; pore; tunnel. *Eorrǫñrǫñ meḷan ānin.* There are lots of holes on the surface of this islet. *Eor rǫñ-jiddik ikilid.* We have pores in our skin.

rǫñ (**r°ag°**). Canoe part, platform over the lee side, opposite the outrigger side.

rǫǫj (**rawaj**). Transitive form of *rrǫǫj* (**rrawaj**).

rǫǫl (**rawal**). 1(*-i*), 2, 3(inf, tr *-e*), 4, 5(*rrǫǫlǫl, rrǫǫlol*), 7. Return; rotate; come back; oscillate; revert; revolve; turn back. *Kwōj rǫǫl ñāāt?* When are you (going) coming back? *Laḷ in ej rrǫǫlǫl.* This earth is spinning.

rǫǫlḷǫk ñan kapijuknen (**rawalḷaq gan kapiyjiqnen**). Repatriate. *Rōnaaj rǫǫlḷǫk ñan kapijuknen eo aer.* They will be repatriated.

rǫǫltōn (**rawalten**). Come back in order to (contraction of *rǫǫltok in* (**rawalteq yin**)).

rǫulep (**rawilep**). Vulgar. 1, 2, 6(*-i*). Testicles, enlarged; elephantiasis.

rōbtak (**rebtak**). Vulgar. 2(inf, tr *-e*), 5(*rrōbtaktak*), 6(*-i*). Scratch anus, to goose.

rōjañ (**rejag**). 1(*-i*), 2(inf, tr *-e*), 3, 4, 7. To encourage, advise; admonish. *Kwōn rōjañe bwe en etal in jikuuḷ.* Encourage him to go to school.

rōjep (**rejep**). 2(inf, tr *-e*), 3, 4, 6(*-i*), 7. Fishing method, line fishing outside lagoon, usually on lee side and fairly close to shore, for flying fish, using sand crab for bait. *Kwōn karōjepe ippaṃ bwe en kkatak.* Take him along so he can learn how to fish for flying fish from you.

rōk (**rẹk**). 1(*rūki-*), 7. South; southern.

rōkeañ (**rẹkyag**). Dial. E, W: *rōña* (**rẹgah**). 7. Southward; directional, enclitic, southward.

rōkka (**rekkah**). Variant form of *rakka* (**rakkah**).

rōḷǫk (**reḷaq**). 1(*-i*), 2, 3, 5(*rrōḷǫkḷǫk*), 7. Slipped by, unite, escape; slide out of hand. *Erōḷǫk bao eo.* The bird slipped by. *Errōḷǫkḷǫk bao eṇ.* That chicken keeps getting away.

rōṃ (**rẹṃ**). Also *lij.* 1(*-i*), 2, 3, 7. To crumble a mound or pile as of sand; fall through; landslide. *Lale erōṃ pāāk in raij kaṇe.* Look out, that (pile of) bags of rice might crumble. *Jab karōṃ bok ṇe.* Don't make that (mound of) sand crumble.

rōṃ (**rẹṃ**). Also *rōṃ* (**reṃ**). From Engl. Rum.

rōnna (**rennah**). From Engl. *rudder, runner* (?). A fish, rudder fish, *Kyphosus vaigiensis* (Eniwetak).

rōnro (**renrew**). They two should.

rōña (**rẹgah**). Dial. W, E: *rōkeañ* (**rẹkyag**). Southward; directional, enclitic, southward. *Ear wārōñawaj wōt.* He walked southward.

rōōj (**rehej**). 2, 5(*rrōōjōj*), 6(*-i*), 8, 9. Loud, of colors, bright. *Ear kōṇak juon uḷa rōōj Būḷāide eo.* He wore a loud aloha shirt on Friday.

rōpin (**rẹpin**). From Engl. 2(inf, tr *-i*), 3, 5(*rrōpinpin*), 6(*-i*). Ribbon. *Ear rōpini bōran.* She wore ribbons in her hair. *Ear karōpini ledik eo nājin.* She put ribbons in her daughter's hair. *Errōpinpin liṃaraṇ.* The ladies always wear ribbons.

rōplen (**replen**). From Engl. 1(*-i*), 2, 3, 4. Minister; reverend.

rōr-. See *rr-*.

rōrāāt (**rerayat**). Vulgar. 1(*-i*). Anus.

rraakak (**rrahakhak**). Dial. W: *erraakak* (**yerrahakhak**), E: *rōraakak* (**rerahakhak**). 1, 2, 3, 6(*-i*). Intense crying, as a baby; bleat; squawk; wail. *Eḷak tutu kaḷ eo an, erraakak ajri eo.* When his diaper got wet, the child wailed.

rran (**rran**). Dial. W: *erran* (**yerran**), E: *rōran* (**reran**). 1(*-i*), 2(inf, tr *rane*), 3, 7, 8, 9, 11(*rranran*). Mark with a pencil; dirty; mar; soil; smudge; smut; soot. *Kwōn jab rane bok ṇe.* Don't mark that book.

rrā (**rray**). Dial. W: *errā* (**yerray**), E: *rōrā* (**reray**). Also *rre* (**rrey**). 1(*-i*), 2, 6(*-i*), 7. Lean against; dodge; move a little sideways to make room; take sides, advocate. *Wōn ṇe kwōj rrā ippān?* Which side are you on?

Kom̧win rrā ŋai turājet. Please move to one side.

rre (**rrȩy**). Dial. W: *erre* (**yȩrrȩy**), E: *rōre* (**rȩrȩy**). Also *rreik* (**rrȩyik**). 1(*-i*), 2, 3, 7(*reitok, ļo̧k, waj*). Wide awake; eyesight; look. *Kwōmaroñ ke rre?* Do you have good eyesight? *Reilo̧k.* Look in that direction.

rre (**rrey**). Variant form of *rrā* (**rray**).

rreik (**rrȩyik**). Variant form of *rre* (**rrȩy**).

rreo (**rreyew, rrȩyȩw**). Dial. W: *erreo* (**yerreyew**), E: *rōreo* rereyew). 1(*-i*), 2, 3(inf, tr *-uk*), 4, 7, 8, 9, 11(*rreoeo*). Clean; pure; sanitary; chaste; clear; neat. *Eļap an rreo meļan in.* This area is clean.

rriabeb (**rriyabyȩb**). Dial. W: *irriabeb* (**yirriyabyȩb**), E: *rūriabeb* (**ririyabyȩb**). From *riab* (**riyab**) "to lie", "to fool someone". 2, 6(*-i*). Fool around.

rrob (**r°r°eb**). Dial. W: *eorrob* (**yer°r°eb**), E: *rorob* (**r°er°eb**). Stock of an anchor.

rrobōlbōl (**rrȩwbȩlbȩl**). Dial. W: *errobōlbōl* (**yȩrrȩwbȩlbȩl**), E: *rōrobōlbōl* (**rȩrȩwbȩlbȩl**). 1(*-i*), 2, 3(inf, tr *-e*), 7. Shimmer; gleam faintly; twinkle; glimmer.

rro̧ñ (**rrag°**). Dial. W: *erro̧ñ* (**yerrag°**), E: *rōro̧ñ* (**rerag°**. 1(*-i*), 2, 3, 7. Ruffling of cocks and dogs before fighting; bristling hair standing on end from terror. *Erro̧ñ kooļan kako eŋ.* That rooster's feathers are bristling.

rro̧o̧j (**rrawaj**). Dial. W: *erro̧o̧j* (**yerrawaj**), E: *rōro̧o̧j* (**rerawaj**). Also *ro̧o̧j.* 1(*-i*), 2(inf, tr *ro̧o̧j(e)*), 4, 6(*-i*), 7. To urge, goad, spur, push. *Ripālle eo ear ro̧o̧je niim̧buun Mājro eo.* The American advised the Majuro laborer to get on the ball. *Kwōn ro̧o̧je ļo̧k ñan jikin jerbal eo an.* Urge him to go back to work. *Ejaje rro̧o̧j armej.* He never goads people.

rrōñ (**rrȩg**). Dial. W: *errōñ* (**yȩrrȩg**), E: *rōrōñ* (**rȩrȩg**). Vulgar. 1(*-i*), 2, 3(st inf *karrōñrōñ,* tr *karrōñ*), 5(*rrōñrōñ*), 7, 8, 9. Erection.

rrwe (**r°r°ey**). Dial. W: *eorrwe* (**yer°r°ey**), E: *rore* (**r°er°ey**). 1, 2(inf, tr *rwe*), 4, 6(*-i*), 7. Stick hand into pocket, hole, or crack. *Koban jeļā bwe kwōjaje rrwe.* You'll never know because you don't know how to fish in crevices. *Kwōn rwe tok kobban.* Stick your hand inside and pull out its contents.

rrwe (**r°r°ȩy**). Dial. W: *eorrwe* (**yȩr°r°ȩy**), E: *rore* (**r°ȩr°ȩy**). 2(inf, tr *-ik(i)*), 3(*karwe*), 4, 6(*-i*), 7. Fishing method, inserting the bare hand into holes nooks or crannies in the reef. *Lale am̧ rrwe bwe m̧aj enāj kij peim̧.* Be careful of poking your bare hand into holes or eels will bite you. *Ej karwe ļeeŋ.* He's putting his hand in the hole on the reef.

ru- (**riw**). Go through; see *ruwaak.*

rualitōk. See *ruwalitōk.*

ruatimjuon. See *ruwatimjuon.*

ruj (**r°ij**). 1(*-i*), 2, 3, 5(*rrujruj*). Wake up; awaken; awake, roused, conscious. *Eorrujruj ajri eŋ.* That child keeps waking up. *Ko̧ruji bwe eawa.* Wake him up because it's time to go.

rujān (**riwjan**). Also *rojān* (**rȩwjan**). Construct form of *roro.*

ruje (**r°ijey**). Transitive form of *rujruj* (**r°ijr°ij**).

rujruj (**r°ijr°ij**). 1(*-i*), 2(inf, tr *ruje*), 3, 4, 5(*rrujruje, rujruje*),6(*-i*), 7. Break; to reef sails. *Iien rujruj.* Time for reefing the sails. *Jen rujruj bwe eļap ļo̧k kōto in.* Let's reef the sail because the wind is picking up.

ruk (**riq**). 1(*-i*), 2, 3, 5(*rrukruk*). Yaws. *Errukruk armej in jem̧aan.* This person used to be covered with sores.

Ruk (**riq**). 4. Place name; Truk.

rukbo (**riqbȩw**). Also *rurbo* (**rir°bȩw**). 1, 2, 6(*-i*), 7. Gather missiles for throwing. *Kwōmake ñak rukbo.* You're sure clumsy at gathering throwing-stones. *Ej rukbuon ñan ta?* What's he collecting missiles for?

rukruk (**r°iqr°iq**). Also *kurkur* (**qir°qir°**). 1(*-i*), 2(inf, tr *-e*), 7. Shake up; gargle; rinse one's mouth; sound of coconut bouncing. *Kwōn rukruke bato ŋe.* Shake up that bottle.

rukut (**riqit**). Also *rukūt* (**riwkit**). Archaic. Two hundred pairs, fish or copra.

RuKwōdo (**riqedew**). Clan name; see *Kwōdo* "Jaluit tract".

ruļa (**riwļah**). From Engl. 6(*-e*). Ruler, straightedge.

rumij (**r°imij**). Dialectal variant of *aļo* (**haļew**).

rum̧wij (**r°im̧ij**). Dial. W, E: *ruñūj* (**r°ig°ij**). 1(*-i*), 2,

3(*kọrrum̧wijm̧wij*), 4, 5(*rrum̧wijm̧wij*), 7. Slow; delay; tarry; late. *Enañūņ rum̧wij am̧ etetal?* Why are you walking so slowly? *Enañin kar rum̧wij am̧ itok?* Why did you come so late? *Ta ņe ear kọrum̧wij eok?* What made you late? *Kwōn jab kōm̧m̧an kọrum̧wijm̧wij.* Don't always delay things. *Jab rrum̧wijm̧wij.* Don't dilly-dally.

ruñļọk (**rig°ļaq**). Also *rūm̧ļọk* (**rim̧ļaq**), *ruññuļọk* (**rig°g°iļaq**), *rūm̧m̧ūļọk* (**rim̧m̧iļaq**). 1(*-i*), 2, 3. Sink; dive under water.

ruñūj (**r°ig°ij**). Dialectal variant of *rum̧wij* (**r°im̧ij**).

ruo (**riwew**). 3(*karruwo*), 7. Two.

ruo m̧ōttan emān (**riwew m̧ettan yeman**). Also *ruo rājetin emān* (**riwew rayjetin yeman**). Two fourths.

ruo m̧ōttan jilu (**riwew m̧ettan jiliw**). Also *juon im rājet* (**jiwen yim rayjet**). Two thirds.

ruo- (**riwe-**). 1. Fault; sin. *Ejjeļọk ruō.* I am innocent. *Ej jab ruom̧.* You are not to blame.

ruokor (**riwewqer**). Also *rukor* (**riwqer**). Archaic. Twenty pairs, fish or copra.

ruorap (**riwerap**). Archaic. 2, 3(inf, tr *-e*), 6(*-i*). Two thousand. *Kwōn karuorape bōnbōn ņe.* Make the count two thousand.

rup (**r°ip**). 2(inf, tr *-e*), 5(*rruprup*), 6(*-i*), 7, 10. Broken; perfective form of *ruprup* (**r°ipr°ip**); ruptured; smash. *Erup bato eo.* The bottle is broken. *Eorruprup.* It's fragile. *Erup atin.* His gall bladder is ruptured.

rup bōro (**r°ip bẹrẹw**). Idiom. Frustrated; worried; broken-hearted. *Erup būruon ke ejab tōprak.* He was frustrated knowing he hadn't made it.

rupe bōkā (**r°ipey bekay**). 4, 6(*-i*). Break a boat in. *Ej kappok rurupe bōkein wa eņ waan.* He's looking for someone to break in his boat.

rupe om̧ (**r°ipẹywẹm̧**). 2(inf, tr *-e*), 3, 4, 6(*-i*), 7. Fishing method, line fishing inside lagoon using hermit crab for bait while at anchor. *Rurupe om̧ ro raņ rōmoottok.* The men who went fishing using the *rupe om̧* method have returned.

ruprup (**r°ipr°ip**). 1(*-i*), 2(inf, tr *rup(e)*), 3, 4, 5(*rruprupe, ruprupe*), 7, 10(*rup*). Break; tear down; demolish. *Em̧ōj rupe m̧weo.* The house has been torn down. *Eor juon kumi in ruprup em̧.* There is a working party for tearing down houses. *Em̧ōj rruprupe m̧weo.* The house has been torn down carelessly (with debris left lying all about).

ruprup (**r°ipr°ip**). 2, 6(*-i*). To hatch. *Eruprup lep ko buļōn mar eņ.* The eggs in the bush have hatched.

ruprupjọkur (**r°ipr°ipjaqir**). Slang. From *ruprup jọkur* (**r°ipr°ip jaqir**). 4, 6(*-i*), 7. To initiate; to begin. *Kwōn ruprupjọkur tok im jino al eo.* You be the initiatior and start the song.

rur (**r°ir°**). 1(*-i*), 2, 3, 4, 7, 8. Pick flowers. *Ledik ro raņ rej rur ut.* The girls are picking flowers.

rurbo (**rir°bẹw**). Variant form of *rukbo* (**riqbẹw**).

ruruwe (**riwriwey**). 1(*-i*), 2, 4, 6(*-i*), 7. Slander; talk about someone behind his back; libel. *Kom̧win jab kōņaan ruruwe armej.* Don't ever say bad things about people. *Aolep iien kōrā rej ruruwe doon.* Women are always slandering one another.

ruum̧ (**riwim̧**). From Engl. 1(*-i*), 2(inf, tr *-i*), 5(*rruum̧um̧*), 7. Room. *Eļap an rruum̧um̧ m̧weeņ.* That house has many rooms.

ruuror (**riwirwẹr**). Assassin. *Rōkōpooļe ruuror eo im buuki.* They chased and shot the assassin.

ruwaak (**riwahak**). Also *raak* (**rahak**), *uraak* (**wirahak**), *jiraak* (**jirahak**). 2, 3, 7. Move (with directional).

ruwaal (**riwahal**). Archaic. 1(*-i*), 2, 3. Twice.

ruwalitōk (**riwahliytẹk**). Also *rualitōk, ralitōk* (**rahliytẹk**), *rwalitōk* (**r°ahliytẹk**). 3, 5(*karruwalitōk*), 7. Eight. *Kōjro ej karruwalitōk.* We have eight each.

ruwamāejet (**riwahmayẹjẹt**). 1(*-i*), 2, 3, 4, 6(*-i*), 7. Stranger; not familiar; alien; foreign; visitor. *Elōñ ruwamāejet raar itok ilo wa eņ.* Many strangers came on that ship. *Ña iruwamāejet kōn kain bōnbōn rot in.* I'm not familiar with this kind of arithmetic.

ruwatimjuon (**riwahtimjiwen**). Also *ruatimjuon, ratimjuon*

(rahtimjiwen). 3,
5(*karruwatimjuon*), 7. Nine.

ruwe (**riwęy**). 2, 6(-*i*), 7. Misfortune due
to breaking of a taboo. *Kwōn jab
ļōke ļadik ņe bwe enāj ruwe.* Don't
walk over the boy because you'll bring
him bad luck.

rūb (**rib**). 2, 3(*karrūbļǫk*), 5(*rrūbrūb*),
6(-*i*). Explosive sound, voiceless
bilabial affricate; fart; break wind.
Errūbrūb ledik eņ. That girl breaks
wind all the time.

Rūbojaar (**ribewjahar**). Clan name.

rūbōb (**ribęb**). Dial. E only; see *dibab*
(**dibab**), *utot* (**witwęt**). 3, 6(-*i*). A fish,
general term for butterfly fish;
including *Chaetodon auriga;
Holocanthus diacanthus; Pygoplites
diacanthus.*

rūbukwi (**ribiqiy**). 3, 5(*karrūbukwi*), 7.
Two hundred.

rūkaanij (**rikahanij**). From *anijnij*
(**hanijnij**). 1(-*i*), 2, 3. Prophesy;
prophet; seer; soothsayer.

rūkaki (**rikakiy**). 1(-*i*), 2, 6(-*i*), 7.
Teacher; preacher; apostle.

rūkaļoor (**rikaļewer**). 1(-*a*), 6(-*a*).
Disciple; follower.

rūkamool (**rikamewel**). Witness;
testifier. *Eor ke aṃ rūkamool ñan
ekajet in.* Have you any witness for
the upcoming trial?

Rūkin-aelōñin (**rikin-hayęylęgyin**). Clan
name.

Rūkipinaelōñin
(**rikipinhayęlęgyin**). Clan name.

Rūkipinbwilujo
(**rikipinbiliwjew**). Clan name.

rūkkatak (**rikkahtak**). Apprentice;
learner. *Ej jañin kaanooj jeļā bwe ej
rūkkatak wōt.* He's not very good at it
because he's still an apprentice.

rūkorea- (**rikewreya-**). Dial. W only; see
wūllepa- (**willepa-**). 1. Uncle,
mother's brother only.

rūkōjerbal armej (**rikejerbal
harmęj**). Employer. *Kwe rūkōjerbal
armej innem kwōj aikuj jeļā kuņaaṃ
ñan rijerbal ro aṃ.* You're an
employer of human beings; therefore
you must know how to treat your
employees as such.

rūkōṃṃan bwebwenato (**rikeṃṃan
beybeynahtew**). Author of stories.
Enañin or ke rūkōṃṃan

bwebwenatoun Ṃajeļ? Are there any
Marshallese authors?

RūṂae (**rimahyey**). Clan name.

RūṂalel (**rimalel**). Clan name.

rūṃļǫk (**rimļaq**). Variant form of
ruñļǫk (**rig°ļaq**).

rūṃṃūļǫk (**riṃṃiļaq**). Variant form of
ruñļǫk (**rig°ļaq**).

rūṃōkarraņ (**rimekarraņ**). Also
rimmenanuwe
(**rimmenahniwęy**). Dwarf; elf;
leprechaun.

rūṃōṃō (**rimehṃeh**). 2. Dirty with
dried matter, especially around mouth
or eyes. *Kwōn aṃwin lǫñiiṃ bwe
erūṃōṃō.* Wash your mouth because it
has something dried on it. *Kwōn etal
ormej bwe erūṃōṃō mejaṃ.* Go wash
your face because you have some dried
matter around your eyes.

RūṂwejoor (**rimeyjewer**). Clan name;
see place name *Ṃwe-joor.*

rūṃwijbar (**rimijbar**). Barber.
Rūṃwijbar kijak ņe. He's a barber.

rūr (**rir**). Vulgar. 1(-*i*). Rectum.

rūr-. See *rr-.*

Rūtōbaaļ (**ritebahaļ**). Clan name.

rūttarinae (**rittariynahyey**). Soldier.

rūtto (**rittew**). 1(-*i*), 2, 3(inf, tr -*ik*,
-*uk*), 7, 8, 9. Old age; old; adult;
mature; of age; ancestor; senior. *Ruo
iiō rūttoun jān ña.* He's two years my
senior.

rūttoļǫk (**rittewļaq**). 1(-*i*), 2. Aging;
mellowed. *Erūttoļǫk jān ṃokta.* He
has aged somewhat since I last saw
him.

rūturi- (**ritir°i-**). 1. Neighbor; spouse.

rwaklep (**r°aklep**). Also *rǫklep*
(**r°aqlep**). 1(-*i*), 2(inf, tr -*e*), 3, 7.
Scoop up by hand.

rwe (**r°ey**). Transitive form of *rrwe*
(**r°r°ey**).

ta (**tah**). What; which. *Ta ņe kijeṃ?*
What are you eating?

ta (**tah**). Dial. W, E: *tak* (**tak**). Eastward;
directional, enclitic, eastward. *Iar lo an
ttōr tawaj iarwaj.* I saw him running
towards the east on the beach.

taaṃbūļo (**tahaṃbiļęw**). From Engl. 2.
Down below; nautical term.

taan (**tahan**). Dial. W only; see *raut*
(**rahwit**). 2(inf, tr -*e*), 4, 6(-*i*), 7. Urine;
urinate.

taanm̧ait (**tahanm̧ahyit**). From Engl. 2(inf, tr *-i*), 4, 6(*-i*), 7. Dynamite. *Raar taanm̧aiti toļ eo.* The mountain was dynamited.

taar (**tahar**). Also *ttaar.* Archaic. Parry; ward off a spear thrust; push away a canoe.

tab (**tab**). 1(*-i*), 2, 3, 7, 8, 9. Obscured, cloudy; unclear weather; fog, dim, haze, blur. *Etab mejatoto rainin.* The air is hazy today.

tab (**tab**). 1, 2, 3, 6(*-i*), 8, 9. High from liquor. *Etab ripade ro.* The party folks got high.

tab (**tab**). From Engl. 6(*-i*). A tub. *Tabin ia ņe am̧?* Where was your tub made?

taboļōn (**tahbewļen**). From Engl. Tarpaulin.

tabōļ (**tabeļ**). From Engl. 1(*-i*), 2(inf, tr *-e, -i*), 3, 7. Double. *Ear tabōļi ek ko im dibōji.* He speared two fish at one time. *En jab tabōļ am̧ m̧ōñā.* Don't eat twice.

tabtab (**tabtab**). 2, 6(*-i*), 7. Trousers; long pants. *Iar tabtabļǫk ñan pade eo.* I wore long pants to the party.

tabu (**tahbiw**). 2(inf, tr *-uk*), 3(*kōtabuuk* (reflex only)). Stranded; a helpless position. *Etabu.* It's too late. *Etabuuk kōj.* We are in a helpless position.

tabuk (**tabiq**). 2(inf, tr *-i*), 4(*rūttabuk*), 5(*ttabukbuk*), 6(*-i*), 7. Medicine, heat-treatment using hot stones wrapped in leaves.

tabur (**tabir°**). 1(*-i*), 2, 3, 5(*ttaburbur*), 7, 8, 9. Hesitate; be reluctant to. *Itabur in kajjitōk wa eņ waan.* I am reluctant to ask him for his vehicle. *Etke kottaburbur in iļǫk ñan m̧weeņ im̧ōn irooj eņ?* Why are you always reluctant to go to the chief's house?

tabur (**tabir°**). 1(*-i*), 2, 7, 8, 9. Slippery, of trees. *Ear wōt im etabur mā eņ.* It rained and that breadfruit tree is slippery.

taburbur (**tabir°bir°**). A fish, parrotfish, *Scarus vetula.*

tabūņņo (**tabiņņew**). Also *tabwiņo* (**tabiyņew**). 2(inf, tr *-ik(i)*), 3, 6(*-i*), 7, 8, 9. Saltspray. *Etabūņņoik(i) tūrak eo im jjo.* Saltspray caused the truck to rust.

tabwil (**tabil**). Fresh egg (see *kune* (**kiwney**)). *Etabwil lep e.* This egg is fresh. *Ekōņaan m̧ōñā tabwil.* He likes to eat fresh eggs.

taeo (**tahyew**). Also *tāeo* (**tayew**). 1(*-i*), 2, 3(inf *kōttaeoeo,* tr *kōttaeoeouk, kōttaeoeoik*), 5(*ttaeoeo*), 8, 9. Pimple; acne. *Ettaeoeo ļeeņ.* He is covered with pimples. *Jab kōettaeoeouk mejam̧.* Don't pick the pimples on your face.

taibuun (**tahyibiwin**). From Engl. 2, 6(*-i*), 7. Typhoon.

taidik (**tahyidik**). 1, 2, 4, 5(*ttaidikdik*), 6(*-i*). Folk dances. *Ettaidikdik riWōjjā.* People from Wotje are always doing folk-dances.

taij (**tahyij**). From Engl. 2, 3(inf, tr *-i*), 4, 6(*-i*). Dice; a game; rolling dice. *Erwōj ar taij inne.* They all were shooting craps yesterday.

Taije (**tahyijey**). From Engl. Thursday.

taikoñ (**tahyikeg°**). From Japn. *daikon*. 2(inf, tr *-e*), 3, 5(*ttaikoñkoñ*), 6(*-i*), 7. Pickled radish. *Kwōn tan kōtaikoñ tok.* Go get us some *daikon*. *Taikoñe juub ņe.* Mix some *daikon* in the soup. *Ettaikoñkoñ.* It smells of pickled radish.

taikō (**tahyikeh**). From Engl. 3, 5(*ttaikōkō*), 6(*-i*). Tiger. *Ettaikōkō buļōn mar in Abdika.* There are tigers all over the African jungles.

taiļa (**tahyiļah**). From Engl. 1(*-i*), 2(inf, tr *-ik*), 3, 4, 6(*-i*). Tailor. *Wōn ņe ear taiļaik jōōt ņe am̧?* Who made your shirt?

taim̧ (**tahyim̧**). From Engl. 1(*-i*), 2(inf, tr *-i*), 4, 5(*ttaim̧im̧*), 6(*-i*), 7. Fight; skirmish; scuffle; tune up. *Erro baj taim̧ wōt jidik.* They almost fought. *Kwōmaroñ ke taim̧i tok injin e?* Could you please give this engine a tune-up?

taim̧oņ (**tahyim̧eņ°**). From Engl. 3, 5(*ttaim̧oņm̧oņ*), 6(*-i*). Diamond. *Ettaim̧oņm̧oņ peiū.* There are lots of diamonds in my hand (in a card game).

taiņam̧ (**tahyiņam̧**). 1(*-i*), 2(inf, tr *-e*), 3, 5(*ttaiņam̧ņam̧*), 6(*-i*). Mosquito net. *Ettaiņam̧ņam̧ riĻora.* The people of Laura always use mosquito nets.

taiñad (**tahyigad**). 1(*-i*), 2, 3. Smell, halitosis; scum, food particles between teeth.

taip (**tahyip**). 2(inf, tr *-i*), 4, 6(*-i*), 7. Type; typewriter. *Kwōjeļā ke taip?* Can you type? *Ear taipi peba eo.* He typed the paper. *An wōn taip in?* Whose typewriter is it?

tak (**tak**). 3, 6(*-i*). A fish, needlefish, *Belone platyura*; *Raphiobelone robusta.*

tak (**tak**). 2(inf, tr *-e*), 7. Use a vehicle or vessel. *Take bajikōļ eņ.* Use the bicycle.

tak (**tak**). Dial. E, W: *ta* (**tah**). Eastward; upward; directional, enclitic, eastward, upward.

take (**takęy**). From Engl. Turkey.

takin (**takin**). Also *jitǫkin* (**jitawkin**). From Engl. *stocking*. 3, 6(*-i*). Socks.

takin aļ (**takin haļ**). Sun-up; sunrise.

takinkin (**takinkin**). From *takin* (**takin**). 1(*-i*), 2, 3(inf, tr *-i*), 7. Wear socks. *Kwōn takinkin kōn takin kā rōkāāl.* Put on these new socks. *Kwōn jab kōtakinkini ippaṃ.* Don't let him use some of your socks in the meantime.

takļǫk (**takļaq**). Variant form of *taļǫk* (**tahļaq**).

taktakōnae (**taktakenhayey**). 2, 6(*-i*). New moon. *Etaktakōnae.* It's new moon out tonight.

taktō (**takteh**). From Engl. 2(inf, tr *-ūk, -ik*), 3, 4, 6(*-i*), 7. Doctor; see a doctor. *Wōn eņ aṃ taktō?* Who is your doctor? *Ta ņe kwaar taktō kake?* What did you go to see the doctor about? *Wōn ņe ear taktōik eok?* Who doctored you? *Iar taktōik neō bwe emetak.* I went to see a doctor about my leg because it hurts.

tal (**tal**). 1(*-i*), 2, 3, 7. Sink; submerge. *Etal wa eo.* The boat sank.

tal (**tal**). Procession of mourners; group of people going to pay respects to a deceased; procession bearing tribute to chief. *Tal eo an bukwōn juon ņe.* That's the procession of mourners from district one. *Tal eo an ṃōñā eņ an Kōppālle ņe ļǫk.* That's the Capelle clan on its way to pay its last respects to the deceased.

talboon (**talbewen**). From Engl. 2(inf, tr *-e*), 4, 5(*ttalboonon*), 6, 7. Telephone. *Iar talboone eok inne.* I telephoned you yesterday. *Ledikin pālle rōttalboonon.* American girls are always on the phone.

tallīñe (**talligey**). Transitive form of *tallōñ* (**talleg**).

tallōñ (**talleg**). 1(*-i*), 2(inf, tr *tallīñe*), 3, 4, 7. Climb up; mount. *Kwōjeļā ke tallōñ?* Do you know how to climb? *Komaroñ ke tallīñe ni eņ?* Can you climb that coconut tree?

taļa (**tahļah**). From Engl. Dollar.

taļe (**taļęy**). From Engl. 2(inf, tr *-ik*), 4, 6(*-i*), 7. Tally; count up.

taļe (**taļęy**). 2, 3(inf *kōttaļeļe*, tr *kōtaļeik(i)*), 5(*ttaļeļe*), 6(*-i*), 8, 9. Have sex appeal.

taļǫk (**tahļaq**). Also *takļǫk* (**takļaq**). Eastward.

taļōn (**taļen**). From Engl. Talent.

taļum. See *tǫļūm.*

tam (**tam**). Variant form of *ļam* (**ļam**).

tampeļ (**tampeļ**). From Engl. 6(*-i*). Temple; altar.

taṃ (**taṃ**). From Engl. 2(inf, tr *-e*), 6(*-i*). Dump; refuse area; discard; reject. *Jǫkpeje ilo taṃ eņ.* Throw it away at the dump. *Rōtaṃe eō.* I was dumped. I got rejected.

taṃbaj (**taṃbaj**). From Japn. *dampatsu.* 1, 2(inf, tr *-e*). Girl's haircut, Japanese style; shingled, cut the hair short.

taṃṃwe (**taṃṃęy**). Dialectal variant of *taṃwe.*

taṃṃwi- (**taṃṃi-**). 1. Mood; disposition.

taṃtaṃ (**taṃtaṃ**). 1(*-i*), 2, 3, 7. Glare; blinded by sunlight. *Eļap an taṃtaṃ im ij jab lo ṃaan.* There is a lot of glare and I can't see ahead.

taṃwe (**taṃęy**). Dial. W, E: *taṃṃwe.* Find something to ride.

tanij (**tanij**). From Engl. 1(*-i*), 2(inf, tr *-i*), 3, 4, 5(*ttanijnij*), 7. Dance, western style. *Ettanijnij rijikuuļ in ae-jikuuļ.* The high school students are always having dances.

tanim (**tanim**). From Engl. 2(inf, tr *-i*), 3, 4(*ttanimnim*), 5(*ttanimnim*), 6(*-i*), 7. Denim; denim trousers, blue jeans, Levis. *Eor ke aṃ tanim?* Have you any denim pants?

taņo (**taņew**). From Japn. *tannoo* "short in ability" or Engl. *doņt know*(?). 2, 5(*ttaņoņo*), 6(*-i*), 8, 9. Kooky; dumb; stupid; eccentricity; loony; mentally unstable.

tañõaļǫk (**taggaļaq**). From "onomatopoeia". 1(*-i*), 2, 3(inf, tr *-e*). Clanging sound.

tap (**tap**). 2, 3, 6(*-i*). Piece of pandanus roots cut and dried to be used as frame in weaving thatch.

tapañ (**tapag**). Archaic. Mortar for making medicine; small piece of rock with hole in it; no one but medicine people may touch.

tape (**tapęy**). Dial. W, E: *peeḷ* (**peyeḷ**). Vulgar. 1(*-i*), 2(inf, tr *-ik*), 3, 4, 5(*ttapepe*), 7. Sexual intercourse.

tapioka (**tapiyewkah**). From Engl. Tapioca.

tar- (**tar-**). 1, 2, 3, 7. Go on a vehicle or sailing canoe (used with directional enclitics (and postpositions)).

tare (**taręy**). 2, 3(inf *kōttarere*, tr *kōttareik(i)*, *kōttarereik(i)*), 4, 8, 9. Hook easily. *Kāāj rot eo etare ṇe.* That's the kind of fish hook that hooks so neatly.

tariṇae (**tariyṇahyey**). 1(*-i*), 2(inf, tr *-ik*), 3, 4(*rūttariṇae*), 7. War; fight a battle; combat. *Ejjañin jeṃḷọk aer tariṇae.* They haven't stopped fighting yet. *Rej tariṇaeik wōt doon.* They are still fighting each other. *Ear pād ilo tariṇae.* He's a combat veteran.

tarkijet (**tarkiyjẹt**). 6(*-i*). Shore; beach; offshore. *Kōpaak tarkijet bwe in kelọk.* Move close to shore so I can jump off.

tarrin (**tarrin**). About; approximately. *Letok wōt tarrin juon bawūnin anien.* Give me about a pound of onions.

tarto-tartak (**tartẹw-tartak**). 2, 3, 4, 6(*-i*). Jaunt, sail, or drive around aimlessly. *Jab tarto-tartak bwe kwōnaaj wōtlọk ilọjet.* Stop running around or you'll fall overboard.

tarukelel (**tariqyelyel**). Archaic. Anxiety. *Etarukelel ije ibūruō.* "There is anxiety in my heart."

tata (**tahtah**). Superlative particle; most.

tawūnin (**tahwinyin**). Also *taunin.* Why?; What is the reason?

tāākji (**tayakjiy**). From Engl. 2(inf, tr *-ik*), 3, 4, 5(*ttāākjiji*), 6(*-i*), 7. Taxicab. *Ear tāākjiik tok kōm.* He brought us in the taxicab.

tāānjen (**tayanjen**). 6(*-i*). Belt keeper.

tāān̄ (**tayag**). From Engl. 6(*-i*). Water container; tank; spout, rain gutter.

tāān̄ (**tayag**). 1(*-i*), 2, 3(inf, tr *-e*), 4, 7, 8, 9. Have sex appeal, of males; lady killer; have a way with women.

tāān̄ (**tayag**). 1(*-i*), 2, 3(inf, tr *-e*), 5(*ttāān̄en̄*), 6(*-i*), 8, 9. Choice coconut tree for collecting sap. *Ni ttāān̄en̄ men ṇe.* That's a choice tree for coconut sap.

tāāp (**tayap**). 1(*-i*), 2(inf, tr *tāāpin*, *-e*), 4, 5(*ttāāpāp*), 7. Provide food for family from local sources (not from the store); provide food for someone. *Ḷadik ro rōmoot in tāāp.* The boys have gone to look for food. *Wōn eo ej tāāpe jinōṃ?* Who provides food for your mother? *Ettāāpāp ḷadik raṇ nājin lieṇ.* Her children always help provide food.

tāṃọṇ (**tayṃẹṇ°**). 1(*-i*), 2, 3, 5(*ttāṃọṇṃọṇ*), 6(*-i*). Graze, as a bullet, chipped; ricochet. *Etāṃọṇ likao eo kōn joot eo.* The young man was grazed by the bullet. *Ettāṃọṇṃọṇ mejān ṇaib eo.* The blade of the knife was chipped in several places.

tāṃọṇ (**tayṃẹṇ°**). Harelip. *Enaaj kar lukkuun deọ eḷañe ear jab tāṃọṇ lọn̄iin.* She would have been very beautiful if she didn't have a harelip.

tāpin (**taypin**). Transitive form of *tāāp* (**tayap**).

tāte (**taytẹy**). Dial. W, E: *tete* (**tẹytẹy**). 1, 2(inf, tr *tāik*), 6(*-i*), 7. Bind; roll up, line or film, spool; coil of coconut sennit. *Eṃōkaj an tāte eo.* He pulls in his line pretty fast. *Tāik eo ṇe ṇa ijeṇe.* Pull in the line and leave it there.

te (**tey**). Also *tete* (**teytey**). Vulgar. 2, 3, 6(*-e*). Sanitary napkin.

teaak (**teyahak**). 2, 5(*teeaake*), 6(*-i*). Provisions for a voyage; make provisions for a journey. *Raar teaak kōn rōn̄oul bao.* They took twenty chickens for provisions. *Eteaake wa eṇ.* That boat picked up a lot of provisions.

tebōḷ (**teybeḷ**). From Engl. 6(*-i*). Table; desk.

tebōḷ jibuun (**teybeḷ jibiwin**). From Engl. Tablespoon.

tebu (**tẹybiw**). From Japn. *debu*. 1(*-i*), 2, 5(*ttebubu*). Fat; overweight, obese.

tebukro (**teybiqrew**). From Japn. *tebukuro*. 2(inf, tr *-ik*), 6, 6(*-i*). Glove. *Ij tebukroiki peiū.* I'm going to wear gloves.

tee- (**teye-**). 1, 2(tr *teek*), 6. What location?; What relation? *Teen eo bok eo ej pād ie?* Where is the book located? *Teen ḷadik eṇ lieṇ?* What relation is that boy to that woman? *Teeṃ ḷeeṇ?* What relation is he to you? *Rej teek doon Tiṃōj im Aḷi?* How are *Tiṃōj* and *Aḷi* related? *Epād bok eo* *iteen tebōļ eo?* Where is the book in relation to the table? *Epād ituteen tūroot eo?* Where is it in relation to the cabinet?

teej (**teyej**). From Engl. 2, 3, 6(*-i*), 7. Test; examination; quiz. *Teejin ta eo kwaar bōk kiiō?* What test did you just take?

teej (**teyej**). 2. Get one's comeuppance.

teejṃōļ (**teyejṃeļ**). From Engl. Decimal.

teek (**teyek**). From Engl. Deck, nautical. *Epād ioon teek.* He's on deck.

teekkiiñ (**tęyękkiyig**). From Engl. (from Japn.). 2(inf, tr *-i*), 4, 6(*-i*), 7. Reinforcing rods.

teeļ (**teyeļ**). Variant form of *teoļ* (**teyeļ°**).

teemjǫǫn (**tęyęmjawan**). From Engl. Large bottle, demijohn.

teeṃbura (**teyeṃbir°ah**). Also *teeṃbūra* (**teyeṃbirah**). From Japn. *tempura* "food dipped in batter and deep fried". 2(inf, tr *-ik*), 6(*-i*). A food, fish, basted in flour and deep fried; tempura. *Teeṃburaik ek kaņe.* Cook those fish tempura style.

teeṃbura (**teyeṃbir°ah**). Vulgar. 2(inf, tr *-ik*), 4, 6(*-i*). Euphemistic reference to illicit sexual relations.

teeñ (**teyeg**). 1, 6(*-i*). Measure; division; class; inning in baseball; grade.

teeñki (**teyegkiy**). 1(*-i*), 2, 3, 6(*-i*), 7. Flashlight; light. *Teeñki jarom.* Electric light.

teep (**tęyęp**). From Engl. 2(inf, tr *-e*), 4, 5(*tteepep*), 6(*-i*), 7. Tape.

teep (**teyep**). 2, 3(inf, *kōtteep,* tr *kōteep(e)*), 5(*tteepep*), 6(*-i*), 3+7. Removed; rooted out; pulled out; extracted. *Eteep juon ñi.* A tooth is extracted.

teiņaļ (**tęyiņaļ**). Variant form of *tenaļ* (**teynaļ**).

teiñ (**tęyig**). Transitive form of *tteiñ* (**ttęyig**).

teiñwa (**tęyigwah**). From Japn. *denwa*. 2(inf, tr *-ik*), 4, 6(*-i*), 7. Telephone; phone. *Kab teiñwa tok ilo ruo awa.* Phone me at two o'clock.

tekōļ (**teykeļ**). From Engl. *tackle*. 2(inf, tr *-e*), 6(*-i*), 7. Raise by rope; lift using crane; block and tackle. *Tekōļe āneļǫk ṃweiuk kaņe.* Unload the merchandise (by crane).

temakil (**tęymakil**). Variant form of *ttemakil* (**ttęymakil**).

tenaļ (**teynaļ**). Also *teiņaļ* (**tęyiņaļ**). 2, 3(*ttenaļnaļ*), 6(*-i*). Get a splinter; sliver. *Jab atartar ijeņe bwe kwōnaaj tenaļ.* Don't lean on that or you might get a splinter. *Ettenaļnaļ aļaļ ņe.* That board is splintered in many spots.

teoļ (**teyeļ°**). Also *teeļ* (**teyeļ**). 1(*-i*), 2, 3, 5(*tteoļeoļ*), 7, 8, 9. Come loose. *Etteoļeoļ ñiū.* My tooth is loose. *Eteoļ ñiū.* My tooth came out.

tepiļ (**teypiļ**). Also *tepiļ* (**tęypiļ**). From Engl. 1(*-i*), 2(inf, tr *-i*), 3, 4, 8, 9. Devil; use bad language; act in a way contrary to missionary teaching. *Ear tepiļi ledik eo.* He tempted (talked provocatively to) the girl.

teroñe (**teyreg°ey**). Unsettle; unnerve; dissilusion.

teru (**tęyriw**). 1(*-i*), 2, 3(inf, tr *-uk*), 4, 5(*tteeruru*), 6(*-i*), 7, 8, 9. Succeed; achieve one's goal. *Koteru ke ilo kkāālel eo?* Did you get elected?

tete (**tęytęy**). Variant form of *tiete* (**tiyęytęy**).

tete (**tęytęy**). Dialectal variant of *tāte* (**taytęy**).

tete (**teytey**). Vulgar. 2, 6(*-i*). Use a sanitary napkin.

ti (**tiy**). 1(*-i*), 2(inf, tr *-ik*), 3. Tea; put tea in. *Wōn e ear tiik tibat e?* Who put tea in this teapot?

tiār (**tiyar**). Variant form of *tūar* (**tihar**).

tiārmān (**tiyarman**). Variant form of *tūar* (**tihar**).

tibat (**tiybat**). From Engl. 6(*-i*). Teapot; tea kettle; coffee pot.

tie (**tiyey**). 1(*tie-*). Lips.

tiek (**tiyek**). 6(*-i*). Rim; molded edge; variant form of *ṃokwōd* (**ṃaqed**).

tiemlo (**tiyemlew**). Idiom. From *tie* (**tiyey**) "lips", *im* (**yim**) "and", *lo* (**lew**) "tongue". 6(*-i*). Someone that people are always talking about; celebrity. *Etiemlo wōt lieņ.* She is the talk of the town.

tiepdǫ (**tiyepdaw**). A fish, black surgeonfish, *Acanthurus nigricans.*

tieta (**tiyetah**). From Engl. Theater; drama.

tiete (**tiyętęy**). Also *tete* (**tęytęy**). Archaic. Formant in place names; reef around a secondary lagoon; end of the reef at a passage.

tiikri (**tiyikriy**). From Engl. Degree, angle measurement; degree, collegiate.

tiin (**tiyin**). From Engl. 3, 5(*ttiinin*), 6(-*i*). Tin; piece of tin roofing. *Ettiinin pia e kōn an m̧or.* This beer has a metallic taste because of its age.

tijeļ (**tiyjeļ**). From Engl. 1(-*i*), 2, 3, 5(*ttijeļjeļ*), 6(-*i*). Diesel; diesel oil. *Ettijeļjeļ jikin injin eo.* The engine room had diesel oil all over.

Tijem̧ba (**tiyjem̧bah**). From Engl. December.

tijem̧ļọk (**tiyjem̧ļaq**). 2. Expert; wiz. *Likao eņ etijem̧ļọk ilo lōkā.* He's a surfing expert. *Ikōņaan tijem̧ļọk ilo kajin Būranij.* I want to be an expert in speaking French.

tijibuun (**tiyjibiwin**). From Engl. Teaspoon.

tijjañ (**tijjag**). 2, 4, 6(-*i*), 8, 9. Have missing teeth. *Jab kalluuk eō bwe kwōnaaj tijjañ.* Don't get me angry or you'll lose your teeth.

tikōn (**tiyken**). From Engl. Deacon. *Tikōn jemān.* His father is a deacon.

til (**til**). Torch.

tilaan (**tilahan**). 2(inf, tr -*e*), 3, 6(-*i*). Pumice stone; basaltic rock which floats.

Tilañ (**tilag**). Clan name.

tilbuuj (**tilbiwij**). 2(inf, tr -*i*), 4, 6(-*i*), 7. Gather followers. *Jijej ear tilbuuji ro rūkaļoran jān riJu ro.* Jesus gathered his followers from among the Jews.

tile (**tiley**). Transitive form of *ttil* (**ttil**).

tilekek (**tilyẹkyẹk**). Also *tiliekek* (**tiliyẹkyẹk**). 2, 3(*kaattilekek*), 4, 5(*ttilekek*), 6(-*i*), 7. Hide; obscured. *Etke kwōj tilekek?* Why are you hiding? *Kwōn jab kōņaan ttilekek.* Don't always hide. *Jeañ ilen kaattilekek.* Let's go play hide and seek. *Rej tiliekek jān rūkadek eo.* They are hiding from the drunk.

tileñeñ (**tilyẹgyẹg**). Also *itileñeñ* (**yitilyẹgyẹg**). 1, 2, 5(*ttileñeñ*), 6(-*i*), 8, 9. Make one's presence felt, especially a group; see *itileoñeoñ*. *Ñe ej or waan Nepi, ettileñeñ jeļa.* When there's a Navy ship in port, sailors are all over the place. *Kumi in al eo jān Ļora ear lukkuun ttileñeñ ilo jebta eo.* The singing group from Laura was the most impressive at the song-fest.

tiliej (**tiliyẹj**). 1(-*i*), 2(inf, tr -*e*), 3, 5(*ttiliejej*), 7. Lines used to reef sails. *Kwōn tilieje wa ņe bwe eļap kōto in.* Reef the sail of your canoe because the wind is strong. *Ettiliejej wa eņ.* The sail of that canoe is always reefed.

tiliekek (**tiliyẹkyẹk**). Variant form of *tilekek* (**tilyẹkyẹk**).

tiljek (**tiljẹk**). 1(-*i*), 2, 3, 4, 8, 9. Thrifty; careful; painstaking; faithful; prudent; frugal.

tilkawor (**tilkawẹr**). Also *tilkọor*. 2(inf, tr -*e*), 3, 4, 6(-*i*), 7. Fishing method, hunting for lobsters at night by means of artificial light, not moonlight. *Jej tilkawor wōt ilo buñūn marok.* We hunt for lobster by the *tilkawor* method only on moonless nights. *Tilkaworin jaje.* The fishing for lobster of an inexperienced person.

tilkōmerā (**tilkemeray**). 2(inf, tr -*ik*), 4, 6(-*i*), 7. Fishing method, torch and machete.

tilmaak (**tilmahak**). 2(inf, tr -*e*), 5, 6(-*i*). To tender; to offer formally; to proffer. *Koñkōrōj enaaj tilmaake tok riboot eo an rainin.* Congress will tender its report today.

tilmaak (**tilmahak**). 2(inf, tr -*e*), 6(-*i*). Spread far and wide. *Raar tilmaake kōjjeļā eo ilo retio.* The message was spread abroad on the radio.

tilpoki (**tilpewkiy**). 1(-*i*), 2, 3, 4, 8, 9. Skin disease.

tiltil (**tiltil**). 1(-*i*), 2, 3, 5(-*i*), 6(-*i*), 8, 9. Embroidery; spotted; dotted. *Ear pikinni kōn juon nuknuk iaļo tiltil.* She wore a yellow polka dot bikini.

tiltil keeañ (**tiltil keyyag**). Wind from the northwest.

timaruk (**timariq**). Also *tōmaruk* (**temariq**). 1(-*i*), 2, 3, 5(*ttimarukruk*), 6(-*i*), 7. Take in water from the top of a canoe; sink; outrigger goes underwater; said of one who finds his former girlfriends are all married. *Jab kallōñlōñ bajinjea bwe kwōnaaj kōtōmaruk wa ņe.* Don't overload the boat or you'll sink it. *Enana wa ņe bwe ettimarukruk.* That boat is no good for it's always going under. *Etōmaruk wa eņ.* The outrigger of that canoe is underwater.

tim̧a (**tiym̧ah**). From Engl. *steamer*. 6(-*i*). Ship; steamer; motorvessel.

timoņ (**tiymeņ°**). From Engl. 5(*ttimoņmoņ*). Ghost; demon; monster; spook. *Ettimoņmoņ ānin.* This island is haunted.

tinaad (**tinahad**). 2(inf, tr *-e*), 3, 6(*-i*), 8, 9. Glare. *Iban lo maan bwe etinaad.* I can't see forward due to the glare.

tinak (**tinak**). Archaic. Rarely used; stay put. *Ļeo etinak ijo.* He just stays there.

tinar (**tinar**). 3, 6(*-i*). A fish, small grouper.

Tipāp (**tipap**). Archaic. Name of a navigational sign; looks like a coconut frond (*pāp*).

tipdik (**tipdik**). Idiom. 2(inf, tr *-i*), 6(*-i*), 7. Analyze; talk in great detail, elaborate. *Kwōn tipdiki tok mōk meļeļein jipij eo am.* Would you elaborate upon your speech? *Inaaj kiiō tipdiki waj meļeļe e.* I will now analyze the meaning.

tipdikdik (**tipdikdik**). 1(*-i*), 2, 3, 5(*ttipdikdik*), 7. Small pieces; fragments; crumbs; bits; chips; particles, scraps. *Ettipdikdik pilawā kā.* These loaves of bread keep crumbling.

tipe- (**tipe-**). 1, 2+1, 6. Way of; seem. *Einwōt kobaj tipen pikōt.* You seem scared. *Etipen naaj wōt.* Looks like rain.

tipen. See *tipe-*.

tipen (**tipen**). From *tipdikdik* "fragments". Piece of. *Tipen wōjke.* Piece cut from a tree.

tipi (**tiypiy**). From Engl. 1(*-i*), 2, 3(inf, tr *-ik*), 4. Tuberculosis.

tipi (**tiypiy**). From Engl. Television.

tipij (**tipij**). Transitive form of *tipjek* (**tipjęk**).

tipjek (**tipjęk**). Dial. W only; see *tūbbǫk* (**tibbaq**). 1(*-i*), 2(inf, tr *tipij(i)*), 3, 4, 5(*ttipjekjek*), 7. Stumble; slip; trip. *Ettōr im tipjek.* He ran and slipped. *Ettipjekjek lieņ.* She's always stumbling. *Ej ettōr wōt ak itipiji.* When he ran I tripped him. *Etipijek.* He stumbled.

tipn̄ōl (**tipgel**). 6(*-i*). Large outrigger canoe, for sailing.

tipn̄ōl (**tipgel**). 1(*-i*), 2, 3. Stumble; fall; offend.

tiptak (**tiptak**). 2(inf, tr *-e*). To trip with the foot.

tirooj (**tiyrewej**). From Engl. "*tea rose*". 3, 6(*-i*). A plant, *Pseuderanthemum atropurpureum* (Bull.) Baily. Cult. Hedge plant. Also applied to other similar hedge plants. Ebon. N.

to (**tęw**). 2, 3, 5(*ttoto*), 7. Disembark; come off of; climb down; strut of a rooster. *Emōj ņe am ttoto.* Why don't you stop getting off (and getting back on).

to (**tęw**). 6(*tou-*). Pit for soaking coconut husks for making sennit.

to (**tęw**). From Engl. Syllable "do" of musical scale.

to (**tęw**). Westward; directional, enclitic, westward. *Kwōn itowaj bar jidik.* Move down a bit more to the west of you.

to (**tew**). 1(*-i*), 2, 3, 6(*-i*), 7, 8, 9. A long time; prolong; last; protracted. *Enañin to am jako?* You were gone quite a while, weren't you? (Give an account of yourself). *Ejjeļǫk wōt toun am jako.* You were gone an awfully long time.

to (**tew**). 6(*-i*). Rope; string; tether.

to (**tew**). Channel; passage into lagoon from ocean.

to jān enōka- (**tęw jan yęnęka-**). Be overdecorated. *Eto jān enōkan ļeeņ.* He is overdecorated.

to-jān-lañ (**tęw-jan-lag**). Idiom. From *to* (**tęw**) "climb down", *jān* (**jan**) "from", *lañ* (**lag**) "heaven". Extremely beautiful woman; a rare beauty; a very beautiful female. *To-jān-lañ men eņ pālen.* His wife is a knock-out.

toeak (**tęwyak**). Feces.

tok (**teq**). 2, 3, 5(*ttoktok*), 6(*-i*). Ignited; catch fire; kindle. *Katoke radikdik kaņe bwe jen jenjen kijek.* Ignite those twigs so we can build a fire. *Ettoktok kiaaj.* Gasoline is flammable.

tok (**teq**). Also *tak* (**tak**) (obligatorily following directional enclitics, and becomes zero following *to* (**tęw**) 'westward' and *tak* (**tak**) or *ta* (**tah**) 'eastward'). Toward the speaker; directional, postposition, toward the speaker. *Iar lo an ttōr niñatak iartak.* I saw him running up eastward on the beach.

tok (**teq**). Variant form of *itok* (**yiteq**).

tokadkad (**tewkadkad**). 1(*-i*), 2(inf, tr *-e*), 3, 7. To tow; string for towing toy canoe in water, held in middle with ends attached to ends of canoe for steering. *Ļadik ro raņ rej bwilbwil tokadkad i ar.* The boys are towing toy canoes along the lagoon beach.

tokake (**tewkakey**). Also *tokañe* (**tewkagey**). Huge lizard, imported from Japan.

tokañe (**tewkagey**). Variant form of *tokake* (**tewkakey**).

tokālik (**teqyalik**). 6(-*i*). Afterwards; later. *Inaaj iioon eok tokālik.* I'll meet you later.

tokja- (**teqja-**). 1, 7. Value; asset; convenient; effect; worth. *Ļap tokja-.* Valuable. *Dik tokja-.* Cheap, of little value. *Jej tokjān.* Of no value. Worthless.

tokkwi (**tẹqqiy, teqqiy**). 2, 3, 5(*ttokkwikwi*), 6(-*i*), 8, 9. Chick. *Ettokkwikwiļọk oror e jān oror ieņ.* This pen's got more chicks in it than that one. *Jen tan katokkwi ippān Ļōbao.* Let's go get chicks from Mr. Chicken.

tokokkok (**tẹqẹqqẹq**). Also *tokokkok* (**teqeqqeq**). 1(-*i*), 2+7, 3(inf, tr -*e*), 6(-*i*), 7. Clucking of a hen.

tokọ (**tewkaw**). Fire logs; of *kōñe* wood, can burn for a week or more.

tokra- (**teqra-**). 1, 7+1. Distance. *Ewi tokran Ṃajeļ jān Awai?* How far are the Marshalls from Hawaii?

tokrak (**teqrak**). 1(-*i*), 2(inf, tr -*e*), 7. Stick used to spread hot stones for earth oven.

toktak (**tẹqtak**). Also *totak* (**tẹwtak**). 1(-*i*), 2(inf, tr -*e*), 3, 4, 7. Dig up; uproot.

toktok (**tẹqtẹq**). 2, 7. Scratch in ground for food, chickens only.

tokubaak (**tewqiwbahak**). 6(-*i*). Canoe part, line from top of mast to outrigger spar (*jojo* (**jewjew**)).

tokwanwa (**teqanwah**). See *tok* "come", *wa* "canoe". Superstition that large waves portend the arrival of a vessel.

tokwiia (**teqiyyah**). 2, 6(-*i*), 8, 9. Incombustible; not flammable; incapable of catching fire and burning; fireproof. (See *tokwiie* (**teqiyyẹy**)). *Eban bwil bwe etokwiia.* It won't burn because it's incombustible.

tokwiie (**teqiyyẹy**). 2, 6(-*i*), 8, 9. Inflammable; combustible (see *tokwiia* (**teqiyyah**)). *Jab kōbaatat iturun bwe etokwiie.* Don't smoke close to it cause it's combustible.

tokwōj (**teqej**). 1(-*i*), 2(inf, tr -*e*), 3, 8, 9. Ignited easily (see *jatokwōj* (**jateqej**)).

tokwōj (**teqej**). Also *tokwōje* (**teqejey**). Accomplish. *Ta ņe kotokwōje?* What good are you? *Eto aō pād ijeņ ak ejjeļọk men eņ itokwōje.* I was there for a while but accomplished nothing. *Ta eo etokwōj ke ear pād i Awai.* What did he accomplish in Hawaii?

tola (**tewlah**). 2(inf, tr -*ik*), 4, 6(-*a*). Knead preserved breadfruit. *Liṃaraņ rej tola bwiro.* The women are kneading preserved breadfruit. *Tolaik bwiro ņe em kapidodouki.* Knead that preserved breadfruit and soften it.

toļ (**teḷ°**). 5(*ttoļtoļ*), 6(-*i*). Hill; mountain. *Eļap an ttoļtoļ ānin.* This island has lots of mountains.

toļaj (**teḷ°aj**). 6(-*i*). Herbs for anointing.

toļoñ (**teḷ°eg°**). Variant form of *tōļoñ* (**teḷeg°**).

toļọk (**tẹwḷaq**). Westward.

toļọk (**tẹwḷaq**). Idiom. 6(-*i*). Such; extreme; so; very. *Baj toļọkun aṃ nana.* You're so bad.

tomede (**tewmedey**). Cable, chain, referred to in Bible; used to bind Samson.

tomewa (**tewmeywah**). Miss the boat. *Itomewa jān tūrep eo bwe iruṃwij.* I missed making the trip because I was late.

tomino (**tewminew**). From Engl. Domino.

tomittori (**tewmittewriy**). From Engl. Dormitory.

tonaaj (**tewnahaj**). From Engl. 1(-*i*), 2, 3, 4, 5(*ttonaajaj*), 6(-*i*). A food, doughnut, with hole. *Ettonaajaj ļam jako ṃwiin.* There are lots of doughnuts in this house.

toņ (**teṇ°**). From Engl. 6(-*i*). A tune; melody.

toņ (**teṇ°**). From Kusaiean. A fish, fresh-water eel; *Anguilla celebesensis*; eel that lives in fresh water, toothless. (Not found in Marshalls but reported from Eastern Carolines.)

toņak (**tẹwṇak**). 1, 2(inf, tr -*e*), 5(*ttoņakņak*). Part, hair; a clearing between trees growing in opposite directions. *Ear toṇake bōran.* He parted his hair. *Ettoṇakṇak likao eṇ.* That young man is always parting his hair.

tonk̄we (**teg°qey**). Contrite.

tonōl (**teg°el**). Get one's comeuppance.

tooj (**tẹwẹj, tewej**). 2, 3, 5(*ttoojoj*), 6(*-i*), 7. Break off of. *Etooj juon wiiḷ.* A wheel came off. *Injinia eo ear katooj injin eo jān kaar eo.* The mechanic took the engine out of the car. *Ettoojoj jebwe in wa eṇ.* The boat's rudder is always falling off.

tooj (**tewej, tẹwẹj**). Dial. W: *tooj* (**tẹwẹj**), E: *tooj* (**tewej**). 1(*-i*), 2, 3(*kattoojoj*), 7, 8, 9. Stand out; be conspicuous; obvious; transparent. *Kwōn jab kattoojoj.* Don't show off. *Eḷap an tooj nuknuk ṇe aṃ.* Your clothes are quite loud.

toojin edwaan (**tẹwẹjin yedwahan**). Idiom. Pretentious; phony; Philistine, hypocrite. *Kwōn jab elḷọk ñan e bwe toojin edwaan bajjek.* Don't bother with him because he's not what he seems.

toon kọuḷaḷo (**tewen kawiwḷahḷẹw**). Spider's web.

toor (**tewer**). Swinging; point in all directions.

toor (**tewer**). Variant form of *tọọr.*

toore (**tewerey**). Transitive form of *ttoor* (**ttewer**).

toorlōñ (**tewerlẹg**). Also *ak* (**hak**), *toollōñ* (**tẹwẹllẹg**). A bird, great frigate bird, *Fregata minor*; a bird, lessor frigate bird, *Fregata ariel.*

toorwa (**tewerwah**). Boat passage on reef; see *tọọr.*

tor (**tẹr°**). 2, 3(inf, tr *-e*), 6(*-i*), 8, 9. Shrink; decreasing in size, as of physique. *Eḷak rọọltok jān kalbuuj etor.* He really shrunk after being in prison.

tor (**ter°**). Dial. E only; see *rot* (**r°et**). Kind; type; sort. *Wa tor?* What kind of boat? *Men tor kaṇ; mettorkaṇ.* Hanky-panky (euphemism).

totak (**tẹwtak**). Also *totak* (**tẹqtak**). 1(*-i*), 2(inf, tr *-e*)), 3, 7. Dig up; uproot.

toto (**tewtew**). Also *allitoto* (**hallitewtew**). 1(*-i*), 2(inf, tr *-uk, -ok*), 3(inf, tr *-uk, -ok*), 4, 7. Hang up; hang on to; hang from. *Kwōn totook jōōt ṇe aṃ.* Hang up your shirt. *Rōḷak loe ej toto ilo bōb eo.* When they found him he was hanging from the pandanus tree.

toul (**tẹwil**). A shell; similar to *di.*

towa (**tewah**). Place for beaching canoes.

towe (**tewey**). 1(*-i*), 2, 5(*ttotowe*), 7. To rub gently; fondle; caress. *Kwōn ttotowe ajri ṇe bwe en mājur.* Keep on caressing the baby so that it goes to sleep.

tọ (**taw**). 3, 5(*ttọtọ*), 6(*-i*). A plant, *Saccharum officinarum* L. Sugar cane (Gramineae). (*Ko* or *to* of Polynesia.)

tọ (**taw**). Pond on reef where fish are caught when tide goes out.

tọ (**taw**). Sail not full; canoe about to capsize.

tọ (**taw**). Glide, of birds.

tọ (**taw**). 2, 6(*-i*), 7. Rain in, as through a window. *Kwōn kiil wūntō ṇe bwe etọ.* Close the window because it is raining in.

tọḷ (**taḷ°**). 6(*-i*). Strips of green coconut branches laid across a fire for warming pandanus leaves. *Jekjek tọḷūn rirar.* Cut branches for singeing.

tọḷ (**taḷ°**). Dialectal variant of *kaḷo* (**kahḷew**).

tọḷe (**tawḷẹy**). From Engl. 6(*-i*). Doll.

tọḷūm (**taḷ°im**). Also *taḷum.* Transitive form of *ttọḷūm* (**ttaḷ°im**).

tọnōt (**tawnet**). From Engl. 1(*-i*), 2(inf, tr *-e*), 4, 5(*ttọnōtnōt*), 6(*-i*), 7. Doughnut. *Tọnōtin wōn in?* Who made this doughnut?

tọọk (**tawak**). From Engl. *dock*. 2(inf, tr *-e*), 3, 6(*-i*). Beach a boat for maintenance purposes; dry-docking, maintain. *Kwōnaaj tọọke ñāāt wa in?* When are you going to do maintenance on this boat?

tọọl (**tawal**). From Engl. 6(*-i*). Towel.

tọọn (**tawan**). 2(inf, tr *-e*), 3. Be away from; be apart. *Jab meḷọkḷọk eō ñe kōjro tọọne doon.* Don't forget me while we're apart. *Jinen edike kōta eo em kōtọọne erro.* Her mother didn't approve so she separated them.

tọọñke (**tawagkẹy**). From Engl. Donkey. *Bōtin wōt tọọñke.* He's as stubborn as a donkey.

tọọr (**tawar**). 1(*-i*), 2, 3, 5(*ttọọror*), 7. Pour out; run, of water; flow; gush; ooze; shed. *Etọọr aebōj eo.* The water is flowing out of the cistern. *Jijej ear* *kōtǫǫrļǫk daan ñan kōj.* Jesus shed his blood for our salvation.

tǫǫr (**tawar**). Also *toor.* Boat passage through a reef; canal; place on an islet where water flows across at high tide; place on reef where water remains at low tide.

tǫǫr pata (**tawar pahtah**). Idiom. 2, 6(*-a*). Entry in net of small groups of fish versus one large group. *Jab kijer in eļļǫk bwe tǫǫr pata.* Don't spread the net out yet for it is just a small group.

tǫǫr pata (**tawar pahtah**). Unexpected streak of luck, windfall. *Tǫǫr pata bajjek.* Just a streak of luck, that's all.

tǫǫt (**tawat**). From Engl. *thwart*. Canoe part, seat on a paddling canoe, usually in the mid-section; canoe part, thwart. *Letok lem ņe iuṃwin tǫǫt ņe.* Hand me the bailer under the seat.

tǫr (**tar°**). Also *tǫrtǫr.* 2(inf, tr *-e*), 6(*-i*), 7. Wash, as a wave or backwash; pull out, as current or undertow. *Raar tǫre rilōkā ro.* The surfers got washed out. *Ebuñ ņo eo im tǫre men ko wōj.* A big wave came and swept everything away.

tǫre (**tar°ey**). Transitive form of *tǫrtǫr* (**tar°tar°**).

tǫrōk (**tawrẹk**). 2, 3, 5(*ttǫrōkrōk*), 6(*-i*). Caught in a trap; get hooked, nabbed. *Lale aṃ jakkōlkōl bwe kwōnaaj tǫrōk.* Stop being indiscrete or you'll get caught. *Ettǫrōkrōk kōn an bwebwe.* He's so stupid he's always walking into traps. *Etǫrōk rūkǫǫt eo.* They nabbed the thief.

tǫrtǫr (**tar°tar°**). 6(*-i*). Eaves; eaves-trough.

tǫrtǫr (**tar°tar°**). 2(inf, tr *tǫre*), 7. Push, move, postponement. *Jenaaj tǫre ṃaanļǫk keemem in.* We'll postpone the birthday party.

tǫrtǫr (**tar°tar°**). Also *tǫr.* 2(inf, tr *tǫke*). Massacre. *Ear tǫre joñoul ṃṃaan.* He wiped out ten men. *Pako tǫrtǫr.* Thresher shark.

tǫujin (**tawijin**). From Engl. 2, 3(inf, tr *-i*), 5(*kōttǫujinjin*), 6(*-i*), 7. One thousand.

tō- (**tẹh**). String.

tōbak (**tebak**). Also *kabbōk* (**kabbẹk**). 3, 5(*ttōbakbak*), 6(*-i*). Male flower of breadfruit; breadfruit bud. *Ettōbakbak eoṃwin mā eņ.* There are lots of buds under that breadfruit tree.

tōbak (**tebak**). From Germ. *Tabak* "tobacco". 3, 5(*ttōbakbak*), 6(*-i*). Cigar.

tōbalbal (**tebalbal**). Also *tōbalbōl* (**tebalbẹl**), *tōbal* (**tebal**). 1(*-i*), 2(inf, tr *tōbale*), 3, 5(*ttōbalbōl*), 6(*-i*), 7. Crawl; creep; slithering. *Ejeļā tōbalbal ajri eņ.* That baby can crawl. *Kōtōbale ajri ņe.* Make the child crawl. *Kiil kōjām ņe bwe ñe eruj enaaj ttōbalbōl.* Close the door for when he gets up he'll be crawling all over the place.

tōbale (**tebaley**). Transitive form of *tōbalbal* (**tebalbal**).

tōbo (**tebew**). Archaic. Smaller eye of sprouted coconut.

tōbo (**tẹbẹw**). Also *tōbu* (**tebiw**). 3, 4+3, 6(*-i*), 3+7. A shell, *Muricidae, Purpura (Manicinella) Armigera.*

tōboļāār (**tebewļayar**). Also *tōboļāār* (**tẹbẹwļayar**). 2. Stage of the coconut seedling in which it is beginning to sprout. *Rōnañin tōboļāār ke ine kaņe?* Have the seedlings begun to sprout?

tōborǫñ (**tẹbẹwrag°**). Also *tōboroñ* (**tebewr°eg°**). Archaic. A shell; similar to *toul* and *di.*

Tōbǫtin (**tebawtin**). 3, 6(*-i*). A plant, pandanus cultigen.

tōbōb (**tebeb**). 1(*-i*), 2, 3(inf, tr *-e*), 6(*-i*), 8, 9. Fat; chubby; robust. *Etōbōb lǫlǫ eņ kijen.* He has a nice and fat chicken.

tōbtōb (**tebteb**). 1(*-i*), 2(inf, tr *tōbwe*), 4, 7. Pull in, as fish on a line; weigh anchor. *Eṃōj aer tōbtōb añkō.* They have weighed anchor. *Añkō eo eņ rej tōbwe.* They are weighing anchor now.

tōbwe (**tebey**). Transitive form of *tōbtōb* (**tebteb**).

tōjin (**tẹhjin**). From Engl. Dozen.

tōkai (**tekahyiy**). From Japn. *takai* "high". 1(*-i*), 2(inf, tr *-ik*), 4, 6(*-i*), 7. Fly ball, in baseball; pop-up, in baseball. *Ear tōkaik ļǫk bǫǫļ eo ñan buļōn mar.* He hit a fly ball right into the bushes.

tōkale (**tekaļẹy**). Also *tōnale* (**tegaļẹy**). 3, 6(*-i*). A shell, killer clam.

tōkā (**tekay**). Also *tōked* (**teked**). Strip of reef; long reef between two islets. *Eike ioon tōkā eņ ñe ej pāāt.* That strip of reef has quite a few fish on it when the tide is low.

tōkeak (**tekyak**). 2, 3, 7. Arrive; come to land; reach destination. *Raar tōkeak tok bon̄.* They arrived last night.

tōl (**tẹl**). 3, 6(*-i*). Larvae of lice; nit.

tōl (**tel**). 1(*-i*), 2(inf, tr *tōle*), 4, 7. To lead, direct, preside.

tōl (**tel**). Transitive form of *tōltōl* (**tẹltẹl**).

tōlien (**teliyen**). So many. *Tōlien ek jeban bwini.* So many fish we can't count them.

tōllọk (**tellaq**). 1(*-i*), 2(inf, tr *-e*). Within the power; within the realm of possibilities; pertain; pertinent; worth. *Ej jab tōllọkū ba iiọkwe eok.* It's not for me to say I love you. *Inaaj kar bōk peiṃ ak ej jab tōllọkū.* I would have married you but I am not worthy. *Ta ṇe kotōlloke kiiō?* What are you worth now? What do you do now?

tōllọkbōd (**tellaqbed**). A fish.

tōlpilo (**tẹlpilẹw**). Also *tōḷpilo* (**teḷpilew**). 2(inf, tr *-uk*), 6(*-i*), 7. Lead astray; blind leading the blind. *Jab po ippān bwe enaaj tōlpilouk eok.* Don't associate with him or he'll lead you astray.

tōltōl (**tẹltẹl**). 1(*-i*), 2(inf, tr *tōl(e)*), 3, 4, 7. Collect; put inside. *Ḷeeṇ ej tōltōl owōj.* He is collecting tax.

tōḷao (**teḷahwew**). 6(*-i*). Sitting mat; coarsely woven. *Tōḷaoun ia ṇe kinieṃ?* Where did your sitting mat come from?

tōḷḷan̄ (**teḷḷag**). Save from a storm.

tōḷon̄ (**teḷeg°**). Also *jeḷon̄* (**jeḷeg°**). 1(*-i*), 2(inf, tr *-e*), 7. Go to the interior of an islet; penetrate to the interior of an islet; pervade. *Raar tōḷon̄e ān eo.* They went to the interior of the island.

tōḷọk (**teḷaq**). Away.

tōmak (**temak**). 1(*-i*), 2(inf, tr *-e*), 3, 4, 5(*ttōmakmak*), 7, 8, 9. Believe, faith, creed, pious. *Ettōmakmak ḷeeṇ.* He is gullible. He's pious. *Etōmak lōḷḷap eṇ.* She's a pious old lady. *Kwōn jab tōmake.* Don't believe him.

tōmak ilo jetōb (**temak yilew jẹtẹb**). Superstition. *Etōmak jetōb.* He's superstitious.

tōmaruk (**temariq**). Variant form of *timaruk* (**timariq**).

tōmean̄ (**temyag**). 2(inf, tr *-e*), 5(*ttōmean̄ean̄*), 6(*-i*), 7. Nautical term; sail downwind with the sail on the south and the outrigger on the north. *Wa ko kaṇ rej tōmean̄ toḷọk.* The canoes are sailing downwind with their sails on the port and the outrigger on the starboard side.

tōmmeḷọk (**temmeḷaq**). 1(*-i*), 2, 3, 5(*ttōmtōm*). Smack the lips. *Wōn in ej ttōmtōm?* Who is that that keeps smacking his lips?

tōmrak (**temrak**). Nautical term; sail with the outrigger on the south.

tōmrok (**temreq**). Also *tōmaruk*, *timaruk*. Nautical term; outrigger sinks because too much weight is placed on it; fall into sin.

tōṃa (**teṃah**). From Japn. *tama* "sphere". 6(*-i*). Lightbulb; pupil of eye. *Kobōk kajoorin tōṃa in meja.* You've taken the light right out of my eyes. (You dazzle me). *Ej likūt ledik eṇ jibwin tōṃa in mejān.* Her granddaughter is the apple of her eye.

tōṃato (**teṃahtew**). From Engl. 2, 3, 5(*ttōṃatoto*), 6(*-i*), 8, 9. Tomato.

tōn (**tẹn**). Also *tōn* (**ten**). From Engl. 6(*-i*). Ton.

tōn̄aak (**tegahak**). Also *ettōn̄aak* (**yettegahak**), *ettōnaak* (**yettenahak**). 7. Porch; veranda; lanai; balcony. *Ejjeḷọk ettōn̄aakin ṃwiin.* This house has no veranda.

tōn̄al (**tegal**). 1(*-i*), 2, 3, 4, 5(*ttōn̄aln̄al*), 7, 8, 9, 11(*tōn̄aln̄al*, *tōn̄aln̄ōl*). Sweet. *Ennọ an ttōn̄aln̄al.* It's pervasive sweetness is delicious.

tōn̄al (**tegal**). 2, 4. Diabetes; diabetic. *Aolep rūtōn̄al rōnaaj taktō.* All those with diabetes will be treated.

tōn̄ale (**tegaḷẹy**). Variant form of *tōkale* (**tekaḷẹy**).

tōn̄n̄ōḷọk (**teggeḷaq**). 2, 3(inf, tr *-e*), 6(*-i*). Sound of a bell or something rung.

tōn̄ōl (**tegel**). 2(inf, tr *tōn̄ōle*), 4(*rūttōn̄ōl*), 5(*ttōn̄ōln̄ōl*), 6(*-i*), 7. Poke; rub. *Tōn̄ōle ṃōk im lale an makōrlep.* Rub her and notice how hypersensitive she is.

tōn̄tōn̄ (**tegteg**). 6(*-i*). Very; the most; intensifier, with great force. *Eḷap n̄ūta ilo bwiltōn̄tōn̄in pata eo.* There was much hunger during the heaviest part of the war. *Ebooḷtōn̄tōn̄ aebōj jimeeṇ eṇ.* That cistern is full to the brim. *Ebōttōn̄tōn̄ ḷadik eṇ.* That boy is the naughtiest.

tōōldepak (tẹhẹldẹpak). 6(-*i*). Garland with flowers set wide apart.

tōōlkut (tẹhẹlqit). 6(-*i*). Garland with flowers set close together.

tōōḷ (tẹhẹḷ). Tooth of a comb; bristle, strand of hair; grain of rice.

tōōm̧ (tehem̧). From Engl. Term.

tōōt (tẹhẹt). Also *tōōt* (tehet). From Engl. Third base.

tōp (tẹp). 5(*ttōptōp*), 6(-*i*). Wood-shavings. *Ettōptōp m̧ōn booj eo.* The boat house had wood-shavings strewn all over the place.

tōp (tẹp). Archaic. Encouragement; incentive. *Jen bōk tōp eo jān ḷeeņ.* Follow the leader, be encouraged, and get the work done.

tōpañ (tepag). Also *tapañ*. Medicine pounding rock.

tōpar (tepar). 2, 3(*kōttōpar*), 7, 10(*tōprak*). Arrive; reach.

tōpdo (tepdew). From Gilb. *te bero*. A plant, tree, *Ficus tinctoria* Forst.

tōpe (tẹpẹy). Transitive form of *tōptōp* (tẹptẹp).

tōplik tōpar (tẹplik tẹphar). 1, 2, 3(inf, tr -*e*), 8, 9. Unbalanced; uneven. *Kajim̧we am̧ jijet bwe etōplik tōpar wa ņe.* Sit properly because the canoe is unbalanced.

tōpḷedik (tẹpḷẹydik). 1, 2, 4, 6(-*i*). To sit up on something high with the feet dangling and moving incessantly. *Ilo m̧antin M̧ajeḷ, em̧o an leddik tōpḷedik.* It's unacceptable for girls to sit with their feet dangling, according to Marshallese custom.

tōprak (teprak). 1(-*i*), 2, 3, 5(*ttōprakrak*), 7. Accomplish; carry out; succeed; netted; achieve; perfective form of *tōpar* (tepar). *Ettōprakrak an jerbal.* He always completes his tasks.

tōpran (tepran). 1(*tōpra-*), 6(*tōpran*). Value; gain; accomplishment; achievement; worth. *Eor ke tōpran jikuuḷ eo am̧?* Did you gain anything from your schooling? *Eor tōpra ņa ilo ānin.* I did much work (planted many things) on this islet.

tōptōp (tẹptẹp). 1(-*i*), 2(inf, tr *tōpe*), 3, 4, 7. Taking gifts to a wedding, funeral, or party for guests to take home. *Elōñ kar nuknuk in tōptōp ilo keemem eo.* There was much cloth brought as gifts to the birthday party. *Ear tōpe*

ruo nuknuk ilo iien keemem eo. He took two pieces of cloth as gifts at the time of the birthday party.

tōptōp (tẹptẹp). 6(-*i*). Chest, trunk; foot locker. *Ia ņe kwaar wiaik tōptōp ņe am̧ ie?* Where did you buy your trunk?

tōptōp (tẹptẹp). A fish, cardinal fish, *Apogon novemfasiatus*; *Paramia quinquekineata*.

tōr (ter). 1(-*i*), 2, 3, 4, 8, 9. Greedy.

tōr (ter). Archaic. 6(*tōran*). Formant in place names; in a certain part. *Tōrrak.* In the south part. *Tōreañ.* In the north part. *Tōrkaņiiene.* On dry land.

tōrak (tẹhrak). Also *kattōrak* (kattẹhrak). 2(inf, tr -*e*), 3, 4, 6(-*i*), 7. Protection in fighting; shield.

tōrak (terak). Ceiling; roof.

tōran (tẹran). Distance. *Tōran ikōtaan Mājro im Jālwōj eḷap.* The distance between Majuro and Jaluit is great.

tōrañ (terag). 2(inf, tr -*e*). Spoil; infect. *Jab kōjjedwawaik kinej eo bwe ḷoñ enaaj torañe.* Don't expose the wound or the flies will infect it.

tōre (tẹrẹy). Time of day or night; the time. *Tōreet in kom̧ro ej ilān eoņōd ie?* What ungodly hour are you two going fishing? *Ej ja tōrein wōt ke ij itok.* I arrived at this time of day. *Enaaj iọkwe eok m̧ae tōreo kobūrook.* She'll love you till you're broke.

tōreej (teryej). Also *tōrej*. From Engl. 3, 6. Thread.

tōreej (teryej). Also *tōrej*. From Engl. 2, 3, 7. Straight, in playing poker.

tōreejab (tereyjab). Also *tōrejab*. From Engl. 2, 3(inf, tr -*e*), 4, 6(-*i*), 7. Dress up. *Ta wūnin am̧ tōrejab?* Why are you all dressed up?

tōreeta (tereytah). Also *tōreta*. From Engl. Trader; merchant.

tōreo (tẹrẹyew). Variant form of *tōrreo* (tẹrrẹyew).

tōrerei- (tẹrẹyrẹyi-). 1, 7, 8, 9. Side; edge; alongside; border; fringe; margin; rim of.

tōrerein iaḷ (tẹrẹyrẹyin yiyaḷ). Roadside.

tōrreo (tẹrrẹyew). Also *tōreo* (tẹrẹyew). All the more. *Iḷak ba en jab jañ, tōrreo ej kab buuḷ im jañ.* When I asked her not to cry, she cried all the more. *Ņe koba en jab idaak, tōrreo ej kab idaak.* If you tell him not to drink, he'll drink all the more.

tōt (**tet**). 1(*-i*), 2, 3(inf, tr *-e*). Stay still; fixed, settled. *Ij katōte joor e ije.* I'm fixing the post in the ground here. *Etōt ioon jikin.* He settled on his homeland.

tōt-. See *tt-*.

tōtaiṃoṇ (**tetahiyṃeṇ°**). 1(*-i*), 2(inf, tr *-e*), 4, 5(*tōtaiṃoṇṃoṇ*), 6(*-i*), 7. A food, taro grated and mixed with coconut oil and coconut sap. *An wōn iien tōtaiṃoṇ.* Whose turn is it to make *tōtaiṃoṇ*? *Etōtaiṃoṇṃoṇ.* It's got *tōtaiṃoṇ* all over it.

tōū (**tẹhih**). Dial. E only; W: *ettōū* (**yẹttẹhih**). A fish, mackerel, *Trachurops crumenopthalmus.*

tta (**ttah**). Dial. W: *etta* (**yettah**), E: *tōta* (**tetah**). 1(*-a*), 2, 4, 6(*-i*). Conceive; become pregnant.

ttabōn (**ttaben**). Dial. W: *ettabōn* (**yettaben**), E: *tōtabōn* (**tetaben**). 1(*-i*), 2(inf, tr *-e*), 4, 8, 9. Occult; black magic; omen.

ttal (**ttal**). Dial. W: *ettal* (**yettal**), E: *tōtal* (**tetal**). 1(*-i*), 2, 3, 7, 8, 9. Leak; puncture. *Ettal ainbat e.* This pot leaks.

ttal (**ttal**). Dial. W: *ettal* (**yettal**), E: *tōtal* (**tetal**). 1(*-i*), 2, 6(*-i*), 8, 9. Loudmouth; blabber-mouth; telltale. *Kwōn jab kōṇaan ttal.* Don't be a blabbermouth.

ttaḷum. See *ttoḷūm.*

ttaorak (**ttahwewrak**). Dial. W: *ettaorak* (**yettahwewrak**), E: *tōtaorak* (**tetahwewrak**). 1, 2(inf, tr *-e*), 3(inf, tr *-e*), 5(*ttaorak*), 6(*-i*), 7, 8, 9. Gritty feeling under the eyelids; sticky, of eyes. *Ej ttaorak wōt meja jān ke iar pilo.* It has felt gritty under my eyelids since I got the eye disease. *Ettaorak meja.* My eyes feel sticky.

ttā (**ttay**). Dial. W: *ettā* (**yettay**), E: *tōtā* (**yetay**). 1(*-i*), 2, 3(inf, tr *kōttāik*), 4, 6(*-i*), 8, 9, 11(*ttāte*). Low; lowly; menial; demote; inferior. *Eḷap an ttā jerbal eṇ an.* He has a menial job. *Eḷap an ttā baḷuun eo.* The plane is very low. *Eṃōj kōttāiki.* He's been demoted.

ttā bōro (**ttay bẹrẹw**). Dial. W: *ettā bōro* (**yettay bẹrẹw**), E: *tōtā bōro* (**tetay bẹrẹw**). 1(*...būruo-*), 2, 3, 4, 7. Humble; modest.

ttein̄ (**ttẹyig**). Dial. W: *ettein̄* (**yẹttẹyig**), E: *tōtein̄* (**yẹtẹyig**). 1(*-i*), 2(inf, tr *tein̄(i)*), 4, 7. Fill with liquid. *Kwōn tein̄i kaar eṇ kōn ḷalem kōḷan in kiaaj.* Please put five gallons of gas in the car. *Kwōn tein̄ bato ṇe kōn aebōj.* Fill that bottle with fresh water.

ttemakil (**ttẹymakil**). Dial. W: *ettemakil* (**yẹttẹymakil**), E: *tōtemakil* (**tẹtẹymakil**). Also *temakil* (**tẹymakil**). 1(*-i*), 2(inf, tr *temakil(i)*), 4, 5(*ttemakilkil*), 6(*-i*), 7. Pluck feathers from a bird; pluck leaves from midrib of coconut fronds; tear apart. *Wōn e ear ttemakilkil kimej ṇa ije?* Who plucked this frond and scattered leaves all over the place?

ttiijij (**ttiyijyij**). Dial. W: *ittiijij* (**yittiyijyij**), E: *tūtiijij* (**titiyijyij**). Sound of grease frying; sizzle. *Ettiij ḷọk ek eo ke emat.* The fish kept sizzling when it was cooked.

ttil (**ttil**). Dial. W: *ittil* (**yittil**), E: *tūtil* (**titil**). 1(*-i*), 2(inf, tr *tile*), 3, 7. Burn; light; set fire to; ignite. *Kwōn tile aḷaḷ ṇe.* Set fire to that piece of wood.

ttino (**ttinẹw**). Dial. W: *ittino* (**yittinẹw**), E: *tūtino* (**titinẹw**). Also *aḷọk* (**halaq**). 1, 2, 3(inf, tr -ik, -uk), 5(*ttinono*), 6(*-i*), 7, 8, 9. Secret; mysterious; camouflaged; obscure; hidden; covert. *Ettino ṃwilin.* He's a wolf in sheep's clothing. *Kattinouk men in.* Keep this a secret. *Ettinono an jerbal.* He's very secretive about his work. *Eḷap an ttino ijo ej kūttiliek ie.* The place he is hiding is secret.

tto (**ttẹw**). Dial. W: *etto* (**yẹttẹw**), E: *tōto* (**yẹtẹw**). 1(*-i*), 2(inf, tr *tuuj(i)*), 3, 4, 7. Dig taro. *Ḷōṃaro raṇ rej tto iaraj ṃōn̄ein jota.* Those fellows are digging taro for supper.

tto (**ttew**). Dial. W: *etto* (**yettew**), E: *tōto* (**yetew**). 2. Fishing method, use fishpole at night with either lure or bait.

ttoḷọk (**ttewḷaq**). Dial. W: *ettoḷọk* (**yettewḷaq**), E: *tōtoḷọk* (**tetewḷaq**). 1(*-i*), 2, 3, 7. Far; distant; remote. *Ettoḷọk Wūjlan̄ jān Mājro.* Ujelang is far from Majuro.

tton̄ (**tteg°**). Dial. W: *etton̄* (**yetteg°**), E: *tōton̄* (**teteg°**). Also *n̄n̄or* (**gger°**). 1, 2, 3, 7. Sleep soundly. *Eḷap aō kar tton̄.* I really slept soundly.

ttoon (**ttẹwẹn**). Dial. W: *ettoon* (**yẹttẹwẹn**), E: *tōtoon* (**yẹtẹwẹn**). 1(*-i*), 2, 3(st inf *kattoonon*, tr *kattoon*), 5(*ttoonon*), 7, 11(*ttoonon*). Dirty; corrupt; foul; nasty; obscene; polluted; unclean, vulgar, gross. *Ekattoonon.* He's sloppy. *Ettoonon nōbjān ṃwiin.* There's litter all around this house. *Ettoon kobban lọñiin.* He's got a foul mouth.

ttoor (**ttewer**). Dial. W: *ettoor* (**yettewer**), E: *tōtoor* (**tetewer**). 2(inf, tr *toore*), 4, 6(*-i*), 7. Fishing method, pole fishing along the beach or shore. *Kwōj ttoor jikōt.* In which direction are you pole fishing?

ttọ (**ttaw**). Dial. W: *ettọ* (**yettaw**), E: *tōtọ* (**tetaw**). 1, 2(inf, tr *tọuk*), 4, 6(*-i*). Mend a net. *Ḷōṃaraṇ rej ttọ ok.* The men are mending nets.

ttọḷ. See *ttọḷūm*.

ttọḷūm (**ttaḷ°im**). Dial. W: *ettọḷūm* (**yettaḷ°im**), E: *tōtọḷūm* (**tetaḷ°im**). Also *ttọḷ* (**ttaḷ°**). 1(*-i*), 2(inf, tr *tọḷūm(i)*), 4, 5(*ttọḷūmḷwūm*), 7. Grope; reach for something in the dark; feel around for something; fumble. *Eṃōj ṇe aṃ ttọḷūmḷwūm.* Control your hands. *Tọḷūmtok juon ni jān lowaan pāāk ṇe.* Get a coconut for me out of the bag.

ttōl (**ttẹl**). Dial. W: *ettōl* (**yẹttẹl**), E: *tōtōl* (**yẹtẹl**). Give preference to.

ttōllōñ (**ttẹllẹg**). Dial. W: *ettōllōñ*, E: *tōtōllōñ*. Look up.

ttōṇak (**tteṇak**). Dial. W: *ettōṇak* (**yetteṇak**), E: *tōtōṇak* (**teteṇak**). 1(*-i*), 2(inf, tr *-e*), 4, 5(*ttōṇakṇak*), 7. Dream; fantasy; day-dream. *Eḷap aō ttōṇakṇak ṇai ṃwiin.* I always dream (when I sleep) in this house. *Eṃōj ṇe aṃ ttōṇak.* Stop your day-dreaming.

ttōñ (**ttẹg**). Dial. W: *ettōñ* (**yẹttẹg**), E: *tōtōñ* (**tẹtẹg**), *rere* (**reyrey**) . 1(*-i*), 2, 3(st inf *kattōñtōñ*, tr *kattōñ*), 5(*ttōñtōñ*), 7. Laugh. *Ettōñtōñ ajri eṇ.* That child is always laughing. *Ekattōñtōñ ledik eṇ.* That girl is charming. *Jab kattōñ eō.* Don't make me laugh.

ttōñ dikdik (**ttẹg dikdik**). Dial. W: *ettōñ dikdik* (**yẹttẹg dikdik**), E: *tōtoñ dikdik* (**yẹtẹg dikdik**). 1(*-i*), 2, 3, 7. Smile; titter; giggle; chuckle.

ttōñtōñ (**ttegteg**). Dial. W: *ettōñtōñ* (**yettegteg**), E: *tōtōñtōñ* (**tetegteg**). 1(*-i*), 2, 3, 7. Rattling of bottle, etc.; chinking; jangling; jingling; clinking.

ttōr (**ttẹr**). Dial. W: *ettōr* (**yẹttẹr**), E: *tōtōr* (**tẹtẹr**). 1(*-i*), 2, 3, 4, 7. Run.

ttōr kālọk (**ttẹr kaylaq**). Dial. W: *ettōr kālọk* (**yẹttẹr kaylaq**), E: *tōtōr kālọk* (**tẹtẹr kaylaq**). 1(*-i*), 2, 4, 7. Run and jump.

ttuuj (**ttiwij**). Dial. W: *ittuuj* (**yittiwij**), E: *tūtuuj* (**titiwij**). 1(*-i*), 2(inf, tr *tuuj(i)*), 4, 7. Dig up.

ttuur (**ttiwir**). Dial. W: *ittuur* (**yittiwir**), E: *tūtuur* (**titiwir**). 1(*-i*), 2(inf, tr *tuur(i)*), 4, 7. Dive down. *Rōmoot in ttuur tok kapoor.* They went to dive for and bring back giant clams. *Kwōn tuur tok bukbuk eṇ.* Dive down and get that helmet shell.

ttuur bōro (**ttiwir bẹrẹw**). Dial. W: *ittuur bōro* (**yittiwir bẹrẹw**), E: *tūtuur bōro* (**titiwir bẹrẹw**). 1(*būruo-*), 2(inf, tr *tuur būruo-*), 4, 6(*-i*). Psychoanalyze; pry into someone's thoughts. *Kwōn tuur būruon.* Find out what is really on his mind. *Jekdọọn ñe kotuur būruō ak iban kwaḷọk aō ḷōmṇak.* Even if you persist on questioning me, I will not say what's on my mind.

ttūṃurṃur (**ttiṃir°ṃir°**). Dial. W: *ittūṃurṃur* (**yittiṃir°ṃir°**), E: *tūtṃurṃur* (**titṃir°ṃir°**). 1, 2, 3(inf, tr *-ki*), 6(*-i*), 7, 8, 9. Fearful; doubtful; hesitant. *Kwōn joḷọk aṃ ttūṃurṃur bwe wūnin aṃ wōtlọk ṇe.* You'd better stop being fearful if you want to get anywhere in life.

tu (**tiw**). A locative, where, there. *Tu ia eo bok eo epād ie?* Where is the book? *Epād tulaḷ.* It's down there somewhere.

tu (**tiw**). Variant form of *tudek* (**tiwdek**).

tubar (**tiwbar**). 1(*-i*), 2(inf, tr *-e*), 3, 4, 7. Headlong; jump to dive, head first; dive.

tudek (**tiwdek**). Also *tu* (**tiw**). 1(*-i*), 3, 6(*-i*). Gizzard; stomach.

tueañ (**tiwyag**). Also *tueñ* (**tiwyẹg**). 1(*-i*), 7. Northern part.

tujiloñloñ (**tiwjileg°leg°**). Variant form of *meḷoktakōn* (**meleqtaken**) and *tuujloñloñ* (**tiwijleg°leg°**).

Tujuon (**tiwjiwen**). From *tu* (**tiwi-**) "dive", *juon* (**jiwen**) "one" (?). A plant, pandanus cultigen (Takeuchi).

tulowa (**tiwlewwah**). 1(-*i*). Inward.
Kwōn wūno waj ñan tulowa. Paint
inward.

tulok̗ (**tiwlaq**). 1(-*i*), 2, 3(inf *kattulok̗*, tr
katulok̗), 4, 5(*ttulok̗lok̗*), 7. Go down;
dive; take a bath; submerge. *Etulok̗
al̗.* The sun has set. *Kwōnañin tulok̗
ke?* Haven't you bathed yet? *Waan
tulok̗.* Submarine. *El̗ap an ttulok̗lok̗
l̗een̗.* He does a lot of diving. He's
always taking baths. *Rej kattulok̗ armej
iar.* They are dunking people in the
lagoon. *Katulok̗ neem̗ ilojet.* Dip your
feet in the water (lagoon).

tulok̗kun al̗ (**tiwlaqin hal̗**). Sundown;
sunset.

tulōñ (**tiwlẹg**). 1(-*i*), 2, 7, 8, 9. At the
upper part.

tul̗aar (**til̗°ahar**). Also *tūl̗aar* (**til̗ahar**).
1(-*i*), 2, 3, 5(*ttul̗aarar*). Burnt;
overcooked; scorched. *Etul̗aar raij eo.*
The rice is scorched.

tumej (**tiwmẹj**). 2, 4, 5(*ttumejmej*),
6(-*i*), 7. Open eyes under water. *Jab
tumej bwe elim̗.* Don't open your eyes
in the water because it's murky.

tum̗al̗ (**tiwm̗al̗**). 1, 2, 4, 6(-*i*). A game,
pulling people from port to starboard
under the keel; keel-haul. *Kom̗ jab
tum̗al̗ bwe kom̗ naaj mal̗oñ.* Don't
play that keel-haul game or you'll
drown.

tuññūlal̗l̗ok̗ (**tig°g°ilal̗l̗aq**). Also
tūm̗m̗wilal̗l̗ok̗ (**tim̗m̗ilal̗l̗aq**). 2, 3.
Sink; go underwater.

tuññūli (**tig°g°iliy**). 2, 7. Poke; pluck.
Ear tuññūli mejān ek eo. He plucked
out the fish's eyes. *Jab tuññūli keek
ne.* Don't poke the cake.

tuo (**tiwew**). Archaic. Formant in place
names.

tuon (**tiwen**). 3(inf, tr -*e*), 4+3, 3+7.
Trick; skill; seem. *Ejel̗ā katuon.* He
knows some tricks. *Etuon wōt tok.* It
looks like rain.

tur (**tir°**). 2(inf, tr -*i*), 6(-*i*). End of an
islet; beam of a house. *Kwōnañin turi
ke m̗ōn̗e?* Have you put up the beams
on the house?

tureeaar (**tiwrẹyyahar**). Dial. W: *ittuur*
(**yittiwir**), E: *tūtuur* (**titiwir**). 1(-*i*),
6(-*i*), 7. Eastward.

turilik (**tiwriylik**). Dial. W, E: *turōtle*
(**tiwrẹtley**). 1(-*i*), 6(-*i*), 7. Westward.

turot (**tir°et**). Dial. Bikini only. Kind;
type; sort. *Bōb turot men n̗e?* What
kind of a pandanus is that?

turoñ (**tiwrag°**). 1(-*i*), 2(inf, tr -*e*), 3, 4,
5(*tturoñroñ*), 7. Skin diving; fishing
method, spear fishing. *Elōñ ikōn
turoñ.* There are many fish to be
caught by spearing. *Kwōj turoñ ke?*
Are you going spear fishing?
Etturoñroñ likao in ānin. The fellows
on this island do a lot of spear fishing.

turōk (**tiwrẹk**). 1(-*i*), 7. Southern part.

turōtle (**tiwrẹtley**). Dialectal variant of
turilik (**tiwriylik**).

turrul̗ok̗ (**tir°r°il̗aq**). Also *turūl̗l̗ok̗*
(**tir°il̗l̗aq**). 1(-*i*), 2, 3, 7. Sink;
swamped. *Eturrul̗ok̗ wa eo.* The boat
sank.

turu- (**tir°i-**). 1(-*i*), 4, 6(-*i*), 7. Next to;
close to; near; beside. *Itōm jijet
turū.* Come sit by me.

turum̗ (**tir°im̗**). From Engl. 1(-*i*),
2(inf, tr -*i*), 5(*tturum̗rum̗*). A game,
trump; a card game. *Etturum̗rum̗ Al̗i
im men.* Ali and his wife are always
playing trump.

turun māj (**tir°in maj**).
1(...*meja*-). Face.

tutu (**tiwtiw**). Dial. W, E: *n̗ok* (**n̗eq**).
1(-*i*), 2, 3(inf, tr *katutuuk(i)*),
5(*ttutu*), 7, 8, 9, 11(*tutu*). Bathe, take
a bath; wet. *Etutu nuknuk kā aō.* My
clothes are wet. *Kwōn tutu m̗okta.*
Take a bath first.

tutu in kwōlej (**tiwtiw yin qẹlyẹj**). 2, 4,
6(-*i*). Rinse oneself off in lieu of
thorough shower. *Kwōn tutu in
kwōlej bwe eawa.* Just rinse yourself
off because it's time (to go).

tutukōp (**tiwtiwkẹp**). Variant form of
jujukōp (**jiwjiwkẹp**).

tuuj (**tiwij**). Transitive form of *tto*
(**ttẹw**).

tuuj (**tiwij**). Transitive form of *ttuuj*
(**ttiwij**).

tuuj bōl (**tiwij bẹl**). Slang. From *tuuj
bōl* (**tiwij bẹl**) "dig up taro patch". 2.
Steal someone's wife (euphemism).
Rōtuuj bōl eo an. Someone stole his
wife.

tuujloñloñ (**tiwijleg°leg°**). Also
mel̗oktakōn (**mel̗ẹqtaken**). Period
between setting of sun and rising of
moon; third moon phase; moon phase
after *mel̗oktak*.

tuuḷ (**tiwiḷ**). From Engl. 6(*-i*). Tool. *Eor ke aṃ tuuḷ rot eṇ ej diklọkḷaplọk?* Have you got an adjustable wrench?

tuuḷbọọk (**tiwiḷbawak**). From Engl. 6(*-i*). Toolbox.

tuur (**tiwir**). Transitive form of *ttuur* (**ttiwir**).

tuwa (**tiwwah**). Also *tuwa* (**tiwah**). Small opening; little space between trees; aisle; gap.

tuwaak (**tiwwahak**). Also *tuwaak* (**tiwahak**). 1(*-i*), 2(inf, tr *tuwaak*), 3(inf, tr *-e*), 6(*-i*), 7. Go into the water; wade in water.

tuwā (**tiwway**). 2(inf, tr *-ik(i)*), 4, 6(*-i*), 7. Fishing method, spear fishing while diving. *Iar tuwāiki ek kā.* I speared these fish while diving.

tuwe (**tiwey**). Archaic. Formant in place names; old form of *to* "westward".

tuwe (**tiwey**). 2. Exploit a fishing grounds; to possess, of evil spirits; possessed by a demon. *Rōtuwe lio.* She was possessed. *Eṃōj tuwe jikin eọñōd in.* Someone has fished out the area.

tuwe (**tiwẹy**). To damage. *Jourur etuwe (etwe) ni eo.* Lighting damaged the coconut tree.

tūaḷ (**tihaḷ**). Charge of a school of fish chasing minnows.

tūar (**tihar**). Also *tiār* (**tiyar**), *tiārmān* (**tiyarman**). 3, 6(*-i*). Pandanus blossom.

tūb (**tib**). Also *tip* (**tip**). Reward; prize; delightful; enjoyment. *Ebōk tūb eo.* He took the prize. He enjoys it very much. *Eḷap tūb eo an rainin.* Today is a happy occasion.

tūbbọk (**tibbaq**). Dial. E, W: *tipjek* (**tipjẹk**). 1(*-i*), 2, 3, 4, 5(*ttūbbọkbọk*), 7. Stumble; slip. *Ettōr im tūbbọk.* He ran and stumbled. *Ettūbbọkbọk ajri eṇ.* That child is always stumbling.

tūbḷotak (**tibḷ°etak**). Also *tūbuḷtak.* 1(*-i*), 2(inf, tr *-e*), 3, 4, 6(*-i*), 7. Eulogize; praise; laud; entreat; beg. *Koṃwin tūbḷotake Anij bwe en jipañ koṃ.* Beg God to help you. *Rej al im tūbḷotake etan Irooj.* They are singing and praising the name of the Lord.

tūbok (**tibeq**). Variant form of *ettōbok.*

tūkjinede (**tikjineydey**). From Engl. 6(*-i*). Dictionary.

tūkōk (**tikẹk**). 6(*-i*), 7. High tide. *Tūkōkin jota eḷap jān jibboñ.* Evening tide is higher than morning.

tūkōt (**tikẹt**). Also *tūkōt* (**tiket**). From Engl. 2(inf, tr *-e*), 6(*-i*). Ticket.

tūḷaar (**tiḷahar**). Variant form of *tuḷaar* (**tiḷ°ahar**).

tūṃ (**tiṃ**). 2, 3, 5(*ttūṃtūṃ*), 7. Be late for and miss a plane, boat, or car, etc. *Itūṃ jān baḷuun eo.* I missed the plane. *Ḷeo ettūṃtūṃ eṇ.* That fellow always misses the boat.

tūṃ kwōd (**tiṃ qed**). Idiom. Severance of a relationship. *Jān wōt aṃ nana, etūṃ kwōd eo ikōtaarro.* Simply because you're a harlot, our relationship is dissolved.

tūṃbōḷ (**tiṃbeḷ**). From Engl. Thimble.

tūṃṃọṇ (**tiṃṃaṇ°**). 2(inf, tr *-e*), 4, 6(*-i*). Pluck feathers; pull out hairs; eradicate. *Jab tūṃṃọṇe bōra.* Don't pull out my hair.

tūṃṃwijkōk (**tiṃṃijkẹk**). Slang. From *tūṃ* (**tiṃ**) "break", *mwijkōk* (**ṃijkẹk**) "break". 2, 3, 6(*-i*). Lose out; miss out; cut off completely. *Kwōj kab āteo tūṃṃwijkōk jān būruō.* Now you're really completely cut off from my heart.

tūṃṃwilaḷḷọk (**tiṃṃilaḷḷaq**). Variant form of *tuññūlaḷḷọk* (**tig°g°ilaḷḷaq**).

tūṃtūṃ (**tiṃtiṃ**). Also *tūṃ* (**tiṃ**). 1(*-i*), 2(inf, tr *tūṃ(wi)*), 3, 5(*ttūṃtūṃwi, tūṃtūṃwi*), 7. To pull and break objects such as string, rope, wire or grass; come loose; severed. *Rej tūṃtūṃ wūjooj.* They are pulling grass. *Rej tūṃwi wūjooj ko.* They are pulling the grass. *Kwōn jab ttūṃtūṃi wūjooj kaṇe.* Don't keep pulling up that grass. *Rej katūṃtūṃ bao.* They're plucking chickens. *Etūṃ to eo.* The rope broke.

Tūṃur (**tiṃir°**). Personal name of legendary figure, eldest son of *Lōktañūr*; a constellation; stars in Scorpius; tau, alpha, sigma; Antares.

tūñad (**tigad**). A fish, porgy, *Gnathodentex aurolineatus.*

tūñañ (**tigag**). Dial. E, W: *kōjṃaal.* Ask for food, a shameful thing to do. *Ekajjookok tūñañ.* It's disgraceful to ask people for food.

tūññūḷọk (**tiggiḷaq**). Also *tūñ* (**tig**). 2, 3. Ringing (in ears); ringing sound.

tūr (**tir**). From *tūrtūr* (**tirtir**). 6(*-i*). Bundle that has been wrapped, sticks or pandanus leaves; bundle of long objects such as spears, fish poles, etc. place for making weapons. *Ewi tūrin kane eo?* Where is the bundle of firewood?

tūraab (**tirahab**). 1(*-i*), 2(inf, tr *-e*), 6(*-i*), 7, 8, 9. Cheat; trick; swindle; bluff. *Ejjeļo̧k wōt tūraabin ļeeņ.* He's full of tricks. *Etūraabe eō inne.* He cheated me yesterday. *Tūraabin ia men ņe?* Where's that swindler from?

tūrabōļ (**tirabeļ**). From Engl. 2, 3, 4, 5(*ttūrabōļbōļ*), 7. Trouble. *Ettūrabōļbōļ jar eņ.* That couple is always fighting.

tūraip (**tirahyip**). From Engl. 2, 4, 5(*ttūraipip*), 7, 8, 9. To drive a car. *Ekadik ttūraipip ļadik eņ nājin Robōt.* Robert's boy drives all over the place. *Inaaj tūraipwōj ñan Rita buñniin.* I'll drive over to Rita tonight.

tūrak (**tirak**). From Engl. 1(*-i*), 2, 3, 6(*-i*), 7. Truck.

tūraṃ (**tiraṃ**). From Engl. 2(inf, tr *-e*), 3, 6(*-i*). Drum; barrel; short punches in boxing, as in the beating of a drum. *Etūraṃe mejān.* He gave him short, quick punches to the face.

tūrāikōn (**tirayiken**). From Engl. Dragon.

tūrep (**tiryep**). Also *tūreep* (**tireyep**). From Engl. 7. Trip; voyage.

tūriaṃo (**tiriyaṃew**). 1(*-i*), 2, 3, 4, 7, 8, 9. Sympathize with; have mercy on; have pity; emotion.

tūrook (**tirewek**). Transitive form of *tūroro* (**tirewrew**).

tūroon (**tirewen**). From Engl. Throne.

tūroot (**tirwet**). Also *tūrwōt.* Cabinet; wardrobe; closet; bureau; locker.

tūroro (**tirewrew**). 1(*-i*), 2(inf, tr *tūrook*), 3, 6(*-i*), 7. Wrap with leaves. *Kwōn tūrook mā ņe.* Wrap that breadfruit with leaves.

tūroro (**tirewrew**). Dial. Ujelang only. Wrap up in a blanket. *Ļeo eņ ej tūroro.* The man you're looking for is wrapped up in a blanket.

tūrowa (**tirewwah**). From Engl. 6(*-i*). Drawer.

tūrtūr (**tirtir**). 1(*-i*), 2(inf, tr *-i*), 3, 7. Wrap in basket or leaves; bundle. *Kwōn tūrtūri ek kaņe.* Wrap those fish with leaves. *Rej tūrtūr ek.* They are wrapping fish in leaves. *Ewi tūrtūr in kane eo?* Where is the bundle of firewood?

tūt-. See *tt-.*

tūttūt (**tittit**). Dialectal variant of *ittūt* (**yittit**).

u (**wiw**). Dial. W only; see *o* (**wẹw**). 1(*-i*), 2, 3, 7, 8, 9. Pale.

u (**wiw**). 6(*-i*). Fish trap.

ub (**wib**). 1(*-i*), 2, 3, 6(*ubnen*), 8, 9. Tender skin of a baby; soft; unripe coconut; tender; fragile; frail. *Eub uror ņe.* That bunch of coconuts isn't ripe yet. *Kwōn jab deñōt ajri ņe bwe eub ānbwinnin.* Don't spank that child because its body is tender. *Ubnen Ni Maro.* An immature nut of the *Ni Maro* variety.

ubaak (**wibahak**). 1(*-i*), 2(inf, tr *-e*), 4, 7. Drive off; scare away; shoo away. *Kwōn ubaki bao kaņe.* Shoo those chickens away.

ubabōj (**wibabej**). 1(*-i*), 2, 3(*-e*), 7. Unchewed food caught in throat; choked; shocked; scandalized. *Ṃantin lio eko̧ubabōje likao eo.* Her actions shocked the young man.

ubatak (**wibahtak**). 1, 2(inf, tr *-e*), 4, 6(*-i*), 7. To hit or slap someone with something, usually flat. *Inaaj kar jako ñe iar jab ṃōkaj in iñtōk jān an ubatake eō kōn jebwe eo.* I'd have been a goner if I hadn't moved when he hit me with the broad side of the canoe paddle.

ubatak (**wibahtak**). 5(*ubatake*), 6(*-i*). Pile of earth; high barrier reef. *Eubatake ānin.* This island has lots of earth piles. *Emake ubatake baal in ānin.* The barrier reef of this island is exceptionally high.

ubļo̧ñ (**wibļag°**). 1(*-i*), 2(inf, tr *-e*), 3, 4, 7. Catch flies; drive off flies; swat flies.

ubnen (**wibnen**). Immature coconut fruit of; construct form of *ub* (**wib**).

ubrar (**wibrar**). 1(*-i*), 2(inf, tr *-e*), 7. Slap; strike; smite; scratch with claws.

ubtak (**wibtak**). 1(*-i*), 2(inf, tr *-e*), 7. Steering method using a paddle.

ubwe (**wibey**). Dial. W, E: *ļukut* (**ļiqit**), *ļuktūr* (**ļiqtir**). 2(inf, tr *ubweik, ļukuti, ļuktūrri*), 6(*-i*), 7. Be smashed against something, of canoes. *Ņo eubweik wa eo ņa ibaal.* The waves smashed the canoe against the reef.

ubweņo (**wibeyņew**). 6(-*i*). Wave-guard on a canoe. *Joñan an ļap ņo ejar ubweņo eo.* The wave-guard couldn't withstand the big waves.

ud. See *wūd.*

ujooj. See *wūjooj.*

uke (**wikey**). 2, 7. Take; bring; lead, people or animals.

ukeļǫk (**wikeyļaq**). 1, 2, 3, 4, 6(-*i*). Confess; repent; change one's ways from bad to good; remorse; regret. *Kwōn ukeļǫk jān kadek.* Give up drinking. *Ear ukeļǫk.* He confessed. *Eṃōj an ukeļǫk jān bōd ko an.* He has repented of his sins. *Iukeļǫk bwe iar tan itok.* I regret that I came.

uklele (**wiqleyley**). From Engl. 1(-*i*), 2, 3, 4, 6(-*i*), 7. Ukulele.

ukok (**wikwęk**). 1(-*i*), 2(inf, tr *ukōj(e)*), 4, 5(*ukukōj*), 6(-*i*), 7, 10(*okjak*). Turn; turn over; upset; overturn; push over; topple; eliminate, in contest; reciprocate. *Ukōj dekā kaņe.* Turn those rocks over. *Raar deļǫñ im ukukōj jea ko.* They went in and threw the chairs around. *Eokjak ni eo.* The coconut tree fell down. *Raar ukok dekā em kalibbukwe.* They turned the rocks over to find shells. *Rūbait eo ear ukōje aolepān ļōṃaro jet.* The boxer beat all the rest of the competitors.

ukok (**wikwęk**). 1(-*i*), 2(inf, tr *ukōt(e), ukot(e)*), 3, 4, 5(*ukukōt, ukukot*), 7, 10(*oktak*). Change; translate; interpret; deflect; deform; reciprocate. *Ukōt ainikien.* Translate what he says. *Jab ukukōt kilen eb ņe.* Stop inserting variations into the dance. *Eoktak an kōnnaan.* He speaks differently. *Kwōn jeļā ukōt jouj.* You have to know how to reciprocate favors. *Wōn ņe ear ukot bok ņe ñan kajin Ṃajeļ?* Who translated that book into Marshallese? *Wōn eņ enaaj ukukot ainikien ilo tūrep in an ñan Ratak?* Who will interpret for him at every place on his trip around the eastern chain?

ukoktak (**wikwęktak**). 1(-*i*), 2, 3(inf, tr -*e*), 6(-*i*). Alternate; fluctuate; changing continually; toss and turn. *Eļap an ukoktak kūtwōn allōñ kein.* These are the months when the wind fluctuates. *Kōto in ej ukoktak ikōtaan eañōm rak.* The wind keeps alternating between north and south.

ukood (**wikewed**). Dial. E, W: *ikood* (**yikewed**). Also *ukwōd* (**wikwed**), *ukood* (**wiqewed**). 1(-*i*), 2(inf, tr -*e*), 3, 4, 7, 8, 9, 11(*ukwōd*). Raw. *Ennǫ ukood in bwebwe.* Raw tuna is delicious.

ukot (**wiqet**). Transitive form of *ukok* (**wikwęk**).

ukōj (**wikej**). Transitive form of *ukok* (**wikwęk**).

ukōt (**wiket**). Transitive form of *ukok* (**wikwęk**).

ukōt bōkā (**wiket bekay**). Idiom. Return a favor; compensate. *Ledik eo ej ukōt bōkā ñan aļap ro raar lale jān ke ear dik.* She's looking after the old folks to repay them for looking after her when she was quite young.

ukōt ṃōōr (**wiket ṃeher**). 1(-*a*), 2. Disguise; change color, of fish; countershading.

ukwōj (**wiqej**). Transitive form of *okjak* (**węqjak**).

ulej. See *wūlej.*

ulik. See *wūlik.*

uļūtļūt (**wiļitļit**). Also *ṃokulkul* (**ṃaqilqil**). 1(-*i*), 2, 3, 7, 8, 9, 11(*uļūtļūt*). Fat and healthy, usually referring to a baby; plump.

uṃ (**wiṃ**). Native oven; earth oven; bake; roast.

uṃjāj (**wiṃjaj**). Also *uñjāj* (**wigjaj**). 1(-*i*), 2(inf, tr -*e*), 7. Wring, clothes. *Eṃōj ke aṃ uṃjāje nuknuk ņe?* Did you wring the clothes?

uṃṃa (**wiṃṃah**). Also *uṃa* (**wiṃah**). 1(-*i*), 2(inf, tr -*ik*), 3, 4, 6(-*i*), 7. Kiss.

uṃtaak (**wiṃtahak**). Variant form of *uñtaak* (**wigtahak**).

uṃuṃ (**wiṃwiṃ**). 1(-*i*), 2(inf tr *uṃwin(i)*), 3(*kǫuṃuṃwi*), 4, 7, 11(*uṃuṃ*). Bake, usually in earth oven. *Mā ko kaņ rej uṃuṃ.* Those breadfruit are baking now. *Emej uṃwini mā ko.* Those breadfruit have been baked. *Piik uṃuṃ.* Roasted pork. *Uṃuṃwin wōn mā kein?* Who baked these breadfruit? *Kwōn kǫuṃuṃi ippaṃ.* Let her share your oven.

uṃwin (**wiṃin**). Transitive form of *uṃuṃ* (**wiṃwiṃ**).

un (**win**). See *wūn.*

unniñ. See *wūnniñ.*

uno (**winew**). See *wūno.*

unōk. See *wūnōk.*

unpej. See *wūnpej.*

untoba. See *wūntoba.*

unuj. See *wūnwūj.*

uṇa (**wiṇah**). Fishing method, between two shoals (*ṇa*), with scarer.

uñ (**wig°**). 2, 3, 7. Complete; whole; total a correct amount; come out even; add up to an expected quantity. *Euñ bōnbōn eo raar aikuji.* The amount they needed has been made up.

uñ (**wig**). Variant form of *oñ* (**weg**).

uñar (**wigar**). Carry, in addition. *Uñar juon.* Carry one.

uñjāj (**wigjaj**). Variant form of *uṃjāj* (**wiṃjaj**).

uññar (**wiggar**). 1(*-i*), 2(inf, tr *-e*), 4, 7. Beg for food.

uññūr (**wiggir**). Also *uñūr* (**wigir**), *añur* (**hag°ir**). 2(inf, tr *-i*), 7. Touch; feel. *Jab uñūri.* Don't touch her.

uñtaak (**wigtahak**). Also *uṃtaak* (**wiṃtahak**). 2(inf, tr *-e*), 4, 6(*-i*), 7. Sponge off; wring.

uñtaak (**wigtahak**). Variant form of *oktaak* (**wẹqtahak**) and *eotaak* (**yẹwtahak**).

upaaj. See *wūpaaj.*

upaajaj. See *wūpaajaj.*

ur (**wir**). Also *wūr.* 1, 5(*-i*). Swollen gland; tumor; abscess. *Euri ānbwinnin ḷōḷḷap eo.* The old man's body was swollen all over.

ura (**wirah**). Archaic. 2(inf, tr *-ik(i)*), 4, 5(*uwurara*), 6(*-i*). Person killed and buried with a deceased chieftain to accompany him on his journey to a different world. *Raan kein ejako ad riṂajeḷ uraiki doon.* Nowadays we Marshallese have ceased killing and burying each other with a deceased chieftain. *Eowurara libōn irooj eo.* The dead chief had a lot of dead companions in his grave.

uraak (**wirahak**). Also *ruwaak* (**riwahak**), *jiraak* (**jirahak**), *raak* (**rahak**). 2, 3(inf, tr *kọuraake*), 7. Move (with directional). *Uraak tok.* Move this way. *Uraak tok joujo iturū.* Move here close to me. *Kọuraaketok jea ṇe.* Move that chair here. *Uraake ḷọk kōbañ ṇe.* Move that suitcase away.

urabbaj (**wirabbaj**). 1, 2(inf, tr *-e*), 3(tr *-e*), 4, 6(*-i*), 7. Shinny up. *Ear urabbaje ni eo.* He shinnied up the coconut tree. *Ear kọurabbaje ajri eo.* He made the child shinny up the tree.

ure (**wirey**). 2, 7. Pound; fall on; hammer.

urjep (**wirjep**). Variant form of *kurjep* (**qirjep**).

urḷọk (**wirḷaq**). Variant form of *urrūḷọk.*

uror (**wirwẹr**). Also *uroor* (**wirẹwẹr**). 1(*-i*), 2(inf, tr *urōt*), 4, 6(*-i*), 8, 9. Murder; lynch; kill. *Emọ uror.* It's forbidden to kill. Don't kill. *Kein ar urōt jatin Ebōḷ.* Cain slew his brother Abel.

uror (**wirwẹr**). Also *uroor* (**wirẹwẹr**). 2, 5(*urore*), 6(*-i, urōn*). Cluster; bunch of ripe and drinkable coconuts; bunch of bananas. *Eurore ni eṇ.* That coconut tree has lots of bunches.

urōk (**wirẹk**). 1(*-i*), 2. Fishing method, to fish from a canoe.

urōn (**wiren**). Construct form of *uror* (**wirwẹr**).

urōt (**wiret**). 2. Be possessed by demons. *Rourōt lieṇ im ewūdeakeak.* They possess her and she is crazy.

urōt (**wiret**). Transitive form of *uror* (**wirwẹr**).

urra (**wirrah**). Dialectal variant of *kōjjaromrom* (**kejjar°emr°em**).

urro (**wirrẹw**). From Engl. *hurrah* (?) 1(*-i*), 2, 7. Cheer; hurray.

urrūḷọk (**wirriḷaq**). Also *urḷọk* (**wirḷaq**). 2, 3(inf, tr *-e*), 6(*-i*), 7. Flare; to catch fire; burst into flame. *Eurrūḷọk ṃweo.* The house burst into flame.

urur (**wirwir**). 1(*-i*), 2, 3, 7. Flame; flash; burning, blaze, lighted.

urur (**wirwir**). An insect, moth or miller.

ut (**wit**). Also *wit, wūt.* 1(*-i*), 6(*-i*). A plant, general term for flower of any hedge plant; esp. *Polyscias guilfoylei* (Bull Bailey) or *P. Scutellaria* (Burm. f.) Fosb. (Araliaceae). Common cultivated hedge, often (mis)called "Panax"; flower; tree with flowers; wreath of flowers.

utak (**witak**). 1(*-i*), 3, 6(*-i*). Coconut shoot. *Eḷḷap utakin ni eṇ.* That coconut tree has big shoots.

utaṃwe (**witaṃẹy**). 1(*-i*), 2, 3, 7, 8, 9, 11(*utaṃweṃwe*). Unhealthy; sick; busy; crank; eccentricity; ill; invalid; morbid; confinement; childbirth; commitment. *Ijāmin iwōj bwe eor aō utaṃwe.* I haven't come to see you yet because I've been busy (or sick). *Lio* *ippa ear utaṃwe iMājro.* My wife gave birth at Majuro. *Ḷeeṇ utaṃwe bajjek.* That guy's just a crackpot. *Utaṃwe ta ear kōṃṃane men in.* What nut did this? *Eor ke aṃ utaṃwe ñan ilju?* Do you have any commitment for tomorrow?

utdikdik (**witdikdik**). 1, 2(inf, tr *-i*), 4, 6(*-i*), 7. To sprinkle. *Ij utdikdiki ut kā bwe ren mmourur.* I'm sprinkling these flowers with water so they can flourish.

ute (**witey**). Transitive form of *wōt* (**wẹt**).

uteṇ (**witye̩ṇ**). A bird, red-footed booby.

utiej (**witiyẹj**). 1(*-i*), 2, 3, 4, 7, 8, 9, 11(*utiej, utiejej*). High; dignity; eminent; grand; height; altitude. *Eḷap an utiej baḷuun eo.* That plane is very high. *Elōñ ruutiej raar itok ilo baḷuun eo.* Many V.I.P.'s came on that plane.

utiej būruo- (**witiyẹj biriwe-**). 1, 2, 3. Pride; egotism; conceited. *Idike bwe eḷap an utiej būruon.* I hate her because she has too high an opinion of herself. *Eutiej būruō kōn ḷadik e nejū.* I'm proud of my son.

util (**witil**). 1, 2, 3(*kọutiltil*), 4, 6(*-i*), 8, 9, 11(*util*). Coordinated, physically; know one's way around; have sharp reflexes; nimble; agile. *Kwōmake util.* You sure know your way around. *Ñe iar jab util, inaaj kar jorrāān.* If I wasn't coordinated, I would have hurt myself. *Ajri raṇ rej kọutiltil buḷōn mar kaṇ.* The children are having an acrobatic contest in the woods.

utilolōb (**wityilẹwlẹb**). From *ut* (**wit**) "flower", *ilo* (**yilẹw**) "at", *lōb* (**lẹb**) "grave". A plant, flower, *Jussiaea suffruticosa* (Takeuchi).

utilomar (**wityilewmar**). A plant, *Guettarda speciosa* L. (Rubiaceae). A white-flowered, square-stemmed common wild tree on Ebon called *bwilkōn-utilomar* (**bilken-wit-yilewmar**). Also called (pat. ig.) *utin-ākōj.*

utilōṃjān (**witiylẹṃjan**). From *uti* (**witiy**) "flower of", *Lōṃjān* (**lẹṃjan**) "woman's name". A plant, flower, *Hemigraphis reptans* (Takeuchi).

utin-ākōj (**witin-yakej**). Variant form of *utilomar.*

Utin-Ḷajjidik (**witin-ḷajjiydik**). See *Ijjidik:* "lajjidik's garland". Legend ties this constellation of the northern hemisphere with the *ijjidik* clan of the northern *Rālik* chain, and contrasts it with the constellation *Utin-Ḷarrūbra* of the southern hemisphere and associated *errūbra* clan stemming from Namorik. A constellation; Corona Borealis.

Utin-Ḷarrūbra (**witin-ḷarribrah**). A constellation; Corona Borealis. See *Errūbra* and *Utin-Ḷajjidik.* A constellation; Corona Australis.

utkōk (**witkẹk**). 1(*-i*), 2(inf, tr *utūk(i)*), 7. Take off; cast off clothes; undress; disrobe; naked.

utlōkḷap (**witlẹkḷap**). Second son or daughter; second child.

utḷaṃ (**witḷaṃ**). Variant form of *utḷōṃ* (**witḷeṃ**).

utḷōṃ (**witḷeṃ**). Also *utḷaṃ* (**witḷaṃ**). From Engl. *hoodlum*. 1(*-i*), 2, 3, 4, 5(*uttaiḷōṃ*), 7, 8, 9. A dandy; a show-off; a vain person. *Kwōn jab po ippān bwe euttaiḷōṃ bajjek.* Don't be taken in by him because he's constantly so vain.

utṃaan (**witṃahan**). First-born.

utoñ (**witeg°**). From Engl. 6(*-i*). Noodles.

utot (**witwẹt**). Dial. W: *dibab* (**dibab**), E: *rūbōb* (**ribẹb**). Also *wūtwōt.* A fish, butterfly fish, *Chaetodon anriga* (Ebon).

utọr (**witar°**). 6(*-i*), 7. Squall.

utō- (**wite-**). 1. Mixture of; basic components of; bathing water of; rain of; possessive classifier, bathing water. *Raij utōn jekaro.* Rice cooked in *jekaro*. *Erọọl utōn.* He's gone crazy. *Etteiñ utōṃ ilo aebōj eṇ.* Draw some water for your bath at the cistern. *Eor ke utōṃ?* Have you got bathing water?

utōn-jekaro (**witen-jekarẹw**). 2(inf, tr *-uk*), 6(*-i*). Use coconut sap for cooking. *Ear utōn-jekarouk raij eo.* He cooked the rice in *jekaro*.

utōttōt (**witettet**). 2(inf, tr *-e*), 3(inf, tr *-e*), 6(*-i*), 7. Gush. *Eutōttōte tok ije.* The water is gushing in this direction.

Utōttōt (**witettet**). 3, 6(*-i*). A plant, *Pandanus fischerianus* cultigen.

utpāj (**witpaj**). 2(inf, tr *-e*), 4, 6(*-i*), 7. Plain flower wreath without other ingredients. *Kwōn utpāj bwe eṃōkaj ḷọk.* Make plain flower wreaths because it's simpler. *Enana utpāj bwe* *rej jab aiboojoj.* Plain flower wreaths are not attractive.

utrooj (**witrewej**). From *ut* (**wit**) "flower", Engl. *rose*. Rosebush.

utut (**witwit**). Also *witwit, wūtwūt.* From *ut* (**wit**). 1(-*i*), 2, 3(inf, tr *kǫutut(i)*), 6(-*i*), 7, 8. Wear flowers or a lei. *Etke rej kǫutut(i) pija eṇ?* Why are they putting flowers around the portrait?

utute (**witwitey**). Stay in the rain; transitive distributive form of *wōt* (**wet**). *Kwōn jab utute eok.* Don't stay in the rain.

utūk (**witik**). Transitive form of *utkōk* (**witkẹk**).

utūkaḷ (**witikaḷ**). From *utkōk* (**witkẹk**) "take off", *kaḷ* (**kaḷ**) "loin cloth". 2(inf, tr *-e*), 4, 6(-*i*). To strip; shed clothing; undress; denude. *Kōm ar alwōj utūkaḷ.* We went to a burlesque show. *Utūkaḷe bwe etutu.* Take off his diapers because they are wet.

uuk (**wiwik**). From Engl. Oak.

uuk (**wiwik**). Also *uuki.* 2, 7. Blow. *Lale kōto in euuk eok.* Be careful the wind doesn't blow you away.

uwa (**wiwah**). Dial. W: *iuwa* (**yiwwah**), E: *uwa* (**wiwwah**). Also *kowa.* 2, 3(inf, tr *-ik, -ūk*), 6(-*a*), 8, 9. Bear much fruit; bear many flowers. *Euwa ni eṇ.* The tree has lots of fruit. *Ear kǫuwaik mā eo kōtkan.* He plucked the fruit off his breadfruit tree (bearing fruit before maturing).

uwaak (**wiwahak**). Dial. W: *iuwaak* (**yiwwahak**), E: *uwaak* (**wiwwahak**). 2(inf, tr *-e*), 7, 8. Reply; answer; consent; respond. *Kwaar uwaake ke kajjitōk eo an?* Did you answer his question?

uwaan (**wiwahan**). Dial. W: *iuwaan* (**yiwwahan**), E: *uwaan* (**wiwwahan**). Kind of; number of; member of. *Ebar or ke uwaan nuknuk e?* Are there any more of this kind of clothing? *Jete uwaan jar eo ej itok?* How many are in the group that's coming?

uwaan kakūtōtō (**wiwahan kakitehteh**). Dial. W: *iuwaan kakūtōtō* (**yiwwahan kakitehteh**), E: *uwaan kakūtōtō* (**wiwwahan kakiteateah**). Idiom. Be of a naughty sort; delinquent. *Ej jab aelǫk uwaan kakūtōtō bwe epedet armej.* He's obviously of a naughty sort because he's too forward in his actions.

uwaanrak (**wiwahanrak**). Dial. W: *iuwaanrak* (**yiwwahanrak**), E: *uwaanrak* (**wiwwahanrak**). 2(inf, tr *-e*)8 8, 9. Laden with summer fruit, usually trees. *Euwaanrake mā ṇe.* That breadfruit tree is full of fruit.

uwaañañ (**wiwahaghag**). Dial. W: *iuwaañañ* (**yiwwahaghag**), E: *uwaañañ* (**wiwwahaghag**). Also *waañañ.* 1(-*i*), 2, 3(inf, tr *-e*), 6(-*i*), 7, 8, 9. Howl; bellow; holler; cry loudly; weak from hunger. *Jab kǫuwaañañe ajri ṇe .* Don't make the child howl. *Ta ṇe kwōj uwaañañ kake.* What are you hollering about. *Ear uwaañañ ke ij deñḷǫke.* He howled when I spanked him.

uwaidikdik (**wiwayidikdik**). Dial. W: *iuwaidikdik* (**yiwwayidikdik**), E: *uwaidikdik* (**wiwwayidikdik**). Also *uwainiññiñ* (**wiwahyinignig**). 1(-*i*), 2, 3, 7, 8, 9, 11(*uwāidikdik*). Slender; skinny; narrow; slim.

uwainiññiñ (**wiwayinignig**). Variant form of *uwaidikdik* (**wiwayidikdik**).

uwaitoktok (**wiwayiteqteq**). Dial. W: *iuwaitoktok* (**yiwwayiteqteq**), E: *uwaitoktok* (**wiwwayiteqteq**). 1(-*i*), 2, 3, 7. Long and oval; cylindrical.

uwaṇ (**wiwaṇ**). Dial. W: *iuwaaṇ* (**yiwwahaṇ**), E: *uwaaṇ* (**wiwwahaṇ**). 1(-*i*), 2, 3, 7, 8, 9. Gray haired.

uwaroñ (**wiwareg°**). Dial. W: *iuwaroñ* (**yiwwarẹg°**), E: *uwaroñ* (**wiwwarẹg°**). 1(-*i*), 2, 3, 5(*kǫuwaroñroñ*), 7, 8, 9. Annoyed or bothered by noise. *Eḷap an kǫuwaroñroñ ainikien injin eo.* The noise of the engine is very disturbing.

uwe (**wiwẹy**). Dial. W: *iuwe* (**yiwwẹy**), E: *uwe* (**wiwwẹy**). 1(-*i*), 2, 3, 4, 7. To board; ride; get on; embark; to mount; to rise, of dough. *Euwe pilawā e.* The dough's rising.

uweo (**wiweyew**). Dial. W: *iuweo* (**yiwweyew**), E: *uweo* (**wiwweyew**). There; that (distant but visible); demonstrative, remote singular, singling out.

uwi (**wwiy**). Dial. W: *iuwi* (**yiwwiy**), E: *uwi* (**wiwwiy**). 1(-*i*), 2, 3, 6(-*i*), 8, 9, 11(*uwiwi uwi*). Smell of cooking fish; delicious (of fish only).

uwǫk (**wiwaq**). Dial. W: *iuwǫk* (**yiwwaq**), E: *uwǫk* (**wiwwaq**). Gee;

wow. *Uwo̧k, āinwōt kwōjeļā injin, ļe.* Gee, I didn't know you were a mechanic. *Ta le uwo̧k!* What in tarnation!

uwōjak (**wiwejak**). Also *uwajak.* Dial. W: *iuwōjak* (**yiwwejak**), E: *uwōjak* (**wiwwejak**). 1(-*i*), 2(inf, tr -*e*), 3, 4, 6(-*i*), 7. Cause a ruckus; commotion; disturbance; leap out of water, of small fish attempting to escape larger fish. *Ekadek em uwōjak ilo kuļab eo.* He got drunk and caused a ruckus in the clubhouse. *Euwajak tōū eņ i ar.* The mackerel are jumping out of the water along the lagoon beach.

uwōta (**wiwetah**). Dial. W: *iuwōta* (**yiwwetah**), E: *uwōta* (**wiwwetah**). 1(-*i*), 2, 3(*ko̧uwōtata*), 4, 5(*uwōtata*), 7, 8, 9. In danger of; afraid of; peril. *Kouwōta ke in uwe ilo baļuun?* Are you afraid of riding on airplanes? *Eko̧uwatata uwe ilo baļuun.* Riding on planes is dangerous. *Euwōtata ļeeņ.* That man scares easily.

uwur (**wwir**). Dial. W: *iuwur* (**yiwwir**), E: *uwur* (**wiwwir**), *ba* (**bah**). 1(-*i*), 2, 3, 4, 7. Coryza; to blow one's nose; nasal mucous.

ūjō (**hijeh**). 1, 2, 7. Grin; snarl; see *baūjō. Eṃōj ņe aṃ ūjō.* Stop grinning. *Taņe kwōj ūjō kake.* What are you grinning about? *Ear ūjō tok ñan eō.* She grinned at me.

ūl (**hil**). 1(-*i*), 6(-*i*). Fin; dorsal fin; larger fish.

Ūlin-raj-eo (**hilin-raj-yew**). See *ūl:* "dorsal fin of the whale (or porpoise)". A star; beta Andromedae.

ūlūl (**hilhil**). 1(-*i*), 2, 3, 6(-*i*), 7. Side; edge. *N̄a ij ūlūl.* I'm lying on my side. *Kwōn kaūlūl jāje ņe.* Put the sharp edge of that machete down.

ūlūl (**hilhil**). 6(-*i*). Axe; hatchet. *Imaroñ ke kōjerbal ūlūlin pālle ņe aṃ?* May I use your axe? *Ūlūlin kowainini eo aṃ e ke?* Is this your copra axe?

ūlūlōt (**hilhilet**). Also *ilūlōt.* 2, 3, 4, 7. Talk back; grumble; retort. *Kwōn jab ūlūlōt aṃ kōnnaan.* Don't talk back.

ūne (**hiney**). Distributive form of *ōn* (**hȩn**).

ūō (**hihȩh**). Dial. W, E: *iā* (**yi'yay**). An exclamation expressing sudden pain; "Ouch!"

ūrōj (**hirej**). 1(-*i*), 2(inf, tr -*e*), 4, 5(*ūrōrmej*), 7, 8, 9. Provoke to a quarrel; bother. *Eṃōj ņe aṃ ūrōrmej.* Why don't you stop picking quarrels all the time. *Kwōn jab ūrōje.* Don't bother him.

ūrōrmej (**hirhȩrmȩj**). Also *lōbbañij* (**lȩbbagij**), *bañij* (**bagij**). A fish, general term for all damsel fish.

ūrōrmej (**hirhȩrmȩj**). Distributive form of *ūrōj* (**hirej**).

wa (**wah**). 1(-*a*). Canoe; ship; boat; vehicle.

wa bweo̧ (**wah beyaw**). 6(-*i*). A toy, boat of half coconut. *Ļadik raņ rej kōṃṃan wa bweo̧.* The boys are making coconut boats.

Wa-eo-waan-Tūṃur (**wah-yew-wahan-timir°**). A constellation; stars in Ursa Major; shaped like *Tūṃur*'s canoe: delta, epsilon, and zeta, the center portion; gamma and eta, the stems; and alpha and beta the tuft decorations hanging from gamma.

waa- (**waha-**). 1. Canoe of; ship of; boat of; vehicle of; possessive classifier, canoe, ship, boat, or vehicle.

waabbilāle (**wahabbilalȩy**). Also *abbwilāle* (**habbilaylȩy**). 1(-*i*), 2(inf, tr -*ik*), 4, 7. Put one's arm across another's shoulders while walking.

waak (**wahak**). 2(inf, tr -*e*), 4, 7. Read. *Ewaake ļo̧k rōjelujen eo ñan rukweilo̧k ro āinwōt aer kar kajjitōk.* He read the resolution to the congressmen as they had asked him to.

waakeļo̧k (**wahakeyļaq**). Transitive form of *waakļo̧k* (**wahakļaq**).

waakļo̧k (**wahakļaq**). 2(inf, tr *waakeļo̧k*). Miss an opportunity. *Ijaje tawūnin aer waakiļo̧k ṃōñā nno̧no ko.* I don't know why they passed up the delicious food.

waan (**wahan**). Trivial; in vain; worthless; common; casual; puny. *Ļōmņak waan.* Just a passing thought. *Kwaar jab eñtaan waan.* You did not suffer in vain. *Ejjeļo̧k tokjān aṃ kakkōt bwe kōrā waan men eņ.* You're wasting your time and she's only a common woman.

waan bwil (**wahan bil**). Launching pad; roller.

waan joñak (**wahan jeg°ak**). 1(-*i*), 2, 3, 4, 6(-*i*), 7. Example; parable; illustration, instance, illustrative story. *Ear waan joñak kōn eok.* He used you as an example. *Jenaaj waan joñak kōn juon* *ṃokta.* We'll use one to test it out first.

waan peḷḷọk (**wahan peḷḷaq**). Canoe ready to sail at any time.

waan tulọk (**wahan tiwlaq**). 6(-*i*). Submarine.

waanikli (**wahanikliy**). 2. Support one another by holding each other's waists. *Rūkadek ro raar waanikli doon.* The drunks has their arms around each other's waists to support themselves.

waañañ (**wahaghag**). Variant form of *uwaañañ.*

waat (**wahat**). Also *waate* (**wahatey**). 2, 7. Spy; observe; look into a trap; reconnoiter.

wab (**wab**). From Engl. 6(-*i*). Pier; wharf; berth; dock. *Eor ke wa iṃaan wab eṇ?* Is there a ship at the pier?

wabanban (**wahbanban**). 1(-*i*), 2, 8. Decay; rot; corrupt, used of dead animals or humans swollen but not yet bad smelling.

wabwilbwil (**wahbilbil**). Variant form of *bwilbwil* (**bilbil**).

wadde (**waddey**). 2. Attack by mother hen. *Bao eo ear wadde ledik eo.* The hen attacked the girl.

wadu (**wadiw**). 1, 2(inf, tr -*uk*), 4, 6(-*i*), 7. Request something by flattery; seduce; call a bet in poker. *Ear waduuk lio.* He seduced the woman. *Ear waduuktok jiip eo waan Eaḷṃar.* He got Halmar to lend us his jeep.

wain (**wahyin**). From Engl. 3, 6(-*i*). Wine.

waini (**wahyiniy**). 3, 5(*owainini*), 6(-*i*). Copra; coconut, ripe for copra. *Jete ṇe aṃ pāāk in waini?* How many bags of copra do you have there? *Koṃwin ae tok waini.* Gather copra to this place.

waj (**waj**). From Engl. 1(-*i*), 2(inf, tr -*e*), 4, 6(-*i*), 7. Watchman; guard; watch; patrol; sentinel. *Bwilijmāāṇ ro rej waje ṃweo ṃōn būreejtōn eo.* The police guard the president's house. *Bwilijmāāṇ ro rej kajjojo waj.* The police take turns standing guard. *Wōpet ej waj Mieko.* Obet is a watchman at MIECO. *Ej waje ṃweiuk kaṇ.* He guards the merchandise.

waj (**waj**). From Engl. Watch. *Kwaar wiaik ia waj ṇe nājiṃ?* Where did you buy your watch?

waj (**waj**). Also *wōj* (**węj**). Toward addressee, away from addressor; directional, postposition, toward addressee. *Emoot waj.* He's left toward you.

waja (**wajah**). Variant form of *wajej* (**wajej**).

wajej (**wajej**). Also *waja* (**wajah**). From Engl. 2(inf, tr -*e*), 6(-*i*). Washer, mechanical.

wajekā (**wahjekay**). 2(inf, tr -*iki*), 4, 6(-*i*), 7. To sail a canoe or boat singlehandedly; do something singlehandedly. *Ear wajekāik ḷọk wa eo waan ñan Likiep.* He sailed his boat to Likiep singlehandedly.

wajerakrōk (**wahjerakręk**). Sailboat.

wajwaj (**wajwaj**). From *waj* (**waj**). 1(-*i*), 2, 3(inf, tr -*e*), 4, 7. Wear a watch. *Baj ña ṃōk wajwaj kōn waj ṇe nājiṃ?* May I borrow your watch now? *Kwōn jab kọwajwaje bwe enaaj loṃaan.* I wouldn't let her wear a watch or she'll get arrogant.

wak (**wak**). Vulgar. 1(-*i*), 2, 5(-*e*, *wakōn*). Pubic hair.

wakōn (**waken**). Distributive form of *wak* (**wak**).

waliklik (**wahliklik**). 6(-*i*). Net made of sennit used for sifting arrowroot starch. *Imaroñ ke kōjerbal waliklik eo aṃ?* May I use your arrowroot sifting net?

waḷañi (**waḷagiy**). Also *oḷañi* (**weḷagiy**). 1(-*i*), 2, 3, 7. Open the mouth.

waḷọk (**wahḷaq**). 1(-*i*), 2, 3(inf *kowaḷọk*, tr *kowaḷọk, kwaḷọk*), 5(*owaḷọkḷọk*), 7. Appear; happen; get up, from lying down; emerge; event; result; exist; occur; outcome; product. *Iuwaḷọkḷọk boñ kōn aō kar abṇōṇō.* I kept getting up all night because I was uncomfortable.

wan- (**wan-**). Also *wāān-* (**wayan-**). 1, 2, 3, 7. Walk toward; go toward (used with directional enclitics). *Wanlikḷọk.* Walk toward ocean side. *Wanarḷọk.* Walk toward the lagoon. *Wanāneḷọk.* Go toward the islet. *Wanmetoḷọk.* Go toward the ocean. *Wāniñaḷọk.* Go northward. *Wārūñaḷọk.* Go southward. *Wātoḷọk.* Go westward. *Wātaḷọk.* Go eastward.

wanar (**wanhar**). Dial. W only; see *wāānar* (**wayanhar**). Also *wōnar* (**wenhar**). 2, 7. Go or come towards the lagoon; see *wan-*.

wanāne (**wanyanęy**). Dial. W only; see *weenāne* (**weyenyanęy**). Also *wanāne* (**wanyanęy**), *wōnāne* (**wenyanęy**), *wāānāne* (**wayanyanęy**). 2, 7. Go or come ashore; toward land; shoreward; see *wan-*.

wanij (**wanij**). From Engl. 2(inf, tr *-i*), 4, 6(*-i*), 7. Varnish; lacquer.

waniñ (**wanig**). From Engl. 6(*-i*). Awning. *Ebwil ilowaan waniñ eṇ.* It's very hot under the awning.

wanlaḷ (**wanlaḷ**). 2, 7. Go or come down; descend; dismount; see *wan-*.

wanlik (**wanlik**). 2, 7. Go or come towards the ocean side of an island; go backward.

wanlōñ (**wanlęg**). 2, 7. Ascend; climb; mount; see *wan-*.

wanmeto (**wanmetew**). 2, 7. Go or come seaward; see *wan-*.

wannabōj (**wannabęj**). Also *wōnnabōj* (**wennabęj**). 2, 7. Exit; go out of a building. *Jen wannabōjḷọk in kōlladikdik.* Let's go out for some fresh air.

wañ (**wag**). To bark, of dogs. *Ewañ kidu eṇ.* The dog is barking.

war (**war**). Also *orañe* (**weragey**). 2, 6(*-i*). Barren; incapable of bearing offspring, of women only; sterile.

war (**war**). Lobster lair.

wat (**wat**). Dial. W only; see *luwap* (**liwap**). 6(*-i*). A fish, puffer fish, *Tetraodon hispidus/meleagris/nigropunctatus/patoca.*

wata (**watah**). Also *ota, wōta* (**wetah**), *weta* (**weytah**). Part of an island. *Wōta ta (wōtaat) ṇe kwōj jukwe ie?* What part of the island do you live in? *Eṃṃan wōta jab ṇe aṃ.* You live in a nice place. *Ta nnaanin wōta ṇe kwōj jokwe ie?* What's the news from your part of the island?

watak (**wahtak**). Stand by a weir waiting for tide.

watōk (**watek**). Transitive form of *watwat* (**watwat**).

watre (**watręy**). From Engl. *watery*. 1(*-i*), 3(inf, tr *kowatreik(i), kowatrereik(i)*), 4, 5(*owatrer e*), 6(*-i*), 7, 8, 9, 10(*watre*). Watery; diluted; thin, of liquids; inexperienced; neophyte; novice; greenhorn; wet behind the ears; partially cooked. *Iar lo aer kowatrereik(i) waini kaṇe rej bọuni.* I saw them dry only superficially the copra they're weighing now. *Iwatre bajjek.* I'm just a novice. *Emake watre ṇe juub.* That soup is really watery. *Ruwatrein ia ṇe?* Where's that greenhorn from?

watwat (**watwat**). 1(*-i*), 2(inf, tr *watōk(e)*), 7. Count up; estimate by counting; consider; evaluate; appraise. *Ij jab watōk kōn oṇān ak ñe eor tokjān inaaj wiaiki.* I'm not counting the cost but if it's valuable, I'll buy it.

wau (**wahwiw**). From Haw. *Oahu*. 2, 7. Mother Hubbard dress, named for Oahu; since the missionaries that introduced it were from Oahu.

wawa (**wahwah**). From *wa* (**wah**). 1(*-i*), 2, 3(inf, tr *-ik*), 4, 6(*-i*), 7. Use a boat; use a canoe; use a ship; use a vehicle. *Ejeḷā wawa.* He's good at taking care of boats. *Waan wōn ṇe (wa) kwōj wawa kake?* Whose canoe are you sailing around with?

wawa (**wahwah**). 2, 3(inf, tr *-ik*). Crosswise. *Ewawa wa ṇe eoon wōd ṇe.* Your canoe is crosswise on the coral there.

wawaa- (**wahwaha-**). 1, 6. Foundation.

wawōj (**wahwęj**). Dialectal variant of *iwōj* (**yiwęj**).

wā (**way**). 1(*-i*), 2(inf, tr *wāik*), 4, 6(*-i*), 7. Injection, receive an injection, give an injection; shot; to spear; stab. *Wā in ta eo raar wāik eok kake?* What kind of shot did they give you?

wāān- (**wayan-**). Variant form of *wan-* (**wan-**).

wāānar (**wayanhar**). Dial. E only; see *wanar* (**wanhar**). 2, 7. Go or come towards the lagoon.

wāānāne (**wayanyanęy**). Dial. E only; see *wōnāne* (**wenyanęy**). 2, 7. Go or come ashore; toward land; go shoreward.

wāāpep (**wayapyęp**). 1(*-i*), 2(inf, tr *wāāpipe*), 4, 7. Stab; pierce, as an unhusked coconut in order to drink.

wāāpipe (**wayapyipey**). Transitive form of *wāāpep* (**wayapyęp**).

wāār (**wayar**). 1(*-i*), 2, 3, 5(*wāārār*), 6(*-i*), 7. Crawl on the belly; slide. *Ejino jeḷā wāār ajri eo.* The baby is beginning to be able to crawl on its stomach. *Wōn eo eṇ ej wāārār āne ḷọk.* That turtle keeps on crawling towards the island. *Ne erūttoḷọk enaaj maroñ wāār.* When he grows up he'll be able to crawl. *Kwōn wāār ṃaanwaj.* Slide forward.

wāik (**wayik**). Transitive form of *wā* (**way**).

wāikōn (**wayiken**). From Engl. 2(inf, tr -*e*), 4, 6(-*i*), 7. Wagon.

wāiñat (**wayigat**). Vulgar. From *wā* (**way**) "pierce", *ñat* (**gat**) "palate". 1, 2(inf, tr -*e*), 4, 6(-*i*). Sexual act, position.

wājepdik (**wayjepdik**). Also *wājāpdik* (**wayjapdik**), *wājepādik* (**wayjepadik**), *wejepādik* (**weyjepadik**). 1(-*i*), 2, 3, 4, 6(-*i*), 8, 9. Intelligent; genius; expert; knowledgeable, resourceful; sharp-witted; tactful; witty, sharp; orate; eloquent; fluent; glib. *Eḷap an wājāpdik ilo kōṃṃan kaṇ an kien.* He is an expert in the affairs of the govenment. *Ewājepdik pein ilo jekjek wa.* He is an expert in building boats.

wākar (**waykar**). Also *wekar* (**weykar**). 2(inf, tr -*e*), 4, 6(-*i*), 7. Pierce; spear; stab. *Ear wākare juon ek.* He speared a fish. *Raar wākare eō kōn penejeḷōn.* They gave me a shot of penicillin.

wālej (**waylẹj**). Also *wālej* (**waylej**). From Engl. *wireless*. 2(inf, tr -*e*), 4, 6(-*i*), 7. Transmit by radio; radio transmitter; talk on the radio. *Iar wālej ñan Ṃajeḷ boñ.* I spoke on the radio to the Marshalls last night. *Kab wālej tok ñe eor jabdewōt.* Call me on the radio if anything happens.

wālel (**waylẹl**). Also *wāleel* (**waylẹyẹl**), *kowāelel* (**kewwayẹlyẹl**). 1(-*i*), 2, 3(inf *kowālellel*), 4, 7, 8, 9. Good marksmanship; spearing; sharpshooter. *Eḷap aō wālel jān kwe.* I can spear better than you. *Kōjro etal in kowālellel.* Let's go have a spearing contest.

wālọk (**waylaq**). Dialectal variant of *ilọk* (**yilaq**); variant form of *welọk* (**weylaq**).

wālọklik (**waylaqlik**). Sacrifice food to the gods.

wāmourur (**waymẹwirwir**). 2, 3, 6(-*i*), 8, 9. Healthy in appearance, as a coconut tree.

wānōk (**waynẹk**). 1(-*i*), 2, 3, 4, 7, 8, 9. Just; righteous; justice; perfect; virtuous. *Ewānōk ke kiiō?* Is it perfect now? Now look what you've done (said negatively and critically).

Wātal-kaṇ (**waytal-kaṇ**). From *wātal* "sign". A constellation; stars in Ursa Major; alpha and beta; two of the four "posts of Polaris" (*Jurōn-Liṃanṃan*); alpha is called *Wātal-kaṇ-rāātle* and beta *Wātal-kaṇ-reeaar; also applied to Ursa Minor, three stars (zeta, epsilon, delta) in Little Dipper handle.*

wāto (**waytẹw**). 6(*wātuon, wātoon, wātuwe*). Land tract.

wāto (**waytẹw**). 1(-*i*), 2, 8, 9. Unable to sail close to the wind.

wāto (**waytẹw**). 2, 7. Go westward.

wātok (**wayteq**). Dial. E only; see *itok* (**yiteq**). 1(-*i*), 2, 8. Come.

wātulik (**waytiwlik**). Vulgar. 1(-*i*), 2(inf, tr -*i*), 3, 4, 6(-*i*). Sexual position.

wāwe (**waywẹy**). 2, 7. Go; walk; negotiate one's way through thick brush or heavy seas or between reefs. *Wa eo ear wāwetok kōtaan wōd ko.* The boat picked its way in between coral heads. *Kwōj wāwe ḷọk ñan ia?* Where are you going?

wāwee- (**waywẹyẹ-**). 1, 7. Form; shape; figure; method of; manner of; how; nature of. *Euwāween?* How?

wea (**weyah**). From Engl. 3, 6(-*i*). Wire.

wea (**weyah**). Water course in the reef; small passage between ocean and lagoon.

weaak (**weyahak**). 1(-*i*), 2, 3, 7. Waft through the air, as a ghost; ride comfortably; wander without using physical effort; glide. *Eṃṃan aō kar weaak eoon wa eṇ.* I rode comfortably in that car. *Ej weaak āinwōt bao.* It's gliding like a bird.

weeak (**weyyak**). Interjection: My goodness!, (women only).

weej (**weyej**). From Engl. 2(inf, tr -*e*), 6(-*i*). Wedge.

weejej (**weyejyej**). 1, 2, 3, 6(-*i*), 8, 9. Lisp, in which a sibilant quality is given to the *j* phoneme. *Kwōn jab kọweejeje aṃ kōnnaan.* Don't lisp when you talk. *Eḷak rọọltok jān Amedka, eweejej an kōnnaan.* When he returned from America he talked with a lisp.

weenāne (**weyenyanęy**). Dialectal variant of *wanāne* (**wanyanęy**).

weeppān (**weyeppan**). 1(*-i*), 2, 3, 4, 7, 8, 9. Complete; perfect; improved; of upright character; well done; deluxe; excellent; ratified; approved. *Eļap an weeppān m̧weeņ raar kaļōke.* The house they built is well made. *Eweeppān ke pepe eo ippān?* Has he approved the plan?

weiļ (**węyiļ**). From Engl. 2(inf, tr *-i*), 4, 5(*oweiļiļ*), 6(*-i*), 8, 9. Oil.

wejeļ (**weyjeļ**). Variant form of *owe* (**wwey**).

wejepādik (**weyjepadik**). Variant form of *wājepdik* (**wayjepdik**).

wekañ (**węykag**). Dialectal variant of *peka* (**peykah**).

wekar (**weykar**). Variant form of *wākar* (**waykar**).

welọk (**weylaq, węylaq**). Also *wālọk* (**waylaq**), *uwe* (**wiwęy**). 2. Go away; ride; mount. *Kom̧wij welọk ñan ia?* Where are you going?

weļọk (**weyļaq**). 1(*-i*), 2, 4, 6(*-i*), 8, 9. Deviate from instructions; overstep one's responsibilities. *N̄e kwōnāj bar weļọk ināj kupiiki eok.* If you're caught again doing what you're not to do, I'll fire you.

wetaa- (**weytaha-**). Dial. W, E: *jetak*. 1. On the east side of; see *rilik*. *Epād iwetaan m̧ōņe.* It's east of the house.

wetak (**weytak**). 2, 7. Go eastward.

wetak (**weytak**). 1(*-i*), 2, 8, 9. Able to sail close to the wind. *Eļap an wetak wa eņ.* That canoe can really sail close to the wind.

wetakļap (**weytakļap**). 2, 6(*-i*). Half-moon. *Ej jab meramin wetakļapin Awaii wōt M̧ajeļ.* It's not as bright in Hawaii during half-moon nights as in the Marshalls.

wewā (**węyway**). 1(*-i*), 2(inf, tr *-ik*), 7. To weave pandanus thatch.

wia (**wiyah**). 1(*-i*), 2(inf, tr *-ik*), 4, 7. Buy; sell; purchase. *Iar wiaik juon jodi.* I bought a pair of zories. *Em̧ōj aō wia aō jodi.* I bought some zories for myself.

wiaake (**wiyahakey**). 2, 7. Push; insert. *Kwōn wiaake ļọk aļaļ ņe.* Push that piece of wood in (under the house).

wiaik būruo- (**wiyahyik biriwe-**). Idiom. 1, 2. Bribe. *Ejim̧we an jerbal im ejjeļọk emaroñ wiaik burwōn.* He's honest and no one can bribe him.

wiawe (**wiyahwęy**). Also *wiọwe* (**wiyawęy**). 6(*-i*). A lizard; small and striped; black and white.

wiā (**wiyay**). Variant form of *wie* (**wiyey**).

wie (**wiyey**). Also *wiā* (**wiyay**). 2(inf, tr *wiik(i)*), 7. To pierce; to prick; to goose. *Ear wie ni eo.* He pierced the coconut. *Em̧ōj an ļōļļap eņ wiā lọjilñin.* The old man has pierced his ears. *Lale ņok ņe ewie mejam̧.* Be careful that coconut midrib doesn't pierce your eye. *Enana wiik armej.* It's impolite to goose anyone.

wiik (**wiyik**). From Engl. 1(*-i*), 2(inf, tr *-ik*). Week. *Eļọk de juon wiikū ņai ānin.* I have been on this islet one week now.

wiik (**wiyik**). From Engl. 6(*-i*). Wick. *Kab pukot tok juoņ wiikin ļaam̧ e.* While you're at it, get a wick for the lantern.

wiik (**wiyik**). Transitive form of *wie* (**wiyey**).

wiik in laļ (**wiyik yin laļ**). Next week.

wiiļ (**wiyiļ**). From Engl. Wheel.

wiin (**wiyin**). From Engl. 1(*-i*), 2(inf, tr *-i*), 3(st inf *kọwiinin*, tr *kọwiin*), 4, 5(*uwiinin*). Win; gain; prize; trophy. *Kumi it eo ewiin ilo iakiu eo?* Which team won at baseball? *Eowiinin kumi eņ.* That team always wins. *Kọwiinin.* Contest. Prize in a contest. *Ekọwiinin kijoñ eņ.* He always contributes to his team's winning.

wiin (**wiyin**). 2. Profitable. *Ewiin peejnej eo an.* His business brought him profits. *Ejọwiin m̧weiuk in Australia.* Australian goods don't bring in the business.

wit. See *ut* or *wōt.*

wiwi (**wiywiy**). Also *wi* (**wiy**). 5(*uwiwi*), 6(*-i*). Fat in turtle shell; delicacy; blubber. *Eowiwi jọkur in.* This turtle shell is covered all over the inside with delicious turtle fat. This turtle shell has fat here and there inside it.

wiwijet (**wiywiyjęt**). 1(*-i*), 2, 3, 4, 7, 8, 9. Lose the direction of; panic.

wōd (**wed**). 5(*wōdwōd*), 6(*wōden, wōde*), 7, 8, 9. Coral reef; coral; coralhead. *Ewōdwōd iarin ānin.* There is lots of coral at the lagoon side of this islet.

Wōd-Wāto-eņ (**wed-waytęw-yeņ**). A star; alpha in Canes Venatici; refers to a reef in the *Aerōk* passage at Ailinglapalap.

wōda (**wedah**). Also *oda*. 2, 4, 8, 9. Able to catch many fish; lucky in fishing. *Eļap an wōda likao eņ.* That young man can catch a lot of fish.

wōde (**wedey**). Transitive form of *wōdwōd* (**wedwed**).

wōdinikek (**wędinyikyęk**). Also *wōdinikeōk*. 2, 4, 6(*-i*). Suicide; commit suicide. *Rej tan kalbwin ruwōdinikek eo.* They're going to bury the suicide. *Jerawiwi wōdinikek ippān Katlik.* It's a sin to commit suicide in the Catholic religion.

wōdwōd (**wedwed**). 1(*-i*), 2(inf, tr *wōde*), 7. Chew pandanus.

wōj (**węj**). 2, 7. Beautiful; see *aiboojoj* (**hayibęwęjwęj**). *Ewōj tok wa eņ ioon lọjet.* The canoe looks beautiful on the ocean.

wōj (**węj**). Dial. E, W: *wūj* (**wij**). Balsa driftwood.

wōj (**węj**). Variant form of *waj* (**waj**).

wōj (**węj**). Variant form of *iwōj* (**yiwęj**).

wōja (**wejah**). Also *oja*. From Japn. *ocha*. 3, 6(*-a*). Tea.

wōja (**wejah**). Archaic. 6(*wōjaan, wōja*). Formant in place names; abode; site; scene; possession.

wōja- (**weja-**). 1. Belonging to; possessive classifier, alienable objects and general possessive.

wōjaan-kōmatōrtōr (**wejahan-kematerter**). 1(*-i*), 2, 4, 7, 8, 9. Odious; not likeable. *Ewōjaan-kōmatōrtōr ļeeņ.* He is not likeable.

wōjak (**wejak**). 1(*-i*), 2(inf, tr *-e*), 7. Do; perform. *Ta ņe kwōj wōjake ijeņe?* What are you doing there? *Kwōn jab wōjak kain ṃanit rot ņe.* Don't behave that way.

wōjej (**węjyęj**). Variant form of *jeej* (**jęyęj**).

wōjek (**wejek**). 2(inf, tr *-e*). Nibble; gnaw, of a rat or a mouse. *Eṃọj wōjeke jōōt e aō.* My shirt's been eaten by a rat.

wōjke (**węjkęy**). 3, 6(*-i*). A plant, general word for tree; log; timber.

wōjke (**węjkęy**). From Engl. 6(*-i*). Whiskey. *Eļap an kajoor wōjke ñan ña.* Whiskey is too strong for me.

wōjke-piik (**węjkęy-piyik**). From *wōjke* (**węjkęy**) "tree"; Engl. *fig*. 3, 6(*-i*). A plant, *Ficus carica* L. (Moraceae); The edible fig. Introd. on Wotje.

wōjļā (**węjļay**). Also *wūjļā* (**wijļay**). 1(*-i*), 3, 6(*-i*). A sail. *Wōjļā in waat ņe?* What canoe does that sail belong to?

Wōjļā (**węjļay**). A constellation, upsilon, mu, psi Centauri; triangle-shaped.

wōl (**węl**). Vulgar. 1(*wūle-*). Penis.

wōla (**welah**). 1(*-i*), 2, 3, 6(*-i*), 7, 8, 9. Out of order, of machines; broken, of engines; run-down, of persons, ruined. *Ewōla injin in wa eo waō.* My car's engine has broken down.

wōlbo (**węlbęw**). 1(*-i*), 2, 3(inf *kọwōlbobo, kọolbo,* tr *kọolbouk*), 4, 7, 8, 9. Lovable; beloved; popular. *Wūno in kọwōlbobo.* Love potion. *Raar kọwōlbouki.* They made him popular.

wōllaañ (**wellahag**). Dial. E, W: *pālep* (**palep**). A fish, Moorish idol, *Zanclus cornutus.*

wōm (**wem**). Transitive form of *wōmwōm* (**wemwem**).

wōmak (**wemak**). Also *wōnak* (**wenak**). 1(*-i*), 2, 3, 4, 7. To duck a blow; duck one's head; to shrink from responsibility.

wōmwōm (**wemwem**). Also *omom, wūjroñ* (**wijreg°**). 2(inf, tr *wōm(e)*), 4, 6(*-i*), 7. Extract; withdraw; pull out. *Ear wōm mejān bato eo.* He pulled the cork out of the bottle. *Ear wōme naṃnoor eo jān bu eo.* He withdrew the ramrod from the gun.

wōn (**węn**). 3(*kawōnwōn*), 6(*-i*). Turtle.

wōn (**węn**). Pit in which fruit is buried to ripen: pandanus, bananas, preserved breadfruit.

wōn (**wen**). Who; whoever; whom.

wōnaji (**wenahjiy**). Also *onaji*. From Japn. *onaji* "the same". 2, 3(inf, tr *-ik*), 6(*-i*). Rental. Even; tie in a game.

wōnak (**wenak**). Variant form of *wōmak* (**wemak**).

wōnar (**wenhar**). Variant form of *wanar* (**wanhar**).

wōnāne (**wenyanęy**). Dialectal variant of *wāānāne* (**wayanyanęy**).

wōneṇak (**wẹṇẹyṇak**). Also *oṇeṇak* (**wẹṇẹyṇak**). Legendary cruel giants who scare and kill people; ghosts that haunt and drive people mad, live in dense forests.

wōnjak (**wenjak**). Dial. W, E: *wōnjake.* 2. Perform flawlessly. *Ejjeḷọk men eṇ eoonjak kōn an bar nana taṃṃwin jeṃṃaan.* Nothing went right due to the boss's bad disposition.

Wōnje (**wenjey**). From Engl. Wednesday.

wōnṃaan (**wenṃahan**). 2, 3, 7. Progress; move forward; move up; champion; spokesman. *Ḷeo enaaj wōnṃaan ñan kōj ṇe.* He'll be our spokesman if we need one. *Kwōj wōnṃaan ñan ñāāt?* How far do you intend to move up?

wōnṃae (**wenṃahyey**). 1(*-i*), 2(inf, tr *-ik*), 4, 7. Go and meet. *Rej etal in wōnṃae Aikaṃ eo.* They are going to meet the High Commissioner.

wōnnabōj (**wennabẹj**). Variant form of *wannabōj* (**wannabẹj**).

wōnōt (**wenet**). 1(*-i*), 2, 3, 5(*owōnōtnōt*), 6(*-i*), 8, 9, 11(*wōnōtnōt*). Newly constructed, of vessels or vehicles. *Ej baj owōnōtnōt wa eo waan.* His canoe certainly looked new. *Wūno eo ekọwōnōt ḷoon eo.* The paint made the motorboat look new. *Wa wōnōtnōt.* An absolutely brand new canoe.

wōṇea-. See *oṇea-*.

wōp (**wẹp**). 3, 6(*-i*). A plant, *Barringtonia asiatica* (L.) Kurz. (Barringtoniaceae). A large tree with large, square fruits; young leaves glabrous, with red midribs; seeds used as a fish-poison.

wōpeñ (**wẹpẹg**). 1(*-i*), 3, 6(*-i*). Empty container; shell; cartridge. *Elōñ wōpeñ in joot.* There are many empty shell casings.

wōpieṃ (**wẹpiyẹṃ**). Also *opieṃ.* From Engl. 6(*-i*). Opium.

wōpij (**wepyij**). Also *opij.* From Engl. Office. *Ej jerbal ilo wōpij eṇ eḷap.* He works in the administration building.

wōpija (**wepiyjah**). Also *opija.* From Engl. 2, 6(*-i*). Officer.

wōr. See *or-* for words often spelled *wōr-*.

wōt (**wẹt**). Also *ot, wit.* 2(inf, tr *ute*), 5(*wōttuot, jjidwōtuot; utute*), 6(*-i*). Rain. *Ewōtuot aelōñ in.* This atoll has lots of rain. *Eute waini kaṇe.* It's raining on the copra.

wōt (**wet**). Only; still; just; mere. *Juon wōt aō peen.* I have only one pen. *Ej pād wōt Ṃajeḷ.* He is still in the Marshalls.

wōt (**wet**). 2, 3(*kawōtwōt*), 6(*-i*), 7. Abscess; boil. *Kwōjeḷā ke kọwōtwōt?* Do you know how to treat boils?

wōt (**wet**). 3, 6(*-i*). A plant, taro variety, *Alocasia macrorrhiza* (L.) Sweet. (Araceae). In the same family as taro and Cyrtosperma; "false taro." Two edible varieties: *Wōtaan* and *Wōtaad,* and two inedible: *Wōt-waan* and *Kubwilkōn.*

wōt-aṃwelōñ (**wẹt-haṃẹylẹg**). Rain that falls straight down; big drops but few and far between.

wōt-atok (**wẹt-hateq**). Rain that falls elsewhere but can be heard.

wōt-dikdik (**wẹt-dikdik**). 2, 7. Sprinkle; drizzle.

wōt-mijeljel (**wẹt-mijẹḷjẹl**). Also *wōt-mejeljel* (**wẹt-mẹjẹḷjẹl**). 2, 7. Heavy rain.

wōt-tọ (**wẹt-taw**). Heavy rain from the northeast; see *aetọ.*

Wōt-waan (**wet-wahan**). A plant, taro variety; inedible (Takeuchi), *Xanthosoma.*

wōta (**wetah**). Variant form of *wata* (**watah**).

Wōtaad (**wethad**). A plant, taro variety; edible.

Wōtaan (**wethan**). A plant, taro variety; edible.

wōtan (**wetan**). 1(*-i*), 2, 4, 5(*kkootantōn*), 6(*-i*), 8, 9. Belligerent; bellicose; pugnacious; saucy. *Kwōn jab wōtan bwe kwōnaaj jorrāān.* Don't be belligerent or you'll get into trouble. *Enaaj jorrāān kōn an kkootantōn.* He'll get into trouble because of his obvious belligerence.

wōtar (**wetar**). From Engl. 2(inf, tr *-e*), 4, 6(*-i*), 7. Order. *Kwōnañin wōtare ke nuknuk eo?* Have you ordered the dress?

wōtbai (**wetbahyiy**). Also *otobai* (**wetewbahiy**). From Engl. 1(*-i*), 2(inf, tr *-ik*), 4, 6(*-i*), 7. Scooter; motorcycle; motorbike.

wōteḷ (**wetyeḷ**). Also *oteeḷ* (**weteyeḷ**). From Engl. Hotel.

Wōtin Kapilōñ (**wetin kapiylęg**). From "Carolinian taro". A plant, taro variety (Takeuchi), *Xanthosoma.*

Wōtin Ruk (**wetin riq**). From "Trukese taro". A plant, taro variety (Takeuchi), *Xanthosoma.*

wōtlǫk (**wętlaq**). Dial. W, E: *buñlǫk* (**big°laq**). 1(*-i*), 2, 3(inf *kǫwōtlǫk*, tr *kǫotlǫk*), 5(*wōttōlǫklǫk*), 7. Fall down; drop down, as from a height; tumble; dishonor. *Ewōttōlǫklǫk ajri eņ.* That child is always falling.

wōtlǫk kōn oņānṃweiuk (**wętlaq kęn weņyanṃęyiq**). Sale. *Ewōtlǫk Wiikwaaṃ kōn oņān ṃweiuk.* The Wigwam store has a big sale going on. *Ewōtlǫk oņān ṃweiuk ilo Aļaṃowana.* There's a sale at Ala Moana.

wōtlǫklañ (**wętlaqlag**). Variant form of *bwilǫklañ.*

wōtmiiļ (**wetmiyiļ**). From Engl. Oatmeal.

wōtojome (**wetewjewmey**). Archaic. Fishing method, using scarer; for catching goatfish (*jome*).

wōtōbai (**wetebahiy**). Variant form of *wōtbai* (**wetbahyiy**).

wōtōdtōd (**wetedted**). 1(*-i*), 2, 3, 4, 6(*-i*), 7, 8, 9. Loose bowels; diarrhea; upset stomach.

wōtōm (**wetem**). Also *otem.* Entirely; absolutely; very. *Ña ij ṃool wōtōm ṃool.* I am telling the absolute truth.

wōtōmjej (**wętęmjęj**). Also *otemjej, otemjeļǫk* (**wętęmjeļaq**)). All; every. *Armej wōtōmjej.* Everybody. *Men wōtōmjeļǫk.* Everything.

wōtōmjeļǫk (**wętęmjeļaq**). Also *otemjeļǫk.* Variant form of *wōtōmjej* (**wętęmjęj**).

wōtōn (**wętęn**). Season for breadfruit and pandanus.

wōttuot (**węttiwęt**). Also *wōttuwōt.* Distributive form of *wōt* (**węt**).

wūd (**wid**). Also *ud.* Piece; smallest unit of something, grain. *Bōk ruo daaṃ wūd ilo bōb ņe.* Take two keys of that pandanus as your portion. *Bōk juon kijeṃ wūdin pinana.* Take a banana for yourself. *Ruo wōt wūd e ilo pakij in jikka e kiiō.* There are only three cigarettes left in this pack. *Juon wūdin raij.* A grain of rice.

wūd (**wid**). Also *wūdde* (**widdęy**). Bear fruit, of pandanus.

wūdādo (**widadew**). Also *wūdādu.* 2, 4, 6(*-i*), 7. A toy, coconut hydroplane; to sail a coconut hydroplane. *Ke iar dik, ikōn wūdādo aolep Jādede.* When I was young I used to sail toy hydroplanes every Saturday. *Eṃōkaj wūdādo eņ waan.* His toy hydroplane is very fast.

wūddik (**widdik**). Also *wūnniñ* (**winnig**). 1(*-i*), 2, 3(inf, tr *-i*), 8, 9. Small; tiny; midget.

wūdeakeak (**widyakyak**). 1(*-i*), 2, 3, 7, 8, 9, 11(*wūdeakeak*). Crazy; delirious; insane; maniac; berserk; lunatic. *Aolep im ko jāne bwe ewūdeakeak.* Everyone ran away from him because he went berserk.

wūdede (**widęydęy**). 1(*-i*), 2, 3(inf, tr *-ik*), 7, 8, 9. Mangled; ragged; frayed, fuzzy. *Ij kkōņak nuknuk wūdede.* I'm wearing ragged clothes.

wūdej (**widęj**). A bird, long-tailed New Zealand cuckoo, *Urodynamis taitensis*; cuckoo.

wūdeñ (**wideg**). 1(*-i*), 2(inf, tr *-e*), 4, 5(*uwūdeñdeñ*), 6(*-i*), 7. A food, cooked and pounded breadfruit, taro, bananas, or nuts mixed with grated coconut. *Wūdeñin Mājej. Wūdeñ* from Mejit. *Eowūdeñdeñ rūṃweeņ.* They always make *wūdeñ* at that house.

wūdiddid (**wididdid**). 1(*-i*), 2, 3, 7, 8, 9. Tremble; quake; chills; shiver; vibrate; tremor; shake.

wūdikke (**widikkęy**). 2, 3(inf, tr *-ik*), 6(*-i*). Writhe in pain; twist in pain; shriek in terror or pain. *Iļak ṃwijit kōnwaan bao eo, ewūdikke.* When I cut the chicken's head off, it writhed in pain. *Joot eo ekǫwūdikkeik ļeo.* The bullet sent him twisting in pain.

wūdiñdiñ (**widigdig**). Also *lǫudiñdiñ.* 1(*-i*), 2, 7, 8, 9. Happy; ecstatic.

wūdkabbe (**widkabbęy**). 2, 6(*-i*), 8, 9, 11(*wūdkabbe*). Stunted growth; idiotic; moron; oaf. *Ewūdkabbe ni eo kōtkan.* The coconut tree he planted did not grow properly. *Iiǫkwe ajri ņe ke ewūdkabbe.* I feel sorry for that child who's going to grow up to be a moron.

wūdmouj (**widmęwij**). Also *wūdmuuj* (**widmiwij**). 2, 4, 6(*-i*), 8, 9, 11(*wūdmouj*). Of light complexion; light skinned. *Ewūdmouj bwe nājin riJepaan.* He's light-skinned because his father is Japanese.

wūdmuuj (**widmiwij**). Variant form of *wūdmouj* (**widmẹwij**).

wūj (**wij**). 2(inf, tr *-i*), 6(*-i*). Drown someone by holding his head under water. *Ear wūji kuuj ko.* He drowned the cats.

wūj (**wij**). 3, 6(*-i*). Cork.

wūj (**wij**). Also *wūji* (**wijiy**). 2, 6(*-i*). Pull out of ground; uproot; transitive form of *wūjwūj* (**wijwij**). *Wūji wūjooj kaṇe.* Pull up those weeds.

wūj (**wij**). Dial. W, E: *wōj.* Balsa driftwood.

wūj (**wij**). Formant in place names; rough, of weather, currents, etc.

wūjaak (**wijahak**). 1(*-i*), 2, 4, 7. Tie coconut leaves together to make fishing chain.

wūjabōj (**wijabẹj**). 7, 8, 9. Narrow, of land (see *wūjaloñ* (**wijaleg°**)). *Ewūjabōj Wūlka.* Uliga is narrow.

wūjaḷoñ (**wijaḷeg°**). 1(*-i*), 2, 3, 7, 8, 9, 11(*wūjaḷoñ*). Breadth of an island; wide, of land (see *wūjabōj* (**wijabẹj**)). *Ewūjaḷoñ ānin.* This islet is wide.

wūje- (**wije-**). Dial. W, E: *wūjjie-*. 6(*wūjen, wūjjien*). Part of. *Pikeel-eañ ej wūjen Jarej. Pikeel-eañ* is part of *Jarej.*

wūjek (**wijẹk**). Archaic. Be proud of. *Ij wūjeke ḷeo.* I'm proud of him.

wūjinleep (**wijinleyep**). Dial. E, W: *wūjilleep* (**wijilleyep**). 6(*-i*). A fish, Pacific sailfish; *Istiophorus greyi.*

wūjlep- (**wijlep-**). 2, 7. Give freely; give in abundance; render (with directional); surrender. *Wūjlepḷọk ñan Jijer men ko ṃweien Jijer.* Render to Caesar the things that are Caesar's. *Wūjlepḷọk būruoṃ ñan Anij.* Surrender your heart to God.

wūjḷā (**wijḷay**). Variant form of *wōjḷā* (**wẹjḷay**).

wūjooj (**wijẹwẹj**). Also *ujooj.* A plant, general term for grass or *Ittaria elongata*, actually an epiphytic, penoulous fern; grass; hay; pasture.

wūjooj-in-eoon-bōl (**wijẹwẹj-yin-yẹwẹn-bẹl**). From "grass of the edge of the taro pit". A plant, marsh grass, *Cyperus javanicus* Houtt.

wūjooj-in-Ep (**wijẹwẹj-yin-yep**). From *Ep* (**yep**) "a legendary island". A plant, *Oplismenus compositus* (L.) Beauv. (Gramineae). A Grass. Ebon.

wūjooj-in-lọjet (**wijẹwẹj-yin-lawjẹt**). From "grass of the ocean". A plant, general term for seaweed. *Thalassia hemprichii* (Ehrenb.) Aschers.; any seaweed.

wūjroñ (**wijreg°**). Also *wōmwōm* (**wemwem**). Extract; withdraw; pull out.

wūjtak (**wijtak**). 2(inf, tr *-e*), 6(*-i*), 7. Praise (religious term only); glorify; worship; honor; revere. *Rej wūjtak Anij.* They worship God.

wūjwūj (**wijwij**). 1(*-i*), 2(inf, tr *wūj(i)*), 3, 7. To pull out; root out. *Kwōn wūj doon ṇe jān ijeṇe.* Pull that husking stick out of the ground there. *Ejaje wūjwūj doon e.* This husking stick can't be pulled out.

wūlej (**wilẹj**). Also *ulej.* 3, 6(*-i*). A plant, *Clerodendrum inerme* (L.) Gaertn. (Verbenaceae). A common sprawling shrub with whitish-purplish tubular flowers, exserted stamens, and opposite simple leaves.

wūliej (**wiliyẹj**). Also *uliej, wūlej* (**wilyẹj**), *wūleej* (**wilẹyẹj**). 1(*-i*), 6(*-i*). Cemetery, graveyard; head.

wūlik (**wilik**). Also *ulik.* 1(*-i*), 2, 3. Belch; burp.

wūlio (**wiliyẹw**). 1(*-i*), 2, 3, 7, 8, 9, 11(*wūlioeo*). Handsome, men only.

wūlleej (**willẹyyẹj**). From Engl. Windlass; capstan; winch. *Ejorrāān wūlleej eo an* Militopi. The Militobi's windlass broke down.

wūllepa- (**willepa-**). Dial. E only; see *rūkorea-* (**rikewreya-**). 1. Uncle, mother's brother only.

wūlṃōd (**wilṃed**). 2, 6(*-i*). Thick husk protecting eyes of coconut; whiskers remaining on a husked coconut. *Ñe jej ddeb ni jej wūlṃōd.* When we husk coconuts to drink we leave some husk at the eyes.

wūlok (**wileq**). Archaic. To excuse.

wūmar (**wimar**). Solid ground on which the game of *kajjeor* is played.

wūn (**win**). Also *un.* 6(*wūnin, wūnjān, wūni*). Base; basis; root; reason; purpose; cause; problem; arithmetic; motive; source; lower part of tree, brush, or grass. *Kanōk jān wūnjān.* Pull from the roots.

wūn (**win**). Also *un.* 3(inf *karwūn*, tr *karwūni*), 6(*-i*). Scale of fish; core of a boil.

wūnaak (**winahak**). Also *la.* 2, 3, 6(-*i*), 7. Birds flying looking for fish; a flock of birds flying over a school of fish.

wūne māj (**winey maj**). 1(...*meja*-). Get some shut-eye; take a nap. *Ij ja itan wūne meja jidik ṃokta jān aō naaj mmej.* I think I'll get some shut-eye for a while before I go on watch.

wūnin tōl (**winin tel**). Moral; lesson; inner meaning; motto.

Wūninnin (**wininnin**). From *ninnin* (**ninnin**) "suck" (?) 3, 6(-*i*). A plant, pandanus cultigen (Takeuchi).

wūnit (**winit**). Wrap up; tie up a bundle. *Wūniti jabōn aḷaḷ kaṇ.* Tie up the ends of those pieces of lumber.

Wūnjeeṃ (**winjeyeṃ**). 3, 6(-*i*). A plant, pandanus cultigen; sterile; with narrow leaves best for weaving.

wūnlọk (**winlaq**). Also *ñijlọk.* 2, 3, 6(-*i*). Dive after getting hooked, of fish. *Ear ban tōbwe ek eo ke ear wūnlọk.* He couldn't pull the fish in because it dived. *Ear kọunlọk ek eo.* He let the fish dive.

Wūnmaañ (**winmahag**). A plant, *Pandanus fischerianus* (or hybrid) cultigen; no fruit; leaves used only for textiles. Same as *kou* or *kounmaañ.*

wūnniñ (**winnig**). Also *unniñ, wūddik* (**widdik**). 1(-*i*), 2, 3, 7, 8, 9, 11(*wūnniññiñ*). Dwarfed; very small. *Eḷap an wūnniñ ajri eṇ ear ḷotak.* That baby that was born is very small.

wūno (**winew**). Also *uno.* 1(*wūnoka*-), 2(inf, tr -*ok*), 3, 4, 6(*wūnokan, wūnoun*), 7. Treat, medically; to paint; paint; medicine; color; drug; hue; potion; cure; panacea; remedy. *Raar wūnook kinej e peiū aujpitōḷ.* They treated the cut on my hand at the hospital. *Kwōn wia tok wūno jen wūnook wa e.* Buy some paint and let's paint this boat. *Erōōj wūnokan jōōt ṇe aṃ.* You have a loud-colored shirt. *Naaj ta wūnoka ke ijorrāān.* What's the remedy for relieving me of this heartache.

wūno in ruprup (**winew yin r°ipr°ip**). Laxative; purgative medicine.

wūnojidikdik (**winẹwjidikdik**). Also *unojidikdik, wūnoojdikdik* (**winewejdikdik**). 1(-*i*), 2, 3, 4, 7. Whisper; speak secretly.

wūnokan (**winewkan**). Construct form of *wūno* (**winew**).

wūnōk (**winẹk**). Also *unōk.* Food laid aside for future use; hoarding of food.

wūnōknōk (**winẹknẹk**). 1(-*i*), 2, 3, 7. To lay aside food for future use; hoard food.

wūnpej (**winpẹj**). Also *unpej.* 3, 6(-*i*). Pandanus key, sprouted; a dry brown key of pandanus fruit that has germinated and bears a seedling of small size (under 6" high; usually) (see *pej*).

wūntoba (**wintewbah**). Also *untoba.* From Japn. *undooba*. Playground.

wūntokai (**wintewkahyiy**). From Japn. *undookai*. 2, 4, 6(-*i*). Track and field events. *Rej wūntokai aolep U. N. Day.* They hold track and field events every U.N. Day.

wūntō (**winteh**). From Engl. Window.

wūntōn (**winten**). Archaic. Formant in place names; cluster of; clump of.

wūnwūj (**winwij**). Also *unuj.* 1(-*i*), 2(inf, tr -*i*). Slander; libel.

wūnwūjriabeb (**winwijriyabyẹb**). 2(inf, tr -*e*), 4, 6(-*i*). Slander.

wūpaaj (**wipahaj**). Also *upaaj.* Fireplace; open fireplace for cooking; ashes.

wūpaajaj (**wipahajhaj**). Also *upaajaj.* 2, 3(inf, tr -*e*), 6(-*i*), 8, 9, 11(*wūpaajaj*). Gray.

wūpeḷ (**wipyeḷ**). 1, 2, 8, 9, 11(*wūpeḷeḷ*). Weak; clumsy; feeble; fragile; frail. *Ewūpeḷ.* He's a weakling.

wūpeñ (**wipẹg**). Shell of smaller clams.

wūt. See *ut.*

yiō. See *iiō.*

yokwe. See *iọkwe.*

yuk. See *eok.*

ENGLISH-MARSHALLESE FINDER LIST

abacus: *jorbañ.*
abandoned: *jojoḷāār.*
abashed: *lo.*
abate: *meraḷọk.*
abdomen: *lọje.*
lower abdomen, triangular area: *baj.*
swollen abdomen: *jeje, jieje.*
abhor: *akkōjdat, dike.*
ability: *maroñ.*
ability to cast spell: *anitta.*
ability to jump far: *ppikaj.*
inability to catch many fish (see *koṇkoṇ* (**qeṇqeṇ**)): *jọkoṇkoṇ.*
inability to catch many fish (see *wōda* (**wedah**)): *joda.*
inability to stay underwater long (see *pakij* (**pakij**)): *jāpakij.*
abjure: *kaarmejjet.*
able
able to catch many fish: *koṇkoṇ, wōda.*
able to keep wits during crisis: *lọḷe.*
able to sail close to the wind: *wetak.*
able to stay under water long: *pakij.*
be able to: *jor, maroñ.*
enable: *kōmaroñ.*
not able to reason: *jaje ḷōmṇak.*
unable: *ban.*
unable to go in shallow water, of vessels: *kapjulaḷ.*
unable to hear (see *roñ* (**reg°**)): *jarroñroñ.*
unable to keep still: *ne ṃakūtkūt.*
unable to sail close to the wind: *wāto.*
unable to throw far: *jiban.*
abode: *wōja.*
about: *tarrin.*
about it: *eake, kake.*
about to: *itōn.*
about, approximately: *ellōkan.*
above: *jiṃa, lōñ.*
abrupt: *jidimkij, jum.*
abrupt decision: *idiñ.*
abscess: *ur, wōt.*
absent: *jako.*
absent-minded: *bōrojoḷọk, kūḷaṃwe, mmālele, ppaḷ.*
absenteeism: *ikirumṃwij.*
mark to show absence: *ọo.*
absolute
absolutely: *wōtōm.*
absorb: *jorom.*
abstain: *jitlọk.*
abstemious
abstemious of food: *mattiie.*
absurd
absurd (see *kkar* (**kkar**)): *jekkar.*
Abudefduf
a fish, *maomao, Abudefduf abdominalis*: *badet.*
a fish, sergeant major, *Abudefduf septemfasciatus*: *badet.*
Abudefduf saxatilis: *bakōj.*
abundant: *buñ-pāḷọk, lōñ, lutōkḷọk.*
give in abundance: *wūjlep-.*
Acanthurus
banded surgeonfish, *Acanthurus triostegus* triostegus Linnaeus: *kupañ.*
black surgeonfish, *Acanthurus nigricans*: *tiepdọ.*
orange spot tang, *Acanthurus olivaceus*: *ael.*
red spot tang, *Acanthurus achilles*: *kinbo, pir.*
surgeonfish, *Acanthurus dussumieri*: *kōpat.*
surgeonfish, *Acanthurus lineatus*: *kuwi, kwi.*
surgeonfish, *Acanthurus nigricans*: *aelmeej.*
accelerate: *kūrōn, ḷọk.*
accept
refuse to accept or take: *ṃakokoun bōk.*
accessible
inaccessible: *akā.*
accident: *jirilọk, jorrāān.*
by accident: *jide.*
lie on back as result of accident: *jedtak.*
accompany: *aililōk, karwaan, rājetak.*
accompany either physically or spiritually while in great danger: *mije.*
accomplish: *tōprak, tokwōj.*
accomplishment: *tōpran.*
rely on children to accomplish errands or chores: *ajriin uwaak.*
unaccomplished: *make.*
accost
waylay, accost: *pāpjel ṃae.*
account
charge on account: *akkọun, jaaj.*
accurate: *jejjet.*
accuse: *kinaak.*
accustom
accustom oneself: *meej.*
accustomed to: *mminene.*
unaccustomed: *jāmminene.*

ache: *metak.*
stomach ache: *jemetak.*

Achernar
a star, possibly Achernar (alpha Eridani): *Ijuun Rak.*

achieve: *tōprak.*
achieve one's goal: *teru.*
achieve prominence: *ļe.*
achieved: *jaak.*
achievement: *tōpran.*

Achyranthes
A thorny-stemmed tree. Also applied to other spiny or thorny plants, such as *Achyranthes aspera* L. on Eniwetok, or, in the shorter variant *lōklōk*: *kālōklōk.*

acid: *ajet.*
acidity: *ajet.*

Acila
a shell, *Solemyidae, Acila schencki*: *kūkōr.*

Acmaea
Acmaea pallida: *jowakin.*

acne: *taeo.*
white acne-like fungus under skin: *karko.*

acquainted
acquainted with: *jiniet.*
unacquainted: *jājiniet.*

acquire: *bōk.*

acronym
acronym for Kwajalein Islands Trading Company: *Kūtko.*
acronym for Marshall Islands Import-Export Company: *Mieko.*

act: *m̧wil.*
act in a certain way: *kain̩n̩e.*
act in a way contrary to missionary teaching: *tepiļ.*
actions: *kōm̧m̧an, m̧ūtō-.*

Actinopyga
sea cucumber, *Holothuroidea, Thelonia* or *Actinopyga*: *piāpe.*

active: *keeñki, mmourur, pātōñtōñ.*
inactive: *mejjeeļ.*
very active person: *kākemo̧o̧j.*

actual: *lukkuun.*

ad lib: *kkōn.*

add: *koba.*
add liquid to substance such as starch: *kapejlo̧k.*
add sand or grated coconut: *penpen.*
add up to an expected quantity: *uñ.*
carry, in addition: *uñar.*
not add up: *jo̧uñ.*

addict
smoking addict: *añūrlep.*

address: *jipij.*
address a letter: *atōrej.*
address someone using *Li-* or *Ļa-* prefix on name: *ātlep.*

adequate: *bwe.*

adhere: *dāpdep, ddāp.*

adjoin
adjoining: *atartar.*

adjustment
period of adjustment: *iien kijone.*

administer: *le-.*

administrator
District Administrator: *kom̧ja.*
Educational Administrator: *kom̧ja.*

admire: *alwōj, nōbar.*

admit: *deļo̧ñ.*

admonish: *kapilōk, kauwe, rōjañ.*

adolescent: *boea.*
adolescent (derogatory): *mānniñ.*
unmarried adolescent girl: *jiroñ.*

adopt
adopt children: *kaajiriri.*

adoration: *kabuñ.*

adorn: *inōknōk.*

adult: *rūtto.*

adultery: *lejān.*
commit adultery: *ļōñ.*

advance
advanced: *ļe.*

advantage
disadvantage: *nana tam̧m̧wi-.*

advertise: *karreelel.*

advise: *kapilōk, kauwe, kipel.*
advise someone to lead a conventionally good clean life: *kabkūbjer.*
to encourage, advise: *rōjañ.*
closest advisor: *jim̧win ñi.*

advocate
take sides, advocate: *rrā.*

adze: *jaļtok, māāl.*

Aetobatus
a fish, spotted eagle ray fish, poisonous, *Aetobatus narinari*: *imen.*

affair: *jerbal.*

affect: *jelōt.*

afflict
afflicted: *liaajlo̧ļ.*

affluent: *jeban.*

afford: *maroñ.*

afraid: *kkūm̧kūm̧, kor, mijak.*
afraid of: *uwōta.*
afraid of ghosts: *abwinmake.*

afraid to: *pikōt.*
afraid, warn: *kkōl.*
be afraid of: *lōļn̄ọn̄.*

African pompano: *aron̄.*

after: *āliki-, ļak, ļọkun, ļokwa-.*
afterwards: *tokālik.*
canoe part, after-part when outrigger is on port side: *jabdik.*
aftermath: *ajāllik, jem̧ļọk.*

afterbirth: *kiliblib.*

again: *bar.*
why again?: *jaam̧.*

against: *m̧ae, ņae.*
a feeling against: *kajjikur.*

age: *ded, epepen.*
cause to come of age: *karūtto.*
of age: *rūtto.*
of good age: *m̧m̧an ded.*
old age: *rūtto.*
one of the same or nearly the same age as another: *peļo.*

aged: *aļapļọk, bwijwoļā.*
fruit of aged trees: *ālkūm̧ur.*

aggravate: *kakūtōtō.*
aggravation: *aplon̄lon̄.*

aggregate: *ejouj.*
congregated, aggregated: *kuk.*

agile: *ppikaj, util.*

aging: *rūttoļọk.*

agitate: *lim̧aajņoņo.*
agitated: *jjeikik.*
excited, agitated, energized: *em̧m̧ōļō.*
agitation of feelings: *lim̧otak.*

ago
a long time ago: *etto.*
a while ago: *kkein.*
some time ago: *jem̧aan.*

agony: *en̄taan.*

agree: *rejetak.*
agree among selves: *bōro-kuk.*
agreement: *bujen, koņ.*
shake the head in disagreement: *jeboulul.*

aground
go aground: *eọr, eoņ.*

ague: *piba.*

ahead: *m̧aa-.*
get ahead: *jibadek jidik.*
go ahead: *m̧m̧ōkaj.*
remain ahead of a wave when sailing following the wind: *bun̄m̧aan.*

aid: *jipan̄.*

aide
health aide: *komen.*

ail
ailing: *lọkmej, nan̄inmej.*

aim
aim a gun: *alej.*
aim at: *alej.*

aimless
jaunt, sail, or drive around aimlessly: *tarto-tartak.*
walk aimlessly: *jam̧bo.*

air: *mejatoto.*
cool air: *aem̧ōļoļo.*
exposed to wind and air: *an̄jerak.*
to air out: *jjedwawa.*

air raid: *kuju.*
shelter pit, air raid: *rọn̄.*

airfield: *pij.*

airmail: *eermeeļ.*

airplane: *baļuun.*
arrive, of sailing vessel or airplane: *po.*
to bank, of airplanes: *lā.*

aisle: *tuwa.*

ajar: *idaaptōk, peļļọk.*

alarm: *iruj.*

albacore
a fish, false albacore or *kawakawa*: *ļooj.*

albatross: *le.*
a bird, black-footed albatross, *Diomedea nigripes*: *le.*
a bird, laysan albatross, *Diomedea immutabilis*: *le.*

album
photo album: *bokun pija.*

alcohol: *arkooļ.*
alcoholic: *ņompe.*
like alcoholic beverages: *ņompe.*
strong liquor, alcoholic beverage: *dānnin kadek.*

Aldebaran
Aldebaran in Taurus: *Ļoojļapļap.*

alert: *kōllejar, pojak.*
be alert: *m̧aanjāppopo.*

Aleutra
Aleutra scripta: *m̧ōņakņak.*

Algedi: *Lim̧anm̧an.*

alien: *ruwamāejet.*

alienable
inalienable rights or property: *addemlōkmej.*
possessive classifier, alienable objects and general possessive: *aa-, wōja-.*

alienate
alienated: *kolōkabwi-, kon̄il, m̧weed.*

alight: *jok.*

alive: *mour.*
all: *aolep, wōtōmjej.*
all gone: *maat.*
all present: *likiio.*
all the more: *tōrreo.*
not all there: *irļọk.*
allergy: *lennab.*
alligator: *aļkita.*
allocate: *kōjjemọọj.*
Allophylus
a plant, tree, *Allophylus timorensis*: *kūtaak.*
allot: *kōjjemọọj.*
allow: *kōtļọk.*
allowance for error: *kijen peto.*
allowed: *mālim.*
alloy: *māāl waan.*
alluring: *kakijdikdik, mmejaja.*
ally: *rejetak.*
almanac: *aļōm̧ņak.*
almost: *baj, eitōn, kiōk, m̧ōttan jidik, nañin.*
Alocasia
a plant, taro variety, *Alocasia macrorrhiza*: *wōt.*
alone: *jojoļāār, make.*
fear of being alone in the dark or at sea: *abwinmake.*
alongside: *tōrerei-.*
come alongside: *atartar.*
go alongside of: *atar.*
put alongside: *apar.*
Alopias
a fish, thresher shark, *Alopias vulpes*: *pako tọrtọr.*
alphabet: *aļbapeet.*
already: *m̧ōj.*
because, already: *dedeinke.*
also: *āinwōt, bar, barāinwōt, kab.*
Altair: *Mājlep.*
altar: *lokatok, tampeļ.*
alternate: *ukoktak.*
although: *amñe, meñe.*
altitude: *ļolōñ, utiej.*
Alutera
a fish, scrawled file fish, *Alutera scripta*: *ikudej.*
always: *aolep iien.*
Amanses
a fish, file fish, *Amanses carolae*: *m̧ōņakņak.*
amateur: *jedañ, ñak.*
amaze: *bwilōñ.*
amazed: *ļọkjenaa-, lōļñọñ.*
amazing: *kabwilōñlōñ, kōppaļpaļ.*

ambiguous: *lōñ m̧weñan.*
ambition: *jibadbad.*
seat of ambition: *at.*
ambush: *apād.*
lie in ambush: *kōppao.*
to ambush: *kōmja.*
amend: *jim̧we.*
America: *Amedka, aelōñin pālle.*
among: *bwilji-.*
amount: *ded, detta-, joña-.*
Amphinerita
Puperita japonica or *Amphinerita polita*: *kaddoļ.*
amuse: *kam̧ōņōņō.*
amusement: *m̧ōņōņō.*
Anadara
a shell, *Arcidae, Anadara (scapharca) satowi/broughtonii*: *kūkōr-in-ar.*
small clam, oyster, a shell, *Arcidae, Scapharca inequivalvis* or *Anadara pilulu*: *kūkōr.*
analogy
analogy, attempt: *mālejjoñ.*
analyze: *tipdik.*
Anampses
Anampses caeruleopunctatus: *alle.*
Anas
a bird, mallard, *Anas platyrhynchos*: *roñanpat.*
a bird, northern shoveler, *Anas clypeata*: *roñanpat.*
ancestor: *rūtto.*
mixed ancestry: *aiņokko.*
anchor: *añkō, emjak.*
anchor line: *emjak.*
anchorage: *aba.*
anchorage on ocean side of islet where one waits for more favorable winds: *metto.*
be at anchor: *mmaan.*
bow line, used to tie up an anchor: *lokm̧aan.*
fastened, of anchors only: *kilōk.*
large stone used as an anchor: *kadkad.*
let anchor line out to allow for tide change: *peaut.*
ride at anchor: *emjak.*
stock of an anchor: *rrob.*
to anchor: *ejjeļā.*
weigh anchor: *tōbtōb.*
ancient: *ennāp.*
ancient times: *etto.*
and: *im, kab.*
and so (in narratives): *em̧ōj.*
Andromeda
beta Andromedae: *Ūlin-raj-eo.*

gamma Andromedae: *Poobin-raj-eo.*

anemone
sea anemone: *ḷọr.*

angel: *enjeḷ.*

Angelonia
a plant, flower, *Angelonia salicariaefolia*: *jab meḷọkḷọk.*

anger: *kōḷo, kōmmatōr, kūtōtō.*
anger through jealousy: *kwi.*
angered: *inepata.*
easily angered: *idimkwi, n̄n̄in̄i.*
not angered easily (see *llu* (**lliw**)): *jāllulu.*
slow to anger in debate (see *kwi* (**qiy**)): *jọkkwikwi.*
slow to anger in debate (see *n̄n̄in̄i* (**ggiygiy**)): *jan̄n̄in̄i.*

angle
angle of the jaw: *ron̄.*
measure joints at an angle in construction work: *alej.*

angry: *in̄, ḷōkatip, llu, paḷ, ro.*
angry about injuries received: *kwi.*
become angry: *kun an ḷaaṃ.*
so angry as to resort to revenge: *n̄i.*
very angry: *kūtōtō, matōrtōr.*

Anguilla
Anguilla celebesensis: *toṇ.*

animal: *menninmour.*
a small black lizard with white stripes: *mājḷwōj.*
centipede: *iie, ṇokwanej.*
green and black lizard, *Dasia smaragdina*: *kiḷij.*
kind of lizard, big tree gecko, *Gehyra oceanica*: *korap kūro.*
kind of lizard, gecko, *Lepidodactylus pelagicus* or *Hemiphyllodactylus typus*: *korap.*
tree lizard, green and black, *Dasia smaragdina*: *aop.*
white land crab: *lemḷat.*
call or entice animals or children to come near: *kkaal.*
die out, of plants, animals, or people: *ḷot.*
duty of taking care of a natural or adopted child or pet or domesticated animal: *nāji.*
female, of animals: *kokōrā.*
horn of an animal: *doon.*
male, of animals: *koṃaan.*
round up fish or animals: *ajāl.*
school of fish on reef, herd of animals: *baru.*
young birds or animals: *koon.*

animate
reanimate: *jaruk.*

animosity: *kōjdat.*

ankle
ankle bones: *lijaakkwōlele.*
band around ankles used in climbing trees: *kae.*
climb coconut tree with ankles tied: *ento.*

annihilate: *jeepepḷọk.*
annihilate one-by-one: *jjon̄jon̄.*

anniversary: *keemem.*

Annona
a plant, *Annona muricata* L. (Annonaceae). The sour-sop: *jojaab.*

announce
announcement: *keean̄.*

annoy: *kakūtōtō.*
annoyed or bothered by noise: *uwaron̄.*

anoint: *kkapit.*
herbs for anointing: *toḷaj.*

anonymous
do something for (or against) someone anonymously: *etale-liktōmān.*

another: *bar juon.*
one another: *doon.*

Anous
a bird, black noddy, *Anous tenuirostris*: *jekad.*
a bird, brown noddy, *Anous stolidus*: *pejwak.*

answer: *uwaak.*
answer someone's question: *ṇawāwee-.*
answer to call: *eọron̄.*

ant: *ḷon̄.*
big black ant: *kallep.*
smallest ant: *kinaḷ.*

antagonize
antagonize by tale-bearing: *kiojaḷjaḷ.*

Antares: *Tūṃur.*

ante
ante, in poker: *laḷ.*

antenna: *antena.*

anti-social: *jememe.*

antic
antics: *ṃūtō-.*

anus: *anri-, kimirmir, poḷ, rōrāāt.*
anus hair: *oḷkūn̄.*
scratch anus, to goose: *rōbtak.*
wash anus after defecating, especially women and children, usually in ocean: *eọreor.*

anvil: *aṃbōḷ.*

anxious: *ikdeelel, inepata, kijerjer.*
overanxious: *ṃṃaelep.*
to lust, overanxious: *ṃōṃ.*
wait for anxiously: *jañnuwaad.*
anxiety: *tarukelel.*

any: *jabdewōt.*

Anyperodon
a fish, rock cod, *Anyperodon leucogrammicus*: *kabro, kōḷaoḷap.*

anything: *jabdewōt.*

anyway: *baj.*

apart: *jepel.*
apart, divided into two parts: *rājet.*
be apart: *tọọn.*
far apart (see *kkut* (**qqit**)): *mmejo, mmeḷo.*
take apart: *jaḷjaḷ.*
tear apart: *ttemakil.*

apathetic: *jememe.*

ape: *ṃañke.*

Apogon
a fish, cardinal fish, *Apogon novemfasiatus*: *tōptōp.*

apologize: *joḷọk bōd.*

apostle: *rijjelōk, rūkaki.*

apparatus: *kein jerbal.*

apparent: *alikkar.*

appeal: *owar.*
appealing: *mmejaja.*
have sex appeal: *taḷe.*

appear: *aloklok, jāde, jo, ṃur, waḷọk.*
a boy or man whose appearance makes everyone smile: *ḷḷajkōnkōn.*
appear before an audience: *paañ.*
appearance: *añōltok, kōjālli-, nemāmei-, pao.*
come into appearance: *buñ.*
disappear: *jeepepḷọk, jetḷọk.*
healthy in appearance, as a coconut tree: *wāmourur.*
outward appearance: *añḷọkwi-.*
put in an appearance: *miro.*

appease: *jojoon bōro, medek.*

appendage
appendage, usually to a house (always used with directional postpositions): *daṃok.*

appendicitis: *ṃojo.*

appetite
have an appetite for: *bōro-kōrkōr, ijoḷ.*
of small appetite: *mattiie.*

applaud: *kabbokbok.*
applause: *kabbokbok.*

apple: *abōḷ.*
apple of one's eye: *ñiejo.*
apple-polishing: *kappok jide.*
coconut "apple": *iu.*

apply
apply constant powerful pressure on a rope: *keepep.*
apply oneself: *kakkōt.*

appoint: *jitōñ.*

appraise: *watwat.*

apprentice: *rūkkatak.*

approach: *jikrōk, jitaak, kepaak.*

appropriate: *kkar.*
appropriate others' property: *aṇokṇak.*
to appropriate: *kōjjemọọj.*

approve
approved: *weeppān.*
disapprove: *dike, kōrraat.*

approximate
about, approximately: *ellōkan.*
approximately: *tarrin.*

April: *Eprōḷ.*

Aprion
a fish, snapper, *Aprion virescens*: *ewae.*
a fish, streaker, *Aprion virescens*: *ḷọom.*

apron: *nuknukun kuk.*

apt: *kkā.*

Aquarius
stars in Aquarius: *Jitata.*

Aquila
alpha, beta, gamma Aquilae: *Mājlep.*
epsilon, zeta, omega Aquilae: *Arin-Mājlep.*

Arabica
Arabica scurra/eglantina/couturiera/asiatica or *Cyraea tigris*: *libbukwe.*

architect: *ripija annañ.*

Arcidae
a shell, *Arcidae, Anadara (scapharca) satowi/broughtonii*: *kūkōr-in-ar.*
small clam, oyster, a shell, *Arcidae, Scapharca inequivalvis* or *Anadara pilulu*: *kūkōr.*

Arcturus
Arcturus in Bootes: *Ad.*
the pair of stars Spica and Arcturus: *Daam-Ad.*

area: *peḷaak.*
clean up an area: *rarō.*

Arenaria
a bird, ruddy turnstone, *Arenaria interpres*: *kōtkōt.*

argue: *akwāāl, dọọj, iakwāāl, kōbọuwe.*
argue against: *juṃae.*

argument: *bowōd, leļǫk-letok.*

Argyrops
a fish, redfin, *Argyrops spinifer*: *m̧ōļejetak.*

Aries: *Elmǫñ.*

arise: *jerkak.*

aristocrat
female aristocrat: *lōkkūk.*
male aristocrat: *ļakkūk.*

arithmetic: *bōnbōn.*
do mental arithmetic: *aņtǫǫn.*

arm: *pā.*
beckon by waving arms: *jeeaaļ.*
carry tucked under arm: *abjāje, albakbōk.*
fold arms in front: *bokpā.*
pain in the arm caused by throwing: *joñ.*
put arm around waist of another while standing side by side: *jelpaak.*
put one's arm across another's shoulders while walking: *waabbilāle.*
swing arms while walking: *jerjer.*
walk swinging the arms: *iliik.*

arm
to arm: *ņam̧aanpāā-.*

Armigera
a shell, *Muricidae, Purpura (Manicinella) Armigera*: *tōbo.*

armpit: *medwañ.*
smell of armpits: *medwañ.*

army: *ami.*

aroma: *mālu.*

Arothron
a fish, puffer, *Arothron meleagris*: *luwap-kilmeej.*
a fish, puffer, *Arothron nigropunctatus*: *luwap-iaļo.*

around: *peļaak.*
anywhere around here: *jekākā.*
go around: *ito-itak, rawūn.*
turn, around and around: *iñiñ.*

arouse: *bab-laļ.*
arouse passion: *buñ-kōļowa-.*
aroused to excitement: *jjeurur.*

arrange: *kkar.*
arranged head to tail, of fish: *jitnen m̧ōm̧ō.*
arrangement: *jepaa-.*
beautifully arranged: *ppānpān.*
rearrange: *ikūr.*

arrest: *po.*

arrival
arrival of many canoes: *lipopo.*
cry an arrival, of ship or plane: *jeļo.*
superstition that large waves portend the arrival of a vessel: *tokwanwa.*

arrive: *jikrōk, jitaak, tōkeak, tōpar.*
arrive at: *itaak, m̧or.*
arrive in full force: *ļooribeb.*
arrive, of sailing vessel or airplane: *po.*
to arrive, of a canoe: *jidaak.*

arrogant: *kabbil, kōbbǫǫjǫj, lom̧aan.*

arrow: *lippǫņ.*
shoot a bow and arrow: *lippǫņ.*

arrowroot
a food, preserved breadfruit mixed with arrowroot and coconut sap or sugar, wrapped in breadfruit leaves and baked: *bwiro iiōk.*
a food, soup, spongy coconut and arrowroot: *aikiu.*
a food, spongy meat of sprouted coconut cooked with arrowroot starch and diluted with water: *peaut.*
a food, three to one combination of arrowroot starch and water cooked together: *likōbla.*
a plant, arrowroot, *Tacca leontopetaloides* (L.) Ktze.: *m̧akm̧ōk.*
arrowroot season: *pāl.*
dirty waste water from arrowroot straining process: *kūbween lǫlǫ.*
harvest time for arrowroot: *añōneañ.*
male arrowroot, of no food value: *aetōktōk.*
molded arrowroot starch: *jibwil.*
net made of sennit used for sifting arrowroot starch: *waliklik.*
net, large-meshed, bag-shaped, for washing arrowroot and soaking breadfruit: *do.*
stalk of arrowroot plant: *aetōktōk.*
stone used for grinding arrowroot: *pukor.*
to die, of arrowroot, signaling time for digging the root: *pāl.*
to sieve arrowroot: *epta.*
to sieve arrowroot: first time: *jepta.*

artery: *eke, iaļan bōtōktōk.*

arthritis: *kūrro.*

article: *bwebwenato.*

articulate: *aejemjem.*

artificial: *kōm̧m̧an.*

artist: *ripija.*

Artocarpus
a plant, general term for the breadfruit, *Artocarpus incisus* (Thunb.) L. F. Moraceae: *mā.*
seedless variety of *Artocarpus incisus* (Thunb.) Linn.: *Petaaktak.*

as: *āindein, ke, kōnke.*
as if: *etan wōt ñe.*
ascend: *wanlōñ.*
Asclepias
a plant, *Asclepias curassavica* (Ebon): *kabbok.*
ash
ashes: *melkwaarar, wūpaaj.*
ashes from fireplace: *kūbween upaaj.*
burn to ashes: *melkwaarar.*
ashamed
always ashamed: *jjookok.*
ashore
go ashore on islands belonging to others: *popo m̧anit.*
Asia: *Eijia.*
Asio
a bird, short-eared owl, *Asio flammeus*: *lijem̧ao, m̧ao.*
ask: *jitōk, kajitūkin, kajjitōk.*
ask for food, a shameful thing to do: *tūñañ.*
askew: *ip, oļā, ppeerir.*
Asplenium
a plant, *Asplenium nidus* L. (Pteridophyta): *kartōp.*
ass: *pid.*
assassin: *ruuror.*
assassinate: *kowadoñ, m̧ōrō.*
assault: *ļatipñōl, nitbwil.*
assemble: *bobo, kōļaak.*
to assemble: *kweiļo̧k.*
assembly: *kweiļo̧k.*
assent
nod assent (distributive only): *m̧ajid.*
assert
assert oneself: *kātōk, kōn̄kōm̧m̧an.*
assess
assess the value of: *joñe aorōkin.*
asset: *tokja-.*
assign: *jitōñ.*
assimilate
assimilated: *peljo.*
assist
to assist: *rejetak.*
associate: *m̧ōtta-.*
associate with: *aililōk, iāetōl.*
association: *doulul.*
assorted: *kkārere.*
assume: *ļōmn̄ak.*
assume responsibility for: *bōk ddo.*
assuming that: *bwe bōta.*
assure: *jiroñ.*
asthma: *orļo̧k.*
astonish: *ppaļ.*
astonished: *ļo̧kjenaa-, raññaļo̧k.*
astound: *ppaļ.*
astounded: *raññaļo̧k.*
astray
lead astray: *tōlpilo.*
astronomy: *jedjed iju.*
astute: *kapeel.*
asylum: *im̧ōn bwebwe, im̧ōn utam̧we.*
at: *i, ilo, lo, lo̧.*
be at (always with directional): *ļo-.*
athletic
not athletic: *jo̧kkurere.*
atmosphere: *mejatoto.*
atoll: *aelōñ.*
island or atoll reserved for food gathering, usually for a chief and his immediate family: *ļārooj.*
leeward side of an atoll: *liklaļ.*
main islet of an atoll: *bōran aelōñ, eoonene.*
name of a section of some atolls, usually the windward, northeast part: *aeto̧.*
western and northwestern island northwestern islands in an atoll: *liklaļ.*
windward side of an atoll: *likiej.*
attach: *dāpijek.*
attached: *kkejel, llok.*
attachment: *kketaak.*
build attachments onto a canoe: *peļo̧ñ.*
pamper a child so as to create undue attachment: *kaerer.*
attack: *nitbwil.*
attack at night: *iaboñ.*
attack by mother hen: *wadde.*
attempt: *jaak, jibadbad, kajjioñ.*
analogy, attempt: *mālejjoñ.*
attempt the impossible: *kadkadajaj.*
attend: *pād.*
attention
pay attention to: *eļ.*
stand at attention: *kankan.*
attitude: *bōklōkōt, ļōmn̄ak.*
attorney: *ļoār.*
attract
attract fish or flies with scraps: *am̧am̧.*
attracted: *añal.*
attraction of big fish to smaller fish: *la.*
attractive: *kōmājmāj, m̧ōtañ, mmejaja.*
attractiveness: *aneptok.*
charismatic, person who is always

attracting people around him or her: *ettōl.*
easily attracted to anyone of the opposite sex: *llolo.*
gullible, attracted to: *reel.*
unattractive: *jakōl.*
attractive: *mmeej.*

attribute: *jinōkjeej.*

audience: *alwōj.*
appear before an audience: *paañ.*

audit: *bōnbōn.*

auger: *kilmij.*

August: *Ọkwōj.*

aunt: *jine-.*

Auricularia
a plant, toadstool, *Auricularia ampla* persoon and other earlike *Basidiomycetes* (fungi). Rogers: *lọjilñin kijdik.*

Auriga
stars in Auriga: *Kōḷein-dipāākāk-eo.*

auspices: *oṇaak.*

austere: *kijñeñe.*

Australia: *Aujtōrōlia.*

authentic: *lukwi.*

author
author of stories: *rūkōṃṃan bwebwenato.*

authority: *maroñ, pepe.*
overstep authority: *bōkjab.*

authorize: *kōmaroñ.*

auto
automobile: *jitoja, ṃootka.*

autumn: *añōneañ.*

avenge: *iden-oṇe.*

avert: *bōbrae, eḷḷọk jān.*

aviation: *kkāke.*

avoid: *bōbrae, jeje, kawiiaea.*
avoid because of unfortunate experience: *je.*
interfere in order to avoid: *jujuurḷọk.*
move fast so as to avoid detection: *miro.*

await: *kattar, kōmḷan.*

awake
awake, roused, conscious: *ruj.*
awaken: *ruj.*
keep awake: *mmej.*
late in awakening: *mājurlep.*
to keep awake during the usual hours of sleep: *kōmja.*
wide awake: *rre.*

award: *kọwiinin.*

aware: *jeḷā, kile.*

away: *jako, tōḷọk.*
be away from: *tọọn.*
drift away: *peḷọk.*
get away clean: *joor.*
go away: *welọk.*
run away: *ko.*
stay away from: *kawiiaea.*
steal away: *dej.*
turn away from: *eḷḷọk jān.*

awe: *lōḷñọñ.*

awful: *nana taṃṃwi-.*

awkward: *jatpe.*

awl: *ddāil.*

awning: *waniñ.*

awry: *ip.*

axe: *māāl, ūlūl.*
stone axe: *jeljel.*

babble: *aplo.*

baby: *niññiñ.*
aboriginal women's skirts, now used as baby's mat: *ed.*
baby bird, sooty tern, *mmej*: *jipila.*
baby birds: *kābwil.*
babysit: *kaajiriri.*
fat and healthy, usually referring to a baby: *ṃọkulkul.*
nurse a baby (or a situation): *kaajiriri.*
short tempered, cry-baby, provoked: *kwi.*
soft spot on baby's head: *ṃọñ.*
stillborn baby: *kọ.*

bachelor: *ḷajinono.*

back: *āliki-.*
back of a fish: *aeṃaan.*
back up: *pāāk.*
backkick in kickball: *jaṃlik.*
carry a person on one's back: *kuku.*
come back: *rọọl.*
come back in order to. (Contraction of *rọọltok in* (**rawalteq yin**)): *rọọltōn.*
directional, enclitic, backward or toward the ocean side: *lik.*
fall on one's back: *jarleplep, jedtak, rotak.*
go backward: *jenliklik, wanlik.*
hunchback: *kkuṃliklik.*
in back of: *lik.*
lie on back as result of accident: *jedtak.*
lie on one's back with no regard to surroundings or people.: *jarleplep.*
look back: *ālokorkor.*
lower sides of back, kidney area: *aeo.*
taken aback: *baaj.*
turn back: *rọọl.*
turn the back on someone: *ālkurkur.*

walk with the hands clasped behind the back: *enliklik.*

back and forth
go back and forth: *ito-itak.*
hop back and forth on both feet: *kōm̧ajoñjoñ.*
roll back and forth: *jabwilbwil.*

backbone: *dilep.*

backwash
wash, as a wave or backwash: *tọr.*

bacteria: *kij.*

bad: *nana.*
bad case of skin disease (*koko* (**kewkew**)): *keļe.*
bad luck: *jerata.*
bad odor: *bwiin-nana, bwiin-puwaļ.*
in a bad mood: *nana tam̧m̧wi-.*
speak taboo words that may bring bad luck: *ļakajem̧.*
talk bad about someone: *kōnana.*
use bad language: *tepiļ.*

baffle
baffled: *pok.*

bag: *pāāk.*
baggy: *pidtoto.*
open a bag or basket: *kōjjād.*
twine for sewing up the mouth of a bag: *enneok.*

baggage: *m̧weiuk.*

bail: *bakkiiñ.*
bail out: *ālur.*
bail out water from canoe or boat: *ānen.*
bailer: *lem.*

bait: *anan.*
fish bait: *m̧ọọr.*
fishing method, line fishing inside lagoon using hermit crab for bait: *rupe om̧.*
fishing method, line fishing outside lagoon, usually on lee side and fairly close to shore, for flying fish, using sand crab for bait: *rōjep.*
fishing method, occasional jerking of line to lure a fish to the bait or jig: *kooral.*
fishing method, use fishpole at night with either lure or bait: *tto.*
give bait: *paane.*
live bait: *jowāmuur.*
prepare bait: *kaatat.*
prepare bait from a plant: *kabūt.*
rinse bait: *lije.*
stone upon which bait or chum is mashed: *jinm̧a.*
to use bait: *m̧ọọrọr.*

bake: *um̧.*
a food, bundled and baked spongy meat of sprouted coconut: *iutūr.*
a food, diluted starch baked in coconut spathe in earth oven: *kōlọwutaktak.*
a food, plain baked ripe breadfruit: *mejāliraan.*
a food, preserved breadfruit boiled or baked without wrapping: *koļeiaat.*
a food, spongy meat of sprouted coconut baked in its shell: *iuwum̧um̧.*
bake, usually in earth oven: *um̧um̧.*
baked breadfruit: *liped.*
baked pandanus: *edoum̧.*

balance: *bwe, peļan.*
unbalanced: *tōplik tōpar.*
well-balanced: *jokkun wōt juon.*

balcony: *tōñaak.*

bald: *piļōļ.*
bald head: *oļūb.*

Balistapus
a fish, reef triggerfish, *Balistapus rectangulus/aculeatus*: *im̧im̧.*

balk: *apañ, itweļọk.*
balking: *perper.*

ball: *bọọļ.*
a food, balls of preserved breadfruit sweetened and boiled in coconut oil: *makillō.*
a game, played with pebbles and ball, similar to dice game: *ļuļu.*
backkick in kickball: *jam̧lik.*
ball made from pandanus leaves: *anidep.*
fly ball, in baseball: *tōkai.*
ground ball in baseball: *kōro.*
make balls: *bobo.*
native ball game: *anidep.*
play kickball: *anidep.*
sidekick in kickball: *jem̧kat.*

ballast: *bọļōj, joon̦.*

balloon: *bujeeñ, bujentōm̧a.*

ballot: *pọļot.*

balsa
balsa driftwood: *wōj, wūj.*

bamboo: *bae, koba.*

ban: *mọ.*

banana: *keepran̄.*
a food, cooked and pounded breadfruit, taro, bananas, or nuts mixed with grated coconut: *wūdeñ.*
a plant, a general term for banana: *pinana.*
bunch of bananas: *āj, uror.*
hand of bananas: *ajjen.*

stalk inside bunch of bananas or breadfruit: *perañ.*

band: *korak.*
band around ankles used in climbing trees: *kae.*
band, used for tying torch made from frond: *ida.*
rubber band: *liko.*

band
musical band: *paan.*

bandage: *kkor, korak, kwarkor, rojroj.*
bandaged, tied up, wrapped up: *korkor.*

bang
bang, as of gun: *bokkoḷọk.*

bangle: *pāāñkōḷ.*

bangs
wear hair in bangs: *kọkwe.*

banish: *kalia, kọbaj.*

bank
to bank, of airplanes: *lā.*

bank
bank, financial: *pāāñ.*

bankrupt: *būrook, pāāñkōrab.*

banquet: *keemem, ṃōñāin kōjab.*

baptize: *peptaij.*

bar
exposed and stony bar: *ṇa.*
sandbar, usually not covered even at high tide: *bok.*

bar: *baar.*

barb: *jalōb, kāāj.*

barbaric: *awiia.*

barbecue: *jinkadool.*

barber: *rūṃwijbar.*

bare: *keelwaan, koḷeiaat, ṃañke.*

barefoot
go barefoot: *jintōb.*

bargain: *pepe.*

barge
flat-bottom barge: *ḷaita.*

bark
outer bark of tree: *kilwōd.*

bark
to bark, of dogs: *rorror, wañ.*

barkentine
a barkentine: *ripitwōdwōd.*

barnacles: *dile.*

barometer: *kein katu.*

barque: *baak.*

barracuda
Sphyraena barracuda: *jujukōp.*
Sphyraena forsteri: *jure, ñiitwa.*

barrel: *jepukpuk, tūraṃ.*
empty gasoline barrel: *kaajliiñ.*

barren: *orañe, war.*

barricade: *me.*

barrier
high barrier reef: *ubatak.*

Barringtonia
a plant, *Barringtonia asiatica*: *wōp.*

barter: *jobai.*

basalt
basaltic rock which floats: *tilaan.*

base: *ḷoñtak, pedped, wūn.*
base, foundation, bottom, stem, trunk: *dāpi-.*

baseball: *iakiu.*
a game, Marshallese women's baseball: *ejjebaō.*
baseball catcher: *kajji, kiaj.*
baseball field: *kūraaṇto.*
baseball glove: *kurob.*
baseball pitcher: *pijja.*
bat, baseball: *bōtta.*
fly ball, in baseball: *tōkai.*
ground ball in baseball: *kōro.*
inning in baseball: *teeñ.*
play baseball: *iakiu.*
pop-up, in baseball: *tōkai.*
runs, in a baseball game: *deḷọñ.*
wear a baseball glove: *kurobrob.*
first base: *bōōj.*
second base: *jekōn.*
third base: *tōōt.*

bashful: *abje, jjookok.*

basic
basic components of: *utō-.*

Basidiomycetes
a plant, toadstool, *Auricularia ampla* persoon and other earlike *Basidiomycetes* (fungi). Rogers: *lọjilñin kijdik.*

basin: *pejin.*

basis: *pedped, wūn.*

basket: *iep.*
a basket: *buwar.*
a basket for bearing tribute to a chief: *kōle.*
basket in which chiefs store left-overs: *perañ.*
braid a handle of a basket: *pirōkrōk.*
carry in a basket with long handle slung over shoulder: *aduwado.*
catch with net or basket: *bọur.*
fishing basket: *ṃṃar.*
hand basket of fine weave: *bōjọ.*
kind of basket: *aduwado, jāli.*
large basket: *iepān ṃaal, kilōk.*
open a bag or basket: *kōjjād.*
possessive classifier, flowers, medals,

necklaces, or fishing baskets: *m̧arō-*.
small basket: *jepe.*
small basket, two handles, made from fronds: *banonoor.*
wrap in basket or leaves: *tūrtūr.*

bass
bass, *Plectropomus truncatus*: *akajin, jo̧we, jowanuro̧ñ.*
bass, *Variola louti*: *ikmid, kanbōk, oļaļo.*
giant sea bass, *Promicrops lanceolatus/truncatus*: *jo̧we.*
giant sea bass, *Promicrops truncatus*: *jowāme.*

bass: *peij.*

bat
bat, baseball: *bōtta.*

Batavian parrotfish: *audam̧.*

batch: *baru.*
a batch: *lelkan.*

bath
bathe, take a bath: *tutu.*
bathing water of: *utō-.*
place for bathing: *jiadel.*
possessive classifier, bathing water: *utō-.*
provide with bathing water: *n̄autō-.*
royal bathing pool in old days: *juwadel.*
seldom bathe: *mijak dān.*
seldom bathe (see *tutu* (**tiwtiw**)): *jattutu.*
take a bath: *tulo̧k.*

Bathybembix
A shell, *Trochidae, Bathybembix aeola*: *jidduul.*

batter: *iiōk.*

battery: *pātōre.*
charge a battery: *jaaj.*

battle
battleship: *m̧ōnwa.*
fight a battle: *tarin̄ae.*
get ready for battle: *jabwea.*
killed in battle: *jak.*
one who flees from battle: *pikōt.*
signal made on the end of the *kie* of a canoe signifying battle: *jubwij.*

bawl: *lim̧ō.*
bawl out: *llu.*

bay: *ļam̧, peñak.*

bayonet: *jāje.*

be: *or.*
be at (always with directional): *ļo-.*
be formerly, used to be: *jo̧.*
be left: *pād.*
be somewhere: *pād.*
to be on both sides: *kōjab.*

beach: *tarkijet.*
at the lagoon beach: *iar.*
beach a boat for maintenance purposes: *to̧o̧k.*
beach a canoe to the water line: *jidaak.*
lagoon beach: *ar, parijet.*
lagoon beach of: *are.*
land edge of beach: *kappe.*
landward side of beach: *ioonkappe.*
place for beaching canoes: *towa.*
the beach borage: *kiden.*
to beach canoe or vessel: *ār.*

beacon: *jatiraito, kōmram.*

bead
foreign beads: *pinid.*
perspiration beads: *būļuuddik.*

beak: *bo̧ti.*

beam
beam of a house: *tur.*
canoe part, two beams to which *apet* (**hapeţ**) are lashed: *kie.*

beam
sunbeam: *koonaļ.*

bean
beans: *piin.*

bear
bear a burden: *inene.*
bear fruit: *jebar, le.*
bear fruit, of pandanus: *wūd.*
bear many flowers: *uwa.*
bear much fruit: *uwa.*
bear offspring: *kaliklik, kōmmour.*
bear tales: *bbōk.*
incapable of bearing offspring, of women only: *orañe, war.*
sporadic in bearing, of trees: *jepāl.*
start to bear fruit, of coconuts: *eo̧.*
to bear some hardship: *kajumej.*

bear: *pāār.*
bear hug: *jiburlep.*

beard: *kwōdeak.*
thick beard: *debo̧kut.*

beat: *kapipā, lij, m̧anm̧an, orā, pejaju, piit.*
beat regular time to music, pace: *buñtōn.*
beat upon: *penpen.*
beating of the waves: *depdep.*
chant and urge someone on by beating on a drum: *piniktak.*
club used for beating coconut husk for sennit: *jidjid.*
eat fish while fishing, beat up someone badly: *kōmennañ.*

fast beating of heart in fear: *kkūṃkūṃ*.
given to wife-beating: *ļaire*.
place for beating coconut husks after soaking in preparation for making sennit: *ṃṃal*.

beat
be beat: *kajjinōk, mejjeeļ*.

beatitude: *lọudiñdiñ*.

beautiful: *deọ, kōjaij, ṃōtañ, oļeọ, wōj*.
a very beautiful female: *to-jān-lañ*.
beautifully arranged: *ppānpān*.
extremely beautiful woman: *to-jān-lañ*.

beauty
a rare beauty: *to-jān-lañ*.
beauty spot: *il meej, ilmeej*.

because: *bwe, kōn, kōnke*.
because of: *kake*.
because, already: *dedeinke*.

beckon
beckon with the hand, downward motion: *jeeaaļ*.

become: *erom, jerkan*.

becoming
unbecoming: *jekkar*.

bed: *peet*.
bed (old word used in Bible): *aoj*.

bedlam: *pok*.

bee: *pi*.

beef: *kanniōkin kau, kau*.
corned beef: *kọọnpiip*.

beer: *pia*.

before: *ṃaa-, ṃṃōkaj, ṃokta*.

befriend: *jerā*.

beg: *owar, tūbļotak*.
beg for food: *kōjṃaal, kōkkau, uññar*.
beg insistently: *akweļap*.

beget: *keotak*.

begin: *bwilik ṃaan, jerkan, jjino*.
beginning: *buñ*.
come about, begin to have: *er-*.
to begin: *ruprupjọkur*.
to begin going: *bweradik*.

behavior: *kōṃṃan, ṃanit, ṃūtō-, ṃwil*.

behead: *jebbar*.

behind: *āliki-, ļokwa-, lik, liki*.

behold: *lo*.

being
human being: *armej*.

belch: *wūlik*.

believe: *lōke*.
"I don't believe it!": *eban*.
believe, faith, creed, pious: *tōmak*.
not believe: *jālōke*.

bell: *peeļ*.
sound of a bell or something rung: *tōññōļọk*.

Bellatrix
Bellatrix in Orion. : *Ļāātbwiinbar*.

bellicose: *wōtan*.

belligerent: *wōtan*.

bellow: *uwaañañ*.

belly: *je*.
crawl on the belly: *wāār*.

Belone
a fish, needlefish, *Belone platyura*: *tak*.

belong
belonging to: *aa-, wōja-*.

beloved: *jitōnbōro, wōlbo*.

below: *iuṃwi-, laļ*.

belt: *kañūr*.
belt keeper: *tāānjen*.
wear a belt: *kañūrñūr*.

bench: *jea*.

bend: *dukwal, kkubōl*.
bend forward and down: *jillọk*.
bend toward: *ṃal-*.
to bend: *ālkwōj, kiel*.
to bend down, of coconut shoots only: *kietak*.

beneath: *iuṃwi-*.

benediction: *jarin kōjeraaṃṃan*.

benefit: *jipañ*.

benevolence: *jouj*.

benign: *ineeṃṃan, jouj*.

bent: *kob*.
bent back: *ālkōk*.
bent over: *ālokjak, kkuṃliklik*.

bequest: *amṇak*.

bereave: *būroṃōj*.
visit the bereaved: *ilomej*.

beriberi: *pere*.

berry: *kwōle, lippiru*.

berserk: *wūdeakeak*.

berth: *wab*.

beseech: *owar*.

beseige
beseige a city: *nitbwil*.

beside: *turu-*.
beside oneself with fear: *ļọkjenaa-*.
stand beside: *kōjab*.

best
do one's best: *kattūkat*.

bet: *peta*.
"You bet!": *ekōjkan*.

call a bet in poker: *wadu.*
raise a bet: *peta.*

Betelgeuse
Betelgeuse in Orion: *Ļōkañebar.*

betray: *ketak, kinaak, liaakļọk.*

betroth: *koba.*

between: *kōtaa-.*
in between: *jāpo, loñ.*

bevel: *pābōļ.*

beverage: *dān.*
a beverage, diluted coconut sap: *jeruru.*
beverage of: *lime-.*
like alcoholic beverages: *ņompe.*
not sweet, of beverages: *jatōk.*
strong liquor, alcoholic beverage: *dānnin kadek.*
yeast beverage: *iij.*

bevy: *baru.*

bewail
bewail one's state: *aoļ.*

beware: *kōjparok.*
interjection: "Beware!": *iọuwọ.*

bewilder
bewildered: *pok.*

bewitch: *kkọọl.*

beyond: *jiṃa.*
beyond the point of: *kōptata.*

Bezoardicella
Morum macandrewi/teramachii or *Bezoardicella decussata/areola* or *Phalium glauca*: *jilel.*

bias: *kalijekļọk.*
biased: *jep.*

bib-overalls: *būrijōōt.*

Bible: *Baibōļ.*
possessive classifier, children, pets, money, watches, or Bible: *nāji-.*

bicker: *akwāāl.*
bickering: *bowōd.*

bicycle: *baajkōļ.*
bicycle pedal: *patōļ.*

bid: *pet.*

bide: *kattar.*

big: *kilep, ļap.*
big toe: *addi-lep.*
biggest: *ļaptata.*

big shot: *kāājāj, ļaikaalal, pālu.*

big wheel: *ļakkūk.*

big-eye
a fish, big-eye or burgy: *kie.*
a fish, big-eye or burgy, *Monotaxis grandoculis*: *ṃōjani, mejọkut.*
a fish, big-eyed or goggle-eyed scad fish or horse mackerel, *Trachurops crumenophthalmus*: *pāti.*

bigot: *jep.*

bike
motorbike: *wōtbai.*

bile: *at.*

bill: *piiļ.*

billiard
billiards: *piliet.*
light touching in billiards: *kij.*

billow: *ñōl.*

bind: *liāp, llok, loklok, pọpo, rojroj, tāte.*
bind with sennit: *eọeo.*

binocular
binoculars: *baiklaaj.*

biography: *bwebwenatoun mour an juon armej.*

biology: *katak kōn mour.*

bird: *bao.*
a big sea bird: *Kwe.*
a bird: *o, rapit.*
a bird that sings at dawn: *lọjiraan.*
a bird, white sea gull: *mānnimuuj.*
Micronesian pigeon, *Ducula oceanica*: *ṃuļe.*
black noddy, *Anous tenuirostris*: *jekad.*
black-footed albatross, *Diomedea nigripes*: *le.*
black-naped tern, *Sterna sumatrana*: *keār.*
blue-faced booby, *Sula dactylatra*: *lōļļap.*
blue-gray noddy, *Procelsterna caerulea*: *lọun Pikaar.*
bristle-thighed curlew, *Numenius tahitiensis*: *kōkkōk.*
brown booby, *Sula leucogaster*: *kaļo.*
brown noddy, *Anous stolidus*: *pejwak.*
crane, black *kabaj*: *melmelea.*
crane, black and white spotted *kabaj*: *kekebuona.*
crane, white *kabaj*: *keke.*
crested tern, *Thalasseus bergii*: *keār.*
found on Midway Island: *kōjat.*
golden plover, *Pluvialis dominica*: *kwōlej.*
golden plover, black variety, in breeding plumage: *ļakeke.*
great frigate bird, *Fregata minor*: *ak, toorlōñ.*
gull: *kūṃake.*
laysan albatross, *Diomedea immutabilis*: *le.*

lessor frigate bird, *Fregata ariel*: *ak, toorlōñ.*
long-tailed New Zealand cuckoo, *Urodynamis taitensis*: *wūdej.*
mallard, *Anas platyrhynchos*: *roñanpat.*
northern shoveler, *Anas clypeata*: *roñanpat.*
red-footed booby: *uteņ.*
red-footed booby, *Sula sula*: *nana.*
red-tailed tropicbird, *Phaethon rubricauda*: *ļokwājek.*
reef heron, *Egretta sacra*: *kabaj.*
ruddy turnstone, *Arenaria interpres*: *kōtkōt.*
sanderling, *Crocethia alba*: *kwōl.*
semi-palmate sandpiper, *Ereunetes pusillus*: *kwōl.*
short-eared owl, *Asio flammeus*: *lijeṃao, ṃao.*
sleeps in holes, similar to *pejwak*: *jādṃūṃ.*
slender-billed shearwater, *Puffinus tenuirostris*: *māntōl.*
small, about the size of a butterfly, lives in rocks around the shores of the Northwest Marshalls, smells sweet: *annañ.*
sooty shearwater, *Puffinus griseus*: *māntōl.*
sooty tern, *Sterna fuscata*: *mmej.*
wandering tattler, *Heteroscelus incanum*: *kidid.*
whimbrel, *Numenius phaeopus*: *kowak.*
white tern, *Gygis alba*: *mejǫ.*
white-tailed tropicbird, *Phaethon lepturus*: *jipkorōj.*
wild duck: *rañ.*
a catch of fish, crabs, or birds: *koņa-.*
a flock of birds flying over a school of fish: *la, wūnaak.*
a legendary bird: *ao.*
a pet bird that flies away and never returns: *lumǫǫrļǫk.*
a white sea bird: *bōrōj.*
baby bird, sooty tern, *mmej*: *jipila.*
baby birds: *kābwil.*
bird just getting first wing feathers and not big enough to eat: *kāwur.*
bird trap: *mejļat.*
birdcall: *kuur.*
birds feeding on surface of the ocean, diving and flying up again: *ṃōt.*
birds flying looking for fish: *wūnaak.*
catch birds at night: *jjǫñ.*
catch sleeping birds by hand: *jjoñ.*
defecate from trees, of birds: *de, edde.*
dive of birds or planes: *lōkā.*
flight of a group of birds or planes: *depouk.*
flock of birds: *iur, kōjwad.*
flock of birds fishing: *ļae.*
look for birds: *juakak.*
pit for bird fight: *nit.*
place where birds, fish, or clams gather: *ajañ.*
pluck feathers from a bird: *ttemakil.*
possessive classifier, fish, crabs, or birds: *koņa-.*
snare for catching birds: *keepep.*
tall tree where seabirds sleep: *joor.*
trap for catching birds: *kūṃōōr.*
tree in which birds roost and defecate: *jade.*
watch birds alight to locate roost: *akajok.*
watch birds to locate roost: *akade, alekǫ.*
young birds or aņimals: *koon.*

birth: *ļotak.*
afterbirth: *kiliblib.*
birthmark, dark: *buwak.*
birthplace dear and inherited: *jānnibadbad.*
childbirth: *utaṃwe.*
contractions during childbirth: *kōļo.*
give birth: *keotak, kōmmour.*
light birthmark: *jao.*
stillbirth: *jibuñ.*
woman who just gave birth: *kūrae.*

birthday: *raanin ļotak.*
birthday party: *keemem.*

biscuit: *petkōj.*
a food, biscuits and flour cooked together in water: *kōpjeļtak.*
biscuits: *būreej.*

bit
bits: *tipdikdik.*
broken in bits: *pedakilkil.*
little bit: *jibbūñ, jibūñ.*

bit
a bit, as used on boats: *pet.*

bitch: *kidu.*

bite: *kkij, kūk.*
bite lips: *aṃtōk.*
bite the dust: *ñarñar.*
eat with oversize bites: *kuborbor.*
not biting, of fish: *jakkūk, jaṃōñā.*

bitter: *meǫ.*
smell or taste sour or bitter, as milk, vinegar, or rice soup, etc.: *meñ.*

bivalve
a clam, bivalve: *jenǫ.*
a shell, small bivalve clam: *kalibok.*

a shell, small bivalve, clam: *ko̧nōt*.
close parts, as bivalve: *kkim*.
muscle in a bivalve: *kōjjem̧*.
sand clam, bivalve: *jukkwe*.

blab
blabber-mouth: *bbōk, ttal*.

black: *ditōb, kilmeej*.
black carbon on lantern chimney, used
to blacken tattoos: *m̧am̧ōj*.
black magic: *kkōpāl, ttabōn*.
black magic performed by a sorcerer
using a husked coconut: *kaurur
jiañ*.
pitch black, said of nights: *innijek*.
pitchblack: *maroklep*.
rub in black carbon on tattoos:
item̧am̧ōj.

bladder: *bok*.

blade
blade of machete: *mejān jāje*.

blame: *kōmmatōr, n̄aruo-*.
blame someone or something: *jekpen*.

bland: *mera*.

blanket: *būļañkōj, ko̧o̧j*.
blanket of: *ko̧je-*.
cuddle under a blanket: *kilbur*.
mat used as blanket or sheet: *kilbur*.
possessive classifier, blankets and other
things used as blankets: *ko̧je-*.
possessive classifier, mat or blanket or
mattress: *kinie-*.
to provide with a blanket: *n̄ako̧je-*.
use a blanket: *ko̧o̧joj*.
wrap up in a blanket: *tūroro*.

blaspheme: *būļaajpiim*.

blast: *bokko̧lo̧k*.

blaze
burning, blaze, lighted: *urur*.

bleach: *jerajko*.
bleached: *eor*.
to bleach pandanus leaves over the
fire: *rar*.

bleacher: *jea*.

bleary
bleary-eyed: *mejkōr*.

bleat: *rraakak*.

bleed: *bōtōktōk*.
bleeding: *pilin̄lin̄*.
nosebleed: *ļōjo*.

blend: *kāre*.
blend in: *peljo*.

blenny
a fish, blenny, *Istiblennius paulus*
(Mejit): *kudo̧kwōl*.
a fish, general term for all blenny:
jibbaļañ.

bless
blessed: *jeraam̧m̧an*.

blind: *kun an ļaam̧, pilo*.
blind leading the blind: *tōlpilo*.
blinded by sunlight: *tam̧tam̧*.
blinded with smoke: *mejko*.

blindfold
a game, with blindfolds: *lijjapillo*.

blink: *mājkun, rom*.

bliss: *lo̧udin̄din̄*.

blister
blister, chicken pox: *bok*.
small blisters from over exposure to
sun: *il*.

bloat
bloated: *m̧aal*.

block
blockade: *bbaar*.
blocked: *boņ*.
to block: *pinej*.

block
concrete block: *būļak, pirōk*.
hat block form, any mold, any form:
m̧ōn̄akjān.

block: *būļak*.
block and tackle: *tekōļ*.

blood: *bōtōktōk, da*.
blood clot: *mekak*.
blood pressure: *aerin bōtōktōk*.
blood vessel: *eke, iaļan bōtōktōk*.
bloodletting: *kadkad*.
covered with blood: *daat*.
mixed blood: *aiņokko*.
smell of blood: *meļļā*.
thick blood: *mekak*.

bloom: *bbōl, bōl*.
start to bloom: *nōr*.

blossom: *bbōl*.
pandanus blossom: *tūar*.

blow: *pāl, uuk*.
blow gently, of wind: *lladikdik*.
blow sharply, of wind: *letōn̄*.
blow the nose: *ba*.
blow, of the wind: *detak*.
blown: *peļļok*.
to blow one's nose: *uwur*.

blow
to duck a blow: *wōmak*.

blowtorch: *pilerab*.

blubber: *kūriij, wiwi*.

blue: *būļu*.

blue jeans
denim trousers, blue jeans, Levis:
tanim.

bluegum: *būļukam̧*.

bluff: *bū̧lab.*

bluing: *bū̧lu.*

blunt: *bwijil, kkōb, lijib.*

blur
fog, dim, haze, blur: *tab.*

blush: *kilbūrōrō.*

board: *rā.*
canoe part, board that runs lengthwise on the leeside, above the *jouj* (the bottom half): *jānel.*
checker board: *jekaboot.*

board
to board: *uwe.*

boast: *jājjāj, kōņkōm̧man, likōmjāje.*
boastful: *jājjāj, kōmmejāje.*

boat: *booj, wa.*
a bit, as used on boats: *pet.*
a toy, boat of half coconut: *wa bweọ.*
bail out water from canoe or boat: *ānen.*
be overcrowded, of boats or vehicles (see *kaddoujuj*): *douj.*
beach a boat for maintenance purposes: *tọọk.*
boat decorations: *ļōb.*
boat of: *waa-.*
boat passage on reef: *toorwa.*
boat passage through a reef: *tọọr.*
break a boat in: *rupe bōkā.*
build a canoe or boat: *jekjek wa.*
design edges of canoes or boats: *n̄adn̄ad.*
drinking water containers on a canoe or boat: *kōb.*
picket boat: *ļoon.*
pitch, of a boat: *m̧m̧ōt, m̧ōt.*
possessive classifier, canoe, ship, boat, or vehicle: *waa-.*
rails of boats: *reeļ.*
repair a boat: *āe.*
riggings of boats: *rikin.*
row a boat: *oru.*
sailboat: *wajerakrōk.*
stranded, of canoes, boats or ships: *eọtōk.*
swift, of canoes or boats, nautical term: *ļļaeoeo.*
to sail a canoe or boat singlehandedly: *wajekā.*
tow, as a boat: *aik.*
use a boat: *wawa.*
wake of a boat: *aod.*

boatswain: *bojin.*

bob
to bob: *m̧m̧ōļeiñiñ.*

bobby pin: *piin.*

body: *ānbwin.*
body odor, disagreeable: *bbū̧laplap.*
body shape, looks: *rọkwōj.*
lift weights to build up body: *kaddipenpen.*
somebody: *juon.*
stretch the body: *makōļkōļ.*
well built body: *bakūk.*

Boerhavia
Boerhavia duffusa: *dāpijdekā.*

boil: *du.*
a food, preserved breadfruit boiled or baked without wrapping: *koļeiaat.*
a food, unleavened dough cooked by boiling: *jāibo.*
boil, of water only: *buļuļļuļ.*
to boil pandanus: *aintiin.*

boil: *wōt.*
core of a boil: *wūn.*

boisterous: *koļap, llejlej, peran.*

bold: *jjọjọ, kijon̄, mejel kil, peran.*
bold water: *jirūm̧le.*
not bold: *mmejọkunkun.*

bolt
to bolt one's food: *kōdālōb, orjin.*

bolt: *jikūru.*

bolt
bolt of cloth: *kap.*

bomb: *baam̧, bọkutan̄.*

bon voyage: *kōjjem̧ļọk.*

bond: *korak.*

bone: *di.*
ankle bones: *lijaakkwōlele.*
backbone: *dilep.*
breastbone of a fowl: *pājen̄.*
fishbone stuck in throat: *paļ.*
remove bones from fish: *iiaak.*

bonito
a fish, bonito, *Katsuwonus pelamis*: *ļōjabwil.*
fishing method, for bonitos: *kōļōjabwil.*
herd of bonitos that enters lagoon and can't find its way out: *ajilowōd.*

bonus: *boņōj.*

booby
a bird, blue-faced booby, *Sula dactylatra*: *lōļļap.*
a bird, brown booby, *Sula leucogaster*: *kaļo.*
a bird, red-footed booby: *uteņ.*
a bird, red-footed booby, *Sula sula*: *nana.*

book: *bok.*

bookworm
damage caused by termites or bookworms: *dile.*

boom: *buuṃ, rojak.*
canoe part, decorations of feathers on masthead, boomtips, and sail: *deñḷọk.*
canoe part, end of yard, boom (*rojak ṃaan*): *baḷ.*
socket for end of boom (one at each end of canoe): *dipāākāk.*

boom: *bokkoḷọk, jañai.*

boondocks: *debọkut, mar.*

boost: *iuun.*

boot: *jibuut.*

Bootes
Arcturus in Bootes: *Ad.*
stars in Bootes (beta, mu, nu) and mu in Corona Borealis: *Ok-an-adik.*

borage
the beach borage: *kiden.*

border: *tōrerei-.*
border on mat or stone edge of road: *apar.*

bore: *ddāil.*
bored: *kidel.*

born
be born: *ḷotak.*
first-born: *ṃaanje, utṃaan.*
high-born person: *arōṃṃan.*
well born: *arōṃṃan.*
contents of newborn's intestines: *jā.*

borrow: *jata.*
procure something by flattery or by "borrowing": *kōrabōl.*

bosom: *diklōñ, ob.*

boss: *bọọj, jeṃṃaan.*
be bossy: *kōbbọọjọj.*

both: *aolep, jiṃor.*

bother: *ikien, ūrōj.*
annoyed or bothered by noise: *uwaroñ.*
be bothered by something: *ikdeelel.*
bothered: *abṇōṇō, aploñloñ.*

Bothus
a fish, flounder, *Bothus mancus*: *badej.*

bottle: *bato.*
bottle used for coconut sap: *jeib.*
large bottle, demijohn: *teemjọọn.*
place a bottle (*kor*) at the end of coconut shoot to collect sap initially: *kajokkor.*
ready for a bottle, of coconut shoots only: *raane-bōkāān.*
small bottle or jar: *bōkā.*
tall bottle: *kude.*
wash bottles: *naṃnaṃ.*

bottom: *epat, ḷokwa-, laḷ.*
base, foundation, bottom, stem, trunk: *dāpi-.*
bottom of: *kapi, kapi-.*
rock bottom: *ikjet.*
scrape bottom: *eoṇ.*
to warm one's bottom by the fire: *rabwij.*

bottoms up: *kodia.*

bough: *ra.*

boulder: *ejṃaan.*

bound: *pọpo.*
boundary line: *kōtaa-.*

bout: *im.*

bow
bow down: *badik.*
bow one's head: *dukwal.*
bow the head, as in prayer: *jillọk.*
to bow: *ṃajid.*

bow: *ḷobōrwa.*
bow line, used to tie up an anchor: *lokṃaan.*
bow spray: *ṇojọ.*
bow waves from a ship: *at.*
bowsprit: *ḷobōrwa.*
steer a course with land on one's bow: *anlọk.*

bow: *lippọṇ.*
shoot a bow and arrow: *lippọṇ.*

bow-legged: *māro, perakrōk.*

bow-wow: *roror.*

bowel
guts, intestines, bowels, offal, innards: *ṃajñal.*
loose bowels: *ilọklọje, wōtōdtōd.*

bower: *jik.*

bowl
a small dug-out bowl for pounding food: *jāpe.*
rice bowl: *jokkwi.*
wooden bowl: *jāpe.*

box: *bọọk.*
cash box: *jiipkako, pāāñ.*
short punches in boxing, as in the beating of a drum: *tūraṃ.*
toolbox: *tuuḷbọọk.*
use a box: *bọọkọk.*

box: *bait.*

boxfish
a fish, boxfish, *Ostracion cubicus*: *būḷ.*
a fish, boxfish, *Ostracion sebae*: *pel.*

boy: *ḷaddik.*
a boy or man whose appearance makes everyone smile: *ḷḷajkōnkōn.*

cabin boy: *buwae.*
that boy (close to neither of us): *ļeeņ, ļeieņ, ļouweo.*
that boy (close to you): *ļōņe, ļōņeņe.*
these boys (close to me): *ļōmarā, ļōmarārā, ļōmaro.*
these boys (close to us both): *ļōmarein.*
this boy: *ļein.*
this boy (close to me): *ļeo, ļōe.*
this boy (close to us both): *ļeiō.*
those boys (close to neither of us): *ļōmarāraņ, ļōmaroro.*
those boys (close to you): *ļōmarārane, ļōmarane.*
vocative to boys: *būrǫ.*
what man? What boy?: *ļōt.*

brace
roof brace: *aninwoļā.*

bracelet: *pāāñkōļ.*
wear a bracelet: *pāāñkōļ.*

brackish
brackish, of water: *kōļaebar.*

brag
brag about one's self: *jājjāj.*

braid: *bujek.*
braid a handle of a basket: *pirōkrōk.*
braid, of hair: *pirōkrōk.*
braid, tie: *bobo.*
clean whiskers off of newly braided sennit: *kōrōnāl.*

brain: *kōmālij.*

brake: *būreek.*

bramble
brambles: *kālōklōk.*

branch: *ra.*
lasso a branch: *rajāl.*
major branch of a tree and its contents: *mwiañ.*
small branches: *radikdik.*
rustling of leaves and branches: *mmewiwi.*
throw a rope over a branch: *rajāl.*

brand: *kakōļļe.*

brash: *mmaelep.*

brass: *būraaj, jiniboǫr.*

brave: *kijoñ, pen būruo-, peran.*
magic to make soldiers brave: *mǫun.*
seat of brave emotions: *at.*
seat of bravery: *aj.*

brawl: *im, ire.*

brawn
brawny: *majeļ.*

bread: *pilawā, pilawā mat.*
a food, coconut bread, from copra and flour and sap or sugar: *jinkōļar.*
loaf of bread: *ļoob.*
rise, of bread: *jib.*

breadfruit
a food, balls of preserved breadfruit sweetened and boiled in coconut oil: *makillō.*
a food, breadfruit baked in earth oven: *kōpjar.*
a food, breadfruit cooked on coals and scraped: *kwanjin.*
a food, breadfruit soup: *jokkwōpin mā.*
a food, cooked and pounded breadfruit, taro, bananas, or nuts mixed with grated coconut: *wūdeñ.*
a food, cooked preserved breadfruit smothered in grated coconut: *kubaļ.*
a food, dried overripe breadfruit: *jāānkun.*
a food, nuts of breadfruit, cooked: *kwōlejiped.*
a food, plain baked ripe breadfruit: *mejāliraan.*
a food, preserved breadfruit: *bwiro.*
a food, preserved breadfruit boiled or baked without wrapping: *koļeiaat.*
a food, preserved breadfruit mixed with arrowroot and coconut sap or sugar, wrapped in breadfruit leaves and baked: *bwiro iiōk.*
a food, preserved breadfruit or *peru* flattened and covered with breadfruit leaves and baked: *kajipedped.*
a food, preserved breadfruit, formed into loaves, wrapped in coconut leaves, and cooked on fire: *maio.*
a food, preserved dried breadfruit: *mōņakjān.*
a food, ripe breadfruit mixed with coconut oil and cooked in pots: *nāpnāpe.*
a food, soup of soft rice or breadfruit: *jokkwōp.*
a food, very ripe breadfruit baked in coconut milk: *pǫļjej.*
a food, very ripe breadfruit baked in coconut oil: *kappokpok, mōjjero.*
a food, very ripe breadfruit mixed with coconut milk: *kaļǫ.*
a gathering of people to celebrate the onset of breadfruit season in summer by making offerings to Jebro, the god of breadfruit: *mama.*
a plant, breadfruit variety: *Mejwaan, Metete, Petaaktak.*
a plant, general term for the

breadfruit, *Artocarpus incisus* (Thunb.) L. F. Moraceae: *mā.*
an insect, small, brown, often found around rotten breadfruit: *māniddik.*
baked breadfruit: *liped.*
breadfruit blown down by the wind: *mābuñ.*
breadfruit bud: *tōbak.*
breadfruit flower: *elme, kabbok.*
collect coconuts or breadfruit: *jinwōd.*
cut tree trunk into pieces, as breadfruit for making canoe: *kabbok.*
harvest first fruit of coconut, breadfruit, or pandanus: *akeo̧.*
inedible portion near stem of pandanus or breadfruit: *m̧ak.*
knead preserved breadfruit: *tola.*
male flower of breadfruit: *tōbak.*
net, large-meshed, bag-shaped, for washing arrowroot and soaking breadfruit: *do.*
not ripe, of breadfruit: *kinbūt.*
overripe breadfruit: *meimed.*
overripe spoiled breadfruit: *mālo̧k.*
overripe, of breadfruit without seeds: *mejbak.*
pick breadfruit with a stick: *kōm̧kōm̧.*
portion of fruit near stem of pandanus or breadfruit: *ainm̧ak.*
pound breadfruit or taro: *jukjuk.*
ripe, of breadfruit: *kalo, kōt.*
season for breadfruit and pandanus: *wōtōn.*
sliced unripe breadfruit cooked in coconut milk: *bwilitudek.*
smallest breadfruit or pandanus remaining on tree at end of season: *ļajdeñ.*
smell of preserved breadfruit: *bbiroro.*
smell of roasting breadfruit: *kkwanjinjin.*
stalk inside bunch of bananas or breadfruit: *perañ.*
stick for picking breadfruit: *kein kōm̧.*
stick for stirring fire, turning breadfruit while cooking, etc.: *jabōn pe.*
to roast breadfruit: *kwanjin.*
unripe fallen breadfruit: *māirrūb.*
very ripe, overripe, of breadfruit only: *mmed.*
windfallen breadfruit: *mābuñ.*

breadth
breadth of an island: *wūjaļoñ.*

break: *bwilo̧k, rujruj, ruprup.*
break a boat in: *rupe bōkā.*
break a fast: *dao.*
break a taboo, desecrate: *kōtrāe.*
break loose, as boat from sand: *jjelo̧k.*
break off of: *tooj.*
break something in: *kkaan.*
break taboos attendant to certain medicines while under treatment: *aļo̧k.*
break through: *deblo̧k.*
break wind: *jiñ, rūb.*
break, as a branch: *kwōj.*
break, as a rope: *m̧wijkōk.*
break, as a stick: *m̧o̧ruj.*
break, sticks or bones: *kwōj.*
breakable: *pidodo.*
breaking of waves: *buñraak, rere.*
breaking waves: *buñn̦o.*
do something that will result in misfortune, such as breaking a taboo: *ļōkajem̧.*
easy to break or tear: *m̧ōdm̧ōd.*
misfortune due to breaking of a taboo: *ruwe.*
not break wind often (see *jiñ* (**jig**)): *jājjiñjiñ.*
smell of breaking wind: *bwiin-jiñ.*
taboo breaker: *neen wūlej.*
take a break: *kakkije.*
to pull and break objects such as string, rope, wire or grass: *tūm̧tūm̧.*

break
take a break: *ibbuku.*

breakfast: *m̧abuñ.*
eat breakfast: *m̧abuñ.*

breast: *ittūt, ninnin.*
breastbone of a fowl: *pājeñ.*
enlargement of breasts at puberty: *bwā.*

breath
breathe quick and hard: *mmenonoun kijdik.*
dying breath: *bōk ob.*
hold one's breath: *dek.*
out of breath: *jabjabmenowa-.*
short of breath: *jabjabmenowa-, jeeklo̧k.*
to breathe: *menono.*
sniff, inhale, breathe: *kōbotuut.*

bred
ill-bred: *pāpijek.*
well-bred: *arōm̧m̧an.*

breed: *ine.*

breeze: *an̄, ḷarere.*
a breeze forecasting calm weather: *an̄inlur.*
coolness of a breeze: *lladikdik.*
easterly breeze: *an̄ōlto.*
fair breeze: *m̧akroro.*
fresh breeze: *m̧akroro.*
shoot the breeze: *kōmāltato.*
steady light breeze: *an̄jānjān.*
westerly breeze: *an̄ōltak.*

breezy: *lladikdik.*

bribe: *wiaik būruo-.*

brick: *būḷak, pirōk.*

bridge
bridge of ship: *būrij.*

brief: *kadu, kanu.*

bright: *kabōlbōl, mālōtlōt, meram.*
bright colored: *ilar, meej.*
loud, of colors, bright: *rōōj.*

brilliant: *jatōltōl.*

brim
full to the brim: *dujejjet, lōn̄ mājidjid.*

bring: *bōk, uke.*
bring food to a chief: *ekkan.*
bring food to a chief or lineage head: *eo̧jek.*
bring forth: *kōmmour.*
spend last moments together, farewell occasion, bring to a finish: *kōjjem̧ḷo̧k.*
to bring foods with songs as refreshments to a group of men building a canoe or house to keep their morale up, usually done by the womenfolk of a community: *jemjem māāl.*

bristle: *aujro̧n̄ro̧n̄.*
bristle, strand of hair: *tōōḷ.*
bristling hair standing on end from terror: *rro̧n̄.*

brittle: *jjem̧, kkōm̧, pidodo.*
dry and brittle: *n̄an̄.*

broad: *depakpak.*
a game, high jump or broad jump: *kappin̄.*
have broadened horizons: *loḷo̧kjeṇ.*
slim-waisted and broad-shouldered: *kāāj in kabwebwe.*

broadcast: *bōōjōj.*

broil
a food, fish eaten half broiled but still raw: *koubub.*
broil, on hot stones: *jinkadool.*
broiler: *jijidiin̄.*

broke: *pāān̄kōrab.*
broke, financially: *būrook, oḷiin̄.*
broke, out of money: *jar.*

broken: *jintanji, jo̧re, jorrāān, m̧o̧ruj, rup.*
broken in bits: *pedakilkil.*
broken-hearted: *rup bōro.*
broken, of engines: *wōla.*

brood: *ro.*

broom: *burum̧.*

brothel: *m̧ōn utḷam̧.*

brother
brother-sister relationship: *jem̧nājin.*
older brother: *jei-.*
relation between two brothers-in-law who are married to two sisters: *jemānji-.*
wife's brother: *m̧m̧aan.*
younger brother: *jati-.*

brow: *dam̧.*
eyebrow: *āt.*

brown: *būrawūn, m̧ōṇakṇak.*
brown coconut leaves which fall: *m̧we.*
multicolored, spotted, usually brownish: *kkaadad.*

brown booby
a bird, brown booby, *Sula leucogaster*: *kaḷo.*

Bruguiera
a plant, mangrove, *Bruguiera conjugata* (L.) Merrill: *jon̄.*

bruise: *buwaj.*
bruised: *mao, obab.*

brunette: *jakmeej.*

brush: *būraj, kutak.*
brush off: *pikūr, popo.*
brush teeth: *kurkur.*

brush
lower part of tree, brush, or grass: *wūn.*

bubble: *buḷuḷḷuḷ.*

bucket: *bakōj.*
bucket or can for drawing water from a well: *keikōb.*
container, usually five-gallon paint bucket: *bat.*

buckle: *bakōḷ.*
buckle down: *lin̄ōr.*
buckled: *ālokjak, kob.*

bud: *albok.*
breadfruit bud: *tōbak.*
bud forth: *juḷ.*
budding: *bōro̧ro.*

buddy: *kom̧bani.*

budge: *m̧m̧akūt.*
budget: *bajet.*
buffet: *ñal.*
steady waves buffeting the shore: *ninārār.*
bug: *kij.*
build: *ejaak, ejej, kajjuur, kkal, kōm̧m̧an.*
build a canoe or boat: *jekjek wa.*
build a platform: *ppe.*
build attachments onto a canoe: *peļoñ.*
build up: *ejej.*
build up a pile of rocks: *ppe.*
building materials: *kōbwebwei-.*
lift weights to build up body: *kaddipenpen.*
well built body: *bakūk.*
building: *em̧.*
go out of a building: *wannabōj.*
new building: *akadik.*
possessive classifier, houses or other buildings: *em̧.*
bulb
lightbulb: *tōm̧a.*
bulge: *bbaļokļok.*
bulging: *buļǫkwōjkwōj.*
bulk
bulky: *buļǫkwōjkwōj.*
bulldozer: *baru.*
bullet: *joot.*
graze, as a bullet, chipped: *tām̧ǫņ.*
bulletin: *kōjjeļā.*
bulwark: *jālitak, reeļ.*
bum
to bum: *bam̧, kañkañ.*
bump
bump a sore or wound: *keeñjak, kkeñaj.*
bump and grind: *kajikia.*
bump into: *itaak.*
bump into each other: *im̧aajaj.*
bumpy: *kajkaj, kkaj.*
to bump: *kkaj.*
bump: *būtti.*
tiny bumps on glans penis: *jarōj.*
bumper: *bam̧bōr.*
occur one after another, consecutively, bumper-to-bumper: *kij-ļokwan-doon.*
bunch
a bunch of dried pandanus leaves for thatch: *jim̧.*
bunch of bananas: *āj, uror.*
bunch of pandanus keys: *ajjen.*
bunch of ripe and drinkable coconuts: *uror.*
bundle: *jepjep, tūrtūr.*
a food, bundled and baked spongy meat of sprouted coconut: *iutūr.*
bundle of goods wrapped with a square of cloth: *būroojki.*
bundle of long objects such as spears, fish poles, etc.,: *tūr.*
bundle of mats: *kōtōm̧.*
bundle that has been wrapped, sticks or pandanus leaves: *tūr.*
cloth for wrapping bundle of goods: *būroojki.*
tie up a bundle: *wūnit.*
bunk: *bañ.*
buoy: *buwae.*
tie up to a buoy: *emjak.*
burden: *ddo, iabuñ.*
be overburdened: *ajjibanban.*
bear a burden: *inene.*
burdensome: *ailparo, parok.*
bureau: *tūroot.*
burglar
burglarize: *kǫǫt.*
burgy
a fish, big-eye or burgy: *kie.*
a fish, big-eye or burgy, *Monotaxis grandoculis*: *m̧ōjani, mejǫkut.*
burial
ceremony performed six days after burial, gravel is spread over grave: *eoreak.*
burlap
burlap sack: *pāāk.*
burn: *bwil, māāņ, ttil.*
burn a tree: *jidep.*
burn hair off: *rirar.*
burn to ashes: *melkwaarar.*
burn, of eyes: *korōt.*
burning, blaze, lighted: *urur.*
burnt: *tuļaar.*
incapable of catching fire and burning: *tokwiia.*
sunburned: *kakilkil.*
burp: *wūlik.*
burst: *ebjak.*
burst into flame: *urrūļǫk.*
loud, as of a burst: *pañijñij.*
bury: *kallib.*
bus: *baj.*
bush: *mar.*
a bush: *debǫkut.*
prune a bush: *jipijuļ.*
rosebush: *utrooj.*
shake a bush or tree: *im̧uk.*
smell of leaves of bushes: *kkumarmar.*

bushed: *orā.*

bushel: *jepukpuk.*

business: *peejnej.*
company, business usage: *kombani.*

bust
wiped out, busted, stoned: *kwōp.*

busy: *bajbaj, ṃad, poub, utaṃwe.*
be busy with: *lokjak, ṃadjake.*
busy man: *ḷowaṇwoṇ.*
busy woman: *lowaṇwoṇ.*
very busy: *ailparo, pālo, parok.*

but: *ak, akō.*
but as: *ijoke.*
but what: *akō.*
but what can I do: *ab in et.*

butt: *pid.*
butt of cigarette: *jablọk.*
butt of pandanus key: *ṃak.*
buttocks: *jepe rūr, lọdiñi, pid.*
posterior, buttocks: *lọk.*

butter: *bōta.*

butterfly: *babbūb.*

butterfly fish
butterfly fish, *Chaetodon anriga* (Ebon): *utot.*
butterfly fish, *Chaetodon ocellatus*: *dibab.*
butterfly fish, *Chaetodon ornatissimus*: *bwine.*
general term for butterfly fish: *rūbōb.*
thread-backed butterfly fish, *Heniochus acuminatus*: *ek-bōlōk.*

button: *batin.*

buy: *wia.*
buy drinks and food for a group: *jọut.*
buy gifts for: *jọut.*

by-pass: *ḷe.*

by-product
a by-product of *jekaro*: *jekajeje.*

cab
taxicab: *tāākji.*

cabbage: *kapej.*

cabin: *kāpin.*
cabin boy: *buwae.*

cabinet: *tūroot.*
food cabinet: *pāāntōre.*

cable: *kebōḷ.*
cable, chain, referred to in Bible: *tomede.*
guy rope or cable: *kae.*

cackle: *dekakkak.*

Cadiidae
a shell, *Cadiidae, Corculum impressum/monstrosum/cardissa*: *kūkōr.*

Caesalpinia
a plant, *Caesalpinia pulcherrima* L.: *jeiṃōta.*

Caesar: *Jijer.*

cafeteria: *ṃōn ṃōñā.*

cajole: *reel.*

cake: *keek.*
a food, cake doughnut: *kōtabañ.*

calamity: *jerata, mariprip.*
distracted by some calamity: *ḷọkjenaa-.*

calculate: *jennade.*

caldron: *kōṃa.*

calendar: *aḷōṃṇak, kōḷọṇta.*

calf
calf of leg: *ajaj.*

call: *kkūr, laṃōj.*
answer to call: *eọroñ.*
birdcall: *kuur.*
call a bet in poker: *wadu.*
call at: *ṃalōk.*
call or entice animals or children to come near: *kkaal.*
call to: *katūbtūb.*
call to come: *āñiñintok.*
calling someone by name: *āñiñin.*
dance call, move: *ṃọo.*
quick when called (see *āñiia* (**yagiyyah**)): *āñiie.*
report when called: *eọroñ.*
slow when called (see *āñiie* (**yagiyyẹy**)): *āñiia.*

callous: *kurbalōklōk.*

Callyodon
parrotfish, *Callyodon bataviensis*: *audaṃ.*
parrotfish, *Callyodon microrhinos*: *alwor.*
parrotfish, *Callyodon pulchellus*: *lala, pālpilikio.*

calm: *jokwane, lur.*
a breeze forecasting calm weather: *āñinlur.*
interim period between stormy seasons, usually a calm spell: *jo.*
onset of calm season: *añkidid.*
smooth and calm, of water: *ḷae.*

Calophyllum
a plant, *Calophyllum inophyllum* L. (Guttiferae): *jijo, lukwej.*

camel: *kameḷ.*

camera: *pija.*

camouflage: *kōjakkōlkōl.*
camouflaged: *ttino.*

camp: *kāām.*
campaign: *pata.*
  campaigning: *karreelel.*
campus: *kāāṃbōj.*
can
  bucket or can for drawing water from a well: *keikōb.*
  can of food: *kuwat.*
  can of meat: *kāān.*
  canned sardines: *jeṃṃa.*
  tin can: *kuwat.*
can: *jor, maroñ.*
canal: *tọọr.*
Canavalia
  a plant, *Canavalia spp.* (Leguminosae): *marḷap.*
cancel: *kāānjeḷ.*
Cancer
  stars in Cancer: *Iju-pilo.*
candidate: *jokālōt.*
candle: *kāāntōḷ.*
candy: *jọkleej, ḷọḷe.*
  coconut candy: *ametōṃa.*
cane: *jokoṇ.*
  use a cane: *jokoṇkoṇ.*
Canes
  alpha in Canes Venatici: *Wōd-Wāto-eṇ.*
Canis
  possibly alpha in Canis Minor: *Bake-eo.*
cannon: *pakke.*
cannot: *ban.*
canoe: *wa.*
  a canoe with its sail flapping: *añōppāl.*
  a game, racing toy outrigger canoes: *kariwutut.*
  a place for fishing canoes on an island: *mien.*
  a toy, canoe made from very light wood: *riwut.*
  arrival of many canoes: *lipopo.*
  bail out water from canoe or boat: *ānen.*
  be smashed against something, of canoes: *ubwe.*
  beach a canoe to the water line: *jidaak.*
  build a canoe or boat: *jekjek wa.*
  build attachments onto a canoe: *peḷọñ.*
  canoe about to capsize: *tọ.*
  canoe keel made from *kōñe* wood: *erer.*
  canoe of: *waa-.*
  canoe part, reinforcement close to both ends: *matātōp.*
  canoe ready to sail at any time: *waan peḷḷọk.*
  canoe that cannot go in shallow water: *kaplep.*
  canoe-surfing, when sailing down wind: *kōttōmāle.*
  crutch used for pushing boom of canoe away: *jeḷọk.*
  cut tree trunk into pieces, as breadfruit for making canoe: *kabbok.*
  decorations made from feathers of frigate birds, one on each tip of the sail on a chief's canoe: *kadulele.*
  design edges of canoes or boats: *ñadñad.*
  dimension of a canoe between hull and outrigger: *kōṃñūr.*
  drinking water containers on a canoe or boat: *kōb.*
  fastest method of righting a canoe after it has capsized in order to escape sharks: *keilupako.*
  fishing method with a canoe and line on the ocean side: *liklọk.*
  fishing method, at night from a canoe near lagoon shore: *eoojjaak.*
  fishing method, to fish from a canoe: *urōk.*
  fishing method, use hand line from canoe in deep ocean for fish other than tuna: *kōddāpilpil.*
  fishing method, using a canoe and drifting with the wind and current in a lagoon, line fishing: *peḷọk.*
  fleet of canoes, ships, or planes: *inej.*
  go on a vehicle or sailing canoe (used with directional enclitics (and postpositions)): *tar-.*
  haul canoe or vessel up on shore: *ār.*
  keep a canoe or boat full-sailing: *kabwijer.*
  large outrigger canoe, for sailing: *tipñōl.*
  large sailing canoe: *jitōñ.*
  lashing technique used on canoes: *inwijet.*
  leeward side of a canoe: *kōja.*
  line used to decrease the sail on a canoe: *lukwar.*
  new canoe: *akadik.*
  not paddle easily, of canoes (see *kōrkaakiie* (**kerkahakiyyẹy**)): *kōrkaakiia.*
  paddle a canoe so as to hold it against current: *kab.*
  paddle easily, of canoes (see

kōrkaakiia (**kerkahakiyyah**)): *kōrkaakiie.*
paddling a canoe for pleasure: *kōrkaak.*
paddling canoe: *kōrkōr.*
paint or chop up to a line in canoe building: *atar.*
place for beaching canoes: *towa.*
plunge of a canoe or ship: *m̧ōt.*
possessive classifier, canoe, ship, boat, or vehicle: *waa-.*
pounding or thudding of canoes together: *ļļwūjļwūj.*
push away a canoe: *taar.*
roller for launching canoe: *ļo̧ñ, ļoñtak.*
ropes that go from top of the mast down to both ends of sailing canoe: *jo̧m̧ur.*
sail model canoes: *bwilbwil.*
sennit used for tying canoes: *ām.*
signal made on the end of the *kie* of a canoe signifying battle: *jubwij.*
small house on canoe: *bo̧ktōk, pelpel.*
something that has fallen from a canoe underway: *enkanaode.*
steer canoe with paddle on right of stern to keep bow straight: *audik.*
stranded, of canoes, boats or ships: *eo̧tōk.*
string for towing toy canoe in water, held in middle with ends attached to ends of canoe for steering: *tokadkad.*
swift, of canoes or boats, nautical term: *ļļaeoeo.*
tack canoe to leeward: *kabbe.*
tack, change sail from one end of canoe to the other to tack: *diak.*
take good care of a canoe: *kkein wa.*
take in water from the top of a canoe: *timaruk.*
the outrigger side of a canoe: *retam.*
to arrive, of a canoe: *jidaak.*
to beach canoe or vessel: *ār.*
to chant while drawing up a canoe or other such cooperative work: *ñijir.*
to dry and become seasoned, of lumber, as in canoe building: *pit.*
to paddle a canoe on the starboard side to change course: *auretam.*
to sail a canoe or boat singlehandedly: *wajekā.*
to sail a toy canoe: *riwut.*
to tip, as of canoe: *ām.*
type of lashing applied to the *kie* section of a canoe: *ļļōko̧.*
use a canoe: *wawa.*
wave-guard on a canoe: *ubwen̦o.*

canoe parts
after-part when outrigger is on port side: *jabdik.*
board that runs lengthwise on the leeside, above the *jouj* (the bottom half): *jānel.*
bottom part of canoe: *jouj.*
cleat for tying sheet: *jirukli.*
curved piece connecting outrigger to hull: *apet.*
decorations of feathers on masthead, boomtips, and sail: *deñļo̧k.*
edge of sail fastened to the gaff: *aem̧aan.*
end of yard, boom (*rojak m̧aan*): *baļ.*
foot of sail, edge fastened to the boom: *aekōrā.*
forward part when outrigger is on port side: *jabļap.*
line from top of mast to outrigger spar (*jojo* (**jewjew**)): *tokubaak.*
mast top: *ļot.*
outrigger platform: *ere, kōm̧ñūr.*
outrigger spar: *jojo.*
piece of wood between *apit* and *jojo, below the kie*: *m̧weiur.*
piece of wood on leeside as guard against rubbing from steering paddle: *eran jebwe.*
place where one sits, just behind middle: *eļ.*
platform over the lee side, opposite the outrigger side: *ro̧ñ.*
seat on a paddling canoe, usually in the mid-section: *to̧o̧t.*
socket for end of boom: *dipāākāk.*
the area around the *bwij*: *lo̧bwij.*
thwart: *to̧o̧t.*
ties between spar and outrigger: *jojo.*
two beams to which *apet* (**hapẹt**) are lashed: *kie.*
two end pieces of canoe: *jim̧.*
two pieces of ironwood support that attach the *kie* to the outrigger: *bwij.*
waveguard on both sides of sailing canoe: *añtūkli.*

Canopus: *Dekā-Lijone.*

canteen: *bōkā.*

Canthigaster
Canthigaster jactator/solandri: *luwap.*

canvas: *kanbōj.*
canvas cover: *kabba.*
canvas drop: *jaññōr.*

cap: *bo̧o̧r, bo̧o̧ror.*

capable: *maroñ.*
incapable of bearing offspring, of women only: *orañe, war.*
incapable of being hurt or embarrassed: *mejel kil.*
mature and capable of taking care of oneself: *keke ṇa ireeaar.*

capacity
great capacity: *kkōt.*

cape
cape of: *būke, būkie, būkien, būkōn.*
cape, geographical: *bōke.*

Capella: *Lōk'tañūr.*

capital: *buoj, peje.*
capital city: *kiāptōḷ.*
capital letters: *kiāptōḷ.*

Capsicum
a plant, pepper, *Capsicum* sp.: *peba.*

capsize: *merā, okjak, pedo.*
canoe about to capsize: *tọ.*
fastest method of righting a canoe after it has capsized in order to escape sharks: *keilupako.*
to capsize: *lā.*

capstan: *wūlleej.*

capsule: *batin.*

captain: *kapen.*

captive
take captive: *jipọkwe.*

capture: *bōk, jebjeb, po.*
a move in game of checkers whereby one jump captures many pieces: *jaṃtiltil.*

car: *kaar, ṃootka.*
drive a car: *kaarar.*
to drive a car: *tūraip.*

Caranx
crevally, *Caranx stellatus*: *ikbwij.*
kingfish, *Caranx fulvoguttatus* forskal: *rewa.*
skip jack, *Caranx lessonii*: *ḷañe, ṃōḷajutak.*
skip jack, *Caranx melampygus*, Hawaiian *ulua*: *deltokrōk.*
skip jack, immature form, *Caranx lessonii*: *kupkup.*

carbon
black carbon on lantern chimney, used to blacken tattoos: *ṃaṃōj.*
rub in black carbon on tattoos: *iteṃaṃōj.*

carburetor: *kaabreta.*

Carcharhinus
a fish, ground shark, *Carcharhinus melanopterus*: *pakoon eoon pedped.*
a fish, shark grouper, *Carcharhinus melanopterus*: *pako mej.*

card: *peba.*
a card game: *juip, peeñka, turuṃ.*
cut cards: *kat.*
pass, in card games: *baaj.*
play cards: *kaaj.*
play cards for stakes: *pile.*
playing cards: *kaaj.*
predict, using cards: *kawūjwūj.*

cardinal
a fish, cardinal fish, *Apogon novemfasiatus*: *tōptōp.*

care
be careless: *kōjelbabō.*
care for: *alal, bōk ddo.*
carefree: *jabde.*
careful: *kōjparok, tiljek.*
careless: *jāṃōd, jabde, jerwaan.*
careless manner: *ortabtab.*
duty of taking care of a father: *jemā.*
duty of taking care of a grandson, granddaughter, a grandparent, or a pet: *jibwi.*
duty of taking care of a mother: *jine.*
duty of taking care of a natural or adopted child or pet or domesticated animal: *nāji.*
handle someone or something with care: *kōṃṃanṃōn.*
know how to take care of: *jeḷāṇae.*
land given to someone who took care of the head of the lineage owning the land during illness before death: *ṃōnkọḷotḷot.*
mature and capable of taking care of oneself: *keke ṇa ireeaar.*
one who has taken care of another's child: *jemānji-.*
pretentious care: *iọkwe in kij.*
put clothes away carelessly: *pānuk.*
someone who has no one to take care of him: *jojoḷāār.*
take care not to spoil a good thing: *kōṃbade.*
take care of: *kōjparok.*
take good care of a canoe: *kkein wa.*
taking care of relatives: *aerṃwe.*

careen: *jepāpe, jepewa.*

career: *jerbal.*

carefree: *ineeṃṃan.*

caress: *eoeo, towe.*
rub back and forth gently or caressingly: *eoeo.*

cargo: *ṃweiuk.*
cargo net: *ṃukko.*

sling for hoisting cargo: *m̧ukko.*

Carica
a plant, papaya, *Carica papaya* L. F.: *keinabbu.*

caricature: *annañ, m̧ōñka.*

carol: *al.*

Caroline
Caroline Islands: *Karoļāin, kapilōñ.*

carpenter: *kaam̧tō.*
carpenter's plane: *pilein.*

carpentry: *kaam̧tō.*

carry: *aljek, bbōk, bōk, leak-.*
carry a child on the hip: *jaja.*
carry a person on one's back: *kuku.*
carry female to or from vessel: *bōkkōrā.*
carry in a basket with long handle slung over shoulder: *aduwado.*
carry in one hand: *arorā, pārājet.*
carry on: *loloorjake.*
carry on shoulders: *inene.*
carry out: *loloorjake, tōprak.*
carry tucked under arm: *abjāje, albakbōk.*
carry with both hands: *pārorā.*
carry, in addition: *uñar.*
carry, of currents: *kinōr.*
to carry things on hips: *kōjerrā.*

cart: *kurm̧a.*
push cart: *diaka.*

cartilage: *kōjjem̧.*

carton: *katin.*

cartoon: *m̧ōñka.*

cartridge: *wōpeñ.*

cartwheel: *ne.*

carve: *āe, eo̧r, jiļait.*

case
case, as of food: *keej.*

case
case, as of legal matter: *keej.*

cash
cash box: *jiipkako, pāāñ.*

casket: *kūtim.*

Cassididae
triton shell: *jilel.*

Cassidula
Cassidula plecotrematoides japonica: *alu.*

Cassiopeia
stars in Cassiopeia: alpha, beta, gamma, delta and epsilon: *Ļokwan-Ļakeke.*

Cassis
a shell, Cassididae, *Cassis cornuta*, helmet shell: *bukbuk, laklak.*

Cassytha
a plant, vine, *Cassytha filiformis* L. (Lauraceae).: *kaōnōn.*

cast
ability to cast spell: *anitta.*
cast a spell on: *anjin.*
cast loose: *jo.*
cast off clothes: *utkōk.*
method of casting lots: *pejao.*

cast
cast for broken bone: *kkaapap.*

Castor
Castor and Pollux in Gemini: *Iju-kuwaj-aiļip.*

castrate: *ko̧kwōle.*

casual: *waan.*

cat: *kuuj.*
smell of cats: *kkuujuj.*
superstition that cat crying at night portends death of someone: *bwijenro.*

catalogue: *katļo̧k.*

cataract: *kōtrāāk.*
eye cataract: *jā.*

catarrh: *mmed.*

catch: *bo̧bo.*
a catch of fish, crabs, or birds: *kon̄a-.*
a hole in a tree for catching water: *m̧m̧ak.*
able to catch many fish: *kon̄kon̄, wōda.*
catch a falling object or fruit: *jjā.*
catch birds at night: *jjo̧ñ.*
catch flies: *ubļo̧ñ.*
catch sleeping birds by hand: *jjoñ.*
catch something in one's windpipe: *po̧k.*
catch up with, overcome, overwhelm: *iabuñ.*
catch up, in a game: *bōktak.*
catch with net or basket: *bo̧ur.*
hold up or catch with both hands: *bo̧ur.*
hole in tree for catching rain water: *m̧ak.*
inability to catch many fish (see *kon̄kon̄* (**qen̦qen̦**)): *jo̧kon̄kon̄.*
inability to catch many fish (see *wōda* (**wedah**)): *joda.*
baseball catcher: *kajji, kiaj.*

catechism: *Baibōļ, katkijm̧uuj.*

category: *ar, kilaj.*

caterpillar: *kūtañtañ, m̧winam̧ōn.*

catharsis: *katoļo̧k.*

Catholic: *Katlik.*
a Catholic: *Katlik.*

catsup: *kōjjeb.*
caudal
caudal fin: *ļokdede.*
caught: *auj, ļorak, po.*
caught in a trap: *tǫrōk.*
caught in the act: *pāte.*
caught on a hook: *kǫjek.*
get caught in crossfire: *ļaanwōtwōt.*
caulk: *kōņ.*
causative
causative prefix: *ka-.*
cause: *wūn.*
caution: *kōjparok.*
cautious: *kōllejar.*
cave
cave under reef shelf: *apā.*
cave, orifice, pit: *rǫñ.*
opening of any container, hole, doorway, or cave, etc.: *māj, meja-.*
cavity
cavity in teeth: *m̧ak.*
cease: *bōjrak.*
Cecapterus
a fish, *opelu, Cecapterus* sp: *kauwe.*
cedar
cedar driftwood: *aik.*
Ceiba
Ceiba pentandra (L.) Gaertn.: *kotin.*
ceiling: *tōrak.*
celebrate
a gathering of people to celebrate the onset of breadfruit season in summer by making offerings to Jebro, the god of breadfruit: *m̧am̧a.*
celebrate an occassion in a rather unceremonial manner: *kōļǫk.*
celebration: *keemem.*
celebrity: *tiemlo.*
female celebrity: *lōkkūk.*
male celebrity: *ļakkūk.*
celestial
any celestial body other than the sun and the moon: *iju.*
celestial navigation: *bōk aļ, bōk iju.*
cell
cell, biological: *jeeļ.*
Cellana
Also *Cellana nigrolineata*: *jidduul.*
Cellana nigrisquamata: *jowakin.*
cement: *jimeeņ.*
cemetery
cemetery, graveyard: *wūliej.*
cent
cent(s): *jāān.*
Centaurus
stars in Centaurus: *Jikut-im-rukut.*
stars in Centaurus (1, 2, 3) or Corvus: *Āl-im-kobban.*
zeta in Centaurus: *ļeepwal.*
a constellation, upsilon, mu, psi Centauri: *Wōjļā.*
Centella
a plant, *Centella asiatica* (L.) Urban (Umbelliferae): *mariko.*
center: *eoļōpa-.*
center of: *buļōn.*
centipede
an animal, centipede: *iie, ņokwanej.*
Cepahalopholis
a fish, blue-spotted grouper, *Cepahalopholis argus*: *kalemeej.*
Cepheus
gamma in Cepheus: *Lim̧anm̧an-eņ-an-Ñinjib.*
ceremony
ceremony performed six days after burial, gravel is spread over grave: *eoreak.*
marrige ceremony: *kwōjkwōjin pālele.*
celebrate an occasion in a rather unceremonial manner: *kōļǫk.*
certain: *lukkuun.*
certainly: *ekōjkan.*
certificate: *kein kam̧ool.*
Chaetodon
a fish, butterfly fish, *Chaetodon anriga* (Ebon): *utot.*
a fish, butterfly fish, *Chaetodon ocellatus*: *dibab.*
a fish, butterfly fish, *Chaetodon ornatissimus*: *bwine.*
including *Chaetodon auriga*: *rūbōb.*
chagrin: *ļōkatip, lotaan.*
chain: *jeen.*
cable, chain, referred to in Bible: *tomede.*
coconut leaf chain used in fishing as scarer: *m̧wio.*
fish that wanders outside coconut leaf chain scarer: *ikōnālkinm̧wio.*
fishing method, many men surround a school in shallow water using a coconut leaf chain as scarer: *aļeļe.*
fishing method, using a coconut leaf chain as a scarer at night to block off exit route of fish and waiting for low tide in order to trap them: *lipaanto.*
fishing method, using coconut leaf chain as scarer on dark nights: *pelpel.*

fishing term, said of a coconut leaf chain used as scarer that is strung out unevenly: *kapijjule.*
tie coconut leaves together to make fishing chain: *wūjaak.*

chain-smoking: *bbaidid.*

chair: *jea.*
lawn chair with canvas back: *joba.*

chalk: *jo̧o̧k.*

challenge: *aod.*

chambered nautilus: *lo̧jilñin jourur.*

champion: *m̧ōkade, wōnm̧aan.*

chance: *iien, jide.*
a chance: *iien m̧m̧an.*

change: *ikūr, iñiñ, kā, kōkāāl, oktak, ukok.*
be changed: *llelo̧k.*
change actions in future: *je.*
change color, of fish: *ukōt m̧ōōr.*
change domicile: *jepjep.*
change from one thing to another: *erom.*
change of plans: *idiñ.*
change one's ways from bad to good: *ukelo̧k.*
make change: *jānij.*
tack, change sail from one end of canoe to the other to tack: *diak.*
to paddle a canoe on the starboard side to change course: *auretam.*
changing continually: *ukoktak.*

channel: *to.*
small man-made channel through coral: *mejā.*

chant: *roro.*
ancient chant: *m̧ur.*
chant and urge someone on by beating on a drum: *piniktak.*
compose songs or chants: *kine.*
mistake in performing a dance, song, or chant: *dujebwābwe.*
to chant: *allōk.*
to chant while drawing up a canoe or other such cooperative work: *ñijir.*

chaperon: *karwaan.*

chapter: *jebta.*

character
of upright character: *weeppān.*

characteristic: *ko̧lmān, ļōma-.*
characteristics: *abōne-.*
inherited characteristics: *bōnja-.*

characterize: *kwaļo̧k kadkadi-.*

charcoal: *mālle.*

charge
charge of a school of fish chasing minnows: *tūaļ.*
charge of larger fish on minnows, sardines, etc: *luwi.*

charge
charge a battery: *jaaj.*

charge
charge on account: *akko̧un, jaaj.*

charisma
charismatic, person who is always attracting people around him or her: *ettōl.*

charitable
uncharitable: *miin.*

charity: *jouj.*

charm
charming: *kattōñtōñ, mmejaja.*

Charonia
Charonia tritonis: *jilel.*

chart: *jaat.*

charter: *jata, jemān-āe.*

chase: *kkōpeļ, kōpļe, kōpooļ, libooror, lukwarkwar.*
a chase: *libooror.*
chase men: *kōm̧m̧aanan.*
chase women: *kōkkōrārā.*

chaste: *rreo.*

chat: *bwebwenato bajjek, kōm̧m̧ao, kōmāltato.*
chat idly: *lekōto.*

chatter: *aeñwāñwā.*
chattering of teeth: *ōļōļ.*

cheap: *dik o̧nea-.*

cheat: *ālikinjepjep, kaammeo̧eo.*
cheat, obtain surreptitiously: *liktak.*
to cheat: *peejnej, tūraab.*

check
check mark: *kakōļļe.*
check, money order: *jāāk.*

check: *jāāk.*
check the weather: *katu.*

checker
a move in game of checkers whereby one jump captures many pieces: *jam̧tiltil.*
be checkered: *jekab.*
checker board: *jekaboot.*
checkers: *jekab.*
play checkers: *jekab.*

cheek: *jāp.*

cheer: *urro.*
cheerful: *lem̧ōņōņō.*
cheerful, resigned: *ineem̧m̧an.*
to cheer on: *pinnik.*

urge on by cheers or other means: *pinnik*.

cheese: *jiij*.

Cheilinus
a fish, hogfish, *Cheilinus undulatus*: *ļappo*.
a fish, wrasse, *Cheilinus* sp: *merā, mao*.
Cheilinus chlorourus/diagrammus/oxcephalus/trilobatus: *po*.

Chelon
a fish, *Chelon vaigiensis*: *ikade*.
a fish, mullet, *Chelon vaigiensis*: *akōr*.
a fish, striped mullet, *Chelon vaigiensis*: *aotak*.

chest: *ob*.
chest measurement: *diklōn̄*.
wrestle chest to chest: *kọob*.

chest
chest, trunk: *tōptōp*.

chew: *meme*.
chew out someone: *jueoonmọn̄*.
chew pandanus: *wōdwōd*.
chew the fat: *kōmāltato*.
chew tobacco: *kolied*.
chewing gum: *bwil*.
to chew food and then throw it out of the mouth: *meliak*.
well chewed: *mālij*.
unchewed food caught in throat: *ubabōj*.

chick: *jojo, tokkwi*.

chicken: *bao*.
chicken that walks upright: *ļajjutak*.
clean a fish or chicken: *jejjet*.
expression, "Chicken!": *pedej*.
old chicken: *jenļap*.
scratch in ground for food, chickens only: *toktok*.
sleep, chickens only: *de*.
smell of chicken manure: *bwiin-kūbween-alōr*.
wild chicken: *mānnimar*.
young chicken: *jendik, kāwur*.

chicken pox
blister, chicken pox: *bok*.

chief: *irooj, jeṃṃaan*.
a basket for bearing tribute to a chief: *kōle*.
a rain storm that is the sign of a chief coming: *ļan̄ōn irooj*.
a taboo place reserved for chiefs: *jiadel*.
basket in which chiefs store left-overs: *peran̄*.
best part of pandanus fruit reserved for chiefs: *ajjipek*.
bring food to a chief: *ekkan*.
bring food to a chief or lineage head: *eọjek*.
certain places for chiefs only and forbidden to the commoner: *mo*.
chief's land: *buoj*.
chief's land for making food: *paaj*.
chief's wife, may or may not be of royal blood: *lejļā*.
chiefly carriage and demeanor: *awi*.
death of a chieftain: *bwilọklan̄*.
decorations made from feathers of frigate birds, one on each tip of the sail on a chief's canoe: *kadulele*.
favorite of a chief: *pāleṃoron*.
first food brought to a chief that has just arrived: *ṃōkajkaj*.
high chieftess: *lerooj*.
island or atoll reserved for food gathering, usually for a chief and his immediate family: *ļārooj*.
land given by a chief to a commoner as a bounty for bailing out the chief's canoe in battle expeditions: *kwōdaelem*.
land reserved for chiefs: *kōtra, mọ*.
land where only chiefs and certain women are allowed: *kul*.
member of a clan a chief is especially fond of: *pāleṃoron*.
person killed and buried with a deceased chieftain to accompany him on his journey to a different world: *ura*.
private place reserved for chiefs: *jaar*.
procession bearing tribute to chief: *tal*.
trusted friend of a chief: *pāleṃoron*.

child: *ajri*.
a child who deserts home through anger over parental coercion: *lumọọrļọk*.
a pampered child: *kaerer*.
adopt children: *kaajiriri*.
call or entice animals or children to come near: *kkaal*.
child of: *nāji-*.
children of a man's sister: *man̄de-*.
duty of taking care of a natural or adopted child or pet or domesticated animal: *nāji*.
favorite child: *n̄iejo*.
one who has taken care of another's child: *jemānji-*.
pamper a child so as to create undue attachment: *kaerer*.
parent-child relationship: *jeṃnājin*.

pet name for male child: *kǫkǫ.*
possessive classifier, children, pets, money, watches, or Bible: *nāji-.*
raise children: *kaajiriri.*
rely on children to accomplish errands or chores: *ajriin uwaak.*
said of female children: *iep jāltok.*
said of male children: *iep jaḷḷǫk.*
second child: *utlōkḷap.*

child speech
dog: *kukkuk.*
eat: *meme.*
eat, food: *m̧wām̧wā.*
grandfather: *jim̧m̧a.*
grandmother: *būbū.*
penis: *kǫkǫ, kukkuk, kulālā.*
spanking: *bam̧bam̧.*
to drink water: *kaka.*

childbirth: *utam̧we.*
contractions during childbirth: *kōḷo.*

chill
chills: *ko tok kili-, wūdiddid.*
chilly: *piǫ.*
fever and chills: *piǫ.*
not get chilly easily (see *piǫ* (**piyaw**)): *jāppiǫeo.*
chilly: *m̧ōleǫ.*

chimney
black carbon on lantern chimney, used to blacken tattoos: *m̧am̧ōj.*
lamp chimney: *jimni.*

chin: *jim̧win n̄i.*
chisel-chin: *n̄iņo.*

China: *Jeina.*

chink: *kōk.*
chinking: *ttōn̄tōn̄.*

chip
chip or scrape rust off: *kajjo.*
chips: *tipdikdik.*
splinter, chip: *naaḷ.*
to chip off rust: *kan̄kan̄.*
graze, as a bullet, chipped: *tām̧oņ.*

chip in: *kuņaņa.*

chisel: *mede.*
cold chisel: *kooḷjejeḷ.*

chocolate: *jǫkleej, koko.*

choice: *kkāālel, m̧m̧an.*
choice coconut tree for collecting sap: *tāān̄.*

choirmaster
choirmaster, director of a choral group: *m̧aajta.*

choke: *kkuul, kkuul bōro.*
choke on something, suffocate: *pǫk.*
choked: *ubabōj.*

choose: *jedkā, kkāālel.*

choosy: *kile.*
be choosy or particular: *kōrkōr ioon kūro.*

chop: *jekjek.*
chop down: *jjuok.*
chopped down: *jokak.*
paint or chop up to a line in canoe building: *atar.*
cut, hack, chop off, split, slash: *jepak.*

choppy
choppy seas: *lim̧aajņoņo.*

chopsticks: *aji.*

choral
choirmaster, director of a choral group: *m̧aajta.*

chore: *jerbal.*
leave a chore undone and start another: *jibwe turin jerbal.*
rely on children to accomplish errands or chores: *ajriin uwaak.*

chorus: *kǫrōj.*

Christ
Jesus Christ: *Jijej Kūraij.*

christen
to christen: *ņaeta-.*

Christian: *Kūrjin.*

Christmas: *Kūrijm̧ōj.*
Christmas song fest (Protestant groups): *jebta.*

chronic
chronically sickly: *addimej.*

chub
a fish, chub mackerel, *Ragistrella*: *akwōlā.*
a fish, chub or rudder fish, *Kyphosus vaigiensis*: *pājrōk.*

chubby: *tōbōb.*

chuckle: *ttōn̄ dikdik.*

chum
stone upon which bait or chum is mashed: *jinm̧a.*
to chum for fish: *anan.*
to chum for fish, usually in deep water: *pitpit.*

chunk: *bukwōn.*

church
church (building): *m̧ōn jar.*
church member in good standing: *Kūrjin.*
church offering: *jabawōt.*
communion, church usage: *kwōjkwōj.*
go to church: *jar.*
members of the church: *eklejia.*

cigar: *tōbak.*

cigarette: *baid, jikka.*
butt of cigarette: *jablọk.*
cigarette paper: *kwarkor.*
cigarettes of: *kije-.*
crave cigarettes: *añūr.*
possessive classifier, food or cigarettes: *kije-.*
roll a cigarette: *kwarkor.*
to puff a cigarette: *koub.*

cinch: *kijen niñniñ.*

cinder
cinders: *kūbween uṃ.*

circle: *doulul, ọo.*
closed circle of fish surrounded by *aḷeḷe* (haḷeyḷey) method: *aḷe.*
encircle: *kōpooḷ.*
encircled: *pooḷ.*

circuit
run a complete circuit around a field: *oṃrawūn.*

circumcise
circumcised: *korjak.*
circumcised penis: *pāj.*
uncircumcised penis: *kōkkōk.*

Cirrhitus
a fish, spotted hawkfish, *Cirrhitus pinnulatus*: *kidiej.*

cirrus
cirrus clouds: *ḷoñanwa.*

cistern: *aebōj jimeeṇ.*

citrus
a plant, citrus, lime: *ḷaiṃ.*

city: *jikinkwelọk.*
capital city: *kiāptōḷ.*

civilian: *jepelien.*

chicken pox: *bok aidik.*

claim: *maroñ.*

clam
a clam, bivalve: *jenọ.*
a food, salted fish guts or clams: *jiookra.*
a shell, a clam, *Tridacnidae*: *mejānwōd.*
a shell, clam: *pejao.*
a shell, giant clam: *kapwor.*
a shell, killer clam: *tōkale.*
a shell, small bivalve clam: *kalibok.*
a shell, small bivalve, clam: *kọnōt.*
clam shell, large: *aded.*
clam, medium large: *dimuuj.*
extricate, as meat from clam: *arar.*
mallet made from clam shell: *dekenin.*
meaty part of the clam: *aḷaḷ.*
organ of giant clam: *lām.*
place where birds, fish, or clams gather: *ajañ.*
sand clam, bivalve: *jukkwe.*
shell of larger clams: *addi.*
shell of smaller clams: *wūpeñ.*
small clam, oyster, a shell, *Arcidae, Scapharca inequivalvis* or *Anadara pilulu*: *kūkōr.*
substance of clam shell: *ajaj.*
to close tight, as a clam shell: *kkim.*

clamor: *aeñwāñwā, kkeroro.*
clamor, noise: *ailuwannañnañ.*

clamp: *kkaapap.*

clan: *jowi.*
clan name: *Dāpdep, Erroja, Erroja-kijeek, Erroja-pakolikaelaḷ, Erroja-rilikin-bwilujo, Erroja-rūbūkien-jekjekeṇ, Errūbra, Ijjidik, Ijjidikin-kapinmeto, Irooj, Jedjed, Jeḷapḷap, Jemāluut, Jibuklik, Jibwiḷuḷ, Jinkabo, Jjed, Joḷ, Jowa, Kaḷọ, Kōtra, Looj, Look, Ṃōkauleej, Mekijko, Pit, Raarṇo, Raej, Rael, Raur, RiEpatōn, RiJelwōj, RiKuwajleen, RiLoojraṇ, RiNaṃo, RiPikaarej, RiPit, RiPitin-Mājro, RiPitin-Naṃdik, RiWōjjā, Riikjet, Rilikijjine, Rilikin Jepakina, Rilobarew', Rilokilōñe, Rilokōlañe, Riloṃaḷo, Rilotọbōn, Rilujien Naṃo, Riluut, Rimatoḷeṇ, Rimeik, Ripako, RuKwōdo, RūṂae, RūṂalel, RūṂwejoor, Rūbojaar, Rūkin-aelōñin, Rūkipinaelōñin, Rūkipinbwilujo, Rūtōbaaḷ, Tilañ.*
member of a clan a chief is especially fond of: *pāleṃoron.*

clang
clanging sound: *taññaḷọk.*

clap: *bokkoḷọk.*
clap hands: *kabbokbok.*

clash: *itaak.*
clash, physical as well as philosophical: *iṃaajaj.*
to clash in a fight: *jibwe doon.*

clasp: *dāpdep.*
unclasp: *mejaḷ.*
walk with the hands clasped behind the back: *enliklik.*

class: *ar, kilaj, teeñ.*
any group of people, as a class, unit or division: *jar.*
high-class person: *arōṃṃan.*

clatter: *keroro.*

claw: *akki.*
claw of crab: *jānit.*
scratch with claws: *ubrar.*
to rake, to claw: *rakutak.*

clean: *kkwōjarjar, rreo.*
advise someone to lead a conventionally good clean life: *kabkūbjer.*
clean a fish or chicken: *jejjet.*
clean up an area: *rarō.*
clean whiskers off of newly braided sennit: *kōrōnāl.*
general clean up: *jotoiñ.*
not well-cleaned: *jālōt.*
plunder, clean out: *ropāj.*
well-cleaned: *lōt.*

cleanse: *katoḷọk.*

clear: *alikkar, rreo.*
clear the throat: *melkwarkwar.*
cleared space: *maaj.*
unclear weather: *tab.*
a clearing between trees growing in opposite directions: *toṇak.*

cleat: *kūḷiit.*
canoe part, cleat for tying sheet: *jirukli.*

cleave
cleave, cut in half: *bōrrā.*

clench: *nukuj.*

Clerodendrum
a plant, *Clerodendrum inerme* (L.) Gaertn. (Verbenaceae): *wūlej.*

clever: *jiṃaat, kapeel.*
immature (see *kapeel* (**kapeyel**)), not clever: *jekapeel.*
not clever (see *jiṃaat* (**jiṃahat**)): *jājiṃaat.*

climate: *mejatoto.*

climb: *wanlōñ.*
A yellow-flowered leguminous vine climbing, or decumbent on beaches: *markinenjojo.*
band around ankles used in climbing trees: *kae.*
climb a ladder or a staircase: *jikin uwe.*
climb coconut tree with ankles tied: *ento.*
climb down: *to.*
climb or descend a rope: *pitto.*
climb up: *tallōñ.*
method of climbing down: *pirūrrūr.*
notches cut in a tree for climbing: *jekāiōōj.*
rope used for climbing trees: *jemājirok.*

clinch: *kūḷinij.*

cling
cling to: *ddāp.*
cling to one another: *kaerer.*
clinging: *bab.*

clinic
health clinic: *ṃōn taktō.*

clink
clinking: *ttōñtōñ.*

clip
clip all of the hair off: *kwōdmat.*

clitoris: *būḷūkkañ, būḷūtteej.*

clobber: *notoñ, pejaju.*
clobber someone: *jinṃa.*

clock: *awa.*

clog
clogged: *boṇ.*
wooden clog, footwear: *jinaketa.*

close
able to sail close to the wind: *wetak.*
close to: *epaak, turu-.*
close together: *kut.*
come very close: *koobob.*
grow close together (see *kkut*): *ṃọkut.*
hot and close: *nitñil.*
move closer: *kepaak.*
move something closer by using a stick: *adebdeb.*
not close together: *jọkkutkut.*
sail close to the wind: *kipeddikdik.*
sit close together: *atartar.*
unable to sail close to the wind: *wāto.*

close: *ddọdo, kkiil.*
close in on: *kōpooḷ.*
close parts, as bivalve: *kkim.*
to close tight, as a clam shell: *kkim.*

closet: *tūroot.*

clot
blood clot: *mekak.*
to clot: *mekak.*

cloth: *nuknuk.*
bolt of cloth: *kap.*
cloth for wrapping bundle of goods: *būroojki.*
coconut cloth: *inpel.*
coconut cloth used to squeeze and extract oil from grated coconut: *jouneak.*
coir fibre, fine, not woven, left over from weaving, used as wash cloth: *bwijinbwije.*
loin cloth: *kaḷ.*
roll of cloth: *kap.*
scrub, using wet cloths: *jokiiñ.*
sew together a rip in cloth: *ait.*
tablecloth: *eran teboḷ.*

clothes: *nuknuk.*
cast off clothes: *utkōk.*
change clothes, from good to dirty: *ekpā.*

clothesline: *roro.*
coconut shell for scrubbing clothes: *kuļatļat.*
outer clothes: *anilik.*
put clothes away carelessly: *pānuk.*
rinse clothes: *ṃukṃuk.*
try on clothes: *jon̄jon̄.*
underclothes: *anilowa.*
wave, of a flag or clothes: *ppālpāl.*
to clothe: *ņaballi-.*

clothing: *balle, nuknuk.*
clothing (in construct only): *el.*
loose, of clothing or rope: *pidtoto.*
mat worn as clothing: *nieded.*
shed clothing: *utūkaļ.*
smell of clothing or mats under sun: *bbidetdet.*
smell of damp clothing: *jatbo.*
wear a piece of clothing for the first time: *lōtlōt.*
wear wet clothing: *ṃōrābōt.*

cloud: *kōdọ.*
cirrus clouds: *ļon̄anwa.*
cloud formation or star: *ad.*
cloud formation preceding storm: *pālmuuj.*
cloud formation predicting a typhoon: *ped in pā.*
cloud formation resembling tip of frond: *jepak.*
cumulus cloud: *kōdọ jutak.*
dark cloudy night: *lianij.*
darkness that follows a cloud coming over the horizon at night: *elianij.*
forecast weather by observing clouds: *kōbbaal.*
obscured, cloudy: *tab.*
pass by, of clouds and rain: *peļaak.*
thick cloud formation of cumulus type covering a large portion of the sky: *jā.*

clown: *kōjak.*

club: *aļaļ in den̄den̄, kuļab.*
club of people: *doulul.*
club used for beating coconut husk for sennit: *jidjid.*
go drinking at a club: *kuļab.*
stick used for clubbing fish: *jeṃōnna.*

cluck
clucking of a hen: *tokokkok.*

clump
clump of: *wūntōn.*

clumsy: *apeltak, aujepaļ, jakōl, jatpe, jokwa, kūļaṃwe, wūpeļ.*

cluster: *bukun, uror.*
cluster of: *wūntōn.*
tight clustering of fish when attracted by bait or chum: *boklọk.*

clutch: *bọkwōj.*

clutter: *menọknọk.*
uncluttered: *meļak.*

coal: *mālle.*
coals of fire: *mālle.*

Coalsack: *Dāp-eo.*

coarse: *kkwelep.*
fine, not coarse: *kkwidik.*

coast
seacoast: *kappe, parijet.*

coat: *kopā.*
coating, of paint: *bōrwaj.*
overcoat: *kabba.*
raincoat: *aļkoot, kabba.*

coax: *medek.*

cobweb
cobwebs: *kadeọeo.*

coccyx: *ļuļ.*

cock: *kako.*
cock-fight, in water: *keiwa.*
cock's comb: *ṃọroj.*
ruffling of cocks and dogs before fighting: *rrọn̄.*
take a rooster to a cock-fight: *keid.*

cockroach: *juwapin.*
an insect, cockroach, roach: *kuļuļ.*
smell of cockroaches: *bwiin-juwapen.*

cocoa: *koko.*

coconut: *ni.*
a food, bundled and baked spongy meat of sprouted coconut: *iutūr.*
a food, coconut bread, from copra and flour and sap or sugar: *jinkōļar.*
a food, coconut eaten with another dish, esp. Salt fish or miso: *jiraal.*
a food, cooked and pounded breadfruit, taro, bananas, or nuts mixed with grated coconut: *wūden̄.*
a food, cooked preserved breadfruit smothered in grated coconut: *kubaļ.*
a food, diluted starch baked in coconut spathe in earth oven: *kōlọwutaktak.*
a food, meat of *mejoub* coconut mixed with sugar or sap: *jekōbwa.*
a food, octopus smothered in grated coconut: *penkwe.*
a food, pandanus pulp and juice mixed with grated coconut and coconut oil (and optionally with arrowroot starch), wrapped in breadfruit leaves and boiled or baked: *peru.*

a food, pounded meat of sprouted coconut: *lukor.*
a food, soup, spongy coconut and arrowroot: *aikiu.*
a food, spongy meat of sprouted coconut baked in its shell: *iuwuṃuṃ.*
a food, spongy meat of sprouted coconut cooked with arrowroot starch and diluted with water: *peaut.*
a food, very ripe breadfruit mixed with coconut milk: *kaḷọ.*
a game, pelting one another with lighted pandanus keys or coconut husks: *buwaddel.*
a pile of coconuts: *jokā.*
a plant, tall coconut palm: *ni kenato.*
a toy, boat of half coconut: *wa bweọ.*
a toy, coconut hydroplane: *wūdādo.*
add sand or grated coconut: *penpen.*
black magic performed by a sorcerer using a husked coconut: *kaurur jian̄.*
bunch of ripe and drinkable coconuts: *uror.*
climb coconut tree with ankles tied: *ento.*
coconut "apple": *iu.*
coconut beginning to form hard meat and turn brown: *man̄bōn.*
coconut beginning to turn brown: *man̄.*
coconut candy: *ametōṃa.*
coconut cloth: *inpel.*
coconut cloth used to squeeze and extract oil from grated coconut: *jouneak, jouneak.*
coconut cup: *jiṃan̄ko.*
coconut fibre: *bweọ.*
coconut juice: *dānnin ni.*
coconut leaf chain used in fishing as scarer: *ṃwio.*
coconut mixed with sap or sugar: *lukor.*
coconut sennit: *kkwaḷ.*
coconut shoot: *utak.*
coconut stump: *debọkut.*
coconut syrup boiled down from sap: *jekṃai.*
coconut tree loaded with nuts: *nimuur.*
coconut, nearly ripe: *mejoub.*
coconut, ripe for copra: *waini.*
coconuts still attached to spathe and lowered from tree by means of a rope: *niiddoor.*
coil of coconut sennit: *tāte.*
collect coconuts or breadfruit: *jinwōd.*
collect coconuts and husk them before making copra: *pinju.*
dust from coconut cloth (*inpel*): *roro.*
eat kernel of coconut out of shell with one's teeth: *kijḷat.*
fall prematurely, of coconuts: *kwaḷṃwe.*
fermented coconut toddy: *jiman̄ūn̄.*
fine, of grated coconut: *kkwidik.*
fish that wanders outside coconut leaf chain scarer: *ikōnālkinṃwio.*
fishing method, many men surround a school in shallow water using a coconut leaf chain as scarer: *aḷeḷe.*
fishing method, using a coconut leaf chain as a scarer at night to block off exit route of fish and waiting for low tide in order to trap them: *lipaanto.*
fishing method, using coconut leaf chain as scarer on dark nights: *pelpel.*
fishing term, said of a coconut leaf chain used as scarer that is strung out unevenly: *kapijjule.*
gateway, usually decorated with flowers and coconut fronds: *ṃon̄.*
grate coconuts, grater: *raanke.*
grated coconut: *jokoojwa, pen.*
group of sprouted coconuts past the eating stage: *debweiu.*
hard coconut meat remaining in half-shall of sprouted coconut after spongy core has been removed: *n̄ar.*
hard, dry coconut meat still in shell: *ṃọṇ.*
harvest coconuts: *kowainini.*
harvest first fruit of coconut, breadfruit, or pandanus: *akeọ.*
heartburn caused by drinking fresh coconut sap on an empty stomach: *mmaḷ.*
huge pile, as of coconuts: *ṃōḷōbbā.*
husk a coconut with one's teeth: *ōjōj.*
husk coconuts: *ddeb.*
immature coconut fruit of: *ubnen.*
kernel of spongy meat inside coconut that has just started to sprout: *bōḷọn̄ar.*
knock down coconuts from tree: *nnōk.*
method of extracting coconut meat out of its shell without breaking the meat: *kōmmālwewe.*
midrib of a coconut leaf: *ṇok.*

overgrown and inedible sprouted coconut: *iupej.*
pandanus juice mixed with grated coconut, cooked into custard: *mokwaņ duul.*
pandanus juice mixed with grated coconut, uncooked: *mokwaņ dada.*
peel off the end of a coconut shoot: *kọudpak.*
pick coconuts: *enōk.*
pick green coconuts from tree: *entak.*
pierce, as an unhusked coconut in order to drink: *wāāpep.*
place a bottle (*kor*) at the end of coconut shoot to collect sap initially: *kajokkor.*
pluck ripe coconuts: *kōpālele.*
possessive classifier, water, soft drinks, or juice of coconuts, etc.: *lime-.*
ready for a bottle, of coconut shoots only: *raane-bōkāān.*
red colored, of reddish coconuts or sky: *mir.*
refuse of scraped coconut after it is squeezed: *o.*
sharp stick for husking coconuts: *doon.*
shoot of coconut, pandanus: *juubub.*
sliced unripe breadfruit cooked in coconut milk: *bwilitudek.*
small flowers of pandanus, coconut, or other plants: *did.*
small sprouted coconut: *per.*
smaller eye of sprouted coconut: *tōbo.*
smell of coconuts: *bwiin-ni.*
sound of coconut bouncing: *rukruk.*
spongy meat of sprouted coconut: *iu.*
spoon made from chip of green coconut husk: *auļakļak.*
sprouted coconut: *iu.*
stage of the coconut seedling in which it is beginning to sprout: *tōboļāār.*
stand a coconut husking stick in the ground: *kat.*
start to bear fruit, of coconuts: *eọ.*
steal and drink coconut toddy (off a tree): *jekeidaak.*
stem of coconut bunch from which nuts have fallen: *jepar, jinnipraṇ̄.*
stems of coconut tree that nuts are attached to: *piraṇ̄raṇ̄.*
string fish, coconuts, flowers, etc: *ilele.*
strips of green coconut branches laid across a fire for warming pandanus leaves: *tọļ.*
sucking noise made in drinking green coconuts: *ṃṃōtṃōt.*
sweet coconut water: *māmet.*
thick husk protecting eyes of coconut: *wūlṃōd.*
tiny coconut not fully grown: *kwaļini, kwaļinni.*
to bend down, of coconut shoots only: *kietak.*
to throw grated coconut or sand at someone or something: *pinik.*
two or more persons sharing one coconut: *ninikoko.*
unripe coconut: *ub.*
use a coconut husker: *doonon.*
use mouth to husk coconuts: *ejej.*
whiskers remaining on a husked coconut: *wūlṃōd.*
young coconut meat: *mede.*
young stage of coconut growth, after *debweiu*: *jokiae.*

coconut crab: *barulep.*
fishing method, hunt lobster or coconut crab when the moon is right: *katooj.*
husking of coconuts by coconut crabs: *ejej.*
place in sand where turtle lays eggs or coconut crab molts: *jọ.*

coconut frond: *kimej, pāp.*
fishing method, using woven brown coconut fronds to catch sardines and minnows as they are chased ashore by bigger fish: *apep.*
green coconut fronds: *pāin ni.*
man's skirt made from coconut fronds: *elmen.*
midrib of coconut frond: *pāp.*
pluck leaves from midrib of coconut fronds: *ttemakil.*
special twine made from skin of coconut frond midrib for climbing coconut trees: *kae.*
tip of coconut frond: *jepak.*
twine made from skin of coconut frond midrib: *mālwe.*
mat woven from coconut fronds: *jeinae.*

coconut husk: *bweọ.*
club used for beating coconut husk for sennit: *jidjid.*
piece of wood on which coconut husk is beaten to yield fibre for sennit: *jebōnmāl.*
pit for soaking coconut husks for making sennit: *to.*
place for beating coconut husks after soaking in preparation for making sennit: *ṃṃal.*
scrub self with coconut husk or oil: *bokwārijet.*

smell of pit for soaking coconut husks: *būto.*
spoon cut from coconut husk: *kūļatļat.*
take coconut husks from water after soaking to make sennit: *jarjar.*

coconut leaves
a food, preserved breadfruit, formed into loaves, wrapped in coconut leaves, and cooked on fire: *m̧aio.*
brown coconut leaves which fall: *m̧we.*
dry pandanus or coconut leaves over fire in preparation for weaving: *katrar.*
tie coconut leaves together to make fishing chain: *wūjaak.*

coconut milk: *eaļ.*
a food, grated taro mixed with coconut milk, wrapped in taro leaves and baked in oven: *jebwatōr.*
a food, very ripe breadfruit baked in coconut milk: *p̧ǫljej.*

coconut oil: *pinneep.*
a food, balls of preserved breadfruit sweetened and boiled in coconut oil: *makillō.*
a food, ripe breadfruit mixed with coconut oil and cooked in pots: *nāpnāpe.*
a food, taro grated and mixed with coconut oil and coconut sap: *tōtaim̧oņ.*
a food, very ripe breadfruit baked in coconut oil: *kappokpok, m̧ōjjero.*
coconut oil used for frying: *jebkwanwūjǫ.*
drift nut, sweet smelling, used with coconut oil to make perfume: *ajet.*
smell of rotten copra or rancid coconut oil: *ļōļ.*

coconut sap
a beverage, diluted coconut sap: *jeruru.*
a food, preserved breadfruit mixed with arrowroot and coconut sap or sugar, wrapped in breadfruit leaves and baked: *bwiro iiōk.*
a food, taro grated and mixed with coconut oil and coconut sap: *tōtaim̧oņ.*
bottle used for coconut sap: *jeib.*
coconut sap, toddy: *jedān, jekaro.*
coconut shell for catching coconut sap, whole and empty: *kor.*
fermented, of coconut sap: *mañūñ.*
old and sour coconut sap: *mañūñ.*
use coconut sap for cooking: *utōn-jekaro.*

coconut shell: *ļat.*
coconut shell for catching coconut sap, whole and empty: *kor.*
coconut shell for scrubbing clothes: *kuļatļat.*
coconut shell, lower half with sharp end: *ļat-jim̧.*
coconut shell, lower half, without eye: *jim̧.*
coconut shell, upper half next to stem, with eyes: *ļat-mej.*
fishing method, line fishing using the front half of a coconut shell, in lagoon area: *mejeļat.*

coconut tree
a coconut tree: *ni.*
a plant, general term for all varieties of coconut trees and fruit: *ni.*
a very tall coconut tree: *kenato.*
choice coconut tree for collecting sap: *tāāñ.*
coconut tree that cannot give more fresh toddy (see *tāāñ* (**tayag**)): *jatāāñ.*
core of coconut tree at upper end: *juļ.*
healthy in appearance, as a coconut tree: *wāmourur.*
open spathe of coconut tree: *jepar, jinnipran̄.*
sap of coconut tree: *dān.*
special twine made from skin of coconut frond midrib for climbing coconut trees: *kae.*

cod
a fish, rock cod, *Anyperodon leucogrammicus*: *kabro, kōļaoļap.*
a fish, rock cod, *Epinephelus flavocaeruleus*: *pooklim̧.*
a fish, rock cod, *Serranus fuscoguttatus*: *kūro.*

coelenterate
a coelenterate, Portuguese man-o-war: *aolōk.*

coffee: *kǫpe.*
coffee pot: *tibat.*

cog
cog, gear, ratchet: *raanke.*

cohabit: *koba.*

coherent
incoherent: *aplo.*

coil: *jālin̄in̄, jāljel, p̧ǫpo.*
coil of coconut sennit: *tāte.*
to coil: *kwōje.*

coin: *jāān dekā.*
coir
coir fibre, fine, not woven, left over from weaving, used as wash cloth: *bwijinbwije.*
coke: *koļa.*
cola: *koļa.*
cold: *m̧ōļo, m̧ōleo̧, pio̧.*
common cold: *mejin.*
Coleman lantern: *ļaam̧ kaaj, pilerab.*
collapse: *penā.*
collapsed: *obab.*
collar: *kōļa.*
collateral: *joortoklik, kōpetaklik.*
collect: *ae, tōltōl.*
collect coconuts and husk them before making copra: *pinju.*
collect coconuts or breadfruit: *jinwōd.*
collide
collide head on: *im̧aajaj.*
collide with: *itaak.*
Collisella
a shell, *Patellidae, Collisella grata*: *jidduul.*
collision
sound of a collision: *okkoļo̧k.*
Colocasia
a plant, taro variety, *Colocasia*: *Jibabwāi.*
Colocasia esculenta The true taro of Polynesia. F: *Kōtak.*
colony: *jukjuk.*
color: *wūno.*
bright colored: *ilar, meej.*
change color, of fish: *ukōt m̧ōōr.*
color of: *m̧ōrōn.*
coloring: *kawūno.*
dark colored: *jil.*
dark in color: *meej.*
fading of color: *eor.*
fading of color or shade: *jjurjur.*
gray colored: *kūbween upaaj, kūre.*
green colored: *maroro.*
light colored (see *meej* (**meyej**)): *jāmeej.*
loud, of colors, bright: *rōōj.*
multicolored, spotted, usually brownish: *kkaadad.*
orange colored: *kio.*
rainbow-colored: *iiaeae.*
red colored, of reddish coconuts or sky: *mir.*
reddish color: *m̧ūrar.*
shell of many colors, used as lure for tuna: *jepet.*
tan colored: *kūbween upaaj.*
column: *joor, kaļan.*
comb: *kuum̧.*
cock's comb: *m̧o̧ro̧j.*
tooth of a comb: *tōōļ.*
use a comb: *kuum̧um̧.*
combat: *tarin̄ae.*
lock in combat: *bab.*
take by surprise in hand combat: *ankōm̧ad.*
ward off using Marshallese hand-to-hand combat defense techniques: *pile.*
combination: *ļōōt.*
of right combination: *m̧m̧an utōn.*
combine: *koba.*
combustible
combustible (see *tokwiia* (**teqiyyah**)): *tokwiie.*
incombustible: *tokwiia.*
come: *atok, wātok.*
call to come: *āñiñintok.*
come about, begin to have: *er-.*
come and: *itōm.*
come back: *ro̧o̧l.*
come back in order to. (Contraction of *ro̧o̧ltok in* (**rawalteq yin**)): *ro̧o̧ltōn.*
come closer: *ārār.*
come directly: *iok-.*
come down with a sickness: *lōbo̧.*
come here (of humans): *itok.*
come in order to: *itōn.*
come off of: *to.*
come one at a time: *iaļ aidik.*
come out of water: *ato.*
come to land: *tōkeak.*
come to you (of humans): *iwōj.*
come up: *m̧ōto.*
go or come ashore: *wāānāne, wanāne.*
go or come down: *wanlaļ.*
go or come seaward: *wanmeto.*
go or come towards the lagoon: *wāānar, wanar.*
go or come towards the ocean side of an island: *wanlik.*
come to: *jeļā ļo̧kjen̄.*
comet: *iju.*
comeuppance: *lle.*
get one's comeuppance: *kipdo, teej, toñōl.*
comfort: *kōjea-.*
discomfort: *aploñloñ.*
padding for comfort or for protection from dirt: *erer.*
uncomfortable: *abn̄ōn̄ō.*
uncomfortable feeling about the

stomach from being overstuffed with food: *akeke.*

comic: *m̧ōñka.*

comma: *kom̧a.*

command
commandant: *kom̧aan̦ta.*
commander: *kom̧aan̦ta.*
commandment: *kien.*
to send a command to: *kaiñ.*

commemorate: *kaļo̧k.*

commence
commencement: *jjino.*

commercial: *reel.*
a commercial: *karreelel.*

commission: *kwamijen.*
out of commission: *jintanji.*

commit: *kilaak.*
be committed to perform a task: *lokjak.*
commit suicide: *kilaba, wōdinikek.*
commitment: *lokjak, utam̧we.*

committee: *kamiti.*

common: *jeeknaan, kkā, makijkij, mmakijkij, pata, waan.*
common people: *kajoor.*
common things: *jenwaan.*
do in common: *almaroñ.*

commoner: *armej waan, jeeknaan, jokko, rijerbal, kajoor.*
certain places for chiefs only and forbidden to the commoner: *mo.*
commoner married to royal woman: *irooj-em̧m̧aan.*
land given by a chief to a commoner as a bounty for bailing out the chief's canoe in battle expeditions: *kwōdaelem.*

commotion: *jjānene, jjeurur, uwōjak.*

communion
communion, church usage: *kwōjkwōj.*

community: *jukjuk.*

compact: *bujen, kon̦, ñūñ.*

companion: *m̧ōtta-.*

company
company, business usage: *kom̧bani.*
company, team, group: *kumi.*
keep company: *kōm̧m̧ao.*

compare: *allo̧k, keid.*
compare oneself with another: *atar.*
compare size: *joñjoñ.*

compass: *kam̧bōj.*

compel: *kipel.*

compensate: *kōļļā on̦ea-, n̦aon̦ea-, ukōt bōkā.*

compete: *aitwerōk, atar, depet-doon, jiāe, kewā.*
compete with each other: *lōkdoon.*
competent: *maroñ.*

competent: *keke.*
incompetent: *jedañ.*

competition: *depet-doon.*
put someone out of a competition: *kupi.*

complain: *abn̦ōn̦ō, aoļ, kkeroro, llotaan.*
complain of others: *kinaak.*

complete: *polel, uñ, weeppān.*
completed: *dede, m̧ōj.*
incomplete: *jipikpik, jo̧uñ.*

complex: *aepokpok, pok.*

complexion
of light complexion: *wūdmouj.*

complicate
complicated: *aepokpok, pok.*

compliment: *nōbar.*

comply: *ļoor(e).*

component
basic components of: *utō-.*

compose: *kkōn.*
compose songs or chants: *kine.*
a musical composition to be sung by all singers together: *ko̧rōj.*

compost
oakum, compost: *kōn̦.*

comprehend: *meļeļe.*

compute: *bōnbōn.*
to compute: *jorbañ.*

comrade: *m̧ōtta-.*

Conasprella
Conasprella praecellea/comatosa/ sowerbii or *Profundiconus profundiconus*: *likaebeb.*

conceal: *n̦n̦ooj, pinej.*
unconcealed: *jjerwawa.*

conceit
conceited: *lom̧aan, utiej būruo-.*
imposing, conceited, inconsiderate: *pedet armej.*

conceive: *tta.*

concentrate: *kōļmānļo̧kjen̦.*

concern
concerned: *jelōt.*
concerning: *kōn.*
unconcerned about consequences: *jjo̧jo̧, mejel kil.*

conch
trumpet, horn, siren, conch: *jilel.*

conciliate
to conciliate: *medek.*

concise: *jejjet.*
conclusion: *jemḷọk.*
concoction: *ḷōōt.*
concrete: *jimeeṇ.*
concrete block: *būḷak, pirōk.*
concur
concurrence: *koṇ.*
to second, concur: *rejetak.*
condemn: *liaakḷọk.*
condition: *kōjea-.*
get into prime running condition: *an.*
negatively conditioned: *mañ.*
run-down condition: *ijurwewe.*
conditional
conditional, contrary to fact: *kar.*
conduct: *ṃanit, ṃwil.*
confer: *pepe.*
conference: *kweilọk.*
confess: *kwaḷọk ṃool, ukeḷọk.*
confession: *kwaḷọk bōro.*
confidence: *lōke.*
confine: *kalbuuj.*
confine because of disease: *lōbọ.*
confinement: *utaṃwe.*
confirm: *kaṃool.*
conflict: *airuwaro, aitwerōk.*
confound: *ppaḷ.*
confront: *jelṃae.*
confuse: *pok.*
confusion: *airuwaro.*
congeal: *kwōj.*
Conger
a fish, eel, *Conger cinereus*: *ṃōjoud.*
congratulation: *jeraaṃṃan.*
congregate: *peḷaak.*
congregated, aggregated: *kuk.*
to congregate: *kweilọk.*
congregation: *jarlepju.*
congress: *kwañkurōj.*
Conidae
a shell, *Conidae*: *likaebeb.*
conjecture: *kajjidede, leḷōmṇak.*
connect
connection: *kōkkeitaak.*
disconnect: *mejaḷ.*
disconnected: *jenolọk.*
Conomurex
Conomurex luhuanus: *lōkeed.*
conquer
conquered: *anjọ.*
conscience: *apaproro, bōklōkōt.*
voice of conscience: *ainikien bōklōkōt.*
conscious: *jeḷā ḷokjeṇ.*
awake, roused, conscious: *ruj.*
consciousness: *ḷoḷātāt.*
unconscious: *jajeḷọkjeṇ, ñakḷọkjeṇ.*
consecutive
occur one after another, consecutively, bumper-to-bumper: *kij-ḷokwan-doon.*
consent: *uwaak.*
consequence: *ajāllik.*
sorry consequences: *amentaklaḷ.*
consequently: *jujen.*
conserve: *kōjparok.*
consider: *ddoor, llik, watwat.*
considerate: *jeḷā kuṇaa-.*
be considerate of others: *jake jibwil.*
imposing, conceited, inconsiderate: *pedet armej.*
inconsiderate: *būruon kūro, jaje ḷōmṇak, jememe, kōṇkōṃṃan, ḷōkajeṃ.*
conspicuous: *jenolọk, jjedmatmat.*
be conspicuous: *tooj.*
conspicuously: *ejjab aelọk.*
constant: *mmakijkij.*
constellation: *bukun iju.*
a constellation: *Āl-im-kobban, Aoḷōt, Arin-Mājlep, Aunwōlān-lañ, Bọro, Būbwin Epoon, Bwā-eṇ-an-Joktak, Dāp-eo, Debwāāl-eo, Elmọñ, Iju-kuwaj-aiḷip, Iju-pilo, Jāli, Jāpe, Jeljel, Jemānuwe, Jepjep-eo-an-Lōktañūr, Jikut-im-rukut, Jitata, Kapi-Ḷak, Kāājejen-Tūṃur, Kāām-anij, Kāām-armej, Kōḷein-dipāākāk-eo, Korak-eṇ-an-Tūṃur, Kouj, Ḷak, Ḷakeke, Ḷōmejdikdik, Ḷōṇa, Ḷokwan-Ḷakeke, Ledik-raṇ-nājin-Jebrọ, Lo-raan-ṃwāṃwā-ko, Ṃade-eo-an-Aoḷōt, Ṃade-eo-an-Tūṃur, Mājetdikdik, Mājlep, Men-kaṇ, Ok-an-adik, Rouk, Tūṃur, Utin-Ḷarrūbra, Utin-Ḷarrūbra, Wa-eo-waan-Tūṃur, Wātal-kaṇ, Wōjḷā.*
the constellations *Jeljel* and *Kouj*: *Jeljel-im-Kouj.*
the constellations *Ḷak* and *Jitata*: *Ḷakmijtata.*
the constellations *Kāām-anij* and *Kāām-armej*: *Kāām-kaṇ.*
constipated: *boṇ.*
construct
newly constructed, of vessels or vehicles: *wōnōt.*
construct particle
construct particle or suffix: *in.*
consume: *amān.*

contact: *kōkkeitaak.*
contact, constant and physical: *irar.*
lose contact with: *jokwōd.*

contagious: *kapopo.*

contain: *kōpooḷ.*
container: *nine.*
container for liquids: *pijja.*
container for liquids, of coconut shell: *bōkā.*
drinking water containers on a canoe or boat: *kōb.*
empty container: *wōpeñ.*
get the last drops of water from a water container: *kajḷor.*
opening of any container, hole, doorway, or cave, etc.: *māj, meja-.*
put in container: *ātet.*
use as a container: *nine.*
water container: *tāāñ.*
container, usually five-gallon paint bucket: *bat.*

contemplate: *kōḷmānḷọkjeṇ.*

contemporary: *peḷo.*

contempt: *akkōjdat.*
draw lips to one side in contempt: *kaū.*

content: *po bōro.*
discontent: *jab po bōro.*

contents
contents of: *kobba-.*
contents (of a book): *kadkad.*

contest: *aitwerōk, jiāe, kōṃṃalijar.*
a game, contest to see who can throw a sharp-pointed piece of dried pandanus root, about a yard long, farthest by skimming it on the ground once: *kajjeor.*
contest, fighting or wrestling: *kāre lọwob.*
eliminate, in contest: *ukok.*
fishing contest: *kāre kāāj.*
heated contest: *bok.*
juggling contest: *ekkokowa.*
shooting contest: *kōjjerọro.*

continue: *etal wōt, pen in deo.*
discontinue: *bōjrak.*
interjection: "If that's so, then continue.": *ekwekwe.*
continuously: *etal in wōt juon.*

contract: *bujen, kooṇtōreak.*
compact, contract: *koṇ.*
contractions during childbirth: *kōḷo.*
wilt, contract: *kuṇōk.*

contrary: *juṃae.*
contrary to: *jekkar.*
quite the contrary: *make.*

contrast: *kōtaa-, oktak.*

contribution: *kuṇaa-.*
contribution, share: *kuṇaṇa.*
monthly contribution: *allōñ iju.*

contrite: *tōñkwe.*

control: *dāpdep, kabwijer.*
desire for something, uncontrolled: *ṃṃaelep.*

controversy: *aitwerōk.*

Conus
Conus marmoreus/bandanus: *likaebeb.*

convenient: *tokja-.*

conversation: *bwebwenato, kōṃṃao.*
adult conversation, informal and possibly trivial: *ṃṃawi.*
to converse: *kōṃṃao.*

convulsions
have convulsions: *du.*

cook
a food, biscuits and flour cooked together in water: *kōpjeḷtak.*
a food, breadfruit cooked on coals and scraped: *kwanjin.*
a food, cooked and pounded breadfruit, taro, bananas, or nuts mixed with grated coconut: *wūdeñ.*
a food, cooked preserved breadfruit smothered in grated coconut: *kubaḷ.*
a food, method of cooking fish: take fish eggs (roe) out and squeeze on fish and cook half done: *jāār.*
a food, nuts of breadfruit, cooked: *kwōlejiped.*
a food, ripe breadfruit mixed with coconut oil and cooked in pots: *nāpnāpe.*
a food, spongy meat of sprouted coconut cooked with arrowroot starch and diluted with water: *peaut.*
a food, three to one combination of arrowroot starch and water cooked together: *likōbla.*
a food, unleavened dough cooked by boiling: *jāibo.*
cook fish on stones: *ikjin.*
cook house: *ṃōn kuk.*
cook in a sea biscuit container: *aintiin.*
cook in a tin pan: *aintiin.*
cook shack: *peḷak.*
cooked: *mat.*
cooked pandanus: *edouṃ.*
cooking and eating fish right after catching them, usually at night: *jinre.*
cooking pan: *nāpe.*
cooking utensil: *ainbat.*

easy to cook: *mattiie.*
half-cooked: *amej.*
hard to cook: *mattiia.*
open fireplace for cooking: *wūpaaj.*
partially cooked: *watre.*
smell of cooking fish: *uwi.*
to cook: *kōmat.*
use coconut sap for cooking: *utōn-jekaro.*
work as a cook: *kuk.*
overcooked: *tuḷaar.*
uncooked: *amej.*

cool: *m̧ōḷo.*
cool air: *aem̧ōḷoḷo.*
cool of the evening: *aemedḷọk.*
cooled off, of food once hot: *med.*
coolness: *aem̧ōḷoḷo, aemed.*
coolness of a breeze: *lladikdik.*
keep one's cool: *kōmmaanwa.*
lose one's cool: *kun an ḷaam̧.*
pleasantly cool: *lladikdik.*

coop: *oror.*
cooped up: *keņaak.*
to fly the coop: *ko.*

cooperate: *ippān doon.*
to cooperate: *rādik doon.*

cooperative: *jake jibwil, rādik doon.*
not cooperative: *bōro-jepel.*
to chant while drawing up a canoe or other such cooperative work: *ñijir.*

coordinated
coordinated, physically: *util.*
uncoordinated: *jokwa.*
uncoordinated in dancing (see *kōl* (**kęl**)): *jakōl.*

copper: *kōba.*
smell of copper: *kkōbaba.*

copra: *waini.*
collect coconuts and husk them before making copra: *pinju.*
copra harvesting period: *aḷ.*
copra pieces, taken out of the shell: *jekak.*
cut out copra meat from shell: *karkar.*
dried copra ready to be weighed: *m̧ọọn.*
dry fish or copra by heat: *atiti.*
gather many husked copra nuts: *pinju.*
make copra: *kowainini.*
platform for drying copra: *jād.*
press oil out of grated copra: *joniak.*
smell of rotten copra on body: *maḷḷipen.*
smell of rotten copra or rancid coconut oil: *ḷōḷ.*
sort out bad copra: *ākūt.*
undried copra: *owatrere.*

copy: *anōk, ar.*

coral: *peḷ, wōd.*
a coral: *jebwā, ḷajjidik.*
a coral which can be used as sandpaper: *paḷ.*
coral finger extending out of a main coral head or reef: *anbwe.*
coral lime: *iawewe.*
coral species: *baal.*
coralhead: *wōd.*
cotton coral: *lijakkwe.*
enter and hide inside coral, said of fish only: *pọ.*
gashes in coral reef: *kōlñe.*
small man-made channel through coral: *mejā.*
soft coral rocks found on beach: *pukor.*

Corculum
a shell, *Cadiidae, Corculum impressum/monstrosum/cardissa*: *kūkōr.*

cord
cord made from coconut fibre: *kkwaḷ.*
lashing cord: *ino.*
tie or fasten with a rope or cord: *ḷajiiñ.*

Cordia
a plant, *Cordia subcordata* Lam. (Boraginaceae): *kōņo.*

core: *boḷ, buḷōn.*
core of a boil: *wūn.*
core of coconut tree at upper end: *juḷ.*
pandanus core: *ār.*

Coris
a fish, wrasse, *Coris gaimardi*: *alle, likōb.*

cork: *bọọr, bọọror, wūj.*

corn: *kọọn.*

corned beef: *kọọnpiip.*

corner: *jabōn, kāpoon, kona.*

cornet
a fish, cornet fish, *Fistularia petimba*: *jepooj.*

cornice
cornice or gable of a Marshallese house: *demāju.*

corns: *kūrkaboņ.*

corona: *kūrawūn.*

Corona
Corona Australis: *Utin-Ḷarrūbra.*
Corona Borealis: *Utin-Ḷajjidik.*
stars in Bootes (beta, mu, nu) and mu in Corona Borealis: *Ok-an-adik.*

corpse
a pile of corpses or fish or people: *ajeḷḷā*.
mat used to cover corpses: *kūtim*.
place from which corpses were floated away to sea: *bōn*.
stiffness of a corpse: *ajeḷkā, kā*.
swollen corpse: *bōj*.

corpsman: *komen*.

corral: *oror*.

correct: *jejjet, jiṃwe, ṃool*.
correct angle of handsaws: *oḷā*.

correspond: *kkar*.

corrugated
corrugated iron: *jinnibọọr*.

corrupt: *ttoon*.
corrupt, used of dead animals or humans swollen but not yet bad smelling: *wabanban*.

Corvus
stars in Centaurus (1, 2, 3) or Corvus: *Āl-im-kobban*.

Coryphoena
a fish, dolphin, *Coryphoena hippurus*: *koko*.

coryza: *uwur*.

cost
cost of: *oṇea-*.

costume: *balle, nuknuk*.

cotton: *kotin*.
cotton coral: *lijakkwe*.

couch: *joba*.

cough: *pokpok*.

council: *kọọnjeḷ, pepe*.

count: *bōnbōn*.
count up: *taḷe, watwat*.
estimate by counting: *watwat*.

counter
counterpart: *rājetak*.
countershading: *ukōt ṃōōr*.

country: *aelōñ*.
country of the world: *laḷ*.
foreign country: *aelōñin pālle*.

couple: *pea*.

courageous: *peran*.

course
be off course: *buñ*.
instrument for plotting courses, nautical: *kein kōttōbalbal*.
nautical course: *kooj*.
plot a course: *kkar, kōttōbalbal*.
steer a course with land on one's bow: *anlọk*.
to paddle a canoe on the starboard side to change course: *auretam*.
academic course: *kooj*.

course
water course in the reef: *wea*.

court
try in court: *ekajet*.

cousin
cross cousin: *riliki-*.
female cousin: *jine-*.
female parallel cousins of a male: *ine-*.
older cousin (parallel): *jei-*.
younger cousin (parallel): *jati-*.

covenant: *kalliṃur*.

cover: *bọto, libobo, pinej*.
canvas cover: *kabba*.
cover a sail: *atro*.
cover an earth oven with stones: *ertak*.
cover pandanus to ripen: *poñpoñ*.
cover up a hole: *jieñ*.
cover up an earth oven with leaves and dirt: *kobal*.
covered: *bọọror, bọrōk, penjak*.
covered over: *bal*.
covered with: *peddejak*.
covering: *balle, erer*.
mat used to cover corpses: *kūtim*.
to cover: *kkūtbuuj*.
to cover with a lid: *mājmāj*.
uncover an earth oven, usually when food therein is cooked: *jukok*.
uncovered: *keelwaan*.

covert: *ttino*.

covet: *addikdik, aṇokṇak*.
covet another's spouse, steal another's spouse: *aelellaḷ*.
covetous: *arōk*.
covetousness: *aṇokṇak, kaḷmarok*.

cow: *kau*.

coward: *oḷaḷo, pikōt, puwaḷ*.
"Coward!": *pedej*.

cowboy: *kaubowe*.

cowlick: *likapijwewe*.

cowling: *abọ*.

cowrie
Any cowrie shell, any shell: *libbukwe*.
money cowrie, a shell, *Cypraeidae*: *likajjid*.

crab
a catch of fish, crabs, or birds: *koṇa-*.
a crab: *jine*.
a land crab: *koḷaṃṃwā*.
an animal, white land crab: *lemḷat*.
coconut crab: *barulep*.
crab, general term: *baru*.
fishing method, hunt lobster or coconut crab when the moon is right: *katooj*.
fishing method, line fishing inside

lagoon using hermit crab for bait: *rupe oṃ.*
fishing method, line fishing outside lagoon, usually on lee side and fairly close to shore, for flying fish, using sand crab for bait: *rōjep.*
hermit crab: *oṃ.*
husking of coconuts by coconut crabs: *ejej.*
land crab, brown: *atūñ.*
land crab, inedible: *baru waan.*
place in sand where turtle lays eggs or coconut crab molts: *jọ.*
poisoned by eating crab: *iabaru.*
possessive classifier, fish, crabs, or birds: *koṇa-.*
prepare hermit crabs for bait: *pajo.*
sand crab: *ṃōḷe.*
sea crab: *mādo.*
shell of a crab: *jọkur.*
trap for crabs: *ajokḷā.*
white sand crab: *kalibbañ, karuk.*

crab louse
crab louse, *Phthirius pubis*: *kijdepak.*

crack
cracked: *kōk.*
cracks in skin of soles of feet: *bōlkōk.*
snapping or cracking sound: *ṇṇōjṇōj.*
stick hand into pocket, hole, or crack: *rrwe.*
to crack: *ḷañ.*

cracker: *petkōj.*
crackers: *būreej.*

craft: *kapeel.*

cramp
cramped: *apañ, apeltak.*

crane: *kabaj.*
a bird, crane, black *kabaj*: *melmelea.*
a bird, crane, black and white spotted *kabaj*: *kekebuona.*
a bird, crane, white *kabaj*: *keke.*
crane, mechanical: *kabaj.*
lift using crane: *tekōḷ.*
to crane the neck to see better: *mū.*

crank: *kein kōjjọ, utaṃwe.*
to crank an engine (with causative prefix): *jọ.*

crave: *batur.*
crave cigarettes: *añūr.*
crave fish: *batur.*
stop craving fish: *kōbbaturtur.*

crawl: *tōbalbal.*
crawl on the belly: *wāār.*

crayfish: *bọkuj pedped.*

crazy: *bwebwe, rowālọk, wūdeakeak.*

cream: *milik.*

crease: *bwilọk.*

create: *kōṃanṃan.*

creature
thing, creature: *māl.*

credit: *lōke, nōbar.*

creed
believe, faith, creed, pious: *tōmak.*

creep: *tōbalbal.*

Crenmugil
a fish, mullet, *Crenmugil crenilabis*: *iōōḷ, jooṃuṃ.*

crevally
a fish, crevally, *Caranx stellatus*: *ikbwij.*

crew: *kūru.*

cricket: *jidjid, juwapin.*

crime: *bōd, jorrāān.*

criminal: *ṃōrō.*

crimp
crimped: *ālokjak.*

cringe
to cringe: *mmālwewe.*

Crinum
a plant, *Crinum asiaticum* : *kieb.*

cripple
crippled: *kūrro.*
crippled, of legs only: *ḷōmmejne.*

criss-cross: *pirañrañ.*

critical
critical in speech: *kkañ loo-.*
stand back and study critically, as an artist: *allọk.*

criticism
invite criticism: *kōmmatōr.*

criticize: *kōrraat, lowaar.*

Crocethia
a bird, sanderling, *Crocethia alba*: *kwōl.*

crocodile: *aḷkita.*

crooked: *ankeke, ip.*

crop
second crop of coconuts: *ḷōruk.*

cross: *ḷḷā, lotaan.*
a cross: *debwāāl.*
criss-cross: *pirañrañ.*
cross cousin: *riliki-.*
cross out writing: *ṃanṃan.*
cross over: *kājoon, ḷōke.*
cross the legs: *kowawa.*
cross-eyed: *aljet.*
cross-stick on ship's mast: *kūrọtiik.*
crosscut saw: *bukduul.*
crossed in weaving or plaiting: *idaaptōk.*
crosswise: *wawa.*

cut crosswise: *bukduul.*
lie crosswise: *jitpeeḷeḷ.*
to cross: *kijoon.*
get caught in crossfire: *ḷaanwōtwōt.*

crotch: *lọtōñā.*

crouch: *dipāl.*

crow: *kkūr.*

crowbar: *baar.*

crowd: *bwij, jar.*
a crowd of: *bwijin.*
a large crowd passing backwards and forwards: *itileoñeoñ.*
crowded: *apañ, idepdep.*
crowded, of people: *kut.*
large crowd: *jarlepju.*
milling about of a crowd: *itileoñeoñ.*
move a crowd: *peḷaak.*
not crowded: *meḷak.*
be overcrowded, of boats or vehicles (see *kaddoujuj*): *douj.*

crown: *kūrawūn.*

crude: *ḷam waan.*

cruel: *lāj.*

crumb: *ṃōraṃrōṃ.*
crumbs: *tipdikdik.*

crumble: *lij, ṃōraṃrōṃ.*
crumble paper: *nukuj.*
crumbled: *pedakilkil.*
to crumble a mound or pile as of sand: *rōṃ.*

crunch: *kañurñur, kor, ññurñur.*

crush: *opene.*
crushed: *peddejọkwe.*
crushed in: *jepdak.*

crutch
crutch used for pushing boom of canoe away: *jeḷọk.*
crutches: *jokoṇ.*
use crutches: *jokoṇkoṇ.*

Crux: *Būbwin Epoon.*

cry: *jañ.*
cry an arrival, of ship or plane: *jeḷo.*
cry announcing the sighting of land: *ḷanno.*
cry loudly: *uwaañañ.*
cry of: *ṃōjaan.*
cry on someone's shoulder: *jabneejej.*
crying sound: *ṃa.*
intense crying, as a baby: *rraakak.*
short tempered, cry-baby, provoked: *kwi.*
slow to cry: *jọkkwikwi.*

crystalline
crystalline style: *lām.*

cuckoo: *wūdej.*

cucumber: *kiudi.*
sea cucumber, *Holothuroidea, Holothuria leucospilota*: *jipenpen.*
sea cucumber, *Holothuroidea, Opheodesoma*: *jāibo.*
sea cucumber, *Holothuroidea, Thelonia* or *Actinopyga*: *piāpe.*

Cucurbita
a plant, vine, *Cucurbita pepo* L. (Cucurbitanceae): *baañke.*

cuddle: *atbọkwōj.*
cuddle under a blanket: *kilbur.*
cuddling: *jjibur.*
cuddly: *ṃọkulkul.*

cue: *kiu.*

cuff: *kobak.*

cuffs
handcuffs: *jakōḷ.*

cult
a cult: *didiiñ.*
cult that tattooed and practiced magic: *eḷ.*

cumbersome: *ailparo, parok.*

cumulus
cumulus cloud: *kōdọ jutak.*
thick cloud formation of cumulus type covering a large portion of the sky: *jā.*

cunning: *jiṃaat.*

cup: *kab.*
coconut cup: *jiṃañko.*
use a cup: *kabkab.*

cupboard: *pāāntōre.*

cure: *kōmour, wūno.*
cured: *mour.*
wound that is easy to cure or heal: *mowiie.*
wound that is hard to cure or heal: *mowiia.*

curious: *kajnōt.*

curl
curly: *ṃōjālūlū.*

curlew: *kowak.*
a bird, bristle-thighed curlew, *Numenius tahitiensis*: *kōkkōk.*

current: *ae, aet.*
carry, of currents: *kinōr.*
current flowing eastward: *aetak.*
current flowing into lagoon: *aear.*
current flowing northward: *aeniñeañḷọk.*
current flowing out: *aelik.*
current flowing southward: *aerōkeañḷọk.*
current flowing westward: *aeto.*

currents around a passage: *aekijek.*
good current: *aeṃṃan.*
name of a current: *ṃōtodān.*
ocean currents nearest to an island: *juae.*
ocean currents that are farther away from an island than the *juae* currents: *dibukae.*
ocean currents that are farther away from an island than the *juae* or *dibukae* currents: *jeḷatae.*
on the current: *jelbōn.*
paddle a canoe so as to hold it against current: *kab.*
pull out, as current or undertow: *tọr.*
the first zone of currents: *juae.*
the second zone of currents: *dibukae.*
the third zone of currents: *jeḷatae.*

curry
curry favor with someone: *kappok jide.*
curry the favor of men or women with gifts: *anbōro.*

curry: *kare.*

curse: *jinjin, kanejnej.*
put a curse on: *kkọọl.*
to curse: *kkōpāl.*

curtain: *katiin.*

curve: *kōōb.*
curved: *jel, kkuṃliklik, kob.*

cuss: *jinjin, kanejnej.*

custard
pandanus juice mixed with grated coconut, cooked into custard: *mokwaṇ duul.*

custom: *kōṃanōt, ṃalik, ṃanit.*
customary reimbursement given by anyone in return or exchange for food, living, or payment for medicine or priest-craft: *kabwijeran.*

cut: *bukwabok, jekjek, ṃwijṃwij.*
cleave, cut in half: *bōrrā.*
cut cards: *kat.*
cut corners: *kipeddikdik.*
cut crosswise: *bukduul.*
cut down: *jjuok.*
cut hair: *ṃwijbar.*
cut into strips: *ōrōr.*
cut it large or thick: *jeklep.*
cut lengthwise: *bōrrā.*
cut off: *el, jepjep.*
cut off completely: *tūṃṃwijkōk.*
cut out copra meat from shell: *karkar.*
cut tree trunk into pieces, as breadfruit for making canoe: *kabbok.*
cut with scissors: *jijāj.*
cut with spurs: *jebwij.*
cut, hack, chop-off, split, slash: *jepak.*
cutting edge: *māj.*
haircut: *ṃwijbar.*
not cut waves well: *ṇojọ.*
shingled, cut the hair short: *taṃbaj.*
small cut, scratch: *kurar.*

cute: *ṃṃan.*

cycle
motorcycle: *wōtbai.*

cylindrical: *uwaitoktok.*

Cymatiidae
a shell, *Cymatiidae*: *jilel.*

Cymolutes
Cymolutes praetextatus: *likōb.*

Cyperus
a plant, *Cyperus ferax*: *būkōr.*
a plant, marsh grass, *Cyperus javanicus* Houtt.: *wūjooj-in-eoon-bōl.*

Cypraeidae
a shell, *Cypraeidae*: *libbukwe.*
money cowrie, a shell, *Cypraeidae*: *likajjid.*

Cyraea
Arabica scurra/eglantina/couturiera/asiatica or *Cyraea tigris*: *libbukwe.*

Cyrtosperma
Cyrtosperma chamissonis: *iaraj.*
a cultigen of *Cyrtosperma* (the large "taro"): *kālōklōk.*

daddy: *baba.*

daily: *aolep raan.*

damage: *mariprip.*
damage caused by termites or bookworms: *dile.*
damaged: *jorrāān.*
to damage: *tuwe.*

dame: *lijjọọn.*

damn
"Damn!": *kōṃōttōṇa.*

damp: *boḷot, ṃōḷọwi.*
smell of damp clothing: *jatbo.*

damsel fish
a fish, general term for all damsel fish: *ūrōrmej.*

dance: *eb.*
a dance: *bwijbwij.*
a dance, using fans: *deelel.*
dance call, move: *ṃọo.*
dance steps: *iṃtō-.*
dance, western style: *tanij.*
folk dances: *taidik.*
gather to dance: *du.*
Marshallese folk dance: *leep.*
Marshallese stick dance: *jebwa.*
Marshallese women's stick dance: *jiṃōkṃōk.*

mistake in performing a dance, song, or chant: *dujebwābwe.*
dancing a jig: *jirōm̧rōm̧.*
dancing place: *jikip.*
move hips from side to side while dancing: *kajikia.*
pull as in dancing: *kkekaak.*
uncoordinated in dancing (see *kōl* (**kẹl**)): *jakōl.*

dandruff: *jekak.*

dandy: *kabbil.*
a dandy: *kabōllaļ, utļōm̧.*

danger
accompany either physically or spiritually while in great danger: *mije.*
dangerous: *kauwōtata.*
in danger of: *uwōta.*

dangle: *allitoto.*

dare base
a game, dare base (two bases): *awiia.*

daring: *peran.*

dark: *ditōb, m̧witok, marok.*
dark cloudy night: *lianij.*
dark colored: *jil.*
dark in color: *meej.*
dark night: *diboñ.*
darkness: *m̧ūtok, m̧witok, marok.*
darkness that follows a cloud coming over the horizon at night: *elianij.*
darkskinned: *jakmeej.*
depths of darkness: *Kapin-marok.*
fear of being alone in the dark or at sea: *abwinmake.*
great fear of ghosts and the dark: *abwinmakelep.*
reach for something in the dark: *ttọļūm.*
thick darkness: *marok jilōñlōñ.*
very dark: *ninjek.*

darling: *jitōnbōro.*

darn
interjection: "Darn!" Or "God forbid!": *ōkkōk.*
interjection: "Oh. Oh my. Darn it." (exclamation of mild surprise or disappointment)": *o.*
interjection: "Darn!" Or "Heck!": *ōrrōr.*
interjection: "Shucks!", "Darn!": *io.*

darn: *āj.*

dash: *jọjo.*

Dasia
an animal, tree lizard, green and black, *Dasia smaragdina*: *aop, kiļij.*

dastard
dastardly: *puwaļ.*

date
day, date: *raan.*

daughter
daughter of: *nāji-.*
daughter of a queen: *lerooj.*
second son or daughter: *utlōkļap.*
son or daughter-in-law of: *nāji-.*

daunted
undaunted: *peran.*

dawn: *jiraan, joraantak, m̧ōjawōnene, okraan, raantak.*
a bird that sings at dawn: *lọjiraan.*
period before dawn: *jimmarok.*

day
birthday: *raanin ļotak.*
day of month when moon comes over the horizon just as sun sets: *jetñōl.*
day-dream: *inọñ, ttōṇak.*
day, date: *raan.*
daybreak: *raantak.*
hottest time of day: *bwiltōñtōñ.*
late, time of day or tide: *jọweej.*
the day after the day after tomorrow: *raan eṇ turun jekļaj.*
the day after tomorrow: *jekļaj.*
the day before yesterday: *inne eo ļọk juon, raan eo turun inne.*
time of day or night: *tōre.*
within the next few days: *ilju im men.*

daze
in a daze: *m̧ōjālūlū.*

deacon: *tikōn.*

dead: *jako, mej.*
as dead matter: *likaakrak.*
mourn the dead: *ilomej.*
rise from the dead: *jerkakpeje.*
smell of dead flesh: *kkōōrōr.*

deaf: *jarroñroñ.*
deafening: *pedañwūjñwūj.*

deal: *pepe.*

dear: *jitōnbōro.*

death: *mej.*
atmosphere in which death is certain: *aitwōnmej.*
death of a chieftain: *bwilọklañ.*
intuition about a future misfortune or death: *lomije-.*
land given to someone who took care of the head of the lineage owning the land during illness before death: *m̧ōnkọļotļot.*
near death: *aū.*
premature death: *mijenatabuñ.*
shadow of death: *annañinmej.*
superstition that cat crying at night

portends death of someone: *bwijenro.*

debate: *kōbọuwe.*
slow to anger in debate (see *n̄n̄in̄i* (ggiygiy)): *jan̄n̄in̄i.*

debris: *menọknọk.*

debt: *likjab, m̧uri.*

decay: *wabanban.*
decayed: *kōt.*
smell of decayed flesh: *bwiin-puwaļ, juon̄.*

decease
live at home of deceased during the week following death, relatives and spouse: *an̄ak.*
mourn a deceased: *āmej.*
pay respects to a deceased: *āmej.*
person killed and buried with a deceased chieftain to accompany him on his journey to a different world: *ura.*

deceit: *ankiliriab.*

deceive: *m̧oņ.*

December: *Tijem̧ba.*

decent: *bwe, karbōb.*

deceptive
deceptively: *jatdik.*

decide: *pepe.*
undecided: *apaproro.*

decimal: *teejm̧ōļ.*

decisive
indecisive: *apaproro, bbōroro, bōro-pejpej.*

deck
deck, nautical: *teek.*
decked out: *inōknōk.*

declare: *kōnnaan, kowaļọk.*

decline: *abōb, m̧akoko.*

decorate: *inōknōk.*
decorate, dress up: *kōkōm̧m̧anm̧ōn.*
be overdecorated: *to jān enōka-.*

decoration: *kino.*
boat decorations: *ļōb.*
canoe part, decorations of feathers on masthead, boomtips, and sail: *den̄ļọk.*
decorations made from feathers of frigate birds, one on each tip of the sail on a chief's canoe: *kadulele.*

decoy: *anan.*

decrease: *dikļọk, meraļọk.*
line used to decrease the sail on a canoe: *lukwar.*
decreasing in size: *mọkun.*
decreasing in size, as of physique: *tor.*

dedicate: *aje.*

deed: *jerbal.*

deep: *ļon̄, m̧wilaļ.*
deep water: *jat.*
having a deep draft: *kapjulaļ.*
the deep: *ikjet.*

defeat: *anjọ.*
loss of royal status through defeat in war: *jipọkwe.*

defecate: *pijek.*
defecate from trees, of birds: *de, edde.*
defecate, of children: *m̧wi.*
habitually defecate on ground: *pektaan.*
tree in which birds roost and defecate: *jade.*

defect: *bōd, irļọk.*

defend: *jojomar.*

defense: *jālitak.*
Marshallese art of self-defense: *m̧aanpā.*
ward off using Marshallese hand-to-hand combat defense techniques: *pile.*

deficit: *likjab.*

define: *alikkar.*
well-defined: *meļeļe.*

definite: *alikkar.*

deflate: *kkun.*

deflect: *ukok.*

deflower: *karūtto, ļwūp.*

deform: *ukok.*

defraud: *ālikinjepjep.*

defy: *jum̧ae, kaarmejjet.*

degenerate: *dọlel.*

degree
degree, angle measurement: *tiikri.*
degree, collegiate: *tiikri.*

dehydrate
dehydrated: *m̧ōrā, nāl.*

delay: *aepedped, aļọkbad, rum̧wij.*

delegate: *jitōn̄.*
delegated: *maron̄.*

delete: *jjeor.*

deliberate: *kọọnjeļ, kōbọuwe.*
move with steady and deliberate purpose: *ijubon̄-ijuraan.*

delicacy: *wiwi.*

delicate: *mera.*

delicious: *nnọ.*
delicious (of fish only): *uwi.*

delight: *lọudin̄din̄.*
delightful: *nnọ, tūb.*
interjection: expression of wonder or delight: *bōranm̧aajidake.*

delinquent: *boea, rijorrāān, uwaan kakūtōtō.*

delirious: *wūdeakeak.*

deliver: *bōkḷamleḷọk.*

delouse: *ākūt.*

Delphinus
dolphin, *Delphinus roseiventris*: *ke.*

Delphinus
stars in Delphinus: *Jāpe.*

deluge: *ibwijleplep, nep.*

deluxe: *weeppān.*

demented: *bwebwe.*
house for the demented: *iṃōn bwebwe.*

demijohn
large bottle, demijohn: *teemjọọn.*

demolish: *kọkkure, ruprup.*

demon: *tiṃoņ.*
be possessed by demons: *urōt.*
playground for demons: *meḷaḷ.*
possessed by a demon: *tuwe.*
sea demon: *kwōjenmeto.*

demonstrate: *kōmmeḷeḷe.*

demonstratives
—first person inclusive singular: *in.*
—first person inclusive plural human: *rein.*
—first person inclusive plural nonhuman: *kein.*
—first person exclusive singular: *e, iiō.*
—first person exclusive plural human: *rā, rārā.*
—first person exclusive plural nonhuman: *kā, kākā.*
—second person singular: *ņe, ņeņe.*
—second person plural human: *raņe, rāraņe.*
—second person plural nonhuman: *kaņe, kākaņe.*
—third person singular: *eņ, iieņ.*
—third person plural human: *raņ, rāraņ.*
—third person plural nonhuman: *kaņ, kākaņ.*
—remote singular: *eo, uweo.*
—remote plural human: *ro, roro.*
—remote plural nonhuman: *ko, koko.*

personal demonstratives
—first person inclusive singular: *liin, ḷein.*
—first person inclusive plural: *liṃarein, ḷōṃarein.*
—first person exclusive singular: *lie, liiō, ḷōe, ḷeiō.*
—first person exclusive plural: *liṃarā, liṃarārā, ḷōṃarā, ḷōṃarārā.*
—second person singular: *lieņe, lieņeņe, ḷōņe, ḷōņeņe.*
—second person plural: *liṃaraņe, liṃarāraņe, ḷōṃaraņe, ḷōṃarāraņe.*
—third person singular: *lieņ, liieņ, ḷeeņ, ḷeieņ.*
—third person plural: *liṃaraņ, liṃarāraņ, ḷōṃaraņ, ḷōṃarāraņ.*
—remote singular: *lio, luweo, ḷeo, ḷouweo.*
—remote plural: *liṃaro, liṃaroro, ḷōṃaro, ḷōṃaroro.*

sentence demonstratives
—interrogative singular: *ewi.*
—interrogative plural human: *erri.*
—interrogative plural nonhuman: *erki.*
—first person inclusive singular: *eñin.*
—first person inclusive plural human: *errein.*
—first person inclusive plural nonhuman: *erkein.*
—first person exclusive singular: *eñe, eñiō.*
—first person exclusive plural human: *errā, errārā.*
—first person exclusive plural nonhuman: *erkā, erkākā.*
—second person singular: *eñņe, eñņeņe.*
—second person plural human: *erraņe, errāraņe.*
—second person plural nonhuman: *erkaņe, erkākaņe.*
—third person singular: *eñeņ, eñieņ.*
—third person plural human: *erraņ, errāraņ.*
—third person plural nonhuman: *erkaņ, erkākaņ.*
—remote singular: *eñeo, eñoweo.*
—remote plural human: *erro, erroro.*
—remote plural nonhuman: *erko, erkoko.*

demote: *ttā.*

den: *jik.*

Dendrochirus
a fish, scorpion fish, *Dendrochirus zebra*: *ōō.*

denim: *tanim.*
denim trousers, blue jeans, Levis: *tanim.*

denomination: *ra.*

dense: *bukwelep.*
dense, as of hair or bushes: *bukwekwe.*

dense, of shrubbery: *kut.*
dent: *opene.*
be dented: *penā.*
dented: *obab.*
denude: *utūkaļ.*
deny: *kaarmejjet.*
lie deny, dishonest: *riab.*
depart: *buñlik.*
custom of spending the last night with people before they depart: *jeboñōn.*
spend the night with friends who are departing: *jebokwōn.*
depend
depend on: *lōke.*
depend on people: *atartar.*
not depend on (see *lōke* (lękęy)): *jālōke.*
deposit: *ddoor, deļoñ, llik.*
depression
valley, depression: *komļaļ.*
small valley or depression: *peta.*
depth: *iļoñ.*
depths of darkness: *Kapin-marok.*
depths of the ocean: *ikjet.*
deride: *kajjirere.*
descend: *wanlaļ.*
climb or descend a rope: *pitto.*
describe: *kōmmeļeļe, kwaļok kadkadi-.*
description: *kadkad, kōjālli-.*
desecrate
break a taboo, desecrate: *kōtrāe.*
deselect: *kọkwōpej.*
desert isle: *āne-jeṃaden.*
desert
a child who deserts home through anger over parental coercion: *lumọọrļọk.*
deserve: *aikuj.*
get what one deserves: *lle.*
deserving of: *āteo.*
feel undeserving: *ppat.*
design: *pija.*
design edges of canoes or boats: *ñadñad.*
designate: *jitōñ.*
designate portions: *kōjjebar.*
desire: *aikuj, ankilaa-, kilaak, kōņaan.*
desire food: *bbūriri.*
desire for something, uncontrolled: *ṃṃaelep.*
desire more, of a delicious food, music, or game: *jaṃjaṃ.*
desire something: *ikdeelel.*
romantic desires: *mejpata.*
uncontrolled desire: *aelellaļ.*
unlawful desire: *kijoñ.*
withdraw from society to follow one's own desires: *paarōr.*
desk: *tebōļ.*
despair: *bbeer.*
despicable: *kajjōjō.*
despise: *llotaan.*
despise people: *kōtrāe.*
despite: *amñe.*
despondency: *ddo.*
dessert: *kōṃaolaļ.*
to receive one's just desserts: *lle.*
destination
miss destination: *peļọk.*
proceeding toward destination: *jibadek.*
reach destination: *tōkeak.*
destiny: *anilen, mejānkajjik.*
destitute: *jojoļāār.*
destitute of: *ejjeļọk.*
destroy: *jeepepļọk.*
destroy and take everything: *rakim.*
to destroy: *kọkkure.*
detail
talk in great detail, elaborate: *tipdik.*
detect: *llo.*
move fast so as to avoid detection: *miro.*
deteriorate: *jintanji.*
determination: *kije.*
determine: *jep, ļam.*
determined: *pen būruo-.*
deuce
deuce of spades: *litōļpi.*
devastation: *mariprip.*
develop: *ddek.*
having well-developed Venus mound: *bọñur.*
deviant: *ikōnālkinṃwio.*
deviate: *ir, jebwābwe, jenliklik, rowālọk.*
deviate from instructions: *weļọk.*
devil: *tepiļ.*
devilfish
a fish, devilfish, giant octopus: *kouj.*
a fish, great devilfish, manta: *boraañ.*
devoid: *āmje.*
head devoid of hair: *kweejej.*
devote
devote presents to the gods: *aje.*
devour: *orañļọk.*
dew: *ṃōļọwi.*
dexterity: *mejādik.*
diabetes: *tōñal.*
diabetic: *tōñal.*

diagnose: *etale.*
diagram: *annañ.*
dial: *anōḷ.*
dialect: *kajin.*
diameter: *depakpak.*
diamond: *taiṃoṇ.*
diaper: *kaḷ.*
wear a diaper: *kaḷkaḷ.*
diarrhea: *ilọklọje, raprap, wōtōdtōd.*
diary: *raan ñan raan.*
dice: *taij.*
a game, played with pebbles and ball, similar to dice game: *ḷuḷu.*
rolling dice: *taij.*
dicker: *jobai.*
dictionary: *tūkjinede.*
die
die out, of plants, animals, or people: *ḷot.*
quick to die: *mejjiie.*
slow to die: *mejjiia.*
to die, of arrowroot, signaling time for digging the root: *pāl.*
diesel: *tijeḷ.*
diet: *ṃōñā.*
differ
difference: *kōtaa-, oktak.*
different: *āinjuon.*
different from: *āi-.*
difficult: *pen.*
dig: *kōb.*
dig taro: *tto.*
dig up: *toktak, totak, ttuuj.*
digging of feet or tires into soft sand: *kōbkōb.*
point beyond which one cannot dig further: *ikjet.*
to die, of arrowroot, signaling time for digging the root: *pāl.*
digest: *lij, liklik.*
dignitary: *kāājāj.*
dignity: *utiej.*
dilapidated: *ijurwewe, ṃadeoñeoñ, ṃōdṃōd, ṃōraṃrōṃ, ṃor.*
get old and dilapidated due to continuous soaking in sea water: *luwajet.*
dilemma
in a dilemma: *apaproro.*
diligent: *kūtarre, niknik.*
dilute: *kāre, kabodān.*
dilute food or drink to make it stretch: *ilọk.*
dilute paint: *kapejlọk.*
diluted: *ppej, watre.*
of right dilution: *ṃṃan utōn.*
dim
eyes dim with age: *arrom.*
fog, dim, haze, blur: *tab.*
dimension: *ded.*
diminish: *apdik.*
dimple
dimples: *libwetōr.*
dinner
farewell dinner: *ṃōñāin kōjab.*
last dinner: *dienbwijro.*
Diodon
a fish, porcupine fish, *Diodon hystrix*: *jabōnke, ṃōjañūr.*
Diodora
Diodora (austroglyphis) sieboldii or *Montfortula pulchra* or *Tugali vadososinuata*: *jowakin.*
Diomedea
a bird, black-footed albatross, *Diomedea nigripes*: *le.*
a bird, laysan albatross, *Diomedea immutabilis*: *le.*
dip
dip food: *kattu.*
dip up water: *itōk.*
diplomacy: *jeḷā kuṇaa-.*
dipper: *kekōb, ḷatōḷ.*
direct: *jiniet, jujāl.*
come directly: *iok-.*
go directly to or towards: *iok-.*
go directly toward: *kajju.*
steer directly for: *kaiok.*
direct
to lead, direct, preside: *tōl.*
direction: *jab.*
direction of: *kijjie-.*
head in a certain direction: *jit.*
in what direction: *jikōt.*
lose direction: *peḷọk.*
lose the direction of: *wiwijet.*
point in all directions: *toor.*
directional enclitics
—northward: *niñeañ.*
—backward or toward the ocean side: *lik.*
—downward: *laḷ.*
—eastward: *ta.*
—eastward, upward: *tak.*
—forward: *ṃaan.*
—interiorward: *nọọj.*
—islandward or shoreward: *āne.*
—northward: *niña.*
—seaward: *meto.*
—southward: *rōkeañ, rōña.*
—toward the lagoon side: *ar.*

—upward: *lōn̄*.
—westward: *to*.

directional postpositions
—toward addressee: *waj*.
—toward the speaker: *tok*.
—toward third party: *ļọk*.

director
choirmaster, director of a choral group: *m̧aajta*.

dirt: *bwidej*.
dirty: *bwiltoonon, rran, ttoon*.
dirty water: *lim̧*.
dirty with dried matter, especially around mouth or eyes: *rūm̧ōm̧ō*.
refill a hole with dirt: *jjion̄*.
scoop, dirt or sand: *eọkur*.
very dirty: *jokdād*.

disadvantage: *an mej eņ, nana tam̧m̧wi-*.

disagree: *bōro-jepel, kiojaļjaļ*.
shake the head in disagreement: *jeboulul*.

disappear: *jako, jeepepļọk, jetļọk, ļot, ļotļọk*.

disappointed: *eddo ippa-, kōrraat, llotaan, ro*.
interjection: surprise or disappointment: *ōjjej*.

disapprove: *dike, kōrraat*.

disaster: *bwijerro, jerata*.
final meal together before an impending disaster: *dienbwijro*.
visual signal such as fire to notify of death or other natural disasters: *jubwij*.

disavow: *kaarmejjet*.

discard: *joļọk, tam̧*.
discarded pandanus key: *ār*.

discharge: *eakto*.
discharged: *diwōj*.

disciple: *rijjelōk, rūkaļoor*.

discipline: *katak*.

discomfort: *aplon̄lon̄*.

disconcerted: *lo*.

disconnect: *mejaļ*.
disconnected: *jenolọk*.

discontent: *jab po bōro*.

discontinue: *bōjrak*.

discount: *dikļọk*.

discouraged: *bbeer, bweetkōn*.

discover: *llo*.

discredit
discredit someone to gain favor with another, or as revenge: *baijin*.

discreet: *jenolọk*.

discuss: *kọọnjeļ*.

disease: *jepa, mej, nan̄inmej*.
bad case of skin disease (*koko* (**kewkew**)): *keļe*.
confine because of disease: *lōbọ*.
disease characterized by emaciated legs: *māro*.
disease characterized by swollen belly and emaciated limbs as a result of malnutrition: *jeje*.
disease, scaly and flaky skin: *koko*.
skin disease: *karko, tilpoki*.
skin disease, white spots on body: *jān*.
venereal disease: *jeplej, mādke*.

disembark: *to*.

disenchanted: *kolōkabwi-, lo, m̧weed*.

disenheartened: *m̧weed*.

disentangle: *kōmmeļeļe, mejaļ*.

disgrace: *jook*.

disguise: *kōjakkōlkōl, ukōt m̧ōōr*.
disguised: *jakkōlkōl*.

disgust
disgusted: *ļļao, m̧ōļan̄ļōn̄*.

dish: *kōnnọ*.

dishonest
lie deny, dishonest: *riab*.

dishonor: *jook, wōtlọk*.

disillusion: *teron̄e*.

disinherit: *kalia*.

disintegrate: *jeepepļọk, m̧adeon̄eon̄, m̧ōram̧rōm̧*.

disk
sand disks: *bok allōn̄*.

dislike: *kajjikur*.
dislike to do: *abwin*.
strongly dislike: *dike*.

dislocate
dislocated: *ir, irļọk*.

dismantle: *jjuok*.
dismantled: *jokak*.

dismay
interjection: dismay: *aiaea*.

dismiss: *jjilōk*.
dismiss, fire: *kupi*.

dismount: *wanlaļ*.

disobedient: *bōt*.
disobedient (see *jilikiie* (**jilikiyyẹy**)): *jilikiia*.
disobedient (see *kipiliie* (**kipiliyyẹy**)): *kipiliia*.
wilful disobedience: *aplep*.

disobey: *kōjelbabō, kōtrāe*.

disorder: *pok.*
dispatch: *jjilōk.*
dispensary: *m̧ōn taktō.*
dispersed: *ajeeded, jeeded.*
displace: *poktak.*
displaced: *ir.*
display: *aloklok.*
displease: *ļōkatip, llotaan.*
displeased: *inepata, llu.*
interjection of displeasure used only by women: *ōjjeti-.*
disposition: *kōjea-, m̧ūtō-, tam̧m̧wi-.*
bad disposition: *m̧m̧aļkaro.*
disprove: *kariab.*
dispute: *aitwerōk, aoļ.*
land dispute: *kōtaan wāto.*
start a dispute: *kōjjarōk.*
disqualify: *kupi.*
disregard: *jekdo̧o̧n, kōjelbabō.*
disrobe: *utkōk.*
dissatisfied: *ikrooļ.*
dissatisfy: *jab po bōro.*
dissolve: *ōnļo̧k.*
distance: *kōtaa-, tōran, tokra-.*
a great distance: *leelle.*
look at a distance: *alluwaļo̧k.*
distant: *ttoļo̧k.*
distant, of sight and sound: *kkwaad.*
distill
to distill: *kōmat.*
distinct: *jenoļo̧k, m̧aeļo̧k.*
Distinguenda/echinata: *lidid.*
distinguish: *kile.*
distinguished: *ļakkūk.*
be indistinguishable: *peljo.*
distort: *ikūr.*
distorted: *ip.*
distract
distracted: *m̧ad.*
distracted by some calamity: *ļo̧kjenaa-.*
distress
distressed: *liaajļo̧ļ.*
distribute: *ajej, jaketo-jaketak.*
district: *bukwōn.*
District Administrator: *kom̧ja.*
District Director of Education: *kom̧ja.*
distrophy
muscular distrophy: *māro.*
distrust: *jālōke, kkōljake.*
disturb: *poktak.*
disturbance: *aploñloñ, uwōjak.*
disturbance caused in water by canoe or fish: *aujo̧jo̧.*
disturbed: *abņōņō, ppeerir.*

ditch: *jikur.*
dive: *tubar, tuļo̧k.*
dive after getting hooked, of fish: *ñijļo̧k, wūnļo̧k.*
dive down: *lōrak, ttuur.*
dive of birds or planes: *lōkā.*
dive under water: *ruñļo̧k.*
dive, of a plane: *juñaidi.*
dive, of boats: *ko̧kweet.*
dive, of planes: *lōrak.*
jump to dive, head first: *tubar.*
diverge: *jepel.*
diverse: *kkārere.*
divest
divest of all property: *katoļo̧k.*
divide: *ajej.*
apart, divided into two parts: *rājet.*
divide among each: *kajjo.*
dividing line: *kōtaa-.*
divination: *bubu.*
divination method, using knots in pandanus leaf: *bubu.*
knot in divination: *bo, bwe.*
place for divination: *bad.*
result of divination: *bwe.*
divine: *kkwōjarjar.*
diving
diving mask: *māj, mejān turo̧ñ.*
fishing method, spear fishing while diving: *tuwā.*
long-winded in diving: *pakij.*
division: *teeñ.*
any group of people, as a class, unit or division: *jar.*
division of a land tract: *alen.*
division of an atoll or islet: *bukwōn.*
divorce
divorced: *jepel.*
dizziness: *ñūt.*
dizzy: *addeboulul, ajjim̧aalal, jim̧alejlej, ñillitok.*
do: *jerbal, kōm̧m̧an, m̧adm̧ōd, wōjak.*
do not: *jab bar.*
do one's best: *kattūkat.*
do one's duty, do one's share: *bōk ko̧naa-, bōk ko̧naa-.*
do something singlehandedly: *wajekā.*
do what?: *et.*
do you hear me?: *eañ.*
doing: *kōm̧anm̧an.*
redo: *āpta.*
do
syllable "do" of musical scale: *to.*
docile: *kipiliie.*

dock: *wab.*
dry-docking, maintain: *tọọk.*

doctor: *taktō.*
see a doctor: *taktō.*
witchdoctor: *ṇakṇōk.*

dodder
doddering: *aḷapḷọk, bwijwōḷā, ppaḷ.*

dodge: *rrā.*

dog: *kidu.*
dog, child speech: *kukkuk.*
ruffling of cocks and dogs before fighting: *rrọñ.*
to bark, of dogs: *rorror, wañ.*

dog-tooth tuna
a fish, dog-tooth tuna, *Gymnosarda nuda*: *jilo.*

doll: *tọḷe.*

dollar: *taḷa.*

dolphin
a fish, dolphin, *Coryphoena hippurus*: *koko.*
dolphin, *Delphinus roseiventris*: *ke.*

domestic
domesticated (see *awiia* (**hawiyyah**)): *awiie.*
duty of taking care of a natural or adopted child or pet or domesticated animal: *nāji.*
undomesticated: *awiia.*

dominate: *peek.*

domino: *tomino.*

done: *jaak, ṃōj.*
half-done, of fish or meat: *koubub.*
leave a chore undone and start another: *jibwe turin jerbal.*
not thoroughly done (see *lōt* (**let**)): *jālōt.*
not well done: *amej.*
well done: *weeppān.*

donkey: *tọọñke.*

door: *aor, kōjām.*
doorway: *kōjām.*
opening of any container, hole, doorway, or cave, etc.: *māj, meja-.*

dormitory: *tomittori.*

dorsal
dorsal fin: *eñ, ūl.*

Dosinia
a shell, *Veneridae, Veremilpa minuta/micra/costellifera/scabra* or *Dosinia histrio/abyssicola*: *kūkōr.*

dot
dotted: *tiltil.*
spotted, dotted, spotty: *bbijinjin.*

double: *piro, tabōḷ.*

doubt: *perper.*
doubtful: *ttūṃurṃur.*

dough: *pilawā.*
a food, unleavened dough cooked by boiling: *jāibo.*
to rise, of dough: *uwe.*

doughnut: *tọnōt.*
a food, cake doughnut: *kōtabañ.*
a food, doughnut, with hole: *tonaaj.*

dove: *ṃuḷe.*

down: *laḷ.*
be down and out: *ḷoktōk.*
canoe-surfing, when sailing down wind: *kōttōmāle.*
climb down: *to.*
down below: *taaṃbūḷo.*
downward: *laḷḷọk.*
go down: *tulọk.*
shot down: *lel.*
shotdown: *balu.*
point head downwards: *kalōlō.*
take downwards: *bōklaḷḷọk.*
sail downwind with the sail on the south and the outrigger on the north: *tōmeañ.*

dozen: *tōjin.*

Draco
stars in Draco: *Aoḷōt, Ṃade-eo-an-Aoḷōt.*

draft
draft (fishing): *jarjar.*
having a shallow draft, of ships (see *kaplep*): *kapdik.*
openings in a house causing drafts: *ajerwawa.*
shallow draft: *okwōjaja.*

drag: *ipep, kkekaak, lōkake.*
easy to drag in water (see *atakiia* (**hatakiyyah**)): *atakiie.*
fishing method, using weight with hook, octopus for bait, and dragging it on sandy bottom: *kōjọlim̧.*
hard to drag in water (see *atakiie* (**hatakiyyẹy**)): *atakiia.*
to drag or tow from lagoon side to ocean side: *lelik.*
to drag or tow from ocean side to lagoon side: *lear.*
walk dragging a leg: *māro.*

dragon: *tūrāikōn.*

dragonfly
an insect, dragonfly: *boub.*
large dragonfly: *bouk in iiep.*

drain: *llutōk.*

drama: *kkure, tieta.*

drape: *katiin.*

draw: *aik.*
  bucket or can for drawing water from a well: *keikōb.*
  draw near: *jikrōk.*
  draw out: *kkekaak.*
  draw water: *itōk.*
  drawing lots: *kūbween kijdik.*
  drawing much water causing it to be hard to paddle or sail, nautical: *añōt.*
  to draw: *lōkake.*

draw
  a draw: *jebo.*

draw: *m̧alen.*
  draw a picture: *pija.*

drawer: *tūrowa, kkekaak.*

dread: *kor, mijak.*

dream: *ttōn̄ak.*
  day-dream: *inǫñ, ttōn̄ak.*
  make a sound of pleasure while sleeping because of good dreams: *jeja.*

dreary: *aeto.*

dregs: *o.*

drench
  drenched: *ļwōjat, m̧oujlep.*
  drenched to the skin: *aen̄ak.*

dress: *jokankan.*
  badly dressed: *keelwaan.*
  decorate, dress up: *kōkōm̧m̧anm̧ōn.*
  dress up: *nuknuk, tōreejab.*
  hem a dress: *kobak.*
  lift dress: *kitak.*
  Mother Hubbard dress, named for Oahu: *wau.*
  undress: *utkōk, utūkaļ.*
  well dressed: *ppānpān.*
  women's full-length dress: *ipep.*

dribble: *pil.*

dried
  a food, preserved dried breadfruit: *m̧ōn̄akjān.*
  undried copra: *owatrere.*

drift
  a drifter: *pejpetok.*
  drift about the sea: *peto-petak.*
  drift ashore: *eǫtōk.*
  drift away: *peļǫk.*
  drift away from: *inojeik.*
  drift eastward: *petak.*
  drift northward: *peniñeañ.*
  drift southward: *perōkeañ.*
  drift westward: *peto.*
  fishing method, using a canoe and drifting with the wind and current in a lagoon, line fishing: *peļǫk.*

driftwood
  balsa driftwood: *wōj, wūj.*
  cedar driftwood: *aik.*
  driftwood (small): *jokwā.*
  pine driftwood: *jeļaar.*

drill: *ddāil, deenju, kilmij.*
  a drill: *debwāāl.*

drink: *idaak.*
  buy drinks and food for a group: *jǫut.*
  dilute food or drink to make it stretch: *ilǫk.*
  drink after or together with another: *koko.*
  drink noisily: *ļwiit.*
  drink of: *lime-.*
  drink up: *jorom.*
  drink while eating: *ninikoko.*
  drinking glass: *kab.*
  drinking straw made from *aetōktōk*: *aetōktōk.*
  drinking water: *aebōj, dānnin idaak.*
  drinking water containers on a canoe or boat: *kōb.*
  go drinking at a club: *kuļab.*
  hard drinking: *kodia.*
  heartburn caused by drinking fresh coconut sap on an empty stomach: *mmaļ.*
  illicit drinking: *kaurur baib.*
  possessive classifier, water, soft drinks, or juice of coconuts, etc.: *lime-.*
  provide drink for: *n̄alime-.*
  share a drink: *nininkoko.*
  soft drink: *koļa.*
  sucking noise made in drinking green coconuts: *m̧m̧ōtm̧ōt.*
  taste food or drink: *edjoñ.*
  to drink from a well or a hole in a tree by bending over and using the mouth directly: *m̧ōt.*
  to drink water, child speech: *kaka.*

drip
  dripping: *bbūtbūt, piliñliñ.*
  dripping wet: *aen̄ak.*

drive: *jitoja.*
  drive a car: *kaarar.*
  drive a jeep: *jiipip.*
  drive off: *ubaak.*
  drive off flies: *ubļǫñ.*
  jaunt, sail, or drive around aimlessly: *tarto-tartak.*
  test drive a new or overhauled vehicle: *likbad.*
  to drive a car: *tūraip.*

drizzle: *m̧ōtǫdik, wōt-dikdik.*

drool: *iādatōltōl.*

droop
to droop: *mọkun.*

drop: *pilin̄lin̄.*
canvas drop: *jan̄n̄ōr.*
drop down, as from a height: *wōtlọk.*
drop of liquid: *pil.*
drops of water: *bbūtbūt.*
get the last drops of water from a water container: *kajḷor.*
sharp drop off on bottom of ocean or lagoon: *jirūṃle.*

drought: *jọwōtwōt.*
season of drought: *an̄ōnean̄.*

drown: *maḷon̄.*
drown someone by holding his head under water: *wūj.*

drowsy: *an̄an̄e, mmadidi, mmejraalal.*

drug: *wūno.*

drum: *aje, tūraṃ.*
chant and urge someone on by beating on a drum: *piniktak.*
oil drum, 50-gallon: *kaajliin̄.*

drunk: *kadek.*

Drupa
Drupa ricina/morum or *Purpura* (mancinella): *lidid.*

dry: *jejjat, ṃōṇakṇak, ṃōrā.*
bone dry: *nāl.*
dry and brittle: *n̄an̄.*
dry fish or copra by heat: *atiti.*
dry hair, not oily: *kuraan̄an̄.*
dry pandanus or coconut leaves over fire in preparation for weaving: *katrar.*
dry season: *an̄ōnean̄.*
dry spell: *jọwōtwōt.*
dry throat: *ṃōrā-bōjbōj.*
dry under sun: *kōjeje.*
dryness, onomatopoetic: *ḷaḷḷaḷ.*
leave to dry: *roro.*
on dry land: *eppānene.*
platform for drying copra: *jād.*
rack for heat or smoke drying: *ati, bwi.*
stranded high-and-dry: *pāāt.*
to dry and become seasoned, of lumber, as in canoe building: *pit.*
to dry leaves by fire: *rar.*
to dry under the sun: *nel.*
dry-docking, maintain: *tọọk.*

dubious: *apaproro.*

duck: *badik, dak.*
a bird, wild duck: *ran̄.*
duck one's head: *wōmak.*
to duck a blow: *wōmak.*
"duck soup": *kijen nin̄nin̄.*

duct: *baib.*

Ducula
a bird, Micronesian pigeon, *Ducula oceanica*: *ṃuḷe.*

due: *likjab.*

duel: *im, ire.*

dug
dug up: *ebjak.*

dull: *jājiṃaat, kkōb.*
dull of hearing: *ron̄ jaṃōṇ.*
dullness (of people): *addiṃakoko.*

dumb: *ikōn̄, ṃōḷọwi, taṇo.*
dumbfounded: *boṇ.*

dump: *jọkpej, taṃ.*
garbage dump: *kōlla.*

dumpling: *jāibo.*

dune: *bwijuwe.*

dunk: *kattu.*

durable: *kije.*

duration
of short duration: *jedkaju.*

dust: *būn̄al.*
dust from coconut cloth (*inpel*): *roro.*
dusty: *būn̄al.*
sawdust: *kijen jidpān.*

duty: *jerbal, kuṇaa-.*
do one's duty, do one's share: *bōk koṇaa-.*
duty of taking care of a father: *jemā.*
duty of taking care of a grandson, granddaughter, a grandparent, or a pet: *jibwi.*
duty of taking care of a mother: *jine.*
duty of taking care of a natural or adopted child or pet or domesticated animal: *nāji.*
duty that a younger sibling is expected to give to older siblings: *jei.*
duty that an older sibling is expected to give to younger siblings: *jati.*
duty towards ones relatives: *nukwi.*

dwarf: *ḷajikaj, rimmenanuwe, rūṃōkarraṇ.*
dwarfed: *wūnnin̄.*

dwell: *jokwe, jukjuk.*
spirit dwelling within a person, good or bad: *juk jetōb.*

dwindle: *kuṇōk.*

dye: *dọọl, kawūno.*

dying
be dying: *aū.*
dying breath: *bōk ob.*
long in dying: *mejjiia.*

dynamic
dynamic voice: *ḷḷaaj.*

dynamite: *abba, bǫkutañ, taanṃait.*

e
name of the letter *e*: *āe.*

each: *jabdewōt, kajjo.*
each other: *doon.*

eager: *ikdeelel, kijerjer.*
eager for revenge: *paḷ.*

eagle: *ikōḷ.*

eagle ray
a fish, spotted eagle ray fish, poisonous, *Aetobatus narinari*: *imen.*

ear: *lǫjilñi.*
eardrum: *juñurñur.*
pierce ears: *il.*
possessive classifier, earrings and other things worn on ear: *die-, die-.*
wear earring: *diede.*

early
an early-bird: *mājinmuur.*
wake up early in the morning: *mājinmuur.*
early tomorrow: *ililju.*

earn: *kōṃṃan.*

earnest: *ellowetak, kijejeto.*

earth: *bwidej, laḷ.*
pile of earth: *ubatak.*

earth oven: *uṃ.*
a food, breadfruit baked in earth oven: *kōpjar.*
a food, diluted starch baked in coconut spathe in earth oven: *kōlǫwutaktak.*
bake, usually in earth oven: *uṃuṃ.*
cover an earth oven with stones: *ertak.*
cover up an earth oven with leaves and dirt: *kobal.*
stick used to spread hot stones for earth oven: *tokrak.*
uncover an earth oven, usually when food therein is cooked: *jukok.*

earthworm: *ṃajkadāl.*

ease
ease something: *kadikdik.*

east: *reeaar.*
eastern side: *likiej.*
facing east: *jaḷtak.*
on the east side of: *jetak, wetaa-.*

Easter: *Ijitō.*

easterly
easterly breeze: *añōlto.*
easterly swell: *buñtokrear.*

eastern: *ej.*
eastern side of a house: *lǫpet, pet.*

eastward: *ta, tak, taḷǫk, tureeaar.*
current flowing eastward: *aetak.*
directional, enclitic, eastward: *ta.*
directional, enclitic, eastward, upward: *tak.*
drift eastward: *petak.*
go eastward: *itakḷǫk, wetak.*
head eastward: *jittak.*

easy: *kijen niñniñ, pidodo.*
easy to break or tear: *ṃōdṃōd.*
easy to cook: *mattiie.*
easy to satisfy with food: *mattiie.*
easy to turn (see *jaḷiia* (**jahḷiyyah**)): *jaḷiie.*
easy-going: *ineeṃṃan, jabde.*
take it easy: *kadikdik.*
uneasy: *nana taṃṃwi-.*
wound that is easy to cure or heal (see *mowiia* (**mẹwiyyah**)): *mowiie.*

easy-going: *raḷǫk.*

eat: *kaikai, ṃōñā.*
drink while eating: *ninikoko.*
eat before working: *kapije.*
eat breakfast: *ṃabuñ.*
eat fish while fishing, beat up someone badly: *kōmennañ.*
eat garbage: *attūkoko.*
eat kernel of coconut out of shell with one's teeth: *kijḷat.*
eat left-overs: *attūkoko.*
eat one kind of food not usually eaten alone: *kolied.*
eat only one food: *jintōb.*
eat or drink while walking: *jotal.*
eat raw fish: *koobub.*
eat secretly: *jinre.*
eat supper: *kōjota.*
eat with oversize bites: *kuborbor.*
eat, child speech: *meme.*
eat, food, child speech: *ṃwāṃwā.*
full after eating: *mat.*
greedy eater: *būrooklep, mattiia.*
light eater: *būrudik, mattiie.*
overeat on fruitful land: *jjāāk.*
possessive classifier, tooth or eating utensils: *ñii-.*

eaves: *tǫrtǫr.*
eaves-trough: *tǫrtǫr.*

eavesdrop: *iaroñroñ.*

ebb
ebb tide: *pāāt, roj.*
lowest ebb tide: *pāāt ṃōṇakṇak.*

eccentric: *kūḷaṃwe.*
eccentricity: *taṇo, utaṃwe.*

ecclesia: *eklejia.*

Echeneis
a fish, shark pilot, *Echeneis naucrates*: *ḷattil pako.*

echo: *ainikien Etao.*

eclipse
eclipse of the moon: *bōtōktōk allōñ.*

economize: *kipeddikdik, kōjparok.*

ecstacy: *lọudiñdiñ.*
ecstatic: *wūdiñdiñ.*

edge: *apar, daṃ, tōrerei-, ūlūl.*
be on edge, of people: *idimkwi.*
border on mat or stone edge of road: *apar.*
cutting edge: *māj.*
cutting edge of: *meja-.*
design edges of canoes or boats: *ñadñad.*
edge of: *deṃwā.*
molded edge: *tiek.*
outer edge of reef where large coral heads are: *bōran baal.*
to weave the edges of a mat or hat: *jekōt.*

edgy: *idimkwi.*

edible
edible portion inside certain nuts or seeds: *jibañūñ.*
overgrown and inedible sprouted coconut: *iupej.*

edit: *jeje.*

educate
educated: *jeḷā ḷọkjeṇ.*
District Director of Education: *koṃja.*

eel
eel with no teeth: *deldelbwij.*
eel, *Conger cinereus*: *ṃōjoud.*
eel, large and black: *dāp.*
fresh-water eel: *toṇ.*
large eel: *pedāp.*
moray eel: *kideddelbwij.*
moray eel, *Gymnothorax flavimarginatus*: *ṃakañ.*
moray eel, *Gymnothorax pictus*: *ṃaj-mouj.*
snake eel, *Myrichthys colubrinus*: *ṃajid.*
eel that lives in fresh water, toothless: *toṇ.*
eel, intestinal worm: *ṃaj.*
moray eel: *dāp.*

effect: *tokja-.*

effeminate: *kōrā.*

effervesce: *jib.*

effort: *kakkōt, kijejeto.*

egg: *lep.*
a food, method of cooking fish: take fish eggs (roe) out and squeeze on fish and cook half done: *jāār.*
abandoned unhatched egg, usually spoiled: *kor.*
egg yolk: *bwibwi, bwibwitakaḷ.*
fertilized egg, ready to hatch: *kune.*
fish eggs: *bwiaea, likipia.*
fresh egg (see *kune* (**kiwney**)): *tabwil.*
place in sand where turtle lays eggs or coconut crab molts: *jọ.*
rob sitting hen of her eggs: *eaklep.*
to lay eggs: *lik.*

ego
egotism: *jājjāj, juwa, utiej būruo-.*

Egretta
a bird, reef heron, *Egretta sacra*: *kabaj.*

eight: *ruwalitōk.*
four eighths: *emān ṃōttan ruwalitōk.*

elaborate: *kōmmeḷeḷe, pok.*
talk in great detail, elaborate: *tipdik.*

Elagatis
a fish, rainbow runner, *Elagatis bipinnulatus*: *ikāidik.*

elastic: *mō.*

elbow: *jiṃwin pā.*

elders
respect elders: *kaaḷapḷap.*

elect: *kkāālel.*
election: *kkāālel.*

electric
electric light: *ḷaaṃ jarom.*
electricity: *jarom.*

electrid
a fish, electrid, *Valenciennesia strigata/violifera*: *ikōlood.*

elegance: *kāilar.*
elegant: *karbōb.*

Eleocharis
refers to both *Fimbristylis atollensis* St. John and *Eleocharis geniculata* (L.) R S.: *pādālijṃaan.*

elephant: *eḷbōn.*

elephantiasis: *rọulep.*

Eleusine
a plant, *Eleusine indica* (L.) Gaertn.: *katejukjuk.*

elevation: *ḷolōñ.*

eleven: *joñouljuon.*

elf: *rimmenanuwe, rūṃōkarraṇ.*

eligible: *kkar.*

eliminate: *jjeor.*
eliminate, in contest: *ukok.*

Ellice
Ellice Islands: *Elej.*

elliptical
elliptical in shape: *jepjep.*

Ellobiidae
a shell, *Ellobiidae*: *alu.*

eloquent: *wājepdik.*

emaciated
disease characterized by emaciated legs: *māro.*
emaciated: *apeñāñā, bbōj, m̧ō.*

embalm: *kōbọrōk.*

embark: *uwe.*
disembark: *to.*

embarrass
be embarrassed: *bwilọk māj.*
be embarrassed for: *ko tok kili-, mejko.*
causing public embarrassment: *kabwilọklọk māj.*
embarrassed: *āliklik, jook, lo, pelọk.*
embarrassment caused by actions of another: *mmālwewe.*
hard to embarrass (see *jjookok* (**jjewekwek**)): *jājjookok.*
incapable of being hurt or embarrassed: *mejel kil.*

embellish: *inōknōk.*

ember
embers: *mālle.*

emblem: *kakōl̦l̦e.*

embrace: *atbọkwōj, bọkwōj, kaerer, kkuul.*
embrace while sleeping: *jjibur.*

embroider: *juwain.*
embroidery: *tiltil.*

embryo: *kọ.*

emerge: *wal̦ọk.*
emerge from water: *mmat.*

emergency
emergency equipment: *m̧aanpā.*
emergency treatment: *kōm̧adm̧ōdin idiñ.*

emigrate: *jepjep.*

eminent: *bōtata, kkwōjarjar, utiej.*

emit: *boutl̦ọk.*

emotion: *eñjake, tūriam̧o.*
emotionally unstable: *anniabeab.*
seat of the emotions: *bōro.*

employ: *jerbal.*
employee: *jerbal, rijerbal.*
employer: *rūkōjerbal armej.*
work on a job, employment: *jọọb.*

empty: *āmje, bar, maat.*
empty container: *wōpeñ.*

emulate: *ari-, kajjioñ.*

enable: *kōmaroñ.*

enchant
enchanting: *mmejaja.*
spell, enchantment: *anijnij.*

disenchanted: *kolōkabwi-, lo, m̧weed.*

encircle: *kōpool̦.*
encircled: *pool̦.*

enclosure: *oror.*
sunken enclosure: *nit.*

encounter: *iioon.*

encourage: *pen.*
encouragement: *tōp.*
to encourage, advise: *rōjañ.*

encumber
encumbered: *abor.*

end: *jem̧l̦ọk.*
at the end of: *jabōn.*
either end of an island: *ajokl̦ā.*
end (used in songs): *jimmil̦ọk.*
end of: *jabwe.*
end of an islet: *kiwūl, tur.*
inner end of a single pandanus key: *kiār.*

endanger: *kauwōtata.*

endeavor: *jibadbad, kajjioñ, kakkōt, kijbadbad.*

endorse: *jain.*

endurance: *kijenmej.*

endure: *kōm̧bade.*
unable to endure physically: *ñatñat.*
enduring: *kije.*
long enduring: *meanwōd.*

enemy: *kōjdat.*

energetic: *ājmuur, keeñki.*
excited, agitated, energized: *em̧m̧ōl̦ō.*

energy: *keeñki.*

enervate: *aploñloñ.*

enforce: *jejjet kūtie-.*

engage
engaged: *koba, pālo, poub.*

engine: *injin.*
broken, of engines: *wōla.*
engineer: *injinia.*
fit together, put together an engine or piece of machinery: *bobo.*
mix sail power with engine power: *kabodān.*
operate an engine: *leinjin.*
run, of engines: *jọ.*
to crank an engine (with causative prefix): *jọ.*
use an engine: *leinjin.*
with outboard engine: *l̦oon.*

England: *Iñlij.*
place name, England: *Iñlen.*

English: *Iñlij.*

engrave: *m̧alen.*

enjoy: *itok-limo, kōṇaan.*
enjoyment: *tūb.*

enlarge
enlargement of breasts at puberty: *bwā.*

enormous: *debbōn.*

enough: *bwe.*
enough, of goods or needs: *keke.*
not enough: *jabwe.*
not enough of counted things: *jọuñ.*

enrage
enraged: *ro.*

enroll: *deḷọñ.*

ensign: *bōḷeak.*

entangle: *pok.*
disentangle: *kōmmeḷeḷe, mejaḷ.*
entangled: *ḷorak.*

enter: *deḷọñ, mọọn.*
enter and hide inside coral, said of fish only: *pọ.*
enter into: *mọk.*
enter lagoon: *ṃweeaar.*
follow a large wave in entering a lagoon: *ḷooribeb.*

enterprise: *būrojāāk, jerbal.*

entertain: *kaṃōṇōṇō.*

enthuse: *bab-laḷ.*
enthusiasm: *ellowetak, itok-limo, limo.*
lose enthusiasm: *ṃweed.*

entice: *kkaal.*
call or entice animals or children to come near: *kkaal.*

entire: *aolep.*
entirely: *ḷam jako, wōtōm.*
entirely finished: *dede.*
entirety: *iio.*

entrance: *aor, kōjām.*

entreat: *añōtñōt, tūbḷotak.*

envelope: *impiḷoob.*

envious: *ban, kaṃo, paḷ.*

environment: *meḷan.*

envy: *juunṃaad, ḷọḷōjjed.*

Epibulus
a fish, wrasse, *Epibulus insidiator*: *katōk, mō.*

epidemic
flu epidemic: *mejin.*

epilepsy: *anen Etao.*
have an epileptic attack: *jib.*

Epinephelus
grouper, *Epinephelus adscenscionis*: *ḷōjepjep.*
grouper, *Epinephelus fuscoguttatus*: *kūro.*
grouper, *Epinephelus hexagonatus*: *ṃōṃō.*
rock cod, *Epinephelus flavocaeruleus*: *pookliṃ.*
rock hind, *Epinephelus albofasciatus*: *ḷōjepjep.*
Epinephelus striatus: *aleañ.*

episode: *bwebwenato.*

equal: *āinwōt, kewa.*

equator: *ikkwetōr.*

equip
be equipped with: *le.*
emergency equipment: *ṃaanpā.*
equipment: *ṃweiuk.*

eradicate: *joḷọk, tūṃṃọṇ.*

erase: *jjeor.*
erase footprints or traces: *jieñ, jjioñ.*

erect: *ejej, ju, kajjuur, kkal.*
erected: *jurōk.*
erection: *rrōñ.*

Ereunetes
a bird, semi-palmate sandpiper, *Ereunetes pusillus*: *kwōl.*

erode: *ṃōñā.*

Erosaria
Erosaria helvola/erosa/flaveola or *Monetaria annulus harmandiniana/moneta rhomboides*: *likajjid.*

errand: *jjilōk.*
rely on children to accomplish errands or chores: *ajriin uwaak.*

error: *bōd, jiriḷọk.*

erupt: *jieb-.*

escape: *deor, jọọr, kōpḷọk.*
escape route: *iaḷan jọọr.*
escape, usually from getting hurt: *joor.*
slipped by, unite, escape: *rōḷọk.*

escort: *āñin, apar, karwaan.*

esophagus: *būri.*

essence: *ḷoḷātāt.*

essential: *aorōk.*

establish: *kajjuur.*

estimate: *aṇtọọn, leḷōmṇak.*
estimate by counting: *watwat.*
underestimate: *perper.*

estrange
be estranged from: *lia.*
estranged: *kolōkabwi-.*

etc.: *āierḷọkwōt.*

eternal: *jānindeeo-ñanindeeo.*

eternity: *jiṃṃūḷọk, jimmiḷọk.*

etiquette: *kōṃanōt.*

eulogize: *tūbḷotak.*

eunuch: *kakōļ.*

euphemism: *naan mera.*
euphemism for sexual position: *jitnen m̧ōm̧ō.*
euphemism for sexual relations: *kōmmerara.*
euphemistic reference to any of a variety of activities, mostly off-color: *mettorkaņ.*

Euphorbia
a plant, *Euphorbia heterophylla* L. (Euphobiaceae): *nukne.*
a plant, *Euphorbia thymifolia* L. (Ebon.): *dāpijbok.*
also a species of *Euphorbia*: *bwilbwilikkaj.*

Europe: *aelōñin pālle.*

evacuate: *jepjep.*

evade: *jeerinbale.*
evade, verbally: *jujuurļọk.*

evaluate: *watwat.*

evaporate: *jako.*

even: *wōnaji.*
come out even: *uñ.*
even out: *iden-oņe.*
uneven: *bwijuwe, jikin uwe, tōplik tōpar.*
uneven, as racing canoes: *jake.*
fishing term, said of a coconut leaf chain used as scarer that is strung out unevenly: *kapijjule.*

even
even if: *amñe, meñe.*
even though: *meñe.*

evening: *jota.*
cool of the evening: *aemedļọk.*
evening of the day after tomorrow: *jọteen jekļaj.*
evening prayers (Protestant): *nokwōn.*
four evenings ago: *jọteen eo turun inne eo ļọk juon.*
last evening: *jota.*
this evening: *jọtiinin.*
three evenings ago: *jọteen inne eo ļọk juon.*
tomorrow evening: *jọteen ilju.*
yesterday evening: *jọteen inne.*
a star (planet), Evening Star, Venus (evenings only): *Maalal.*

event: *waļọk.*

ever: *nañin.*
everlasting: *jānindeeo-ñanindeeo.*
forever: *indeeo, kōbo.*
live forever: *juknen.*

every: *aolep, jabdewōt, wōtōmjej.*

evidence: *kam̧ool, kein kam̧ool.*

evil: *nana.*
to possess, of evil spirits: *tuwe.*

evolve: *ejaak.*

exact: *jejjet, lukkuun.*
not exactly: *ejjabdaan.*

exaggerate: *añļap, kōļļapļap.*

exalt
exalted above another: *lijekļọk.*

exam
examination day at end of term: *jem̧nājin.*
examination: *teej.*

examine: *etale, iaļan juon, idajoñjoñ, jāāk, kakōlkōl.*
examine, physically: *kakōlkōl.*
scrutinize, examine: *allọk.*

example: *annañ, jemān-āe, waan joñak.*
take as example, experiment: *mālejjoñ.*

excell
excellent: *weeppān.*

except: *ijellọkwi-.*

excess: *bwe.*
excessive: *bōlej.*

exchange: *jānij, kōrrā.*
customary reimbursement given by anyone in return or exchange for food, living, or payment for medicine or priest-craft: *kabwijeran.*

excite
aroused to excitement: *jjeurur.*
be excited: *jeparujruj.*
excited: *ellowetak, jjeikik, jjeurur.*
excited, agitated, energized: *em̧m̧ōļō.*
excitement: *iruj, jjānene, jeparujruj.*

exclamation
an exclamation expressing sudden pain: *ūō.*
exclamation, of surprise: *bōram̧m̧aanō.*
exclamation: "Goodness!": *ijā.*
exclamation: "Wow!": *ekōļōk.*

excommunicate: *jarin kōtļọk, joļọk.*
be excommunicated: *buñ.*

excrement: *kūbwe.*

excursion: *jam̧bo, kōkajoor.*

excuse
make false excuses: *jekpen.*
to excuse: *joļọk bōd, wūlok.*

execute: *kōm̧m̧an.*
execute an order: *loloorjake.*

execution: *m̧anm̧an.*

executive: *mānija.*

exercise: *kōmmālmel.*

exert
exert oneself: *kakkōt.*

exhaust
exhausted: *m̧ōk, maat, orā.*

exhibit: *kaalwōjwōj.*

exist: *mour, or, pād, waļọk.*
existence: *meļọ, mour.*
manage to exist: *kipeddikdik.*

exit: *diwōj, wannabōj.*

Exocoetidae
a fish, flying fish, family *Exocoetidae*: *jojo.*

exorbitant: *bōlej.*

expand: *m̧ōñāñe.*
expand, as a balloon: *bbool.*

expect: *bōklōkōt, katmāne.*
as expected: *āteo.*
expectant: *aelellaļ.*
unexpected streak of luck, windfall: *tọọr pata.*

expectorate: *kaplo.*

expel: *joļọk, kọbaj.*
to expel: *kakkije.*

expensive: *bōlej, dejeñ.*

experience: *eñjake.*
experienced: *mminene.*
inexperienced (see *mminene* (**mminẹynẹy**)): *jāmminene.*
inexperienced: *watre.*

experiment: *elmọkot.*
take as example, experiment: *mālejjoñ.*

expert: *m̧ōkade, moot, ņakņōk, tijem̧ļọk, wājepdik.*
good in fishing, expert in fishing: *aewanlik.*
intuition and knowledge possessed by certain expert Marshallese navigators using traditional methods: *kabuñpet.*

explain: *kōmmeļeļe.*
explain something in detail: *iiaak.*
explanation of meaning of words: *rāpeļta-.*

explode: *bokkoļọk, deboklọk.*

exploit: *ājļor.*
exploit a fishing grounds: *tuwe.*

explore: *jatoļ.*

explosion
sound of an explosion: *bokkoļọk.*
explosive sound, voiceless bilabial affricate: *rūb.*

expose: *jjedwawa, kowaļọk.*
expose one's faults before his face: *jeklep.*
exposed: *jjerwawa, keelwaan.*
exposed to wind and air: *añjerak.*
spoiled from overexposure to air and sun: *m̧ōņakņak.*

express: *kowaļọk.*

expression
expression: "Chicken": *pedej.*
expression: "Impossible!": *eban.*

expurgate: *katoļọk.*

extend: *m̧ōñāñe.*
extended: *mō.*

extent: *joña-.*

exterior: *lik, nabōj.*

external: *anilik, lik.*

extinct
become extinct: *ļot.*

extinguish: *kkun, m̧anm̧an.*

extort: *kowadoñ.*

extra: *dam̧ok.*

extract: *wōmwōm, wūjroñ.*
a food, juice extracted from fresh pandanus: *jowaanroñ.*
coconut cloth used to squeeze and extract oil from grated coconut: *jouneak.*
extracted: *teep.*
method of extracting coconut meat out of its shell without breaking the meat: *kōmmālwewe.*
method of extracting pudding from cooked pandanus: *kilọk.*

extraordinary: *kōppaļpaļ.*

extravagant: *bōlej.*

extreme: *jabōn, toļọk.*
extremely: *ātin, dọlin, ļam jako, lukkuun.*

extricate
extricate, as meat from clam: *arar.*

eye: *māj.*
apple of one's eye: *ñiejo.*
bleary-eyed: *mejkōr.*
burn, of eyes: *korōt.*
cross-eyed: *aljet.*
eye cataract: *jā.*
eye of: *meja-.*
eye-catching: *kōmājmāj.*
eyeball: *ijuun māj.*
eyebrow: *āt.*
eyes dim with age: *arrom.*
eyes wide open: *kabūrōrō.*
eyesight: *rre.*
get something in one's eye: *pelọk.*

gritty feeling under the eyelids: *ttaorak.*
have sore eyes: *mejmetak.*
inflamed eye: *pilo.*
keep an eye on: *o̧naak.*
look out of the corner of the eye: *addikdik.*
open eyes under water: *tumej.*
pie-eyed: *aljet.*
pluck out eyes: *itūk.*
possessive classifier, eyes, lids, openings, eyeglasses, masks, or goggles: *meja-.*
pupil of eye: *tōm̧a.*
pupil of the eye: *ijuun māj.*
rub ones eye: *itūn̄.*
slimy-eyed: *mejkōr.*
smaller eye of sprouted coconut: *tōbo.*
sticky, of eyes: *ttaorak.*
sty on the eye: *ātbwe.*
wide-eyed: *kabūrōrō.*
possessive classifier, eyes, lids, openings, eyeglasses, masks, or goggles: *meja-.*

eyeglasses: *māj, māj kilaaj.*
eyeglasses of: *meja-.*

fa
syllable "fa" of musical scale: *ba.*

fabric: *ed.*

fabrication: *ļōōt.*

fabulous: *kōppaļpaļ.*

face: *māj, turun māj.*
face away from: *jeļļo̧k.*
face of: *meja-.*
face to face: *jelm̧ae.*
fall on face: *pedo.*
lift up the face: *m̧ajed.*
lose face: *bwilo̧k māj, pelo̧k.*
make a face: *kaū.*
make a sour face: *kōmmen̄.*
put on a long face: *kōjjeram̧ōlm̧ōl.*
to face (with directional): *jaļ.*
turn face up: *kōjjād.*
wash one's face: *ormej.*
facing: *de-.*
facing east: *jaļtak.*

fact: *bwe, lukwi, m̧ool.*
true to fact: *ātin.*

faculty: *ankilaa-.*

fad: *limo.*

fade: *mājkun.*
fade away: *kkwaad.*
fading of color: *eor.*
fading of color or shade: *jjurjur.*

fail: *likjab.*

faint: *ļotļo̧k, n̄illitok, parōk.*

fair: *bwe.*
fair breeze: *m̧akroro.*
fairly: *jaad.*
time of fair weather: *iien rak.*
treat unfairly: *ālikinjepjep.*

fairy: *lōrro̧, n̦oonniep.*

faith: *lōke.*
believe, faith, creed, pious: *tōmak.*
faithful: *m̧ool, tiljek.*
unfaithful, as of spouse: *llo.*

fake: *ļōnan̄, riab.*

fall: *tipn̄ōl.*
cause someone to fall: *ļatipn̄ōl.*
fall and get squashed: *pedej.*
fall apart: *jeepepļo̧k.*
fall down: *bun̄, bun̄lo̧k, olo̧k, wōtlo̧k.*
fall face downward: *bun̄-pedo.*
fall flat: *pedej.*
fall head down: *lōrak.*
fall headlong, in wrestling: *jun̄aidi.*
fall into sin: *tōmrok.*
fall off, of ripe pandanus keys: *po.*
fall on: *ure.*
fall on face: *pedo.*
fall on one's back: *jarleplep, jedtak, rotak.*
fall on one's bottom: *n̄adn̄ad.*
fall prematurely, of coconuts: *kwaļm̧we.*
fall short of, in length: *jen.*
fall through: *rōm̧.*
fall with a thud: *puruk.*
fall, as a tree: *o̧lo̧k.*
fall, from erect position: *okjak.*
fallen prostrate: *o̧lo̧k.*
falling of words from lips: *bun̄raak.*
falling star: *iju rabōļļo̧k.*
pull together, on rope, almost falling: *bun̄ kake.*
something that has fallen from a canoe underway: *enkanaode.*
sound of someone falling: *po̧kwi.*

false: *bōd, riab.*
false love: *io̧kwe in kij.*
false promise: *pepe riab.*
false promises: *naan jekdo̧o̧n.*
false teeth: *n̄in̄at.*
false-hearted: *ankiliriab.*
make false excuses: *jekpen.*

false albacore
a fish, false albacore or *kawakawa*: *ļooj.*

falter: *itweļo̧k.*

fame: *bun̄bun̄.*

familiar: *jiniet, moot.*
familiar with: *kile, m̧ōm̧ō in.*

not familiar: *ruwamāejet.*
family: *baaṃle, bwij, erṃwe, nukwi.*
famine: *kwōle, ñūta.*
food in time of famine: *kūrwaan.*
famous: *buñbuñ.*
fan
a dance, using fans: *deelel.*
a fan: *deel.*
to fan: *deelel.*
use a fan: *deelel.*
fancy: *ilar.*
superficially fancy: *kōmjedeọ.*
fang: *ñi.*
fantastic: *kōppaḷpaḷ.*
fantasy: *ttōṇak.*
far: *leelle, ttoḷọk.*
far apart (see *kkut* (**qqit**)): *mmejo, mmeḷo.*
spread far and wide: *tilmaak.*
fare: *oṇea-.*
farewell
bid farewell: *iọkwe, kōjjājet.*
bid farewell to: *iọkiọkwe.*
farewell dinner: *ṃōñāin kōjab.*
spend last moments together, farewell occasion, bring to a finish: *kōjjemḷọk.*
farm: *atake, jikin kallib.*
fart: *jiñ, rūb.*
fascinating: *kōppaḷpaḷ.*
fascination: *ppaḷ.*
fashion: *ḷōma-.*
fast: *iiṃ, iur, ḷḷaeoeo, ṃōkaj.*
do it fast: *menḷọk.*
faster: *ḷọk.*
go fast: *jetñak, jorñak.*
move fast so as to avoid detection: *miro.*
not fast: *jāiur, jāiurjet.*
tie or fasten with a rope or cord: *ḷajiiñ.*
walk fast: *jorjor.*
fast
break a fast: *dao.*
to fast: *jitlọk.*
fast
fasten: *dāpijek, kōbobo.*
fastened: *kijek.*
fastened, of anchors only: *kilōk.*
fat: *matōk, tebu, tōbōb.*
chew the fat: *kōmāltato.*
fat and healthy, usually referring to a baby: *ṃọkulkul, uḷūtḷūt.*
fat in turtle shell: *wiwi.*
fat, of meat: *kūriij.*
fatso: *ḷōttekōḷkōḷ.*
fatten: *matōk.*
roll of fat around waist: *maḷūttōk.*
short and fat, of people: *depetdoul.*
fate: *anilen, jide, kilaak.*
father: *baba, jema-.*
duty of taking care of a father: *jemā.*
fathom: *ñeñe.*
fatigue: *ṃōk.*
fatigued: *kajjinōk.*
faucet: *bọjet.*
fault: *bōd, ṇota, ruo-.*
expose one's faults before his face: *jeklep.*
find fault with: *kkọbōl.*
favor: *jouj.*
curry favor with someone: *kappok jide.*
curry the favor of men or women with gifts: *anbōro.*
force someone to do some favor for one: *kōṃakoko.*
give gift to win favor, to opposite sex: *kōbōjbōj.*
return a favor: *ukōt bōkā.*
favorable: *ṃakroro, ṃṃan.*
unfavorable tide, neither high nor low: *jatloñ.*
favorite: *makmake.*
favorite child: *ñiejo.*
favorite of a chief: *pālemoron.*
favorite one: *jitōnbōro.*
hurt feelings of some by showing favoritism to others: *kabwilọklọk māj.*
fear: *kor, lōḷñọñ, mijak.*
beside oneself with fear: *ḷọkjenaa-.*
fear of being alone in the dark or at sea: *abwinmake.*
fearful: *ttūṃurṃur.*
fearless: *pen būruo-, peran.*
fearless (see *mijak* (**mijak**)): *jāmmijakjak.*
great fear of ghosts and the dark: *abwinmakelep.*
feast: *keemem, kwōjkwōj.*
marriage feast: *kwōjkwōjin pālele.*
feat
perform a feat: *lukor.*
feather: *kooḷ.*
canoe part, decorations of feathers on masthead, boomtips, and sail: *deñḷọk.*
decorations made from feathers of frigate birds, one on each tip of the sail on a chief's canoe: *kadulele.*
not hairy, not feathery: *nemwak.*

pluck feather or hair (Ralik only): *imkilkil.*
pluck feathers: *tūm̧m̧ǫn̦.*
pluck feathers from a bird: *ttemakil.*
rooster tail feather: *ļōb.*
snipe that has lost its feathers: *m̧ōdkowak.*

feature: *ļōma-, pao.*

February: *Pāpode.*

feces: *kūbwe, toeak.*
hard feces: *m̧ǫn̦.*
smell of feces: *kūñ.*
smell of feces on body or clothing: *ñoño.*
soft bits of feces: *m̧wi.*

fed
be fed up: *m̧weed.*
underfed: *kwōle.*

fee: *ǫnea-.*

feeble: *addimej, m̧ōjņǫ, wūpeļ.*

feed: *paane.*
feed a fire: *ankaan.*
feed off a surface: *ñarñar.*
to feed: *naajdik.*

feel: *eñjake, uññūr.*
a feeling against: *kajjikur.*
a raspy feeling in the throat, especially after a cold: *mmelkwarkwar.*
agitation of feelings: *lim̧otak.*
feel around for something: *ttǫļūm.*
feel undeserving: *ppat.*
feel unworthy: *ppat.*
make someone feel welcome: *karuwanene.*

feet
cracks in skin of soles of feet: *bōlkōk.*
feet sink in sand making for difficult walking: *neen kōbkōb.*
sound of treading feet: *m̧m̧ūn̦m̧ūn̦.*

feign: *jekpen.*
feign sickness: *riab nañinmej.*

fell
felling of a tree: *oļǫk.*

fellow: *kijak.*
fellowship: *kom̧bani, ikueaak.*

female: *kōrā.*
a female married to a chief or householder: *iep jāltok.*
a very beautiful female: *to-jān-lañ.*
carry female to or from vessel: *bōkkōrā.*
female of quarter royal descent: *lejjibjib.*
female whose father is a chief and whose mother is a commoner: *lōbdak.*
female, of animals: *kokōrā.*
said of female children: *iep jāltok.*

fence: *oror.*

fencing
art of fencing: *kilen jāje.*

fender: *abǫ.*

ferment
fermented: *meñ.*
fermented coconut toddy: *jimañūñ.*
fermented, of coconut sap: *mañūñ.*

fern
a plant, fern, *Microsorium scolopendria* Burm. F. Copeland: *kino.*
shoot of the bird's nest fern (*kartōp*): *m̧ūļōñ.*

ferocious: *lāj.*

ferry: *leak-, llik.*

fertile: *kimuur.*
fertile soil: *kōl.*

fertilize: *kōn̦.*
fertilized egg, ready to hatch: *kune.*

fetus: *kǫ.*

feud: *an armeje doon, kōtaan wāto.*

fever: *bwil, piba.*
fever and chills: *piǫ.*
feverish: *piba.*

few: *iiet, jejjo, jet.*
known by only a few: *anjejjo.*

fibre: *iden.*
coconut fibre: *bweǫ.*
coir fibre, fine, not woven, left over from weaving, used as wash cloth: *bwijinbwije.*
cord made from coconut fibre: *kkwaļ.*
husk fibre: *kwōd.*

fickle: *bbōroro, bōro-pejpej, m̧m̧aļkaro.*

fiction: *inǫñ.*

Ficus
a plant, *Ficus carica* L. (Moraceae): *wōjke-piik.*
a plant, tree, *Ficus tinctoria* Forst: *tōpdo.*

field: *meļaaj.*
airfield: *pij.*
baseball field: *kūraan̦to.*
open field: *enne, maaj.*
run a complete circuit around a field: *om̧rawūn.*
track and field events: *wūntokai.*

field trip: *piiļ tūrep.*
field trip ship: *piiļ tūrep.*
go on a field trip ship: *rawūn.*

fierce: *lāj.*

fifteen: *joñouļļalem.*

fifth
fifth moon phase: *marokiddik.*
the fifth: *kein kaḷalem.*

fifty: *lemñoul.*
fifty pairs, fish or copra: *limakor.*

fig
The edible fig: *wōjke-piik.*

fight: *kōṃṃaejek, taiṃ.*
cause to fight: *keid.*
cock-fight, in water: *keiwa.*
contest, fighting or wrestling: *kāre lọwob.*
fight a battle: *tariṇae.*
fight between relatives: *an armeje doon.*
fighter plane: *jeṇtoki.*
fighting stance: *joorkatkat.*
pit for bird fight: *nit.*
protection in fighting: *tōrak.*
return to fight again after having been repulsed: *kotūbtūb.*
ruffling of cocks and dogs before fighting: *rrọñ.*
start fighting: *ṃur.*
to clash in a fight: *jibwe doon.*
to fight: *ire.*

figure: *kā, kea-, nōṃba, wāwee-.*
figure (used negatively): *kōjālli-.*

filch: *pānāpnep.*

file: *baeḷ, ḷā.*

file fish
a fish, file fish, *Amanses carolae*: *ṃōṇakṇak.*
a fish, scrawled file fish, *Alutera scripta*: *ikudej.*

fill
fill with liquid: *tteiñ.*
filled up: *booḷ.*
filled up, of a hole: *jeñak.*
refill a hole with dirt: *jjioñ.*
space-filling: *kaddoujuj.*
to fill: *kanne.*

film: *piliṃ.*
roll of film: *jāljel.*
roll up, line or film, spool: *tāte.*

filter: *liklik.*

filth
filthy: *bwiltoonon, jokdād, kkōr.*

Fimbristylis
refers to both *Fimbristylis atollensis* St. John and *Eleocharis geniculata* (L.) R S.: *pādālijṃaan.*

fin: *eñ, pā, ūl.*
caudal fin: *ḷọkdede.*

final: *āliktata.*
final meal together before an impending disaster: *dienbwijro.*
finally: *āliktata, kab.*

finance: *bajet, jāān.*

find: *llo, ppok.*
easy to find (see *aḷakiia* (**haḷakiyyah**)): *aḷakiie.*
find out: *eọroñ.*
find out about: *kajitūkin.*
find something to ride: *taṃwe.*
hard to find (see *aḷakiie* (**haḷakiyyẹy**)): *aḷakiia.*

fine
fine, not coarse: *kkwidik.*
fine, of grated coconut: *kkwidik.*

fine: *bakkiiñ.*

fine: *ṃṃan.*

finger: *addi, jānit.*
coral finger extending out of a main coral head or reef: *anbwe.*
fingernail: *akki, akkiin pā.*
fingerprint: *jenok.*
index finger: *addi-kọọtot.*
little finger: *addi-dik.*
make marks with the fingernails: *rakutak.*
middle finger: *addi-eoḷap.*
pinch with fingernails: *kinji.*
to flick someone or something with the fingers: *libbūṇōj.*

finish: *jeṃḷọk.*
entirely finished: *dede.*
finish a task: *ñijlọk.*
finished: *ṃōj.*
partially finished: *jipikpik.*
spend last moments together, farewell occasion, bring to a finish: *kōjjeṃḷọk.*

fire: *kijeek.*
catch fire: *tok.*
coals of fire: *mālle.*
feed a fire: *ankaan.*
feed a fire with firewood: *ṇakaan.*
fire logs: *tokọ.*
fire out of control: *kōḷọk.*
fire starting slowly: *jatokwōj.*
firebrands: *buwaddel.*
firecracker: *kabbokbok.*
fireplace: *wūpaaj.*
fireproof. (See *tokwiie* (**teqiyyẹy**)): *tokwiia.*
fireworks: *kōmram.*
forest fire: *kōḷọk.*
groove in piece of wood, for *etōñ* firemaking: *kin.*

incapable of catching fire and burning: *tokwiia.*
make fire: *itkaap.*
make fire by rubbing sticks: *etoñ, it.*
open fireplace for cooking: *wūpaaj.*
put out a fire: *kkun.*
put something over a fire: *perar.*
refuel a fire: *anekane.*
set fire to: *ttil.*
sleep close to fire all night, especially old people: *eọwilik.*
speed up when rubbing sticks to make fire: *jorjor.*
start a fire: *jenjen, kenọkwōl.*
start, of fire: *jọ.*
stick for stirring fire, turning breadfruit while cooking, etc.: *jabōn pe.*
stir food or fire with a stick: *arar.*
strips of green coconut branches laid across a fire for warming pandanus leaves: *tọļ.*
take off of fire: *ato.*
to catch fire: *urrūļọk.*
to warm one's bottom by the fire: *rabwij.*
to warm oneself by the fire: *rañrañ.*

fire
dismiss, fire: *kupi.*

firewood: *kane.*
feed a fire with firewood: *ṇakaan.*
firewood, for keeping warm only: *jitōñ.*

firm: *dem, kijñeñe, mājojo, ñūñ, pen.*

first: *ṃṃōkaj.*
first aid: *kōṃadṃōdin idiñ.*
first base: *bōōj.*
first moon phase: *jetmar.*
first-born: *ṃaanje, utṃaan.*
the first: *kein kajuon.*
the first zone of currents: *juae.*
use for the first time: *kkaan.*
wear a piece of clothing for the first time: *lōtlōt.*

fish: *ek.*
a catch of fish, crabs, or birds: *koṇa-.*
names of unidentified fish: *āpil, adipā, aelbūrōrō, aikūtōkōd, aujwe, aunel, autak, ddep, didak, dokweer, ek-bōļāāk, ekpā, ikallo, ikōn-ae, jāpek, jaad, kāāntōļ, kaallo, kawal, kilkil, kọde, kōpādel, kūbur, kūtkūtijet, kudiil, ļōjjeptaktak, ļouj, loļ, ṃaj-waan, ṃaļokļok, mānnōt, manōt, mejeik, melea, mijjebwā, mọk, ṇo, ñoñ, peekdu, tōllọkbōd.*
African pompano: *aroñ.*
Chelon vaigiensis: *ikade.*
Lethrinus sp: *mejabbe.*
Lutjanus gibbus: *jato.*
Pomacentrid: *bakōj.*
Seriola purpurascens: *ṃanoļ.*
maomao, Abudefduf abdominalis: *badet.*
moi, Polydactylus sexfilis: *atkadu.*
opelu, Cecapterus sp: *kauwe.*
piha, Spratelloides delicatulus: *aol.*
uu or *panu*: *ṃōn-kiden.*
Moorish idol (?): *pedeọ.*
Moorish idol, *Zanclus canescens*: *jourur.*
Moorish idol, *Zanclus cornutus*: *pālep, wōllañ.*
Pacific sailfish: *wūjinleep.*
Pacific sea perch, *Kuhlia taeniura* (Mejit.): *kōnān.*
a shark: *arōnpe.*
a species of skate: *jiṃjọ.*
banded surgeonfish, *Acanthurus triostegus* triostegus Linnaeus: *kupañ.*
barracuda, *Sphyraena barracuda*: *jujukōp.*
barracuda, *Sphyraena forsteri*: *jure, ñiitwa.*
bass, *Plectropomus truncatus*: *akajin, jọwe, jowanurọñ.*
bass, *Variola louti*: *ikmid, kanbōk, oļaļo.*
big-eye or burgy: *kie.*
big-eye or burgy, *Monotaxis grandoculis*: *ṃōjani, mejọkut.*
big-eyed or goggle-eyed scad fish or horse mackerel, *Trachurops crumenophthalmus*: *pāti.*
black surgeonfish, *Acanthurus nigricans*: *tiepdọ.*
black triggerfish, *Melichthys ringens*: *būb.*
blenny, *Istiblennius paulus* (Mejit): *kudọkwōl.*
blue-spotted grouper, *Cepahalopholis argus*: *kalemeej.*
bonito, *Katsuwonus pelamis*: *ļōjabwil.*
boxfish, *Ostracion cubicus*: *būļ.*
boxfish, *Ostracion sebae*: *pel.*
butterfly fish, *Chaetodon anriga* (Ebon): *utot.*
butterfly fish, *Chaetodon ocellatus*: *dibab.*
butterfly fish, *Chaetodon ornatissimus*: *bwine.*

cardinal fish, *Apogon novemfasiatus*: *tōptōp.*
chub mackerel, *Ragistrella*: *akwōlā.*
chub or rudder fish, *Kyphosus vaigiensis*: *pājrōk.*
convict tang or banded surgeonfish, *Hepatus triostegus*: *kupañ.*
cornet fish, *Fistularia petimba*: *jepooj.*
crevally, *Caranx stellatus*: *ikbwij.*
devilfish, giant octopus: *kouj.*
dog-tooth tuna, *Gymnosarda nuda*: *jilo.*
dolphin, *Coryphoena hippurus*: *koko.*
eel with no teeth: *deldelbwij.*
eel, *Conger cinereus*: *m̧ōjoud.*
eel, large and black: *dāp.*
electrid, *Valenciennesia strigata/violifera*: *ikōlood.*
false albacore or *kawakawa*: *ļooj.*
file fish, *Amanses carolae*: *m̧ōņakņak.*
flounder, *Bothus mancus*: *badej.*
flying fish, family *Exocoetidae*: *jojo.*
fresh-water eel: *toņ.*
general term for all blenny: *jibbaļañ.*
general term for all damsel fish: *ūrōrmej.*
general term for all goby: *jippuļe.*
general term for butterfly fish: *rūbōb.*
general term for shark: *pako.*
giant sea bass, *Promicrops lanceolatus/truncatus*: *jo̧we.*
giant sea bass, *Promicrops truncatus*: *jowāme.*
goatfish, *Mulloidichthys auriflama*: *jome.*
goatfish, *Mulloidichthys samoensis*: *jo.*
goatfish, *Parupeneus barberinus*: *m̧ōtal.*
goatfish, *Parupeneus sp*: *jorobbā.*
goatfish, *Upeneus tragula*: *joļo̧km̧ōōr.*
goby (Mejit): *kūtōk, kwōpra.*
goggle-eye, *Priacanthus cruentatus*: *ļwōl.*
great devilfish, manta: *boraañ.*
ground shark, *Carcharhinus melanopterus*: *pakoon eoon pedped.*
grouper: *aleañ, ļakkūrae.*
grouper, *Epinephelus adscenscionis*: *ļōjepjep.*
grouper, *Epinephelus fuscoguttatus*: *kūro.*
grouper, *Epinephelus hexagonatus*: *m̧ōm̧ō.*
halfbeak, *Hemiramphus depauperatus*: *buwaj.*
halfbeak, *Hyporhamphus laticeps*: *kūbu.*
hogfish, *Cheilinus undulatus*: *ļappo.*
jellyfish: *jañij.*
kind of shark: *jepāp.*
kind of shark, no teeth: *bab.*
kingfish: *al.*
kingfish, *Caranx fulvoguttatus* forskal: *rewa.*
large eel: *pedāp.*
leather-jack, *Scomberoides lysan*: *aoļōt.*
lionfish, *Pterois volitans*: *ōō.*
mackerel, *Grammatorcynus bicarinatus*: *ikabwe.*
mackerel, *Scomber japonicus*: *m̧ōlm̧ōl.*
mackerel, *Trachurops crumenopthalmus*: *ettōū, tōū.*
moray eel: *kideddelbwij.*
moray eel, *Gymnothorax flavimarginatus*: *m̧akañ.*
moray eel, *Gymnothorax pictus*: *m̧aj-mouj.*
mullet, *Chelon vaigiensis*: *akōr.*
mullet, *Crenmugil crenilabis*: *iōōļ.*
mullet, *Crenmugil crenilabis* (Eniwetak): *joom̧um̧.*
needlefish, *Belone platyura*: *tak.*
needlefish, *Strongylura marina*: *m̧ak.*
orange spot tang, *Acanthurus olivaceus*: *ael.*
parrotfish, *Callyodon bataviensis*: *audam̧.*
parrotfish, *Callyodon microrhinos*: *alwor.*
parrotfish, *Callyodon pulchellus*: *lala, pālpilikio.*
parrotfish, *Scarus harid*: *ekmouj.*
parrotfish, *Scarus jonesi/sordidus*: *merā.*
parrotfish, *Scarus jonesi/sordidus*: *mao.*
parrotfish, *Scarus vetula*: *taburbur.*
perch, *Lutjanus fulviflamma*: *kālikrōk.*
pilot fish, *Naucrates ductor*: *ikuut.*
pompano, *Trachinotus bailloni*: *m̧ōļojetak.*
pompano, *Trachinotus bailloni*: *kauwe.*
porcupine fish, *Diodon hystrix*: *jabōnke, m̧ōjañūr.*
porgy, *Gnathodentex aurolineatus*: *tūñad.*
puffer fish, *Tetraodon hispidus*: *luwap.*
puffer fish, *Tetraodon hispidus/*

meleagris/nigropunctatus/patoca: *wat.*
puffer, *Arothron meleagris*: *luwap-kilmeej.*
puffer, *Arothron ŋigropunctatus*: *luwap-iaļo.*
rabbitfish, *Siganus* sp.: *m̧orm̧or.*
rabbitfish, *Siganus rostratus*: *m̧o̧le.*
rabbitfish, *Siganus rostratus/puellus*: *ellōk.*
rainbow runner, *Elagatis bipinnulatus*: *ikāidik.*
ray fish (poisonous): *āibukwi.*
red snapper, *Lutjanus bohar*: *paan.*
red snapper, *Lutjanus vaigiensis*: *jaap.*
red spot tang, *Acanthurus achilles*: *kinbo, pir.*
redfin, *Argyrops spinifer*: *m̧ōļejetak.*
reef triggerfish, *Balistapus rectangulus/aculeatus*: *im̧im̧.*
rock cod, *Anyperodon leucogrammicus*: *kabro, kōļaoļap.*
rock cod, *Epinephelus flavocaeruleus*: *pooklim̧.*
rock cod, *Serranus fuscoguttatus*: *kūro.*
rock hind, *Epinephelus albofasciatus*: *ļōjepjep.*
rudder fish, *Kyphosus vaigiensis* (Eniwetak): *rōnna.*
salmon: *jam̧ōņ.*
sardine, *Sardine sardinella* (small): *mimuul.*
sardine, *Sardinella* sp.: *kwarkwar, mamo.*
scavenger, *Lethrinus* sp: *ņamāni.*
scavenger, *Lethrinus kallopterus*: *perak.*
scavenger, *Lethrinus microdon*: *mejmej.*
scavenger, *Lethrinus miniatus*: *jaļiia.*
scavenger, *Lethrinus variegatus*: *dijiñ, nōt.*
scorpion fish, *Dendrochirus zebra*: *ōō.*
scrawled file fish, *Alutera scripta*: *ikudej.*
sea horse, *Hippocampus kuda*: *kidudujet.*
sergeant major, *Abudefduf septemfasciatus*: *badet.*
shark grouper, *Carcharhinus melanopterus*: *pako mej.*
shark pilot, *Echeneis naucrates*: *ļattil pako.*
shark, *Trisenodon obesus*: *pako korak.*
silverfish, *Gerres baconensis*: *ilmek.*
skip jack, *Caranx lessonii*: *ļañe, m̧ōļajutak.*
skip jack, *Caranx melampygus*, Hawaiian *ulua*: *deltokrōk.*
skip jack, immature form, *Caranx lessonii*: *kupkup.*
small grouper: *tinar.*
snake eel, *Myrichthys colubrinus*: *m̧ajid.*
snapper, *Aprion virescens*: *ewae.*
snapper, *Gymnocranius microndon/griseus*: *mejmej.*
snapper, *Lutjanus flavipes*: *jāj.*
snapper, *Lutjanus kasmira forskal*: *jetaar.*
snapper, *Lutjanus monostigmus*: *juwajo.*
snapper, *Lutjanus vitta*: *bōnej.*
snapper, *Scolopsis cancellatus*: *kwōlej.*
spot snapper, *Lutjanus fulviflamma*: *kalikūrōk.*
spotted eagle ray fish, poisonous, *Aetobatus narinari*: *imen.*
spotted hawkfish, *Cirrhitus pinnulatus*: *kidiej.*
squirrel fish: *mālij.*
squirrel fish, *Holocentrus* sp.: *jera.*
squirrel fish, *Holocentrus binotatus/scythrops*: *kur.*
squirrel fish, *Holocentrus microstoma*: *kañkōñ.*
squirrel fish, *Myripristis berndti*: *m̧ōn.*
starry flounder, *Platichthys stellatus*: *bale.*
streaker, *Aprion virescens*: *ļo̧om.*
striped mullet, *Chelon vaigiensis*: *aotak.*
stripey, *Kuhlia taeniura*: *jerwōt.*
surgeonfish, *Acanthurus dussumieri*: *kōpat.*
surgeonfish, *Acanthurus lineatus*: *kuwi, kwi.*
surgeonfish, *Acanthurus nigricans*: *aelmeej.*
surgeonfish, *Naso unicornis*: *eañrōk, m̧o̧ņe.*
swordfish, *Xiphia gladius*: *ļōjkaan.*
thread-backed butterfly fish, *Heniochus acuminatus*: *ek-bōlōk.*
thresher shark, *Alopias vulpes*: *pako to̧rto̧r.*
tiger shark, *Galeocerdo arcticus*: *pako tiltil.*
tiny surface minnow: *ņaņ.*

trigger fish, *Rhinecanthus aculeatus*: *liele.*
trunkfish, *Ostracion tuberculatus*: *pel.*
tuna, *Neothunus macropterus*: *bwebwe.*
unicorn fish, *Hepatus olivaceus Schneider Bloch*: *ael.*
unicorn fish, *Naso brevirostris*: *batakļaj.*
unicorn fish, *Naso lituratus*: *bwilak.*
wrasse: *mao.*
wrasse, *Cheilinus* sp: *merā.*
wrasse, *Coris gaimardi*: *alle, likōb.*
wrasse, *Epibulus insidiator*: *katōk, mō.*
wrasse, *Halichoeres trimaculatus*: *po.*
wrasse, *Thalashona vitidum*: *lo.*
wrasse, *Thalassoma lunare*: *ikōn-wōd.*
wrasse, *Thalassoma umbrostigma*: *bōkkāāj.*
a flock of birds flying over a school of fish: *la, wūnaak.*
a food, fish eaten half broiled but still raw: *koubub.*
a food, fish, basted in flour and deep fried: *teeṃbura.*
a food, method of cooking fish: take fish eggs (roe) out and squeeze on fish and cook half done: *jāār, jāār.*
a food, raw fish: *jaajmi.*
a food, salted fish guts or clams: *jiookra.*
a pile of corpses or fish or people: *ajeļļā.*
able to catch many fish: *koņkoņ, wōda.*
any large fish: *jomām.*
arranged head to tail, of fish: *jitnen ṃōṃō.*
attract fish or flies with scraps: *aṃaṃ.*
attraction of big fish to smaller fish: *la.*
back of a fish: *aeṃaan.*
birds flying looking for fish: *wūnaak.*
change color, of fish: *ukōt ṃōōr.*
charge of a school of fish chasing minnows: *tūaļ.*
charge of larger fish on minnows, sardines, etc: *luwi.*
clean a fish or chicken: *jejjet.*
closed circle of fish surrounded by *aļeļe* (**haļeyļey**) method: *aļe.*
cook fish on stones: *ikjin.*
cooking and eating fish right after catching them, usually at night: *jinre.*
coral weir to trap fish: *me.*
crave fish: *batur.*
dive after getting hooked, of fish: *n̄ijlọk, wūnlọk.*
dry fish or copra by heat: *atiti.*
eat fish while fishing, beat up someone badly: *kōmennan̄.*
eat raw fish: *koobub.*
enter and hide inside coral, said of fish only: *pọ.*
entry in net of small groups of fish versus one large group: *tọọr pata.*
exceptionally big fish: *ajorṃaan.*
fish bait: *ṃọọr.*
fish eggs: *bwiaea, likipia.*
fish gills: *or.*
fish odor: *jon̄ọ.*
fish out an area in order to spite those coming later: *ļōbọtin.*
fish pole: *bwā.*
fish roe: *pia.*
fish that aren't sufficient for the next day: *ekin bon̄ jab lo raan.*
fish that wanders outside coconut leaf chain scarer: *ikōnālkinṃwio.*
fish trap: *u.*
fish's stomach: *petōk.*
fishbone stuck in throat: *paļ.*
fishing method, fishing for squirrel fish in small holes on reef during low tide using a two or three-foot-long leader fastened onto a piece of wood about the same length: *diil.*
fishing method, pole fishing for goatfish: *kadjo.*
fishing method, use fishpole at the reef edge and fish for *kidiej*: *kakidiej.*
front half of fish: *jebbar.*
get spoiled, of fish: *ekļọk.*
hives, from eating spoiled fish: *judu.*
inability to catch many fish (see *koņkoņ* (**qeņqeņ**)): *jọkoņkoņ.*
inability to catch many fish (see *wōda* (**wedah**)): *joda.*
leap out of water, of small fish attempting to escape larger fish: *uwōjak.*
legendary fish banished by Jebro to be eaten by other fish: *aoļ.*
long fish trap, for sprats, net with handle: *bọro.*
look for fish: *jore.*
lucky in fishing: *wōda.*
many, as a school of fish: *doom.*
mill around, of small fish: *auļeļe.*
movement of fish near surface: *boklọk.*
nibble, as fish on bait: *ļļijļij.*

not biting, of fish. (See *m̧õñã* (**m̧egay**)): *jam̧õñã.*
not many fish, of a place (see *ek* (**yȩk**)): *jãike.*
not tasty, of fish (see *uwi* (**wwiy**)): *jo̧uwi.*
place where birds, fish, or clams gather: *ajañ.*
poisonous fish: *ikaarar.*
possessive classifier, fish, crabs, or birds: *kon̄a-.*
pull in, as fish on a line: *tõbtõb.*
remove bones from fish: *iiaak.*
round up fish or animals: *ajãl.*
scale fish: *karwũn.*
scale of fish: *wũn.*
scarcity of fish (see *ike* (**yikey**)): *jaike.*
school of fish: *bwijin.*
school of fish on reef, herd of animals: *baru.*
slime from slugs and fish: *medaekek.*
smell of cooking fish: *uwi.*
smell of fish, lingering on hands, body, or utensils: *aelel.*
smoked fish: *ek m̧õn̄akn̄ak.*
spines on fish: *iñ.*
spoiled fish or meat: *kõt.*
stick used for clubbing fish: *jem̧õnna.*
stone fortress for trapping fish: *kõjjoal.*
stop craving fish: *kõbbaturtur.*
string fish, coconuts, flowers, etc: *ilele.*
stunned, of fish: *kõjļo̧r.*
tail half of fish: *jablo̧k.*
tend fish traps: *bbã.*
tight clustering of fish when attracted by bait or chum: *booklo̧k.*
to chum for fish: *anan.*
to chum for fish, usually in deep water: *pitpit.*
to fish before everyone else and also before it is the right time to start: *akļañ.*
to tire a fish after it is hooked: *kaddejdej.*
too fresh to be tasty, said of fish just caught that has not been allowed to settle sufficiently before being eaten raw: *ļļeoeo.*
wire for stringing fish: *ile.*

fishing

a place for fishing canoes on an island: *mien.*
coconut leaf chain used in fishing as scarer: *m̧wio.*
exploit a fishing grounds: *tuwe.*
fishing basket: *m̧m̧ar.*
fishing contest: *kãre kããj.*
fishing method, spear fishing: *turo̧ñ.*
fishing method, spear fishing while diving: *tuwã.*
fishing term, said of a coconut leaf chain used as scarer that is strung out unevenly: *kapijjule.*
go fishing: *eo̧ñõd.*
go fishing frequently: *eeo̧ñõdñwõd.*
good in fishing, expert in fishing: *aewanlik, aewanlik.*
long fishing net: *okaetok.*
possessive classifier, flowers, medals, necklaces, or fishing baskets: *m̧arõ-.*
pull fishing line rhythmically while trolling: *koraal.*
seldom go fishing: *jeeo̧ñõd.*
tie coconut leaves together to make fishing chain: *wũjaak.*
tripod for fishing: *okwa.*
wire leader, used in fishing: *atad, ļõļ.*

fishing methods

—involving fruit of the *wõp* (*Barringtonia asiatica* tree): *obbar.*
—with a canoe and line on the ocean side: *liklo̧k.*
—at night from a canoe near lagoon shore: *eoojjaak.*
—between two shoals (*n̄a*), with scarer: *un̄a.*
—bottom fishing in lagoon: *eolaļ.*
—catching flying fish when they enter lagoon at a certain location at Namu: *jibadede.*
—chasing fish into weir: *kõtto̧o̧r.*
—chasing mackerel into a throw net held upon one side: *kõtaltõl.*
—fish with a pole: *kõbwãbwe.*
—fishing for squirrel fish in small holes on reef during low tide using a two or three-foot-long leader fastened onto a piece of wood about the same length: *diil.*
—fishing with a torch: *kabwil.*
—flying fish at night with torch and net: *bo̧bo.*
—for bonitos: *kõļõjabwil.*
—for needlefish (*m̧ak*): *kõm̧m̧ak.*
—for porpoises: *jibke.*
—hanging on to reef while spearing: *kiijbaal.*
—hunt lobster or coconut crab when the moon is right: *katooj.*
—hunting for lobsters at night by means of artificial light, not moonlight: *tilkawor.*

—inserting the bare hand into holes nooks or crannies in the reef: *rrwe.*

—line fishing at night, jerking the line to cause phosphorescence in water to attract fish to the bait: *kōjjaromrom.*

—line fishing in lagoon from canoe at night: *ettōbok.*

—line fishing inside lagoon using hermit crab for bait: *rupe om̧.*

—line fishing outside lagoon, usually on lee side and fairly close to shore, for flying fish, using sand crab for bait: *rōjep.*

—line fishing using floats: *kōppel̗o̧k.*

—line fishing using the front half of a coconut shell, in lagoon area: *mejel̗at.*

—long line, deep ocean, for tuna: *l̗atippān.*

—many men surround a school in shallow water using a coconut leaf chain as scarer: *al̗el̗e.*

—occasional jerking of line to lure a fish to the bait or jig: *kooral.*

—pole fishing along the beach or shore: *ttoor.*

—pole fishing for goatfish: *kadjo.*

—pole fishing from a raised platform or tripod used for fishing: *okwa.*

—pole fishing on barrier reef edge at low tide on dark nights: *juunboñ.*

—pole or line fishing using no bait but simply jerking the line in the hope of hooking a fish by chance: *kāājrabōl.*

—search for fish on the reef at low tide: *kaikikūt.*

—searching for fish at low tide over the reef: *etalpeet.*

—spear fishing: *turo̧ñ.*

—spear fishing while diving: *tuwā.*

—spearfishing on reef: *aubō.*

—stand beside weir and watch for mackerel: *jo.*

—striking needlefish with a long piece of wood or a paddle as they float on the surface of the water on moonlit nights: *deñtak.*

—surround a school of rainbow runners with plain sennit: *ekkoonak.*

—surrounding edges of shoals with net: *kun̗a.*

—throw out line from lagoon beach: *eojojo.*

—to fish from a canoe: *urōk.*

—torch and machete: *tilkōmerā.*

—troll at night: *kōrkaak.*

—trolling inside lagoon: *kōkko̧jekjek.*

—trolling outside lagoon: *ilarak.*

—use fishpole at night: *kappej.*

—use fishpole at night with either lure or bait: *tto.*

—use fishpole at the reef edge and fish for *kidiej*: *kakidiej.*

—use hand line from canoe in deep ocean for fish other than tuna: *kōddāpilpil.*

—use long net and *m̧wio* (m̧iyew) during high tide and wait for low: *jurōk.*

—use throwing net: *kadkad.*

—using a canoe and drifting with the wind and current in a lagoon, line fishing: *pel̗o̧k.*

—using a coconut leaf chain as a scarer at night to block off exit route of fish and waiting for low tide in order to trap them: *lipaanto.*

—using coconut leaf chain as scarer on dark nights: *pelpel.*

—using diving mask and fishline outside: *jāāk.*

—using long net at day time along reef ridge: *jabuk.*

—using scarer: *wōtojome.*

—using scarer and weir: *kwōmej.*

—using surrounding net on dark nights: *aejek.*

—using weight with hook, octopus for bait, and dragging it on sandy bottom: *kōjo̧lim̧.*

—using woven brown coconut fronds to catch sardines and minnows as they are chased ashore by bigger fish: *apep.*

—waiting along the usual path of fish on the reef to spear them, usually done at the beginning of ebb and flow tide: *kōkkāāl̗āl̗.*

—with spear at reef edge: *bbō.*

stones used in *jibke* fishing method for porpoises: *dekā in jibke.*

fishline: *eo.*

fishing method, using diving mask and fishline outside: *jāāk.*

fishline, on a pole: *mejje.*

jerk a fishline to hook a fish: *dimtak.*

nylon fishline: *eke, eo eke.*

reel for fishline: *kurjep.*

yank a fishline: *liit.*

Fissurellidae

a shell, *Fissurellidae*: *jowakin.*

fist

clenched fist: *dukwal̗.*

hit with fists: *bait.*

put up fists: *pañ.*

Fistularia
a fish, cornet fish, *Fistularia petimba*: *jepooj.*

fit: *koṇ, ḷḷaak.*
fit poorly (see *koṇ* (**qeṇ**)): *jọkoṇ.*
fit tightly: *bab.*
fit together, put together an engine or piece of machinery: *bobo.*
force to fit: *obar.*
poorly fitting: *booḷoḷ.*
to fit: *ḷaak.*

fit: *kkar.*
fit for (always followed by construct particle *in*): *āj.*
it is fitting: *kkar.*
look fitting: *joto.*

five: *ḷalem.*
five hundred: *limabukwi.*
five pairs, fish or copra: *jabjet.*
five thousand: *limādep.*

fix: *āe, kōṃṃan, ṃadṃōd.*
fixed, settled: *tōt.*

fizz: *buḷuḷḷuḷ, jib.*

flabby
flabby, of skin: *pidtoto.*

flag: *bōḷeak.*
flagpole: *juron bōḷeak.*
wave, of a flag or clothes: *ppālpāl.*

flaky
disease, scaly and flaky skin: *koko.*

flame: *urur.*
burst into flame: *urrūḷọk.*
old flame: *kōba.*

flammable
inflammable: *tokwiie, jọwiie.*
not flammable: *tokwiia, jọwiia.*

flap: *jopāl, pikpik, ppālpāl.*
a canoe with its sail flapping: *añōppāl.*

flare: *urrūḷọk.*

flash: *meram, urur.*
flashing light: *jjoram.*

flashlight: *ḷaaṃ jarom, teeñki.*
reflector of flashlight or spotlight: *ḷat.*

flat: *eọọn wōt juon.*
flat, of land only: *pikin.*
flatten: *jjiped.*
flatten pandanus leaves: *karere.*

flat
flat music or voice, usually out of tune: *būḷāāt.*
flat, music: *bōna.*

flatter
procure something by flattery or by "borrowing": *kōrabōl.*
request something by flattery: *wadu.*

flavor: *nām.*

flaw: *bōd, irḷọk.*
perform flawlessly: *wōnjak.*

flea: *kij.*

flee: *dej, ko.*
one who flees from battle: *pikōt.*

fleece
to fleece someone: *kwōdmat, reja.*

fleet
fleet of canoes, ships, or planes: *inej.*
fleeting: *jedkaju.*

flesh: *kanniōk.*
smell of dead flesh: *kkōōrōr.*
smell of decayed flesh: *bwiin-puwaḷ, juoñ.*

Fleurya
a plant, *Fleurya ruderalis* (Forst. F.) Gaudichaud. (Urticaceae): *neen kōtkōt.*

flex
flexed muscles: *jar ṃajeḷ.*
flexible: *mañōtñōt, pedañōtñōt.*
inflexible: *kajjiṃwe.*

flick
to flick someone or something with the fingers: *libbūṇōj.*

flies
attract fish or flies with scraps: *aṃaṃ.*
swat, drive off, or catch flies: *ubḷọñ.*

flight
flight of a group of birds or planes: *depouk.*
flighty: *anniabeab.*

flimsy: *kōmjedeọ, māni.*

fling: *jekad-.*

flint: *dekā.*

flip: *kōrabōl.*

flirt: *kattoojoj.*
flirting: *abje.*

float: *ppej, ppepe.*
basaltic rock which floats: *tilaan.*
fishing method, line fishing using floats: *kōppeḷọk.*
float loose: *jjeḷọk.*
float loose, of ships: *jo.*
float upwards to the surface of the water: *pelōñ.*
float used in fishing: *kōppeḷọk.*

flock: *bwijin.*
a flock of birds flying over a school of fish: *la, wūnaak.*

flock of birds: *iur, kōjwad.*
flock of birds fishing: *ḷae.*
flock, school: *m̧ur.*

flood: *ibwijleplep.*
flooded: *ppej.*

floor
floor mat, coarse: *jepkọ.*
floor of house: *pedped.*

flop: *jālirara, ñadñad.*
flop around: *ddipikpik.*

flounder
a fish, flounder, *Bothus mancus*: *badej.*
a fish, starry flounder, *Platichthys stellatus*: *bale.*

flour: *pilawā.*

flourish: *didbōlbōl, jebar.*

flow: *eọọḷ, ōḷ, tọọr.*
flow, series of larger waves: *ibeb.*
overflow: *jieb-, llutōk.*
overflow, water: *booḷtōñtōñ.*
overflowing: *lutōkḷọk.*

flower: *ut.*
a plant, flower, *Hemigraphis reptans*: *utilōm̧jān.*
a plant, flower, *Jussiaea suffruticosa*: *utilolōb.*
a plant, flower, *Nerium oleander*. L: *oḷiaanta.*
a plant, general term for flower of any hedge plant: *ut.*
bear many flowers: *uwa.*
breadfruit flower: *elme.*
Common cult hedge. Often (mis-) called "panax." Flower: *ut.*
flower, about to bloom: *albok.*
fragrant, of flowers: *mālu.*
garland with flowers set close together: *tōōlkut.*
garland with flowers set wide apart: *tōōldepak.*
gateway, usually decorated with flowers and coconut fronds: *m̧oñ.*
hibiscus flower: *rooj.*
male flower of breadfruit: *tōbak.*
pick flowers: *rur.*
plain flower wreath without other ingredients: *utpāj.*
possessive classifier, flowers or wreaths worn on head: *pālli-.*
possessive classifier, flowers, medals, necklaces, or fishing baskets: *m̧arō-.*
skin parts of a plant to ensure its bearing of fruit or flowers: *kōnar.*
small flowers of pandanus, coconut, or other plants: *did.*
string fish, coconuts, flowers, etc: *ilele.*
to flower: *didbōlbōl.*
wear a rose or hibiscus flower: *roojoj.*
wear flowers on head: *pālpel.*
wear flowers or a lei: *utut.*
weave flowers or shells into a lei: *ḷōḷō.*
wreath of flowers: *ut.*
tree with flowers: *ut.*

flu: *būḷu.*
flu epidemic: *mejin.*

fluctuate: *ukoktak.*

fluent: *kkañ loo-, wājepdik.*

fluid: *dān.*

flunk: *būḷañ.*

flush: *kilbūrōrō.*
a flush in poker: *peḷaj.*

flute: *robba.*

flutter: *ddipikpik, jopāl, ppālpāl.*
flutter, as of wings: *pikpik.*
in a flutter: *jeparujruj.*

fly: *kā-, kālọk, kkāke.*
fly a kite: *lim̧aakak.*
fly a pandanus rocket: *didim̧akōl.*
fly away: *kālọk.*
fly ball, in baseball: *tōkai.*
fly low: *jokwadikdik, kōttāte, kōttadede.*
fly off: *piklọk.*
fly off towards the sea: *pikmeto.*
fly to the lagoon side: *keeaar.*
fly up and down: *kātilmaak.*
legendary flying woman: *lōrrọ.*
to fly: *pik.*
wings outstretched in flying: *jepeḷā.*

fly
a fly: *ḷọñ.*

flying fish
a fish, flying fish, family *Exocoetidae*: *jojo.*
a food, flying fish with pandanus stuffing: *ḷatum̧a.*
fishing method, catching flying fish when they enter lagoon at a certain location at Namu: *jibadede.*
fishing method, line fishing outside lagoon, usually on lee side and fairly close to shore, for flying fish, using sand crab for bait: *rōjep.*

foam: *bukwaarar, lijem̧ōrm̧ōr, m̧ōrm̧ōr, meme.*
foaming: *m̧ōrm̧ōr.*

fog
fog, dim, haze, blur: *tab.*

fold: *lemlem.*
fold arms in front: *bokpā.*
fold in a sloppy manner: *nukuj.*

folded: *limek.*
to fold: *ālkwōj.*

folk: *armej.*
folk dances: *taidik.*

follow: *ļoor(e).*
always following people around: *aemọkkwe.*
follow a large wave in entering a lagoon: *ļooribeb.*
follow after: *etal ļore.*
follow through: *loloorjake.*
follow trail or track: *anōk.*
follow with the eyes: *jjāāl.*
follower: *rūkaļoor.*
followers: *doon.*
gather followers: *tilbuuj.*

fond: *kālọk.*
have fond memories of: *emļọk.*
speak fondly of a person or place where one has been: *emļọk.*

fondle: *jebjeb, towe.*
fondle sexually: *lijjukul.*

foods or dishes
—*peru* cooked in certain shapes: *likaaļļaj.*
—balls of preserved breadfruit sweetened and boiled in coconut oil: *makillō.*
—biscuits and flour cooked together in water: *kōpjeļtak.*
—breadfruit baked in earth oven: *kōpjar.*
—breadfruit cooked on coals and scraped: *kwanjin.*
—breadfruit soup: *jokkwōpin mā.*
—bundled and baked spongy meat of sprouted coconut: *iutūr.*
—cake doughnut: *kōtabañ.*
—coconut bread, from copra and flour and sap or sugar: *jinkōļar.*
—coconut eaten with another dish, esp. Salt fish or miso: *jiraal.*
—cooked and pounded breadfruit, taro, bananas, or nuts mixed with grated coconut: *wūdeñ.*
—cooked preserved breadfruit smothered in grated coconut: *kubaļ.*
—diluted starch baked in coconut spathe in earth oven: *kōlọwutaktak.*
—doughnut, with hole: *tonaaj.*
—dried overripe breadfruit: *jāānkun.*
—fish eaten half broiled but still raw: *koubub.*
—fish, basted in flour and deep fried: *teeṃbura.*
—flying fish with pandanus stuffing: *ļatuṃa.*
—grated taro mixed with coconut milk, wrapped in taro leaves and baked in oven: *jebwatōr.*
—juice extracted from fresh pandanus: *jowaanroñ.*
—meat course: *jālele.*
—meat of *mejoub* coconut mixed with sugar or sap: *jekōbwa.*
—method of cooking fish: take fish eggs (roe) out and squeeze on fish and cook half done: *jāār.*
—nuts of breadfruit, cooked: *kwōlejiped.*
—octopus smothered in grated coconut: *penkwe.*
—pandanus chips: *jekaka.*
—pandanus custard mixed with water: *jennōb.*
—pandanus juice cooked and preserved: *mokwaṇ.*
—pandanus juice mixed with grated coconut: *mokwaṇ dada, mokwaṇ duul.*
—pandanus pudding cooked in hot rocks: *del.*
—pandanus pulp and juice mixed with grated coconut and coconut oil (and optionally with arrowroot starch), wrapped in breadfruit leaves and boiled or baked: *peru.*
—plain baked ripe breadfruit: *mejāliraan.*
—pounded meat of sprouted coconut: *lukor.*
—preserved breadfruit: *bwiro.*
—preserved breadfruit, cooked: *dukwaļ booļọļ.*
—preserved breadfruit boiled or baked without wrapping: *koļeiaat.*
—preserved breadfruit mixed with arrowroot and coconut sap or sugar, wrapped in breadfruit leaves and baked: *bwiro iiōk.*
—preserved breadfruit or *peru* flattened and covered with breadfruit leaves and baked: *kajipedped.*
—preserved breadfruit, formed into loaves, wrapped in coconut leaves, and cooked on fire: *ṃaio.*
—preserved dried breadfruit: *ṃōṇakjān.*
—raw fish: *jaajmi.*
—ripe breadfruit mixed with coconut oil and cooked in pots: *nāpnāpe.*
—salted fish guts or clams: *jiookra.*

—sliced unripe breadfruit cooked in coconut milk: *bwilitudek.*
—soup of soft rice or breadfruit: *jokkwōp.*
—soup, spongy coconut and arrowroot: *aikiu.*
—spongy meat of sprouted coconut baked in its shell: *iuwumum̧.*
—spongy meat of sprouted coconut cooked with arrowroot starch and diluted with water: *peaut.*
—taro grated and mixed with coconut oil and coconut sap: *tōtaim̧on̦.*
—three to one combination of arrowroot starch and water cooked together: *likōbla.*
—unleavened dough cooked by boiling: *jāibo.*
—very ripe breadfruit baked in coconut milk: *p̧ol̦jej.*
—very ripe breadfruit baked in coconut oil: *kappokpok, m̧ōjjero.*
—very ripe breadfruit mixed with coconut milk: *kal̦o̧.*
—watered down pandanus preserves: *ro̧krok.*

food: *kkan, m̧ōñā.*
a tasty combination of foods: *kane.*
ashamed, concerning food: *āliklik.*
ask for food, a shameful thing to do: *tūñañ.*
beg for food: *kōjm̧aal, kōkkau, uññar.*
bring food to a chief: *ekkan.*
bring food to a chief or lineage head: *eo̧jek.*
buy drinks and food for a group: *jo̧ut.*
cooked food: *kanmat.*
cooled off, of food once hot: *med.*
desire food: *bbūriri.*
dilute food or drink to make it stretch: *ilo̧k.*
dip food: *kattu.*
easy to satisfy with food: *mattiie.*
eat, food, child speech: *m̧wām̧wā.*
first food after fast: *dao.*
first food brought to a chief that has just arrived: *m̧ōkajkaj.*
food cabinet: *pāāntōre.*
food given with love: *kanio̧kwe.*
food in time of famine: *kūrwaan.*
food laid aside for future use: *wūnōk.*
food of: *kije-.*
food or drink eaten while walking: *jotal.*
foods prepared for visitors before their arrival: *kabwijeran.*
gather food: *ennōk, kakijen.*
hard to satisfy with food: *mattiia.*
hoard food: *wūnōknōk.*
hoarding of food: *wūnōk.*
illegal gathering of food on another's property: *l̦e eoon em̧.*
island or atoll reserved for food gathering, usually for a chief and his immediate family: *l̦ārooj.*
ladle, scoop food: *nam̧ōl̦.*
land used for preserving food, esp. Pandanus: *jepāde.*
legendary food: *mel̦añūr.*
possessive classifier, food or cigarettes: *kije-.*
pound food: *kapipā, lijlij.*
provide food for family from local sources (not from the store): *tāāp.*
provide food for someone: *tāāp.*
provide with food: *n̦akije-.*
sacrifice food to the gods: *wālo̧klik.*
scum, food particles between teeth: *taiñad.*
share food equally: *aikiu.*
share of food: *kōj.*
small tray, made from fronds for food: *enrā.*
smothered, of food: *jitable.*
stir food or fire with a stick: *arar.*
taste food or drink: *edjoñ.*
to bolt one's food: *kōdālōb, orjin.*
to bring foods with songs as refreshments to a group of men building a canoe or house to keep their morale up, usually done by the womenfolk of a community: *jemjem māāl.*
to chew food and then throw it out of the mouth: *meliak.*
to lay aside food for future use: *wūnōknōk.*
unchewed food caught in throat: *ubabōj.*
uncomfortable feeling about the stomach from being overstuffed with food: *akeke.*

fool: *bwebwe.*
fool around: *rriabeb.*
foolish: *bwebwe.*

foot: *ne.*
canoe part, foot of sail, edge fastened to the boom: *aekōrā.*
foot race: *iāllulu.*
go on foot: *etal lal̦.*
set foot on: *jjuur.*
sole of foot: *lo̧piden ne.*
to trip with the foot: *tiptak.*
wooden clog, footwear: *jinaketa.*

foot locker: *tōptōp.*

football
a game, underwater football using a rock for a ball: *ninnin̄.*

footprint
erase footprints: *jien̄.*
erase footprints or traces: *jjion̄.*
footprints: *jenok, kin, maalkan ne.*

footstep
footsteps in gravel or dry leaves: *m̧m̧ōjānjān.*

for: *bwe, in, kōn, m̧ae.*

forbid: *bōbrae, kipel.*
forbidden: *bwinimjaad, m̧o̧.*
interjection: "Darn!" Or "God forbid!": *ōkkōk.*

force: *kajoor, kipel.*
force into: *kipin.*
force someone to do some favor for one: *kōm̧akoko.*
force to fit: *obar.*

fore: *m̧aan.*

forecast
forecast predicting the onset of prevailing northeast trade winds: *den̄den̄in mājlep.*
forecast weather: *katu.*
forecast weather by observing clouds: *kōbbaal.*

forehead: *dam̧.*
having a protruding forehead: *kkodam̧dam̧.*

foreign: *ruwamāejet.*
foreign country: *aelōn̄in pālle.*

foresight: *lo̧l̦o̧kjen̦.*

foreskin
pull back the foreskin: *kuraj, ore.*

forest: *bukun, bul̦ōn mar.*
forest fire: *kōl̦o̧k.*

foretell: *kajjimalele, kawūjwūj.*

forever: *indeeo, kōbo.*
live forever: *juknen.*

forget: *mel̦o̧kl̦o̧k.*
forgetful: *bōrojol̦o̧k, mmālele.*

forgive: *jol̦o̧k bōd.*

fork: *bo̧o̧k, jibuun, kapel.*
use a fork: *bo̧o̧ko̧k.*

form: *wāwee-.*
form of, shape of: *lo̧l̦in.*
hat block form, any mold, any form: *m̧ōn̄akjān, m̧ōn̄akjān.*
well-formed: *karbōb.*

formal: *kijn̄en̄e.*

Formalhaut
Formalhaut in Pisces Austrinus: *Mejabwil.*

formant
formant in place names: *Le, ā, al̦o, apa, aut, den̄, ej, ilel, iō, ja, jekāān, jekar, jo̧, ka, kul, lok, m̧ōre, maro, or, pāl, pāl, peje, pek, pieo, pik, ra, ror, tiete, tōr, tuo, tuwe, wōja, wūj, wūntōn.*

formation
cloud formation preceding storm: *pālmuuj.*
cloud formation predicting a typhoon: *ped in pā.*
cloud formation resembling tip of frond: *jepak.*

former: *m̧okta.*
be formerly, used to be: *jo̧.*
former lover: *m̧or.*

formulate: *n̦al̦ōma-.*

fornicate: *l̦ōn̄.*

forsake: *jol̦o̧k, lumo̧o̧rl̦o̧k.*

fort: *me.*
fortified place: *me.*

forth
issue forth: *boutl̦o̧k.*

fortress
stone fortress for trapping fish: *kōjjoal.*

fortunate: *jeraam̧m̧an, m̧aju.*
unfortunate: *jedao, jerata.*

fortune
misfortune: *jerata.*
tell fortunes: *bubu.*

forty: *en̄oul.*
forty pairs, fish or copra: *ākor.*

forward: *m̧aan, mejel kil, pedet armej.*
canoe part, forward part when outrigger is on port side: *jabl̦ap.*
directional, enclitic, forward: *m̧aan.*
move forward: *wōnm̧aan.*

foul: *jokdād, ttoon.*
foul odor stench: *bwiin-puwal̦.*
foul-mouthed: *nana kobban lo̧n̄ii-.*
foul, in games: *pet.*

foundation: *l̦ōn̄tak, pedped, wawaa-.*
base, foundation, bottom, stem, trunk: *dāpi-.*

fountain: *būtto̧o̧r.*

fountain pen: *bo̧o̧ntōn peen.*

four: *emān.*
four eighths: *emān m̧ōttan ruwalitōk.*
four hundred: *eabukwi.*
four thousand: *earap.*
fourteen: *jon̄oul emān.*
have four of a kind in poker: *l̦āān.*
the fourth: *kein kāāmen.*

two fourths: *ruo m̧ōttan emān.*
fourth moon phase: *meļokļok.*

fowl: *bao.*
breastbone of a fowl: *pājeñ.*

fraction: *m̧ōtta-.*

fracture: *bwilǫk.*

fragile: *kkōm̧, kōmjedeǫ, om̧oja, pidodo, ub, wūpeļ.*

fragment
fragments: *tipdikdik.*

fragrant
fragrant smell: *ñaj.*
fragrant, of flowers: *mālu.*

frail: *pidodo, ub, wūpeļ.*

framboesia
ulcerated framboesia: *rajjiia.*

frame: *ānbwin, kā.*
frame of a house: *kādikdik.*
piece of pandanus roots cut and dried to be used as frame in weaving thatch: *tap.*
provide a framework for: *ņaļōma-.*

France: *Būranij.*

frank: *m̧ool.*

frantic: *ikdeelel.*

fraud: *kǫǫt.*
defraud: *ālikinjepjep.*
to strip of money or property by fraud or threat: *kwōdmat, reja.*

fray
frayed: *m̧ōdm̧ōd.*
frayed, fuzzy: *wūdede.*

freak: *kūļam̧we.*

freckles: *kūbween ļǫñ.*

free
carefree: *ineem̧m̧an.*
give freely: *wūjlep-.*
to free: *kōtļǫk.*
freedom: *anemkwōj.*

freeze: *kwōj.*

Fregata
a bird, great frigate bird, *Fregata minor*: *ak, toorlōñ.*
a bird, lessor frigate bird, *Fregata ariel*: *ak, toorlōñ.*

freight: *būreit.*

frequent: *kut, makijkij, mmakijkij.*
not frequent (see *kut* (**qit**)): *jǫkkutkut.*
to frequent: *kkeini.*

fresh: *kāāl.*
fresh breeze: *m̧akroro.*
fresh water: *māmet.*
go away for some fresh air: *kōkajoor.*
too fresh to be tasty, said of fish just caught that has not been allowed to settle sufficiently before being eaten raw: *ļļeoeo.*

friction: *irir.*

Friday: *Bōraide.*

friend: *jerā, kom̧bani.*
be friends: *jem̧jerā.*
befriend: *jerā.*
friendly relationship: *jem̧jerā.*
friendship: *jem̧jerā.*
trusted friend of a chief: *pālem̧oron.*

frigate: *baak.*

frigate bird
a bird, great frigate bird, *Fregata minor*: *ak, toorlōñ.*
a bird, lessor frigate bird, *Fregata ariel*: *ak, toorlōñ.*
decorations made from feathers of frigate birds, one on each tip of the sail on a chief's canoe: *kadulele.*
place where frigate birds sleep in trees: *m̧wilik.*

fright: *lōļñǫñ.*
frightened: *kor.*
frightening: *kaammijak.*

frill: *kūm̧aļm̧aļ.*

fringe: *tōrerei-.*

frisky
frisky, sound, vigorous: *ājmuur.*

frog: *būrǫk.*

frolic: *ikien, kōņaanikien.*

from: *in, jān.*

frond
band, used for tying torch made from frond: *ida.*
bed of fronds on which the tails of porpoises are placed: *kin.*
coconut frond: *kimej, pāp.*
gateway, usually decorated with flowers and coconut fronds: *m̧oñ.*
make torches from brown fronds: *bǫk.*
midrib of coconut frond: *pāp.*
small tray, made from fronds for food: *enrā.*
special twine made from skin of coconut frond midrib for climbing coconut trees: *kae.*
torch made from dried fronds: *pāle.*
twine made from skin of coconut frond midrib: *mālwe.*
green coconut fronds: *pāin ni.*
man's skirt made from coconut fronds: *elmen.*
mat woven from coconut fronds: *jeinae.*
pluck leaves from midrib of coconut fronds: *ttemakil.*

front: *ṃaan.*
a place in front of: *ṃaa-.*
front half of fish: *jebbar.*

frost: *aij.*

froth: *ṃōrṃōr.*

frown: *kōmmeñ.*

frugal: *tiljek.*

fruit: *kwōle, le.*
a plant, general term for all varieties of coconut trees and fruit: *ni.*
bear fruit, of pandanus: *wūd.*
bear much fruit: *uwa.*
catch a falling object or fruit: *jjā.*
fruit of *kōṇṇat, kkōñ, kitaak,* and *jidkok*: *lippiru.*
fruit of aged trees: *ālkūṃur.*
fruit-laden: *kowa.*
harvest first fruit of coconut, breadfruit, or pandanus: *akeọ.*
harvest fruit: *jele.*
laden with summer fruit, usually trees: *uwaanrak.*
last fruits: *ḷajdeñ.*
orange, the fruit: *oran.*
pit in which fruit is buried to ripen: *wōn.*
pluck, of fruit: *ḷotḷot.*
portion of fruit near stem of pandanus or breadfruit: *ainṃak.*
ripe fruit, fallen to the ground: *atabuñ.*
skin parts of a plant to ensure its bearing of fruit or flowers: *kōnar.*
start to bear fruit, of coconuts: *eọ.*
stem of a fruit: *kōḷā.*
wait for fruit to ripen: *kōmmako.*

frustrate
frustrated: *bbeer, rup bōro.*
frustration: *dikāāḷāḷ.*

fry: *būrae.*
sound of grease frying: *ttiijij.*

fuel: *kaan, kane.*
provide fuel for: *ṇakaan.*
refuel a fire: *anekane.*
use as fuel: *kaan.*

fulfill: *kaṃool.*
fulfill someone's request: *ṇawāwee-.*
fulfill, as a prophecy: *kūrṃool.*

full: *bab, booḷ, kōlōk, lōñ, mājidjid, obrak.*
full after eating: *mat.*
full of: *jab, jjuurore.*
full sail, nautical: *kankan, lōtlōt.*
full to the brim: *dujejjet, lōñ mājidjid.*
keep a canoe or boat full-sailing: *kabwijer.*
less than half full: *jakapen.*
night after full moon: *jetmar.*
night of full moon: *jetñōl.*
sail not full: *tọ.*
arrive in full force: *ḷooribeb.*

fumble: *ttọḷūm.*

fun
make fun: *kōjak.*
make fun of: *lowaar.*

function: *jerbal.*

fund: *jāān.*

funeral: *kallib.*
taking gifts to a wedding, funeral, or party for guests to take home: *tōptōp.*

fungus: *kito, lirọuwe.*
white acne-like fungus under skin: *karko.*

funnel: *banōḷ.*

funny: *kōjak, liāp.*

fur
smooth like fur: *meoeo.*

furious: *kūtōtō, matōrtōr, paḷ.*

furnish: *ṇaṃweie-.*

fury: *llu.*

fuse: *piwūj.*

fuss: *kkeroro.*

future
future tense marker: *naaj.*
intuition about a future misfortune or death: *lomije-.*
near future: *ilju im men.*

fuzz
frayed, fuzzy: *wūdede.*
fuzzy-haired: *pirañrañ.*
fuzzy, of hair: *kweejej.*

gabble: *aeñwāñwā.*

gable: *daṃ.*
cornice or gable of a Marshallese house: *demāju.*

gadget: *kūḷaabreej.*

gaff: *ankeke, kāāj, kaab, rojak.*
canoe part, edge of sail fastened to the gaff: *aeṃaan.*

gain: *tōpran, wiin.*

gal: *lijā, lijjọọn.*

Galeocerdo
a fish, tiger shark, *Galeocerdo arcticus*: *pako tiltil.*

gall
gall bladder: *at.*

galley: *kiaḷe.*

gallon: *kaḷan.*

gamble: *pile.*

game: *kkure.*
a card game: *juip, peeñka.*
a game: *iaļan juon, jaañke, ṃwina, taij.*
a game, Marshallese women's baseball: *ejjebaō.*
a game, child's play using pebbles and shells as imaginary objects and characters: *lijjikin.*
a game, contest to see who can throw a sharp-pointed piece of dried pandanus root, about a yard long, farthest by skimming it on the ground once: *kajjeor.*
a game, dare base (one base): *eub.*
a game, dare base (two bases): *awiia.*
a game, diving for pandanus: *lijunaṃnaṃ.*
a game, hide behind a mat and have another guess: *kōļōnwa.*
a game, hide-and-seek: *ṃwijju.*
a game, high jump or broad jump: *kappiñ.*
a game, holding a child up with one's feet while flat on one's back (parent-child game): *jippapa.*
a game, hop-scotch: *kappetpet.*
a game, jacks: *kiiñkiiñ.*
a game, juggling: *leje"ñje"ñ, lejọñjọñ.*
a game, king of the mountain: *kojuwa.*
a game, making holes in sand and covering them: *kūttūk.*
a game, pelting one another with lighted pandanus keys or coconut husks: *buwaddel.*
a game, played with pebbles and ball, similar to dice game: *ļuļu.*
a game, pulling people from port to starboard under the keel: *tuṃaļ.*
a game, racing toy outrigger canoes: *kariwutut.*
a game, scissors, paper, and stone: *jaañke.*
a game, similar to "drop the handkerchief": *arot.*
a game, skip-rope: *kutiñ.*
a game, slight-of-hand using shell and three holes in sand: *ṃōjjā.*
a game, tag: *anoot.*
a game, to play house: *ļōkōṃ.*
a game, trump: *turuṃ.*
a game, underwater football using a rock for a ball: *niñniñ.*
a game, with blindfolds: *lijjapillo.*
catch up, in a game: *bōktak.*
foul, in games: *pet.*
pass, in card games: *baaj.*
solid ground on which the game of *kajjeor* is played: *wūmar.*
tie in a game: *jebo, wōnaji.*
warmed up, in games: *pet pā.*

gang: *kāāñ.*
to gang up on someone or something: *ṃaijek.*
work gang: *kumi.*

gangling: *aujepaļ.*

gangrene: *jiṇo.*

gap: *tuwa.*

gape: *aļļañ, ppaļ.*

garage: *kūraaj.*

garbage: *kwōpej.*
eat garbage: *attūkoko.*
garbage dump: *kōlla.*

garden: *atake, jikin kallib.*

gargle: *kurkur, rukruk.*

garland
garland with flowers set close together: *tōōlkut.*
garland with flowers set wide apart: *tōōldepak.*
strands for weaving garlands or stringing leis: *id.*

garment: *nuknuk.*

gash
gashes in coral reef: *kōlñe.*
long gashes in the outside reef: *mejā.*

gasoline: *kiaj.*

gate: *kōjām.*
gateway: *aor.*
gateway, usually decorated with flowers and coconut fronds: *ṃoñ.*

gather: *ae, pānuk.*
a gathering of people to celebrate the onset of breadfruit season in summer by making offerings to Jebro, the god of breadfruit: *ṃaṃa.*
gather fallen pandanus leaves from ground for thatch or handicraft: *ppel.*
gather followers: *tilbuuj.*
gather food: *ennōk, kakijen.*
gather green pandanus leaves from trees: *bōlbōl.*
gather in a certain spot: *peļaak.*
gather many husked copra nuts: *pinju.*
gather missiles for throwing: *rukbo.*
gather news or information: *eọroñ naan.*
gather to dance: *du.*
gathered together: *kuk.*
illegal gathering of food on another's property: *ļe eoon eṃ.*

gay: *m̧ōn̄ōn̄ō.*
gaze
to gaze at: *kallimjek.*
gear
cog, gear, ratchet: *raanke.*
gecko
an animal, kind of lizard, big tree gecko, *Gehyra oceanica*: *korap kūro.*
an animal, kind of lizard, gecko, *Lepidodactylus pelagicus* or *Hemiphyllodactylus typus*: *korap.*
gee: *uwo̧k.*
Gehenna: *kena.*
Gehyra
an animal, kind of lizard, big tree gecko, *Gehyra oceanica*: *korap kūro.*
gem: *dekā aorōk.*
Gemini
Castor and Pollux in Gemini: *Iju-kuwaj-aiļip.*
genealogy: *kadkad.*
study one's genealogy: *jitdam̧.*
generation: *epepen.*
generous: *m̧m̧ool.*
genital
smell of unwashed genitals: *kūtkūt.*
genius: *n̄akn̄ōk, wājepdik.*
gentle: *ineem̧m̧an, meanwōd.*
genuflect: *juubkwe.*
genuine: *lukwi.*
germ: *kij.*
Germany: *Jāmne.*
germinate: *ddek.*
Gerres
a fish, silverfish, *Gerres baconensis*: *ilmek.*
get: *bōk, llo.*
get away clean: *joor.*
get by: *kipeddikdik.*
get hooked, nabbed: *to̧rōk.*
get into prime running condition: *an.*
get something in one's eye: *pelo̧k.*
get the last drops of water from a water container: *kajļor.*
get up: *jerkak.*
get up, from lying down: *waļo̧k.*
ghost: *eakeak, m̧ōkade, timo̧n̄.*
a ghost, haunts and drives people mad, lives in dense forests: *on̄en̄ak.*
afraid of ghosts: *abwinmake.*
great fear of ghosts and the dark: *abwinmakelep.*
possessed by ghosts: *mejatoto.*
put on heads or chests of those allegedly attacked by ghosts to repel later attacks: *kūm̧ur.*
sickness, believed caused by sea-ghosts: *rilojet.*
waft through the air, as a ghost: *weaak.*
ghosts that haunt and drive people mad, live in dense forests: *wōnen̄ak.*
giant: *ineea, rimakaiio.*
a shell, giant clam: *kapwor.*
giant lobster: *bo̧kuj pedped.*
giant size: *debbōn.*
legendary cruel giants who scare and kill people: *wōnen̄ak.*
organ of giant clam: *lām.*
giant sea bass
a fish, giant sea bass, *Promicrops lanceolatus/truncatus*: *jo̧we.*
giddy: *addeboulul, baūjō, bwebwe, jim̧alejlej, m̧ōļo̧wi.*
gift: *joortak.*
buy gifts for: *jo̧ut.*
curry the favor of men or women with gifts: *anbōro.*
gift (with directional postpositions): *menin le-.*
gift land: *im̧ōn aje.*
gifts: *m̧weiuk.*
give gift to someone: *n̄am̧weie-.*
give gift to win favor, to opposite sex: *kōbōjbōj.*
laying gifts under a Christmas tree (at a Christmas song fest): *jin̄ap.*
reciprocating of gifts: *kabbōjrak.*
return gift: *kabbōjrak.*
taking gifts to a wedding, funeral, or party for guests to take home: *tōptōp.*
visit home of dead person with gifts: *ilomej.*
giggle: *ttōn̄ dikdik.*
Gilbert
Gilbert (Islands): *Kilbōt.*
Gilbertese: *Pit.*
gills: *bōro.*
fish gills: *or.*
gimlet: *kilmij.*
gin: *jiin.*
girdle
to girdle a plant: *kōnar.*
girl: *leddik.*
a girl or woman whose appearance makes everyone smile: *llejkōnkōn.*
girl hunting: *jawōd.*
nickname for baby girl: *jiron̄.*
that girl (close to neither of us): *lien̄, luweo.*

that girl (close to you): *lieņe, lieņeņe.*
these girls (close to me): *limarā, limarārā, limaro.*
these girls (close to us both): *limarein.*
this girl (close to me): *lie, lio.*
this girl (close to us both): *liin, liiō.*
those girls (close to neither of us): *limarāraņ, limaraņ, limaroro.*
those girls (close to you): *limarāraņe, limaraņe.*
unmarried adolescent girl: *jiroñ.*

give: *le-.*
give (polite form): *jake.*
give as present and ask for its return: *ajejin Jowa, ajejin Ļōktab.*
give away: *leļǫk.*
give away freely: *ankilaak.*
give away without remuneration: *aje.*
give birth: *keotak, kōmmour.*
give freely: *wūjlep-.*
give gift to win favor, to opposite sex: *kōbōjbōj.*
give in abundance: *wūjlep-.*
give shape to: *ņaļōma-.*
give to the speaker: *letok.*
give to you: *lewōj.*
give up: *baaj, bbetok, ṃaal, ṃweed.*
give up hope: *bweetkōn.*
give up, as in war: *bbeer.*
surrender, give up: *jatōptōp.*

gizzard: *tudek.*

glad: *ṃōņōņō.*

glance: *animro-, miro.*
glance by: *ļļā.*
glance off: *jājļǫk.*

gland
sickness, swollen lymph glands: *bbūra.*
swollen gland: *ur.*

glare: *taṃtaṃ, tinaad.*

glass: *kilaj.*
broken glass: *bato.*
drinking glass: *kab.*

glasses
eyeglasses: *māj, māj kilaaj.*
eyeglasses of: *meja-.*
sunglasses: *māj.*
sunglasses of: *meja-.*
to wear glasses: *mājmāj.*

gleam: *romaak.*
gleam faintly: *rrobōlbōl.*

glee: *lǫudiñdiñ.*

glib: *wājepdik.*

glide: *weaak.*
glide in the air: *jepeļā.*
glide, of birds: *tǫ.*

glimmer: *rrobōlbōl.*

glimpse: *animro-.*
catch a glimpse of, because of fast motion: *iiṃ.*

glitter: *rabōlbōl.*

gloat: *juwaļōñļōñ.*

gloom: *marok.*
gloomy: *lianij.*

glorify: *nōbar, wūjtak.*

glory: *aibooj.*

glove: *tebukro.*
baseball glove: *kurob.*
wear a baseball glove: *kurobrob.*

glow: *kabōlbōl, meram.*

glue: *kūļu.*

glutton: *būrooklep, mattiia.*

gnat: *jokwajok.*

Gnathodentex
a fish, porgy, *Gnathodentex aurolineatus*: *tūñad.*

gnaw: *ajoļjoļ.*
gnaw, of a rat or a mouse: *wōjek.*

go: *etal, jeblaak, wāwe.*
go aground: *ṃwitaak.*
go ahead: *ṃṃōkaj.*
go alongside of: *atar.*
go and meet: *wōnṃae.*
go around: *ito-itak.*
go around with: *aililōk.*
go as a passenger: *bajinjea.*
go ashore on islands belonging to others: *popo ṃanit.*
go away: *kodaaj, weļǫk.*
go away (of humans): *ilǫk.*
go away for a change of scene: *jaṃbo.*
go away for some fresh air: *kōkajoor.*
go back and forth: *ito-itak.*
go backward: *jenliklik, wanlik.*
go directly to or towards: *iok-.*
go directly toward: *kajju.*
go drinking at a club: *kuļab.*
go eastward: *itakļǫk, wetak.*
go from sea side of an island to lagoon side: *kear.*
go in a passage: *ṃweeaar.*
go into the water: *tuwaak.*
go on a vehicle or sailing canoe (used with directional enclitics (and postpositions)): *tar-.*
go on foot: *etal laļ.*
go one at a time: *iaļ aidik.*
go or come ashore: *wāānāne, wanāne.*
go or come down: *wanlaļ.*
go or come seaward: *wanmeto.*

go or come towards the lagoon: *wāānar, wanar.*
go or come towards the ocean side of an island: *wanlik.*
go out: *diwōj.*
go out a passage: *m̧welik.*
go out of a building: *wannabōj.*
go over: *etale.*
go shoreward: *wāānāne.*
go through: *deblo̧k, dibuk, l̦ipdel̦o̧k, pejlo̧k, ru-.*
go to and fro: *jebwāālel.*
go to the interior of an islet: *tōl̦oñ.*
go to the lagoon side: *keeaar.*
go to the ocean side: *kālik.*
go to the ocean side on the southern end of an island: *kālikrōk.*
go to you: *iwōj.*
go toward: *kaiok.*
go toward (used with directional enclitics): *wan-.*
go westward: *ito, wāto.*
keep going: *etal wōt.*
step or go over: *l̦ōke.*
to begin going: *bweradik.*

go-ahead: *jodi.*

goad
to urge, goad, spur, push: *rro̧o̧j.*

goal: *mejānkajjik.*
achieve one's goal: *teru.*
reach a goal: *auj.*

goat: *koot.*

goatfish: *jo.*
Mulloidichthys auriflama: *jome.*
Mulloidichthys samoensis: *jo.*
Parupeneus barberinus: *m̧ōtal.*
Parupeneus sp: *jorobbā.*
Upeneus tragula: *jol̦o̧km̧ōōr.*
fishing method, pole fishing for goatfish: *kadjo.*

goby
a fish, general term for all goby: *jippul̦e.*
a fish, goby (Mejit): *kūtōk, kwōpra.*

god
a god of fish: *irooj rilik.*
half gods, literally "those gods.": *anij ran̦.*
interjection: "Darn!" Or "God forbid!": *ōkkōk.*
sacrifice food to the gods: *wālo̧klik.*
God: *Anij.*
Almighty God: *Anij L̦apl̦ap.*
interjection: "By God!": *m̧ajidak.*

goggle
possessive classifier, eyes, lids, openings, eyeglasses, masks, or goggles: *meja-.*
goggles: *mejān turo̧ñ.*

goggle-eye
a fish, big-eyed or goggle-eyed scad fish or horse mackerel, *Trachurops crumenophthalmus*: *pāti.*
a fish, goggle-eye, *Priacanthus cruentatus*: *l̦wōl.*

gold: *kool̦.*

golden plover
a bird, golden plover, *Pluvialis dominica*: *kwōlej.*
a bird, golden plover, black variety, in breeding plumage: *l̦akeke.*

Goliath: *Kol̦eiaat.*

Gomphrena
a plant, *Gomphrena globosa*: *abl̦ajtiiñ.*

gone: *jako.*
all gone: *maat.*
gone for a long time: *lino̧k.*
gone forth: *m̧ōre, moot.*

gonorrhea: *jeplej.*

goo
gooey, as bread not fully cooked: *depñat.*

good: *m̧m̧an.*
good for nothing: *pata.*
good in fishing, expert in fishing: *aewanlik.*
good looking: *kōjaij.*
interjection: "Good grief!": *aia.*
looks good but won't last: *kōmjedeo̧.*
make good: *kōm̧anm̧an.*
no good: *jettokja-.*
of good age: *m̧m̧an ded.*
of good mixture: *m̧m̧an utōn.*
of good size: *m̧m̧an ded.*
put in good shape: *kwadikdik.*
taste good: *nno̧.*

goodbye
wave goodbye: *jokutbae.*

goods: *m̧weiuk.*
land or goods put away for future use or need: *kōpetaklik.*
security, land or goods or money put away for future use or for children: *joortoklik.*

goose
scratch anus, to goose: *rōbtak.*
to goose: *wie.*

goose pimple
goose pimples: *ko tok kili-.*

gorgeous: *aiboojoj.*

gorilla: *kuriḷa.*

gossip: *arōk naan, bbōk, naan jekdọọn.*

Gossypium
a plant, *Gossypium barbadense* L. (Malvaceae): *kotin.*

gourd
the gourd: *baañke.*

gout: *kūrro.*

government: *kien.*
head of a governmental organization: *kom̧ja.*

governor: *kabna.*

gown: *likko.*

grab
grab, squeeze: *kkuul.*

grace: *jouj.*
graceful: *kattōñtōñ.*

gracious
interjection: "Gracious!": *m̧ajō.*

grade: *teeñ.*

gradual
gradually, little by little, piecemeal: *jidik illoķ jidik.*

graduate: *diwōjḷọk.*

grain
grain of rice: *tōōḷ.*
smallest unit of something, grain: *wūd.*

gram: *kūraam̧.*

Grammatorcynus
a fish, mackerel, *Grammatorcynus bicarinatus*: *ikabwe.*

gramophone: *jukoñki.*

grand: *m̧m̧an, utiej.*

grandchild: *būbū.*
granddaughter: *lijjibūbū.*
grandson, affectionate term: *ḷajjibūbū.*
duty of taking care of a grandson, granddaughter, a grandparent, or a pet: *jibwi.*

grandparent
grandfather (with possessive suffixes): *jim̧m̧a.*
grandfather, child speech: *jim̧m̧a.*
grandmother: *obajañ.*
affectionate term for grandmother: *lijjibūbū.*
grandmother, child speech: *būbū.*
grandmother, grandchild, of: *jibwi-.*
duty of taking care of a grandson, granddaughter, a grandparent, or a pet: *jibwi.*

grandstander
a grandstander: *kabōllaḷ.*

grant: *jake, le-.*
take for granted: *ālikinjepjep.*

grape: *kūreep.*

grapple
to grapple with: *ñijlọk.*

grasp: *jebjeb, kkuul.*

grass: *wūjooj.*
a plant, a grass: *pādālijm̧aan.*
a plant, a grass, prickly: *lōklōk.*
a plant, grass, *Thuarea involuta*: *kakkūm̧kūm̧.*
grass skirt: *in, inin, ōr.*
grass skirt boys put on at puberty: *kiōk.*
lower part of tree, brush, or grass: *wūn.*
pull up weeds or grass: *kintak.*
to pull and break objects such as string, rope, wire or grass: *tūm̧tūm̧.*

grasshopper: *jidjid.*
an insect, grasshopper: *jeḷo.*

grate
grate coconuts, grater: *raanke, raanke.*
grate one's teeth: *kaōrōr.*
grated coconut: *pen.*

grated coconut: *jokoojwa.*
a food, cooked and pounded breadfruit, taro, bananas, or nuts mixed with grated coconut: *wūdeñ.*
a food, cooked preserved breadfruit smothered in grated coconut: *kubaḷ.*
a food, octopus smothered in grated coconut: *penkwe.*
a food, pandanus pulp and juice mixed with grated coconut and coconut oil (and optionally with arrowroot starch), wrapped in breadfruit leaves and boiled or baked: *peru.*
add sand or grated coconut: *penpen.*
coconut cloth used to squeeze and extract oil from grated coconut: *jouneak.*
fine, of grated coconut: *kkwidik.*
pandanus juice mixed with grated coconut, cooked into custard: *mokwaņ duul.*
pandanus juice mixed with grated coconut, uncooked: *mokwaņ dada.*
to throw grated coconut or sand at someone or something: *pinik.*

grateful: *m̧m̧ool.*
be grateful: *kam̧m̧oolol.*

gratify
to gratify: *ñiājo.*

grave: *lōb.*
cemetery, graveyard: *wūliej.*
ceremony performed six days after burial, gravel is spread over grave: *eoreak.*

gravel: *dekā, ļā.*
ceremony performed six days after burial, gravel is spread over grave: *eoreak.*
footsteps in gravel or dry leaves: *m̧m̧ōjānjān.*
rattling of gravel: *ļļāārār.*

gravy: *jāle-, jālele, kūrepe.*

gray: *wūpaajaj.*
gray colored: *kūbween upaaj, kūre.*
gray haired: *uwaņ.*

graze: *anōr, ļāān.*
graze, as a bullet, chipped: *tām̧oņ.*

grease: *kūriij.*
sound of grease frying: *ttiijij.*

great: *ļap, m̧m̧an.*
greatest: *ļaptata, lijekļọk.*
intensifier, with great force: *tōn̄tōn̄.*
very great: *bōtata, lijekļọk.*

greed: *koņak.*
greedy: *arōk, tōr.*
greedy eater: *būrooklep, mattiia.*
greedy for food: *mattiia.*
not greedy (see *tōr* (**ter**)): *jatōr.*

green: *kūriin, owatrere.*
green colored: *maroro.*
greenhorn: *watre.*

greet: *iọkiọkwe, iọkwe.*

grief: *būrom̧ōj, ilomej.*
recall with grief: *ajļọk.*
sobbing because of grief: *m̧ōtato.*

grieve: *kōmmen̄.*

grill: *jinkadool.*
grill verbally: *kajitūkin.*
to grill someone: *ekajet.*

grim: *kijn̄en̄e, lāj.*

grimace: *jememe, kōmmen̄.*

grin: *ūjō.*

grind: *lij.*
bump and grind: *kajikia.*
grind with the teeth, noisily: *kan̄urn̄ur.*
stone used for grinding arrowroot: *pukor.*

grip: *dāpdep, m̧ūt.*

gripe: *abņōņō, llotaan.*

grit
grit the teeth: *ōļōļ.*
gritty feeling under the eyelids: *ttaorak.*

groan: *n̄ijlọk, n̄n̄ūr.*
groaning: *n̄ijlọk.*

groggy: *an̄an̄e, arun̄ijn̄ij.*

groove: *kom̧laļ.*
groove in piece of wood, for *etōn̄* firemaking: *kin.*

grope: *jatoļ, ttọļūm.*

gross: *iio.*
unclean, vulgar, gross: *ttoon.*

grotesque: *kōjak.*

grouch
grouchy: *m̧m̧aļkaro, nana tam̧m̧wi-.*

ground: *bwidej.*
a fish, ground shark, *Carcharhinus melanopterus*: *pakoon eoon pedped.*
go aground: *eọr, m̧witaak.*
ground ball in baseball: *kōro.*
ground wire: *kūrawūn.*
habitually defecate on ground: *pektaan.*
on the ground: *laļ.*
playground: *wūntoba.*
pull out of ground: *wūj.*
slip under ground or sand: *jọ.*
solid ground on which the game of *kajjeor* is played: *wūmar.*

group: *bwijin.*
a group of people going to a place for a specific purpose: *aktal.*
any group of people, as a class, unit or division: *jar.*
company, team, group: *kumi.*
group of people going to pay respects to a deceased: *tal.*
group within a Protestant congregation: *jebta.*
make one's presence felt, especially a group: *tilen̄en̄.*
work on something as a group: *kumit.*

grouper: *alean̄, ļakkūrae.*
blue-spotted grouper, *Cepahalopholis argus*: *kalemeej.*
Epinephelus adscenscionis: *ļōjepjep.*
Epinephelus fuscoguttatus: *kūro.*
Epinephelus hexagonatus: *m̧ōm̧ō.*
shark grouper, *Carcharhinus melanopterus*: *pako mej.*
small grouper: *tinar.*

grove: *bukun.*

grow: *ddek, eọn̄, jebar.*
grow close together (see *kkut*): *m̧okut.*
grow slowly: *ļūbbat.*
grow smaller: *jen.*
grow together as plants: *idepdep.*
grow well: *didbōlbōl.*

grown over: *jel.*
grown together: *piro.*
growth from old root or branch: *juḷ.*
heavy growth: *debọkut.*
plant or tree growth from old root or after old branch of tree has been cut down: *ḷor.*
stage of growth: *ded.*
stunted growth: *ḷūbbat, wūdkabbe.*

growl: *ññūr.*

grub: *kapije, kkan, ṃōñā.*

grudge: *ṇota.*

grumble: *kkeroro, ūlūlōt.*

grunt: *ññūr.*

Grus: *Bwā-eṇ-an-Joktak.*

guarantee: *joortoklik, kalliṃur.*

guard: *baar, baṃpe, bwilijmāāṇ, waj.*
canoe part, piece of wood on leeside as guard against rubbing from steering paddle: *eran jebwe.*
canoe part, waveguard on both sides of sailing canoe: *añtūkli.*
guardian: *likōpejñak.*
wave-guard on a canoe: *ubweṇo.*

guess: *kajjidede, kajjimalele, leḷōmṇak.*
a game, hide behind a mat and have another guess: *kōḷōnwa.*

guest: *riitok, rilotok.*

Guettarda
a plant, *Guettarda speciosa* L. (Rubiaceae): *utilomar.*

guide: *jiniet.*

guilty: *bōd.*

guitar: *kūta.*

gull: *keār.*
a bird, gull: *kūṃake.*

gullible
gullible, attracted to: *reel.*

gulp: *orañḷọk.*

gum
chewing gum: *bwil.*
cover with gum: *bwilbwil.*
gummy: *bwilbwil.*

gums: *ñad.*

gun: *bu, likajik.*
aim a gun: *alej.*
be shaken by recoil of a gun: *ṃweiur.*
big gun: *pakke.*
gunpowder: *bọurok.*
machine gun: *kikanju.*
not good marksman, with gun, slingshot, or by throwing stones (see *jerọ* (**jeraw**)): *jerta.*
shotgun: *lijjukwōlkwōl.*
tremor or vibration caused by sound of gun or thunder: *pañijñij.*

gurgle
shake a liquid so that it gurgles: *kọkkorōjrōj.*

gush: *bbūtūktūk, tọọr, utōttōt.*

gust: *añijwiwi.*
gusty wind: *añjarjar, ḷadikin eoon ere, okjānlañ.*

gut
guts, intestines, bowels, offal, innards: *ṃajñal.*

gutter
spout, rain gutter: *tāāñ.*

guy: *kijak.*
guy rope or cable: *kae.*

Gygis
a bird, white tern, *Gygis alba*: *mejọ.*

Gymnocranius
a fish, snapper, *Gymnocranius microndon/griseus*: *mejmej.*

Gymnosarda
a fish, dog-tooth tuna, *Gymnosarda nuda*: *jilo.*

Gymnothorax
moray eel, *Gymnothorax flavimarginatus*: *ṃakañ.*
moray eel, *Gymnothorax pictus*: *ṃaj-mouj.*
Gymnothorax sp.: *dāp.*
Gymnothorax rupelli/petelli: *kideddelbwij.*

gyp: *ajej in kabwebwe.*

habit: *abja, meej, mminene.*
habitually defecate on ground: *pektaan.*
have the habit of: *mminene.*

hack
cut, hack, chop-off, split, slash: *jepak.*

hacksaw: *jidpān aen.*

had: *kar.*

Hades: *Kapin-marok.*

hail: *katūbtūb.*

hair: *kooḷ.*
anus hair: *oḷkūñ.*
be hairy: *kooḷoḷ.*
braid, of hair: *pirōkrōk.*
bristle, strand of hair: *tōōḷ.*
bristling hair standing on end from terror: *rrọñ.*
burn hair off: *rirar.*
clip all of the hair off: *kwōdmat.*
cut hair: *ṃwijbar.*
dry hair, not oily: *kuraañañ.*
fuzzy-haired: *pirañrañ.*

fuzzy, of hair: *kweejej.*
girl's haircut, Japanese style: *taṃbaj.*
grey haired: *uwaṇ.*
hair pomade: *kūriijin kkapit.*
hair smoothed with oil: *medọḷ.*
haircut: *ṃwijbar.*
hairsplitting: *kajjiṃwe.*
having a receding hairline: *kkodaṃdaṃ.*
head devoid of hair: *kweejej.*
kinky, of hair: *iñiñ.*
knot of hair, women: *bujek.*
lose hair: *ṃōd.*
not hairy (see *kooḷ* (**qeweḷ**)): *jọkooḷoḷ.*
not hairy, not feathery: *nemwak.*
part, hair: *toṇak.*
pluck feather or hair (Ralik only): *imkilkil.*
pubic hair: *wak.*
pull out hairs: *tūṃṃọṇ.*
shingled, cut the hair short: *taṃbaj.*
small mole with a hair sticking out: *būttiwoḷ.*
straight hair: *maḷko.*
trim hair with a razor: *jeor.*
twist and pull hair: *dāde.*
twist the hair into a knot: *bujek.*
wear hair in bangs: *kọkwe.*
wear hair loose on one's back, of women: *aleak.*

half: *jeblokwa-, jimattan.*
be half full: *jeblokwa-.*
front half of fish: *jebbar.*
half-moon: *wetakḷap.*
left half of human body: *anmiiñ.*
less than half full: *jakapen.*
right half of human body: *anmooṇ.*
tail half of fish: *jablọk.*

half-caste: *apkaaj.*

half-cooked
half-cooked (as rice when inadequate water is used): *bbūkbūk.*

half-done
half-done, of fish or meat: *koubub.*

halfbeak
a fish, halfbeak, *Hemiramphus depauperatus*: *buwaj.*
a fish, halfbeak, *Hyporhamphus laticeps*: *kūbu.*

Halichoeres
a fish, wrasse, *Halichoeres trimaculatus*: *po.*

halitosis
smell, halitosis: *taiñad.*

hall
mess hall: *ṃōn ṃōñā.*

halo: *ao.*

halt: *bōjrak.*
halted: *baaj.*

ham: *aṃ.*

hammer: *aṃa, ḷwūj, ure.*
pound with a mallet or hammer: *penḷwūj.*

hammock: *aṃak.*

hand: *pā.*
carry in one hand: *arorā, pārājet.*
carry with both hands: *pārorā.*
clap hands: *kabbokbok.*
do something singlehandedly: *wajekā.*
fishing method, inserting the bare hand into holes nooks or crannies in the reef: *rrwe.*
hand of bananas: *ajjen.*
hand over: *jake.*
hand something to the rear or back: *lelik.*
hold hands while walking: *ijjurpe.*
hold up or catch with both hands: *bọur.*
inquisitive, of hands only: *pānāpnep.*
left hand: *anbwijban, anmiiñ.*
open-handed: *ṃṃool.*
palm of hand: *ḷọpiden pā.*
right hand: *anbwijmaroñ, anmooṇ.*
scoop up by hand: *rwaklep.*
shake hands to make a promise binding: *jeep.*
stand on one's hands: *ju.*
take by the hand: *kabwijer.*
throw by handfuls: *eọkur.*
use one hand: *jalenpā.*
walk hand in hand: *ijjurpe.*
walk with the hands clasped behind the back: *enliklik.*
wash hands: *aṃwin.*
water for washing hands: *aṃwin.*

hand line
fishing method, use hand line from canoe in deep ocean for fish other than tuna: *kōddāpilpil.*

handcuff
handcuffs: *jakōḷ.*

handicap
handicapped: *jipikpik.*

handicraft: *amiṃōṇo.*
gather fallen pandanus leaves from ground for thatch or handicraft: *ppel.*
make handicraft: *amiṃōṇo.*

handkerchief: *añkijep.*

handle
braid a handle of a basket: *pirōkrōk.*

handle, as of a knife or shovel: *juro-*.
make a handle for a spear: *buñi*.
spear handle: *buñ*.
handle someone or something with care: *kōm̧m̧anm̧ōn*.

handsome: *kōjaij, m̧ōtañ*.
handsome, men only: *wūlio*.

hang: *allijāljāl*.
hang from: *toto*.
hang on: *ekkejel, jirok, m̧ūt*.
hang on the line: *roro*.
hang on to: *toto*.
hang up: *toto*.
hang upon: *kkejel*.

Hansen's disease: *lōba*.

haphazard: *ortabtab*.

happen: *waļọk*.
happen to: *ļokwan*.

happy: *buñ-bōro, kam̧ōņōņō, m̧ōņōņō, wūdiñdiñ*.
be very happy: *jab juur laļ*.
walk in a happy mood: *alijerļọk*.

harass: *apañ, kkọbōl*.

harbor: *aba, ejja, ja, mājik*.

hard: *pen*.
hard to cook: *mattiia*.
hard to embarrass (see *jjookok* (**jjewekwek**)): *jājjookok*.
hard to scare: *jāmmijakjak*.
hard to turn (see *jaļiie* (**jahļiyyẹy**)): *jaļiia*.
hard working: *owan, niknik*.
hard, ground: *ñūñ*.
hardening of starch or tallow or lead: *kwōj*.
wound that is hard to cure or heal (see *mowiie* (**mẹwiyyẹy**)): *mowiia*.

hardship
withstand hardships: *kajumej*.

hardwood: *kije*.

harelip: *tām̧oņ*.

Harengula
Harengula kinzei: *mamo*.

harm: *jorrāān, mariprip*.
harmful substances: *baijin*.

harmonica: *am̧onika*.

harmony: *koņkōtaa-*.

harpoon: *m̧ade*.

harsh: *lāj*.
talk harshly: *būroñ*.

harvest: *m̧adm̧ōd*.
copra harvesting period: *aļ*.
harvest coconuts: *kowainini*.
harvest first fruit of coconut, breadfruit, or pandanus: *akẹọ*.
harvest fruit: *jele*.
harvest pandanus: *jowe*.
harvest time for arrowroot: *añōneañ*.

hasp: *injej*.

hassle: *apañ, im*.

haste: *m̧m̧ōkaj*.
hasty: *iiōk dakdak*.

hat: *at*.
hat block form, any mold, any form: *m̧ōņakjān*.
to weave the edges of a mat or hat: *jekōt*.
wear a hat: *atat*.

hatch: *aj*.
abandoned unhatched egg, usually spoiled: *kor*.
fertilized egg, ready to hatch: *kune*.
to hatch: *ruprup*.

hatchet: *māāl, ūlūl*.

hate: *abōb, akkōjdat, dike, kōjdat, kūtōtō*.
hateful: *kōmatōrtōr*.
very hateful: *kajjōjō*.

haughty: *lom̧aan*.

haul: *ektak, ipep*.
haul by cart: *kurm̧a*.
haul canoe or vessel up on shore: *ār*.
keel-haul: *tum̧aļ*.

haunch
sit on one's haunches: *pijļẹļẹ*.

haunt: *kkeini*.
a ghost, haunts and drives people mad, lives in dense forests: *oņeņak*.
haunted: *aeto, mọņmọņ*.

have: *or*.
have it made: *jeban*.
have something on one's mind: *ikdeelel*.

Hawaii: *Awai*.
Hawaiian *humu-humu nuku-nuku a-puaa*: *im̧im̧*.

hawkfish
a fish, spotted hawkfish, *Cirrhitus pinnulatus*: *kidiej*.

hay: *wūjooj*.

hazard
hazardous: *kauwōtata*.

haze
fog, dim, haze, blur: *tab*.

he: *e*.
he, away from the speaker: *ļeeņ*.

head: *pet, wūliej*.
bald head: *oļūb*.
behead: *jebbar*.
bow one's head: *dukwal*.
coralhead: *wōd*.
duck one's head: *wōmak*.

head eastward: *jittak.*
head in a certain direction: *jit.*
head man: *karo.*
head northward: *jitniñeañ.*
head of: *bōrā, jeban.*
head of a governmental organization: *komja.*
head of a household: *karo.*
head part in lying down, as the head of the bed: *jebbar.*
head southward: *jitrōkeañ.*
head westward: *jitto.*
head wreath of: *pālli-.*
head, top, tip: *bar.*
headlong: *tubar.*
land given to someone who took care of the head of the lineage owning the land during illness before death: *m̧ōnkǫļotļot.*
level-headed: *lǫļe.*
lineage head: *aļap.*
lower the head, humble oneself: *badik.*
pate of head: *m̧ǫñ.*
point head downwards: *kalōlō.*
possessive classifier, flowers or wreaths worn on head: *pālli-.*
put wreath on one's head: *pālpel.*
shake the head in disagreement: *jeboulul.*
shaven head: *oļūb.*
slap on the back of the head: *jepwaļ.*
stand on one's head: *ju, lōlō.*
turn the head slowly from side to side: *jeboulul.*
wear flowers on head: *pālpel.*

heal
extraordinary healing powers, as in Marshallese native medicine: *kōbbōkakkak.*
having healing powers: *mālkwōj.*
healing together of a wound: *ik.*
to heal: *mo.*
wound that is easy to cure or heal (see *mowiia* (**mẹwiyyah**)): *mowiie.*
wound that is hard to cure or heal (see *mowiie* (**mẹwiyyẹy**)): *mowiia.*

health
fat and healthy, usually referring to a baby: *m̧ǫkulkul, uļūtļūt.*
good health: *keeñki.*
health aide: *komen.*
health clinic: *m̧ōn taktō.*
healthy: *ājmuur.*
healthy in appearance, as a coconut tree: *wāmourur.*
unhealthy: *utam̧we.*

heap: *ejaak.*
heap of stones: *ajokļā.*
heaping up of waves: *jetak.*

hear
do you hear me?: *eañ.*
dull of hearing: *roñ jam̧ǫņ.*
good hearing (see *roñiia* (**reg°iyyah**)): *roñiie.*
hard of hearing (see *roñiie* (**reg°iyyẹy**)): *roñiia.*
hear well: *roñļǫkjeņ.*
quick of hearing: *roñļǫkjeņ.*
to hear: *roñ.*
unable to hear (see *roñ* (**reg°**)): *jarroñroñ.*

heart: *bam̧, menono.*
"heart": *bōro.*
broken-hearted: *rup bōro.*
fast beating of heart in fear: *kkūm̧kūm̧.*
heart of palm: *jiab.*
heart of tree: *boļ.*
know by heart: *kkiil.*
soft-hearted: *ineem̧m̧an, meanwōd.*
stouthearted: *pen būruo-.*
stronghearted: *pen būruo-.*
heartburn: *bwilmeleeñ.*
heartburn caused by drinking fresh coconut sap on an empty stomach: *mmaļ.*
disenheartened: *m̧weed.*

hearty: *keeñki.*

heat: *māāņāņ.*
dry fish or copra by heat: *atiti.*
heated contest: *bok.*
medicine, heat-treatment using hot stones wrapped in leaves: *tabuk.*
prickly heat, heatrash: *bok aidik.*

heathen: *peikan.*

heave: *kiliblib.*
heave to: *iptu.*

heaven: *aelōñin-lañ, lañ.*

heavy: *ddo.*
heavy growth: *debǫkut.*

heck
interjection: "darn!" Or "heck!": *ōrrōr.*

heckle: *kūtōtō.*

hedge
common cultivated hedge, often (mis)called "Panax": *ut.*

heebie-jeebies
the heebie-jeebies: *mmāālel.*

heel: *jim̧win ne.*
walk on heels: *juknene.*

height: *ļolōñ, utiej.*
hell: *kena.*
helmet shell
a shell, Cassididae, *Cassis cornuta*, helmet shell: *bukbuk, laklak.*
help: *jipañ, rejetak.*
a helpless position: *tabu.*
to help one another: *ṃaijek.*
hem: *kitak.*
hem a dress: *kobak.*
hem in: *apañ.*
hemmed in: *keṇaak.*
Hemigaleops
holotype of *Hemigaleops fosteri*: *bab.*
Hemigraphis
a plant, flower, *Hemigraphis reptans* (Takeuchi): *utilōṃjān.*
Hemiphyllodactylus
an animal, kind of lizard, gecko, *Lepidodactylus pelagicus* or *Hemiphyllodactylus typus*: *korap.*
Hemiramphus
a fish, halfbeak, *Hemiramphus depauperatus*: *buwaj.*
hemorrhoid
hemorrhoids: *ṃaj.*
hen: *ļọļọ.*
attack by mother hen: *wadde.*
brood hen: *jenļap.*
clucking of a hen: *tokokkok.*
rob sitting hen of her eggs: *eaklep.*
to set, of hens: *lik.*
Heniochus
a fish, thread-backed butterfly fish, *Heniochus acuminatus*: *ek-bōlōk.*
Hepatus
a fish, convict tang or banded surgeonfish, *Hepatus triostegus*: *kupañ.*
a fish, unicorn fish, *Hepatus olivaceus Schneider Bloch*: *ael.*
Hepatus bariene: *kōpat.*
her: *an.*
him, her, it: *e.*
herb: *kūṃur.*
A red-stemmed weedy herb: *neen kōtkōt.*
a yellow-flowered herb: *kio.*
herbs for anointing: *toļaj.*
herd
herd of bonitos that enters lagoon and can't find its way out: *ajilowōd.*
school of fish on reef, herd of animals: *baru.*
here: *ije, ijeko, ijin, ijjiiō, ijo.*
anywhere around here: *jekākā.*
here he or it is: *eñe, eñiō.*
here it is: *eñeo, eñin, eo, iiō.*
here it is (close to me): *ieñe.*
here they are: *erko, erro.*
here they are (people close to me): *errā, errārā.*
here they are (people close to us both): *errein.*
here they are (things close to both of us): *erkein.*
here they are (things close to me): *erkā, erkākā.*
here they are, nonhumans only: *irko.*
hereabouts: *ijekā, ijekākā.*
right here: *joujo.*
here and there
to be here and there: *kākemọọj.*
hereabouts: *ijekein.*
heredity: *bōdañ.*
heritage: *bōnja-.*
heritage of land: *ļāṃoran.*
hermaphrodite: *kakōļ.*
Hermes
Hermes mitratus/cylindraceus/auriconus/clavus: *likaebeb.*
hermit crab: *oṃ.*
fishing method, line fishing inside lagoon using hermit crab for bait: *rupe oṃ, kōppajojo.*
prepare hermit crabs for bait: *pajo.*
Hernandia
a plant, tree, *Hernandia nymphaeifolia* (Presl) Kubitzki (Hernandiaceae): *piñpiñ.*
hernia: *iñ lọjien.*
hero
heroic: *peran.*
heron
a bird, reef heron, *Egretta sacra*: *kabaj.*
hesitant: *ttūṃurṃur.*
hesitate: *aepedped, tabur.*
hesitate (reflexive): *itweļọk.*
Heteroscelus
a bird, wandering tattler, *Heteroscelus incanum*: *kidid.*
hew: *jekjek.*
hibiscus
a plant, hibiscus, *Hibiscus tiliaceus* L. (Malvaceae).: *ļọ.*
hibiscus flower: *rooj.*
wear a rose or hibiscus flower: *roojoj.*
hiccough: *ṃajoñjoñ.*
hidden
having hidden qualities: *jatdik.*
hidden: *aelọk, ṇojak, ttino.*

watch with evil interest or hidden
purpose: *kōppao.*

hide: *kaattilōklōk, m̧ōjjo, ņņooj, pinej,*
tilekek.
  a game, hide behind a mat and have
another guess: *kōļōnwa.*
  a game, hide-and-seek: *m̧wijju.*
  enter and hide inside coral, said of fish
only: *po̧.*
  hide from work: *kona.*
  hide-and-seek: *kaattilōklōk,*
kūttiliek, m̧ōjjo.
  to hide: *kūttiliek.*

high: *lōñ, utiej.*
  a game, high jump or broad jump:
kappiñ.
  be stranded high-and-dry: *pāte.*
  high from liquor: *tab.*
  high tide: *ibwij, tūkōk.*
  high-born person: *arōm̧m̧an.*
  high-class person: *arōm̧m̧an.*
  high-pitched sound: *ļļaaj.*
  highest tide: *ibwijleplep.*
  make high: *būļak.*
  neither high nor low: *loñ.*
  ride high in water because not
loaded: *okwōjaja.*

high-and-dry
  stranded high-and-dry: *pāāt.*

hike: *jam̧bo.*

hill: *bat, toļ.*
  hill of: *bati.*
  top of the hill: *raanbat.*

him
  him, her, it: *e.*

hind: *ļokwa-.*

hinder: *bōbrae.*
  hindered: *apañ.*

hinge: *injej.*

hint: *kakōļļe.*

hip: *doñ, ep, m̧ur.*
  carry a child on the hip: *jaja.*
  hips: *ip.*
  move hips from side to side while
dancing: *kajikia.*
  movement of hips during sexual
intercourse: *aelaļ.*
  to carry things on hips: *kōjerrā.*
  wear pants high on hips: *m̧uriej.*

Hippocampus
  a fish, sea horse, *Hippocampus kuda*:
kidudujet.

hire: *o̧ņea-.*

his: *an.*

history: *bwebwenato.*

hit: *jarom, lel, m̧anm̧an, notoñ.*
  be hit by mistake as a bystander:
ļaanwōtwōt.
  hit the mark: *ļaj, lel.*
  hit with fists: *bait.*
  to hit or slap someone with something,
usually flat: *ubatak.*

hives: *lennab.*
  hives, from eating spoiled fish: *judu.*

hoard: *ko̧kko̧ņko̧ņ.*
  hoard food: *wūnōknōk.*
  hoarding of food: *wūnōk.*

hoarse: *ppoñ.*

hobgoblin: *eakeak.*

hog: *piik.*

hogfish
  a fish, hogfish, *Cheilinus undulatus*:
ļappo.

hoist: *jirab.*
  hoist by sling: *m̧ukko.*
  hoist sails: *jerak.*
  sling for hoisting cargo: *m̧ukko.*

hold: *dāpdep, jebjeb, kabwijer.*
  a game, holding a child up with one's
feet while flat on one's back (parent-
child game): *jippapa.*
  hold back, not do one's best: *jenliklik.*
  hold hands while walking: *ijjurpe.*
  hold on to: *kkejel.*
  hold on to keep from falling: *jirok,*
kabbōjrak.
  hold one's breath: *dek.*
  hold open and up: *kōjjāl.*
  hold out, as a baby for another to
take: *jake.*
  hold something tightly: *kōkki.*
  hold tight: *kkuul.*
  hold up: *jepak.*
  hold up from water: *akake.*
  hold up or catch with both hands:
bo̧ur.
  paddle a canoe so as to hold it against
current: *kab.*

hole: *ro̧ñ.*
  a hole in a tree for catching water:
m̧m̧ak.
  cover up a hole: *jieñ.*
  hole in tree for catching rain water:
m̧ak.
  make a hole: *ddāil, il.*
  opening of any container, hole,
doorway, or cave, etc.: *māj, meja-.*
  refill a hole with dirt: *jjioñ.*
  stick hand into pocket, hole, or
crack: *rrwe.*
  to drink from a well or a hole in a tree

by bending over and using the mouth directly: *m̧ōt.*
to poke into a hole persistently at something, usually an octopus: *lekōn.*

holiday: *kakkije.*

holler: *kkeiļǫk, kōkkeiļǫk, lam̧ōj, uwaañañ.*

Holocanthus
Holocanthus diacanthus: *rūbōb.*

Holocentrus
a fish, squirrel fish, *Holocentrus* sp.: *jera.*
a fish, squirrel fish, *Holocentrus binotatus/scythrops*: *kur.*
a fish, squirrel fish, *Holocentrus microstoma*: *kañkōñ.*

Holothuroidea
sea cucumber, *Holothuroidea, Holothuria leucospilota*: *jipenpen.*
sea cucumber, *Holothuroidea, Opheodesoma*: *jāibo.*
sea cucumber, *Holothuroidea, Thelonia* or *Actinopyga*: *piāpe.*

holy: *kkwōjarjar.*

home: *em̧.*
home of: *kapijukune-.*

home run: *om̧rawūn.*

homely: *dakke, dakōlkōl, jepa, jokwa, kōnana.*

homesick: *oñ.*
be homesick for: *ļokwanwa.*

honest: *jim̧we, m̧ool.*
interjection: "Honestly, I swear it's so.": *mejāro.*
lie deny, dishonest: *riab.*

honey: *ōne.*

honor: *buñbuñ, wūjtak.*
dishonor: *wōtlǫk.*
honored: *ñiājo.*

hood: *abǫ.*

hoof: *juuj.*

hook: *kāāj.*
caught on a hook: *kǫjek.*
dive after getting hooked, of fish: *ñijlǫk, wūnlǫk.*
get hooked: *kǫjek.*
get hooked, nabbed: *tǫrōk.*
hook and pull: *ankiij.*
hook easily: *tare.*
hooked: *kijek.*
jerk a fishline to hook a fish: *dimtak.*

hoop: *roñ.*

hop: *kājoon, kālǫk.*
a game, hop-scotch: *kappetpet.*
hop back and forth on both feet: *kōm̧ajoñjoñ.*
hop on one foot: *ajjuknene.*

hope: *kōjatdikdik.*
give up hope: *bweetkōn.*
hope, trust, look forward to: *katmāne.*
lose hope: *bbeer.*

horizon: *kapin lañ.*
have broadened horizons: *loļǫkjeņ.*

horn: *bōke.*
horn of an animal: *doon.*
trumpet, horn, siren, conch: *jilel.*

horrible: *kaammijak.*

horror: *kor, mijak.*

horse: *ǫǫj.*
horse play: *kōņaanikien.*
ride a horse: *ǫǫjǫj.*
horse around: *kǫbōk.*

horse mackerel
a fish, big-eyed or goggle-eyed scad fish or horse mackerel, *Trachurops crumenophthalmus*: *pāti.*

hose: *ooj.*

hospital: *aujpitōļ, m̧ōn taktō.*

hospitality: *karuwanene.*

host: *jem̧m̧aan.*

hostile: *jememe, lāj.*

hot: *bwil.*
hot and close: *nitñil.*
hot tempered: *jidimkij.*
hottest time of day: *bwiltōñtōñ.*
piping hot: *bwiltōñtōñ.*

hotel: *wōteļ.*

hour: *awa.*

house: *em̧, m̧ōjab-, m̧we, m̧weieņ, m̧weiō, pāl.*
beam of a house: *tur.*
cook house: *m̧ōn kuk.*
cornice or gable of a Marshallese house: *demāju.*
frame of a house: *kādikdik.*
head of a household: *karo.*
house for the demented: *im̧ōn bwebwe.*
house, demonstrative first person inclusive singular: *m̧wiin.*
house, demonstrative second person singular: *m̧ōņe.*
house, demonstrative third person singular: *m̧weeņ.*
house, demonstrative third person singular abstract: *m̧weo.*
house, demonstrative third person singular, singling out: *m̧ouweo.*
household: *em̧, eoonļā.*

houses, demonstrative first person exclusive plural: *m̧ōkā*.
houses, demonstrative first person exclusive plural, singling out: *m̧ōkākā*.
houses, demonstrative first person inclusive plural: *m̧ōkein*.
houses, demonstrative second person plural: *m̧ōkaņe*.
houses, demonstrative second person plural, singling out: *m̧ōkākaņe*.
houses, demonstrative second person singular, singling out: *m̧ōņeņe*.
houses, demonstrative third person plural: *m̧ōkaņ*.
houses, demonstrative third person plural abstract: *m̧ōko*.
houses, demonstrative third person plural, singling out: *m̧ōkākaņ*.
houses,demonstrative third person plural, singling out: *m̧ōkoko*.
lighthouse: *miade*.
meeting house: *m̧ōn kweiļọk*.
men's house (?): *ja*.
openings in a house causing drafts: *ajerwawa*.
possessive classifier, houses or other buildings: *em̧*.
side of a house: *kii-*.
small house on canoe: *bọktōk, pelpel*.
storehouse: *joko*.
temporary house, shack: *m̧ōn kōppād*.
that house (close to neither of us): *m̧ouweo, m̧weeņ, m̧weieņ*.
that house (close to you): *m̧ōņe, m̧ōņeņe*.
the house (often not present): *m̧weo*.
the houses (often not present): *m̧ōko*.
these houses (close to me): *m̧ōkā, m̧ōkākā, m̧ōko*.
these houses (close to us both): *m̧ōkein*.
this house (close to me): *m̧we, m̧weiō, m̧weo*.
this house (close to us both): *m̧wiin*.
those houses (close to neither of us): *m̧ōkākaņ, m̧ōkaņ, m̧ōkoko*.
those houses (close to you): *m̧ōkākaņe, m̧ōkaņe*.
townhouse: *m̧ōn kweiļọk*.
two-story house: *nikāi*.
upper story of house: *po*.
warehouse: *joko*.
what house?: *m̧ōt*.
whore house: *m̧ōn utļam̧*.
low-cost housing: *kāām*.

how: *ekōjka-, wāwee-*.
"And how!": *ekōjkan*.
but how about: *baj ke*.
how about: *akō*.
how many?: *jete*.
how much?: *ewi*.
how?: *ia*.

however: *bōtab, ijoke*.

howl: *uwaañañ*.

huddle: *kuk*.

hue: *wūno*.

hug: *bọkwōj, jjibur*.
bear hug: *jiburlep*.

huge: *debbōn, depdep, kilep*.

hull: *ānbwin*.

human
human being: *armej*.

humble: *ttā bōro*.
lower the head, humble oneself: *badik*.

humid: *m̧ōļọwi*.

humiliate: *jook*.

humor: *kōjak*.

hunch: *kkōljake*.

hunchback: *kkum̧liklik*.

hundred
five hundred: *limabukwi*.
four hundred: *eabukwi*.
hundreds of: *bukwi*.
one hundred: *jibukwi*.
one hundred pairs, fish or copra: *jikut*.
three hundred: *jilubukwi*.
two hundred: *rūbukwi*.
two hundred pairs, fish or copra: *rukut*.

hung up
hung up on, sold on: *reel*.

hunger
weak feeling, usually from hunger: *ajeļkā*.
weak from hunger: *uwaañañ*.

hungry: *añañe, bōro-kōrkōr, eañden, kwōle, okļe*.

hunt
fishing method, hunt lobster or coconut crab when the moon is right: *katooj*.
hunt for: *kappok, ppok*.
to hunt lobsters: *kalwor*.
turn over rubbish hunting for something: *okpej*.

hurray: *urro*.

hurry: *abōbbōb, bwijọkorkor, ļọk*.
hurry up: *jab rum̧wij, menļọk*.
hurry up (with directional): *jarōb*.
in a hurry: *jidimkij, kijerjer*.
to hurry someone: *lipjerjer*.

hurt: *metak.*
hurt as result of rejection: *balu.*
hurt feelings of some by showing favoritism to others: *kabwilọklọk māj.*
talk that hurts the feelings: *añjarjar.*

husband: *pālee-, rii-.*

husk
coconut husk: *bweọ.*
collect coconuts and husk them before making copra: *pinju.*
gather many husked copra nuts: *pinju.*
husk a coconut with one's teeth: *ōjōj.*
husk coconuts: *ddeb.*
husk fibre: *kwōd.*
husking of coconuts by coconut crabs: *ejej.*
piece of wood on which coconut husk is beaten to yield fibre for sennit: *jebōnmāl.*
pierce with husking stick or spear: *ddeb.*
pile of husks near husking stick: *bweo.*
scrub self with coconut husk or oil: *bokwārijet.*
sharp stick for husking coconuts: *doon.*
spoon made from chip of green coconut husk: *auḷakḷak.*
stand a coconut husking stick in the ground: *kat.*
thick husk protecting eyes of coconut: *wūlṃōd.*
use a coconut husker: *doonon.*
use mouth to husk coconuts: *ejej.*
pit for soaking coconut husks for making sennit: *to.*
place for beating coconut husks after soaking in preparation for making sennit: *ṃṃal.*
smell of pit for soaking coconut husks: *būto.*
take coconut husks from water after soaking to make sennit: *jarjar.*

husky: *dipen.*
husky voice: *ṃōrā-bōjbōj.*
husky, and usually quite tall: *peñpeñ.*

hustle: *lipjerjer.*

hut: *ajjuur, peḷak.*

hybrid: *apkaaj, kakōḷ.*

Hydra
possibly stars in *Hydra*: *Debwāāl-eo.*

hydroplane
a toy, coconut hydroplane: *wūdādo.*

Hydrus: *Ḷōṇa.*

hymen: *jā.*

Hymenocallis
a plant, *Hymenocallis littoralis*: *kiebin wau.*

hymn: *alin jar.*

Hynnis
Hynnis cubensis: *aroñ.*

hypersensitive
hypersensitive, sexually: *makōrlep.*

hypocrisy: *ankiliriab.*

hypocrite
Philistine, hypocrite: *toojin edwaan.*
hypocritical: *ṃwil in jiip.*

Hyporhamphus
a fish, halfbeak, *Hyporhamphus laticeps*: *kūbu.*

hysterical
laugh hysterically: *leea.*

I: *ña.*

ice: *aij.*
ice cream: *aij kudiiṃ.*
ice-box: *bọọk aij.*

idea: *ḷōmṇak.*

ideal: *po ḷōma-.*

identical: *āinwōt juon.*

identification
identification of: *kijjie-.*

identify: *kile.*

idiom: *kaj.*

idiot
idiotic: *wūdkabbe.*

idle: *jowan, pād bajjek.*

idol: *ekjab.*
idols: *anij raṇ.*

if: *eḷañe, ñe.*

ignite: *jọ, ttil.*
ignited: *tok.*
ignited easily: *tokwōj.*
not ignited easily: *jatokwōj.*
ignition switch: *kein kōjjọ.*

ignorant: *jajeḷọkjeṇ.*
ignorance: *ñakḷọkjeṇ.*

ignore: *inojeik, jekdọọn, kajukur, kōjool.*
ignored: *jool.*

ill: *lọkmej, nañinmej, utaṃwe.*
ill-bred: *pāpijek.*
illness: *mej.*
land given to someone who took care of the head of the lineage owning the land during illness before death: *ṃōnkọḷotḷot.*
serious illness: *dọlel.*

illegal
illegal gathering of food on another's property: *ḷe eoon eṃ.*

illicit
euphemistic reference to illicit sexual relations: *teeṃbura.*
illicit drinking: *kaurur baib.*
illicit sexual intercourse: *paarōr.*
smoke illicitly: *lijāludik.*
illogical: *jaje ļōmņak.*
illuminate: *meram, romaak.*
illusion
mirage, optical illusion, illusion: *jāmilur, jāmilur.*
illustration
illustration, instance, illustrative story: *waan joñak.*
image: *annañ, ar, nemāmei-.*
imagine: *etan wōt ñe, ļam, ļōkōṃ.*
imbecile: *bwebwe, kūļaṃwe.*
imitate: *anōk, ari-, kajjioñ.*
imitate actions of others: *ar.*
immaculate: *kkwōjarjar.*
immature
immature (see *kapeel* (**kapeyel**)), not clever: *jekapeel.*
immature coconut fruit of: *ubnen.*
immediate: *epaak, iur.*
immediately: *jab ruṃwij, kiiō-kiiō.*
immigrant: *pejpetok.*
immoral: *kijoñ.*
immorality: *kijoñ.*
immune: *pojak.*
impatient: *atebar, kijerjer.*
impede
impeded: *abor.*
impertinent: *nōṃaiki.*
impetuous: *aelellaļ, ṃōṃlep.*
implement: *kein jerbal.*
implemented: *dede.*
implicate: *jelōt.*
imply: *kowaļọk.*
import: *deļọñ.*
smell of imported goods: *bwiin-ppāllele.*
important: *aorōk, ļaikaalal.*
important person: *ļakkūk, pālu.*
importunate: *añōtñōt.*
imposing
imposing, conceited, inconsiderate: *pedet armej.*
impossible: *ban.*
attempt the impossible: *kadkadajaj.*
expression: "Impossible!": *eban.*
impotent: *ṃōjņọ.*
sexually impotent (male) (see *rrōñ* (**rręg**)): *jarrōñrōñ.*
impound: *ātet.*
impress: *bwilōñ.*
imprint: *kkal.*
imprinted: *kōn.*
improper: *jekkar.*
improve
improved: *weeppān.*
improvise: *kkōn.*
in: *i, ilo, ilowa.*
go in a passage: *ṃweeaar.*
in a certain part: *tōr.*
inside: *ilowa.*
stick in: *duuj.*
inability
inability to catch many fish (see *koņkoņ* (**qeņqeņ**)): *jọkoņkoņ.*
inability to catch many fish (see *wōda* (**wedah**)): *joda.*
inability to stay underwater long (see *pakij* (**pakij**)): *jāpakij.*
inaccessible: *akā.*
inactive: *mejjeeļ.*
inalienable
inalienable rights or property: *addemlōkmej.*
incantation: *katok.*
perform an incantation: *allōk.*
incapable
incapable of bearing offspring, of women only: *orañe, war.*
incapable of being hurt or embarrassed: *mejel kil.*
incense: *ijur.*
incentive: *tōp.*
incest: *kōpa.*
inch: *inij.*
incision: *ṃwijṃwij.*
incline
inclined to: *kkā.*
include: *kōpooļ.*
incoherent: *aplo.*
incombustible: *tokwiia.*
income: *deļọñ.*
incompetent: *jedañ.*
incomplete: *jipikpik, jọuñ.*
inconsiderate: *būruon kūro, jaje ļōmņak, jememe, kōņkōṃṃan, ļōkajeṃ.*
imposing, conceited, inconsiderate: *pedet armej.*
incorporate: *koba.*
increase: *būļak, koorļọk, ṃōñāñe, orļọk.*
indecisive: *apaproro, bbōroro, bōro-pejpej.*

indeed: *lukkuun.*
indelible: *ban jjeor, kōn.*
independence: *anemkwōj.*
index
  index finger: *addi-kọọtot.*
Indian giver
  be an Indian giver: *ajejin Jowa, ajejin Ḷōktab.*
indicate: *kowaḷọk.*
  indication: *kakōḷḷe.*
indigestion: *boṇ.*
indistinguishable: *peljo.*
individual: *armej.*
indulge
  to indulge: *ñiājo.*
industrious: *niknik, owan.*
  not industrious: *jāniknik.*
inebriated: *kadek.*
inedible
  inedible portion near stem of pandanus or breadfruit: *ṃak.*
  overgrown and inedible sprouted coconut: *iupej.*
inertia: *jālirara.*
inexperienced
  inexperienced: *watre.*
  inexperienced (see *mminene* (**mminẹynẹy**)): *jāmminene.*
infant: *niññiñ.*
infatuation: *iọkwe in kij.*
infect: *tōrañ.*
  infected: *anilen.*
inferior: *ttā.*
infiltrate: *dibuk.*
inflame
  inflamed eye: *pilo.*
inflammable: *tokwiie.*
  inflammable (see *jọwiia* (**jawiyyah**)): *jọwiie.*
inflate
  inflated: *bbool.*
inflexible: *kajjiṃwe.*
inform: *keeañ.*
  to inform: *kaiñ.*
  well-informed: *jeḷā.*
informal: *ḷam waan.*
information: *kōjjeḷā, meḷeḷe.*
  gather news or information: *eọroñ naan.*
infuriate
  infuriated: *ro.*
ingrate: *kabbil.*
ingredient: *kāre, kino.*
inhabit: *jokwe, jukjuk.*
  uninhabited land: *rārōk.*
inhale: *koub.*
  sniff, inhale, breathe: *kōbotuut.*
inherit
  disinherit: *kalia.*
  inherit, physical or mental characteristics: *bōdañ.*
  inherited characteristics: *bōnja-.*
  land inherited by: *kapijukune-.*
  inheritance: *ājinkōj, amṇak, jolōt.*
inhibit: *bbaar.*
initial: *jjino.*
initiate: *bwilik ṃaan, jjino.*
  initiate sexually: *karūtto.*
  to initiate: *ruprupjọkur.*
injection
  injection, receive an injection, give an injection: *wā.*
injure: *kọkkure.*
ink: *inik.*
innards: *je.*
  guts, intestines, bowels, offal, innards: *ṃajñal.*
inning: *deḷọñ.*
  inning in baseball: *teeñ.*
innocent: *jajeḷọkjeṇ.*
Inocarpus
  a plant, *Inocarpus edulus*: *kūrak.*
inquire: *kajjitōk.*
  inquire of an authority: *jitdaṃ.*
inquisitive: *kajnōt.*
  inquisitive, of hands only: *pānāpnep.*
insane: *bwebwe, wūdeakeak.*
inscrutable: *ṃwilaḷ bōro.*
insects
  big black ant: *kallep.*
  dragonfly: *boub.*
  grasshopper: *jeḷo.*
  moth: *mānnikiden, jourur.*
  moth or miller: *urur.*
  small, brown insect, often found around rotten breadfruit: *māniddik.*
  smallest ant: *kinaḷ.*
insert: *deḷọñ, duuj, ppāin, wiaake.*
inside: *lowa.*
insignia: *kūṃaḷṃaḷ.*
  metal insignia, military: *baar.*
  uniform insignia: *kakōḷḷe.*
insist: *akweḷap.*
  beg insistently: *akweḷap.*
inspect: *etale, idajoñjoñ.*
inspire: *bab-laḷ.*
  inspired: *ellowetak, iruj lọjie-.*
  inspiring: *kakōṃkōṃ.*

install: *ddoor, kōļaak.*
instance
illustration, instance, illustrative story: *waan joñak.*
instant
instantaneous: *idiñ.*
instantly: *ṃōkaj.*
instead
instead of: *bwiden, ijellọkwi-.*
institute: *jjino, kajjuur.*
instruct
deviate from instructions: *weļọk.*
instruction: *kipel, katak.*
instrument: *kein jerbal.*
instrument for plotting courses, nautical: *kein kōttōbalbal.*
instrumental: *kein.*
musical instrument: *kōjañjañ.*
insufficient: *jabwe.*
insufficient knowledge: *jeļā jabjab.*
insult: *jeklep, kajjirere.*
insulted: *eddo ippa-.*
insurance: *joortoklik.*
intact: *iio, jañin kkaan, likiio.*
integrate: *koba.*
integrated: *peljo.*
integrity: *ṃṃool.*
intellect: *bōklōkōt, ļoļātāt.*
intelligent: *jiṃaat, wājepdik.*
intend: *itōn, ļōmṇak.*
intensifier
intensifier used with demonstratives: *jab.*
intensifier, of limited use: for time, tide, or weather: *jelōñlōñ.*
intensifier, with great force: *tōñtōñ.*
intentionally
unintentionally: *jirilọk.*
intercede: *jojomar.*
intercourse
illicit sexual intercourse: *paarōr.*
not have intercourse often (see *tape* (**tapẹy**)): *jattapepe.*
sexual intercourse: *ijij, peeļ, peru, tape.*
interest: *limo.*
arouse interest: *itok-limo.*
interest money: *orļọk.*
not interesting (see *ṃōṇōṇō* (**ṃẹṇehṇeh**)): *jaṃōṇōṇō.*
showing interest: *ekwekwe.*
interfere: *juṃae.*
interfere in order to avoid: *jujuurļọk.*
interim
interim period between stormy seasons, usually a calm spell: *jo.*
interior: *lowa.*
directional, enclitic, interiorward: *nọọj.*
go to the interior of an islet: *tōļoñ.*
interior of an island: *iooj, lọjien āne.*
interiorward of an island and from lagoon side only: *nọọj.*
interjections
"My goodness!" (Women only): *weeak.*
"Wow!" (Expression of surprise): *bōkkōk.*
"Beware!": *iọuwọ.*
"By God!": *ṃajidak.*
"Darn!" Or "God forbid!": *ōkkōk.*
"Good grief!": *aia.*
"Gracious!": *ṃajō.*
"Heck!": *jeej.*
"Honestly, I swear it's so.": *mejāro.*
"How about that!": *kōjaṃṃōk.*
"If that's so, then continue.": *ekwekwe.*
"No wonder!" "It stands to reason.": *jebata.*
"Ouch!": *iā.*
"Ouch!" (Pain or sexual pleasure): *ōttōt.*
"See what you've done!" (Always used with personal demonstratives): *io-.*
"Stupid!": *bōkāro.*
"Ugh!": *ōrrōr.*
"You don't say!": *kwōjabṃōk.*
"Darn!" Or "Heck!": *ōrrōr.*
connotes unwillingness: *ōļļōļ, ōṇṇōṇ.*
dismay: *aiaea.*
expression of sexual pleasure: *ōrrōr.*
expression of wonder or delight: *bōranṃaajidake.*
surprise or disappointment: *ōjjej.*
displeasure, used only by women: *ōjjeti-.*
intermediate: *kōtaa-.*
intermission: *bōjrak.*
internal: *lowa.*
interpret: *ukok.*
interrogate: *kajitūkin.*
interrogative
interrogative generally countering previous statements: *baj ke.*
interrupt
interruption: *bōjrak.*
intersect
intersection of roads: *kāpoon.*
intestine
contents of newborn's intestines: *jā.*
guts, intestines, bowels, offal, innards: *ṃajñal.*
eel, intestinal worm: *ṃaj.*

intimate: *bwil.*
intimidate
intimidated: *kor.*
into
go into: *m̧o̧o̧n.*
intoxicate
intoxicated: *kadek.*
intoxicating: *kadek.*
intrepid: *pen būruo-.*
intricate: *pok.*
intrigue
intrigued: *iruj lo̧jie-.*
introduce: *ba kajjie-.*
introversion: *jememe.*
Intsia
a plant, tree, *Intsia bijuga*: *kubōk.*
intuition
intuition about a future misfortune or death: *lomije-.*
intuition and knowledge possessed by certain expert Marshallese navigators using traditional methods: *kabun̄pet.*
invade
to invade: *jodik.*
invalid: *ārpej, banban, m̧ōjn̦o̧, o̧la̧lo, ppal̦, utam̧we.*
invasion: *kuju.*
invent: *kkōn.*
invest
invested money: *orl̦o̧k.*
investigate: *eded, etale, iaron̄ron̄, idajon̄jon̄.*
invisible: *aelo̧k.*
invitation: *kkūr.*
invite: *jiron̄.*
invoke: *owar.*
invoke a spirit: *allōk.*
involve: *koba.*
be involved: *lokjak.*
deeply involved: *kōptata.*
get involved accidently: *l̦aanwōtwōt.*
involved: *jelōt.*
inward: *tulowa.*
Ipomoea
a plant, sweet potato, *Ipomoea batatas*: *piteto.*
a plant, vine, *Ipomoea tuba*: *marpel̦e.*
Ipomoea pes-caprae: *markinenjojo.*
Ipomoea tuba: *marl̦ap.*
iron: *aen, māāl.*
corrugated iron: *jinnibo̧o̧r.*
smell of iron: *mmāālāl.*
iron pot: *ainbat.*
irresponsible: *jabde.*
irritate
smart, irritated: *korōt.*
irritation: *kūtōtō.*
island: *āne, aelōn̄.*
breadth of an island: *wūjal̦on̄.*
directional, enclitic, islandward or shoreward: *āne.*
either end of an island: *ajokl̦ā.*
go ashore on islands belonging to others: *popo m̧anit.*
go or come towards the ocean side of an island: *wanlik.*
interior of an island: *iooj, lo̧jien āne.*
island or atoll reserved for food gathering, usually for a chief and his immediate family: *l̦ārooj.*
middle of an island: *iooj.*
ocean side of an island: *jablik.*
walk between islands at low tide: *etal iene.*
western and northwestern island northwestern islands in an atoll: *liklal̦, liklal̦.*
part of an island: *wata.*
islet: *āne.*
desert isle: *āne-jem̧aden.*
end of an islet: *kiwūl, tur.*
go to the interior of an islet: *tōl̦on̄.*
main islet of an atoll: *bōran aelōn̄, eoonene.*
small islets of an atoll: *aeto̧.*
stony islet without trees: *bokom̧n̦a.*
the opening between islets: *mej, mejje.*
this islet: *ānin.*
isolate: *jenolo̧k.*
Istiblennius
a fish, blenny, *Istiblennius paulus* (Mejit): *kudo̧kwōl.*
Istiophorus
Istiophorus greyi: *wūjinleep.*
it: *e.*
"It can't be!": *eban.*
him, her, it: *e.*
its: *an.*
itch: *m̧ōn̦ōjn̦ōj.*
itchy: *bbōn̦ōjn̦ōj, dim̧ōm̧.*
itinerary: *ial̦.*
Ittaria
a plant, general term for grass or *Ittaria elongata*, actually an epiphytic, penoulous fern: *wūjooj.*
Ixora
a plant, tree, *Ixora carolinensis* (Val.) Hosokawa (Rubiaceae): *kajdo.*

jab: *duuj.*
jabbing: *ddeb.*
jack
a game, jacks: *kiiñkiiñ.*
jack up: *kotak, jāāk.*
jacket: *kopā.*
life jacket: *kein aō.*
jag
jagged: *pirañrañ.*
jail: *kalbuuj.*
to be in jail: *kalbuuj.*
to be thrown in jail: *kalbuuj.*
jam: *jaaṃ.*
jangle: *kkorkor.*
jangling: *ttōñtōñ.*
January: *Jānwōde.*
Japan: *Jepaan, Nibboñ.*
jar: *bato.*
small bottle or jar: *bōkā.*
jarred
be jarred: *kajkaj.*
jarred: *ṃweiur.*
jargon: *kaj.*
jaunt
jaunt, sail, or drive around aimlessly: *tarto-tartak.*
jaw
angle of the jaw: *roñ.*
lower jaw: *atlaḷ.*
upper jaw: *atlōñ.*
jealous: *arōk kōrā, atebar, kaṃo, kōmmọ, paḷ, ro.*
anger through jealousy: *kwi.*
jealousy: *juunṃaad.*
protect with jealousy: *jetṇaak.*
jeans
denim trousers, blue jeans, Levis: *tanim.*
jeep: *jiip.*
drive a jeep: *jiipip.*
jello: *kapejlọk.*
jelly: *jaaṃ.*
jellyfish
a fish, jellyfish: *jañij.*
jeopardize: *kauwōtata.*
jerk: *liit, lleṃaj.*
fishing method, line fishing at night, jerking the line to cause phosphorescence in water to attract fish to the bait: *kōjjaromrom.*
fishing method, occasional jerking of line to lure a fish to the bait or jig: *kooral.*
jerk a fishline to hook a fish: *dimtak.*
jerky: *lleṃaj.*
Jesus
Jesus Christ: *Jijej Kūraij.*
jettison: *eakpel.*
jig
dancing a jig: *jirōṃrōṃ.*
fishing method, occasional jerking of line to lure a fish to the bait or jig: *kooral.*
jingle: *kkorkor.*
jingling: *ttōñtōñ.*
jitterbug: *jurbak.*
job
get a job: *jọọb.*
jog: *kakiaaj.*
join: *dāpijek, koba.*
join in: *almaroñ.*
joined: *piro.*
joining: *ik.*
joint: *kketaak.*
joint, body: *mọkwōj.*
measure joints at an angle in construction work: *alej.*
out of joint: *ir.*
stiffness in joints: *akā.*
joke: *liāp.*
play practical jokes: *ikien.*
to joke: *kōjak.*
jolly: *kaṃōṇōṇō.*
jolt
jolted: *ṃajōjō, ṃweiur.*
jostling: *itileoñeoñ.*
jot: *jibūñ.*
journey: *iaḷ, ito-itak.*
see off on a journey: *kōjjājet.*
jovial: *kaṃōṇōṇō.*
joy: *jibbūñ, lañlōñ, ṃōṇōṇō.*
judge: *ekajet, jāj.*
jug: *bōkā.*
juggle: *ekkokowa, kejau.*
a game, juggling: *lejoñjoñ, lejọñjọñ.*
juggling contest: *ekkokowa.*
juice: *dān.*
a food, juice extracted from fresh pandanus: *jowaanroñ.*
coconut juice: *dānnin ni.*
July: *Juḷae.*
jumble: *pānuk.*
jumbled: *pok.*
jump: *kālọk, pāl-.*
a game, high jump or broad jump: *kappiñ, kappiñ.*
ability to jump far: *ppikaj.*
jump down: *kālọk.*
jump into the sea: *kālọk.*
jump into the water: *ro.*

jump on: *kāik.*
jump out of: *kenabōj.*
jump over: *kājoon.*
jump over, transitive form of *kkāke* (**kkaykẹy**): *kāik.*
jump to dive, head first: *tubar.*
jump up: *katiej.*
jump up and down: *kkāke.*
run and jump: *ttōr kālọk.*

jun ken po: *jaañke.*

June: *Juun.*

jungle: *buḷōn mar.*

junk: *kwōpej.*

Jussiaea
a plant, flower, *Jussiaea suffruticosa*: *utilolōb.*

just: *baj, bajjek, de, kab, wānōk, wōt.*
just as: *āindein.*
just sufficient: *bōka-.*
justice: *wānōk.*

jut
jutting out from the rest: *daṃok.*

KITCO: *Kūtko.*

kahuna: *rijọubwe.*

Kanaka
Kanaka, derogatory: *kōṇakō.*

Katsuwonus
a fish, bonito, *Katsuwonus pelamis*: *ḷōjabwil.*

kawakawa
a fish, false albacore or *kawakawa*: *ḷooj.*

keel: *kiiḷ.*
canoe keel made from *kōñe* wood: *erer.*
keel over: *jepewa.*
low keel: *kaplep.*
keel-haul: *tuṃaḷ.*

keen: *kkañ.*
keen vision: *loḷọkjeṇ.*

keep: *dāpdep.*
able to keep wits during crisis: *lọḷe.*
belt keeper: *tāānjen.*
keep going: *etal wōt.*
keep in touch with: *kkeini.*
keep on: *ekwekwe, pen in deo.*
keep one's cool: *kōmmaanwa.*
keeping a ball in the air by kicking (*anidep* (**haniydep**)): *jaja.*
keepsake: *jolōt.*
not able to keep secrets: *bbōk.*
to keep as a pet: *nājnej.*
to keep awake during the usual hours of sleep: *kōmja.*
unable to keep still: *ne ṃakūtkūt.*
understand how to keep temper: *kōmmaanwa.*

keg: *jepukpuk.*

kernel: *kwōle.*
kernel of spongy meat inside coconut that has just started to sprout: *bōḷoñar.*

kerosene: *karjin.*
smell of kerosene: *kkarjinjin.*
use kerosene: *lekarjin.*

ketch: *jikuna.*

kettle: *kōṃa.*
tea kettle: *tibat.*

key
also a ripe key of pandanus: *bōb.*
bunch of pandanus keys: *ajjen.*
butt of pandanus key: *ṃak.*
discarded pandanus key: *ār.*
dry key of pandanus fruit: *pej.*
inner end of a single pandanus key: *kiār.*
pandanus key, sprouted: *wūnpej.*
pull keys off pandanus: *ḷotḷot.*
two pandanus keys joined together: *piro.*

key
off key, voice: *bōna.*

key: *ki.*

khaki: *kaki.*

kick: *bwijbwij, bwijjik, jaṃ, jebwij, jjuur, juuj.*
backkick in kickball: *jaṃlik.*
kick feet in swimming: *bwijeae.*
kick out: *joḷọk.*
play kickball: *anidep.*
sidekick in kickball: *jeṃkat.*

kid: *ajri.*
to kid: *kōjak.*

kidney: *deke in jibke.*
lower sides of back, kidney area: *aeo.*

kill: *ṃanṃan, uror.*
kill in the night: *jjọñ.*
kill singly: *jjoñjoñ.*
kill someone during a typhoon in anticipation of shortage of food: *okjānḷañ.*
killed in battle: *jak.*
to kill: *ṃōrō.*
a kill-joy: *jaṃṃōṇōṇō.*

killer clam
a shell, killer clam: *tōkale.*

kin: *erṃwe, nukwi.*
matrilineal kin: *jowi.*

kind: *jouj, kain, rot, tor, turot.*
be kind to: *jeḷāṇae.*
kind of: *uwaan.*

kindhearted: *jouj.*
kindness: *jouj.*
please, would you kindly: *m̧ōk.*
unkind: *jememe.*
kindle: *tok.*
king: *bwio, irooj, kiiñ.*
a game, king of the mountain: *kojuwa.*
kingdom: *aelōñin kiiñ.*
kingfish: *al.*
Caranx fulvoguttatus Forskal: *rewa.*
kink: *jāliñiñ.*
kinky: *m̧ōjālūlū.*
kinky, of hair: *iñiñ.*
kiss: *mejenma, um̧m̧a.*
French kiss: *lojojo.*
kitchen: *m̧ōn kuk.*
kite: *lim̧aakak.*
fly a kite: *lim̧aakak.*
kleptomania: *pānāpnep.*
knack: *jeḷā kuņaa-, kapeel, mejādik.*
knead: *ñal.*
knead preserved breadfruit: *tola.*
to roll in a kneading way: *m̧abwil.*
knee: *bukwe.*
knock-kneed: *māro.*
kneel: *bukwelōlō, juubkwe.*
kneel or bend over: *kapijpij.*
knife: *di.*
knife, small, not folding: *bakbōk.*
long knife: *jāje.*
pierce with knife: *bwiār.*
pocket knife: *ņaib.*
smooth with a knife: *eǫr.*
stick with spear, knife, or needle, etc.: *lōlō.*
knit: *āj.*
knock
almost knocked out: *m̧ajōjō.*
knock down coconuts from tree: *nnōk.*
knock off: *depdep.*
knocking: *ḷḷaḷḷaḷ.*
to knock: *kaḷḷaḷḷaḷ.*
knock-kneed: *māro.*
knock-out, pretty: *kōjaij.*
knoll: *bat.*
knot: *booj.*
a knot: *boḷan.*
a special kind of knot: *annor.*
be knotted: *booj.*
knot in divination: *bo, bwe.*
knot of hair, women: *bujek.*
knot, in wood: *bōke.*
shoestring knot: *korak.*
tie a knot in string or rope: *bubu.*
twist the hair into a knot: *bujek.*

know: *jeḷā.*
know better: *mañ.*
know by heart: *kkiil.*
know how to: *jeḷā.*
know how to maneuver: *jeḷā kōppeḷak.*
know how to take care of: *jeḷāņae.*
know one's way around: *m̧ōm̧ō in, util.*
known by only a few: *anjejjo.*
not know: *jaje, ñak.*
not know which way to go: *añjebwāālel.*
knowledge: *jeḷā ḷokjeņ.*
insufficient knowledge: *jeḷā jabjab.*
intuition and knowledge possessed by certain expert Marshallese navigators using traditional methods: *kabuñpet.*
knowledgeable, resourceful: *wājepdik.*
seek knowledge: *jitdam̧.*
knuckle: *m̧ọkwōj.*
kooky: *taņo.*
Kuhlia
a fish, Pacific sea perch, *Kuhlia taeniura* (Mejit.): *kōnān.*
a fish, stripey, *Kuhlia taeniura*: *jerwōt.*
kwashiorkor: *jeje.*
Kyphosus
a fish, chub or rudder fish, *Kyphosus vaigiensis*: *pājrōk.*
a fish, rudder fish, *Kyphosus vaigiensis* (Eniwetak): *rōnna.*
la
syllable "la" of musical scale: *la.*
labor: *jerbal, m̧adm̧ōd.*
laborer: *niim̧bu.*
lace: *juwain*
lack: *aikuj.*
lacking: *jej.*
lacquer: *wanij.*
lad: *kijak.*
ladder: *jikin uwe.*
climb a ladder or a staircase: *jikin uwe.*
laden: *iabuñ.*
fruit-laden: *kowa.*
laden with summer fruit, usually trees: *uwaanrak.*
ladle: *ḷatōḷ.*
ladle, scoop food: *nam̧ōḷ.*
lady: *kōrā.*
lady killer: *tāāñ.*
ladies' man (derogatory sense): *mejpata.*

lag: *jenliklik.*
Lagenaria
  Lagenaria siceraria (Molina) Standley: *baañke.*
lagoon: *loṃaḷo, ṃaḷo.*
  at the lagoon beach: *iar.*
  current flowing into lagoon: *aeȧr.*
  enter lagoon: *ṃweeaar.*
  follow a large wave in entering a lagoon: *ḷooribeb.*
  go or come towards the lagoon: *wāānar, wanar.*
  lagoon beach: *ar, parijet.*
  lagoon beach of: *are, arōn.*
  lagoon shore: *parijet.*
  leave lagoon: *ṃwelik.*
  passage into lagoon from ocean: *to.*
  reef around a secondary lagoon: *tiete.*
  reef in the lagoon just under the surface: *medde.*
  secondary lagoon: *mājik, naṃ.*
lagoon side
  fly to the lagoon side: *keeaar.*
  go from sea side of an island to lagoon side: *kear.*
  go to the lagoon side: *keeaar.*
  interiorward of an island and from lagoon side only: *nọọj.*
  lagoon side of an island: *jabar.*
  to drag or tow from lagoon side to ocean side: *lelik.*
  to drag or tow from ocean side to lagoon side: *lear.*
lair
  lobster lair: *war.*
laity: *eklejia.*
lamb: *ḷaaṃ.*
Lambis
  Lambis crocata/scorpius/lambis: *aorak.*
lame: *kūrro.*
lament: *ilomej, jañ, liaajlọḷ.*
  lamentation: *liaajlọḷ.*
lamp: *ḷaaṃ.*
  lamp chimney: *jimni.*
  use a lamp: *ḷaaṃaṃ.*
lanai: *maḷto, tōñaak.*
land: *āne, aelōñ, jānnibadbad.*
  breadth of an island: *wūjaḷoñ.*
  chief's land: *buoj.*
  chief's land for making food: *paaj.*
  come to land: *tōkeak.*
  division of a land tract: *alen.*
  flat, of land only: *pikin.*
  gift land: *iṃōn aje.*
  land dispute: *kōtaan wāto.*
  land given by a chief to a commoner as a bounty for bailing out the chief's canoe in battle expeditions: *kwōdaelem.*
  land given by a king to a commoner woman as a bounty for suckling a royal baby: *limen ninnin.*
  land given to someone who took care of the head of the lineage owning the land during illness before death: *ṃōnkọḷotḷot.*
  land inherited by: *kapijukune-.*
  land of: *jiki-.*
  land or goods put away for future use or need: *kōpetaklik.*
  land reserved for chiefs: *kōtra, mọ.*
  land tract: *wāto, ḷain.*
  land used for preserving food, esp. Pandanus: *jepāde.*
  land, sailing vessel: *po.*
  go ashore on islands belonging to others: *popo ṃanit.*
  landing of soldiers: *kuju.*
  landmark: *kakōḷḷe.*
  narrow, of land (see *wūjaloñ* (**wijaleg°**)): *wūjabōj.*
  on dry land: *eppānene.*
  own much land: *amḷap.*
  own much land or real estate: *amṇak.*
  remove from land: *kalia.*
  security, land or goods or money put away for future use or for children: *joortoklik.*
  sight land: *ḷanno.*
  small land tract: *bwiddik.*
  small piece of land: *oḷōt.*
  to land: *jidaak, jodik, jok.*
  toward land: *wāānāne, wanāne.*
  uninhabited land: *rārōk.*
  wasteland: *jeṃaden.*
  part of an island: *wata.*
  wide, of land (see *wūjabōj* (**wijabẹj**)): *wūjaḷoñ.*
land crab
  an animal, white land crab: *lemḷat.*
  land crab, inedible: *baru waan.*
landslide: *ṃōraṃrōṃ, rōṃ.*
landward
  landward side of beach: *ioonkappe.*
lane: *iaḷ.*
language: *kaj, kajin.*
  use bad language: *tepiḷ.*
lanky: *aujepaḷ.*
lantana
  a plant, lantana: *ḷaṇtōna.*
lantern: *ḷantōn.*
  black carbon on lantern chimney, used to blacken tattoos: *ṃaṃōj.*

Coleman lantern: *ļaam̧ kaaj, pilerab.*

lard: *kūriij.*

large: *debbōn, kilep, ļap.*
cut it large or thick: *jeklep.*
enlargement of breasts at puberty: *bwā.*

larva
larvae of lice: *tōl.*
wiggler larvae of mosquitoes: *lijeljelm̧ak.*

lascivious
lasciviousness: *aplep.*

lash: *deñdeñ, eo̧eo.*
lashing cord: *ino.*
lashing technique used on canoes: *inwijet.*
type of lashing applied to the *kie* section of a canoe: *ļļōko̧.*

lass: *lijā.*

lasso
lasso a branch: *rajāl.*
to lasso: *kōjjāl.*

last: *āliki-, to.*
come in last in a race: *piditte.*
last night: *boñ.*
last part: *perañ.*
last supper: *m̧ōñāin kōjab.*
spend last moments together, farewell occasion, bring to a finish: *kōjjem̧ļo̧k.*
the last: *ļo̧k.*
very last: *āliktata.*

lasting
everlasting: *jānindeeo-ñanindeeo.*

latch: *ļak.*
latch on to: *ekkejel, kkejel.*

late: *aļo, bbat, rum̧wij.*
always late: *aļokbad.*
be late for and miss a plane, boat, or car, etc.: *tūm̧.*
be too late: *likjab.*
late in awakening: *mājurlep.*
late, time of day or tide: *jo̧weej.*
later: *ālik, tokālik.*
too late: *jerakiaarļap, kōptata.*
too late for something: *bbat.*

latrine: *m̧ōn bwidej, m̧ōn kōppojak.*

laud: *tūbļotak.*

laugh: *llejkakkak, rere, ttōñ.*
always smiling or laughing: *baūjō.*
laugh at: *kajjirere.*
laugh hysterically: *leea.*
laugh long and loudly: *leea.*
outburst of laughter: *dekakļo̧k.*
provoking laughter: *kattōñtōñ.*
sorrowful laughter: *rereenak.*

launch: *kōkālo̧k.*
launch forth: *bwillo̧k.*
launching: *bwil.*
launching pad: *waan bwil.*
roller for launching canoe: *ļo̧ñ, ļoñtak.*

launder: *kwaļkoļ.*

lava-lava: *ļobļoba.*

law: *kien.*
a law-making body: *nitijeļā.*
lawful: *mālim.*
lawyer: *ļoār.*

laxative: *wūno in ruprup.*

lay
lay away: *kōttōn.*
lay out: *eļļo̧k.*
lay to, nautical: *iptu.*
to lay eggs: *lik.*

layer: *alen, pik.*

laysan albatross
a bird, laysan albatross, *Diomedea immutabilis*: *le.*

lazy: *jāniknik, mejjeeļ.*
lazy (see *owan*): *jowan.*

lead: *āñin, kipel, kkaal, leet.*
blind leading the blind: *tōlpilo.*
lead astray: *tōlpilo.*
lead, people or animals: *uke.*
to lead, direct, preside: *tōl.*
leader: *bo̧o̧j.*
wire leader, used in fishing: *atad, ļōļ.*

leaf: *bōlōk.*
pandanus leaf: *maañ.*
stalk, leafstem, petiole: *kōļā.*

leak: *ttal.*
not leak: *jettal.*

lean: *atōrak.*
lean against: *rrā.*
lean back: *atartar.*
lean toward: *m̧al-.*
lean upon: *atartar.*

lean-to: *peļak, ajjuur.*

leap: *pāl-.*
able to leap well: *ppiñ.*
leap out of water, of small fish attempting to escape larger fish: *uwōjak.*

learn: *katak.*
learn not to: *mañ.*
learner: *rūkkatak.*
quick to learn: *penawiie.*
slow to learn: *penawiia.*

leather: *kilin kau.*

leather-jack
a fish, leather-jack, *Scomberoides lysan*: *aoḷōt.*

leave: *jeblaak.*
leave a chore undone and start another: *jibwe turin jerbal.*
leave lagoon: *ṃwelik.*
leave marks: *kōn.*
leave so that it...(Contraction of *likūt bwe en* (**likit bey yen**)): *likūtōn.*
leave to dry: *roro.*
leave unnoticed: *deor.*
leave vehicle or vessel: *llik.*
rustling of leaves and branches: *mmewiwi.*

leaven: *kauwe.*
a food, unleavened dough cooked by boiling: *jāibo.*
unleavened pancake: *minor.*

leaves
dry or decayed leaves used in fertilizing: *kōṇ.*
footsteps in gravel or dry leaves: *ṃṃōjānjān.*
leaves near pandanus stem: *ainṃak.*
lose leaves, of trees: *ṃōd.*
smell of leaves of bushes: *kkumarmar.*
turn pages or leaves: *ālāl.*
wrap in basket or leaves: *tūrtūr.*
wrap with leaves: *tūroro.*
yellow or brown leaves: *aerar.*

lecture: *jipij, kwaḷọk naan.*

lee
canoe part, platform over the lee side, opposite the outrigger side: *rọñ.*
leeward side of a canoe: *kōja.*
leeward side of an atoll: *liklaḷ.*
leeward side where there is no wind: *jablur.*
tack canoe to leeward: *kabbe.*
leeway: *kijen peto, peto.*

left: *anbwijban.*
left half of human body: *anmiiñ.*
left hand: *anbwijban, anmiiñ.*

left
left over: *bwe.*
left-overs of a shark: *anpakolu.*
what is left: *ko (ro) jet.*
basket in which chiefs store left-overs: *perañ.*
eat left-overs: *attūkoko.*

leg: *ne.*
calf of leg: *ajaj.*
crippled, of legs only: *ḷōmmejne.*
cross the legs: *kowawa.*
disease characterized by emaciated legs: *māro.*
spread legs wide open: *bōḷñak.*
weak in the legs: *lijjipdo.*
weak-legged: *māro.*
bow-legged: *māro, perakrōk.*

legal
illegal gathering of food on another's property: *ḷe eoon eṃ.*

legend: *bwebwenatoon etto, inọñ.*
a legendary bird: *ao.*
a legendary hero: *Jebrọ.*
a legendary turtle: *Lijebake.*
legendary cruel sea men with long fingernails: *kakwōj.*
legendary fairies who fished for red snappers and sometimes fed people: *ṇoonniep.*
legendary fish banished by Jebro to be eaten by other fish: *aoḷ.*
legendary food: *meḷañūr.*
legendary game played by young women: *marere.*
legendary monster: *kidudujet.*
legendary pile of copra brought to Mwineak on Ebon by man from the Gilbert Islands: *eak.*
legendary place where human spirits are said to go after death: *Ewerōk.*
legendary power given by Jebro to Jekad: *ao.*
legendary turtle: *Ajjuunun.*
name of legendary bird banished by *Jebrọ* along with the *aol* fish because of their tardiness: *Le.*
name of legendary man: *aḷak.*
name of legendary trickster: *Etao.*

legible: *alikkar.*

legislate
to legislate: *nitijeḷā.*
legislature: *nitijeḷā.*

lei
make leis: *pit.*
strands for weaving garlands or stringing leis: *id.*
wear flowers or a lei: *utut.*
weave flowers or shells into a lei: *ḷōḷō.*

length: *aetok.*
lengthen: *dde.*

lenient: *meoeo.*

Lent: *iien kijone.*

Lentigo
a shell, *Strombidae, Lentigo lentiginosus* or *Tricornis sinuatus/thersites/latissimus*: *eañ.*

Leo
stars in Leo Minor: *Men-kaŋ.*

leper: *lōba.*

Lepidodactylus
an animal, kind of lizard, gecko, *Lepidodactylus pelagicus* or *Hemiphyllodactylus typus*: *korap.*

leprechaun: *rimmenanuwe, rūṃōkarraŋ.*

leprosy: *lōba.*

Leptoconus
Leptoconus kawamurai/ammiralis: *likaebeb.*

less: *iiet.*
less in quantity: *apdik.*
less than: *likjab.*
less than half full: *jakapen.*
lessen: *apdik.*

lesson: *katak, wūnin tōl.*

let
bloodletting: *kadkad.*
let anchor line out to allow for tide change: *peaut.*
let down: *ddoor.*
let down carefully: *ddoor.*
let go: *kōtļọk.*
let out: *kōtļọk.*
let out a rope to slacken it: *peaut.*
let's the two of us: *jeŋro.*
let's, we are to: *jen.*

lethargic: *addiṃakoko, addimej, mejjani, mejjeeļ.*

Lethrinus
scavenger, *Lethrinus* sp.: *ŋamāni, mejabbe.*
scavenger, *Lethrinus kallopterus*: *perak.*
scavenger, *Lethrinus microdon*: *mejmej.*
scavenger, *Lethrinus miniatus*: *jaļiia.*
scavenger, *Lethrinus variegatus*: *dijiñ, nōt.*

letter: *lōta.*
capital letters: *kiāptōļ.*
name of the letter *e*: *āe.*
name of the letter *o*: *ọo.*

level: *eọọn wōt juon.*
carpenter's level: *ļābōļ.*
level off: *eoreak.*
level-headed: *lọļe.*

lever: *ļoñtak.*
raise by lever: *ļakilulu, ļōbat.*

Levis
denim trousers, blue jeans, Levis: *tanim.*

liability: *likjab, ṃuri.*

liar: *ļaanriab, riab.*

libel: *ruruwe, wūnwūj.*

liberal: *ṃṃool.*

liberty: *anemkwōj.*

Libra
sigma in Sagitarius and beta Librae: *Aunwōlān-lañ.*

library: *ļāibrāre.*

lice
larvae of lice: *tōl.*
popping sound made when squashing lice: *noñ.*

license: *mālim.*

licentious
live licentiously: *paarōr.*

lick: *daṃdeṃ.*

lid: *libobo, māj.*
lid of: *meja-.*
possessive classifier, eyes, lids, openings, eyeglasses, masks, or goggles: *meja-.*
to cover with a lid: *mājmāj.*

lie: *eļļọk.*
always lie down: *alebabu.*
lie crosswise: *jitpeeļeļ.*
lie down: *babu.*
lie face up: *jedelañ.*
lie in ambush: *kōppao.*
lie in wait for: *kōjjaad.*
lie in wait to grab an opportunity: *kōppao.*
lie in waiting: *kōppao.*
lie on back as result of accident: *jedtak.*
lie on one's back with no regard to surroundings or people.: *jarleplep.*
lie on stomach: *pedo.*
lie with head propped on elbow: *jepdak.*

lie: *ṃoŋ.*
lie deny, dishonest: *riab.*
lies: *naan jekdọọn.*
tell a lie: *māār.*

life: *mour.*
advise someone to lead a conventionally good clean life: *kabkūbjer.*
give life to: *kōmmour.*
life jacket: *kein aō.*
life preserver: *kein aō.*

lift: *bọur, kotak, lelōñ.*
lift by lever: *ļōbat.*
lift by rope: *jirab.*
lift dress: *kitak.*
lift up the face: *ṃajed.*

lift using crane: *tekōḷ.*
lift weights to build up body: *kaddipenpen.*

ligament: *kōjjeṃ.*

light: *meram, teeñki, ttil.*
blinded by sunlight: *taṃtaṃ.*
burning, blaze, lighted: *urur.*
electric light: *ḷaaṃ jarom.*
fishing method, hunting for lobsters at night by means of artificial light, not moonlight: *tilkawor, tilkawor.*
flashing light: *jjoram.*
flashlight: *ḷaaṃ jarom, teeñki.*
go out, of a light: *kkun.*
light colored (see *meej* (**meyej**)): *jāmeej.*
light skinned: *wūdmouj.*
lightbulb: *tōṃa.*
lighter: *ḷait, ḷaita.*
lighthouse: *miade.*
lights on: *bbōl.*
moonlight: *meramin allōñ.*
of light complexion: *wūdmouj.*
searchlight: *jatiraito.*
sunlight: *meramin aḷ.*
to have light: *romrom.*
to light: *romaak.*

light
light in weight: *bōḷaḷ, mera.*
lighten ship: *eakpel.*

lightning: *jarom.*
lightning as a sign of fair weather: *jetḷādik.*

like: *ijoḷ, kōņaan.*
dislike: *kajjikur.*
dislike to do: *abwin.*
not likeable: *wōjaan-kōmatōrtōr.*
strongly dislike: *dike.*

like: *āinwōt, ari-.*
alike: *āinwōt juon.*
almost alike: *āinḷọk.*
likeness: *āindein, nemāmei-.*
likewise: *barāinwōt.*
unlike: *āinjuon.*

lily: *lele.*

limb: *ra.*
have one limb shorter than the other: *jipijuḷ.*

limber: *pidodo.*

lime
a plant, citrus, lime: *ḷaiṃ.*
coral lime: *iawewe.*

limit: *jeṃḷọk.*

limp: *ajjukub, jjipdodo, kuņōk.*
walk with a limp: *jipijuḷ.*

limpet
limpet snails with nonconical shells: *jidduul.*

line: *eo, ḷain, laajrak.*
anchor line: *emjak.*
boundary line: *kōtaa-.*
bow line, used to tie up an anchor: *lokṃaan.*
canoe part, line from top of mast to outrigger spar (*jojo* (**jewjew**)): *tokubaak.*
clothesline: *roro.*
fishing method with a canoe and line on the ocean side: *liklọk.*
fishing method, line fishing at night, jerking the line to cause phosphorescence in water to attract fish to the bait: *kōjjaromrom.*
fishing method, line fishing in lagoon from canoe at night: *ettōbok.*
fishing method, line fishing inside lagoon using hermit crab for bait: *rupe oṃ.*
fishing method, line fishing outside lagoon, usually on lee side and fairly close to shore, for flying fish, using sand crab for bait: *rōjep.*
fishing method, line fishing using floats: *kōppeḷọk.*
fishing method, line fishing using the front half of a coconut shell, in lagoon area: *mejeḷat.*
fishing method, long line, deep ocean, for tuna: *ḷatippān.*
fishing method, occasional jerking of line to lure a fish to the bait or jig: *kooral.*
fishing method, pole or line fishing using no bait but simply jerking the line in the hope of hooking a fish by chance: *kāājrabōl.*
fishing method, throw out line from lagoon beach: *eojojo.*
fishing method, use hand line from canoe in deep ocean for fish other than tuna: *kōddāpilpil.*
fishing method, using a canoe and drifting with the wind and current in a lagoon, line fishing: *peḷọk.*
fishline: *eo.*
fishline, on a pole: *mejje.*
hang on the line: *roro.*
in line with: *kijjie-.*
jerk a fishline to hook a fish: *dimtak.*
let anchor line out to allow for tide change: *peaut.*
line used to decrease the sail on a canoe: *lukwar.*

lines used to reef sails: *tiliej.*
not in line: *jake.*
nylon fishline: *eke, eo eke.*
paint or chop up to a line in canoe building: *atar.*
pull in, as fish on a line: *tōbtōb.*
reel for fishline: *kurjep.*
roll up, line or film, spool: *tāte.*
stretched tight, of lines, ropes, etc.: *lōtlōt.*
toss a line by means of weight tied to end: *iñjālle.*
yank a fishline: *liit.*

lineage: *bwij.*
bring food to a chief or lineage head: *eọjek.*
land given to someone who took care of the head of the lineage owning the land during illness before death: *ṃōnkọḷotḷot.*
lineage head: *aḷap.*

linger: *dāpdep.*

lingo: *kaj.*

link: *dāpijek, kkejel.*

lion: *ḷaiōōn.*

lionfish
a fish, lionfish, *Pterois volitans*: *ōō.*

lip
bite lips: *aṃtōk.*
draw lips to one side in contempt: *kaū.*
harelip: *tāṃoṇ.*
lips: *tie.*
smack the lips: *tōmmeḷọk.*

liquid: *dān.*
add liquid to substance such as starch: *kapejlọk.*
container for liquids: *pijja.*
container for liquids, of coconut shell: *bōkā.*
drop of liquid: *pil.*
fill with liquid: *tteiñ.*
shake a liquid so that it gurgles: *kọkkorōjrōj.*

liquor
high from liquor: *tab.*
strong liquor, alcoholic beverage: *dānnin kadek.*

lisp
lisp, in which a sibilant quality is given to the *j* phoneme: *weejej.*

list: *laajrak.*
to list: *jepāpe, lā.*

listen: *roñjake.*
listen intently: *kāroñjak.*

listless
listless, melancholy: *addiṃakoko.*

Lithoconus
Lithoconus eburneus/litteratus/pardus: *likaebeb.*

litter: *kwōpej, kwōpejpej, menọknọk, ro.*

little: *dik, niñ.*
a little: *bajjek.*
a little more: *bar jidik.*
gradually, little by little, piecemeal: *jidik illọk jidik.*
in a little bit: *ṃōttan jidik.*
little bit: *jibbūñ, jibūñ.*
little finger: *addi-dik.*
very little: *jebōñ.*

live: *mour.*
live at home of deceased during the week following death, relatives and spouse: *añak.*
live forever: *juknen.*
live somewhere: *jokwe.*
live with: *jukjuk.*

lively: *kaṃōṇōṇō, keeñki, mmourur.*
not lively: *jāmmourur.*

liver: *aj.*

living: *mmourur.*
living things: *menninmour.*

lizard: *mānnueaḷ, wiawe.*
a small black lizard with white stripes: *mājḷwōj.*
green and black lizard, *Dasia smaragdina*: *kiḷij.*
kind of lizard, big tree gecko, *Gehyra oceanica*: *korap kūro.*
kind of lizard, gecko, *Lepidodactylus pelagicus* or *Hemiphyllodactylus typus*: *korap.*
tree lizard, green and black, *Dasia smaragdina*: *aop.*
huge lizard, imported from Japan: *tokake.*
ugly-looking lizard: *kutiltil.*

load
coconut tree loaded with nuts: *nimuur.*
heavily loaded boat: *jok.*
to load: *ektak.*
unload: *eakpel, eakto.*

loaf: *pād bajjek.*
loaf of bread: *ḷoob.*

loathe: *jjō.*

lobster: *or.*
fishing method, hunt lobster or coconut crab when the moon is right: *katooj.*
fishing method, hunting for lobsters at night by means of artificial light, not moonlight: *tilkawor.*

lobster lair: *war.*
tail of lobster: *m̧ōjañ.*
to hunt lobsters: *kalwor.*

locate: *kajjuur, kowaļo̧k.*
watch birds to locate roost: *akade, aleko̧.*

location
location of: *kijjie-.*
what location?: *tee-.*

locative demonstratives
—first person inclusive singular: *ijin.*
—first person inclusive plural: *ijekein.*
—first person exclusive singular: *ije, ijjiiō.*
—first person exclusive plural: *ijekā, ijekākā.*
—second person singular: *ijen̦e, ijen̦en̦e.*
—second person plural: *ijekan̦e, ijekākan̦e.*
—third person singular: *ijen̦, ijjien̦.*
—third person plural: *ijekan̦, ijekākan̦.*
—remote singular: *ijo, ijjuweo.*
—remote plural: *ijeko, ijekoko.*

locative particles: *jo̧, lo, lo̧, n̦a, tu.*

lock
lock in combat: *bab.*
oarlock: *piin.*
padlock: *ļak.*
to lock: *ļak.*
use an oarlock: *piinin.*

locker: *tūroot.*
foot locker: *tōptōp.*

locust: *jidjid.*

loft: *po.*

log: *wōjke.*
fire logs: *toko̧.*

logged
waterlogged: *ļwōjat.*

logic: *meļeļe.*
illogical: *jaje ļōmn̦ak.*

loin: *ep, m̧ur.*
loin cloth: *kaļ.*
loins: *baj.*
wear a loin cloth: *kaļkaļ.*

loiter: *m̧ad.*

lone
lonely: *jeram̧ōl, make.*
lonesome: *jañnuwaad.*

long: *aetok.*
a long time ago: *etto.*
long and oval: *uwaitoktok.*
long-winded in diving: *pakij.*

long
long for: *jañnuwaad.*
longing for: *oñ.*
to long: *likakōj.*
watch and long for a bite of food while another is eating: *kōjm̧aal.*

look: *jujāl, lale, rre.*
go around looking for something: *allo.*
good looking: *kōjaij.*
hope, trust, look forward to: *katmāne.*
look after: *lale, on̦aak.*
look after a sick person: *kau.*
look at: *alwōj.*
look at a distance: *alluwaļo̧k.*
look at steadfastly: *kallimjek.*
look back: *ālokorkor, reilik.*
look fitting: *joto.*
look for: *jejer, kappok, ppok.*
look for a vehicle: *luwa.*
look for birds: *juakak.*
look for fish: *jore.*
look for the true pedigree: *jitdam̧.*
look in a mirror: *kilaj.*
look into: *liñōr.*
look into a trap: *waat.*
look out of the corner of the eye: *addikdik.*
look over: *etale.*
look over one's shoulder: *mū.*
look up: *jjed, ttōllōñ.*
look up after nodding, sleeping, or reading: *bōk bar.*
looks good but won't last: *kōmjedeo̧.*
weather lookout: *katu.*
looks: *kōjālli-.*
body shape, looks: *ro̧kwōj.*

loony: *kūļam̧we, tan̦o.*

loose: *booļoļ, jālōt.*
break loose, as boat from sand: *jjelo̧k.*
cast loose: *jo.*
come loose: *teoļ, tūm̧tūm̧.*
float loose: *jjelo̧k.*
float loose, of ships: *jo.*
loose bowels: *ilo̧klo̧je.*
loose, of clothing or rope: *pidtoto.*
loosen: *jaļjaļ.*

loot: *ropāj.*
ravage, ransack, loot: *rakim.*

Lord
Lord of Hosts: *Anij in Inelep.*

lore: *bwebwenato, ino̧ñ.*

lose: *luuj.*
lose contact with: *jokwōd.*
lose direction: *peļo̧k.*
lose face: *bwilo̧k māj, peļo̧k.*
lose hair: *m̧ōd.*
lose hope: *bbeer, bbetok.*

lose leaves, of trees: *m̧ōd.*
lose one's cool: *kun an ļaam̧.*
lose out: *tūm̧m̧wijkōk.*
lose temper: *kun an ļaam̧.*
lose the direction of: *wiwijet.*

loss
loss of royal status through defeat in war: *jipǫkwe.*

lost: *añjebwāālel, jako.*
be lost: *jebwābwe.*

lot: *lōñ.*

lotion: *bōkā.*
possessive classifier, perfume or lotion, or containers thereof: *kapitō-.*

lots
drawing lots: *kūbween kijdik.*

loud: *koļap, ļļaaj, ļļaaj, peran.*
cry loudly: *uwaañañ.*
loud nonsense talk: *llejlej.*
loud, as of a burst: *pañijñij.*
loud, of colors, bright: *rōōj.*
loudmouth: *ttal.*

louse: *kij.*
crab louse, *Phthirius pubis*: *kijdepak.*
delouse: *ākūt.*
large louse: *kijlep.*
young louse: *mānniñ.*

louver
louver, fixed and opaque: *kājōjō.*
louver, movable and opaque or transparent: *ļubōr.*

lovable: *wōlbo.*
unlovable: *pāpijek.*

love
false love: *iǫkwe in kij.*
food given with love: *kaniǫkwe.*
head over heels in love: *bwil.*
love song: *alin m̧aina.*
lovesick: *mejkaiie, kālǫk.*
nurture a love affair: *jetņaak.*
place for making love, usually in bushes: *jik.*
puppy love: *iǫkwe in kij.*
to love: *iǫkwe, kkōņak.*
true love: *iǫkwe in eǫ.*
unsuccessful in one's love advances: *bokbok.*
beloved: *wōlbo.*

lovely: *aiboojoj, mmejaja.*

lover
former lover: *m̧or.*
secret lover: *batin.*

low: *ttā.*
fly low: *kōttāte, kōttadede.*
low salary: *dik oņea-.*
lowest ebb tide: *pāāt m̧ōņakņak.*
lowly: *ttā.*
neither high nor low: *loñ.*
low-class people: *jeeknaan.*
coconut shell, lower half with sharp end: *ļat-jim̧.*
lower part of tree, brush, or grass: *wūn.*

lower
lower sail: *po.*
lower the head, humble oneself: *badik.*
to lower something: *ddǫdo.*

loyal: *m̧ool.*

lubrication: *jjir.*

luck: *jeraam̧m̧an.*
bad luck: *jerata.*
lucky: *jeraam̧m̧an, kankan kōj, m̧aju.*
lucky in fishing: *wōda.*
person or thing that causes trouble or bad luck: *jona.*
push one's luck: *kadkadajaj.*
speak taboo words that may bring bad luck: *ļakajem̧.*
stretched luck: *kankan kōj.*
unexpected streak of luck, windfall: *tǫǫr pata.*

luff: *bwābwe.*

lug
to lug: *ajjibanban.*

luggage: *kōbañ.*

lumber: *aļaļ.*
a type of imported lumber from the bluegum (eucalyptus) tree: *būļukam̧.*
to dry and become seasoned, of lumber, as in canoe building: *pit.*

luminous: *meram, romaak.*

Lumnitzera
a plant, *Lumnitzera littorea*: *kimeme.*

lump: *bbōj, bwijuwe.*

lunacy: *m̧ōjǫliñōr.*

lunatic: *m̧ōjǫliñōr, wūdeakeak.*

lung: *ār.*

lure: *anan, kkaal.*
fishing method, occasional jerking of line to lure a fish to the bait or jig: *kooral.*
fishing method, use fishpole at night with either lure or bait: *tto.*
shell of many colors, used as lure for tuna: *jepet.*

lurk: *kaattilōklōk.*

luscious: *kaijoļjoļ, nnǫ.*

lush: *bukwekwe.*

lust: *ļōñ.*
lust for: *mejkaiie.*
lustful: *mejkaiie.*

lustful, males only: *booļ.*
lusty: *m̧ōm̧.*
to lust in vain: *mejkaiie.*
to lust, overanxious: *m̧ōm̧.*

luster: *rabōlbōl.*

Lutjanus
a fish, *Lutjanus gibbus*: *jato.*
perch, *Lutjanus fulviflamma*: *kālikrōk.*
red snapper, *Lutjanus bohar*: *paan.*
red snapper, *Lutjanus vaigiensis*: *jaap.*
snapper, *Lutjanus flavipes*: *jāj.*
snapper, *Lutjanus kasmira forskal*: *jetaar.*
snapper, *Lutjanus monostigmus*: *juwajo.*
snapper, *Lutjanus vitta*: *bōnej.*
spot snapper, *Lutjanus fulviflamma*: *kalikūrōk.*

luxuriant: *bukwelep.*

lymph: *medaekek.*
sickness, swollen lymph glands: *bbūra.*

lynch: *uror.*

Lythraceae
growing on the hottest open sandy beaches. (*Lythraceae*: *kōn̄e.*

MIECO: *Mieko.*

ma'am: *la, le.*

machete: *jāje.*
blade of machete: *mejān jāje.*
fishing method, torch and machete: *tilkōmerā.*
slash with machete: *kabwil.*

machine
fit together, put together an engine or piece of machinery: *bobo.*
sewing machine: *mejin.*
machine gun: *kikanju.*

mackerel
big-eyed or goggle-eyed scad fish or horse mackerel, *Trachurops crumenophthalmus*: *pāti.*
mackerel, *Grammatorcynus bicarinatus*: *ikabwe.*
mackerel, *Scomber japonicus*: *m̧ōlm̧ōl.*
mackerel, *Trachurops crumenopthalmus*: *ettōū, tōū.*
fishing method, chasing mackerel into a throw net held upon one side: *kōtaltōl.*
fishing method, stand beside weir and watch for mackerel: *jo.*

Macrophragma
a shell, *Macrophragma tokyeense* (*Turritellidae*): *likarkar.*

mad: *bwebwe, llu, rowālǫk.*

maggot
have maggots: *likaakrak.*
worm, maggot: *likaakrak.*

magic: *anijnij, rojak.*
black magic: *kkōpāl, ttabōn.*
cult that tattooed and practiced magic: *eļ.*
magic to make soldiers brave: *mǫun.*
magic trick: *jibai.*
magical power: *ļǫun, mǫun.*
magical power of speech: *atlo.*
make magic: *kapāl.*
magician: *rijǫubwe.*

magistrate: *joonjo, kom̧ja.*

magnet: *jitūūl, m̧akneet.*

magnificent: *aiboojoj.*

mahogany: *m̧aōkōni.*

maid: *jiron̄, lejnono.*

mail: *lōta.*

maim
maimed: *jipikpik.*

main: *lukkuun.*
main islet of an atoll: *bōran aelōn̄, eoonene.*

maintain: *dāpdep.*
dry-docking, maintain: *tǫǫk.*

maintenance
beach a boat for maintenance purposes: *tǫǫk.*

majestic: *bōtata.*

majority: *jarlepju.*

make: *kōm̧m̧an.*
make a face: *kaū.*
make a handle for a spear: *bun̄i.*
make balls: *bobo.*
make believe: *ļōkōm̧.*
make clear: *kōmmeļeļe.*
make do: *kkōn.*
make do with what one has: *kipeddikdik.*
make food: *m̧adm̧ōd.*
make good: *kōm̧anm̧an.*
make handicraft: *amim̧ōn̄o.*
make leis: *pit.*
make out: *bōktak.*
make quick sharp turns: *jeerinbale.*
make room for: *jeje.*
make sennit: *kkwaļ.*
make the grade: *bōktak.*
make weapons: *nōļ.*
make well: *kōmour.*

male: *m̧m̧aan.*
male arrowroot, of no food value: *aetōktōk.*
male flower of breadfruit: *tōbak.*

male of one-fourth royal descent: *ļajjibjib*.
male, of animals: *koṃaan*.
said of male children: *iep jaļļǫk*.

malice: *kūtōtō*.

malignant
a sore, painful and malignant, usually located on the hands or feet: *jiṇo*.

malinger: *riab nañinmej*.
malingering: *kona*.

mallard
a bird, mallard, *Anas platyrhynchos*: *roñanpat*.

mallet: *ļwūj*.
mallet made from clam shell: *dekenin*.
pound with a mallet or hammer: *penļwūj*.

malnutrition
disease characterized by swollen belly and emaciated limbs as a result of malnutrition: *jeje*.

man: *ṃṃaan*.
a boy or man whose appearance makes everyone smile: *ļļajkōnkōn*.
busy man: *ļowaṇwoṇ*.
manly: *ṃṃaanan*.
old man: *ļaļļap*.
old man, term of respect: *aļap*.
that man (close to neither of us): *ļeeṇ, ļeieṇ, ļouweo*.
that man (close to you): *ļōṇe, ļōṇeṇe*.
the man (often not present): *ļeo*.
this man (close to me): *ļeo, ļōe*.
this man (close to us both): *ļein, ļeiō*.
top man in organization: *jeṃṃaan*.
unmarried man: *ļajinono*.
what man? What boy?: *ļōt*.
wise man: *kanpil*.
young man: *likao*.

manage: *lale*.
manage to exist: *kipeddikdik*.
manager: *mānija*.

maneuver: *kōttōbalbal*.
know how to maneuver: *jeļā kōppeļak*.
to maneuver: *jekaboot*.
wrestling maneuver, Marshallese style only: *ektak*.

mangle
mangled: *peddejǫkwe, wūdede*.

mango: *mañko*.

mangrove
Bruguiera conjugata (L.) Merrill: *joñ*.
Sonneratia caseolaris. In mangrove depressions: *kōnpat*.

maniac: *wūdeakeak*.

Manicinella
a shell, *Muricidae, Purpura (Manicinella) Armigera*: *tōbo*.

manifest: *alikkar*.

manipulate: *iṇoṇooj*.

manner: *ṃwil*.
manner of: *wāwee-*.
manners: *kōṃanōt*.
sultry mannerisms: *ikiddik*.
way or manner of doing something: *ap, kōl*.

manta
a fish, great devilfish, manta: *boraañ*.

manure: *kōṇ, kūbwe*.
smell of chicken manure: *bwiin-kūbween-alōr*.

manuscript
print by hand with manuscript style: *kiāptōļ*.

many: *bwijin, lōñ*.
many times: *lōñ alen*.
many, as a school of fish: *doom*.
not many: *ejjabdaan*.
so many: *tōlien*.

maomao
a fish, *maomao, Abudefduf abdominalis*: *badet*.

map: *mab*.

mar: *rran*.
marred: *kinejnej*.

marble: *ajaj*.
play marbles: *kōjjobaba*.
play marbles for keeps: *lukkuun*.
shooter marble: *ļōttekōļkōļ*.

march
to march, parade: *ṃaaj*.

March: *Ṃaaj*.

margin: *tōrerei-*.

Mariana Islands: *kapilōñ*.

marijuana
smoking marijuana: *kaurur baib*.

mark
check mark: *kakōļļe*.
good marksmanship: *wālel*.
good marksmanship in shooting or throwing: *jerǫ*.
hit the mark: *ļaj*.
landmark: *kakōļļe*.
leave marks: *kōn*.
make marks with the fingernails: *rakutak*.
mark to show absence: *ǫo*.
mark with a pencil: *rran*.
not good marksman with spear (see *wālel* (**waylȩl**)): *jowālel*.

not good marksman, with gun,
slingshot, or by throwing stones (see
jero̧ (**jeraw**)): *jerta.*

market: *m̧akūt.*

marlin: *l̗ōjkaan.*

marlinespike: *m̧aanjibaik.*

marriage: *pālele.*
marriage ceremony: *kwōjkwōjin
pālele.*
marriage feast: *kwōjkwōjin pālele.*
witness in marriage ceremony:
kōjab.
witnesses in marriage: *apar.*

married: *pālele.*
single, unmarried: *jalen.*
unmarried man: *l̗ajinono.*
unmarried woman: *lejnono.*

marrow
bone marrow: *n̗on̗n̗on̗meej.*

marry
to marry: *m̧are.*

marsh grass
a plant, marsh grass, *Cyperus javanicus*
Houtt: *wūjooj-in-eoon-bōl.*

marvelous: *aiboojoj.*

mash: *kapipā, lij, lijlij.*
mashed: *mālij.*
mashed taro or potato: *kōmālij.*
stone upon which bait or chum is
mashed: *jinm̧a.*

mask
diving mask: *māj, mejān turo̧ñ.*
fishing method, using diving mask and
fishline outside: *jāāk.*
possessive classifier, eyes, lids,
openings, eyeglasses, masks, or
goggles: *meja-.*

mass: *depiio.*

mass service: *mija.*

massacre: *to̧rto̧r.*

massage: *jukjuk, pitpit.*

mast: *kaju, kiju.*
canoe part, decorations of feathers on
masthead, boomtips, and sail:
deñl̗o̧k.
canoe part, line from top of mast to
outrigger spar (*jojo* (**jewjew**)):
tokubaak.
canoe part, mast top: *l̗ot.*
cross-stick on ship's mast: *kūro̧tiik.*
let sail and mast fall while tacking:
merā.

master
choirmaster, director of a choral
group: *m̧aajta.*

masturbate: *l̗ajikmeed, lepā, lukwōj.*

mat: *erer, jaki.*
a game, hide behind a mat and have
another guess: *kōl̗ōnwa.*
a mat for wearing: *ed.*
border on mat or stone edge of
road: *apar.*
bundle of mats: *kōtōm.*
floor mat, coarse: *jepko̧.*
large bundle of mats: *kūtōm.*
mat of: *kinie-.*
mat used as blanket or sheet: *kilbur.*
mat used to cover corpses: *kūtim.*
mat worn as clothing: *nieded.*
mat woven from coconut fronds:
jeinae.
pandanus mat for sail cover: *atro.*
provide a mat for: *n̗akinee-.*
roll up mats, etc.: *āle.*
sitting mat: *era-, tōl̗ao.*
sleeping mat: *jañiñi.*
small sitting mat: *miar.*
smell of clothing or mats under sun:
bbidetdet.
spread mats: *erōk.*
to weave the edges of a mat or hat:
jekōt.

match: *atar, kewa, kkar.*
ill matched: *jekkar.*

match: *mājet.*
strike a match: *it.*

mate
ship's mate: *meej.*

material
building materials: *kōbwebwei-.*
material quality: *añōltok.*

mathematics: *bōnbōn.*

matrimony: *kwōjkwōjin pālele.*

matter: *men.*
as dead matter: *likaakrak.*
not matter: *jekdo̧o̧n.*
what's the matter: *ebajeet.*

mattress: *būtoñ, mātōrej.*
possessive classifier, mat or blanket or
mattress: *kinie-.*
sleep on mattress: *būtoñtoñ.*

mature: *kalo, keke, rūtto.*
immature (see *kapeel* (**kapeyel**)), not
clever: *jekapeel.*
immature coconut fruit of: *ubnen.*
make mature: *karūtto.*
mature and capable of taking care of
oneself: *keke n̗a ireeaar.*
to mature, of poultry: *jenl̗ap.*

maturity: *m̧m̧an ded.*

maximum: *kilep.*

may: *maroñ.*

May: *Māe.*

maybe: *bōlen, ijoke.*

me: *eō.*

meager
meager (see *bwe* (**bey**)): *jabwe.*

meal: *m̧ōñā.*
final meal together before an impending disaster: *dienbwijro.*

mean: *itōn, ļōmņak.*
inner meaning: *wūnin tōl.*
meaning: *meļeļe.*

mean: *kajjōjō, lāj, m̧ōrō.*

measles: *bok aidik.*

measure: *joñak, joñjoñ, teeñ.*
chest measurement: *diklōñ.*
measure joints at an angle in construction work: *alej.*

meat: *kanniōk.*
a food, meat course: *jālele.*
can of meat: *kāān.*
half-done, of fish or meat: *koubub.*
meat course to go with rice or other staple: *jāle-.*
meaty part of the clam: *aļaļ.*
smell and taste of uncooked meat: *bbūramejmej.*
spoiled fish or meat: *kōt.*
whale meat: *itok.*
young coconut meat: *mede.*

mechanic: *injinia.*

medal: *m̧arm̧ar, m̧ōttaalia.*
medallion: *m̧ōttaalia.*
medallion of: *m̧arō-.*
possessive classifier, flowers, medals, necklaces, or fishing baskets: *m̧arō-.*

meddlesome: *doebeb.*

medical
medical treatment by members of the cult (*didiiñ*): *didiiñ.*
phases in medical treatment starting with the second: *bōrwaj.*
rub with oil as medical treatment: *pitpit.*
treat, medically: *wūno.*

medicine: *wūno.*
break taboos attendant to certain medicines while under treatment: *aļok.*
customary reimbursement given by anyone in return or exchange for food, living, or payment for medicine or priest-craft: *kabwijeran.*
extraordinary healing powers, as in Marshallese native medicine: *kōbbōkakkak.*
medicine pounding rock: *tōpañ.*
medicine women: *didiiñ.*
medicine, heat-treatment using hot stones wrapped in leaves: *tabuk.*
mortar for making medicine: *tapañ.*
place for making medicine: *pieo.*
purgative medicine: *wūno in ruprup.*
sorcery in medicine: *m̧adm̧ōd.*

meditate: *kōļmānļokjeņ.*

meek: *ineem̧m̧an.*

meet: *allolo, iioon, jelm̧ae.*
go and meet: *wōnm̧ae.*
meet and stop: *pāpjel m̧ae.*
meeting: *kweilok.*
meeting house: *m̧ōn kweiļok.*
meeting place: *out, peje.*
to meet together: *kweiļok.*

Melampus
Melampus fasciatus: *alu.*
used in head leis. Also *Melampus nuxcastanea*: *alu.*

melancholy: *ddo.*
listless, melancholy: *addim̧akoko.*

Melichthys
a fish, black triggerfish, *Melichthys ringens*: *būb.*

mellow: *ineem̧m̧an, kalo.*
mellowed: *rūttoļok.*

melodious
melodious sound: *ļļaaj.*

melody: *ainikie-, toņ.*

melt: *ōnļok.*

member: *m̧ōtta-.*
member of: *uwaan.*
members of the church: *eklejia.*

membrane: *jā.*

memorandum: *kein kakeememej.*

memorize: *kkiil.*

memory: *ememej.*
have fond memories of: *emļok.*
memories of those little things we used to do: *kiddik.*

men
chase men: *kōm̧m̧aanan.*
men's house: *ja.*
the men (often not present): *ļōm̧aro.*
these men (close to me): *ļōm̧arā, ļōm̧arārā, ļōm̧aro.*
these men (close to us both): *ļōm̧arein.*
those men (close to neither of us): *ļōm̧arāraņ, ļōm̧araņ, ļōm̧aroro.*
those men (close to you): *ļōm̧arārāņe, ļōm̧araņe.*

mend: *karpen.*
mend a net: *kanwōd, ttǫ.*
menehune: *rimmenanuwe.*
menial: *ttā.*
menstruation: *bōtōktōk, mejen allōn̄.*
mental: *ļōmņak.*
do mental arithmetic: *aņtǫǫn.*
mentally unstable: *m̧ōjǫlin̄ōr, taņo.*
mention: *kōnono.*
merchandise: *m̧weiuk.*
merchant: *tōreeta.*
mercy
have mercy on: *tūriam̧o.*
mere: *wōt.*
merge
merged: *koba, peljo.*
merit: *jinōkjeej.*
merry: *kam̧ōņōņō, lem̧ōņōņō.*
merriment: *lan̄lōn̄.*
mesh: *dāde, dāpijek.*
extra mesh in a net: *mejkōnkōn.*
mess
be messed up: *poktak.*
messed up: *pok.*
messy: *kkōr.*
mess hall: *m̧ōn m̧ōn̄ā.*
message: *nnaan.*
Messerschmidia
a plant, *Messerschmidia argentea* (L.F.) I. Johnston: *kiden.*
metal: *māāl.*
meteor: *iju rabōļļǫk.*
method: *ap, kōl.*
a method of tying sennit on the *m̧weiur* of a canoe: *n̄iinpako.*
fastest method of righting a canoe after it has capsized in order to escape sharks: *keilupako.*
method of: *wāwee-.*
method of casting lots: *pejao.*
method of climbing down: *pirūrrūr.*
method of doing something: *rāpeļta-.*
method of doing something step by step: *kiltōn.*
method of extracting coconut meat out of its shell without breaking the meat: *kōmmālwewe.*
meticulous: *kile.*
mi
syllable "mi" of musical scale: *mi.*
Micronesian pigeon
a bird, Micronesian pigeon, *Ducula oceanica*: *m̧uļe.*
microscopic: *jibbatūn̄tūn̄, jibbūn̄.*
Microsorium
a plant, fern, *Microsorium scolopendria* Burm. F. Copeland: *kino.*
middle: *ioļap.*
middle of: *buļōn, eoļōpa-, lukwō-.*
middle of an island: *iooj.*
middle of many things or people: *bwilji-.*
midget: *ļajikaj, rimmenanuwe, wūddik.*
midnight: *lukwōn bon̄.*
midrib
midrib of a coconut leaf: *ņok.*
midrib of coconut frond: *pāp.*
midrib of frond stripped for tying or for sewing copra sacks: *mālwe.*
midst
in the midst of: *buļōn.*
miff
miffed: *lotaan.*
might: *kajoor.*
might as well: *jujen.*
migrate: *jepjep, m̧m̧akūt.*
Mikadotrochus
Perotrochus teramachii or *Mikadotrochus schmalzi*: *likaabdoulul, likōppejdat.*
mild: *mera.*
mildew: *m̧ōļǫwi, menādik.*
mile: *m̧aiļ.*
military
stripes showing military rank: *iem̧a.*
milk: *milik.*
coconut milk: *eaļ.*
Milky Way
dark spot in the Milky Way beside theta in Ophiuchus: *Dāp-eo.*
mill
mill around, of small fish: *auļeļe.*
milling about of a crowd: *itileon̄eon̄.*
miller
an insect, moth or miller: *urur.*
million: *milien.*
mimic: *ari-, lowaar.*
mind: *bōklōkōt, kokōro, ļoļātāt.*
absent-minded: *bōrojoļǫk, kūļam̧we, mmālele, ppaļ.*
never mind: *āinwōt juon, jekdǫǫn.*
mine: *aō.*
mingle: *koba, peljo.*
minister: *rōplen.*
minnow: *aol.*
a fish, tiny surface minnow: *ņaņ.*
charge of a school of fish chasing minnows: *tūaļ.*

fishing method, using woven brown coconut fronds to catch sardines and minnows as they are chased ashore by bigger fish: *apep.*

minor: *jiddik, m̧aina, m̄anniñ.*

minute: *jibbatūñtūñ, jibbūñ, minit.*

Mirabilis
a plant, *Mirabilis jalapa* L. (Nyctaginaceae): *emān-awa.*

miracle: *kakōl̦l̦e.*

mirage
mirage, optical illusion, illusion: *jāmilur.*

mirror: *kapjer, kilaj.*
look in a mirror: *kilaj.*
signal with a mirror: *kakkilaajaj.*

miscellaneous: *jabdewōt, kkārere.*

mischievous: *ājāj, bōt, doebeb, kakūtōtō, l̦ōkatip.*

miser
miserly: *arōk, miin.*
miserly, even of worthless objects: *arōk menoknok.*
very miserly: *kūbbon̦.*

misfortune: *jerata.*
do something that will result in misfortune, such as breaking a taboo: *l̦ōkajem̧.*
intuition about a future misfortune or death: *lomije-.*
misfortune due to breaking of a taboo: *ruwe.*

misgiving: *lel̦ok-letok.*

mislead: *jebwābwe.*

miss: *l̦e.*
be late for and miss a plane, boat, or car, etc.: *tūm̧.*
miss an opportunity: *waakl̦ok.*
miss constantly: *jokwōd.*
miss destination: *pel̦ok.*
miss out: *tūm̧m̧wijkōk.*
miss the boat: *tomewa.*
missing: *jako.*

miss: *lijā.*

Missa
Roman Catholic Missa: *mija.*

missile: *mijel̦.*
gather missiles for throwing: *rukbo.*
missile, for throwing only: *bo.*

mission: *mijen.*
missionary: *mejinede.*

mist: *m̧ōtodik.*

mistake: *bōd.*
mistake in performing a dance, song, or chant: *dujebwābwe.*

Mister: *al̦e.*

mistrust: *jālōke.*

mix: *iiōk.*
mix in: *peljo.*
mix sail power with engine power: *kabodān.*
mix together a variety of ingredients: *jitable.*
mix with water: *kāre, kabodān.*
mixed: *kkārere.*
mixed ancestry: *ainokko.*
mixed blood: *ainokko.*
mixture: *iiōk.*
mixture of: *utō-.*
of good mixture: *m̧m̧an utōn.*

moan: *ññūr.*

mob: *jarlepju.*

mobilize
mobilize (military): *joorkatkat.*

mock: *ar, kajjioñ, kajjirere, lowaar.*

model: *jemān-āe.*
sail model canoes: *bwilbwil.*

modest: *mmejokunkun, ttā bōro.*

moi
a fish, *moi, Polydactylus sexfilis*: *atkadu.*

moist: *m̧ōl̦owi.*
moisture: *m̧ōl̦owi.*

molar: *ñilep.*

mold
hat block form, any mold, any form: *m̧ōn̦akjān.*
molded arrowroot starch: *jibwil.*

mold: *lirouwe.*
moldy: *l̦ōl̦.*
moldy taste: *nnān.*

mole: *il meej.*
mole on the skin: *ilmeej.*
mole, hairy: *buwak.*
small mole with a hair sticking out: *būttiwol̦.*

molt: *orjib.*
place in sand where turtle lays eggs or coconut crab molts: *jo.*
place where turtles molt: *mej.*

momento: *kein kakeememej.*

momma: *m̧am̧a.*

Monday: *M̧ande.*

Monetaria
Erosaria helvola/erosa/flaveola or *Monetaria annulus harmandiniana/moneta rhomboides*: *likajjid.*

money: *bajet, jāān, m̧aak, m̧ani.*
broke, out of money: *jar.*
check, money order: *jāāk.*
interest money: *orl̦ok.*

invested money: *orḷọk.*
money of: *nāji-.*
out of money: *būrook, oḷiin̄.*
possessive classifier, children, pets, money, watches, or Bible: *nāji-.*
security, land or goods or money put away for future use or for children: *joortoklik.*
short of money: *jiban.*
to strip of money or property by fraud or threat: *kwōdmat, reja.*

money cowrie
money cowrie, a shell, *Cypraeidae: likajjid.*

monitor: *kāron̄jak.*
monitor secretly: *iaron̄ron̄.*

monkey: *ṃan̄ke.*

monkey wrench: *ṃan̄ke jibana.*

Monotaxis
a fish, big-eye or burgy, *Monotaxis grandoculis: ṃōjani, mejọkut.*
Monotaxis grandoculis: kie.

monster: *eakeak, tiṃoṇ.*
legendary monster: *kidudujet.*
roar, as of the wind or a monster: *rorror.*

Montfortula
Diodora (austroglyphis) sieboldii or *Montfortula pulchra* or *Tugali vadososinuata: jowakin.*

month: *allōn̄.*
day of month when moon comes over the horizon just as sun sets: *jetn̄ōl.*
monthly contribution: *allōn̄ iju.*
next month: *allōn̄ in laḷ.*

monument: *kakōḷḷe.*

mood: *taṃṃwi-.*
in a bad mood: *nana taṃṃwi-.*
moody: *ṃṃaḷkaro, nana taṃṃwi-.*

moon: *allōn̄.*
eclipse of the moon: *bōtōktōk allōn̄.*
fifth moon phase: *marokiddik.*
first moon phase: *jetmar.*
first quarter of the moon: *adik.*
fishing method, hunting for lobsters at night by means of artificial light, not moonlight: *tilkawor.*
fourth moon phase: *meḷọkḷọk.*
half-moon: *wetakḷap.*
moon phase after *jetmar: meḷoktak.*
moon phase after *marokiddik: maroklep.*
moon phase after *meḷọkḷọk: marokiddik.*
moon phase after *meḷoktak: meḷoktakōn, tuujlon̄lon̄.*
moon phase after *meḷoktakōn: meḷọkḷọk.*
moonless: *maroklep.*
moonlight: *meramin allōn̄.*
new moon: *taktakōnae.*
night after full moon: *jetmar.*
night of full moon: *jetn̄ōl.*
period between setting of sun and rising of moon: *meḷọkḷọk, meḷoktakōn, tuujlon̄lon̄.*
period between setting of sun and rising or moon: *meḷoktak.*
second moon phase: *meḷoktak.*
sickness believed to be caused by sleeping at night under the moon: *ṃōjọlin̄ōr.*
sixth moon phase: *maroklep.*
third moon phase: *meḷoktakōn, tuujlon̄lon̄.*

moonrise: *iiaḷan̄e.*

moor: *emjak.*

Moorish idol
a fish, Moorish idol, *Zanclus canescens: jourur.*
a fish, Moorish idol, *Zanclus cornutus: pālep, wōllaan̄.*

mop: *ṃaab.*

moral: *katak, wūnin tōl.*

morale: *kōḷo.*

moray eel: *dāp.*
a fish, moray eel: *kideddelbwij.*
a fish, moray eel, *Gymnothorax flavimarginatus: ṃakan̄.*
a fish, moray eel, *Gymnothorax pictus: ṃaj-mouj.*

morbid: *utaṃwe.*

more: *bar.*
a little more: *bar jidik.*
all the more: *tōrreo.*
desire more, of a delicious food, music, or game: *jaṃjaṃ.*
more like it: *ebajjeet.*
more than: *jiṃa.*
take more than one's share: *bōkḷap.*

Morinda
a plant, *Morinda citrifolia* L. (Rubiaceae): *kalenen, nen.*

morning: *jibbon̄, okraan.*
morning of the day after tomorrow: *jibbon̄ōnin jekḷaj.*
this morning: *jibbon̄ōniin.*
three mornings ago: *jibbon̄ōn eo turun inne, jibbon̄ōn inne eo ḷọk juon.*
tomorrow morning: *jibbon̄ōn ilju.*
yesterday morning: *jibbon̄ōn inne.*
a star (planet), Morning Star, Venus

(mornings only): *Jurōn-Jemān-Kurlōñ.*
moron: *kūḷaṃwe, likjab, rowālọk, wūdkabbe.*
mortal
mortal sin: *jerọwiwiin mej.*
mortar
mortar for making medicine: *tapañ.*
mortgage: *joortoklik.*
Morum
Morum macandrewi/teramachii or *Bezoardicella decussata/areola* or *Phalium glauca*: *jilel.*
mosquito: *jokwajok, ṇaṃ.*
mosquito coil: *ḷwaar.*
mosquito net: *taiṇaṃ.*
wiggler larvae of mosquitoes: *lijeljelṃak.*
moss: *liṃliṃ.*
slimy moss: *kūbween aḷ.*
most: *tata.*
the most: *tōñtōñ.*
usually, mostly: *epliklik.*
moth: *babbūb, menādik.*
an insect, moth: *mānnikiden.*
an insect, moth or miller: *urur.*
mother: *jine-, ṃaṃa.*
duty of taking care of a mother: *jine.*
Mother Hubbard: *ipep.*
Mother Hubbard dress, named for Oahu: *wau.*
motion: *ṃṃakūt.*
motion sickness: *ḷḷao.*
motive: *wūn.*
motor: *injin.*
motorbike: *wōtbai.*
motorcycle: *wōtbai.*
outboard motor: *injin ḷọk.*
motto: *kaj, wūnin tōl.*
mound: *bat.*
mound of stones: *ajokḷā.*
to crumble a mound or pile as of sand: *rōṃ.*
mount: *tallōñ, wanlōñ, welọk.*
dismount: *wanlaḷ.*
to mount: *uwe.*
mountain: *toḷ.*
a game, king of the mountain: *kojuwa.*
mourn: *būroṃōj, jañ.*
mourn a deceased: *āmej.*
mourn the dead: *ilomej.*
mourning: *liaajlọḷ.*
procession of mourners: *tal.*
mouse: *kijdik.*
gnaw, of a rat or a mouse: *wōjek.*

mouth: *lọñi.*
big-mouth: *koḷap.*
blabber-mouth: *bbōk, ttal.*
foul-mouthed: *nana kobban lọñii-.*
loudmouth: *ttal.*
open the mouth: *waḷañi.*
palate of mouth: *ñat.*
rinse one's mouth: *kurkur, rukruk.*
to chew food and then throw it out of the mouth: *meliak.*
use mouth to husk coconuts: *ejej.*

move: *ṃṃakūt.*
a move in game of checkers whereby one jump captures many pieces: *jaṃtiltil.*
a smart move: *jeḷā kōppeḷak.*
move (with directional): *jiraak-, raak, ruwaak, uraak.*
move a crowd: *peḷaak.*
move a little sideways to make room: *rrā.*
move at highest possible speed: *buuḷtōñtōñ.*
move away: *jepjep.*
move closer: *kepaak.*
move fast so as to avoid detection: *miro.*
move forward: *wōnṃaan.*
move hips from side to side while dancing: *kajikia.*
move out swiftly: *kōplọk.*
move slowly, snail's pace: *ṃōkaj jān oṃ.*
move something closer by using a stick: *adebdeb.*
move up: *wōnṃaan.*
move with steady and deliberate purpose: *ijuboñ-ijuraan.*
movement of fish near surface: *boklọk.*
movement of hips during sexual intercourse: *aelaḷ.*
movement of pelvis: *doñ.*
moving: *jjānene.*
moving from one place to another: *ne ṃakūtkūt.*
push, move, postponement: *tọrtọr.*

movie: *pija ṃakūtkūt.*
a movie: *ṃupi.*
to see a movie: *ṃupi.*
moving picture: *pija ṃakūtkūt.*

mow: *jepjep.*

much: *kuborbor, lōñ.*
not much: *ejjabdaan.*
not so very much: *daan.*
too much: *bōlej.*

mucous: *ba.*
  nasal mucous: *uwur.*
mud: *pedkat.*
  muddy: *jo.*
muffler: *baib.*
mullet
  mullet, *Crenmugil crenilabis*: *iōōļ,*
    joomum.
  striped mullet, *Chelon vaigiensis*:
    akōr, aotak.
Mulloidichthys
  goatfish, *Mulloidichthys auriflama*:
    jome.
  goatfish, *Mulloidichthys samoensis*: *jo.*
multiple: *bwijin.*
multiplication
  times, in multiplication: *alen.*
  multiply: *koorļok.*
multitude: *inelep, jarlepju.*
mum: *ikōñ.*
mumble: *alñūrñūr.*
mumps: *ļōpper.*
munch: *kañurñur.*
municipality: *jukjuk.*
murder: *kowadoñ, m̧ōrō, uror.*
  murderer: *m̧ōrō.*
  murderous: *m̧ōrō.*
murex shell: *lōkeed.*
Muricidae
  a shell, *Muricidae*: *lidid.*
  a shell, *Muricidae, Purpura*
    (Manicinella) Armigera: *tōbo.*
murk
  murky water: *lim̧.*
murmur: *alñūrñūr.*
Musa
  a plant, general term for bananas,
    Musa sapientum L. (Musaceae):
    keeprañ.
muscle: *m̧ajeļ, keeļ.*
  flexed muscles: *jar m̧ajeļ.*
  muscle in a bivalve: *kōjjem̧.*
  possessing control of vaginal
    muscles: *kkweetet.*
  strain one's abdominal muscles: *iñ*
    ļojien.
  muscular: *peñpeñ.*
  muscular distrophy: *māro.*
music: *al.*
  a musical composition to be sung by all
    singers together: *kọrōj.*
  beat regular time to music, pace:
    buñtōn.
  flat music or voice, usually out of
    tune: *būļāāt.*
  flat, music: *bōna.*

musical band: *paan.*
musical instrument: *kōjañjañ.*
organ, musical: *ọkwōn.*
play music: *kōjañjañ.*
play music on radio or phonograph:
  jañ.
musical scale syllables: *to, re, mi, ba,*
  jooļ, la, ji.
muss
  mussed up: *nokjek.*
must: *aikuj.*
mustache: *kwōdeak.*
musty
  musty taste: *nnān.*
mute: *ikōñ, kejakļọkjeņ.*
mutter: *alñūrñūr.*
my: *aō.*
Myrichthys
  a fish, snake eel, *Myrichthys*
    colubrinus: *m̧ajid.*
  Myrichthys bleekeri: *kideddelbwij.*
Myripristis
  squirrel fish, *Myripristis berndti*:
    m̧ōn.
  Myripristis sp.: *jera.*
  Myripristis bowditchae/murdjan:
    m̧ōn-kiden.
mysterious: *ttino.*
myth: *bwebwenato, inọñ.*
nab
  get hooked, nabbed: *tọrōk.*
  get nabbed: *auj.*
  nabbed: *po.*
nag
  nagged: *abņōņō, aploñloñ.*
  nagging: *kakōl, kile.*
nail: *dila.*
  fingernail: *akki, akkiin pā.*
  pinch with fingernails: *kinji.*
  toenail: *akki, akkiin ne.*
naive: *jedañ.*
naked: *keelwaan, m̧añke, utkōk.*
name: *āt.*
  a person, unnamed: *men.*
  address someone using *Li-* or *Ļa-*
    prefix on name: *ātlep.*
  be named after: *ātņak.*
  be named for a person: *etņake.*
  calling someone by name: *āñiñin.*
  name of the letter *e*: *āe.*
  name of the letter *o*: *ọo.*
  name of the youngest son (tenthborn)
    of *Lōktañūr* (ļektagir), legendary:
    Jeļeilōñ.
  name with *Li-* or *Ļa* prefix: *ātlep.*
  namesake: *etņake.*

nickname: *ātdik*.
nickname for baby girl: *jiroñ*.
pet name: *ātdik*.
pet name for male child: *kǫkǫ*.
prefix to feminine names: *Li-*.
prefix to masculine names: *Ḷa-*.
take the name of another: *ātṇak*.
to name: *ṇaeta-*.

nap: *pipi*.
take a nap: *wūne māj*.

napkin
sanitary napkin: *te*.
use a sanitary napkin: *tete*.

narrow: *aidik, ainiñ, uwaidikdik*.
narrow, of land (see *wūjaloñ* (**wijaleg°**)): *wūjabōj*.

nasal
nasal mucous: *uwur*.

Naso
a fish, surgeonfish, *Naso unicornis*: *eañrōk, ṃǫṇe*.
a fish, unicorn fish, *Naso brevirostris*: *batakḷaj*.
a fish, unicorn fish, *Naso lituratus*: *bwilak*.

nasty: *ttoon*.

nation: *laḷ*.

native: *kōṇakō*.

nature
nature of: *wāwee-*.

Naucrates
a fish, pilot fish, *Naucrates ductor*: *ikuut*.

naughty: *ājāj, bōt, ḷōkatip, rinana*.
be of a naughty sort: *uwaan kakūtōtō*.

nausea: *ṃōḷañḷōñ*.
get nauseated by: *jjō*.
nauseated: *ṃōḷañḷōñ*.
nauseating: *kajjōjō*.
not nauseated easily: *jājjō*.

nautical
be underway, nautical: *jerak*.
deck, nautical: *teek*.
drawing much water causing it to be hard to paddle or sail, nautical: *añōt*.
full sail, nautical: *kankan, lōtlōt*.
instrument for plotting courses, nautical: *kein kōttōbalbal*.
lay to, nautical: *iptu*.
nautical course: *kooj*.
nautical term: *jjeraak, taaṃbūḷo, tōmeañ, tōmrak, tōmrok*.
pay out, nautical: *peaut*.
ribs, nautical: *eḷḷa*.
sheet, nautical: *iep*.
swift, of canoes or boats, nautical term: *ḷḷaeoeo*.
tiller, nautical: *jila*.

Nautilidae
a shell, *Nautilidae*: *lǫjilñin jourur*.

nautilus
chambered nautilus, *Nautilus pompilius*: *lǫjilñin jourur*.

navel: *bwije-*.

navigate: *meto*.
navigation: *meto*.
celestial navigation: *bōk aḷ, bōk iju*.
name of a navigational sign: *Ejje, Erra, Jarkul, Kwe, Tipāp*.
navigation "knot" where two waves meet: *buoj*.
navigational sign in Marshallese navigation: *kōkḷaḷ*.
name of a navigational sign: *Nakwōpe*.
name of two navigational signs: *Kobal*.
intuition and knowledge possessed by certain expert Marshallese navigators using traditional methods: *kabuñpet*.

navy: *nepi*.

ne'er-do-well
a ne'er-do-well: *ikōn aḷe*.

neap
period of neap tides: *idik*.

near: *epaak, turu-*.
draw near: *jikrōk*.
nearly: *epaak*.

nearly: *baj, kiōk, nañin*.

neat: *karbōb, meḷak, rreo*.
not neat: *jǫkoṇ*.

necessary: *aikuj*.

necessity: *aikuj*.

neck: *kōnwa*.
neck of the penis: *ṃǫkwōd*.
stretch the neck: *mōōbōb*.
to crane the neck to see better: *mū*.
wear around the neck: *ṃarṃar*.

necklace: *ṃarṃar*.
little stones used to make necklaces: *kāāj*.
necklace of: *ṃarō-*.
possessive classifier, flowers, medals, necklaces, or fishing baskets: *ṃarō-*.
wear a necklace: *ṃarṃar*.

need: *aikuj*.

needle: *iie, niiḷ, nitōḷ*.
stick with spear, knife, or needle, etc.: *lōlō*.

needlefish
a fish, needlefish, *Belone platyura*: *tak.*
a fish, needlefish, *Strongylura marina*: *ṃak.*
fishing method, for needlefish (*ṃak*): *kōṃṃak.*
fishing method, striking needlefish with a long piece of wood or a paddle as they float on the surface of the water on moonlit nights: *deñtak.*

negative: *dāpdep.*
negative future tense: *ban.*
negative prefix: *ja-.*
negatively conditioned: *mañ.*

neglect: *jāniknik, jokwōd, kajukur.*
neglect one's primary responsibilty: *kadkadmootot.*
neglect the commoners: *kwōje dunen meļaaj.*
neglected: *jool.*

negotiate: *pepe.*
negotiate one's way through thick brush or heavy seas or between reefs: *wāwe.*

negro: *niikro.*

neighbor: *rūturi-.*
neighborhood: *peļaak.*

neophyte: *watre.*

Neothunus
a fish, tuna, *Neothunus macropterus*: *bwebwe.*

nephew: *mañde-.*

Nephrolepis
a plant, *Nephrolepis acutifolia* similar to the familiar "Boston fern": *anṃōkadede.*
a plant, *Nephrolepis biserata* (Sw.) Schott. Namorik. Boston fern: *baidik.*

nepotism: *jep.*

Neritidae
a shell, *Neritidae*: *jinenpokpok, kaddoļ.*

Neritipsis
Neritipsis radula: *kobal.*

Nerium
a plant, flower, *Nerium oleander*. L: *oļiaanta.*

nerve: *nōōb.*

nervous: *abņōņō, kkūṃkūṃ.*

nest: *el.*
turtle nest: *karōk.*

nestle: *jjibur.*

net: *ok.*
cargo net: *ṃukko.*
catch with net or basket: *bọur.*
entry in net of small groups of fish versus one large group: *tọọr pata.*
extra mesh in a net: *mejkōnkōn.*
fishing method, chasing mackerel into a throw net held upon one side: *kōtaltōl.*
fishing method, use long net and *ṃwio* (**ṃiyew**) during high tide and wait for low: *jurōk.*
fishing method, use throwing net: *kadkad.*
long fish trap, for sprats, net with handle: *bọro.*
long fishing net: *okaetok.*
mend a net: *kanwōd, ttọ.*
mosquito net: *taiņaṃ.*
net made of sennit used for sifting arrowroot starch: *waliklik.*
net, large-meshed, bag-shaped, for washing arrowroot and soaking breadfruit: *do.*
netted: *tōprak.*
netting: *ok.*
part of a net: *jak.*
part of net where weights are attached: *jeklaļ.*
raise fish net from water: *jarjar.*

never: *jañin.*
never mind: *jekdọọn.*
never will do: *ban.*

nevertheless: *bōtab, ijoke, makarta.*

new: *kāāl.*
new moon: *taktakōnae.*
newly constructed, of vessels or vehicles: *wōnōt.*
renew: *kōkāāl.*
smell of new things: *bwiin-ppāllele.*

New Zealand cuckoo
a bird, long-tailed New Zealand cuckoo, *Urodynamis taitensis*: *wūdej.*

news: *keeañ, nnaan, nuuj.*
gather news or information: *eọroñ naan.*
newspaper: *nuujpeba.*

next
next to: *epaak, turu-.*

nibble: *wōjek.*
nibble, as fish on bait: *ļļijļij.*

nice: *ṃṃan.*

nickel: *nikōļ.*

nickname: *ātdik.*
nickname for baby girl: *jiroñ.*

niece: *mañde-.*

night: *boñ.*
attack at night: *iaboñ.*
catch birds at night: *jjọñ.*

custom of spending the last night with people before they depart: *jeboñōn.*
dark cloudy night: *lianij.*
four nights ago: *boñōn eo turun inne eo ļọk juon.*
kill in the night: *jjọñ.*
midnight: *lukwōn boñ.*
night after *jetñil* (**jeţgil**): *jetmar.*
night after full moon: *jetmar.*
night before last: *buñūn inne.*
night of full moon: *jetñōl.*
night of the day after tomorrow: *buñūn jekļaj.*
pitch black, said of nights: *innijek.*
raid at night: *iaboñ.*
three nights ago: *buñūn inne eo ļọk juon.*
time of day or night: *tōre.*
tomorrow night: *buñūn ilju.*
tonight: *buñniin.*

nil: *ejej, ejjeļọk.*

nimble: *buñ-peltak, util.*

nine: *ruwatimjuon.*

nip: *apap, kūk.*

nipple: *ittūt.*

nit: *liññar, mānniñ, tōl.*

nit-pick: *kakūtōtō.*

no: *eaab, jaab.*
no more: *jej, maat.*

noble: *bwio.*

nobody: *ejjeļọk.*

nod: *ajjiṃaalal.*
look up after nodding, sleeping, or reading: *bōk bar.*
nod assent (distributive only): *ṃajid.*
nods: *buñtōn.*

noddy
a bird, black noddy, *Anous tenuirostris*: *jekad.*
a bird, blue-gray noddy, *Procelsterna caerulea*: *lọun Pikaar.*
a bird, brown noddy, *Anous stolidus*: *pejwak.*
white spot on the head of the brown noddy (*pejwak*) bird: *ao.*

noise: *aeñwāñwā, ainikie-, kkeroro.*
annoyed or bothered by noise: *uwaroñ.*
clamor, noise: *ailuwannañnañ.*
sucking noise made in drinking green coconuts: *ṃṃōtṃōt.*
noisy: *airuwaro, dekōṃkōṃ, koļap, peran.*
be noisy: *keroro.*

nomad: *bwijteoļeoļ.*

none: *ejej, ejjeļọk, jej.*

nonsense
loud nonsense talk: *llejlej.*

noodle
noodles: *utoñ.*

noon: *raelep.*

noose: *allok.*

normal
normally: *kkā.*

north: *eañ.*
north side: *eañtak.*
northern part: *tueañ.*
on the north side of: *aikne.*
sail downwind with the sail on the south and the outrigger on the north: *tōmeañ.*
wind from the north: *jokļā.*
North Star: *Liṃanṃan.*
two pairs of stars that point to the North Star: *Jurōn-Liṃanṃan.*

northeast: *eñ-rear.*
forecast predicting the onset of prevailing northeast trade winds: *deñdeñin mājlep.*
heavy rain from the northeast: *wōttọ.*
northeast trade wind: *kọto.*

northerly
northerly swell: *buñtokeañ.*

northern shoveler
a bird, northern shoveler, *Anas clypeata*: *roñanpat.*

northward: *niña.*
current flowing northward: *aeniñeañļọk.*
directional, enclitic northward: *niñeañ.*
directional, enclitic, northward: *niña.*
head northward: *jitniñeañ.*

northwest
northwestern sky: *kapilōñ iōñ.*
western and northwestern island northwestern islands in an atoll: *liklaļ.*
wind from the northwest: *tiltil keeañ.*
western and northwestern island northwestern islands in an atoll: *liklaļ.*

nose: *bọti.*
nosebleed: *ļōjo.*
nosey: *eded, bbōk.*
runny nose: *ba.*
sickness, constant running nose: *anjilik.*
take a nose dive: *ñarñar.*

talk through the nose: *kajņoņ.*

nostalgia: *emļǫk, oñ.*

not: *jab.*
not able to see well (see *llo* (**llew**)): *jāllo.*
not add up: *jǫuñ.*
not again: *jab bar.*
not angered easily (see *llu* (**lliw**)): *jāllulu.*
not any: *ejej.*
not at all: *podem.*
not athletic: *jǫkkurere.*
not believe: *jālōke.*
not biting, of fish (see *kūk* (**kik**)): *jakkūk.*
not biting, of fish. (See *m̧ōñā* (**m̧egay**)): *jam̧ōñā.*
not break wind often (see *jiñ* (**jig**)): *jājjiñjiñ.*
not clever (see *jim̧aat* (**jim̧ahat**)): *jājim̧aat.*
not depend on (see *lōke* (**lękęy**)): *jālōke.*
not enough: *jabwe.*
not enough of counted things: *jǫuñ.*
not even: *podem.*
not fast: *jāiur, jāiurjet.*
not flammable: *tokwiia.*
not flammable (see *jǫwiie* (**jawiyyęy**)): *jǫwiia.*
not frequent (see *kut* (**qit**)): *jǫkkutkut.*
not get chilly easily (see *piǫ* (**piyaw**)): *jāppiǫeo.*
not good marksman with spear (see *wālel* (**waylęl**)): *jowālel.*
not greedy (see *tōr* (**ter**)): *jatōr.*
not hairy (see *kooļ* (**qeweļ**)): *jǫkooļoļ.*
not have intercourse often (see *tape* (**tapęy**)): *jattapepe.*
not have the ability to: *ban.*
not ignite easily (see *tokwōj* (**teqej**)): *jatokwōj.*
not in line: *jake.*
not industrious: *jāniknik.*
not interesting (see *m̧ōņōņō* (**m̧enehņeh**)): *jam̧ōņōņō.*
not know: *jaje, ñak.*
not know which way to go: *añjebwāālel.*
not leak: *jettal.*
not lively: *jāmmourur.*
not many fish, of a place (see *ek* (**yęk**)): *jāike.*
not matter: *jekdǫǫn.*
not nauseated easily: *jājjō.*
not often: *jǫkkutkut.*
not paddle easily, of canoes (see *kōrkaakiie* (**kerkahakiyyęy**)): *kōrkaakiia.*
not paired off (see *uñ* (**wig**)): *jǫuñ.*
not perservering (see *niknik* (**niknik**)): *jāniknik.*
not quick (see *iur* (**yir°**)): *jāiur.*
not quick in action (see *iurjet* (**yir°jęt**)): *jāiurjet.*
not rainy: *jǫwōtwōt.*
not recognize (see *kile* (**kiley**)): *jakile.*
not satisfied: *jam̧jam̧.*
not scare easily (see *kkōl* (**kkęl**)): *jakkōl.*
not scare easily (see *uwōta* (**wiwetah**)): *jǫuwōta.*
not serviceable (see *keiie* (**kęyiyyęy**)): *jakeiie.*
not smart: *jājim̧aat.*
not so very much: *daan.*
not speedy: *jāiurjet.*
not start easily: *jǫwiia.*
not strong: *jakeiie.*
not strong physically (see *dipen* (**diypęn**)): *jādipen.*
not tasty, of fish (see *uwi* (**wwiy**)): *jǫuwi.*
not thoroughly done (see *lōt* (**let**)): *jālōt.*
not trust in: *jālōke.*
not useful: *jakeiie.*
not well-cleaned: *jālōt.*
not well-sifted: *jālōt.*
not yet: *jañin.*
will not, determination or simple future: *jāmin.*

notable
person who is notable: *kāājāj.*

Notadusta
also *Notadusta martini katsuae*: *likajjid.*

notch
notches cut in a tree for climbing: *jekāiōōj.*

nothing: *ejej, ejjeļǫk.*
good for nothing: *pata.*

notice: *kile, kōjjeļā, mejek.*

notify: *jiroñ, keeañ.*

notion: *ļōmņak.*

Notoacmea
Notoacmea gloriosa/concinna and *Patelloida saccharina* lanx: *jidduul.*

notorious: *buñbuñ.*

nourish: *naajdik.*
nourishing: *ōn.*
undernourished: *kwōle.*

November: *Nobōm̧ba.*

novice: *ñak, watre.*

now: *ja, kiin, kiiō.*

nude: *koļeiaat, m̧añke.*
denude: *utūkaļ.*

Nudibranchs
Nudibranchs, Onchidium sp: *pedobar.*

numb: *mej.*

number: *nōm̧ba.*
number of: *ora-, uwaan.*
word used to form phrases and ordinal numbers: *kein.*

Numenius
a bird, bristle-thighed curlew, *Numenius tahitiensis*: *kōkkōk.*
a bird, whimbrel, *Numenius phaeopus*: *kowak.*

numerous: *pata.*
numerous (of insects): *ju.*

nun: *bōjin.*

nurse: *nōōj.*
nurse a baby (or a situation): *kaajiriri.*
nurse a patient: *kau.*

nurture: *kaajiriri.*
nurture a love affair: *jetņaak.*

nut: *kwōle.*
a food, cooked and pounded breadfruit, taro, bananas, or nuts mixed with grated coconut: *wūdeñ.*
a food, nuts of breadfruit, cooked: *kwōlejiped.*
drift nut, sweet smelling, used with coconut oil to make perfume: *ajet.*
edible portion inside certain nuts or seeds: *jibañūñ.*
"Nuts!": *aia.*

nutrition: *m̧ōñā, ōn.*

nylon
nylon fishline: *eke, eo eke.*

o
name of the letter *o*: *o̧o.*

oaf: *wūdkabbe.*

oak: *uuk.*

oakum
oakum, compost: *kōņ.*

oar: *jebwe.*
oarlock: *piin.*
use an oarlock: *piinin.*

oath: *kallim̧ur.*

oatmeal: *wōtmiiļ.*

obdurate: *bōt, kijñeñe, kipiliia.*

obedience: *pokake.*
wilful disobedience: *aplep.*
disobedient: *jilikiia, kipiliia.*
obedient: *jilikiie, kipiliie.*

obese
overweight, obese: *tebu.*

obey: *pokake.*
disobey: *kōjelbabō, kōtrāe.*
obey readily and cheerfully: *jilikiie.*
slow to obey: *jilikiia.*

object: *men.*
objection: *kein jum̧ae.*
objectionable: *kōmmatōr.*
objective: *mejānkajjik.*

obligate
obligated: *aikuj, kallim̧ur.*

oblige: *kipel.*

obliterate: *jjeor.*

oblivious: *meļo̧kļo̧k, mmālele.*

obnoxious: *kōmatōrtōr.*

obscene: *ttoon.*

obscure: *aelo̧k, ttino.*
obscured: *ņojak, tilekek.*
obscured, cloudy: *tab.*

observe: *jjāāl, kōjjaad, lale, waat.*
observe from a distance: *jedjed.*
forecast weather by observing clouds: *kōbbaal.*
observing stars: *jedjed iju.*

obsess
become an obsession: *jiktok.*
obsessed: *lokjak, pālo.*
obsession: *ikdeelel.*

obsolescent: *m̧or.*

obsolete: *m̧or.*

obstacle: *kino̧wea-.*

obstinate: *bōt, kipiliia.*

obstruct: *pinej.*
obstructed: *boņ, jeddam̧.*

obtain: *bōk.*
cheat, obtain surreptitiously: *liktak.*

Obtusifolia: *kaar.*

obvious: *alikkar, jjedmatmat, tooj.*
obviously: *ejjab aelo̧k.*

occasion: *alen, iien.*

occult: *ttabōn.*

occupation: *jerbal.*

occupied: *m̧ad, pālo, poub.*

occupy: *bōk.*
occupy a lot of space: *koobob.*

occur: *waļo̧k.*
occur one after another, consecutively, bumper-to-bumper: *kij-ļo̧kwan-doon.*
occur to: *eñak.*
occurrence: *buñ.*

ocean: *lo̧jet, lo̧meto, meto.*
depths of the ocean: *ikjet.*
ocean swell: *ñōl.*
passage into lagoon from ocean: *to.*

surface of the ocean: *aejet.*

ocean side
anchorage on ocean side of islet where one waits for more favorable winds: *metto.*
fishing method with a canoe and line on the ocean side: *liklọk.*
go or come towards the ocean side of an island: *wanlik.*
go to the ocean side: *kālik.*
go to the ocean side on the southern end of an island: *kālikrōk.*
ocean side of: *lik, liki.*
ocean side of an island: *jablik.*
to drag or tow from lagoon side to ocean side: *lelik.*
to drag or tow from ocean side to lagoon side: *lear.*

Ochrosia
a plant, *Ochrosia oppositifolia* (Lam.) K. Schum. (Apocynaceae): *kōjbar.*

Ocimum
a plant, *Ocimum sanctum* L. (Labiatae). A cult. mint: *katriiñ.*

Octans
stars in Octans: *Lo-raan-ṃwāṃwā-ko.*

October: *Oktoba.*

octopus: *kweet.*
a fish, devilfish, giant octopus: *kouj.*
a food, octopus smothered in grated coconut: *penkwe.*
fishing method, using weight with hook, octopus for bait, and dragging it on sandy bottom: *kōjọliṃ.*
octopus tentacles: *ko-in-kweet.*
to poke into a hole persistently at something, usually an octopus: *lekōn.*

odd: *bwe, kūḷaṃwe.*

odious: *wōjaan-kōmatōrtōr.*

odor: *bwii-, nām.*
bad odor: *bwiin-nana, bwiin-puwaḷ.*
body odor, disagreeable: *bbūḷapḷap.*
foul odor stench: *bwiin-puwaḷ.*
make odorous: *kōnāmnām.*
smell, body odor, disagreeable: *ajjiḷapḷap.*

of: *in.*

off: *jān.*
be off course: *buñ.*
come off of: *to.*
euphemistic reference to any of a variety of activities, mostly off-color: *mettorkaṇ.*
off beat: *kūḷaṃwe.*
off key, voice: *bōna.*
take off of fire: *ato.*

off and on: *pād o.*

offal: *kwōpej.*
guts, intestines, bowels, offal, innards: *ṃajñal.*

offend: *tipñōl.*
offended: *llu, lotaan, matōrtōr.*
offensive: *kōmatōrtōr, kōmmatōr.*

offer: *aje, jake, le-.*
a gathering of people to celebrate the onset of breadfruit season in summer by making offerings to Jebro, the god of breadfruit: *ṃaṃa.*
church offering: *jabawōt.*
offer sacrifice: *katok.*
offerings: *menin aje.*
to offer formally: *tilmaak.*

office: *wōpij.*

officer: *wōpija.*
officer of high rank: *kapen.*

offshoot: *ajāllik.*

offshore: *tarkijet.*

offspring
incapable of bearing offspring, of women only: *orañe, war.*
offspring of: *nāji-.*

often: *kut, lōñ alen, makijkij, mmakijkij.*
not often: *jọkkutkut.*
very often: *kkā.*

ogle: *kōmmāidik.*

oh
interjection: "Oh. Oh my. Darn it." (exclamation of mild surprise or disappointment)": *o.*
exclamation: "Oh my!": *edded.*

oil: *weiḷ.*
coconut cloth used to squeeze and extract oil from grated coconut: *jouneak.*
coconut oil: *pinneep.*
container of oil or water for use with royal whetstone: *ṇop.*
diesel oil: *tijeḷ.*
dry hair, not oily: *kuraañañ.*
hair smoothed with oil: *medọḷ.*
oil belonging to: *kapitō-.*
oil found under the shell of a turtle: *ao.*
oil oneself: *kkapit.*
oily: *maḷḷipen.*
oily hair: *medọḷ.*
press oil out of grated copra: *joniak.*
rub with oil as medical treatment: *pitpit.*
scrub self with coconut husk or oil: *bokwārijet.*

ointment: *kkapit.*
ointment of leaves and oil: *kūm̧ur.*

okay: *ekwe.*

old: *rūtto.*
get old and dilapidated due to continuous soaking in sea water: *luwajet.*
old chicken: *jenļap.*
old man: *ļaļļap.*
old man, term of respect: *aļap.*
old woman: *obajañ.*
old-fashioned: *m̧antin etto.*
old, of things: *m̧or.*
olden times: *ennāp, etto.*

omen: *bwijerro, kakōļļe, ttabōn.*

Omphalius
trochus, a shell, *Trochidae, Omphalius pfeifferi* or *Tristichotrochus haliarchus*. A shell, *Pleurotomariidae*: *likōppejdat.*

on: *ewe, i, ioo-.*
get on: *uwe.*
off and on: *pād o.*

once: *juon alen, juon iien.*

Onchidium
Nudibranchs, Onchidium sp: *pedobar.*

one: *juon.*
come one at a time: *iaļ aidik.*
go one at a time: *iaļ aidik.*
one another: *doon.*
one hundred pairs, fish or copra: *jikut.*
one thousand: *toujin.*
someone: *juon.*

onion: *anien.*

only: *wōt.*
only, indicating relative unimportance of activity: *bajjek.*

onrush: *ibeb.*

onset: *ibeb.*

onslaught: *ibeb.*

onward: *m̧aan.*

ooze: *tǫǫr.*
oozy: *kkōr.*

opelu
a fish, *opelu, Cecapterus* sp: *kauwe.*

open: *erļǫk, peļļǫk.*
eyes wide open: *kabūrōrō.*
hold open and up: *kōjjāl.*
open a bag or basket: *kōjjād.*
open a crack: *ļañ.*
open air: *nabōj.*
open eyes under water: *tumej.*
open the mouth: *waļañi.*
open-handed: *m̧m̧ool.*
spread legs wide open: *bōļñak.*

opening
opening of any container, hole, doorway, or cave, etc.: *māj, meja-.*
openings in a house causing drafts: *ajerwawa.*
possessive classifier, eyes, lids, openings, eyeglasses, masks, or goggles: *meja-.*
small opening: *tuwa.*
the opening between islets: *mej, mejje.*

operate: *bukwabok, jerbal, kōm̧m̧an, m̧adm̧ōd.*
operate an engine: *leinjin.*

Opheodesoma
sea cucumber, *Holothuroidea, Opheodesoma*: *jāibo.*

Ophiuchus
dark spot in the Milky Way beside theta in Ophiuchus: *Dāp-eo.*
gamma in Ophiuchus: *Bake-eo.*
stars in Ophiuchus: *Debwāāl-eo, M̧ade-eo-an-Tūm̧ur.*

opinion: *ļōmņak.*
have an opinion: *baab.*

opium: *wōpiem̧.*

Oplismenus
a plant, *Oplismenus compositus* (L.) Beauv: *wūjooj-in-Ep.*

opportune: *m̧m̧an.*

opportunity: *iien m̧m̧an.*
lie in wait to grab an opportunity: *kōppao.*
miss an opportunity: *waakļǫk.*

oppose: *dem̧ak, jum̧ae, pāpjel m̧ae.*

oppress
oppressed: *orā.*
oppression: *jjiped.*

optical
mirage, optical illusion, illusion: *jāmilur.*

optimism: *kijenmej.*
optimistic: *kije.*

option: *kkāālel.*

opulent: *m̧weiie.*

or: *ak.*

oral: *kōnono.*

orange
orange colored: *kio.*
orange, the fruit: *oran.*

orange spot tang
a fish, orange spot tang, *Acanthurus olivaceus*: *ael.*

orate: *wājepdik.*
oration: *kwaļǫk naan.*

orchestra: *paan.*

ordeal: *etalju.*
order: *laajrak.*
disorder: *pok.*
in good order: *meḷak.*
not in order: *ppeerir.*
orderliness: *koṇ.*
orderly: *koṇ.*
out of order, of machines: *wōla.*
put in order: *kkar, kwadikdik.*
well-ordered: *meḷeḷe.*
order: *wōtar.*
ordinal
word used to form phrases and ordinal numbers: *kein.*
ordinance: *kien.*
ordination: *kapitōn būriij.*
organ
organ of giant clam: *lām.*
organ, musical: *ọkwōn.*
organization: *doulul.*
head of a governmental organization: *koṃja.*
organize: *kkar.*
well-organized: *koṇ.*
orgasm: *diṃōṃ.*
orifice
cave, orifice, pit: *rọñ.*
origin: *jjino.*
original sin: *jerọwiwiin jolōt.*
originate: *jebar, jjino.*
Orion
Betelgeuse in Orion: *Ḷōkañebar.*
delta, epsilon, zeta, sigma Orionis.: *Jeljel.*
lambda, phi 1, phi 2 Orionis: *Jāli.*
stars in Orion: *Kouj.*
Bellatrix in Orion: *Ḷāātbwiinbar.*
ornament
ornament, trimmings: *inōknōk.*
ornaments: *kūṃaḷṃaḷ.*
ornery: *ṃṃaḷkaro.*
orphan: *atajinemjen.*
oscillate: *rọọl.*
osculate: *mejenma.*
osteopathy: *pitpit.*
Ostracion
a fish, boxfish, *Ostracion cubicus*: *būḷ.*
a fish, boxfish, *Ostracion sebae*: *pel.*
a fish, trunkfish, *Ostracion tuberculatus*: *pel.*
ostracize: *kalia.*
other: *bar jet, juon.*
a few others: *jet.*
each other: *doon.*
otherwise: *āinjuon.*
others: *bar jet.*
ouch
"Ouch!": *ekōḷōk, iā, ūō.*
interjection: "Ouch!" (pain or sexual pleasure): *ōttōt.*
ought to
ought to have: *kar.*
ounce: *aunij.*
our
our, dual inclusive: *arro.*
our, exclusive: *am.*
our, inclusive: *ad.*
ours: *ad, am, arro.*
oust: *kōkālọk.*
out: *jako.*
broke, out of money: *jar.*
come out of water: *ato.*
current flowing out: *aelik.*
get out: *diwōj.*
go out a passage: *ṃwelik.*
go out, of a light: *kkun.*
out of commission: *jorrāān.*
out of joint: *ir.*
out of order: *jorrāān.*
out of order, of machines: *wōla.*
out of reach: *jabjab.*
out of sight: *penjak.*
outside: *āliki-.*
put out a fire: *kkun.*
put someone out of a competition: *kupi.*
outboard
outboard motor: *injin ḷọk.*
with outboard engine: *ḷoon.*
outburst
outburst of laughter: *dekakḷọk.*
outcast: *rinana.*
outcome: *waḷọk.*
outdated: *ṃor.*
outdo: *ḷe.*
outdoors: *meḷaaj.*
outer
outer clothes: *anilik.*
outfit: *kōbwebwei-, koṃbani.*
outlandish: *kōjak.*
outlaw: *rinana.*
outline: *annañ.*
outnumber: *lōñ.*
outrageous: *kōmmatōr.*
outrigger: *kubaak.*
a game, racing toy outrigger canoes: *kariwutut.*
canoe part, line from top of mast to outrigger spar (*jojo* (**jewjew**)): *tokubaak.*

canoe part, outrigger platform: *ere, kōm̧ñūr.*
canoe part, outrigger spar: *jojo.*
canoe part, ties between spar and outrigger: *jojo.*
dimension of a canoe between hull and outrigger: *kōm̧ñūr.*
large outrigger canoe, for sailing: *tipñōl.*
outrigger goes underwater: *timaruk.*
outrigger sinks because too much weight is placed on it: *tōmrok.*
sail downwind with the sail on the south and the outrigger on the north: *tōmeañ.*
sail with outrigger out of water: *ām.*
sail with the outrigger on the south: *tōmrak.*
the outrigger side of a canoe: *retam.*
to bring up outrigger and hold it at 45 degrees while sailing: *kakkiāmem.*

outside: *lik, liki, nabōj.*

outsmart
outsmart, swindle: *Etao.*

outwit: *Etao.*

oval
long and oval: *uwaitoktok.*

ovation: *kabbokbok.*

oven: *obwin.*
a food, breadfruit baked in earth oven: *kōpjar.*
a food, diluted starch baked in coconut spathe in earth oven: *kōlo̧wutaktak.*
bake, usually in earth oven: *um̧um̧.*
cover an earth oven with stones: *ertak.*
cover up an earth oven with leaves and dirt: *kobal.*
earth oven: *um̧.*
native oven: *um̧.*
small oven or stove: *paaj.*
stick used to spread hot stones for earth oven: *tokrak.*
uncover an earth oven, usually when food therein is cooked: *jukok.*

over: *ioo-, ļo̧k, lōñ.*
kneel or bend over: *kapijpij.*
overflow: *llutōk.*
overhead: *lōñ.*
repeat over and over: *ālijinmen.*

overalls
bib-overalls: *būrijōōt.*

overanxious: *m̧m̧aelep.*
to lust, overanxious: *m̧ōm̧.*

overbearing: *kōbbo̧o̧jo̧j.*

overcast: *kōdo̧.*

overcoat: *kabba, kopā.*

overcome: *anjo̧, ibeb.*
be overcome: *raññaļo̧k.*
catch up with, overcome, overwhelm: *iabuñ.*

overcook
overcooked: *tuļaar.*

overcrowd
be overcrowded, of boats or vehicles (see *kaddoujuj*): *douj.*

overdecorate
be overdecorated: *to jān enōka-.*

overeat
overeat on fruitful land: *jjāāk.*

overexposure
spoiled from overexposure to air and sun: *m̧ōņakņak.*

overflow: *budeñ, ibeb, jieb-.*
overflow, water: *booļtōñtōñ.*
overflowing: *lutōkļo̧k.*

overhang: *maļtu.*

overhaul: *āe, an.*
test drive a new or overhauled vehicle: *likbad.*
test sail a new or overhauled vessel: *likbad.*

overlay
windward overlay of sail: *jā.*

overripe
overripe breadfruit: *meimed.*
overripe spoiled breadfruit: *māļo̧k.*
overripe, of breadfruit with seeds: *meimed.*
overripe, of breadfruit without seeds: *mejbak.*
very ripe, overripe, of breadfruit only: *mmed.*

overrun: *ibeb.*

oversee: *oņaak, peet.*

overshoot: *ļe.*

oversleep: *mājurlep.*

overstep
overstep authority: *bōkjab.*
overstep one's responsibilities: *weļo̧k.*

overthrow: *jeepepļo̧k.*

overtime: *obataim.*
work overtime: *ailparo.*

overturn: *okjak, ukok.*

overweight
overweight, obese: *tebu.*

overwhelm
catch up with, overcome, overwhelm: *iabuñ.*
overwhelmed (usually with negative emotion): *lañm̧wijidjid.*

overwork
overworked: *parōk.*
Ovula
Ovula costellatum: *libbukwe.*
Ovulidae
a shell, *Ovulidae*: *libbukwe.*
owe: *likjab, ṃuri.*
owl
a bird, short-eared owl, *Asio flammeus*: *lijeṃao, ṃao.*
own: *peek.*
own much land: *amḷap.*
own much land or real estate: *amṇak.*
own up: *kwaḷọk ṃool.*
oxygen: *akjijen.*
oyster: *di, eọr.*
small clam, oyster, a shell, *Arcidae, Scapharca inequivalvis* or *Anadara pilulu*: *kūkōr.*
pace
beat regular time to music, pace: *buñtōn.*
move slowly, snail's pace: *ṃōkaj jān oṃ.*
Pacific sailfish
a fish, Pacific sailfish: *wūjinleep.*
pacify: *jojomar, jojoon, jojoon bōro.*
pacify the winds and cause winds favorable for a sailing expedition: *kaurur jiañ.*
pacified: *aenōṃṃan, jokwane.*
pack: *ātet, limek, pakij.*
pack bags tightly: *ḷattuñ.*
packed: *lemlem, ñilñil.*
packed solid: *ñūñ.*
packet: *pakij.*
packing up: *limek.*
package: *jepjep, lemlem, limek, pakij.*
pad: *matmat.*
padding for comfort or for protection from dirt: *erer.*
paddle: *aōṇōṇ, jebwe, kiped.*
canoe part, piece of wood on leeside as guard against rubbing from steering paddle: *eran jebwe.*
drawing much water causing it to be hard to paddle or sail, nautical: *añōt.*
not paddle easily, of canoes (see *kōrkaakiie* (**kerkahakiyyẹy**)): *kōrkaakiia.*
paddle a canoe so as to hold it against current: *kab.*
paddle easily, of canoes (see *kōrkaakiia* (**kerkahakiyyah**)): *kōrkaakiie.*
steer canoe with paddle on right of stern to keep bow straight: *audik.*
steering method using a paddle: *ubtak.*
to paddle a canoe on the starboard side to change course: *auretam.*
use a paddle: *jebwebwe.*
paddling a canoe for pleasure: *kōrkaak.*
paddling canoe: *kōrkōr.*
padlock: *ḷak.*
pagan: *peikan.*
page: *alen, peij.*
turn pages or leaves: *ālāl.*
paid
get paid: *kōḷḷā.*
pail: *bakōj.*
pain: *metak.*
a sore, painful and malignant, usually located on the hands or feet: *jiṇo.*
interjection: "Ouch!" (Pain or sexual pleasure): *ōttōt.*
pain in testicles: *liklep.*
pain in the arm caused by throwing: *joñ.*
sharp pain as from a whip or a burn: *ṇṇōk.*
shriek in terror or pain: *wūdikke.*
writhe in pain: *iñimmaḷ, wūdikke.*
painstaking: *tiljek.*
paint: *wūno.*
coating, of paint: *bōrwaj.*
container, usually five-gallon paint bucket: *bat.*
dilute paint: *kapejlọk.*
paint or chop up to a line in canoe building: *atar.*
to paint: *wūno.*
pair: *pea.*
fifty pairs, fish or copra: *limakor.*
five pairs, fish or copra: *jabjet.*
forty pairs, fish or copra: *ākor.*
not paired off (see *uñ* (**wig**)): *jọuñ.*
one hundred pairs, fish or copra: *jikut.*
sixty pairs, fish or copra: *jiljinokor.*
ten pairs, fish or copra: *jọkden.*
thirty pairs, fish or copra: *jilikor.*
twenty pairs, fish or copra: *ruokor.*
two hundred pairs, fish or copra: *rukut.*
pal: *ṃōtta-.*
palate
palate of mouth: *ñat.*
pale: *o, u.*
pallet: *paḷōt.*
palm
a plant, tall coconut palm: *ni kenato.*

heart of palm: *jiab.*

palm
palm of hand: *lọpiden pā.*

Palmadusta
Palmadusta lutea: *likajjid.*

palpitation: *kkūṃkūṃ.*

palsy: *akā, mej ānbwin.*

pamper
a pampered child: *kaerer.*
be spoiled, of a pampered child: *kakōl.*
pamper a child so as to create undue attachment: *kaerer.*

pan
cook in a tin pan: *aintiin.*
cooking pan: *nāpe, paan.*

panacea: *wūno.*

Panax
common cultivated hedge, often (mis)called "Panax": *ut.*

pancake: *baankeek.*
unleavened pancake: *minor.*

pandanus
a bunch of dried pandanus leaves for thatch: *jiṃ.*
a food, flying fish with pandanus stuffing: *ḷatuṃa.*
a food, juice extracted from fresh pandanus: *jowaanroñ.*
a food, pandanus chips: *jekaka.*
a food, pandanus custard mixed with water: *jennōb.*
a food, pandanus juice cooked and preserved: *mokwaṇ.*
a food, pandanus pudding cooked in hot rocks: *del.*
a food, pandanus pulp and juice mixed with grated coconut and coconut oil (and optionally with arrowroot starch), wrapped in breadfruit leaves and boiled or baked: *peru.*
a food, watered down pandanus preserves: *rọkrok.*
a game, contest to see who can throw a sharp-pointed piece of dried pandanus root, about a yard long, farthest by skimming it on the ground once: *kajjeor.*
a game, diving for pandanus: *lijunaṃnaṃ.*
a game, pelting one another with lighted pandanus keys or coconut husks: *buwaddel.*
a plant, pandanus variety: *Ḷipjenkur.*
a plant, pandanus, a general name for any pandanus plant: *bōb.*
aerial roots of the pandanus: *liok.*
any wild pandanus: *edwaan.*
baked pandanus: *edouṃ.*
ball made from pandanus leaves: *anidep.*
be pricked by pandanus thorns: *ṃake.*
bear fruit, of pandanus: *wūd.*
best part of pandanus fruit reserved for chiefs: *ajjipek.*
bunch of pandanus keys: *ajjen.*
bundle that has been wrapped, sticks or pandanus leaves: *tūr.*
butt of pandanus key: *ṃak.*
cause pandanus to ripen: *okaliklik.*
chew pandanus: *wōdwōd.*
cooked pandanus: *edouṃ.*
cover pandanus to ripen: *poñpoñ.*
discarded pandanus key: *ār, pej.*
divination method, using knots in pandanus leaf: *bubu.*
dry key of pandanus fruit: *pej.*
dry pandanus or coconut leaves over fire in preparation for weaving: *katrar.*
fall off, of ripe pandanus keys: *po.*
flatten pandanus leaves: *karere.*
gather fallen pandanus leaves from ground for thatch or handicraft: *ppel.*
gather green pandanus leaves from trees: *bōlbōl.*
harvest first fruit of coconut, breadfruit, or pandanus: *akeọ.*
harvest pandanus: *jowe.*
in Ralik Chain, dried pandanus paste: *jāānkun.*
inedible portion near stem of pandanus or breadfruit: *ṃak.*
inner end of a single pandanus key: *kiār.*
land used for preserving food, especially pandanus: *jepāde.*
leaves near pandanus stem: *ainṃak.*
method of extracting pudding from cooked pandanus: *kilọk.*
pandanus blossom: *tūar.*
pandanus core: *ār.*
pandanus juice mixed with grated coconut, cooked into custard: *mokwaṇ duul.*
pandanus key, sprouted: *wūnpej.*
pandanus leaf: *maañ.*
pandanus leaf used for rolling cigarettes: *kwarkor.*
pandanus mat for sail cover: *atro.*
pandanus of: *daa-.*
pandanus rocket: *didiṃakōl.*
pandanus stump: *debọkut.*

pick pandanus: *okok.*
pick unripe pandanus: *okabur.*
pick wild pandanus: *kakidwaan.*
piece of pandanus roots cut and dried to be used as frame in weaving thatch: *tap.*
portion of fruit near stem of pandanus or breadfruit: *ainm̧ak.*
pounded stack of processed pandanus leaves: *noonon.*
pull keys off pandanus: *ļotļot.*
remove thorns from pandanus leaves: *iiaak.*
ripe, of pandanus: *owat.*
roll up, as dried pandanus leaves: *jāļjel.*
scraper for pandanus with three wooden legs and bowl set beneath: *peka.*
season for breadfruit and pandanus: *wōtōn.*
shoot of coconut, pandanus: *juubub.*
small flowers of pandanus, coconut, or other plants: *did.*
smallest breadfruit or pandanus remaining on tree at end of season: *ļajdeñ.*
strips of green coconut branches laid across a fire for warming pandanus leaves: *toļ.*
sweet smell, of ripe pandanus fruit: *bwiin-tōñal.*
thorns in a pandanus leaf: *m̧ake, m̧akur.*
to bleach pandanus leaves over the fire: *rar.*
to boil pandanus: *aintiin.*
to weave pandanus thatch: *wewā.*
tripod for juicing pandanus: *peka.*
two pandanus keys joined together: *piro.*
wrap pandanus fruit with coconut leaves to make it ripen: *kūtōb.*
a plant, *Pandanus carolinianus* cultigen: *Jọm̧win-atak, Ļōjokdād, Aelok, M̧aidikdik.*
a plant, *Pandanus fischerianus* (or hybrid) cultigen: *Wūnmaañ.*
a plant, *Pandanus fischerianus* X *Pandanus carolinianus* (hybrid) cultigen. (Stone): *Kūbwejeñōn.*
a plant, *Pandanus fischerianus* cultigen: *Ajbwirōk, Anm̧ōden, Annānu, Annenep, Anperia, Antakļōñar, Bōb-irooj, Būkōr, Buñbuñ, Edm̧am̧o, Edwaan-eṇ-an-Nelu, Jabloed, Jabōn-bok, Jorobbā, Jọibeb, Jọilokwaar, Kōmālij, Kōpnaan, Kūm̧lujen, Lañlōñ, Lepni, Lipjinmede, Lotọọn, Ļam̧tōr, Ļeikm̧aan, Ļōjepkọ, Ļōkōtwa, Ļōm̧ōeṇ, Ļōpo, Lōrro, Ļōtōl, M̧ōjāl, M̧ōjjelwōj, Maañurun, Nibuñ, Utōttōt.*
a plant, probably *Pandanus fischerianus* cultigen: *Joonmāāṇ, Kou, Loarm̧we.*

pang: *ṇṇōk.*

panic: *lōļñọñ, wiwijet.*

panties
women's panties: *jakkōlkōl.*

pantry: *pāāntōre.*

pants: *jedọujij.*
long pants: *tabtab.*
roll up pants: *kitak.*
underpants, men's: *jorm̧ōta.*
wear pants high on hips: *m̧uriej.*

panu
a fish, *uu* or *panu*: *m̧ōn-kiden.*

papaya: *keinabbu.*

paper: *peba.*
cigarette paper: *kwarkor.*
newspaper: *nuujpeba.*
toilet paper: *pij in kwiir.*

par: *joña-.*

parable: *būrabōļ, mālejjoñ, waan joñak.*

parachute: *rakka.*

parade
to march, parade: *m̧aaj.*

paradise: *pedetaij.*

paragraph: *pārokōrāāp.*

paralleled
unparalleled: *jej uwaan.*

paralyze
paralyzed: *mej ānbwin.*

Paramia
Paramia quinquekineata: *tōptōp.*

paraphernalia: *kōbwebwei-.*

parasite: *kij.*

parasol: *am̧bwidilā.*

parcel: *pakij.*

parch: *atiti.*

pare: *eọr.*

parent
a parent-in-law: *jelpa-.*
parent-child relationship: *jem̧nājin.*

park
to park: *baak.*

parrot: *kọkwe.*

parrotfish
Callyodon bataviensis: *audam̧.*
Callyodon microrhinos: *alwor.*

Callyodon pulchellus: *lala, pālpilikio.*
Scarus harid: *ekmouj.*
Scarus jonesi/sordidus: *mao, merā.*
Scarus vetula: *taburbur.*

parry: *pile, taar.*

part: *awetak, jabok, m̧ōtta-, matoļ.*
apart, divided into two parts: *rājet.*
at the upper part: *tulōn̄.*
fall apart: *jeepepļo̧k.*
lower part of tree, brush, or grass: *wūn.*
northern part: *tuean̄.*
part of: *wūje-.*
part, hair: *tono̧k.*
partly: *rājet.*
southern part: *turōk.*
supplementary part: *rejeta-.*
part of an island: *wata.*

partial: *jep, kalijekļo̧k.*
partially finished: *jipikpik.*

participate: *bōk kon̄aa-.*

particle
particles, scraps: *tipdikdik.*

particular: *kile.*
be choosy or particular: *kōrkōr ioon kūro.*
particularly: *ļaptata.*

partner: *kom̧bani, m̧ōtta-.*
partner of opposite sex: *kubaak.*

party
birthday party: *keemem.*
party, Marshallese style: *kam̧ōļo.*
taking gifts to a wedding, funeral, or party for guests to take home: *tōptōp.*
working party: *okun bade.*

Parupeneus
a fish, goatfish, *Parupeneus barberinus*: *m̧ōtal.*
a fish, goatfish, *Parupeneus sp*: *jorobbā.*

pass: *kiibbu, ļe.*
pass across: *kijoon.*
pass away: *bōk kakkije, jako.*
pass by: *ļļā.*
pass by, of clouds and rain: *peļaak.*
pass out: *jem̧ļo̧k.*
pass over: *kijoon.*
pass something around: *jaketo-jaketak.*
pass something to someone: *jjaak.*
pass thatch to one tying: *jemān aj.*
pass through: *deblo̧k.*
pass, in card games: *baaj.*
passed: *ļļā.*
to pass a crucial stage: *llemej.*

passage
boat passage on reef: *toorwa.*
boat passage through a reef: *to̧o̧r.*
currents around a passage: *aekijek.*
end of the reef at a passage: *tiete.*
go in a passage: *m̧weeaar.*
go out a passage: *m̧welik.*
passage into lagoon from ocean: *to.*
small passage between ocean and lagoon: *wea.*

passenger: *bajinjea.*

passion
arouse passion: *bun̄-kōļowa-.*

past
past tense: *ar, kar.*
past tense subordinate clause introducer: *ke.*

pasture: *maaj, meļaaj, wūjooj.*

pat
to pat gently: *boboor.*

patch: *karpen.*

pate
pate of head: *m̧o̧n̄.*

Patellidae
a shell, *Patellidae*: *jowakin.*
a shell, *Patellidae, Collisella grata*: *jidduul.*

path: *iaļ.*
path from house to beach: *mejeto.*
path from house to either beach: *mejate.*

pathetic: *kabbūrom̧ōjm̧ōj.*

patience: *kijenmej, meanwōd.*
patient: *kūtarre.*
impatient: *atebar.*
stay where one is at patiently: *likatōttōt.*
to watch patiently: *akade.*

patrol: *waj.*

pattern: *anōk, jon̄ak.*

pause: *bōjrak.*
pause to admire: *allo̧k.*

Pavo
Rediculus (alpha Pavonis): *Likin-Buwame.*

paw: *ne.*

pay: *kōļļā, ņaon̄ea-, peo̧o̧b.*
customary reimbursement given by anyone in return or exchange for food, living, or payment for medicine or priest-craft: *kabwijeran.*
group of people going to pay respects to a deceased: *tal.*
pay for: *kōļļā on̄ea-.*
pay out, nautical: *peaut.*
pay respects to a deceased: *āmej.*

pea-shooter: *lijjukwōlkwōl.*

peace: *aenōṃṃan.*
peaceful: *aenōṃṃan.*

peak: *ṃaan.*

peanut: *pinōt.*

pearl: *bōōr.*

pebble
a game, child's play using pebbles and shells as imaginary objects and characters: *lijjikin.*
a game, played with pebbles and ball, similar to dice game: *ḷuḷu.*

peck: *kūk.*

peculiar: *oktak.*
peculiarity: *abja.*

pedal
bicycle pedal: *patōḷ.*

peddle: *jobai.*

pedigree: *kadkad.*
look for the true pedigree: *jitdaṃ.*

peek: *allimōmō, kōjjaad.*

peel: *orjib.*
peel off the end of a coconut shoot: *kọudpak.*
strip or peel off one layer at a time: *ejej.*
to peel: *ākilkil, kakilkil.*

peep: *allimōmō, kōjjaad, rere.*

peer: *arrom, kewa, peḷo.*
to peer at: *kōlọtuwawa.*

peeve
peeved: *lotaan.*

Pegasus
stars in Pegasus: *Ḷak.*

pelvis: *doñ.*
movement of pelvis: *doñ.*

Pemphis
a plant, *Pemphis acidula* Forst: *kiej, kiejor, kōñe.*

pen: *peen.*
fountain pen: *bọọntōn peen.*
penmanship: *eḷtan pā.*
use a pen: *peenen.*

pen: *oror.*

penalize: *kaje.*

penalty: *kaje.*

pencil: *pinjeḷ.*
mark with a pencil: *rran.*

penetentiary: *kalbuuj.*

penetrate: *deblọk, dibuk, kapejlọk, mọọn, pejlọk.*
penetrate to the interior of an islet: *tōḷoñ.*

penicillin: *penejeḷōn.*

penis: *wōl.*
circumcised penis: *pāj.*
neck of the penis: *ṃọkwōd.*
penis, child speech: *kọkọ, kukkuk, kulālā.*
string under penis: *lil.*
tiny bumps on glans penis: *jarōj.*
uncircumcised penis: *kōkkōk.*

penny: *juon jāān.*
penny-pinching: *miin.*

pension: *jipañ.*

pensive
be silent and pensive: *kejakḷọkjeṇ.*

people: *armej.*
a group of people going to a place for a specific purpose: *aktal.*
a pile of corpses or fish or people: *ajeḷḷā.*
any group of people, as a class, unit or division: *jar.*
club of people: *doulul.*
common people: *armej waan, kajoor.*
die out, of plants, animals, or people: *ḷot.*
low-class people: *jeeknaan.*
those people (close to neither of us): *errāraṇ, erraṇ, erroro.*

pep: *keeñki.*

Peperomia
a plant, *Peperomia volkensii* C.: *dāpijdekā.*

pepper: *pepa.*
a plant, pepper, *Capsicum* sp.: *peba.*

perceive: *kile.*
perceive correctly: *bōbtowa.*
perceive indistinctly: *arrom.*

percent: *bōjjāān.*

perception
sensitive in perception: *loḷọkjeṇ.*

perch
a fish, Pacific sea perch, *Kuhlia taeniura* (Mejit.): *kōnān.*
a fish, perch, *Lutjanus fulviflamma*: *kālikrōk.*
perched: *jok.*

perfect: *karbōb, po ḷōma-, polel, wānōk, weeppān.*

perfective forms
—of *ālāl* (**yalyal**): *ālkōk.*
—of *ālkwōj* (**yalqej**): *ālokjak.*
—of *atartar* (**hatartar**): *atōrak.*
—of *baar* (**bahar**): *bbaar.*
—of *bobo* (**bęwbęw**) and of *bubu* (**biwbiw**): *bobo.*
—of *bubu* (**biwbiw**): *bujek.*
—of *dāpdep* (**dapdẹp**): *dāpijek.*
—of *ebeb* (**yebyeb**): *ebjak.*

—of *ejej* (yejyej)): *ejaak.*
—of *erer* (yeryer): *erōk.*
—of *iñiñ* (yigyig): *iñrōk, iñtōk.*
—of *jaļjaļ*: *mejaļ.*
—of *jebjeb* (jębjęb): *po.*
—of *jjioñ* (jjiyęg°): *jeñak.*
—of *jjuok* (jjiwek): *jokak.*
—of *kabwijer* (kabijęr): *bōjrak.*
—of *kajjuur* (kajjiwir): *jurōk.*
—of *keke* (kęykęy): *kijek.*
—of *kkiil* (kkiyil): *kilōk.*
—of *kōpopo* (kepewpew): *pojak.*
—of *kwarkor* (qarqęr): *korkor.*
—of *kwarkor* (qarqęr): *korak.*
—of *ļukut* (ļiqit): *ļoktōk.*
—of *lemlem* (lęmlęm): *limek.*
—of *loklok* (lęqlęq): *lokjak.*
—of *ņņooj* (ņņewej): *ņojak.*
—of *nukuj* (niqij): *nokjek.*
—of *obar* (webar) and of *koobob* (kewebweb): *obrak.*
—of *peoeo* (pewewyew): *potak.*
—of *peoeo* (peyewyew): *peo.*
—of *pinej* (pinęj): *penjak.*
—of *pok* (pęq): *poktak.*
—of *romrom* (r°emr°em): *romaak.*
—of *ruprup* (r°ipr°ip): *rup.*
—of *tōpar* (tepar): *tōprak.*
—of *ukok* (wikwęk): *okjak.*
—of *ukok* (wikwęk): *oktak.*

perforate: *karroņroņ.*

perform: *kōmman, madmōd, wōjak.*
mistake in performing a dance, song, or chant: *dujebwābwe.*
perform a feat: *lukor.*
perform a trick: *jibai.*
perform flawlessly: *wōnjak.*

perfume: *bōkā.*
drift nut, sweet smelling, used with coconut oil to make perfume: *ajet.*
make perfume: *kiloottōr, kōļotōr.*
perfume, imported only: *bōkāñaj.*
possessive classifier, perfume or lotion, or containers thereof: *kapitō-.*
put on perfume: *kkapit.*

perhaps: *bōlen.*

peril: *mej, uwōta.*

period
interim period between stormy seasons, usually a calm spell: *jo.*
period before dawn: *jimmarok.*
period between setting of sun and rising of moon: *meļokļok, meļoktakōn, tuujloñloñ.*
period between setting of sun and rising or moon: *meļoktak.*
period between tides: *aemman.*
period of adjustment: *iien kijone.*

period: *pidiiet.*

permission: *anemkwōj, mālim.*

permit: *kiibbu, kōtļok.*
permitted: *mālim.*

Perotrochus
Perotrochus teramachii or *Mikadotrochus schmalzi*: *likaabdoulul, likōppejdat.*

perpendicular: *ju.*
out of perpendicular: *oļā.*

perpetual: *indeeo.*

perplexed: *pok.*

persecution: *eñtaan.*

perservering
not perservering (see *niknik* (niknik)): *jāniknik.*

Perseus
a constellation: stars in Perseus: *Kapi-Ļak.*
nebula in Perseus: *Iju-māj-roumum.*

persevere: *kakkōt, kattūkat, kijejeto, kijenmej, mijmijelaļ.*
perseverance: *kūtarre, likōk.*

persist: *kakkōt.*
why persist...?: *jaam.*
persistent: *kiliddāp.*
do something persistently: *ijuboñ-ijuraan.*

person: *armej.*
a person, unnamed: *men.*
a vain person: *utļōm.*
high-born person: *arōmman.*
high-class person: *arōmman.*
person from: *ri-.*
person killed and buried with a deceased chieftain to accompany him on his journey to a different world: *ura.*
person or thing that causes trouble or bad luck: *jona.*
person who: *ri-.*
person who carries weight in his speech due to social status: *ļajjuur.*
person who is not "in" or "with it": *ikōnālkinmwio.*
person who is notable: *kāājāj.*

personality: *bōnja-.*

personnel: *rijerbal.*

perspire: *menokadu.*
perspiration: *menokadu.*
perspiration beads: *būļuuddik.*

Perstolida
Perstolida coffea/ursellus: *likajjid.*

persuade: *kipel.*
persuaded: *reel.*
persuasive: *aejemjem.*
pertain: *tōllọk.*
pertinent: *tōllọk.*
perturb
perturbed: *inepata.*
pervade: *tōḷoñ.*
pervert
perverted: *jebwābwe.*
pessimism: *bbeer.*
pessimistic: *kajjikur, kōrraat, perper.*
pest: *ḷōkatip, rinana.*
pester: *ikien.*
pet: *jibwi, nājnej.*
a pet bird that flies away and never returns: *lumọọrḷọk.*
duty of taking care of a natural or adopted child or pet or domesticated animal: *nāji.*
pet name: *ātdik.*
pet of: *jibwi-, nāji-.*
possessive classifier, children, pets, money, watches, or Bible: *nāji-.*
to keep as a pet: *nājnej.*
petiole
stalk, leafstem, petiole: *kōḷā.*
petite: *kādik.*
petition: *kajjitōk, owar.*
petticoat: *likko.*
petty: *jiddik.*
pew: *jea.*
Phaethon
a bird, red-tailed tropicbird, *Phaethon rubricauda*: *ḷokwājek.*
a bird, white-tailed tropicbird, *Phaethon lepturus*: *jipkorōj.*
Phalium
Morum macandrewi/teramachii or *Bezoardicella decussata/areola* or *Phalium glauca*: *jilel.*
phase: *alen.*
fifth moon phase: *marokiddik.*
first moon phase: *jetmar.*
fourth moon phase: *meḷọkḷọk.*
moon phase after *jetmar*: *meḷoktak.*
moon phase after *marokiddik*: *maroklep.*
moon phase after *meḷọkḷọk*: *marokiddik.*
moon phase after *meḷoktak*: *meḷoktakōn, tuujloñloñ.*
moon phase after *meḷoktakōn*: *meḷọkḷọk.*
phases in medical treatment starting with the second: *bōrwaj.*
second moon phase: *meḷoktak.*
sixth moon phase: *maroklep.*
third moon phase: *meḷoktakōn, tuujloñloñ.*
Philistine
Philistine, hypocrite: *toojin edwaan.*
phlebotomy: *kadkad.*
phlegm: *medaekek, melkwarkwar, mmed.*
phlegmatic: *mejjeeḷ.*
phone: *teiñwa.*
phonograph: *jukoñki, kūrababboon.*
phonograph record: *deekto.*
phony: *toojin edwaan.*
phosphate: *bọọjpet, diiñko.*
phosphorescence
fishing method, line fishing at night, jerking the line to cause phosphorescence in water to attract fish to the bait: *kōjjaromrom.*
phosphorescent: *aḷak.*
photo: *pija.*
photo album: *bokun pija.*
Phsalis
a plant, herb, *Phsalis angulata*: *kaōrōr.*
Phthirius
crab louse, *Phthirius pubis*: *kijdepak.*
Phyllantus
a plant, flower, *Phyllantus niruri* (Takeuchi): *jiljino awa.*
physical: *ānbwin.*
coordinated, physically: *util.*
examine, physically: *kakōlkōl.*
physical stimulation: *kōḷo.*
physically strong: *dejeñ, dipen.*
unable to endure physically: *ñatñat.*
physique: *rọkwōj.*
decreasing in size, as of physique: *tor.*
piano: *piano.*
play piano: *piano.*
pick: *ḷotḷot.*
pick breadfruit with a stick: *kōṃkōṃ.*
pick coconuts: *enōk.*
pick flowers: *rur.*
pick green coconuts from tree: *entak.*
pick out: *kkāālel.*
pick out food from teeth: *arar.*
pick out splinters: *arar.*
pick pandanus: *okok.*
pick unripe pandanus: *okabur.*
pick up bits of rubbish: *kintak.*
pick wild pandanus: *kakidwaan.*
pick off someone: *jjoñjoñ.*
pick-up
pick-up truck: *pekab.*

picket: *dumej.*
picket boat: *ļoon.*
pickle: *pikōļ.*
pickled radish: *taikoñ.*
picnic: *ļōppekañkūr, piknik.*
picture: *annañ, pija.*
draw a picture: *pija.*
moving picture: *pija m̧akūtkūt.*
pidgin: *pijin.*
pie: *bae.*
piece: *m̧ōtta-, wūd.*
piece of: *tipen.*
small pieces: *tipdikdik.*
tear into fine pieces: *imkilkil.*
gradually, little by little, piecemeal: *jidik illo̧k jidik.*
pier: *wab.*
pierce: *dibuk, il, kapejlo̧k, lōlō, pejlo̧k, wākar.*
pierce ears: *il.*
pierce with husking stick or spear: *ddeb.*
pierce with knife: *bwiār.*
pierce, as an unhusked coconut in order to drink: *wāāpep.*
to pierce: *wie.*
piercing
piercing sound: *ļļaaj.*
pig: *piik.*
pigeon: *m̧uļe.*
a bird, Micronesian pigeon, *Ducula oceanica*: *m̧uļe.*
piha
a fish, *piha, Spratelloides delicatulus*: *aol.*
pile: *ejouj.*
a pile of coconuts: *jokā.*
a pile of corpses or fish or people: *ajeļļā.*
build up a pile of rocks: *ppe.*
huge pile, as of coconuts: *m̧ōļōbbā.*
pile of coconuts knocked down from tree: *nnōk.*
pile of earth: *ubatak.*
pile of husks near husking stick: *bweo.*
pile of stones: *eakļe.*
pile up: *ejaak, ejej, jojoon, pānuk.*
pile up plant materials: *m̧uuj.*
to crumble a mound or pile as of sand: *rōm̧.*
pilfer: *jam̧, ko̧o̧t.*
pill: *batin.*
pillar: *joor.*
pillow: *pet.*
provide a pillow for: *ņapitō-.*
use a pillow: *petpet.*
pilot: *baiļat.*
a fish, pilot fish, *Naucrates ductor*: *ikuut.*
a fish, shark pilot, *Echeneis naucrates*: *ļattil pako.*
pimple: *taeo.*
goose pimples: *ko tok kili-.*
pin
bobby pin: *piin.*
safety pin: *piin.*
straight pin: *niiļ.*
wear a pin: *piinin.*
windmill, pinwheel: *lodideañ.*
pincers: *peenjej.*
pinch
pinch with fingernails: *kinji.*
pinching, with finger: *apap.*
pine
pine driftwood: *jeļaar.*
pine
pine after someone or something: *ļokwanwa.*
to pine: *likakōj.*
to pine after: *kālo̧k iļo̧kwan.*
pineapple: *peinabōļ.*
pink: *kōn̦o, piiñ.*
pinky: *addi-dik.*
pious
believe, faith, creed, pious: *tōmak.*
pipe: *baib.*
smoking pipe: *baid.*
Pipturus
a plant, tree *Pipturus argenteus* (Forst. F.) Weddell. (Urticaceae): *arm̧we.*
Pisces
Formalhaut in Pisces Austrinus: *Mejabwil.*
stars in Pisces: *Bo̧ro.*
Pisonia
a plant, tree, *Pisonia grandis* R. Br. (Nyctaginaceae). A large hard wood tree. N: *kañal.*
pistol: *lijjukwōlkwōl, likajik.*
piston: *pijtoñ.*
pit
cave, orifice, pit: *ro̧ñ.*
pit for bird fight: *nit.*
pit for soaking coconut husks for making sennit: *to.*
pit in which fruit is buried to ripen: *wōn.*
shelter pit, air raid: *ro̧ñ.*
smell of pit for soaking coconut husks: *būto.*
pitch
high-pitched sound: *ļļaaj.*

pitch
  pitch-black: *diboñ, innijek, maroklep.*
pitch: *kadkad.*
  baseball pitcher: *pijja.*
pitch
  pitch, of a boat: *m̧m̧ōt, m̧ōt.*
  toss and pitch on the sea: *kōm̧te, m̧witaak.*
pitcher: *pijja.*
pith: *bol̗.*
pitiful: *kabbūrom̧ōjm̧ōj.*
pitter-patter
  pitter-patter of rain: *m̧m̧ōn̗m̧ōn̗.*
pity: *būrom̧ōj.*
  have pity: *tūriam̧o.*
  seek pity: *kōjjeram̧ōlm̧ōl.*
place: *llik, pek.*
  a place for fishing canoes on an island: *mien.*
  a place in front of: *m̧aa-.*
  a taboo place reserved for chiefs: *jiadel.*
  at that place (close to neither of us): *ijekoko, ijjiien̗, ijjuweo.*
  certain places for chiefs only and forbidden to the commoner: *mo.*
  displace: *poktak.*
  place for making love, usually in bushes: *jik.*
  place name: *Bōl̗au, Boonpe, Iaab, Iñlen, Jāipaan, Jam̧uwa, Karol̗āin, Kujjae, L̗ora, M̧adianna, Nawōdo, Nukne, Rita, Ruk.*
  place of: *jiki-.*
  place where frigate birds sleep in trees: *m̧wilik.*
  replace: *bōk jikin.*
  take the place of: *bōk jikin.*
  that place (close to neither of us): *ijen̗.*
  this place: *ije, ijin.*
  this place (close to me): *ijjiiō.*
  those places: *ijoko.*
  those places (close to neither of us): *ijekākan̗, ijekan̗.*
placenta: *kiliblib, pej.*
plague: *mej, nañinmej.*
plain: *alikkar, jepa, mel̗el̗e.*
plait: *pirōkrōk.*
  crossed in weaving or plaiting: *idaaptōk.*
plan: *annañ, jekaboot, kkar, kōllejar, pepe.*
plans: *l̗ōmn̗ak.*
plane: *bal̗uun.*
  a toy, coconut hydroplane: *wūdādo.*

dive of birds or planes: *lōkā.*
dive, of planes: *lōrak.*
fighter plane: *jen̗toki.*
fleet of canoes, ships, or planes: *inej.*
propeller of plane or ship: *pikpik.*
ride on a plane: *kā-.*
waves of ships or planes: *ibeb.*

plane
  carpenter's plane: *pilein.*
  plane surface: *pik.*
planet: *iju.*
  a star (planet), Evening Star, Venus (evenings only): *Maalal.*
  a star (planet), Morning Star, Venus (mornings only): *Jurōn-Jemān-Kurlōñ.*
plank: *al̗al̗, rā.*
plant: *kallib.*
plants
  Annona muricata L. (Annonaceae). The sour-sop: *jojaab.*
  Asclepias curassavica (Ebon): *kabbok.*
  Asplenium nidus L. (Pteridophyta): *kartōp.*
  Barringtonia asiatica (L.) Kurz. (Barringtoniaceae): *wōp.*
  Caesalpinia pulcherrima L.: *jeimōta.*
  Calophyllum inophyllum L. (Guttiferae): *jijo, lukwej.*
  Canavalia spp. (Leguminosae): *marl̗ap.*
  Centella asiatica (L.) Urban (Umbelliferae): *mariko.*
  Clerodendrum inerme (L.) Gaertn. (Verbenaceae): *wūlej.*
  Cordia subcordata Lam. (Boraginaceae): *kōn̗o.*
  Crinum asiaticum L. (Amaryllidacea). The large common spider lily cult. As hedges: *kieb.*
  Cyperus ferax: *būkōr.*
  Edwaan: *edwaan.*
  Eleusine indica (L.) Gaertn: *katejukjuk.*
  Euphorbia heterophylla L. (Euphobiaceae): *nukne.*
  Euphorbia thymifolia L. (Ebon): *dāpijbok.*
  Ficus carica L. (Moraceae): *wōjke-piik.*
  Fleurya ruderalis (Forst. F.) Gaudichaud. (Urticaceae): *neen kōtkōt.*
  Gomphrena globosa: *abl̗ajtiiñ.*
  Gossypium barbadense L. (Malvaceae): *kotin.*

Guettarda speciosa L. (Rubiaceae): *utilomar.*
Hymenocallis littoralis: *kiebin wau.*
Inocarpus edulus: *kūrak.*
Lumnitzera littorea: *kimeme.*
Messerschmidia argentea (L.F.) I. Johnston: *kiden.*
Mirabilis jalapa L. (Nyctaginaceae): *emān-awa.*
Morinda citrifolia L. (Rubiaceae): *kalenen.*
Morinda citrifolia L. (Rubiaceae): *nen.*
Nephrolepis acutifolia similar to the familiar "Boston fern": *anm̧ōkadede.*
Nephrolepis biserata (Sw.) Schott. Namorik. Boston fern: *baidik.*
Ochrosia oppositifolia (Lam.) K. Schum. (Apocynaceae): *kōjbar.*
Ocimum sanctum L. (Labiatae). A cult. Mint: *katriin̄.*
Oplismenus compositus (L.) Beauv: *wūjooj-in-Ep.*
Pandanus carolinianus, see *pandanus.*: *wūjooj-in-Ep.*
Pandanus fischerianus, see *pandanus.*: *wūjooj-in-Ep.*
Pemphis acidula Forst.: *kiej, kiejor, kōn̄e.*
Peperomia volkensii C.: *dāpijdekā.*
Plumeria acuminata Ait. (Apocynaceae): *meria.*
Portulaca: *kūran̄.*
Pseuderanthemum atropurpureum (Bull.) Baily. Cult. Hedge plant: *tirooj.*
Psilotum nudum: *martok.*
Russelia juncea (Scrophulariaceae): *albokbōr̨or̨o.*
Scaevola frutescens (Mill.) Krause: *kōņņat.*
Sida fallax Walpers: *kio.*
Sonneratia caseolaris: *buļaboļ.*
Sophora tomentosa L. (Leguminosae): *kille.*
Soulamea amara Lam. (Simarubaceae): *kabwijlōn̄.*
Suriana maritima L. (Simarubaceae): *n̄en̄e.*
Sybedrella nodiflora (L.) Gaertn: *bwilbwilikkaj.*
Synedrella nodiflora, a small yellow fld. Composite weed: *kinwōj.*
Terminalia catappa L. (Combretaceae): *kotōl.*
Vernocia cinerea (L.) Less.: *jān-aelōn̄-n̄an-aelōn̄.*
Vigna marina (Burm.) Merrill. (Leguminosae): *markinenjojo.*
Wedelia biflora (L.) DC. (Compositae): *markūbwebwe.*
Ximenia americana L. (Oclacaceae): *kālōklōk.*
Saccharum officinarum L. Sugar cane (Gramineae).: *tǫ.*
a general term for banana: *pinana.*
a grass: *pādālijm̧aan.*
a grass, prickly: *lōklōk.*
a shrub with red flowers: *kōtōmānlimpok.*
a tree: *peļo.*
arrowroot, *Tacca leontopetaloides* (L.) Ktze.: *m̧akm̧ōk.*
banana variety: *Abōļ, Jilubukwi, Jǫǫk, Jǫrukwōd, Ļōktaan, M̧ōkadkad.*
banana variety (Takeuchi): *Aelōn̄-kein, Jeina, Kilbōt, Ļōjennom̧aj, Mile.*
breadfruit variety: *Bukdǫļ, Mākinono, Mejenwe, Mejwaan, Metete, Petaaktak.*
breadfruit variety (Takeuchi): *Kūbwedoul, Kūtroro, Mābat, Mādak, Mādik, Māikwe, Mākwōle, Mām̧we, Māron̄, Mejidduul, Mejwa, Nōn̄nōn̄.*
citrus, lime: *ļaim̧.*
coconut: *Ni Iaļo.*
coconut variety: *Kōņǫuwe, Ni Bōn, Ni Būrōrō, Ni Kadu, Ni Lǫurō, Ni M̧ōl, Ni Maro, Ni Mir.*
coconut variety (Takeuchi): *Ni Lōklōk, Ni Mouj, Ni Ram.*
fern, *Microsorium scolopendria* Burm. F. Copeland: *kino.*
flower, *Angelonia salicariaefolia*: *jab meļǫkļǫk.*
flower, *Hemigraphis reptans*: *utilōm̧jān.*
flower, *Jussiaea suffruticosa*: *utilolōb.*
flower, *Nerium oleander*. L: *oļiaanta.*
flower, *Phyllantus niruri*: *jiljino awa.*
general term for all varieties of coconut trees and fruit: *ni.*
general term for bananas, *Musa sapientum* L. (Musaceae): *keepran̄.*
general term for flower of any hedge plant: *ut.*
general term for grass or *Ittaria elongata*, actually an epiphytic, penoulous fern: *wūjooj.*
general term for seaweed. *Thalassia*

hemprichii (Ehrenb.) Aschers.: *wūjooj-in-lọjet.*
general term for the breadfruit, *Artocarpus incisus* (Thunb.) L. F. Moraceae: *mā.*
general word for tree: *wōjke.*
grass, *Thuarea involuta*: *kakkūm̧kūm̧.*
herb, *Phsalis angulata*: *kaōrōr.*
hibiscus, *Hibiscus tiliaceus* L. (Malvaceae).: *ḷọ.*
lantana: *ḷaņtōna.*
mangrove, *Bruguiera conjugata* (L.) Merrill: *joñ.*
mangrove, *Sonneratia caseolaris*. In mangrove depressions: *kōnpat.*
marsh grass, *Cyperus javanicus* Houtt: *wūjooj-in-eoon-bōl.*
miscellaneous plants: *Būkien, Jọliō, jidkok, kāmeñ, kaatat, pedọḷ.*
pandanus cultigen: *Aij, Ajoḷ, Aḷḷañinwa, Aḷḷorkaņ, Anbūri, Anbwilwa, Anidep, Anjeer, Anjiio, Ankōnār, Anlojet, Anuujjeep, Anuwōt, Aojañ, Atinek, Bōb-bōņwa, Bōjbōj, Bōrọk, Edinij, Edwaan-eņ-an-Lōḷtok, Luwaju, Edwaan-in-likin-M̧ōnkwōlej, Edwaan-in-lọurō, Ekeņ, Elpeekdu, Jabroñjake, Jabtōkā, Jidpān, Jikōpeo, Jiḷōbbar, Jilelwōj, Jọinin, Jọlije, Jọm̧ōdān, Jọm̧win-jekad, Jọm̧win-joñ, Kabaj, Kapjulaḷ, Kilin-ek, Kinwum̧, Kōbbok, Koperwa, Kūrañ, Ḷakiwa, Lim̧aan, Lọjikōt, Lọpiñpiñ, Luwaju, Ḷawōden, Ḷipjenkur, Ḷōjm̧ao, Ņadepak, Pānuk, Tōbọtin, Wūnjeem̧, kūborbor.*
pandanus cultigen (Takeuchi): *Būrōk, Edwaan-eņ-an-Limaan, Edwaan-in-Būkōr, Edwaan-in-Jọibeb, Edwaan-in-M̧wejok, Edwaan-in-Matoḷej, Ėkke, Innintok, Jakōmen, Jatūrwe, Julele, Juriātak, Korōjjaak, Ḷapukor, Ḷōjoor, Ḷokwakōj, Lijepen, Mānnikkiden, Metaat, Pilele, Tujuon, Wūninnin.*
pandanus, a general name for any pandanus plant: *bōb.*
papaya, *Carica papaya* L. F.: *keinabbu.*
pepper, *Capsicum* sp.: *peba.*
plant with a single leaf: *aijo.*
sweet potato, *Ipomoea batatas*: *piteto.*
tall coconut palm: *ni kenato.*
taro variety: *Kōtak, Kubwilkōn, Wōt-waan, Wōtaad, Wōtaan.*
taro variety, *Xanthosoma*: *Wōtin Kapilōñ, Wōtin Ruk.*
taro variety, *Alocasia macrorrhiza* (L.) Sweet. (Araceae). In the same family as taro and Cyrtosperma: *wōt.*
taro variety, *Colocasia*: *Jibabwāi.*
taro, general term: *iaraj.*
toadstool, *Auricularia ampla* Persoon and other earlike *Basidiomycetes* (fungi). : *lọjilñin kijdik.*
tree *Pipturus argenteus* (Forst. F.) Weddell. (Urticaceae): *arm̧we.*
tree, *Allophylus timorensis* (DC.): *kūtaak.*
tree, *Ficus tinctoria* Forst: *tōpdo.*
tree, *Hernandia nymphaeifolia* (Presl) Kubitzki (Hernandiaceae): *piñpiñ.*
tree, *Intsia bijuga*: *kubōk.*
tree, *Ixora carolinensis* (Val.) Hosokawa (Rubiaceae): *kajdo.*
tree, *Pisonia grandis* R. Br. (Nyctaginaceae). A large hard wood tree. N: *kañal.*
tree, *Premna corymbosa* (Burm. F.) Rottl: *kaar.*
tree, *Terminalia litoralis*: *kkōñ.*
vine, *Cassytha filiformis* L. (Lauraceae).: *kaōnōn.*
vine, *Cucurbita pepo* L. (Cucurbitanceae): *baañke.*
vine, *Ipomoea tuba*: *marpeḷe.*
vine, *Triumfetta procumbens* Forst. F. (Tiliaceae): *atat.*
die out, of plants, animals, or people: *ḷot.*
immature taro plant: *il.*
pile up plant materials: *m̧uuj.*
plant of: *kōtka-.*
plant or tree growth from old root or after old branch of tree has been cut down: *ḷor.*
plantation plantings: *jitlọk.*
plants: *keinikkan.*
prepare bait from a plant: *kabūt.*
rich, of soil or plant: *kimuur.*
smell of dead plants in water: *juoñ.*
to girdle a plant: *kōnar.*
to plant: *kkat.*
underground section of a plant: *debọkut.*

plastic: *bōd, būḷajtiik.*

plate: *kōnnọ, pileij.*

platform
build a platform: *ppe.*
canoe part, outrigger platform: *ere, kōm̧ñūr.*
canoe part, platform over the lee side, opposite the outrigger side: *rọñ.*

fishing method, pole fishing from a raised platform or tripod used for fishing: *okwa.*
platform for drying copra: *jād.*

Platichthys
a fish, starry flounder, *Platichthys stellatus*: *bale.*

play: *ikien, kkure.*
a game, child's play using pebbles and shells as imaginary objects and characters: *lijjikin.*
play baseball: *iakiu.*
play cards: *kaaj.*
play cards for stakes: *pile.*
play checkers: *jekab.*
play kickball: *anidep.*
play marbles: *kōjjobaba.*
play marbles for keeps: *lukkuun.*
play music: *kōjañjañ.*
play music on radio or phonograph: *jañ.*
play piano: *piano.*
play poker: *pile.*
play practical jokes: *ikien.*
play volleyball: *baļeboo̧ļ.*
playing cards: *kaaj.*
seldom play (see *kkure* (**qqirẹy**)): *jo̧kkurere.*

playboy: *mejpata.*

playground: *kūraaņto, wūntoba.*
playground for demons: *meļaļ.*

plea: *kajjitōk.*

plead: *owar.*

pleasant: *kaṃōņōņō, kattōñtōñ, ļļajkōnkōn, llejkōnkōn.*
pleasantly cool: *lladikdik.*
unpleasant sensation: *mmāālel.*

please: *kōņaan.*
displease: *ļōkatip, llotaan.*
please, would you kindly: *ṃōk.*
displeased: *inepata.*
pleasing: *ṃṃan, mmejaja.*
pleasing to the eye: *ppānpān.*
pleasure: *ṃōņōņō.*
interjection of displeasure used only by women: *ōjjeti-.*
interjection: "Ouch!" (pain or sexual pleasure): *ōttōt.*
interjection: expression of sexual pleasure: *ōrrōr.*
make a sound of pleasure while sleeping because of good dreams: *jeja.*

pleat: *kobak.*

Plectropomus
a fish, bass, *Plectropomus truncatus*: *akajin, jo̧we, jowanuro̧ñ.*

pledge: *kalliṃur.*

Pleiades
a star, eta in Taurus (Pleiades): *Jebro̧, Jeļeilōñ.*

plenty: *ļap, lōñ.*
plentiful: *aļakiie, eojaļ, lutōkļo̧k.*

Pleurotomariidae
trochus, a shell, *Pleurotomariidae*: *likaabdoulul.*
trochus, a shell, *Trochidae, Omphalius pfeifferi* or *Tristichotrochus haliarchus*. A shell, *Pleurotomariidae*: *likōppejdat.*

pliable: *mañōtñōt, pedañōtñōt.*

pliant: *mañōtñōt.*

pliers: *peenjej.*

plot: *ļam.*
instrument for plotting courses, nautical: *kein kōttōbalbal.*
plot a course: *kkar, kōttōbalbal.*

plover
a bird, golden plover, *Pluvialis dominica*: *kwōlej.*
a bird, golden plover, black variety, in breeding plumage: *ļakeke.*

pluck: *tuññūli.*
pluck feather or hair (Ralik only): *imkilkil.*
pluck feathers: *tūṃṃo̧ņ.*
pluck feathers from a bird: *ttemakil.*
pluck leaves from midrib of coconut fronds: *ttemakil.*
pluck out eyes: *itūk.*
pluck ripe coconuts: *kōpālele.*
pluck, of fruit: *ļotļot.*

plug: *bo̧o̧r.*
plugged: *bo̧rōk.*

plumeria: *meria.*

plump: *uļūtļūt.*

plunder
plunder after battle: *rakōm.*
plunder, clean out: *ropāj.*
to plunder: *rakim.*

plunge
plunge into the sea: *roļo̧k.*
plunge of a canoe or ship: *ṃōt.*

plus: *koba.*

Pluvialis
a bird, golden plover, *Pluvialis dominica*: *kwōlej.*

plywood: *būļāwut.*

poach: *ļe eoon eṃ.*

pocket: *bōjo̧.*
stick hand into pocket, hole, or crack: *rrwe.*
pocket knife: *ņaib.*

poem: *boem̧.*

point: *jabōn.*
point head downwards: *kalōlō.*
point in all directions: *toor.*
point of: *jabwe.*
point of no return: *jerakiaarļap.*
point out: *ba kajjie-.*
point out something (to someone): *jitōñ.*
pointed: *kkañ.*

poise
poised: *jeļā kōppeļak.*

poison: *baijin.*
poisoned by eating crab: *iabaru.*
poisonous fish: *ikaarar.*
poisonous, of fish: *kadek.*

poke: *ddāil, debdeb, iuun, tōñōl, tuññūli.*
poke with something: *arar.*
to poke into a hole persistently at something, usually an octopus: *lekōn.*

poker
a flush in poker: *peļaj.*
ante, in poker: *laļ.*
call a bet in poker: *wadu.*
have four of a kind in poker: *ļāān.*
play poker: *pile.*
straight, in playing poker: *tōreej.*

Polaris: *Dunen-eañ, Lim̧anm̧an.*
posts of Polaris: *Jurōn-Lim̧anm̧an.*

pole: *joor.*
bundle of long objects such as spears, fish poles, etc.,: *tūr.*
fish pole: *bwā.*
fishing method, fish with a pole: *kōbwābwe.*
fishing method, pole fishing along the beach or shore: *ttoor.*
fishing method, pole fishing for goatfish: *kadjo.*
fishing method, pole fishing from a raised platform or tripod used for fishing: *okwa.*
fishing method, pole fishing on barrier reef edge at low tide on dark nights: *juunboñ.*
fishing method, pole or line fishing using no bait but simply jerking the line in the hope of hooking a fish by chance: *kāājrabōl.*
fishing method, use fishpole at night: *kappej.*
fishing method, use fishpole at night with either lure or bait: *tto.*
fishing method, use fishpole at the reef edge and fish for *kidiej*: *kakidiej.*
fishline, on a pole: *mejje.*
flagpole: *juron bōļeak.*
pole for poling in shallow water: *kōbōj.*
poling in shallow water with a pole: *kōbōjbōj.*

police: *bwilijmāāņ.*

policy: *kien, kōl.*

polio: *boļio.*

polish: *kāilar.*
polish (with causative prefix): *jatōltōl.*

politics: *kien.*

pollute
polluted: *ttoon.*

Pollux
Castor and Pollux in Gemini: *Iju-kuwaj-aiļip.*

Polydactylus
a fish, *moi, Polydactylus sexfilis*: *atkadu.*

Polyscias
esp: *Polyscias guilfoylei* (Bull Bailey) or *P. Scutellaria* (Burm. F.) Fosb. (Araliaceae): *ut.*

Pomacentrid
a fish, *Pomacentrid*: *bakōj.*

pomade
hair pomade: *kūriijin kkapit.*

pompadour: *kōbbǫk.*

pompano
a fish, pompano, *Trachinotus bailloni*: *m̧ōļojetak.*
a fish, pompano, *Trachinotus bailloni*: *kauwe.*

pompous: *jājjāj.*

pond
pond on reef where fish are caught when tide goes out: *tǫ.*
pond with many fish: *lōb.*

ponder: *ļōmņak.*

pontoon: *baantuun.*

pool: *ae.*
royal bathing pool in old days: *juwadel.*
shallow pool on reef: *jalōb.*
small pool on reef at low tide, or in interior of island: *ļwe.*

pool: *piliet.*

pooped: *orā.*

poor: *jeram̧ōl.*
of poor quality: *ļam waan.*
poor quality: *om̧oja.*
poor soil: *ļǫurō.*

pop: *bokkoļǫk.*
popping sound: *ņǫb.*
popping sound made when squashing lice: *noñ.*

pop-up
pop-up, in baseball: *tōkai.*

popular: *kattōñtōñ, ļļajkōnkōn, llejkōnkōn, wōlbo.*
popularity: *aneptok.*

porch: *maļto, tōñaak.*

porcupine fish
a fish, porcupine fish, *Diodon hystrix*: *jabōnke, ṃōjañūr.*

pore: *rǫñ.*

porgy
a fish, porgy, *Gnathodentex aurolineatus*: *tūñad.*

pork: *kanniōkin piik, piik.*

porpoise: *ke.*
bed of fronds on which the tails of porpoises are placed: *kin.*
fishing method, for porpoises: *jibke.*

port: *aba.*
canoe part, after-part when outrigger is on port side: *jabdik.*
canoe part, forward part when outrigger is on port side: *jabļap.*
port side (see *retam* (**reytam**)): *kōja.*
port tack: *jabļap.*
sailing port to wind: *jabdik.*

portend
superstition that large waves portend the arrival of a vessel: *tokwanwa.*

portion: *ṃōtta-.*
designate portions: *kōjjebar.*

portrait: *pija.*

portray: *kwaļǫk kadkadi-.*

Portuguese man-o-war
a coelenterate, Portuguese man-o-war: *aolōk.*

Portulaca
a plant, *Portulaca*: *kūrañ.*

position: *jiki-, kadkad, ļōmņak.*
position of: *jellen.*
slip down out of position, of things: *pir.*

possess
be possessed by demons: *urōt.*
be possessive: *kōmmǫ.*
possessed: *rijekā.*
possessed by a demon: *tuwe.*
possessed by ghosts: *mejatoto.*
possessive of women: *arōk kōrā.*
take possession of: *mǫk.*
to possess, of evil spirits: *tuwe.*
possession: *wōja.*

possessive classifiers
—alienable objects and general possessive: *aa-, wōja-.*
—bathing water: *utō-.*
—blankets and other things used as blankets: *kǫje-.*
—boundary or difference: *kōtaa-.*
—canoe, ship, boat, or vehicle: *waa-.*
—children, pets, money, watches, or Bible: *nāji-.*
—earrings and other things worn on ear: *die-.*
—eyes, lids, openings, eyeglasses, masks, or goggles: *meja-.*
—fish, crabs, or birds: *koņa-.*
—flowers or wreaths worn on head: *pālli-.*
—flowers, medals, necklaces, or fishing baskets: *ṃarō-.*
—food or cigarettes: *kije-.*
—grandmother or grandchild or pet: *jibwi-.*
—houses or other buildings: *eṃ.*
—mat or blanket or mattress: *kinie-.*
—perfume or lotion, or containers thereof: *kapitō-.*
—plant or seedling: *kōtka-.*
—position or property: *jiki-.*
—sauces: *jāle-.*
—tooth or eating utensils: *ñii-.*
—water, soft drinks, or juice of coconuts, etc.: *lime-.*

possible: *maroñ.*
expression: "Impossible!": *eban.*
impossible: *ban.*
within the realm of possibilities: *tōllǫk.*

post: *joor.*
posts of Polaris: *Jurōn-Liṃanṃan.*

posterior: *lǫdiñi, pid.*
posterior, buttocks: *lǫk.*

postpone
push, move, postponement: *tǫrtǫr.*

pot
a food, ripe breadfruit mixed with coconut oil and cooked in pots: *nāpnāpe.*
coffee pot: *tibat.*
iron pot: *ainbat.*
large pot: *kōṃa.*
teapot: *tibat.*

potato: *piteto.*
a plant, sweet potato, *Ipomoea batatas*: *piteto.*
mashed taro or potato: *kōmālij.*

potent: *mālkwōj.*
impotent: *ṃōjņǫ.*

sexually impotent (male) (see *rrōñ*
(**rręg**)): *jarrōñrōñ.*
potential: *kōjatdikdik.*
potion: *wūno.*
pouch: *bōjo̧, pāāk.*
poultry
to mature, of poultry: *jenḷap.*
pound: *ddipiñpiñ, deñdeñ, lij, nin, nono,
notoñ, pejaju, ure.*
medicine pounding rock: *tōpañ.*
pound breadfruit or taro: *jukjuk.*
pound food: *kapipā, lijlij.*
pound something or someone: *jinṃa.*
pound with a mallet or hammer:
penḷwūj.
pounded stack of processed pandanus
leaves: *noonon.*
pounding or thudding of canoes
together: *ḷḷwūjḷwūj.*
sound of waves pounding on reef:
lijeñūrñūr.
pound: *bo̧un.*
pour: *llutōk.*
pour out: *to̧o̧r.*
pout: *jememe, kaū.*
poverty: *jeraṃōl.*
powder: *bo̧uta.*
gunpowder: *bo̧urok.*
power: *kajoor, maroñ.*
extraordinary healing powers, as in
Marshallese native medicine:
kōbbōkakkak.
having healing powers: *mālkwōj.*
having supernatural powers:
mo̧nṃo̧n.
legendary power given by Jebro to
Jekad: *ao.*
magical power: *ḷo̧un.*
magical power of speech: *atlo.*
place where members of the *Ripako*
clan exercise their power to control
storms: *bōn.*
powerful in speech: *aejemjem.*
powerless: *ṃōjṇo̧.*
spiritual power: *abōn.*
within the power: *tōllo̧k.*
pox
blister, chicken pox: *bok.*
ckicken pox: *bok aidik.*
practically: *kiōk.*
practice: *deenju, kōmmālmel, mminene.*
practiced: *mminene.*
target practice: *kōjjero̧ro.*
praise: *nōbar, ro̧ḷo̧k, tūbḷotak.*
praise (religious term only): *wūjtak.*
praised: *ñiājo.*

prance: *alijerḷo̧k.*
pray: *jar.*
evening prayers (Protestant): *nokwōn.*
preach: *kowaḷo̧k, kwaḷo̧k naan.*
preacher: *rūkaki.*
precede: *ṃokta.*
precede, be in time for: *ṃṃōkaj.*
precious: *aorōk.*
precipitous: *jirūṃle, ju.*
precise: *jejjet, jiṃwe.*
precocious
precocious, of children: *ṃṃawi.*
predict: *bōklōkōt, kajjimalele.*
predict something and thereby cause it
to happen: *ajjimālele.*
predict, using cards: *kawūjwūj.*
preempt: *kkotaak, kōbbat.*
preemptive: *nib.*
preference
give preference to: *ttōl.*
prefix
prefix to feminine names: *Li-.*
prefix to masculine names: *Ḷa-.*
pregnant: *bōro̧ro, nañinmej.*
become pregnant: *tta.*
pregnant woman: *kūrae.*
prejudice: *kalijekḷo̧k.*
prejudiced: *jep.*
premature: *jum.*
premature death: *mijenatabuñ.*
Premna
a plant, tree, *Premna corymbosa*
(Burm. F.) Rottl: *kaar.*
prepare: *kōpopo.*
be prepared for the task at hand:
lōkōk.
prepare bait: *kaatat.*
prepare hermit crabs for bait: *pajo.*
prepare to strike: *pañ.*
prepared: *dede, pojak.*
to prepare for the unexpected:
ṃaanjāppopo.
preparedness: *likōk.*
prescribe: *kkar.*
presence: *pād.*
make one's presence felt, especially a
group: *tileñeñ.*
present: *joortak.*
devote presents to the gods: *aje.*
preserve: *kōbo̧rōk, kōjparok.*
a food, balls of preserved breadfruit
sweetened and boiled in coconut
oil: *makilḷō.*
a food, cooked preserved breadfruit
smothered in grated coconut:
kubaḷ.

a food, preserved breadfruit: *bwiro.*
a food, preserved breadfruit mixed with arrowroot and coconut sap or sugar, wrapped in breadfruit leaves and baked: *bwiro iiōk.*
a food, preserved breadfruit or *peru* flattened and covered with breadfruit leaves and baked: *kajipedped.*
a food, preserved breadfruit boiled or baked without wrapping: *koļeiaat.*
life preserver: *kein aō.*
smell of preserved breadfruit: *bbiroro.*

preserves
a food, watered down pandanus preserves: *ŗokrok.*

preside
to lead, direct, preside: *tōl.*

president: *būreejtōn.*

press: *kkeeņ(e).*
apply constant powerful pressure on a rope: *keepep.*
blood pressure: *aerin bōtōktōk.*
press down on: *jjiped, joon.*
press oil out of grated copra: *joniak.*
pressure: *aer.*
pressurized: *n̄iln̄il.*

prestige: *bun̄bun̄.*

presume: *ļōmņak.*

presumptuous: *mejel kil, pedet armej.*

pretend: *jekpen, ļōkōm̧.*
pretend that: *etan wōt n̄e.*
pretend to be satisfied: *ļōnan̄.*
pretense: *ankiliriab.*
pretentious: *toojin edwaan.*
pretentious care: *ioķwe in kij.*

pretty: *aiboojoj, ilar, kakijdikdik.*
knock-out, pretty: *kōjaij.*
look pretty at sunset: *aļkōnar.*
pretty, of women: *deo̧.*

prevail: *anjo̧.*

prevent: *baar, bōbrae, dem̧ak.*

Priacanthus
a fish, goggle-eye, *Priacanthus cruentatus*: *ļwōl.*

price
price of: *oņea-.*

prick: *lōklōk.*
a plant, a grass, prickly: *lōklōk.*
be pricked by pandanus thorns: *m̧ake.*
pricking sensation of body limbs: *kkinaļnaļ.*
prickly heat: *bok aidik.*
to prick: *wie.*

pride: *kabbil, utiej būruo-.*

priest: *bata, būrij.*
customary reimbursement given by anyone in return or exchange for food, living, or payment for medicine or priest-craft: *kabwijeran.*

primp: *kōmmāidik.*

prince
half prince, royal father but commoner mother: *bwidak.*
quarter prince, royal father but mother half-princess: *bwidak irooj.*

princess
quarter princess, royal father but mother half-princess: *bwidak lerooj.*

principal: *būrinjibōļ.*

principle: *abja.*

print: *jenok.*
imprint: *kkal.*
print by hand with manuscript style: *kiāptōļ.*
imprinted: *kōn.*
erase footprints: *jien̄.*
erase footprints or traces: *jjion̄.*
footprints: *jenok, kin, maalkan ne.*

prison: *būreek, kalbuuj.*

prize: *ko̧wiinin, mejānkajjik, tūb, wiin.*

probably: *bōlen.*

problem: *kajjitōk, wūn.*

procedure: *kōl.*

proceed: *etal wōt.*
proceeding toward destination: *jibadek.*

Procelsterna
a bird, blue-gray noddy, *Procelsterna caerulea*: *lo̧un Pikaar.*

procession
a steady procession: *jepekōļan.*
procession bearing tribute to chief: *tal.*
procession of mourners: *tal.*

proclaim: *kowaļo̧k.*
proclamation: *keean̄.*

procrastinate: *aepedped.*

procure
procure something by flattery or by "borrowing": *kōrabōl.*

prod: *debdeb.*
prodding: *adebdeb.*

prodigal: *bōro-ļap, jām̧ōd, jerwaan.*

produce: *jebar.*
product: *waļo̧k.*
unproductive coconut tree (see *kimuur* (**kimiwir**)): *jakimuur.*

profane: *kōtrāe.*

proffer
to proffer: *tilmaak.*
profile: *annañ.*
profit: *orļǫk.*
profitable: *wiin.*
unprofitable: *jettokja-.*
profound: *m̧wilaļ.*
Profundiconus
Conasprella praecellea/comatosa/ sowerbii or *Profundiconus profundiconus*: *likaebeb.*
program: *būrookraam̧.*
review day program: *jem̧nājin.*
progress: *ddek, wōnm̧aan.*
progress slowly but steadily: *kipeddikdik.*
prohibit
prohibited: *m̧ǫ.*
project: *būrojāāk, jerbal.*
projection: *būtti.*
prolong: *to.*
promenade: *ikueaak.*
Promicrops
a fish, giant sea bass, *Promicrops lanceolatus/truncatus*: *jǫwe.*
a fish, giant sea bass, *Promicrops truncatus*: *jowāme.*
prominence
achieve prominence: *ļe.*
promiscuous: *kidu, kijoñ.*
promise: *kallim̧ur.*
false promise: *pepe riab.*
false promises: *naan jekdǫǫn.*
prompt: *iur, m̧ōkaj.*
pronoun
—absolute and object: *kōj.*
—absolute and object, first person plural exclusive: *kōm.*
—absolute and object, second person plural: *kom̧.*
—absolute, first person singular: *ña.*
—absolute, second person singular: *kwe.*
—absolute, third person plural, them: *er.*
—absolute, third person singular: *e.*
—object, first person singular: *eō.*
—object, second person singular: *eok.*
—object, third person plural: *er.*
—object, third person singular: *e.*
proof: *kam̧ool, kein kam̧ool.*
prop: *apar.*
prop up: *kowawa.*
propaganda: *karreelel.*
propagate: *orļǫk.*
propeller
propeller of plane or ship: *pikpik.*
proper: *ebajjeet, jejjet, kkar.*
improper: *jekkar.*
property: *m̧weiuk.*
appropriate others' property: *aņokņak.*
divest of all property: *katoļǫk.*
inalienable rights or property: *addemlōkmej.*
property of: *jiki-, kapijukune-.*
to strip of money or property by fraud or threat: *kwōdmat, reja.*
prophecy
fulfill, as a prophecy: *kūrm̧ool.*
prophesy: *kanaan, rūkaanij.*
prophet: *rūkaanij.*
propose
propose to do: *katmāne.*
proposition
to proposition: *lekōto.*
prosper
prosperous wind: *m̧akroro.*
prostrate
fallen prostrate: *oļǫk.*
protect: *kōjparok, oņaak.*
padding for comfort or for protection from dirt: *erer.*
protect from rain or spray at sea with mat: *boktak.*
protect from rain or wind: *bǫto*
protect with jealousy: *jetņaak.*
protected: *barōk.*
protection: *jālitak, likōpejñak.*
protector: *erer, penja-.*
something that is put under something else to protect, lift, or support it: *ļoñtak.*
protection in fighting: *tōrak.*
protest: *jum̧ae.*
Protestant: *mijen.*
Protestant, religion: *Būrotijen.*
protract
protracted: *to.*
protrude
protrude out from a surface thereby showing: *mmat.*
having a protruding forehead: *kkodam̧dam̧.*
proud: *buñ-bōro, juwa.*
be proud: *kōņkōm̧m̧an.*
be proud of: *wūjek.*
prove: *mālejjoñ.*
proverb: *jabōnkōnnaan.*
provide
provide a framework for: *ņaļoma-.*

provide a mat for: *ņakinee-.*
provide a pillow for: *ņapitō-.*
provide drink for: *ņalime-.*
provide food for family from local sources (not from the store): *tāāp.*
provide for: *oņaak.*
provide fuel for: *ņakaan.*
provide wherewithal: *ņawāwee-.*
provide with a wage or salary: *ņaoņea-.*
provide with bathing water: *ņautō-.*
provide with food: *ņakije-.*
to provide with a blanket: *ņakǫje-.*

province: *bukwōn.*

provision
provisions: *ale, ṃweiuk.*
provisions for a voyage: *ṃṃōd, ṃōd, nnōk, teaak.*

provoke
provoke to a quarrel: *ūrōj.*
provoked: *llu.*
short tempered, cry-baby, provoked: *kwi.*
provocation: *liṃotak.*
provoking laughter: *kattōn̄tōn̄.*

prow: *ļobōrwa.*

prudent: *tiljek.*

prune
prune a bush: *jipijuļ.*
to prune: *jekjek.*

pry: *ļakilulu, ļōbat.*
pry into someone's thoughts: *ttuur bōro.*
prying: *eded.*

Psalms
the Psalms: *Jaaṃ.*

Pseuderanthemum
a plant, *Pseuderanthemum atropurpureum* (Bull.) Baily. Cult. Hedge plant: *tirooj.*

Psilotum
a plant, *Psilotum nudum*: *martok.*

psoriasis: *jān.*

psychoanalyze: *ttuur bōro.*

psychosis
psychosis, of a latent nature: *ṃṃaļkaro.*

Pterois
a fish, lionfish, *Pterois volitans*: *ōō.*

puberty
grass skirt boys put on at puberty: *kiōk.*

pubic
pubic hair: *wak.*
pubis: *bǫn̄ur.*

public
in public: *lǫbwilej, lueaļ.*
in the public eye: *jarlepju.*
publicity: *lǫbwilej.*

pucker
puckered: *nokjek.*

puff: *mmenonoun kijdik.*
puffed-up: *kōmmejāje.*
to puff a cigarette: *koub.*

puffer fish
Tetraodon hispidus: *luwap.*
Tetraodon hispidus/meleagris/nigropunctatus/patoca: *wat.*
Arothron meleagris: *luwap-kilmeej.*
Arothron nigropunctatus: *luwap-iaļo.*

Puffinus
a bird, slender-billed shearwater, *Puffinus tenuirostris*: *māntōl.*
a bird, sooty shearwater, *Puffinus griseus*: *māntōl.*

pugnacious: *ļaire, wōtan.*

pull: *aik, atak, kankan, kkāālel, nnōōr.*
hook and pull: *ankiij.*
pull as in dancing: *kkekaak.*
pull at it: *eolǫk.*
pull back the foreskin: *kuraj, ore.*
pull down: *eolǫk.*
pull fishing line rhythmically while trolling: *koraal.*
pull in, as fish on a line: *tōbtōb.*
pull keys off pandanus: *ļotļot.*
pull out: *ālāl, kkekaak, wōmwōm, wūjron̄.*
pull out hairs: *tūṃṃoņ.*
pull out of ground: *wūj.*
pull out, as current or undertow: *tǫr.*
pull together, on rope, almost falling: *bun̄ kake.*
pull up: *ļōbat.*
pull up stakes: *ṃṃakūt.*
pull up weeds or grass: *kintak.*
pulled out: *teep.*
to pull and break objects such as string, rope, wire or grass: *tūṃtūṃ.*
to pull out: *wūjwūj.*
twist and pull hair: *dāde.*

pulley: *būļak.*

pulse: *baṃ.*

pulverize: *kapipā.*

pumice
pumice stone: *tilaan.*

pump: *baṃ.*

pumpkin: *baan̄ke.*

pun: *kaj.*
punch: *bait, dukwaḷ, jarom.*
short punches in boxing, as in the beating of a drum: *tūraṃ.*
punch
punch, beverage: *ban.*
punctuation: *kakōḷḷe.*
puncture: *lōlō, ttal.*
punish: *eṇọ, iden-oṇe, kaje, kauwe, kōmanñmañ.*
punish (with causative prefix): *je.*
punk: *jit.*
puny: *ṃōjṇọ, niñ, waan.*
Puperita
Puperita japonica or *Amphinerita polita*: *kaddoḷ.*
pupil
pupil of eye: *tōṃa.*
pupil of the eye: *ijuun māj.*
purchase: *wia.*
pure: *kkwōjarjar, rreo.*
purgative
purgative medicine: *wūno in ruprup.*
purge: *katoḷọk.*
purify: *katoḷọk.*
purpose: *wūn.*
move with steady and deliberate purpose: *ijuboñ-ijuraan.*
Purpura
a shell, *Muricidae, Purpura (Manicinella) Armigera*: *tōbo.*
Drupa ricina/morum or *Purpura* (mancinella): *lidid.*
purse: *jiipkako.*
purser: *jiipkako.*
purser, ship: *baja.*
pus: *medaekek.*
push: *iuun, jipeḷḷọk, jiraak-, wiaake.*
push away a canoe: *taar.*
push forth: *bwillọk.*
push one's luck: *kadkadajaj.*
push out: *kọbaj.*
push over: *ukok.*
push up soil, of roots: *pādāl.*
push, move, postponement: *tọrtọr.*
to urge, goad, spur, push: *rrọọj.*
push cart: *diaka.*
pushover: *kijen niñniñ, mejjani.*
pussy: *kuuj.*
put: *ddoor, llik.*
fit together, put together an engine or piece of machinery: *bobo.*
put alongside: *apar.*
put aside: *kōttōn.*
put clothes away carelessly: *pānuk.*
put down: *ddoor.*
put in: *ṃalōk.*
put in container: *ātet.*
put in good shape: *kwadikdik.*
put in order: *kkar, kwadikdik.*
put inside: *tōltōl.*
put on: *kōḷaak.*
put on a long face: *kōjjeraṃōlṃōl.*
put on top of: *jojoon.*
put out a fire: *kkun.*
put something on top of: *ertak.*
put something over a fire: *perar.*
put things away: *kọkkoṇkoṇ.*
put things in place: *kọkkoṇkoṇ.*
put up: *kajjuur.*
put wreath on one's head: *pālpel.*
putting the forearm on the forehead while lying down: *eoonpālōñ.*
putty: *bate.*
Pygoplites
Pygoplites diacanthus: *rūbōb.*
Pythia
Pythia cecillei: *alu.*
quake: *ṃweiur, wūdiddid.*
qualify
disqualify: *kupi.*
qualified: *kkar.*
quality: *bōnja-.*
material quality: *añōltok.*
poor quality: *oṃoja.*
quantity: *detta-, joña-, ora-.*
add up to an expected quantity: *uñ.*
quarrel: *akwāāl, aoḷ, iakwāāl, kōtaan wāto, leḷọk-letok.*
a quarrel between two related persons which will result in misfortune: *bwijerro.*
quarreling: *airuwaro.*
quarreling among siblings: *bowōd.*
quarter: *kuwata.*
first quarter of the moon: *adik.*
queasy: *jjō.*
queen: *kwiin, lerooj.*
daughter of a queen: *lerooj.*
query: *kajitūkin.*
quest: *jibadbad, ppok.*
question: *kajjitōk.*
answer someone's question: *ṇawāwee-.*
yes-no question particle: *ke.*
quick: *iur, ṃōkaj.*
not quick (see *iur* (**yir°**)): *jāiur.*
not quick in action (see *iurjet* (**yir°jẹt**)): *jāiurjet.*
quick in action: *iurjet.*
quick of hearing: *roñḷọkjeṇ.*

quick to die (see *mejjiia* (**mẹjjiyyah**)): *mejjiie.*
quick to learn (see *penawiia* (**pẹnhawiyyah**)): *penawiie.*
quick when called (see *āñiia* (**yagiyyah**)): *āñiie.*
quick-minded: *lọḷe.*
quickly: *abōbbōb, jarōb.*

quiet: *ikōñ, jjeḷọk an naan, lur.*
talk very quietly: *ajjinono.*

quit: *bōjrak, ṃōj.*

quite: *kakkōt.*

quiz: *teej.*

quote: *ālij.*

rabbit: *rapit.*

rabbitfish
Siganus sp.: *ṃorṃor.*
Siganus rostratus: *ṃọle.*
Siganus rostratus/puellus: *ellōk.*

race: *iāekwōj, jowi.*
come in last in a race: *piditte.*
foot race: *iāllulu.*
relay race: *dide.*
a game, racing toy outrigger canoes: *kariwutut.*

rack: *jād.*
rack for heat or smoke drying: *ati, bwi.*

racket: *keroro, kkeroro.*

radar: *retaar.*

radio: *retio.*
radio transmitter: *wālej.*
receive by radio: *bọur.*
talk on the radio: *wālej.*
transmit by radio: *wālej.*

radish
pickled radish: *taikoñ.*

raffle: *kūbween kijdik.*

raft: *raab.*

rafter
rafters: *jekpād, kattal.*

rag: *bōro.*
ragged: *wūdede.*

rage: *kūtōtō, matōrtōr.*

Ragistrella
a fish, chub mackerel, *Ragistrella*: *akwōlā.*

raid
air raid: *kuju.*
raid at night: *iaboñ.*
shelter pit, air raid: *rọñ.*
to raid: *jodik.*

rail
railings: *reeḷ.*
rails of boats: *reeḷ.*

railroad
be railroaded: *liaakḷọk.*

rain: *wōt.*
a rain storm that is the sign of a chief coming: *ḷañōn irooj.*
heavy rain: *wōt-mijeljel.*
heavy rain from the northeast: *wōt-tọ.*
hole in tree for catching rain water: *ṃak.*
not rain: *jato.*
not rainy: *jọwōtwōt.*
pass by, of clouds and rain: *peḷaak.*
pitter-patter of rain: *ṃṃōṇṃōṇ.*
protect from rain or spray at sea with mat: *boktak.*
rain in, as through a window: *tọ.*
rain of: *utō-.*
rain that falls elsewhere but can be heard: *wōt-atok.*
rain that falls straight down: *wōt-aṃwelōñ.*
rain water: *aebōj, dānnin aebōj, dānnin wōt.*
raincoat: *aḷkoot, kabba.*
seldom rains (see *wōt* (**wẹt**)): *jọwōtwōt.*
stay in the rain: *utute.*
take shelter from the rain or sun: *kōjato.*
time between rain showers: *meḷa.*
wait for rain to subside: *kōḷọk.*
wait under shelter for rain to stop: *kaḷọk.*

rainbow: *iia, jemāluut.*
rainbow-colored: *iiaeae.*

rainbow runner
a fish, rainbow runner, *Elagatis bipinnulatus*: *ikāidik.*
fishing method, surround a school of rainbow runners with plain sennit: *ekkoonak.*

raise: *ālāl, būḷak, kotak, ḷōbat.*
raise a bet: *peta.*
raise by lever: *ḷakilulu, ḷōbat.*
raise by rope: *tekōḷ.*
raise children: *kaajiriri.*
raise fish net from water: *jarjar.*
raise up: *ḷabuk.*

raisin: *rejin.*

rake: *kutak, reek.*
to rake, to claw: *rakutak.*

ram: *debdeb, kipin.*

ramble: *jaṃbo.*

ramrod: *naṃnoor.*

rancid: *nnān.*
smell of rotten copra or rancid coconut oil: *ļōļ.*
random
at random: *jabdetakwōt.*
range
within range: *allọk.*
rank: *laajrak.*
stripes showing military rank: *iemṃa.*
ransack
ravage, ransack, loot: *rakim.*
ransom: *pinmuur.*
rape: *ļatipñōl.*
Raphiobelone
Raphiobelone robusta: *tak.*
rapid: *iur, iurjet.*
rappel
rappelling: *pitto.*
rapture: *lọudiñdiñ.*
rare: *jeja.*
exceedingly rare: *bōtata.*
rarely used: *tinak.*
rascal: *boea, raajkōļ, rijorrāān.*
rash: *ļakajeṃ, lennab.*
be rash: *ļōkajeṃ.*
heatrash: *bok aidik.*
rasp
a raspy feeling in the throat, especially after a cold: *mmelkwarkwar.*
rasping sound: *rap.*
rat
gnaw, of a rat or a mouse: *wōjek.*
rat, *Rattus rattus* or *Rattus exulans*: *kijdik.*
ratchet
cog, gear, ratchet: *raanke.*
rate: *ded.*
rather: *jaad.*
rather than: *bwiden.*
ratified: *weeppān.*
ration: *aikiu, kōj.*
rational: *meļeļe.*
ratline: *jikin uwe.*
rattle: *kkorkor, kor.*
rattling
rattling of bottle, etc.: *ttōñtōñ.*
rattling of gravel: *ļļāārār.*
Rattus
rat, *Rattus rattus* or *Rattus exulans*: *kijdik, kijdik.*
ravage
ravage, ransack, loot: *rakim.*
raw: *amej, ukood.*
a food, fish eaten half broiled but still raw: *koubub.*
a food, raw fish: *jaajmi.*
eat raw fish: *koobub.*
ray
a fish, ray fish (poisonous): *āibukwi.*
a fish, spotted eagle ray fish, poisonous, *Aetobatus narinari*: *imen.*
sting ray: *boraañ, ṃaļokļok.*
ray
rays of the sun: *ko-in-aļ.*
sunray: *koonaļ.*
razor: *reja.*
trim hair with a razor: *jeor.*
re
syllable "re" of musical scale: *re.*
reach: *po, tōpar.*
not reach: *likjab.*
out of reach: *jabjab.*
reach a goal: *auj.*
reach destination: *tōkeak.*
reach for something in the dark: *ttọļūm.*
reached: *jaak.*
to reach: *jeb-.*
try to reach: *jibadek.*
read: *kōnono, waak.*
look up after nodding, sleeping, or reading: *bōk bar.*
reread: *āpta.*
ready: *dede, pojak.*
ready for a bottle, of coconut shoots only: *raane-bōkāān.*
stand ready: *joorkatkat.*
real: *lukwi.*
realistic: *ṃool.*
really: *ātin, dọlin, kāājej, lukkuun.*
really (only in negative usage): *kakkōt.*
real estate: *bwidej.*
own much land or real estate: *amṇak.*
realize: *eñak, kile.*
realm
within the realm of possibilities: *tōllọk.*
reanimate: *jaruk.*
reap: *ṃadṃōd.*
rear: *lik.*
rearrange: *ikūr.*
reason: *wūn.*
interjection: "No wonder!" "It stands to reason.": *jebata.*
not able to reason: *jaje ļōmṇak.*
what is the reason: *tawūnin.*
rebuff
rebuffed: *balu, bokbok, jeddaṃ.*
rebuke: *kkọbōl.*

recall: *ememej.*
recall with grief: *ajḷǫk.*

receding
having a receding hairline: *kkodaṃdaṃ.*

receipt: *rijjiit.*

receive: *bōk.*
receive by radio: *bǫur.*

recent
recently: *kiin jeṃaanḷǫk.*
the most recent: *ḷǫk.*

recess: *ibbuku, kakkije.*

recipe: *ḷōōt.*

reciprocate: *ukok, ukok.*
to reciprocate: *ṇaoṇea-.*
reciprocating of gifts: *kabbōjrak.*

recite: *ālij, kōnono.*

reckless: *jabde, jakkōl, jeḷmāne.*

reckon: *aṇtǫǫn, lōke.*

recline
inclined to recline: *alebabu.*
recline, stretched out: *jitṃanṃan.*

recognize: *kile.*
not recognize (see *kile* (**kiley**)): *jakile.*
refuse to recognize: *kaarmejjet.*
try to recognize: *kakōlkōl.*
unrecognizable: *jakkōlkōl.*

recoil
be shaken by recoil of a gun: *ṃweiur.*

recollect: *ememej.*

recommend: *nōbar.*

recompense: *kōḷḷā oṇea-.*
recompense for evil deed: *iden-oṇe.*

reconcile: *medek.*
reconciled: *koṇkōtaa-.*
reconciliation: *medek.*

reconnoiter: *iaroñroñ, waat.*

record: *jeje.*
phonograph record: *deekto.*
record player: *jukoñki.*

recover: *llo, mour.*
be recovering: *mour-tak.*

rectum: *poḷ, rūr.*

recumbent: *eḷḷǫk.*

red: *būrōrō.*
become red, of leaves: *ed.*
red colored, of reddish coconuts or sky: *mir.*
reddish color: *ṃūrar.*

red snapper
a fish, red snapper, *Lutjanus bohar*: *paan.*
a fish, red snapper, *Lutjanus vaigiensis*: *jaap.*

redeem: *lǫmǫǫr, pinmuur.*

redfin
a fish, redfin, *Argyrops spinifer*: *ṃōḷejetak.*

Rediculus
Rediculus (alpha Pavonis): *Likin-Buwame.*

redo: *āpta.*

reduce: *kaddikdik.*

redwood: *kāmeej.*

reef: *pedped.*
a reef separate from main reef: *ñe.*
boat passage on reef: *toorwa.*
boat passage through a reef: *tǫǫr.*
cave under reef shelf: *apā.*
coral reef: *wōd.*
edge of reef: *ḷakej.*
fishing method, searching for fish at low tide over the reef: *etalpeet.*
gashes in coral reef: *kōlñe.*
high barrier reef: *ubatak.*
long gashes in the outside reef: *mejā.*
outer edge of reef where large coral heads are: *bōran baal.*
pond on reef where fish are caught when tide goes out: *tǫ.*
reef around a secondary lagoon: *tiete.*
reef edge: *baal.*
reef in the lagoon just under the surface: *medde.*
small pool on reef at low tide, or in interior of island: *ḷwe.*
smell of exposed reef: *bbilwōdwōd.*
sound of waves pounding on reef: *lijeñūrñūr.*
strip of reef: *tōkā.*
water course in the reef: *wea.*

reef heron
a bird, reef heron, *Egretta sacra*: *kabaj.*

reef
lines used to reef sails: *tiliej.*
to reef sails: *rujruj.*

reel: *addeboulul, jāljel.*
reel for fishline: *kurjep.*

referee: *aṃbai.*

refill
refill a hole with dirt: *jjioñ.*

reflect: *kōḷmānḷǫkjeṇ.*
reflect a bright light: *kakkilaajaj.*
reflection: *annañ.*
reflector of flashlight or spotlight: *ḷat.*

reflex
have sharp reflexes: *util.*

refreshment
to bring foods with songs as
refreshments to a group of men
building a canoe or house to keep
their morale up, usually done by the
womenfolk of a community: *jemjem
māāl.*

refrigerator: *bọọk aij.*

refugee: *jipọkwe.*

refund: *peọọb.*

refurbish: *kōkāāl.*

refuse: *abōb, abwin.*
always refuse: *abōblep, ṃakokolep.*
refuse to accept or take: *ṃakokoun
bōk.*
refuse to do something: *ṃakoko.*
refuse to recognize: *kaarmejjet.*

refuse: *kwōpej.*
refuse area: *taṃ.*
refuse of scraped coconut after it is
squeezed: *o.*

refute: *kariab.*

regard: *kallimjek.*
disregard: *jekdọọn, kōjelbabō.*
regarding: *kijjie-.*
regardless: *jekdọọn.*

regret: *ajḷọk, ukeḷọk.*

regulation
regulations: *kien.*

Regulus: *Ḷōkoojṇo.*

rehearse: *kōmmālmel.*

reimburse: *kōḷḷā likjab.*
customary reimbursement given by
anyone in return or exchange for
food, living, or payment for
medicine or priest-craft: *kabwijeran.*

reinforce
canoe part, reinforcement close to
both ends: *matātōp.*
reinforcing rods: *teekkiiñ.*

reiterate: *ālij.*

reject: *abwin bōk, dike, jọkpej,
ṃakokoun bōk, taṃ.*
rejected: *balu, jeddaṃ.*

relation
brother-sister relationship: *jeṃnājin.*
family relationship: *kadkad.*
friendly relationship: *jemjerā.*
parent-child relationship: *jeṃnājin.*
relation between two brothers-in-law
who are married to two sisters:
jemānji-.
severance of a relationship: *tūṃ
kwōd.*
taboo relationship: *jeṃnājin, jore.*
what relation?: *tee-.*

relative
duty towards ones relatives: *nukwi.*
fight between relatives: *an armeje
doon.*
relatives: *erṃwe, nukwi.*
taboo female relatives of the same
generation: *ine-.*
taking care of relatives: *aerṃwe.*
related to each other: *jenokwōn.*

relay
relay race: *dide.*

release: *kōtḷọk.*
be released from: *jọọr.*

relevant: *kkar.*

relieve
euphemism used on sailing vessels to
notify men to stay out of sight when
women need to relieve
themselves: *inọñ.*
need to relieve oneself: *batbat.*

religion: *kabuñ.*
religious instruction: *Baibōḷ.*
religious period: *iien kijone.*
religious retreat: *jitḷọk.*

relinquish: *kōtḷọk.*

relish
to relish something: *ijoḷ.*

reluctant
be reluctant to: *tabur.*

rely
rely on: *lōke.*
rely on children to accomplish errands
or chores: *ajriin uwaak.*

remain: *pād.*
remain ahead of a wave when sailing
following the wind: *buñṃaan.*
remainder: *bwe, ko (ro) jet.*

remains
remains of a tree especially if covered
with fern growth: *debọkut.*

remedy: *wūno.*

remember: *ememej, keememej.*
remember with sorrow:
ememḷọkjeṇ.

remind: *kakememej.*
reminder: *kein kakeememej.*

reminisce: *ememḷọkjeṇ, emḷọk.*

remnant: *ṃōtta-.*
remnants: *būrar.*

remorse: *ukeḷọk.*

remote: *ttoḷọk.*

removable: *maroñ ṃṃakūt.*
not removable: *kōn.*

remove
remove bones from fish: *iiaak.*
remove from land: *kalia.*

remove thorns from pandanus leaves: *iiaak*.
removed: *teep*.
remunerate: *kōḷḷā oṇea-*.
rend: *kekeel, peoeo*.
render: *le-*.
render (with directional): *wūjlep-*.
rendezvous
a rendezvous: *jikin ioon doon*.
renew: *kōkāāl*.
renounce: *kaarmejjet*.
renovate: *kōkāāl*.
renown: *buñbuñ*.
renowned: *akaje*.
rent: *jata*.
rental: *oṇān jata, wōnaji*.
repair: *ṃadṃōd*.
repair a boat: *āe*.
repatriate: *rọọḷḷọk ñan kapijuknen*.
repay: *kōḷḷā likjab*.
repeat: *ālij*.
repeat over and over: *ālijinmen*.
repeatedly: *kkā*.
repel
repelled: *jeddaṃ*.
repent: *ukeḷọk*.
repetitious: *ālijinmen*.
replace: *bōk jikin, pinej jenkwa-*.
replace the bottom part (*jouj*) of a canoe: *jeḷañ*.
replete: *booḷ, obrak*.
replete with: *peddejak*.
replica: *annañ*.
reply: *uwaak*.
report: *kōnnaan*.
report of official matters: *keeañ*.
report when called: *eọroñ*.
represent: *pinej jenkwa-*.
reprimand: *jueoonmọñ, kauwe*.
reproach: *kauwe, kinaak, kipel*.
reprove: *kauwe*.
repudiate: *kaarmejjet, kalia*.
reputation: *āt*.
request: *añōtñōt, kajjitōk*.
fulfill someone's request: *ṇawāwee-*.
request something by flattery: *wadu*.
reread: *āpta*.
rescue: *lọmọọr*.
resemble: *āinwōt*.
resemble, parent and child: *bōdañ*.
resemblance: *nemāmei-*.
resent: *dike, llotaan*.
reserve
reserved: *jememe*.
reside: *jokwe*.
residence: *jukjuk*.
residue: *bwe*.
resign: *kaṃōj*.
cheerful, resigned: *ineeṃṃan*.
to resign: *kakkije*.
resin: *bwilbwil*.
resist: *dāpdep, juṃae*.
resound
resounding: *pedañwūjñwūj*.
resource
knowledgeable, resourceful: *wājepdik*.
resourceful: *mejādik*.
respect
respect elders: *kaaḷapḷap*.
pay respects to a deceased: *āmej*.
respiration: *menono*.
respond: *uwaak*.
respond to: *eọroñ*.
responsibility: *ddo, kuṇaa-*.
assume responsibility for: *bōk ddo*.
take responsibility: *loloorjake*.
to shrink from responsibility: *wōmak*.
neglect one's primary responsibility: *kadkadmootot*.
be responsible for: *bōk ddo, kilaak*.
rest: *ibbuku*.
rest on: *atartar*.
restless: *kijerjer*.
to rest: *kakkije*.
rest: *ko (ro) jet*.
restaurant: *kọpe jọọb, ṃōn ṃōñā*.
restore: *jaruk*.
restrict
restricted: *ṃọ*.
result: *ajāllik, kilaak, waḷọk*.
resume: *jjino*.
resurrect: *jaruk*.
resurrection: *jerkakpeje*.
resuscitate: *jaruk*.
retain: *dāpdep*.
retaliate: *iden-oṇe*.
retard
retarded: *ṃōḷọwi*.
retort: *bokkoḷọk, ūlūlōt*.
retreat: *jenliklik*.
religious retreat: *jitlọk*.
retreat in war: *eọwilik*.
return: *jepḷaak, rọọl*.
no return: *kōptata*.
point of no return: *jerakiaarḷap*.
return a favor: *ukōt bōkā*.
return to fight again after having been repulsed: *kotūbtūb*.

reunion: *iiāio.*
reveal: *kōnnaan, kowaļọk.*
revenge: *bwil-bōro, iden-oņe.*
eager for revenge: *paļ.*
so angry as to resort to revenge: *n̄i.*
revere: *nōbar, wūjtak.*
reverend: *rōplen.*
reverie: *emļọk.*
reverse: *pāāk.*
revert: *rọọl.*
review: *ālij.*
review day program: *jem̧nājin.*
revive: *jaruk.*
revolting: *kajjōjō.*
revolting person: *pāpijek.*
revolve: *rọọl.*
revolver: *lijjukwōlkwōl, likajik.*
reward: *jinōkjeej, tūb.*
negative reward: *lle.*
reward for: *kijin.*
rewrite: *āpta.*
rheumatism: *kūrro.*
Rhinecanthus
a fish, trigger fish, *Rhinecanthus aculeatus*: *liele.*
rhythm: *piit.*
lack rhythm: *jokwa.*
shout rhythmically while doing a job requiring team work, as carrying a canoe: *roro.*
rib: *diin kat.*
ribs, nautical: *eļļa.*
ribbon: *rōpin.*
rice: *raij.*
a food, soup of soft rice or breadfruit: *jokkwōp.*
grain of rice: *tōōļ.*
wash rice: *patpat.*
rice bowl: *jokkwi.*
rich: *jeban, m̧weiie.*
rich, of soil or plant: *kimuur.*
to enrich: *ņam̧weie-.*
rickety: *om̧oja.*
ricochet: *jājjāj, ļāān, tām̧oņ.*
rid
to get rid of: *jujuurļọk.*
riddle: *lōn̄n̄a.*
ride: *uwe, weļọk.*
find something to ride: *tam̧we.*
ride a horse: *ọọjọj.*
ride at anchor: *emjak.*
ride back and forth: *ikueaak.*
ride comfortably: *weaak.*
ride high in water because not loaded: *okwōjaja.*
ride on a plane: *kā-.*
ride the waves: *m̧ōt.*
ridge
roof ridge: *bōrwaj.*
ridicule: *kajjirere.*
ridiculous: *jekkar, kōjak.*
riffraff: *armej waan, edwaan, ikōn aļe.*
rifle: *bu.*
rig
riggings of boats: *rikin.*
right: *anbwijmaron̄, jejjet, jim̧we, lukkuun, m̧ool.*
fastest method of righting a canoe after it has capsized in order to escape sharks: *keilupako.*
inalienable rights or property: *addemlōkmej.*
of right combination: *m̧m̧an utōn.*
of right dilution: *m̧m̧an utōn.*
right half of human body: *anmooņ.*
right hand: *anbwijmaron̄, anmooņ.*
right here: *joujo.*
rightly: *jim̧we.*
that is all right: *āinwōt juon.*
that's right: *eeo.*
righteous: *kkwōjarjar, wānōk.*
rigid: *kajjim̧we, kijn̄en̄e, pen.*
rigorous: *kajjim̧we.*
rile
riled: *llu.*
rim: *apar, tiek.*
rim of: *tōrerei-.*
ring: *riin̄.*
possessive classifier, earrings and other things worn on ear: *die-.*
wear a ring: *riin̄in̄.*
wear earring: *diede.*
ring
ringing (in ears): *tūn̄n̄ūļọk.*
ringing sound: *tūn̄n̄ūļọk.*
ringworm: *kito, koko.*
rinse: *m̧okm̧ok.*
rinse bait: *lije.*
rinse clothes: *m̧ukm̧uk.*
rinse one's mouth: *kurkur, rukruk.*
rinse oneself off in lieu of thorough shower: *tutu in kwōlej.*
riot: *im.*
rip: *kekeel, lim̧aajņoņo, merrōļọk, peoeo.*
ripped: *peo, potak.*
sew together a rip in cloth: *ait.*
ripe
cause pandanus to ripen: *okaliklik.*
coconut, ripe for copra: *waini.*
cover pandanus to ripen: *pon̄pon̄.*
not ripe: *owatrere.*

not ripe, of breadfruit: *kinbūt.*
not ripe, of fruit: *kūk.*
overripe breadfruit: *meimed.*
overripe spoiled breadfruit: *mālọk.*
overripe, of breadfruit with seeds: *meimed.*
overripe, of breadfruit without seeds: *mejbak.*
pick unripe pandanus: *okabur.*
pit in which fruit is buried to ripen: *wōn.*
ripe, of breadfruit: *kalo, kōt.*
ripe, of pandanus: *owat.*
ripen: *mād.*
unripe: *bur, kūk.*
unripe coconut: *ub.*
very ripe, overripe, of breadfruit only: *mmed.*
wait for fruit to ripen: *kōmmako.*
ripen: *ertak.*
wrap pandanus fruit with coconut leaves to make it ripen: *kūtōb.*

ripple: *liṃaajṇoṇo.*

rise: *ṃōto.*
moonrise: *iialañe.*
rise from the dead: *jerkakpeje.*
rise, of bread: *jib.*
stumble and rise again to run: *buñpeltak.*
to rise, of dough: *uwe.*
water rises in a well or swamp: *jib.*

risk
risky: *kakkūṃkūṃ, kauwōtata.*
to risk: *kōjelbabō.*

rite: *kabuñ.*

rival
rivalry: *jiāe.*

river: *reba.*

roach: *juwapin.*
an insect, cockroach, roach: *kuḷuḷ.*
smell of cockroaches: *bwiin-juwapen.*

road: *iaḷ.*
border on mat or stone edge of road: *apar.*
intersection of roads: *kāpoon.*

roadside: *tōrerein iaḷ.*

roam: *ṃṃōkadkad.*

roar
roar of an animal: *kōṃñūr.*
roar, as of the wind or a monster: *rorror.*

roast: *uṃ.*
smell of roasting breadfruit: *kkwanjinjin.*
to roast breadfruit: *kwanjin.*

rob: *kowadoñ.*
rob sitting hen of her eggs: *eaklep.*

robe
disrobe: *utkōk.*

robust: *ājmuur, tōbōb.*

rock: *bar, dekā, ejṃaan.*
basaltic rock which floats: *tilaan.*
build up a pile of rocks: *ppe.*
hard rock: *ajaj.*
heavy volcanic rocks: *dekā lọḷ.*
medicine pounding rock: *tōpañ.*
rocky: *dekāke.*
soft coral rocks found on beach: *pukor.*
turn over small rocks when searching: *okḷā.*

rock cod
Anyperodon leucogrammicus: *kabro, kōḷaoḷap.*
Epinephelus flavocaeruleus: *pookliṃ.*
Serranus fuscoguttatus: *kūro.*

rock hind
Epinephelus albofasciatus: *ḷōjepjep.*

rock: *ṃṃōḷeiñiñ, ṃwitaak.*
to rock something: *jeballe.*

rock-happy: *kidel.*

rocket: *rakōt.*
pandanus rocket: *didiṃakōl.*

rod
reinforcing rods: *teekkiiñ.*

roe: *likipia.*
fish roe: *pia.*

roil
roiḷed: *liṃ.*

roll: *dāpilpil, ṃṃōḷeiñiñ.*
roll a cigarette: *kwarkor.*
roll back and forth: *jabwilbwil.*
roll of a ship: *llāle.*
roll of cloth: *kap.*
roll of fat around waist: *maḷūttōk.*
roll of film: *jāljel.*
roll up mats, etc.: *āle.*
roll up pants: *kitak.*
roll up shirt sleeves or trousers: *limtak.*
roll up sloppily, wrinkled: *ḷukut.*
roll up, as dried pandanus leaves: *jāljel.*
roll up, line or film, spool: *tāte.*
rolled: *poktak.*
rolled, as by surf: *ḷukut.*
rolling dice: *taij.*
swaying from side to side, as a ship rolling: *jepliklik.*
to roll in a kneading way: *ṃabwil.*
to roll, of ships: *lā.*

roller: *kōro, waan bwil.*
roller for launching canoe: *ļọñ, ļoñtak.*

roly-poly: *depetdoul.*

romantic
romantic desires: *mejpata.*

roof: *maļtu, tōrak.*
piece of tin roofing: *tiin.*
put thatch on roof: *kōtak.*
roof brace: *añinwoļā.*
roof ridge: *bōrwaj.*
roofing: *jinnibọọr.*
tin roofing: *jinibọọr.*

rookery: *akade, de.*

room: *ruuṃ.*
make room for: *jeje, ṇajiki-.*
move a little sideways to make room: *rrā.*

roost: *edde.*
roost of: *jipkōn.*
roosting place of birds: *akade.*
tree in which birds roost and defecate: *jade.*
watch birds alight to locate roost: *akajok.*
watch birds to locate roost: *akade, alekọ.*

rooster: *kako.*
rooster tail feather: *ļōb.*
strut of a rooster: *adpā, to.*
take a rooster to a cock-fight: *keid.*

root: *okar, wūn.*
aerial roots of the pandanus: *liok.*
push up soil, of roots: *pādāl.*
root of matter: *boļ.*
root out: *wūjwūj.*
rooted out: *teep.*
rooty soil: *ibnene.*
uproot: *toktak, totak, wūj.*

rope: *to.*
a game, skip-rope: *kutiñ.*
break, as a rope: *ṃwijkōk.*
climb or descend a rope: *pitto.*
coconuts still attached to spathe and lowered from tree by means of a rope: *niiddoor.*
guy rope or cable: *kae.*
let out a rope to slacken it: *peaut.*
loose, of clothing or rope: *pidtoto.*
raise by rope: *tekōļ.*
rope from sheet line forward and aft: *ieplik.*
rope used for climbing trees: *jemājirok.*
ropes that go from top of the mast down to both ends of sailing canoe: *jọṃur.*
strand of rope or wire: *ko.*
stretched tight, of lines, ropes, etc.: *lōtlōt.*
throw a rope over a branch: *rajāl.*
tie or fasten with a rope or cord: *ļajiiñ.*
to pull and break objects such as string, rope, wire or grass: *tūṃtūṃ.*
use a rope: *leto.*

rosary: *rojeri.*

rose: *rooj.*
wear a rose or hibiscus flower: *roojoj.*

rosebush: *utrooj.*

rot: *kōt, wabanban.*
rotten: *kōt.*
rotten (of wood): *ajjiļapļap.*
smell of rotten copra on body: *maļļipen.*
smell of rotten copra or rancid coconut oil: *ļōļ.*

rotate: *addeboulul, rọọl.*

rotten: *ṃor.*

rough: *kkaj, kurbalōklōk, kurere.*
rough skin: *bbadede.*
rough, of weather, currents, etc.: *wūj.*
roughness around penis: *kūļarōj.*

round: *doulul.*
anything small and round: *lijadoul.*
round up fish or animals: *ajāl.*

rouse
awake, roused, conscious: *ruj.*

route: *iaļ.*
escape route: *iaļan jọọr.*

row: *aeñwāñwā, aōṇōṇ.*
row a boat: *oru.*
row of houses: *alen.*

rowdy: *ṃṃaļkaro, nana taṃṃwi-.*

royal
commoner married to royal woman: *irooj-eṃṃaan.*
container of oil or water for use with royal whetstone: *ṇop.*
female of quarter royal descent: *lejjibjib.*
lesser royal rank: *ātōk.*
loss of royal status through defeat in war: *jipọkwe.*
male of one-fourth royal descent: *ļajjibjib.*
royal bathing pool in old days: *juwadel.*

rub: *irir, ṃabwil, tōñōl.*
canoe part, piece of wood on leeside as

guard against rubbing from steering paddle: *eran jebwe.*
make fire by rubbing sticks: *etoñ, it.*
rub back and forth gently or caressingly: *eoeo.*
rub clothes in washing: *ṃukṃuk.*
rub in black carbon on tattoos: *iteṃaṃōj.*
rub ones eye: *itūk, itūñ.*
rub with oil as medical treatment: *pitpit.*
speed up when rubbing sticks to make fire: *jorjor.*
to rub gently: *boboor, towe.*

rubber: *roba.*
rubber band: *liko.*
shoot with a rubber band: *lippin.*
small rubber tube: *kumi.*

rubbish: *jọkpej, kwōpej, menọknọk.*
pick up bits of rubbish: *kintak.*
turn over rubbish hunting for something: *okpej.*

rubble
pile of rubble: *ilel.*

ruckus
cause a ruckus: *uwōjak.*

rudder: *jebwe.*

rudder fish
chub or rudder fish, *Kyphosus vaigiensis*: *pājrōk.*
rudder fish, *Kyphosus vaigiensis* (Eniwetak): *rōnna.*

ruddy
a bird, ruddy turnstone, *Arenaria interpres*: *kōtkōt.*

rude: *jakōl.*

ruffle
ruffled: *ḷoktōk.*
ruffling of cocks and dogs before fighting: *rrọñ.*

rug: *erer.*

rugged: *kije.*

ruin: *jeepepḷọk, kọkkure.*
ruined: *jorrāān.*
run-down, of persons, ruined: *wōla.*

rule: *kien.*
rule over: *peek.*

rule
ruler, straightedge: *ruḷa.*

rum: *rōṃ.*

rumble: *ññūr.*
distant rumbling of waves: *lijeñūrñūr.*

rummage: *eded.*

rummy: *rami.*

rump: *pid.*

rumple
rumpled: *ḷoktōk.*

run: *ttōr.*
be running over: *jieb-.*
get into prime running condition: *an.*
home run: *oṃrawūn.*
run a complete circuit around a field: *oṃrawūn.*
run and jump: *ttōr kāḷọk.*
run at full speed: *kọkleejej.*
run away: *ko, kōpḷọk.*
run away far after losing a fight or because afraid: *koñil.*
run in a zigzag fashion: *jeerinbale.*
run into: *iioon.*
run lightly: *kakiaaj.*
run over: *jjiped.*
run, of engines: *jọ.*
run, of water: *tọọr.*
runny nose: *ba.*
runs, in a baseball game: *deḷọñ.*

run-down
run-down condition: *ijurwewe.*
run-down, of persons, ruined: *wōla.*

runner
a fish, rainbow runner, *Elagatis bipinnulatus*: *ikāidik.*

runt: *oḷar.*

rupture
ruptured: *rup.*

rush: *bwijọkorkor.*
onrush: *ibeb.*

Russelia
a plant, *Russelia juncea* (scrophulariaceae): *albokbōrọro.*

Russia: *Rojia.*

rust: *ḷōjo.*
chip or scrape rust off: *kajjo.*
make rusty: *kajjo.*
rusty: *jjo.*
to chip off rust: *kañkañ.*

rustle
rustling of leaves and branches: *mmewiwi.*

Sabbath
the Sabbath: *Jabōt.*

sabotage
to sabotage: *kōmmatōr.*

Saccharum
a plant, *Saccharum officinarum* L. Sugar cane (Gramineae). (Ko: *tọ.*

sack
burlap sack: *pāāk.*

sacrament: *jakkūramen.*

sacred: *kkwōjarjar.*

sacrifice: *joortak, katok.*
sacrifice food to the gods: *wālǫklik.*

sacrilegious: *kōtrāe.*

sacrum: *ļuļ.*

sad: *būroṃōj.*
saddening: *kabbūroṃōjṃōj.*
sadness: *būroṃōj.*

safe: *jaruk, koņ, pāāñ.*

safety pin: *piin.*

sag: *pidtoto.*

sage: *kanpil.*

Sagittarius
sigma in Sagittarius and beta Librae: *Aunwōlān-lañ.*
stars in Sagittarius: *Mājetdikdik.*

sail
a canoe with its sail flapping: *añōppāl.*
a sail: *wōjļā.*
able to sail close to the wind: *wetak.*
arrive, of sailing vessel or airplane: *po.*
canoe part, decorations of feathers on masthead, boomtips, and sail: *deñļǫk.*
canoe part, edge of sail fastened to the gaff: *aeṃaan.*
canoe part, foot of sail, edge fastened to the boom: *aekōrā.*
canoe part, waveguard on both sides of sailing canoe: *añtūkli.*
canoe-surfing, when sailing down wind: *kōttōmāle.*
cover a sail: *atro.*
decorations made from feathers of frigate birds, one on each tip of the sail on a chief's canoe: *kadulele.*
drawing much water causing it to be hard to paddle or sail, nautical: *añōt.*
full sail, nautical: *kankan, lōtlōt.*
go on a vehicle or sailing canoe (used with directional enclitics (and postpositions)): *tar-.*
go sailing: *jerakrōk.*
hoist sails: *jerak.*
jaunt, sail, or drive around aimlessly: *tarto-tartak.*
keep a canoe or boat full-sailing: *kabwijer.*
land, sailing vessel: *po.*
large outrigger canoe, for sailing: *tipñōl.*
large sailing canoe: *jitōñ.*
let sail and mast fall while tacking: *merā.*
line used to decrease the sail on a canoe: *lukwar.*
lines used to reef sails: *tiliej.*
lower sail: *po.*
mix sail power with engine power: *kabodān.*
pacify the winds and cause winds favorable for a sailing expedition: *kaurur jiañ.*
remain ahead of a wave when sailing following the wind: *buñṃaan.*
sail away: *jeblaak, jerak.*
sail close to the wind: *kipeddikdik.*
sail downwind with the sail on the south and the outrigger on the north: *tōmeañ.*
sail into the wind, tacking often: *jeje.*
sail model canoes: *bwilbwil.*
sail not full: *tǫ.*
sail of a certain shape: *ṃōjbwe.*
sail onto land: *ṃor.*
sail out to sea: *buñlik.*
sail westward: *kabbe.*
sail with outrigger out of water: *ām.*
sail with the outrigger on the south: *tōmrak.*
sail with the wind: *kabbe.*
sailboat: *wajerakrōk.*
sailing port to wind: *jabdik.*
sailing starboard to wind: *jabļap.*
shake, of a sail in the wind: *jopāl.*
spar of sail: *rojak.*
tack, change sail from one end of canoe to the other to tack: *diak.*
tacks in sailing: *ālu.*
test sail a new or overhauled vessel: *likbad.*
to bring up outrigger and hold it at 45 degrees while sailing: *kakkiāmem.*
to reef sails: *rujruj.*
to sail a canoe or boat singlehandedly: *wajekā.*
to sail a coconut hydroplane: *wūdādo.*
to sail a toy canoe: *riwut.*
to sheet sails in: *ņatoon.*
unable to sail close to the wind: *wāto.*
uneven sailing wind in lee of an islet: *añinene.*
use a sail: *lewōjļā.*
windward overlay of sail: *jā.*

sailfish
a fish, Pacific sailfish: *wūjinleep.*

sailor: *jeļa, juwape.*

salary
low salary: *dik oņea-.*
provide with a wage or salary: *ņaoņea-.*

salary of: *oṇea-*.

sale: *wōtlok̦ kōn oṇānṃweiuk.*

saliva: *iādatōltōl, kaplo, ṃṃōj.*

salmon
a fish, salmon: *jaṃōṇ.*

saloon: *baar.*

salt: *jool̦.*
a food, salted fish guts or clams: *jiookra.*
not salty: *aebōjbōj.*
salt water: *dānnin lojet.*
saltspray: *tabūṇṇo.*
salty: *jatōk.*

salute
salute with the hands: *jekjek.*
salutation: *al̦e.*

salvation: *lomoor.*

same: *āinwōt, āinwōt juon.*
at the same level: *pen in deo.*
same as: *āi-.*
the same: *barāinwōt.*

sampan: *jempaan.*

sample: *elṃok̦ot, jaṃbōl̦, edjoñ.*

sanctified: *kkwōjarjar.*

sanction: *mālim.*

sanctum: *lokatok.*

sand: *bok.*
add sand or grated coconut: *penpen.*
be sandy: *bokbok.*
coarse sand: *bok ajaj, bokkwelep.*
digging of feet or tires into soft sand: *kōbkōb.*
feet sink in sand making for difficult walking: *neen kōbkōb.*
fine sand: *bokkwidik.*
fine sand in sea: *liṃ.*
fishing method, using weight with hook, octopus for bait, and dragging it on sandy bottom: *kōjol̦iṃ.*
sand disks: *bok allōñ.*
sand hardened together: *barl̦ok.*
sandbank: *ppe.*
sandbar, usually not covered even at high tide: *bok.*
sandspit: *bok.*
scoop, dirt or sand: *eok̦ur.*
slip under ground or sand: *jo.*
throw sand at: *bor.*
to throw grated coconut or sand at someone or something: *pinik.*

sand clam
sand clam, bivalve: *jukkwe.*

sand crab: *ṃōl̦e.*
fishing method, line fishing outside lagoon, usually on lee side and fairly close to shore, for flying fish, using sand crab for bait: *rōjep.*
white sand crab: *kalibbañ, karuk.*

sanderling
a bird, sanderling, *Crocethia alba*: *kwōl.*

sandpaper: *jaanpeba.*
a coral which can be used as sandpaper: *pal̦.*

sandpiper
a bird, semi-palmate sandpiper, *Ereunetes pusillus*: *kwōl.*

sandspit
sandspit of: *bokwā, bokwan.*

sandwich: *jāānwūj.*

sandworm
small sandworm: *būttiwal̦.*

sane: *jel̦ā l̦okjeṇ.*

sanitary: *rreo.*
sanitary napkin: *te.*
use a sanitary napkin: *tete.*

sap: *bwil.*
a food, preserved breadfruit mixed with arrowroot and coconut sap or sugar, wrapped in breadfruit leaves and baked: *bwiro iiōk.*
bottle used for coconut sap: *jeib.*
choice coconut tree for collecting sap: *tāāñ.*
coconut mixed with sap or sugar: *lukor.*
coconut sap, toddy: *jedān, jekaro.*
coconut shell for catching coconut sap, whole and empty: *kor.*
fermented, of coconut sap: *mañūñ.*
old and sour coconut sap: *mañūñ.*
place a bottle (*kor*) at the end of coconut shoot to collect sap initially: *kajokkor.*
sap of coconut tree: *dān.*
use coconut sap for cooking: *utōn-jekaro.*

Sarda
Sarda sarda: *l̦ōjabwil.*

sardine
a fish, sardine, *Sardine sardinella* (small): *mimuul.*
a fish, sardine, *Sardinella* sp.: *kwarkwar, mamo.*
canned sardines: *jeṃṃa.*
fishing method, using woven brown coconut fronds to catch sardines and minnows as they are chased ashore by bigger fish: *apep.*
sardines: *jatiin.*

satiate
satiated: *ṃaal, mat.*

satisfied: *ju-bōro, mat.*
dissatisfied: *ikrooḷ.*
not satisfied: *jaṃjaṃ.*
pretend to be satisfied: *ḷōnañ.*
satisfy: *po bōro, polel.*
dissatisfy: *jab po bōro.*
easy to satisfy with food: *mattiie.*
hard to satisfy with food: *mattiia.*

saturate
saturated: *eo, ḷwōjat.*
saturated with water: *bok.*

Saturday: *Jādede.*

sauce: *jāle-, jālele.*
possessive classifier, sauces: *jāle-.*
soy sauce: *joiu.*

saucy: *wōtan.*

saunter: *jaṃbo, kōkajoor.*

sausage: *jọjej.*

savage
savage (see *awiie* (**hawiyyẹy**)): *awiia.*

save: *ijellọkwi-, kōjparok, lọmọọr.*
save from a storm: *tōḷḷañ.*

savings: *joortoklik.*

savor: *edjoñ.*
savory smell: *bwiin-ennọ.*

saw: *jidpān.*
correct angle of handsaws: *oḷā.*
crosscut saw: *bukduul.*
hacksaw: *jidpān aen.*
ripsaw: *bōrrā.*
sawdust: *kijen jidpān.*

say: *ba, bōḷa, kōmlōt.*
interjection: "You don't say!": *kwōjabṃōk.*
say in vain: *ba pata.*
what do you say?: *eañ.*

saying: *jabōnkōnnaan, kaj.*

scab
scabby: *kwōdkwōdi.*

scad
a fish, big-eyed or goggle-eyed scad fish or horse mackerel, *Trachurops crumenophthalmus*: *pāti.*

Scaevola
a plant, *Scaevola frutescens* (Mill.) Krause: *kōṇṇat.*

scaffold: *okwa.*

scale
scale fish: *karwūn.*
scale of fish: *wūn.*

scales: *bọun.*

scaly
disease, scaly and flaky skin: *koko.*
scaly skin: *kwōdkwōdi.*

scan
scanning: *kakōlkōl.*

scandal: *kajjookok.*
scandalize: *kabwilọklọk māj.*
scandalized: *ubabōj.*

Scapharca
small clam, oyster, a shell, *Arcidae, Scapharca inequivalvis* or *Anadara pilulu*: *kūkōr.*

scar: *kinej.*

scarce: *aḷakiia, jeja.*
scarcity of fish (see *ike* (**yikey**)): *jaike.*

scare
coconut leaf chain used in fishing as scarer: *ṃwio.*
fish that wanders outside coconut leaf chain scarer: *ikōnālkinṃwio.*
fishing method, between two shoals (*ṇa*), with scarer: *uṇa.*
fishing method, many men surround a school in shallow water using a coconut leaf chain as scarer: *aḷeḷe.*
fishing method, using a coconut leaf chain as a scarer at night to block off exit route of fish and waiting for low tide in order to trap them: *lipaanto.*
fishing method, using coconut leaf chain as scarer on dark nights: *pelpel.*
fishing method, using scarer: *wōtojome.*
fishing method, using scarer and weir: *kwōmej.*
fishing term, said of a coconut leaf chain used as scarer that is strung out unevenly: *kapijjule.*
form a triangle shape with scarer (*ṃwieo*) in fishing by the *jurōk* method: *juḷḷwe.*
hard to scare: *jāmmijakjak.*
not scare easily (see *kkōl* (**kkẹl**)): *jakkōl.*
not scare easily (see *uwōta* (**wiwetah**)): *jọuwōta.*
scare away: *ubaak.*
scared: *ilbōk, kkōl, kor, mijak.*

scarf: *ḷokkorbar.*

Scarus
a fish, parrotfish, *Scarus harid*: *ekmouj.*
a fish, parrotfish, *Scarus jonesi/ sordidus*: *merā.*
a fish, parrotfish, *Scarus jonesi/ sordidus*: *mao.*
a fish, parrotfish, *Scarus vetula*: *taburbur.*

scatter: *ebeb, lij.*
scattered: *ajeeded, ebjak, eojaḷ, jeeded, jekadkad, jeplōklōk.*

scavenge: *okpej.*

scavenger fish
Lethrinus sp: *ņamāni.*
Lethrinus kallopterus: *perak.*
Lethrinus microdon: *mejmej.*
Lethrinus miniatus: *jaļiia.*
Lethrinus variegatus: *dijiñ, nōt.*

scene: *wōja.*

scent: *nām.*
trace scent: *kāātet.*

scheme: *jekaboot, kkar, kōllejar, kōttōbalbal, ļam.*

school
a flock of birds flying over a school of fish: *la, wūnaak.*
charge of a school of fish chasing minnows: *tūaļ.*
flock, school: *m̧ur.*
many, as a school of fish: *doom.*
school of fish: *bwijin.*
school of fish on reef, herd of animals: *baru.*

school: *jikuuļ.*
schoolhouse: *m̧ōn jikuuļ.*

schooner: *jikuna.*

scientist: *jaintiij.*

scissors: *jijāj.*
a game, scissors, paper, and stone: *jaañke.*
cut with scissors: *jijāj.*

scold: *būroñ, eņọ, jueoonmọñ, kauwe, kipel, llu.*

Scolopsis
a fish, snapper, *Scolopsis cancellatus*: *kwōlej.*

Scomber
a fish, leather-jack, *Scomberoides lysan*: *aoļōt.*
a fish, mackerel, *Scomber japonicus*: *m̧ōlm̧ōl.*

scoop
ladle, scoop food: *nam̧ōļ.*
scoop up: *rọkrok.*
scoop up by hand: *rwaklep.*
scoop up more than one's share: *rọklep.*
scoop, dirt or sand: *eọkur.*

scooter: *wōtbai.*

scorch
scorched: *aerar, tuļaar.*

score: *bōnbōn.*

scorn: *akkōjdat, kōjdat.*

Scorpaenopsis
scorpion fish or stone fish, *Scorpaenopsis diabolus/gibbosa/novaeguineae/macadamsi/cacopsis/albobrunnea/guamensis/parvipinnis*: *ņo.*

scorpion: *mādepep.*

scorpion fish
a fish, scorpion fish, *Dendrochirus zebra*: *ōō.*
scorpion fish or stone fish, *Scorpaenopsis diabolus/gibbosa/novaeguineae/macadamsi/cacopsis/albobrunnea/guamensis/parvipinnis*: *ņo.*

Scorpius
stars in Scorpius: *Kāājejen-Tūm̧ur, Korak-eņ-an-Tūm̧ur, Ļōmejdikdik, Tūm̧ur.*

scourge
scourged: *eñtaan.*

scramble: *jitable.*

scrap
particles, scraps: *tipdikdik.*

scrape: *irir, kar, kutak, kwekwe.*
chip or scrape rust off: *kajjo.*
scrape bottom: *eoņ.*
scraper for pandanus with three wooden legs and bowl set beneath: *peka.*

scratch: *jukkwe, kar, kutak, kwekwe, rọkrok.*
scratch anus, to goose: *rōbtak.*
scratch in ground for food, chickens only: *toktok.*
scratch with claws: *ubrar.*
scratch, as a cat: *rakutak.*
scratch, of chickens: *ebeb.*
scratchy: *kurere.*
small cut, scratch: *kurar.*

scream: *kōkkeilọk.*

screen: *ok.*

screw: *jikūru.*

scribe: *jikraip.*

script: *m̧alen.*

scrotum: *rọ.*
smell of scrotum: *bbūrọrọ.*

scrounge
scrounge around: *okpej.*

scrub: *būraj.*
coconut shell for scrubbing clothes: *kuļatļat.*
scrub self with coconut husk or oil: *bokwārijet.*
scrub, using wet cloths: *jokiiñ.*

scrumptious: *nnọ.*

scrupulous: *jim̧we.*
unscrupulous: *jām̧ōd, jeļmāne.*

scrutinize
scrutinize, examine: *allọk.*

scrutinizing: *kakōlkōl.*

scuba
scuba tank: *akjijen.*

scuffle: *taiṃ.*

scull: *oru.*

scum
scum, food particles between teeth: *taiñad.*

sea: *lọjet, lọmeto, meto.*
choppy seas: *liṃaajṇọṇọ.*
drift about the sea: *peto-petak.*
fear of being alone in the dark or at sea: *abwinmake.*
fly off towards the sea: *pikmeto.*
go from sea side of an island to lagoon side: *kear.*
go or come seaward: *wanmeto.*
plunge into the sea: *roḷọk.*
seacoast: *parijet.*
seashore: *parijet.*
seasick: *ḷḷao, ṃōḷañḷōñ.*
smell of the sea: *bbijetjet.*

sea anemone: *ḷọr.*

sea bass
a fish, giant sea bass, *Promicrops lanceolatus/truncatus*: *jọwe.*
a fish, giant sea bass, *Promicrops truncatus*: *jowāme.*

sea cucumber
Holothuroidea, Holothuria leucospilo ta: *jipenpen.*
Holothuroidea, Opheodesoma: *jāibo.*
Holothuroidea, Thelonia or *Actinopyga*: *piāpe.*

sea demon: *kwōjenmeto.*

sea gull
a bird, white as sea gull: *mānnimuuj.*

sea horse
a fish, sea horse, *Hippocampus kuda*: *kidudujet.*

sea perch
a fish, Pacific sea perch, *Kuhlia taeniura* (Mejit.): *kōnān.*

sea slug: *pedobar, piāpe.*

sea snail: *jinenpokpok.*
sea snail, top shell: *kaddoḷ.*

sea water
get old and dilapidated due to continuous soaking in sea water: *luwajet.*

search: *allo.*
search for: *kappok, ppok.*
search in a large area: *peet.*
searchlight: *jatiraito.*
turn over small rocks when searching: *okḷā.*

season: *buñ.*
a gathering of people to celebrate the onset of breadfruit season in summer by making offerings to Jebro, the god of breadfruit: *ṃaṃa.*
arrowroot season: *pāl.*
dry season: *añōneañ.*
onset of calm season: *añkidid.*
onset of the windy season: *añkwōl.*
season for breadfruit and pandanus: *wōtōn.*
season of drought: *añōneañ.*
windy season: *añōneañ.*

seasoned
to dry and become seasoned, of lumber, as in canoe building: *pit.*

seat: *jea.*
canoe part, seat on a paddling canoe, usually in the mid-section: *tọọt.*

seaward: *metoḷọk.*
directional, enclitic, seaward: *meto.*

seaweed
a plant, general term for seaweed. *Thalassia hemprichii* (Ehrenb.) Aschers.: *wūjooj-in-lọjet.*
any seaweed: *wūjooj-in-lọjet.*

secede: *diwōj.*

second
second base: *jekōn.*
second child: *utlōkḷap.*
second moon phase: *meḷoktak.*
second son or daughter: *utlōkḷap.*
second-hand: *jekōnāān.*
the second: *kein karuo.*
the second zone of currents: *dibukae.*
to second, concur: *rejetak.*

second
a second of time: *jekōn.*

secret: *ttino.*
eat secretly: *jinre.*
monitor secretly: *iaroñroñ.*
not able to keep secrets: *bbōk.*
speak secretly: *wūnojidikdik.*

section
section of: *ṃōtta-.*

secure: *pojak.*
secured: *koṇ.*
tie securely: *boḷan.*

security: *kōpetaklik.*
security, land or goods or money put away for future use or for children: *joortoklik.*

seduce: *jawōd, wadu.*
seduce a woman: *kōrabōl.*

see: *allolo, lale, llo.*
let's see: *jaṃṃōk.*
not able to see well (see *llo* (**llew**)): *jāllo.*
not see well: *pilo.*
oversee: *oṇaak.*
see off on a journey: *kōjjājet.*
see off on a voyage: *juwōne.*
see something pass by: *jjāāl.*
see, in Biblical usage: *lo.*
sight-seeing: *alwōj bajjek.*
to see a movie: *ṃupi.*
to see someone passing between clumps of trees: *kōlọtuwawa.*

see-saw: *abōṇtọun.*

seed: *ine, kwōle.*
edible portion inside certain nuts or seeds: *jibañūñ.*
seedling: *ine.*

seek: *ppok.*
seek knowledge: *jitdaṃ.*
seek news: *eọroñ.*
seek pity: *kōjjeraṃōlṃōl.*

seem: *āinwōt, tipe-, tuon.*

seer: *rūkaanij.*

segment: *ar.*

segregate
segregated: *jenolọk.*

seize: *jebjeb.*
seized: *po.*

seldom: *jeja.*
seldom bathe: *mijak dān.*
seldom bathe (see *tutu* (**tiwtiw**)): *jattutu.*
seldom go fishing: *jeeọñōd.*
seldom play (see *kkure* (**qqirẹy**)): *jọkkurere.*
seldom rains (see *wōt* (**wẹt**)): *jọwōtwōt.*
seldom tire (see *kkijeje* (**kkijẹyjẹy**)): *jakkijeje.*

select: *kkāālel.*
deselect: *kọkwōpej.*
selection: *kkāālel.*

self: *ḷoḷātāt, make.*
brag about one's self: *jājjāj.*
Marshallese art of self-defense: *ṃaanpā.*
self-willed: *jeḷṃāne.*
selfish: *būruon kūro, kūbboṇ.*

sell: *jobai, wia.*
not to sell oneself short: *jab dodoorḷọk.*
set, sell oneself short: *ddoor.*
soft sell: *lekōto.*

semblance: *ḷōma-.*

semen: *pek.*

send: *jjilōk.*
send another to do one's work: *kōmādodo.*
send by airmail: *eermeeḷ.*
to send a command to: *kaiñ.*

senile: *ppaḷ.*

senior: *rūtto.*

sennit
bind with sennit: *eọeo.*
clean whiskers off of newly braided sennit: *kōrōnāl.*
club used for beating coconut husk for sennit: *jidjid.*
coconut sennit: *kkwaḷ.*
coil of coconut sennit: *tāte.*
fishing method, surround a school of rainbow runners with plain sennit: *ekkoonak.*
make sennit: *kkwaḷ.*
net made of sennit used for sifting arrowroot starch: *waliklik.*
piece of wood on which coconut husk is beaten to yield fibre for sennit: *jebōnmāl.*
pit for soaking coconut husks for making sennit: *to.*
place for beating coconut husks after soaking in preparation for making sennit: *ṃṃal.*
sennit used for tying canoes: *ām.*
take coconut husks from water after soaking to make sennit: *jarjar.*
twist sennit: *pit.*

sensation
stinging sensation: *idid.*
unpleasant sensation: *mmāālel.*

sense: *eñjake.*
come to one's senses: *iañak.*

sensitive
hypersensitive, sexually: *makōrlep.*
sensitive in perception: *loḷọkjeṇ.*

sentence: *jāntōj, jaṇtōj.*

sentinel: *baṃpe, waj.*

sentry: *baṃpe.*

separate: *jenolọk, jepel.*
separate from: *jājḷọk.*
separately: *kajjojo.*

September: *Jeptōṃba.*

serene: *ineeṃṃan, lur.*

sergeant major
a fish, sergeant major, *Abudefduf septemfasciatus*: *badet.*

series: *lelkan.*

Seriola
a fish, *Seriola purpurascens*: *m̧anoļ.*

serious
seriously: *dọlin.*
take seriously (with directionals): *eļ.*

serpent: *jabōn, jedpānit.*

Serranus
a fish, rock cod, *Serranus fuscoguttatus*: *kūro.*

servant: *buwae, kuli, rijjelōk.*
servant (with person prefix *rū-*): *kōm̧akoko.*

serve: *buwae, jerbal.*
be served right: *lle.*
not serviceable: *jakeiie.*
serviceable: *keiie.*

set
set fire to: *ttil.*
set, sell oneself short: *ddoor.*
to set, of hens: *lik.*

settle: *jukjuk.*
fixed, settled: *tōt.*
settle, of liquids: *jok.*
settlement, village: *jukjuk.*

seven: *jiljilimjuon.*
seventeen: *joñouljiljilmjuon.*
seventy: *jiljilimjuonñoul.*

sever
severance of a relationship: *tūm̧ kwōd.*
severed: *m̧wijkōk, tūm̧tūm̧.*

several: *iiet, jejjo, jet.*

severe: *dejeñ, pen.*

sew: *keke.*
sew or tie on thatch: *kōtak.*
sew together a rip in cloth: *ait.*
sewing machine: *mejin.*
sewn: *kijek.*
twine for sewing up the mouth of a bag: *enneok.*

sex appeal
have sex appeal: *taļe.*
have sex appeal, of males: *tāāñ.*
lacking sex appeal: *jatāāñ.*
lacking sex appeal (see *taļe* (**taļ̧ey**)): *jataļe.*

sextant: *bōk aļ, bōk iju.*

sexual
euphemism for sexual position: *jitnen m̧ōm̧ō.*
euphemism for sexual relations: *kōmmerara.*
euphemistic reference to illicit sexual relations: *teem̧bura.*
fondle sexually: *lijjukul.*
have sexual relations: *letak.*
hypersensitive, sexually: *makōrlep.*
illicit sexual intercourse: *paarōr.*
initiate sexually: *karūtto.*
interjection: "Ouch!" (Pain or sexual pleasure): *ōttōt.*
interjection: expression of sexual pleasure: *ōrrōr.*
movement of hips during sexual intercourse: *aelaļ.*
said of a male who ejaculates prematurely in sexual intercourse: *kako.*
sexual act: *aelaļ, katro.*
sexual act, position: *wāiñat.*
sexual intercourse: *ijij, peeļ, peru, tape.*
sexual position: *wātulik.*
sexual technique: *kọkkwidikdik.*
smell of unwashed sexual organs: *būn̦o.*

shabby: *pidtoto.*

shack: *peļak.*
cook shack: *peļak.*
temporary house, shack: *m̧ōn kōppād.*

shackle
shackles: *jakōļ.*

shade: *aelor, aemed, jabalur, llor.*
shadow, shade: *kallor.*
to shade the eyes with the hand and watch for a school of fish: *jjor.*
countershading: *ukōt m̧ōōr.*

shadow: *annañ, llor.*
shadow of death: *annañinmej.*
shadow, shade: *kallor.*

shake: *idik, wūdiddid.*
be shaken: *kajkaj.*
be shaken by recoil of a gun: *m̧weiur.*
shake a bush or tree: *im̧uk.*
shake a liquid so that it gurgles: *kọkkorōjrōj.*
shake down a container to pack more solidly: *ļattuñ.*
shake hands to make a promise binding: *jeep.*
shake off: *pikpikūr.*
shake out: *pikpikūr.*
shake pebbles and ball or dice: *ļuļu.*
shake the head in disagreement: *jeboulul.*
shake up: *rukruk.*
shake, of a sail in the wind: *jopāl.*

shall: *naaj.*

shallow: *pejpej.*
canoe that cannot go in shallow water: *kaplep.*
having a shallow draft, of ships (see *kaplep*): *kapdik.*

shallow draft: *okwōjaja.*
shallow place in the water: *kōppāāt.*
unable to go in shallow water, of vessels: *kapjulaḷ.*

shaman: *ṇakṇōk.*

shame: *jook.*
ashamed: *jook, lo.*
ashamed, concerning food: *āliklik.*
be ashamed: *pelọk.*
shameful behavior: *kajjookok.*
shameless: *jājjookok.*

shanty: *peḷak.*

shape: *annañ, kea-, ḷōma-, wāwee-.*
body shape, looks: *rọkwōj.*
form of, shape of: *lọḷin.*
give shape to: *ṇaḷōma-.*
shapeless: *jejḷōma-.*
to shape: *ḷam.*

share: *ded, jaketo-jaketak.*
a share: *ājinkōj.*
contribution, share: *kuṇaṇa.*
do one's duty, do one's share: *bōk koṇaa-.*
make shares, of food, work, etc: *kōjjebar.*
scoop up more than one's share: *rọklep.*
share a drink: *ninninkoko.*
share food equally: *aikiu.*
share of food: *kōj.*
take more than one's share: *ṃṃaelep.*
two or more persons sharing one coconut: *ninikoko.*

shark
a shark: *arōnpe.*
general term for shark: *pako.*
ground shark, *Carcharhinus melanopterus*: *pakoon eoon pedped.*
kind of shark: *jepāp.*
kind of shark, no teeth: *bab.*
shark grouper, *Carcharhinus melanopterus*: *pako mej.*
shark pilot, *Echeneis naucrates*: *ḷattil pako.*
shark, *Trisenodon obesus*: *pako korak.*
thresher shark, *Alopias vulpes*: *pako tọrtọr.*
tiger shark, *Galeocerdo arcticus*: *pako tiltil.*
a giant red shark: *Ejje.*
a giant shark: *Jarkul.*
fastest method of righting a canoe after it has capsized in order to escape sharks: *keilupako.*
left-overs of a shark: *anpakolu.*

sharp: *kkañ.*
sharp pain as from a whip or a burn: *ṇṇōk.*
sharp-tongued: *kkañ loo-.*
sharp-witted: *wājepdik.*
sharpen: *jemjem.*
sharpshooter: *wālel.*
witty, sharp: *wājepdik.*

shatter
shattered: *pedakilkil.*

shave: *āl, reja.*
shaven head: *oḷūb.*
wood-shavings: *tōp.*

she: *e.*

shear
shears: *jijāj.*
to shear: *ṃwijbar.*

shearwater
a bird, slender-billed shearwater, *Puffinus tenuirostris*: *māntōl.*
a bird, sooty shearwater, *Puffinus griseus*: *māntōl.*

sheath: *nine.*

shed: *tọọr.*
a temporary shed: *peḷak.*
shed clothing: *utūkaḷ.*

sheep: *jiip.*

sheet: *jiit.*
canoe part, cleat for tying sheet: *jirukli.*
mat used as blanket or sheet: *kilbur.*
rope from sheet line forward and aft: *ieplik.*
sheet of paper: *alen.*
sheet, nautical: *iep.*
to sheet sails in: *ṇatoon.*
use a sheet: *jiitit.*

shelf: *po.*

shell
a food, spongy meat of sprouted coconut baked in its shell: *iuwumuṃ.*
a game, child's play using pebbles and shells as imaginary objects and characters: *lijjikin.*
a game, slight-of-hand using shell and three holes in sand: *ṃōjjā.*
a shell: *bake, dimuuj, tōborọñ, toul.*
a shell, *Acmaeidae*: *jowakin.*
a shell, *Arcidae, Anadara (scapharca) satowi/broughtonii*: *kūkōr-in-ar.*
a shell, *Cadiidae, Corculum impressum/monstrosum/cardissa*: *kūkōr.*
a shell, *Conidae*: *likaebeb.*
a shell, *Cymatiidae*: *jilel.*
a shell, *Cypraeidae*: *libbukwe.*

a shell, *Ellobiidae*: *alu.*
a shell, *Fissurellidae*: *jowakin.*
a shell, *Macrophragma tokyeense (Turritellidae)*: *likarkar.*
a shell, *Muricidae*: *lidid.*
a shell, *Muricidae, Purpura (Manicinella) Armigera*: *tōbo.*
a shell, *Nautilidae*: *lọjilñin jourur.*
a shell, *Neritidae*: *jinenpokpok, kaddoḷ.*
a shell, *Neritipsidae*: *kobal.*
a shell, *Ovulidae*: *libbukwe.*
a shell, *Patellidae*: *jowakin.*
a shell, *Patellidae, Collisella grata*: *jidduul.*
a shell, *Siphonaridae*: *jowakin.*
a shell, *Solemyidae, Acila schencki*: *kūkōr.*
a shell, *Strombidae*: *aorak, lōkeed.*
a shell, *Strombidae, Lentigo lentiginosus* or *Tricornis sinuatus/thersites/latissimus*: *eañ.*
a shell, *Tellinidae, Tellinella philippii/staurella/virgata*: *kūkōr.*
a shell, *Trochidae, Bathybembix aeola*: *jidduul.*
a shell, *Veneridae, Veremilpa minuta/micra/costellifera/scabra* or *Dosinia histrio/abyssicola*: *kūkōr.*
a shell, Cassididae, *Cassis cornuta*, helmet shell: *bukbuk, bukbuk, laklak, laklak.*
a shell, a clam, *Tridacnidae*: *mejānwōd.*
a shell, clam: *pejao.*
a shell, conical and longer than trochus: *jibbin-bōran-bōb, luo.*
a shell, giant clam: *kapwor.*
a shell, killer clam: *tōkale.*
a shell, small bivalve clam: *kalibok.*
a shell, small bivalve, clam: *kọnōt.*
a toy, of shells or wood: *likaebeb.*
any cowrie shell, any shell: *libbukwe, libbukwe.*
ammunition shell casing: *wōpeñ.*
clam shell, large: *aded.*
coconut shell: *ḷat.*
coconut shell for catching coconut sap, whole and empty: *kor.*
coconut shell for scrubbing clothes: *kuḷatḷat.*
coconut shell, lower half with sharp end: *ḷat-jiṃ.*
coconut shell, lower half, without eye: *jiṃ.*
coconut shell, upper half next to stem, with eyes: *ḷat-mej.*
cone shell: *likaebeb.*
conical shell, larger than trochus: *luwo.*
cut out copra meat from shell: *karkar.*
fat in turtle shell: *wiwi.*
limpet shell: *jowakin.*
mallet made from clam shell: *dekenin.*
method of extracting coconut meat out of its shell without breaking the meat: *kōmmālwewe.*
money cowrie, a shell, *Cypraeidae*: *likajjid.*
sea snail, top shell: *kaddoḷ.*
shell of a crab: *jọkur.*
shell of larger clams: *addi.*
shell of many colors, used as lure for tuna: *jepet.*
shell of smaller clams: *wūpeñ.*
small clam, oyster, a shell, *Arcidae, Scapharca inequivalvis* or *Anadara pilulu*: *kūkōr.*
small empty shells that wash up and pile up on beach: *lōrro.*
spider shell: *aorak.*
substance of clam shell: *ajaj.*
top shell: *jidduul.*
triton shell. A shell, *Cassididae*: *jilel.*
trochus, a shell, *Pleurotomariidae*: *likaabdoulul.*
trochus, a shell, *Trochidae, Omphalius pfeifferi* or *Tristichotrochus haliarchus*. A shell, *Pleurotomariidae*: *likōppejdat, likōppejdat.*
turtle shell: *bōd, jọkur.*
weave flowers or shells into a lei: *ḷōḷō.*

shelter
shelter pit, air raid: *rọñ.*
shelter with mat at sea: *boktak.*
sheltered: *jablur.*
take shelter from the rain or sun: *kōjato.*
temporary shelter: *iṃōn kōppād.*
unsheltered: *jjerwawa.*
wait under shelter for rain to stop: *kaḷọk.*

shepherd: *jabōt.*

shield: *likōpejñak, tōrak.*
shielded: *barōk.*

shift: *kā.*

shimmer: *rrobōlbōl.*

shin: *bọtin nee-.*
shinny up: *urabbaj.*

shine: *kāilar, romaak.*
shine in the distance: *kabōlbōl.*
shiny: *jatōltōl, rabōlbōl.*

shingle
shingled, cut the hair short: *taṃbaj.*

ship: *baak, tim̧a, wa.*
battleship: *m̧ōnwa.*
bridge of ship: *būrij.*
field trip ship: *piil̦ tūrep.*
fleet of canoes, ships, or planes: *inej.*
go on a field trip ship: *rawūn.*
having a shallow draft, of ships (see *kaplep*): *kapdik.*
lighten ship: *eakpel.*
plunge of a canoe or ship: *m̧ōt.*
possessive classifier, canoe, ship, boat, or vehicle: *waa-.*
propeller of plane or ship: *pikpik.*
roll of a ship: *llāle.*
ship of: *waa-.*
ship's mate: *meej.*
shipwrecked: *eo̧tōk.*
stranded, of canoes, boats or ships: *eo̧tōk.*
to roll, of ships: *lā.*
to ship water: *douj.*
use a ship: *wawa.*
warship: *m̧ōnwa.*
waves of ships or planes: *ibeb.*

ship worm: *dile.*

shirk: *kōmādodo.*

shirt: *jōōt.*
shirtless: *kol̦eiaat, m̧an̄ke.*
T-shirt: *jiin̄lij.*
undershirt: *jiin̄lij.*
wear a shirt: *jōōtōt.*

shiver: *ebeb, kebeban, wūdiddid.*
have a shiver sent up one's spine: *mmāālel.*

shoal: *kina, kōppāāt, ņa.*
fishing method, between two shoals (*ņa*), with scarer: *uņa.*
fishing method, surrounding edges of shoals with net: *kuņa.*
shoal, of fish: *baru.*
strike a shoal: *eoņ.*

shock: *kūm̧m̧ūl̦o̧k, m̧ajōjō.*
electric shock: *jarom.*
shocked: *ilbōk, kūran̄, m̧weiur, ubabōj.*

shoe
shoes: *juuj.*
shoestring knot: *korak.*
wear shoes: *juujuj.*

shoo
shoo away: *ubaak.*

shoot: *bu.*
good marksmanship in shooting or throwing: *jero̧.*
sharpshooter: *wālel.*
shoot a bow and arrow: *lippo̧ņ.*
shoot the breeze: *kōmāltato.*
shoot with a rubber band: *lippin.*
shoot with a sling: *kōpin.*
shoot with rubber and spear: *lippin.*
shooting contest: *kōjjero̧ro.*

shoot the breeze: *lekōto.*

shoot
coconut shoot: *utak.*
shoot of coconut, pandanus: *juubub.*
shoot of the bird's nest fern (*kartōp*): *m̧ūl̦ōn̄.*
young shoot: *l̦or.*
young shoot. (Not used for coconuts or pandanus): *jul̦.*

shooter
pea-shooter: *lijjukwōlkwōl.*
shooter marble: *l̦ōttekōl̦kōl̦.*

shop: *m̧ōn wia.*

shore: *kappe, tarkijet.*
ashore: *iāne.*
directional, enclitic, islandward or shoreward: *āne.*
drift ashore: *eo̧tōk.*
go or come ashore: *wanāne.*
go shoreward: *wāānāne.*
haul canoe or vessel up on shore: *ār.*
lagoon shore: *parijet.*
offshore: *tarkijet.*
on the shore: *ioonkappe.*
seashore: *parijet.*
set ashore: *leāne.*
shoreward: *wanāne.*
steady waves buffeting the shore: *ninārār.*
washed ashore: *l̦ukut.*

short: *kadu, kanu.*
be short of: *jabjab.*
fall short of: *likjab.*
fall short of, in length: *jen.*
have one limb shorter than the other: *jipijul̦.*
kill someone during a typhoon in anticipation of shortage of food: *okjānl̦an̄.*
not to sell oneself short: *jab dodoorl̦o̧k.*
of short duration: *jedkaju.*
short and fat, of people: *depetdoul.*
short of breath: *jabjabmenowa-, jeekl̦o̧k.*
short of money: *jiban.*
short tempered, cry-baby, provoked: *kwi.*
short winded: *kkijeje.*
shortcoming: *an mej en̦.*
shortcut: *ial̦ kadu.*
shorten: *jepjep.*
shortly: *m̧ōttan jidik.*

shot: *wā.*
a shot of whiskey: *jaat.*
shot down: *lel.*
shotdown: *balu.*
shotgun: *lijjukwōlkwōl.*

should: *aikuj, ļokwan.*

shoulder: *aerā, kōp.*
carry in a basket with long handle slung over shoulder: *aduwado.*
carry on shoulders: *inene.*
put one's arm across another's shoulders while walking: *waabbilāle.*
slim-waisted and broad-shouldered: *kāāj in kabwebwe.*
touch shoulders: *aerār.*

shout: *kkeilọk, kōkkeilọk.*
shout rhythmically while doing a job requiring team work, as carrying a canoe: *roro.*
to shout: *laṃōj.*

shove
shove a person: *jipeļļọk.*

shovel: *jabōļ.*

shoveler
a bird, northern shoveler, *Anas clypeata*: *roñanpat.*

show: *ba kajjie-, jāde, kaalwōjwōj, kowaļọk.*
please show it to me: *jaṃṃōk.*
show off: *juwaļōñļōñ.*
show where to go: *āñin.*

show-off: *jājjāj, kabbil, kabōllaļ, kakōl, kōņkōṃṃan, likōmjāje.*
a show-off: *utļōṃ.*
show-off before the opposite sex: *kattoojoj.*
show-off one's possessions or achievements: *kōmmejāje.*

shower
time between rain showers: *meļa.*

shoyu: *joiu.*

shrewd: *jiṃaat, mejādik.*

shriek: *kkeilọk, kōkkeilọk.*
shriek in terror or pain: *wūdikke.*

shrimp: *libbūņōj.*

shrine: *lokatok.*

shrink: *jen, kuņōk, pit, tor.*
to shrink from responsibility: *wōmak.*

shrivel: *kuņōk.*

shroud
shrouds: *rikin.*

shrub: *ļor, mar.*
a shrub: *debọkut.*

shucks
"Shucks!": *kōṃōttōņa.*
interjection: "Shucks!" "Darn!": *io.*

shudder: *ebeb.*
shudder, as with cold: *kebeban.*

shut: *kilōk, kkiil.*

shut-eye
get some shut-eye: *wūne māj.*

shuttle: *booj.*

shy: *abje, jook.*

sibling
duty that a younger sibling is expected to give to older siblings: *jei.*
duty that an older sibling is expected to give to younger siblings: *jati.*
older sibling: *jei-.*
quarreling among siblings: *bowōd.*
younger sibling: *jati-.*
siblings: *jemjati.*

sick: *nañinmej, utaṃwe.*
a sickness supposed to come from eating *kọnet* (**kawnet**): *ppārijet.*
chronically sickly: *addimej.*
come down with a sickness: *lōbọ.*
homesick: *oñ.*
look after a sick person: *kau.*
lovesick: *kāļọk, mejkaiie.*
motion sickness: *ļļao.*
seasick: *ļļao, ṃōļañļōñ.*
sickly: *lọkmej.*
sickly (see *mour* (**mẹwir**)): *jāmmourur.*
sickness: *ñūt, nañinmej.*
sickness believed to be caused by sleeping at night under the moon: *ṃōjọliñōr.*
sickness, believed caused by sea-ghosts: *rilojet.*
sickness, constant running nose: *anjilik.*
sickness, swollen lymph glands: *bbūra.*

sickle: *jikōļ.*

Sida
a plant, *Sida fallax* Walpers: *kio.*

side: *tōrerei-, ūlūl.*
alongside: *tōrerei-.*
come alongside: *atartar.*
leeward side of an atoll: *liklaļ.*
move a little sideways to make room: *rrā.*
north side: *eañtak.*
on the east side of: *jetak, wetaa-.*
on the north side of: *aikne.*
on the south side of: *eọọtle.*
on the west side of: *rāātle, rilik.*
one-sided: *rājet.*
side of a house: *kii-.*
side of man or animal: *kat.*

sidekick in kickball: *jeṃkat.*
take sides, advocate: *rrā.*
to be on both sides: *kōjab.*
windward side of an atoll: *likiej.*

sideburns: *jeor.*

sieve: *kein liklik.*
to sieve arrowroot: *epta.*
to sieve arrowroot: first time: *jepta.*

sift: *liklik.*
net made of sennit used for sifting arrowroot starch: *waliklik.*
not well-sifted: *jālōt.*
well-sifted: *lōt.*

Siganus
a fish, rabbitfish, *Siganus* sp.: *ṃorṃor.*
a fish, rabbitfish, *Siganus rostratus*: *ṃọle.*
a fish, rabbitfish, *Siganus rostratus/ puellus*: *ellōk.*

sight
be in sight: *jāde.*
distant, of sight and sound: *kkwaad.*
euphemism used on sailing vessels to notify men to stay out of sight when women need to relieve themselves: *inọn̄.*
eyesight: *rre.*
foresight: *loḷọkjeṇ.*
out of sight: *penjak.*
receive sight: *loḷọkjeṇ.*
sight along a board to see if it is straight: *allọk.*
sight land: *ḷanno.*
sight-seeing: *alwōj bajjek.*
sightless: *kun an ḷaaṃ.*

sign: *jain, kakōḷḷe.*
a rain storm that is the sign of a chief coming: *ḷan̄ōn irooj.*
name of two navigational signs: *Kobal.*
navigational sign in Marshallese navigation: *kōkḷaḷ.*
signal: *kakōḷḷe.*
signal with a mirror: *kakkilaajaj.*
signify: *kakōḷḷe.*

signal
signal made on the end of the *kie* of a canoe signifying battle: *jubwij.*
visual signal such as fire to notify of death or other natural disasters: *jubwij.*

silent
be silent and pensive: *kejaklọkjeṇ.*
keep silent: *ikōn̄.*
silence: *ikōn̄.*

silhouette: *annan̄.*

silk: *jelōk.*

silly: *bwebwe, jajeḷọkjeṇ.*

silver: *jelba.*

silverfish
a fish, silverfish, *Gerres baconensis*: *ilmek.*

similar
more similar to: *āinḷọk.*
similar to: *āi-, ari-.*

simmer: *du.*

simple: *ḷam waan, pidodo.*

simulate: *ari-.*

sin: *bōd, jerọwiwi, ruo-.*
fall into sin: *tōmrok.*
mortal sin: *jerọwiwiin mej.*
original sin: *jerọwiwiin jolōt.*

since: *jān, kōnke.*

sincere: *ṃool.*

sing: *al.*
a musical composition to be sung by all singers together: *kọrōj.*
sing upon trees or in places above: *aluej.*

singe: *rirar.*

single
single, unmarried: *jalen.*

singlehanded: *jalenpā.*
to sail a canoe or boat singlehandedly: *wajekā.*

singly: *kajjojo.*

sink: *pelaḷ, run̄ḷọk, tal, timaruk, tun̄n̄ūlaḷḷọk, turruḷọk.*
feet sink in sand making for difficult walking: *neen kōbkōb.*
outrigger sinks because too much weight is placed on it: *tōmrok.*
sink into something: *ṃọọn.*
sink something in water: *kōtal.*

sinus
characterized by chronic sinusitis: *rijekā.*

siphon: *ṇomṇom.*

Siphonaridae
a shell, *Siphonaridae*: *jowakin.*

sir: *ḷe.*

siren: *jaidin̄.*
trumpet, horn, siren, conch: *jilel.*

sister
older sister: *jei-, jine-.*
sisters of a male: *ine-.*
younger sister: *jati-.*

sit
babysit: *kaajiriri.*
sit close together: *atartar.*
sit down: *jijet.*

sit on one's haunches: *pijļeļe.*
sitting mat: *era-, tōļao.*
small sitting mat: *miar.*
to sit up on something high with the feet dangling and moving incessantly: *tōpļedik.*

site: *wōja.*

six: *jiljino.*
sixteen: *joñouljiljino.*
sixty: *jiljinoñoul.*
sixty pairs, fish or copra: *jiljinokor.*
sixth moon phase: *maroklep.*

size: *ded, detta-, jaij, joña-.*
compare size: *joñjoñ.*
decreasing in size: *mǫkun.*
decreasing in size, as of physique: *tor.*
giant size: *debbōn.*
of good size: *m̧m̧an ded.*

sizzle: *ttiijij.*

skate: *jikeet.*
a fish, a species of skate: *jim̧jǫ.*

skeptical: *kōrraat.*

ski: *jājjāj.*

skid: *jājjāj, jirilǫk, midij.*

skiff: *booj.*

skill: *mejādik, tuon.*
skillful: *kapeel, ņakņōk.*
unskilled person: *jedañ.*
unskillful: *jekapeel.*

skim
skim across a surface: *jājjāj.*

skin: *kil.*
bad case of skin disease (*koko* (**kewkew**)): *keļe.*
cracks in skin of soles of feet: *bōlkōk.*
darkskinned: *jakmeej.*
disease, scaly and flaky skin: *koko.*
flabby, of skin: *pidtoto.*
get under one's skin: *kiliddāp.*
light skinned: *wūdmouj.*
mole on the skin: *ilmeej.*
rough skin: *bbadede.*
scaly skin: *kwōdkwōdi.*
skin disease: *karko, tilpoki.*
skin disease, white spots on body: *jān.*
skin diving: *turǫñ.*
skin parts of a plant to ensure its bearing of fruit or flowers: *kōnar.*
skin ulcer: *dekā, eakeak.*
tender skin of a baby: *ub.*
to skin: *ākilkil, kakilkil.*
twine made from skin of coconut frond midrib: *mālwe.*
thick-skinned: *mejel kil.*

skinny: *aidik, uwaidikdik.*

skip: *jājjāj, kijoon.*
a game, skip-rope: *kutiñ.*
skip over: *kājoon.*

skip jack
Caranx lessonii: *ļañe, m̧ōļajutak.*
Caranx melampygus, Hawaiian *ulua*: *deltokrōk.*
immature form, *Caranx lessonii*: *kupkup.*

skirmish: *taim̧.*
a skirmish: *im.*

skirt: *likko.*
aboriginal women's skirts, now used as baby's mat: *ed.*
grass skirt: *in, inin, ōr.*
grass skirt boys put on at puberty: *kiōk.*
man's skirt made from coconut fronds: *elmen.*
wear a skirt: *inin.*

skull: *ļat.*

sky: *lañ.*
northwestern sky: *kapilōñ iōñ.*
red colored, of reddish coconuts or sky: *mir.*
southwestern sky: *kapilōñ rōk.*
western sky: *kapilōñ.*

slab: *pedped.*

slack
let out a rope to slacken it: *peaut.*

slam
slam, as of a door: *okkoļǫk.*

slander: *ruruwe, wūnwūj, wūnwūjriabeb.*

slang: *kaj.*

slap: *deñdeñ, depdep, jeptak, ubrar.*
slap on the back of the head: *jepwaļ.*
to hit or slap someone with something, usually flat: *ubatak.*
waves receding from shore slapping against incoming waves: *jipikra.*

slash: *ōrōr.*
cut, hack, chop-off, split, slash: *jepak.*
slash with machete: *kabwil.*

slaughter: *m̧anm̧an.*

slave: *kuli.*

slay: *kowadoñ, m̧anm̧an.*

sleek: *meoeo, metal.*

sleep: *kiki, mājur.*
asleep: *kiki, mājur.*
fall asleep: *m̧adenļǫk.*
look up after nodding, sleeping, or reading: *bōk bar.*
make a sound of pleasure while

sleeping because of good dreams: *jeja.*
oversleep: *mājurlep.*
see a vision in sleep: *m̧adenļǫk.*
sleep close to fire all night, especially old people: *eǫwilik.*
sleep on mattress: *būtoñtoñ.*
sleep soundly: *joņak, leņak, m̧adenļǫk, mājurlep, ñakļǫkjeņ, ttoñ.*
sleep, chickens only: *de.*
sleeping mat: *jañiñi.*
sleeping place of: *lǫrun.*
sleepy: *aruñijñij, mejki, mmadidi, mmejraalal.*
talk or walk in one's sleep: *jja.*

sleeve
roll up shirt sleeves or trousers: *limtak.*

slender: *kādik, uwaidikdik.*

slice: *jiļait.*

slick: *meoeo, metal.*

slide: *midij, wāār.*
slide accidentally: *jirilǫk.*
slide out of hand: *rōļǫk.*

slight: *jiniñniñ.*
slightly: *jaad.*

slim: *kādik, uwaidikdik.*
slim-waisted and broad-shouldered: *kāāj in kabwebwe.*

slime
slime from slugs and fish: *medaekek.*
slimy: *dāndān, kkōr, korōt.*
slimy-eyed: *mejkōr.*

sling
hoist by sling: *m̧ukko.*
not good marksman, with gun, slingshot, or by throwing stones (see *jerǫ* (**jeraw**)): *jerta.*
shoot with a sling: *kōpin.*
sling for hoisting cargo: *m̧ukko.*
slingshot: *buwat.*
stones in a sling: *bo.*

slip: *jājļǫk, jikeet, jirilǫk, midij, tipjek, tūbbǫk.*
slip down a tree or pole: *pirūrrūr.*
slip down out of position, of things: *pir.*
slip out: *kkekaak.*
slip under ground or sand: *jǫ.*
slipped by, unite, escape: *rōļǫk.*
slippery: *jjir.*
slippery, of trees: *tabur.*

slip: *jemej, likko.*
wear a slip: *jemej.*

slipper: *jodi.*

slipshod: *jabde.*

slit: *m̧wijm̧wij.*

slither
slithering: *tōbalbal.*

sliver: *tenaļ.*

slobber: *iādatōltōl, kaplo.*

slogan: *kaj.*

sloop: *ioot.*
a sloop: *jibūkbūk.*

slop
slop out: *llutōk.*
sloppy: *iiōk dakdak, jabde, jakōl.*

slope: *jepāpe.*
steep slope: *jirūm̧le.*

slovenly: *iiōk dakdak.*
a slovenly person: *ikōn aļe.*

slow: *bat, jāiur, kadikdik, mejjeeļ, ppedikdik, raļǫk, rum̧wij.*
be slow to decide: *aepedped.*
be slow witted: *aļļañ.*
move slowly, snail's pace: *m̧ōkaj jān om̧.*
slow moving: *ikirum̧wij.*
slow to anger in debate (see *kwi* (**qiy**)): *jǫkkwikwi.*
slow to anger in debate (see *ññiñi* (**ggiygiy**)): *jaññiñi.*
slow to cry: *jǫkkwikwi.*
slow to die (see *mejjiie* (**mẹjjiyyẹy**)): *mejjiia.*
slow to learn (see *penawiie* (**pẹnhawiyyẹy**)): *penawiia.*
slow to obey: *jilikiia.*
slow when called (see *āñiie* (**yagiyyẹy**)): *āñiia.*
very slow: *ikirum̧wij.*

slug
sea slug: *pedobar, piāpe.*
slime from slugs and fish: *medaekek.*

slug: *dukwaļ.*

sluggish: *ddo, jāmmourur.*
sluggishness: *addim̧akoko.*

slumber: *kiki.*

slur
slur one's words: *aplo.*

slurp
to slurp: *ļwiit.*

sly: *Etao.*

smack
smack the lips: *tōmmeļǫk.*

small: *dik, jiddik, niñ, wūddik.*
anything small and round: *lijadoul.*
general term for small things: *oļar.*
small fry: *mānniñ.*
small pieces: *tipdikdik.*
small pox: *bokļap.*
small thing: *ja.*

very small: *jibbatūñtūñ, jiniñniñ, wūnniñ.*
very small amount: *jebōñ.*

smart: *jiṃaat, mālōtlōt, penawiie.*
a smart move: *jeḷā kōppeḷak.*
not smart: *jājiṃaat.*

smart
smart, as medicine on a sore: *māāṇ.*
smart, irritated: *korōt.*

smash: *jjiped, rup.*
be smashed against something, of canoes: *ubwe.*
get smashed in: *penā.*
smash into each other: *iṃaajaj.*
smash-up: *iṃaajaj.*
smashed: *kwōp, mālij, obab, peddejọkwe.*

smear: *būrar.*

smegma: *ṇaṇ.*

smell: *ātāt, bbūḷapḷap, bwii-, kāātet, kōnāmnām, nām, nāmnām.*
fragrant smell: *ñaj.*
savory smell: *bwiin-ennọ.*
smell and taste of uncooked meat: *bbūramejmej.*
smell moldy: *ḷōḷ.*
smell of a swamp: *juoñ.*
smell of armpits: *medwañ.*
smell of blood: *meḷḷā.*
smell of breaking wind: *bwiin-jiñ.*
smell of cats: *kkuujuj.*
smell of chicken manure: *bwiin-kūbween-alōr.*
smell of clothing or mats under sun: *bbidetdet.*
smell of cockroaches: *bwiin-juwapen.*
smell of coconuts: *būbnini, bwiin-ni.*
smell of cooking fish: *uwi.*
smell of copper: *kkōbaba.*
smell of damp clothing: *jatbo.*
smell of dead flesh: *kkōōrōr.*
smell of dead plants in water: *juoñ.*
smell of decayed flesh: *bwiin-puwaḷ, juoñ.*
smell of exposed reef: *bbilwōdwōd.*
smell of feces: *kūñ.*
smell of feces on body or clothing: *ñoño.*
smell of fish, lingering on hands, body, or utensils: *aelel, joñọ.*
smell of imported goods: *bwiin-ppāllele.*
smell of iron: *mmāālāl.*
smell of kerosene: *kkarjinjin.*
smell of leaves of bushes: *kkumarmar.*
smell of new things: *bwiin-ppāllele.*
smell of pit for soaking coconut husks: *būto.*
smell of preserved breadfruit: *bbiroro.*
smell of roasting breadfruit: *kkwanjinjin.*
smell of rotten copra on body: *maḷḷipen.*
smell of rotten copra or rancid coconut oil: *ḷōḷ.*
smell of scrotum: *bbūrọrọ.*
smell of smoke on breath, body, or clothing, etc.: *bbaidid.*
smell of the sea: *bbijetjet.*
smell of turtles: *bbilwōnwōn.*
smell of unwashed genitals: *kūtkūt.*
smell of unwashed sexual organs: *būṇo.*
smell of urine: *kūḷōj, mieñ.*
smell or taste sour or bitter, as milk, vinegar, or rice soup, etc.: *meñ.*
smell, body odor, disagreeable: *ajjiḷapḷap.*
smell, halitosis: *taiñad.*
smelly: *nām.*
sweet smell, of ripe pandanus fruit: *bwiin-tōñal.*

smile: *ttōñ dikdik.*
a boy or man whose appearance makes everyone smile: *ḷḷajkōnkōn.*
smile, showing the white of the teeth: *rere.*
always smiling or laughing: *baūjō.*

smite: *ubrar.*

smithereens: *pedakilkil.*

smoke: *atiti, baat, baatat, boutḷọk.*
blinded with smoke: *mejko.*
chain smoke: *baidtōñtōñ.*
rack for heat or smoke drying: *ati, bwi.*
smell of smoke on breath, body, or clothing, etc.: *bbaidid.*
smoke illicitly: *lijāludik.*
smoke out: *jinbaat.*
smoked fish: *ek ṃōṇakṇak.*
to smoke: *kōbaatat.*
smoking addict: *añūrlep.*
smoking marijuana: *kaurur baib.*

smooth: *metal.*
hair smoothed with oil: *medọḷ.*
not smooth: *kurere.*
smooth and calm, of water: *ḷae.*
smooth like fur: *meoeo.*
smooth surf after a succession of rollers: *mooḷ.*
smooth with a knife: *eọr.*

smother
smothered: *jabjen menowa-.*
smothered, of food: *jitable.*

smudge: *jinbaat, rran.*
smuggle: *kōrabōl.*
smut: *rran.*
snack: *m̧ōñein kōtaan awa.*
snag
snagged: *kijek.*
snail
common snail: *lidid.*
limpet snails with nonconical shells: *jidduul.*
move slowly, snail's pace: *m̧ōkaj jān om̧.*
sea snail: *jinenpokpok.*
sea snail, top shell: *kaddoļ.*
snake: *jabōn, jedpānit.*
a fish, snake eel, *Myrichthys colubrinus*: *m̧ajid.*
snap: *kwōj.*
snap up: *kkubōl.*
snap, as a branch: *dokwōj.*
snapping or cracking sound: *ņņōjņōj.*
snapping sound: *ņoj.*
snapper
red snapper, *Lutjanus bohar*: *paan.*
red snapper, *Lutjanus vaigiensis*: *jaap.*
snapper, *Aprion virescens*: *ewae.*
snapper, *Gymnocranius microndon/griseus*: *mejmej.*
snapper, *Lutjanus flavipes*: *jāj.*
snapper, *Lutjanus kasmira forskal*: *jetaar.*
snapper, *Lutjanus monostigmus*: *juwajo.*
snapper, *Lutjanus vitta*: *bōnej.*
snapper, *Scolopsis cancellatus*: *kwōlej.*
spot snapper, *Lutjanus fulviflamma*: *kalikūrōk.*
snare: *allok, aujiid, jān.*
snare for catching birds: *keepep.*
snarl: *ūjō.*
snarled: *pok.*
unsnarl: *jaļjaļ, mejaļ.*
unsnarl a tangled fishline: *kōmmeļeļe.*
unsnarled: *meļeļe.*
sneak: *ajādik, ajjādikdik.*
sneak away: *iaļ aidik.*
sneak away from: *kona.*
sneak out: *ajjiwewe.*
sneer: *kajjirere.*
sneeze: *m̧aje.*
constant sneezing: *anjilik.*
sniff: *kāātet, kōnāmnām.*
sniff around: *kāātet.*
sniff, inhale, breathe: *kōbotuut.*
snipe: *kwōlej.*
snipe that has lost its feathers: *m̧ōdkowak.*
snitch: *kinaak, kōrabōl, kona.*
snitch: *kiltōn.*
snob
snobbish: *kappok jide.*
snoop: *apād.*
snooping: *eded.*
snore: *ñortak.*
snout: *bo̧ti.*
snow: *jiņo.*
snuff: *kāātet.*
so: *āindein, jemļam, toļo̧k.*
and so: *jujen.*
and so (in narratives): *em̧ōj.*
so that: *bwe.*
so what: *makarta.*
soak: *jojo.*
get old and dilapidated due to continuous soaking in sea water: *luwajet.*
pit for soaking coconut husks for making sennit: *to.*
smell of pit for soaking coconut husks: *būto.*
soaked: *m̧oujlep.*
soap: *joob.*
use soap: *joobob.*
soar: *pāl-.*
sob: *batoñtoñ.*
sobbing because of grief: *m̧ōtato.*
sober: *jeļā ļo̧kjen̄, jememe.*
social
anti-social: *jememe.*
society: *jarlepju.*
socket
socket for end of boom (one at each end of canoe): *dipāākāk.*
socks: *jito̧kin, takin.*
wear socks: *takinkin.*
sod
surface, sod: *jat.*
sofa: *joba.*
soft: *jjipdodo, pidodo, ub.*
soft drink: *koļa.*
soft sell: *lekōto.*
soft spoken: *naan mera.*
soft spot on baby's head: *m̧on̄.*
soft to touch: *meoeo.*
soft-hearted: *ineem̧m̧an, meanwōd.*
soggy: *ļwōjat.*
soil: *bwidej, rran.*
area from which soil has been taken: *anil.*
fertile soil: *kōl.*

good soil: *ijo.*
poor soil: *ḷọurō.*
push up soil, of roots: *pādāl.*
rich, of soil or plant: *kimuur.*

sol
syllable "sol" of musical scale: *jooḷ.*

solace: *jojoon.*

sold
hung up on, sold on: *reel.*

soldier: *rūttarinae.*
magic to make soldiers brave: *mọun.*

sole
cracks in skin of soles of feet: *bōlkōk.*
sole of foot: *lọpiden ne.*

Solemyidae
a shell, *Solemyidae, Acila schencki*: *kūkōr.*

solid: *mājojo, ñilñil, pen.*
packed solid: *ñūñ.*
shake down a container to pack more solidly: *ḷattuñ.*
solidify: *kwōj.*

solitaire: *kawūjwūj.*

solitary: *make.*

somber: *lianij.*

some: *jet, jiṃa.*
somebody: *juon.*
someone: *juon.*
something: *juon men.*
sometime: *juon iien.*
sometimes: *jet ien.*
somewhat: *jaad.*
somewhere here around me: *ijekā, ijekākā.*
somewhere here around us: *ijekein.*
someone that people are always talking about: *tiemlo.*

somersault: *juñaidi.*

somnolent: *mmadidi.*

son
second son or daughter: *utlōkḷap.*
son of: *nāji-.*
son or daughter-in-law of: *nāji-.*
sonny: *būrọ.*

song: *al.*
christmas song fest (Protestant groups): *jebta.*
compose songs or chants: *kine.*
love song: *alin ṃaina.*
mistake in performing a dance, song, or chant: *dujebwābwe.*
start a song: *jarjar.*
steering song: *alin ṃur.*
to bring foods with songs as refreshments to a group of men building a canoe or house to keep their morale up, usually done by the womenfolk of a community: *jemjem māāl.*

Sonneratia
a plant, *Sonneratia caseolaris*: *buḷaboḷ.*
a plant, mangrove, *Sonneratia caseolaris*. In mangrove depressions: *kōnpat.*

sonorous: *ḷḷaaj.*

soon: *epaak, ṃōttan jidik.*
very soon: *kiiō-kiiō.*

soot: *rran.*

soothsayer: *rūkaanij.*

sooty tern
a bird, sooty tern, *Sterna fuscata*: *mmej.*
baby bird, sooty tern, *mmej*: *jipila.*

Sophora
a plant, *Sophora tomentosa* L. (Leguminosae): *kille.*

soprano: *jebrano.*

sorcerer: *rijọubwe.*
black magic performed by a sorcerer using a husked coconut: *kaurur jiañ.*
sorcerer whose speech has magical power: *atlo.*

sorcery: *anijnij, rojak.*
sorcery in medicine: *ṃadṃōd.*

sore: *metak.*
a sore, painful and malignant, usually located on the hands or feet: *jiṇo.*
bump a sore or wound: *keeñjak, kkeñaj.*
have sore eyes: *mejmetak.*

sorrow: *būroṃōj.*
remember with sorrow: *ememḷọkjeṇ.*
sorrowful: *kabbūroṃōjṃōj.*
sorrowful laughter: *rereenak.*
sorrowful looking: *kōmjaaḷaḷ.*

sorry: *būroṃōj.*
sorry consequences: *amentaklaḷ.*

sort: *kain, rot, tor, turot.*
sort of: *kaiṇṇe.*
sort out: *kọkwōpej.*
sort out bad copra: *ākūt.*

sortie
a sortie of planes: *ibeb.*

soul: *ḷọḷātāt.*
her soul: *aṇ.*
his soul: *an.*
my soul: *aō.*
our soul: *ad, am.*
our souls: *arro.*

your soul: *aṃ.*
your souls: *ami.*

Soulamea
a plant, *Soulamea amara* Lam. (Simarubaceae): *kabwijlōñ.*

sound: *ainikie-, ñil.*
clanging sound: *taññaļọk.*
crying sound: *ṃa.*
distant, of sight and sound: *kkwaad.*
explosive sound, voiceless bilabial affricate: *rūb.*
frisky, sound, vigorous: *ājmuur.*
high-pitched sound: *ļļaaj.*
make a sound of pleasure while sleeping because of good dreams: *jeja.*
melodious sound: *ļļaaj.*
piercing sound: *ļļaaj.*
popping sound: *ṇọb.*
popping sound made when squashing lice: *noñ.*
rasping sound: *rap.*
ringing sound: *tūññūļọk.*
sleep soundly: *ñakļọkjeṇ.*
snapping or cracking sound: *ṇṇōjṇōj.*
snapping sound: *ṇoj.*
sound of a bell or something rung: *tōññōļọk.*
sound of a collision: *okkoļọk.*
sound of an explosion: *bokkoļọk.*
sound of coconut bouncing: *rukruk.*
sound of grease frying: *ttiijij.*
sound of someone falling: *pọkwi.*
sound of stamping: *puruk.*
sound of treading feet: *ṃṃūṇṃūṇ.*
sound of waves pounding on reef: *lijeñūrñūr.*
thudding sound: *pọkwi.*
tremor or vibration caused by sound of gun or thunder: *pañijñij.*
voiceless bilabial affricate with a sudden, audible expulsion of sound (low): *rap.*

soundly
sleep soundly: *joṇak, leṇak, ṃadenļọk, mājurlep, ttoñ.*

soup: *juub.*
a food, breadfruit soup: *jokkwōpin mā.*
a food, soup of soft rice or breadfruit: *jokkwōp.*
a food, soup, spongy coconut and arrowroot: *aikiu.*

sour: *meọ.*
make a sour face: *kōmmeñ.*
old and sour coconut sap: *mañūñ.*
smell or taste sour or bitter, as milk, vinegar, or rice soup, etc.: *meñ.*
sour faced: *jaṃṃōṇōṇō.*
sour toddy: *jimañūñ.*

source: *wūn.*

south: *rak, rōk.*
on the south side of: *eọọtle.*
sail with the outrigger on the south: *tōmrak.*
southern part: *turōk.*
the Southern Cross: *Būbwin Epoon.*

southerly
southerly swell: *buñtokrōk.*

southward: *rōkeañ, rōña.*
current flowing southward: *aerōkeañļọk.*
directional, enclitic, southward: *rōkeañ, rōña.*
drift southward: *perōkeañ.*
head southward: *jitrōkeañ.*

southwest
southwestern sky: *kapilōñ rōk.*
wind from southwest: *kūtak.*

souvenir: *jolōt, kein kakeememej.*

sow
to sow: *kkat.*

soy sauce: *joiu.*

space: *mejatoto.*
cleared space: *maaj.*
little space between trees: *tuwa.*
occupy a lot of space: *koobob.*
open space: *meļaaj.*
space-filling: *kaddoujuj.*

spade: *jipeit.*
deuce of spades: *litōļpi.*

Spain: *Jipein.*

spank: *deñdeñ, depdep, eṇọ, kapipā, ļwōjā, notoñ, pejaju.*
spanking, child speech: *baṃbaṃ.*

spar
canoe part, line from top of mast to outrigger spar (*jojo* (**jewjew**)): *tokubaak.*
canoe part, outrigger spar: *jojo.*
canoe part, ties between spar and outrigger: *jojo.*
spar of sail: *rojak.*

spat: *leļọk-letok.*

spathe
a food, diluted starch baked in coconut spathe in earth oven: *kōlọwutaktak.*
open spathe of coconut tree: *jepar, jinnipraň.*

spawn: *ine.*

speak: *kōmlōt, kōnnaan, kōnono.*
speak secretly: *wūnojidikdik.*
speak taboo words that may bring bad luck: *ļakajeṃ.*
directional, postposition, toward the speaker: *tok.*

spear: *ṃade, wākar.*
bundle of long objects such as spears, fish poles, etc.,: *tūr.*
fishing method, hanging on to reef while spearing: *kiijbaal.*
fishing method, spear fishing: *turoñ.*
fishing method, spear fishing while diving: *tuwā.*
fishing method, spearfishing on reef: *aubō.*
fishing method, waiting along the usual path of fish on the reef to spear them, usually done at the beginning of ebb and flow tide: *kōkkāāļāļ.*
fishing method, with spear at reef edge: *bbō.*
make a handle for a spear: *buñi.*
not good marksman with spear (see *wālel* (**waylęl**)): *jowālel.*
pierce with husking stick or spear: *ddeb.*
shoot with rubber and spear: *lippin.*
spear handle: *buñ.*
spearing: *wālel.*
stick with spear, knife, or needle, etc.: *lōlō.*
to spear: *debdeb, wā.*
use a spear: *ṃadede.*
ward off a spear thrust: *taar.*

special
especially: *ļaptata.*

specialist: *ņakņōk.*

specific: *jejjet.*

spectacles: *māj kilaaj.*

spectacular: *kōppaļpaļ.*

speculate: *kajjidede, kajjimalele, leļōmņak.*

speech: *jipij, kwaļok naan.*
critical in speech: *kkañ loo-.*
magical power of speech: *atlo.*
make a speech: *jipij.*
powerful in speech: *aejemjem.*

speed: *ṃōkaj.*
Marshallese goddess of speed: *Lippidjowe.*
move at highest possible speed: *buuļtōñtōñ.*
not speedy: *jāiurjet.*
run at full speed: *kokleejej.*
speed up: *kūrōn.*
speed up when rubbing sticks to make fire: *jorjor.*
speedy: *ṃōkaj.*

spell
ability to cast spell: *anitta.*
cast a spell on: *anjin.*
spell, enchantment: *anijnij.*

spell: *jipeeļ.*
spelling: *jipeeļ.*

spend: *amān.*
custom of spending the last night with people before they depart: *jeboñōn.*
spend last moments together, farewell occasion, bring to a finish: *kōjjeṃļok.*
spend the night with friends who are departing: *jebokwōn.*

spendthrift: *bōro-ļap.*

sperm: *pek.*

spew
spew out chewed food: *burak.*

Sphyraena
a fish, barracuda, *Sphyraena barracuda*: *jujukōp.*
a fish, barracuda, *Sphyraena forsteri*: *jure, ñiitwa.*

Spica
Spica in Virgo: *Da.*
the pair of stars Spica and Arcturus: *Daam-Ad.*

spider: *kadeoeo, kauļaļo.*
giant spider: *kūrkūrbale, kūrūble.*
spider's web: *toon kouļaļo.*

spider shell: *aorak.*

spigot: *bojet.*

spike: *jibaik.*
marlinespike: *ṃaanjibaik.*

spill: *llutōk.*

spin: *jet, kajet, likaebeb.*

spine: *dilep.*
spines on fish: *iñ.*

spinster: *lejnono.*

spiral: *kilmij.*

spirit: *jetōb.*
invoke a spirit: *allōk.*
spirit dwelling within a person, good or bad: *juk jetōb.*
spiritual power: *abōn.*
to possess, of evil spirits: *tuwe.*

spit: *iādatōltōl, ṃṃōj.*
spit out something: *pejmām.*
spittle: *kaplo.*
to spit: *kaplo.*

spit
sandspit: *bok.*

splash: *bbūtūktūk, jjelōblōb.*
  splash water on: *jǫjo.*
spleen: *aj.*
splendid: *aiboojoj.*
splendor: *kāilar.*
splice: *dde.*
splinter
  get a splinter: *tenaḷ.*
  pick out splinters: *arar.*
  splinter, chip: *naaḷ.*
  splintered: *kurbalōklōk.*
split: *bōrrā, jar, kōk.*
  cut, hack, chop-off, split, slash: *jepak.*
  split open: *bōḷñak.*
spoil: *kǫkkure, tōrañ.*
  abandoned unhatched egg, usually
    spoiled: *kor.*
  be spoiled, of a pampered child:
    kakōl.
  get spoiled, of fish: *ekḷǫk.*
  hives, from eating spoiled fish: *judu.*
  overripe spoiled breadfruit: *māḷǫk.*
  spoiled fish or meat: *kōt.*
  spoiled from overexposure to air and
    sun: *mōṇakṇak.*
  take care not to spoil a good thing:
    kōṃbade.
spoke
  soft spoken: *naan mera.*
  spokesman: *jiṃwin ñi, wōnṃaan.*
spokeshave: *jibǫkjeep.*
Spondius: *bake.*
sponge: *matmat, oñoñ.*
  sponge off: *uñtaak.*
  to sponge off of someone: *kañkañ,*
    kwōdmat, reja.
spook: *timǫṇ.*
  spooky: *aeto.*
spool
  roll up, line or film, spool: *tāte.*
spoon: *jibuun.*
  spoon cut from coconut husk:
    kūḷatḷat.
  spoon made from chip of green
    coconut husk: *auḷakḷak.*
  tablespoon: *tebōḷ jibuun.*
  teaspoon: *tijibuun.*
sporadic
  sporadic in bearing, of trees: *jepāl.*
sport: *kkure.*
  be a good sport: *kaṃōṇōṇō.*
spot: *buwaj.*
  beauty spot: *il meej, ilmeej.*
  multicolored, spotted, usually
    brownish: *kkaadad.*
  spot, as on dog: *buwak.*

spotless: *kkwōjarjar.*
spotted: *tiltil.*
spotted, dotted, spotty: *bbijinjin.*
  striped or spotted, as in ancient
    tattoo: *eǫt.*
  white spot on the head of the brown
    noddy (*pejwak*) bird: *ao.*
spouse: *kuṇaa-, pālee-, rii-, rūturi-.*
  covet another's spouse, steal another's
    spouse: *aelellaḷ, aelellaḷ.*
  spouse of: *ippa-.*
  steal another's spouse: *jebbōro, kkuul*
    bōro.
spout
  spout, rain gutter: *tāāñ.*
sprain: *iñiñ, iñrōk, jānruk, jidpaḷ.*
  sprained: *ir.*
sprat
  long fish trap, for sprats, net with
    handle: *bǫro.*
Spratelloides
  a fish, *piha, Spratelloides*
    delicatulus: aol.
spray: *bbūtūktūk, boutḷǫk,*
  jādbūtūktūk.
  bow spray: *ṇojǫ.*
  protect from rain or spray at sea with
    mat: *boktak.*
  saltspray: *tabūṇṇo.*
  wet with spray: *jādbūtūktūk.*
spread
  spread about: *jeplōklōk.*
  spread abroad: *peddejak.*
  spread eagle: *perakrōk.*
  spread far and wide: *tilmaak.*
  spread legs wide open: *bōḷñak.*
  spread mats: *erōk.*
  spread one's thighs: *ḷañ.*
  spread out: *eḷḷǫk, eojaḷ, erḷǫk, jeeded.*
  spread the word: *bōōjōj.*
sprightly: *alijerḷǫk, iurjet, kākemǫǫj,*
  mmourur.
spring: *jibriiñ.*
  spring tide: *iaḷap.*
  swamp spring: *keiiuiu.*
  to spring: *kā-.*
sprinkle: *bbūtbūt, wōt-dikdik.*
  to sprinkle: *utdikdik.*
sprit
  bowsprit: *ḷobōrwa.*
sprout: *eǫñ, juḷ, ḷor.*
  a food, bundled and baked spongy
    meat of sprouted coconut: *iutūr.*
  a food, pounded meat of sprouted
    coconut: *lukor.*
  hard coconut meat remaining in half-
    shall of sprouted coconut after

spongy core has been removed: *ñar.*
kernel of spongy meat inside coconut that has just started to sprout: *bōļoñar.*
overgrown and inedible sprouted coconut: *iupej.*
pandanus key, sprouted: *wūnpej.*
small sprouted coconut: *per.*
smaller eye of sprouted coconut: *tōbo.*
spongy meat of sprouted coconut: *iu.*
sprout, of leaves: *jebar.*
sprouted coconut: *iu.*
stage of the coconut seedling in which it is beginning to sprout: *tōboļāār.*
taro sprout: *il.*
a food, spongy meat of sprouted coconut baked in its shell: *iuwumųmų.*
a food, spongy meat of sprouted coconut cooked with arrowroot starch and diluted with water: *peaut.*
group of sprouted coconuts past the eating stage: *debweiu.*

spur: *jebwij.*
to urge, goad, spur, push: *rrǫǫj.*

spurt: *bbūtūktūk, būttūk.*

sputum: *mmed.*

spy: *iaroñroñ, jibai, kōjjaad, waat.*

spyglass: *baiklaaj.*

squab: *koon.*

squall: *utǫr.*
wind squall: *mowi.*

square: *jukwẹea.*

square off
to square off: *jibwe doon.*

squash: *baañke.*
fall and get squashed: *pedej.*

squat: *pijļeļe.*
squat with legs wide apart: *kōļtak.*

squawk: *rraakak.*

squeamish: *arrukwikwi, jjō.*
not squeamish: *jājjō.*

squeeze: *kkeeņ(e).*
coconut cloth used to squeeze and extract oil from grated coconut: *jouneak.*
grab, squeeze: *kkuul.*
squeeze into: *obar.*
squeeze into a seat: *koobob.*

squid: *nōt.*

squint: *addikdik, aljet.*

squirm: *iñtōk.*

squirrel fish: *mālij.*
Holocentrus sp.: *jera.*
Holocentrus binotatus/scythrops: *kur.*
Holocentrus microstoma: *kañkōñ.*
Myripristis berndti: *m̧ōn.*
fishing method, fishing for squirrel fish: *diil.*

squirt: *būttūk.*

stab: *bwiār, ōrōr, wā, wāāpep, wākar.*

stable
emotionally unstable: *anniabeab.*
mentally unstable: *m̧ōjǫliñōr, taņo.*
unstable: *bbōroro, bōro-pejpej, m̧m̧akūt.*
stabilized: *jokkun wōt juon.*

stack: *ejouj.*
stack up: *jojoon.*

staff: *jokoņ, joor.*

stage
group of sprouted coconuts past the eating stage: *debweiu.*
stage of growth: *ded.*
stage of the coconut seedling in which it is beginning to sprout: *tōboļāār.*
young stage of coconut growth, after *debweiu*: *jokiae.*

stagger: *jebwāālel, jepāppāp, m̧m̧al.*

stain
stained: *māār.*
stains: *būrar.*

stair
climb a ladder or a staircase: *jikin uwe.*
staircase: *jikin uwe.*
stairway: *jikin uwe.*

stake: *dumej.*

stake
play cards for stakes: *pile.*

stale: *nānnān, nnān.*

stalk
stalk inside bunch of bananas or breadfruit: *perañ.*
stalk of arrowroot plant: *aetōktōk.*
stalk, leafstem, petiole: *kōļā.*

stalk
stalk someone or something: *apād.*

stall
to stall: *m̧oņ.*

stalwart: *kije.*

stammer: *allo.*

stamp
sound of stamping: *puruk.*
stamping: *m̧m̧ūņm̧ūņ.*

stamp: *jitaam̧.*

stance
fighting stance: *joorkatkat.*

stand: *jurōk, kajjuur, kowawa.*
stand a coconut husking stick in the ground: *kat.*

stand a torch in the ground: *kwōn.*
stand at attention: *kankan.*
stand back and study critically, as an artist: *allọk.*
stand beside: *kōjab.*
stand by a weir waiting for tide: *watak.*
stand on one's hands: *ju.*
stand on one's head: *ju, lōlō.*
stand on tiptoes: *ajjuknene.*
stand out: *tooj.*
stand ready: *joorkatkat, kakkōt.*
stand still: *bōjrak.*
stand up: *jutak.*
stand upward from below (seen from above, as looking down in water): *jitlōñ.*
standing: *jurōk.*

stanza: *eoon.*

star: *iju.*
a star: *Ad, Bad, Bake-eo, Da, Dekā-Lijone, Dipāākāk, Iju-ilo-bok-ajaj, Iju-ilo-raan-kubōk, Iju-māj-roum̧um̧, Jeļeilōñ, Jurōn-aodet-kaņ-rilik, Ļāātbwiinbar, Ļakelōñ, Ļōkañebar, Ļōkoojņo, Ļōmānkōto, Ļoojļapļap, Ledikdik, Likin-Buwame, Lim̧anm̧an-eņ-an-Ñinjib, Lōk'tañūr, Mejabwil, Poobin-raj-eo, Ūlin-raj-eo, Wōd-Wāto-eņ, ļeepwal.*
a star (planet), Evening Star, Venus (evenings only): *Maalal.*
a star (planet), Morning Star, Venus (mornings only): *Jurōn-Jemān-Kurlōñ.*
a star, Vega: *Elm̧ad.*
a star, eta in Taurus (Pleiades): *Jebrọ.*
a star, possibly Achernar (alpha Eridani): *Ijuun Rak.*
cloud formation or star: *ad.*
falling star: *iju rabōļļọk.*
North Star: *Lim̧anm̧an.*
observing stars: *jedjed iju.*
the pair of stars Spica and Arcturus: *Daam-Ad.*
two pairs of stars that point to the North Star: *Jurōn-Lim̧anm̧an.*

starboard
sailing starboard to wind: *jabļap.*
starboard tack: *jabdik.*
to paddle a canoe on the starboard side to change course: *auretam.*

starch: *m̧akm̧ōk.*
a food, diluted starch baked in coconut spathe in earth oven: *kōlọwutaktak.*
a food, spongy meat of sprouted coconut cooked with arrowroot starch and diluted with water: *peaut.*
a food, three to one combination of arrowroot starch and water cooked together: *likōbla.*
add liquid to substance such as starch: *kapejlọk.*
molded arrowroot starch: *jibwil.*
net made of sennit used for sifting arrowroot starch: *waliklik.*

stare
stare after: *alluwaļọk.*
stare at: *kallimjek.*
stare open-mouthed: *aļļañ.*

starry flounder
a fish, starry flounder, *Platichthys stellatus*: *bale.*

start: *jjino.*
not start easily: *jọwiia.*
start a fire: *jenjen.*
start a song: *jarjar.*
start easily: *jọwiie.*
start fighting: *m̧ur.*
start, of fire: *jọ.*

startle
startled: *ilbōk, kūrañ, m̧weiur.*

starve
starved: *kwōle.*
starvation: *ñūta.*

state: *kōnnaan.*

statue: *annañ, ekjab.*

stature
of great stature: *ineea.*

status: *kadkad.*
loss of royal status through defeat in war: *jipọkwe.*
person who carries weight in his speech due to social status: *ļajjuur.*

status quo
tamper with the status quo: *iuiuun dekein jinme.*

stay: *pād.*
inability to stay underwater long (see *pakij* (**pakij**)): *jāpakij.*
stay away from: *kawiiaea.*
stay in the rain: *utute.*
stay put: *likatōttōt, tinak.*
stay up: *mmej.*
stay where one is at patiently: *likatōttōt.*

steady
keep a boat steady: *jok.*
move with steady and deliberate purpose: *ijuboñ-ijuraan.*
steadily: *etal in wōt juon.*

steal: *jam̧, kǫǫt, kōjjen, pānāpnep.*
covet another's spouse, steal another's spouse: *aelellaļ.*
steal and drink coconut toddy (off a tree): *jekeidaak.*
steal another's spouse: *jebbōro, kkuul bōro.*
steal away: *dej.*
steal someone's wife (euphemism): *tuuj bōl.*

steam: *baatat, boutļǫk.*

steamer: *tim̧a.*

steel: *jitūūl, māāl.*

steep: *ju.*
steep close to shore: *jirūm̧le.*

steer: *jebwebwe, kōjbwe.*
canoe part, piece of wood on leeside as guard against rubbing from steering paddle: *eran jebwe.*
steer a course with land on one's bow: *anlǫk.*
steer canoe with paddle on right of stern to keep bow straight: *audik.*
steer directly for: *kaiok.*
steering method using a paddle: *ubtak.*
steering song: *alin m̧ur.*
steering wheel: *jebwe.*

stem
base, foundation, bottom, stem, trunk: *dāpi-.*
stalk, leafstem, petiole: *kōļā.*
stem from: *jebar.*
stem of a fruit: *kōļā.*
stem of coconut bunch from which nuts have fallen: *jepar, jinnipran̄.*
stems of coconut tree that nuts are attached to: *piran̄ran̄.*

stench: *kūļōj.*
foul odor stench: *bwiin-puwaļ.*

step
footsteps in gravel or dry leaves: *m̧m̧ōjānjān.*
method of doing something step by step: *kiltōn.*
overstep one's responsibilities: *weļǫk.*
quick short steps: *netūbtūb.*
step on: *etetal, jjuur.*
step or go over: *ļōke.*
steps: *bun̄tōn, bun̄tōn ne.*

sterile: *oran̄e, war.*

stern: *kajjim̧we.*

Sterna
a bird, black-naped tern, *Sterna sumatrana*: *keār.*
a bird, sooty tern, *Sterna fuscata*: *mmej.*

stevedore: *okun bade.*

stew: *juub.*

stick: *aļaļ.*
a pointed stick rubbed up and down on another stick to make a fire: *jolǫk.*
bundle that has been wrapped, sticks or pandanus leaves: *tūr.*
long stick placed on shoulders of two persons to carry burden suspended between: *ine.*
make fire by rubbing sticks: *eton̄, it.*
Marshallese stick dance: *jebwa.*
Marshallese women's stick dance: *jim̧ōkm̧ōk.*
move something closer by using a stick: *adebdeb.*
pick breadfruit with a stick: *kōm̧kōm̧.*
sharp stick for husking coconuts: *doon.*
speed up when rubbing sticks to make fire: *jorjor.*
stand a coconut husking stick in the ground: *kat.*
stick for picking breadfruit: *kein kōm̧.*
stick for stirring fire, turning breadfruit while cooking, etc.: *jabōn pe.*
stick used for clubbing fish: *jem̧ōnna.*
stick used to spread hot stones for earth oven: *tokrak.*
stir food or fire with a stick: *arar.*
walking stick: *jokoņ.*

stick
stick something into the ground: *kōtlaļ.*
stick hand into pocket, hole, or crack: *rrwe.*
stick in: *duuj.*
stick up, on head or canoe: *aujrǫn̄rǫn̄.*
stick with spear, knife, or needle, etc.: *lōlō.*

stick
stick to: *ddāp.*
sticky: *ddāp.*
sticky, of eyes: *ttaorak.*
viscid, sticky, of food: *depn̄at.*

stiff
stiffen: *kwōj.*
stiffness in joints: *akā.*
stiffness of a corpse: *ajeļkā, kā.*

stifle
stifled: *jabjen menowa-.*

still: *ja, lur, wōt.*
stand still: *bōjrak.*

stay still: *tōt.*
unable to keep still: *ne m̧akūtkūt.*
why still?: *jaam̧.*

stillbirth: *jibuñ.*
stillborn baby: *kǫ.*

stimulation
physical stimulation: *kōļo.*

sting: *ņņōk.*
stinging sensation: *idid.*
to sting: *idid.*

sting ray: *boraañ, m̧aļokļok.*

stingy: *arōk, kūbboņ, miin.*

stink: *bwiin-puwaļ.*

stipend: *oņea-.*

stir: *aujek, poktak.*
stick for stirring fire, turning breadfruit while cooking, etc.: *jabōn pe.*
stir food or fire with a stick: *arar.*
stir up: *iiōk, jjeurur, kiojaļjaļ.*
stirred up: *lim̧, poktak.*

stir-crazy: *kidel.*

stitch: *keke.*

stock
stock of an anchor: *rrob.*

stockade: *kalbuuj.*

stockings: *jitǫkin.*

stomach: *je, lǫje, tudek.*
fish's stomach: *petōk.*
lie on stomach: *pedo.*
stomach ache: *jemetak.*
uncomfortable feeling about the stomach from being overstuffed with food: *akeke.*
upset stomach: *wōtōdtōd.*

stone: *dekā.*
cook fish on stones: *ikjin.*
cover an earth oven with stones: *ertak.*
heap of stones: *ajokļā.*
large stone: *ejm̧aan.*
large stone used as an anchor: *kadkad.*
little stones used to make necklaces: *kāāj.*
luau stones: *dekā lǫļ.*
not good marksman, with gun, slingshot, or by throwing stones (see *jerǫ* (**jeraw**)): *jerta.*
pile of stones: *eakļe.*
pumice stone: *tilaan.*
select stones for missiles: *jemān bo.*
stone axe: *jeljel.*
stone fortress for trapping fish: *kōjjoal.*
stone upon which bait or chum is mashed: *jinm̧a.*
stone used for grinding arrowroot: *pukor.*
stones in a sling: *bo.*
stones used in *jibke* fishing method for porpoises: *dekā in jibke.*
throw stones at: *jemān bo, kijbo.*
throw stones repeatedly at an object or person: *ajjikad.*
tombstone: *jebwe.*
wiped out, busted, stoned: *kwōp.*

stone fish
scorpion fish or stone fish, *Scorpaenopsis diabolus/gibbosa/novaeguineae/macadamsi/cacopsis/albobrunnea/guamensis/parvipinnis*: *ņo.*

stony: *dekāke.*
stony islet without trees: *bokom̧ņa.*

stoop: *m̧al-.*
stooped: *kob.*

stop: *bōbrae, bōjrak, ļǫk, pāpjel m̧ae.*
meet and stop: *pāpjel m̧ae.*
stop craving fish: *kōbbaturtur.*
stop, in the sense of stay: *pād.*

stopper: *bǫǫr, penja-.*

store: *m̧ōn wia.*

store
to store: *kōttōn.*

storehouse: *ale, joko.*

storm: *ibeb, kior, kōtteepiņa, ļañ, ññat.*
a big storm: *jeļañ.*
a rain storm that is the sign of a chief coming: *ļañōn irooj.*
a storm: *aere.*
cloud formation preceding storm: *pālmuuj.*
interim period between stormy seasons, usually a calm spell: *jo.*
name of a storm that usually comes in the summer: *Likabwiro.*
period of storms: *Dāpeij.*
place where members of the *Ripako* clan exercise their power to control storms: *bōn.*
save from a storm: *tōļļañ.*
storms associated with the ascendancy of *Jeljel* (stars in Orion): *Jeljeltak.*
tropical storm similar to typhoon in strength: *kapiļak.*
violent storm: *aññat.*

story: *bwebwenato.*
folkloristic story: *inǫñ.*
illustration, instance, illustrative story: *waan jonak.*

story
story of a house: *alen.*
two-story house: *nikāi.*

upper story of house: *po.*

stout: *pen.*
stouthearted: *pen būruo-*

stove: *jitoob, obwin.*
small oven or stove: *paaj.*

stow: *pānuk.*

straddle: *perakrōk.*

straggle: *jeplōklōk.*

straight: *jejjet, jiṃwe.*
straight hair: *maḷko.*
straight up, of tall trees: *ju.*
straight, in playing poker: *tōreej.*
straighten one's self up: *mōōbōb.*
straightforward: *jiṃwe.*
straightlaced: *jaṃṃōṇōṇō.*
ruler, straightedge: *ruḷa.*

strain: *atbọkwōj, kkeeṇ(e), liklik.*
strain one's abdominal muscles: *iñ lọjien.*

strand
bristle, strand of hair: *tōōḷ.*
strand of rope or wire: *ko.*
strands: *iden.*
strands for weaving garlands or stringing leis: *id.*

stranded: *tabu.*
stranded high-and-dry: *pāāt, pāte.*
stranded, of canoes, boats or ships: *eọtōk.*

strange: *kōjak.*
stranger: *ruwamāejet.*
stranger, tramp, vagabond: *armej jeedwa.*

strangle
strangle, to throttle: *kkuul bōro.*

strap: *kañūr.*

strategy: *kōllejar.*
good strategy: *jeḷā kōppeḷak.*

stratum: *pik.*

straw
drinking straw made from *aetōktōk*: *aetōktōk.*

stray: *jebwābwe.*
lead astray: *tōlpilo.*

streak
unexpected streak of luck, windfall: *tọọr pata.*

streaker
a fish, streaker, *Aprion virescens*: *ḷọom.*

stream
stream running out of swamp: *kōḷ.*

street: *iaḷ.*

strength: *kajoor.*

stretch: *eḷḷọk, kankan.*
dilute food or drink to make it stretch: *ilọk.*
recline, stretched out: *jitṃanṃan.*
stretch out: *erḷọk.*
stretch the body: *makōḷkōḷ.*
stretch the neck: *mōōbōb.*
stretched: *aer.*
stretched luck: *kankan kōj.*
stretched tight, of lines, ropes, etc.: *lōtlōt.*
stretchy: *mō.*

strict: *kajjiṃwe, kijñeñe, pen.*

strife: *akwāāl.*

strike: *notoñ, ubrar.*
strike a match: *it.*
strike a shoal: *eoṇ.*
strike a wave: *ṃwitaak.*
strike against: *itaak.*
strike aginst each other: *iṃaajaj.*
strike the trunk of a tree so that the flowers may blossom forth quickly: *kōnar.*

string: *ile, to, tō-.*
shoestring knot: *korak.*
strands for weaving garlands or stringing leis: *id.*
string fish, coconuts, flowers, etc: *ilele.*
string for towing toy canoe in water, held in middle with ends attached to ends of canoe for steering: *tokadkad.*
string under penis: *lil.*
to pull and break objects such as string, rope, wire or grass: *tūṃtūṃ.*
wire for stringing fish: *ile.*
wrapped around, of string: *jāliñiñ.*

strip
cut into strips: *ōrōr.*
strip of reef: *tōkā.*
strip or peel off one layer at a time: *ejej.*
strips of green coconut branches laid across a fire for warming pandanus leaves: *tọḷ.*
weaving strips: *iden.*

strip
to strip: *utūkaḷ.*
to strip of money or property by fraud or threat: *kwōdmat, reja.*

stripe
striped or spotted, as in ancient tattoo: *eọọt.*
stripes showing military rank: *ieṃa.*

striped mullet
a fish, striped mullet, *Chelon vaigiensis*: *aotak.*

stripey
a fish, stripey, *Kuhlia taeniura*: *jerwōt.*

strive: *kakkōt.*
strive toward: *pinnitto.*

stroke: *eoeo.*

stroll: *alwōj bajjek, jaṃbo.*

Strombidae
a shell, *Strombidae*: *aorak, lōkeed.*
a shell, *Strombidae, Lentigo lentiginosus* or *Tricornis sinuatus/thersites/latissimus*: *eañ.*

strong: *kajoor, keiie, keke, kijñeñe, kkōt, kūtarre, mājojo, pen, peñpeñ.*
having strong stomach (see *jjō* (**jjẹh**)): *jājjō.*
not strong: *jakeiie.*
not strong physically (see *dipen* (**diypẹn**)): *jādipen.*
physically strong: *dejeñ, dipen.*
strong, of wind or storm: *dejeñ.*
stronghearted: *pen būruo-.*

Strongylura
a fish, needlefish, *Strongylura marina*: *ṃak.*

struck: *lel.*

structure: *kkal.*

struggle: *kakkōt, kōpkōp.*
to struggle for: *pinnitto.*

strut: *kōmmāidik, ḷakḷak.*
strut of a rooster: *adpā, to.*

stubborn: *būruon kūro, dejeñ, kiliddāp.*

stuck: *kōn.*
fishbone stuck in throat: *paḷ.*
stuck on to: *kkejel.*

stuck-up: *kabbil, kakōl, loṃaan.*

study: *katak, liñōr.*
stand back and study critically, as an artist: *allọk.*
study one's genealogy: *jitdaṃ.*

stuff
uncomfortable feeling about the stomach from being overstuffed with food: *akeke.*

stuffy: *nitñil.*

stumble: *tipjek, tipñōl, tūbbọk.*
stumble and fall while carrying: *buñ kake.*
stumble and rise again to run: *buñ-peltak.*
stumble but not fall: *jepāppāp.*

stump: *dāpdep, ibnene.*
coconut stump: *debọkut.*
pandanus stump: *debọkut.*
stump of any tree: *debọkut.*

stun
stunned: *kūrañ, ṃaal, ṃajōjō, ṃōjālūlū.*
stunned, of fish: *kōjḷọr.*

stunt
stunted growth: *ḷūbbat, wūdkabbe.*

stupid: *bwebwe, kūḷaṃwe, penawiia, taṇo.*
interjection: "Stupid!": *bōkāro.*

sturdy: *kije.*

stutter: *allo.*

sty
sty on the eye: *ātbwe.*

style: *ṃūtō-.*
style (clothes): *joñak.*
style-setter: *kakōl.*

stymied: *boṇ.*

subdue: *anjọ.*

subjects: *doon.*

submarine: *waan tulọk.*

submerge: *tal, tulọk.*

subside: *dikḷọk, meraḷọk.*

substance: *ōn.*

substitute
substitute for: *bōk jikin, pinej jenkwa-.*

subtle: *mera.*

subtract: *bōk.*

succeed: *pinej jenkwa-, teru, tōprak.*
succeed in work, play, school, or with the opposite sex: *bōktak.*
successful: *jeraaṃṃan.*
unsuccessful in one's love advances: *bokbok.*

such: *toḷọk.*
such a: *jemḷam.*

suck: *ninnin.*
land given by a king to a commoner woman as a bounty for suckling a royal baby: *limen ninnin.*
suck in hard: *ṇomṇom.*
suck up: *jorom.*
sucking noise made in drinking green coconuts: *ṃṃōtṃōt.*
suckle: *ninnin.*
two babies suckling from the same woman: *limenkoko.*

sudden: *idiñ, jedkaju, jidimkij, jum.*
suddenly: *idiñ.*

suffer
longsuffering: *meanwōd.*
suffering: *eñtaan.*

sufficient: *bwe.*
fish that aren't sufficient for the next day: *ekin boñ jab lo raan.*
just sufficient: *bōka-.*

sufficient even if it's little, of food: *kaniọkwe.*

suffocate: *jabjen menowa-.*
choke on something, suffocate: *pọk.*

sugar: *jukwa.*
a food, preserved breadfruit mixed with arrowroot and coconut sap or sugar, wrapped in breadfruit leaves and baked: *bwiro iiōk.*
sugar cane: *tọ.*

suggest
suggestion: *ḷōmṇak.*

suicide: *kilaba, wōdinikek.*
commit suicide: *wōdinikek.*

suit
suitable: *kkar.*
unsuitable: *jekkar.*

suitcase: *kōbañ.*

Sula
a bird, blue-faced booby, ***Sula dactylatra***: *lōḷḷap.*
a bird, brown booby, ***Sula leucogaster***: *kaḷo.*
a bird, red-footed booby, ***Sula sula***: *nana.*

sulk
sulky: *ṃṃaḷkaro.*

sultry
appear sultry: *kōmmāidik.*
sultry mannerisms: *ikiddik.*

sum: *koba.*

summer: *jeṃar, rak.*
a gathering of people to celebrate the onset of breadfruit season in summer by making offerings to Jebro, the god of breadfruit: *ṃaṃa.*
laden with summer fruit, usually trees: *uwaanrak.*
name of a storm that usually comes in the summer: *Likabwiro.*
summertime: *iien rak.*

summon: *kkūr, lale.*

sun: *aḷ.*
blinded by sunlight: *taṃtaṃ.*
look pretty at sunset: *aḷkōnar.*
period between setting of sun and rising of moon: *meḷọkḷọk, meḷoktakōn, tuujloñloñ.*
period between setting of sun and rising or moon: *meḷoktak.*
rays of the sun: *ko-in-aḷ.*
small blisters from over exposure to sun: *il.*
smell of clothing or mats under sun: *bbidetdet.*
sun-up: *takin aḷ.*
sunbathe: *kōjeje.*
sunbathing: *aḷkwōjeje.*
sunbeam: *koonaḷ.*
sunburned: *kakilkil.*
sundown: *tulọkun aḷ.*
sunglasses: *māj.*
sunlight: *meramin aḷ.*
sunny day without wind: *detñil.*
sunray: *koonaḷ.*
sunrise: *takin aḷ.*
sunset: *tulọkun aḷ.*
sunshine: *det.*
take shelter from the rain or sun: *kōjato.*
to dry under the sun: *nel.*
to sun: *kōjeje.*

Sunday: *Jabōt.*

sunk
sunken in: *kōn.*

sup
to sup: *kōjota.*

supercargo: *baja, jiipkako.*

superficial: *pejpej.*
superficially fancy: *kōmjedeọ.*

superlative
superlative particle: *tata.*

supernatural
having supernatural powers: *mọṇmọṇ.*

supersede: *pinej jenkwa-.*

superstition: *tōmak ilo jetōb.*
superstition that cat crying at night portends death of someone: *bwijenro.*
superstition that large waves portend the arrival of a vessel: *tokwanwa.*

supervise: *lale.*

supine: *jedelañ.*

supper: *kōjota.*
last supper: *ṃōñāin kōjab.*

supplant: *bōk jikin.*

supple: *jjipdodo.*

supplement
supplementary part: *rejeta-.*

supplied
well supplied with food and property: *jeban.*

support: *jepak.*
something that is put under something else to protect, lift, or support it: *ḷoñtak.*
support one another by holding each other's waists: *waanikli.*

suppose: *baab.*
supposing: *jen ba.*

sure: *ṃool.*
make sure: *loloorjake.*

surely: *lukkuun.*
surety: *joortoklik.*

surf: *ņo.*
canoe-surfing, when sailing down wind: *kōttōmāle.*
high surf: *buñņo.*
rolled, as by surf: *ļukut.*
smooth surf after a succession of rollers: *mooļ.*
surf-boarding: *lōkā, lōkōr.*

surface: *ioo-.*
be on top of a plane surface, water or land: *mmat.*
float upwards to the surface of the water: *pelōñ.*
land surface: *meļan.*
plane surface: *pik.*
surface of: *ewe.*
surface of the ocean: *aejet.*
surface, sod: *jat.*

surgeonfish: *bwilak.*
banded surgeonfish, *Acanthurus triostegus* triostegus Linnaeus: *kupañ.*
black surgeonfish, *Acanthurus nigricans*: *tiepdǫ.*
convict tang or banded surgeonfish, *Hepatus triostegus*: *kupañ.*
surgeonfish, *Acanthurus dussumieri*: *kōpat.*
surgeonfish, *Acanthurus lineatus*: *kuwi, kwi.*
surgeonfish, *Acanthurus nigricans*: *aelmeej.*
surgeonfish, *Naso unicornis*: *eañrōk, m̧ǫņe.*

surgery: *m̧wijm̧wij.*

Suriana
a plant, *Suriana maritima* L. (Simarubaceae): *ñeñe.*

surmise: *kajjimalele, leļōmņak.*

surpass: *ļe.*

surplus: *budeñ, bwe.*

surprise: *bwilōñ.*
exclamation, of surprise: *bōram̧m̧aanō.*
interjection: surprise or disappointment: *ōjjej.*
surprised: *ilbōk.*
take by surprise in hand combat: *ankōm̧ad.*
surprising: *kabwilōñlōñ.*
surprisingly: *jatdik.*

surrender: *baaj, bbeer, wūjlep-.*
surrender, give up: *jatōptōp.*

surreptitious
cheat, obtain surreptitiously: *liktak.*

surround: *kōpooļ, nitbwil.*
be surrounded by: *kkōņak.*
fishing method, many men surround a school in shallow water using a coconut leaf chain as scarer: *aļeļe.*
fishing method, surrounding edges of shoals with net: *kuņa.*
fishing method, using surrounding net on dark nights: *aejek.*
surrounded: *pooļ.*
surrounding: *peļaak.*
surroundings: *meļan.*

survey: *joñak.*
survey critically: *allǫk.*
to survey: *peet.*

susceptible
susceptible to: *kkā.*

suspect: *eņak, eņǫ, kkōljake.*

suspense
suspenseful: *kakkūm̧kūm̧.*

suspicion: *kkōljake.*

sustenance: *kkan.*

swabby: *juwape.*

swaddle: *kūtimtim.*

swagger: *ļakļak.*

swallow: *kōdālōb, orañļǫk.*

swamp: *pat.*
smell of a swamp: *juoñ.*
stream running out of swamp: *kōļ.*
swamp spring: *keiiuiu.*
swamped: *turruļǫk.*
water rises in a well or swamp: *jib.*

swap: *jānij.*

swat
swat flies: *ubļǫñ.*

sway: *m̧al-, m̧m̧ōļeiñiñ.*
sway back and forth: *ajjim̧aalal, buñto-buñtak.*
swaying from side to side, as a ship rolling: *jepliklik.*

swear: *jinjin, kanejnej.*
interjection: "Honestly, I swear it's so.": *mejāro.*
to swear by: *kajje.*

sweat: *menokadu.*
sweaty: *kkōr.*

sweep: *popo.*
to sweep: *burum̧.*

sweet: *māmet, tōñal.*
not sweet, of beverages: *jatōk.*
sweet coconut water: *māmet.*
sweet smell, of ripe pandanus fruit: *bwiin-tōñal.*
sweetish taste: *māmet.*

sweet potato
a plant, sweet potato, *Ipomoea batatas*: *piteto.*

sweetheart: *batin, jitōnbōro.*

swell: *bbǫk, bbōj, bbool.*
swell up: *jib.*
swelling: *ļōpper, per.*

swell
easterly swell: *buñtokrear.*
northerly swell: *buñtokeañ.*
ocean swell: *ñōl.*
southerly swell: *buñtokrōk.*
westerly swell: *buñtokrilik.*

swell: *m̧m̧an.*

swift: *iim̧, iur.*
move out swiftly: *kōplǫk.*
swift, of canoes or boats, nautical term: *ļļaeoeo.*

swim: *aō.*
kick feet in swimming: *bwijeae.*
tow while swimming: *akake.*

swindle: *kǫǫt.*
outsmart, swindle: *Etao.*

swing: *jālirara.*
a swing: *lijjidwaļǫk.*
swing arms while walking: *jerjer.*
swing something or someone around in a circle, as a child: *jelpaak.*
swinging: *toor.*
to swing at someone wildly: *depdep.*
walk swinging the arms: *iliik.*

swipe: *jam̧, kiltōn, kǫǫt, kōrabōl.*

switch: *jānij.*
ignition switch: *kein kōjjǫ.*

swivel: *juwabōļ.*

swollen: *bbǫk, bbōj.*
swollen abdomen: *jeje, jieje.*
swollen corpse: *bōj.*

sword: *jāje.*

swordfish
a fish, swordfish, *Xiphia gladius*: *ļōjkaan.*

Sybedrella
a plant, *Sybedrella nodiflora* (L.) Gaertin: *bwilbwilikkaj.*

syllables of musical scale: *to, re, mi, ba, jooļ, la, ji.*

symbol: *bwe, kakōļļe.*

sympathize: *iǫkwe.*
sympathize with: *tūriam̧o.*

symptom: *kakōļļe.*

Synanceja
Synanceja verrucosa: *ņo.*

Synedrella
a plant, *Synedrella nodiflora*, a small yellow fld. Composite weed: *kinwōj.*

syphilis: *jeplej.*

syrup: *jurub.*
coconut syrup boiled down from sap: *jekm̧ai.*

system: *kkar.*

T-shirt: *jiiñlij.*

table: *tebōļ.*
tablecloth: *eran tebōļ.*
tablespoon: *tebōļ jibuun.*

tablet
tablet, medicine: *batin.*

taboo: *bwinimjaad, jabwi, m̧ǫ, m̧ǫņm̧ǫņ.*
a taboo place reserved for chiefs: *jiadel.*
break a taboo, desecrate: *kōtrāe.*
break taboos attendant to certain medicines while under treatment: *aļok.*
do something that will result in misfortune, such as breaking a taboo: *ļōkajem̧.*
misfortune due to breaking of a taboo: *ruwe.*
speak taboo words that may bring bad luck: *ļakajem̧.*
taboo breaker: *neen wūlej.*
taboo relationship: *jem̧nājin, jore.*

Tacca
a plant, arrowroot, *Tacca leontopetaloides* (L.) Ktze.: *m̧akm̧ōk.*

taciturn: *ikōñ, jjeļǫk an naan.*

tack
correct point for tacking in order to reach an island: *jjeraak.*
let sail and mast fall while tacking: *merā.*
port tack: *jabļap.*
starboard tack: *jabdik.*
tack canoe to leeward: *kabbe.*
tack windward: *bwābwe.*
tack, change sail from one end of canoe to the other to tack: *diak.*
tacking: *jenwōd.*
tacks in sailing: *ālu.*

tackle
block and tackle: *tekōļ.*
tackle someone, pulling their knees together like ripped cloth: *ait.*

tact
tactful: *jeļā kōppeļak, mejādik, wājepdik.*

tactic
good tactic: *jeḷā kōppeḷak.*
tactics: *kōllejar, kōttōbalbal.*

tag
a game, tag: *anoot.*

tail: *ḷokwa-.*
rooster tail feather: *ḷōb.*
tail half of fish: *jablọk.*
tail of lobster: *ṃōjañ.*
wave tail above surface, of fish: *lọklọk.*

tailor: *taiḷa.*

take: *bbōk, bōk, leak-, lōkake, uke.*
take a nose dive: *ñarñar.*
take a rooster to a cock-fight: *keid.*
take as much as possible from a person: *ājḷor.*
take by force that which one does not own: *aṇokṇak.*
take by surprise in hand combat: *ankōṃad.*
take by the hand: *kabwijer.*
take care of: *lale.*
take coconut husks from water after soaking to make sennit: *jarjar.*
take downwards: *bōklaḷḷọk.*
take for granted: *ālikinjepjep.*
take in water from the top of a canoe: *timaruk.*
take it: *eo.*
take it easy: *kōṃṃanṃōn.*
take more than one's share: *bōkḷap, ṃṃaelep.*
take off: *kōplọk, utkōk.*
take off of fire: *ato.*
take part in: *bōk koṇaa-.*
take part of: *kkaan.*
take possession of: *mọk.*
take seriously (with directionals): *eḷ.*
take sides: *jep.*
take sides, advocate: *rrā.*
take something from the mouth: *meliak.*
take turns: *kajjojo.*
take upward: *bōklōñḷọk.*

take-off: *kā-.*

tale: *bwebwenato.*
antagonize by tale-bearing: *kiojaḷjaḷ.*
bear tales: *bbōk.*
telltale: *kinaak, ttal.*

talent: *taḷōn.*

talk: *bwebwenato, kōnnaan, kōnono.*
loud nonsense talk: *llejlej.*
not talkative: *jjeḷọk an naan.*
someone that people are always talking about: *tiemlo.*
talk about someone behind his back: *ruruwe.*
talk back: *ūlūlōt.*
talk bad about someone: *kōnana.*
talk harshly: *būroñ.*
talk in great detail, elaborate: *tipdik.*
talk of something one is not certain about: *ajjimālele.*
talk on the radio: *wālej.*
talk or walk in one's sleep: *jja.*
talk that hurts the feelings: *añjarjar.*
talk through the nose: *kajṇoṇ.*
talk very quietly: *ajjinono.*
talkative: *kajnōt, ṃṃawi.*

tall: *aetok, ineea.*
husky, and usually quite tall: *peñpeñ.*

tally: *taḷe.*

talon: *akki.*

tame: *awiie.*

tamper
tamper with: *iṇoṇooj.*
tamper with the status quo: *iuiuun dekein jinme.*

tan
tan colored: *kūbween upaaj.*

tang
a fish, convict tang or banded surgeonfish, *Hepatus triostegus*: *kupañ.*
a fish, orange spot tang, *Acanthurus olivaceus*: *ael.*
a fish, red spot tang, *Acanthurus achilles*: *kinbo, pir.*

tangle
entangle: *pok.*
tangled: *dāde, dapitōk, idaaptōk.*
untangle: *kōmmeḷeḷe.*

tank: *tāāñ.*
scuba tank: *akjijen.*

tantalize
tantalize or tease, of food only: *kaijoḷjoḷ.*

tap
tap on: *penpen.*
tap-dance: *jurbak.*
taps: *buñtōn.*
wiretap: *iaroñroñ.*

tape: *teep.*

tapioca: *tapioka.*

tar: *pij.*

tardy: *bbat, ppedikdik.*
chronically tardy: *ikiruṃwij.*

target
on target: *allọk, ḷaj.*
target practice: *kōjjerọro.*

taro: *iaraj.*
a food, cooked and pounded breadfruit, taro, bananas, or nuts mixed with grated coconut: *wūdeñ.*
a food, grated taro mixed with coconut milk, wrapped in taro leaves and baked in oven: *jebwatōr.*
a food, taro grated and mixed with coconut oil and coconut sap: *tōtaiṃoṇ.*
a plant, taro variety: *Wōtaad, Wōtaan.*
dig taro: *tto.*
immature taro plant: *il.*
mashed taro or potato: *kōmālij.*
pound breadfruit or taro: *jukjuk.*
taro patch: *bōl.*
taro residue, used for seedling after the edible portion has been cut off, usually of a mature taro: *pak.*
taro sprout: *il.*

tarpaulin: *taboḷōn.*

tarry: *aepedped, ruṃwij.*

task: *jerbal.*
finish a task: *ñijlọk.*

taste: *nām, nāmnām.*
moldy taste: *nnān.*
musty taste: *nnān.*
smell and taste of uncooked meat: *bbūramejmej.*
smell or taste sour or bitter, as milk, vinegar, or rice soup, etc.: *meñ.*
sweetish taste: *māmet.*
taste food or drink: *edjoñ.*
taste good: *nnọ.*
tasteless: *aebōjbōj.*

tasty: *nnọ.*
a tasty combination of foods: *kane.*
not tasty, of fish (see *uwi* (**wwiy**)): *jọuwi.*
too fresh to be tasty, said of fish just caught that has not been allowed to settle sufficiently before being eaten raw: *ḷḷeoeo.*

tatter
tattered: *potak.*

tattle: *kinaak.*

tattler
a bird, wandering tattler, *Heteroscelus incanum*: *kidid.*

tattoo: *eọ.*
black carbon on lantern chimney, used to blacken tattoos: *ṃaṃōj.*
cult that tattooed and practiced magic: *eḷ.*
rub in black carbon on tattoos: *iteṃaṃōj.*
striped or spotted, as in ancient tattoo: *eọọt.*

taunt: *kakūtōtō.*

Taurus
a star, eta in Taurus (Pleiades): *Jebrọ, Jeḷeilōñ.*
Aldebaran in Taurus: *Ḷoojḷapḷap.*
stars in Taurus: *Jepjep-eo-an-Lōktañūr, Ledik-raṇ-nājin-Jebrọ.*

taut: *kankan.*

tavern: *baar.*

tax: *owōj.*

taxicab: *tāākji.*

tea: *ti, wōja.*
put tea in: *ti.*
tea kettle: *tibat.*
teapot: *tibat.*

teach: *jikuuḷ.*
teacher: *rūkaki.*
to teach: *katak.*

team
company, team, group: *kumi.*
shout rhythmically while doing a job requiring team work, as carrying a canoe: *roro.*

Teanianotus
Teanianotus triacanthus: *ṇo.*

tear: *kekeel, merrōḷọk, peoeo, potak.*
easy to break or tear: *ṃōdṃōd.*
tear apart: *ttemakil.*
tear down: *ruprup.*
tear into fine pieces: *imkilkil.*

tears: *dānnin kōmjaaḷaḷ.*
have tears in the eyes: *kōmmeñ.*

tease
tantalize or tease, of food only: *kaijoḷjoḷ.*
to tease: *ḷōkatip.*
teasing: *kakūtōtō, ḷōkatip.*

teaspoon: *tijibuun.*

teat: *ittūt.*

technique: *kōl.*
ward off using Marshallese hand-to-hand combat defense techniques: *pile.*

teem: *obrak.*
teeming with: *doom, jure.*

teeter-totter: *abōṇtọun.*

teeth
brush teeth: *kurkur.*
cavity in teeth: *ṃak.*
chattering of teeth: *ōḷōḷ.*
false teeth: *ñiñat.*
grind with the teeth, noisily: *kañurñur.*

grit the teeth: *ōļōļ.*
have missing teeth: *tijjañ.*
husk a coconut with one's teeth: *ōjōj.*
pick out food from teeth: *arar.*
scum, food particles between teeth: *taiñad.*
smile, showing the white of the teeth: *rere.*
weak teeth: *ñiban.*

telephone: *talboon, teiñwa.*

telescope: *baiklaaj.*

television: *tipi.*

tell: *jiroñ, kōnnaan.*
tell fortunes: *bubu.*
tell on someone: *kinaak.*
tell the truth: *kwaļọk ṃool.*
telltale: *kinaak, ttal.*

Tellinella
a shell, *Tellinidae, Tellinella philippii/staurella/virgata*: *kūkōr.*

temper
hot tempered: *jidimkij.*
lose temper: *kun an ļaaṃ.*
short tempered: *bōro-kadu.*
short tempered, cry-baby, provoked: *kwi.*
slow to lose temper: *jarōjrōj.*
understand how to keep temper: *kōmmaanwa.*
variable in temper: *ṃṃaļkaro.*

temperature: *bwil.*

temple: *tampeļ.*

temporary: *peļļọk.*
a temporary shed: *peļak.*
temporary house, shack: *ṃōn kōppād.*

tempt: *kapo, ļatipñōl.*
temptation: *kapo.*

tempura: *teeṃbura.*

ten: *joñoul.*
ten pairs, fish or copra: *jọkden.*

tend
tend fish traps: *bbā.*
tend to: *kkā.*

tender: *pidodo, ub.*

tender
to tender: *tilmaak.*

tense: *atebar, kijñeñe.*
tensed up: *ddo.*

tent: *eṃ nuknuk.*

tentacle: *ko.*
octopus tentacles: *ko-in-kweet.*
tentacles: *joko.*

term: *tōōṃ.*

Terminalia
a plant, *Terminalia catappa* L. (Combretaceae): *kotōl.*
a plant, tree, *Terminalia litoralis*: *kkōñ.*

terminate: *kaṃōj.*

termite: *dile.*
damage caused by termites or bookworms: *dile.*

tern
black-naped tern, *Sterna sumatrana*: *keār.*
crested tern, *Thalasseus bergii*: *keār.*
sooty tern, *Sterna fuscata*: *mmej.*
white tern, *Gygis alba*: *mejọ.*
baby bird, sooty tern, *mmej*: *jipila.*

terrify
terrifying: *kaammijak.*
terrified: *kor.*

territory: *jiki-.*

terror: *lōļñọñ.*
bristling hair standing on end from terror: *rrọñ.*
shriek in terror or pain: *wūdikke.*

test: *iaļan juon, mālejjoñ, teej.*
acid test: *mālejjoñ.*
test drive a new or overhauled vehicle: *likbad.*
test sail a new or overhauled vessel: *likbad.*

testament: *kalliṃur.*

testicle: *kwōle, rọ.*
pain in testicles: *liklep.*
testicles, enlarged: *rọulep.*

testify: *kaṃool, kōnnaan.*
testifier: *rūkaṃool.*

tether: *to.*

Tetraodon
a fish, puffer fish, *Tetraodon hispidus*: *luwap.*
a fish, puffer fish, *Tetraodon hispidus/meleagris/nigropunctatus/patoca*: *wat.*

Thalashona
a fish, wrasse, *Thalashona vitidum*: *lo.* *Thalashona ballieui*: *alle.*

Thalasseus
a bird, crested tern, *Thalasseus bergii*: *keār.*

Thalassia
a plant, general term for seaweed. *Thalassia hemprichii* (Ehrenb.) Aschers.: *wūjooj-in-lọjet.*

Thalassoma
a fish, wrasse, *Thalassoma lunare*: *ikōn-wōd.*
a fish, wrasse, *Thalassoma umbrostigma*: *bōkkāāj.*

than: *jān.*

thank
thank you: *koṃṃool.*
to be thanked: *ṃṃool.*
to thank: *kaṃṃoolol.*

that: *ke, me.*
so that: *bwe.*
that (close to neither of us): *eṇ, iieṇ.*
that (close to you): *eñṇe, ṇe, ṇeṇe.*
that (close to you), singling out: *eñṇeṇe.*
that (distant but visible): *uweo.*
that over there: *eñeṇ, eñieṇ.*
that's it: *eñin, eñṇe, ieñṇe.*

thatch: *aj.*
a bunch of dried pandanus leaves for thatch: *jiṃ.*
gather fallen pandanus leaves from ground for thatch or handicraft: *ppel.*
pass thatch to one tying: *jemān aj.*
piece of pandanus roots cut and dried to be used as frame in weaving thatch: *tap.*
put thatch on roof: *kōtak.*
put thatch on walls: *katnok.*
sew or tie on thatch: *kōtak.*
to weave pandanus thatch: *wewā.*

the
the (often for entities not present): *eo, ko, ro.*

theater: *tieta.*

their
theirs: *aer.*
theirs (five or more persons): *aerwōj.*
theirs (four persons): *aereañ.*
theirs (three persons): *aerjeel.*
theirs (two persons): *aerro.*

Thelonia
sea cucumber, *Holothuroidea, Thelonia* or *Actinopyga*: *piāpe.*

them
pronoun, absolute, third person plural, them: *er.*

then: *innām, jujen.*
then after: *ḷak.*
then when: *ḷak.*
then, denoting diversion from one activity, person, or situation to another: *baj.*

there: *ijekākaṇ, ijekaṇ, ijeko, ijeṇ, ijo, uweo.*
a locative, where, there: *tu.*
over there: *ijekoko, ijjuweo.*
there are: *or.*
there by you: *ijeṇe, ijeṇeṇe.*
there is: *or.*
there it is: *eñṇe, eñoweo.*
there they are: *erkoko, erroro.*
there they are (people close to neither of us): *errārаṇe.*
there they are (people close to you): *erraṇe.*
there they are (things close to you): *erkākaṇe, erkaṇe.*
thereabouts: *ijekākaṇe.*
thereabouts (close to you): *ijekaṇe.*
therefore: *āindein, kōn menin.*

these
these (individuals close to me): *rā, rārā.*
these (individuals close to us both): *rein.*
these (people close to me): *erro.*
these (things close to me): *kā, kākā.*
these (things close to us both): *kein.*

they: *er.*
they should: *ren.*
they two should: *rōnro.*
they, progressive: *rej.*
they, two people: *erro.*

thick: *bukwekwe, bukwelep, kut, mijel.*
cut it large or thick: *jeklep.*
thick beard: *debọkut.*
thick blood: *mekak.*
thick, of long and round objects: *aiḷip.*
thicken: *kwōj.*
thickness: *mijel.*
thick-headed: *bwebwe.*
thick-skinned: *mejel kil.*

thicket: *mar.*

thigh
inside of thigh: *lọtōñā.*

thimble: *tūṃbōḷ.*

thin: *ainiñ, bbōj, māni.*
thin of body: *aidik.*
thin, of animals or men: *ṃō.*
thin, of liquids: *watre.*
very thin: *apeñāñā.*

thing: *men.*
something: *juon men.*
these things (close to me): *erko.*
thing for doing something: *kein.*
thing, creature: *māl.*
those things (close to neither of us): *erkākaṇ, erkaṇ, erkoko.*

think: *baab, kōḷmānḷọkjeṇ, ḷōmṇak.*

third
a third: *matoḷ.*
the third: *kein kajilu.*
the third zone of currents: *jeḷatae.*
third base: *tōōt.*
third moon phase: *meḷoktakōn, tuujloñloñ.*
two thirds: *ruo ṃōttan jilu.*

thirst: *maro.*
thirsty: *maro.*

thirteen: *joñoul jilu.*

thirty: *jilñuul.*
thirty pairs, fish or copra: *jilikor.*

this: *e, eñeo.*
this (close to me): *iiō.*
this (thing close to us both): *in.*
this thing here between us: *eñin.*

Thliostyra
Thliostyra albicilla: *jinenpokpok.*

thorax: *ob.*

thorn
remove thorns from pandanus leaves: *iiaak.*
thorns: *kālōklōk.*
thorns in a pandanus leaf: *ṃake, ṃakur.*
thorny: *kurbalōklōk.*

thorough
not thoroughly done (see *lōt* (**let**)): *jālōt.*
thoroughly done: *lōt.*

those
those (individuals close to neither of us): *rāraņ, raņ.*
those (individuals close to you): *rāraņe, raņe.*
those (individuals distant but visible): *roro.*
those (things close to neither of us): *kākaņ, kaņ.*
those (things close to you): *kākaņe, kaņe.*
those (things distant but visible): *koko.*
those places: *ijoko.*

though: *meñe.*

thought: *ļōmņak.*
pry into someone's thoughts: *ttuur bōro.*
thoughtful: *jeḷā kuņaa-.*
thoughtless: *jaje kuņaa-.*

thousand: *jerapen.*
five thousand: *limādep.*
four thousand: *earap.*
one thousand: *toujin.*
three thousand: *jilirap.*
two thousand: *ruorap.*

thrash: *deñdeñ, pejaju.*
thrash the arms and legs around while in water: *bwijeae.*

thread: *tōreej.*

threat
to strip of money or property by fraud or threat: *kwōdmat, reja.*
threatened: *mijak.*
threatening: *nana taṃṃwi-.*

three: *jilu.*
three hundred: *jilubukwi.*
three thousand: *jilirap.*

thresher shark
a fish, thresher shark, *Alopias vulpes*: *pako toŗtoŗ.*

threshold: *aor.*

thrift
thrifty: *tiljek.*

thrill
thrilled: *iruj loįie-.*

throat: *bōro.*
a raspy feeling in the throat, especially after a cold: *mmelkwarkwar.*
clear the throat: *melkwarkwar.*
dry throat: *ṃōrā-bōjbōj.*
fishbone stuck in throat: *paḷ.*
to clear one's throat: *mmelkwarkwar.*
unchewed food caught in throat: *ubabōj.*

throb: *ddipiñpiñ.*

throne: *tūroon.*

throng: *jarlepju.*

throttle
strangle, to throttle: *kkuul bōro.*

through: *buḷōn.*
break through: *deblọk.*
go through: *ḷipdeḷọk, pejlọk.*
pass through: *deblọk.*

throw: *kadkad.*
a game, contest to see who can throw a sharp-pointed piece of dried pandanus root, about a yard long, farthest by skimming it on the ground once: *kajjeor.*
able to throw hard: *elmaroñ.*
fishing method, use throwing net: *kadkad.*
gather missiles for throwing: *rukbo.*
good marksmanship in shooting or throwing: *jerọ.*
throw (always with directional postpositions): *jo.*
throw a line with a weight attached to the end: *kōjjāl.*
throw a rope over a branch: *rajāl.*
throw away: *joḷọk.*

throw by handfuls: *eo̧kur.*
throw down: *ebeb.*
throw down, as in wrestling: *ekbab, patpat.*
throw far: *jimaroñ.*
throw in a wide sweeping motion: *kōjjāl.*
throw on the ground: *patpat.*
throw sand at: *bor.*
throw stones at: *jemān bo, kijbo.*
throw stones repeatedly at an object or person: *ajjikad.*
throw waste food or trash somewhere: *kwōpejpej.*
to be thrown in jail: *kalbuuj.*
to throw grated coconut or sand at someone or something: *pinik.*
unable to throw far: *jiban.*
wild, in throwing: *boor.*
fishing method, chasing mackerel into a throw net held upon one side: *kōtaltōl.*

Thuarea
a plant, grass, *Thuarea involuta*: *kakkūm̧kūm̧.*

thud
fall with a thud: *puruk.*
pounding or thudding of canoes together: *ļļwūjļwūj.*
thudding sound: *po̧kwi.*

thumb: *addi-lep.*

thunder: *jourur.*
tremor or vibration caused by sound of gun or thunder: *pañijñij.*

Thursday: *Taije.*

thus: *āindein, eñin.*

thwart: *dikāāļāļ.*
canoe part, thwart: *to̧o̧t.*

ti
syllable "ti" of musical scale: *ji.*

ticket: *kiibbu, tūkōt.*

tickle
to tickle: *kūrkūr.*
ticklish: *arrukwikwi, kilperakrōk.*

tide: *bōkā.*
ebb tide: *pāāt, roj.*
fishing method, searching for fish at low tide over the reef: *etalpeet.*
high tide: *ibwij, tūkōk.*
highest tide: *ibwijleplep.*
intensifier, of limited use: for time, tide, or weather: *jelōñlōñ.*
late, time of day or tide: *jo̧weej.*
let anchor line out to allow for tide change: *peaut.*
lowest ebb tide: *pāāt m̧ōn̦akn̦ak.*
period between tides: *aemm̧an.*
period of great tidal variations: *iaļap.*
period of neap tides: *idik.*
spring tide: *iaļap.*
unfavorable tide, neither high nor low: *jatloñ.*
walk between islands at low tide: *etal iene.*

tidy: *karbōb, meļak.*

tie: *joobn̦ōj, kkor, kōbobo, korak, llok, po̧po.*
bandaged, tied up, wrapped up: *korkor.*
be tied down by a task: *lokjak.*
braid, tie: *bobo.*
canoe part, ties between spar and outrigger: *jojo.*
climb coconut tree with ankles tied: *ento.*
sew or tie on thatch: *kōtak.*
tie a knot in string or rope: *bubu.*
tie coconut leaves together to make fishing chain: *wūjaak.*
tie in a game: *jebo, wōnaji.*
tie on: *loklok.*
tie or fasten with a rope or cord: *ļajiiñ.*
tie securely: *boļan.*
tie up: *kwarkor.*
tie up a bundle: *wūnit.*
tie up a person or animal: *liāp.*
tie up a vessel: *mmaan.*
tie up to a buoy: *emjak.*
untie: *mejaļ.*

tiger: *taikō.*

tiger shark
a fish, tiger shark, *Galeocerdo arcticus*: *pako tiltil.*

tight: *aer, bab, dim, kankan, kon̦, ñilñil.*
hold something tightly: *kōkki.*
pack bags tightly: *ļattuñ.*
stretched tight, of lines, ropes, etc.: *lōtlōt.*
tight, not used with liquids: *obrak.*
to close tight, as a clam shell: *kkim.*
water-tight (see *ttal* (**ttal**)): *jettal.*

tiller
tiller, nautical: *jila.*

timber: *wōjke.*
the large cross timbers forming foundation work of the outrigger in a canoe: *kie.*

time: *awa, iie, iien.*
a long time: *to.*
a long time ago: *etto.*
a second of time: *jekōn.*

ancient times: *etto.*
for the time being: *ja.*
hottest time of day: *bwiltōn̄tōn̄.*
intensifier, of limited use: for time, tide, or weather: *jelōn̄lōn̄.*
late, time of day or tide: *jo̧weej.*
olden times: *ennāp, etto.*
one time: *juon iien.*
overtime: *obataim.*
precede, be in time for: *m̧m̧ōkaj.*
some time ago: *jem̧aan.*
sometime: *juon iien.*
sometimes: *jet ien.*
the time: *tōre.*
time between rain showers: *meļa.*
time of day or night: *tōre.*
time of fair weather: *iien rak.*
untimely: *jum.*
work overtime: *ailparo.*

time: *alen.*
many times: *lōn̄ alen.*
one more time: *annen.*
times, in multiplication: *alen.*
use for the first time: *kkaan.*
wear a piece of clothing for the first time: *lōtlōt.*

timid: *mijak.*

tin: *tiin.*
cook in a tin pan: *aintiin.*
piece of tin roofing: *tiin.*
tin can: *kuwat.*
tin roofing: *jinibo̧o̧r.*

tinder: *jit.*

Tinea
Tinea versicolor: *jān.*

tiny: *jibbatūn̄tūn̄, jibbūn̄, jinin̄nin̄, nin̄, oļar, wūddik.*

tip
head, top, tip: *bar.*
tip of: *jabōn, jabwe.*
tip of coconut frond: *jepak.*
tiptoe: *ajjādikdik.*
stand on tiptoes: *ajjuknene.*

tip
tipped over: *oļo̧k.*
to tip, as of canoe: *ām.*

tire
seldom tire (see *kkijeje* (**kkijẹyjẹy**)): *jakkijeje.*
tire easily: *kkijeje.*
tired: *m̧ōk, orā.*
tired of staying in one place: *kidel.*
tired out: *kajjinōk, pālo.*
to tire a fish after it is hooked: *kaddejdej.*

tithe: *allōn̄ iju.*

titter: *ttōn̄ dikdik.*

to: *in, n̄an.*

to and fro
go to and fro: *jebwāālel.*
traverse to and fro: *ikueaak.*

toadstool: *lo̧jiln̄in kijdik.*
a plant, toadstool, *Auricularia ampla* persoon and other earlike *Basidiomycetes* (fungi). Rogers: *lo̧jiln̄in kijdik.*

tobacco: *jepaake.*
chew tobacco: *kolied.*

today: *rainin.*

toddler: *ajri.*

toddy
coconut sap, toddy: *jedān, jekaro.*
coconut tree that cannot give more fresh toddy (see *tāān̄* (**tayag**)): *jatāān̄.*
fermented coconut toddy: *jiman̄ūn̄.*
steal and drink coconut toddy (off a tree): *jekeidaak.*

toe: *addi.*
big toe: *addi-lep.*
tiptoe: *ajjādikdik.*
toenail: *akki, akkiin ne.*
stand on tiptoes: *ajjuknene.*

together: *ippān doon, jim̧or.*
close together: *kut.*
coming together: *ik.*
fit together, put together an engine or piece of machinery: *bobo.*
gathered together: *kuk.*
get together: *koba, likiio.*
get together happily: *lioeo.*
grown together: *piro.*
not close together: *jo̧kkutkut.*
put together: *koba.*

toilet: *m̧ōn bwidej, m̧ōn kōppojak.*
toilet paper: *pij in kwiir.*

tomato: *tōm̧ato.*

tomb: *lōb.*
tombstone: *jebwe.*

tomorrow: *ilju.*
early tomorrow: *ililju.*
tomorrow night: *bun̄ūn ilju.*

ton: *tōn.*

tongue: *lo.*
sharp-tongued: *kkan̄ loo-.*
tongue-tied: *allo.*

tonight: *bun̄niin.*

too: *āinwōt, kab.*
too much: *bōlej.*

tool: *kein jerbal, tuuļ.*
toolbox: *tuuļbo̧o̧k.*

tooth: *n̄i.*
tooth of: *n̄ii-.*
tooth of a comb: *tōōḷ.*
wisdom tooth: *n̄ilep.*

top: *bọọror, ioo-, likaebeb.*
at the top of: *jeban.*
be on top of a plane surface, water or land: *mmat.*
canoe part, mast top: *ḷot.*
head, top, tip: *bar.*
on top of: *raan.*
put on top of: *jojoon.*
put something on top of: *ertak.*
top man in organization: *jem̧m̧aan.*
top of the hill: *raanbat.*
top shell: *jidduul.*

top shell
sea snail, top shell: *kaddoḷ.*

topple: *bun̄lọk, ukok.*
topple over: *oḷọk.*

torch: *til.*
band, used for tying torch made from frond: *ida.*
blowtorch: *pilerab.*
fishing method, fishing with a torch: *kabwil.*
fishing method, torch and machete: *tilkōmerā.*
make torches from brown fronds: *bọk.*
stand a torch in the ground: *kwōn.*
torch made from dried fronds: *pāle.*

torment: *en̄taan.*

torn: *peo, potak.*
torn off: *jar.*

tornado: *aire.*

torso: *kā.*
torso of a person: *kāān.*

toss
toss a line by means of weight tied to end: *in̄jālle.*
toss and pitch on the sea: *kōm̧te.*
toss and turn: *ukoktak.*

tot: *mānnin̄.*

total: *aolep.*
total a correct amount: *un̄.*

touch: *un̄n̄ūr.*
just touch: *anōr.*
keep in touch with: *kkeini.*
light touching in billiards: *kij.*
soft to touch: *meoeo.*
to touch sand: *jidaak.*
touch only part of something: *kōtrar.*
touch shoulders: *aerār.*
touch unexpectedly by accident: *jelōt.*

tough: *pen.*
tough, of people: *kijon̄.*

tow: *atak.*
pull out, as current or undertow: *tọr.*
string for towing toy canoe in water, held in middle with ends attached to ends of canoe for steering: *tokadkad.*
to drag or tow from lagoon side to ocean side: *lelik.*
to drag or tow from ocean side to lagoon side: *lear.*
to tow: *tokadkad.*
tow while swimming: *akake.*
tow, as a boat: *aik.*

toward: *m̧ae.*
bend toward: *m̧al-.*
go toward: *kaiok.*
toward a third party, neither speaker nor addressee: *ḷọk.*
toward addressee, away from addressor: *waj.*
toward the speaker: *tok.*

towel: *tọọl.*

tower
watch-tower: *miade.*

town: *bukwōn, jikinkwelọk.*
townhouse: *m̧ōn kweiḷọk.*

toy
a game, racing toy outrigger canoes: *kariwutut.*
a toy: *didim̧akōl.*
a toy, boat of half coconut: *wa bweọ.*
a toy, canoe made from very light wood: *riwut.*
a toy, coconut hydroplane: *wūdādo.*
a toy, of shells or wood: *likaebeb.*
string for towing toy canoe in water, held in middle with ends attached to ends of canoe for steering: *tokadkad.*
to sail a toy canoe: *riwut.*
toy of: *nāji-.*

trace: *anōk, miro.*
erase footprints or traces: *jjion̄.*
trace scent: *kāātet.*
traces: *būrar, jenok.*
turtle traces: *popo.*

Trachinotus
a fish, pompano, *Trachinotus bailloni*: *kauwe, m̧ōḷọjetak.*

trachoma: *pilo.*

Trachurops
a fish, big-eyed or goggle-eyed scad fish or horse mackerel, *Trachurops crumenophthalmus*: *pāti.*

a fish, mackerel, *Trachurops crumenopthalmus*: *ettōū, tōū.*

track
follow trail or track: *anōk.*
track and field events: *wūntokai.*
tracks: *jenok.*

tract
division of a land tract: *alen.*
land tract: *wāto, ḷain.*
small land tract: *bwiddik.*

tractor: *baru.*

trade: *jānij, jobai.*
trader: *tōreeta.*

trade wind
forecast predicting the onset of prevailing northeast trade winds: *deñdeñin mājlep.*
northeast trade wind: *kọto.*

tragedy: *bwijerro, jerata.*

trail
follow trail or track: *anōk.*

train: *kipel.*
training: *kōmmālmel.*

tramp: *jokko.*
stranger, tramp, vagabond: *armej jeedwa.*

trance
be in a trance: *kejakḷọkjeṇ.*

transfer: *leak-.*

transitory: *jedkaju.*

translate: *ukok.*

transmit
radio transmitter: *wālej.*
transmit by radio: *wālej.*

transparent: *tooj.*

transport: *aljek, leak-.*
transportation: *iaḷ.*

trap: *aujiid.*
bird trap: *mejḷat.*
caught in a trap: *tọrōk.*
coral weir to trap fish: *me.*
fish trap: *u.*
long fish trap, for sprats, net with handle: *bọro.*
look into a trap: *waat.*
stone fortress for trapping fish: *kōjjoal.*
tend fish traps: *bbā.*
trap for catching birds: *kūṃōōr.*
trap for crabs: *ajokḷā.*
trapped: *keṇaak.*

trash: *jọkpej, kwōpej, menọknọk.*
pile of trash: *ḷokot.*
throw waste food or trash somewhere: *kwōpejpej.*

travel: *ito-itak.*
travel on a vacation: *jaṃbo.*

traverse
traverse to and fro.: *jaṃbo.*

tray: *oboñ.*
small tray, made from fronds for food: *enrā.*

tread
sound of treading feet: *ṃṃūṇṃūṇ.*
tread on: *jjuur.*
tread water: *aō in kijdik, bwijeae.*
treading: *ṃṃūṇṃūṇ.*

treat: *jọut.*
break taboos attendant to certain medicines while under treatment: *aḷok.*
emergency treatment: *kōṃadṃōdin idiñ.*
medical treatment by members of the cult (*didiiñ*): *didiiñ.*
medicine, heat-treatment using hot stones wrapped in leaves: *tabuk.*
phases in medical treatment starting with the second: *bōrwaj.*
rub with oil as medical treatment: *pitpit.*
treat unfairly: *ālikinjepjep.*
treat, medically: *wūno.*

treble: *ḷḷaaj.*

tree: *kāān.*
a clearing between trees growing in opposite directions: *toṇak.*
a hole in a tree for catching water: *ṃṃak.*
a plant, general word for tree: *wōjke.*
a plant, tree, *Ficus tinctoria* Forst: *tōpdo.*
a tree: *kāmeñ, kimā.*
band around ankles used in climbing trees: *kae.*
burn a tree: *jidep.*
cut tree trunk into pieces, as breadfruit for making canoe: *kabbok.*
defecate from trees, of birds: *de, edde.*
felling of a tree: *oḷọk.*
fruit of aged trees: *ālkūṃur.*
heart of tree: *boḷ.*
hole in tree for catching rain water: *ṃak.*
large tree: *kōtabtab.*
little space between trees: *tuwa.*
lose leaves, of trees: *ṃōd.*
lower part of tree, brush, or grass: *wūn.*
major branch of a tree and its contents: *ṃwiañ.*

notches cut in a tree for climbing: *jekāiōōj.*
outer bark of tree: *kilwōd.*
place where frigate birds sleep in trees: *m̧wilik.*
plant or tree growth from old root or after old branch of tree has been cut down: *l̗or.*
remains of a tree especially if covered with fern growth: *deboķut.*
rope used for climbing trees: *jemājirok.*
shake a bush or tree: *im̧uk.*
sing upon trees or in places above: *aluej.*
slip down a tree or pole: *pirūrrūr.*
slippery, of trees: *tabur.*
stump of any tree: *deboķut.*
tall tree where seabirds sleep: *joor.*
tree in which birds roost and defecate: *jade.*
tree with flowers: *ut.*
trunk of a tree: *dāpdep, kāān.*
trunk of a young tree: *kōneo.*

tremble: *wūdiddid.*

tremor: *wūdiddid.*
tremor or vibration caused by sound of gun or thunder: *pañijñij.*

trench: *jikur.*

trespass: *l̗e eoon em̧.*

trial: *mālejjoñ.*
a trial: *ial̗an juon.*

triangle
form a triangle shape with scarer (*m̧wieo*) in fishing by the *jurōk* method: *jul̗l̗we.*

tribe: *bwij.*

tribute: *ekkan, eo̧jek, owōj.*
a basket for bearing tribute to a chief: *kōle.*
procession bearing tribute to chief: *tal.*

trick: *mo̧ņ, tuon.*
magic trick: *jibai.*
name of legendary trickster: *Etao.*
to trick: *liktak.*

trickle: *pil.*

Tricornis
a shell, *Strombidae, Lentigo lentiginosus* or *Tricornis sinuatus/thersites/latissimus*: *eañ.*

Tridacna
small *Tridacna*: *aded.*
Tridacna (chametrachea) crocea: *mejānwōd.*

trigger: *kāāp.*

triggerfish
black triggerfish, *Melichthys ringens*: *būb.*
reef triggerfish, *Balistapus rectangulus/aculeatus*: *im̧im̧.*
triggerfish, *Rhinecanthus aculeatus*: *liele.*

trim: *m̧wijbar.*
ornament, trimmings: *inōknōk.*
trim hair with a razor: *jeor.*

trip: *tipjek.*
to trip with the foot: *tiptak.*
trip someone: *l̗atipñōl.*
tripped: *rotak.*

trip: *tūrep.*
field trip: *piil̗ tūrep.*
field trip ship: *piil̗ tūrep.*

tripod
fishing method, pole fishing from a raised platform or tripod used for fishing: *okwa.*
tripod for fishing: *okwa.*
tripod for juicing pandanus: *peka.*

Trisenodon
a fish, shark, *Trisenodon obesus*: *pako korak.*

Tristichotrochus
trochus, a shell, *Trochidae, Omphalius pfeifferi* or *Tristichotrochus haliarchus*. A shell, *Pleurotomariidae*: *likōppejdat.*

trite: *mor.*

triton
triton shell. A shell, *Cassididae*: *jilel.*

Triumfetta
a plant, vine, *Triumfetta procumbens* Forst. F. (Tiliaceae): *atat.*

triumph: *anjo̧.*

trivial: *waan.*
trivial (see *tokja-* (**teqja-**)): *jettokja-.*

trochus
a shell, *Trochidae, Bathybembix aeola*: *jidduul.*
conical shell, larger than trochus: *luwo.*
trochus, a shell, *Pleurotomariidae*: *likaabdoulul.*
trochus, a shell, *Trochidae, Omphalius pfeifferi* or *Tristichotrochus haliarchus*. A shell, *Pleurotomariidae*: *likōppejdat.*

troll
fishing method, troll at night: *kōrkaak.*
fishing method, trolling inside lagoon: *kōkkojekjek.*
fishing method, trolling outside lagoon: *ilarak.*

pull fishing line rhythmically while trolling: *koraal.*
trolling: *ilarak.*

trophy: *kọwiinin, wiin.*

tropical storm
tropical storm similar to typhoon in strength: *kapiḷak.*

tropicbird
a bird, red-tailed tropicbird, *Phaethon rubricauda*: *ḷokwājek.*
a bird, white-tailed tropicbird, *Phaethon lepturus*: *jipkorōj.*

trouble: *airuwaro, jorrāān, mariprip, pok, tūrabōḷ.*
person or thing that causes trouble or bad luck: *jona.*
stir up trouble: *kiojaḷjaḷ.*
troubled: *inepata.*
troublesome: *ailparo, parok.*

trough
eaves-trough: *tọrtọr.*

trousers: *jedọujij, tabtab.*
denim trousers, blue jeans, Levis: *tanim.*
roll up shirt sleeves or trousers: *limtak.*

truck: *jitoja, ṃootka, tūrak.*
pick-up truck: *pekab.*

true: *lukkuun, ṃool.*
true to fact: *ātin.*
untrue: *riab.*

trump
a game, trump: *turuṃ.*

trumpet: *robba.*
trumpet, horn, siren, conch: *jilel.*

trunk: *kā, kea-.*
base, foundation, bottom, stem, trunk: *dāpi-.*
cut tree trunk into pieces, as breadfruit for making canoe: *kabbok.*
its trunk: *jekāān.*
trunk of a tree: *dāpdep, kāān.*
trunk of a young tree: *kōneo.*

trunk
chest, trunk: *tōptōp.*

trunkfish
a fish, trunkfish, *Ostracion tuberculatus*: *pel.*

trust
hope, trust, look forward to: *katmāne.*
not trust in: *jālōke.*
trust in: *lōke.*
trusted friend of a chief: *pālemoron.*

truth: *ṃool.*
tell the truth: *kwaḷọk ṃool.*

try: *idajoñjoñ, kajjioñ, mālejjoñ.*
try hard: *jibadbad, kakkōt, kattūkat.*
try hard to reach: *kijbadbad.*
try in court: *ekajet.*
try on clothes: *joñjoñ.*
try to reach: *jibadek.*
try to recognize: *kakōlkōl.*
trying: *jatdik.*

tub
a tub: *tab.*
wooden tub: *jāpe.*

tube
small rubber tube: *kumi.*

tuberculosis: *tipi.*

tuck
carry tucked under arm: *abjāje.*
tuck in: *kkūtbuuj.*

Tuesday: *Juje.*

tug: *kankan.*
tug of war: *kankan to.*

Tugali
Diodora (austroglyphis) sieboldii or *Montfortula pulchra* or *Tugali vadososinuata*: *jowakin.*

tumble: *wōtlọk.*
tumble over: *oḷọk.*

tumor: *ḷōpper, ṃaj, per, ur.*

tuna
a fish, dog-tooth tuna, *Gymnosarda nuda*: *jilo.*
a fish, tuna, *Neothunus macropterus*: *bwebwe.*
fishing method, long line, deep ocean, for tuna: *ḷatippān.*
shell of many colors, used as lure for tuna: *jepet.*

tune
a tune: *toṇ.*
flat music or voice, usually out of tune: *būḷāāt.*
tune up: *taiṃ, an.*

tunnel: *rọñ.*

turbid: *liṃ.*

turbulence: *aeñwāñwā.*

turkey: *take.*

turmoil: *aeñwāñwā.*

turn: *alen, jeor, kā, ukok.*
easy to turn: *jaḷiie.*
hard to turn: *jaḷiia.*
overturn: *okjak.*
take turns: *kajjojo.*
to turn: *jeik.*
toss and turn: *ukoktak.*
turn a vehicle: *jaaḷ.*
turn around: *oktak.*
turn away from: *eḷḷọk jān.*

turn back: *rǫǫl.*
turn face up: *kōjjād.*
turn for worse: *iñiñ.*
turn over: *jedtak, pedo, ukok.*
turn over or up: *ālāl.*
turn over rubbish hunting for something: *okpej.*
turn over small rocks when searching: *okļā.*
turn pages or leaves: *ālāl.*
turn the back on someone: *ālkurkur.*
turn the head slowly from side to side: *jeboulul.*
turn toward (always used with directional postpositions): *jujāl.*
turn, around and around: *iñiñ.*

turpentine: *jerpentain.*

Turritellidae
a shell, *Macrophragma tokyeense (Turritellidae)*: *likarkar.*

turtle: *wōn.*
fat in turtle shell: *wiwi.*
kind of turtle: *jebake.*
legendary turtle: *Ajjuunun.*
oil found under the shell of a turtle: *ao.*
place in sand where turtle lays eggs or coconut crab molts: *jǫ.*
place where turtles molt: *mej.*
turtle nest: *karōk.*
turtle shell: *bōd, jǫkur.*
turtle traces: *popo.*
turtles off *Wōja* islet of Ailinglapalap atoll: *Kobal.*
smell of turtles: *bbilwōnwōn.*

twelve: *joñoul ruo.*

twenty: *roñoul.*
twenty pairs, fish or copra: *ruokor.*

twice: *ruwaal.*
do something twice: *āpta.*

twig: *radikdik.*

twilight: *okraan.*

twin
twins: *bo, piro.*

twine
special twine made from skin of coconut frond midrib for climbing coconut trees: *kae.*
twine for sewing up the mouth of a bag: *enneok.*
twine made from skin of coconut frond midrib: *mālwe.*

twinkle: *rrobōlbōl.*
twinkle, as stars: *kabōlbōl.*

twirl: *iñiñ.*

twist
twist and pull hair: *dāde.*
twist around: *kōpooļ.*
twist in pain: *wūdikke.*
twist sennit: *pit.*
twist the hair into a knot: *bujek.*
twisted: *iñrōk, iñtōk.*

two: *ruo.*
two fourths: *ruo m̧ōttan emān.*
two hundred: *rūbukwi.*
two hundred pairs, fish or copra: *rukut.*
two thirds: *ruo m̧ōttan jilu.*
two thousand: *ruorap.*
two-faced: *m̧wil in jiip.*
two-story house: *nikāi.*

type: *kain, rot, tor, turot.*

type: *taip.*
typewriter: *taip.*

typhoon: *ļañ, taibuun.*
kill someone during a typhoon in anticipation of shortage of food: *okjānļañ.*
name of waves caused by typhoon: *Likkūr, Lim̧jeed, Lōbjañwūjooj, Lōņomeme, Lōtbar, Lōttǫr.*
tropical storm similar to typhoon in strength: *kapiļak.*

typical: *koļmān.*

ugh
interjection: "Ugh!": *ōrrōr.*

ugly: *dakōlkōl, jepa, kōnana, nabbe.*
ugly, of people: *dakke.*
very ugly: *kajjōjō.*

ukulele: *uklele.*

ulcer: *aļjer.*
skin ulcer: *dekā, eakeak.*
ulcerated framboesia: *rajjiia.*

ulua
a fish, skip jack, *Caranx melampygus*, Hawaiian *ulua*: *deltokrōk.*

umbrella: *am̧bwidilā.*

umpire: *am̧bai.*

unable: *ban.*
unable to endure physically: *ñatñat.*
unable to go in shallow water, of vessels: *kapjulaļ.*
unable to hear (see *roñ* (**reg°**)): *jarroñroñ.*
unable to keep still: *ne m̧akūtkūt.*
unable to sail close to the wind: *wāto.*
unable to stomach something: *ñatñat.*
unable to throw far: *jiban.*

unaccomplished: *make.*
unaccustomed: *jāmminene.*
unacquainted: *jājiniet.*
unattractive: *jakōl.*
unbalanced: *tōplik tōpar.*
unbecoming: *jekkar.*
unceremonial
celebrate an occassion in a rather unceremonial manner: *kōļọk.*
uncharitable: *miin.*
unchewed
unchewed food caught in throat: *ubabōj.*
uncircumcised
uncircumcised penis: *kōkkōk.*
unclasp: *mejaļ.*
uncle
uncle on the mother's side: *aļap.*
uncle, father's brother: *jema-.*
uncle, mother's brother only: *rūkorea-, wūllepa-.*
unclean
unclean, vulgar, gross: *ttoon.*
unclear
unclear weather: *tab.*
uncluttered: *meļak.*
uncomfortable: *abņōņō.*
uncomfortable feeling about the stomach from being overstuffed with food: *akeke.*
unconcerned
unconcerned about consequences: *jjọjọ, mejel kil.*
unconscious: *jajeļọkjeņ, ñakļọkjeņ.*
uncontrolled
desire for something, uncontrolled: *m̧m̧aelep.*
uncooked: *amej.*
uncoordinated
uncoordinated: *jokwa.*
uncoordinated in dancing (see *kōl* (**kẹl**)): *jakōl.*
uncover
uncover an earth oven, usually when food therein is cooked: *jukok.*
uncovered: *keelwaan.*
undaunted: *peran.*
undecided: *apaproro.*
under: *ium̧wi-, jọm̧win, lọrun.*
underneath: *ium̧wi-.*
underclothes: *anilowa.*
underestimate: *perper.*
underestimate one's potential: *jab dodoorlọk.*
underfed: *kwōle.*
underground
underground section of a plant: *debọkut.*
undernourished: *kwōle.*
underpants
underpants, men's: *jorm̧ōta.*
undershirt: *jiiñlij.*
understand: *meļeļe.*
understand how to keep temper: *kōmmaanwa.*
understandable: *alikkar.*
undertake: *jaak.*
undertaking: *jerbal.*
undertow
pull out, as current or undertow: *tọr.*
underwater
ability to stay underwater long: *pakij.*
go underwater: *tuññūlaļļọk.*
inability to stay underwater long: *jāpakij.*
outrigger goes underwater: *timaruk.*
underway
be underway, nautical: *jerak.*
something that has fallen from a canoe underway: *enkanaode.*
underwear: *anilowa.*
undeserving
feel undeserving: *ppat.*
undomesticated: *awiia.*
undone
leave a chore undone and start another: *jibwe turin jerbal.*
undress: *utkōk, utūkaļ.*
undried
undried copra: *owatrere.*
uneasiness: *addim̧akoko.*
uneasy: *nana tam̧m̧wi-.*
uneven: *bwijuwe, jikin uwe, tōplik tōpar.*
fishing term, said of a coconut leaf chain used as scarer that is strung out unevenly: *kapijjule.*
uneven, as racing canoes: *jake.*
unexpected
unexpected streak of luck, windfall: *tọọr pata.*
unfair
treat unfairly: *ālikinjepjep.*
unfaithful
unfaithful, as of spouse: *llo.*
unfavorable
unfavorable tide, neither high nor low: *jatloñ.*

unfortunate: *jedao, jerata.*
unhealthy: *utaṃwe.*
unicorn fish
Hepatus olivaceus Schneider Bloch: *ael.*
Naso brevirostris: *batakļaj.*
Naso lituratus: *bwilak.*
unified: *koba.*
uniform
uniform insignia: *kakōļļe.*
uninhabited
uninhabited land: *rārōk.*
unintentional
unintentionally: *jirilọk.*
unit
any group of people, as a class, unit or division: *jar.*
smallest unit of something, grain: *wūd.*
unite: *koba.*
form a united group: *bōro-kuk.*
slipped by, unite, escape: *rōļọk.*
to unite with: *kkejel.*
unkempt: *pirañrañ.*
unkind: *jememe.*
unleavened
unleavened pancake: *minor.*
unlike: *āinjuon.*
unload: *eakpel, eakto.*
unlovable: *pāpijek.*
unmarried
single, unmarried: *jalen.*
unmarried adolescent girl: *jiroñ.*
unmarried man: *ļajinono.*
unmarried woman: *lejnono.*
unnerve: *teroñe.*
unparalleled: *jej uwaan.*
unpleasant
unpleasant sensation: *mmāālel.*
unproductive
unproductive coconut tree (see ***kimuur*** **(kimiwir)**): *jakimuur.*
unprofitable: *jettokja-.*
unravel: *mejaļ.*
unrecognizable: *jakkōlkōl.*
unripe: *bur, kūk.*
pick unripe pandanus: *okabur.*
unripe coconut: *ub.*
unripe fallen breadfruit: *māirrūb.*
unruly: *jāṃōd, jeļmāne.*
unscrupulous: *jāṃōd, jeļmāne.*
unsettle: *teroñe.*
unskilled
unskilled person: *jedañ.*
unskillful: *jekapeel.*
unsnarl: *jaļjaļ, mejaļ.*
unsnarl a tangled fishline: *kōmmeļeļe.*
unsnarled: *meļeļe.*
unstable: *bbōroro, bōro-pejpej, ṃṃakūt.*
emotionally unstable: *anniabeab.*
mentally unstable: *ṃōjọliñōr, taṇo.*
unsuccessful
unsuccessful in one's love advances: *bokbok.*
unsuitable: *jekkar.*
untangle: *kōmmeļeļe.*
untie: *mejaļ.*
until: *ṃae, oom.*
untimely: *jum.*
untrue: *riab.*
unused: *jañin kkaan.*
unusual: *oktak.*
unwanted: *jool.*
unwashed
smell of unwashed genitals: *kūtkūt.*
unwieldy: *aujepaļ.*
unwilling: *ṃakoko.*
interjection: connotes unwillingness: *ōļļōļ, ōṇṇōṇ.*
wake up, unwillingly: *aruñijñij.*
unwind: *jaļjaļ.*
unworthy
feel unworthy: *ppat.*
up: *lōñ.*
directional, enclitic, upward: *lōñ.*
get up: *jerkak.*
stick up, on head or canoe: *aujrọñrọñ.*
take upward: *bōklōñļọk.*
up to: *oom.*
Upeneus
a fish, goatfish, *Upeneus tragula*: *joļọkṃōōr.*
upon: *ioo-.*
upper: *ej.*
at the upper part: *tulōñ.*
coconut shell, upper half next to stem, with eyes: *ļat-mej.*
upper story of house: *po.*
upright
of upright character: *weeppān.*
uproot: *toktak, totak, wūj.*
upset: *abṇōṇō, okjak, ukok.*
upset stomach: *wōtōdtōd.*
upside down: *lōrak, okjak.*
turn upside down: *kalōlō.*

upward: *tak.*
directional, enclitic, eastward, upward: *tak.*

urge: *loloorjake.*
chant and urge someone on by beating on a drum: *piniktak.*
strongly urge: *akweḷap.*
to urge, goad, spur, push: *rrọọj.*
urge on by cheers or other means: *pinnik.*

urinate: *kōmmatōr, raut, taan.*
urinate on: *ṃōjọ.*
urinate, of children only: *eañ.*

urine: *raut, taan.*
smell of urine: *kūḷōj, mieñ.*

Urodynamis
a bird, long-tailed New Zealand cuckoo, *Urodynamis taitensis*: *wūdej.*

Ursa
alpha Ursae Minoris: *Liṃanṃan.*
possibly 2 in Ursa Minor: *Jurōn-aodet-kaṇ-rilik.*
stars in Ursa Major: *Kāām-anij, Kāām-armej, Wa-eo-waan-Tūṃur, Wātal-kaṇ.*
stars in Ursa Minor: *Jemānuwe.*

us: *kōj.*
us (excl.): *kōm.*

use: *amān, le.*
to use bait: *mọọrọr.*
use a blanket: *kọọjoj.*
use a boat: *wawa.*
use a cane: *jokoṇkoṇ.*
use a canoe: *wawa.*
use a comb: *kuuṃuṃ.*
use a cup: *kabkab.*
use a fan: *deelel.*
use a lamp: *ḷaaṃaṃ.*
use a pen: *peenen.*
use a pillow: *petpet.*
use a rope: *leto.*
use a sail: *lewōjḷā.*
use a sanitary napkin: *tete.*
use a sheet: *jiitit.*
use a ship: *wawa.*
use a spear: *ṃadede.*
use a vehicle: *wawa.*
use a vehicle or vessel: *tak.*
use an engine: *leinjin.*
use an oarlock: *piinin.*
use as a container: *nine.*
use as fuel: *kaan.*
use bad language: *tepiḷ.*
use coconut sap for cooking: *utōn-jekaro.*
use crutches: *jokoṇkoṇ.*
use for the first time: *kkaan.*
use kerosene: *lekarjin.*
use one's head: *aṇtọọn.*
use part of: *kkaan.*
use soap: *joobob.*
unused: *jañin kkaan.*

use
not useful: *jakeiie.*
useful: *keiie.*
useless: *jettokja-, pata.*

used to: *kkein, mminene.*
be formerly, used to be: *jọ.*

usual
unusual: *oktak.*
usually: *kkā.*
usually do something: *kōṇaan.*
usually, mostly: *epliklik.*

utensil
cooking utensil: *ainbat.*
possessive classifier, tooth or eating utensils: *ñii-.*

uterus: *jikin niñniñ.*

uu
a fish, *uu* or *panu*: *ṃōn-kiden.*

uvula: *būri.*

V.I.P.: *akaje, kāājāj, ḷakkūk, pālu.*

vacate: *jepjep.*

vacation: *kakkije.*
summer vacation: *jeṃar.*
travel on a vacation: *jaṃbo.*

vagabond
stranger, tramp, vagabond: *armej jeedwa.*

vagina: *bōḷbōḷ, kōd, pipi.*
possessing control of vaginal muscles: *kkweetet.*

vain
a vain person: *utḷōṃ.*
in vain: *pata, waan.*
say in vain: *ba pata.*

Valenciennesia
a fish, electrid, *Valenciennesia strigata/violifera*: *ikōlood.*

valiant: *peran.*

valley
small valley or depression: *peta.*
valley, depression: *koṃlaḷ.*

valuable: *aorōk.*

value: *tōpran, tokja-.*
assess the value of: *joñe aorōkin.*

vampire: *mejenkwaad.*

vanish: *jako.*
to vanish over the horizon: *jetḷọk.*
vanished: *jako.*

vapor: *menokadu.*

varicose
varicose veins: *jar eke.*

Variola
a fish, bass, *Variola louti*: *ikmid, kanbōk, oļaļo.*

varnish: *wanij.*

vast: *kilep.*

Vega
a star, Vega: *Elṃad.*

vegetables
green vegetables: *nōbba.*

vehicle: *wa.*
go on a vehicle or sailing canoe (used with directional enclitics (and postpositions)): *tar-.*
leave vehicle or vessel: *llik.*
look for a vehicle: *luwa.*
newly constructed, of vessels or vehicles: *wōnōt.*
possessive classifier, canoe, ship, boat, or vehicle: *waa-.*
test drive a new or overhauled vehicle: *likbad.*
turn a vehicle: *jaaļ.*
use a vehicle: *wawa.*
use a vehicle or vessel: *tak.*
vehicle of: *waa-.*

vein: *eke, iaļan bōtōktōk.*

velvet
velvety: *ṃọkulkul, meoeo.*

venereal
venereal disease: *jeplej, mādke.*

Veneridae
a shell, *Veneridae, Veremilpa minuta/ micra/costellifera/scabra* or *Dosinia histrio/abyssicola*: *kūkōr.*

ventilate: *jjedwawa.*

Venus
a star (planet), Evening Star, Venus (evenings only): *Maalal.*
a star (planet), Morning Star, Venus (mornings only): *Jurōn-Jemān-Kurlōñ.*

veranda: *maļto, tōñaak.*

verbal
verbalize: *kōnono.*

Veremilpa
a shell, *Veneridae, Veremilpa minuta/ micra/costellifera/scabra* or *Dosinia histrio/abyssicola*: *kūkōr.*

Vernocia
a plant, *Vernocia cinerea* (L.) Less.: *jān-aelōñ-ñan-aelōñ.*

verse: *eoon.*

vertical: *ju.*

very: *jelōñlōñ, kakkōt, kanooj, tōñtōñ, toļọk, wōtōm.*
a very tall coconut tree: *kenato.*
not so very much: *daan.*
very great: *bōtata.*

vessel
arrive, of sailing vessel or airplane: *po.*
blood vessel: *eke, iaļan bōtōktōk.*
haul canoe or vessel up on shore: *ār.*
land, sailing vessel: *po.*
leave vehicle or vessel: *llik.*
motorvessel: *tiṃa.*
newly constructed, of vessels or vehicles: *wōnōt.*
superstition that large waves portend the arrival of a vessel: *tokwanwa.*
test sail a new or overhauled vessel: *likbad.*
tie up a vessel: *mmaan.*
to beach canoe or vessel: *ār.*
use a vehicle or vessel: *tak.*

vex: *kōmmatōr.*
vexed: *aplonlon.*

vibrate: *ebeb, wūdiddid.*
tremor or vibration caused by sound of gun or thunder: *pañijñij.*

vicinity: *peļaak.*

vicious: *ājāj.*

victory: *anjọ.*

view
come into view after being hidden: *mmat.*
taking in the view: *alwōj bajjek.*

vigilance: *likōk.*

Vigna
a plant, *Vigna marina* (Burm.) Merrill. (Leguminosae): *markinenjojo.*

vigor
frisky, sound, vigorous: *ājmuur.*
vigorous: *pātōñtōñ, peñpeñ.*

village: *bukwōn.*
settlement, village: *jukjuk.*

vine
a plant, vine, *Ipomoea tuba*: *marpeļe.*
a plant, vine, *Triumfetta procumbens* Forst. F. (Tiliaceae): *atat.*
A yellow-flowered leguminous vine climbing, or decumbent on beaches: *markinenjojo.*

vinegar: *penkō.*

violet: *piolōt.*

violin: *baeoliin.*

viper: *jabōn.*

virgin: *bōjin.*
lose virginity: *buñ.*

virtuous: *wānōk.*

viscid
viscid, sticky, of food: *depñat.*

viscous: *bōjbōj.*

vise: *baij.*

visible: *alikkar.*
invisible: *aelọk.*

vision
keen vision: *loḷọkjeṇ.*
long vision: *loḷọkjeṇ.*
see a vision in sleep: *ṃadenḷọk.*

visit: *lo-.*
visit home of dead person with gifts: *ilomej.*
visit the bereaved: *ilomej.*
visitor: *riitok, rilotok, ruwamāejet.*
foods prepared for visitors before their arrival: *kabwijeran.*

vital: *aorōk.*

vitamin: *ōn.*

vivacious: *keeñki.*

vocative
—to boys: *būrọ.*
—to girls: *jiroñ.*
—familiar, feminine plural: *liṃarārā, liṃaroro.*
—familiar, feminine singular: *liiō.*
—familiar, masculine plural: *ḷōṃarārā, ḷōṃaroro.*
—familiar, masculine singular: *ḷeiō.*
—feminine plural: *liṃa.*
—feminine singular: *la, le.*
—masculine plural: *ḷōṃa.*
—masculine singular: *ḷe.*

vociferous: *dekōṃkōṃ.*

voice: *ainikie-.*
dynamic voice: *ḷḷaaj.*
husky voice: *ṃōrā-bōjbōj.*

void
devoid: *āmje.*
head devoid of hair: *kweejej.*

volcano: *booḷkeno.*
heavy volcanic rocks: *dekā lọḷ.*

volleyball: *baḷebọọḷ.*

voluminous: *kobbā.*

vomit: *ṃṃōj.*

voodoo: *kkōpāl.*

voracious: *būrooklep, mattiia.*

vortex: *likapijwewe.*

vote
vote, vote for: *bout.*

vow: *kalliṃur.*

voyage: *tūrep.*
bon voyage: *kōjjemḷọk.*
provisions for a voyage: *ṃṃōd, ṃōd, nnōk, teaak.*
see off on a voyage: *juwōne.*

vulgar
unclean, vulgar, gross: *ttoon.*

vulva: *bōḷbōḷ, bōlōk.*

wade
wade in water: *tuwaak.*

waft: *jāālel.*
waft through the air, as a ghost: *weaak.*
waft, of waves: *kinōr.*

wag: *kōjjaaḷaḷ.*

wage
provide with a wage or salary: *ṇaoṇea-.*
wages of: *oṇea-.*

waggle: *kōjjaaḷaḷ.*

wagon: *kurṃa, wāikōn.*

wail: *jañ, liṃō, rraakak.*

waist: *ip, lukwō-.*
put arm around waist of another while standing side by side: *jelpaak.*
roll of fat around waist: *maḷūttōk.*
slim-waisted and broad-shouldered: *kāāj in kabwebwe.*
small waisted: *kādik.*
support one another by holding each other's waists: *waanikli.*

wait
await: *kattar, kōmḷan.*
lie in wait for: *apād, kōjjaad.*
lie in waiting: *kōppao.*
wait a spell: *kōmḷan.*
wait for: *kattar.*
wait for anxiously: *jañnuwaad.*
wait for fruit to ripen: *kōmmako.*
wait for rain to subside: *kōḷọk.*
wait under shelter for rain to stop: *kaḷọk.*

waiter: *buwae.*

waitress: *buwae.*

wake: *jebokwōn.*
wake of a boat: *aod.*
wake, ship or fish: *bukwaarar.*

wake up: *ruj.*
wake up early in the morning: *mājinmuur.*
wake up, unwillingly: *aruñijñij.*

walk: *etal laḷ, etetal, wāwe.*
eat or drink while walking: *jotal.*
feet sink in sand making for difficult walking: *neen kōbkōb.*
put one's arm across another's shoulders while walking: *waabbilāle.*
swing arms while walking: *jerjer.*

talk or walk in one's sleep: *jja.*
walk aimlessly: *jam̧bo.*
walk back and forth: *ikueaak.*
walk between islands at low tide: *etal iene.*
walk dragging a leg: *māro.*
walk fast: *jorjor.*
walk hand in hand: *jjurpe.*
walk in a happy mood: *alijerḷọk.*
walk in an excited mood: *jjeikik.*
walk on hands: *ju.*
walk on heels: *juknene.*
walk slowly: *ajādik.*
walk swinging the arms: *iliik.*
walk toward: *wan-.*
walk with a limp: *jipijuḷ.*
walk with the hands clasped behind the back: *enliklik.*
walking stick: *jokoņ.*

wall: *kii-.*
coral wall: *me.*
put thatch on walls: *katnok.*

wallet: *jiipkako.*

walrus: *kiduun lọjet.*

wan: *o.*

wander: *jebwābwe, m̧m̧ōkadkad.*
fish that wanders outside coconut leaf chain scarer: *ikōnālkinm̧wio.*
wander without using physical effort: *weaak.*

wandering tattler
a bird, wandering tattler, *Heteroscelus incanum*: *kidid.*

wane: *mājkun, mọkun.*

want: *kōņaan.*
want more: *jam̧jam̧.*
unwanted: *jool.*

war: *pata, tariņae.*
loss of royal status through defeat in war: *jipọkwe.*
retreat in war: *eọwilik.*

ward
ward off a spear thrust: *taar.*
ward off using Marshallese hand-to-hand combat defense techniques: *pile.*

wardrobe: *tūroot.*

warehouse: *joko.*

warm: *māāņāņ.*
to warm one's bottom by the fire: *rabwij.*
to warm oneself by the fire: *rañrañ.*
warm up: *deenju.*
warmed up, in games: *bok.*
warmed up, in games: *pet pā.*
warmth: *māāņāņ.*

warn: *kabroñḷọk, kauwe, kipel.*
afraid, warn: *kkōl.*

warp
warped: *bok.*

warship: *m̧ōnwa.*

wart: *būtti, būttiwoḷ.*
wart, bushy type: *būtti kakūtōtō.*

wash: *kwaḷkoḷ.*
coir fibre, fine, not woven, left over from weaving, used as wash cloth: *bwijinbwije.*
rub clothes in washing: *m̧ukm̧uk.*
smell of unwashed sexual organs: *būņo, kūtkūt.*
wash anus after defecating, especially women and children, usually in ocean: *eọreor.*
wash bottles: *nam̧nam̧.*
wash hands: *am̧win.*
wash one's face: *ormej.*
wash private parts, female: *ḷokḷok.*
wash rice: *patpat.*
wash, as a wave or backwash: *tọr.*
washed ashore: *ḷukut.*
water for washing hands: *am̧win.*

washer
washer, mechanical: *wajej.*

waste: *jerwaan, kwōpej.*
dirty waste water from arrowroot straining process: *kūbween lọlọ.*
throw waste food or trash somewhere: *kwōpejpej.*
wasted away: *apeñāñā.*
wasteful: *bōro-ḷap.*
wasteland: *jem̧aden.*

watch: *alwōj, kōmja, mejek, waj.*
keep watch all the time, as on board a ship or at a bedside, without taking a rest: *kajumej.*
keep watching: *mejek.*
possessive classifier, children, pets, money, watches, or Bible: *nāji-.*
to watch patiently: *akade.*
watch and long for a bite of food while another is eating: *kōjm̧aal.*
watch birds alight to locate roost: *akajok.*
watch birds to locate roost: *akade, alekọ.*
watch for enemies: *kawal.*
watch over: *alal.*
watch with evil interest or hidden purpose: *kōppao.*
watch-tower: *miade.*
watchman: *waj.*

watch: *waj.*

water: *dān.*
  a hole in a tree for catching water: *m̧m̧ak.*
  ability to stay underwater long: *pakij.*
  bathing water of: *utō-.*
  brackish, of water: *kōļaebar.*
  bucket or can for drawing water from a well: *keikōb.*
  come out of water: *ato.*
  container of oil or water for use with royal whetstone: *n̄op.*
  deep water: *jat.*
  dip up water: *itōk.*
  disturbance caused in water by canoe or fish: *auj̧o̧j̧o̧.*
  draw water: *itōk.*
  drawing much water causing it to be hard to paddle or sail, nautical: *añōt.*
  drinking water: *aebōj, dānnin idaak.*
  drinking water containers on a canoe or boat: *kōb.*
  drops of water: *bbūtbūt.*
  fresh water: *māmet.*
  get the last drops of water from a water container: *kajļor, kajļor.*
  go into the water: *tuwaak.*
  go underwater: *tuññūlaļļok.*
  jump into the water: *ro.*
  mix with water: *kāre.*
  no water: *jej̧j̧at.*
  open eyes under water: *tumej.*
  outrigger goes underwater: *timaruk.*
  place on an islet where water flows across at high tide: *to̧o̧r.*
  place on reef where water remains at low tide: *to̧o̧r.*
  possessive classifier, bathing water: *utō-.*
  possessive classifier, water, soft drinks, or juice of coconuts, etc.: *lime-.*
  provide with bathing water: *n̄autō-.*
  rain water: *aebōj, dānnin aebōj, dānnin wōt.*
  run, of water: *to̧o̧r.*
  salt water: *dānnin ļo̧jet.*
  splash water on: *jojo.*
  take in water from the top of a canoe: *timaruk.*
  to drink water, child speech: *kaka.*
  wade in water: *tuwaak.*
  water container: *tāāñ.*
  water course in the reef: *wea.*
  water down: *ilo̧k.*
  water for washing hands: *am̧win.*
  water rises in a well or swamp: *jib.*
  water-tight (see *ttal* (**ttal**)): *jettal.*
  waterlogged: *ļwōjat.*

watery: *dāndān, kkōr, ppej, watre.*
well water: *aebōj laļ, dānnin laļ.*

waters
  the waters between Jaluit and Ailinglaplap atolls: *Metwan Al.*

wave
  a wave: *n̄o.*
  beating of the waves: *depdep.*
  bow waves from a ship: *at.*
  breaking of waves: *buñraak, rere.*
  breaking waves: *buñn̄o.*
  canoe part, waveguard on both sides of sailing canoe: *añtūkli.*
  distant rumbling of waves: *lijeñūrñūr.*
  flow, series of larger waves: *ibeb.*
  follow a large wave in entering a lagoon: *ļooribeb.*
  heaping up of waves: *jetak.*
  mounting wave which does not break: *ñōl.*
  name of waves caused by typhoon: *Likkūr, Lim̧jeed, Lōbjañwūjooj, Lōn̄omeme, Lōtbar, Lōtto̧o̧r.*
  navigation "knot" where two waves meet: *buoj.*
  not cut waves well: *n̄o̧j̧o̧.*
  period between series of larger waves: *mo̧o̧l.*
  remain ahead of a wave when sailing following the wind: *buñm̧aan.*
  ride the waves: *m̧ōt.*
  sound of waves pounding on reef: *lijeñūrñūr.*
  steady waves buffeting the shore: *ninārār.*
  strike a wave: *m̧witaak.*
  superstition that large waves portend the arrival of a vessel: *tokwanwa.*
  waft, of waves: *kinōr.*
  wash, as a wave or backwash: *to̧r.*
  wave ready to break: *jatak.*
  wave-guard on a canoe: *ubwen̄o.*
  waves caused by something: *lim̧aajn̄o̧n̄o.*
  waves of ships or planes: *ibeb.*
  waves receding from shore slapping against incoming waves: *jipikra.*

wave
  wave goodbye: *jokutbae.*
  wave tail above surface, of fish: *ļokļok.*
  wave, of a flag: *jopāl.*
  wave, of a flag or clothes: *ppālpāl.*

waver: *itweļok.*

wavy: *m̧ōjālūlū.*

way: *iaḷ.*
a way made clear for escaping: *iaḷan jọọr.*
be on one's way: *jibadek jidik.*
know one's way around: *util.*
not know which way to go: *añjebwāālel.*
something in one's way or place: *penjak.*
way of: *tipe-.*
way or manner of doing something: *ap, kōl.*

waylay: *apād, kōmja.*
waylay, accost: *pāpjel ṃae.*

we
let's, we are to: *jen.*
we (excl.): *kōm.*
we (incl.): *kōj.*
we two are to: *jeṇro.*

weak: *ban, ṃōjṇọ, wūpeḷ.*
weak feeling, usually from hunger: *ajeḷkā.*
weak from hunger: *uwaañañ.*
weak in the legs: *lijjipdo.*
weak teeth: *ñiban.*
weak-legged: *māro.*
weak, permanent condition: *banban.*
weakened from a blow: *ṃaal.*
weakling: *ārpej, mejjani, oḷaḷo.*
weakness: *an mej eṇ.*

wealth: *jeraaṃṃan, ṃaju, ṃweiuk.*
wealthy: *ṃweiie.*

wean: *liktūt.*

weapon: *aḷaḷ in deñdeñ.*
make weapons: *nōḷ.*
place for making weapons: *tūr.*

wear: *kkōṇak.*
a mat for wearing: *ed.*
wear a baseball glove: *kurobrob.*
wear a belt: *kañūrñūr.*
wear a bracelet: *pāāñkōḷ.*
wear a diaper: *kaḷkaḷ.*
wear a hat: *atat.*
wear a lava-lava: *ḷobḷoba.*
wear a loin cloth: *kaḷkaḷ.*
wear a necklace: *ṃarṃar.*
wear a piece of clothing for the first time: *lōtlōt.*
wear a pin: *piinin.*
wear a ring: *riiñiñ.*
wear a rose or hibiscus flower: *roojoj.*
wear a shirt: *jōōtōt.*
wear a slip: *jemej.*
wear a towel as a lava-lava: *ḷobḷoba.*
wear a watch: *wajwaj.*
wear a zori: *jodi.*
wear around the neck: *ṃarṃar.*
wear earring: *diede.*
wear flowers on head: *pālpel.*
wear flowers or a lei: *utut.*
wear pants high on hips: *ṃuriej.*
wear shoes: *juujuj.*
wear socks: *takinkin.*
wear wet clothing: *ṃōrābōt.*

weary: *kajjinōk, ṃōk, pālo.*

weather: *lañ.*
a breeze forecasting calm weather: *añinlur.*
check the weather: *katu.*
forecast weather: *katu.*
forecast weather by observing clouds: *kōbbaal.*
intensifier, of limited use: for time, tide, or weather: *jelōñlōñ.*
lightning as a sign of fair weather: *jetḷādik.*
time of fair weather: *iien rak.*
unclear weather: *tab.*

weave: *āj.*
to weave pandanus thatch: *wewā.*
to weave the edges of a mat or hat: *jekōt.*
weave flowers or shells into a lei: *ḷōḷō.*
crossed in weaving or plaiting: *idaaptōk.*
strands for weaving garlands or stringing leis: *id.*
weaving strips: *iden.*

web
spider's web: *toon kọuḷaḷo.*

wedding: *kwōjkwōjin pālele.*
taking gifts to a wedding, funeral, or party for guests to take home: *tōptōp.*

Wedelia
a plant, *Wedelia biflora* (L.) DC. (Compositae): *markūbwebwe.*

wedge: *weej.*

Wednesday: *Wōnje.*

weed
A red-stemmed weedy herb: *neen kōtkōt.*
pull up weeds or grass: *kintak.*
a plant, general term for seaweed. *Thalassia hemprichii* (Ehrenb.) Aschers.: *wūjooj-in-lọjet.*

week: *wiik.*
next week: *wiik in laḷ.*

weep: *jañ.*
weep loudly: *liṃō.*

weigh: *bọun.*
dried copra ready to be weighed: *ṃọọn.*

weigh anchor: *tōbtōb.*
weigh down: *jjiped.*

weight: *bọun.*
lift weights to build up body: *kaddipenpen.*
light in weight: *bōļaļ, mera.*
overweight, obese: *tebu.*
person who carries weight in his speech due to social status: *ļajjuur.*
toss a line by means of weight tied to end: *iñjālle.*
weighted down, of people only: *ajjibanban.*
weighty in words: *aejemjem.*

weir
coral weir to trap fish: *me.*
fishing method, chasing fish into weir: *kōttọọr.*
fishing method, stand beside weir and watch for mackerel: *jo.*
fishing method, using scarer and weir: *kwōmej.*
stand by a weir waiting for tide: *watak.*

welcome: *karuwanene.*

weld
welded: *ddāp.*

well: *ekwe.*
make well: *kōmour.*
not well done: *amej.*
well born: *arōṃṃan.*
well done: *weeppān.*
well dressed: *ppānpān.*
well-cleaned: *lōt.*
well-organized: *koṇ.*
well-to-do: *ṃweiie.*

well
a well: *aebōj.*
bucket or can for drawing water from a well: *keikōb.*
to drink from a well or a hole in a tree by bending over and using the mouth directly: *ṃōt.*
water rises in a well or swamp: *jib.*
well water: *aebōj laļ, dānnin laļ.*

well-bred: *arōṃṃan.*

wen: *per.*

west: *rālik.*
on the west side of: *rāātle, rilik.*
west side of: *kapi.*
western and northwestern island northwestern islands in an atoll: *liklaļ.*
western sky: *kapilōñ.*
westernized: *pālle.*

westerly
westerly breeze: *añōltak.*
westerly swell: *buñtokrilik.*

westward: *to, toļok, turilik.*
current flowing westward: *aeto.*
directional, enclitic, westward: *to.*
drift westward: *peto.*
go westward: *ito, wāto.*
head westward: *jitto.*
sail westward: *kabbe.*

wet: *ṃōļọwi, ṇok, tutu.*
dripping wet: *aeṇak.*
very wet: *eo, ṃoujlep.*
wear wet clothing: *ṃōrābōt.*
wet behind the ears: *watre.*
wet with spray: *jādbūtūktūk.*

whale: *raj.*
one of a pair of whales: *Erra, Kerara.*
whale meat: *itok.*
whaling: *kōrajraj.*

wharf: *wab.*

what: *ta.*
do what?: *et.*
in what direction: *jikōt.*
somewhat: *jaad.*
to do what: *jikōt.*
what do you say?: *eañ.*
what for?: *enta.*
what if: *ļak.*
what is the reason: *tawūnin.*
what man? What boy?: *ļōt, ļōt.*
what's the matter: *ebajeet.*

whatever: *jabdewōt.*

wheel: *ne, wiiļ.*
steering wheel: *jebwe.*
wheel and deal: *kōppao.*
windmill, pinwheel: *lodideañ.*

when: *ñe.*
when?: *ñāāt.*

where: *ijeko, ijo.*
a locative, where, there: *tu.*
somewhere here around me: *ijekā, ijekākā.*
somewhere here around us: *ijekein.*
where are they? (Of humans): *erri.*
where are they? (Of things): *erki.*
where?: *ewi, ia.*
wherefore: *kōn menin.*

wherewithal
provide wherewithal: *ṇawāwee-.*

whet: *jemjem.*

whetstone
container of oil or water for use with royal whetstone: *ṇop.*

which: *me, ta.*

while
a while ago: *kkein.*

whimbrel
a bird, whimbrel, *Numenius phaeopus*: *kowak.*

whip: *deñdeñ, lij.*

whirl: *addeboulul.*
whirlpool: *likapijwewe.*
whirlwind: *añijwiwi.*

whisker
whiskers: *kwōdeak.*
clean whiskers off of newly braided sennit: *kōrōnāl.*
whiskers remaining on a husked coconut: *wūlṃōd.*

whiskey: *wōjke.*
a shot of whiskey: *jaat.*

whisper: *ajjinono, ṃṃaidikdik, wūnojidikdik.*

whistle: *ajwewe, owe.*
whistling, long continued: *ajwewe.*

white: *mouj.*
a bird, white as sea gull: *mānnimuuj.*
smile, showing the white of the teeth: *rere.*
white spot on the head of the brown noddy (*pejwak*) bird: *ao.*

whittle: *eọr.*

who: *me, wōn.*

whoever: *wōn.*

whole: *depiio, iio, likiio, uñ.*

whom: *wōn.*

whoop: *kkeilọk.*

whore
whore house: *ṃōn utḷaṃ.*

whorl: *likapijwewe.*

why
why?: *bwe, enta, etke, tawūnin.*

wick: *wiik.*

wicked: *nana.*

wide: *depakpak.*
wide-eyed: *kabūrōrō.*
wide, of land (see *wūjabōj* (**wijabẹj**)): *wūjaḷoñ.*
width: *depakpak.*

wieldy
unwieldy: *aujepaḷ.*

wife: *pālee-, rii-.*
chief's wife, may or may not be of royal blood: *lejḷā.*
given to wife-beating: *ḷaire.*
steal someone's wife (euphemism): *tuuj bōl.*

wiggle: *bbōōlōl, iñiñtōk.*

wiggler
wiggler larvae of mosquitoes: *ḷijeljelṃak.*

wild: *awiia, mānnimar.*
a bird, wild duck: *rañ.*
wild, in throwing: *boor.*

wilderness: *āne-jeṃaden, buḷōn mar.*

will: *ankilaa-.*
will be: *naaj.*

willing
unwilling: *ṃakoko.*
wake up, unwillingly: *aruñijñij.*
interjection: connotes unwillingness: *ōḷḷōḷ, ōṇṇōṇ.*

wilt
wilt, contract: *kuṇōk.*

win: *wiin.*
win a victory: *anjọ.*

winch: *jirab, wūlleej.*

wind: *añ, kōto.*
a sudden wind: *ṃweawi.*
able to sail close to the wind: *wetak.*
anchorage on ocean side of islet where one waits for more favorable winds: *metto.*
blow gently, of wind: *lladikdik.*
blow sharply, of wind: *letōñ.*
blow, of the wind: *detak.*
canoe-surfing, when sailing down wind: *kōttōmāle.*
catch something in one's windpipe: *pọk.*
exposed to wind and air: *añjerak.*
forecast predicting the onset of prevailing northeast tra de winds: *deñdeñin.*
gusty wind: *añjarjar, ḷadikin eoon ere, okjānlañ.*
northeast trade wind: *kọto.*
onset of the windy season: *añkwōl.*
pacify the winds and cause winds favorable for a sailing expedition: *kaurur jiañ.*
prosperous wind: *ṃakroro.*
roar, as of the wind or a monster: *rorror.*
sail close to the wind: *kipeddikdik.*
sail downwind with the sail on the south and the outrigger on the north: *tōmeañ.*
sail following the wind: *kōllōkā.*
sail with the wind: *kabbe.*
short winded: *kkijeje.*
strong wind: *okjānlañ.*
unable to sail close to the wind: *wāto.*

uneven sailing wind in lee of an islet: *añinene.*
unexpected streak of luck, windfall: *tọọr pata.*
whirlwind: *añijwiwi.*
wind from southwest: *kūtak.*
wind from the east: *itok reeaar.*
wind from the north: *jokḷā.*
wind from the northwest: *tiltil keeañ.*
wind from the west: *itak kipilōñ.*
wind squall: *mowi.*
wind that gathers strength as it reaches the treetops: *añinraanjitbōnmar.*
windbreak: *jaññōr.*
windfallen breadfruit: *mābuñ.*
windmill, pinwheel: *lodideañ.*
windward side of an atoll: *likiej.*
windy season: *añōneañ.*

wind: *iñiñ.*
unwind: *jaḷjaḷ.*

winded: *kajjinōk.*

windlass: *wūlleej.*

window: *wūntō.*
sliding window: *kājōjō.*

wine: *wain.*

wing: *pā.*
flutter, as of wings: *pikpik.*
wings outstretched in flying: *jepeḷā.*

wink: *rom.*

winter
wintertime: *añōneañ.*

wipe: *irir.*
to wipe oneself after defecating: *kwiir.*
wiped out, busted, stoned: *kwōp.*

wire: *wea.*
ground wire: *kūrawūn.*
strand of rope or wire: *ko.*
strong wires twisted together: *kebōḷ.*
to pull and break objects such as string, rope, wire or grass: *tūṃtūṃ.*
wire for stringing fish: *ile.*
wire leader, used in fishing: *atad, ḷōḷ.*
wiretap: *iaroñroñ.*

wisdom: *jeḷā ḷọkjeṇ, ḷoḷātāt.*

wisdom tooth: *ñilep.*

wise: *kapeel.*
wise man: *kanpil.*

wish: *kōṇaan.*
wish for: *ḷōkōṃ.*

wit
able to keep wits during crisis: *lọḷe.*
be slow witted: *aḷḷañ.*
sharp-witted: *wājepdik.*
witty, sharp: *wājepdik.*

witch
bewitch: *kkọọl.*
use witchcraft: *anji.*
witch who eats people: *mejenkwaad.*
witchcraft: *anijnij.*
witchdoctor: *ṇakṇōk.*

with: *ippa-, kōn, le.*
be with: *karwaan.*
with it: *eake, kake.*
with someone: *iaa-.*

withdraw: *kkekaak, nnōōr, wōmwōm, wūjroñ.*
withdraw from society to follow one's own desires: *paarōr.*

wither
withered: *ṃōṇakṇak, ṃōrā.*

within
within the realm of possibilities: *tōllọk.*

without: *ejjeḷọk.*

withstand
withstand hardships: *kajumej.*

witness: *lo, rūkaṃool.*
witness in marriage ceremony: *kōjab.*
witnesses in marriage: *apar.*

wiz: *moot, tijeṃḷọk.*

wizard: *ṃōkade, ṇakṇōk.*
wizardism: *bubu.*

wobble: *bbōōlōl.*

woe: *o.*

wolf: *oḷip.*

woman: *kōrā.*
a girl or woman whose appearance makes everyone smile: *llejkōnkōn.*
busy woman: *lowaṇwoṇ.*
easy woman: *kōba.*
extremely beautiful woman: *to-jān-lañ.*
legendary flying woman: *lōrrọ.*
old woman: *lōḷḷap, obajañ.*
pregnant woman: *kūrae.*
that woman (close to neither of us): *lieṇ, liieṇ, luweo.*
that woman (close to you): *lieṇe, lieṇeṇe.*
the woman (often not present): *lio.*
this woman (close to me): *lie, lio.*
this woman (close to us both): *liin, liiō.*
unmarried woman: *lejnono.*
what woman?: *lōt.*
woman who flies after loss of love or departure of loved one: *lōrrọ.*

woman who just gave birth: *kūrae.*
chase women: *kōkkōrārā.*
have a way with women: *tāān.*
medicine women: *didiiñ.*
the women (often not present): *limaro.*
these women (close to me): *limarā, limarārā, limaro.*
these women (close to us both): *limarein.*
those women (close to neither of us): *limarāraņ, limaraņ, limaroro.*
those women (close to you): *limarārane, limarane.*
you, to many women in general, not specific: *lima.*

womb: *jikin niñniñ.*

wonder: *bwilōñ, ļokjenaa-.*
interjection: "No wonder!" "It stands to reason.": *jebata.*
interjection: expression of wonder or delight: *bōranmaajidake.*
wonderful: *aiboojoj.*

woo: *jawōd.*

wood: *aļaļ.*
piece of wood on which coconut husk is beaten to yield fibre for sennit: *jebōnmāl.*
wood-shavings: *tōp.*

woods: *buļōn mar.*

word: *naan.*
falling of words from lips: *buñraak.*
spread the word: *bōōjōj.*
weighty in words: *aejemjem.*

work: *jerbal.*
eat before working: *kapije.*
hard working: *owan.*
send another to do one's work: *kōmādodo.*
shout rhythmically while doing a job requiring team work, as carrying a canoe: *roro.*
to chant while drawing up a canoe or other such cooperative work: *ñijir.*
work alone: *ajerre.*
work gang: *kumi.*
work on a boat to make it sail fast: *an.*
work on a job, employment: *joob.*
work on something as a group: *kumit.*
work overtime: *ailparo.*
work together: *atanijo.*
worker: *rijerbal.*
working by some contrivance or other: *madmōd.*
working party: *okun bade.*
working place: *jep.*
workmanship: *eļtan pā.*
overworked: *parōk.*
hard working: *niknik.*

world: *laļ.*
country of the world: *laļ.*

worm
earthworm: *majkadāl.*
eel, intestinal worm: *maj.*
ship worm: *dile.*
worm, maggot: *likaakrak.*
damage caused by termites or bookworms: *dile.*

worn
worn out: *mor, pālo.*
worn-out woven things: *mwid.*

worry: *inepata, llotaan.*
worried: *rup bōro.*

worse
turn for worse: *iñiñ.*

worship: *buñ-pedo, kabuñ, wūjtak.*

worth: *tōllok, tōpran, tokja-.*
worthless: *jettokja-, waan.*
worthless person or thing: *iupej.*

worthy
feel unworthy: *ppat.*

wound: *kinej.*
bump a sore or wound: *keeñjak, kkeñaj.*
healing together of a wound: *ik.*
wound that is easy to cure or heal: *mowiie.*
wound that is hard to cure or heal: *mowiia.*
wounded: *kinejnej.*

wow: *uwok.*
exclamation: "Wow!": *ekōļōk.*

wrap: *lemlem, lokor, rojroj.*
a food, preserved breadfruit boiled or baked without wrapping: *koļeiaat.*
bandaged, tied up, wrapped up: *korkor.*
bundle of goods wrapped with a square of cloth: *būroojki.*
bundle that has been wrapped, sticks or pandanus leaves: *tūr.*
cloth for wrapping bundle of goods: *būroojki.*
wrap in basket or leaves: *tūrtūr.*
wrap pandanus fruit with coconut leaves to make it ripen: *kūtōb.*
wrap the body: *kūtimtim.*
wrap up: *kkor, korak, kwarkor, kwōje, wūnit.*
wrap up in a blanket: *tūroro.*
wrap with leaves: *tūroro.*
wrapped around, of string: *jāliñiñ.*
wrapped sloppily: *buļokwōjkwōj.*

wrapping: *limek.*

wrasse
Cheilinus sp: *mao, merā.*
Coris gaimardi: *alle, likōb.*
Epibulus insidiator: *katōk, mō.*
Halichoeres trimaculatus: *po.*
Thalashona vitidum: *lo.*
Thalassoma lunare: *ikōn-wōd.*
Thalassoma umbrostigma: *bōkkāāj.*

wrath: *mej.*

wreath
head wreath of: *pālli-.*
plain flower wreath without other ingredients: *utpāj.*
possessive classifier, flowers or wreaths worn on head: *pālli-.*
put wreath on one's head: *pālpel.*
wreathe: *ļōļō.*
wreath of flowers: *ut.*

wreck
shipwrecked: *eǫtōk.*

wrench
a wrench: *jibana.*
monkey wrench: *m̧añke jibana.*

wrestle: *kǫbōk, kopāp.*
wrestle chest to chest: *kǫob.*
wrestling: *eotaak, oktaak.*
contest, fighting or wrestling: *kāre lǫwob.*
fall headlong, in wrestling: *juñaidi.*
throw down, as in wrestling: *ekbab, patpat.*
wrestling hold for throwing over shoulder: *buñūnpāp.*
wrestling maneuver, Marshallese style only: *ektak.*

wretch
wretched: *nana tam̧m̧wi-, pāpijek.*

wriggle: *iñiñtōk.*

wring: *uñtaak.*
wring, clothes: *um̧jāj.*

wrinkle
roll up sloppily, wrinkled: *ļukut.*
wrinkled: *ļoktōk, nokjek.*

wrist: *m̧ǫkwōj.*

write: *jeje, m̧alen.*
rewrite: *āpta.*
typewriter: *taip.*

writhe
writhe in pain: *iñimmaļ, wūdikke.*

wrong: *bōd.*

Xanthosoma
a plant, taro variety (Takeuchi), *Xanthosoma*: *Wōtin Kapilōñ, Wōtin Ruk, Wōt-waan.*

Ximenia
a plant, *Ximenia americana* L. (Oclacaceae): *kālōklōk.*

Xiphia
a fish, swordfish, *Xiphia gladius*: *ļōjkaan.*

Xyrichthys
Xyrichthys taeniouris: *likōb.*

yacht: *iǫǫt.*

yam: *iaam̧.*

yank: *keepep.*
yank a fishline: *liit.*

Yap
place name, Yap: *Iaab.*

yard: *iaat.*
canoe part, end of yard, boom (*rojak m̧aan*): *baļ.*

yaw: *m̧witaak.*

yawn: *mebbōļa.*

yaws: *dekā, rajjiia, ruk.*
yaws, ulcerated: *bakke, bakkito.*

year: *iiō.*

yearn: *likakōj.*
yearn for: *jañnuwaad.*

yeast: *iij.*
yeast beverage: *iij.*

yell: *kkeilǫk, kōkkeilǫk.*

yellow: *iaļo.*
"Yellow!": *pedej.*
a yellow-flowered herb: *kio.*
yellowish: *māār.*

yes: *aaet, iiūñ, iññā.*

yesterday: *inne.*
the day before yesterday: *inne eo ļǫk juon.*

yet
not yet: *kijer.*

yolk
egg yolk: *bwibwi, bwibwitakaļ.*

yonder: *ijekoko, ijjiieņ, ijjuweo.*

you: *eok, kom̧, kwe.*
interjection: "You don't say!": *kwōjabm̧ōk.*
you, plus particle of past tense singular: *kwaar.*
you, singular progressive: *kwōj.*
you, to many men in general, not specific: *ļōm̧a.*
you, to many women in general, not specific: *lim̧a.*
you, two persons: *kom̧ro.*
yourself: *kwe make.*
yourselves: *kom̧ make.*

young: *dik, niñ.*
young birds or animals: *koon.*
young chicken: *jendik.*

young man: *likao.*
youngster: *boea, jokko.*

your: *aṃ, ami, amiiañ, amijel, amiro, amiwōj.*
yours (four persons): *amiiañ.*
yours (three or more persons): *amiwōj.*
yours (three persons): *amijel.*
yours (two persons): *amiro.*
yours, plural: *ami.*
yours, singular: *aṃ.*

youth
youthful: *ṃṃan ded.*

Zanclus
a fish, Moorish idol, *Zanclus canescens*: *jourur.*
a fish, moorish idol, *Zanclus cornutus*: *pālep, wōllaañ.*

zeal: *kijejeto.*

zero: *ọo.*

zigzag
follow a zigzag course in running past obstacles: *kōttadede.*

zip
to zip: *jibōr.*
zipper: *jibōr.*

zone
the first zone of currents: *juae.*
the second zone of currents: *dibukae.*
the third zone of currents: *jeḷatae.*

zoo: *jikin menin mour.*

zoology: *katak kōn menin mour.*

zori
wear a zori: *jodi.*
zorie(s): *jodi.*

PLACE NAMES OF THE MARSHALL ISLANDS

A-eañ (**hah-yag**). Recur. form. See *Ajeltak, Aej.* Ailinglapalap district; Ailuk district; Mili district.

A-eañ-eņ (**hah-yag-yeņ**). Recur. form. Rongelap district; Rongerik district; Wotho district; Ujae district; Kwajalein district; Majuro district.

Abak (**habak**). Unanalyz. Mejit tract.

Abņōņō (**habņehņeh**). Gramm. See *abņōņō* "uncomfortable". Wotje tract.

Adbūb (**hadbib**). Reminisc. gramm. See *ad, būb:* "triggerfish cloud formation"; see *Būbwin Epoon.* Namorik tract.

Addeb-kaņ (**haddẹb-kaņ**). Gramm. See *addeb* "exchange". Utirik household.

Addi-eņ (**haddiy-yeņ**). Gramm. See *addi* "finger; clam shell". Kwajalein tract.

Addi-kaņ (**haddiy-kaņ**). Gramm. Bikini islet.

Addokwōj (**haddeqej**). Part. recur. form. See *ad, dokwōj:* "sign of a storm that snaps branches". Likiep tract.

Adjekik (**hadjekyik**). Part. recur. form. See *jjeikik* "excitement". Ailinglapalap islet.

Ae (**hayey**). Gramm. Jaluit islet.

Aebōj (**hayẹbẹj**). Gramm. See *aebōj* "well". Rongelap tract; Wotho tract; Lae tract; Ujae tract; three Kwajalein tracts; Ailinglapalap tract; four Jaluit tracts; Likiep tract; Maloelap tract; Aur tract; two Majuro tracts; eight Arno tracts; Mili tract.

Aebōj-eņ (**hayẹbẹj-yeņ**). Gramm. Bikini tract.

Aedetdet (**hayedetdet**). Gramm. See *ae, detdet* "current heated by sun". Arno tract.

Aej (**hayẹj**). Recur. form. Eniwetak islet; Ebon tract; Likiep islet.

Aej-kaņ (**hayẹj-kaņ**). Recur. form. Rongelap islet.

Aejelti (**hayẹjẹltiy**). Reminisc. gramm. Arno tract.

Aelok (**hayẹlẹq**). Reminisc. gramm. Ratak atoll; Ailuk; Mejit tract; Ailuk islet.

Aeloķlap-eņ (**hayẹlẹqļap-yeņ**). Reminisc. gramm. Aur tract.

Aelōñ-eo (**hayẹlẹg-yew**). Gramm. See *aelōñ* "island". Majuro tract; Mili islet; Knox islet.

Aelōñ-jab-eņ (**hayẹlẹg-jab-yeņ**). Gramm.: "that atoll". Kwajalein so large it can be considered to be more than one atoll. Kwajalein district.

Aelōñin-ae (**hayẹlẹgin-hayey**). Gramm. See *aelōñ, ae:* "island of current". Ralik atoll; Ailinginae.

Aelōñin-waan (**hayẹlẹgin-wahan**). Part. reminisc. gramm. See *aelōñ, waan:* "worthless island". Bikini tract.

Aelōñļapļap (**hayẹlẹgļapļap**). Gramm. See *aelōñ, ļap:* "large atoll". Ralik atoll; Ailinglapalap.

Aeoļ (**hayeweļ°**). Reminisc. gramm. See *aoļ:* "tract said to be the home of a spirit named *Tarkōm̧kōm̧* who guards all food preparation utensils to prevent disputes over food". Maloelap tract.

Aer-Epoon (**hayẹr-yepẹwẹn**). Reminisc. gramm. See *Epoon:* "their Ebon (perhaps colonized by Ebon people)". Arno islet.

Aerkōj (**hayẹrkẹj**). Gramm. Bikini islet.

Aerkōj-laļ (**hayẹrkẹj-laļ**). Gramm. See *aer, kōj, laļ:* "their share of the earth". Bikini islet.

Aerōk (**hayẹrẹk**). Reminisc. gramm. See *ae, rōk:* "southern current". Ailinglapalap district; Ailinglapalap district; Ailinglapalap islet; Mejit tract; Maloelap district.

Aerōk-eņ (**hayẹrẹk-yeņ**). Reminisc. gramm. Ailinginae islet.

Aerrōk (**hayẹrrẹk**). Reminisc. gramm. Maloelap islet.

Aetọ (**hayetaw**). Recur. form. See *aetọ* "small islets, northeast side". Ujelang district; Rongelap district; Rongerik district; Ailinginae district; Wotho district; Lae district; Ujae district; Kwajalein district; Namu district; Likiep district; Erikub district; Wotje district; Aur district.

Aetọ-in-aelōñ-jab-eņ (**hayetaw-yin-hayelẹg-jab-yeņ**). Recur. form. Kwajalein district.

Aidik (**hayidik**). Gramm. See *aidik* "narrow". Rongelap islet.

Aikne (**hayikney**). Recur. form. See *aikne* "north". Likiep islet.

Ainbōl (**hayinbẹl**). Part. recur. form. See *ain* "gather", *bōl* "taro patch". Mejit tract.

Aitle-eņ (**hayitlẹy-yeņ**). Part. recur. form. See *ait, le:* "tackle the *le* bird". Kwajalein tract.

Aj-eņ-lik (**haj-yeņ-lik**). Gramm. See *aj:* "that outer thatch". Arno islet.

Aj-kaņ (**haj-kaņ**). Gramm. See *aj* "thatch". Kwajalein islet.

Ajabōn (**hajaben**). Part. recur. form. See *jabōn* "end of". Mili tract.

Ajaļto (**hajaļtęw**). Reminisc. gramm. Namorik district.

Ajañ-eņ (**hajag-yeņ**). Gramm. See *ajañ* "place for harvesting food". Utirik islet.

Ajād (**hajad**). Part. recur. form. See *jād* "drying rack". Ailinglapalap tract.

Ajālto-rōk (**hajaltęw-ręk**). Recur. form. Arno district.

Ajbwirōk-kaņ (**hajbiyręk-kaņ**). Gramm. See *Ajbwirōk* "a pandanus cultigen". Likiep tract.

Aje-eañ (**hajey-yag**). Gramm. See *iṃōn aje* "gift land". Mili islet.

Aje-eañ-iōñ (**hajey-yag-yiyęg**). Gramm. Mili tract.

Aje-eañ-rōk (**hajey-yag-ręk**). Gramm. Mili tract.

Ajej-eņ (**hajyęj-yeņ**). Gramm. See *ajej* "divide". Jaluit islet.

Ajeltak (**hajęltak**). Reminisc. gramm. Mili tract.

Ajeltake (**hajęltakęy**). Part. reminisc. gramm. Majuro district.

Ajeļļāran (**hajeļļayran**). Gramm. See *ajeļļā* "pile of corpses". Mili islet.

Ajiddik (**hajiddik**). Reminisc. gramm. See *jidik:* "small". Ailuk islet.

Ajille (**hajillęy**). Reminisc. gramm. See *aj, le:* "liver of the *le* bird". Namorik tract.

Ajillep (**hajillep**). Reminisc. gramm. See *Ellep:* "this land was taken from the pond at Lib according to a legend". Ailuk islet.

Ajiltakōņ (**hajiltakeņ**). Part. reminisc. gramm. Eniwetak tract.

Ajjatak (**hajjahtak**). Reminisc. gramm. See *jatak* "wave ready to break". Ailuk islet.

Ajjekadkad-eņ-ebokbok (**hajjekadkad-yeņ-yebeqbeq**). Recur. form. See *jekad* "black noddy", *bokbok* "sandy". Mili islet.

Ajjekadkad-eņ-edekāke (**hajjekadkad-yeņ-yedekaykęy**). Recur. form. See *dekāke* "stony". Mili islet.

Ajlik-eņ (**hajlik-yeņ**). Gramm. See *aj, lik* "that outer thatch". Maloelap islet.

Ajṃanoļ (**hajṃaneļ°**). Part. recur. form. See *aj, ṃanoļ:* "liver of the *ṃanoļ* fish". Arno islet.

Ajoļ (**hajeļ°**). Gramm. See *Ajol* "a pandanus cultigen". Rongelap tract.

Ajoļā (**hajeļ°ay**). Part. reminisc. gramm. See *ajokļā* "end of the island". Majuro islet.

Ajpeļļọk (**hajpeļļaq**). Gramm. See *aj* "thatch", *peļļọk* "open" or "blown". Likiep tract.

Ajrak (**hajrak**). Gramm. Majuro tract.

Ajwāān (**hajwayan**). Part. reminisc. gramm. See *aj, wā* "pierced thatch". Mili islet.

Ak-eo (**hak-yew**). Gramm. See *ak* "frigate bird". Wotje islet.

Akade (**hakadęy**). Gramm. See *akade* "rookery". Majuro coral head.

Akadik (**hakahdik**). Gramm. See *akadik* "new construction". Ujelang tract.

Akadik-eņ (**hakahdik-yeņ**). Gramm. Rongelap tract; Lib tract; three Kwajalein tracts; Namu tract; Ailinglapalap tract; two Ebon tracts; Maloelap tract; three Arno tracts; Mili tract.

Akadik-kaņ (**hakahdik-kaņ**). Gramm. Mejit tract.

Akatal (**hakatal**). Part. reminisc. gramm. See *ak, tal* "frigate bird dives". Arno islet.

Akeọ-eañ (**hakyaw-yag**). Gramm. See *akeọ* "harvest first fruit". Arno tract.

Akeọ-rak (**hakyaw-rak**). Gramm. Arno tract.

Akmej (**hakmęj**). Gramm. See *ak, mej:* "dead frigate bird". Wotje islet.

Akob-eņ (**haqęb-yeņ**). Recur. form. See *kob* "bent". Rongerik tract.

Aktil-kaņ (**haktil-kaņ**). Recur. form. See *ak, ttil:* "place to hunt frigate birds with torches". Mili islet.

Akulwe (**haqilwey**). Unanalyz. Ailuk islet.

Akulwe-eañ (**haqilwey-yag**). Unanalyz. Ailuk tract.

Akulwe-rak (**haqilwey-rak**). Unanalyz. Ailuk tract.

Alen-kaņ (**halen-kaņ**). Gramm. See *alen:* "those divisions". Knox district.

Alkarkar (**halkarkar**). Gramm. See *alikkar* "clear". Arno tract.

Alkarkar-kaņ (**halkarkar-kaņ**). Gramm. Likiep tract.

Alle (**hallęy**). Gramm. See *alle* "wrasse". Ujae islet.

Alliiej (**halliyyẹj**). Reminisc. gramm. See *alle, ej:* "eastern wrasse". Ailuk islet.

Alliiej-eañ (**halliyyẹj-yag**). Reminisc. gramm. Ailuk tract.

Alliiej-rak (**halliyyẹj-rak**). Reminisc. gramm. Ailuk tract.

Allirōk (**halliyrẹk**). Reminisc. gramm. See *alle, rōk, Alliiej:* "southern wrasse". Ailuk islet.

Alloron (**hallẹr°ẹn**). Gramm. See *allor:* "its shade". Arno tract.

Alñan (**halgan**). Part. recur. form. See *al, ñan:* "sing to". Ailinglapalap tract.

Aļajka (**haļajkah**). From Engl. *Alaska*. Two Arno tracts.

Aļakod (**haļakwed**). Recur. form. See *aļak, wōd.* Mili tract.

Aļampel (**haļampẹl**). Part. recur. form. See *ļam, pel:* "shape of the boxfish". Eniwetak islet.

Aļārār (**haļyaryar**). Part. recur. form. See *al, ārār.* Mili islet.

Aļeļap-eṇ (**haļeyļap-yeṇ**). Gramm. distort. See *aļe:* "large catch of fish". Bikini tract.

Aļkadik (**haļkahdik**). Part. recur. form. Lae islet.

Aļļañ-kaṇ (**haļļag-kaṇ**). Gramm. See *aļļañ:* "those gapings". Ailuk tract.

Aļļañan-eṇ (**haļļagan-yeṇ**). Part. recur. form. Jaluit tract.

Aļļe-eṇ (**haļļey-yeṇ**). Recur. form. See *aļ, ļe:* "the sun passes". Arno tract.

Aļļoñwetak (**haļļeg°weytak**). Part. reminisc. gramm. Ebon tract.

Aļmāni (**haļmaniy**). Unanalyz. Bikar islet.

Aļñaden (**haļgaden**). Pers. name, legendary monster with gums (*ñad*) bloody like the rising sun (*aļ*). Rongelap islet; Maloelap islet.

Aļǫkwōd (**haļaqed**). Unanalyz. See *Oraļǫk* "Maloelap tract". Mili tract.

Aļwal (**haļwal**). From Gilb. *aroaro* (?) "name of a fish" (?) Majuro tract.

Amo (**hamew**). Reminisc. gramm. See *mo* "taboo land". Ailuk islet.

Aṃbo (**haṃbẹw**). Recur. form. See *aṃ; bo:* "your missiles". Mejit tract; two Kwajalein islets.

Ananij (**hanhanij**). Gramm. See *anij:* "belonging to a god". Eniwetak islet.

Anboklep (**hanbeqlep**). Recur. form. See *bok* "sand". Bikini tract.

Anbōr (**hanbẹr**). Unanalyz. Jaluit islet; Jaluit tract.

Anbwil-eṇ (**hanbil-yeṇ**). Recur. form. See *bwil* "hot, burn". Wotho islet.

Anel (**hanel**). Unanalyz. See *el:* "cut off (trees)". Namu islet; Likiep islet; Mili tract.

Aneppooļ (**haneppeweļ**). Unanalyz. Majuro islet; Majuro tract.

Anibuk (**hanibiq**). Part. reminisc. gramm. Ailinginae islet.

Aniddik (**haniddik**). Reminisc. gramm. Namu islet.

Anil (**hanil**). Gramm. See *anil* "soilless". Majuro islet; Mili islet.

Anillep (**hanillep**). Gramm. See *anil* "large area without soil". Namu islet; Jaluit islet.

Anjarōj (**hanjarej**). Recur. form. See *jarōjrōj, Jarōj.* Likiep islet.

Anjāje-kaṇ (**hanjayjẹy-kaṇ**). Recur. form. See *jāje* "sword". Rongelap islet.

Ankeke-jāiōñ (**hankẹykẹy-jayiyẹg**). Gramm. See *ankeke* "crooked". Wotje islet.

Ankeke-jāirōk (**hankẹykẹy-jayirẹk**). Gramm. Wotje islet.

Ankōt (**hanket**). Reminisc. gramm. See *kōt:* "ripe breadfruit". Aur tract.

Anmarut (**hanmarwit**). Recur. form. See *mar* "bush", *ut* "flower", *utilomar:* "land of flowering trees growing among bushes". Majuro tract.

Anṃaan (**hanṃahan**). Recur. form. See *ṃṃaan* "men". Jaluit islet.

Annañ (**hannag**). Gramm. See *annañ* "picture" or "shadow (of a tree)"; also "name of a bird". Majuro tract.

Annejāāñ (**hannejayag**). Gramm. distort. See *annañ, Jāāñ:* "shadow of *Jāāñ*". Maloelap islet.

Annudik (**hanniwdik**). Unanalyz. Jaluit islet; Jaluit tract.

Anokṇak (**haneqṇak**). Gramm. distort. See *aṇokṇak, ankoṇak:* "appropriated property". Utirik household.

Anooļ (**haneweļ**). Unanalyz. Namorik tract.

Anoontak (**hanewentak**). Unanalyz. Jaluit tract.

Anōkṇā (**hanekṇay**). Recur. form. See *anōk* "follow a pattern". Mejit tract.

Anpeļļǫk (**hanpeļļaq**). Recur. form. See *waan peļļǫk:* "temporary abode". Namu tract.

Antak (**hantak**). Recur. form. Arno tract.

Antoṇia (**hanteṇ°iyah**). From Germ. *Antonia*. Mili tract.

Anuuj (**haniwij**). Unanalyz. Jaluit tract.

Aṇwūj (**haṇ°ij**). Unanalyz. Ujae islet.

Añinene (**haginyẹnẹy**). Gramm. See *añinene* "uneven breeze in lee of islet". Two Arno tracts.

Añtak (**hagtak**). Gramm. See *añ* "breeze", *tak* "eastward". Aur tract.

Añtak-kaṇ (**hagtak-kaṇ**). Gramm. See *añ, tak:* "places where the breeze sometimes comes from the west". Ebon tract.

Ao-eṇ (**hahwew-yeṇ**). Gramm. See *ao* "legendary power". Lib tract.

Aojañ (**hawejag**). Part. recur. form. See *ao, jañ.* Ebon tract.

Aojo (**hawejew**). Part. recur. form. See *ao, jo.* Namu islet.

Aomrā (**hawemray**). Part. recur. form. See *merā* "capsize". Wotje islet.

Aomrā-dik (**hawemray-dik**). Part. recur. form. Wotje islet.

Aoṃaṇ (**hawẹṃaṇ**). Unanalyz. Eniwetak islet.

Aoṃwen (**haweṃen**). Unanalyz. Bikini islet.

Aon (**hawen**). Gramm. Utirik islet.

Aonep (**hawenep**). Unanalyz. Ujae tract.

Aooṃ-eṇ (**hawewẹṃ-yeṇ**). Unanalyz. Bikini islet.

Aoroñ (**hawereg°**). Unanalyz. Ebon tract.

Aotle (**hawẹtlẹy**). Reminisc. gramm. Arno islet.

Aōj (**hahej**). Unanalyz. Kwajalein islet.

Apaanke (**hapahankẹy**). Recur. form. Wotho tract.

Apaliklik (**hapahliklik**). Recur. form. Kwajalein tract.

Apanke (**hapankẹy**). Recur. form. See *apa, ke* "the *apa* of porpoises". Wotho tract.

Apatutu (**hapahtiwtiw**). Recur. form. Wotho tract; Kwajalein tract; Ailinglapalap tract.

Apādto (**hapadtẹw**). Gramm. See *apād:* "westward ambush". Rongerik tract.

Apjutak (**hapjiwtak**). Gramm. See *ap, jutak:* "way of standing". Arno tract.

Ar-ej (**har-yẹj**). Gramm. See *ar* "lagoon beach". Ailinglapalap islet.

Ar-kaṇ (**har-kaṇ**). Gramm. Majuro tract.

Ar-kaṇ-in-lo-kabwijlōñ (**har-kaṇ-yin-lew-kabijlẹg**). Part. recur. form. Arno tract.

Arar-eṇ (**harhar-yeṇ**). Gramm. See *arar* "stirring". Ailinglapalap tract.

Arbar (**harbar**). Part. recur. form. See *bar* "rock". Rongelap islet; Mili district; Mili islet.

Arbwā (**harbay**). Part. recur. form. See *bwā* "fishpole". Kwajalein islet; Jaluit islet.

Are-Ḷōmato (**harey-ḷematẹw**). Pers. name. Mili tract.

Are-tọ-jāiiōñ (**harey-taw-jayiyyẹg**). Recur. form. See *are, aetọ:* "lagoon side facing wind and current". Erikub islet.

Are-tọ-jāirōk (**harey-taw-jayiyrẹk**). Recur. form. Erikub islet.

Areañ (**haryag**). Gramm. See *ar, eañ:* "northern lagoon beach". Mili tract.

Arejebōn (**hareyjeben**). Recur. form. See *are, jabōn.* Jaluit tract.

Ari-jo (**hariy-jew**). Reminisc. gramm. See *are, jo* "lagoon beach of goatfish". Kwajalein tract.

Ari-rā-eṇ (**hariy-ray-yeṇ**). Unanalyz. Ujae tract.

Arjaḷtok (**harjaḷteq**). Gramm. See *ar, jaḷ, tok:* "lagoon beach facing this way". Wotje tract.

Arjāl (**harjal**). Part. recur. form. Jaluit tract; Mejit tract.

Arjāltak (**harjaltak**). Gramm. See *ar, jāl, tak:* "lagoon beach facing eastward". Ailinglapalap tract; Likiep tract; Wotje tract.

Arjekik (**harjekyik**). Gramm. distort. See *ar, jjeikik:* "beach of excitement". Ailinglapalap tract.

Arjel (**harjẹl**). Reminisc. gramm. Aur islet.

Arjeltak (**harjeltak**). Reminisc. gramm. Lae tract.

Arḷap (**harḷap**). Gramm. See *ar, ḷap:* "large lagoon beach". Jaluit islet.

Arṇo (**harṇew**). Also *Aṇṇo* (**haṇṇew**). Recur. form. See *ar* "lagoon beach", *ṇo* "wave". Ratak atoll; Arno district; Arno islet.

Arṇo-eañ (**harṇew-yag**). Part. recur. form. Arno tract.

Arṇo-rak (**harṇew-rak**). Part. recur. form. Arno tract.

Arōjeboṇ (**harẹjebeṇ°**). Reminisc. gramm. Jaluit tract.

Arōn-an (**haren-han**). Recur. form. Majuro tract.

Arōn-elenej (**haren-yẹlẹnẹj**). Recur. form. Lib tract.

Arōn-or (**haren-wer**). Gramm. See *or:* "lagoon beach of fish gills". Majuro tract.

Arōn-pako-eañ (**haren-pakew-yag**). Gramm. See *ar* "lagoon beach", *pako* "shark": "northern lagoon beach of sharks". Majuro tract.

Arōn-pako-rak (**haren-pakew-rak**). Gramm. Majuro tract.

Arōn-peje (**haren-pẹjẹy**). Recur. form. See *ar, peje:* "lagoon beach of the capital". Majuro tract.

Arōn-wōj (**haren-wẹj**). Gramm. See *wōj* "balsa driftwood". Kwajalein tract.

Arōppok (**harẹppẹq**). Reminisc. gramm. See *ppok* "look for". Ailinglapalap tract.

Arpat (**harpat**). Part. recur. form. See *pat* "swamp". Namorik tract.

Arrak (**harrak**). Gramm. See *rak* "south". Wotho tract; Majuro district; Arno tract.

Arro-eṇ (**harrẹw-yeṇ**). Gramm. See *ro* "jump into the water". Jaluit islet.

Artōb (**hartẹb**). Part. reminisc. gramm. Wotho tract.

Arweeañ-eañ (**har°eyyag-yag**). Part. recur. form. Arno tract.

Arweeañ-rak (**har°eyyag-rak**). Part. recur. form. Arno tract.

Atarḷain (**hatarḷahyin**). Gramm. See *atar, ḷain:* "chop up to the line". Kili tract.

Atartar (**hatartar**). Gramm. See *atartar* "adjoin". Utirik household.

Atat-eṇ-eḷip (**hathat-yeṇ-yeḷip**). Gramm. See *atat* "a vine". Majuro tract.

Atotak (**hatẹwtak**). Gramm. See *ato* "come out of water", *tak* "eastward". Likiep islet.

Atotok (**hatẹwteq**). Gramm. Maloelap household.

Atūñ-kaṇ (**hatig-kaṇ**). Gramm. See *atūñ* "land crab". Arno tract.

Aubnen (**hawibnen**). Recur. form. See *ubnen* "immature coconut fruit". Majuro tract.

Aujarōj (**hawiwjarej**). Recur. form. Likiep islet.

Aujiblōñ (**hawijiblẹg**). Recur. form. See *jib, lōñ:* "rise up". Arno tract.

Aujke (**hawijkẹy**). Reminisc. gramm. See *aujek:* "stir it". Majuro tract.

Aur (**hawir**). Unanalyz. Ratak atoll; Aur; Kwajalein tract; Aur district; Aur islet.

Aut-eañ (**hawit-yag**). Unanalyz. Arno tract.

Aut-rak (**hawit-rak**). Recur. form. Arno tract.

Autle (**hawitlẹy**). Recur. form. Two Mili islets; Mili tract.

Autle-eṇ (**hawitlẹy-yeṇ**). Recur. form. Kwajalein tract.

Ā-eṇ (**yay-yeṇ**). Recur. form. Maloelap islet; Majuro tract; Knox tract.

Ādapoot (**yadahpewet**). Unanalyz. Rongelap islet.

Ādkup (**yadqip**). Unanalyz. Ratak atoll; Erikub; Erikub islet.

Ādpā (**yadpay**). Unanalyz. Aur islet.

Ājā-eṇ (**yajay-yeṇ**). Unanalyz. Majuro tract.

Ājej (**yajyẹj**). Reminisc. gramm. Aur islet; Majuro islet.

Ājo-eṇ (**yajẹw-yeṇ**). Unanalyz. Mejit tract.

Ājo-iōñ (**yajẹw-yiyẹg**). Unanalyz. Aur tract.

Ājo-rōk (**yajẹw-rẹk**). Unanalyz. Aur tract.

Ālālen-iōñ (**yalyalen-yiyẹg**). Recur. form. Also the name of one of a pair of navigational signs, two 'turtles' about 20 miles off Ebon. Ebon tract.

Ālālen-irōk (**yalyalen-yirẹk**). Recur. form. Name of the other navigational sign off Ebon (see *ālālen-iōñ*). Ebon tract.

Āleen-ak (**yaleyen-hak**). Gramm. distort. See *el, ak:* "frigate bird nest". Rongelap tract.

Ālele-roon (**yalẹylẹy-rẹwẹn**). Unanalyz. Eniwetak islet.

Ālkukur (**yalqiwqir°**). Also *ālkurkur.* Gramm. See *ālkurkur* "face away from each other". Mejit tract.

Ālle (**yalley**). Gramm. distort. See *alle* "a fish". Eniwetak islet.

Āllep (**yallep**). Reminisc. gramm. Kwajalein islet.

Ālli (**yalliy**). Gramm. Eniwetak islet.

Āllok (**yallẹq**). Recur. form. See *lok* "middle". Utirik islet; Taka islet; Wotje islet.

Āllokļap (**yallẹqļap**). Gramm. See *llok* "tie up". Eniwetak islet.

Ālu-eņ (**yaliw-yeņ**). Gramm. See *ālu* "a tack in sailing". Mili tract.

Āne-aetok (**yanẹy-hayeteq**). Gramm. See *aetok* "long". Rongelap islet; two Arno islets.

Āne-aidik (**yanẹy-hayidik**). Gramm. See *aidik* "narrow". Wotho islet; Majuro tract; Arno islet.

Āne-aļ (**yanẹy-haļ**). Gramm. See *aļ* "sun". Mili islet.

Āne-aļo (**yanẹy-haļew**). Recur. form. See *aļo* "late". Kwajalein islet.

Āne-aļǫ (**yanẹy-haļaw**). Unanalyz. Bikini islet.

Āne-anij (**yanẹy-hanij**). Gramm. See *anijnij* "sorcery". Two Namu islets; Ailuk islet; Wotje islet.

Āne-anijņa (**yanẹy-hanijņah**). Part. recur. form. Mili islet.

Āne-ao (**yanẹy-hahwew**). Gramm. See *ao* "legendary power". Ailuk islet.

Āne-ar (**yanẹy-har**). Gramm. Arno islet.

Āne-armej (**yanẹy-harmẹj**). Gramm. See *armej* "people". Jaluit islet; Ebon islet; Utirik islet; Ailuk islet; Likiep islet; Wotje islet; Majuro islet; Arno islet; Mili islet.

Āne-audik (**yanẹy-hawidik**). Gramm. See *audik* "steer canoe with paddle on right". Ailuk islet.

Āne-awi (**yanẹy-hawiy**). Gramm. See *awi* "chiefly demeanor". Wotje islet.

Āne-ā-eo (**yanẹy-yay-yew**). Recur. form. Namu tract.

Āne-barbar (**yanẹy-barbar**). Gramm. See *bar* "rock". Rongelap islet; Wotho islet.

Āne-bōn (**yanẹy-bẹn**). Gramm. See *bōn* "place for floating corpses away". Kwajalein islet; Maloelap islet.

Āne-bubu (**yanẹy-biwbiw**). Gramm. See *bubu* "divination". Aur islet.

Āne-buoj (**yanẹy-biwẹj**). Gramm. See *buoj* "capital". Kwajalein islet.

Āne-bwilij-jāiōn̄ (**yanẹy-bilij-jayiyẹg**). Gramm. See *bwilji-* "in the midst". Wotje islet.

Āne-bwilij-jāirōk (**yanẹy-bilij-jayirẹk**). Gramm. Wotje islet.

Āne-debǫkut (**yanẹy-debaqit**). Gramm. See *debǫkut* "stump". Majuro islet.

Āne-dik (**yanẹy-dik**). Gramm. See *dik* "small". Bikini district; two Rongelap islets; Aur islet; Majuro tract; Arno tract.

Āne-dikdik (**yanẹy-dikdik**). Gramm. Ujae tract; Kwajalein islet; Kwajalein tract.

Āne-dikdik-iar (**yanẹy-dikdik-yiyhar**). Gramm. Ebon tract.

Āne-dikdik-ilik (**yanẹy-dikdik-yilik**). Gramm. Ebon tract.

Āne-doul (**yanẹy-dẹwil**). Gramm. distort. See *doulul* "round". Eniwetak sandspit; Jaluit islet; Arno islet; Mili islet.

Āne-doulul (**yanẹy-dẹwilwil**). Gramm. Rongelap islet.

Āne-eak (**yanẹy-yak**). Gramm. distort. See *eakeak* "ghost". Ailinglapalap islet.

Āne-eņ-aetok (**yanẹy-yeņ-hayeteq**). Gramm. Ailinglapalap islet.

Āne-eņ-edik (**yanẹy-yeņ-yedik**). Gramm. Arno islet; two Arno tracts.

Āne-jabaru (**yanẹy-jabariw**). Part. reminisc. gramm. See *baru:* "we can catch many fish". Majuro islet.

Āne-jabrok (**yanẹy-jabrẹq**). Unanalyz. Ailuk islet.

Āne-jaōeōe (**yanẹy-jahẹyhẹy**). Unanalyz. Demon said to live there and make the noise "*ōeōe*". Maloelap islet.

Āne-jā (**yanẹy-jay**). Also *Enejā*. Gramm. See *jā* "capsize". Ailuk islet.

Āne-jāij (**yanẹy-jayij**). Gramm. distort. Likiep islet.

Āne-jāiōn̄ (**yanẹy-jayiyẹg**). Gramm. Jaluit islet.

Āne-jāltak (**yanẹy-jaltak**). Gramm. See *jaļ, tak:* "facing eastward". Jaluit tract.

Āne-jāltak-rālik (**yanẹy-jaltak-raylik**). Gramm. Jaluit tract.

Āne-jāltak-reeaar (**yanẹy-jaltak-reyyahar**). Gramm. Jaluit tract.

Āne-jālto (**yanẹy-jaltẹw**). Gramm. See *jaļ, to:* "facing westward". Wotho islet; Lae islet; Jaluit tract.

Āne-jālto (**yanẹy-jaltew**). Reminisc. gramm. Namorik tract.

Āne-Jebrǫ (**yanẹy-jebraw**). Pers. name. Kwajalein islet.

Āne-jebwā (**yanẹy-jebay**). Gramm. See *jebwā* "a coral". Wotje islet.

Āne-jeeaaļ (**yanẹy-jeyyahaļ**). Gramm. See *jeeaaļ* "beckon". Likiep islet.

Āne-jeij (**yanęy-jęyij**). Unanalyz. Namu islet.

Āne-jelaļ (**yanęy-jeylaļ**). Gramm. distort. Likiep islet.

Āne-jeļaar (**yanęy-jeļahar**). Gramm. See *jeļaar* "pine". Ailuk islet.

Āne-jeļtak (**yanęy-jeļtak**). Reminisc. gramm. Wotje islet; Arno tract; Mili tract.

Āne-jeṃaden (**yanęy-jeṃaden**). Gramm. See *āne-jeṃaden* "wilderness". Ailuk islet.

Āne-jet (**yanęy-jet**). Gramm. See *jet* "miscellaneous". Rongelap islet; Jaluit islet; Mili district; Mili islet.

Āne-jo-eņ (**yanęy-jew-yeņ**). Gramm. See *jo* "goatfish". Majuro tract.

Āne-jore (**yanęy-jęwręy**). Gramm. See *jore* "look for fish". Kwajalein islet; Ailuk islet.

Āne-jǫ (**yanęy-jaw**). Gramm. See *jǫ* "place where turtle lays eggs". Ailinglapalap islet.

Āne-ju (**yanęy-jiw**). Gramm. See *ju:* "perpendicular wind from the islet, requiring tack". Wotho islet; Majuro islet.

Āne-kallep (**yanęy-kallep**). Gramm. See *kallep* "black ants". Majuro islet; Majuro tract.

Āne-kaliṃur (**yanęy-kalliṃir°**). Gramm. See *kalliṃur* "covenant". Majuro islet.

Āne-kaņ (**yanęy-kaņ**). Gramm. Rongelap islet.

Āne-kaņ-jidik (**yanęy-kaņ-jidik**). Gramm. Jaluit tract; Mili tract.

Āne-kaņ-lik (**yanęy-kaņ-lik**). Gramm. Namu islet; Ailinglapalap islet.

Āne-kaņ-liklaļ (**yanęy-kaņ-liklaļ**). Gramm. Kwajalein islet.

Āne-kaņ-lo-to (**yanęy-kaņ-lew-tew**). Gramm. See *to* "passage". Ailinglapalap islet.

Āne-kaņ-raittok (**yanęy-kaņ-rahyitteq**). Gramm. distort. Ailinglapalap islet.

Āne-kaņ-rōddik (**yanęy-kaņ-reddik**). Gramm. distort. Kwajalein islet.

Āne-kaņ-rōk (**yanęy-kaņ-ręk**). Gramm. Erikub district.

Āne-karan (**yanęy-karan**). Unanalyz. Kwajalein islet.

Āne-kartōp (**yanęy-kartep**). Gramm. See *kartōp* "fern". Knox islet.

Āne-kā-ej (**yanęy-kay-yęj**). Gramm. Arno islet.

Āne-kā-lik (**yanęy-kay-lik**). Gramm. Majuro tract; two Arno islets.

Āne-kāāṃ (**yanęy-kayaṃ**). Part. recur. form. See *kea-:* "your trunk". Wotje islet.

Āne-kāiiōn̄ (**yanęy-kayiyyęg**). Gramm. Majuro district.

Āne-kāilik (**yanęy-kayilik**). Gramm. Aur islet.

Āne-kio (**yanęy-kiyew**). Gramm. See *kio* "a plant". Wotje islet.

Āne-ko (**yanęy-kęw**). Recur. form. Erikub islet; Majuro islet.

Āne-ko-iōn̄ (**yanęy-kęw-yiyęg**). Recur. form. Ebon islet.

Āne-kowak (**yanęy-qewwak**). Gramm. See *kowak* "whimbrel". Ujae tract; Namu islet.

Āne-kōjbar (**yanęy-kęjbar**). Gramm. See *kōjbar* "a tree". Arno islet.

Āne-kōmkwaņ (**yanęy-kemqaņ**). Gramm. See *mokwaņ* "a food". Wotje islet.

Āne-kōņņat (**yanęy-kęņņat**). Gramm. See *kōņņat* "a shrub". Wotje islet.

Āne-kōņo (**yanęy-keņew**). Gramm. See *kōņo* "a tree". Wotje islet.

Āne-kōņoņo (**yanęy-keņewņew**). Gramm. Namu tract.

Āne-kōn̄e (**yanęy-kęgęy**). Gramm. See *kōn̄e* "a tree". Ujelang tract.

Āne-kōpļe (**yanęy-qepļey**). Gramm. See *kōpļe* "chase away". Wotje islet.

Āne-Kōrea (**yanęy-kęryah**). From Gilb. *Kuria Atoll*. Arno islet.

Āne-kōtkōt (**yanęy-ketket**). Gramm. See *kōtkōt* "ruddy turnstone". Wotje islet; Majuro islet; Majuro tract; Arno islet.

Āne-kūbwebwe (**yanęy-kibeybey**). Gramm. See *kūbwe* "feces". Bikini tract.

Āne-kūra (**yanęy-kirah**). Unanalyz. An islet of birds; *kūra* perhaps a bird cry. Likiep islet.

Āne-laṃōj (**yanęy-laṃęj**). Gramm. See *laṃōj* "shout". Jaluit tract.

Āne-Lijek (**yanęy-lijęk**). Pers. name. Wotje islet.

Āne-lik (**yanęy-lik**). Gramm. Arno islet; Arno tract.

Āne-lokļap (**yanęy-lęqļap**). Recur. form. See *lukwōn, lok* "middle". Likiep islet; Maloelap islet; Arno islet.

Āne-lur-arōn (**yanẹy-lir°-haren**). Gramm. See *lur* "calm", *arōn* "its beach". Arno islet.

Āne-Ḷaṃōj (**yanẹy-ḷaṃẹj**). Pers. name. Ujae islet.

Āne-ḷap (**yanẹy-ḷap**). Gramm. Rongelap islet.

Āne-ḷokrā (**yanẹy-ḷeqray**). Unanalyz. Majuro islet.

Āne-makij (**yanẹy-makij**). Gramm. distort. See *mmakijkij* "frequent". Majuro islet.

Āne-maro (**yanẹy-mahrew**). Gramm. See *maroro* "green". Mili islet.

Āne-mājik-eṇ (**yanẹy-majik-yeṇ**). Gramm. See *mājik* "harbor". Maloelap islet.

Āne-meḷap (**yanẹy-meḷap**). Part. reminisc. gramm. Namu islet.

Āne-meḷap-jāiiōñ (**yanẹy-meḷap-jayiyyẹg**). Part. reminisc. gramm. Namu islet.

Āne-mọ (**yanẹy-maw**). Gramm. See *mọ* "taboo". Arno islet.

Āne-mọmo (**yanẹy-mawmẹw**). Gramm. See *mọ* "taboo". Jaluit islet.

Āne-mọọn (**yanẹy-mawan**). Reminisc. gramm. See *mọ:* "his taboo islet". Ebon islet.

Āne-ṃaan (**yanẹy-ṃahan**). Gramm. distort. See *ṃṃaan:* "male, virile, fruitful isle". Wotje islet; Maloelap islet; Arno islet.

Āne-ṃak (**yanẹy-ṃak**). Gramm. See *ṃak* "needlefish" or *ṃṃak* "hole in tree for catching rain". Namu islet.

Āne-ṃanṃan (**yanẹy-ṃanṃan**). Gramm. See *ṃanṃan* "slaughter". Lae islet; Ailinglapalap tract; Ailuk islet.

Āne-ṃanōt (**yanẹy-ṃanet**). Gramm. distort. See *ṃanit* "custom". Ujelang islet; Kwajalein islet; Namorik tract; Majuro islet.

Āne-paaj-eṇ (**yanẹy-pahaj-yeṇ**). Gramm. See *paaj* "chief's kitchen". Aur islet.

Āne-paroro (**yanẹy-parewrew**). Reminisc. gramm. See *ailparo* "work overtime". Majuro islet.

Āne-pedo (**yanẹy-pedew**). Gramm. See *pedo* "capsize". Wotje islet.

Āne-piñ (**yanẹy-pig**). Reminisc. gramm. See *piñpiñ* "a tree". Kwajalein islet.

Āne-piro (**yanẹy-pirew**). Gramm. See *piro* "twin". Jaluit islet.

Āne-raj (**yanẹy-raj**). Gramm. See *raj* "whale". Ujelang islet; Mili islet.

Āne-rā-eṇ (**yanẹy-ray-yeṇ**). Recur. form. See *rā* "board". Jabwot tract; Arno islet.

Āne-reen (**yanẹy-rẹyẹn**). Gramm. distort. Wotje islet.

Āne-rein (**yanẹy-rẹyin**). Gramm. Lae islet.

Āne-rukrukun-jāiiōñ (**yanẹy-r°iqr°iqin-jayiyyẹg**). Gramm. See *rukruk* "shake, sound of coconut bouncing". Likiep islet.

Āne-rukrukun-jāirōk (**yanẹy r°iqr°iqin jayiyrẹk**). Gramm. Likiep islet.

Āne-ruo (**yanẹy-r°iwew**). Gramm. See *ruo* "two". Kwajalein islet.

Āne-tatabuk (**yanẹy-tahtahbiq**). Unanalyz. Mili tract.

Āne-tōp (**yanẹy-tẹp**). Also *Āne-tōb* (**yanẹy-tẹb**). Gramm. See *tōp* "encouragement". Ebon tract.

Āne-ut (**yanẹy-wit**). Gramm. See *ut* "flower". Namorik tract.

Āne-wa (**yanẹy-wah**). Gramm. See *wa* "canoe". Mili islet.

Āne-wā (**yanẹy-way**). Gramm. See *wā* "to spear". Ailinglapalap islet.

Āne-wātak (**yanẹy-waytak**). Gramm. distort. Ralik atoll; Eniwetak; Ujelang large district; Rongerik islet; Ailinglapalap tract; Eniwetak islet.

Āne-wāto (**yanẹy-waytẹw**). Gramm. distort. Arno islet.

Āne-wetak (**yanẹy-weytak**). Gramm. Kwajalein islet.

Āne-wetak-kaṇ (**yanẹy-weytak-kaṇ**). Gramm. Ailinginae islet.

Āne-wōd (**yanẹy-wed**). Gramm. See *wōd* "coral". Wotje islet.

Āne-wōpñak (**yanẹy-wepgak**). Unanalyz. Wotje islet.

Āne-wūdoḷ (**yanẹy-wideḷ°**). Unanalyz. Namu islet.

Āneed-dik-kaṇ (**yaneyed-dik-kaṇ**). Gramm. distort. Wotho islet; Namu islet.

Āneḷḷap (**yanẹyẹḷḷap**). Gramm. distort. Ujelang islet.

Āneḷḷap-kaṇ (**yanẹyẹḷḷap-kaṇ**). Gramm. distort. Rongelap islet; Kwajalein islet.

Ānen-bubu-eṇ (**yanyen-biwbiw-yeṇ**). Gramm. See *bubu* "divination". Majuro islet.

Ānen-eṃṃaan (**yanyen-yeṃṃahan**). Gramm. See *ṃṃaan* "men". Jaluit islet; Likiep islet; Ailuk islet.

Ānen-kōñe (**yanyen-kęgęy**). Gramm. See *kōñe* "a tree". Two Ailuk islets.

Ānen-kōñe (**yaneyen-kegęy**). Gramm. distort. Ailuk islet.

Ānen-kōrā (**yanyen-keray**). Gramm. See *kōrā* "women". Ailuk islet.

Ānen-kwōl (**yanyen-qel**). Gramm. See *kwōl* "sandpiper". Arno islet.

Ānen-lik (**yanyen-lik**). Gramm. Ailuk islet.

Ānen-lokļap (**yaneyen-leqļap**). Recur. form. Knox islet.

Ānen-oṃ (**yanyen-węṃ**). Gramm. See *oṃ* "hermit crab". Ailinglapalap islet; Ailuk islet; Wotje islet.

Ānen-ta-eo (**yanyen-tah-yew**). Part. recur. form. See *ta eo* "what for?" Majuro tract.

Ānen-uwa (**yanyen-wiwah**). Gramm. See *uwa* "bear much fruit". Likiep islet.

Ānen-uwaan (**yanyen-wiwahan**). Gramm. See *uwaan:* "islet of sorts and types". Likiep islet.

Ānen-wūdej (**yanyen-widęj**). Gramm. See *wūdej* "cuckoo". Majuro islet.

Āneņ (**yanyeņ**). Gramm. Mejit district.

Āneņ-edik (**yanyeņ-yedik**). Gramm. Wotje islet; Mili tract.

Āneņ-eutiej-kāān (**yanyeņ-yęwitiyęj-kayan**). Gramm. Mili islet; Mili tract.

Āneņ-iar (**yanyeņ-yiyhar**). Gramm. Mili islet.

Āneņ-iōk (**yanyeņ-yiyęk**). Reminisc. gramm. See *ek* "fish". Namu islet.

Āneņ-iōñ (**yanyeņ-yiyęg**). Gramm. Lae islet.

Āneņ-lik (**yanyeņ-lik**). Gramm. Mili islet.

Āneņ-rilik (**yanyeņ-riylik**). Gramm. Majuro islet.

Āneo (**yanyęw**). Unanalyz. Bikini district; Bikini islet.

Āneppool (**yanęppewel**). Reminisc. gramm. See *pooļ* "surrounded". Majuro tract.

Ānerer (**yanyeryer**). Reminisc. gramm. See *erer* "protector". Ailinglapalap islet.

Āni-buk (**yaniy-biq**). Reminisc. gramm. See *bukbuk* "helmet shell". Ailinginae islet.

Āni-dik (**yaniy-dik**). Gramm. distort. Bikini islet; Arno islet; two Arno tracts.

Āni-dik-jāiiōñ (**yaniy-dik-jayiyyęg**). Gramm. distort. Maloelap islet.

Āni-dik-jāirōk (**yaniy-dik-jayiyręk**). Gramm. distort. Maloelap islet.

Āni-dikdik (**yaniy-dikdik**). Gramm. distort. Bikini islet.

Āni-eōñ (**yaniy-yęg**). Gramm. distort. Arno islet.

Āni-juon (**yaniy-jiwen**). Part. recur. form. Maloelap islet.

Āni-la (**yaniy-lah**). Unanalyz. Mejit tract.

Āni-look (**yaniy-lęwęk**). Unanalyz. Ebon district; Ebon islet.

Āni-ne (**yaniy-nęy**). Unanalyz. Ailuk islet.

Āni-piñ (**yaniy-pig**). Reminisc. gramm. See *piñpiñ* "a tree"; see also *Āne-piñ*. Ailinglapalap islet and district; Wotje islet.

Āniiej (**yaniyyęj**). Gramm. distort. Likiep islet.

Āniiiaak (**yaniyyiyahak**). Gramm. distort. See *ak* "frigate bird". Ailinglapalap islet.

Āniin-kūro (**yaniyin-kiręw**). Gramm. distort. See *kūro* "a fish". Majuro household.

Ānlook (**yanlęwęk**). Unanalyz. Likiep islet.

Ānṃō (**yanṃeh**). Unanalyz. Eniwetak sandspit.

Ānṃō (**yanṃęh**). Unanalyz. Eniwetak islet.

Ānōṃṃaan (**yaneṃṃahan**). Gramm. distort. See *ṃṃaan* "men". Bikini islet.

Āpen (**yapen**). Unanalyz. Maloelap tract.

Āpta (**yaptah**). Also *Epta.* Gramm. See *āpta* "do twice". Ailuk islet.

Āreppok (**yaryęppęq**). Recur. form. See *ār, ppok:* "look for a beaching place". Two Ailinglapalap tracts.

Ārtok (**yarteq**). Gramm. See *ār, tok:* "beach it hither". Jaluit islet.

Ātoñtoñ-eņ-ebokbok (**yateg°teg°-yeņ-yebeqbeq**). Gramm. See *ātoñ* "smell something", *bokbok* "sandy". Mili islet.

Ātoñtoñ-eņ-edekāke (**yateg°teg°-yeņ-yedekaykęy**). Gramm. See *dekāke* "stony". Mili islet.

Ātōk (**yatek**). Gramm. See *ātōk* "a royal rank". Bikini tract.

Baaj-kaņ (**bahaj-kaņ**). From Japn. *basu* "bath". Wotje tract.

Bad-eņ (**bad-yeņ**). Gramm. See *bad* "place for divination". Jaluit tract.

Badabōden (**badabeden**). Recur. form. Arno islet.

Badik (**bahdik**). Unanalyz. Namu islet.

Baidik (**bahyidik**). Gramm. See *baidik* "Boston fern". Ebon tract.

Bakaļōj (**bakaļęj**). Unanalyz., see *Baklej* "Majuro tract". Wotje tract.

Bakkūr (**bakkir**). Unanalyz. Lae tract.

Baklej (**baklęj**). Unanalyz., see *Bakaļōj* "Wotje tract". Majuro tract.

Ballōklōk (**ballęklęk**). Gramm. distort. See *bar, lōklōk:* "prickly rock". Two Ailinglapalap tracts.

Baļap (**bahļap**). Unanalyz. Namu islet.

Banep (**bahnep**). Recur. form. Ebon tract.

Bar (**bar**). Gramm. See *bar* "rock". Mili islet.

Bar-aetoktok (**bar-hayeteqteq**). Gramm. See *bar, aetok* "long rock". Ebon tract.

Bar-eņ (**bar-yeņ**). Gramm. Bikini tract; Rongelap islet; Ujae tract; Kili tract; Knox islet.

Bar-kaņ (**bar-kaņ**). Gramm. Two Majuro tracts.

Bar-ko (**bar-kew**). Gramm. Mejit tract.

Bar-Ļōperu (**bar-ļepeyriw**). Pers. name. Ailuk islet.

Bar-mej (**bar-męj**). Part. recur. form. Lib tract.

Barbaran (**barbaran**). Unanalyz. Arno tract.

Barbarbuñ (**barbarbig°**). Unanalyz. Mejit tract.

Bareǫ-ireeaar (**baryaw-yiręyyahar**). Reminisc. gramm. See *bar, eǫ:* "tattoo rock". Lae tract.

Bareǫ-irilik (**baryaw-yiriylik**). Reminisc. gramm. Lae tract.

Barļap (**barļap**). Also *Baļļap* (**baļļap**). Gramm. See *bar, ļap:* "big rock". Ebon rock.

Barōņ (**bareņ**). Gramm. distort. Eniwetak shoal.

Barror (**barrer°**). Part. recur. form. See *bar, ror* "roaring rock". Ebon tract.

Baru (**bariw**). Gramm. See *baru* "crab". Mejit tract.

Barukuk (**barwikwik**). Reminisc. gramm. See *uuk* "blow". Ailinglapalap tract.

Bat-doulul (**bat-dęwilwil**). Gramm. See *bat, doulul:* "round hill". Rongelap tract.

Bat-eņ (**bat-yeņ**). Gramm. Ujae tract; Kwajalein tract; Namu tract; three Ailinglapalap tracts; Jaluit tract; Kili tract; Mejit tract; Aur tract.

Bat-Itōn (**bat-yiten**). From Engl. *Eden.* Bikini tract; Kili tract.

Bat-kaņ (**bat-kaņ**). Gramm. Majuro tract.

Bat-kaņ-ioļap (**bat-kaņ-yiyewļap**). Gramm. Mili tract.

Bat-kaņ-iōñ (**bat-kaņ-yiyęg**). Gramm. Mili tract.

Bat-kaņ-rōk (**bat-kaņ-ręk**). Gramm. Mili tract.

Bat-Lukpe (**bat-liqpęy**). Pers. name. Utirik tract.

Bat-rāirōk (**bat-rayiyręk**). Gramm. Kwajalein tract.

Bat-wetak (**bat-węytak**). Gramm. See *wetak* "go eastward". Ailinglapalap tract; Arno tract.

Bat-wi (**bat-wiy**). Unanalyz. Rongelap tract.

Batbōtōn (**batbęten**). Part. reminisc. gramm. Mejit tract.

Batbūt-eņ (**batbit-yeņ**). Part. reminisc. gramm. Rongelap islet.

Bati-dān-maaj (**batiy-dan-mahaj**). Part. recur. form. See *bati* "hill of", *dān* "water", *maaj* "clearing". Majuro tract.

Bati-jabwea (**batiy-jabeyah**). Gramm. See *jabwea* "get ready for battle". Maloelap household.

Bati-jilauwā (**batiy-jilahwiway**). Unanalyz. Lib tract.

Bati-jiṃaal (**batiy-jiṃahal**). Unanalyz. Aur tract.

Bati-joñļǫk (**batiy-jeg°ļaq**). Unanalyz. Aur tract.

Bati-jǫkjok (**batiy-jaqjeq**). Gramm. distort. See *jokwajok* "gnat". Erikub tract.

Bati-Lijablo (**batiy-lijablew**). Pers. name. See *jab, llo:* Mrs. Blind's hill. Wotje tract.

Bati-Lijarroñ (**batiy-lijarreg°**). Pers. name. See *jarroñroñ:* Mrs. Deaf's hill. Wotje tract.

Bati-Liktōmān (**batiy-likteman**). Pers. name. See *etale-liktōmān.* Majuro household.

Bati-Litakdikin (**batiy-litakdikin**). Pers. name. Majuro household.

Bati-Ļanej (**batiy-ļanyęj**). Pers. name. Ujae tract.

Bati-Ļōjkab (**batiy-ļejkab**). Pers. name. Arno tract.

Bati-tiṃoŋ (**batiy-tiyṃeŋ°**). Gramm. See *tiṃoŋ* "demon". Utirik household.

Batiddǫǫl (**batiddawal**). Gramm. distort. See *batin, dǫǫl:* "hill of dyes". Eniwetak tract.

Batin (**batin**). Gramm. See *batin* "sweetheart" or "button". Ailinglapalap tract; Mejit tract.

Batin-anij (**batin-hanij**). Pers. name. See *anijnij* "sorcery". Mili tract.

Batin-Awe (**batin-hawẹy**). Pers. name. Maloelap tract.

Batin-bōkāļap (**batin-bekayļap**). Gramm. See *bōkā* "tide" or "oil container". Majuro tract.

Batin-bubu (**batin-biwbiw**). Gramm. See *bubu* "divination". Majuro tract.

Batin-dek (**batin-dek**). Unanalyz. Jaluit tract.

Batin-denļap (**batin-dẹnļap**). Reminisc. gramm. See *dān* "water". Majuro tract.

Batin-kañal (**batin-kahgal**). Gramm. See *kañal* "a tree". Kwajalein tract; Likiep tract.

Batin-kāmeej (**batin-kaymeyej**). Gramm. See *kāmeej* "redwood". Jaluit tract.

Batin-kijeek (**batin-kijeyek**). Gramm. See *kijeek* "fire". Wotje tract.

Batin-kio (**batin-kiyew**). Gramm. See *kio* "a plant". Ailinglapalap tract; Majuro tract.

Batin-Kotmeiñ (**batin-qetmẹyig**). Pers. name. Kwajalein tract.

Batin-Kūtmiiñ (**batin-kitmiyig**). Gramm. distort. Bikini tract.

Batin-Ļwōjrwe (**batin-ļ°ejr°ey**). Pers. name. Namorik tract.

Batin-mirmir (**batin-mirmir**). Gramm. See *mir* "red". Majuro tract.

Batin-ṃaļok (**batin-ṃaļẹq**). Unanalyz. Majuro tract.

Batin-ṃōļañ (**batin-ṃeļag**). Unanalyz. Mejit tract.

Batin-nen (**batin-nẹn**). Gramm. See *nen* "a tree". Jaluit tract.

Batin-or (**batin-wer**). Gramm. See *or* "fish gills". Namu tract.

Batin-orļap (**batin-werļap**). Gramm. Majuro tract.

Batin-ut (**batin-wit**). Gramm. See *ut* "flower". Maloelap tract.

Batin-utkōk (**batin-witkẹk**). Gramm. See *utkōk* "disrobe". Jaluit tract.

Batō (**bateh**). Unanalyz. Two Ailinglapalap tracts.

Batōn (**baten**). Gramm. distort. Eniwetak tract.

Bo (**bẹw**). Gramm. See *bo* "twin". Namorik tract.

Bok (**beq**). Gramm. Rongelap islet; Rongerik islet; Ujae islet; Namu islet; Ailinglapalap islet; Wotje islet; Maloelap islet.

Bok-addel (**beq-haddel**). Also *Bokwā-del.* Unanalyz. See *del* "a food". Maloelap islet; Majuro islet.

Bok-aetoktok (**beq-hayeteqteq**). Gramm. See *aetok* "long". Bikini islet.

Bok-aidik (**beq-hayidik**). Gramm. See *aidik* "narrow". Eniwetak islet.

Bok-aitoktok (**beq-hayiteqteq**). Gramm. distort. Majuro islet.

Bok-ajaj (**beq-hajhaj**). Gramm. See *ajaj* "clam shell, hard rock". Ebon tract.

Bok-ak (**beq-hak**). Gramm. See *ak* "frigate bird". Ratak atoll; Taongi; Kwajalein islet; Taongi islet.

Bok-allōñlōñ (**beq-hallẹglẹg**). Gramm. distort. See *allōñ* "moon". Arno tract.

Bok-alwōj (**beq-halwẹj**). Gramm. See *alwōj* "look at". Rongelap islet.

Bok-anij (**beq-hanij**). Gramm. See *anijnij* "sorcery". Maloelap islet; Mili islet.

Bok-armej (**beq-harmẹj**). Gramm. See *armej* "people". Utirik islet.

Bok-atil-kaṇ (**beq-hatil-kaṇ**). Unanalyz. Maloelap tract; Majuro tract.

Bok-dikdik (**beq-dikdik**). Gramm. See *dik* "small". Arno islet; Mili islet; Mili tract.

Bok-doulul (**beq-dẹwilwil**). Gramm. See *doulul* "round". Bikini islet.

Bok-eañ (**beq-yag**). Gramm. Maloelap islet.

Bok-ed (**beq-yed**). Gramm. distort. See *eded* "rummage". Wotho islet; Kwajalein islet.

Bok-ed-rālik (**beq-yed-raylik**). Gramm. distort. Jaluit tract.

Bok-ed-rear (**beq-yed-rẹyhar**). Gramm. distort. Jaluit tract.

Bok-edda (**beq-yeddah**). Part. reminisc. gramm. Wotje islet.

Bok-edik (**beq-yedik**). Gramm. Bikini sandspit.

Bok-ejej-eṇ (**beq-yejyej-yeṇ**). Gramm. See *ejej* "husk with the teeth". Maloelap islet.

Bok-eleọṃo (**beq-yelyawṃew**). Unanalyz. Ailinglapalap islet.

Bok-ellāāp (**beq-yellayap**). Unanalyz. Rongelap islet.

Bok-ellu (**beq-yelliw**). Gramm. See *llu* "angry". Erikub islet.

Bok-eṇ (**beq-yeṇ**). Gramm. Eniwetak islet; Rongelap islet; Ailinginae islet; Kwajalein islet; Ailinglapalap islet; three Jaluit islets; Namorik tract; Taka sandspit; Likiep islet; Likiep tract; Maloelap islet; Maloelap tract; Majuro islet; Majuro tract; Arno islet; Arno tract; Mili tract.

Bok-eṇ-dik (**beq-yeṇ-dik**). Gramm. Arno tract.

Bok-eṇ-eḷap (**beq-yeṇ-yeḷap**). Gramm. Eniwetak islet.

Bok-erreo (**beq-yerreyew**). Gramm. See *rreo* "clean". Ujelang tract.

Bok-jā-ej (**beq-jay-yẹj**). Gramm. See *jā* "sail falling toward outrigger". Majuro sandspit.

Bok-jā-laḷ (**beq-jay-laḷ**). Gramm. Majuro sandspit.

Bok-jālto (**beq-jaltẹw**). Gramm. See *jaḷ, to:* "face westward". Rongelap islet.

Bok-kalilala (**beq-kalilahlah**). Unanalyz. Namu islet.

Bok-kaṇ (**beq-kaṇ**). Gramm. Kwajalein sandspit; Kwajalein islet; Namu islet; three Jaluit islets; Mejit tract; two Ailuk islets; Arno islet.

Bok-kaṇ-raittok (**beq-kaṇ-rahyitteq**). Gramm. distort. See *aetok* "long". Jaluit islet.

Bok-kaṇ-rokkut (**beq-kaṇ-reqqit**). Gramm. See *kkut* "close together". Rongelap islet.

Bok-kā (**beq-kay**). Gramm. Rongelap islet.

Bok-kooṃṃaan (**beq-kewemṃmahan**). Gramm. See *koṃaan* "male". Eniwetak sandspit.

Bok-Lemjān (**beq-lẹmjan**). Pers. name, legendary woman. Erikub islet.

Bok-Limaallọk (**beq-limahallaq**). Pers. name. Erikub sandspit.

Bok-Limāiddik (**beq-limayiddik**). Pers. name. Lae islet.

Bok-Ḷajkūt (**beq-ḷajkit**). Pers. name; see *jikut.* Wotje islet.

Bok-Ḷajulik (**beq-ḷajiwlik**). Pers. name, legendary man who died on this islet. Maloelap islet.

Bok-ḷañ (**beq-ḷag**). Gramm. See *ḷañ* "storm". Ailinglapalap islet; Likiep islet; Mili tract.

Bok-ḷañ-eañ (**beq-ḷag-yag**). Gramm. Arno tract.

Bok-ḷañ-ioḷap (**beq-ḷag-yiyewḷap**). Gramm. Jaluit tract.

Bok-ḷañ-rak (**beq-ḷag-rak**). Gramm. Arno tract.

Bok-ḷañ-rālik (**beq-ḷag-raylik**). Gramm. Jaluit tract.

Bok-ḷañ-reeaar (**beq-ḷag-reyyahar**). Gramm. Jaluit tract.

Bok-ḷap (**beq-ḷap**). Gramm. See *ḷap* "large". Eniwetak sandspit; two Kwajalein islets; Maloelap islet.

Bok-ḷapḷap (**beq-ḷapḷap**). Gramm. Bikini sandspit; Jaluit islet; Likiep islet.

Bok-ḷapwea (**beq-ḷapweyah**). Gramm. See *ḷap, wea:* "big sandspit by the passage". Maloelap islet.

Bok-ḷā (**beq-ḷay**). Gramm. See *ḷā* "gravel". Taongi islet.

Bok-Ḷeaju (**beq-ḷeyahjiw**). Pers. name. Kwajalein sandspit.

Bok-ḷipḷip-eṇ (**beq-ḷipḷip-yeṇ**). Gramm. distort. See *ḷap* "big". Kwajalein islet.

Bok-Ḷoje (**beq-ḷewjey**). Pers. name. Maloelap islet.

Bok-Ḷōjoon (**beq-ḷejewen**). Pers. name. Aur islet.

Bok-Ḷōḷḷaaj (**beq-ḷeḷḷahaj**). Pers. name. Arno sandspit.

Bok-ḷuḷu (**beq-ḷiwiḷiw**). Gramm. See *ḷuḷu* "a game". Lae islet.

Bok-ḷwūj (**beq-ḷ°ij**). Unanalyz. Ailinginae islet.

Bok-meej (**beq-meyej**). Gramm. See *meej* "bright colored". Ailinglapalap islet; Majuro islet.

Bok-mekak (**beq-mekak**). Gramm. See *mekak* "blood clot". Wotje islet.

Bok-ṃọruj (**beq-ṃar°ij**). Gramm. See *ṃọruj* "break". Kwajalein sandspit.

Bok-na-eañ (**beq-nah-yag**). Unanalyz. Aur islet.

Bok-Nāik (**beq-nayik**). Pers. name. Erikub islet.

Bok-nejān (**beq-nejan**). Unanalyz. Bikini islet.

Bok-ṇauwo (**beq-ṇawiwew**). Part. recur. form. See *ṇa* "shoal", *uwo* "name of a bird (?)". Maloelap islet.

Bok-oḷḷap-kaṇ (**beq-weḷḷap-kaṇ**). Gramm. distort. Bikini islet.

Bok-Oḷṃanuno (**beq-weḷṃaniwnew**). Pers. name: *Ḷōṃanuno,* a legendary man who tried to weaken the power of medicine (*ṃan uno*). Wotje islet.

Bok-orḷap (**beq-werḷap**). Gramm. See *or, ḷap:* "large gill". Majuro islet.

Bok-papa (**beq-pahpah**). Unanalyz. Ailinglapalap tract.

Bok-pata (**beq-pahtah**). Gramm. See *pata* "useless". Bikini islet.

Bok-Rilōñ (**beq-rilęg**). Pers. name, chief who invaded Mili, first landing at this islet. Mili islet.

Bok-ro (**beq-rẹw**). Gramm. See *ro* "angry". Ailinglapalap islet.

Bok-tal (**beq-tal**). Part. recur. form. See *tal* "sink". Wotho islet.

Bok-tañ (**beq-tag**). From Japn. *bakudan* "bomb". Ailinglapalap tract.

Bok-tọọḷ (**beq-tawaḷ**). Unanalyz. Eniwetak sandspit.

Bok-ur (**beq-wir**). Part. recur. form. See *urur* "flame". Majuro islet.

Bok-wārooj (**beq-wayrewej**). Unanalyz. Aur islet.

Bok-we-raj (**beq-wey-raj**). Reminisc. gramm. See *wā* "to spear", *raj* "whale". Rongerik islet; Namu islet.

Bokḷewōj (**bẹqḷẹywẹj**). Unanalyz. Wotje islet.

Boktañ (**beqtag**). Gramm. See *boktañ* "bomb". Ailinglapalap tract.

Bokwalijmuuj (**beqahlijmiwij**). Part. reminisc. gramm. See *lij* "crumble, wash down, of sand", *mouj* "white, bright". Mejit tract.

Bokwalijṃaan (**beqahlijṃahan**). Part. reminisc. gramm. See *lij* "crumble, wash down, of sand", *ṃaan* "forward"; see also *Liṃanṃan,* with variant name *Lijṃaan.* Jaluit islet.

Bokwalijrak (**beqahlijrak**). Part. reminisc. gramm. See *lij* "crumble, wash down, of sand", *rak* "south". Mejit tract.

Bokwan-aetok (**beqan-hayeteq**). Gramm. See *ae* "current", *tok* "hither". Lae islet.

Bokwan-aitok (**beqan-hayiteq**). Gramm. distort. Aur islet.

Bokwan-ajbwirōk (**beqan-hajbiyręk**). Gramm. See *Ajbwirōk* "pandanus variety". Maloelap islet.

Bokwan-ake (**beqan-hakey**). Gramm. distort. See *akā* "inaccessible". Jaluit islet.

Bokwan-alejwa (**beqan-halęjwah**). Part. recur. form. See *alej, wa:* "aim a canoe (at it)". Mili islet.

Bokwan-aolōk (**beqan-hawęlęk**). Gramm. See *aolōk* "Portuguese man-o-war". Ailinglapalap tract.

Bokwan-ājdeṃ (**beqan-yajdeṃ**). Unanalyz. Maloelap islet.

Bokwan-ājin-or (**beqan-yajin-wẹr**). Part. recur. form. See *āj, or:* "lobster weaving pattern". Maloelap islet.

Bokwan-āllu (**beqan-yalliw**). Reminisc. gramm. See *iāllulu* "race". Maloelap islet.

Bokwan-baru (**beqan-bariw**). Gramm. See *baru* "crab". Two Namu tracts.

Bokwan-bōtōn (**beqan-bẹtẹn**). Unanalyz. Majuro islet.

Bokwan-detak (**beqan-dẹytak**). Gramm. See *detak* "blow, of wind". Eniwetak sandspit.

Bokwan-eeaḷ (**beqan-yeyyaḷ**). Unanalyz. Mili islet.

Bokwan-ejṃaan (**beqan-yejṃahan**). Gramm. See *ejṃaan* "boulder". Aur islet.

Bokwan-ejṃaan-dik (**beqan-yejṃahan-dik**). Gramm. Aur islet.

Bokwan-eṃṃaan (**beqan-yeṃṃahan**). Gramm. See *ṃṃaan* "men". Ailinglapalap islet.

Bokwan-Etao (**beqan-yetahwew**). Gramm. See *Etao* "legendary trickster". Rongelap islet.

Bokwan-ibeb (**beqan-yibyẹb**). Gramm. See *ibeb* "overflow". Ujelang islet.

Bokwan-ibeb-dik (**beqan-yibyẹb-dik**). Gramm. Ujelang islet.

Bokwan-iiaak (**beqan-yiyahak**). Gramm. See *iiaak* "remove bones from fish". Two Arno islets.

Bokwan-ikabwe (**beqan-yikabẹy**). Gramm. See *ikabwe* "mackerel". Arno islet.

Bokwan-ilel (**beqan-yilyẹl**). Recur. form. See *ilel* "rubble". Mili islet.

Bokwan-iōñ (**beqan-yiyẹg**). Gramm. Eniwetak sandspit.

Bokwan-iurjeņ (**beqan-yir°jeņ**). Gramm. See *iur, jeņ* "hurry there". Eniwetak sandspit.

Bokwan-je (**beqan-jęy**). Gramm. See *je* "stomach". Majuro tract.

Bokwan-jinre (**beqan-jinręy**). Gramm. See *jinre* "cook and eat fish right after catching". Ailinginae islet.

Bokwan-jǫ-iwōj (**beqan-jaw-yiwęj**). Gramm. See *jǫ, iwōj:* "formerly coming to you". Eniwetak islet.

Bokwan-juakak (**beqan-jiwhakhak**). Gramm. See *juakak* "hunt birds". Ujelang islet.

Bokwan-juwi (**beqan-jiwiy**). Gramm. See *juwi* "white tern". Ujelang islet.

Bokwan-kadid (**beqan-kadid**). Unanalyz. Bikini sandspit.

Bokwan-kallep (**beqan-kallep**). Gramm. See *kallep* "black ants". Maloelap islet.

Bokwan-kaṃōj (**beqan-kaṃęj**). Gramm. See *kaṃōj* "terminate". Ailuk tract.

Bokwan-kāmeej (**beqan-kaymęyęj**). Gramm. distort. See *kāmeej* "redwood". Rongerik islet.

Bokwan-kāmeej (**beqan-kaymeyej**). Gramm. Ujelang islet.

Bokwan-keer (**beqan-keyyer**). Gramm. distort. See *keār* "gull". Mili tract.

Bokwan-kiden (**beqan-kidęn**). Gramm. See *kiden* "beach borage". Lae islet.

Bokwan-kidu (**beqan-kidiw**). Gramm. See *kidu* "dog". Ujae islet.

Bokwan-kidudujet (**beqan-kidiwdiwjęt**). Gramm. See *kidudujet* "sea monster". Rongelap islet.

Bokwan-kio (**beqan-kiyew**). Gramm. See *kio* "a plant". Jaluit islet; Jaluit tract; Arno islet.

Bokwan-kiped (**beqan-kiped**). Gramm. See *kiped* "paddle". Jaluit tract.

Bokwan-kowak (**beqan-qewwak**). Gramm. See *kowak* "whimbrel". Likiep islet; Erikub islet; Maloelap islet; Arno islet.

Bokwan-kōṃanṃan (**beqan-keṃanṃan**). Gramm. See *kōṃanṃan* "create". Mili islet.

Bokwan-kōṃtāān̄ (**beqan-keṃtayag**). Part. reminisc. gramm. See *kōmte, ean̄:* "tossing at the north end". Aur islet.

Bokwan-kōn (**beqan-kęn**). Gramm. See *kōn* "indelible, not removable". Maloelap islet.

Bokwan-kōrā (**beqan-keray**). Gramm. See *kōrā* "women". Arno islet; Mili islet.

Bokwan-kwōmarōj (**beqan-qemarej**). Unanalyz. *Kwōmarōj* felt to be an old word whose meaning has been lost. Namu islet.

Bokwan-Lepeea (**beqan-lępęyyah**). Also *Boka-Lepeea* (**beqah-lępęyyah**). Pers. name, a woman who left everyone and went to seek food during a period of famine. Jaluit islet.

Bokwan-Liaanjepel (**beqan-liyahanjępęl**). Pers. name. Eniwetak sandspit.

Bokwan-lokļap (**beqan-lęqļap**). Recur. form. See *lok* "middle". Knox tract.

Bokwan-Ļapidka (**beqan-ļapidkah**). Pers. name. Kwajalein islet.

Bokwan-mar (**beqan-mar**). Gramm. See *mar* "bushes". Mili tract.

Bokwan-ṃaj (**beqan-ṃaj**). Gramm. See *ṃaj* "eel". Namu tract.

Bokwan-ṃak (**beqan-ṃak**). Gramm. See *ṃak* "needlefish". Majuro islet.

Bokwan-ṃwio-kaņ (**beqan-ṃiyew-kaņ**). Gramm. See *ṃwio:* "sandspits for making scarers". Ailuk islet.

Bokwan-ņa (**beqan-ņah**). Gramm. See *ņa* "shoal". Maloelap islet.

Bokwan-pako (**beqan-pakew**). Gramm. See *pako* "shark". Eniwetak islet.

Bokwan-peeļ (**beqan-peyeļ**). Gramm. See *peeļ* "intercourse". Jaluit islet.

Bokwan-pel (**beqan-pęl**). Also *Bokoppel.* Gramm. See *pel* "boxfish". Eniwetak sandspit.

Bokwan-pido (**beqan-pidew**). Gramm. distort. See *pidodo* "fragile". Ailinglapalap islet.

Bokwan-pit (**beqan-pit**). Gramm. See *Pit* "Gilbertese". Ailinglapalap islet; two Arno islets.

Bokwan-raj (**beqan-raj**). Gramm. See *raj* "whale". Eniwetak islet.

Bokwan-tariņae (**beqan-tariyņahyey**). Gramm. See *tariņae* "war". Maloelap islet; Arno islet.

Bokwan-tōrak (**beqan-tęhrak**). Gramm. See *tōrak* "shield". Jaluit islet.

Bokwan-tuwaak (**beqan-tiwahak**). Gramm. See *tuwaak* "wade". Bikini islet.

Bokwan-uṃ (**beqan-wiṃ**). Gramm. See *uṃ* "oven". Jaluit islet.

Bokwan-utkōk (**beqan-witkęk**). Gramm. See *utkōk* "naked". Namu islet.

Bokwan-utōk (**beqan-witęk**). Gramm. distort. See *utūk* "take off apparel". Maloelap islet.

Bokwan-watmān (**beqan-watman**). Unanalyz. Eniwetak sandspit.

Bokwan-wōtwōt (**beqan-wetwet**). Gramm. distort. See *wōt* "wild taro". Knox islet.

Bokwā-depto (**beqay-dęptęw**). Gramm. See *depdep, to:* "waves beating it westward". Mili islet.

Bokwā-dik (**beqay-dik**). Gramm. Arno islet.

Bokwā-jaḷwaj (**beqay-jaḷwaj**). Gramm. See *jaḷ, waj:* "facing you". Mili tract.

Bokwā-jeḷo (**beqay-jeyḷew**). Gramm. See *jeḷo* "sail ho!" Mili tract.

Bokwā-Jenmọọn (**beqay-jenmawan**). Part. reminisc. gramm. See *mọọn:* "*jenmọọn* is the name of a legendary woman who came here and sank in the sand. Mili islet.

Bokwā-jenwaan (**beqay-jenwahan**). Gramm. See *jenwaan* "common things". Arno islet.

Bokwā-jine (**beqay-jiynęy**). Gramm. See *jine* "sand crab". Maloelap islet.

Bokwā-Ledde (**beqay-lęddęy**). Pers. name. Mili islet.

Bokwā-Lijekāān (**beqay-lijekayan**). Pers. name. Arno islet.

Bokwā-Lijeñjeñ (**beqay-lijegjeg**). Pers. name. Mili islet.

Bokwā-Lijṃwā (**beqay-lijṃay**). Pers. name. Majuro islet.

Bokwā-Lijoorlọbwij (**beqay-lijęwęrlawbij**). Pers. name. Mili islet.

Bokwā-Likij (**beqay-likij**). Pers. name. Mili tract.

Bokwā-Likōrwa (**beqay-likerwah**). Pers. name. Arno islet.

Bokwā-Liṃjok (**beqay-liṃjeq**). Pers. name. Arno tract.

Bokwā-lōrro (**beqay-lęrręw**). Gramm. See *lōrro* "small empty shells". Maloelap islet.

Bokwā-luo (**beqay-liwew**). Gramm. See *luo* "a shell". Eniwetak islet.

Bokwā-Lurito (**beqay-lir°iytew**). Pers. name. Maloelap islet.

Bokwā-Luwuṃ (**beqay-liwwiṃ**). Pers. name. Kwajalein islet.

Bokwā-Ḷatulik (**beqay-ḷatiwlik**). Pers. name or name of a school of fish. Majuro islet.

Bokwā-ḷōdde (**beqay-ḷęddęy**). Unanalyz. Mili islet.

Bokwā-Ḷōjaōn (**beqay-ḷejahen**). Pers. name. Arno islet.

Bokwā-Ḷōjā-eṇ (**beqay-ḷejay-yeṇ**). Pers. name. Mili islet; Mili tract.

Bokwā-Ḷōjokdọ (**beqay-ḷejeqdaw**). Pers. name. Aur islet.

Bokwā-Ḷōkāājḷō (**beqay-ḷekayajḷeh**). Pers. name, a legendary man. Two Majuro islets.

Bokwā-Neimej (**beqay-nęyimęj**). Pers. name. Mili islet.

Bokwā-riPit (**beqay-ripit**). Gramm. See *Pit* "Gilbertese". Wotje islet.

Bokwā-rok-kaṇ (**beqay-req-kaṇ**). Also *Bokwā-robbaṇ*. Unanalyz. "Land where people store food." Mili islet.

Bokwā-ron (**beqay-r°en**). Unanalyz. Ailinglapalap islet.

Bokwā-tariṇae (**beqay-tariyṇahyey**). Gramm. See *tariṇae* "war". Arno islet; Arno tract; Mili islet.

Bokwā-til-kaṇ (**beqay-til-kaṇ**). Gramm. See *ttil* "burn". Maloelap tract.

Bokwā-to (**beqay-tęw**). Gramm. See *to* "to land". Erikub islet.

Bokwā-tuon-aḷ (**beqay-tiwen-haḷ**). Gramm. See *tuon, aḷ:* "the way of the sunrise". Majuro islet.

Bokwe-jabuñ (**beqey-jabig°**). Unanalyz. Wotje islet.

Bokwōn (**beqen**). Reminisc. gramm. Eniwetak islet.

Bokwōn-alo (**beqen-halęw**). Gramm. distort. See *alu* "a shell". Ailinglapalap islet.

Bokwōn-alọk (**beqen-halaq**). Gramm. distort. See *alọk* "obscure". Mili islet.

Bokwōn-aujjọr (**beqen-hawijjar°**). Unanalyz. Kwajalein islet.

Bokwōn-āneeḷap-kaṇ-ruo (**beqen-yanęyęḷap-kaṇ-riwew**). Gramm. distort. Ujelang islet.

Bokwōn-ār (**beqen-yar**). Gramm. See *ār* "to beach". Ujelang islet.

Bokwōn-eḷap (**beqen-yeḷap**). Gramm. Ujelang islet.

Bokwōn-keār (**beqen-keyyar**). Gramm. See *keār* "gull". Mili islet.

Bokwōn-keer (**beqen-keyyer**). Gramm. distort. Ailinginae islet.

Bokwōppel (**beqeppęl**). Reminisc. gramm. See *pel* "boxfish". Eniwetak islet.

Boḷañ (**bęwḷag**). Gramm. See *bubu, ḷañ:* "divination concerning storms". Namorik tract; Majuro tract.

Boobwa (**bęwębwah**). Unanalyz. Namu tract.

Boojbake (**bewejbakey**). Unanalyz. Namu tract.

Boojḷañ (**bęwęjḷag**). Reminisc. gramm. See *buoj* "capital", *ḷañ* "storm". Namu tract.

Boojmetoon (**bewejmetewen**). Part. recur. form. See *meto* "ocean". Eniwetak tract.

Boollikōn (**bewelliken**). Unanalyz. Eniwetak tract.

Boon-alen (**bewen-halen**). From Engl. *Bonin Islands*. Ebon tract.

Botuon (**bewtiwen**). Unanalyz. Eniwetak sandspit.

Bour (**bęwir**). Unanalyz. Ebon tract.

Bǫrorōn (**bawręwręn**). Unanalyz. Arno tract.

Bōdao (**bedahwew**). Part. recur. form. See *bōd* "turtle shell", *ao* "oil under turtle shell". Wotje islet; Ebon tract.

Bōk-ņa-ilik (**bek-ņah-yilik**). Part. recur. form. See *bōk:* "take outside". Kwajalein tract.

Bōkā-eņ (**bekay-yeņ**). Gramm. See *bōkā* "tide" or "oil container". Ujelang tract; Eniwetak tract; Wotho tract; Ailinglapalap tract; Ebon tract.

Bōkā-rōk (**bekay-ręk**). Gramm. Ujae islet.

Bōkāāḷkouj (**bekayaḷqęwij**). Unanalyz. Jaluit tract.

Bōkāān (**bekayan**). Unanalyz. Aur tract.

Bōkbar (**bekbar**). Gramm. See *bōk bar* "look around after sleeping". Mili islet; Mili tract.

Bōke-dikdik (**bękęy-dikdik**). Gramm. See *bōke* "cape", *dik* "small". Arno islet.

Bōke-eņ (**bękęy-yeņ**). Gramm. Rongelap tract; two Namu tracts; four Ailinglapalap tracts; three Jaluit tracts; two Namorik tracts; Ebon tract; three Majuro tracts; three Arno tracts; Mili tract; Knox tract.

Bōke-in-māllen (**bękęy-yin-mallen**). Unanalyz. Aur tract.

Bōke-juwaḷōñḷōñ (**bękęy-jiwahḷęgḷęg**). Gramm. See *bōke, juwaḷōñḷōñ:* "show-off cape". Wotje tract.

Bōke-liklǫk (**bękęy-liklaq**). Gramm. See *liklǫk* "a fishing method". Kwajalein tract.

Bōkḷapḷap (**bękḷapḷap**). Reminisc. gramm. Aur islet.

Bōl (**bęl**). Gramm. See *bōl* "taro pit". Namu tract; Ailinglapalap tract.

Bōl-eņ (**bęl-yeņ**). Gramm. Arno tract.

Bōle-eañ (**bęlęy-yag**). Unanalyz. Aur tract.

Bōlkōk (**belkek**). Unanalyz. Maloelap household.

Bōlōk-kaņ (**bęlęk-kaņ**). Gramm. See *bōlōk* "leaf". Likiep tract.

Bōlwōj (**bęlwęj**). Part. recur. form. See *bōl* "taro pit". Mejit tract.

Bōḷadek (**beḷadek**). Unanalyz. Namorik tract.

Bōḷḷañ (**bęḷḷag**). Unanalyz. Ailinglapalap tract.

Bōn-eņ (**bęn-yeņ**). Gramm. See *bōn* "place for floating corpses away". Two Jaluit tracts; Aur tract.

Bōn-kaņ (**bęn-kaņ**). Gramm. Kwajalein tract.

Bōnlik-bōnar (**benlik-benhar**). Gramm. distort. Rongelap tract.

Bōnto (**bentew**). Part. reminisc. gramm. See *to* "passage". Maloelap channel.

Bōran-aelōñ-eņ (**beran-hayęlęg-yeņ**). Gramm. See *bōran aelōñ* "main islet". Likiep district; Maloelap district; Mili district.

Bōran-aelōñ-in (**beran-hayęlęg-yin**). Gramm. Rongelap district.

Bōran-ailiñ-in (**beran-hayilig-yin**). Gramm. distort. Majuro district.

Bōran-bōl (**beran-bęl**). Gramm. See *bōran* "head of", *bōl* "taro pit". Ujae tract; Lib tract; Jabwot tract.

Bōran-ekmouj-reeaar (**beran-yękmęwij-reyyahar**). Gramm. See *bōran* "head of", *ek-mouj* "parrotfish". Ailinglapalap tract.

Bōran-ekmouj-riilik (**beran-yękmęwij-riyilik**). Gramm. Ailinglapalap tract.

Bōrā-jojoon (**beray-jewjewen**). Gramm. See *jojoon* "pile up". Majuro tract.

Bōrā-Lōbo (**beray-lębęw**). Pers. name. See *Lōbo,* another Ailinglapalap tract. Ailinglapalap islet.

Bōre-jebǫuwe (**berey-jebawiwwey**). Unanalyz. Jaluit tract.

Bōreǫ (**bereyaw**). Reminisc. gramm. Majuro tract.

Bōro (**berẹw**). Reminisc. gramm. See *bōro* "throat, heart". Arno tract.

Bōro (**berew**). Reminisc. gramm. Aur tract; Arno islet.

Bōro-eṇ-iōñ (**berẹw-yeṇ-yiyẹg**). Reminisc. gramm. Arno household.

Bōro-eṇ-rōk (**berẹw-yeṇ-rẹk**). Reminisc. gramm. Arno household.

Bōrọ (**beraw**). Reminisc. gramm. See *būrọ* "sonny". Mejit tract.

Bōrọk (**beraq**). Unanalyz. Rongelap islet.

Bōrta (**bertah**). Unanalyz. Ailinglapalap tract.

Bōtōktōkinniṃṃaan (**betektekinniṃṃahan**). Gramm. distort. Mili tract.

Bōtto (**bettew**). Unanalyz. Jaluit islet.

Bu (**biw**). Gramm. See *bu* "gun". Wotje islet.

Bubu-eṇ (**biwbiw-yeṇ**). Gramm. See *bubu* "divination". Maloelap tract; Maloelap household; Aur tract.

Bubu-eṇ-jāiōñ (**biwbiw-yeṇ-jayiyẹg**). Gramm. Arno tract.

Bubu-eṇ-jārōk (**biwbiw-yeṇ-jayrẹk**). Gramm. Arno tract.

Bubu-kaṇ (**biwbiw-kaṇ**). Gramm. Mejit tract.

Bujen-eṃ (**biwjen-yeṃ**). Recur. form. See *bujen* "agreement", *eṃ* "house". Ailinglapalap tract.

Buk (**biq**). Unanalyz. Ailinglapalap islet.

Bukoṃ (**biqwẹṃ**). Reminisc. gramm. See *bukbuk* "helmet shell, *oṃ* "hermit crab". Ujelang islet.

Bukwe-eṇ (**biqẹy-yeṇ**). Gramm. See *bukwekwe* "lush". Arno tract.

Bukwe-kaṇ (**biqẹy-kaṇ**). Gramm. Maloelap tract; two Aur tracts.

Bukwe-Ḷōpo (**biqey-ḷepew**). Pers. name. Majuro tract.

Bukwi-naṃ (**biqiy-naṃ**). Part. recur. form. See *bukwi, ṇaṃ:* "hundreds of mosquitoes". Eniwetak tract.

Bukwi-til (**biqiy-til**). Part. recur. form. See *til:* "hundreds of torches". Majuro tract.

Bukwōn-eṇ-ioḷap (**biqen-yeṇ-yiyewḷap**). Gramm. See *bukwōn* "district". Likiep tract.

Bukwōn-jāej (**biqen-jayyẹj**). Gramm. Likiep islet.

Bukwōn-jālik (**biqen-jaylik**). Gramm. Likiep islet.

Bukwōn-kaṇ (**biqen-kaṇ**). Gramm. Eniwetak islet.

Bukwōn-kio (**biqen-kiyew**). Gramm. distort. See *kio* "a plant". Ailinglapalap tract.

Bukwōn-kūr (**biqen-kir**). Gramm. See *kūr* "call". Majuro tract.

Buñmelōñ-rālik (**big°mẹlẹg-raylik**). Unanalyz. Kwajalein tract.

Buñmelōñ-rear (**big°meleg-reyhar**). Reminisc. gramm. Kwajalein tract.

Buoj (**biwẹj**). Gramm. See *buoj* "capital". Bikini tract; Wotho tract; two Ujae tracts; four Kwajalein tracts; two Namu tracts; Ailinglapalap district; Ailinglapalap district; Ailinglapalap islet; two Jaluit tracts; Mejit tract; Ailuk tract; two Wotje tracts.

Buoj-ar (**biwẹj-har**). Gramm. Namu household; Maloelap tract.

Buoj-dik (**biwej-dik**). Gramm. Majuro tract.

Buoj-iōñ (**biwẹj-yiyẹg**). Gramm. Aur tract; Mili tract.

Buoj-kōp (**biwẹj-kẹp**). Part. recur. form. See *kōpkōp* "struggle". Jaluit tract.

Buoj-ḷañ-iōñ (**biwẹj-ḷag-yiyẹg**). Part. recur. form. Ebon tract.

Buoj-ḷañ-irōk (**biwẹj-ḷag-yirẹk**). Part. recur. form. Ebon tract.

Buoj-ḷap (**biwej-ḷap**). Gramm. Maloelap islet; Majuro tract.

Buoj-raiōñ (**biwẹj-rahyiyẹg**). Gramm. Kwajalein tract.

Buoj-rairōk (**biwẹj-rahyirẹk**). Gramm. Kwajalein tract.

Buoj-rōk (**biwẹj-rẹk**). Gramm. Aur tract; Mili tract.

Buron (**bir°en**). Unanalyz. Majuro islet.

Buru-ku-lik (**bir°iw-kiw-lik**). Unanalyz. Mili islet.

Buru-niu (**bir°iw-niyiw**). Unanalyz. Namorik tract.

Buruo-eṇ (**bir°iwẹh-yeṇ**). Gramm. See *bōro:* "my heart". Ailinglapalap tract.

Buruon (**bir°iwen**). Gramm. See *bōro:* "his heart, her heart". Majuro islet; Mili islet.

Butaritari (**biwtariytariy**). From Gilb. *Butaritari*. Mejit tract.

Buwaj (**biwaj**). Gramm. See *buwaj* "halfbeak" or "bruise". Wotje tract.

Buwajaj (**biwajhaj**). Gramm. Arno tract.

Buwame (**biwamẹy**). Unanalyz. Jaluit tract.

Buwar (**biwar**). Gramm. See *buwar* "a basket". Mejit tract.

Buwar-iōn̄ (**biwar-yiyęg**). Gramm. Mejit tract.

Buwar-rōk (**biwar-ręk**). Gramm. Mejit tract.

Buwe (**biwęy**). Unanalyz. Aur islet.

Buwe (**biwey**). Unanalyz. Mili islet.

Buwun̄i (**biwwig°iy**). Unanalyz. Arno tract.

Būbnini (**bibniyniy**). Gramm. See *būbnini* "smell of coconuts". Majuro tract.

Būke-loon (**bikęy-lęwęn**). Unanalyz. Majuro tract.

Būke-Ļōjowōn (**bikey-ļęjęwwęn**). Pers. name. Arno islet.

Būkie-Ruwa (**bikiyey-riwah**). Pers. name. Arno tract.

Būkien (**bikiyen**). Gramm. See *bōke:* "its cape". Knox tract.

Būkien-kālōn̄ (**bikiyen-kaylęg**). Gramm. See *bōke, kā-:* "cape of jumping up". Kwajalein tract.

Būkien-kidu (**bikiyen-kidiw**). Gramm. See *bōke, kidu:* "dog cape". Arno islet.

Būkien-kōmej (**bikiyen-kęmęj**). Gramm. distort. See *kimej* "frond". Kwajalein tract.

Būkien-kūtaak-eņ (**bikiyen-kitahak-yeņ**). Gramm. See *kūtaak* "a tree". Jaluit tract.

Būkien-Ļakūrwaan (**bikiyen-ļakirwahan**). Pers. name. See *kūrwaan:* "he who can find something to eat in a period of famine". Arno tract.

Būkin-out (**bikin-węwit**). Gramm. See *out* "meeting place". Majuro tract.

Būkje-Ļapoāne (**bikjey-ļapewyanęy**). Pers. name. Arno tract.

Būkōn (**biken**). Gramm. See *bōke* "cape". Majuro tract.

Būkōn-aļo (**biken-haļew**). Recur. form. See *aļo* "late". Majuro tract.

Būkōn-jekjekōn (**biken-jękjękęn**). Gramm. See *jekjek* "chop". Ailinglapalap tract.

Būkōn-laletak (**biken-lahleytak**). Gramm. See *lale, tak:* "look eastward". Ebon tract.

Būkōn-ļooj (**biken-ļewej**). Unanalyz. Kwajalein tract.

Būkōn-n̄ijo (**biken-gijew**). Unanalyz. Ailinglapalap tract.

Būkōn-paotok (**biken-pahwewteq**). Gramm. See *pao, tok:* "appearance from here". Rongelap tract.

Būkōr (**bikęr**). Gramm. See *būkōr* "a plant". Bikini islet; Aur tract.

Būļadek (**biļadek**). Unanalyz. Likiep tract.

Būļaļa (**biļahļah**). Unanalyz. Jaluit tract.

Būn̄būn̄-eņ (**bigbig-yeņ**). Unanalyz. Aur tract.

Būrjin (**birjin**). Unanalyz. Mejit tract.

Būroto (**birewtew**). Unanalyz. Kwajalein tract.

Būrukulik (**biriwkiwlik**). Unanalyz. Majuro coral head.

Būtbūtļon̄ (**bitbitļeg°**). Unanalyz. Arno tract.

Bwe (**bęy**). Gramm. See *bwe* "divination knot". Lae islet.

Bweradik (**beyrahdik**). Unanalyz. Arno tract.

Bwibwi (**biybiy**). Gramm. See *bwibwi* "yolk". Maloelap islet.

Bwiddik-ean̄ (**biddik-yag**). Reminisc. gramm. See *bwiddik* "small tract". Majuro tract.

Bwiddik-rak (**biddik-rak**). Reminisc. gramm. Majuro tract.

Bwideje (**bidęjęy**). Part. reminisc. gramm. See *bwidej* "soil". Taongi islet.

Bwijin-mar (**bijin-mar**). Gramm. See *bwijin, mar:* "lots of bushes". Maloelap tract.

Bwijm̧weerer (**bijm̧ęyęryęr**). Also *Bwijm̧weereor* (**bijm̧eyeryer°**). Reminisc. gramm. Jaluit tract.

Bwil-eņ (**bil-yeņ**). Gramm. See *bwil* "heat". Rongelap tract; Namu tract; three Namorik tracts.

Bwilaklaktak (**bilaklaktak**). Part. recur. form. See *bwilak* "unicorn fish". Maloelap islet.

Bwilār-eņ (**bilyar-yeņ**). Gramm. See *bwil* "to launch", *ār* "to beach". Aur tract.

Bwilel (**bilęl**). Unanalyz. Ebon islet.

Bwinnaat (**binnahat**). Unanalyz. Arno islet.

Dabǫkut-kaņ (**dabaqit-kaņ**). Gramm. See *debǫkut* "stumps". Mili islet.

Damā (**dahmay**). Unanalyz. Bikini tract.

Dame (**dahmey**). Unanalyz. Lae islet.

Dame-dik (**dahmey-dik**). Unanalyz. Lae islet.

Dame-rilik (**dahmey-riylik**). Unanalyz. Lae islet.

Dān (**dan**). Gramm. See *dān* "water". Jaluit islet.

Dān-or-kūbwe (**dan-wer-kibey**). Gramm. See *dān, or, kūbwe:* "water has feces". Aur tract.

Dānm̧ūkil (**danm̧ikil**). Also *Dānm̧ūkūñ*. Part. reminisc. gramm. See *kūñ* "smell of feces". Utirik household.

Dāpdep (**dapdẹp**). Gramm. See *dāpdep* "control, retain". Knox tract.

Dāpdep-eņ (**dapdẹp-yeņ**). Gramm. Mili islet.

Dāwiļǫk (**daywiylaq**). Unanalyz. Wotho tract.

Debļǫkun (**dẹblaqin**). Gramm. See *debļǫk* "penetration". Mili tract.

Debǫkut-eņ (**debaqit-yeņ**). Gramm. See *debǫkut* "stump". Aur islet.

Debwe-iu (**dẹbẹy-yiw**). Gramm. distort. See *debweiu* "old sprouted coconuts". Majuro tract.

Debwe-iu (**debey-yiw**). Gramm. Kwajalein islet.

Debwe-iu-eņ (**debey-yiw-yeņ**). Gramm. Namu tract; Ailinglapalap islet; Jaluit islet.

Debweǫ-eņ (**dẹbyaw-yeņ**). Part. reminisc. gramm. Arno islet.

Debweǫ-eņ (**debeyaw-yeņ**). Part. reminisc. gramm. Mili islet; Mili tract.

Dede (**deydey**). Unanalyz. Jaluit islet.

Dedm̧weeņ (**dedm̧eyeņ**). Part. reminisc. gramm. See *m̧weeņ* "that house". Aur tract.

Dekā-eņ (**dekay-yeņ**). Gramm. See *dekā* "stone". Ailinglapalap islet; Utirik channel.

Dekā-eņ-edik (**dekay-yeņ-yedik**). Gramm. Maloelap islet.

Dekā-mer-kaņ (**dekay-mẹr-kaņ**). Gramm. distort. See *mir* "red". Mejit tract.

Deldelbwij (**deldelbij**). Gramm. See *deldelbwij* "a fish". Eniwetak islet.

Demaļōp (**demaļep**). Unanalyz. Majuro tract.

Demar (**demar**). Unanalyz. Namu islet.

Demdǫļ (**demdaļ°**). Unanalyz. Ebon islet; Ebon tract.

Dem̧jelañ (**dem̧jeylag**). Part. reminisc. gramm. See *dem̧wā, jeļañ* "edge of a big storm". Majuro tract.

Dem̧wājoñ (**dem̧ayjeg°**). Gramm. See *dem̧wā, joñ:* "edge of the mangroves". Majuro tract; two Arno tracts; Mili tract.

Den-ar (**den-har**). Reminisc. gramm. See *dān* "water". Majuro tracṭ.

Den-lik (**den-lik**). Reminisc. gramm. Majuro tract.

Denijo (**deniyjẹw**). Reminisc. gramm. See *dān* "water", *jo* "float loose". Kwajalein tract.

Denikden (**dẹnikdẹn**). Part. reminisc. gramm. See *kiden* "beach borage". Arno tract.

Denjab (**denjab**). Reminisc. gramm. Mejit tract.

Denkipinōr (**dẹnkipiner**). Gramm. distort. See *dān, kapin, ōr:* "damp bottoms of grass skirts (from walking in swamp)". Mejit tract.

Denmeo (**dẹnmeyew**). Gramm. distort. See *dān* "water", *meǫ* "bitter". Majuro islet.

Deñjān (**degjan**). Part. reminisc. gramm. Arno tract.

Deñōj-eņ (**degej-yeņ**). Part. reminisc. gramm. See *deñdeñ*. Lib tract.

Deñōjeen (**degejeen**). Part. reminisc. gramm. Rongerik tract.

Deñōn-ae (**degen-hahyey**). Recur. form. See *ae* "current". Kwajalein sandspit.

Deñōn-m̧ōt (**degen-m̧ẹt**). Part. reminisc. gramm. See *m̧ōt* "ride the waves". Arno tract.

Depae (**dephahyey**). Part. reminisc. gramm. See *ae:* "name of a current". Namorik tract.

Detñil (**detgil**). Gramm. See *detñil* "sunny and calm". Arno tract.

Di-lep (**diy-lep**). Gramm. See *dilep* "backbone". Ailinglapalap tract.

Diboñ (**dibẹg°**). Gramm. distort. See *diboñ* "dark night". Lae islet; Jaluit islet.

Dibwāwōn (**dibaywen**). Gramm. distort. See *dibōj, aeo:* "spear his lower back". Eniwetak islet.

Didbōl (**didbel**). Gramm. distort. See *didbōlbōl* "to flower and flourish". Arno tract.

Didej (**didẹj**). Unanalyz. Majuro islet.

Didi (**diydiy**). Gramm. See *di:* "bony" or "teeming with oysters". Ailinglapalap tract; Ebon islet; Likiep islet; Wotje islet; Knox tract.

Didmej-jāiōñ (**didmẹj-jayiyẹg**). Gramm. See *didmej* "stake". Majuro tract.

Didmej-jārōk (**didmẹj-jayrẹk**). Gramm. Majuro tract.

Dik-tata (**dik-tahtah**). Gramm. See *dik, tata:* "smallest". Arno tract.

Dikiañ-iōñ (**dikiyag-yiyẹg**). Recur. form. Kwajalein tract.

Dikiañ-rōk (**dikiyag-rẹk**). Recur. form. Kwajalein tract.

Doñōjen (**deg°ejyen**). Unanalyz. Rongerik tract.

Doot (**dẹwẹt**). Unanalyz. Lae tract.

Dọuk-eṇ (**dawik-yeṇ**). Gramm. See *dọuk* "lower it". Jaluit tract.

Du (**diw**). Gramm. See *du* "boiling". Erikub islet.

Eakūūl-kaṇ (**yakihil-kaṇ**). Unanalyz. Mili islet.

Eaḷḷeen (**yaḷḷeyen**). Unanalyz. Arno tract.

Eaḷḷwōj (**yaḷ°ḷ°ẹj**). Unanalyz. Ebon tract.

Eañ-detdet (**yag-detdet**). Gramm. See *eañ, det:* "sunny north". Majuro tract.

Eañi-to (**yagiy-tẹw**). Gramm. distort. See *eañ, to:* "north of the husk soaking pit". Majuro tract.

Eañin-bok-eṇ (**yagin-beq-yeṇ**). Gramm. See *eañ, bok:* "north of the sandspit". Mejit tract.

Eañin-bōl (**yagin-bẹl**). Gramm. Ujae tract.

Eañin-ene (**yagin-yẹnẹy**). Gramm. See *āne:* "north part of the islet". Arno tract.

Ed-eṇ (**yed-yeṇ**). Gramm. See *ed* "become red". Mili islet.

Edbūb (**yedbib**). Part. recur. form. Namorik tract.

Eded (**yedyed**). Gramm. See *eded* "rummage". Ailinglapalap islet.

Eded-iōñ (**yedyed-yiyẹg**). Gramm. Wotje tract.

Eded-rōk (**yedyed-rẹk**). Gramm. Wotje tract.

Edjekāān (**yedjekayan**). Gramm. distort. See *ed, jekāān:* "its trunk becomes red". Wotje islet; Maloelap islet; Arno islet; Arno tract.

Eika-eṇ (**yẹyikah-yeṇ**). From Engl. *acre*. Ailinglapalap tract.

Ejbad (**yejbad**). Part. reminisc. gramm. See *bad* "place for divination". Utirik tract.

Ejel (**yẹjẹl**). Gramm. See *jel:* "it is grown over". Kwajalein islet.

Ejel-wawaan (**yẹjẹl-wahwahan**). Gramm. See *jel, wawaa-:* "its foundation is curved". Mili islet.

Ejelpen (**yejelpen**). Gramm. distort. See *jelpa* "parent-in-law". Maloelap islet.

Ejjaruk (**yejjariq**). Gramm. See *jaruk:* "it is safe". Kwajalein tract.

Ejje (**yẹjjẹy**). Gramm. See *ejje* "navigational sign". Jaluit tract.

Ejjeḷā (**yejjeḷay**). Gramm. See *ejjeḷā* "to anchor". Kwajalein islet.

Ejjepo (**yẹjjẹpẹw**). Reminisc. gramm. See *ajjen, po:* "cluster of pandanus keys falls off". Bikini islet.

Ejṃaan (**yejṃahan**). Gramm. See *ejṃaan* "boulder". Arno coral head.

Ejwa (**yejwah**). Unanalyz. Mili islet.

Ek-mouj (**yẹk-mẹwij**). Gramm. See *ekmouj* "parrotfish". Wotje tract.

Ekalur (**yekalir°**). Gramm. See *lur:* "it makes for serenity". Majuro tract.

Ekjab (**yekjab**). Gramm. Aur tract.

Ekjab-eṇ (**yekjab-yeṇ**). Gramm. See *ekjab* "idol". Majuro tract.

Ekkat-kaṇ (**yekkat-kaṇ**). Gramm. See *kkat:* "those plantings". Kwajalein coral head.

Ekọ-eṇ (**yekaw-yeṇ**). Unanalyz. Kwajalein tract.

Ekōj (**yẹkẹj**). Reminisc. gramm. See *kōj:* "it is us". Rongelap islet.

Ekōjab (**yekejab**). Gramm. See *ekjab* "idol". Arno tract.

El-ak (**yel-hak**). Part. recur. form. See *el* "nest", *ak* "frigate bird". Bikini tract; Jaluit tract.

El-bōd (**yel-bed**). Part. recur. form. See *bōd* "turtle shell". Majuro tract.

El-buñbuñ (**yel-big°big°**). Gramm. distort. See *buñbuñ* "famous". Jaluit tract; Ebon tract.

El-eṇ (**yẹl-yeṇ**). Gramm. See *el* "nest". Kwajalein tract; two Jaluit tracts.

El-eṇ (**yel-yeṇ**). Gramm. distort. Rongelap tract; Ujae tract; two Kwajalein tracts; two Ailinglapalap tracts; two Jaluit tracts; Likiep tract; Wotje tract; Aur tract.

El-eo (**yel-yew**). Reminisc. gramm. Ailinglapalap tract.

El-eọ (**yel-yaw**). Reminisc. gramm. See *eọ* "tattoo". Mili tract.

El-jar (**yel-jar**). Unanalyz. The demon *Laaneo* had a baby born here, according to legend. Ebon tract.

El-kwaat (**yel-qahat**). Unanalyz. Kwajalein tract.

El-me (**yel-mey**). Unanalyz. Maloelap tract.

El-mej (**yel-mẹj**). Part. recur. form. See *mej:* "place where the dead are taken". Namorik tract.

El-m̧ad (**yel-m̧ad**). Part. recur. form. See *m̧ad* "busy". Maloelap tract.

El-pāl (**yel-pal**). Recur. form. See *pāl* "house". Ailuk tract.

El-pālu (**yel-paliw**). Reminisc. gramm. See *eḷ, pālu* "a club of big shots". Ebon tract.

El-pāp (**yel-pap**). Reminisc. gramm. See *pāp* "frond". Namu tract.

El-pene (**yel-pẹnẹy**). Part. recur. form. See *pen* "encourage him". Ebon tract.

El-tutu (**yel-tiwtiw**). Part. recur. form. See *tutu* "bathe". Majuro tract.

Ele (**yẹlẹy**). Gramm. See *ele* "fish string". Jaluit islet.

Ele-jibukwi (**yeley-jibiqiy**). Gramm. See *jibukwi:* "one hundred on the fish string". Ailuk tract.

Ele-jibukwi-iar (**yeley-jibiqiy-yiyhar**). Gramm. Ailuk household.

Ele-jibukwi-lik (**yeley-jibiqiy-lik**). Gramm. Ailuk household.

Ele-lōn̄ (**yẹlẹy-lẹg**). Gramm. See *ele, lōn̄:* "upper part of fish string". Mejit tract; Wotje tract; Arno tract.

Ele-ḷwe (**yẹlẹy-ḷ°ẹy**). Part. recur. form. See *el, ḷwe:* "this nest is a pond". Majuro tract.

Ele-rōk (**yẹlẹy-rẹk**). Gramm. Arno tract.

Elelan̄ (**yelyelag**). Unanalyz. Majuro tract.

Elelen (**yelyelen**). Unanalyz. Eniwetak tract.

Elen-ak (**yelen-hak**). Gramm. distort. Majuro tract.

Elen-m̧ao (**yelen-m̧ahwew**). Gramm. distort. See *el, m̧ao* "owl nest". Arno tract.

Eleņak (**yeleyņak**). Gramm. See *leņak* "he is sleeping soundly". Kwajalein islet.

Elladikdik-raiiōn̄ (**yellahdikdik-rahiyyẹg**). Gramm. See *lladikdik* "pleasantly cool". Kwajalein tract.

Elladikdik-rairōk (**yellahdikdik-rahiyrẹk**). Gramm. Kwajalein tract.

Ellep (**yellep**). Reminisc. gramm. See *el, ḷap:* "big nest". Ralik island; Lib.

Ellōkan (**yellekan**). Gramm. See *ellōkan* "about". Majuro islet.

Elmen (**yẹlmẹn**). Gramm. The skirt of the legendary god of good fortune *Ḷakidid* brought many tuna to the lagoon off *Elmen.* See *elmen* "skirt". Ebon tract.

Elm̧ad (**yẹlm̧ad**). Gramm. See *elm̧ad* "Vega". Maloelap tract.

Elōkeo-ean̄ (**yelekyew-yag**). Unanalyz. Majuro tract.

Elōkeo-rak (**yelekyew-rak**). Unanalyz. Majuro tract.

Eḷe (**yeḷey**). Unanalyz. See *eḷ* "a cult". Kwajalein islet.

Eḷḷap (**yeḷḷap**). Reminisc. gramm. See *ār, ḷap:* "big place for beaching". Mejit tract; Majuro tract.

Eḷm̧oņ (**yeḷm̧eņ°**). Unanalyz. Namorik district.

Em-maan̄-eņ (**yẹmh-mahag-yeņ**). Gramm. Likiep tract.

Emej (**yẹmẹj**). Gramm. See *emej* "to moor". Utirik household.

Emejwa (**yẹmẹjwah**). Gramm. See *emej, wa:* "moor a canoe". Likiep islet; Arno tract; Mili tract.

Ememe (**yẹmyẹmẹy**). Gramm. distort. See *ememej* "memory". Lae tract.

Emjak-kaņ (**yẹmjak-kaņ**). Gramm. See *emjak:* "the moorings". Arno tract.

Emjān-wa (**yemjan-wah**). Gramm. See *emjak, wa:* "canoe anchorage". Ujae tract.

Emḷọk (**yemḷaq**). Gramm. See *emḷọk* "nostalgia". Mili tract.

Emmeej (**yemmeyej**). Gramm. See *mmeej:* "it is attractive". Ebon islet.

Em̧-maan̄-eņ (**yẹm̧-mahag-yeņ**). Gramm. See *em̧, maan̄* "pandanus leaf house". Likiep tract.

Em̧m̧al (**yem̧m̧al**). Gramm. distort. See *em̧, m̧al:* "swaying house" or *m̧m̧al* "place for beating husks". Namu islet.

Enbar (**yenbar**). Part. reminisc. gramm. See *āne, bar:* "rock isle". Ebon tract.

Ene-eņ (**yẹnẹy-yeņ**). Gramm. See *āne* "islet". Ailuk tract.

Enea (**yeneyah**). Reminisc. gramm. See *āne, ia* "where is the islet with a cistern to fill our containers, asked two legendary girls". Wotje islet; Maloelap islet; Arno tract.

Enejā (**yeneyjay**). Also *Āne-jā*. Reminisc. gramm. See *āne, jā:* "islet where sails fall toward outrigger". Ailuk islet.

Eneo̧r (**yenyar°**). Reminisc. gramm. See *āne, eo̧r:* "islet of going aground (a British ship went aground here)". Ebon islet.

Enjepe (**yȩnjȩpȩy**). Part. recur. form. See *Āne, jepe:* "basket isle". Eniwetak district; Eniwetak islet.

Enm̧aat (**yenm̧ahat**). Unanalyz. Kwajalein islet.

Ennak (**yennak**). Unanalyz. Ailinglapalap islet.

Enne (**yȩnnȩy**). Gramm. See *enne* "field". Namorik tract.

En̄op (**yen̄°ep**). Part. recur. form. See *n̄op* "whetstone". Aur islet.

Eo (**yew**). Gramm. Namu islet.

Eokko̧r-en̄ (**yeqqar°-yen̄**). Pers. name. Ailinglapalap tract.

Eokwōjaja (**yeweqejahjah**). Gramm. See *okwōjaja:* "it is high above the water". Kwajalein tract.

Eolo̧k (**yewlaq**). Gramm. See *eolo̧k* "pull down". Maloelap islet.

Eoļap (**yewļap**). Gramm. See *eoļap* "middle". Maloelap tract; Majuro district.

Eoļap-en̄ (**yewļap-yen̄**). Gramm. Ujae district; Ailinglapalap tract.

Eoļļwōj (**yeļ°ļ°ej**). Unanalyz. Arno tract.

Eomeļan̄ (**yewmeļag**). Gramm. See *eomeļan̄* "land reserved for chiefs". Bikini islet.

Eoon-ale (**yewen-haley**). Unanalyz. Bikini tract.

Eoon-awi (**yewen-hawiy**). Recur. form. Arno tract.

Eoon-ene (**yȩwȩn-yȩnȩy**). Gramm. See *eoonene* "main islet". Rongelap district; Rongerik district; Ailinginae district.

Eoon-ene (**yewen-yȩnȩy**). Gramm. Two Eniwetak districts; Lae district; Ujae district; Kwajalein district; Namu district; Namorik district; Mejit district; Ailuk district; Erikub district; Majuro district.

Eoon-epeje (**yewen-yȩpȩjȩy**). Reminisc. gramm. See *eoo-, epje:* "main meeting place". Aur islet.

Eoon-epje (**yewen-yepjȩy**). Reminisc. gramm. Maloelap islet; Lae islet; Arno islet.

Eoon-ipije (**yewen-yipijȩy**). Reminisc. gramm. Wotje islet.

Eoon-jo (**yewen-jew**). Gramm. See *eoo-, jo:* "surface for fishing by the *jo* method". Ailinglapalap tract.

Eoon-kōjeej (**yewen-kȩjȩyȩj**). Unanalyz. Rongerik tract.

Eoon-kōjeej (**yewen-kejeyej**). Unanalyz. Ailinglapalap tract.

Eoon-ļā (**yewen-ļay**). Gramm. See *eoo-, ļā:* "gravel surface". Kili district.

Eoon-maaj (**yewen-mahaj**). Gramm. See *eoo-, maaj:* "clear surface". Wotho tract; two Kwajalein tracts; Namu tract; three Jaluit tracts; two Ebon tracts; two Mejit tracts; Wotje tract; five Majuro tracts; four Arno tracts.

Eoon-meto-in (**yewen-metew-yin**). Gramm. See *meto:* "this ocean surface". Wotho tract; Lib tract.

Eoon-peje (**yȩwȩn-pȩjȩy**). Gramm. Rongelap islet.

Eoon-peje (**yewen-pȩjȩy**). Gramm. See *peje:* "main meeting place". Wotho tract; Kwajalein tract.

Eoon-rak (**yewen-rak**). Gramm. See *rak:* "southern surface". Wotje district.

Eoon-toļ (**yewen-teļ°**). Gramm. See *eoo-, toļ:* "mountain top". Ailinglapalap tract.

Eorrob (**yer°r°eb**). Unanalyz. Kwajalein islet.

Eowo (**yewwew**). Unanalyz. Jaluit islet.

Eo̧m̧o (**yawm̧ew**). Unanalyz. Ailinglapalap islet.

Eo̧m̧ōlōn̄ (**yawm̧ȩlȩg**). Reminisc. gramm. See *Eo̧m̧we-lan̄*. Ailinglapalap tract.

Eo̧m̧ōn-mā (**yawm̧ȩn-may**). Gramm. distort. See *ium̧wi-, mā:* "under the breadfruit tree". Arno tract.

Eo̧m̧we-lan̄ (**yawm̧ȩy-lag**). Gramm. distort. See *ium̧wi-, lan̄:* "under the sky". Majuro tract.

Eo̧n̄ōn (**yag°en**). Unanalyz. Mejit tract.

Eo̧o̧tle (**yawatlȩy**). Recur. form. See *eo̧o̧tle* "south". Likiep islet.

Eo̧werōk (**yawȩyrȩk**). Gramm. See *Ewerōk* "land of departed spirits, beyond the River Styx". Mili tract.

Eōōļ (**yeheļ**). Gramm. See *ōļ:* "it flows". Namorik tract.

Epatōn (**yepaten**). Recur. form. See *epat:* "its bottom or west end". Kwajalein islet.

Epāju (**yepajiw**). Unanalyz. Ujae islet.

Epe-eañ (**yepey-yag**). From Gilb. *Abaiang*. Arno tract.

Epjā (**yepjay**). Also *Ibae* (**yibahyey**). Reminisc. gramm. See *epje,* or *epliklik jā:* "usually capsize". Kwajalein islet; Ebeye.

Epjā-dik (**yepjay-dik**). Reminisc. gramm. Kwajalein islet.

Epḷañ (**yepḷag**). Reminisc. gramm. See *epliklik, ḷañ:* "usually storm". Ebon tract.

Epni (**yepniy**). Reminisc. gramm. See *iep* "basket", *ni* "coconut". Jaluit tract.

Epoon (**yepewen**). Reminisc. gramm. See *iep waan* "a type of basket which the atoll is thought to be shaped like". Ralik atoll; Ebon; Ebon islet; Utirik tract.

Epōnūn (**yephenhin**). Unanalyz. Namu islet.

Eppān-ene (**yeppan-yẹnẹy**). Gramm. See *eppānene* "dry land". Ailinglapalap tract.

Epta (**yeptah**). Also *Āpta.* Gramm. See *epta* "sieve arrowroot second time (see sister islet *Jepta*)". Ailuk islet.

Epwaj (**yepwaj**). Reminisc. gramm. See *iep* "basket", *waj* "to you". Kwajalein islet.

Eram (**yeram**). Gramm. See *era-:* "our sitting mat". Ebon tract; Majuro tract; Mili tract.

Erbar (**yerbar**). Also *Ārbar.* Unanalyz. Maloelap islet.

Erḷañ (**yerḷag**). Part. reminisc. gramm. See *er-, ḷañ:* "getting a storm". Kwajalein tract; Jabwot tract.

Ero (**yẹrẹw**). Gramm. See *ro* "he is disappointed". Kwajalein islet.

Erra (**yẹrrah**). Gramm. See *Erra* "navigational sign". Namorik tract.

Etaañ (**yetahag**). Part. reminisc. gramm. See *añ* "wind". Arno tract; Mili tract.

Ettar-kaṇ (**yettar-kaṇ**). Unanalyz. Rongelap tract.

Ewe-ṇa (**yewey-ṇah**). Gramm. distort. See *ewe, ṇa:* "on a shoal". Maloelap tract.

Ewe-ṇo (**yewey-ṇ°ew**). Gramm. distort. See *ewe, ṇo:* "on the waves". Ujae tract.

Ewerōk (**yẹwẹyrẹk**). Gramm. See *Ewerōk* "land of departed spirits". Likiep tract; Arno tract.

Iakjo (**yiyakjẹw**). From Japn. *yakusho* "town house". Ujelang tract.

Iio (**yiyẹw**). Gramm. See *iio* "the whole". Ebon islet.

Ijo-eṇ (**yijẹw-yeṇ**). Gramm. See *ijo* "good soil". Namu tract; Ailinglapalap tract; Arno district; Arno islet.

Ijo-kaṇ (**yijẹw-kaṇ**). Gramm. Erikub islet.

Ilel-eṇ (**yilyẹl-yeṇ**). Recur. form. Ailinglapalap islet; Majuro islet.

Ilel-kaṇ (**yilyẹl-kaṇ**). Recur. form. Two Arno islets; Mili islet; Knox islet.

Ilel-lañin-ato (**yilyẹl-lagin-hatew**). Part. reminisc. gramm. Arno islet.

Ilelen-ñe (**yilyẹlẹn-gẹy**). Gramm. See *ilel, ñe:* "pile of rubble of the separate reef". Arno islet.

Iṃroj (**yiṃr°ej**). Reminisc. gramm. See *eṃ, roj:* "ebb tide house". Jaluit islet.

Iṃweelel (**yiṃeyelyẹl**). Unanalyz. Arno islet.

Iṃwej (**yiṃyẹj**). Reminisc. gramm. See *eṃ, ej:* "eastern house" or *iṃ, ej* "glimpse to the east". Jaluit district; Jaluit islet.

Iṃwin-juwi (**yiṃin-jiwiy**). Gramm. See *juwi:* "house of terns". Two Ujelang tracts.

Iṃwin-keotak (**yiṃin-kẹyẹwtak**). Gramm. See *keotak* "give birth". Ujelang tract.

Iṃwin-kūbwe (**yiṃin-kibey**). Gramm. See *kūbwe:* "house of feces". Ujelang tract.

Iṃwin-wiawe (**yiṃin-wiyahwẹy**). Gramm. See *wiawe:* "house of lizards". Ujelang tract.

Ine (**yinẹy**). Gramm. See *ine* "carrying stick". Arno district; Arno islet.

Ineekto (**yineyektẹw**). Gramm. See *inene, to:* "carry on shoulders westward". Likiep tract.

Intiia (**yintiyiyah**). From Engl. *India*. Arno tract.

Iñlen (**yiglen**). From Engl. *England*. Majuro tract.

Iojrwe (**yiyẹwẹjr°ẹy**). Reminisc. gramm. See *io, jore:* "here it is, a taboo relationship". Arno tract.

Irooj (**yirẹwẹj**). Gramm. See *irooj* "chief". Majuro islet.

Irooj-eṃṃaan (**yirewej-yemṃahan**). Gramm. See *irooj-eṃṃaan* "commoner married to royal woman". Wotho islet; Namu islet.

It-kaṇ (**yit-kaṇ**). Gramm. See *it* "make fire". Rongelap islet.

Itōbana (**yitebanah**). From Japn. (?) Jaluit islet.

Iukden (**yiqdẹn**). Gramm. See *iu, kiden* "small beach borage, just sprouted". Eniwetak islet.

Iukkure-kaṇ (**yiqqirẹy-kaṇ**). Gramm. See *kkure* "play". Two Ailinglapalap tracts.

Ja-doul (**jah-dẹwil**). Gramm. See *ja, doulul:* "round harbor"; see also *lijadoul* "small and round". Arno islet.

Ja-eo (**jah-yew**). Gramm. See *ja:* "harbor" or "the place for men". Ailuk islet; Arno tract.

Jaapañ (**jahapag**). Gramm. See *apañ:* "we are hindered". Aur tract.

Jaar (**jahar**). Gramm. See *jaar* "chief's sanctuary". Jaluit islet.

Jab-ajeej (**jab-hajẹyẹj**). Gramm. See *jab, ajej:* "do not divide". Maloelap household.

Jab-ej (**jab-yẹj**). Reminisc. gramm. See *jab, ej:* "not above (do not get your heads above the bushes as you watch the approaching fleet from the shore)" or *jabōn, ej:* "eastern corner". Ebon tract; Maloelap tract; Aur tract.

Jab-eṇ (**jab-yeṇ**). Gramm. See *jab:* "that direction". Arno tract.

Jab-ilo-ae (**jab-yilew-hayey**). Gramm. See *ae:* "not in the current". Namu tract.

Jab-ilo-ae-iōñ (**jab-yilew-hayey-yiyẹg**). Gramm. Namu tract.

Jab-lo-buoj (**jab-lẹw-biwẹj**). Reminisc. gramm. See *buoj:* "not see the navigation junction". Knox tract.

Jab-lu-iaḷ (**jab-liw-yiyaḷ**). Reminisc. gramm. See *iaḷ:* "not on the path". Ujae tract.

Jab-toḷoñ-eṇ (**jab-teḷ°eg-yeṇ**). Gramm. See *toḷoñ:* "cannot pass through". Bikini tract.

Jab-toḷoñe (**jab-teḷ°egey**). Gramm. See *toḷoñ:* "cannot penetrate it". Ujae tract; Kwajalein tract; Namorik tract.

Jabalur (**jabalir°**). Gramm. See *jabalur* "shade". Kwajalein tract.

Jabat (**jabat**). Gramm. distort. See *Jebat* "ralik island", *jabōt* "shepherd", *Jabōt* "Sabbath, *bat:* "we are late"(?) Majuro tract.

Jabbe (**jabbẹy**). Gramm. distort. See *bwe:* "not enough". Mejit tract; Ailuk islet.

Jabjabōn (**jabjaben**). Gramm. See *jabjab* "out of reach". Mili islet.

Jabjatete (**jabjatẹytẹy**). Reminisc. gramm. See *tiete:* "end of the reef". Maloelap islet.

Jabjedoñe (**jabjedeg°ey**). Unanalyz. Namorik tract.

Jabkaṃan (**jabkaṃan**). Unanalyz. Arno tract.

Jabkōl (**jabkel**). Gramm. See *jab, kōl:* "not fertile". Majuro tract; Mili tract.

Jabkwōl (**jabqel**). Gramm. distort. Ebon tract.

Jabkwōn (**jabqen**). Gramm. See *jabok:* "part of it". Rongelap tract.

Jable (**jablẹy**). Part. recur. form. See *le* "a bird", "not estranged". Kwajalein tract; Namu tract; Mili tract.

Jabḷeen-kijdik (**jabḷeyen-kijdik**). Gramm. See *ḷeen kijdik:* "toadstool point". Knox islet.

Jabnodān (**jabnewdan**). Part. reminisc. gramm. See *jabōn, wōd* "the tip of its coral". Jaluit islet.

Jabṇae (**jabṇahyey**). Part. reminisc. gramm. See *jab, ṇae:* "not against (me but for me, referring to an argument)". Ujae tract.

Jabọọn (**jabawan**). Reminisc. gramm. See *jab, owan* "not lazy"; see also place names *Jabwan* and *Jebwan.* Aur tract.

Jabōjjaat (**jabejjahat**). Part. reminisc. gramm. See *jabōn, jaat:* "end of the chart". Namorik tract.

Jabōjjirooj (**jabejjirewej**). Reminisc. gramm. See *irooj* "chief". Ebon tract.

Jabōḷḷā (**jabeḷḷay**). Gramm. See *ḷḷā:* "cannot pass by". Kili tract.

Jabōn-aidikdik (**jaben-hayidikdik**). Gramm. See *aidik:* "narrow tip". Jaluit tract; Arno tract.

Jabōn-āneo (**jaben-yanyew**). Gramm. distort. See *āne:* "end of the islet". Jaluit tract.

Jabōn-ānin (**jaben-yanyin**). Gramm. See *āne:* "end of this isle". Ailinglapalap islet; Ailinglapalap tract.

Jabōn-bar (**jaben-bar**). Gramm. See *bar:* "tip of the rock". Bikini tract; Majuro tract.

Jabōn-bar-eņ (jaben-bar-yeņ). Gramm.
Aur tract; Majuro tract.

Jabōn-bok (jaben-beq). Gramm. See *bok:*
"tip of the sandspit". Rongelap tract;
Lae tract; Ujae tract; Lib tract;
Kwajalein tract; Ailinglapalap tract;
Jaluit tract; Namorik tract; Likiep
tract; Maloelap tract; Aur tract; Majuro
tract; Arno tract.

Jabōn-bok-ioḷap (jaben-beq-yiyewḷap).
Gramm. Jaluit tract.

Jabōn-bok-iōñ (jaben-beq-yiyęg).
Gramm. Aur tract.

Jabōn-bok-rālik (jaben-beq-raylik).
Gramm. Jaluit tract.

Jabōn-bok-reeaar (jaben-beq-reyyahar).
Gramm. Jaluit tract.

Jabōn-bok-rōk (jaben-beq-ręk). Gramm.
Aur tract.

Jabōn-bōl (jaben-bęl). Gramm. See *bōl:*
"end of the taro pit". Jaluit tract.

Jabōn-ekeke (jaben-yękęykęy). Gramm.
distort. See *eke* "vein" or *keke* "sew".
Mili tract.

Jabōn-Etao (jaben-yetahwew). Gramm.
See *Etao* "legendary trickster".
Rongelap tract.

Jabōn-jāāp (jaben-jayap). Gramm. Loan
from Germ.(?) Arno tract.

Jabōn-kiwūl (jaben-kiywil). Recur. form.
See *kiwūl:* "end of the islet". Arno
tract; Mili tract.

Jabōn-kōnnaan (jaben-kennahan).
Gramm. See *jabōnkōnnaan*
"proverb". Arno tract.

Jabōn-kūrañrañ (jaben-kiragrag).
Reminisc. gramm. See *kūrañ* "a plant"
or *rañrañ* "get warm by a fire". Ebon
tract.

Jabōn-laḷ (jaben-laḷ). Gramm. See *laḷ:*
"tip of the earth", "low or western
tip". Maloelap household.

Jabōn-looj (jaben-lęwęj). Recur. form.
See *lo, wōj:* "see beauty" or *Looj* "an
islet and a clan name (*RiLoojraņ*).
Jaluit tract.

Jabōn-Ḷare (jaben-ḷaręy). Pers. name.
Mili tract.

Jabōn-na (jaben-nah). Reminisc. gramm.
See *ņa* "shoal". Ailinglapalap tract.

Jabōn-pāāt (jaben-payat). Gramm. See
pāāt "low tide". Lib tract;
Ailinglapalap tract; two Jaluit tracts;
Wotje tract.

Jabōn-welǫk-eņ (jaben-weylaq-yeņ).
Gramm. See *welǫk:* "go up on an islet
from the reef". Arno tract.

Jabōn-wōd (jaben-wed). Gramm. See
wōd "coral". Ujae district; Kwajalein
islet; two Kwajalein tracts; Erikub islet;
Arno district; Arno tract; Mili islet.

Jabōn-wōj (jaben-wej). Unanalyz. Wotho
tract.

Jabrok (jabręq). Gramm. See *rok* "not
disappointed". Majuro tract.

Jabtiete (jabtiyetey). Reminisc. gramm.
See *tiete:* "end of the reef". Majuro
tract.

Jabuknǫk (jabiqnaq). Part. reminisc.
gramm. See *jabuk* "fishing method".
Namorik tract.

Jabuknǫk (jabiqnaq). Part. reminisc.
gramm. Namu tract.

Jabukwi (jabiqiy). Gramm. See *jabuk:*
"catch them with the long net". Jaluit
tract.

Jabwan (jabwan). Reminisc. gramm.
Mili tract.

Jabwe-jād-eņ (jabey-jad-yeņ). Gramm.
distort. See *jād:* "end of the drying
rack". Arno tract.

Jabwe-jorjoron (jabęy-jęr°jęr°en).
Gramm. distort. See *jorjor:* "point of
his walking fast". Arno tract.

Jabwe-ņo (jabey-ņew). Gramm. distort.
See *ņo* "waves". Two Aur tracts.

Jabwe-ro (jabwęy-ręw). Reminisc.
gramm. See *ro* "jump into the water".
Ailinglapalap tract.

Jabwi-ņa-eņ (jabiy-ņah-yeņ). Gramm.
distort. See *ņa:* "tip of the shoal".
Rongelap tract.

Jabwi-roñ (jabiy-reg°). Gramm. distort.
See *rǫñ:* "point of the hole (of a
legendary eel (*Lijinolōr*) who came
here from Jemo. Likiep tract.

Jade-eņ (jahdęy-yeņ). Gramm. See *jade*
"roost". Namu tract; Ailinglapalap
tract; Ebon tract.

Jade-ko (jahdęy-kew). Gramm. Mejit
tract.

Jaerpit (jahyerpit). Reminisc. gramm. See
pit: "seasoned lumber". Namu tract.

Jake-pǫ (jakęy-paw). Part. reminisc.
gramm. Lib tract.

Jako-ḷǫkjeņ (jakęw-ḷaqjeņ). Reminisc.
gramm. See *jako:* "go away from
there". Arno islet.

Jakǫuj (jakawij). Unanalyz. Kwajalein
sandspit.

Jakroot (**jakrẹwẹt**). Unanalyz. Kwajalein islet.

Jaļto (**jaļtẹw**). Gramm. See *jaļ, to:* "facing westward". Arno tract.

Jaļto-rōk-eņ (**jaļtẹw-rẹk-yeņ**). Gramm. Ebon tract.

Jaļtokwōn-eņ (**jaļteqen-yeņ**). Gramm. See *jaļtok:* "his adze". Arno tract.

Jaļtoon-ej (**jaļtẹwẹn-yẹj**). Reminisc. gramm. See *jaļ, to:* "facing westward, on the east". Likiep islet.

Jaļtu-ej (**jaļtiw-yẹj**). Gramm. distort. See *jaļ, to:* "facing westward, on the east". Mili islet.

Jaṃo (**jahṃew**). Unanalyz. Mili tract.

Jaṃuwa (**jahṃiwwah**). From Samoa. Arno islet.

Jañai (**jahgahyiy**). From Engl. *Shang-Hai*. Bikini tract; Namu tract.

Jañi-dekā (**jagiy-dekay**). Reminisc. gramm. Aur tract.

Jarebuñ (**jarẹybig°**). Also *Jadebuñ* (**jadẹybig°**). Reminisc. gramm. See *jade, buñ:* "roost and fall". Maloelap tract.

Jarkul (**jarqil**). Gramm. See *jarkul* "a navigational sign". Arno islet.

Jarōj (**jarej**). Also *Rita* (**riytah**). Gramm. See *jarōj*. Majuro district; Majuro islet.

Jatakā (**jatakay**). Reminisc. gramm. See *jatak* "wave ready to break". Kwajalein coral head.

Jatloñ (**jatleg°**). Gramm. See *jatlōñ* "unfavorable tide". Utirik tract; Maloelap tract.

Jatļoñ (**jatļeg°**). Also *Jatloñ*. Reminisc. gramm. See *jat, ļoñ:* "deep water". Utirik tract.

Jato (**jatew**). Gramm. Lib tract.

Jatōptōp (**jateptep**). Gramm. See *jatōptōp* "stand firm". Rongerik tract.

Jattimlij (**jattimlij**). Pers. name. Name of a legendary messenger. Ebon tract.

Jā (**jay**). Gramm. See *jā* "falling sail". Kwajalein islet; Ailinglapalap islet.

Jāāļtō (**jayaļteh**). Reminisc. gramm. See *jāālel, tok:* "waft this way". Majuro district.

Jāāñ (**jayag**). Reminisc. gramm. See *jā, eañ* "capsize in the north". Maloelap district; Maloelap islet.

Jāār-eņ (**jayar-yeņ**). Gramm. See *jāār* "method of cooking fish". Three Arno tracts.

Jāātṃwiin (**jayatṃiyin**). Gramm. See *ātāt:* "we smell this house". Ailinglapalap tract.

Jāden (**jaden**). Unanalyz. Kwajalein tract.

Jādkinļat (**jadkinļat**). Part. reminisc. gramm. See *jād, kōn, ļat:* "drying rack with coconut shell". Jaluit tract.

Jādkul (**jadqil**). Part. recur. form. See *jād, kul.* Jaluit islet.

Jādoor (**jadewer**). Unanalyz. Eniwetak islet.

Jāidboñ (**jayidbẹg°**). Reminisc. gramm. See *jā, diboñ:* "cumulus clouds cover the sky on a dark night". Lae sandspit.

Jāiliñin (**jayiligin**). Reminisc. gramm. See *jā, lōñ:* "cumulus clouds above it". Ailinglapalap tract.

Jāina (**jayinah**). From Engl. *China.* Ebon tract; Mili tract.

Jāioon (**jayiyewen**). From Bibl. *Zion*. Namorik district.

Jālik (**jaylik**). Recur. form. See *jā, lik:* "sail falls on the ocean side". Eniwetak sandspit.

Jāloklap (**jaleqļap**). Recur. form. Ailuk islet; Majuro district.

Jālooj (**jalẹwẹj**). Also *Jalwōj* (**jalwẹj**), *jelwōj* (**jẹlwẹj**). Recur. form. See *jāl, wōj:* "facing you" or "facing beauty". Ralik atoll; Jaluit; Jaluit district; Jaluit islet.

Jālōte (**jaletey**). Gramm. See *jālōt:* "not well sifted, not thoroughly done". Bikini islet.

Jāltokwōn-eņ (**jalteqen-yeņ**). Gramm. Arno tract.

Jālturōk (**jaltiwrẹk**). Gramm. See *jāl, tu, rōk:* "face southward". Arno tract.

Jāltuweņo (**jaltiweyņew**). Reminisc. gramm. See *jāl* "facing", *tuwe* "westward", *ņo* "waves". Wotho tract; Mejit tract.

Jālukra (**jaliqrah**). Unanalyz. Likiep tract.

Jāmne (**jamney**). From Engl. *Germany*. Wotje tract.

Jāmǫ (**jaymaw**). Reminisc. gramm. See *mǫ* "taboo". Ratak island; Jemo; Aur tract.

Jāneed (**janẹyẹd**). Recur. form. See *ed* "skirt mat". Namu islet.

Jānlā (**janlay**). Part. recur. form. See *jān, ļā* "from the gravel". Bikini tract.

Jānmā (**janmay**). Part. recur. form. See *jān, mā* "from the breadfruit". Wotje tract.

Jānm̧a-eņ (**janm̧ah-yeņ**). Unanalyz. Arno tract.

Jāpeej (**japęyęj**). Unanalyz. Maloelap tract.

Jāpik (**japik**). Gramm. distort. See *jāpek* "a fish". Kwajalein islet.

Jāple (**japlęy**). Pers. name. A legendary woman. Majuro tract.

Jāpo (**japęw**). Unanalyz. Arno district; Arno islet.

Je (**jey**). Unanalyz. Ailinglapalap district; Ailinglapalap islet.

Jebaeañ-eañ (**jebahyag-yag**). Unanalyz. Arno tract.

Jebaeañ-rak (**jebahyag-rak**). Unanalyz. Arno tract.

Jebal (**jeybal**). Reminisc. gramm. See *jeballe* "to rock". Majuro tract.

Jebañōt (**jębangęt**). Unanalyz. Ailuk islet.

Jebat (**jebat**). Reminisc. gramm. See *bat* "hill". Ralik island; Jabwot.

Jebjaan (**jebjahan**). Unanalyz. Ailinglapalap tract.

Jebļotak (**jebļewtak**). Gramm. distort. See *jab, ļotak:* "not born". Jaluit tract.

Jebņa (**jebņah**). Gramm. See *jeb-, ņa:* "reach the shoal". Jaluit islet; Arno islet.

Jeboojia (**jębęwęjiyah**). Gramm. See *booj:* "which knot are we in?", "which constitution do we obey?", "where do we live?" Namorik tract.

Jebōtjaat (**jebetjahat**). See *Jabōjjaat.* Namorik tract.

Jebrǫ (**jebraw**). Pers. name. See *Jebrǫ.* Maloelap islet.

Jebrǫ-rālik (**jebraw-raylik**). Gramm. Ailinglapalap tract.

Jebrǫ-rear (**jebraw-reyhar**). Gramm. Ailinglapalap tract.

Jebtōkā (**jebtekay**). Gramm. See *jeb-, tōkā:* "reach the long reef". Rongelap tract.

Jebwad (**jebwad**). Unanalyz. See *Jebņa* and *Jebtōkā.* Jaluit district; Jaluit islet; Arno islet.

Jebwan (**jebwan**). Unanalyz. Ailinglapalap district; Ailinglapalap islet.

Jebwā (**jebay**). Gramm. See *jebwā* "a coral"; *jebwābwe* "be lost". Ebon tract.

Jedeju (**jedejiw**). Reminisc. gramm. See *jedjed iju* "look up at the stars". Mejit tract; Majuro tract.

Jedelañ (**jedeylag**). Gramm. See *jedelañ* "supine; observe the heavens; look up at the sky". Ailinglapalap tract; Jaluit tract.

Jedko (**jedkew**). Loan from Bibl. *Jericho.* Ujelang islet; Mejit tract; Likiep tract; Maloelap islet; Arno islet.

Jedkul (**jedqil**). Recur. form. See *kul.* Likiep tract.

Jeerkǫǫj (**jeyerkawaj**). Unanalyz. Ujae tract.

Jei-iōñ (**jęyiy-yiyęg**). Reminisc. gramm. See *je, ije:* "here in the north". Erikub district.

Jei-rōk (**jęyiy-ręk**). Reminisc. gramm. See *je, ije:* "here in the south". Erikub district; Majuro district.

Jeik (**jęyik**). Gramm. See *jeik* "tack around them; turn". Namu islet; Majuro tract.

Jeiñ (**jęyig**). Gramm. See *iñ:* "we are angry". Majuro tract.

Jejeik (**jęyjęyik**). Gramm. Majuro tract.

Jejem̧ (**jejem̧**). Gramm. See *jjem̧* "brittle". Maloelap islet.

Jejerwa (**jęjęrwah**). Gramm. See *jejer, wa* "look for a canoe". Utirik household.

Jekar (**jekar**). Recur. form. See *jekar.* Ebon tract; Mejit tract; Ailuk tract; Maloelap tract; Arno tract; Mili islet.

Jekar-aidikdik (**jekar-hayidikdik**). Recur. form. Ailuk tract.

Jekar-iōñ (**jekar-yiyęg**). Recur. form. Aur tract.

Jekar-rōk (**jekar-ręk**). Recur. form. Aur tract.

Jekiik-tok (**jekiyik-teq**). Gramm. See *jjeikik* "excited". Lae tract.

Jekkōto-in (**jękkętęw-yin**). Gramm. See *jek, kōto:* "cut the wind". Majuro tract.

Jeklikin (**jęklikin**). Reminisc. gramm. See *jek, likin:* "cut his back", "chop at the ocean side". Bikini tract.

Jeklikin-rāirōk (**jęklikin-rayiręk**). Reminisc. gramm. Bikini tract.

Jekņak (**jekņak**). Gramm. See *kōņak:* "we love". Utirik tract.

Jekrak (**jekrak**). Unanalyz. Ebon tract.

Jelbōn (**jẹlben**). Gramm. Mili islet.

Jele (**jẹlẹy**). Gramm. See *jele* "harvest fruit". Aur islet.

Jelleḷọk (**jelleyḷaq**). Gramm. See *llelọk:* "we are changed". Mili tract.

Jeḷā-eṇ (**jeḷay-yeṇ**). Gramm. See *jeḷā:* "that knowledge". Ailinginae islet.

Jeḷeiwa (**jeḷẹyiywah**). Part. reminisc. gramm. See *Jeḷeilōñ, wa.* Namu tract.

Jeḷo (**jeyḷew**). From Engl. *sail ho!.* Mejit tract.

Jeḷtoon-ej (**jeḷtẹwẹn-yẹj**). Reminisc. gramm. See *jaḷ, to, ej:* "facing its eastern pass". Erikub islet.

Jemājirok-ej (**jemajirẹq-yẹj**). Gramm. See *jemājirok* "climbing rope". Arno tract.

Jemāluut (**jemayliwit**). Pers. name. A legendary man. Utirik household.

Jemān-iōñ (**jeman-yiyẹg**). Recur. form. See *jema-, iōñ.* Arno tract.

Jemān-meñ (**jeman-mẹg**). Part. recur. form. See *jema-, meñ.* Arno islet.

Jemān-rōk (**jeman-rẹk**). Recur. form. Arno tract.

Jemeja-eṇ (**jemejah-yeṇ**). Pers. name. Younger brother of *Jemāluut.* Arno tract.

Jemene (**jemeney**). From Engl. *Germany.* Mejit tract.

Jeṃaan (**jeṃahan**). Part. reminisc. gramm. See *ṃaan* "forward". Mejit tract.

Jenbōn-kaṇ (**jẹnbẹn-kaṇ**). Part. reminisc. gramm. See *Jelbōn* "Mili islet"; *bōn* "place for making magic". Ebon tract.

Jenkā (**jẹnkay**). Also *Jenokkwā* (**jẹnẹqqay**). Gramm. See *jenok:* "these footprints". Likiep islet.

Jenliklik (**jenliklik**). Gramm. See *jenliklik* "retreat". Bikar islet.

Jenmaanlọk (**jenmahanlaq**). Part. reminisc. gramm. See *jen, anlọk:* "let's put it on our bow". Maloelap islet.

Jenmọun (**jenmawin**). Part. recur. form. See *mọun:* "let's make magic." Ailinglapalap islet.

Jennepnep (**jennepnep**). Unanalyz. Majuro tract.

Jenokkwā (**jẹnẹqqay**). Variant form of *Jenkā* (**jẹnkay**).

Jeṇ-ioḷap (**jeṇ-yiyewḷap**). Gramm. See *jeṇ* "there in the middle". Utirik tract.

Jeṇ-iōñ (**jeṇ-yiyẹg**). Gramm. See *jeṇ* "there in the north". Kwajalein tract; three Wotje tracts.

Jeṇ-irōk (**jeṇ-yirẹk**). Gramm. See *jeṇ* "there in the south". Jaluit tract.

Jeṇrōk (**jeṇrẹk**). Reminisc. gramm. See *jeṇ* "there, *rōk* "south". Kwajalein tract; four Jaluit tracts; Utirik tract; Ailuk tract; three Wotje tracts; Majuro tract.

Jepaan (**jepahan**). From Engl. *Japan.* Jaluit tract.

Jepakina (**jepahkinah**). Reminisc. gramm. See *jepa, kina:* "ugly shoal". Arno islet.

Jepaḷ (**jepaḷ**). Gramm. See *paḷ:* "we are angry". Likiep islet.

Jepao (**jepahwew**). Gramm. distort. See *pao:* "we appear". Namorik tract.

Jepāde (**jepadẹy**). Gramm. See *jepāde* "cannery". Utirik tract.

Jepāl (**jẹypal**). Gramm. See *jepāl* "bear sporadically". Majuro tract.

Jepān-or (**jepan-wer**). Reminisc. gramm. See *jāp* "cheek", *or* (a formant): "cheek of the *or*". Namorik tract.

Jepeet (**jepeyet**). Unanalyz. Jaluit islet.

Jepeik (**jepeyik**). Reminisc. gramm. See *jepe, ek:* "fish basket". Ailuk islet.

Jepet-eṇ (**jepet-yeṇ**). Gramm. See *jepet* "lure". Majuro tract.

Jepjowe (**jẹpjewwey**). Gramm. See *jep, jowe* "place of the pandanus harvest". Ailuk tract.

Jepjowe (**jepjewey**). Gramm. distort. Arno tract.

Jepḷaakin-pako (**jepḷahakin-pakew**). Gramm. See *jepḷaak, pako:* "return of the shark". Ailinglapalap tract.

Jepṇa (**jepṇah**). Reminisc. gramm. See *ṇa* "shoal". Jaluit islet.

Jepñọo (**jepgawẹw**). Also *Jepño* (**jepgẹw**). Unanalyz. Arno tract.

Jepo (**jepẹw**). Reminisc. gramm. See *po:* "we land". Ailinglapalap islet.

Jepta (**jeptah**). Gramm. See *jepta* "sieve arrowroot first time (see sister islet *Epta*)". Ailuk islet.

Jeptaan (**jeptahan**). Gramm. See *jepta:* "its first time through the strainer". Eniwetak islet.

Jeraak (**jerahak**). Gramm. See *raak:* "we move". Kwajalein islet.

Jeraakto (**jerahaktẹw**). Gramm. See *raak:* "we move westward". Mejit tract.

Jerata-kaṇ (**jerahtah-kaṇ**). Gramm. See *jerata:* "those misfortunes". Arno tract.

Jerea (**jereyah**). From Bibl. *Syria*. Ailinginae islet.

Jerḷañ (**jerlan**). Recur. form. See *ḷañ* "storm". Jaluit islet.

Jetakin-iaḷ (**jetakin-yiyaḷ**). Gramm. See *jetak:* "east side of the road". Mili tract.

Jetā (**jetay**). Unanalyz. Lib tract.

Jibatur (**jibatir°**). Unanalyz. Namorik tract.

Jibkōn-wūdej (**jibken-widẹj**). Part. reminisc. gramm. See *wūdej* "cuckoo"; see *jipkōn-ak-eṇ,* Namorik tract. Ujelang tract.

Jibokra (**jibẹqrah**). Reminisc. gramm. See *jipikra* "slapping of waves". Rongelap tract.

Jibwin-men (**jibin-men**). Reminisc. gramm. See *jibwi-, men* "grandmother of things or animals" or "his pet creature". Rongelap tract, Mili islet.

Jidaakin-ej (**jidahakin-yẹj**). Gramm. See *jidaak, ej:* "landing on the east". Mejit tract.

Jidaakin-wa (**jidahakin-wah**). Gramm. See *jidaak:* "canoe landing". Taka tract.

Jidbokbok-kaṇ (**jidbẹqbẹq-kaṇ**). Part. reminisc. gramm. See *bokbok* "sandy". Jaluit islet.

Jidiia (**jidiyiyah**). From Bibl. *Syria*. Mili tract.

Jien-pel (**jiyen-pẹl**). Gramm. See *je* "belly of the boxfish". Majuro tract; Arno tract.

Jiiaḷ (**jiyyaḷ**). Part. reminisc. gramm. Maloelap tract; Maloelap household.

Jijo-kaṇ (**jijẹw-kaṇ**). Gramm. Majuro tract.

Jikako (**jikakẹw**). From Engl. *Chicago*. Lae tract.

Jikin-jerbal (**jikin-jerbal**). Gramm. Bikini tract.

Jikin-wa-iōñ (**jikin-wah-yiyẹg**). Gramm. Mili tract.

Jikin-wa-irōk (**jikin-wah-yirẹk**). Gramm. Mili tract.

Jikipdu (**jikipdiw**). Gramm. See *jikip, du:* "many people gather to dance". Wotje tract.

Jikke (**jikkẹy**). Gramm. Likiep tract.

Jikōpeo (**jikepyew**). Gramm. See *Jikōpeo* "pandanus variety". Mejit tract.

Jilañ (**jilag**). Gramm. See *lañ* "middle of the sky". Arno islet.

Jilej (**jilẹj**). Gramm. See *jilej* "where the *wūlej* grows". Maloelap tract.

Jilel (**jilẹl**). Gramm. Jaluit tract.

Jilñid (**jilgid**). Unanalyz. Jaluit tract.

Jiḷoon (**jiḷewen**). From Engl. *Ceylon*. Lae tract; Jaluit islet; Arno islet; Arno tract.

Jiṃ-eṇ (**jiṃ-yeṇ**). Gramm. See *jiṃ* "tip of the canoe". Knox tract.

Jiṃṃūḷọk (**jiṃṃiḷaq**). Gramm. See *jiṃṃūḷọk* "eternity". Mili tract.

Jiṃwin-ne (**jiṃin-ney**). Gramm. See *jiṃwin ne* "heel". Ailinglapalap tract; Arno islet.

Jinai (**jinahiy**). From Bibl. *Sinai*. Namorik district.

Jinbaad-kaṇ (**jinbahad-kaṇ**). Unanalyz. Majuro tract.

Jinbwi (**jinbiy**). Unanalyz. Bikini tract; Namu tract.

Jinimjedu (**jinimjẹdiw**). Unanalyz. Arno household.

Jinimnọñ (**jinimnag°**). Unanalyz. Arno household.

Jinme (**jinmey**). Unanalyz. Eniwetak islet.

Jinok (**jineq**). Gramm. distort. See *jenok* "footprint". Majuro tract.

Jinokme (**jineqmey**). Part. reminisc. gramm. Arno islet.

Jinọkoṇ (**jinaqeṇ**). Gramm. distort. Eniwetak tract.

Jinōro (**jinerew**). Unanalyz. Eniwetak islet.

Jinpaḷ (**jinpaḷ**). Reminisc. gramm. See *bwijin paḷ* "lots of sandpaper coral". Jaluit islet.

Jintao (**jintahwew**). From Chinese place name *Ching-tao*. Maloelap tract.

Jinwōd (**jinwed**). Gramm. See *jinwōd* "collect fruit". Arno tract.

Jiped-kūbwe (**jiped-kibey**). Gramm. See *jiped, kūbwe* "flatten feces". Aur tract.

Jiped-pọ (**jiped-paw**). Part. reminisc. gramm. See *jiped, pọ* "flatten entering the coral". Rongerik islet.

Jipein (**jipẹyin**). From Engl. *Spain*. Mili islet; Likiep tract.

Jipila (**jipilah**). Gramm. See *jipila* "baby tern". Taongi islet.

Jipkōn-ak-eṇ (**jipken-hak-yeṇ**). Gramm. See *jipkōn, ak:* "roost of the frigate bird". Namorik tract.

Jiroñ (**jireg°**). Gramm. See *jiroñ* "maiden". Jaluit tract.

Jiroñ-kaṇ (**jireg°-kaṇ**). Gramm. Ailuk islet.

Jiruujlem (**jiriwijlem**). From Bibl. *Jerusalem*. Arno islet.

Jiruullōñ (**jiriwillęg**). Pers. name, a demon who inhabits this tract. Mili tract.

Jitlǫk-kaṇ (**jitlaq-kaṇ**). Gramm. See *jitḷok:* "those plantation plantings". Ailinglapalap tract; Jaluit tract; Majuro tract.

Jitlōñḷǫk (**jitlęgḷaq**). Gramm. See *jitolōñ* "stand up straight". Mili tract.

Jitni (**jitniy**). From Engl. *Sydney*. Jaluit tract; Utirik household; Maloelap household; Majuro tract; Mili islet.

Jitniñeañ-eṇ (**jitnigyag-yeṇ**). Gramm. See *jitniñeañ* "lies straight northward". Wotho district; Lib district; Likiep trac.

Jitniñiañ (**jitnigyiyag**). Gramm. Rongelap district.

Jitōn-or (**jiten-wer**). Part. reminisc. gramm. See *Jepān-or, jit, jitnen ṃōṃō:* "head or point of the *or* (?)". Rongerik tract.

Jitrōkeañ (**jitrękyag**). Gramm. See *jitrōkeañ* "lies straight southward". Wotho district.

Jitrōkeañ-eṇ (**jitrękyag-yeṇ**). Gramm. Lib district; two Likiep tracts; Arno tract.

Jitrōkiañ (**jitrękyiyag**). Gramm. Rongelap district.

Jitto-eṇ (**jittęw-yeṇ**). Gramm. See *jitto* "head westward". Ujelang district; Ujelang tract; Bikini district; three Rongelap districts; Rongerik district; Ailinginae district; Ujae district; Kwajalein district; four Namu districts; three Ailinglapalap tracts; Likiep district; Ebon district; Ebon tract; Utirik district; Utirik tract; two Ailuk districts; four Likiep tracts; Wotje tract; two Maloelap tracts; two Aur tracts; Majuro tract; six Arno tracts; seven Mili tracts.

Jittok-eṇ (**jitteq-yeṇ**). Gramm. See *tok* "head in this direction". Bikini tract; Jaluit district; Mili tract.

Jo-eṇ-ḷap (**jew-yeṇ-ḷap**). Gramm. See *jo:* "that large fishing place". Namu tract; Majuro tract.

Joba (**jewbah**). From Engl. *sofa*. Wotje tract.

Jobōran (**jewberan**). Gramm. See *jo, bar* "its head appears". Ailinglapalap tract.

Jokdik (**jeqdik**). Part. recur. form. See *jok:* "small perch". Rongelap islet.

Jokiae (**jewkiyhayey**). Gramm. See *jokiae* "young stage of coconut growth". Ebon tract.

Jokoojwa (**jęqęwęjwah**). Gramm. See *jokoojwa* "grated coconut". Ebon tract.

Jolen (**jęwlęn**). Unanalyz. Wotje islet.

Jolen-iōñ (**jęwlęn-yiyęg**). Unanalyz. Wotje islet.

Joñ-eṇ (**jeg°-yeṇ**). Gramm. See *joñ* "mangrove". Kwajalein tract.

Joñ-eṇ-dik (**jeg°-yeṇ-dik**). Gramm. Arno islet.

Joñ-kaṇ (**jeg°-kaṇ**). Gramm. Majuro tract.

Joñain (**jeg°ahyin**). Unanalyz. Mejit tract.

Joñǫk (**jeg°aq**). Also *joñak.* Gramm. See *joñak* "measure". Majuro tract.

Joonmej (**jewenmęj**). Recur. form. See *joon, mej:* "nearly die". Namorik tract.

Joor-kaṇ (**jęwęr-kaṇ**). Gramm. See *joor:* "those posts", "those tall trees". Rongelap islet.

Joorjāne (**jewerjanęy**). Also *Jeorjāne* (**jeyer°janęy**). Gramm. distort. See *jeor, joor, jān:* "escape from him", "turn from it". Likiep tract.

Joraan (**jęr°ahan**). Pers. name. Mejit district.

Joranikiōk (**jer°hanikiyęk**). Gramm. distort. See *jor, an, kiōk* "how he can wear his grass skirt". Ailuk tract.

Jorñak (**jer°gak**). Gramm. See *jorñak* "go fast". Mili tract.

Jotōṃ (**jewteṃ**). From Bibl. *Sodom.* Namu tract; Ailinglapalap tract.

Jounbar (**jęwinbar**). Part. reminisc. gramm. Eniwetak islet.

Jowapin (**jewahpin**). Gramm. See *juwapin* "cricket". Ailinglapalap tract.

Jǫ (**jaw**). Gramm. See *jǫ* "place where turtle lays eggs and coconut crab hides". Ailinglapalap tract.

Jǫ-Likiep (**jaw-likiyep**). Recur. form. See *jǫ* "at Likiep". Likiep tract.

Jǫ-lo-pat (**jaw-lęw-pat**). Recur. form. See *jǫ, pat:* "be in the swamp", "sink in the swamp". Arno tract.

Jǫkur (**jaqir**). Gramm. See *jǫkur* "turtle shell". Utirik household.

Jǫm̧win-ak (**jawm̧in-hak**). Recur. form. See *ak:* "under the frigate bird". Ujae tract.

Jǫrwe (**jawr°ęy**). Gramm. See *jǫre* "ruined". Majuro tract.

Jōḷan̄ (**jęhḷag**). Unanalyz. Lae tract; Ebon tract.

Jujelto (**jiwjęltęw**). Part. recur. form. See *ju, jāl, to:* "vertical facing westward". Mili tract.

Juknen (**jiqnen**). Gramm. Mili islet; Mili tract.

Jukur (**jiqir°**). Gramm. See *jikur* "ditch". Mejit tract.

Julel (**jiwlel**). Also *Julel* (**jiwlęl**). Unanalyz. Likiep tract.

Juḷ-eņ (**jiḷ°-yeņ**). Gramm. See *juḷ:* "that sprout". Arno islet.

Juḷḷwe (**jiḷ°ḷ°ęy**). Gramm. See *juḷḷwe* "form a triangle with fish scarer". Maloelap tract.

Juḷu (**jiwḷ°iw**). From Sulu (*Sea*). Namorik district.

Juolik-iōn̄ (**jiwelik-yiyęg**). Unanalyz. Eniwetak tract.

Juroj (**jir°ęj**). Unanalyz. Ebon islet.

Jurujlem (**jir°ijlem**). From Bibl. *Jerusalem.* Namorik tract.

Jutak-eņ (**jiwtak-yeņ**). Gramm. See *jutak:* "stand up, a fighting stance". Mejit tract; Aur tract.

Jutokwōn-bon̄ (**jiwteqęn-bęg°**). Part. recur. form. See *jutak, tok, bon̄:* "someone stands up at night". Arno tract.

Jutōnkwaar (**jiwtenqahar**). Pers. name. Ailinglapalap tract.

Juwi (**jiwwiy**). Gramm. See *juwi* "white tern". Arno tract.

Kaat-eḷap (**kahat-yeḷap**). Gramm. See *kaatat:* "large *kaatat* plant". Arno islet.

Kabbijer (**kabbijęr**). Reminisc. gramm. See *kabwijer* "keep a canoe full sailing", *kabbe* "sail with the wind". Ailinglapalap tract.

Kabbil-ko (**kabbil-kew**). Gramm. See *bwil:* "places for burning". Mejit tract.

Kabbok (**kabbeq**). Gramm. See *kabbok* "breadfruit flower". Ailuk islet.

Kabjeran-kam̧o (**kabjeran-kam̧ew**). Gramm. See *kabwijeran, kam̧o:* "feast preparations that cause jealousy, as with the prodigal son". Namorik tract.

Kabjeri (**kabjeriy**). Gramm. See *kabwijer:* "control them". Namorik tract.

Kabokbok (**kabeqbeq**). Gramm. See *bokbok:* "covered with sand". Ailinglapalap tract.

Kabokbok-eņ (**kabeqbeq-yeņ**). Gramm. Jaluit tract.

Kabōdkōj (**kabędkęj**). Gramm. See *bōd:* "causes us to err". Maloelap tract.

Kabron̄ḷọk (**kabreg°ḷaq**). Gramm. See *kabron̄ḷọk* "warn". Majuro tract.

Kabtejo-reeaar (**kabteyjew-reyyahar**). Gramm. See *kabwit, jo:* "place where a plant grows that is used to prepare bait for goatfish". Wotje tract.

Kabtejo-rōtle (**kabteyjew-rętley**). Gramm. Wotje tract.

Kajāduḷot (**kajadiḷ°et**). Unanalyz. Lae tract.

Kajidkaallo (**kajidkahallęw**). Part. reminisc. gramm. See *kaallo* "a fish". Mejit tract.

Kaju-kaņ (**kajiw-kaņ**). Gramm. See *kaju:* "those masts". Arno tract.

Kakkije (**kakkijęy**). Gramm. See *kakkije* "rest". Mili tract.

Kakko (**kakkęw**). From Japn. *gakkoo* "school". Namu tract.

Kakōm̧ (**kakem̧**). Reminisc. gramm. See *kein kōm̧:* "look for a breadfruit picking stick"; see also *kakōm̧kōm̧* "inspiring, full of ideas". Mejit tract.

Kalboonea (**kalbewenyah**). From Engl. *California*. Mejit tract.

Kalbōk (**kalbek**). Pers. name. Arno islet; Arno tract.

Kalenen (**kahlęynęn**). Gramm. See *kalenen* "female *nen* tree". Wotje tract.

Kalo (**kalew**). Gramm. See *kalo* "ripe". Ujelang islet.

Kalo-eņ (**kalew-yeņ**). Gramm. Mili tract.

Kaḷaebar (**kaḷahyebar**). Gramm. distort. See *kōḷaebar* "brackish". Kwajalein tract.

Kaḷap (**kaḷap**). Unanalyz. Namorik tract.

Kaḷeḷe (**kaḷęyḷęy**). From Bibl. *Galilee*. Arno islet.

Kaḷoonia (**kaḷeweniyah**). From Germ. *Kolonia*. Arno tract.

Kaṃome (**kaṃewmey**). From Japn. *kamome* "sea gull". Taongi islet.

Kane (**kaney**). Gramm. See *kane* "tasty". Arno tract.

Kanel (**kanel**). Gramm. See *nel:* "place for drying under the sun", or possibly a loan from Engl. *gunwale.* Majuro tract.

Kañal (**kahgal**). Gramm. See *kañal* "a tree". Kwajalein tract; Maloelap tract.

Kañal-eṇ (**kahgal-yeṇ**). Gramm. Bikini tract; Kili tract; Utirik tract.

Kañkōto (**kagkẹtẹw**). Gramm. See *kañ, kōto:* "eats the wind". Jaluit tract.

Kapale (**kapaley**). Gramm. See *kapāl* "make magic for him". Rongelap islet.

Kapen (**kapen**). Reminisc. gramm. See *kapi-* "its bottom". Wotho islet; Ailuk islet; Likiep islet; Wotje islet; Maloelap district; Maloelap islet.

Kapi-jabḷot (**kapiy-jabḷ°et**). Gramm. See *ḷot:* "west side is not missing". Ujae tract; Maloelap tract.

Kapi-jabwan (**kapiy-jabwan**). Reminisc. gramm. See *Jabwan* "place name": "west of Jabwan". Rongelap tract.

Kapi-jebwan (**kapiy-jebwan**). Reminisc. gramm. Lae tract.

Kapi-joñ (**kapiy-jeg°**). Gramm. See *joñ:* "west of the mangrove". Arno tract.

Kapi-le (**kapiy-lẹy**). Recur. form. See *le* "a bird". Majuro tract.

Kapi-lem-eṇ (**kapiy-lẹm-yeṇ**). Gramm. See *lem:* "bottom of the bailer or dipper". Arno tract.

Kapi-ḷae (**kapiy-ḷahyey**). Gramm. See *ḷae:* "west of calm water". Majuro tract.

Kapi-ḷǫ (**kapiy-ḷaw**). Gramm. See *ḷǫ* "hibiscus". Majuro tract.

Kapi-ḷwe (**kapiy-ḷ°ẹy**). Gramm. See *ḷwe* "pond". Two Maloelap tracts; Majuro tract.

Kapi-ṇa (**kapiy-ṇah**). Gramm. distort. See *ṇa* "shoal". Ujelang tract.

Kapi-rǫñ (**kapiy-rag°**). Gramm. distort. See *rǫñ:* "bottom of the pit". Ailinglapalap tract.

Kapi-to (**kapiy-tẹw**). Gramm. See *to:* "bottom of the husk soaking pit". Lib tract; Arno tract.

Kapi-towa (**kapiy-tewah**). Gramm. distort. See *towa* "west of; the beaching spot". Jaluit tract.

Kapin-aelōñ-eṇ (**kapin-hayẹlẹg-yeṇ**). Gramm. See *kapi-:* "bottom (west side) of the atoll". Likiep district; Maloelap district.

Kapin-aelōñ-in (**kapin-hayẹlẹg-yin**). Gramm. Ailinginae district; Rongelap district; Kwajalein district; Mili district.

Kapin-āne (**kapin-yanẹy**). Gramm. See *kapi-:* "bottom (west side) of the islet". Eniwetak tract; Bikini tract; Kwajalein tract; Namu tract; six Wotje tracts; Majuro tract; Arno tract.

Kapin-āne-eṇ (**kapin-yanẹy-yeṇ**). Gramm. Kwajalein tract.

Kapin-ānin (**kapin-yanyin**). Gramm. Three Kwajalein tracts.

Kapin-bok (**kapin-beq**). Gramm. See *bok:* "west side of the sandspit". Jaluit islet; Arno islet.

Kapin-bōl (**kapin-bẹl**). Gramm. See *bōl:* "bottom of the taro pit". Ujae tract; Lib tract; Kwajalein tract; Namu tract.

Kapin-eṃṃal (**kapin-yeṃṃal**). Gramm. See *ṃṃal* "west of the husk-beating place". Namu islet.

Kapin-kor (**kapin-qẹr**). Gramm. See *kor:* "bottom of the coconut shell". Lib tract.

Kapin-maaj (**kapin-mahaj**). Gramm. See *maaj* "west side of the clearing". Bikini tract; Lib household.

Kapin-mar (**kapin-mar**). Gramm. See *mar:* "west of the boondocks". Kwajalein tract.

Kapin-mej (**kapin-mẹj**). Gramm. See *mej:* "west of the opening between islets". Rongerik tract.

Kapin-mejje-eṇ (**kapin-mẹjjẹy-yeṇ**). Gramm. See *mejje:* "west of the opening between islets". Eniwetak tract.

Kapin-naṃ (**kapin-naṃ**). Gramm. See *naṃ* "bottom of the secondary lagoon". Namorik tract.

Kapin-pat (**kapin-pat**). Gramm. See *pat* "bottom (west side) of the swamp". Eniwetak tract; Rongelap tract; Ailinglapalap tract; Arno tract; Mili tract.

Kapin-pat-rālik (**kapin-pat-raylik**). Gramm. Ailinglapalap tract.

Kapin-pat-reeaar (**kapin-pat-reyyahar**). Gramm. Ailinglapalap tract.

Kapin-wōd (**kapin-wed**). Gramm. See *wōd* "bottom of the coral". Likiep islet.

Kapitto (**kapittew**). Gramm. See *kkapit, to:* "rub rope", "twist and make sennit by rubbing on thighs". Maloelap tract.

Kapjor (**kapjẹr°**). Gramm. See *kapjer* "mirror". Arno tract.

Karoro (**karẹwrẹw**). Gramm. See *ro:* "cause disappointment for lack of food". Majuro tract.

Karwe (**kar°ey**). Gramm. See *rrwe* "put one's hand in a hole in the reef. Ailinginae islet.

Kati-ej (**katiy-yẹj**). Gramm. See *katiej* "jump up"; a legend tells how Needlefish (*Tak*) who lived on this islet jumped on Hermit Crab (*Oṃ*) who lived on the next islet (*Oḷar*) and called the other crabs to race. Ailinglapalap islet.

Katḷoñ-kaṇ (**katḷ°eg°-kaṇ**). Gramm. See *toḷoñ:* "cause to go ashore". Arno tract.

Katḷoñ-kaṇ-rāātle (**katḷ°eg°-kaṇ-rayatley**). Gramm. Arno household.

Katḷoñ-kaṇ-reeaar (**katḷ°eg°-kaṇ-reyyahar**). Gramm. Arno household.

Katnokḷapḷap (**katneqḷapḷap**). Gramm. See *katnok* "put thatch on walls". Erikub tract.

Katooj (**katẹwẹj**). Gramm. See *katooj* "hunt lobster or coconut crab at night". Majuro tract.

Katooj-kaṇ (**katẹwẹj-kaṇ**). Gramm. Maloelap tract.

Katoonno (**katẹwẹnnew**). Gramm. See *to, nnọ* "bring down tasty things (from the trees)". Arno tract.

Katōtō-eṇ (**katehteh-yeṇ**). Unanalyz. Arno islet; Arno tract.

Katrar (**katrar**). Gramm. See *katrar* "to dry leaves". Maloelap tract.

Kattar (**kattar**). Gramm. distort. See *kattar* "wait". Likiep tract.

Kawao (**kawahwew**). From Japn. *kawauwo* "river fish" (?). Wotje tract.

Kā (**kay**). Gramm. See *kā* "turn or change". Kwajalein islet.

Kā-meej (**kay-meyej**). Gramm. See *kā, meej:* "bright-colored trunks". Rongerik tract.

Kāājṃarṃar (**kayajṃarṃar**). Gramm. See *kāāj, ṃarṃar:* "necklace stones". Wotje tract.

Kāān-aerōk (**kayan-hayẹrẹk**). Gramm. See *kāān:* "trees that grow like those at Aerok". Maloelap islet.

Kāān-Mājro (**kayan-majrẹw**). Gramm. See *kāān:* "trees that grow like those at Majuro". Maloelap islet.

Kāārlik (**kayarlik**). Gramm. See *ār:* "beach canoes on the ocean side". Jaluit tract.

Kāet (**kayẹt**). Unanalyz. Ailinglapalap islet.

Kāijen (**kayijẹn**). Unanalyz. Jaluit islet; Wotje islet.

Kāiuiu (**kayiwyiw**). Gramm. See *kaiuiu* "gather sprouted coconut". Lae tract.

Kājoni (**kayjewniy**). Gramm. See *kājoon:* "skip over them". Kwajalein tract.

Kālik-kear (**kaylik-keyhar**). Gramm. See *kālik* "go back and forth from lagoon side to oceanside". Two Jaluit tracts.

Kāmeej-eṇ (**kaymeyej-yeṇ**). Gramm. See *kā, meej:* "that bright colored tree". Majuro tract.

Kāmeñ (**kaymẹg**). Gramm. See *kāmeñ* "a tree". Wotje tract.

Kārokā (**kayrẹwkay**). Unanalyz. Rongelap islet; Rongerik islet.

Kātilmaak (**kaytilmahak**). Gramm. See *kātilmaak* "fly up and down". Mejit tract.

Ke (**kẹy**). Gramm. Wotje islet.

Ke-eṇ (**kẹy-yeṇ**). Gramm. See *ke* "porpoise". Rongelap islet.

Ke-jaiiōñ (**kẹy-jahiyyẹg**). Gramm. Wotje islet.

Ke-jairōk (**kẹy-jahiyrẹk**). Gramm. Wotje islet.

Keār-kaṇ (**keyyar-kaṇ**). Gramm. See *keār:* "those terns". Mili islet.

Keeja (**keyejah**). Gramm. See *jeja* "causes pleasant dreams". Wotje tract.

Keeṃ-kein (**kẹyẹṃ-kẹyin**). Gramm. distort. See *kii-, eṃ* "walls of these houses". Mejit tract.

Keeṃṃaan (**kẹyẹṃṃahan**). Gramm. See *ke, ṃṃaan:* "man porpoise" or *kāān* "torso of a man". Majuro islet; Arno islet.

Keena (**keyenah**). Unanalyz. Eniwetak tract.

Keenaij (**keyenhayij**). Gramm. distort. See *kāān, Aij* "trunk of the Aij variety of pandanus". Maloelap islet.

Keepepli (**kẹyẹpyẹpliy**). Part. reminisc. gramm. See *keepep* "bird snare". Jaluit tract.

Kein-den (**kẹyin-dẹn**). Gramm. distort. See *kein, dān* "thing for water". Maloelap islet.

Kein-mọkwaṇ (**kẹyin-maqaṇ**). Gramm. See *kein, mokwaṇ* "thing for making *mokwan*". Maloelap islet.

Kejān (**keyjan**). Gramm. distort. See *kelọk, jān* "fly away from". Majuro tract.

Keju (**keyjiw**). Pers. name. Mejit district.

Keko (**keykew**). Gramm. See *keke* "white crane". Kwajalein islet.

Kerara (**kẹyrahrah**). Gramm. See *Kerara* "a navigational sign". Namorik tract.

Kewūnilañ (**keywiniylag**). Reminisc. gramm. See *wūn, lañ:* "form the base of the sky". Kwajalein tract.

Kiabōl (**kiyahbẹl**). Gramm. See *kābwil* "baby birds". Knox islet.

Kid-eṇ (**kid-yeṇ**). Recur. form. Arno sandspit.

Kidāpej (**kidapẹj**). Unanalyz. Arno tract.

Kiden-eṇ (**kidẹn-yeṇ**). Gramm. See *kiden* "beach borage". Ujelang islet; two Eniwetak islets; Kwajalein islet; Namu islet; Majuro islet; three Arno islets; Knox islet.

Kiden-kaṇ (**kidẹn-kaṇ**). Gramm. Kili tract; Erikub islet; Wotje islet; two Maloelap islets; Aur islet; two Mili islets; Knox islet.

Kiden-ḷapḷap (**kidẹn-ḷapḷap**). Gramm. Rongelap tract.

Kieb-eṇ (**kiyẹb-yeṇ**). Gramm. See *kieb* "spider lily". Maloelap tract.

Kiejej (**kiyẹjyẹj**). Gramm. See *kiej "Pemphis acidula"*, or a distortion of *kāājej* "really". Rongelap islet.

Kiijen (**kiyijẹn**). Unanalyz. Two Jaluit islets.

Kiijen-iōñ (**kiyijẹn-yiyẹg**). Unanalyz. Jaluit tract.

Kiijen-irōk (**kiyijẹn-yirẹk**). Unanalyz. Jaluit tract.

Kijinṃūk (**kijinṃik**). Gramm. distort. See *kijin, ṃōk* "reward for fatigue (in fighting)". Jaluit tract.

Kijjinbwi (**kijjinbiy**). Unanalyz. Kwajalein islet.

Kijmelañ (**kijmelag**). Unanalyz. Maloelap tract.

Kijoon (**kijewen**). Gramm. See *kijoon* "skip over". Arno tract.

Kikō (**kiykeh**). From "name of legendary bird". Ailinglapalap tract.

Kilañe (**kilagẹy**). Gramm. See *kil, kilōñe, kōlñe* "gashes in reef". Arno district; Arno islet.

Kilbōt (**kilbet**). From Engl. *Gilbert (Islands)*. Likiep tract.

Kilenbōr (**kilenber**). Unanalyz. Maloelap islet.

Killen (**killen**). Unanalyz. Ailinglapalap tract.

Kilo-rōk (**kilẹw-rẹk**). Unanalyz. Eniwetak tract.

Kilọk-eṇ (**kilaq-yeṇ**). Gramm. See *kilọk* "to juice pandanus". Rongelap islet; Kwajalein tract; Ailinglapalap islet.

Kilọkwōn (**kilaqen**). Unanalyz. Ujelang islet.

Kilōk (**kilẹk**). Gramm. See *kilōk* "large basket". Majuro islet.

Kilōk-eṇ (**kilẹk-yeṇ**). Gramm. Ailinglapalap islet.

Kilōṃṃan (**kileṃṃan**). Reminisc. gramm. See *kil, ṃṃan* "good passage". Arno islet.

Kilōṃṃar (**kileṃṃar**). Reminisc. gramm. See *kil, ṃṃar* "fish basket passage". Likiep islet.

Kilōñe-eṇ (**kilẹgẹy-yeṇ**). Gramm. See *kilōñe, kōlñe* "gashes in reef". Arno tract.

Kimājo-iōñ (**kimajew-yiyẹg**). Recur. form. See *kimā* "a tree". Wotje islet.

Kimej-eṇ (**kimẹj-yeṇ**). Gramm. See *kimej* "frond". Ebon tract.

Kimej-kaṇ (**kimẹj-kaṇ**). Gramm. Rongelap islet.

Kimeme-kaṇ (**kimeymey-kaṇ**). Gramm. See *kimeme* "a tree". Ailinglapalap tract.

Kina-eṇ (**kinah-yeṇ**). Gramm. See *kina* "shoal". Majuro tract.

Kina-joñ (**kinah-jeg°**). Gramm. See *kina, joñ:* "mangrove shoal". Jaluit islet; Arno district; Arno islet.

Kināden (**kinaden**). Unanalyz. Likiep islet.

Kināden-kaṇ (**kinaden-kaṇ**). Unanalyz. Likiep islet.

Kinej-eṇ (**kinẹj-yeṇ**). Gramm. See *kinej:* "that scar". Jaluit tract.

Kinep-eañ (**kinep-yag**). Recur. form. Maloelap tract.

Kinep-rōk (**kinep-rẹk**). Recur. form. Kwajalein tract.

Kinetak (**kineytak**). Recur. form. See *kine, tak.* Ujelang tract.

Kinilọkwe (**kiniylaqẹy**). Part. recur. form. See *kin, lọk* "bed for its tail". Majuro tract.

Kinniñi (**kinnigiy**). Unanalyz. Arno tract.

Kinọwā (**kinaway**). Gramm. distort. See *kinọwea-* "obstacle". Majuro tract.

Kio (**kiyew**). Gramm. See *kio* "a plant". Kwajalein islet.

Kio-kaṇ (**kiyew-kaṇ**). Gramm. Kwajalein tract.

Kiole (**kiyẹwlẹy**). From Span. (?). Namorik tract.

Kioto (**kiyewtew**). From Japn. *Kyooto.* Namu tract; Wotje tract; Arno tract.

Kipin-maaj (**kipin-mahaj**). Gramm. distort. See *kapin, maaj:* "west of the clearing". Mejit tract.

Kipliia (**kipliyyah**). Gramm. See *kipiliia* "disobedient". Mili tract.

Kiur (**kiywir**). Gramm. See *kior* "storm". Jaluit islet.

Kob-eṇ (**qẹb**). Gramm. See *kob* "bent, curved". Ailinginae islet.

Kobal-raiiōñ (**qebal-rahiyyẹg**). Gramm. See *Kobal:* "navigational signs; turtles". Ailinglapalap tract.

Kobal-rairōk (**qebal-rahiyrẹk**). Gramm. Ailinglapalap tract.

Kobban (**qebban**). Gramm. See *kobba-:* "its contents". Aur tract.

Kobūkōr (**qebikẹr**). Part. recur. form. See *ko* "separate, *būkōr* "a plant": "the *būkōr* plants separate this tract from the next one". Ebon tract.

Kobwā (**qebay**). Recur. form. See *koba, bwā:* possible blend; "bamboo fishpole". Arno tract.

Koiie (**kewiyyẹy**). Gramm. See *ko, awiie:* "easy to run away". Namu tract.

Kokbal (**keqbal**). Gramm. See *ka-* "causative prefix", *kobal* "a shell": "find *kobal* shells". Majuro tract.

Kokoonpit (**qẹwqẹwẹnpit**). Gramm. See *koko, Pit:* "Gilbertese dolphin" or "Gilbertese ringworm". Kwajalein tract.

Koḷaṃṃwā (**qeḷaṃṃay**). Gramm. See *koḷaṃṃwā* "land crab". Majuro tract.

Koṃlaḷ (**qẹṃlaḷ**). Gramm. See *koṃlaḷ* "valley". Majuro tract.

Koṃle (**qẹṃlẹy**). Pers. name, a demon. Kwajalein islet.

Koñil (**qẹwgil**). Gramm. distort. See *koñil* "alienated". Arno tract.

Koto (**qẹwtẹw**). Gramm. distort. See *ko, to:* "flee westward". Ailinglapalap islet; Ebon tract.

Kotōn-kadikdik (**qẹtẹn-kadikdik**). Also *kōttōn-kwadikdik* (**kẹttẹn-qadikdik**). Gramm. distort. See *itōn, kadikdik:* "you ought to take it easy" or *kōttōn, kwadikdik:* "secure everything and put it in good shape". Maloelap tract.

Kowa-eṇ (**qẹwwah-yeṇ**). Gramm. See *kowa* "laden with fruit". Kwajalein tract.

Kowak-kaṇ (**qewak-kaṇ**). Gramm. See *kowak:* "those curlews". Kwajalein islet.

Kowatōtō (**qewatehteh**). Unanalyz. Namu tract.

Kọbajia (**kawbajyiyah**). Gramm. See *kọbaj, ia* "banish where?" Arno tract.

Kọdej (**qawdẹj**). Unanalyz. Arno tract.

Kọkleejej (**qaqleyejyej**). Gramm. See *kọkleejej* "run at full tilt". Kwajalein tract.

Kọlọḷḷọḷ-kaṇ (**kaḷ°ẹḷ°ḷ°ẹḷ°-kaṇ**). Gramm. See *kaḷḷaḷḷaḷ* "knock". Likiep tract.

Kọrere-iōñ (**qar°ẹyrẹy-yiyẹg**). Part. recur. form. See *rere* "peep". Ebon tract.

Kọrere-irōk (**qar°ẹyrẹy-yirẹk**). Part. recur. form. Ebon tract.

Kọrujlañ (**qar°ijlag**). Gramm. See *ruj, lañ:* "wake up the sky", done by someone other than member of Ripako clan trespassing on a *bōn,* thereby bringing rain and wind. Arno islet.

Kōbjeje (**kebjeyjey**). Unanalyz. Namorik tract.

Kōdọ-rōk (**kedaw-rẹk**). Gramm. See *kōdọ* "cloud". Mili tract.

Kōjañ-dekā (**kejag-dekay**). Gramm. See *kōjañjañ, dekay:* "(play a) stone instrument". Arno tract.

Kōjañ-kwōleej (**kejag-qẹlẹyẹj**). Gramm. See *jañ, kwōlej:* "causes the plover to sing". Majuro tract.

Kōjāltok (**kejalteq**). Gramm. See *jāl:* "causes one to face this way". Wotje tract.

Kōjbar-kaṇ (**kẹjbar-kaṇ**). Gramm. See *kōjbar* "a tree". Ebon tract; Mili tract.

Kōjbwā (**kẹjbay**). Gramm. distort. See *kōjbwe* "steer". Maloelap islet.

Kōjbwe (**kẹjbey**). Gramm. distort. See *kōjbwe* "steer". Arno islet.

Kōjjen (**kẹjjẹn**). Gramm. See *kōjjen* "steal". Likiep islet.

Kōjjọuj (**kejjawij**). Gramm. See *jọ* "push down". Wotje islet.

Kōkeār (**kekeyyar**). Gramm. See *keār* "hunt tern". Ailuk tract.

Kōkōm̧m̧anm̧ōn (**kekem̧m̧anmẹn**). Gramm. See *kōkōm̧m̧anm̧ōn* "decorate". Ailinglapalap tract.

Kōle (**kẹlẹy**). Gramm. See *kōle* "a basket". Ralik island: Kili. Likiep islet; Arno islet; Arno tract.

Kōlladikdik (**kellahdikdik**). Gramm. See *lladikdik:* "find a cooler place". Utirik household.

Kōḷ-eṇ (**keḷ-yeṇ**). Gramm. See *kōḷ* "stream running out of swamp". Ailinglapalap tract.

Kōḷaebar (**keḷahyeybar**). Gramm. See *kōḷaebar* "brackish". Ailinglapalap islet.

Kōḷaḷ-eṇ (**keḷaḷ-yeṇ**). Reminisc. gramm. See *kōkḷaḷ* "navigational sign". Majuro islet; Arno islet.

Kōḷḷapḷañ (**keḷḷapḷag**). Part. recur. form. See *ḷañ* "storm". Kwajalein tract.

Kōḷomi (**keḷewmiy**). Unanalyz. Majuro tract.

Kōḷotōr (**kẹḷẹwtẹr**). Gramm. See *kōḷotōr* "make perfume". Likiep tract.

Kōḷọbōk (**keḷawbẹk**). Recur. form. See *kōḷọ* "a food". Knox tract.

Kōḷōjjab (**keḷejjab**). Unanalyz. Lae tract.

Kōḷōn (**keḷen**). Pers. name. Mejit district.

Kōmājo-rōk (**kemajew-rẹk**). Unanalyz. Wotje islet.

Kōmje-kaṇ (**kẹmjẹy-kaṇ**). Unanalyz. Namu tract.

Kōmjedeọ (**kemjedyaw**). Gramm. See *kōmjedeọ* "superficially fancy". Arno tract.

Kōm̧ade (**kem̧adey**). Gramm. See *m̧ad:* "occupies him; distracts him". Kwajalein tract.

Kōm̧adkōj (**kem̧adkẹj**). Gramm. See *m̧ad:* "occupies us; distracts us". Wotje tract.

Kōm̧anm̧ankōj (**kem̧anm̧ankẹj**). Gramm. See *kōm̧anm̧an* "make peace with/ among us". Ebon tract.

Kōm̧kōm̧ḷañōn (**kem̧kem̧ḷagen**). Part. recur. form. See *kōm̧kōm̧* "pick breadfruit", *ḷañon irooj* "sign of a chief coming". Mejit tract.

Kōm̧ñūr (**kem̧gir**). Gramm. See *kōm̧ñūr* "outrigger platform" or "a roaring sound". Mejit tract; Arno tract.

Kōm̧weej (**kẹm̧ẹyẹj**). Gramm. distort. See *kom̧, ej* "you are up". Arno tract.

Kōnañ (**kenag**). Unanalyz. Majuro tract; three Mili tracts.

Kōnañin (**kenagin**). Unanalyz. Mili tract.

Kōnnaanḷọk (**kennahanḷaq**). Gramm. See *kōnnaan:* "keep on talking". Majuro tract.

Kōṇakkā (**keṇakkay**). Reminisc. gramm. See *kōṇak* "these surroundings". Mejit tract.

Kōṇṇat-kaṇ (**kẹṇṇat-kaṇ**). Gramm. See *kōṇṇat* "a shrub". Mili islet.

Kōṇo-eṇ (**keṇew-yeṇ**). Gramm. See *kōṇo* "a tree". Bikini tract; Wotho tract; Kwajalein tract; Kili tract.

Kōṇoon (**keṇewen**). Reminisc. gramm. See *kōṇo:* "its *kōṇo* tree". Ailuk islet.

Kōñe-eṇ-iōñ (**kẹgẹy-yeṇ-yiyẹg**). Gramm. See *kōñ* "*Pemphis acidula*". Kili tract.

Kōñe-eṇ-irōk (**kẹgẹy-yeṇ-yirẹk**). Gramm. Kili tract.

Kōñe-jekāān-eṇ (**kẹgẹy-jekayan-yeṇ**). Gramm. See *kōñe, jekāān:* "that *Pemphis* trunk". Kwajalein islet.

Kōñe-kaṇ (**kẹgẹy-kaṇ**). Gramm. Ailinginae islet; two Ailinglapalap tracts; Ebon tract; Majuro tract.

Kōpālpāl-kaṇ (**kepalpal-kaṇ**). Gramm. distort. See *ppālpāl:* "those blowings". Likiep islet; Mejit tract.

Kōpālto-bok (**kepaltẹw-beq**). Gramm. distort. See *ppālpāl* "blow sand westward". Arno tract.

Kōpin-le (**kepin-lẹy**). Gramm. See *kepin, le:* "shoot albatross with a sling". Lae islet.

Kōpin-nam̧ (**kepin-nam̧**). Gramm. distort. See *kapin nam̧* "bottom of the secondary lagoon". Ailinglapalap household.

Kōpjeje (**kẹpjeyjey**). Unanalyz. Namorik tract.

Kōpjeltak (**kẹpjeltak**). Reminisc. gramm. See *kōpjeḷtak* "a food". Arno district.

Kōrara (**kerahrah**). Unanalyz. Namorik tract.

Kōrā (**keray**). Gramm. See *kōrā* "woman". Majuro islet.

Kōrmaō (**kermaheh**). Reminisc. gramm. See *kōrkōr, im, aō* "(see a drift) canoe and swim (to it)". Arno tract.

Kōta-eņ (**ketah-yeņ**). Gramm. See *kōtaa-* "boundary". Utirik household; Mili tract.

Kōta-kaņ (**ketah-kaņ**). Gramm. Arno tract.

Kōtabtab (**ketabtab**). Gramm. See *kōtabtab* "large tree". Ailuk tract.

Kōtabur (**ketabir°**). Gramm. See *tabur* "causes slipperiness". Mejit tract.

Kōtan-bar (**ketan-bar**). Gramm. distort. See *kōtaa-, bar:* "between rocks". Majuro tract.

Kōtļaļ-eņ (**ketļaļ-yeņ**). Gramm. distort. See *kōtlaļ* "stick something into the ground". Majuro tract.

Kōtñañ-eņ (**ketgag-yeņ**). Gramm. See *tūñañ:* "causes to beg for food". Utirik household.

Kōtooj-rālik (**ketewej-raylik**). Gramm. See *kōtooj:* "pull up the husking stick". Ailinglapalap tract.

Kōtooj-rear (**ketewej-reyhar**). Gramm. Ailinglapalap tract.

Kōtra (**ketrah**). Gramm. See *kōtra* "land reserved for chiefs". Ailinglapalap tract.

Kōtrar-eņ (**ketrar-yeņ**). Gramm. See *kōtrar* "touch part of it". Kwajalein tract; two Arno tracts.

Kōtteepiņa (**ketteyepiņah**). Gramm. See *kōtteepiņa* "storm". Kwajalein islet.

Kōttǫǫr (**kettawar**). Also *kōtǫǫr*. Gramm. See *kōttǫǫr:* "chase fish into the weir" or "cause to flow". Mili tract.

Kōttōke (**kęttękęy**). Unanalyz. See *tōkā*. Likiep tract.

Kōttūbab (**kęttibab**). Unanalyz. Ailinglapalap tract.

Kōtwale (**ketwalęy**). Unanalyz. Bikini tract.

Kubōk-eņ (**qibęk-yeņ**). Gramm. See *kubōk* "a tree". Ebon tract.

Kubur-jāirōk (**qibir°-jayiyręk**). Gramm. distort. See *kūbur* "a fish". Likiep tract.

Kudiil-eņ (**qidiyil-yeņ**). Gramm. See *kudiil* "a fish". Jaluit tract.

Kuṃkuṃļap (**qiṃqiṃļap**). Unanalyz. Ebon islet.

Kuoj (**qiwej**). Unanalyz. Ebon tract.

Kur-eņ (**qir-yeņ**). Gramm. See *kur* "squirrel fish". Rongelap tract.

Kuria (**qiriyah**). From Gilb. *Kuria* (*Atoll*). Arno tract; Mili tract.

Kurob (**kir°ęb**). Unanalyz. Ebon islet.

Kurōr (**qirer**). Unanalyz. Kwajalein islet.

Kuruno (**qir°inęw**). Unanalyz. Eniwetak sandspit.

Kuteuñ (**qiteywig°**). Unanalyz. Mejit tract.

Kuwajleen (**qiwajleyen**). Recur. form. See *waj* "to you", *leen* "its fruit"; legend says that after a typhoon its only fruit was flowers which the people took to the chief as the only available tribute. Ralik atoll; Kwajalein; Kwajalein islet; Namu tract; two Arno tracts.

Kuwalañ (**qiwalag**). Unanalyz. Maloelap tract.

Kuwaro (**qiwarew**). Unanalyz., although this tract is said to have a valley inhabited by a huge lizard called *Jǫ-Kuwaro.* Ebon tract.

Kuwato (**qiwatęw**). Unanalyz. Jaluit tract.

Kuwatōp (**qiwatep**). Unanalyz. Kwajalein islet.

Kūbur (**kibir°**). Gramm. See *kūbur* "a fish". Ailinglapalap islet.

Kūbūt (**kibit**). Reminisc. gramm. See *kūbwij* "dig", *kinbūt* "not ripe". Arno tract.

Kūbween-eañ (**kibeyen-yag**). Gramm. See *kūbwe:* "feces of the north". Aur islet.

Kūbween-uṃ (**kibeyen-wiṃ**). Gramm. See *kūbwe; uṃ:* "cinders". Majuro tract.

Kūkṃoņ (**kikṃeņ°**). Recur. form. See *kūk* "bite", *ṃoņ* "lie". Knox tract.

Kūṃake (**kiṃakęy**). Gramm. See *kūmake* "a gull". Likiep islet.

Kūṃar (**kiṃar**). Recur. form. See *ṃarṃar* "necklace". Maloelap islet.

Kūṃōōr (**kiṃeher**). Gramm. See *kūṃōōr* "bird trap"; *Jemāluut* is said to have made a trap on this tract. Majuro tract.

Kūrañ-kaņ (**kirag-kaņ**). Gramm. See *kurañ* "those startlings (by the demons that inhabit these tracts)". Arno islet; two Arno tracts; Mili tract.

Kūrooļ (**kireweļ**). Reminisc. gramm. See *ikrooļ* "dissatisfied". Maloelap tract.

Kūtaak-eṇ (**kitahak-yeṇ**). Gramm. See *kūtaak* "a tree". Aur tract.

Kūtoob (**kiteweb**). Unanalyz. Lib tract.

Kūttaño (**kittagew**). Unanalyz. Likiep tract.

Kūttiij (**kittiyij**). Also *Ṃwin-kūtiij.* Reminisc. gramm. See *ttiijij* "place for cooking greasy fish". Ebon tract.

Kūttūke (**kittikey**). Gramm. See *kūttūk* "cover it up". Likiep tract.

Kwaroñ (**qareg°**). Reminisc. gramm. See *kwōn, rọñ:* "stick a torch in the hole". Wotje islet.

Kwaroñ-dik (**qareg°-dik**). Reminisc. gramm. Wotje islet.

Kwe-eṇ (**qẹy-yeṇ**). Gramm. See *kwe* "a navigational sign". Ailinglapalap tract.

Kwōderaj (**qedeyraj**). Recur. form. See *raj* "whale". Kwajalein tract.

Kwōdo (**qedew**). Recur. form. See *RuKwōdo* "clan name". Jaluit tract.

Kwōdu (**qediw**). Unanalyz. Erikub islet.

Kwōjāām (**qejayam**). Gramm. See *kwōje, ām:* "coil sennit". Mili tract.

Kwōjebwāān (**qejebayan**). Gramm. See *kwōj, bwā:* "break his fishpole". Maloelap islet.

Kwōmijen (**qemiyjen**). Loan from Engl. *commission,* or possibly from *mijen:* "you get sick from it". Ujae tract.

Kwōmokwa (**qemeqwah**). Unanalyz. Ailinglapalap tract.

Laaṃ (**lahaṃ**). Unanalyz. Jaluit islet.

Lae (**lahyey**). Reminisc. gramm. See *ḷae* "calm water". Ralik atoll; Lae; Lae islet.

Laeto (**lahyeytew**). Recur. form. See *la* "birds fishing, *ae* "current, *to* "passage". Majuro tract.

Lano (**lahnew**). Pers. name: legendary woman who watches all the fish in the pass. Maloelap channel.

Lañjo (**lagjew**). Pers. name. Two Mejit districts.

Lā-eṇ (**lay-yeṇ**). Gramm. See *lā* "capsize". Namu tract.

Ledeọtok (**lẹdyawteq**). Pers. name. See *deọ* "beautiful". Arno islet.

Ledik-raṇ (**ledik-raṇ**). Gramm. See *leddik:* "those girls". Majuro tract; two Arno tracts.

Ledik-ro (**ledik-rew**). Gramm. Erikub tract.

Ledikdik (**leydikdik**). Gramm. See *Ledikdik* "a star". Two Wotje tracts; two Majuro tracts.

Ledpāp (**ledpap**). Part. reminisc. gramm. See *pāp* "frond". Rongerik tract.

Leep (**leyep**). Gramm. See *leep* "folk dance". Lae islet; Ailinglapalap islet; Namorik tract.

Lejoni (**lejewniy**). Pers. name: a legendary woman. Ailinglapalap tract.

Lejraak-jāiiōñ (**lẹjrahak-jayiyyẹg**). Pers. name. Arno tract.

Lejraak-jāirōk (**lẹjrahak-jayiyrẹk**). Pers. name. Arno tract.

Lejroñ (**lẹjreg°**). Pers. name. Jaluit islet.

Lejroñ (**lejreg°**). Pers. name: a demon. Ebon tract.

Lejrwe (**lẹjr°ẹy**). Pers. name. See *jore* "taboo relationship". Wotje tract; Arno tract.

Lejwama (**lẹjwamah**). Also *Lewamā.* Recur. form. See *le-, wa, mā:* "use a canoe made from breadfruit wood". Mili tract.

Leleen (**leyleyen**). Gramm. See *le-, leen* "gives its fruit". Mejit tract.

Leḷā-eṇ (**lẹyḷay-yeṇ**). Gramm. distort. See *le-, ḷā* "put on gravel". Mili tract.

Lemmetal (**lẹmmetal**). Gramm. See *lem, metal* "smooth bailer". Arno tract.

Lepjer (**lẹpjẹr**). Unanalyz. Jaluit islet.

Leppejeṇ (**lẹppẹjeṇ**). Unanalyz. Arno islet.

Leppọṇ (**lẹppeṇ°**). Gramm. distort. See *lippọṇ* "arrow". Arno islet.

Letọ-eañ (**lẹytaw-yag**). Gramm. See *le-, wōt-tọ:* "render a heavy rain from the northeast". Majuro tract.

Letọ-rak (**lẹytaw-rak**). Gramm. Majuro tract.

Letōñ (**lẹytẹṇ°**). Gramm. See *letōñ* "sharp wind". Aur tract.

Liājke (**liyajkẹy**). Pers. name. Mejit tract.

Libar (**libar**). Pers. name. See *libar* "rock". Arno tract.

Lieormeto (**liyewermetew**). Pers. name. Mejit district.

Lijaro (**lijarew**). Unanalyz. Rongelap tract.

Lijebōro (**lijẹbẹrẹw**). Also *Lijebbōro.* Pers. name. See *jebbōro:* "Mrs. Spouse-stealer". Majuro islet.

Lijedkā (**lijẹdkay**). Pers. name. See *jedkā:* "Mrs. Choose". Jaluit tract.

Lijeerpit (**lijeyerpit**). Unanalyz. Rongelap tract.

Lijinen (**lijinẹn**). Gramm. See *lijlij* "pound", *nen* "*Morinda citrifolia*". Majuro tract.

Lijjadiñdiñ (**lijjahdigdig**). Pers. name. Mejit tract.

Lijjiṃwe (**lijjiṃẹy**). Pers. name. Mili tract.

Lijkōbwa (**lijkẹbwah**). Also *Lijkōbwā* (**lijkẹbay**). Pers. name. Mili islet.

Lijukidej (**lijiwkidẹj**). Pers. name, a spirit. Mejit tract and rock.

Lik-ej (**lik-yẹj**). Gramm. See *lik, ej:* "ocean side on the east". Mejit tract.

Lik-iolap (**lik-yiyewḷap**). Gramm. See *lik, ioḷap:* "ocean side in the middle". Kwajalein tract.

Lik-jorme (**lik-jer°mey**). Gramm. See *jorom:* "absorb it". Bikini tract.

Lik-kaṇ (**lik-kaṇ**). Gramm. Mejit tract; Arno tract.

Lik-laḷ (**lik-laḷ**). Gramm. See *liklaḷ* "leeward side of atoll". Ujelang district; Eniwetak district; Rongelap district; Rongerik district; Ailinginae district; Lae district; Ujae district; Kwajalein district; Jaluit district; Namorik district; Utirik household; Mejit tract; Likiep district; Aur district.

Lik-ḷōp (**lik-ḷep**). Reminisc. gramm. See *ḷap* "big". Mili islet.

Lik-rōk (**lik-rẹk**). Gramm. See *rōk* "south". Ujae tract; Ailinglapalap tract; Jaluit tract; Maloelap tract; Maloelap household.

Likabrowa (**likabrewah**). Also *Likin-Kabroñḷọk*. Unanalyz. Majuro tract.

Likajeer (**likajeyer**). Pers. name. See *jeer:* "Mrs. Cause-to-turn-away". Kwajalein tract.

Likakōṃ (**likakeṃ**). Also *Likakōñ*. Pers. name. Knox islet.

Likañūññūñ (**likagiggig**). Pers. name. See *ñūñ:* "Mrs. Pack-the-ground-hard". Majuro tract.

Likarñij (**likargij**). Also *Likarṃij*. Pers. name. Arno islet.

Likaroaro (**likarewharew**). Pers. name. Ailinglapalap islet.

Liki-eōñ (**likiy-yẹg**). Gramm. distort. See *eañ* "north". Mejit tract.

Liki-jaḷtok (**likiy-jaḷteq**). Gramm. See *jaḷtok* "adze". Kwajalein tract.

Liki-jāl-eṇ (**likiy-jal-yeṇ**). Unanalyz. Mejit tract.

Liki-jeḷo (**likiy-jeyḷew**). Gramm. See *liki, jeḷo:* "on the ocean side of 'sail ho!'". Likiep tract.

Liki-jemọ (**likiy-jemaw**). Recur. form. See *Jemọ* "Ratak island". Majuro tract.

Liki-jepakina (**likiy-jepakinah**). Unanalyz. Arno tract.

Liki-jinre (**likiy-jinrẹy**). Gramm. See *jinre* "cook and eat fish right after catching". Mili tract.

Liki-joñ (**likiy-jeg°**). Gramm. See *joñ* "mangrove". Arno tract.

Liki-lo-bok (**likiy-lew-beq**). Gramm. See *bok* "sand". Wotho tract.

Liki-lo-mar (**likiy-lew-mar**). Gramm. See *mar* "bushes". Mejit tract.

Liki-lo-ṇo (**likiy-lew-ṇew**). Gramm. See *ṇo* "waves". Ujae tract.

Liki-Lo-pat (**likiy-lẹw-pat**). Gramm. distort. See *Lo-pat* "mejit tract". Mejit tract.

Liki-lọ-Ḷwōj (**likiy-law-ḷ°ẹj**). Unanalyz. See *Ḷwōj* "Ailinglapalap tract". Ailinglapalap tract.

Liki-lōk-ej (**likiy-lẹk-yẹj**). Gramm. distort. Majuro tract.

Liki-ḷe-eo (**likiy-ḷẹy-yew**). Gramm. distort. See *ḷwe* "pond", or *eakḷe* "pile of stones". Ailinglapalap tract.

Liki-rakōm (**likiy-rakẹm**). Gramm. See *rakōm* "plunder". Mejit tract.

Liki-tōmrak (**likiy-temrak**). Part. reminisc. gramm. See *tōmrak* "sail with outrigger on south". Mejit tract.

Likiej (**likiyẹj**). Gramm. See *likiej* "windward side of atoll". Ujae tract; Namorik district; Mili islet; Mili tract.

Likiep (**likiyep**). Recur. form. See *iep* "basket". Ratak atoll; Likiep; Likiep district; Likiep islet; Majuro tract.

Likijjine (**likijjinẹy**). Pers. name, legendary woman. Kwajalein islet.

Likin-aemat (**likin-hayemat**). Recur. form. See *mat* "cooked", *mmat* "emerge". Majuro tract.

Likin-aj-eṇ-lik (**likin-haj-yeṇ-lik**). Gramm. See *aj* "thatch". Arno tract.

Likin-aojañ (**likin-hawejag**). Gramm. See *Aojañ* "a pandanus variety". Majuro tract.

Likin-apñak (**likin-hapgak**). Unanalyz. Ebon tract.

Likin-Arōn-or (**likin-haren-wer°**). Gramm. See *Arōn-or* "Majuro tract". Majuro household.

Likin-Arōn-peje (**likin-haren-pęjęy**). Recur. form. See *Arōn-peje* "Majuro tract". Majuro household.

Likin-arraj (**likin-harraj**). Gramm. See *ar, raj* "whale beach". Aur tract.

Likin-atbwā (**likin-hatbay**). Unanalyz. Majuro tract.

Likin-awe (**likin-hawęy**). Unanalyz. Namorik tract.

Likin-batō (**likin-bateh**). Part. reminisc. gramm. See *Batō* "Ailinglapalap tracts", also *bat* "hill". This tract is on the ocean side of a hill. Mejit tract.

Likin-Boļañ (**likin-bęwļag**). Part. reminisc. gramm. See *Boļañ* "Majuro tract". Majuro household.

Likin-bōn (**likin-bęn**). Gramm. See *bōn* "place for floating corpses away". Kwajalein tract; Arno tract.

Likin-Bōreọ (**likin-bereyaw**). Unanalyz. See *Bōreọ* "Majuro tract". Majuro tract.

Likin-bōt-kaṇ (**likin-bęt-kaṇ**). Gramm. See *bōt* "naughty". Aur tract.

Likin-bukwōj (**likin-biqęj**). Unanalyz. Mejit tract.

Likin-Bwiddik (**likin-biddik**). Reminisc. gramm. See *Bwiddik-ean, Bwiddik-rak* "Majuro tracts". Majuro household.

Likin-Ekalur (**likin-yekalir°**). Gramm. See *Ekalur* "Majuro tract". Majuro household.

Likin-elōkeo (**likin-yelekyew**). Unanalyz. Majuro household.

Likin-Eoon-maaj (**likin-yewen-mahaj**). Gramm. See *Eoon-maaj* "Majuro tract". Majuro tract.

Likin-Eōōļ (**likin-yeheļ**). Gramm. See *Eōōļ* "Namorik tract". Namorik tract.

Likin-ilọk (**likin-yilaq**). Gramm. See *ilọk* "go away". Jaluit tract.

Likin-Jabōn-wōd (**likin-jaben-wed**). Gramm. See *Jabon-wōd* "tract name". Namorik tract.

Likin-Kabroñļọk (**likin-kabreg°ļaq**). Also *Likabrowa.* Unanalyz. See *Kabroñļọk* "Majuro tract". Majuro tract.

Likin-kade (**likin-kadey**). Gramm. See *kade* "large stone used as anchor". Mejit tract.

Likin-Kamrōk (**likin-kamręk**). Pers. name, a demon. Mejit tract.

Likin-kane (**likin-kaney**). Gramm. See *kane* "tasty". Arno tract.

Likin-Kapi-joñ (**likin-kapiy-jeg°**). Gramm. See *Kapi-joñ* "tract name". Majuro tract.

Likin-Kapi-ļae (**likin-kapiy-ļahyey**). Gramm. See *Kapi-ļae* "Majuro tract". Majuro household.

Likin-korear (**likin-qer°eyhar**). Unanalyz. Namorik tract.

Likin-Kōpnaan-iar (**likin-kepnahan-yiyhar**). Gramm. See *Kōpnaan* "a pandanus variety". Maloelap household.

Likin-Kōpnaan-lik (**likin-kepnahan-lik**). Gramm. Maloelap household.

Likin-kūṃ-ej (**likin-kiṃ-yęj**). Unanalyz. Aur tract.

Likin-kūṇu (**likin-kiṇiw**). Gramm. distort. See *kōṇo* "a tree". Majuro tract.

Likin-kūñ-eṇ (**likin-kig-yeṇ**). Gramm. See *kūñ* "smell of feces". Majuro tract.

Likin-lobajre (**likin-lewbajrey**). Unanalyz. Majuro tract.

Likin-lọļinṃak (**likin-lawļinṃak**). Gramm. See *lọļin, ṃak* "ocean side of the shape of a needlefish; see also *Lọ-ļeenṃak* "Ailinglapalap tract" and *Lọļinṃak* "Knox tract". Majuro tract.

Likin-ļọotōl (**likin-ļawętęl**). Unanalyz. Namorik tract.

Likin-Ļōjọkubōk (**likin-ļejawqibęk**). Pers. name. See *kubōk* "a tree". Majuro tract.

Likin-maro (**likin-maręw**). Gramm. See *maro* "thirst". Majuro tract.

Likin-meļeo (**likin-męļyew**). Unanalyz. Kwajalein tract.

Likin-Mọon (**likin-mawen**). Unanalyz. See *Mọon* "Majuro tract". Majuro tract.

Likin-Ṃaļok (**likin-ṃaļęq**). Unanalyz. See *Ṃaļok* "tract name". Majuro tract.

Likin-Ṃōn-aļļañ (**likin-ṃen-haļļag**). Gramm. See *Ṃōn-aļļañ* "tract name". Majuro tract.

Likin-Ṃōn-bok (**likin-ṃen-beq**). Gramm. See *Ṃōn-bok* "Majuro tract". Majuro tract.

Likin-Ṃōn-kwōleej (**likin-ṃen-qeleyej**). Gramm. See *Ṃōn-kwōleej* "Ebon tract". Ebon tract.

Likin-ṃōtodān (**likin-ṃetewdan**). Gramm. See *ṃwō* "house", *to* "passage", *dān* "water". Majuro tract.

Likin-M̧we-jak (**likin-m̧ey-jak**). Part. recur. form. See *M̧we-jak* "Majuro tract". Majuro tract.

Likin-M̧we-joor (**likin-m̧ey-jewer**). Recur. form. See *M̧we-joor* "Majuro tract". Majuro tract.

Likin-M̧we-nen (**likin-m̧ẹy-nẹn**). Gramm. See *M̧we-nen* "Majuro tract". Majuro household.

Likin-M̧we-tooj (**likin-m̧ẹy-tẹwẹj**). Gramm. See *M̧we-tooj* "Majuro tract". Majuro household.

Likin-M̧widu (**likin-m̧idiw**). Reminisc. gramm. See *M̧widu* "Majuro tract". Majuro household.

Likin-M̧win-ijo (**likin-m̧in-yijẹw**). Recur. form. See *M̧win-ijo* "tract name". Majuro tract.

Likin-oļeep (**likin-weļeyep**). Reminisc. gramm. See *ņoonniep:* "place for fairies". Majuro tract.

Likin-Pikaar (**likin-pikahar**). Gramm. See *Pikaar* "place name". Mejit tract.

Likin-Uti-jabōn-or (**likin-witiy-jaben-wer**). Recur. form. See *Uti-jabōn-wōd* "Majuro tract". Majuro household.

Likin-Wa-eņ (**likin-wah-yeņ**). Gramm. See *Wa-eņ* "Namu tract". Namu household.

Likin-Welǫk-eņ (**likin-weylaq-yeņ**). Gramm. See *Welǫk-eņ* "tract name". Majuro tract.

Likjāp (**likjap**). Unanalyz. Namu tract.

Likōm̧m̧an (**likem̧m̧an**). Gramm. See *lik, m̧m̧an:* "good ocean side". Rongelap islet.

Likreo (**likreyew**). Reminisc. gramm. See *rreo* "clean", or *lōkōr, eo:* "the surfing spot". Two Maloelap households.

Liktalkupañ (**liktalqipag**). Reminisc. gramm. See *lik, tal, kupañ* "oceanside where the surgeonfish are under the water". Arno tract.

Likūm̧m̧an-eņ (**likim̧m̧an-yeņ**). Gramm. distort. See *lik, m̧m̧an:* "good ocean side". Mejit tract.

Limar (**limar**). Pers. name. See *mar:* "Mrs. Bush". Majuro tract.

Limarpe (**limarpey**). Pers. name. Ebon tract.

Limādbōb (**limadbeb**). Pers. name. See *mād, bōb:* "Mrs. Breadfruit-ripening". Mili islet.

Limen-rālik (**limen-raylik**). Gramm. See *lime-* "his beverage"; name of one of two legendary wells that are navigational signs. Namorik tract.

Limen-rear (**limen-reyhar**). Gramm., see *Limen-rālik.* Namorik tract.

Limǫǫj (**limawaj**). Pers. name, a woman who came from the Eastern Carolines during German times. Ujelang tract.

Lim̧-eņ (**lim̧-yeņ**). Gramm. See *lim̧* "murky water". Ailuk tract.

Lim̧ōnkoko (**lim̧enkewkew**). Gramm. distort. See *limenkoko* "two babies nursing from the same woman (this tract was probably *limen ninnin*)"; blend with *im̧ōn* "house of". Mili tract.

Lim̧wijlǫk (**lim̧ijlaq**). Pers. name. Eniwetak tract.

Lionen (**liyẹwnẹn**). Pers. name. See *nen* "a tree". Bikini household.

Liopeaan (**liyẹwpẹyahan**). Unanalyz. Bikini household.

Lipaakdik (**lipahakdik**). Reminisc. gramm. See *lep, ak* "small frigate bird egg". Arno tract.

Lipoojļā (**lipewejļay**). Pers. name. See *po, wōjļā:* "Mrs. Take-down-sail". Jaluit tract.

Lippiruk-kaņ (**lippiriq-kaņ**). Gramm. See *lippiru:* "those berries". Rongelap islet.

Lippuņ-anij (**lippiņ°-hanij**). Pers. name. Mejit tract.

Lo-aj (**lew-haj**). Gramm. See *aj* "thatch". Arno tract.

Lo-ani (**lew-haniy**). Gramm. See *anan:* "chum for them". Ujae islet.

Lo-arm̧we (**lew-harm̧ey**). Gramm. See *arm̧we:* "at the *arm̧we* tree". Mejit tract.

Lo-ākā (**lew-yakay**). Gramm. See *ākā* "pile of stones; crab trap". Lae tract; Kwajalein tract; Ailinglapalap tract; Mejit tract.

Lo-āne (**lew-yanẹy**). Gramm. See *āne* "islet". Mili tract.

Lo-āpep (**lew-yapyẹp**). Gramm. Ebon tract.

Lo-bar (**lew-bar**). Gramm. See *bar* "rock". Arno tract.

Lo-bōkā (**lew-bekay**). Gramm. See *bōkā* "tide" or "oil container". Arno tract.

Lo-bōkā-eņ (**lew-bekay-yeņ**). Gramm. Ujelang tract.

Lo-debǫkut (**lew-debaqit**). Gramm. See *debǫkut* "stump". Mejit tract.

Lo-dekā (**lew-dekay**). Gramm. See *dekā* "stones". Kwajalein tract; Namu tract; Mejit tract.

Lo-ekā (**lew-yekay**). Gramm. distort. See *Lo-ākā* "place name". Ujelang tract; Wotje tract; Maloelap tract; Aur tract; Arno tract.

Lo-iaḷ (**lew-yiyaḷ**). Gramm. See *iaḷ* "path". Lib tract.

Lo-iemaaj (**lew-yiyemahaj**). Part. reminisc. gramm. See *maaj* "clearing". Jaluit tract.

Lo-jaar (**lew-jahar**). Gramm. See *jaar* "chief's sanctuary". Mejit tract.

Lo-jabwāetoḷe (**lew-jabayețewḷey**). Unanalyz. Kwajalein tract.

Lo-jade (**lew-jahdey**). Gramm. See *jade* "roost". Bikini tract.

Lo-jaḷap (**lew-jahḷap**). Gramm. See *ja* "big harbor". Mejit tract; Majuro tract.

Lo-jāār (**lew-jayar**). Gramm. See *jāār* "method of cooking fish". Arno tract.

Lo-jāpe (**lew-japey**). Unanalyz. Aur tract.

Lo-jekar (**lew-jekar**). Recur. form. See *jekar.* Jaluit tract; Arno tract.

Lo-joñe (**lew-jeg°ey**). Gramm. See *joñ:* "lots of mangroves". Majuro tract.

Lo-kaar (**lew-kahar**). Gramm. See *kaar* "a tree". Ujelang tract; Ujae tract; Ailinglapalap tract; Mejit tract; Arno tract.

Lo-kabbil (**lew-kabbil**). Gramm. See *kabbil* "pride" or *bwil* "set fire to". Two Kwajalein tracts; Arno tract.

Lo-kabbok (**lew-kabbeq**). Gramm. See *kabbok* "a plant". Kwajalein tract.

Lo-kabok (**lew-kabeq**). Gramm. See *bokbok* "sandy". Kwajalein tract.

Lo-kabōlbōl (**lew-kabęlbęl**). Gramm. See *kabōlbōl* "shiny". Erikub channel.

Lo-kabwijlōñ (**lew-kabijlęg**). Gramm. See *kabwijlōñ* "a shrub". Wotho tract; Arno tract.

Lo-kajdo (**lew-kajdęw**). Gramm. See *kajdo* "a tree". Arno tract.

Lo-kañal (**lew-kahgal**). Gramm. See *kañal* "a tree". Namorik tract.

Lo-karōn (**lew-karen**). Unanalyz. Ujelang tract.

Lo-katok (**lew-kateq**). Gramm. See *katok* "sacrifice". Rongelap tract; Rongerik tract; two Jaluit tracts; Mili tract.

Lo-kābwil (**lew-kaybil**). Gramm. See *kābwil* "baby birds". Bikini tract; Wotje tract.

Lo-kālōklōk (**lew-kaylęklęk**). Gramm. See *kālōklōk:* "at the thorny tree". Lae tract.

Lo-kōjab-eañ (**lew-kejab-yag**). Gramm. See *kōjab* "stand beside". Majuro tract.

Lo-kōjab-rak (**lew-kejab-rak**). Gramm. Majuro tract.

Lo-kōtra (**lew-ketrah**). Gramm. See *Kōtra* "a clan". Namu tract.

Lo-kūtaak-ko (**lew-kitahak-kew**). Gramm. See *kūtaak* "a tree". Mejit tract.

Lo-lur-eṇ (**lew-lir°-yeṇ**). Gramm. See *lur* "calm". Mili tract.

Lo-Ḷaat (**lew-ḷahat**). Recur. form. See *Ḷaat* "name of a cape on *Piñlep* islet. Jaluit tract.

Lo-ḷam (**lew-ḷam**). Gramm. See *ḷam* "bay". Wotje tract.

Lo-ḷam-eṇ (**lew-ḷam-yeṇ**). Gramm. Ebon tract.

Lo-Ḷōpako (**lew-lepakew**). Pers. name. See *pako:* "Mr. Shark". Ebon tract.

Lo-maaj (**lew-mahaj**). Gramm. See *maaj* "clearing". Ujelang tract; Eniwetak tract; Lae tract; Ailinglapalap tract; Jaluit tract; Namorik tract.

Lo-mar (**lew-mar**). Gramm. See *mar* "bushes". Likiep tract; Wotje tract; Majuro district; Majuro tract; Arno tract.

Lo-mar-eṇ (**lew-mar-yeṇ**). Gramm. Kili tract.

Lo-mar-in-ṃalel (**lew-mar-yin-ṃalel**). Gramm. See *Ṃalel* "Arno district and islet". Arno district.

Lo-mar-kaṇ (**lew-mar-kaṇ**). Gramm. Bikini tract.

Lo-marok (**lew-mareq**). Gramm. See *marok* "darkness". Namorik tract.

Lo-matoḷ (**lew-mateḷ°**). Gramm. See *matoḷ* "one third". Mejit tract.

Lo-mādo (**lew-madew**). Gramm. See *mādo* "sea crab" or *kōmādodo* "shirk". Arno tract.

Lo-mādo-eañ (**lew-madew-yag**). Gramm. Arno tract.

Lo-mādo-rak (**lew-madew-rak**). Gramm. Arno tract.

Lo-mekā (**lew-mekay**). Reminisc. gramm. See *Lo-ṃōkā* "place name". Majuro tract.

Lo-meḷaḷ (**lew-meḷaḷ**). Gramm. See *meḷaḷ* "demon playground". Maloelap tract.

Lo-ṃaju-rōk (**lew-ṃajiw-rẹk**). Gramm.
See *ṃaju* "at southern good fortune".
Majuro tract.

Lo-ṃōkā (**lew-ṃekay**). Gramm. See
ṃōkā "these houses". Ujelang tract;
Ailinglapalap tract; Jaluit tract; Arno
islet; Arno tract.

Lo-ṃōkā-ireeaar (**lew-ṃekay-
yirẹyyahar**). Gramm. Lae tract.

Lo-ṃōkā-irilik (**lew-ṃekay-yiriylik**).
Gramm. Lae tract.

Lo-naṃōn-ke (**lew-naṃen-kẹy**). Gramm.
See *naṃ, ke:* "secondary lagoon of
porpoises". Majuro tract.

Lo-nen-ko (**lew-nẹn-kew**). Gramm. See
nen: "at the *nen* trees". Mejit tract.

Lo-ṇa-kaṇ (**lew-ṇah-kaṇ**). Gramm. See
ṇa: "at the shoals". Mejit tract.

Lo-pat (**lew-pat**). Gramm. See *pat* "at
the swamp". Bikini tract; Wotho tract;
Kwajalein tract; Namu tract;
Ailinglapalap tract; Jaluit tract; Ebon
tract; Mejit tract; Wotje tract; Majuro
district; Arno islet.

Lo-pat-eṇ (**lew-pat-yeṇ**). Gramm. Kili
tract.

Lo-peñak (**lew-pegak**). Gramm. See
peñak "bay". Majuro tract.

Lo-ran (**lew-ran**). Reminisc. gramm. See
raan "on top of it". Kwajalein tract.

Lo-ran-ej (**lew-ran-yẹj**). Reminisc.
gramm. Kwajalein tract.

Lo-rōreo (**lew-rereyew**). Gramm. See *rreo*
"clean". Knox tract.

Lo-taat (**lew-tahat**). Unanalyz. Rongerik
tract.

Lo-to (**lew-tew**). Gramm. See *to*
"passage". Majuro tract.

Lo-to-eṇ (**lew-tew-yeṇ**). Gramm. Jaluit
tract.

Lo-tokǫ-eṇ (**lew-teqaw-yeṇ**). Reminisc.
gramm. See *tōkā.* Ujae tract.

Lo-tōbak (**lew-tebak**). Gramm. See
tōbak "breadfruit bud". Arno islet.

Lo-tupit (**lew-tiwpit**). Part. reminisc.
gramm. See *tu* "direction", *pit* "Gilbert
Islands", "massage", "make leis". Arno
tract.

Lo-ut (**lew-wit**). Gramm. See *ut*
"flower". Rongerik tract; Aur tract.

Loeaañ (**lẹwyahag**). Part. reminisc.
gramm. Knox tract.

Lokjāiiōñ (**leqjayiyyẹg**). Unanalyz.
Kwajalein tract.

Lokjāirōk (**leqjayirẹk**). Unanalyz.
Kwajalein tract.

Lokḷap (**lẹqḷap**). Recur. form. See *lok,
ioḷap:* "middle". Jaluit tract; Arno
tract.

Lokobbar (**leqebbar**). Unanalyz. Arno
tract.

Lokor (**lẹqẹr°**). Gramm. See *lokor*
"wrap". Ailinglapalap tract.

Lometo (**lẹwṃẹtẹw**). Gramm. distort. See
lo, meto "see the sea". Majuro tract.

Looj (**lẹwẹj**). Pers. name. See *Looj* "clan
name". Eniwetak islet; Rongelap islet;
Lae islet; Erikub islet; Arno tract; Mili
islet.

Looj (**lewej**). Gramm. See *Looj* "islet
name" and *riLoojraṇ* "clan name".
Arno tract.

Loojwa (**lẹwẹjwah**). Pers. name, a
demon. Ailuk islet.

Loojwa (**lewejwah**). Gramm. distort.
Wotje islet.

Looṃkōlaak (**leweṃkelahak**). Part.
reminisc. gramm. Aur tract.

Loonmejaar (**lẹwẹnmejahar**). Unanalyz.
Arno tract.

Lori-Lejṃaan (**lewriy-lẹjṃahan**). Gramm.
See *lǫrun:* "sleeping place of
Lejṃaan, a legendary woman (and
star)". Majuro tract.

Lowalōb (**lewalẹb**). Gramm. See *lōb:* "in
the pond with many fish". Arno tract.

Lowaṇwon (**lẹwaṇwẹṇ**). Gramm. See
lowaṇwoṇ "busy woman". Mejit tract.

Lǫ-aik-eṇ (**law-hayik-yeṇ**). Gramm. See
aik: "at the boat towing place". Jaluit
tract.

Lǫ-alitōk (**law-haliytẹk**). Reminisc.
gramm. See *ruwalitōk* "eight". Wotho
tract; Wotje tract.

Lǫ-apā (**law-hapay**). Gramm. See *apā*
"cave under reef". Arno tract.

Lǫ-ākā (**law-yakay**). Recur. form. See
ākā "mound of stones; crab trap".
Ujae tract; Majuro tract.

Lǫ-āne (**law-yanẹy**). Gramm. See *āne*
"islet". Three Majuro tracts.

Lǫ-bok-eṇ-rālik (**law-beq-yeṇ-raylik**).
Gramm. See *bok* "sandspit". Jaluit
tract.

Lǫ-bok-eṇ-reeaar (**law-beq-yeṇ-
reyyahar**). Gramm. Jaluit tract.

Lǫ-bokwe (**law-bẹqẹy**). Gramm. distort.
See *bōke* "cape". Kwajalein tract;
Namorik tract.

Lọ-bōl (**law-bẹl**). Gramm. See *bōl* "taro pit". Kwajalein tract; Utirik household.

Lọ-bōn (**law-bẹn**). Gramm. See *bōn* "place for floating away corpses". Kwajalein islet.

Lọ-bōro (**law-bẹrẹw**). Gramm. See *bōro* "throat, heart": "favorite place". Mejit tract.

Lọ-bōt (**law-bẹt**). Gramm. See *bōt* "naughty". Mejit tract; two Majuro tracts.

Lọ-buñ (**law-big°**). Gramm. See *buñ:* "where things are always falling off the trees". Lib tract.

Lọ-būkōr (**law-bikẹr**). Gramm. See *būkōr* "a plant". Kwajalein tract; Ailinglapalap tract; Ebon tract.

Lọ-būkōr-eṇ (**law-bikẹr-yeṇ**). Gramm. Rongerik tract.

Lọ-bwiddik (**law-biddik**). Gramm. See *bwiddik* "small piece of land". Jabwot tract.

Lọ-bwidej (**law-bidẹj**). Gramm. See *bwidej* "soil": "lots of soil". Ailinglapalap tract.

Lọ-debọkut (**law-debaqit**). Gramm. See *debọkut* "stump". Mili tract.

Lọ-dekā (**law-dekay**). Gramm. See *dekā* "stones". Likiep tract.

Lọ-dinaaj (**law-dinahaj**). Reminisc. gramm. See *di, aj:* "bone of the thatch (thatch frame; see *tap*)". Arno tract.

Lọ-ejja-eṇ (**law-yejjah-yeṇ**). Gramm. See *ejja* "harbor". Ujae tract.

Lọ-ekā (**law-yekay**). Recur. form. See *Lọ-ākā*. Wotho tract.

Lọ-el-eṇ (**law-yẹl-yeṇ**). Gramm. See *el* "nest". Majuro tract.

Lọ-el-eṇ (**law-yel-yeṇ**). Reminisc. gramm. Arno islet; Arno tract.

Lọ-ene (**law-yẹnẹy**). Gramm. See *āne* "islet". Majuro tract.

Lọ-ene-eṇ (**law-yẹnẹy-yeṇ**). Gramm. Maloelap tract; Maloelap household.

Lọ-ene-eṇ-lik (**law-yẹnẹy-yeṇ-lik**). Gramm. Maloelap household.

Lọ-eo-eṇ (**law-yẹw-yeṇ**). Reminisc. gramm. See *eo* "at the wet place". Three Jaluit tracts; three Mejit tracts.

Lọ-ibwij (**law-yibij**). Gramm. See *ibwij* "high tide". Majuro tract.

Lọ-ie-eañ (**law-yiyey-yag**). Recur. form. See *Lọ-iō-eṇ.* Eniwetak tract; Majuro tract; Likiep tract; Aur tract; two Maloelap households; two Majuro tracts; seven Arno tracts; Mili tract.

Lọ-ien-eo (**law-yiyen-yew**). Gramm. See *iien* "occasion (of war)". Mejit tract.

Lọ-ijo (**law-yijẹw**). Gramm. See *ijo* "good soil". Majuro tract.

Lọ-iō-eḷap (**law-yiyeh-yeḷap**). Recur. form. Maloelap household.

Lọ-iō-eṇ (**law-yiyẹh-yeṇ**). Recur. form. Ujae tract; Kwajalein tract; Utirik household.

Lọ-iō-eṇ (**law-yiyeh-yeṇ**). Recur. form. See *iō* "sprouted coconut". Kwajalein tract; Lib tract; Ailinglapalap tract; Namorik tract; two Arno tracts.

Lọ-iō-eṇ-ar (**law-yiyeh-yeṇ-har**). Recur. form. Arno tract.

Lọ-iō-eṇ-lik (**law-yiyeh-yeṇ-lik**). Recur. form. Majuro tract; Arno tract.

Lọ-iō-eṇ-rak (**law-yiyeh-yeṇ-rak**). Recur. form. Majuro tract.

Lọ-irooj (**law-yirewej**). Gramm. See *irooj* "chief". Ujae tract.

Lọ-jānjen (**law-janjẹn**). Also *Lojānjen.* Gramm. distort. See *lo, jān, ijin:* "see from here". (Main islet can be seen from here.) Majuro tract.

Lọ-jekar (**law-jekar**). Recur. form. See *jekar.* Namu tract.

Lọ-jewōd (**law-jẹywed**). Gramm. See *je, wōd* "at the stomach (deep part) of a coral head". Ujae tract.

Lọ-jiaḷ (**law-jiyaḷ**). Unanalyz. Bikini tract.

Lọ-jiādel (**law-jiyadel**). Gramm. See *jiādel:* "at the chief's bath". Ailinglapalap tract.

Lọ-jidep (**law-jidep**). Gramm. See *jidep:* "at the burnt tree". Bikini tract.

Lọ-jilel (**law-jilẹl**). Gramm. See *jilel* "trumpet shell". Arno tract.

Lọ-jiraan (**law-jirahan**). Gramm. See *jiraan* "dawn". Arno tract.

Lọ-jiroñ (**law-jireg°**). Gramm. See *jiroñ* "assurance". Taka islet.

Lọ-jitak (**law-jitak**). Reminisc. gramm. See *jitaak:* "arrival spot". Eniwetak tract.

Lọ-jo-eṇ (**law-jew-yeṇ**). Gramm. See *jo* "weir fishing". Two Kwajalein tracts; Erikub tract; Arno tract.

Lọ-jo-eṇ-jāiiōñ (**law-jew-yeṇ-jayiyyẹg**). Gramm. Aur tract.

Lọ-jo-eṇ-jāirōk (**law-jew-yeṇ-jayiyrẹk**). Gramm. Aur tract.

Lọ-jokoṃlaak (**law-jẹqẹṃlahak**). Unanalyz. Kwajalein tract; Ailinglapalap tract.

Lo̧-jon̄-en̦ (**law-jeg°-yen̦**). Gramm. See *jon̄* "mangrove". Lae tract; two Kwajalein tracts.

Lo̧-Jowa (**law-jewah**). Gramm. See *Jowa* "a clan". Eniwetak islet.

Lo̧-jurōk-en̦ (**law-jiwrȩk-yen̦**). Gramm. See *jurōk* "net fishing". Rongerik tract.

Lo̧-kaar (**law-kahar**). Gramm. See *kaar* "a tree". Namu tract.

Lo̧-kaar-rāiiōn̄ (**law-kahar-rayiyyȩg**). Gramm. Namu tract.

Lo̧-kaļ-en̦ (**law-kaļ-yen̦**). Gramm. See *kaļ* "loincloth", *kōļ* "stream running out of swamp". Namorik tract.

Lo̧-kan̄al (**law-kahgal**). Gramm. See *kan̄al* "a tree". Bikini tract; Ailinglapalap tract.

Lo̧-kapit (**law-kapit**). Gramm. See *kapit* "anoint". According to legend, Jebro's mother anointed him king here after he won a race. Ailinglapalap tract.

Lo̧-keim̧ (**law-kȩyim̧**). Gramm. distort. See *kii-, em̧:* "at the house wall". Wotje tract.

Lo̧-kied-kan̦ (**law-kiyed-kan̦**). Gramm. See *kien:* "our commandments". Bikini tract.

Lo̧-kiep (**law-kiyȩp**). Gramm. See *kieb* "spider lily". Namorik tract; Ebon tract; Likiep tract.

Lo̧-kijato (**law-kijatew**). Gramm. distort. See *kōjato:* "at the shelter". Lib tract.

Lo̧-kijeek (**law-kijeyek**). Gramm. See *kijeek* "fire". Majuro tract; Arno islet; Arno tract.

Lo̧-kil (**law-kil**). Gramm. See *kil* "skin". Ailinglapalap tract.

Lo̧-kilib (**law-kilib**). Unanalyz. Mili islet.

Lo̧-kille (**law-killȩy**). Gramm. See *kille* "a shrub". Ujae tract; Arno tract.

Lo̧-kilōn̄e (**law-kilegey**). Gramm. See *kōln̄e* "gashes in the reef". Maloelap tract.

Lo̧-kimā (**law-kimay**). Gramm. See *kimā* "a tree". Utirik tract.

Lo̧-kio (**law-kiyew**). Gramm. See *kio* "a plant". Namorik tract.

Lo̧-kobwijlōn̄ (**law-qebijlȩg**). Unanalyz. Mili tract.

Lo̧-kōjbar (**law-kȩjbar**). Gramm. See *kōjbar* "a tree". Ujelang tract; two Eniwetak tracts; Lib tract; two Kwajalein tracts; Namu tract; three Ailinglapalap tracts; three Jaluit tracts; two Majuro tracts.

Lo̧-kōjbar-ean̄ (**law-kȩjbar-yag**). Gramm. Arno tract.

Lo̧-kōjbar-rak (**law-kȩjbar-rak**). Gramm. Arno tract.

Lo̧-kōļ-en̦ (**law-keļ-yen̦**). Gramm. See *kōļ* "stream running out of swamp". Wotho tract; Namorik tract.

Lo̧-kōmje (**law-kȩmjȩy**). Reminisc. gramm. See *kōm* "we", *je* "here". Namorik tract.

Lo̧-kōn̦o (**law-ken̦ew**). Gramm. See *kōn̦o* "a tree". Lib tract; Ailinglapalap tract; Jaluit tract; Ebon tract; Namorik tract.

Lo̧-kōn̄e (**law-kȩgȩy**). Gramm. See *kōn̄e* "a tree". Bikini tract; two Ailinglapalap tracts; Jaluit tract.

Lo̧-kōn̄e-iōn̄ (**law-kegȩy-yiyȩg**). Gramm. distort. Wotho tract.

Lo̧-kōn̄e-rōk (**law-kegȩy-rȩk**). Gramm. distort. Wotho tract.

Lo̧-kūbwe (**law-kibey**). Gramm. See *kūbwe* "feces". Ailinglapalap tract; Utirik tract; Arno tract.

Lo̧-kūbwe-iaar (**law-kibey-yiyahar**). Gramm. Utirik household.

Lo̧-kūbwe-iooj (**law-kibey-yiyȩwȩj**). Gramm. Utirik household.

Lo̧-kūļōn̄e (**law-kiļȩgȩy**). Gramm. distort. See *kōln̄e* "gashes in the reef". Majuro tract.

Lo̧-kūn̦n̦at (**law-kin̦n̦at**). Gramm. distort. See *kōn̦n̦at* "a shrub". Namu tract; Ailinglapalap tract.

Lo̧-kūran̄ (**law-kirag**). Gramm. See *Kūran̄* "a pandanus variety". Ailinglapalap tract.

Lo̧-kūtaak (**law-kitahak**). Gramm. See *kūtaak* "a tree". Ailinglapalap tract; Jaluit tract; Namorik tract.

Lo̧-kūtak (**law-kitak**). Gramm. See *kūtak* "wind from southwest". Lib tract.

Lo̧-kwelo (**law-qeylȩw**). Also *Ļo̧klo* (**ļaqlew**). Unanalyz. Namorik tract.

Lo̧-kwiieb (**law-qiyyeb**). Gramm. distort. See *kieb* "spider lily". Eniwetak tract.

Lo̧-lem (**law-lȩm**). Gramm. See *lem* "bailer". Likiep tract.

Lo̧-libōn (**law-liben**). Gramm. See *lōb:* "at his (her) grave". Arno tract.

Lo̧-lim-en̦ (**law-lim-yen̦**). Gramm. See *lim* "fold". Arno tract.

Lo̧-lim̧-en̦ (**law-lim̧-yen̦**). Gramm. See *lim̧* "murky water". Jaluit tract; Likiep tract; Wotje tract; Aur tract; Arno tract.

Lo̧-lim̧-eņ-jāirōk (**law-lim̧-yeņ-jayiyrȩk**). Gramm. Wotje tract.

Lo̧-lim̧we (**law-lim̧ȩy**). Recur. form. See *Lo̧-lim̧-eņ.* Two Knox islets.

Lo̧-lur-eņ (**law-lir°-yeņ**). Gramm. See *lur* "calm". Ailuk tract.

Lo̧-Ļanej (**law-ļanȩj**). Pers. name, legendary man. Ailinglapalap tract; Ailinglapalap household.

Lo̧-ļeenbadet (**law-ļeyenbadet**). Gramm. distort. See *ļwe, badet:* "pond of the *maomao* fish". Ailinglapalap tract.

Lo̧-ļeenm̧ak (**law-ļȩyȩnm̧ak**). Gramm. distort. See *ļwe, m̧ak:* "pond of needlefish"; see also *lo̧ļin* "shape of" and *Lo̧ļinm̧ak* "Knox tract": "shape of a needlefish". Ailinglapalap tract.

Lo̧-ļejeįjat (**law-ļȩyjejjat**). Gramm. See *ļwe, jeįjat* "at the pond of no water". Kwajalein tract.

Lo̧-ļoore (**law-ļȩwȩrȩy**). Also *Lo̧-lorā* (**law-lȩwray**). Unanalyz. Ujae tract.

Lo̧-ļo̧ (**law-ļaw**). Gramm. See *ļo̧* "hibiscus". Ailinglapalap tract; Mejit tract.

Lo̧-ļwe (**law-ļ°ȩy**). Gramm. See *ļwe* "pond". Kwajalein tract; Namorik tract; Namu tract; Majuro tract.

Lo̧-ļwūjpenpen (**law-ļ°ijpȩnpȩn**). Gramm. distort. See *ļwe, jipenpen* "at sea cucumber pond". Ailinglapalap tract.

Lo̧-me-eņ (**law-mȩy-yeņ**). Gramm. See *me* "weir". Ailinglapalap tract; two Aur tracts.

Lo̧-meej (**law-meyej**). Gramm. See *meej:* "at the accustomed place". Rongelap tract.

Lo̧-mej (**law-mȩj**). Gramm. See *mej* "opening between two islets". Wotho tract; two Ailinglapalap tracts.

Lo̧-mej-eņ (**law-mȩj-yeņ**). Gramm. Kwajalein tract; Majuro tract; Mili tract.

Lo̧-mejate (**law-mejatȩy**). Gramm. See *mejate* "path to the beach". Ebon tract.

Lo̧-mejādik (**law-mejaydik**). Gramm. See *meja:* "at the small gash in the reef". Ailinglapalap tract.

Lo̧-mejenkeiiuiu (**law-mejenkȩyiyyiwyiw**). Gramm. distort. See *meja-, keiiuiu* "at the eye of the swamp spring". Namu tract.

Lo̧-mejeto (**law-mȩjetew**). Gramm. distort. See *mejeto* "path to the beach". Kwajalein tract.

Lo̧-mejeto (**law-mejetew**). Gramm. Kwajalein tract.

Lo̧-mejje-eņ (**law-mȩjjȩy-yeņ**). Gramm. See *mejje* "opening between islets". Jaluit tract.

Lo̧-mejto (**law-mȩjtȩw**). Gramm. distort. See *mejeto* "path to the beach". Lae tract.

Lo̧-meļaļ (**law-meļaļ**). Gramm. See *meļaļ* "demon playground". Arno tract.

Lo̧-metto (**law-mettew**). Gramm. See *metto* "ocean anchorage". Arno tract.

Lo̧-mien (**law-miyen**). Gramm. See *mien:* "at the canoe storage". Arno tract.

Lo̧-mō (**law-mȩh**). Unanalyz. Utirik tract.

Lo̧-m̧ōk (**law-m̧ȩk**). Gramm. See *m̧ōk* "fatigue". Majuro tract.

Lo̧-m̧ōk (**law-m̧ek**). Gramm. Mili tract.

Lo̧-m̧ōk-rāātle (**law-m̧ek-rayatley**). Gramm. Arno tract.

Lo̧-m̧ōk-rālik (**law-m̧ek-raylik**). Gramm. Jaluit tract.

Lo̧-m̧ōk-reeaar (**law-m̧ek-reyyahar**). Gramm. Jaluit tract; Arno tract.

Lo̧-m̧ōkā (**law-m̧ekay**). Gramm. See *m̧ōkā* "these houses". Majuro tract.

Lo̧-m̧ōkādik (**law-m̧ekaydik**). Gramm. See *m̧ōkā:* "at these small houses". Ailinglapalap tract; Jaluit tract.

Lo̧-m̧we-eņ (**law-m̧ȩy-yeņ**). Gramm. See *m̧we:* "at that place of brown fronds". Majuro tract.

Lo̧-m̧wilaļ (**law-m̧ilaļ**). Gramm. See *m̧wilaļ:* "in the depths". Rongelap islet.

Lo̧-m̧wilik (**law-m̧ilik**). Also *Lo̧o̧m̧lik.* Gramm. See *m̧wilik* "place where frigatebirds sleep". Bikini district; Bikini islet.

Lo̧-m̧wilik-eņ (**law-m̧ilik-yeņ**). Gramm. Ebon tract; Maloelap tract.

Lo̧-m̧wilik-eņ-iōñ (**law-m̧ilik-yeņ-yiyȩg**). Gramm. Aur tract.

Lo̧-m̧wilik-eņ-rōk (**law-m̧ilik-yeņ-rȩk**). Gramm. Aur tract.

Lo̧-nen (**law-nȩn**). Gramm. See *nen* "a tree". Utirik household.

Lo̧-ni-eņ (**law-niy-yeņ**). Gramm. See *ni* "coconut tree". Kili tract.

Lo̧-nit (**law-nit**). Gramm. See *nit* "sunken enclosure". Ailuk tract.

Lo̧-nit-eañ (**law-nit-yag**). Gramm. Arno tract.

Lọ-nit-rak (**law-nit-rak**). Gramm. Arno tract.

Lọ-nōt (**law-nẹt**). Gramm. See *nōt* "squid". Wotje tract.

Lọ-ṇo (**law-ṇew**). Gramm. See *ṇo* "waves". Two Kwajalein tracts.

Lọ-or (**law-wer**). Gramm. See *or.* Namorik tract; Ebon tract; Arno tract.

Lọ-paaj (**law-pahaj**). Gramm. See *paaj* "chief's kitchen". Majuro tract.

Lọ-pat (**law-pat**). Gramm. See *pat* "swamp". Eniwetak tract; Rongelap tract; Likiep tract.

Lọ-pat-rālik (**law-pat-raylik**). Gramm. Kwajalein tract.

Lọ-pat-reeaar (**law-pat-reyyahar**). Gramm. Kwajalein tract.

Lọ-Peen (**law-pẹyẹn**). Reminisc. gramm., *Peen* is the name of a cape here, possibly from *pein* "its arm". Maloelap tract.

Lọ-pele (**law-peley**). Gramm. distort. See *marpeḷe* "a plant". Eniwetak tract.

Lọ-pet (**law-pet**). Gramm. See *pet* "foul". Namu tract.

Lọ-pikaere (**law-pikahyẹrẹy**). Reminisc. gramm. See *pikpik* "flapping", *aere* "a storm". Majuro islet.

Lọ-piñpiñ (**law-pigpig**). Gramm. See *piñpiñ* "a tree". Ujae tract; Lae tract; Kwajalein tract; Namu tract; three Ailinglapalap tracts; Ebon tract; Likiep tract; Maloelap tract.

Lọ-piñpiñ-ko (**law-pigpig-kew**). Gramm. Mejit tract.

Lọ-piti (**law-pitiy**). Gramm. See *piti* "twist it": "place for making sennit". Bikini tract.

Lọ-pooḷ (**law-peweḷ**). Gramm. See *pooḷ* "encircled". Two Arno tracts.

Lọ-pooḷ-iaar (**law-peweḷ-yiyahar**). Gramm. Arno household.

Lọ-pooḷ-ilik (**law-peweḷ-yilik**). Gramm. Arno household.

Lọ-pooḷ-iooj (**law-peweḷ-yiyẹwẹj**). Gramm. Arno household.

Lọ-poon-ire (**law-pewen-yirey**). Gramm. See *poon, ire* "land to fight". Aur tract.

Lọ-ro-eṇ (**law-rew-yeṇ**). Unanalyz. Rongelap tract.

Lọ-roñroñ (**law-r°eg°r°eg°**). Recur. form. Mili tract.

Lọ-ror-eṇ (**law-r°er°-yeṇ**). Gramm. See *ror* "at the roaring place". Two Rongelap tracts; Wotho tract.

Lọ-roro (**law-rẹwrẹw**). Gramm. See *roro* "chanting" or "dust blowing down from the coconut cloth (*inpel*)". Mejit tract.

Lọ-taar (**law-tahar**). Gramm. See *taar* "the place of warding off". Namu tract.

Lọ-taat (**law-tahat**). Unanalyz. Bikini tract.

Lọ-tiaerōk (**law-tiyhayẹrẹk**). Recur. form. See *tiete, aerōkeañḷọk:* "end of the reef where the current flows southward". Arno tract.

Lọ-tilaan (**law-tilahan**). Gramm. See *tilaan* "basaltic rock which floats ashore". Namu tract; Jabwot tract; Ailinglapalap tract; Arno tract.

Lọ-tilañ (**law-tilag**). Unanalyz. See *Tilañ* "a clan". Kwajalein tract.

Lọ-to (**law-tẹw**). Gramm. See *to* "pit for soaking husks". Arno tract.

Lọ-to (**law-tew**). Gramm. See *to* "passage". Bikini tract; Ujae tract; Likiep islet; Majuro tract; two Arno tracts; Knox tract.

Lọ-to-eṇ (**law-tew-yeṇ**). Gramm. Rongelap tract; Namorik tract; Majuro tract; Arno tract.

Lọ-toṇak (**law-tẹwṇak**). Gramm. See *toṇak:* "at the parting of the trees". Lae tract; Kwajalein tract; Namu tract; Ailinglapalap tract; two Jaluit tracts; Maloelap tract.

Lọ-toonwa (**law-tewenwah**). Gramm. See *to, wa:* "at the canoe passage". Maloelap tract; Knox tract.

Lọ-toor (**law-tẹwẹr**). Gramm. distort. See *toor* "pool or channel on reef". Arno tract.

Lọ-toor-eṇ (**law-tewer-yeṇ**). Gramm. See *toor:* "at the channel on the reef". Namorik tract.

Lọ-tọ-dik (**law-taw-dik**). Gramm. See *tọ* "pond on reef". Majuro tract.

Lọ-tọ-ej (**law-taw-yẹj**). Gramm. See *tọ, ej:* "at the eastern passage". Namorik tract.

Lọ-tọ-eṇ (**law-taw-yeṇ**). Gramm. Bikini tract; Likiep tract.

Lọ-tọḷā (**law-taḷ°ay**). Part. reminisc. gramm. See *to, ḷā* "gravel pond on reef". Majuro tract.

Lọ-tujo (**law-tiwjew**). Part. recur. form. Arno tract.

Lọ-tuon-pako (**law-tiwen-pakew**). Gramm. See *tuon, pako:* "skill of the shark". Jaluit tract.

Lǫ-u (law-wiw). Gramm. See *u* "fish trap". Kwajalein tract.

Lǫ-ut (law-wit). Gramm. See *ut* "flowers". Arno tract.

Lǫ-ut-kaṇ (law-wit-kaṇ). Gramm. Bikini tract; Wotho tract; Wotje tract.

Lǫ-wōne (law-wẹnẹy). Gramm. See *wōn:* "at the place of this turtle". Ebon tract.

Lǫ-wōt-ko (law-wẹt-kew). Gramm. See *wōt* "place of the rains". Mili tract.

Lǫ-wūj (law-wij). Gramm. See *wūj* "balsa driftwood". Namorik household; Ailinglapalap tract.

Lǫ-wūj-kaṇ (law-wij-kaṇ). Gramm. Arno tract.

Lǫ-wūjooj (law-wijẹwẹj). Gramm. See *wūjooj* "grass". Mejit tract.

Lǫ-wūleej (law-wilẹyẹj). Gramm. See *wūliej* "cemetery". Bikini tract.

Lǫ-wūlej (law-wilẹj). Gramm. See *wūlej* "a shrub". Namu tract.

Lǫ-wūnmaañ (law-winmahag). Gramm. See *wūnmaañ* "a pandanus variety". Maloelap tract.

Lǫli-ṇa-eṇ (lawḷiy-ṇah-yeṇ). Gramm. See *ḷǫlin, ṇa* "shape of that shoal". Mili tract.

Lǫḷinṃak (lawḷinṃak). Gramm. See *ḷǫlin, ṃak* "shape of a needlefish". Knox tract.

Lǫmǫǫr-iōñ (lawmawar-yiyẹg). Gramm. See *ḷǫmǫǫr* "rescue". Wotje tract.

Lǫmǫǫr-rōk (lawmawar-rẹk). Gramm. Wotje tract.

Lǫñba (lag°bah). Unanalyz. Ujae islet.

Lǫñloñ (lag°lẹg°). Reminisc. gramm. See *lañlōñ* "joy". Mejit tract.

Lǫǫrkā-eṇ (lawarkay-yeṇ). Unanalyz. Ebon tract.

Lǫri-den (lawr°iy-dẹn). Gramm. distort. See *ḷǫri, kiden* "under the *kiden* "tree". Majuro tract.

Lǫri-to (lawr°iy-tew). Gramm. See *ḷǫri, to* "under the passage". Arno tract.

Lǫrun-kōṇo (lawr°in-keṇew). Gramm. See *ḷǫrun, kōṇo:* "under the *kōṇo* tree". Arno islet.

Lǫulōro (lawilerew). Also *Lawūlōro* (lahwilerew). Unanalyz. Arno islet.

Lōbañ-eṇ (lebag-yeṇ). Unanalyz. Arno tract.

Lōbo (lẹbẹw). Pers. name. Ailinglapalap tract.

Lōbrar (lebrar). Unanalyz. Rongerik tract.

Lōkea (lẹkẹyah). Gramm. See *lōke, ia:* "put trust where". Mili tract.

Lōkkalik (lẹkkalik). Unanalyz. See *kaliklik* "bear babies". Majuro tract; Arno tract.

Lōkōn-eṃ (leken-yeṃ). Gramm. distort. See *lik, eṃ* "behind the house". Mejit tract.

Lōkōt (lẹkẹt). Gramm. distort. See *likūt* "deposit". Ebon tract.

Lōḷḷaḷ (leḷḷaḷ). Part. recur. form. See *ḷaḷ* "down to earth". Jaluit islet.

Lōrro (lẹrrew). Gramm. See *lōrrǫ.* Arno tract.

Lōtbar (lẹtbar). Gramm. See *Lōtbar* "waves caused by typhoon". Arno tract.

Lujoor (liwjewer). Pers. name. Eniwetak islet.

Lukoḷpān-eṇ (liqeḷpan-yeṇ). Gramm. distort. See *lukwōn eoḷapān:* "in the middle of the middle". Namu tract.

Lukoon (liqẹwen). Reminisc. gramm. See *lukwōn wōn* "in the middle of the ripening pit". Rongelap islet.

Lukottōkkā (liqettekkay). Reminisc. gramm. See *lukwō-, tōkā:* "in the middle of the long reef". Rongelap islet.

Lukun-ut (liqin-wit). Gramm. distort. See *lukwō-, ut* "in the midst of flowers". Aur tract.

Lukwaḷḷōj (liqaḷḷej). Pers. name. Mili tract.

Lukweej-eṇ (liqeyej-yeṇ). Gramm. See *lukwej* "a tree". Ujelang tract.

Lukwōj (liqej). Gramm. See *lukwōj* "tie". Bikini islet; Namu islet; Arno islet.

Lukwōj-kōj (liqej-kẹj). Gramm. See *lukwōj, kōj:* "ties us". Majuro tract; Arno tract.

Lukwōn (liqen). Gramm. See *lukwōn* "middle". Wotje tract; three Maloelap tracts; Majuro tract; Arno tract.

Lukwōn-ānin (liqen-yanyin). Gramm. See *lukwōn, āne:* "middle of this islet". Ujelang tract.

Lukwōn-ene (liqen-yẹṇey). Gramm. See *lukwōn, āne:* "middle of the islet". Aur tract.

Lukwōn-maajaj (liqen-mahajhaj). Gramm. See *maaj:* "clear middle". Aur tract.

Lukwōn-wōd (**liqen-wed**). Gramm. See *wōd:* "middle of the coral". Likiep islet; Mili district; Mili islet.

Lukwōn-wōj (**liqen-wẹj**). Gramm. See *lukwōn, wōj:* "balsa driftwood in the middle". Majuro tract.

Luoj-jāiōn̄ (**liwẹj-jayiyyẹg**). Pers. name. Kwajalein islet.

Luoj-jāirōk (**liwẹj-jayiyrẹk**). Pers. name. Kwajalein islet.

Lur-ene (**lir°-yẹnẹy**). Gramm. See *lur* "calm", *āne* "islet". Rongelap tract; Aur tract.

Lur-eṇ (**lir°-yeṇ**). Gramm. Namorik tract.

Luuj-rōk (**liwij-rẹk**). Pers. name. Ailuk islet.

Luwabar-jāltak-kaṇ (**liwahbar-jaltak-kaṇ**). Recur. form. See *luwa, bar.* Kwajalein coral head.

Luwajerak (**liwahjerak**). Pers. name, legendary woman. Mili islet.

Luwallan̄ (**liwallag**). Pers. name. Majuro tract.

Luweej-eṇ (**liweyej-yeṇ**). Pers. name. See *lukwej* "a tree". Two Mili tracts.

Ḷaaj-Mājro (**ḷahaj-majrẹw**). Pers. name, *Ḷaaj* and *Ḷodejilu* were two famous warriors in battle between Majuro and Maloelap. Majuro tract.

Ḷaak (**ḷahak**). Gramm. See *ḷaak* "to fit". Maloelap islet.

Ḷaakul (**ḷahaqil**). Pers. name, a demon. Utirik household.

Ḷaannōn̄ (**ḷahanneg**). Pers. name. See *annan̄* "Mr. Shadow". Arno tract.

Ḷaarej (**ḷaharyej**). Unanalyz. Eniwetak tract.

Ḷaatdik (**ḷahatdik**). Pers. name. Mejit district.

Ḷabarej (**ḷabaryẹj**). Pers. name, an ancient chief. Rongelap islet.

Ḷabo (**ḷabew**). Unanalyz. Kwajalein islet.

Ḷadudu-rāātle (**ḷadiwdiw-rayatley**). Reminisc. gramm. Arno tract.

Ḷadudu-reeaar (**ḷadiwdiw-reyyahar**). Reminisc. gramm. Arno tract.

Ḷajbwe (**ḷajbẹy**). Gramm. See *ḷaj, bwe:* "hit the mark". Arno tract.

Ḷajden̄ (**ḷajdeg**). Gramm. See *ḷajden̄* "last fruits". Aur tract.

Ḷaje (**ḷajẹy**). Unanalyz. Ailinglapalap tract.

Ḷajibwe (**ḷajibẹy**). Unanalyz. Arno tract.

Ḷajilel (**ḷajilẹl**). Unanalyz. See *jilel* "conch shell". Arno tract.

Ḷajiḷaḷip (**ḷajiyḷaḷip**). Pers. name, a spirit. Wotje tract.

Ḷajinej (**ḷajinej**). Pers. name. Mili islet.

Ḷajjidik (**ḷajjidik**). Gramm. See *ḷajjidik* "a coral". Ailinglapalap household.

Ḷajọutoḷ (**ḷajawiwteḷ°**). Pers. name, a legendary man. Wotje tract.

Ḷajumājjen (**ḷajiwmajjẹn**). Pers. name, a man who was brave in battle. Wotje tract.

Ḷajuṃaat (**ḷajiwṃahat**). Pers. name. Likiep tract.

Ḷakelōn̄ (**ḷakẹylẹg**). Gramm. See *Ḷakelōn̄* "a star". Mili tract.

Ḷakne (**ḷaknẹy**). Pers. name. Ailinglapalap islet; Arno tract.

Ḷakubaak (**ḷakiwbahak**). Pers. name. See *kubaak:* "Mr. Outrigger". Mejit tract.

Ḷakūḷḷij (**ḷakiḷḷij**). Pers. name. See *kiḷij:* "Mr. Lizard". Majuro tract.

Ḷalikiiōn̄ (**ḷalikiyyẹg**). Pers. name. Mejit tract.

Ḷam-eṇ (**ḷam-yeṇ**). Gramm. See *ḷam* "bay". Ebon tract; two Likiep tracts; Arno household.

Ḷaṃwin-ijo (**ḷaṃin-yijẹw**). Recur. form. See *ijo* "good soil". Wotje tract.

Ḷaneej (**ḷanẹyẹj**). Pers. name, legendary man who tattooed people and fish, brother of *Ḷewōj.* Maloelap tract.

Ḷaṇtōn (**ḷaṇten**). From Engl. *London.* Wotje tract; Mili islet.

Ḷan̄idaan (**ḷagidahan**). Pers. name. Jaluit islet.

Ḷan̄ḷan̄ (**ḷagḷag**). Gramm. See *ḷan̄* "storm". Ailinglapalap tract.

Ḷappo (**ḷappẹw**). Gramm. See *ḷappo* "hogfish". Bikini tract.

Ḷarere (**ḷarẹyrẹy**). Gramm. See *ḷarere* "breeze". Jaluit islet.

Ḷarōktak (**ḷarektak**). Unanalyz. Ujelang tract.

Ḷatjiṃ (**latjiṃ**). Gramm. See *ḷatjiṃ* "lower half of coconut shell". Ailinglapalap household.

Ḷatmij (**latmij**). Gramm. distort. See *ḷatmej* "upper half of coconut shell". Ailinglapalap household.

Ḷatōṃṃan (**ḷateṃṃan**). Pers. name. Mejit district.

Ḷā-dik (**ḷay-dik**). Gramm. See *ḷā* "gravel". Mili islet.

Ļā-eņ (**ļay-yeņ**). Gramm. Two Bikini tracts.

Ļāārpep (**ļayarpep**). Pers. name. See *ār, pāp:* "Mr. Beaching-frond". Mili islet.

Ļārooj (**ļayręwęj**). Gramm. See *ļārooj* "chief's reservation". Erikub district; Maloelap islet.

Ļeeded (**ļeyedyed**). Reminisc. gramm. See *ļe eoon eṃ* "trespass", *eded* "rummage". Ailinglapalap tract.

Ļeen (**ļeyen**). Unanalyz. Likiep islet.

Ļeeoon (**ļeyyewen**). Gramm. See *ļe eoon eṃ* "poach". Ailinglapalap tract.

Ļele (**ļeyley**). Pers. name. Bikini islet.

Ļipdeļǫk (**ļipdęyļaq**). Gramm. See *ļipdeļǫk* "go through". Mili tract.

Ļipjenkur (**ļipjenqir**). Gramm. Ujae tract.

Ļobōlǫk-rāiōñ (**ļęwbelaq-rayiyęg**). Unanalyz. Kwajalein tract.

Ļobōlǫk-rāirōk (**ļęwbelaq-rayiyręk**). Unanalyz. Kwajalein tract.

Ļojelañ (**ļ°ejeylag**). Unanalyz. Ailuk tract.

Ļokadik (**ļewkadik**). Pers. name. Arno tract.

Ļokleej (**ļ°ęqlęyęj**). Pers. name. See *kwōlej:* "Mr. Plover". Majuro tract.

Ļokool-eņ (**ļ°eqewel-yeņ**). Pers. name, a magician. Arno tract.

Ļoñane (**ļ°eg°anęy**). Unanalyz. Jaluit islet; Jaluit tract.

Ļookalik (**ļ°ewekalik**). Pers. name. See *okaliklik:* "Mr. Pandanus-storer". Wotje tract.

Ļooñ (**ļ°eweg**). Unanalyz. Arno tract.

Ļoorjep (**ļ°ewerjep**). Unanalyz. Ujelang tract.

Ļotōnaļ (**ļ°etęnhaļ**). Gramm. See *ļot, aļ:* "sunset". Ujae tract.

Ļowa (**ļ°ewah**). Pers. name, a famous navigator. Maloelap islet.

Ļǫ-ed (**ļaw-yed**). Gramm. See *ļǫ, ed* "red-leaved hibiscus". Namorik tract.

Ļǫ-eņ (**ļaw-yeņ**). Gramm. Namu district; Namu islet; Ailinglapalap tract.

Ļǫjipā (**ļawjipay**). Unanalyz. Rongelap tract.

Ļǫkko (**ļaqqew**). Gramm. distort. Eniwetak tract.

Ļǫkurjeban (**ļaqirjeban**). Pers. name. See *kur, jeban:* "Mr. Plentiful-squirrel-fish". Majuro tract.

Ļǫoje (**ļawejey**). Also *Ļawōje.* Unanalyz. Mejit tract.

Ļǫuwe (**ļawiwęy**). Also *Ļauwe.* Pers. name, a chief. Jaluit tract.

Ļōbǫtin (**ļebawtin**). Pers. name, and name of fishing method named after man with this name. See *bǫti:* "Mr. Nose". Majuro tract.

Ļōbweeaan (**ļębęyyahan**). Unanalyz. Bikini tract.

Ļōjele (**ļęjęlęy**). Pers. name. Ailinglapalap tract; Arno tract.

Ļōjemwā (**ļejemway**). Pers. name. Majuro tract.

Ļōjjoodiōñ (**ļejjewedyiyęg**). Pers. name. Mili tract.

Ļōjkad (**ļejkad**). Pers. name. See *jekad:* "Mr. Noddy". Majuro tract.

Ļōjolep (**ļejewlep**). Pers. name. Likiep tract.

Ļōjomām (**ļejęwmam**). Pers. name. See *jomām:* "Mr. Giant-fish". Arno tract.

Ļōjonaañ (**ļejewnahag**). Also *Ļōjoknahag* (**ļejeqnahag**). Pers. name. Mili tract.

Ļōjorñak (**ļejer°gak**). Pers. name. See *jorñak:* "Mr. Speedy". Arno islet.

Ļōjorōk (**ļejewręk**). Pers. name. Majuro tract.

Ļōjǫliṃ-eņ (**ļejawliṃ-yeņ**). Pers. name. See *jǫ, ļiṃ:* "Mr. Push-into-the-sandy-beach". Majuro tract.

Ļōjǫuddik (**ļejawiddik**). Pers. name. Majuro tract.

Ļōjǫunbar (**ļejawinbar**). Pers. name. See *jǫ, wūn, bar:* "Mr. Push-under-the-rock". Majuro tract.

Ļōkanij (**ļekhanij**). Gramm. See *ļōkatip, anij:* "displease the gods". Arno tract.

Ļōkeae (**ļekeyhayey**). Gramm. See *ļōke, ae:* "cross over the currents (*jukae, dibukae,* and *jeļatae*) and see land". Namorik tract.

Ļōkļañ (**ļekļag**). Pers. name. See *ļañ:* "Mr. Storm-maker". Bikini tract.

Ļōkōbo (**ļękębęw**). Pers. name, a Gilbertese man who drifted here and lived here. Ebon tract.

Ļōkōbǫñ (**ļekebwag°**). Unanalyz. Arno islet.

Ļōkōnmǫk (**ļekenmaq**). Pers. name. See *kan, mǫk:* "Mr. Surgeonfish-eater". Majuro tract.

Ḷōlwe (**ḷelwey**). Pers. name. See *llo, loe:* "Mr. See-him, an important man". Mili islet.

Ḷōmǫoj (**ḷemawej**). Also *Ḷōmawōj.* Pers. name, related to *lemawōji tok* "harvest and bring all foods to the house". Arno tract.

Ḷōm̧dā-lik (**ḷem̧day-lik**). Pers. name. Mili tract.

Ḷōn̄ar (**ḷegar**). Pers. name, a legendary man who lived here and went on voyage with wife. Mejit tract; Arno district; Arno islet.

Ḷōpako (**ḷepakew**). Pers. name. See *pako:* "Mr. Shark". Arno tract.

Ḷōplon̄ (**ḷepleg°**). Reminisc. gramm. See *lep, ḷon̄:* "ant egg". Majuro islet.

Ḷōpņa (**ḷepņah**). Pers. name, legendary man. Ailinglapalap islet.

Ḷōrkōm̧ (**ḷerkem̧**). Pers. name. Wotje tract.

Ḷōruk (**ḷeriq**). Gramm. See *ḷōruk* "second crop". Jaluit tract; Mejit tract; Aur tract.

Ḷōtoonke (**ḷetewenkẹy**). Pers. name. See *to, ke:* "Mr. Porpoise-pass". Likiep tract.

Ḷōtran̄ (**ḷetrag**). Pers. name. See *tōran̄.* Majuro tract.

Ḷuḷupi (**ḷiwḷiwpiy**). Unanalyz. Utirik household.

Ḷwe-eņ (**ḷ°ẹy-yeņ**). Gramm. See *ḷwe* "pond". Ailuk tract; Arno tract.

Ḷwe-jab (**ḷ°ẹy-jab**). Part. recur. form. See *ḷwe* "pond". Lae islet.

Ḷwōj (**ḷ°ẹj**). Unanalyz. Ailinglapalap tract.

Ḷwōjāde (**ḷ°ejadẹy**). Reminisc. gramm. See *ḷwe* "pond", *jāde* "in sight". Mili tract.

Ḷwūj-kaņ (**ḷ°ij-kaņ**). Gramm. See *ḷwūj:* "those mallets". Arno tract.

Maaj (**mahaj**). Gramm. See *maaj* "clearing". Rongelap tract.

Maaj-dikdik (**mahaj-dikdik**). Gramm. See *maaj, dik:* "small clearing". Mejit tract.

Maaj-eņ (**mahaj-yeņ**). Gramm. See *maaj:* "the clearing". Bikini tract; three Kwajalein tracts; Mili islet; Mili tract.

Maaj-kaņ (**mahaj-kaņ**). Gramm. Two Maloelap tracts.

Maajatutu (**mahajatiwtiw**). Part. recur. form. See *maaj* "clearing", *tutu* "bathing". Mejit tract.

Maajin-wūd (**mahajin-wid**). Gramm. See *maaj, wūd:* "clearing of bits and pieces". Ebon tract.

Maajno (**mahajnew**). Unanalyz. Ailinglapalap tract.

Maaklōn̄ (**mahaklẹg**). Part. recur. form. See *lōn̄* "above". Kwajalein tract.

Maan (**mahan**). Part. recur. form. See *mmaan* "at anchor". Kwajalein islet.

Maan̄rar (**mahagrar**). Gramm. See *maan̄, rar:* "bleached pandanus leaf". Arno islet.

Madidi (**mahdiydiy**). Reminisc. gramm. See *mmadidi* "drowsy". Mili tract.

Maira (**mahyirah**). Pers. name. Mejit tract.

Majoḷ (**mahjeḷ°**). Unanalyz. Jaluit tract.

Maḷkā (**maḷkay**). Unanalyz. Mili islet.

Maḷkā-eoḷap (**maḷkay-yewḷap**). Unanalyz. Mili tract.

Maḷkā-iiōn̄ (**maḷkay-yiyyẹg**). Unanalyz. Mili tract.

Maḷkā-irōk (**maḷkay-yiyrẹk**). Unanalyz. Mili tract.

Maḷkwōn (**maḷqẹn**). Unanalyz. See *Maḷkwōn* "Rongelap tract". Wotje tract.

Maḷkwōn (**maḷqen**). Unanalyz. See *Maḷkwōn* "Wotje tract", *Maḷkwōn* "Rongelap tract". Ebon tract.

Maḷǫǫn (**maḷawan**). Reminisc. gramm. See *m̧aḷo* "lagoon". Ujelang tract.

Manōt (**mahnet**). Gramm. See *manōt* "a fish". Mili tract.

Man̄bōn-rālik (**magben-raylik**). Gramm. See *man̄bōn* "ripening coconut". Kwajalein tract.

Man̄bōn-reeaar (**magben-reyyahar**). Gramm. Kwajalein tract.

Man̄in-bōōt (**magin-behet**). Part. reminisc. gramm. See *man̄* "ripening coconut". Bikini tract.

Mar (**mar**). Gramm. See *mar* "thicket". Majuro tract.

Mar-atat (**mar-hathat**). Gramm. See *mar:* "thicket of *atat* vines". Ujae tract.

Mar-eņ (**mar-yeņ**). Gramm. Rongelap tract; Aur tract; Majuro tract.

Marere (**mareyrey**). Gramm. See *marere* "legendary game". Maloelap islet; Aur islet.

Marere-dik (**mareyrey-dik**). Gramm. Aur islet.

Marip (**marip**). Gramm. See *mariprip* "damage". Ailuk islet.

Marjāj-eṇ (**marjaj-yeṇ**). Gramm. See *marjāj* "a plant". Maloelap tract.

Markūñ (**markig**). Gramm. See *mar, kūñ* "thicket that smells of feces". Mili tract.

Marme (**marmey**). Gramm. distort. See *mar, jome:* "bushes whose leaves are used as bait for goatfish". Ailuk islet.

Marmer (**marmẹr**). Reminisc. gramm. See *mar* "bushes". Ebon tract.

Marok-eṇ (**mareq-yeṇ**). Gramm. See *marok* "darkness". Mili islet.

Marōbōn (**mareben**). Unanalyz. Arno tract.

Marut (**marwit**). Gramm. See *mar, ut* "flower bush". Aur tract.

Matḷan (**matḷan**). Gramm. See *matoḷ:* "a third of it", or distortion of *meḷan* "surroundings". Aur tract.

Matoḷ-ej (**mateḷ°-yẹj**). Gramm. See *matoḷ* "third part". Majuro tract.

Matoḷ-eṇ (**mateḷ°-yeṇ**). Gramm. Arno district; Arno islet.

Matte-eṇ (**mattey-yeṇ**). Unanalyz. Ailinglapalap islet.

Māānwa (**mayanwah**). Gramm. See *mā, wa:* "breadfruit (wood) for a canoe". Ebon tract.

Māddebōn (**maddeben**). Unanalyz. Arno islet.

Māddeen (**maddeyen**). Gramm. distort. See *medde* "reef under surface of lagoon". Eniwetak islet.

Mādejje (**madẹjjẹy**). Unanalyz. Ailinglapalap tract.

Mādikio (**maydikiyew**). Unanalyz. Namorik tract.

Mādjāj-eṇ (**madjaj-yeṇ**). Gramm. distort. See *marjāj* "a plant". Maloelap tract.

Mādo-eṇ (**maydew-yeṇ**). Gramm. See *mādo* "breadfruit soaking net". Ailuk tract.

Mājān-bu (**majan-biw**). Gramm. See *māj, bu:* "bore of the gun". Mili islet.

Mājān-iōñ (**majan-yiyẹg**). Gramm. See *māj:* "its northern opening". Mejit tract.

Mājeej (**majẹyẹj**). Also *Mejeej* (**mẹjyẹj**). Reminisc. gramm. See *māj, ej* "eastern opening". Ratak island; Mejit; Kwajalein tract; Utirik household.

Mājel (**majẹl**). Reminisc. gramm. See *mejel* "dense". Ailinglapalap islet.

Mājjen (**majjẹn**). Unanalyz. Wotje islet.

Mājo (**majẹw**). Recur. form. See *mājojo* "firm". Arno tract.

Mājro (**majrẹw**). Reminisc. gramm. See *māj, ruo* "two openings"; see also *Mājruon* and *Mājrwi-rōk.* Ratak atoll; Majuro; Mejit tract; Majuro islet.

Mājroṇ (**majr°eṇ°**). Part. reminisc. gramm. Maloelap islet.

Mājruon (**majriwen**). Part. reminisc. gramm. Wotho islet; Aur islet.

Mājruon-dik (**majriwen-dik**). Part. reminisc. gramm. Aur islet.

Mājrwi-rōk (**majr°iy-rẹk**). Part. reminisc. gramm.: *Mājro-i-rōk* "Majuro in the south". Jaluit islet.

Mālila (**maliylah**). From Phil. *Manila.* Jaluit tract.

Mālkūñ (**malkig**). Part. reminisc. gramm. See *kūñ* "smell of feces". Mili tract.

Mālle (**malley**). Gramm. See *mālle* "coals". Likiep islet.

Mālletọọr (**mallẹytawar**). Reminisc. gramm. See *māl, tọọr:* "thing for pouring out". Utirik household.

Mālu (**maliw**). Gramm. See *mālu* "fragrant". Rongelap islet.

Māniddik-rāiiōñ (**maniddik-rayiyyẹg**). Gramm. See *māniddik.* Ailinglapalap tract.

Māniddik-rāirōk (**maniddik-rayiyrẹk**). Gramm. Ailinglapalap tract.

Mānjeb (**manjẹb**). Unanalyz. Namorik tract.

Mānne (**mannẹy**). Reminisc. gramm. See *māni* "thin". Two Mejit tracts.

Mānniplak (**manniplak**). Unanalyz. Jaluit tract.

Me-dettak (**mey-dettak**). Gramm. distort. See *me* "fortress"; *dej, tak:* "flee eastward"; see also *Meinko* "Arno tract". Mejit tract.

Me-kaṇ (**mẹy-kaṇ**). Gramm. See *me* "those weirs". Kwajalein tract.

Mede-kaṇ (**medey-kaṇ**). Gramm. Arno tract.

Meeṇ-aidik (**meyeṇ-hayidik**). Gramm. See *me, aidik* "that narrow weir". Eniwetak tract.

Meik (**mẹyik**). Reminisc. gramm. See *me, ik:* "closed weir". Kwajalein islet.

Meikkōñ (**mẹyikkẹg**). Reminisc. gramm. See *me, kkōñ:* "weir at the *Terminalia* tree". Wotje islet.

Mein (**męyin**). Unanalyz. Ailinglapalap tract.

Meinko (**męyinkew**). Gramm. See *me, ko:* "fortress for fleeing"; see also *Me-dettak* "Mejit tract". Arno tract.

Mej-eṇ (**męj-yeṇ**). Gramm. See *mej* "open reef between islets". Kwajalein tract.

Mej-kadu-eṇ (**męj-kadiw-yeṇ**). Gramm. See *kadu* "that short reef". Ebon tract.

Mejatin-wōn (**mejatin-węn**). Part. reminisc. gramm. See *mejate, wōn:* "turtle path to the beach". Kwajalein tract.

Mejatto (**mejattew**). Part. reminisc. gramm. See *mejatoto* "possessed by ghosts", or *mejān to* "eye of the passage". Rongelap islet; Kwajalein islet; Jaluit islet.

Mejā-eṇ (**mejay-yeṇ**). Gramm. See *mejā:* "the gash in the reef". Maloelap tract.

Mejān-atūn̄ (**mejan-hatig**). Gramm. See *māj, atūn̄:* "eye of the land crab". Jabwot tract.

Mejān-wōte (**mejan-wętęy**). Reminisc. gramm. See *māj.* Arno tract.

Meje-Tabo (**mejey-tabew**). Recur. form. See *meja-, Tabo* "eye of Tabo, a coral head in the lagoon". Mili tract.

Mejej (**męjyęj**). Reminisc. gramm. See *mejje, ej:* "eastern opening". Wotho tract.

Mejejān (**mejeyjan**). Reminisc. gramm. See *mejje, jān* "snare line". Majuro tract.

Mejejjok (**mejejjeq**). Unanalyz. Ailinglapalap islet.

Mejeto (**mejetew**). Gramm. See *mejeto* "path to the beach". Maloelap tract.

Mejetool (**męjętęwęl**). Unanalyz. Ailinglapalap tract.

Mejjae (**mejjahyey**). Reminisc. gramm. See *meja-, ae:* "eye of the current". Jaluit district; Jaluit islet.

Mejjak (**mejjak**). Unanalyz. Ujae tract.

Mejje-eṇ (**męjjęy-yeṇ**). Gramm. See *mejje* "opening between islets". Namu tract.

Mejjen (**męjjęn**). Reminisc. gramm. See *mejje.* Mejit tract.

Mejjǫto (**mejjawtęw**). Unanalyz. See *Mejoto-eṇ* "Jaluit tract". Ailinglapalap tract.

Mejoto-eṇ (**męjęwtęw-yeṇ**). Reminisc. gramm. See *jo, to* "float loose westward". Jaluit tract.

Mellem (**mellem**). Unanalyz., although a story tells of a man named *Lām* who liked to eat breadfruit (*mā*)". Maloelap tract.

Melōke (**męlękęy**). From Ponapean *mel ke* "Is it true?" (?). Mili tract.

Meḷaḷ-eṇ (**meḷaḷ-yeṇ**). Gramm. See *meḷaḷ* "demon playground". Rongelap tract; Namu tract.

Meḷan̄ (**meḷag**). Gramm. distort. See *eomeḷan̄* "land reserved for chiefs". Likiep islet.

Meḷoktakōn (**meḷeqtaken**). Gramm. See *Meḷoktakōn* "moon phase". Arno tract.

Meḷǫ (**meḷaw**). Gramm. See *meḷǫ* "existence". Wotje tract.

Menanuon (**menahniwęn**). Reminisc. gramm. See *rimmenanuwe* "elves". Ebon tract.

Menanuwe (**menahniwwęy**). Reminisc. gramm. See *rimmenanuwe* "elves". Maloelap tract; three Maloelap households.

Menmao (**menmahwew**). Part. reminisc. gramm. See *menninmour* "animal", *ṃao* "owl" or *mao* "parrotfish". Bikini tract.

Menǫknǫk-eṇ (**menaqnaq-yeṇ**). Gramm. See *menǫknǫk* "debris". Arno district.

Men̄ā (**megay**). Reminisc. gramm. See *ṃōn̄ā* "food". Jaluit islet.

Merake (**merakęy**). From Gilb. *Marakei* (*Atoll*). Majuro tract; Arno tract; see also *Merraki.*

Merake (**merakey**). From Gilb. *Marakei* (*Atoll*). Mili tract; see also *Merraki.*

Meram-jān-ḷōn̄ar (**meram-jan-ḷegar**). Gramm. See *meram* "light", *jān* "from", *Ḷōn̄ar* "personal and place name". Wotje tract.

Merraki (**merrakiy**). From Gilb. *Marakei* (*Atoll*). Bikini tract; see also *Merake.*

Metete (**meteytey**). Gramm. distort. See *Metete* "breadfruit variety"; see also *tiete.* Mili tract.

Metete-kaṇ (**metęytęy-kaṇ**). Gramm. Eniwetak tract.

Metḷan-ene (**metḷan-yęnęy**). Gramm. distort. See *Matḷan* "Aur tract", see also *matoḷ, āne:* "third part of the islet". Majuro tract.

Metḷanel (**metḷanyel**). Reminisc. gramm. See *matoḷ, el:* "third part of the nest". Ebon tract.

Metoonkōn (**metewenkẹn**). Gramm. See *meto, kōn:* "sea that leaves its imprint". Majuro tract.

Metto-eṇ (**mettew-yeṇ**). Gramm. See *metto* "ocean anchorage". Likiep tract.

Mettool (**mettẹwẹl**). Unanalyz. Ailinglapalap tract.

Metwe (**mẹtwẹy**). From Engl. *Midway* (*Island*). Likiep tract.

Mien-wa (**miyen-wah**). Gramm. See *mien* "canoe storage". Ailuk islet; Arno tract.

Mijijak (**mijiyjak**). Unanalyz. Ujae tract.

Mijjinem (**mijjinem**). Gramm. distort. See *mej, jine-:* "our mother is dead". Namorik tract.

Mile (**milẹy**). Unanalyz. Ratak atoll; Mili; Mejit tract; Majuro tract; Mili district; Mili islet.

Milu (**miliw**). Unanalyz. Kwajalein islet.

Minṃa (**minṃah**). Unanalyz., next to a tract named *Ṃūttūṃa*. Mili tract.

Mitwanbad (**mitwanbad**). Part. reminisc. gramm. See *meto* "navigation", *Bad* "a star". Arno tract.

Mokḷanej (**meqḷanẹj**). Unanalyz. Bikini tract; Kili tract.

Moonwaan (**mewenwahan**). Gramm. See *mo, waan:* "forbidden part of his vessel"; stern portion of schooners owned by chiefs has been taboo to others. Arno islet.

Moottoonpād (**mewettewenpad**). Unanalyz. Jaluit tract.

Morjoroje (**mer°jer°ejey**). Gramm. distort. See *mar, ruje:* "break shrubs into small pieces for burning". Arno tract.

Morkwā-eṇ (**mer°qay-yeṇ**). Unanalyz. Ebon tract.

Motok-ej (**mewteq-yẹj**). Unanalyz. Ailinglapalap coral head.

Motok-laḷ (**mewteq-laḷ**). Unanalyz. Ailinglapalap coral head.

Mour-taḷọk (**mẹwir-tahḷaq**). Part. recur. form. See *mour* "live eastward". Ailinglapalap tract.

Mọkwōjḷaṇ (**maqejḷag**). Gramm. See *mọkwōj, ḷañ* "joints crack". Aur tract.

Mọon (**mawen**). Also *Mawōn*. Reminisc. gramm. See *mọ:* "its forbiddenness". Majuro tract.

Ṃaaj (**ṃahaj**). Unanalyz. Rongerik tract; Kwajalein sandspit.

Ṃaajḷañ (**ṃahajḷag**). Recur. form. See *ḷañ* "storm". Majuro tract.

Ṃaajṇa (**ṃahajṇah**). Recur. form. See *ṇa* "shoal". Bikini tract.

Ṃaaklōñ (**ṃahaklẹg**). Unanalyz. Namorik tract.

Ṃaan-āneṇ (**ṃahan-yanyeṇ**). Gramm. See *ṃaan:* "front of that islet". Majuro tract.

Ṃaanwa (**ṃahanwah**). Gramm. See *ṃaan, wa* "canoe front". Mili tract.

Ṃaat (**ṃahat**). Recur. form., as in *Ḷajuṃaat* "name of a demon". Namu islet; Likiep islet.

Ṃaatdik (**ṃahatdik**). Recur. form. Mili tract.

Ṃabuñbuñ (**ṃabig°big°**). Part. reminisc. gramm. See *buñbuñ* "famous". Wotje tract.

Ṃadike (**ṃadikey**). Part. recur. form. See *dike* "dislike". Mili islet.

Ṃadṃad (**ṃadṃad**). Gramm. See *ṃad* "busy". Namorik tract.

Ṃadooṃ (**ṃadeweṃ**). Gramm. See *ṃad, oṃ:* "busy with hermit crabs". Ujelang islet.

Ṃadooṃ-dik (**ṃadeweṃ-dik**). Gramm. Two Ujelang islets.

Ṃae (**ṃahyey**). Recur. form. See *rūṂae* "clan name". Namu district; Namu islet.

Ṃaeḷọk (**ṃahyelaq**). Gramm. See *ṃaeḷok* "distinct". Namorik tract.

Ṃaetoktok (**ṃahyeteqteq**). Reminisc. gramm. See *eṃ, aetok* "long house". Arno tract.

Ṃaiddik (**ṃahyiddik**). Reminisc. gramm. See *eṃ, aidik* "narrow house". Majuro tract.

Ṃaidik (**ṃahyidik**). Reminisc. gramm. Bikini tract; Ailinglapalap tract; Kili tract.

Ṃaidik-kaṇ (**ṃahyidik-kaṇ**). Reminisc. gramm. Arno tract.

Ṃaidikdik (**ṃahyidikdik**). Gramm. See *eṃ aidik:* "narrow house", also *ṃṃaidikdik* "whisper". Lib tract; Ailinglapalap tract; Jaluit tract; Ebon tract; Likiep tract; Wotje tract; Aur tract; Arno tract.

Ṃaikeeḷ (**ṃahyikeyeḷ**). Pers. name. Mejit district.

Ṃaiḷ (**ṃahyiḷ**). Loan from Engl. *mile.* Mejit tract.

M̧ajaej (**m̧ajhayẹj**). Recur. form. See *m̧aj* "eel", *Aej* "island on which members of the *raej* clan live". Wotje islet.

M̧ajeļ (**m̧ahjeļ**). From Engl. *Marshall*. Ujelang tract; Namorik district.

M̧ajjoļañ (**m̧ajjẹwļag**). Unanalyz. Jabwot tract.

M̧ajjoorļañ (**m̧ajjẹwẹrļag**). Unanalyz. Ailinglapalap tract.

M̧ajjor (**m̧ajjer°**). Recur. form. See *m̧aj* "eel", *jjor* "shade the eyes while looking for fish". Jaluit tract.

M̧ajkōn (**m̧ajkẹn**). Recur. form. See *m̧aj* "eel", *lekōn* "poke into a hole". Namu district; Namu islet.

M̧akil (**m̧akil**). From Mokil (Atoll in Eastern Caroline Islands). Ailinginae islet; Lib tract; Mejit tract.

M̧akin (**m̧akin**). From Gilb. *Makin*. Jaluit tract; Ebon tract; Arno islet.

M̧akkije (**m̧akkijẹy**). Gramm. See *m̧ak, kije:* "hard parts of pandanus". Majuro tract.

M̧akūt (**m̧ahkit**). From Engl. *market*. Ailinglapalap tract; Ailuk tract.

M̧alel (**m̧alel**). Gramm. See *rūM̧alel* "clan name". Arno district; Arno islet.

M̧alik (**m̧alik**). Gramm. See *m̧alik* "custom". Kwajalein islet.

M̧alū-eņ (**m̧alih-yeņ**). Pers. name, a legendary demon. Three Arno tracts; Mili tract.

M̧aļkwōn (**m̧aļqẹn**). Reminisc. gramm. See *m̧aļokļok:* "sting ray". Rongelap tract.

M̧aļo-eļap (**m̧aļew-yeļap**). Gramm. See *m̧aļo:* "large lagoon". Ratak atoll; Maloelap.

M̧aļok (**m̧aļẹq**). Reminisc. gramm. See *m̧aļokļok* "sting ray". Ailuk islet; Majuro tract.

M̧an-to (**m̧an-tẹw**). Part. recur. form. See *to* "husk soaking pit". Jaluit tract.

M̧an-ut (**m̧an-wit**). Gramm. distort. See *M̧ōn-ut* "house of flowers". Namu tract.

M̧an-wōt (**m̧an-wẹt**). Gramm. distort. See *wōt* "rain". Namorik tract.

M̧an-wōtwōt (**m̧an-wetwet**). Gramm. distort. See *M̧ōn-wōt.* Namorik tract.

M̧andik (**m̧andik**). Unanalyz. Ailinglapalap tract.

M̧andik-kaņ (**m̧andik-kaņ**). Unanalyz. Ebon tract.

M̧anit (**m̧anit**). Gramm. See *m̧anit* "custom". Jaluit tract.

M̧anjen-kaņ (**m̧anjen-kaņ**). Unanalyz. Ailinginae islet.

M̧ankōn (**m̧ankẹn**). Unanalyz. Ebon tract.

M̧anneen (**m̧anneyen**). Unanalyz. Three Ailinglapalap tracts; Jaluit tract; Namorik tract; Ebon tract.

M̧anom̧a (**m̧anewm̧ah**). Unanalyz. Jaluit tract.

M̧anōkkōñ (**m̧anekkẹg**). Gramm. distort. See *M̧ōn-ekkōñ* "house of the *Terminalia* tree". Namorik tract.

M̧anōt (**m̧anet**). Gramm. distort. See *m̧anit* "custom". Wotje islet.

M̧aņe (**m̧ahņey**). Unanalyz. Ebon tract.

M̧ao (**m̧ahwew**). Gramm. See *m̧ao* "owl". Mili islet.

M̧atteen (**m̧atteyen**). Unanalyz. Likiep islet.

M̧o-raiiōñ (**m̧ew-rahyiyyẹg**). Reminisc. gramm. Lae tract.

M̧o-rairōk (**m̧ew-rahyiyrẹk**). Reminisc. gramm. Lae tract.

M̧ojā (**m̧ewjay**). Unanalyz. Lae tract.

M̧okm̧ok (**m̧eqm̧eq**). Gramm. See *m̧okm̧ok* "rinse". Arno islet.

M̧okrara (**m̧eqrahrah**). Unanalyz. Mejit tract.

M̧ool-eņ (**m̧ewel-yeņ**). Gramm. See *m̧ool* "truth". Lib tract.

M̧oonbōd (**m̧ewenbed**). Reminisc. gramm. See *wōn* "turtle", *bōd* "turtle shell". Maloelap tract.

M̧orunna (**m̧er°innah**). Also *M̧oriņa.* Reminisc. gramm. See *m̧or, ņa:* "land on the shoal". Ujelang islet.

M̧o̧kut-kaņ (**m̧aqit-kaņ**). Gramm. See *m̧o̧kut* "grow close together". Arno tract.

M̧o̧ļwōjļwōj (**m̧aļ°ejļ°ej**). Gramm. See *m̧o̧ļwōjļwōj* "soak". Arno tract.

M̧ōdānļo̧k (**m̧edanļaq**). Gramm. See *m̧ōdānļo̧k* "sleep and dream". Utirik household.

M̧ōjaankul (**m̧ejahanqil**). Gramm. distort. See *m̧ōjaan:* "cry of the *kul,* or perhaps *kwōl* "sanderling". Jaluit tract.

M̧ōjabbe-rōk (**m̧ejabbẹy-rẹk**). Reminisc. gramm. See *m̧ōjab-, rōk:* "house in the south". Majuro tract.

Ṃōjajo (**ṃejahjęw**). Unanalyz. Wotje tract.

Ṃōjalomar (**ṃejahlewmar**). Part. reminisc. gramm. See *ilo, mar:* "in the bushes". Mili tract.

Ṃōjaḷto (**ṃejaḷtęw**). Gramm. See *jaḷ, to:* "house facing westward". Arno tract.

Ṃōjañ (**ṃejag**). Gramm. See *ṃōjañ* "lobster tail". Wotje tract.

Ṃōjañin-bōd (**ṃejagin-bed**). Gramm., referring to the resonating sound (*jañ*) of a turtle shell (*bōd*). When such a creature is caught at night, it is tapped on the back to make sure it is a turtle rather than the poisonous eagle ray fish (*imen*). Mejit tract.

Ṃōjañjañ (**ṃejagjag**). Gramm. See *jañ:* "crying house". Majuro tract.

Ṃōjat (**ṃejat**). Gramm. See *jat* "under the surface of the water". Lae tract.

Ṃōjālto (**ṃejaltęw**). Gramm. See *jāl, to:* "house facing westward". Rongelap tract.

Ṃōjānjen (**ṃejanjęn**). Reminisc. gramm. See *jān:* "snare house". Namu tract.

Ṃōjbwe (**ṃęjbęy**). Gramm. See *ṃōjbwe* "a sail". Wotje tract.

Ṃōjeltak-rālik (**ṃęjęltak-raylik**). Gramm. distort. See *jāl, tak:* "western portion of the house facing eastward". Kwajalein tract.

Ṃōjeltak-reeaar (**ṃęjęltak-reyyahar**). Gramm. distort. Kwajalein tract.

Ṃōjeḷañ (**ṃejeḷag**). Gramm. See *jeḷañ* "replace the bottom part of a canoe". Wotje tract.

Ṃōjeḷḷañ (**ṃęjęḷḷag**). Part. reminisc. gramm. See *Ṃōjeḷañ;* also possibly *ṃōj, ḷañ* "after the storm". Mili tract.

Ṃōjen-eṇ (**ṃęjęn-yeṇ**). Reminisc. gramm. See *ṃōj:* "its completion". Ailinglapalap tract.

Ṃōjen-kaṇ (**ṃęjęn-kaṇ**). Reminisc. gramm. Majuro tract.

Ṃōjetōnpat (**ṃęjętenpat**). Gramm. distort. See *ṃwijit:* "cutting of the swamp (one swamp cuts across another here to form the shape of a cross)". Likiep tract.

Ṃōjjālniñeañ (**ṃejjalnigyag**). Gramm. See *jāl, niñeañ:* "house facing northward". Namu tract.

Ṃōjjālto (**ṃejjaltęw**). Gramm. See *to* "westward". Kwajalein tract; Ailinglapalap tract.

Ṃōjjāltok (**ṃejjalteq**). Gramm. See *tok* "hither". Kwajalein tract.

Ṃōjjebaak (**ṃejjebahak**). Gramm. distort. See *jebjeb, ak:* "catch frigate birds". Ailinglapalap tract.

Ṃōjjekad (**ṃejjekad**). Gramm. distort. See *jekad:* "house of the noddy bird". Namu tract.

Ṃōjjel-ar (**ṃejjel-har**). Gramm. distort. See *jāl, ar:* "face the lagoon". Kwajalein tract.

Ṃōjjeraak (**ṃejjerahak**). Gramm. See *jjeraak:* "house where it is time to tack". Jaluit tract.

Ṃōjjero (**ṃęjjęyręw**). Gramm. See *ṃōjjero* "a food". Kili tract; Namorik tract; Ebon tract.

Ṃōjjetōp (**ṃęjjętęp**). Gramm. distort. See *jetōp:* "house of spirits". Ebon tract.

Ṃōjjipāl (**ṃejjipal**). Reminisc. gramm. See *pāl* "dying arrowroot". Ailinglapalap tract.

Ṃōjjokḷā (**ṃejjęqḷay**). Gramm. distort. See *jokḷā* "north wind". Namu tract.

Ṃōjjokoḷā (**ṃejjeqeḷay**). Gramm. distort. Ailinglapalap tract.

Ṃōjjōjō (**ṃęjjęhjęh**). Gramm. distort. See *jjō:* "ugly house". Ebon tract.

Ṃōjkōnkōn (**ṃęjkęnkęn**). Gramm. distort. See *mejkōnkōn* "extra mesh". Arno tract.

Ṃōjṃōjin (**ṃęjṃęjin**). Reminisc. gramm. See *ṃōj* "finish". Jaluit tract.

Ṃōjñap (**ṃejgap**). Reminisc. gramm. See *ṃajñal* "intestines. Legend says people formerly had no intestines until they killed and ate the *Ṃōjñap* creatures. Maloelap tract.

Ṃōjoñ (**ṃejeg°**). Also *Ṃōn-joñ.* Gramm. See *joñ* "mangrove". Namorik household.

Ṃōk-eo (**ṃęk-yew**). Gramm. See *ṃōk* "fatigue". Majuro tract.

Ṃōkaṇ-aidik (**ṃekaṇ-hayidik**). Gramm. See *aidik:* "those narrow houses". Ailinglapalap tract.

Ṃōkaṇ-reeaar (**ṃekaṇ-reyyahar**). Gramm. Arno tract.

Ṃōkaṇ-rōk (**ṃekaṇ-ręk**). Gramm. Namu tract.

Ṃōkar (**ṃekar**). Gramm. See *rūṃōkarraṇ* "elves". Maloelap islet; Arno tract.

Ṃōkkōñ (**ṃękkęg**). Gramm. distort. See *kkōñ* "a tree". Eniwetak tract.

Ṃōlaar (**ṃelahar**). Reminisc. gramm. See *ṃal, ar:* "lean toward the lagoon". Wotje tract.

Ṃōlaetọ (**ṃelhayetaw**). Reminisc. gramm. See *ṃal, aetọ:* "lean towards the northeast, into the trade winds". Mili tract.

Ṃōlala (**ṃelahlah**). Gramm. See *lala:* "hen house", or possibly *kūbween lọlọ:* "house of dirty waste water". Jaluit tract.

Ṃōle (**ṃeḷẹy**). Unanalyz. Arno tract.

Ṃōleọ (**ṃeleyaw**). Gramm. See *ṃōleọ* "chilly". Arno islet.

Ṃōllokḷap (**ṃẹllẹqḷap**). Gramm. See *Lokḷap:* "house right in the middle". Taka tract; five Wotje tracts; two Aur tracts; two Majuro tracts; Arno tract.

Ṃōllokḷap-rāātle (**ṃẹllẹqḷap-rayatley**). Gramm. Majuro tract.

Ṃōllokḷap-reeaar (**ṃẹllẹqḷap-reyyahar**). Gramm. Majuro tract.

Ṃōllokmar (**ṃẹllẹqmar**). Reminisc. gramm. See *lok, mar:* "house in the midst of the bushes". Ailinglapalap tract.

Ṃōllomar (**ṃẹllẹwmar**). Reminisc. gramm. See *ilo, mar:* "house in the bushes". Wotje tract.

Ṃōllōñ (**ṃẹllẹg**). Gramm. distort. See *lōñ:* "top house". Aur tract.

Ṃōḷajjila (**ṃeḷajjilah**). Unanalyz. Bikini tract; Kili tract.

Ṃōḷañ (**ṃeḷag**). Gramm. See *ḷañ* "storm"; see also *ṃōḷañḷọṇ:* "nausea". Jaluit tract.

Ṃōḷap (**ṃeḷap**). Gramm. See *ḷap:* "big house". Ebon tract.

Ṃōḷaplej (**ṃeḷaplẹj**). Recur. form., from *eṃ ḷap lọbwilej:* "large house where many live". Ebon tract.

Ṃōḷapḷap (**ṃeḷapḷap**). Gramm. Jabwot tract; Ailinglapalap tract.

Ṃōḷetaklōñ (**ṃeḷeytaklẹg**). Gramm. See *ṃōḷe:* "sand crab coming up". Likiep tract.

Ṃōḷḷoñ (**ṃẹḷḷẹg°**). Gramm. distort. See *ḷoñ:* "house of ants". Jaluit tract.

Ṃōḷōbbā-jāiiōñ (**ṃeḷebbay-jayiyyẹg**). Gramm. See *ṃōḷōbbā* "pile of coconuts". Aur islet.

Ṃōḷōbbā-jāirōk (**ṃeḷebbay-jayiyrẹk**). Gramm. Aur islet.

Ṃōṃak-eṇ (**ṃeṃak-yeṇ**). Gramm. See *ṃṃak* "hole in tree for catching water". Majuro tract.

Ṃōṃak-kaṇ (**ṃeṃak-kaṇ**). Gramm. See *ṃṃak:* "those hollow trees". Arno rock.

Ṃōṃōt (**ṃẹṃẹt**). Gramm. See *ṃṃōt* "pitch of a boat on the waves". Mejit tract.

Ṃōn-aden (**ṃen-haden**). Gramm. See *aden* "clam shell". Kwajalein tract; Namorik tract.

Ṃōn-aebōj (**ṃen-hayẹbẹj**). Gramm. See *aebōj* "cistern". Aur tract.

Ṃōn-aeden (**ṃen-hayeden**). Gramm. distort. See *ae, dān* "collect water". Arno tract.

Ṃōn-ael-eañ (**ṃen-hayel-yag**). Unanalyz. Majuro tract.

Ṃōn-ael-rak (**ṃen-hayel-rak**). Unanalyz. Majuro tract.

Ṃōn-aetōktōk (**ṃen-hayetẹktẹk**). Gramm. See *aetōktōk* "male arrowroot". Mili tract.

Ṃōn-aidik (**ṃen-hayidik**). Gramm. See *aidik* "narrow". Ujae tract; Kwajalein tract; Jaluit tract; three Wotje tracts; Maloelap tract; two Arno tracts.

Ṃōn-aitwe-eṇ (**ṃen-hayitwey-yeṇ**). Gramm. See *aitwe:* "that house of conflict". Maloelap tract.

Ṃōn-ajej (**ṃen-hajyẹj**). Gramm. See *ajej* "divide". Mili tract.

Ṃōn-ajerre (**ṃen-hajẹrrẹy**). Gramm. See *ajerre* "work alone". Majuro tract.

Ṃōn-Ajjuunun-iōñ (**ṃen-hajjiwinwin-yiyẹg**). Gramm., Ajjuunun is the name of a legendary turtle who dug its nest on these tracts; nest remains today as valley. Majuro tract.

Ṃōn-Ajjuunun-rōk (**ṃen-hajjiwinwin-rẹk**). Gramm. Majuro tract.

Ṃōn-ak (**ṃen-hak**). Gramm. See *ak* "frigate bird". Ujae tract; three Ailinglapalap tracts; three Jaluit tracts; Namorik tract; Wotje tract; Majuro tract; two Arno tracts; Mili tract.

Ṃōn-ak-eṇ (**ṃen-hak-yeṇ**). Gramm. Knox islet.

Ṃōn-ak-jāiiōñ (**ṃen-hak-jayiyyẹg**). Gramm. Likiep tract.

Ṃōn-ak-jāirōk (**ṃen-hak-jayiyrẹk**). Gramm. Likiep tract.

Ṃōn-ak-rāātle (**ṃen-hak-rayatley**). Gramm. Majuro tract.

Ṃōn-ak-reeaar (**ṃen-hak-reyyahar**). Gramm. Majuro tract.

M̧ōn-aktal (**m̧en-haktal**). Gramm. See *aktal* "group of people going with a purpose". Wotje tract; Majuro tract.

M̧ōn-aktū (**m̧en-haktih**). Reminisc. gramm. Arno tract.

M̧ōn-akūtm̧ur (**m̧en-hakitm̧ir°**). Recur. form. See *m̧ur.* Knox tract.

M̧ōn-alikkar (**m̧en-halikkar**). Gramm. See *alikkar* "clear". Maloelap tract.

M̧ōn-alle (**m̧en-hallẹy**). Gramm. See *alle* "wrasse". Arno tract.

M̧ōn-allǫk (**m̧en-hallaq**). Gramm. See *allǫk* "examine". Eniwetak tract; Rongelap tract.

M̧ōn-alooj (**m̧en-halẹwẹj**). Gramm. See *alwōj* "look at". Ujae tract; Lib tract; Kwajalein tract; Mejit tracts; Ailuk tract; Wotje tract; Arno tract.

M̧ōn-alwa (**m̧en-halwah**). Part. recur. form. See *al* "sing", *wa* "canoe". Majuro tract.

M̧ōn-aļ (**m̧en-haļ**). Gramm. See *aļ* "sun". Kwajalein tract; Ailinglapalap tract.

M̧ōn-aļā (**m̧en-haļay**). Unanalyz. Arno tract.

M̧ōn-aļļañ (**m̧en-haļļag**). Gramm. See *aļļañ* "gape". Ailuk tract; Arno tract; Mili tract; Knox tract.

M̧ōn-anij (**m̧en-hanij**). Gramm. See *anijnij* "sorcery". Kwajalein tract; Ailinglapalap household; Majuro tract; two Arno tracts.

M̧ōn-añ (**m̧en-hag**). Gramm. See *añ* "wind". Mejit tract; Maloelap tract.

M̧ōn-añkō (**m̧en-hagkeh**). Gramm. See *añkō* "anchor". Mejit tract.

M̧ōn-aññat (**m̧en-haggat**). Gramm. See *aññat* "violent storm". Eniwetak tract.

M̧ōn-aorōk (**m̧en-hawẹrẹk**). Gramm. See *aorōk* "value". Arno tract.

M̧ōn-apap (**m̧en-haphap**). Gramm. See *apap* "pinch". Aur tract.

M̧ōn-apet (**m̧en-hapẹt**). Gramm. See *apet* "canoe part". Jaluit tract.

M̧ōn-arar (**m̧en-harhar**). Gramm. See *arar* "stir fire or food"; "pick meat from clam shell". Ebon tract; Mili tract.

M̧ōn-arm̧we (**m̧en-harm̧ey**). Gramm. See *arm̧we* "a tree". Lib tract.

M̧ōn-Arņo (**m̧en-harņew**). Recur. form. Aur tract; Arno tract.

M̧ōn-arot (**m̧en-har°et**). Gramm. See *arot* "a game". Lib household.

M̧ōn-arōpje (**m̧en-harepjẹy**). Recur. form. See *Arōn-peje* "Majuro tract". Arno tract.

M̧ōn-arrweļwe (**m̧en-harr°ẹyļ°ẹy**). Gramm. distort. See *arōn, ļwe:* "house on the lagoon side of the pond". Arno tract.

M̧ōn-arwele (**m̧en-har°ẹylẹy**). Gramm. distort. Arno tract.

M̧ōn-atartar (**m̧en-hatartar**). Gramm. See *atartar* "adjoin". Wotje tract.

M̧ōn-atat (**m̧en-hathat**). Gramm. See *atat* "a vine". Maloelap tract.

M̧ōn-atm̧ōd (**m̧en-hatm̧ẹd**). Part. recur. form. See *m̧ōd* "lose leaves". Arno tract.

M̧ōn-atūñ (**m̧en-hatig**). Gramm. See *atūñ* "land crab". Ailinglapalap tract.

M̧ōn-ājeto (**m̧en-yajẹtẹw**). Unanalyz. Arno tract.

M̧ōn-ājirañ (**m̧en-yajirag**). Reminisc. gramm. See *āj, keeprañ* "a bunch of bananas". Mili tract.

M̧ōn-ājo (**m̧en-yajẹw**). Recur. form. See *āj* "banana bunch"; legend says bananas on this tract belonged to the daughters of Etao. Majuro tract.

M̧ōn-bad-eņ (**m̧en-bad-yeņ**). Gramm. See *bad* "divination site". Wotho tract.

M̧ōn-baļ (**m̧en-baļ**). Gramm. See *baļ* "canoe part". Arno tract.

M̧ōn-ban (**m̧en-ban**). Gramm. See *ban* "cannot": "cannot work it alone", "it cannot produce", or "we are tired of coming here". Wotje tract; Maloelap tract.

M̧ōn-bar (**m̧en-bar**). Gramm. See *bar* "rock". Kwajalein tract.

M̧ōn-baru (**m̧en-bariw**). Gramm. See *baru* "crab". Ujelang tract; Ailinglapalap tract; Utirik tract; Wotje tract; Maloelap tract; Majuro tract.

M̧ōn-barwat (**m̧en-barwat**). Gramm. See *bar, wat:* "head of the puffer fish". Ebon tract.

M̧ōn-bat (**m̧en-bat**). Gramm. See *bat* "hill". Mili tract.

M̧ōn-bok (**m̧en-beq**). Gramm. See *bok* "sand". Majuro tract.

M̧ōn-bok-iaar (**m̧en-beq-yiyahar**). Gramm. Mili tract.

M̧ōn-bok-iiōñ (**m̧en-beq-yiyyẹg**). Gramm. Ebon tract.

M̧ōn-bok-iooj (**m̧en-beq-yiyẹwẹj**). Gramm. Mili tract.

M̧ōn-bok-irōk (**m̧en-beq-yiyrȩk**). Gramm. Ebon tract.

M̧ōn-boñ (**m̧en-bȩg°**). Gramm. See *boñ* "night". Majuro tract.

M̧ōn-bǫ (**m̧en-baw**). Unanalyz. Two Ailinglapalap tracts.

M̧ōn-bōd (**m̧en-bed**). Gramm. See *bōd* "turtle shell". Jaluit tract; Aur tract; Majuro tract; Arno tract.

M̧ōn-bōd-iōñ (**m̧en-bed-yiyȩg**). Gramm. Wotje tract.

M̧ōn-bōd-rōk (**m̧en-bed-rȩk**). Gramm. Wotje tract.

M̧ōn-bōjrak (**m̧en-bȩjrak**). Gramm. See *bōjrak* "stop". Mejit tract.

M̧ōn-bōl (**m̧en-bȩl**). Gramm. See *bōl* "taro pit". Arno tract.

M̧ōn-bōlbōl (**m̧en-bȩlbȩl**). Gramm. Arno tract.

M̧ōn-bōōjōj (**m̧en-behejhej**). Gramm. See *bōōjōj* "broadcast". Arno tract.

M̧ōn-bōrōj (**m̧en-berej**). Gramm. See *bōrōj* "white sea bird". Arno tract.

M̧ōn-Bukdǫļ (**m̧en-biqdaļ°**). Gramm. See *Bukdǫļ* "breadfruit variety". Arno tract.

M̧ōn-bwidej (**m̧en-bidȩj**). Gramm. See *bwidej* "soil". Jaluit tract.

M̧ōn-bwilōñ (**m̧en-bileg**). Gramm. See *bwilōñ* "surprise". Jaluit tract.

M̧ōn-bwine (**m̧en-biney**). Gramm. distort. See *bwine* "butterfly fish". Namorik tract.

M̧ōn-dekā (**m̧en-dekay**). Gramm. See *dekā* "stones". Namorik tract.

M̧ōn-dool-kaņ (**m̧en-dȩwȩl-kaņ**). Unanalyz. Wotho tract.

M̧ōn-eaļapen (**m̧en-yaļapen**). Unanalyz. Ailinglapalap tract.

M̧ōn-eb (**m̧en-yeb**). Gramm. See *eb* "dance". Mejit tract.

M̧ōn-edǫ (**m̧en-yedaw**). Reminisc. gramm. See *dǫǫj* argue. Arno tract.

M̧ōn-ekkōñ (**m̧en-yȩkkȩg**). Gramm. See *kkōñ* "a tree". Wotho tract; Namu tract.

M̧ōn-ekkōr (**m̧en-yekkȩr**). Gramm. See *kkōr* "slimy". Ujae tract.

M̧ōn-ele (**m̧en-yȩlȩy**). Gramm. See *ele* "fish string". Arno tract.

M̧ōn-elokor (**m̧en-yelȩqȩr**). Gramm. distort. See *ālokorkor* "look back". Mili tract.

M̧ōn-eļǫr (**m̧en-yeļar°**). Gramm. See *ļǫr* "black anemone". Aur tract.

M̧ōn-em̧m̧aan (**m̧en-yem̧m̧ahan**). Gramm. Arno tract.

M̧ōn-eor (**m̧en-yȩr°**). Gramm. See *eor:* "house of faded colors". Wotho tract.

M̧ōn-eǫkļe (**m̧en-yaqļȩy**). Gramm. distort. See *okļe* "hungry. Arno tract.

M̧ōn-epāl (**m̧en-yepal**). Reminisc. gramm. See *pāl* "dying arrowroot". Namorik tract.

M̧ōn-eppej (**m̧en-yȩppȩj**). Gramm. See *ppej* "flooded". Mejit tract.

M̧ōn-erōk-wa (**m̧en-yerek-wah**). Gramm. See *ārōk, wa* "beach canoes". Mili tract.

M̧ōn-erran (**m̧en-yerran**). Gramm. See *rran* "dirty". Jaluit tract.

M̧ōn-iep (**m̧en-yiyep**). Gramm. See *iep* "basket". Majuro tract.

M̧ōn-ijo (**m̧en-yijȩw**). Recur. form. See *ijo* "good soil". Taka tract.

M̧ōn-ire (**m̧en-yirȩy**). Gramm. See *ire* "fight". Ujae tract.

M̧ōn-itōk (**m̧en-yitȩk**). Gramm. See *itōk* "draw water". Kwajalein tract.

M̧ōn-iu (**m̧en-yiw**). Gramm. See *iu* "sprouted coconut". Jaluit tract.

M̧ōn-jabuk (**m̧en-jabiq**). Gramm. See *jabuk* "fish with net on reef". Wotho tract.

M̧ōn-jaļto (**m̧en-jaļtȩw**). Gramm. See *jaļ, to:* "facing west". Kwajalein tract.

M̧ōn-jebōñ (**m̧en-jȩbȩg**). Gramm. See *jebōñ* "very little". Kwajalein tract.

M̧ōn-jetōb (**m̧en-jȩtȩb**). Gramm. See *jetōb* "spirit". Wotho tract; Maloelap tract.

M̧ōn-jokļā (**m̧en-jeqļay**). Gramm. See *jokļā* "wind from the north". Kwajalein tract.

M̧ōn-joorur (**m̧en-jewerwir**). Gramm. See *jourur* "thunder; a fish; an insect". Kwajalein tract.

M̧ōn-jorme (**m̧en-jer°mey**). Gramm. See *jorom* "drink up". Knox tract.

M̧ōn-joto (**m̧en-jȩwtȩw**). Gramm. See *jo:* "throw westward". Ujelang tract; Ailinglapalap tract.

M̧ōn-juwi (**m̧en-jiwiy**). Gramm. See *juwi* "white tern". Eniwetak tract.

M̧ōn-kajet (**m̧en-kajet**). Gramm. See *kajet* "spin". Aur tract.

M̧ōn-kañal (**m̧en-kahgal**). Gramm. See *kañal* "a tree". Two Kwajalein tracts; Namu tract; Ailinglapalap tract; Jaluit tract; Maloelap tract; Majuro tract.

M̧ōn-kaōnōn (**m̧en-kahenhen**). Gramm. See *kaōnōn* "a parasitic vine". Utirik household; Wotje tract.

M̧ōn-kappe (**m̧en-kappẹy**). Gramm. See *kappe* "bank". Ujelang tract.

M̧ōn-karuk (**m̧en-kariq**). Gramm. See *karuk* "sand crab". Ujae tract; Kwajalein tract; Aur tract.

M̧ōn-Katlik (**m̧en-katlik**). From Engl. or Germ. Catholic. Arno tract.

M̧ōn-kawal (**m̧en-kahwal**). Gramm. See *kawal* "a fish; watch for enemies". Maloelap tract.

M̧ōn-kābwil (**m̧en-kaybil**). Gramm. distort. See *kābwil* "baby birds". Wotje tract.

M̧ōn-kāden (**m̧en-kayden**). Reminisc. gramm. See *dān* "water". Wotho tract.

M̧ōn-kāmeej (**m̧en-kaymeyej**). Gramm. See *kāmeej* "redwood driftwood". Ailinglapalap tract.

M̧ōn-ke (**m̧ẹn-kẹy**). Gramm. See *ke* "porpoise". Namu tract; Utirik tract.

M̧ōn-ke (**m̧en-kẹy**). Gramm. See *ke* "porpoise". Kwajalein tract; Ailinglapalap tract; Wotje tract; Arno tract.

M̧ōn-kear (**m̧en-keyhar**). Gramm. Jaluit tract.

M̧ōn-keār (**m̧en-keyyar**). Gramm. See *keār* "tern". Ailinglapalap tract; two Jaluit tracts; Maloelap tract; Aur tract.

M̧ōn-keer (**m̧en-keyyer**). Gramm. distort. Maloelap tract.

M̧ōn-keo (**m̧en-kẹyẹw**). Gramm. distort. See *kio* "a plant". Arno tract.

M̧ōn-keotak (**m̧en-kẹyẹwtak**). Gramm. See *keotak* "give birth". Eniwetak tract.

M̧ōn-kewā (**m̧en-kẹyway**). Gramm. See *kewā* "compete". Knox tract.

M̧ōn-kid-eņ (**m̧en-kid-yeņ**). Recur. form. Wotje tract.

M̧ōn-kiden (**m̧en-kidẹn**). Gramm. See *kiden* "beach borage"; see also *m̧ōn-kiden* "a fish". Ujae tract; Ailinglapalap tract.

M̧ōn-kiep (**m̧en-kiyẹp**). Gramm. See *kieb* "spider lily". Kwajalein tract; Ailinglapalap tract; Jaluit tract.

M̧ōn-kilabōd (**m̧en-kilahbed**). Part. recur. form. See *bōd* "turtle shell". Jaluit tract.

M̧ōn-kino (**m̧en-kinew**). Gramm. See *kino* "fern". Ailinglapalap tract; Ebon tract; Likiep tract.

M̧ōn-kio (**m̧en-kiyew**). Gramm. See *kio* "a plant". Bikini tract; Rongelap tract; Jaluit tract.

M̧ōn-kior (**m̧en-kiyẹr°**). Gramm. See *kior* "a storm". Kwajalein tract.

M̧ōn-ko (**m̧en-qew**). Gramm. See *ko* "flee". Arno tract.

M̧ōn-ko-eņ (**m̧en-qẹw-yeņ**). Reminisc. gramm. See *koko* "dolphin". Mili tract.

M̧ōn-kodaaj (**m̧en-kewdahaj**). Gramm. See *kodaaj* "go away". Jabwot tract.

M̧ōn-koobob (**m̧en-qewebweb**). Gramm. See *koobob* "squeeze into a small space". Jaluit tract.

M̧ōn-koobub (**m̧en-qewebwib**). Gramm. See *koobub* "eat raw fish". Kwajalein tract.

M̧ōn-koot (**m̧en-qẹwẹt**). Reminisc. gramm. See *ko, wōt* "flee rain". Mili tract.

M̧ōn-kowak (**m̧en-kewwak**). Gramm. See *kowak* "curlew". Majuro tract.

M̧ōn-kọkweet (**m̧en-kaqẹyẹt**). Gramm. See *kweet:* "catch octopus". Ujae tract; Wotho tract.

M̧ōn-kọob (**m̧en-kawẹb**). Gramm. See *kọob* "wrestle". Wotje tract.

M̧ōn-kọoṃ (**m̧en-kawẹṃ**). Gramm. See *oṃ:* "find hermit crabs". Namorik tract.

M̧ōn-kōjbar (**m̧en-kẹjbar**). Gramm. See *kōjbar* "a plant". Arno tract.

M̧ōn-kōkkōk (**m̧en-kekkek**). Gramm. See *kōkkōk* "curlew". Arno tract.

M̧ōn-kōlōk (**m̧en-kẹlẹk**). Gramm. See *kōlōk* "full". Lae tract.

M̧ōn-kōḷọk (**m̧en-keḷaq**). Gramm. See *kōḷọk* "wait for rain to subside". Wotho tract.

M̧ōn-kōmālij (**m̧en-kemalij**). Gramm. See *kōmālij* "mashed taro". Mejit tract.

M̧ōn-kōmko (**m̧en-kemkew**). Unanalyz. See *ko:* "we flee". Arno tract.

M̧ōn-kōṃṃan (**m̧en-keṃṃan**). Gramm. See *kōṃṃan* "make, do". Arno tract.

M̧ōn-kōṃṃan-iōñ (**m̧en-keṃṃan-yiyẹg**). Gramm. Mili tract.

M̧ōn-kōṃṃan-rōk (**m̧en-keṃṃan-rẹk**). Gramm. Mili tract.

M̧ōn-kōņ (**m̧en-keņ**). Gramm. See *kōņ* "fertilizer". Wotho tract; Ailinglapalap tract.

M̧ōn-kōn̄n̄at (**m̧ęn-kęn̄n̄at**). Gramm. Arno tract.

M̧ōn-kōn̄n̄at (**m̧en-kęn̄n̄at**). Gramm. See *kōn̄n̄at* "a shrub". Two Jaluit tracts; Kili tract; Namorik tract; Maloelap tract.

M̧ōn-kōn̄o (**m̧en-ken̄ew**). Gramm. See *kōn̄o* "a tree". Bikini tract; Ujae tract; three Kwajalein tracts; Namu tract; Ailinglapalap tract; three Jaluit tracts; Kili tract; Maloelap tract; three Majuro tracts; Arno tract; Mili tract.

M̧ōn-kōñe (**m̧en-kęgęy**). Gramm. See *kōñe* "a tree". Lib tract; Arno tract.

M̧ōn-kōñe (**m̧en-kegęy**). Gramm. distort. Arno islet.

M̧ōn-kōpeel (**m̧en-kepeyel**). Gramm. See *kapeel* "skillful". Arno tract.

M̧ōn-kōpļaak (**m̧en-kepļahak**). Gramm. See *peļaak:* "cause to assemble". Mili tract.

M̧ōn-kōppao (**m̧en-keppahwew**). Gramm. See *kōppao* "ambush". Ujae tract; Likiep tract.

M̧ōn-kūro (**m̧en-kirew**). Gramm. distort. See *kūro* "grouper". Arno tract.

M̧ōn-kōt (**m̧en-ket**). Unanalyz. Bikini tract.

M̧ōn-kōtak (**m̧en-ketak**). Gramm. See *kōtak* "Kusaiean taro". Ebon household.

M̧ōn-kōto (**m̧ęn-kętęw**). Gramm. See *kōto* "wind". Jaluit tract.

M̧ōn-kōtooj (**m̧en-kętęwęj**). Gramm. See *tooj* "cause to break off". Mejit tract.

M̧ōn-kōtōm̧ (**m̧en-kętęm̧**). Gramm. See *kōtōm̧* "bundle of mats". Majuro tract.

M̧ōn-kubōk (**m̧en-qibęk**). Gramm. See *kubōk* "a tree". Two Kwajalein tracts.

M̧ōn-kupañ (**m̧en-qipag**). Gramm. See *kupañ* "surgeonfish". Jaluit tract.

M̧ōn-kure (**m̧en-qiręy**). Reminisc. gramm. See *kkure* "play". Ailinglapalap tract.

M̧ōn-kūbwe (**m̧en-kibey**). Gramm. See *kūbwe* "feces". Rongerik tract; Lae tract; three Jaluit tracts.

M̧ōn-kūbwijlōñ (**m̧en-kibijlęg**). Gramm. See *kūbwij, lōñ* "dig up the top". Aur tract.

M̧ōn-kūñ (**m̧en-kig**). Gramm. See *kūñ* "smell of feces". Kwajalein tract.

M̧ōn-kūrao (**m̧en-kirhahwew**). Part. recur. form. See *kūr* "call, *ao* "legendary bird". Ailinglapalap tract.

M̧ōn-kūtak (**m̧en-kitak**). Gramm. See *kūtak* "wind from southwest". Kwajalein tract.

M̧ōn-kūtiij (**m̧en-kitiyij**). Unanalyz. Jaluit tract; Ebon tract.

M̧ōn-kwekwe (**m̧en-qęyqęy**). Gramm. See *kwekwe* "scratch". Mili tract.

M̧ōn-kweļǫk (**m̧en-qęylaq**). Gramm. See *kweļǫk* "meeting". Mejit tract.

M̧ōn-kwōleej (**m̧en-qęlęyęj**). Gramm. See *kwōlej* "plover". Wotje tract; Maloelap tract; Aur tract; Majuro tract; Arno tract.

M̧ōn-kwōleej (**m̧en-qeleyej**). Gramm. Lae tract; two Kwajalein tracts; Jaluit tract; Ebon tract.

M̧ōn-kwōmej (**m̧en-qęmęj**). Gramm. See *kwōmej* "fishing method". Erikub tract.

M̧ōn-kwōpej (**m̧en-qępęj**). From Engl. *garbage* (?). Lae tract.

M̧ōn-kwōpoup (**m̧en-qępęwip**). Reminisc. gramm. See *poub:* "you are busy". Utirik tract.

M̧ōn-ladikdik (**m̧en-lahdikdik**). Gramm. See *lladikdik* "breeze". Arno tract.

M̧ōn-lañ (**m̧en-lag**). Gramm. See *lañ* "sky, heaven". Maloelap tract; Mili tract.

M̧ōn-lalok-eañ (**m̧en-lahleq-yag**). Pers. name, pond on this and adjoining tract shaped like face of demon named **Ļōm̧ōnlalok* and grass growing at one edge is called his beard: *kwōdeak kan̄ an Ļōm̧ōnlalok.* Arno tract.

M̧ōn-lalok-rak (**m̧en-lahleq-rak**). Pers. name. Arno tract.

M̧ōn-lik-ej (**m̧en-lik-yęj**). Gramm. Namu tract.

M̧ōn-lo-ak (**m̧en-lew-hak**). Gramm. See *ak* "frigate bird". Ailinglapalap tract.

M̧ōn-lo-bar (**m̧en-lew-bar**). Gramm. See *bar* "rock". Kwajalein tract.

M̧ōn-lo-bōl (**m̧en-lęw-bęl**). Gramm. See *bōl:* "house at the taro pit". Kwajalein tract; Mejit tract.

M̧ōn-lo-mar (**m̧en-lęw-mar**). Gramm. Jaluit tract.

M̧ōn-lo-mar (**m̧en-lew-mar**). Gramm. See *mar:* "house in the bushes". Wotho tract; Arno tract.

M̧ōn-lo-mar-rālik (**m̧en-lęw-mar-raylik**). Gramm. Kwajalein tract.

M̧ōn-lo-mar-reeaar (**m̧ęn-lęw-mar-reyyahar**). Gramm. Kwajalein tract.

M̧ōn-lo-mā (**m̧en-lȩw-may**). Gramm. See *mā:* "house at the breadfruit tree". Kwajalein tract.

M̧ōn-lokļap (**m̧ȩn-lȩqļap**). Recur. form. Kili tract; Majuro tract; Knox tract.

M̧ōn-lokļap (**m̧en-lȩqļap**). Recur. form. Two Kwajalein tracts; two Namu tracts; three Ailinglapalap tracts; two Jaluit tracts; two Likiep tracts; Maloelap tract; Majuro tract; five Arno tracts; Arno household.

M̧ōn-lokļap (**m̧en-leqļap**). Recur. form. Lae tract.

M̧ōn-lokļap-reeaar (**m̧en-lȩqļap-reyyahar**). Recur. form. Majuro tract.

M̧ōn-lokļap-rōtle (**m̧en-lȩqļap-rȩtley**). Recur. form. Majuro tract.

M̧ōn-lǫ-to (**m̧en-law-tew**). Gramm. See *to:* "house at the passage". Mili tract.

M̧ōn-lu-eaļ (**m̧en-liw-yaļ**). Gramm. distort. Ailuk tract; Arno tract.

M̧ōn-lu-iaļ (**m̧en-liw-yiyaļ**). Gramm. distort. See *iaļ:* "house at the road". Namu tract; Mejit tract; Mili tract.

M̧ōn-lu-ni (**m̧en-liw-niy**). Gramm. See *ni:* "house at the coconut tree". Ujae tract.

M̧ōn-lu-to (**m̧en-liw-tew**). Gramm. See *to* "passage". Arno tract.

M̧ōn-ļam-eņ (**m̧en-ļam-yeņ**). Gramm. See *ļam* "bay". Ailinglapalap household.

M̧ōn-ļañ (**m̧en-ļag**). Gramm. See *ļañ* "storm". Jaluit tract.

M̧ōn-ļomā (**m̧en-ļewmay**). Gramm. distort. See *mā* "breadfruit". Wotho tract.

M̧ōn-maaj (**m̧en-mahaj**). Gramm. See *maaj* "clearing". Kwajalein tract.

M̧ōn-maañ (**m̧en-mahag**). Gramm. See *maañ* "pandanus leaf". Utirik tract.

M̧ōn-mañ (**m̧en-mag**). Gramm. See *mañ* "coconut turning brown". Mili tract.

M̧ōn-mā (**m̧en-may**). Gramm. See *mā* "breadfruit". Maloelap tract; Arno tract.

M̧ōn-mājto (**m̧en-majtew**). Gramm. distort. See *mejeto* "path". Utirik tract.

M̧ōn-me (**m̧en-mȩy**). Gramm. See *me* "weir". Ailuk tract.

M̧ōn-mejeto (**m̧en-mejetew**). Gramm. See *mejeto* "path". Likiep tract.

M̧ōn-mejwaan (**m̧en-mȩjwahan**). Gramm. See *mejwaan* "breadfruit variety". Aur tract.

M̧ōn-mǫ-eņ (**m̧en-maw-yeņ**). Gramm. See *mǫ* "taboo". Ebon tract; Arno tract; two Mili tracts.

M̧ōn-mǫr (**m̧en-mar°**). Unanalyz. Jabwot tract.

M̧ōn-m̧aam̧ (**m̧en-m̧aham̧**). Gramm. See *m̧aa-* "in front of you". Ailinglapalap tract.

M̧ōn-m̧ōto (**m̧en-m̧ȩtȩw**). Unanalyz. Namorik tract.

M̧ōn-nen (**m̧ȩn-nȩn**). Gramm. See *nen* "a tree". Ailinglapalap tract.

M̧ōn-nen (**m̧en-nȩn**). Gramm. Kwajalein tract.

M̧ōn-ņooniep (**m̧en-ņeweniyep**). Gramm. See *ņoonniep* "fairies". Ailinglapalap tract.

M̧ōn-o (**m̧en-wew**). Gramm. See *o* "a bird". Kwajalein tract; Ailinglapalap tract.

M̧ōn-o-eņ (**m̧ȩn-wȩw-yeņ**). Gramm. See *o* "the dregs". Mili tract.

M̧ōn-okar (**m̧en-wekar**). Gramm. See *okar* "roots". Maloelap tract.

M̧ōn-om̧ (**m̧en-wȩm̧**). Gramm. See *om̧* "hermit crab". Mili tract.

M̧ōn-om̧-eņ (**m̧en-wȩm̧-yeņ**). Gramm. Ujae tract.

M̧ōn-om̧a (**m̧en-wem̧ah**). Reminisc. gramm. See *um̧a* "kiss". Ebon tract.

M̧ōn-oror (**m̧en-werwer**). Gramm. See *oror* "fence". Majuro tract.

M̧ōn-owe (**m̧en-wewwey**). Gramm. See *owe* "whistle". Majuro tract.

M̧ōn-pako (**m̧en-pakew**). Gramm. See *pako* "shark". Rongelap tract.

M̧ōn-pat (**m̧en-pat**). Gramm. distort. See *pat* "swamp". Majuro tract; Arno tract.

M̧ōn-pāl (**m̧en-pal**). Gramm. See *pāl* "house of dying arrowroot". Arno tract.

M̧ōn-pej (**m̧en-pȩj**). Gramm. See *pej* "placenta; discarded pandanus key; tar". Ailinglapalap tract.

M̧ōn-pele (**m̧en-pȩļȩy**). Gramm. distort. Arno tract.

M̧ōn-peļe (**m̧en-peļey**). Gramm. See *marpeļe* " a plant". Bikini tract; Wotho tract; two Kwajalein tracts; Namu tract; Ailinglapalap tract; Utirik household; Arno tract.

M̧ōn-peleǫ (**m̧en-peleyaw**). Gramm. See *peleǫ* "Moorish idol". Arno tract.

M̧ōn-penna (**m̧en-pennah**). Unanalyz. Arno islet.

M̧ōn-perap (**m̧en-perap**). Reminisc. gramm. See *pedāp* "large eel". Arno tract.

M̧ōn-perar (**m̧en-perar**). Gramm. See *perar* "put over fire". Namorik tract.

M̧ōn-pit (**m̧en-pit**). Gramm. See *pit* "twist sennit". Ebon tract.

M̧ōn-po (**m̧en-pew**). Gramm. See *po* "lower sail". Namu tract.

M̧ōn-po-iōn̄ (**m̧en-pew-yiyęg**). Gramm. Namu tract.

M̧ōn-raanbat (**m̧en-rahanbat**). Gramm. See *raanbat:* "house on top of the hill". Wotho tract.

M̧ōn-rūkin-aebōj (**m̧en-rikin-hayębęj**). Gramm. See *aebōj* "house south of the cistern". Kwajalein tract.

M̧ōn-tain (**m̧en-tahyin**). Part. recur. form. See *ta:* "what's this?" Kwajalein tract.

M̧ōn-turun-bōkā (**m̧en-tir°in-bekay**). Gramm. See *bōkā:* "house near the tide". Bikini tract.

M̧ōn-turun-bōl (**m̧en-tir°in-bęl**). Gramm. See *bōl:* "house near the taro pit". Wotho tract; Kwajalein tract.

M̧ōn-um̧ (**m̧en-wim̧**). Gramm. See *um̧* "earth oven". Jaluit tract.

M̧ōn-un̄ar (**m̧en-wigar**). Gramm. See *un̄n̄ar, un̄ar:* "beg for food", "carry in addition". Ailinglapalap tract; Maloelap tract; Arno tract.

M̧ōn-un̄n̄ar (**m̧en-wiggar**). Gramm. See *un̄n̄ar* "beg for food". Ailuk tract.

M̧ōn-ut (**m̧en-wit**). Gramm. See *ut* "flowers". Ailinglapalap tract; Kili tract.

M̧ōn-wa (**m̧en-wah**). Gramm. See *wa* "canoe". Two Wotje tracts.

M̧ōn-waaktak (**m̧en-wahaktak**). Unanalyz. Ebon tract.

M̧ōn-Waju (**m̧en-wajiw**). Pers. name, legendary woman *Luwaju.* Majuro tract.

M̧ōn-watak (**m̧en-wahtak**). Gramm. See *watak* "stand by weir waiting for tide". Jaluit tract.

M̧ōn-wōd-dik (**m̧en-wed-dik**). Gramm. See *wōd* "coral". Two Arno tracts.

M̧ōn-wōdwōd (**m̧en-wedwed**). Gramm. See *wōd* "coral". Arno tract.

M̧ōn-wōme (**m̧en-wemey**). Gramm. See *wōme* "pull it out". Arno tract.

M̧ōn-wōt (**m̧en-wet**). Gramm. See *wōt* "wild taro". Kwajalein tract; Jaluit tract; Ebon tract; two Arno tracts.

M̧ōn-wūjek (**m̧en-wijęk**). Gramm. See *wūjek* "be proud of". Jaluit tract.

M̧ōn-wūjooj (**m̧en-wijęwęj**). Gramm. See *wūjooj* "grass". Ujae tract; Kwajalein tract; Jaluit tract.

M̧ōn-wūliej (**m̧en-wiliyęj**). Gramm. See *wūliej* "cemetery". Eniwetak tract; Bikini tract; Lae tract; Kwajalein tract; Ailinglapalap tract; Namorik tract; Maloelap tract; Aur tract; three Arno tracts; two Mili tracts.

M̧ōnellok (**m̧ęnęlleq**). Reminisc. gramm. See *llok* "tie up". Arno tract.

M̧ōnikkūn̄ (**m̧enikkig**). Gramm. distort. See *kkōn̄* "a tree"; see also *kūn̄* "smell of feces". Ailuk tract.

M̧ōnon̄n̄o (**m̧eneg°g°ew**). Gramm. distort. See *n̄on̄o* "smell of feces". Wotje tract.

M̧ōnōbbō (**m̧enebbeh**). Gramm. See *bbō* "fish with spear on reef". Mili tract.

M̧ōnōkkan (**m̧enekkan**). Gramm. distort. See *kkan* "sustenance". Likiep tract.

M̧ōnōkkar-iaar (**m̧enekkar-yiyahar**). Gramm. distort. See *kkar* "arrange". Aur tract.

M̧ōnōkkar-iooj (**m̧enekkar-yiyęwęj**). Gramm. distort. Aur tract.

M̧ōnōkkōn̄ (**m̧ęnękkęg**). Gramm. distort. See *kkōn̄* "a plant". Ailinglapalap tract.

M̧ōnōn̄n̄aj (**m̧eneggaj**). Gramm. distort. See *n̄aj* "fragrant". Arno tract.

M̧ōnōn̄n̄at (**m̧eneggat**). Gramm. distort. See *n̄n̄at* "storm". Ailuk tract; Wotje tract.

M̧ōn̗akn̗ak (**m̧en̗akn̗ak**). Gramm. See *m̧ōn̗akn̗ak* "withered". Majuro tract.

M̧ōn̗ooļļap (**m̧ęn̗ewelļļap**). Also *M̧ōļooļļap* (**m̧eļewelļļap**), *M̧aļo-eļap* (**m̧aļew-yeļap**). 4. Atoll; Ratak; Maloelap.

M̧ōn̄ādik (**m̧egaydik**). Gramm. See *m̧ōn̄ā, dik:* "eat little". Jaluit tract.

M̧ōn̄āļapen (**m̧egayļapen**). Pers. name, a legendary monster who eats too much. Ailinglapalap tract.

M̧ōre-ean̄ (**m̧erey-yag**). Reminisc. gramm. See *m̧ōre* "gone northward". Arno tract.

M̧ōre-ear (**m̧ęręy-yehar**). Recur. form. Three Arno tracts.

M̧ōre-ear-iaar (**m̧ẹrẹy-yehar-yiyahar**). Recur. form. Arno household.

M̧ōre-ear-ilik (**m̧ẹrẹy-yehar-yilik**). Recur. form. Arno household.

M̧ōre-ear-iooj (**m̧ẹrẹy-yehar-yiyẹwẹj**). Recur. form. Arno household.

M̧ōre-tak (**m̧ẹrey-tak**). Recur. form. Arno tract.

M̧ōrōn-kul (**m̧eren-qil**). Recur. form. See *m̧ōrōn:* "color of the *kul,* or of the *kwōl* "sanderling". Kwajalein islet; Arno tract.

M̧ōrrōto (**m̧erretew**). Unanalyz. Jaluit tract.

M̧ōt (**m̧et**). Gramm. See *m̧ōt* "what house?" Mili tract.

M̧ōtab-lōn̄ (**m̧etab-lẹg**). Gramm. See *tab* "mist", *lōn̄* "above". Kwajalein tract.

M̧ōtbaru (**m̧etbariw**). Part. recur. form. See *baru* "crab". Arno tract.

M̧ōtļoļ-eņ (**m̧etl̦°el̦°-yeņ**). Also *M̧ōttoļ.* Recur. form. See *toļ:* "mountain house". Aur tract.

M̧ōtoeǫ (**m̧ẹtẹwyaw**). Recur. form. See *to* "taro pit", *eǫ* "begin to bear fruit". Arno tract.

M̧ōtoļǫk-raj (**m̧etẹwl̦aq-raj**). Gramm. See *m̧ōto, raj:* "whales rise", or *em̧, to, raj:* "house where whales go westward". Namu tract.

M̧ōtōļļan̄ (**m̧etel̦l̦ag**). Also *M̧ōttōļļan̄, M̧we-tōļļan̄.* Gramm. See *tōļļan̄:* "house safe from storms". Wotje tract.

M̧ōtōrkan-iiene (**m̧eterkan-yiyyẹnẹy**). Gramm. See *tōr:* "house on dry land". Majuro tract.

M̧ōtōrrak (**m̧eterrak**). Gramm. See *tōr:* "house in the south part". Arno tract.

M̧ōtran-el (**m̧etran-yel**). Gramm. See *tōr, el:* "house in the part cut off". Arno tract.

M̧ōtran-ut (**m̧etran-wit**). Gramm. See *tōr, ut:* "house in the flowery part". Arno tract.

M̧ōtta (**m̧ettah**). Gramm. See *m̧ōtta-:* "my portion". Mejit tract.

M̧ōttam̧wij (**m̧ettam̧ij**). Pers. name, legendary woman *lim̧ōttam̧wij.* Namu islet; Namorik tract.

M̧ōttǫ-eņ (**m̧ettaw-yeņ**). Reminisc. gramm. See *tǫ* "wind not full in sail". Namorik tract.

M̧ōttōllōn̄ (**m̧ettẹllẹg**). Reminisc. gramm. See *ttōlōn̄* "look up". Ebon household.

M̧uri-jilo (**m̧ir°i-jilẹw**). Gramm. See *m̧ur, jilo:* "school of albacore tuna". Utirik channel.

M̧urilik (**m̧ir°iylik**). Gramm. See *m̧ur* "appear at the ocean side". Majuro tract.

M̧urle (**m̧ir°lẹy**). Gramm. See *m̧ur, le:* "albatross appears", or short for *m̧urun le* "flock of albatross". Kwajalein islet; Jaluit tract.

M̧uujilen (**m̧iwijyilen**). Reminisc. gramm. See *m̧uuj, el* "pile up plant materials for its nest". Ebon tract.

M̧ūk-eņ (**m̧ik-yeņ**). Reminisc. gramm. See *m̧ōk* "fatigue". Majuro tract.

M̧ūkil (**m̧ikil**). Recur. form. See *kil* "skin". Likiep islet.

M̧ūkōn (**m̧iken**). Unanalyz. Lae tract.

M̧ūļe (**m̧il̦ẹy**). Reminisc. gramm. Namorik tract.

M̧ūļōn̄ (**m̧il̦ẹg**). Gramm. See *mūļōn̄* "fern shoot". Mejit tract.

M̧ūm̧ōt (**m̧im̧et**). Gramm. See *m̧m̧ōt* "pitching". Aur islet.

M̧ūrar (**m̧irar**). Gramm. See *m̧ūrar* "reddish color". Jaluit tract.

M̧ūt (**m̧it**). Gramm. See *m̧ūt* "hang on". Eniwetak islet.

M̧ūt-dikdik (**m̧it-dikdik**). Gramm. Eniwetak islet.

M̧ūtbōro (**m̧itbẹrẹw**). Gramm. See *m̧ūt, bōro* "hang on to the throat". Arno tract.

M̧ūtinōrro (**m̧itinerrẹw**). Unanalyz. Majuro tract.

M̧ūtok (**m̧iteq**). Gramm. See *m̧ūtok* "dark". Maloelap islet.

M̧ūtoņ-bar (**m̧iteņ°-bar**). Part. reminisc. gramm. Arno tract.

M̧ūtti-eņ (**m̧ittiy-yeņ**). Recur. form. Ailinglapalap tract.

M̧ūtti-laļ (**m̧ittiy-lal̦**). Recur. form. See *laļ* "earth". Majuro tract.

M̧ūttin-kuuj (**m̧ittin-qiwij**). Recur. form. See *kuuj* "cat". Mejit tract.

M̧ūttoon (**m̧ittẹwẹn**). Gramm. distort. See *ttoon:* "dirty house". Utirik tract.

M̧ūttūm̧a (**m̧ittim̧ah**). Recur. form., next to a tract named *Minm̧a.* Mili tract.

M̧ūtutu (**m̧itiwtiw**). Gramm. See *tutu* "bathe". Ebon tract.

M̧ūtwelōn̄ (**m̧itwẹylẹg**). Gramm. See *tuwe, lōn̄:* "house of damaged tops (of trees, due to lightning)". Majuro tract.

M̧we-dedmo̧o̧n (**m̧ey-dedmawan**). Gramm. See *ded, mo̧o̧n* "amount of dried copra". Arno tract.

M̧we-dekā (**m̧ęy-dekay**). Gramm. See *dekā* "house of stones". Majuro tract.

M̧we-det (**m̧ey-det**). Gramm. See *det* "house of sunshine". Namorik tract; Jaluit tract; Maloelap tract.

M̧we-deto (**m̧ęy-dęytęw**). Gramm. See *de, to* "house facing westward". Maloelap tract; Maloelap household.

M̧we-diktak (**m̧ęy-diktak**). Recur. form. See *dik, tak:* "this small house (facing) toward the east". Likiep tract.

M̧we-jaarar (**m̧ey-jaharhar**). Gramm. See *arar:* "we stir the fire with a stick and turn the breadfruit while it cooks". Arno tract.

M̧we-jak (**m̧ey-jak**). Gramm. See *jak* "net string". Jaluit tract; Namorik tract; Aur tract; Majuro tract.

M̧we-jak-rālik (**m̧ey-jak-raylik**). Gramm. Ailinglapalap tract.

M̧we-jak-reeaar (**m̧ey-jak-reyyahar**). Gramm. Ailinglapalap tract.

M̧we-jeban (**m̧ey-jeban**). Gramm. See *jeban* "rich". Majuro tract.

M̧we-jeboñōn (**m̧ęy-jębęg°ęn**). Gramm. See *jeboñon* "spend the night before departure". Arno tract.

M̧we-jed (**m̧ey-jed**). Reminisc. gramm. See *jjed* "look up". Arno tract.

M̧we-Jeepden (**m̧ey-jeyepdęn**). From *Severin* "name of a European trader who lived on this tract during German times". Arno tract.

M̧we-jeer (**m̧ey-jeyer**). Reminisc. gramm. See *jeer* "turn". Mejit tract.

M̧we-jeļañ (**m̧ey-jeyļag**). Gramm. See *jeļañ:* "storm". Kwajalein tract; Arno tract.

M̧we-jeļoñ (**m̧ęy-jeļeg°**). Gramm. See *toloñ* "go ashore, penetrate". Majuro tract.

M̧we-jeļo̧k (**m̧ey-jeļaq**). Gramm. See *ejjeļo̧k* "nothing to do". Majuro tract.

M̧we-jen (**m̧ey-jen**). Unanalyz. See *jān* "snare". Majuro tract.

M̧we-jera (**m̧ey-jerah**). Gramm. See *jera* "squirrel fish". Arno tract.

M̧we-jerkā (**m̧ey-jerkay**). Also *M̧we-jertak.* Gramm. See *jerjer:* "walk eastward swinging arms". Wotje tract.

M̧we-jerto (**m̧ęy-jęrtęw**). Gramm. See *jerjer:* "walk westward swinging arms". Wotje tract.

M̧we-jo (**m̧ey-jew**). Gramm. See *jo* "a fish". Kwajalein tract.

M̧we-jokden (**m̧ey-jeqden**). Gramm. See *jo̧kden* "ten pairs of fish or copra nuts". Ailinginae islet.

M̧we-joñ (**m̧ey-jeg°**). Gramm. See *joñ* "mangrove". Maloelap tract; Majuro household.

M̧we-joñļo̧k (**m̧ey-jeg°ļaq**). Gramm. See *joñ:* "lots of mangroves". Majuro tract.

M̧we-joor (**m̧ey-jewer**). Gramm. See *joor* "escape"; see also *Rūm̧wejoor* "name of clan said to have escaped from *Raarņo.* Likiep tract; Majuro tract; Arno tract.

M̧we-jorjor (**m̧ey-jer°jer°**). Gramm. See *jorjor* "walk fast". Majuro tract.

M̧we-joto (**m̧ęy-jęwtęw**). Unanalyz. Majuro tract.

M̧we-jo̧kjok (**m̧ey-jaqjeq**). Gramm. See *jokwajok* "mosquito". Arno tract.

M̧we-jurļo̧ņ (**m̧ęy-jir°ļ°aņ°**). Unanalyz. Arno tract.

M̧we-Liam̧ (**m̧ey-liyam̧**). Pers. name, a legendary woman. Wotje tract.

M̧we-loron (**m̧ęy-lęr°ęn**). Gramm. See *llor:* "its shade, his shadow". Arno tract.

M̧we-Ļakne (**m̧ey-ļaknęy**). Pers. name, a legendary man. Arno tract.

M̧we-Ļarwōj (**m̧ey-ļarwej**). Pers. name. Arno tract.

M̧we-Ļōm̧weed (**m̧ey-ļem̧eyed**). Pers. name. Arno tract.

M̧we-nen (**m̧ęy-nęn**). Gramm. See *nen* "a tree". Majuro tract.

M̧we-ņo (**m̧ey-ņew**). Gramm. See *ņo* "waves". Majuro tract.

M̧we-ra (**m̧ey-rah**). Gramm. See *ra* "branches". Mili tract.

M̧we-ro̧ñ (**m̧ey-rag°**). Gramm. See *ro̧ñ* "hole". Arno tract.

M̧we-tejek (**m̧ęy-tęyjęk**). Unanalyz. Majuro tract.

M̧we-terā (**m̧ey-teyray**). Gramm. See *tterā.* Four Arno tracts. (**m̧ey-teļ°eg°**). Gramm. See *toļoñ* "go ashore, penetrate". Majuro tract.

M̧we-tooj (**m̧ęy-tęwęj**). Gramm. See *tooj* "conspicuous". Maloelap tract; Majuro tract.

M̧we-toon (**m̧ęy-tęwęn**). Reminisc. gramm. See *to:* "his taro pit", ttoon "dirty". Arno tract.

M̗we-tọrtọr (**m̗ey-tar°tar°**). Gramm. See *tọrtọr* "eaves". Majuro tract.

M̗we-tōp (**m̗ẹy-tẹp**). Gramm. See *tōp* "wood shavings". Arno tract.

M̗weej (**m̗ẹyẹj**). Gramm. See *ej:* "high, eastern". Lae tract.

M̗weejej (**m̗ẹyẹjyẹj**). Unanalyz. Wotho tract.

M̗weejkāān-eņ (**m̗eyejkayan-yeņ**). Gramm. See *jekāān* "house of trunks". Namu islet.

M̗weenjelọk (**m̗eyenjeylaq**). Reminisc. gramm. See *jelọk* "push away the sail". Maloelap tract.

M̗weeņ (**m̗eyeņ**). Gramm. See *m̗weeņ* "that house". Mili tract.

M̗weeņ-aidik (**m̗eyeņ-hayidik**). Gramm. See *aidik:* "that narrow house". Eniwetak tract.

M̗weeņ-eaitok-jurōn (**m̗eyeņ-yehayiteq-jiwren**). Gramm. See *aetok, joor:* "that house that has tall pillars". Kwajalein tract.

M̗weeņ-edik (**m̗eyeņ-yedik**). Gramm. See *dik* "small". Two Ebon tracts; Arno islet.

M̗weeņ-elip (**m̗eyeņ-yelip**). Gramm. distort. See *ļap* "large". Jaluit tract.

M̗weeņ-eļip (**m̗eyeņ-yeļip**). Gramm. distort. Mili tract.

M̗weeņ-eōn̄ (**m̗eyeņ-yẹg**). Gramm. See *ean̄* "north". Likiep tract.

M̗weeņ-iaar (**m̗eyeņ-yiyahar**). Gramm. See *ar:* "that house at the lagoon beach". Jaluit tract.

M̗weeņ-iiōn̄ (**m̗eyeņ-yiyyẹg**). Gramm. Mili tract.

M̗weeņ-ioļap (**m̗eyeņ-yiyewļap**). Gramm. See *ioļap* "in the middle". Four Jaluit tracts; Ebon tract; three Wotje tracts; Arno tract; five Mili tracts.

M̗weeņ-iooj (**m̗eyeņ-yiyẹwẹj**). Gramm. See *iooj:* "that house in the interior". Two Jaluit tracts.

M̗weeņ-irōk (**m̗eyeņ-yiyrẹk**). Gramm. Mili tract.

M̗weeņ-lik (**m̗eyeņ-lik**). Gramm. See *lik:* "that house on the ocean side". Kwajalein tract; Ailuk tract; Likiep tract; Aur tract.

M̗weeņ-lo-aebōj-eņ (**m̗eyeņ-lew-hayẹbẹj-yeņ**). Gramm. See *lọ, aebōj:* "that house at the cistern". Mili tract.

M̗weeņ-lọ-jon̄ (**m̗eyeņ-law-jeg°**). Gramm. See *lọ, jon̄:* "that house at the mangrove". Jaluit tract.

M̗weeņ-ļap (**m̗eyeņ-ļap**). Gramm. See *ļap* "large". Bikini tract; two Rongelap tracts; Ailinglapalap tract; Jaluit tract; Kili tract; Wotje tract; two Maloelap tracts.

M̗weeņ-rōk (**m̗eyeņ-rẹk**). Gramm. See *rōk* "south". Ailinglapalap tract; two Mili tracts.

M̗weeņ-tur (**m̗eyeņ-tir°**). Gramm. See *tur* "end of islet". Maloelap tract.

M̗weertak-rālik (**m̗eyertak-raylik**). Gramm. See *ertak* "cover oven with stones"; "ripen". Kwajalein tract.

M̗weertak-reeaar (**m̗eyertak-reyyahar**). Gramm. Kwajalein tract.

M̗weetdik (**m̗eyetdik**). Reminisc. gramm. See *Nam̗wi.* Rongerik islet; Arno islet.

M̗weetļap (**m̗eyetļap**). Reminisc. gramm. Rongerik islet.

M̗weetļon̄ (**m̗eyetļeg°**). Gramm. See *M̗we-toļon̄.* Arno tract.

M̗weo-tak (**m̗eyew-tak**). Gramm. See *tak* "eastward". Wotho tract.

M̗were-eaar (**m̗ẹyrẹy-yahar**). Unanalyz. Arno tract.

M̗weta (**m̗eytah**). Gramm. See *ta:* "what house?" Majuro tract.

M̗wi-dukwal (**m̗iy-diqal**). Gramm. See *dukwal* "bow one's head". Arno tract.

M̗wi-jilo (**m̗iy-jilẹw**). Recur. form. See *jilo* "a fish". Arno tract.

M̗wi-jukok (**m̗iy-jiqẹq**). Recur. form. See *jukok* "uncover an oven". Majuro tract.

M̗wi-lukwōn (**m̗iy-liqen**). Recur. form. See *lukwō-* "middle". Arno tract.

M̗wi-rōkin-ut (**m̗iy-rẹkin-wit**). Gramm. See *ut:* "house south of the flowers". Majuro tract.

M̗wi-tete (**m̗iy-tẹytẹy**). Recur. form. See *tete* "roll of sennit". Majuro tract.

M̗wi-tilaan (**m̗iy-tilahan**). Recur. form. See *tilaan* "basaltic rock". Maloelap tract.

M̗wi-tinōro (**m̗iy-tinẹrẹw**). Unanalyz. Two Arno tracts.

M̗wi-tuon (**m̗iy-tiwen**). Recur. form. See *tuon* "skill". Maloelap tract.

M̗wi-tuonbar (**m̗iy-tiwenbar**). Reminisc. gramm. See *tuon, bar:* "tricks of the rock (where magic is practiced)". Arno tract.

M̗wi-tuwaak (**m̗iy-tiwahak**). Recur. form. See *tuwaak* "wade". Majuro tract.

M̧wi-tūb (**m̧iy-tib**). Gramm. See *tūb* "delightful house". Mili tract.

M̧wi-tūñañ (**m̧iy-tigag**). Recur. form. See *tūñañ* "beg for food". Aur tract; Arno tract.

M̧wi-tūr (**m̧iy-tir**). Recur. form. See *tūr* "place for making weapons". Two Mejit tracts.

M̧widdik-kaņ (**m̧iddik-kaņ**). Gramm. See *dik:* "those small houses". Ujae tract; Jaluit tract.

M̧widikdik (**m̧idikdik**). Gramm. See *dik:* "small house". Arno tract.

M̧widu (**m̧idiw**). Gramm. See *em̧, du* "house where they gather to dance". Ebon tract; Likiep tract; Majuro tract.

M̧widu-eņ (**m̧idiw-yeņ**). Part. recur. form. Two Mili tracts.

M̧wiiañ (**m̧iyyag**). Recur. form. See *m̧we, ean:* "this house in the north". Two Arno islets.

M̧wiiañ-dik (**m̧iyyag-dik**). Recur. form. Arno islet.

M̧wiilji (**m̧iyiljiy**). Recur. form. See *lije, liji:* "house for rinsing bait". Wotho tract.

M̧wijdaat (**m̧ijdahat**). Recur. form. See *m̧wij, daat:* "cut and covered with blood". Wotho tract.

M̧wiji-ļwe (**m̧ijiy-ļ°ęy**). Gramm. See *m̧ōj, m̧wiji, ļwe:* "after the pond". Maloelap tract; Maloelap household; Mili tract.

M̧wiji-ņa (**m̧ijiy-ņah**). Gramm. See *m̧ōj, ņa:* "after the shoal". Wotho tract.

M̧wijin-ene (**m̧ijin-yęnęy**). Gramm. See *āne:* "after the islet". Arno tract.

M̧wijin-ene-kaņ (**m̧ijin-yęnęy-kaņ**). Gramm. Majuro tract; Arno tract.

M̧wijin-eñōn (**m̧ijin-yegęn**). Gramm. distort. See *m̧ōj, enin:* "end of the fin". Utirik tract.

M̧wijin-kadek (**m̧ijin-kadek**). Recur. form. Eniwetak islet.

M̧wijin-karok (**m̧ijin-kareq**). Reminisc. gramm. See *karōk:* "after arranging (the family from eldest to youngest and giving land to each)". Arno tract.

M̧wijin-ni (**m̧ijin-niy**). Recur. form. See *ni:* "after the coconut". Ebon tract.

M̧wijit-eņ (**m̧ijit-yeņ**). Gramm. See *m̧wijit* "cut it". Ujae tract.

M̧wijjilej (**m̧ijjilęj**). Reminisc. gramm. See *wūliej:* "after the cemetery (?)". Mejit tract.

M̧wijjinep (**m̧ijjinep**). Unanalyz. Jaluit tract.

M̧wijjirabōd (**m̧ijjirabed**). Part. reminisc. gramm. See *bōd* "turtle shell". Ailinglapalap tract.

M̧wijjuurur (**m̧ijjiwirwir**). Recur. form. See *jjuurore* "full of something". Ailinglapalap tract.

M̧wilbar (**m̧ilbar**). Recur. form. See *libar* "rock". Majuro tract.

M̧wilkōk (**m̧ilkęk**). Recur. form. See *kōk, likōk:* "cracked house". Ailinglapalap tract.

M̧willukubwe (**m̧illiqibey**). Reminisc. gramm. See *ilo, kūbwe:* "house among feces". Arno tract.

M̧win-bar (**m̧in-bar**). Gramm. See *bar* "rock". Rongelap tract.

M̧win-bukwe (**m̧in-biqęy**). Gramm. See *bukwekwe:* "thick (from lagoon to ocean)". Majuro tract.

M̧win-buojļap-ar (**m̧in-biwęjļap-har**). Gramm. See *buoj:* "lagoon side of the large capital house". Arno tract.

M̧win-buojļap-lik (**m̧in-biwęjļap-lik**). Gramm. Arno tract.

M̧win-buut (**m̧in-biwit**). Unanalyz. Bikini tract; Majuro tract.

M̧win-būkōr (**m̧in-bikęr**). Gramm. See *būkōr* "a plant". Two Maloelap tracts; Majuro tract.

M̧win-bwijenro (**m̧in-bijenręw**). Gramm. See *bwijenro* "superstition". Majuro tract.

M̧win-eak (**m̧in-yak**). Gramm. See *eak* "legendary pile of copra". Ebon tract.

M̧win-ekkōñ (**m̧in-yekkęg**). Gramm. See *kkōñ* "a tree". Likiep tract.

M̧win-iaļ (**m̧in-yiyaļ**). Gramm. See *iaļ* "road". Aur tract.

M̧win-idaak (**m̧in-yidahak**). Gramm. See *idaak* "drink". Kwajalein tract.

M̧win-iie (**m̧in-yiyyęy**). Gramm. See *iie* "centipede". Maloelap tract; Maloelap household.

M̧win-ijo (**m̧in-yijęw**). Recur. form. See *ijo* "house of good soil". Utirik tract; Wotje tract; Maloelap tract; Maloelap household; Arno tract; Mili tract.

M̧win-ijo-ar (**m̧in-yijęw-har**). Recur. form. Arno household.

M̧win-ijo-lik (**m̧in-yijęw-lik**). Recur. form. Arno household.

M̧win-ijoļ (**m̧in-yijeļ°**). Gramm. See *ijoļ* "appetite". Aur tract.

M̧win-inem (**m̧in-yinem**). Gramm. See *ine-:* "our sisters". Namu tract.

M̧win-iōn̄ (**m̧in-yiyęg**). Gramm. Mejit tract.

M̧win-ire (**m̧in-yirey**). Gramm. See *ire* "fight". Namu tract.

M̧win-ito (**m̧in-yitęw**). Gramm. See *ito* "go west". Jabwot tract.

M̧win-iwaņ (**m̧in-yiwaņ**). Reminisc. gramm. See *uwaņ* "gray haired". Eniwetak tract.

M̧win-ke (**m̧in-kęy**). Gramm. See *ke* "porpoise". Ujae tract.

M̧win-kiār (**m̧in-kiyar**). Gramm. distort. See *keār* "tern". Erikub tract.

M̧win-kid-eņ (**m̧in-kid-yeņ**). Reminisc. gramm. Arno tract.

M̧win-kiden (**m̧in-kidęn**). Gramm. See *kiden* "beach borage". Ailinglapalap tract; Maloelap tract; three Majuro tracts; Arno tract; Mili tract; Knox tract.

M̧win-kiej (**m̧in-kiyęj**). Gramm. See *kiej* "a tree". Arno tract.

M̧win-kiep (**m̧in-kiyęp**). Gramm. See *kiep* "spider lily". Maloelap tract; Majuro tract.

M̧win-kiio (**m̧in-kiyyew**). Gramm. distort. Two Maloelap tracts; Arno tract; Mili tract.

M̧win-kijdik-eņ (**m̧in-kijdik-yeņ**). Gramm. See *kijdik* "rat". Rongelap tract.

M̧win-kiju (**m̧in-kijiw**). Gramm. See *kiju* "mast". Arno tract.

M̧win-kille (**m̧in-killęy**). Gramm. See *kille* "a shrub". Mili tract.

M̧win-kinep-rōk (**m̧in-kinep-ręk**). Gramm. See *Kinep-rōk* "Kwajalein tract". Majuro tract.

M̧win-kino (**m̧in-kinew**). Gramm. See *kino* "fern". Ujae tract; Kwajalein tract; Maloelap tract; two Majuro tracts; Arno tract.

M̧win-kio (**m̧in-kiyew**). Gramm. See *kio* "a plant". Wotho tract; Namu tract; Majuro tract; Arno tract.

M̧win-kio-rāātle (**m̧in-kiyew-rayatley**). Gramm. Arno household.

M̧win-kio-reeaar (**m̧in-kiyew-reyyahar**). Gramm. Arno household.

M̧win-kipillo (**m̧in-kipillęw**). Part. reminisc. gramm. See *kapin* "bottom of", *lo* "disenchantment". Mejit tract.

M̧win-kipin-pat (**m̧in-kipin-pat**). Gramm. distort. See *kapin:* "house west of the swamp". Arno tract.

M̧win-kōņo (**m̧in-keņew**). Gramm. See *kōņo* "a tree". Arno tract.

M̧win-kubōk (**m̧in-qibęk**). Gramm. See *kubōk* "a tree". Ailinglapalap tract; Mili tract.

M̧win-kude (**m̧in-qidey**). From Japn. *tokkuri* "sake bottle" (?) Knox tract.

M̧win-kur (**m̧in-qir°**). Gramm. See *kur* "squirrel fish". Arno islet.

M̧win-kūbwe (**m̧in-kibey**). Gramm. See *kūbwe* "feces". Wotho tract; Namu tract; Ebon tract; Maloelap tract; Maloelap tract; two Arno tracts.

M̧win-kūbwe-iiōn̄ (**m̧in-kibey-yiyyęg**). Gramm. Mili tract.

M̧win-kūbwe-irōk (**m̧in-kibey-yiyręk**). Gramm. Mili tract.

M̧win-kūbwi-jekar (**m̧in-kibiy-jekar**). Recur. form. See *jekar:* "house of *jekar* feces. Arno tract.

M̧win-kūn̄ (**m̧in-kig**). Gramm. See *kūn̄* "smell of feces". Ailinglapalap tract; Likiep tract; Wotje tract; Erikub tract; Arno tract; Mili tract.

M̧win-kūra (**m̧in-kirah**). Reminisc. gramm. See *kūrak* "a plant". Ujae tract.

M̧win-kūtaak (**m̧in-kitahak**). Gramm. See *kūtaak* "a tree". Two Maloelap tracts; Majuro tract; two Arno tracts.

M̧win-kūtaak-rāātle (**m̧in-kitahak-rayatley**). Gramm. Arno tract.

M̧win-kūtaak-reeaar (**m̧in-kitahak-reyyahar**). Gramm. Arno tract.

M̧win-kūtak (**m̧in-kitak**). Gramm. See *kūtak* "wind from southwest". Ailinglapalap tract.

M̧win-kūtōtō (**m̧in-kitęhtęh**). Gramm. See *kūtōtō* "angry". Arno tract.

M̧win-Limǫǫr (**m̧in-limawar**). Pers. name. See *mǫǫr:* "Mrs. Bait's house". Eniwetak tract.

M̧win-lu-eaļ (**m̧in-liw-yaļ**). Reminisc. gramm. See *iaļ:* "house at the road". Two Kwajalein tracts.

M̧win-lu-iaļ (**m̧in-liw-yiyaļ**). Gramm. Eniwetak tract.

M̧win-Luāl (**m̧in-liwyal**). Pers. name. Rongelap tract.

M̧win-lukubwe (**m̧in-liqibey**). Gramm. distort. See *kūbwe:* "house among feces". Two Arno tracts.

M̧win-m̧wide (**m̧in-m̧idęy**). Reminisc. gramm. See *m̧wid* "worn-out woven things". Arno tract.

M̧win-m̧wijlōñ (**m̧in-m̧ijlęg**). Gramm. See *m̧wij, lōñ:* "cut off the top". Mejit tract.

M̧win-nen (**m̧in-nęn**). Gramm. See *nen* "a tree". Ailinglapalap tract.

M̧win-niñ-aebōj (**m̧in-nig-hayębęj**). Gramm. distort. See *niñ, aebōj* "house with a small cistern". Namu tract.

M̧win-Pit-raiiōñ (**m̧in-pit-rahyiyyęg**). Gramm. See *Pit* "Gilbertese". Kwajalein tract.

M̧win-Pit-rairōk (**m̧in-pit-rahyiyręk**). Gramm. Kwajalein tract.

M̧win-pukor (**m̧in-piqęr**). Gramm. See *pukor* "coral rocks". Ailinglapalap tract.

M̧win-tūb (**m̧in-tib**). Gramm. See *tūb* "reward; delight". Eniwetak tract.

M̧win-ukok (**m̧in-wikwęk**). Gramm. See *ukok* "turn over". Rongelap tract.

M̧win-um̧ (**m̧in-wim̧**). Gramm. Maloelap tract.

M̧win-uñar (**m̧in-wigar**). Gramm. See *uññar* "beg for food", *uñar* "carry in addition". Arno tract.

M̧win-ut (**m̧in-wit**). Gramm. See *ut* "flowers". Bikini tract; Namu tract; Wotje tract.

M̧win-utot (**m̧in-witwęt**). Gramm. See *utot* "butterfly fish". Mili tract.

M̧win-watak (**m̧in-wahtak**). Gramm. See *watak* "stand by a weir". Ailinglapalap tract.

M̧win-wi (**m̧in-wiy**). Reminisc. gramm. See *uwi* "smell of fish cooking". Majuro tract.

M̧win-wūdej (**m̧in-widęj**). Gramm. See *wūdej* "a bird". Ailinglapalap tract.

M̧win-wūjjien (**m̧in-wijjiyen**). Gramm. See *wūje-:* "house that is part of it". Arno tract.

M̧win-wūjooj (**m̧in-wijęwęj**). Gramm. See *wūjooj* "grass". Maloelap tract; Arno tract.

M̧win-wūjroñ (**m̧in-wijreg°**). Gramm. See *wūjroñ* "pull out". Arno tract.

M̧win-wūlej (**m̧in-wilęj**). Gramm. See *wūlej* "a shrub". Wotje tract; Arno tract.

M̧win-wūliej (**m̧in-wiliyęj**). Gramm. See *wūliej* "cemetery". Bikini tract; Namu tract; Arno tract.

M̧win-wūllep (**m̧in-willep**). Gramm. See *wūllepa-* "mother's brother". Knox tract.

M̧win-wūlok (**m̧in-wileq**). Gramm. See *wūlok* "excuse". Namu tract.

M̧win-wūmatoļ (**m̧in-wimateļ°**). Part. recur. form. See *matoļ* "part". Arno tract.

M̧winikōd (**m̧iniked**). Reminisc. gramm. See *ainikied* "our voice". Arno tract.

M̧wininñij (**m̧iniggij**). Gramm. See *ññij* "groan". Eniwetak tract.

M̧winnuiaļ (**m̧inniwyiyaļ**). Reminisc. gramm. See *M̧win-lu-iaļ.* Maloelap tract.

M̧wintaļañ (**m̧intahļag**). Unanalyz. Maloelap tract.

Naajaj (**nahajhaj**). Gramm. See *naaj, aj:* "will be thatched". Arno islet.

Naajbōl (**nahajbęl**). Gramm. See *naaj, bbōl* "will bloom". Likiep islet.

Naaļ (**nahaļ**). Gramm. See *naaļ* "splinter". Arno islet.

Nabbe (**nabbęy**). Gramm. See *nabbe* "ugly". Jaluit islet.

Nakwōpe (**nahqepey**). Recur. form. See *Nakwōpe* "a navigational sign". Ailinglapalap tract.

Naļwōj (**nahļ°ej**). Unanalyz. Wotho tract.

Naṃ (**naṃ**). Gramm. Bikini district; Bikini islet.

Naṃ-en (**naṃ-yen**). Gramm. See *naṃ* "secondary lagoon". Rongelap islet; Arno tract; two Mili islets.

Naṃ-ke (**naṃ-kęy**). Gramm. See *naṃ, ke:* "porpoise lagoon". Ujelang tract.

Naṃ-oļar (**naṃ-weļar**). Gramm. See *oļar:* "small secondary lagoon". Jaluit islet.

Naṃdān (**naṃdan**). Reminisc. gramm. Jaluit tract; see *Nōṃdān.*

Naṃdik (**naṃdik**). Gramm. See *naṃ, dik:* "small secondary lagoon". Ralik atoll; Namorik; Ailinglapalap tract; Namorik islet.

Naṃdike (**naṃdikey**). Part. recur. form. See *dike* "dislike". Ailinglapalap tract.

Naṃo (**naṃęw**). Unanalyz. Ralik atoll; Namu; Kwajalein tract; Namu islet.

Naṃwi (**naṃiy**). Gramm. See *naṃ* "secondary lagoon". Legend says this islet and nearby *Mweetdik* were brought here from Namorik (*Naṃdik*), hence the first and last portions of their names. Arno islet.

Naṃwijlel-eañ (**naṃijlęl-yag**). Gramm. See *naṃ, jilel:* "lagoon of trumpet shells". Majuro tract.

Naṃwijlel-rak (**naṃijlẹl-rak**). Gramm. Majuro tract.

Nanajellen (**nahnahjellen**). Gramm. See *nana, jellen:* "out of position". Erikub tract.

Nanij (**nahnij**). Pers. name, a god. Jaluit islet.

Natọuj (**nahtawij**). Unanalyz. Jaluit islet.

Nawōdo (**nahwewdew**). Loan from *Nawōdo* "Nauru". Ailinglapalap islet.

Ne-wōt-juon (**ney-wet-jiwen**). Gramm.: "follow the footprint (of the owner of the land)". Kwajalein tract.

Neen-ek (**neyen-yẹk**). Gramm. See *ne, ek:* "fish legs: bottom fins of fish such as the grouper (*ḷakkūrae*) or turtles. Namu islet.

Neen-oṃ (**neyen-wẹṃ**). Gramm. See *ne, oṃ:* "legs of the hermit crab". Namu islet.

Neiobwā (**nẹyiyewbay**). Pers. name. Majuro tract.

Nemā (**nemay**). Gramm. See *nām:* "smell of". Bikini tract; Namu tract.

Nemā-aidikdik (**nemay-hayidikdik**). Gramm. See *aidik:* "narrow *Nemā*". Namu tract.

Nemmā (**nemmay**). Reminisc. gramm. See *nām, mā:* "smell of breadfruit". Arno tract.

Nennōr (**nenner**). Reminisc. gramm. See *nen, nōr:* "the *Morinda* starts to bloom". Kwajalein islet.

Nenwa (**nenwah**). Reminisc. gramm. See *nen, wa:* "canoe bearing *Morinda* fruit". Likiep tract.

Nepdān (**nepdan**). Gramm. See *nep, dān:* "lots of water". Wotje islet.

Ni (**niy**). Gramm. See *ni* "coconut". Ailuk islet.

Ni-eṇ (**niy-yeṇ**). Gramm. See *ni:* "that coconut". Kili tract.

Ni-kaṇ (**niy-kaṇ**). Gramm. See *ni:* "those coconuts". Bikini tract; Ailinglapalap tract; Arno tract.

Ni-ṃōtṃōt (**niy-ṃẹtṃẹt**). Gramm. See *ṃṃōtṃōt:* "coconuts drank noisily". Bikini tract.

Nibuñ (**nibig°**). Part. recur. form. See *Nibuñ* "pandanus variety". Wotje islet.

Niiḷ (**niyiḷ**). From Engl. *needle*. Mejit tract.

Niin-mar-eañ (**niyin-mar-yag**). Gramm. See *ni, mar:* "coconuts of the bushes". Ebon tract.

Niin-mar-eṇ (**niyin-mar-yeṇ**). Gramm. Namu islet.

Nilep (**niylep**). Gramm. distort. See *ni, ḷap:* "big coconuts". Jaluit islet.

Nimuur (**niymiwir**). Gramm. See *nimuur* "coconut tree loaded with nuts". Aur tract.

Nimuur-kaṇ (**niymiwir-kaṇ**). Gramm. Kili tract.

Niṃur (**niṃir°**). Unanalyz. Kwajalein islet.

Nin-eṇ (**nin-yeṇ**). Gramm. See *nin:* "place for pounding pandanus leaves". Arno tract.

Nini (**niyniy**). Gramm. See *ni:* "many coconuts". Kwajalein islet.

Niñilep (**nigiylep**). Part. recur. form. See *ñilep* "molar". Namorik tract.

Nokwat (**neqat**). Unanalyz. Kwajalein tract.

Nōḷ (**neḷ**). Gramm. See *nōḷ* "make weapons". Kwajalein islet; Mili tract.

Nōḷḷe (**neḷḷey**). Also *Ḷōḷḷe*. Unanalyz. Ujelang islet.

Nōḷpi (**neḷpiy**). Unanalyz. Lae tract.

Nōṃdān (**neṃdan**). Also *Naṃdān*. Reminisc. gramm. See *naṃ, dān:* "lagoon water". Jaluit islet.

Nōṃḷaḷ (**neṃḷaḷ**). Reminisc. gramm. See *naṃ, ṃwilaḷ:* "deep secondary lagoon"; see also *meḷaḷ*. Likiep tract.

Nukḷāiḷāi (**niqḷayiḷayiy**). From Ellice *Nukulaelae*. Ailinglapalap tract.

Nukne (**niqnẹy**). From Engl. *New Guinea*. Kwajalein islet; Namu tract; Utirik tract; Mejit tract.

Nukne-rāātle (**niqney-rayatley**). From Engl. *New Guinea*. Arno islet.

Nukne-reeaar (**niqney-reyyahar**). From Engl. *New Guinea*. Arno islet.

Nukut (**niqit**). Reminisc. gramm. See *nukuj* "fold sloppily". Kwajalein tract.

Nuṃakūt (**niwṃahkit**). Loan from Engl. *New Market*. Arno tract.

Nupidkōn (**niwpidkẹn**). From Engl. *New Britain*. Arno tract.

Nuwe (**niwẹy**). From Ellice *Nui, or from Niue in Polynesia*. Majuro tract.

Nuwiọọk (**niwiyawak**). From Engl. *New York*. Wotje tract.

Ṇa-boñ (**ṇah-bẹg°**). Gramm. See *boñ:* "night shoal". Lae islet.

Ṇa-bọkore (**ṇah-baqer°ẹy**). Gramm. This is the Ratak equivalent of the Ralik *ṇaṇaambokbok* "gravel and sand mixed together". Majuro coral head.

Ṇa-dedeen (**ṇah-deydeyen**). Recur. form. See *Dede* "Jaluit islet". Mejit tract.

Ṇa-dik (**ṇah-dik**). Gramm. Likiep islet; Majuro tract.

Ṇa-dikdik (**ṇah-dikdik**). Gramm. See *dik:* "small shoal". Ratak atoll; Knox; Knox islet.

Ṇa-eṇ (**ṇah-yeṇ**). Gramm. See *eṇ:* "the shoal". Rongelap islet; Kwajalein tract; Jaluit islet; Arno tract.

Ṇa-eṇ-ḷap (**ṇah-yeṇ-ḷap**). Gramm. Ujae islet.

Ṇa-eṇjāiiōñ (**ṇah-yeṇjayiyyẹg**). Gramm. Arno tract.

Ṇa-eṇjārōk (**ṇah-yeṇjayrẹk**). Gramm. Arno tract.

Ṇa-in (**ṇah-yin**). Gramm. See *ṇa, in:* "this shoal". Likiep tract.

Ṇa-jā (**ṇah-jay**). Gramm. See *jā* "falling sail". Utirik islet.

Ṇa-jebake (**ṇah-jebakey**). Gramm. See *jebake* "turtle with beautiful shell". Arno islet.

Ṇa-jib-eṇ (**ṇah-jib-yeṇ**). Gramm. See *jib:* "the rising shoal". Ailinginae islet.

Ṇa-kaṇ (**ṇah-kaṇ**). Gramm. See *kaṇ:* "those shoals". Majuro tract.

Ṇa-kaṇ-ej (**ṇah-kaṇ-yẹj**). Gramm. See *ṇa, ej:* "those shoals on the east". Arno sandspit; Mili islet.

Ṇa-ko (**ṇah-kew**). Gramm. See *ko:* "the shoals". Knox islet.

Ṇa-kor (**ṇah-qẹr**). Gramm. See *kor* "coconut shell". Ebon islet.

Ṇa-kullep (**ṇah-qillep**). Gramm. distort. See *kur, ḷap:* "shoal of large squirrel fish". Erikub tract.

Ṇa-Limaadik (**ṇah-limahdik**). Pers. name. Arno shoal.

Ṇa-ḷap (**ṇah-ḷap**). Gramm. See *ḷap:* "large shoal". Namu islet; Namu tract; Ailinglapalap islet; Utirik islet; Ailuk tract; Likiep islet; Mili islet.

Ṇa-ḷap-iōñ (**ṇah-ḷap-yiyẹg**). Gramm. Arno tract; Mili tract.

Ṇa-ḷap-rōk (**ṇah-ḷap-rẹk**). Gramm. Arno tract; Mili tract.

Ṇa-meej (**ṇah-meyej**). Gramm. See *meej:* "dark-colored shoal". Arno islet.

Ṇa-ṃōj (**ṇah-ṃẹj**). Gramm. See *ṃōj:* "finished (forming) shoal". Mili tract.

Ṇa-pejpej (**ṇah-pẹjpẹj**). Gramm. See *pejpej:* "shallow shoal". Majuro tract.

Ṇa-rā (**ṇah-ray**). Gramm. See *rā:* "these shoals (using the human form of the demonstrative rather than the expected nonhuman *kā*)". Arno islet; Mili islet.

Ṇa-rur-eṇ (**ṇah-r°ir°-yeṇ**). Gramm. See *rur:* "the flower picking shoal". Arno islet.

Ṇa-tutu (**ṇah-tiwtiw**). Gramm. See *tutu:* "wet shoal". Utirik islet.

Ṇa-wāto (**ṇah-waytẹw**). Gramm. See *wāto* "go westward". Majuro tract.

Ṇa-wetak (**ṇa-weytak**). Gramm. See *wetak* "go eastward". Jaluit islet.

Ṇa-wōj (**ṇah-wej**). Reminisc. gramm. See *wōj* "driftwood". Maloelap islet.

Ṇaajbōl (**ṇahajbẹl**). Unanalyz. Likiep islet.

Ṇaallo (**ṇahallẹw**). Recur. form. See *ṇa, allo:* "searching shoal". Mili district; Mili islet.

Ṇaan-alle (**ṇahan-hallẹy**). Gramm. See *alle:* "wrasse shoal". Aur islet.

Ṇaan-jade (**ṇahan-jahdẹy**). Gramm. See *jade:* "roosting shoal". Ailinglapalap islet.

Ṇaan-kalle (**ṇahan-kalley**). Gramm. See *alle:* "shoal for catching wrasse". Knox tract.

Ṇaan-kāmeej (**ṇahan-kaymeyej**). Gramm. See *kāmeej:* "redwood driftwood shoal". Jaluit islet.

Ṇaan-ke (**ṇahan-kẹy**). Gramm. See *ke:* "porpoise shoal". Majuro islet.

Ṇaan-kōjeje (**ṇahan-kẹjẹyjẹy**). Gramm. distort. See *kōjeje* "dry under sun". Jaluit islet.

Ṇaan-kōjeje (**ṇahan-kejeyjey**). Gramm. Jaluit islet.

Ṇaan-kōtkōt (**ṇahan-ketket**). Gramm. See *kōtkōt* "ruddy turnstone". Knox islet.

Ṇaan-kwekwe (**ṇahan-qẹyqẹy**). Gramm. See *kwekwe* "scratch". Maloelap tract.

Ṇaan-men (**ṇahan-men**). Gramm. See *men* "things, creatures". Ebon islet.

Ṇaan-merā (**ṇahan-meray**). Gramm. See *merā:* "parrotfish shoal". Ujae islet.

Ṇaan-ut (**ṇahan-wit**). Gramm. See *ut:* "flowery shoal". Ailinglapalap tract.

Ṇaan-uwaṇ (**ṇahan-wiwaṇ**). Gramm. See *uwaṇ:* "gray-haired shoal". Knox tract.

Ṇaaneōñ (**ṇahanẹyẹg**). Gramm. distort. See *eañ* "north". Wotje islet.

Ṇaarmej (**ṇaharmẹj**). Also *Naarmej* (**naharmẹj**). Gramm. See *armej:* "people shoal". Jaluit islet.

Ṇaṃakke (**ṇahṃakkęy**). Recur. form. See *ṇa, ṃak, ke.* Mili islet.

Ṇamṇōṃ (**ṇamṇẹm**). Gramm. See *ṇaṃ:* "swarming with mosquitoes". Jaluit islet.

Ṇaniktal (**ṇahniktal**). Reminisc. gramm. See *ṇa, ek, tal* "shoal of procession bearing fish as tribute". Knox islet.

Ṇauweej (**ṇahwiweyej**). From Engl. *northwest.* Ailinglapalap islet; Ebon household.

Ṇonmeea (**ṇ°enmeyyah**). From Ellice *Nanumea*. Jaluit tract.

Ṇoṇmeea (**ṇ°eṇ°meyyah**). From Ellice *Nanumea*. Ebon tract; Majuro tract.

Ṇōnouj (**ṇenewij**). From Gilb. *Nonouti (Atoll).* Wotje tract.

N̄ad (**gad**). Gramm. See *n̄ad* "gums". Mili islet.

N̄an̄tain (**gagtahyin**). Reminisc. gramm. See *n̄an̄, ta, in:* "what brittleness is this?" Mili islet.

N̄e (**gęy**). Gramm. See *n̄en̄e* "a plant". Ailuk islet.

N̄en̄e (**gęygęy**). Gramm. See *n̄en̄e* "a plant". Kwajalein islet.

N̄i-ej (**giy-yẹj**). Gramm. See *n̄i, ej* "high (eastern) tooth". Ailinglapalap islet.

N̄i-ej-reeaar (**giy-yẹj-reyyahar**). Gramm. Ailinglapalap tract.

N̄i-ej-relik (**giy-yẹj-reylik**). Gramm. Ailinglapalap tract.

N̄illiṇo (**gilliyṇew**). Gramm. See *n̄il, ṇo:* "sound of the waves". Mili tract.

N̄on̄ (**g°eg°**). Gramm. See *n̄on̄* "a fish". Jaluit islet.

O (**wẹw**). Gramm. See *o* "the dregs". Arno tract.

O-dik (**wew-dik**). Gramm. See *o:* "small *o* bird". Bikini islet.

O-eṇ (**wew-yeṇ**). Gramm. See *o* "a bird". Majuro tract.

Obbar (**webbar**). Gramm. See *obbar* "fishing method". Rongelap tract.

Okok (**wekwek**). Gramm. See *okok* "pick pandanus". Majuro tract.

Oḷabkōn (**weḷabkẹn**). Unanalyz. Jaluit tract.

Oḷar (**weḷar**). Gramm. See *oḷar:* "tiny things". Ailinglapalap islet.

Oḷbwe (**weḷbey**). Unanalyz. Jaluit islet.

Oḷouj (**weḷẹwij**). Reminisc. gramm. See *ḷouj* "a fish". Aur tract.

Oḷōt (**weḷet**). Gramm. See *oḷōt* "land of no value". Maloelap islet.

Oḷūr-eṇ (**weḷir-yeṇ**). Unanalyz. Mili tract.

Oṇṇa-eṇ (**weṇṇah-yeṇ**). Part. recur. form. See *ṇa* "shoal". Lib tract.

Oṇojo (**weṇewjew**). Part. recur. form. See *ṇo, jo:* "waves cause to float loose"; see also *Wōnejo-eṇ* "Namorik tract". Arno tract.

On̄ (**weg°**). Gramm. See *on̄* "nostalgia". Maloelap islet.

On̄-in (**weg°-yin**). Gramm. See *on̄, ijin:* "homesickness here". Arno tract.

On̄i (**weg°iy**). Unanalyz. Arno islet.

On̄ḷā (**weg°ḷay**). Reminisc. gramm. See *on̄, eoonḷā:* "homesick household". Namorik tract.

Or-eṇ (**wer-yeṇ**). Gramm. See *or.* Jaluit tract; Ebon tract.

Oralo (**werhalẹw**). Unanalyz. Namu tract.

Oraḷok (**werhaḷaq**). Unanalyz. See *Aḷọkwōd* "Mili tract". Maloelap tract.

Orarōn (**werharen**). Gramm. distort. See *or, ar:* "has a lagoon beach". Mili tract.

Orbwilọk (**werbilaq**). Part. recur. form. See *bwilọk* "broken". Ebon tract.

Orkā-eṇ (**werkay-yeṇ**). Gramm. See *or, kā:* "has trunks". Bikini islet.

Orkilo (**werkilew**). Reminisc. gramm. See *or* "has", *kilo* "ordinary sights (?)". Majuro tract.

Orḷap (**werḷap**). Gramm. See *or, ḷap:* "big *or*". Kwajalein tract; Ailinglapalap tract; Jaluit tract; Ebon tract.

Oror (**werwer**). Gramm. See *oror* "fence". Aur tract.

Orpāl (**werpal**). Part. recur. form. See *pāl* "dying arrowroot". Majuro tract.

Orpāp (**wẹrpap**). Part. reminisc. gramm. See *pāp* "frond". Kwajalein islet.

Out (**wẹwit**). Gramm. See *out* "meeting place". Erikub tract.

Ọu (**wawiw**). From Haw. *Oahu*. Mili islet.

Paaneraj (**pahaneyraj**). Gramm. See *paane, raj:* "give bait to whales". Bikini tract.

Paarōr-kaṇ (**paharher-kaṇ**). Gramm. See *paarōr* "where a couple go for illicit intercourse". Ailuk islet.

Paarōr-kaṇ-ean̄ (**paharher-kaṇ-yag**). Gramm. Ailuk tract.

Paarōr-kaṇ-rak (**paharher-kaṇ-rak**). Gramm. Ailuk tract.

Paojān (**pahwewjan**). Part. reminisc. gramm. See *pao, jān:* "appear from (that cape)". Aur islet; Majuro tract; Mili tract.

Paojen (**pahwewjen**). Gramm. distort. Ailuk islet.

Parij-eṇ (**parij-yeṇ**). Gramm. See *parij* "starry flounder". Ebon tract.

Pat-dik (**pat-dik**). Gramm. See *pat* "swamp". Lib tract; Jaluit tract.

Pat-eṇ (**pat-yeṇ**). Gramm. distort. Likiep tract; two Wotje tracts.

Pat-eṇ-lik (**pat-yeṇ-lik**). Gramm. distort. Lib tract.

Pata-eṇ-ḷap (**pahtah-yeṇ-ḷap**). Gramm. See *pata:* "the big war". Majuro coral head.

Patiddik (**patiddik**). Gramm. distort. See *pat, dik:* "wee swamp". Jaluit tract.

Patleem (**patleyem**). From Bibl. *Bethlehem*. Mejit tract.

Patlōñ (**patlęg**). Recur. form. See *pat* "swamp", *lōñ* "above". Majuro tract.

Patpat (**patpat**). Gramm. See *pat:* "swampy". Rongerik islet.

Patpat-rōk (**patpat-rẹk**). Gramm. Aur tract.

Patto (**pattẹw**). Gramm. See *pat, to:* "swamp soaking pit". Jaluit tract.

Pāāllin-eañ (**payallin-yag**). From Germ. *Berlin.* Ailuk tract.

Pāāllin-rak (**payallin-rak**). From Germ. *Berlin*. Ailuk tract.

Pādāl (**padal**). Gramm. See *pādāl* "roots push up the soil". Rongelap tract.

Pādọḷ (**padaḷ°**). Gramm. distort. See *pedọḷ* "a plant". Namorik tract.

Pāidjo (**payidjew**). Unanalyz. Utirik household.

Pāl-wōj (**pal-wẹj**). Gramm. See *pāl, wōj* "blow to you". Rongelap tract.

Pālkōn (**palken**). Reminisc. gramm. See *pālōk* "donning of leis". Arno tract.

Pālle (**palley**). Part. recur. form. See *pāl* "dying arrowroot". Mejit tract.

Pāllep (**pallep**). Part. recur. form. See *pāl* "dying arrowroot". Namorik tract.

Pāpañ (**papag**). Unanalyz. Arno tract.

Pedi-Kaḷōḷe (**pediy-kaḷẹḷẹy**). Gramm. distort. See *pād:* "stay in Galilee". Mejit tract.

Pedowan (**pedewan**). Also *Pedewan.* Gramm. distort. See *pedowan* "capsize", or *pād, ewan:* "stay and engage in activities". Wotho tract; Namu tract.

Pedọḷ (**pedaḷ°**). Gramm. distort. See *pedọḷ* "a plant". Rongelap tract.

Pein-wōn (**pẹyin-wẹn**). Gramm. distort. See *pā, wōn:* "turtle flippers". Arno tract.

Peinmen (**pẹyinmẹn**). Reminisc. gramm. See *pā, imen* "fins of the eagle ray"; see *Pein-wōn.* Ujae tract.

Pejej (**pẹjyẹj**). Part. reminisc. gramm. See *pej, ejej:* "a pandanus key which has been stripped (by a crab)". Majuro tract.

Pejio (**pẹyjiyẹw**). From Gilb. *Betio Islet* in *Tarawa Atoll.* Wotje tract.

Pek (**pẹk**). Recur. form. See *pek* "place". Ujae islet.

Pekāt (**pẹkyat**). Recur. form. See *pek:* "These islets are said to be the haunts of demons." Maloelap islet; Aur islet.

Pekjā (**pẹkjay**). Recur. form. See *pek, jā:* "capsizing place". Jaluit islet.

Pekrak (**pẹkrak**). Recur. form. See *pek, rak:* "southern place". Utirik islet.

Pekram (**pẹkram**). Recur. form. Kwajalein islet; Ailinglapalap islet.

Pelae (**pelahyey**). Part. recur. form. See *ae* "current". Lae tract.

Peljeṃ (**peljeṃ**). From Engl. *Belgium*. Mejit tract.

Pelpel-eṇ (**pẹlpẹl-yeṇ**). Gramm. See *pelpel* "house on canoe" or "place for fishing with a scarer at night". Arno islet.

Peḷaak (**peḷahak**). Gramm. See *peḷaak* "congregate". Mejit tract; Majuro tract.

Peḷaakdik-aidikdik (**peḷahakdik-hayidikdik**). Gramm. See *peḷaak, dik:* "cloud passes by a little". Ebon tract.

Peḷaakdik-ḷapḷap (**peḷahakdik-ḷapḷap**). Gramm. Ebon tract.

Peḷak (**peḷak**). Gramm. See *peḷak* "cook shack". Majuro tract.

Peḷe (**peḷey**). Gramm. See *marpeḷe* "a vine". Maloelap tract.

Peḷe-eṇ (**peḷey-yeṇ**). Gramm. Utirik household.

Peḷkā (**peḷkay**). Gramm. See *peḷ:* "these *peḷ* coral". Ebon tract.

Peḷo (**peḷew**). Gramm. See *peḷo* "a tree". Ebon tract.

Peḷọñ-eṇ (**peḷag°-yeṇ**). Gramm. Mili tract.

Penaṃ (**pęynaṃ**). Reminisc. gramm. See *ppepe, naṃ:* "float in the secondary lagoon". Wotho tract; two Jaluit tracts.

Penaṃ (**peynaṃ**). Part. reminisc. gramm. Likiep tract.

Penām (**pęynam**). Part. reminisc. gramm. See *Penaṃ* "tract name". Jaluit tract.

Peniaḷ (**penyiyaḷ**). Part. recur. form. See *iaḷ* "road"; see also *Pepen-wōd* "Aur tract name". Jaluit tract.

Penpat (**penpat**). Part. recur. form. See *pat* "swamp". Jaluit tract.

Peñak (**pegak**). Gramm. See *peñak* "bay". Jaluit tract.

Pepen-wōd (**pepen-wed**). Gramm. distort. See *pepa-, wōd:* "with coral". Aur tract.

Perake (**perakey**). Loan from Gilb. *Merake* (?) Maloelap islet.

Perañ (**perag**). Gramm. See *perañ* "left-over basket". Ailinglapalap islet; Ailinglapalap tract.

Perrọkot (**perraqet**). Unanalyz. Majuro tract.

Peru (**pęriw**). Gramm. See *peru* "a food". Arno tract.

Peta-dik (**petah-dik**). Gramm. See *peta* "small depression". Arno tract.

Petaaktak (**petahaktak**). Gramm. See *Petaaktak* "breadfruit variety". Kwajalein tract; Aur tract.

Petañe (**petagey**). Unanalyz. See *peta.* Bikini tract.

Peto-eṇ (**peytew-yeṇ**). Gramm. distort. See *peto* "drift westward". Bikini tract.

Petōḷ (**peteḷ**). From Bibl. *Bethel.* Namorik district.

Piddik (**piddik**). Gramm. See *pid, dik:* "small rump". Ebon tract.

Pienḷwe (**piyenḷ°ęy**). Recur. form. See *pieo, ḷwe.* Jaluit tract.

Pienmej (**piyenmęj**). Recur. form. See *pieo, mej.* Ailinglapalap tract; Jaluit tract; Arno tract.

Pienmen (**piyenmęn**). Part. recur. form. See *pieo.* Jaluit tract.

Piepe (**piyępęy**). Gramm. See *ppe* "sandbank". Likiep islet.

Pieto (**piyętęw**). Gramm. See *peto* "drift westward". Two Arno tracts.

Pieto (**piyetew**). Gramm. distort. Ujelang islet.

Pietto (**piyettęw**). Reminisc. gramm. Jaluit tract.

Pietto (**piyettew**). Reminisc. gramm. Kwajalein tract.

Piieoḷḷe (**piyyeweḷḷęy**). Recur. form. See *pieo, ḷwe.* Jaluit tract.

Piieoṇḷwe-rālik (**piyyeweṇḷ°ęy-raylik**). Recur. form. See *pieo, ḷwe.* Jaluit tract.

Piieoṇḷwe-reeaar (**piyyeweṇḷ°ęy-reyyahar**). Recur. form. Jaluit tract.

Pijeto (**pijeytew**). From Engl. *potato.* Mejit tract.

Piji (**piyjiy**). From Fiji. Arno tract.

Pijidọọj (**pijidawaj**). Unanalyz. Jaluit tract.

Pijin-kur (**pijin-qir°**). Gramm. See *pej, kur:* "squirrel fish waste". Kwajalein islet.

Pijle (**pijlęy**). Part. recur. form. See *le* "albatross". Eniwetak islet.

Pik-ajaj (**pik-hajhaj**). Gramm. See *pik, ajaj:* "layer of hard rock". Majuro islet.

Pik-dik (**pik-dik**). Gramm. Kwajalein islet; Ailinglapalap islet.

Pik-dikdik (**pik-dikdik**). Gramm. See *pik, dik:* "small surface". Majuro tract.

Pik-eṇ (**pik-yeṇ**). Gramm. distort. Wotho islet.

Pik-nuunun (**pik-niwinwin**). Reminisc. gramm. See *pik, nono* "pounded surface". Arno tract.

Pik-ut (**pik-wit**). Gramm. See *ut:* "flowery surface". Arno tract.

Pikaajḷā (**pikahajḷay**). Unanalyz. Ailinglapalap islet; Ailinglapalap tract.

Pikaar (**pikahar**). Gramm. See *pik, ar* "fly lagoonward". Atoll; Ratak; Bikar; Bikar islet.

Pikaar-ej (**pikahar-yęj**). Gramm. Arno district; Arno islet.

Pikaar-iaar (**pikahar-yiyahar**). Gramm. Arno tract.

Pikaar-ilik (**pikahar-yiylik**). Gramm. Arno tract.

Pikadet (**pikadet**). Part. reminisc. gramm. See *badet* "a fish". Jaluit tract; Aur islet.

Pikaṃōj (**pikaṃęj**). Unanalyz. Arno tract.

Pikanoḷ (**pikaneḷ°**). Unanalyz. Wotje islet.

Pikden (**pikdȩn**). Gramm. distort. See *dān* "watery surface". Bikini islet; Rongelap islet; Kwajalein islet.

Pike (**pikȩy**). Gramm. distort. See *pikin* "its surface". Utirik islet; Mejit tract.

Pike-eņ-dik (**pikey-yeņ-dik**). Gramm. See *pik:* "that small surface". Aur islet.

Pike-tōkeak (**pikey-tekyak**). Gramm. See *pike, tōkeak* "surface of arrival". Likiep islet.

Pike-tōļoñ (**pikey-teļeg°**). Gramm. distort. See *pike, tōļoñ* "surface of penetration". Likiep islet.

Pikeed (**pikeyed**). Recur. form. See *pik, tōked.* Ailinglapalap islet.

Pikeed-rālik (**pikeyed-raylik**). Recur. form. Jaluit tract.

Pikeed-reeaar (**pikeyed-reyyahar**). Recur. form. Jaluit tract.

Pikeedat (**pikeyedat**). Part. recur. form. Majuro islet.

Pikeedda (**pikeyeddah**). Part. recur. form. Namorik tract.

Pikeej (**pikeyej**). Gramm. distort. See *pike, ej* "high (eastern) surface". Kwajalein islet; Wotje islet.

Pikeel-eañ (**pikeyel-yag**). Reminisc. gramm. See *pik, eañ:* "flying northward". Majuro islet.

Pikien (**pikiyen**). Gramm. distort. Jaluit tract.

Pikijil (**pikijil**). Unanalyz. Arno tract.

Pikinni (**pikinniy**). Reminisc. gramm. See *pik, ni:* "surface of coconuts". Ralik atoll; Bikini; Eniwetak tract; Bikini large district; Bikini islet; Wotho tract; Namorik tract.

Pikjin (**pikjin**). Reminisc. gramm. See *pik, ijin:* "the surface here". Jaluit islet.

Pikjinjin (**pikjinjin**). Reminisc. gramm. See *jinjin:* "surface of swearing", or "the surface here" as in *Pikjin.* Majuro tract.

Pikoṃōn (**pikȩwṃȩn**). Reminisc. gramm. See *pik, iuṃwi-:* "layer under it". Arno tract.

Pikooj (**pikȩwȩj**). Reminisc. gramm. See *pik, wōj:* "fly to you". Arno islet.

Pikooj-jā-iōñ (**pikȩwȩj-jay-yiyȩg**). Reminisc. gramm. Arno tract.

Pikooj-jā-rōk (**pikȩwȩj-jay-rȩk**). Reminisc. gramm. Arno tract.

Pikoon (**pikewen**). Unanalyz. Namu islet.

Pikōlāpet (**pikȩlapet**). Unanalyz. Lae islet.

Pikōṃṃan (**pikeṃṃan**). Gramm. distort. See *ṃṃan:* "good surface". Kwajalein tract; Ailinglapalap tract; Aur islet.

Pikōn (**piken**). Gramm. See *pik:* "its surface". Eniwetak islet; Ailuk islet.

Pikōn-aden (**piken-haden**). Gramm. distort. See *pikin, aden:* "surface of tridachna shells". Rongerik islet.

Pikōn-aj (**pikȩn-haj**). Gramm. See *aj:* "surface of thatch". Lae islet.

Pikōn-aj (**piken-haj**). Gramm. Kwajalein tract.

Pikōn-arar (**piken-harhar**). Gramm. See *arar;* "poke with a stick". Rongelap islet.

Pikōn-āle (**piken-yalȩy**). Gramm. See *pikin, āle:* "surface for rolling up". Arno islet.

Pikōn-ār (**pikȩn-yar**). Gramm. distort. See *ār:* "beaching surface". Maloelap islet.

Pikōn-bar (**pikȩn-bar**). Gramm. distort. See *bar:* "surface of the rock". Aur islet.

Pikōn-dik (**piken-dik**). Gramm. Majuro islet.

Pikōn-eņ (**piken-yeņ**). Gramm. Aur district; Aur islet.

Pikōn-eñwōd (**piken-yeg°ed**). Gramm. distort. See *pikin, eǫñōd:* "fishing surface". Wotje islet.

Pikōn-eōñ (**piken-yȩg**). Gramm. See *eañ:* "northern surface". Mili islet.

Pikōn-erjab (**piken-yerjab**). Unanalyz. Jaluit islet.

Pikōn-kar (**piken-kar**). Gramm. See *pikin, kar:* "surface for scraping". Ujae islet.

Pikōn-karere (**piken-kareyrey**). Gramm. See *pik, karere:* "surface for flattening pandanus leaves". Namorik tract.

Pikōn-keke (**piken-keykey**). Gramm. See *pik, keke:* "surface of cranes". Ebon tract.

Pikōn-kōļañe (**piken-keļagȩy**). Gramm. distort. See *pik, kōlñe:* "surface of coral holes". Wotje islet.

Pikōn-ļip (**piken-ļip**). Gramm. distort. See *ļap:* "its big surface". Majuro islet.

Pikōn-mao (**piken-mahwew**). Gramm. See *mao:* "parrotfish surface". Arno islet.

Pikōn-marļǫk (**piken-marļaq**). Gramm. distort. See *mar:* "too many bushes". Ailuk islet.

Pikōn-nōḷ (**piken-neḷ**). Gramm. See *pikin, nōḷ:* "surface for making weapons". Kwajalein islet.

Pikōn-o (**piken-wew**). Gramm. See *pikin, o:* "surface of the *o* bird". Kwajalein islet.

Pikōn-ōbbōn (**piken-hebben**). Reminisc. gramm. See *bbō* "spear fishing on the reef". Rongelap islet.

Pikōn-wōt (**piken-wet**). Gramm. See *pik, wōt:* "surface of wild taro". Kwajalein sandspit.

Pikōne (**pikęnęy**). Part. reminisc. gramm. Arno islet.

Pikōṇṇo (**pikeṇṇew**). Gramm. See *pik, ṇo:* "surface of waves". Rongelap islet.

Pikre (**pikręy**). Reminisc. gramm. See *rre* "look". Ebon islet.

Pikro (**pikręw**). Reminisc. gramm. See *ro* "anger". Mili islet.

Pillae (**pillahyey**). Part. recur. form. See *pil* "trickle", *lae* "still water". Eniwetak islet.

Pinaotak (**pinhawetak**). Reminisc. gramm. See *pā; aotak:* "mullet fin". Ujelang tract.

Pinejrak (**pinejrak**). Gramm. See *pinej, rak:* "hide the south". Ailuk islet.

Piñlep (**piglep**). From *Pingelap* (Atoll in Eastern Caroline Islands), or see *ppiñ* "big leap" or *piñpiñ* "a tree". Ailinglapalap tract; Jaluit islet.

Piñpiñ-eṇ (**pigpig-yeṇ**). Gramm. See *piñpiñ:* "that *Hernandia* tree". Kwajalein tract; Majuro tract.

Piñpiñ-kaṇ (**pigpig-kaṇ**). Gramm. Majuro tract.

Piñpiñin-jāi-eōñ (**pigpigin-jayiy-yęg**). Gramm. Likiep islet.

Piñpiñin-jāi-rōk (**pigpigin-jayiy-ręk**). Gramm. Likiep islet.

Pio (**piyęw**). Recur. form. See *pieo.* Wotje islet.

Pio (**piyew**). Recur. form. Ailuk islet.

Pioḷe-eṇ (**piyęwḷęy-yeṇ**). Recur. form. See *pieo, ḷwe, Pieoṇḷwe.* Mili islet.

Pipi (**piypiy**). Gramm. See *pipi* "nap". Jaluit tract; Ebon tract; Maloelap tract.

Pipi-kwōdeak (**piypiy-qedyak**). Gramm. See *pipi, kwōdeak.* Majuro sandspit.

Po-ḷapḷap (**pew-ḷapḷap**). Gramm. See *po, ḷap:* "big arrival" or "big capture". Ailinglapalap tract.

Pokwat (**pęqwat**). Reminisc. gramm. See *pek, wat:* "place of puffer fish". Wotje islet.

Pokwat-dik (**pęqwat-dik**). Reminisc. gramm. Wotje islet.

Pookluuj (**pewekliwij**). Part. recur. form. See *pook* "sweep something". Bikini islet.

Pooḷ (**peweḷ**). Gramm. See *pooḷ* "surrounded". Ailinglapalap tract; Aur tract.

Pooḷ-aidikdik (**peweḷ-hayidikdik**). Gramm. Ailinglapalap tract; Aur tract.

Pooḷ-iaar (**peweḷ-yiyahar**). Gramm. Mili tract.

Pooḷ-ilik (**peweḷ-yilik**). Gramm. Mili tract.

Poonpe (**pęwęnpęy**). From *Ponape.* Arno tract.

Pǫpo (**pawpęw**). Gramm. See *pǫpo* "coil". Mili tract.

Pukor-eañ (**piqęr-yag**). Gramm. See *pukor* "coral rocks". Namu islet.

Pukor-eṇ (**piqęr-yeṇ**). Gramm. Mili tract.

Ra-ej (**rah-yęj**). Gramm. See *ra, ej:* "eastern branch"; see also *Raej* "clan name". Ujelang islet; Erikub district.

Raadkōneo (**rahadkenyew**). Gramm. See *ra, kōneo:* "our branch (youthful offspring) is beginning to be (strong) like a tree". Mejit tract.

Raanbat (**rahanbat**). Gramm. See *raanbat:* "on top of the hill". Namorik household.

Raantak (**rahantak**). Gramm. See *raantak* "daybreak". Namorik district.

Rabōltak (**rabeltak**). Gramm. See *rabōlbōl:* "eastward glitter". Kwajalein tract.

Radik-kaṇ (**rahdik-kaṇ**). Gramm. See *ra, dik:* "those small branches". Bikini tract.

Rairōk (**rahyiyręk**). Gramm. See *ra, rōk:* "branch in the south". Utirik household; Majuro district; Majuro tract.

Raki-jāār (**rakiy-jayar**). Reminisc. gramm. See *rak, ār:* "south of (where) we beach". Arno sandspit.

Rakin-matoḷ (**rakin-mateḷ°**). Gramm. See *rak, matoḷ:* "south of the one-third portion". Mejit tract.

Raktak (**raktak**). Gramm. See *rak, tak:* "southeast". Majuro district; Mili district.

Ranel (**rahnel**). Gramm. See *ra, nel:* "branch dried under the sun". Majuro tract.

Raprap (**raprap**). Gramm. See *raprap* "diarrhea". Namu tract.

Ratak (**rahtak**). 4. Eastern chain of the Marshall Islands; Ratak.

Rā-eo (**ray-yew**). Gramm. See *rā:* "the board". Mejit tract.

Rālik (**raylik**). 4. Western chain of the Marshall Islands; Ralik.

Rālikin-to (**raylikin-tew**). Gramm. See *rālik, to:* "west of the pass". Ebon district.

Rārōk (**rayrẹk**). Recur. form. See *rārōk* "uninhabited land". Arno tract.

Rārōk-eañ (**rayrẹk-yag**). Recur. form. Kwajalein district.

Rārōk-eṇ (**rayrẹk-yeṇ**). Recur. form. Ujelang district; Jaluit tract.

Rārōk-kaṇ (**rayrẹk-kaṇ**). Recur. form. Namu district; Ailinglapalap islet; Ebon district.

Re-ḷap (**rẹy-ḷap**). Reminisc. gramm. See *rre, ḷap:* "big surveillance". Mejit tract.

Rear (**reyhar**). Recur. form. See *reeaar* "east". Majuro tract.

Rear-ḷapḷap (**reyhar-ḷapḷap**). Recur. form. Arno district.

Reeañ (**reyyag**). Recur. form. See *eañ* "north". Majuro tract; Arno tract.

Reirōkeañ (**rẹyirẹkyag**). Gramm. See *reilik:* "look southward". Majuro tract.

Reito (**rẹyitẹw**). Gramm. See *reilik:* "look westward". Arno tract.

Reo (**reyew**). Reminisc. gramm. See *rreo* "clean". Rongelap tract.

Rere-bajjek (**rẹyrẹy-bajjẹk**). Gramm. See *rre, bajjek:* "just looking around". Arno tract.

Retak-eṇ (**rẹytak-yeṇ**). Gramm. See *reilik:* "look eastward". Maloelap tract.

Riabwin (**riyabin**). Gramm. See *riab:* "his dishonesty". Arno tract.

Rijuut (**rijiwit**). Unanalyz. Ebon tract.

Rirōk (**riyrẹk**). Reminisc. gramm. See *rārōk* "uninhabited land". Ailinglapalap tract.

Roā (**rẹwyay**). Unanalyz. Ebon islet; Wotje islet.

Roā-dik (**rẹwyay-dik**). Unanalyz. Namu islet.

Roā-lep (**rẹwyay-lep**). Unanalyz. Namu islet.

Rokwōp (**r°eqep**). Unanalyz. Ailinglapalap tract.

Roñaeo (**r°eg°ahyew**). Reminisc. gramm. See *rọñ:* "my hole". Namorik tract.

Roñbar (**r°eg°bar**). Reminisc. gramm. See *rọñ,* "hole on rock". Two Majuro tracts.

Roñdik (**r°eg°dik**). Gramm. See *roñ, dik:* "small hoop". Ralik atoll; Rongerik; Rongerik islet; Arno tract.

Roñḷap (**r°eg°ḷap**). Gramm. Ralik atoll; Rongelap; Rongelap islet.

Roñoḷḷap (**r°eg°eḷḷap**). Gramm. Likiep islet.

Roñōddik (**r°eg°eddik**). Gramm. Likiep islet.

Roñōnnōbban (**r°eg°ennebban**). Reminisc. gramm. See *rọñ, bbō:* "hole for spear fishing". Majuro tract.

Roñre (**r°eg°rẹy**). Reminisc. gramm. See *roñ, de:* "heard already". Ailuk tract.

Roñroñ (**r°eg°r°eg°**). Reminisc. gramm. See *rọñ:* "holes". Majuro tract.

Rooj-kōrā (**rewej-keray**). Pers. name. See *rooj* "flower", *kōrā* "woman". Bikini islet.

Rooklik (**r°eweqlik**). Unanalyz. Namorik tract.

Ror-ej-aetok (**r°er°-yej-hayeteq**). Part. reminisc. gramm. See *aetok:* "the long *ror*". Mili islet.

Ror-eṇ (**r°er°-yeṇ**). Gramm. See *ror.* Lib tract; Namu tract; Mili tract.

Ror-eṇ-rālik (**r°er°-yeṇ-raylik**). Gramm. Ailinglapalap tract.

Ror-eṇ-reeaar (**r°er°-yeṇ-reyyahar**). Gramm. Namu tract; Ailinglapalap tract.

Ror-kaṇ (**r°er°-kaṇ**). Gramm. Arno tract.

Rọñ (**r°ag°**). Gramm. See *rọñ* "hole". Two Arno tracts.

Rọọl-kōmālij (**rawal-kemalij**). Gramm. See *rọọl, kōmālij:* "brain turns". Ailinglapalap tract.

Rōmālim (**remalim**). Gramm. See *mālim:* "they are permitted". Ailinglapalap islet.

Rubad (**r°iwbad**). Reminisc. gramm. See *ru-, bar:* "go through rocks". Majuro tract.

Rukut (**r°iqit**). Gramm. Two Ailinglapalap tracts.

Runit (**r°iwnit**). Gramm. See *ru-, nit:* "go through the pit". Eniwetak islet.

Ruot (**r°iwet**). Reminisc. gramm. See *ru-, wōt:* "go through wild taro". Ujae islet; Kwajalein islet.

Rupe (**r°iwpęy**). Gramm. distort. See *rup:* "break it". Kili tract; Ebon tract.

Rupe-kōj (**r°iwpęy-kęj**). Gramm. distort. See *rup, kōj:* "smash us". Arno tract; Mili islet.

Ruujia (**r°iwijyiyah**). From Engl. *Russia*. Eniwetak tract.

Ruwa (**r°iwah**). Gramm. See *ri-, wa:* "crew". Jaluit islet.

Taar (**tahar**). Gramm. See *taar* "parry". Maloelap islet.

Taarwa (**taharwah**). Gramm. See *taar, wa:* "push away a canoe". Jaluit tract.

Tabo (**tabew**). Unanalyz. Mili coral head.

Tabtūb (**tabtib**). Reminisc. gramm. See *tab:* "misty". Wotje tract.

Tabwi-ņo (**tabiy-ņew**). Gramm. See *tabūņņo* "salt spray". Wotje islet.

Tae (**tahyey**). Reminisc. gramm. See *ta, e:* "what's this?" Arno islet.

Taij (**tahyij**). Unanalyz. Namorik islet.

Taiti (**tahyitiy**). From Tahiti. Wotje tract.

Takadik (**takahdik**). Reminisc. gramm. See *tōkā, dik:* "small strip of reef". Wotje tract.

Takan (**takhan**). Reminisc. gramm. See *tak, an:* "his soul rises". Likiep tract; Majuro tract.

Takijab (**takiyjab**). Recur. form. See *tak, jab:* "not (see the sun)rise (?)". Ebon tract.

Takin-allōñ (**takin-hallęg**). Gramm. See *tak, allōñ:* "moonrise". Maloelap islet.

Takinej (**takinęj**). Pers. name. Two Mejit districts.

Taklep (**taklep**). Gramm. See *tak, ļap:* "big needlefish". Arno islet.

Taklep-ej (**taklep-yęj**). Gramm. Arno islet.

Taklep-laļ (**taklep-laļ**). Gramm. Arno islet.

Taļto (**taļtęw**). Reminisc. gramm. See *tal, to:* "westward procession". Maloelap islet.

Tamād (**tamad**). Gramm. See *tam:* "our shape". Arno tract.

Taṃ (**taṃ**). Gramm. See *taṃ* "dump". Utirik household.

Taṃōl (**taṃęl**). Reminisc. gramm. See *ṃōlṃōl* "mackerel". Likiep islet.

Taṃwe (**taṃwęy**). Gramm. See *taṃwe* "find something to ride". Arno tract.

Tapañ (**tapag**). Also *tōpañ*. Gramm. See *tapañ* "medicine mortar". Arno tract.

Tar-wōj (**tar-węj**). Gramm. See *tar, wōj:* "sail to you". Kwajalein islet.

Tar-wōj-iōñ (**tar-węj-yiyęg**). Gramm. Kwajalein tract.

Tar-wōj-rōk (**tar-węj-ręk**). Gramm. Kwajalein tract.

Tarep (**taryep**). Recur. form. See *tar, iep:* "go (weave) baskets (as elves did here according to legend)". Aur islet.

Taruk (**tariq**). Reminisc. gramm. See *tarukelel* "anxiety". Arno tract.

Tataar-wōj (**tatahar-węj**). Reminisc. gramm. See *taar, wōj:* "parry toward you". Mejit tract.

Tawūno (**tahwinew**). Gramm. See *ta, wūno:* "what medicine?" Jaluit tract.

Teepñat (**teyepgat**). Gramm. See *teep, niñat:* "remove false teeth" or *ñat* "remove palate". Mili islet.

Tekooļ (**teyqeweļ**). Gramm. See *te* "sanitary napkin", *kooļ* "hair". Arno islet.

Teļap (**teyļap**). Gramm. See *te, ļap:* "large sanitary napkin". Ailinglapalap tract; Majuro district; Majuro islet.

Teroñ (**teyreg°**). Reminisc. gramm. See *teroñe* "shake him up". Majuro tract; two Arno tracts.

Teteļabuk (**tęytęyļabiq**). Gramm. See *tiete, ļabuk:* "reef raises up". Majuro tract.

Teteļañ-eañ (**tęytęyļag-yag**). Recur. form. See *tiete, ļañ:* "storm reef". Majuro tract.

Teteļañ-rak (**tęytęyļag-rak**). Recur. form. Majuro tract.

Tiete (**tiyętęy**). Recur. form. See *tiete* "reef". Majuro tract.

Tiete-eņ (**tiyętęy-yeņ**). Recur. form. Arno tract.

Tietlu (**tiyetliw**). Unanalyz. Mejit tract.

Tile (**tilęy**). Reminisc. gramm. See *tile* "burn it". Ebon islet.

Tiliej (**tiliyęj**). Gramm. See *tiliej* "reef the sail". Likiep tract.

Tilo (**tilew**). Unanalyz. Ebon tract.

Tilwañ-eņ (**tilwag-yeņ**). Unanalyz. Mili tract.

Tinak (**tinak**). Gramm. See *tinak* "stay put". Jaluit tract; Arno district; Arno islet.

Tinar (**tinar**). Gramm. See *tinar* "small grouper". Majuro tract.

Tipāp (**tipap**). Recur. form. See *Tipāp* "navigational sign". Wotje islet.

Tipen-wōd (**tipen-wed**). Gramm. See *tipen, wōd:* "piece of coral". Ailinginae islet.

Titi-dik (**tiytiy-dik**). Reminisc. gramm. See *tiete:* "small reef". Majuro tract.

To (**tew**). Gramm. See *to* "channel, passage". Jaluit islet; Ebon channel; Utirik channel; five Likiep channels; Majuro tract.

To-āje (**tew-yajey**). Also *Toon-Āne-jā.* Unanalyz. Ailuk channel.

To-bukbuk (**tew-biqbiq**). Gramm. See *to, bukbuk:* "helmet shell channel". Arno channel.

To-dik-kaņ (**tew-dik-kaņ**). Gramm. See *dik:* "those small channels". Ujae channel.

To-eņ (**tęw-yeņ**). Gramm. See *to:* "the soaking pit". Two Wotho tracts.

To-eņ (**tew-yeņ**). Gramm. See *to:* "the channel". Lae islet.

To-eņ-an-Etao (**tew-yeņ-han-yetahwew**). Gramm. See *Etao:* "Etao's passage". Majuro channel.

To-eņ-edik (**tew-yeņ-yedik**). Gramm. See *dik:* "that small channel". Ujelang channel; Eniwetak channel.

To-eņ-eļap (**tew-yeņ-yeļap**). Gramm. See *ļap:* "that large channel". Ujelang channel; Ujelang tract.

To-kaņ (**tęw-kaņ**). Gramm. See *to:* "those soaking pits". Two Kwajalein tracts.

To-kaņ (**tew-kaņ**). Gramm. Ebon tract; two Aur tracts.

To-kaņ-o (**tew-kaņ-wew**). Recur. form. Maloelap tract.

To-ļap (**tew-ļap**). Gramm. See *ļap:* "big passage". Ujae channel; Kwajalein channel; Bikar channel; Utirik channel; Ailuk channel; Erikub channel; Wotje channel; Maloelap channel; Majuro channel; Arno channel.

To-ļapļap (**tew-ļapļap**). Gramm. Eniwetak channel; Ailinglapalap channel.

To-Ļowa (**tew-ļewah**). Pers. name. Maloelap channel.

To-Ļowakaņle (**tew-ļewahkaņlęy**). Also *To-Ļowakalle.* Pers. name, a man eaten by sharks when he tried to swim this pass ca. 1880. Arno channel.

To-mej (**tew-męj**). Gramm. See *mej:* "open reef channel". Wotje channel.

To-mekak (**tew-mekak**). Gramm. See *mekak:* "blood clot channel". Kwajalein channel.

To-mettōr (**tew-męttęr**). Part. reminisc. gramm. See *ttōr* "run". Wotje channel.

To-mouj (**tew-męwij**). Gramm. See *mouj:* "white channel". Utirik channel.

To-pikōn (**tew-piken**). Recur. form. See *pikin.* Majuro tract.

Toālem̧ (**tewyalyęm̧**). Reminisc. gramm. See *(kō)to (ej) āl (jān ājin) m̧weo* "the wind blows the thatch from the house", or *to, ālim* "bail it out for a long time", blended with *em̧* "house": "land given as reward for faithful service bailing the chief's canoe". Arno tract.

Toeak (**tęwyak**). Gramm. See *toeak* "feces". Majuro tract.

Tokoup (**tewqęwip**). Unanalyz. Mejit tract.

Tokǫ (**tewkaw**). Gramm. See *tokǫ:* "fire log". Namorik tract.

Tola (**tewlah**). Gramm. See *tola* "knead preserved breadfruit". Arno islet.

Toļ-eņ (**teļ°-yeņ**). Gramm. See *toļ:* "the mountain". Bikini tract; Ailinglapalap islet.

Toļ-eņ-ioļap (**teļ°-yeņ-yiyewļap**). Gramm. See *toļ:* "the mountain, middle section". Kwajalein tract.

Toļ-eņ-rālik (**teļ°-yeņ-raylik**). Gramm. See *toļ:* "the mountain, west section". Kwajalein tract.

Toļ-eņ-reeaar (**teļ°-yeņ-reyyahar**). Gramm. See *toļ:* "the mountain, east section". Kwajalein tract.

Toļ-kaņ (**teļ°-kaņ**). Gramm. See *toļ:* "those mountains". Two Arno islets.

Toļej (**teļ°yej**). Part. recur. form. See *toļ* "mountain". Wotje islet.

Toļoļļoļ (**teļ°eļ°ļ°eļ°**). Reminisc. gramm. See *toļ:* "many mountains". Ailinglapalap islet.

Toļońtok (**teļ°eg°teq**). Gramm. See *tōļoń, tok:* "penetrate hither". Mejit tract.

Tomewa (**tewmeywah**). Gramm. See *tomewa* "miss the boat". Arno tract.

Toņak (**tęwņak**). Gramm. See *toņak* "part". Kwajalein tract: Wotje tract.

Tońal (**tewgal**). Part. recur. form. See *to, ńal:* "kneading pass"; former sandspit; perhaps a passage (*to*) even earlier. Jaluit islet.

Toñkwe (**teg°qęy**). Gramm. See *toñkwe* "contrite". Mili tract.

Toodda (**teweddah**). Gramm. distort. See *da:* "bloody channel". Bikini channel; Arno channel; Mili channel.

Toojlǫk (**tęwęjlaq**). Gramm. See *tooj:* "quite conspicuous". Likiep tract.

Toojlǫk (**tewejlaq**). Gramm. Utirik household.

toon- (**tewen**). A common generic in place names, construct form of *to* meaning "channel of, passage of", often combined with the name of a specific adjoining islet or sandspit.

Toon-aelōñ (**tewen-hayęlęg**). Also *Toon-aelōṃ*. Gramm. (distort.) See *to, aelōñ:* "pass of the atoll", or *ae, liṃ:* "pass of murky current". Arno tract.

Toon-aerār (**tewen-hayeryar**). Gramm. See *aerār:* "touching-shoulders pass". Wotje channel.

Toon-Aidik (**tewen-hayidik**). Recur. form. Rongelap channel.

Toon-Aikne (**tewen-hayiknęy**). Recur. form. Likiep channel.

Toon-aj (**tewen-haj**). Gramm. See *to, aj:* "small pond for soaking thatch". Ebon tract; Arno tract; Mili islet.

Toon-Ajwāān (**tewen-hajwayan**). Recur. form. Mili channel.

Toon-Anbwil-eņ (**tewen-hanbil-yeņ**). Recur. form. Wotho channel.

Toon-Anel (**tewen-hanel**). Recur. form. Namu channel.

Toon-Anibuk (**tewen-hanibiq**). Recur. form. Ailinginae channel.

Toon-Arbwā (**tewen-harbay**). Recur. form. Kwajalein channel.

Toon-Arjel (**tewen-harjęl**). Recur. form. Aur channel.

Toon-Atartar (**tewen-hatartar**). Recur. form. Wotje channel.

Toon-Āne-anijņa (**tewen-yanęy-hanijņah**). Recur. form. Mili channel.

Toon-Āne-bōn (**tewen-yanęy-bęn**). Recur. form. Maloelap channel.

Toon-Āne-buoj (**tewen-yanęy-biwęj**). Recur. form. Kwajalein channel.

Toon-Āne-doulul (**tewen-yanęy-dęwilwil**). Recur. form. Rongelap channel.

Toon-Āne-jā (**tewen-yanęy-jay**). Also *To-āje*. Recur. form. Ailuk channel.

Toon-Āne-jet (**tewen-yanęy-jet**). Recur. form. Rongelap channel.

Toon-Āne-kaņ (**tewen-yanęy-kaņ**). Recur. form. Rongelap channel.

Toon-Āne-piñ (**tewen-yanęy-pig**). Recur. form. Kwajalein channel.

Toon-Āne-wātak (**tewen-yanęy-waytak**). Recur. form. Rongerik channel.

Toon-Ānen-eṃṃaan (**tewen-yanyen-yeṃṃahan**). Recur. form. Ailuk channel.

Toon-Āni-juon (**tewen-yaniy-jiwen**). Recur. form. Kwajalein channel; Maloelap channel.

Toon-Āni-piñ (**tewen-yaniy-pig**). Recur. form. Ailinglapalap channel.

Toon-Ānōṃṃaan (**tewen-yanęṃṃahan**). Recur. form. Bikini channel.

Toon-Bok (**tewen-beq**). Gramm. Rongerik channel; Ujae channel; Namu channel.

Toon-Bok-aetoktok (**tewen-beq-hayeteqteq**). Recur. form. Bikini channel.

Toon-Bok-anij (**tewen-beq-hanij**). Recur. form. Maloelap channel.

Toon-Bok-doulul (**tewen-beq-dęwilwil**). Gramm. Bikini channel.

Toon-Bok-ellāāp (**tewen-beq-yellayap**). Recur. form. Rongelap channel.

Toon-Bokwā-Lurito (**tewen-beqay-lir°iytew**). Recur. form. Maloelap channel.

Toon-Buwe (**tewen-biwey**). Recur. form. Mili channel.

Toon-Bwibwi (**tewen-biybiy**). Recur. form. Maloelap channel.

Toon-Eded (**tewen-yedyed**). Recur. form. Ailinglapalap channel.

Toon-Eorrob (**tewen-yer°r°eb**). Recur. form. Kwajalein channel.

Toon-Ero (**tewen-yęręw**). Recur. form. Kwajalein channel.

Toon-Ilel-kaņ (**tewen-yilyęl-kaņ**). Recur. form. Mili channel.

Toon-Jabōn-wōd (**tewen-jaben-wed**). Recur. form. Mili channel.

Toon-Jabwan (**tewen-jabwan**). Recur. form. Rongelap channel.

Toon-Jatōptōp (**tewen-jateptep**). Recur. form. Rongerik channel.

Toon-Jā (**tewen-jay**). Recur. form. Kwajalein channel; Ailinglapalap channel.

Toon-Jālōte (**tewen-jaletey**). Recur. form. Bikini channel.

Toon-Jāpek (**tewen-japęk**). Recur. form. Kwajalein channel.

Toon-Jure (**tewen-jiwręy**). Unanalyz. Ujae channel.

Toon-kabbar (**tewen-kabbar**). Part. recur. form. See *kab, bar:* "another one" (*kab bar juon*). Erikub channel.

Toon-Kati-ej (**tewen-katiy-yęj**). Recur. form. Ailinglapalap channel.

Toon-kaerer (**tewen-kahyęryęr**). Gramm. See *kaerer:* "channel of embracing (currents)". Wotje channel.

Toon-Kā (**tewen-kay**). Recur. form. Kwajalein channel.

Toon-Kārokā (**tewen-kayręwkay**). Recur. form. Rongelap channel.

Toon-ke (**tewen-kęy**). Gramm. See *ke:* "porpoise pass". Majuro tract.

Toon-Kiden-eṇ (**tewen-kidęn-yeṇ**). Recur. form. Kwajalein channel.

Toon-Kiejej (**tewen-kiyęjyęj**). Recur. form. Rongelap channel.

Toon-Kijjinbwi (**tewen-kijjinbiy**). Recur. form. Kwajalein channel.

Toon-Koṃle (**tewen-qęṃlęy**). Recur. form. Kwajalein channel.

Toon-koobob (**tewen-kewebweb**). Gramm. See *koobob:* "coming-very-close channel". Wotje channel.

Toon-Kọrujlañ (**tewen-qar°ijlag**). Recur. form. Arno channel.

Toon-kōṃṃaejek (**tewen-keṃṃahyęjęk**). Gramm. See *kōṃṃaejek:* "fighting channel". Wotje channel.

Toon-Kūbur (**tewen-kibir°**). Recur. form. Ailinglapalap channel.

Toon-kūtim (**tewen-kitim**). Gramm. See *kūtim* "casket". (There is a small passage at this tract from which corpses were floated away.) Mejit tract.

Toon-Likijjine (**tewen-likijjinęy**). Recur. form. Kwajalein channel.

Toon-Lukwōj (**tewen-liqej**). Recur. form. Bikini channel.

Toon-Lukwōnwōd (**tewen-liqenwed**). Recur. form. Mili channel.

Toon-ḷọunlep (**tewen-ḷawinlep**). Recur. form. See *ḷọun, ḷap:* "passage of great magical power". Bikini tract.

Toon-Māĳen (**tewen-majjęn**). Recur. form. Wotje channel.

Toon-Mājruon (**tewen-majriwen**). Recur. form. Wotho channel.

Toon-Mālu (**tewen-maliw**). Recur. form. Rongelap channel.

Toon-Meik (**tewen-męyik**). Recur. form. Kwajalein channel.

Toon-mej (**tewen-męj**). Gramm. See *mej:* "passage of the open reef between islets". Kwajalein channel.

Toon-Mejĳok (**tewen-mejejjeq**). Recur. form. Ailinglapalap channel.

Toon-mertak (**tewen-mertak**). Unanalyz. Kwajalein channel.

Toon-Milu (**tewen-miliw**). Recur. form. Kwajalein channel.

Toon-Ṃakil (**tewen-ṃakil**). Recur. form. Ailinginae channel.

Toon-Ṃaḷọk (**tewen-ṃaḷaq**). Recur. form. Ailuk channel.

Toon-Ṃur (**tewen-ṃir°**). Gramm. Arno channel.

Toon-Ṃurle (**tewen-ṃir°lęy**). Recur. form. Kwajalein channel.

Toon-Na-kaṇ-ej (**tewen-nah-kaṇ-yęj**). Recur. form. Mili channel.

Toon-naṃ (**tewen-naṃ**). Gramm. See *naṃ:* "secondary lagoon channel". Ailinglapalap channel.

Toon-Nini (**tewen-niyniy**). Recur. form. Kwajalein channel.

Toon-Nōḷ (**tewen-neḷ**). Recur. form. Kwajalein channel.

Toon-Ṇa-ḷap (**tewen-ṇah-ḷap**). Recur. form. Mili channel.

Toon-Ṇaan-jāde (**tewen-ṇahan-jadęy**). Recur. form. Ailinglapalap channel.

Toon-Ṇamok (**tewen-ṇameq**). Part. reminisc. gramm. See *ṇa, mọk:* "shoal of *mọk* fish" or "possession shoal". Mili channel.

Toon-Orkā-eṇ (**tewen-werkay-yeṇ**). Recur. form. Bikini channel.

Toon-Pekram (**tewen-pękram**). Recur. form. Kwajalein channel.

Toon-Pik (**tewen-pik**). Recur. form. Namu channel.

Toon-Pik-eṇ (**tewen-pik-yeṇ**). Recur. form. Wotho channel.

Toon-Pikden (**tewen-pikdęn**). Recur. form. Kwajalein channel.

Toon-Pikeej (**tewen-pikeyej**). Recur. form. Kwajalein channel.

Toon-riPit (**tewen-ripit**). Gramm., from adjoining islet called *Bokwā-riPit.* Wotje channel.

Toon-Tar-wōj (**tewen-tar-węj**). Recur. form. Kwajalein channel.

Toon-Totǫǫn (**tewen-tewtawan**). Recur. form. Wotje channel.

Toon-Tōke-wa (**tewen-tekey-wah**). Recur. form. Mili channel.

Toon-Tōn̄le (**tewen-tęglęy**). Recur. form. Kwajalein channel.

Toon-turǫn̄ (**tewen-tiwr°ag°**). Gramm. See *turon̄:* "spear-fishing channel". Ujelang channel.

Toon-Wōje-kaņ (**tewen-węjęy-kaņ**). Recur. form., from flanking islets called *Wōje-jāiiōn̄* and *Wōje-jāirōk,* meaning "pass of those *wōje*'s. Kwajalein channel.

Toon-Wōnwōt (**tewen-wenwet**). Recur. form. Kwajalein channel.

Toon-wūj-kaņ (**tewen-wij-kaņ**). Gramm. See *to, wūj:* "those ropes for uprooting". Majuro tract.

Toorwa (**tęwęrwah**). From Gilb. *Tarawa*. Jaluit tract.

Toorwa (**tewerwah**). Loan from Gilb. *Tarawa;* see also *toorwa* "boat passage on reef". Ebon tract; Arno tract; Mili tract.

Topi (**tewpiy**). Unanalyz. Taka tract.

Toretok (**ter°eyteq**). Gramm. distort. See *tǫr:* "wash hither". Mili tract.

Totak (**tęwtak**). Gramm. See *totak* "dig up". Arno tract.

Totǫǫn (**tewtawan**). Gramm. See *to, tǫǫn:* "long separation", or may refer to the many channels (*to*) this islet lies among. Wotje islet.

Toul (**tęwil**). Gramm. See *toul* "a shell". Ailuk islet.

Towa-kaņ (**tewah-kaņ**). Gramm. See *towa* "those canoe beaching places". Arno tract.

Tǫ-dik (**taw-dik**). Gramm. distort. See *to:* "small channel". Ujae channel; Wotje channel.

Tǫ-ej (**taw-yęj**). Gramm. distort. See *to:* "eastern channel". Erikub channel.

Tǫ-eņ (**taw-yeņ**). Gramm. See *tǫ:* "that reef pond". Arno islet; Mili islet.

Tǫ-lokm̧aan (**taw-lęqm̧ahan**). Gramm. See *tǫ, lokm̧aan:* "bow line pond", or gramm. distort.: "bow line rope". Arno tract.

Tǫ-nimle (**taw-nimlęy**). Gramm. distort. See *to, in, Mile:* "Mili pass". Majuro tract.

Tǫ-pikle (**taw-piklęy**). Reminisc. gramm. See *tǫ, pikpik, le:* "the albatross glides and flaps its wings". Kwajalein tract; Arno tract.

Tǫǫk (**tawak**). Gramm. See *tǫǫk* "dry-dock". Jaluit tract.

Tǫǫn-wōd (**tawan-wed**). Gramm. distort. See *to, wōd:* "coral channel". Bikini channel.

Tǫǫr-eņ (**tawar-yeņ**). Gramm. See *tǫǫr:* "that place with water on the reef". Ebon tract.

Tǫǫr-kōto (**tawar-kętęw**). Gramm. See *kōto:* "windy pond". Ebon tract.

Tǫǫrin-māntōl (**tawarin-mantęl**). Gramm. See *tǫǫr, māntōl:* "a stream of (flying) shearwater". Ailinglapalap tract.

Tǫǫrļǫk-booj-eņ (**tawarļaq-bęwęj-yeņ**). Gramm. See *tǫǫr, booj:* "the navigational wave knot flows outward". Kwajalein tract.

Tǫro-kaņ (**tawręw-kaņ**). Part. recur. form. See *to, ro:* "those angry channels". Namu channel.

Tōbaaļ (**tebahaļ**). Reminisc. gramm. See *tōb, aļ:* "pull up the sun". Jaluit tract; Ebon tract; Mejit tract; Aur district; Aur district; Aur islet.

Tōbar (**tęhbar**). Recur. form. See *tō* "string", *bar* "rocks". Ebon tract.

Tōbo (**tębęw**). Gramm. See *tōbo* "a shell". Ailinglapalap islet.

Tōbom̧aro (**tębęwm̧arew**). Part. recur. form. See *tōbo* "a shell". Ailinglapalap islet.

Tōboron̄ (**tebewr°eg°**). Gramm. See *tōboron̄* "a shell". Arno tract.

Tōbu (**tebiw**). Gramm. See *tōbo* "a shell". Ailuk islet.

Tōkā (**tekay**). Gramm. Two Bikini coral heads; Jaluit islet; Jaluit tract; Ebon district; Ebon islet; Ratak atoll; Taka; Taka islet.

Tōkā-dikdik (**tekay-dikdik**). Gramm. See *tōkā, dik:* "small strip of reef". Bikini coral head.

Tōkā-eņ (**tekay-yeņ**). Gramm. Likiep islet.

Tōkā-iōn̄ (**tekay-yiyęg**). Gramm. Eniwetak district.

Tōkā-jeltak (**tekay-jęltak**). Gramm. distort. See *jāl, tak:* "reef facing east". Ujelang tract.

Tōkā-Look (**tekay-lęwęq**). Recur. form. See *Look:* "reef of the Look clan". Arno tract.

Tōkā-muuj-kaṇ (**tekay-miwij-kaṇ**). Gramm. distort. See *tōkā, mouj:* "those white strips of reef". Kwajalein channel.

Tōkdik (**tekdik**). Reminisc. gramm. See *tōkā, dik:* "small strip of reef". Namu islet.

Tōke-wa (**tekey-wah**). Reminisc. gramm. See *tōkā, wa:* "canoe reef". Mejit tract; Mili islet.

Tōklep (**teklep**). Reminisc. gramm. See *Tōkdik.* Namu islet.

Tōlien (**teliyen**). Gramm. See *tōlien* "so many". Wotje tract.

Tōlmọñ-eṇ (**tẹlmag°-yeṇ**). Recur. form. See *tōl, mọñ:* "nits (on) pate". Ujae tract.

Tōlñan (**tẹlgan**). Gramm. See *tōl, ñan:* "lead to". Wotje tract.

Tōlwañ (**tẹlwag**). Recur. form. See *tōl* "nit", *wañ* "to bark". Mili tract.

Tōḷā (**tẹhḷay**). Recur. form. See *tō, ḷā:* "string of gravel". Wotje tract.

Tōḷoñtak (**teḷeg°tak**). Gramm. distort. See *tōḷoñ, tak:* "penetrate eastward". Majuro tract; Arno tract.

Tōḷoñūn-et (**teḷeg°in-yẹt**). Gramm. See *tōḷoñ, et:* "go to the interior to do what?" Mili tract.

Tōḷọkjān (**teḷaqjan**). Gramm. See *tōḷọk, jān:* "stay away from". Arno tract.

Tōmeiñ (**temẹyig**). Unanalyz. Jaluit tract; Mejit tract.

Tōñle (**tẹglẹy**). Gramm. distort. See *tōnale* "killer clam". Kwajalein islet.

Tōññōḷọk (**teggeḷaq**). Gramm. See *tōññōḷọk* "ringing sound". Aur tract.

Tōpa-joñ (**tepah-jeg°**). Part. reminisc. gramm. See *joñ* "mangrove". Arno tract.

Tōpañ-eṇ (**tepag-yeṇ**). Gramm. See *tōpañ* "medicine rock". Namu islet.

Tōpta (**teptah**). Reminisc. gramm. See *tōpran, ta:* "accomplish what" (a blend). Kwajalein islet.

Tōran (**tẹran**). Gramm. See *tōran* "distance". Majuro tract.

Tōrkọ (**terkaw**). Unanalyz. Wotje tract.

Tōrwa (**terwah**). From Gilb. *Tarawa.* Maloelap islet; Arno tract.

Tuo (**tiwew**). Unanalyz. Ebon tract.

Tuo-kaṇ (**tiwew-kaṇ**). Unanalyz. Kwajalein tract.

Tur (**tir°**). Recur. form. See *tur* "end of islet". Ailinglapalap tract; Jaluit tract; two Likiep tracts; two Majuro tracts; Mili tract; Knox tract.

Tur-eṇ (**tir°-yeṇ**). Recur. form. See *tur:* "the tip". Three Kwajalein tracts.

Tur-iōñ (**tir°-yiyẹg**). Recur. form. See *tur, iōñ:* "northern tip". Aur tract.

Turun-to (**tir°in-tew**). Gramm. See *turu-, to:* "near the pass". Likiep district; Majuro district.

Tutu (**tiwtiw**). Gramm. See *tutu* "bathe". Namu islet; Arno district; Arno islet; Arno tract.

Tutu-ḷañ-ari-jet (**tiwtiw-ḷag-hariy-jet**). Recur. form. See *lọjet:* "wet storm on the beach of the sea". Rongelap tract.

Tuun-ke (**tiwin-kẹy**). Gramm. See *tulọk, ke:* "diving of porpoises". Utirik household.

Tuwa-eṇ (**tiwah-yeṇ**). Gramm. See *tuwa:* "the gap". Kwajalein tract.

Tuwa-kaṇ (**tiwah-kaṇ**). Gramm. See *tuwa:* "the gaps". Majuro tract.

Tuwaak-eṇ (**tiwahak-yeṇ**). Gramm. See *tuwaak:* "the wading place". Mili islet.

Tuwaakḷọk (**tiwahakḷaq**). Gramm. See *tuwaak:* "wade away". Aur tract.

Tuwaakḷọk-eṇ (**tiwahakḷaq-yeṇ**). Gramm. Kwajalein tract; two Wotje tracts.

Tuwaṇ (**tiwaṇ**). Unanalyz. Two Eniwetak tracts.

Tūbab (**tibab**). Unanalyz. See *bab* "a shark". Wotho tract; Lib household; Namu tract; two Ailinglapalap tracts.

Tūbuuj (**tibiwij**). Unanalyz. Kwajalein islet.

Tūbwiene (**tibiyyẹnẹy**). Gramm. See *tūb* "enjoy", *āne* "islet"; possibly from *ej joktok tūbiene* "it alights to enjoy the islet". Jaluit tract.

Tūkar-eṇ (**tikar-yeṇ**). Unanalyz. See *tūar.* Bikini tract.

Tūñañtak (**tigagtak**). Gramm. See *tuñañ, tak:* "wind brings the odor of food eastward". Mejit tract.

Tūñōñtak (**tigẹgtak**). Gramm. distort. Likiep tract.

Tūrabōḷ (**tirabeḷ**). Loan from Engl. *trouble.* Likiep tract.

Ubaklej (**wibaklẹj**). Unanalyz., see *Baklej* "Majuro tract". Lae tract.

Ukoktak-kaṇ (**wiqwẹqtak-kaṇ**). Gramm. See *ukoktak:* "those fluctuations". Jaluit tract; two Arno tracts.

Ukoon (**wikęwęn**). Part. reminisc. gramm. See *koon* "squab". Wotje islet.

Ukōj (**wikej**). Gramm. See *ukōj* "turn". Maloelap islet; Arno islet.

Ukōjjak (**wikejjak**). Gramm. See *ukōj, jak:* "turn the bottom of the net up". Kwajalein tract.

Umattōn (**wimatten**). Reminisc. gramm. See *mat:* possible shortening of *ukōt ñan matten* "turn (fish over fire) so it will be well-cooked". Erikub tract.

Uṃ-eṇ (**wiṃ-yeṇ**). Gramm. See *uṃ:* "the oven". Arno tract.

Uṇa (**wiṇah**). Gramm. See *uṇa* "fish between shoals with scarer". Maloelap tract; Maloelap household.

Uṇṇa (**wiṇṇah**). Reminisc. gramm. See *wūn, ṇa:* "shoal base". Two Ebon tracts.

Urbaj (**wirbaj**). Gramm. See *ur, baj:* "pubic abscess", or distortion of *urabbaj* "shinny up". Jaluit islet.

Urōk-eṇ (**wiręk-yeṇ**). Gramm. See *urōk* "fish from a canoe". Mejit tract; Maloelap tract; Aur tract.

Urōt-būkōr (**wiret-bikęr**). Gramm. See *urōt* "kill", *būkōr* "a plant". Two Arno tracts; Mili tract.

Uti-jabōn-or (**witiy-jaben-wer**). Recur. form. See *ut, jabōn, or:* "flower at the tip of the *or*". Majuro tract.

Utiddik-kaṇ (**witiddik-kaṇ**). Gramm. distort. See *utdikdik:* "those sprinklings". Majuro tract.

Utiej (**witiyęj**). Gramm. See *utiej* "high". Wotho islet.

Utiete (**witiyętęy**). Part. reminisc. gramm. See *tiete* "reef", or possibly *ut, iiet, e:* "these few flowers". Arno islet.

Utin-paañ (**witin-pahag**). Gramm. See *ut, paañ:* "lei for appearing before many people". Majuro tract.

Utrōk (**witręk**). Gramm. See *ut, rōk:* "southern flower". Atoll; Ratak; Utirik; Ebon tract; Utirik islet.

Uttin-ene (**wittin-yęnęy**). Part. reminisc. gramm. See *āne* "islet". Rongelap tract.

Uttōn-ke (**witten-kęy**). Part. reminisc. gramm. See *ke* "porpoise". Bikini tract; Ailinglapalap tract.

Utute (**witwitey**). Gramm. See *utute* "stay in the rain". Majuro tract.

Uwe (**wiwęy**). Gramm. See *uwe* "get on board". Wotje islet.

Ūl-eṇ (**hil-yeṇ**). Gramm. See *ūl* "dorsal fin". Arno district; Arno islet.

Wa-eṇ (**wah-yeṇ**). Gramm. See *wa:* "the canoe". Namu tract; Jaluit tract.

Wa-kāmeej (**wah-kaymeyej**). Gramm. See *wa, kāmeej:* "redwood canoe". Eniwetak islet.

Wab-eṇ (**wab-yeṇ**). Gramm. See *wab* "pier". Ebon tract.

Waikiki (**wahyikiykiy**). From Haw. *Waikiki*. Jaluit tract.

Waito (**wahyitew**). Gramm. See *wa, to:* "canoe in the pass". Two Mili islets.

Wajelke (**wahjelkęy**). Gramm. See *wa, lōke:* "canoe we depend on". Bikini tract.

Wajlukwatōlempel (**wajliqatelempęl**). Also *Luwatelempel* (**liwatęlęmpęl**), *Uwatelempel* (**wiwatelempęl**). Part. reminisc. gramm. See *tōl im pel:* "nit and boxfish"; see also *Aḷampel* "Eniwetak islet". Eniwetak tract.

Warwor (**warwęr**). Gramm. See *war, or:* "lobster haven". Arno tract.

Watwaidikdik (**watwahyidikdik**). Reminisc. gramm. See *wāto, aidik:* "narrow tract"; see also *Wāto-aidikdik* "another Wotho tract name". Wotho tract.

Wā (**way**). Gramm. See *wā* "stab". Ebon tract.

Wāātwerōk (**wayatwęyręk**). Gramm. distort. See *wāto, rōk:* "southern tract" or "go westward in the south". Taka islet; Wotje islet.

Wājutak (**wayjiwtak**). Reminisc. gramm. See *wā, jutak:* "stab standing". Majuro tract.

Wālọk-eṇ (**waylaq-yeṇ**). Gramm. See *wālọk* "go away". Four Ailinglapalap tracts; Jaluit tract; Namorik tract; Ebon tract.

Wālọklik-eṇ (**waylaqlik-yeṇ**). Gramm. See *wālọklik:* "the place of sacrifice". Aur tract.

Wāto (**waytęw**). Gramm. See *wāto* "land tract". Ujae tract.

Wāto-aidik (**waytęw-hayidik**). Gramm. distort. Kwajalein tract.

Wāto-aidikdik (**waytęw-hayidikdik**). Gramm. See *wāto, aidik:* "narrow tract". Bikini tract; Wotho tract; three Kwajalein tracts.

Wāto-eņ (**waytęw-yeņ**). Gramm. See *wāto:* "the tract". Ujae tract; Namu tract; Ailuk tract.

Wāto-jeb-ej (**waytęw-jęb-yęj**). Reminisc. gramm. See *wāto, jeb, ej:* "tract reaches the east". Ailinglapalap tract.

Wātoon-aļ (**waytęwęn-haļ**). Gramm. See *aļ:* "sun tract". Kwajalein tract.

Wātoon-bōl (**waytęwęn-bęl**). Gramm. See *bōl:* "taro pit tract". Kwajalein tract.

Wātoon-eṃṃaan (**waytęwęn-yeṃṃahan**). Gramm. See *ṃṃaan:* "tract of men". Wotho tract; Lae tract.

Wātoon-pel (**waytęwęn-pęl**). Gramm. See *pel:* "boxfish tract". Namu tract.

Wātuon (**waytiwen**). Gramm. See *wāto:* "his tract". Aur tract; Arno tract.

Wātuon-aidik (**waytiwen-hayidik**). Gramm. See *wāto, aidik:* "tract of thinness". Two Majuro tracts; Arno tract.

Wātuon-ke (**waytiwen-kęy**). Gramm. See *ke:* "porpoise tract". Arno tract.

Wātuon-ke-eañ (**waytiwen-kęy-yag**). Gramm. Arno tract.

Wātuon-ke-rak (**waytiwen-kęy-rak**). Gramm. Arno tract.

Wātuon-pel (**waytiwen-pęl**). Gramm. See *pel:* "boxfish tract". Majuro tract.

Wātuon-piñpiñ (**waytiwen-pigpig**). Gramm. See *piñpiñ:* "tract of *Hernandia* trees". Arno tract.

Wātuwe-lōñ (**waytiwey-lęg**). Gramm. See *wāto, lōñ:* "high tract". Arno tract.

Weļok-eņ (**węylaq-yeņ**). Gramm. See *weļok* "go away". Arno tract.

Weļok-eņ (**weylaq-yeņ**). Gramm. Bikini tract; Jaluit tract.

Weļok-kaņ (**weylaq-kaņ**). Gramm. Ujelang tract.

Weļokun-wōj (**węylaqin-węj**). Gramm. See *weļok, wōj:* "beautiful journey". Likiep tract.

Wetaan-bōl (**weytahan-bęl**). Gramm. See *wetaa-, bōl:* "on the east side of the taro pit". Jaluit tract.

Wetaan-mar (**weytahan-mar**). Gramm. See *mar:* "on the east side of the bushes". Kwajalein tract.

Wetaan-ti (**weytahan-tiy**). Part. reminisc. gramm. See *tiete:* "on the east side of the reef". Wotje tract.

Wetaan-to (**weytahan-tew**). Gramm. See *wetaa-, to:* "on the east side of the pass". Ebon district.

Wetak-iōñ (**weytak-yiyęg**). Gramm. See *wetak:* "go eastward in the north". Aur tract.

Wōd-alo (**wed-halęw**). Also *Wōdālo.* Part. reminisc. gramm. See *wōd* "coral". Ailinglapalap tract.

Wōd-jebwā (**wed-jebay**). Gramm. See *wōd, jebwā:* "coral of the *jebwā* variety". Arno tract.

Wōd-jepāp (**wed-jepap**). Gramm. See *wōd, jepāp:* "*Jepāp* shark coral reef". Namu islet.

Wōd-ko-lik (**wed-qew-lik**). Pers. name, *Luodkolik, a navigational sign in the form of a giant female shark about 15 miles offshore.* Arno coral head.

Wōd-meej (**wed-meyej**). Gramm. See *wōd, meej:* "bright-colored coral. Wotje islet.

Wōd-wātuon (**wed-waytiwen**). Recur. form. See *wōd, wāto:* "coral in its tracts". Ailinglapalap islet.

Wōda (**wedah**). Gramm. See *wōda* "successful in fishing". Jaluit islet.

Wōdaajji-kaņ (**wedahajjiy-kaņ**). Part. reminisc. gramm. See *wōda, ajjikad:* "repeated success in fishing", or see *wōd:* "those *Ajji* coral heads". Kwajalein coral head.

Wōdaṃōj (**wedahṃęj**). Reminisc. gramm. See *wōda, ṃōj:* "success in fishing finished", or see *wōd:* "*Aṃōj* coral head". Arno coral head.

Wōde-ņa (**wedey-ņah**). Reminisc. gramm. See *wōd, ņa:* "shoal of much coral". Arno islet.

Wōden-el-kaņ (**weden-yęl-kaņ**). Gramm. See *wōd, el:* "those nest corals". Arno tract.

Wōden-iōñ (**weden-yiyęg**). Gramm. See *wōd, iōn:* "coral of the north". Mejit tract.

Wōden-katoļok (**weden-katęwļaq**). Gramm. See *katoļok:* "catharsis coral". (People used to come here for cleansing from sickness.) Ailuk tract.

Wōdeñ (**wedeg**). Part. reminisc. gramm. See *wōd* "coral". Eniwetak district.

Wōja (**wejah**). Recur. form. See *wōja* "abode". Ailinglapalap district; Ailinglapalap islet; Majuro district.

Wōja-armej (**wejah-harmęj**). Gramm. See *wōja, armej:* "abode of people". Mejit tract.

Wōja-jak (**wejah-jak**). Gramm. See *wōja, jak:* "scene of killing in battle". Two Mejit tracts.

Wōja-jekad (**wejah-jekad**). Gramm. See *wōja, jekad:* "where the noddy lives". Majuro tract.

Wōja-kaņ (**wejah-kaņ**). Recur. form. See *wōja:* "those abodes". Arno tract.

Wōja-likōk-eañ (**wejah-likęk-yag**). Gramm. See *wōja, likōk:* "site of preparedness". Majuro tract.

Wōja-likōk-rak (**wejah-likęk-rak**). Gramm. Majuro tract.

Wōja-ļapļap (**wejah-ļapļap**). Recur. form. See *wōja:* "large abode". Arno tract.

Wōja-niñniñ (**wejah-nignig**). Gramm. See *niñniñ:* "abode of babes". Majuro tract.

Wōjaan-bajbaj (**wejahan-bajbaj**). Gramm. See *wōja, bajbaj:* "scene of busyness". Namorik tract.

Wōjaan-Etao (**wejahan-yetahwew**). Pers. name. See *wōja, Etao:* "Etao's abode". Majuro tract.

Wōjaan-kōlōk (**wejahan-kelek**). Gramm. See *kōlōk:* "scene of fullness". Ebon tract.

Wōjaan-kōtak (**wejahan-ketak**). Gramm. See *kōtak:* "site of roof thatching". Ailinglapalap tract.

Wōjaan-Mile (**wejahan-milęy**). Recur. form. See *Mile* "Mili atoll". Ailinglapalap tract.

Wōjālaerōk (**wejalhayęręk**). Pers. name: "abode of *Laerōk*". (Note that other islets in the atoll include *Wōja* and *Aerōk.)* Ailinglapalap islet.

Wōjāle (**wejalęy**). Reminisc. gramm. See *le:* "albatross abode". Majuro tract.

Wōje-jāiiōñ (**węjęy-jayiyyęg**). Unanalyz. Kwajalein islet.

Wōje-jāirōk (**węjęy-jayiyręk**). Unanalyz. Kwajalein islet.

Wōjjak (**wejjak**). Unanalyz. Ujae islet.

Wōjjā (**wejjay**). Reminisc. gramm. See *jjāāk:* "land on which one can overeat". Ratak atoll; Wotje; Wotje islet; Majuro tract; Arno tract.

Wōjļā-eņ (**węjļay-yeņ**). Gramm. Arno tract.

Wōlōr (**węlęr**). Unanalyz. Arno islet.

Wōnaeo (**wenahyęw**). Reminisc. gramm. See *wōn, eo:* "who?" Arno tract.

Wōnaerro (**wenahyerrew**). Gramm. distort. See *wōn, iaa-:* "which of the two of them?" Namorik tract.

Wōndik (**węndik**). Gramm. See *wōn:* "small turtle". Ebon tract.

Wōnejo-eņ (**węnęjew-yeņ**). Part. reminisc. gramm. See *wōn, jọ:* "turtle lays eggs". Namorik tract.

Wōnenwe (**wenenwey**). Unanalyz. Lib household.

Wōnmak (**wenmak**). Unanalyz. Kwajalein islet; Maloelap islet.

Wōnmej (**węnmęj**). Gramm. See *wōn, mej:* "turtle molting site". Wotje islet.

Wōnoot (**wenewet**). Pers. name, a vampire who ate the reef and made the passes on both sides of this islet, and who still demands provisions from passing canoes to ensure against their capsizing. Kwajalein islet.

Wōp-eņ (**węp-yeņ**). Gramm. See *wōp:* "the *Barringtonia* tree". Arno tract.

Wōple (**węplęy**). Unanalyz. Kwajalein islet.

Wōtaan-kaņ-jāiiōñ (**wetahan-kaņ-jayiyyęg**). Gramm. See *wōtaan:* "those wild taro". Maloelap tract.

Wōtaan-kaņ-jāirōk (**wetahan-kaņ-jayiyręk**). Gramm. Maloelap tract.

Wōtare (**wetaręy**). Gramm. distort. See *watre:* "partially cooked". Mejit tract.

Wōtbūkōr (**wetbikęr**). Part. recur. form. See *būkōr* "a plant". Mejit tract; Majuro tract.

Wōte-jabuk (**wetey-jabiq**). Part. recur. form. See *jabuk* "fishing method". Kwajalein tract.

Wōtle (**wętlęy**). Unanalyz. Jaluit islet; Jaluit tract.

Wōtmwā (**wętmay:**). Pers. name, Whitmer, a German sea captain for Jaluit Gesellschaft (1904-1913) on motorized schooners Aelous and Triton; once found the reef called Limjalele northeast of Arno and east of Aur. Aur tract.

Wōtojome (**wetewjewmey**). Gramm. See *wōtojome* "fish for goatfish". Ailinglapalap tract.

Wōtōnnọ (**wętęnnaw**). Reminisc. gramm. See *wōtōn, nnọ:* "tasty season". Maloelap tract.

Wōtōnnọ-eņ (**wętennaw-yeņ**). Reminisc. gramm. Majuro tract.

Wōtto (**wettew**). Unanalyz. Ralik atoll; Wotho; Wotho islet; Utirik household; Arno tract; Mili tract.

Wūdde (**widdęy**). Reminisc. gramm. See *wūd* "pandanus bears". Arno islet.

Wūdde-kaṇ (**widdẹy-kaṇ**). Reminisc. gramm. See *wūd:* "those bearing pandanus". Ailinglapalap tract.

Wūj-kaṇ (**wij-kaṇ**). Gramm. See *wūj:* "those balsa driftwood". Mili tract.

Wūjae (**wijahyey**). Reminisc. gramm. See *wūj, ae:* "rough currents". Ralik atoll; Ujae; Ujae islet.

Wūjen (**wijen**). Reminisc. gramm. See *wūje-* "part of (it)". Lib tract.

Wūjenel (**wijenel**). Reminisc. gramm. See *wūje-, el:* "part of the nest". Aur tract.

Wūji-tak (**wijiy-tak**). Reminisc. gramm. See *wūj:* "pull it up". Eniwetak tract.

Wūjji-eṇ (**wijjiy-yeṇ**). Unanalyz. Ailinglapalap tract.

Wūjjuon-eṇ (**wijjiwen-yeṇ**). Unanalyz. Ailinginae islet.

Wūjlañ (**wijlag**). Recur. form. See *wūj, lañ:* "rough, cloudy sky". Ralik atoll; Ujelang; Aur large district; Ujelang islet; Jaluit tract; Namorik tract; Arno tract.

Wūjtak (**wijtak**). Gramm. See *wūjtak* "praise". Mejit district; Arno tract.

Wūleej (**wilẹyẹj**). Gramm. See *wūliej* "cemetery". Kwajalein tract.

Wūleej-eṇ (**wilẹyẹj-yeṇ**). Gramm. Jaluit islet; two Likiep tracts; Arno tract; Mili islet; Mili tract.

Wūleej-kaṇ (**wilẹyẹj-kaṇ**). Gramm. Knox islet.

Wūleej-rak (**wilẹyẹj-rak**). Gramm. Jaluit islet.

Wūlej-eṇ (**wilẹj-yeṇ**). Gramm. See *wūlej* "a shrub". Arno tract.

Wūlej-kaṇ (**wilẹj-kaṇ**). Gramm. Kwajalein tract.

Wūleo (**wilẹyẹw**). Gramm. distort. See *wūlio* "handsome". Majuro tract.

Wūlka (**wilkah**). Unanalyz. Jaluit tract; Ailuk islet; Majuro district; Majuro islet.

Wūlka-eañ (**wilkah-yag**). Unanalyz. Ailuk tract.

Wūlka-rak (**wilkah-rak**). Unanalyz. Ailuk tract.

Wūlkā (**wilkay**). Unanalyz. Jaluit tract.

Wūnbar (**winbar**). Reminisc. gramm. See *wūn, bar:* "rock base". Eniwetak islet; Lae tract; Namu tract; four Ailinglapalap tracts; Wotje tract; two Mili tracts.

Wūnbar-eṇ (**winbar-yeṇ**). Reminisc. gramm. Two Jaluit tracts; Namorik tract.

Wūnejjo (**winejjew**). Unanalyz. Namu tract; Ailinglapalap tract.

Wūni (**winiy**). Gramm. See *wūn:* "its base". Two Mejit tracts.

Wūni-ej (**winiy-yẹj**). Gramm. Majuro tract.

Wūni-ḷwe-kaṇ (**winiy-ḷ°ẹy-kaṇ**). Gramm. See *wūn, ḷwe:* "base of those ponds". Arno tract.

Wūni-ṇa (**winiy-ṇah**). Gramm. See *wūn, ṇa:* "shoal base". Namu tract; Maloelap tract; Majuro tract.

Wūni-ṇa-eṇ (**winiy-ṇah-yeṇ**). Gramm. Mili islet.

Wūni-ṇa-eo (**winiy-ṇah-yew**). Gramm. Mejit tract.

Wūni-tọọr-kaṇ (**winiy-tawar-kaṇ**). Gramm. See *wūn, tọọr:* "base of those streams". Arno tract.

Wūnin-ekjab (**winin-yekjab**). Gramm. See *wūn, ekjab:* "base of the idol". Majuro tract.

Wūnittūr (**winittir**). Reminisc. gramm. See *wūnit, tūr:* "wrap up a bundle". Ailinglapalap islet.

Wūnoon-kaṇ (**winẹwẹn-kaṇ**). Reminisc. gramm. See *wūn, wōn:* "ripening pit bases". Arno tract.

Wūntō (**winteh**). From Engl. *window.* Mejit tract; Majuro tract.

Wūntōn-Ajoḷ (**winten-hajeḷ°**). Gramm. See *wūntōn, Ajoḷ:* "clump of *Ajoḷ* pandanus". Lae tract.

Wūntōn-bar (**winten-bar**). Gramm. See *wuntōn, bar:* "cluster of rocks". Ujae tract.

Wūntōn-kāmeej (**winten-kaymeyej**). Gramm. See *kāmeej:* "cluster of redwood driftwood". Lae tract.

Wūntōnwa (**wintenwah**). Gramm. See *wa:* "cluster of canoes". Ujae tract.